WITHDRAWN

Critical Survey of Science Fiction & Fantasy Literature

Third Edition

Critical Survey of Science Fiction & Fantasy Literature

Third Edition

Volume 1

Edited by
Paul Di Filippo

Stafford Library
Columbia College
1001 Rogers Street
Columbia, MO 65216

SALEM PRESS
A Division of EBSCO Information Services, Inc.
Ipswich, Massachusetts

GREY HOUSE PUBLISHING

Cover photo: iStock

Copyright © 2017, by Salem Press, A Division of EBSCO Information Services, Inc., and Grey House Publishing, Inc.

All rights reserved. No part of this work may be used or reproduced in any manner whatsoever or transmitted in any form or by any means, electronic or mechanical, including photocopy, recording, or any information storage and retrieval system, without written permission from the copyright owner. For information contact Grey House Publishing/Salem Press, 4919 Route 22, PO Box 56, Amenia, NY 12501

Critical Survey of Science Fiction & Fantasy Literature, Third Edition, published by Grey House Publishing, Inc., Amenia, NY, under exclusive license from EBSCO Publishing, Inc.

∞ *The paper used in these volumes conforms to the American National Standard for Permanence of Paper for Printed Library Materials, Z39.48 1992 (R2009).*

Publisher's Cataloging-In-Publication Data
(Prepared by The Donohue Group, Inc.)

Names: Di Filippo, Paul, 1954- editor.
Title: Critical survey of science fiction and fantasy literature / edited by Paul Di Filippo

Other Titles: Magill's guide to science fiction and fantasy literature.

Description: Third edition. | Pasadena, California ; Hackensack, New Jersey : Salem Press, Inc. ; Amenia, NY : Grey House Publishing, Inc., [2017] | Originally published as: Magill's guide to science fiction and fantasy literature. ©1996. | Includes bibliographical references and index.

Identifiers: ISBN 978-1-68217-278-0 (set) | ISBN 978-1-68217-282-7 (v.1) | ISBN 978-1-68217-283-4 (v.2) | ISBN 978-1-68217-284-1 (v.3)

Subjects: LCSH: Science fiction—History and criticism. | Fantasy literature—History and criticism.

Classification: LCC PN3433.8 .M34 2017 | DDC 809.38762—dc23

PRINTED IN THE UNITED STATES OF AMERICA

Contents

Publisher's Note xi
Contributors xiii
List of Genres xxi
Introduction xxv
Science Fiction and Fantasy xxix
Complete List of Contents xxxvii

The Absolute at Large 1
Accelerando 2
Adam and Eve 4
Adventures of Vlad Taltos 5
Aegypt, Love and Sleep, Daemonomania and Endless Things 8
Against Infinity 10
Air 12
Aladore 14
Alas, Babylon 15
Alice's Adventures in Wonderland and Through the Looking-Glass 16
Alif the Unseen 19
All Hallow's Eve 20
All Times Possible 22
Alraune 23
The Alteration 25
Always Coming Home 26
The Amber Series 28
Amnesia Moon 30
Among Others 31
Analogue Men 33
The Andromeda Strain 35
Animal Farm 36
Anno Dracula 38
The Anthony Villiers Novels 39
The Anubis Gates 41
Ape and Essence 43
Arachne 44
Area X: The Southern Reach Trilogy 46

Arthur Rex 48
The Artificial Kid 50
At the Back of the North Wind 51
At the Mountains of Madness and Other Novels 53
The Atlan Series 54
Babel 17 57
Barefoot in the Head 58
Baron Munchausen's Narrative of His Marvellous Travels and Campaigns in Russia 60
The Barsoom Series 61
Beauty and the Beast and Song of Orpheus 63
Beggars in Spain and Beggars and Choosers 65
The Beginning Place 67
A Beleaguered City 69
The Belgariad 70
The Berserker Series 72
The Best of C. M. Kornbluth 74
The Best of Cordwainer Smith 76
The Best Short Stories of J. G. Ballard 77
Beyond Apollo 79
Beyond the Aquila Rift 81
Beyond the Golden Stair 82
Big Planet and Showboat World 84
The Big Time 86
The Bill, the Galactic Hero Series 87
The Birthgrave Trilogy 89
The Black Cloud 91
Black Easter and The Day After Judgment 93
Black Empire 95
Black Flame 96
Black No More 98
Black Oxen 99

Black Trillium	101
Black Unicorn and Gold Unicorn	103
Blood Music	105
The Blood of Roses	106
The Blue Hawk	108
The Blue Star	109
The Blue Sword and The Hero and the Crown	111
Bone Dance	113
Bone Forest	114
The Book of the Dun Cow	116
The Book of the New Sun	117
The Book of Wonder	119
Born to Exile and In the Red Lords Reach	121
The Borrowers Series	123
The Boys from Brazil	125
Boy's Life	126
Brain Rose	128
Brain Wave	129
Brasyl	131
Brave New World	133
The Breast	134
Briar Rose	136
The Brick Moon	137
The Bridge	139
The Brigadier Ffellowes Stories	140
Bring the Jubilee	142
Brokedown Palace	144
The Broken Land	145
The Broken Sword	147
Brood of the Witch Queen	148
Brother to Dragons	150
Brute Orbits	151
Bug Jack Barron	153
Burn Witch Burn	154
Burning Chrome	156
The Burning Court	157
Camp Concentration	159
Canopus in Argos	160
A Canticle for Leibowitz	162
Carnacki the Ghost Finder	164
Carrie	165
A Case of Conscience	167
The Castle of Otranto	168
Cat's Cradle	170
The Caves of Steel and The Naked Sun	171
Celestis	173
The Centaur	175
The Child Garden	176
The Childe Cycle	178
Childhood's End	180
Children of the Atom	182
Chimera	183
China Mountain Zhang	185
The Chronicles of Clovis	187
The Chronicles of Narnia	188
The Chronicles of the Deryni	191
The Chronicles of Thomas Covenant the Unbeliever and The Second Chronicles of Thomas Covenant the Unbeliever	193
The Chronicles of Tornor	195
The Chrysalids	197
The Chymical Wedding	199
The Circus of Dr Lao	200
Cities in Flight	202
City	204
The City and the Stars	205
Clarke County, Space	207
The Clockwork Man	208
A Clockwork Orange	210
Cloned Lives	211
The Cloning of Joanna May	213
The Cloud Walker	214
The Collected Ghost Stories of M. R. James	216
The Colossus Trilogy	217
The Coming Race	220
The Conan Series	221
Conjure Wife	223

A Connecticut Yankee in King Arthur's Court ... 225
The Cornelius Chronicles ... 226
Counterfeit World ... 229
The Course of the Heart ... 230
Crash ... 232
The Crock of Gold ... 233
Crown of Stars ... 234
A Crystal Age ... 236
Crystal Express ... 237
The Culture Series ... 239
The Cyberiad ... 241
Cyteen ... 242
Cythera ... 244
Dagon and Other Macabre Tales ... 246
The Dancers at the End of Time Series ... 247
The Dark Elf Trilogy ... 249
The Dark Is Rising Sequence ... 251
Dark Universe ... 253
Darker than You Think ... 255
Darkover Landfall ... 256
Davy ... 258
The Day of the Triffids ... 259
The Dead Father ... 261
The Dead Zone ... 262
A Deal with the Devil ... 263
The Death of Grass ... 265
Death Qualified and The Best Defense ... 267
The Deathworld Trilogy ... 269
Deerskin ... 271
The Demolished Man ... 272
The Demon Princes Series ... 274
Descent into Hell ... 276
The Devil Is Dead ... 277
The Devil Rides Out ... 279
Devil's Tor ... 281
Dhalgren ... 282
The Diamond Age; or, a Young Lady's Illustrated Primer ... 284
The Difference Engine ... 285

A Different Flesh ... 287
A Different Kingdom ... 288
Dimension of Miracles ... 290
Dinner at Deviant's Palace ... 291
Dirk Gently's Holistic Detective Agency and The Long Dark Tea Time of the Soul ... 293
The Disappearance ... 295
The Discworld Series ... 296
The Dispossessed ... 298
Do Androids Dream of Electric Sheep? ... 300
Dr. Bloodmoney ... 301
Doctor Rat ... 303
Donovan's Brain ... 304
Doomsday Book ... 306
A Door into Ocean ... 307
The Door into Summer ... 309
Door Number Three ... 310
Dorothea Dreams ... 311
Double Star ... 313
Downbelow Station ... 314
Downward to the Earth ... 316
Dracula ... 317
The Dracula Series ... 319
Dracula Unbound ... 320
The Dragon in the Sea ... 322
The Dragon Knight Series ... 323
The Dragon Masters ... 325
The Dragon Waiting ... 327
The Dragonbone Chair ... 328
The Dragonriders of Pern ... 330
Dragonsbane ... 332
Dream ... 333
The Dream Master ... 335
A Dreamer's Tales ... 336
Dreamsnake ... 338
Drink Down the Moon ... 339
The Drowned World ... 340
The Duncton Chronicles and The Book of Silence ... 342

The Dune Series	344
The Dunwich Horror and Others	346
Durdane	347
The Dying Earth Series	350
Dying Inside	352
E Pluribus Unicorn	354
Earth	355
Earth Abides	357
Earthfasts	358
The Earth's Children Series	360
Earthsea	362
Earthseed	364
Echoes from the Macabre	365
Eden	367
Edison's Conquest of Mars	368
The Einstein Intersection	370
The Elenium	371
Elidor	374
The Elric Saga	375
The Embedding	377
The Empire of Fear	379
Empire of the East	380
The Enchanted Castle	381
The End of Eternity	383
The Ender Series	384
The Ends of the Earth	387
Engine Summer	388
Eon and Eternity	390
The E. T. Novels	392
Eternal Light	394
Evolution's Darling	395
The Exorcist	397
Eye in the Sky	399
The Face in the Abyss	401
The Face in the Frost	402
Fafhrd and the Gray Mouser	403
Fahrenheit 451	405
Fairyland	407
Falling Free	409
The Falling Woman	411
The Famished Road and Songs of Enchantment	412
Fancies and Goodnights	414
The Fantasy Worlds of Peter Beagle	416
Fantazius Mallare and The Kingdom of Evil	417
Fata Morgana	419
The Fates of the Princes of Dyfed and Book of the Three Dragons	421
Fear and Typewriter in the Sky	423
Fearful Pleasures	424
Feersum Endjinn	426
The Female Man	427
Fevre Dream	429
The Fifth Head of Cerberus	430
Fire and Hemlock	432
A Fire upon the Deep	433
The First Men in the Moon	435
The Fisher King Trilogy	436
The Flandry Series	438
Flow My Tears, the Policeman Said	440
Flowers for Algernon	441
The Forever King	443
The Forever War	444
The Forge of God and Anvil of Stars	446
The Forgotten Beasts of Eld	448
The Foundation Series	449
Fountains of Paradise	451
Frankenstein	453
Frankenstein Unbound	454
From the Earth to the Moon	456
Frontera	458
The Fury	459
Fury	461
The Future Los Angeles Series	462
A Game of Dark	465
The Gap Series	466
The Gate to Women's Country	468
Gene Wolfe's Book of Days	470
The Genesis Machine	471
Ghost Story	473

Contents

A Gift from Earth	474
Giles Goat-Boy	476
The Girl the Gold Watch and Everything	477
Gladiator at Law	479
Glass Soup and White Apples	480
The Glimmering	482
Glimpses	484
Glory Road	485
Glory Season	487
The Godhead Trilogy	488
The Gods Themselves	490
Golden Witchbreed	491
The Golem	493
The Golem and The Jinni	494
Good News from Outer Space	496
Gravity's Rainbow	498
Gray Matters	499
The Great God Pan	501
The Great Sky River Trilogy	502
Green Eyes	504
The Green Isle of the Great Deep	505
The Green Man	507
The Green Man	508
Green Mansions	510
Greenmantle	511
Grendel	513
Greybeard	514
Grimus	516
Gulliver's Travels	517
Gunner Cade	519
Half Past Human	521
The Hampdenshire Wonder	523
The Handmaid's Tale	524
Hard to Be a God	526
Hardwired	528
Hasan	529
The Haunting of Hill House	531
The Haunting of Toby Jugg	532
The Heads of Cerberus	533
The Healer's War	535
Heart of a Dog	536
The Heechee Series	538
Heinrich von Ofterdingen	540
Hell House	542
The Helliconia Trilogy	543
Her Smoke Rose Up Forever	545
The Heritage Universe Series	546
Herovit's World	549
The High Crusade	550
High-Rise	552
The Hitchhiker's Guide to the Galaxy Series	553
The Hobbit	555
The Holy Ground Trilogy	557
Homunculus and Lord Kelvin's Machine	559
Hothouse	561
The House Next Door	563
The House on the Borderland	564
The House on the Strand	566
A House Boat on the Styx and The Pursuit of the House Boat	567
Humour and Fantasy	569
Hyperborea	571
The Hyperion Cantos	572

Publisher's Note

This new edition of the *Critical Survey of Science Fiction & Fantasy Literature* is a three-volume set offering plot summaries and analyses of 842 of the most popular and frequently taught science fiction and fantasy books and series. Articles are alphabetically arranged by titles and range from such childhood fantasy classics as Lewis Carroll's *Alice's Adventures in Wonderland* (1865) and L. Frank Baum's *The Wonderful Wizard of Oz* (1900) to such pioneering science-fiction works as H. G. Wells's *The War of the Worlds* (1898) and modern science-fiction and fantasy classics as Robert Heinlein's *The Moon Is a Harsh Mistress* (1966) and J. R. R. Tolkien's *Lord of the Rings* trilogy (1954-1955). Among other prominent writers whose works are included are Isaac Asimov, Arthur C. Clarke, Frank Herbert, John Crowley, Ellen Kushner, and C. S. Lewis.

The front matter includes a broad survey of developments in the science fiction and fantasy fields by scholar T. A. Shippey, editor of the 2002 edition, and an introduction by Paul Di Filippo, editor of this revised edition.

The content in these volumes combines material updated from Salem Press's 1996 *Magill's Guide to Science Fiction and Fantasy Literature* with brand new, recently published works by writers such as China Miéville, Howard V. Hendrix, and David Brin.

Each article discusses an individual book or series and often comments on other works by the same author. Individual articles open with basic reference information in a ready-reference format: author's name, birth and death dates, identification of the work as either science fiction or fantasy, subgenre, type of work (such as drama, novel, novella, series, or story), time and location of plot, and date of first publication. The main body of each essay contains "The Story" which summarizes the work's plot and identifies major characters, and "Analysis" which offers a critical interpretation of the title and identifies literary devices and themes used in the work.

Readers will find several reference tools at the end of Volume 3:

- Annotated bibliography arranged by subject;
- Up-to-date lists of major science fiction and fantasy award winners;
- Timeline of works discussed;
- Annotated website list;
- Indexes: Author, Title, and Genre.

All essays are signed by their contributors. A list of these academicians, freelance writers, and independent scholars appear with their affiliations at the beginning of Volume 1. Salem Press thanks the set's contributors and especially, Editor Paul Di Filippo, whose biography appears at the end of Volume 3.

Contributors

Amy Adelstein
Independent Scholar

Walter Albert
University of Pittsburgh

A. Owen Aldridge
University of Illinois

Emily Alward
Greenwood, Indiana, Public Library

Steve Anderson
University of Arkansas at Little Rock

Ronnie Apter
Central Michigan University

Stanley Archer
Texas A&M University

Gerald S. Argetsinger
Rochester Institute of Technology

Mike Ashley
Independent Scholar

Bryan Aubrey
Independent Scholar

Charles Avinger
Washtenaw Community College

Mary Bagley
Missouri Baptist College

Jim Baird
University of North Texas

Barbara L. Baker
Central Missouri State University

Neal Baker
Dickinson College

James J. Balakier
University of South Dakota

Jerry L. Ball
Arkansas State University

Paul J. Baltes
Brigham Young University

Henry J. Baron
Calvin College

David Barratt
Independent Scholar

Martha A. Bartter
Northeast Missouri State University

Margaret W. Batschelet
University of Texas at San Antonio

Elizabeth H. Battles
Texas Wesleyan University

Margaret D. Bauer
Texas A&M University

Paulina L. Bazin
Loyola University

Karen S. Bellinfante
Independent Scholar

Cynthia Breslin Beres
Independent Scholar

Donna Berliner
Southern Methodist University

Cynthia A. Bily
Adrian College

Margaret Boe Birns
The New School for Social Research

Nicholas Birns
New School University

Russell Blackford
Independent Scholar

Tim Blackmore
University of Western Ontario

Franz G. Blaha
University of Nebraska—Lincoln

Richard Bleiler
University of Connecticut

Pette Bochynsky
Salem State College

Edra C. Bogle
University of North Texas

Janice M. Bogstad
University of Wisconsin—Eau Claire

Bernadette Lynn Bosky
Independent Scholar

Wendy Bousfield
Syracuse University

Kevin Boyle
Elon College

C. K. Breckenridge
Independent Scholar

John P. Brennan
Indiana University—Purdue University at Fort Wayne

Peter Brigg
University of Guelph

Wesley Britton
Grayson County College

David Bromige
Sonoma State University

Carroll Brown
Independent Scholar

Siobhan Craft Brownson
University of South Carolina—Columbia

Sam Bruce
Independent Scholar

Paul Buchanan
Biola University

CRITICAL SURVEY OF SCIENCE FICTION & FANTASY LITERATURE

Mary A. Burgess
Borgo Press

Edmund J. Campion
University of Tennessee

Peter Cannon
Independent Scholar

David B. Carroll
California State University, Los Angeles

Shawn Carruth
Concordia College

Erskine Carter
Black Hawk College

Sonya Cashdan
East Tennessee State University

Jeffrey Cass
Texas A&M International University

Christine R. Catron
St. Mary's University

Karen Rose Cercone
Indiana University of Pennsylvania

Edgar L. Chapman
Bradley University

Daniele Chatelain
University of Redlands

Amy Clarke
St. Mary's College of California

Daryl R. Coats
Northwestern State University of Louisiana

David W. Cole
University of Wisconsin—Baraboo

Tammy S. Conard
Texas Tech University

Gary William Crawford
Independent Scholar

Peter Crawford
Independent Scholar

C. K. Breckenridge
Independent Scholar

Don D'Ammassa
Independent Scholar

Shira Daemon
Independent Scholar

Susan Jaye Dauer
Austin Community College

Clark Davis
Northeast Louisiana University

Mary V. Davis
Independent Scholar

Radford B. Davis
Independent Scholar

Frank Day
Clemson University

Dennis R. Dean
Independent Scholar

Mary Jo Deegan
University of Nebraska—Lincoln

Bill Delaney
Independent Scholar

Paul Dellinger
Independent Scholar

Francine Dempsey
College of St. Rose

Paul Di Filippo
Independent Scholar

Mike Dickinson
Independent Scholar

Frank Dietz
University of Texas at Austin

Gene Doty
University of Missouri—Rolla

Catherine Doyle
Christopher Newport University

H. L. Drake
Millersville University

Lawrence Driscoll
University of Southern California

Thomas DuBose
Louisiana State University—Shreveport

Joyce Duncan
East Tennessee State University

Stefan Dziemianowicz
Independent Scholar

Bernard J. Farber
Illinois Institute of Technology

Jo N. Farrar
San Jacinto College

James Feast
Baruch College, City University of New York

Tom Feller
Independent Scholar

John Fiero
University of Southwestern Louisiana

David Marc Fischer
Independent Scholar

James O. Foster
Baylor University

Ronald Foust
Loyola University in New Orleans

Diana Pharaoh Francis
Ball State University

D. Douglas Fratz
Independent Scholar

June M. Frazer
Western Illinois University

Kelly Fuller
The Claremont Graduate School

Jean C. Fulton
Landmark College

Contributors

Robert Galbreath
University of North Carolina at Greensboro

Robert L. Gale
University of Pittsburgh

Jeffrey Galle
Northeast Louisiana University

Charles Gannon
Fordham University

Ann D. Garbett
Averett College

Tanya Gardiner-Scott
Mount Ida College

C. A. Gardner
Independent Scholar

Gayle Gaskill
College of St. Catherine

Victoria Gaydosik
East Central University

Diana L. Gerow
Niagara County Community College

Craig Gilbert
Portland State University

Marjorie Ginsberg
William Paterson College

Beaird Glover
Independent Scholar

Marc Goldstein
Independent Scholar

Lewis L. Gould
University of Texas

Carla Graham
University of Wisconsin—La Crosse

Charles A. Gramlich
Xavier University

Kenneth B. Grant
University of Wisconsin Center—Baraboo/Sauk County

David Griffin
Carnage Hall Magazine

John L. Grigsby
Independent Scholar

Elizabeth A. Hait
McNeese State University

James C. Hall
University of Illinois at Chicago

Peter C. Hall
Independent Scholar

Paul Hansom
University of Southern California

William H. Hardesty III
Miami University

Betsy P. Harfst
Kishwaukee College

Michael Harper
Scripps College

Gregory Harris
Independent Scholar

June Harris
University of Arizona

Maverick Marvin Harris
East Texas Baptist University

Darren Harris-Fain
Shawnee State University

Katie Harse
University of Calgary

Donald M. Hassler
Kent State University

A. Waller Hastings
Northern State University

Gary Layne Hatch
Brigham Young University

Len Hatfield
Virginia Polytechnic Institute and State University

John C. Hawley
Santa Clara University

Robert W. Haynes
Texas A&M International University

Charles Heffelfinger
Independent Scholar

Karen Hellekson
University of Kansas

Terry Heller
Coe College

Suzette J. Henderson
University of South Florida

Karin U. Hermann
University of Arkansas

Richard A. Hill
Taylor University

David Hinckley
University of California, Riverside

Joseph W. Hinton
Independent Scholar

Arthur D. Hlavaty
Independent Scholar

James L. Hodge
Bowdoin College

W. Kenneth Holditch
University of New Orleans

John R. Holmes
Franciscan University of Steubenville

Joan Hope
Indiana University at Bloomington

Kenneth L. Houghton
Independent Scholar

Mary Hurd
East Tennessee State University

Susan Hwang
Independent Scholar

xv

Earl G. Ingersoll
State University of New York College, Brockport

Alex Irvine
Independent Scholar

Archibald E. Irwin
Indiana University Southeast

Charles Israel
Columbia College of South Carolina

John Jacob
Northwestern University

Jeff Johnson
Independent Scholar

Eunice Pedersen Johnston
North Dakota State University

Paul Joseph
Nova Southeastern University Law Center

Donald P. Kaczvinsky
Louisiana Tech University

Anne K. Kaler
Gwynedd Mercy College

Daven M. Kari
California Baptist College

Cynthia Lee Katona
Ohlone College

U. Milo Kaufmann
University of Illinois at Urbana—Champaign

Philip E. Kaveny
University of Wisconsin—Madison

James D. Keeline
Prince and the Pauper Collectible Children's Books

Kara K. Keeling
Christopher Newport University

Richard Keenan
University of Maryland—Eastern Shore

Fiona Kelleghan
University of Miami

Richard Kelly
University of Tennessee

Howard A. Kerner
Polk Community College

Paul Kincaid
Independent Scholar

Jeff King
University of North Texas

Susan S. Kissell
Northern Kentucky University

Katharine Kittredge
Ithaca College

E. Laura Kleiner
Indiana State University

Kim G. Kofmel
University of Western Ontario

Grove Koger
Boise Public Library

David C. Kopaska-Merkel
Dreams & Nightmares Magazine

Dennis M. Kratz
University of Texas at Dallas

Eugene Larson
Pierce College

William Laskowski
Jamestown College

Dianna Laurent
Southeastern Louisiana University

William T. Lawlor
University of Wisconsin—Stevens Point

Benjamin S. Lawson
Albany State College

L. L. Lee
Western Washington University

Steven Lehman
John Abbott College

Elisabeth Anne Leonard
Kent State University

Leon Lewis
Appalachian State University

Rania Lisas
Virginia Polytechnic Institute and State University

Janet Alice Long
Independent Scholar

Steven R. Luebke
University of Wisconsin—River Falls

R. C. Lutz
University of the Pacific

Janet McCann
Texas A&M University

Robert McClenaghan
Independent Scholar

Jean McConnell
New Mexico Military Institute

Andrew Macdonald
Loyola University, New Orleans

Gina Macdonald
Loyola University, New Orleans

Ron McFarland
University of Idaho

James M. McGlathery
University of Illinois at Urbana–Champaign

Edythe M. McGovern
West Los Angeles College

S. Thomas Mack
University of South Carolina—Aiken

Edgar V. McKnight, Jr.
Gardner-Webb University

Contributors

Kevin McNeilly
University of British Columbia

Willis E. McNelly
California State University, Fullerton

Samuel Maio
San Jose State University

Daryl F. Mallett
Independent Scholar

Edward A. Malone
University of Missouri–Rolla

Lawrence K. Mansour
University of Maryland

Joseph J. Marchesani
Pennsylvania State University—McKeesport

Tony A. Markham
Fitchburg State College

Louis Markos
Houston Baptist University

Wayne Martindale
Wheaton College

Charles E. May
California State University, Long Beach

Laurence W. Mazzeno
Ursuline College

Patrick Meanor
State University of New York—Oneonta

Marvin E. Mengeling
University of Wisconsin—Oshkosh

Carole F. Meyers
Georgia Institute of Technology

Julia Meyers
Duquesne University

Michael R. Meyers
Shaw University

Vasa D. Mihailovich
University of North Carolina

Larisa Mihaylova
Moscow State University

Joseph Milicia
University of Wisconsin—Sheboygan

B. Diane Miller
Independent Scholar

Debra G. Miller
Eastern New Mexico University

P. Andrew Miller
Independent Scholar

Paula M. Miller
Biola University

Timothy C. Miller
Millersville University of Pennsylvania

Joseph Minne
Independent Scholar

Carla Mall Minor
Independent Scholar

Catherine Mintz
Independent Scholar

Scott E. Moncrieff
Andrews University

Chris Morgan
Independent Scholar

Trevor J. Morgan
Independent Scholar

Bernard E. Morris
Independent Scholar

Robert E. Morsberger
California State Polytechnic University, Pomona

Sherry Morton-Mollo
Independent Scholar

Stephanie Moss
University of South Florida

Kevin P. Mulcahy
Rutgers University

Roark Mulligan
Christopher Newport University

Wayne Narey
Arkansas State University

Joseph M. Nassar
Rochester Institute of Technology

Keith Neilson
California State University, Fullerton

Jörg C. Neumann
University of Texas, Austin

George E. Nicholas
Benedictine College

John Nizalowski
Mesa State College

George T. Novotny
University of South Florida

David Oakes
Texas Christian University

Bruce Olsen
Alabama State University

James M. O'Neil
The Citadel

Twila Yates Papay
Rollins College

D. Barrowman Park
Western Washington University

Margaret E. Parks
Independent Scholar

Joseph F. Patrouch
University of Dayton

David Peck
California State University, Long Beach

Dennis R. Perry
University of Missouri—Rolla

Lawrence Person
Nova Express

Jefferson M. Peters
Kagoshima University

Thomas D. Petitjean, Jr.
Louisiana State University—Eunice

John R. Pfeiffer
Central Michigan University

Karsten Piper
Independent Scholar

Allene Phy-Olsen
Austin Peay State University

Clifton W. Potter, Jr.
Lynchburg College

Victoria Price
Lamar University

Norman Prinsky
Augusta College

Charles Pullen
Queen's University

Christian L. Pyle
University of Kentucky

R. Kent Rasmussen
Independent Scholar

Alan I. Rea, Jr.
Bowling Green State University

Robert Reginald
California State University, San Bernadino

Mark Rich
Independent Scholar

Janine Rider
Mesa State College

Stephen L. Robbins
Dickinson State University

Robin Roberts
Louisiana State University

Claire Robinson
Independent Scholar

Larry Rochelle
Johnson County Community College

Carl Rollyson
Baruch College, City University of New York

Natalie M. Rosinsky
Independent Scholar

Michael-Anne Rubenstien
Independent Scholar

Nicholas Ruddick
University of Regina

Willard J. Rusch
University of Southern Maine

Todd H. Sammons
University of Hawaii at Manoa

Scott Samuelson
Ricks College

Joe Sanders
Lakeland Community College

W. A. Senior
Broward Community College

Roberta Sharp
California State Polytechnic University, Pomona

Bill Sheehan
Independent Scholar

T. A. Shippey
St. Louis University

R. Baird Shuman
University of Illinois at Urbana—Champaign

Charles L. P. Silet
Iowa State University

Carl Singleton
Fort Hays State University

Amy Sisson
Independent Scholar

Ira Smolensky
Monmouth College

Maureen Speller
Independent Scholar

William C. Spruiell
Western Carolina University

Andrew Sprung
D'Youville College

Brian Stableford
King Alfred's College

Michael Stuprich
Ithaca College

Roy Arthur Swanson
University of Wisconsin—Milwaukee

Raymond H. Thompson
Acadia University

John H. Timmerman
Calvin College

Michael J. Tolley
The University of Adelaide

Samuel Umland
University of Nebraska–Kearney

Jeff VanderMeer
Independent Scholar

Mary E. Virginia
Independent Scholar

Janeen Webb
Australian Catholic University

Quinn Weller
University of Indianapolis

James M. Welsh
Salisbury State University

Donna Glee Williams
North Carolina Center for the Advancement of Teaching

Philip F. Williams
Arizona State University

Contributors

Judith Barton Williamson
Sauk Valley Community College

John Wilson
Independent Scholar

Michael Witkoski
University of South Carolina

Clifton Yearley
State University of New York—Buffalo

Carl B. Yoke
Kent State University

Beth Rapp Young
University of Alabama in Huntsville

Mary Young
The College of Wooster

Gary Zacharias
Palomar College

Marc Zaldivar
Virginia Polytechnic Institute and State University

Alan Ziskin
Independent Scholar

List of Genres

The ready-reference top matter in each article identifies a primary genre—science fiction or fantasy—and a secondary classification of a narrower genre. Definitions of the latter classifications are provided below.

Alien civilization: Centers on an attempt to present an alien (nonhuman, nonartificial) intelligence or civilization.

Alternate History: Sometimes also called "counterfactual," this type of science fiction is concerned with detailing the events on any continuum where, due to a historical incident happening otherwise than in our consensus records, the path of history has gone differently. Often, real-life characters appear with the fictional ones.

Animal Fable: This mode of fantasy is distinguishable from two other types of imaginative narratives involving beasts. In a novel such as *Watership Down*, animals are treated naturalistically, but disclosed to possess a hidden sapience. In novels such as the *Redwall* series, animals have a technic culture and civilization all their own. But an Animal Fable is an allegory and a satire in which animals more or less stand in for humans, living similar lives but with a literally different "skin" that allows covert points to be made and lessons to be drawn that reflect on humanity.

Animal fantasy: A genre going back to Aesop, it often functions as allegory. Distinguished from **animal fable**.

Apocalypse: Deals with the end of the world as known, often but not always through nuclear holocaust. This is a more dramatic form of the catastrophe story. Post-holocaust fiction, in contrast, discusses the aftermath of the apocalyptic event more than the event itself.

Artificial intelligence: Plots deal with human-created forms of intelligence such as "thinking" computers, robots, androids, and cyborgs.

Catastrophe: Usually set on Earth, involving various natural disasters and attempts to deal with them.

Cautionary: Attempts to warn of some current or extrapolated danger, seriously and without amusement. May overlap with apocalypse fiction.

Closed universe: Protagonists are in some type of closed environment that they perceive as natural and complete; they discover the "outside" during the plot action.

Cosmic Horror: Stories which posit a malign universe, usually filled with many races of alien beings superior to humanity and inimical to our species. The terror effects of these tales often derive from actual scientific paradigms concerning the vastness and unknowability of the universe. The work of H. P. Lovecraft is the prime specimen.

Cosmic voyage: Begins with early "voyage to the moon" stories and continues through longer space travels.

Cultural exploration: Works affected by anthropological theory. Cultures are different because of different cultural decisions, not different physical characteristics.

Cyberpunk: Characterized by extensive use of computers or artificial intelligences, often with a state of streetwise anarchy among the protagonists.

Dystopia: The opposite of utopia; an imagined world that is horrific rather than ideal. Differs from cautionary works through an element of relish or deliberate exaggeration.

Evolutionary fantasy: Concerns attempts to demonstrate, disprove, or modify evolutionary theory. Some works deal with mutations. Overlaps to some extent with superbeing stories.

Exploratory: "To boldly go where no man has gone before." The credo of *Star Trek* is exemplified in stories of this type. Wehter visiting new planets, new dimensions, new galaxies, or lost worlds, SF of this stripe is concerned with the introduction of humanity into new realms.

Extrapolatory: Takes a feature of contemporary society and projects it into the future as increasingly dominant. May overlap with the **cautionary** tale.

Extrasensory powers: Characters possess some form of ESP. The society may be based on control and development of such powers. Overlaps with superbeing stories.

Fairytale: A retelling or repurposing of a classical fairytale, or a new original work which exemplifies the themes and motifs and characters of the classical mode.

Feminist: Characterized by a concern for altered female roles or by future gender war.

Future history: Extensive histories of the future, often in series form and often cyclic.

Future war: Central interest is on the nature of war rather than war as a threat or as part of the background.

Galactic empire: The plot is interstellar. A future history may contain a galactic empire; the galactic empire story will not be as encompassing in its span of time.

Heroic fantasy: Set in a fantasy world in which characters approach the scale of epic or romance; encompasses "sword and sorcery" plots.

High fantasy: Little or no connection with the current world, set "elsewhere." Many works of heroic fantasy are also high fantasy, but not all high fantasy is heroic fantasy.

Historical Fantasy: This type of story employs canonical, real-life venues and characters, but inserts fictional, unrecorded events and personages, mainly supernatural or otherworldly, into the interstices of the written records.

Inner space: Stresses internal alterations of consciousness rather than external technological control.

Interplanetary romance: Like **planetary romance**, an old category of fiction motivated by a desire to extend the travels and adventures of nineteenth and twentieth century adventurers into space. This genre perhaps is the most recognizable as science fiction to readers who are relatively unfamiliar with the field.

Invasion story: Alien beings attack a planet.

Life Extension: Stories which examine the technological or fantastical prolongation of the normal human lifespan, extending even to immortality.

Magical Realism: A relatively realistic plot is disturbed by figures of myth or fantasy.

Magical world: A type of heroic fantasy with emphasis not on characters' quests but instead on social organization based on a technology that does not conform to current science.

Marvelous Invention: A type of tale in which the plot is precipitated, enlarged and complicated mainly by the introduction of a new gadget or new technology, often involving paradigm-altering upsets to the accepted science of the time.

Medieval future: A future era reverts to medieval social structures, which then are exposed to change. These works often are set on an alien planet with civilizations of some medieval type.

Metaphysical Fantasy: A type of fantasy in which the epistemological and ontological bases for the nature of reality are investigated, frequently resulting in surreal scenarios such as found in David Lindsay's classic *A Voyage to Arcturus* or Damon Knight's *Humpty Dumpty: An Oval*.

Mythological: Depends on the characters and settings of some established system of mythology.

New Wave: Imagistic and highly metaphoric, inclined toward psychology and the soft sciences, and often similar to works of dystopia. The New Wave, largely contained in works of the 1960's, attempted to turn science fiction more toward mainstream literature. New Wave overlaps to a large extent with inner space fiction, and cyberpunk can be seen as a resurgence of the New Wave.

Occult: A mode of fantasy characterized by interest in the practices of magic and the supernatural, often with an element of the macabre.

Planetary romance: A type of heroic fantasy but with scientific trappings, often set on Venus or Mars.

Post-holocaust: Set in a world recovering from a (usually nuclear) holocaust, often characterized by anarchy, mutations, and an attempt to struggle toward some form of civilization. Differs from apocalypse stories in dealing with the aftermath of the holocaust rather than the holocaust itself.

Singularity: Stories embodying the concept that the creation and perfection of artificial intelligence will transform the human world beyond all knowing by merely human intelligences, sometimes leading to an apocalypse, but sometimes leading to a utopia.

Steampunk: A mode of mock-Victorian story, either science-fictional or purely fantastical, in which the global culture of the historical Victorian period—technology, fashion, politics, economics, et al—is utilized, either in extant form or radically altered form, providing adventures which either slot neatly into the consensus timeline or occur in divergent and parallel worlds.

Space Opera: Large-scale, baroque, melodramatic adventures of a galactic magnitude, frequently involving star empires spread across many worlds and featuring races, human and alien. *Star Wars* is the most familiar instance of space opera, along with classics such as *Dune* and *The Foundation Trilogy*.

Superbeing: Conjectures on the next stage of evolution, usually rejecting the idea of greater intelligence in favor of some exaggerated physical characteristic or a new form of mental power; the latter type overlaps with extrasensory power stories.

Superhero: Attempting to capture and complexify the tropes of superhero comics, the well-done Superhero science fiction novel adds depth of character and some level of plausibility to the scenario while preserving the thrills and action of the graphic novel.

Technocratic: a technological object or idea is the dominant plot element. Much of science fiction has technocratic elements, particularly that known as "hard" science fiction, but if these elements do not dominate the plot, the work falls into another classification.

Theological romance: Often involves a divinely ruled universe within the framework of a post-scientific society. Such works are seen as "antiscience" fiction.

Time travel: Characters are able to move forward or backward in time and often attempt to use this power to create or maintain an acceptable stream of history.

Urban Fantasy: Blending naturalistic settings, characters and culture with eruptions of the supernatural, this type of tale differs from MAGICAL REALISM in that surrealism and absurdity and the inexplicable are eschewed in favor of a rigorous, almost scientific treatment of the occult elements of the tale.

Utopia: Describes an ideal society.

INTRODUCTION

Welcome to the pages of Salem Press's *Critical Survey of Science Fiction & Fantasy Literature,* one of the most comprehensive and wide-ranging guides for teachers, students and general readers of fantastical literature available today, featuring plot synopses and critical analyses for nearly one thousand milestone books in the genre, selected from the field's distant inception to the present. This edition, updated and expanded, combines the wealth of material in the set's first appearance—published as *Magill's Guide to Science Fiction and Fantasy Literature* (1996), edited by T. A. Shippey—with entries from *Magill's Choice: Classics of Science Fiction and Fantasy Literature* (2002), edited by Fiona Kelleghan. Entries from both these editions have been revised in light of new publications and developments, while fifty additional books or series have been brought onboard to cover the interval since prior editions. All tables and charts are fully contemporaneous with our date of publication, while online resources and the bibliography have received a burnishing. The "List of Genres" underwent some changes as well, to reflect new concepts and modes. Debuting essay writers indeed bring their fresh insights, but the essence of this work still relies on the immense contributions made by editors Shippey and Kelleghan and the scores of earlier essay writers who represent the best of independent and academic scholarship.

The fifty new titles have been chosen for a variety of reasons. First, above all, for the sheer high quality of their writing, storytelling and ideation. Second, for serving as examples of unprecedented modes and methods within the genre not previously seen or covered. Third, for contributing a mix of new voices and fresh effusions from the old masters. Five of the new additions backfill gaps in the coverage for the earlier part of the twentieth century, but most new titles have appeared since 1996.

As publication dates approach closer to the present-day, books have hardly begun to stretch their legs with their audience, so to speak, making it harder to weigh their durability and eventual place in the canon, and, therefore, worthiness for inclusion in this guide. Certain titles that seemed faddish, tied to topical controversies, or have already faded from the peak of their acclaim, were easily rejected. Readers will seek in vain here for an exegesis of *Abraham Lincoln: Vampire Hunter,* or the *Twilight* series. Likewise, on the opposite end of the spectrum, highly valuable and important books, such as the J. K. Rowling's *Harry Potter* series or Suzanne Collins's *The Hunger Games* saga, escape coverage here due somewhat paradoxically to their coverage in other sources. Readers interested in Harry and Katniss have no dearth of alternate resources to consult. We have also omitted some worthy series which have not yet reached their conclusion and, therefore, lack a full-fledged estimation and analysis. Falling into this category is George R. R. Martin's famous and accomplished cycle, *A Song of Ice and Fire,* known to TV viewers as *A Game of Thrones,* and Patrick Rothfuss's *The Kingkiller Chronicle.*

Despite these small lacunae, however, the up-to-date portrait of the field presented in this guide remains comprehensive and undimmed. The majority of the older entries deal with undeniable immortal classics from the linked genres of science fiction and fantasy (to which, along with the horror genre and a dozen smaller non-mimetic sub-genres, famous critic John Clute has applied the umbrella term "fantastika"), and the new titles stand a fair chance, in our estimation, of assuming the same stature as the giants.

* * *

The first two editions of this work felt it necessary to explain science fiction and fantasy up front, and to make a case for the worth of these louche pulpish "para-literatures" when opposed to the mainstream of naturalistic literature as defined by the academy, an institution commercial, educational, and journalistic, which quite often has offered disdain for these genres since the birth of the categories. This edition retains some of that defense and attempt at definition, in the form of Tom Shippey's valuable essay, "Science Fiction and Fantasy" which follows this introduction. But in the year 2017, it no longer seems strictly necessary to defend the worth and vitality of these genres with quite the same level of aggressiveness, nor to attempt to nail them down as if they were exotic beasts. In fact, so potently have the tropes and toolkit of SF and fantasy diffused into the mainstream that many, many authors marketed as mainstream—Jennifer Egan, Gary Shteyngart, Lev Grossman, Karen Russell—are really fantasists and speculators at heart, who serve usefully to obliterate or smudge the old boundaries and definitions.

This new self-assured stance derives from one simple fact: nowadays, science fiction and fantasy are more popular than they have ever been, primarily due to their incarnations in the cinema and on television, but also to several blockbuster novels. It might almost be argued that fantastika is the dominant story-telling mode these days, on screen and on the page. The battle between fantastika and naturalism has reached a victory—or at least a ceasefire—and it can be argued that fantastika is the winner. Penetration and adoption is universal. Op-ed political commentators use examples from Philip K. Dick and J. G. Ballard without explanation, while pop musicians incorporate the tropes of fantasy and SF into their videos. Visionary businessmen pioneers like Elon Musk daily enact scenarios out of Heinlein and Asimov.

The tipping point for this condition might very well be traced to the years 2001-2002 – exactly when the last edition of this work was being prepared. Hence, the old-fashioned defensive attitude long maintained by the partisans of SF and fantasy was still in effect when Fiona Kelleghan wrote her bold paean to the genres.

What changed in that period? December of 2001 saw the release of Peter Jackson's *The Fellowship of the Ring*. In 2002 the first immensely successful and revolutionary *Spider-Man* movie appeared. If we incorporate Spider-Man and his superhero peers into science fiction—not too much of a stretch—then these two films heralded the double triumph of SF and fantasy over more "realistic" modes of storytelling. The marketplace, audience and readership never looked back.

While printed literature cannot match the box office income of media spectacles, it has nonetheless marched in parallel with its more glamorous siblings, achieving new heights of sales and creativity, attracting and becoming a home to a flock of more diverse writers and readers who bring to the table their unique viewpoints and experiences. When a complex and intellectually challenging and unabashedly science-fictional book such as Neal Stephenson's *Anathem* hits the bestseller lists, the revolution is over.

Two eminent anthologists in the field, the husband and wife team of Ann and Jeff VanderMeer, have chronicled this revolution in two massive anthologies: *The Big Book of Science Fiction* (2016) and *The Weird* (2012). The former covers the whole gamut of SF; the latter anthology looks only at a certain potent subset of fantasy, but nonetheless reaches conclusions that apply more broadly.

The following quotes from each introduction demonstrate the current-day reach and influence that make science fiction and fantasy so popular and important, so impressive and dominant. The astute VanderMeer team put it perfectly:

Since the days of Mary Shelley, Jules Verne, and H. G. Wells, science fiction has not just helped define and shape the course of literature but reached well beyond fictional realms to influence our perspectives on culture, science, and technology. Ideas like electric cars, space travel, and forms of advanced communication comparable to today's cell phone all first found their way into the public's awareness through science fiction. In stories like Alicia Yincz Cossio's "The IWM 1000" from the 1970s you can even find a clear prediction of Information Age giants like Google and when Neil Armstrong set foot on the moon, the event was a very real culmination of a yearning already expressed through science fiction for many decades. Science fiction has allowed us to dream of a better world by creating visions of future societies without prejudice or war. Dystopias, too, like Ray Bradbury's Fahrenheit 451, *have had their place in science fiction, allowing writers to comment on injustice and dangers to democracy. Where would Eastern Bloc writers have been without the creative outlet of science fiction, which by seeming not to speak about the present day often made it past the censors? For many under Soviet domination during those decades, science fiction was a form of subversion and a symbol of freedom. Today, science fiction continues to ask "What if?" about such important topics as global warming, energy*

Introduction

dependence, the toxic effects of capitalism, and the uses of our modern technology, while also bringing back to readers strange and wonderful visions. No other form of literature has been so relevant to our present yet been so filled with visionary and transcendent moments. No other form has been as entertaining, either.

The following, from the VanderMeers' introduction to *The Weird*, deliberately does not cover every virtue of every type of fantasy (epic fantasy is not mentioned, nor are humorous fantasists Terry Pratchett and Tom Holt, or the kinky appeal of urban fantasy)—but nonetheless their description hints at fantasy's universal allure:

> With unease and the temporary abolition of the rational, can also come the strangely beautiful, intertwined with terror. Reverie or epiphany, yes, but dark reverie or epiphany—not the lightness of "I wandered lonely as a cloud" but the weight of, for example, seminal early twentieth-century weird writer and artist Alfred Kubin's sensation of being "overcome…by a dark power that conjured up before my mind strange creatures, houses, landscapes, grotesque and frightful situations." [Fantasy] can be transformative—sometimes literally—entertaining monsters while not always seeing them as monstrous. It strives for a kind of understanding even when something cannot be understood, and acknowledges failure as sign and symbol of our limitations.

Combining the parallel insights of the VanderMeers into one basket appraisal of the worth and functions of the twin genres, we see then that science fiction encourages and demands the application of the intellect and the reasoning and speculative facilities—while not precluding emotions and a sense of adventure—in order to chart the progress of civilization down a million alternate avenues of the multiverse. And we also see that fantasy allows the unfettered imagination to confront humanity's deepest dreams and fears, hopes and aspirations, and nightmares in whatever wild, allegorical, emblematic and decidedly unrealistic forms are best suited to punch our hardwired buttons. You might say that SF is all Superego, while fantasy is all Id, with Ego serving as the interface territory where they meet and share their findings.

Given these fresh insights into the eternal importance and vitality and uses of science fiction and fantasy, and given the high profile of these genres in the marketplace, a volume such as the one you hold in your hands is an essential Baedeker, *vade mecum*, roadmap and Bible for any eager traveler venturing "beyond the fields we know."

—Paul Di Filippo

Excerpts from *The Big Book of Science Fiction* (2016) and *The Weird* (2012) reprinted courtesy of Ann and Jeff VanderMeer.

Science Fiction and Fantasy

The urge to tell tales of wonder is at least as old as any records human beings possess, and almost certainly older. Although modern literary criticism tends to downplay that urge, or to assign it a lower seniority than other narrative forms, one could properly claim that there are in essence three different provinces of the realm of story, all of equal value and all of equal age. Most obvious is the urge to record what actually happened, or what people believe actually happened. This is called not story but "history." Next is the urge to make up stories about events that did not actually happen, and about people who may be complete inventions of the storyteller. This is called "fiction," a genre that extends from the anecdotes people still tell about things that (allegedly) happened to their (perhaps imaginary) friends all the way through to the great and developed complexity of the written novel.

Third and last in this progression is the urge to tell stories not only about invented events and invented people but also about invented creatures, such as werewolves and vampires, or invented worlds, such as Middle-earth or Atlantis or the Earthly Paradise, or to tell any kind of tale that invents not only the people who exist in it but also the conditions under which they exist. Perhaps it is significant that there is no generally accepted label in our culture for this final category of story. One might suggest the word "fantasy," a word related to both "phantom" and "fancy" and having a root meaning of "making (something) visible," specifically imagining or making images of something that is not actually there. Fantasy, however, has an established meaning in the parlance of modern literary marketing. Part of that meaning is "not the same as science fiction," a difference further discussed below.

The International Association for the Fantastic in the Arts has proposed "the fantastic" as a broader label to set against the very large categories of "history" and "fiction." This label covers both modern fantasy and modern science fiction, taking in as well the ancestor genres of fairy tale, romance, myth, legend, ghost story, and many others. Stories of "the fantastic" may be defined as including any set in a world different from our own or that include elements recognized as alien to our own, things that are not true or not yet true. The dominant modern branches of the fantastic are fantasy and science fiction, but the fantastic includes genres older than either of them.

These three very broadly defined types of story—history, fiction, and the fantastic—did not, as far as is known, develop out of one another. All three were present at the dawn of European literature more than two thousand years ago and no doubt existed earlier on other continents. As an example of history, one can point to Herodotus's *The History of the Persian Wars* (c. 430 b.c.e.), an account of the Greek and Persian wars and all that led up to them in the fifth and sixth centuries b.c.e. For fiction, one could cite Homer's epic poem *The Iliad* (c. 800 b.c.e.), an account of an even older war between Greeks and Trojans, possibly with a historical basis but clearly composed to tell a story of adultery and revenge, not to list dates and events. Finally, Homer's *The Odyssey* (c. 800 b.c.e.) is in many ways a classic example of the fantastic, with its much loved and still much imitated tales of one-eyed, man-eating giants and witches who can turn people into beasts.

These three cases should provide a salutary reminder that there is no seniority in literary modes and that the fantastic, far from being a junior partner to history and fiction, is as old as either of them. The examples also show how difficult it is to keep the basic distinctions between story types absolutely clear. Many historians, Herodotus included, have been called liars and writers of fiction. By contrast, much fiction has been, and sometimes still is, thought by many people to be literally true. To switch from early Greek to early British literature, Geoffrey of Monmouth, the author of *History of the Kings of Britain* (1718; first published as *Historia regum Britanniae*, c. 1136), was dismissed as a total fabricator by some of his contemporaries, and most modern scholars have agreed with that assessment. Geoffrey's retelling of the legend of King Arthur, however, was accepted as absolute fact by many readers from the twelfth century to the early sixteenth, when the first historian to cast serious doubt on Arthur's reality was dismissed by English patriots as a crazy and jealous Italian.

At present, books about King Arthur may be produced by professional historians, by writers of historical fiction, and by writers of the fantastic such as T. H. White, author of *The Once and Future King* (1958). One of the earliest references to the Arthur story is an incident that crept into real history when, in 1113, a Frenchman visiting Cornwall told a local resident that his belief that King Arthur was not dead but would return again was utter nonsense, or as one might now say, "completely fantastic." A fracas began when the Cornishman defended the truth of his belief, and it was the fracas, not the legend, that found its way into recorded history.

Arguments about literary genres usually are not taken as far as that, but the incident serves to demonstrate that one person's fantasy may be another person's history. Just the same, although figures such as King Arthur, Odysseus, and Beowulf may be very hard or even impossible to categorize, the basic idea of the three modes, with their different relationships to literal truth, remains valid. It also can be said that as time has gone by, the differences generally have become more marked and the distinctions have become clearer. One of C. S. Lewis's characters, the scholarly Dr. Dimble in *That Hideous Strength* (1945), the last work of Lewis's Space Trilogy, says at one point:

> if you dip into any college, or school, or parish—anything you like—at a given point in its history, you always find that there was a time before that point when there was more elbow-room and contrasts weren't so sharp; and that there's going to be a point after that time when there is even less room for indecision and choices are more momentous.... The whole thing is sorting itself out all the time, coming to a point, getting sharper and harder.

Dimble says this only to excuse his own side's resurrection of Merlin from the past and its use of a kind of magic that would now be unlawful but in the old days was not yet categorized, not yet ruled out. What he says has a kind of force, however, for literary genres as well. Even the well-publicized efforts of modern avant-garde writers to mix literary genres depend for their effect on awareness of what the genres are. When it comes to fiction and the fantastic especially, and beyond them to the modern division of the fantastic into fantasy and science fiction, the tendency of present-day readers to draw sharp lines of distinction has become very strong.

This is a result of the major social and psychological development that marks off modern times from all previous eras and that (however much one may complain about it) most people see as a process of continuous acceleration: The rise of science. It entirely confirms Dr. Dimble's theory to note that although "science" is a word of great age— *scientia* is only the Latin word for "knowledge"—the highly specialized meaning now given to the word has been traced by the *Oxford English Dictionary* no further than 1725, and then not very convincingly. As late as 1834, that dictionary recorded objections to the use of the newly invented word "scientist." Only in the later nineteenth century does one find the words "science," "scientist," and "scientific" being given their modern meaning. From then on, however, one can see the ideas of science and the scientific method taking hold in more and more minds, with ever increasing power, as tools for establishing human control over nature and as particularly reliable guides for systematizing some kinds of knowledge. This immense physical, mental, and semantic change has had its effect on literature, in particular on the whole realm of the fantastic and on its two major modern divisions of fantasy and science fiction.

To consider first the history of science fiction alone, one may say in brief that as human beings began to do things in sober reality that no human being had ever done before, storytellers began to wonder what limits on novelty there were and what in the world might happen next. This impulse intersected with the ancient urge toward telling tales of wonder but also tended radically to alter it. For example, stories had been told for countless generations about raising the dead. In Homer's *The Odyssey*, Odysseus calls up the ghost of Achilles to give him advice. In the Bible, one reads of Jesus' raising of Lazarus. The first is a matter of magic, the second of religion. In *Frankenstein* (1818), however, MaryWollstonecraft Shelley imagines the creation of new life from the dead by scientific method, by means of a kind of electricity.

The speculation nowadays would be classified as fantasy, because scientists are fairly sure that her method would not work. In Mary Shelley's time, this cannot have been so obvious. Scientists had made the legs of dead frogs react by stimulating them electrically. Who was to say that the method could not be extended and perfected?

In exactly the same way, but eighty years later, H. G. Wells in *The Island of Dr. Moreau* (1896) put forward the idea that human beings could create not life but intelligence, by taking animals and altering them surgically through "vivisection." After his book was published, Wells carried on an indignant correspondence designed to show that his idea was not impossible but had a basis in scientific fact. Although nowadays it appears certain that he was wrong, as with Mary Shelley this was not so obvious at the time. Michael Crichton's *Jurassic Park* (1990), with its dinosaurs revived from blood samples, probably will pass into the same area of "disproved theses" in even less time than Mary Shelley's or Wells's speculations, but for the moment at least a few of his conjectures appear plausible. The point is that science fiction in particular, whether *Frankenstein* or *The Island of Dr. Moreau* or *Jurassic Park*, tends to follow the frontier of scientific possibility. This frontier, effectively static for hundreds if not thousands of years, expanded with growing acceleration all through the nineteenth and twentieth centuries. Its expansion has created an ever increasing area of speculation and possibility in which science fiction can flourish.

Most modern definitions of science fiction accordingly make some reference both to the need for novelty and the use of the imagination (an ancient requirement of all forms of the fantastic) and to the need for logic, rigor, and control by the strict requirements of science (a distinctively modern demand). Robert Heinlein thus declared, in an essay printed in *The Science Fiction Novel* (1969), edited by Basil Davenport, that science fiction is:

> a realistic speculation about possible future events, based solidly on adequate knowledge of the real world, past and present, and on a thorough understanding of the nature and significance of the scientific method.

One notes, on one hand, words such as "speculation" and "possible," but on the other, the words "realistic," "adequate," "thorough," and "scientific." Kingsley Amis, another distinguished practitioner in the field, asserted in his *New Maps of Hell* (1961) that:

> Science Fiction is that class of prose narrative treating of a situation that could not arise in the world that we know, but which is hypothesized on the basis of some innovation in science or technology, or pseudo-science or pseudo-technology, whether human or extraterrestrial in origin.

There is a sense in this definition that Amis is rather "hedging his bet" by careful use of the term "pseudo," and one can see why. Who is to say that the science of *Jurassic Park* is not as unreal as that of *Frankenstein*? Nevertheless, one sees once again the element of "not-truth" ("could *not* arise in the world that we know," emphasis added), qualified and even opposed by "science," "technology," "innovation," and "hypothesized."

One can sum up both Heinlein and Amis, and most other definitions of the genre, by saying that science fiction takes place in a world or setting that its contemporary readers know for certain is not true but that they are also prepared to accept as not impossible.

It may seem that this last requirement acts as a kind of restraint on the imagination, but to think that is to ignore the deep and powerful effect that real scientific innovation has had on the lives and attitudes of many modern readers. It is, after all, still possible for living memory to reach back to a time when it was generally accepted that human beings would never be able to fly. Many old people of the late twentieth century, as well as most of the early writers of American science fiction, grew up in a world that swept with unbelievable speed from the Wright brothers' flight in 1903 to dueling fighter planes in 1915, to transatlantic flights in 1919 and thousand-bomber raids in 1943, and then on to the *Enola Gay*— which dropped the atomic bomb on Hiroshima in 1945—the Strategic Air Command, everyday commercial traffic, and supersonic passenger jets. In the same way, the very idea of "wireless" transmission seemed in its beginnings eerie, almost ghostly, in the way that radio waves could be transmitted invisibly, impalpably, and apparently with nothing for them to transmit through. Technological advance led in quick succession to the radio becoming a normal household appliance, followed in turn by television and satellite links, accompanied by all the innovations of film technology from the first "cinema" to modern video.

It has been remarked often by science-fiction writers themselves that although many of them had imagined the first flight to the moon, none of them had ever thought that the first flight would be watched live on television by a mass world audience. In such cases, the progress of science outstripped even the range of imagination. One result has been the creation of a mass audience sensitized to the idea of unpredictable but nevertheless possible, or plausible, technological change. The modern subgenre of "cyberpunk" could not exist without an audience aware of the progress from vacuum tube to transistor to silicon chip, and from the giant computers of older science fiction, such as John Brunner's *Stand on Zanzibar* (1968), to the personal computers of today, the Internet, and the "hacker culture" that technology instantly if inadvertently created.

Science fiction thus differs from its ancestor forms of the past, such as the "utopia" or the "imaginary voyage," in containing within itself an element of belief, or at any rate something stronger than the "suspended disbelief" of older theories of ordinary fiction. Many, if not most, sciencefiction readers firmly believe that there are alien intelligent races, simply because of what astronomy seems to say about the number of stars and planets in the real universe. It does not follow that one needs to believe that any of these races has contacted humans, and many popular stories of UFOs would be met with some scorn as scientifically implausible.

One might note the way in which intelligent Martians have drifted slowly out of the area of plausibility, or possible belief, as astronomy and space probes have increased knowledge of the planet Mars. Wells's *The War of theWorlds* (1898) drew on the theories of his own time, which saw Mars as an Earth-like but ancient and hence further-evolved planet. Edgar Rice Burroughs's Barsoom series, beginning in 1917 with *A Princess of Mars*, added to that the idea of reduced gravity and hence greater strength and speed for his Earth-born human hero. By the time of Kim Stanley Robinson's Mars trilogy (1992-1996), both these scenarios had become untenable, and the Mars of Robinson's imagination (which is also that of contemporary knowledge) is a different, less populated, but not less fascinating place. Scientific progress once again has ruled out some speculations and at the same time created completely different ones. Although these too may one day be ruled out in their turn, the Mars trilogy, like *The War of the Worlds* or *A Princess of Mars*, will remain science fiction as originally conceived, drawing on a deep well of belief and real knowledge, though such knowledge is always known and admitted to be incomplete.

Science fiction's modern companion genre, fantasy, has been less obviously but no less deeply affected by the triumph of rationalism and the accelerating awareness of science. It might seem that stories about dragons could be much the same in modern times as in the tenth century. Indeed, Smaug, in J. R. R. Tolkien's *The Hobbit* (1937), has an ancestry that stretches back to the Norse Fafnir and the nameless dragon that is the bane of Beowulf in the epic that carries his name, dating from about the eleventh century. Even if the creatures are the same, however, the context of belief in which they are embedded cannot help being different. To put it simply, although people find it much easier now to believe in voyages to Mars, they find it much less easy to believe in the existence of dragons on Earth.

To the audiences of Old Norse or Old English poems, it might not seem at all impossible that dragons existed, perhaps somewhere outside the rather small patch of territory they had explored. The *Anglo-Saxon Chronicle*, a work every bit as historical in its intentions as Herodotus's, and one that remains highly respected by modern historians, nevertheless records the appearance of flying dragons in Northumbria in the year 793 and shows no sign of intending to be "fantastic." The case is quite different now. It is reasonably certain that there are no canals on Mars, but it is 100 percent certain that there are no dragons (as traditionally described) on Earth. The world is too well explored to leave a place for them. In any case, the sheer mechanics of imagining a beast that could breathe fire, somehow insulate its own internal organs, and also find a means of ignition appears impossible. This has not prevented author after author from trying to create a situation in which the impossible dragon of tradition could become possible, whether through Tolkien's device of distancing the creature into a far-past world where all kinds of things appear to be different or Ursula Le Guin's method of creating "a world where magic works," governed, it seems, by a different set of physical laws.

Both Tolkien and Le Guin were well aware that they could not simply bring a dragon into the story and expect the skeptical and well-informed modern reader to accept it as a fact. If one wishes to continue to use the creatures of humanity's oldest fears and imaginings—such as dragons, elves, werewolves, and vampires—these creatures have to be given some kind of explanation, some kind of apparently rational setting. At the very least, the challenge of rationality has to be faced, not ignored. One can say, then, that if science fiction deals with what is known not to be true, but not known to be beyond possibility, fantasy in its modern sense deals with what is known or very generally thought to be impossible. A common method of doing this is to set the tale in a different universe or an alternative reality, as is done in Stephen Donaldson's Chronicles of Thomas Covenant (1977-1983). One should note that this is not the same as setting it on an alien planet within this universe, for in that case the laws of physical causation as understood would still apply. In a different universe, the world and the characters may be ruled by magic, not science, and the problem (as, for example, in L. Sprague de Camp and Fletcher Pratt's Incomplete Enchanter series, 1941-1954) may be for the characters to understand the different logic of magic. Despite the appearance of Norse gods, giants, enchanters, werewolves, and other such beings, de Camp and Pratt's universe does run on logic: It is only the premises of the logic that have changed. Works of this nature demonstrate at once both the urge to escape from the confines of the real and accepted and an inability to let go of the cause-and-effect beliefs so thoroughly part of modern everyday life.

Modern definitions of fantasy accordingly often find difficulty in being both broad enough to take in what is an extremely prolific genre and narrow enough to say anything useful. It is hard to improve on Kathryn Hume's statement, in her book *Fantasy and Mimesis* (1984), that *"Fantasy is any departure from consensus reality*, an impulse native to literature and manifested in innumerable variations." This definition, however, needs to be filled out by a long discussion of the "variations" and leaves open the distinction between ancient examples of the fantastic such as *The Odyssey* and its modern mutations.

To understand the latter point, one needs only to look at some fantasy works. The fantastic is an ancient mode; fantasy (at least as defined by bookstores) is a modern genre. As a result, one often can find pairs or comparisons, with a traditional work of a kind that goes back to antiquity on one hand, and on the other a self-conscious modern version of the same thing. Thus, ghost stories are as old as literature, and no doubt older, but in the nineteenth century M. R. James (a famous classical scholar) still was capable of exploiting the ancient fears from his great depth of learning. Kingsley Amis's *The Green Man* (1969) also is very clearly a ghost story, but one that cannot rely on old assumptions about the afterlife and one whose agnostic hero finds it hard to have any belief in the afterlife at all. Argument about the very nature of ghosts and of religious belief becomes, accordingly, a vital part of Amis's tale.

In a similar way, *Baron Münchausen's Narrative* (1785) represents the old "traveler's tale" or "tall story." These are re-created in Sterling Lanier's Brigadier Ffellowes stories (collected in 1972 and 1986), made plausible not only by their far-off settings but also by the cool and matter-of-fact narrative of the brigadier himself. Both *Dracula* (1897) and *Frankenstein* are rewritten by Brian Aldiss; Kenneth Grahame's animal fable of *The Wind in the Willows* (1908) is reshaped by modern knowledge of ecology and animal behavior in Richard Adams's *Watership Down* (1972); Angela Carter, Tanith Lee, and Jane Yolen have created among them a new genre of modern (and often both feminist and Freudian) fairy tale, related but also ideologically opposed to old tales like those of the Brothers Grimm; the almost contextless romance narratives of William Morris and E. R. Eddison are pulled firmly into shape with maps, calendars, languages, and appendices by Tolkien; traditional ballad is made into realistic narrative by Ellen Kushner's *Thomas the Rhymer* (1990) and Diana Wynne Jones's *Fire and Hemlock* (1985).

In all these cases, one can see a sense of argument, of explanation, one might almost say of discipline, falling on the old genres that once had no need to justify themselves. That sense of discipline parallels the growth of science fiction, as *Unknown* was for a while the partner fantasy magazine to science fiction's *Astounding* (note the implications of the two adjectives), and as joint audience interest created twin-track publications such as *The Magazine of Fantasy and Science Fiction* (still in existence) and *Science Fantasy* (unfortunately extinct).

Modern fantasy authors in particular are often eager to model their work on, to rewrite, or to reply to works of the past in which they see some element of the fantastic. John Gardner's *Grendel* (1971) is a retelling of the Old English epic of Beowulf from the point of view of the monster, not the hero; T. H. White's *The Once and Future King* passionately rehandles the story of Sir Thomas Malory's Middle English romance *Le Morte d'Arthur* (c. 1469); the medieval Welsh anthology of wonder-tales known as *The Mabinogion* provides the basis for Alan Garner's *The Owl Service* (1967) and for several other modern works; and the de Camp and Pratt Incomplete Enchanter series works its way through settings as diverse as the Icelandic *Prose Edda*, the Finnish *Kalevala*, Irish mythology, and English and Italian romantic epic.

The existence of horror stories indirectly raises an interesting question. Why are so many people prepared to write and to read pure fantasy in the modern day, when "consensus reality" is so strong and readers in a way have to be coaxed outside it? The answer, in the case of horror stories, is clear. These stories have an obvious motivation, which is to frighten their readers, duplicating in literary form the controlled fear of, for example, a fairground ride. Science fiction also can justify itself eas- ily, as an "early warning system" or education in possibility. But fantasy? Is it not a kind of nostalgia, a reluctance to let go of old images, perhaps learned and loved in childhood, before the defenses of skepticism were raised?

Arguments against this "escapist" accusation are common and powerful. It has been pointed out that authors as different as J. R. R. Tolkien and C. S. Lewis, Kurt Vonnegut and Ursula Le Guin, and Stephen Donaldson and Gene Wolfe are all clearly addressing through their fantasies (just as much as through their works of science fiction) such grim and vital issues for the twentieth century and beyond as the origins of evil, the nature of war, and the future of the planet—topics that seem to be outside the scope of realistic fiction. It is also possible that "heroic fantasy" in particular—a mode that seemed dead until revived by Tolkien but now perhaps is among the most commercially successful and popular form of writing to be found in America—draws its impetus from deliberate rejection of the prevailingly unheroic, ironic, self-doubting attitudes of much realistic fiction: It is not an escape so much as a defiance. What cannot be denied is the present competitiveness, one might almost say dominance, of the current fantasy/science-fiction field. Hundreds or thousands of titles are published each year in each genre. Some authors—among them Greg Bear, Gregory Benford, David Eddings, and Terry Brooks—figure consistently in best-seller lists. Both science fiction and fantasy have made the transition to film and television, with series as popular as *Star Trek* and *Star Wars*. In a more academic mode, authors such as Angela Carter are recognized subjects of study in universities across the world. Science fiction especially has been an immensely influential vehicle for feminist thought, through authors such as Joanna Russ, Suzy McKee Charnas, Marge Piercy, and James Tiptree, Jr. (the pen name of Alice Sheldon).

Experimental writing is represented by such tours de force as Russell Hoban's *Riddley Walker* (1980). Furthermore, in this situation of commercial success and commercial exploitation, although the line between fantasy and science fiction remains in most cases clear, there is a sense of continuous probing of the boundaries of both forms by several authors, prominent among them Tim Powers, Michael Swanwick, and Gene Wolfe. At the same time, if there is a shift of weight discernible, it is on the whole from science fiction toward fantasy. A number of established "hard science fiction" authors, among them Gordon R. Dickson, Orson Scott Card, and Piers Anthony, have shown themselves ready to move sideways into the writing of fantasy. Commercial considerations likely play a part in this move, but one may well believe that in the same way that science fiction earned public respect and won its way to literary favor through the middle of the twentieth century, so practitioners of fantasy have shown the world what can be done within that genre toward the end of the century, making their case not by argument but by example.

There is a further and final point that may be made about the nature of both modern genres, fantasy and science fiction, and about their joint relationship to the dominating principle of science. This is that there are many disciplines that aspire to the dignity of being scientific. The core disciplines remain, no doubt, physics, chemistry, biology, and mathematics: No one doubts that these, and their modern offshoots or specializations such as genetics and astronomy, are sciences in every sense of the term. At the other extreme, traditional humanities subjects such as history and literary study have ceased, after a sometimes brief flirtation with "scientificity," to make any claims of this nature. There remain what are often described as the "soft sciences," which include sociology, political science, economics, anthropology, and others. It is not often realized how fertile some of these fields have been for creative writers, nor how radically new they may be, developing over much the same relatively short period as the "hard sciences."

Just as one could see an "epistemic break" or major transformation between, say, medieval alchemy and modern chemistry, or medieval astrology and modern astronomy, so there are clear developments from the ancient habits of treasure hunting and grave robbing to systematic archaeology; from dilettante ethnography to modern anthropology; from belletristic philology to the nineteenth century science of comparative philology and through it to computational linguistics; from the antiquarian sketching of stones and monuments to the recovery of hieroglyphs, cuneiform, and the code-breaking ability to read totally lost and forgotten scripts such as Cretan "Linear B." All these "soft sciences" have provided major inspiration for creative writers. The dream of inventing the mathematical hard science of "psychohistory" is at the heart of Isaac Asimov's famous Foundation series.

Ursula K. (for Kroeber) Le Guin is herself the daughter of two of the most prominent American anthropologists of the twentieth century, Alfred and Theodora Kroeber. Tolkien has a fair claim to being one of the most influential ancient philologists of the twentieth century, even disregarding the effect of his fantasies. The power and lure of archaeology (a subject that filled the nineteenth and twentieth centuries with glittering discoveries from Mycenae to Babylon to Ur and Egypt's Valley of the Tombs) have given inspiration to authors as different as H. P. Lovecraft, Gregory Benford, and Larry Niven.

Perhaps the most dramatic development of recent years has been the sudden interest taken in the idea of alternative (or alternate) history, an idea that goes back at least as far as 1931, when the American novelist Winston Churchill wrote his provocatively titled essay "If Lee Had Not Won the Battle of Gettysburg," and that has led to such complex works as Philip K. Dick's *The Man in the High Castle* (1962), Ward Moore's *Bring the Jubilee* (1953), and Kingsley Amis's *The Alteration* (1976). In the late 1990's, more than a dozen well-known authors were working busily in the field, including at least one prominent American politician (Newt Gingrich) and the prolific Harry Turtledove, once a professional historian. Is this particular subgenre fantasy or science fiction?

If one looks at Mark Twain's *A Connecticut Yankee in King Arthur's Court* (1889) or L. Sprague de Camp's *Lest Darkness Fall* (1941), one would probably decide for fantasy: Neither work makes any serious effort to explain how the modern-day heroes find themselves suddenly "back in the past." Both of them, however, and Turtledove's stories as well, show a keen interest in the history of technology that gives them a claim to "not impossible" status. In cases such as these, the distinctions between fantasy and science fiction, between hard and soft sciences, lose their usual force. One may add that such works also are a powerful argument against a kind of ethnocentrism that could be called "chronocentrism," the belief that the way history did happen is the only way it could have happened, that the arrow of time points unerringly and inevitably to the world as it stands.

Both science fiction and fantasy functioned during the twentieth century, and continue to function during the twenty-first, as major explanatory tools that have provided meaning and insight to millions of readers, often about vital issues such as the origins of war and the nature of humanity, and often to readers who have been failed by all older and more traditional forms of writing (such as history and mainstream fiction). They also can be seen as the main indicators of radical shifts of attitude and understanding in the population at large. In the process, they have acted as powerful if unrecognized forces against prejudice and ethnocentrism, and they have served as guides to and recruiters for both hard and soft sciences. It has been acknowledged many times that there would have been no ventures into space, no moon landings or planetary flybys, without the stimulus of decades of space fiction. Both fantasy and science fiction have opened unexplored territories of the imagination.

—*T. A. Shippey*

Complete List of Contents

Volume 1

Publisher's Note xi
Contributors xiii
List of Genres xxi
Introduction xxv
Science Fiction and Fantasy xxix

The Absolute at Large 1
Accelerando 2
Adam and Eve 4
Adventures of Vlad Taltos 5
Aegypt, Love and Sleep, Daemonomania
    and Endless Things 8
Against Infinity 10
Air 12
Aladore 14
Alas, Babylon 15
Alice's Adventures in Wonderland and
    Through the Looking-Glass 16
Alif the Unseen 19
All Hallow's Eve 20
All Times Possible 22
Alraune 23
The Alteration 25
Always Coming Home 26
The Amber Series 28
Amnesia Moon 30
Among Others 31
Analogue Men 33
The Andromeda Strain 35
Animal Farm 36
Anno Dracula 38
The Anthony Villiers Novels 39
The Anubis Gates 41
Ape and Essence 43
Arachne 44

Area X: The Southern Reach Trilogy 46
Arthur Rex 48
The Artificial Kid 50
At the Back of the North Wind 51
At the Mountains of Madness and
    Other Novels 53
The Atlan Series 54
Babel 17 57
Barefoot in the Head 58
Baron Munchausen's Narrative of His
    Marvellous Travels and Campaigns in
    Russia 60
The Barsoom Series 61
Beauty and the Beast and Song of Orpheus 63
Beggars in Spain and Beggars and
    Choosers 65
The Beginning Place 67
A Beleaguered City 69
The Belgariad 70
The Berserker Series 72
The Best of C. M. Kornbluth 74
The Best of Cordwainer Smith 76
The Best Short Stories of J. G. Ballard ... 77
Beyond Apollo 79
Beyond the Aquila Rift 81
Beyond the Golden Stair 82
Big Planet and Showboat World 84
The Big Time 86
The Bill, the Galactic Hero Series 87
The Birthgrave Trilogy 89
The Black Cloud 91
Black Easter and The Day After Judgment 93
Black Empire 95
Black Flame 96
Black No More 98

Title	Page
Black Oxen	99
Black Trillium	101
Black Unicorn and Gold Unicorn	103
Blood Music	105
The Blood of Roses	106
The Blue Hawk	108
The Blue Star	109
The Blue Sword and The Hero and the Crown	111
Bone Dance	113
Bone Forest	114
The Book of the Dun Cow	116
The Book of the New Sun	117
The Book of Wonder	119
Born to Exile and In the Red Lords Reach	121
The Borrowers Series	123
The Boys from Brazil	125
Boy's Life	126
Brain Rose	128
Brain Wave	129
Brasyl	131
Brave New World	133
The Breast	134
Briar Rose	136
The Brick Moon	137
The Bridge	139
The Brigadier Ffellowes Stories	140
Bring the Jubilee	142
Brokedown Palace	144
The Broken Land	145
The Broken Sword	147
Brood of the Witch Queen	148
Brother to Dragons	150
Brute Orbits	151
Bug Jack Barron	153
Burn Witch Burn	154
Burning Chrome	156
The Burning Court	157
Camp Concentration	159
Canopus in Argos	160
A Canticle for Leibowitz	162
Carnacki the Ghost Finder	164
Carrie	165
A Case of Conscience	167
The Castle of Otranto	168
Cat's Cradle	170
The Caves of Steel and The Naked Sun	171
Celestis	173
The Centaur	175
The Child Garden	176
The Childe Cycle	178
Childhood's End	180
Children of the Atom	182
Chimera	183
China Mountain Zhang	185
The Chronicles of Clovis	187
The Chronicles of Narnia	188
The Chronicles of the Deryni	191
The Chronicles of Thomas Covenant the Unbeliever and The Second Chronicles of Thomas Covenant the Unbeliever	193
The Chronicles of Tornor	195
The Chrysalids	197
The Chymical Wedding	199
The Circus of Dr Lao	200
Cities in Flight	202
City	204
The City and the Stars	205
Clarke County, Space	207
The Clockwork Man	208
A Clockwork Orange	210
Cloned Lives	211
The Cloning of Joanna May	213
The Cloud Walker	214
The Collected Ghost Stories of M. R. James	216
The Colossus Trilogy	217
The Coming Race	220
The Conan Series	221

Complete List of Contents

Conjure Wife 223
A Connecticut Yankee in King Arthur's Court 225
The Cornelius Chronicles 226
Counterfeit World 229
The Course of the Heart 230
Crash 232
The Crock of Gold 233
Crown of Stars 234
A Crystal Age 236
Crystal Express 237
The Culture Series 239
The Cyberiad 241
Cyteen 242
Cythera 244
Dagon and Other Macabre Tales 246
The Dancers at the End of Time Series 247
The Dark Elf Trilogy 249
The Dark Is Rising Sequence 251
Dark Universe 253
Darker than You Think 255
Darkover Landfall 256
Davy 258
The Day of the Triffids 259
The Dead Father 261
The Dead Zone 262
A Deal with the Devil 263
The Death of Grass 265
Death Qualified and The Best Defense 267
The Deathworld Trilogy 269
Deerskin 271
The Demolished Man 272
The Demon Princes Series 274
Descent into Hell 276
The Devil Is Dead 277
The Devil Rides Out 279
Devil's Tor 281
Dhalgren 282
The Diamond Age; or, a Young Lady's Illustrated Primer 284

The Difference Engine 285
A Different Flesh 287
A Different Kingdom 288
Dimension of Miracles 290
Dinner at Deviant's Palace 291
Dirk Gently's Holistic Detective Agency and The Long Dark Tea Time of the Soul 293
The Disappearance 295
The Discworld Series 296
The Dispossessed 298
Do Androids Dream of Electric Sheep? 300
Dr. Bloodmoney 301
Doctor Rat 303
Donovan's Brain 304
Doomsday Book 306
A Door into Ocean 307
The Door into Summer 309
Door Number Three 310
Dorothea Dreams 311
Double Star 313
Downbelow Station 314
Downward to the Earth 316
Dracula 317
The Dracula Series 319
Dracula Unbound 320
The Dragon in the Sea 322
The Dragon Knight Series 323
The Dragon Masters 325
The Dragon Waiting 327
The Dragonbone Chair 328
The Dragonriders of Pern 330
Dragonsbane 332
Dream 333
The Dream Master 335
A Dreamer's Tales 336
Dreamsnake 338
Drink Down the Moon 339
The Drowned World 340

The Duncton Chronicles and The Book of Silence	342
The Dune Series	344
The Dunwich Horror and Others	346
Durdane	347
The Dying Earth Series	350
Dying Inside	352
E Pluribus Unicorn	354
Earth	355
Earth Abides	357
Earthfasts	358
The Earth's Children Series	360
Earthsea	362
Earthseed	364
Echoes from the Macabre	365
Eden	367
Edison's Conquest of Mars	368
The Einstein Intersection	370
The Elenium	371
Elidor	374
The Elric Saga	375
The Embedding	377
The Empire of Fear	379
Empire of the East	380
The Enchanted Castle	381
The End of Eternity	383
The Ender Series	384
The Ends of the Earth	387
Engine Summer	388
Eon and Eternity	390
The E. T. Novels	392
Eternal Light	394
Evolution's Darling	395
The Exorcist	397
Eye in the Sky	399
The Face in the Abyss	401
The Face in the Frost	402
Fafhrd and the Gray Mouser	403
Fahrenheit 451	405
Fairyland	407
Falling Free	409
The Falling Woman	411
The Famished Road and Songs of Enchantment	412
Fancies and Goodnights	414
The Fantasy Worlds of Peter Beagle	416
Fantazius Mallare and The Kingdom of Evil	417
Fata Morgana	419
The Fates of the Princes of Dyfed and Book of the Three Dragons	421
Fear and Typewriter in the Sky	423
Fearful Pleasures	424
Feersum Endjinn	426
The Female Man	427
Fevre Dream	429
The Fifth Head of Cerberus	430
Fire and Hemlock	432
A Fire upon the Deep	433
The First Men in the Moon	435
The Fisher King Trilogy	436
The Flandry Series	438
Flow My Tears, the Policeman Said	440
Flowers for Algernon	441
The Forever King	443
The Forever War	444
The Forge of God and Anvil of Stars	446
The Forgotten Beasts of Eld	448
The Foundation Series	449
Fountains of Paradise	451
Frankenstein	453
Frankenstein Unbound	454
From the Earth to the Moon	456
Frontera	458
The Fury	459
Fury	461
The Future Los Angeles Series	462
A Game of Dark	465
The Gap Series	466
The Gate to Women's Country	468

Gene Wolfe's Book of Days 470
The Genesis Machine 471
Ghost Story 473
A Gift from Earth 474
Giles Goat-Boy 476
The Girl the Gold Watch and Everything 477
Gladiator at Law 479
Glass Soup and White Apples 480
The Glimmering 482
Glimpses 484
Glory Road 485
Glory Season 487
The Godhead Trilogy 488
The Gods Themselves 490
Golden Witchbreed 491
The Golem 493
The Golem and The Jinni 494
Good News from Outer Space 496
Gravity's Rainbow 498
Gray Matters 499
The Great God Pan 501
The Great Sky River Trilogy 502
Green Eyes 504
The Green Isle of the Great Deep 505
The Green Man 507
The Green Man 508
Green Mansions 510
Greenmantle 511
Grendel 513
Greybeard 514
Grimus 516
Gulliver's Travels 517
Gunner Cade 519

Half Past Human 521
The Hampdenshire Wonder 523
The Handmaid's Tale 524
Hard to Be a God 526
Hardwired 528
Hasan 529
The Haunting of Hill House 531
The Haunting of Toby Jugg 532
The Heads of Cerberus 533
The Healer's War 535
Heart of a Dog 536
The Heechee Series 538
Heinrich von Ofterdingen 540
Hell House 542
The Helliconia Trilogy 543
Her Smoke Rose Up Forever 545
The Heritage Universe Series 546
Herovit's World 549
The High Crusade 550
High-Rise 552
The Hitchhiker's Guide to the Galaxy
  Series 553
The Hobbit 555
The Holy Ground Trilogy 557
Homunculus and Lord Kelvin's Machine 559
Hothouse 561
The House Next Door 563
The House on the Borderland 564
The House on the Strand 566
A House Boat on the Styx and The
  Pursuit of the House Boat 567
Humour and Fantasy 569
Hyperborea 571
The Hyperion Cantos 572

Volume 2

I Am Legend 575
I Have No Mouth and I Must Scream 576
I Will Fear No Evil 578

Ice 579
The Icewind Dale Trilogy 581
The Illusionist 583

Title	Page
The Illustrated Man	585
Imajica	586
The Immortals	588
Imperial Earth	589
In the Ocean of Night and Across the Sea of Suns	591
In Yana, the Touch of Undying	593
The Incomplete Enchanter	594
The Infernal Desire Machines of Doctor Hoffman	596
The Inheritors	598
The Innkeepers Song	599
The Instrumentality of Mankind	600
Inter Ice Age 4	602
The Invention of Morel	603
Inverted World	605
The Invisible Man	606
The Iron Dragon's Daughter	608
The Iron Heel	609
Island	611
The Island of Doctor Death and Other Stories	612
The Island of Dr. Moreau	614
Islands in the Net	615
Ixion in Heaven	617
Jack of Shadows	619
Jack the Giant Killer	620
The Jagged Orbit	622
The Jaguar Hunter	623
The Jewels of Aptor	625
Jirel of Joiry	626
John the Balladeer	628
The Jonathan Bing Series	629
Jonathan Livingston Seagull	631
Jonathan Strange and Mr Norrell	632
Journey to the Center of the Earth	634
Julian Comstock: a Story of 22nd-Century America	635
Julius Le Vallon and The Bright Messenger	637
The Jungle Books	639
Jurassic Park	641
Kafka on the Shore	642
The Khaavren Romances	645
Khaled	647
Kiln People	648
The King in Yellow	650
The King of Elfland's Daughter	652
The King of the Golden River	653
Kingdoms of Elfin	654
Kwaidan	656
The Labyrinth Key	658
The Lair of the White Worm	659
Lanark	661
Land of Dreams	663
The Land of Laughs	664
The Land of Mist	666
Land of Unreason	667
The Land That Time Forgot	669
Last and First Men	670
The Last Man	671
The Last Starship from Earth	673
The Left Hand of Darkness	674
The Legion of Space	676
The Lensman Series	678
Lest Darkness Fall	680
Level 7	682
The Life and Opinions of Kater Murr	683
Life During Wartime	685
The Light Ages	686
The Lights in the Sky Are Stars	688
Lilith	689
Limbo	691
Lincoln's Dreams	692
The Listeners	694
Little, Big	695
The Little Country	697
The Little Prince	698
Logan's Run	699
The Long Loud Silence	701
The Long Tomorrow	702
The Long Walk	704

Title	Page
Looking Backward	705
Lord Darcy	707
Lord of Light	709
Lord of the Flies	710
The Lord of the Rings	712
Lost Horizon	714
The Lost Traveller	715
The Lost World	717
Love in the Ruins and The Thanatos Syndrome	718
The Lovers	721
Lud-in-the-Mist	722
Lumen	724
The Lyonesse Trilogy	725
Lythande	727
The Mabinogion Tetralogy	730
Macrolife	732
Macroscope	733
The Magic Series	735
Make Room! Make Room!	737
The Malacia Tapestry	738
The Malloreon	740
The Man in the High Castle	742
Man Plus	744
The Man who Awoke	745
The Man Who Folded Himself	747
The Man Who Was Thursday	748
Many Dimensions	750
The Mars Trilogy	751
The Martian Chronicles	753
Martian Time-Slip	755
The Mask of Circe	757
The Master and Margarita	758
The Master Li Series	760
The M.D.	762
Melmoth the Wanderer	763
Melusine	765
Memoirs of a Spacewoman	766
Merlin	768
The Merlin Trilogy	769
Merlin's Godson and Merlin's Ring	771
Merlin's Wood	773
The Merman's Children	775
Metropolis	776
Midas World	778
The Midwich Cuckoos	779
The Mightiest Machine	781
Millennium	782
The Mind Parasites	784
Mindbridge	785
Mindswap	787
The Minotaur Trilogy	788
The Mirage	790
The Mirror	792
A Mirror for Observers	794
Mission of Gravity and Star Light	795
Mr. George and Other Odd Persons	797
Mistress Mashams Repose	798
The Mists of Avalon	800
Mockingbird	801
Moderan	802
The Monk	804
Monk's Magic	805
The Moon Is a Harsh Mistress	807
The Moon Is Hell!	808
Moon of Three Rings	810
The Moon Pool	811
Moonheart	813
More than Human	814
The Mortgage on the Brain	816
The Mote in God's Eye and The Gripping Hand	817
The Motherlines Series	819
The Mount	821
Moving Mars	823
Mutant	824
The Mythago Cycle	826
Naked Lunch	829
The Napoleon of Notting Hill	830
The Narrative of Arthur Gordon Pym	832

Title	Page
Necroville	833
Nerves	835
The Neuromancer Trilogy	836
Nifft the Lean	838
The Night Land	840
The Night Mayor	841
Nightfall	843
Nightflyers	845
Nightmare Journey	846
Nights at the Circus	847
Nightwings	849
Nineteen Eighty-Four	850
The Nitrogen Fix	852
No Enemy but Time	853
Non-Stop	855
Norstrilia	856
Nova	858
Nova Express	859
Nova Swing	861
The Novarian Series	863
The Null A Trilogy	865
Oath of Fealty	868
The October Country	869
Odd John	871
Of Men and Monsters	872
Ole Doc Methuselah	873
Omega: The Last Days of the World	875
On Stranger Tides	877
On the Beach	878
On Wings of Song	880
The Once and Future King	881
Only Begotten Daughter	883
Operation Chaos	884
The Ophiuchi Hotline	886
The Orange County Trilogy	887
Orbital Decay	890
Orbitsville	891
Orlando	893
The Other	894
Other Days, Other Eyes	896
The Other Passenger	897
The Other Side of the Mountain	898
Other Worlds	900
Our Lady of Darkness	902
The Owl Service	904
The Paper Grail	906
The Paper Menagerie and Other Stories	907
The Paradox Men	909
The Parasite	911
The Passion of New Eve	912
The Past Through Tomorrow	913
The Patternist Series	915
Patterns	917
Pavane	918
Perdido Street Station	920
Peregrine: Primus and Peregrine: Secundus	922
Perfume	923
Permutation City	925
Pet Sematary	926
Peter Schlemihl	928
Phantasmion	929
Phantastes	931
The Phantom Ship	932
The Phoenix and the Mirror	934
Picnic on Paradise	935
The Picture of Dorian Gray	937
Pilgrimage and The People	938
Planet of Adventure	940
Planet of the Apes	943
Player Piano	944
The Polesotechnic League Series	946
Portrait of Jennie	948
The Postman	949
The Prestige	951
The Princess and the Goblin and The Princess and Curdie	952
The Princess Bride	954
Proteus Manifest	956
The Prydain Chronicles	958
The Psammead Trilogy	960

The Puppet Masters	962
The Purple Cloud	963
Radiance	966
Ralph 124C 41+	967
The Rama Series	969
Rashomon and Other Stories	971
Rats and Gargoyles and The Architecture of Desire	973
Red Dust	975
The Red Tree	976
A Rendezvous in Averoigne	978
Replay	979
The Restoration Game	981
The Return	982
The Revolt of the Angels	984
Riddle of Stars	985
Riddley Walker	987
The Riftwar Saga	989
Ring Around the Sun	991
Ringworld and The Ringworld Engineers	993
Rite of Passage	995
The Riverworld Series	996
The Roads of Heaven	998
The Robot Stories	1000
The Robots of Dawn and Robots and Empire	1002
Roderick and Roderick at Random	1004
Rogue Moon	1006
The Roots of the Mountains	1007
The Rose	1009
The Rose and the Ring	1010
Rosemary's Baby	1012
R.U.R.	1013
The Saga of Pliocene Exile	1016
Salem's Lot	1018
Salt	1019
Sandkings	1021
Sarah Canary	1022
The Sardonyx Net	1023
The Satanist	1025
The Scarecrows	1026
Schismatrix	1028
The Scholars of Night	1029
The Science Fiction of Mark Twain	1031

Volume 3

The Seedling Stars	1033
Seeklight	1034
The Shadow Year	1035
Shadows in the Sun	1037
Shardik	1038
This Shared Dream	1040
Shatterday	1041
She and Ayesha	1043
The Shining	1045
The Ship of Ishtar	1046
The Ship Who Sang	1048
The Shockwave Rider	1049
The Shrinking Man	1051
The Silmarillion	1052
Silverlock and The Moon's Fire Eating Daughter	1054
Silver Screen	1056
Sinister Barrier	1058
The Sirens of Titan	1059
Sirius	1061
Slan	1062
Slaughterhouse-Five	1064
Slaves of Sleep	1066
The Snail on the Slope	1067
Snow Crash	1069
The Snow Queen Trilogy	1070
So Love Returns	1072
Solaris	1073

Title	Page
Soldier of the Mist and Soldier of Arete	1075
Something Wicked This Way Comes	1077
Song of Kali	1079
Songs of Earth and Power	1080
The Sorcerer's Ship	1082
Sorcerer's Son and The Crystal Palace	1084
The Sorcery Hall Trilogy	1086
The Sound of His Horn	1088
The Space Merchants and The Merchants' War	1090
The Space Odyssey Series	1092
The Space Trilogy	1094
The Spiral Series	1096
The Stainless Steel Rat Series	1098
The Stand	1101
Stand on Zanzibar	1102
Star Maker	1104
Star Man's Son, 2250 A.D.	1105
Starplex	1107
The Star Trek Series	1108
The Star Wars Trilogy	1111
Stars in My Pocket Like Grains of Sand	1113
The Stars My Destination	1114
Starship Troopers	1116
Stations of the Tide	1117
Steel Beach	1119
The Stepford Wives	1120
Steppenwolf	1122
The Strange Case of Dr. Jekyll and Mr. Hyde	1123
Strange Relations	1125
Stranger in a Strange Land	1126
The Stress of Her Regard	1128
A String in the Harp	1129
The Sundering Flood	1131
The Sword Of Shannara Trilogy And The Heritage Of Shannara	1132
Sword and Sorceress	1134
The Sword of Rhiannon	1137
Sword of the Demon	1138
Swordspoint	1140
Synners	1141
The Synthetic Man	1143
Take Back Plenty	1145
Tales from the Flat Earth	1146
The Tales of Alvin Maker	1148
Tales of Horror and the Supernatural	1150
Tales of Known Space	1152
Tales of Nevèrÿon	1153
Tau Zero	1155
Tehanu	1156
There Are Doors	1158
These Mortals	1159
They'd Rather Be Right	1161
The 13 Clocks	1162
This Immortal	1164
This Is the Way the World Ends	1165
Thomas the Rhymer	1167
The Three Damosels	1168
Three Hainish Novels	1170
Three Hearts and Three Lions	1172
334	1173
The Three Stigmata of Palmer Eldritch	1175
Tigerman	1176
Till We Have Faces	1178
Time and Again and From Time to Time	1180
Time Enough for Love	1182
The Time Machine	1183
A Time of Changes	1185
The Time Patrol Series	1186
Timescape	1188
The Titus Groan Trilogy	1190
To the Devil—A Daughter	1192
The Tom Swift Series	1194
A Touch of Sturgeon	1196
Tower of Glass	1197
Toxicology	1199
The Transmigration of Timothy Archer	1201
The Traveler in Black	1202
Trilby	1204

Complete List of Contents

Triton	1205
The Tritonian Ring	1206
Trouble and Her Friends	1208
Tuf Voyaging	1209
Twenty Thousand Leagues Under the Sea	1211
The Twilight of the Gods and Other Tales	1212
2018 A.D.: Or, The King Kong Blues	1214
Ubik	1216
The Unconquered Country	1217
Undine	1219
The Universal Baseball Association, Inc., J. Henry Waugh, Prop.	1220
The Unlimited Dream Company	1222
The Uplift Sequence	1223
Uprooted	1226
Upsidonia	1227
Vacuum Diagrams	1230
Vacuum Flowers	1231
VALIS	1233
Vampire Chronicles	1234
The Vampire Tapestry	1237
The Vampires of Alfama	1238
Varney the Vampyre	1240
Vathek	1241
The Venetian Glass Nephew	1243
Venus Plus X	1244
The Viagens/Krishna Series	1246
The Viriconium Sequence	1248
Virtual Light	1250
Volkhavaar	1252
The Vorkosigan Series	1253
The Voyage of the Space Beagle	1255
A Voyage to Arcturus	1257
Wagner and the Wehr-Wolf	1259
Waldo and Magic, Inc.	1260
The Wanderer	1262
Wandering Ghosts	1263
The War Against Chaos	1265
War for the Oaks	1267
War in Heaven	1268
The War of Don Emmanuel's Nether Parts	1270
The War of the Worlds	1271
War with the Newts	1272
The Ware Tetralogy	1274
The Wasp Factory	1276
Watch the North Wind Rise	1278
Watchers	1279
The Water-Babies	1281
Watership Down	1282
Way Station	1284
The Way to Babylon	1285
We	1287
Weaveworld	1288
The Weigher of Souls	1289
The Weirdstone of Brisingamen and The Moon of Gomrath	1291
The Well at the World's End	1293
The Well of the Unicorn	1294
Werenight and Prince of the North	1296
The Werewolf of Paris	1298
The West of Eden Trilogy	1299
What Dreams May Come	1302
The Wheel of Time Series	1303
When Gravity Fails	1305
When Harlie Was One	1307
When the Birds Fly South	1308
When the Sleeper Wakes	1310
When Worlds Collide and After Worlds Collide	1311
Where Late the Sweet Birds Sang	1313
Where The Blue Begins	1315
The White Abacus	1316
The White Deer	1318
The White Hotel	1319
Who?	1321
Wieland	1322
The Wind Eye	1324
The Wind in the Willows	1325

Title	Page
The Windrose Chronicles	1327
The Windsinger Series	1329
The Windup Girl	1331
The Wine of Violence	1333
The Winter of the World Trilogy	1334
The Witch of Prague	1336
Witch World	1338
The Witches of Karres	1339
The Witching Hour	1341
Wizard World	1342
The Wolf-Leader	1344
Wolfbane	1346
The Wolfen	1347
Woman on the Edge of Time	1349
The Wonderful Wizard of Oz	1350
The Wood Beyond the World	1352
The Word for World Is Forest	1353
The World of Tiers	1355
The World's Desire	1357
The Worlds Trilogy	1358
The Worm Ouroboros	1360
A Wrinkle in Time	1362
The Xanth Series	1364
Xélucha and Others	1366
Xenogenesis	1368
The Year of the Quiet Sun	1370
The Years of the City	1371
The Yiddish Policemen's Union	1373
You Shall Know Them	1375
You're All Alone	1377
Ysabel	1378
Zoo City	1380
Zothique	1381
Zotz!	1383
Selected Science-Fiction and Fantasy Awards	1385
Timeline	1396
Bibliography	1399
Science Fiction and Fantasy Websites	1426
Title Index	1429
Author Index	1451
Genre Index	1469

CRITICAL SURVEY OF SCIENCE FICTION & FANTASY LITERATURE

Third Edition

The Absolute at Large

The unleashing of nuclear power leads to merciless religious wars on a global scale, each sect identifying the new power as justification for its dogmas

Author: Karel Čapek (1890-1938)
Genre: Science fiction—extrapolatory
Type of work: Novel
Time of work: 1943-1953
Locale: Primarily Czechoslovakia
First published: *Továrna na absolutno* (1922; English translation, 1927)

The Story

Karel Čapek published *The Absolute at Large* at the beginning of his career, showing early his fascination with futurology. The interest manifested itself in several other works. The story concerns a young Czech engineer, Rudolph Marek, who invents a machine called the Karburator, which uses atomic energy without any residue, which he calls the Absolute. A manufacturer, G. H. Bondy, inspects the machine and is overcome by a strange euphoria resembling that of religious ecstasy. This absolute, godlike power of the machine made the inventor anxious to sell it. Whatever it is—an intoxicating, stimulating gas developed by the process of complete combustion, a form of X ray, or some hitherto unknown power—it affects everyone coming in contact with it and transports them into religious ecstasy. Concerned only with profit and seeing in the Karburator the realization of a centuries-old dream of a cheap, pure source of energy, Bondy buys the machine and sells it worldwide.

After Karburators have been installed throughout the world, their impact becomes evident. Because they enhance religious fervor, people love one another more, factory owners become philanthropists, and religious fanaticism increases everywhere. These developments are offset by opposite effects. Workers protest insane overproduction, the loss of jobs as the machines take over, and the depletion of raw materials. Unnecessary work is undertaken because the machines demand work. Church authorities worry that the "new god" may replace them. Moreover, the Karburators may result in a loss of control, as in the case of the workers on a dredge who are transformed into religious zealots and the riders on a merry-go-round who suddenly sense that they are embarking on a flight into an unknown land.

More important, various religious groups identify with the Absolute and use it as a proof that only their dogmas are correct. This leads to rivalry among them and ultimately to full-scale skirmishes. The entire planet becomes engulfed in a war of all against all. The widespread religious war results in tremendous damage and bodily harm. Not only are the two main religions—Protestants and Catholics—at war; so are other religions as well as nationalities. The Chinese fight in Czechoslovakia, Russian Cossacks in the Sahara, Macedonians and Senegalese in Finland, and the French in Tibet. African blacks fight Mongolians in Europe while North America is invaded by Japan. This so-called "Greatest War" lasts from February, 1944, to the fall of 1953. Only thirteen people survive a war that engages 198 million participants.

Years later, several survivors get together and argue about the war, bemoaning the lack of tolerance. Bondy, who along with Marek started it all, finds refuge on a Pacific island. He concludes succinctly that every nation insists on its own absolute truth and each person thinks he or she has the whole of God; when others claim the same, they have to be killed so that God and truth can belong only to one person, or group, or nation.

Analysis

Čapek started his literary career by writing short stories in a pessimistic vein. He would later soften his pessimism and write with humor, even cheerfulness, yet he was always drawn to the dark secrets of human nature. In *The Absolute at Large*, he tried to illuminate some of those secrets on a cosmic scale. Although he often wrote to entertain, he combined entertainment with a warning against the negative impulses of human behavior. In doing so, he was often philosophical in his approach, in the tradition of liberal humanism of European intellectuals between the two world wars.

The Absolute at Large is a satire not only on human mores but also on some of the most pressing dilemmas of the twentieth century. The most obvious satire is on the common belief in steady progress brought on by scientific achievements such as atomic energy. The novel reflects somewhat skeptically on the beneficial effects of the splitting of the atom, treating it as an example of the "genie out of the bottle" syndrome. Instead of bringing only benefits, it creates problems such as how to control the unleashed energy, overproduction, alienation, and ultimately war. Although Čapek did not foresee the horrors of nuclear bombs (he would do that in a 1924 novel, *Krakatit*), he predicted the divisions, enmity, and war among various nations. To be sure, the wars in *The Absolute at Large* are based on religious differences and intolerance dating back thousands of years, but the discovery of atomic energy increased the ferocity of the divisions.

The religious wars serve Čapek only as a pretext for lashing out at fanaticism of any kind. Čapek speaks as a true humanist immediately after World War I, having witnessed a catastrophe involving many nations and causing almost as much suffering as the fictitious wars of his novel. The novel appeared on the eve of the rise of totalitarian systems in Italy and Germany that gave rise to as much intolerance as in *The Absolute at Large*. By musing that if annihilating conflicts can happen in the realm of religion, Čapek warns of dangers in other areas.

Because of its societal and semiphilosophical overtones, the novel is not science fiction in the classical sense. Čapek uses the framework of the genre to hint at, and warn of, possibilities for the future. Although not everything from the novel has come true, Čapek did predict important happenings: the power of the atom, often difficult to control; another world conflagration; and warfare fanned by religious intolerance. In this sense, the novel is a moral story, a parable, a satire, and a fictionalized philosophical essay, with enough science-fiction traits to make it a potential vision of the future.

—*Vasa D. Mihailovich*

Accelerando

A series of nine stories follows the adventures of a family in a post-singularity future in which artificial intelligences are sentient, humans are able to upload their personalities into data networks, and initial contact is made with an alien civilization

Author: Charles Stross (1964–)
Genre: Science Fiction—singularity
Type of Work: Novel
Time of Work: Future
Location: Earth & Outer Space
First published: 2005

The Story

Manfred Macx is an entrepreneur in a future that has seen a breakdown of the traditional capitalistic models. Artificial intelligences have become self-aware, and the borders between government and commerce are more blurred than ever. The interface between humans and their computers is even murkier. Manfred believes that human society is in the process of change so rapid that the supposed current problems—national debt, underemployment, etc.—are transitory and unimportant. Although he has initiated many profitable ventures and holds numerous patents, he donates all of the proceeds to nonprofits and other entities, to the chagrin of the IRS. He sees his role as making life better for other people.

In the first episode, Manfred is contacted by an artificial intelligence generated by the nervous systems of lobsters who have been uploaded into a Russian network and who want to defect. He arranges for them to become the "crew" of a deep-space exploratory vessel. The story jumps forward a few years. Manfred is facing a messy divorce and myriad lawsuits for copyright infringement and other activities. He is actively pursuing a strategy to protect the rights of uploaded personalities because he anticipates that humans will soon acquire a kind of immortality by digitizing themselves. At the end of the first set of three episodes, Manfred has been mugged and has lost his memory, while the lobster intelligences have thrived and proliferated in space.

Radio contact with alien intelligences has been established. Manfred's brief marriage has resulted in a daughter, Amber, who eventually uploads herself into the data stream and, in that form, goes off to explore the stars. As part of the virtual crew of a space vessel, she makes contact with an alien race, but rather than the super-intelligent and altruistic species speculated about early in the cycle, these aliens turn out to be essentially human-style confidence tricksters who victimize the races they encounter. The explorers encounter another virtual civilization, which has been parasitized by various intelligences and are briefly trapped there.

Since Amber is essentially a datafile, there can be multiple versions of her, and when she returns to Earth, she encounters the son of one of an alternate version of herself. The two of them are caught up in the battle caused in part by her parents' varying opinions about the optimal form of human society. The final third of the novel describes the emergence of a kind of group consciousness encompassing all of the human beings in the solar system, along with the dismantling of most of its planets, but while this may be viewed as a positive result given the many benefits described in the earlier installments, Manfred and his family begin to have second thoughts about surrendering their individuality and finally decide to leave the solar system rather than be incorporated into the evolving meta-mind. They further explore the alien matrix, which Amber encountered during her earlier adventures.

ANALYSIS
This novel originally appeared as a series of nine short stories—five of which were nominated for one or more awards—so it is necessarily episodic, although arguably its effect is greater when read as a single narrative spanning generations than as a series of snapshots. It is set in a post-singularity future, that is, following a point in time where technological change has had a fundamental impact on human society and psychology, and artificial intelligence have reached the point where artificial minds will exceed human intelligence. Stross employs neologisms to create the atmosphere of a radically changed future and introduces a large number of unusual concepts, many of them never explained, which can sometimes be bewildering. There are throwaway concepts introduced just for atmosphere, without ever being explained, and even human motivations are often unclear and seemingly irrational. The text is so information-rich that, at times, it requires close attention to be comprehended.

There are strong elements of satire throughout, despite the superficially serious subplots. Individuals and agencies act in exaggerated ways, sometimes with humorous consequences. Not all of it is frivolous, however. The story makes valid arguments about the desirability of removing the concept of money from human society, which would theoretically eliminate many of the distinctions between rich and poor. The author's focus on economic concerns, particularly in the first half of the book, is quite unusual in the genre. He raises more questions than he answers, however. For example, while the copied personalities are functionally identical, Stross largely ignores the issue of continuity of consciousness. Some of his speculative side trips contain enough ideas for an entire shelf of new books.

Stross employs the present tense throughout. This technique is often used as a method of suggesting immediacy and volatility to a story, sometimes at the expense of revealing too much of the author's presence and thereby making it more difficult for the reader to become immersed in the narrative. Stross handles this tightrope-walking act with more skill than most of his peers. The text is also interspersed with infodumps in the form of news-feed summaries, whose details provide context rather than advance the plot. The complexity of the actual story lines is disguised somewhat by the density of peripheral material. Events that may seem trivial in the early segments are eventually revealed to have great importance later in the series.

The novel is something of a throwback despite its cutting-edge technological speculation because there is little room left for character development, which is typical of earlier science fiction. Similarly, we only see the immediate environment of a few exceptional characters. There is little sense of how the world in general functions. Amber is reasonably well drawn, but Manfred, his wife, and the subsidiary characters are more archetypes than real people. Despite these apparent literary shortcomings, the novel is rich in speculation and inventive in its construction of a future that has changed so dramatically that the very nature of humanity must adapt.

—Don D'Ammassa

ADAM AND EVE

Dialogue, domestic scenes, and another woman combine to reduce Adam and Eve's status from that of biblical icons to that of an average couple

Author: John Erskine (1879–1951)
Genre: Fantasy—alternate history
Type of work: Novel
Time of work: The origin of humankind
Locale: Paradise
First published: 1927

THE STORY

The novel's action is limited to the characters' observation of the flora, fauna, and elements that surround them. The plot focuses on the characters' gradual appreciation of the cause-and-effect relationships inherent among all natural phenomena. The main theme is the conflict between carnal and spiritual love, which John Erskine dramatizes by involving the biblical couple in a romantic triangle with the provocative Lilith. Adam's attention vacillates between the sensual Lilith and the more mystical Eve.

In the novel's first of five parts, Adam encounters various animals, including a dog that helps to lighten the tone of this philosophical novel. Adam also observes the beauty of nature and meets Lilith. In part 2, Adam and Lilith milk a cow and learn how to kiss. Part 3 begins with Adam's realization that he has invented love. Adam and Lilith go swimming, and Adam discovers that love alters the physical senses.

The cow bears a calf at about the time Eve appears in the novel. In the same way that part 2 had ended with Adam kissing Lilith, Adam kisses Eve at the end of part 3, and she slaps him in response. In part 4, Lilith assumes the form of a serpent and offers Adam and Eve the forbidden fruit. Adam builds a wall around the garden and teaches Eve to swim. By the end of part 4, Adam has become confused about whether he is happier with Lilith or with Eve.

In part 5, Eve begins to wear clothes for modesty and learns to cook with fire. She becomes pregnant and bears a son. The novel concludes with Adam resolving to teach his son so he will not repeat his father's mistakes. Adam's experiences have taught him that intelligence is fundamental to happiness.

ANALYSIS

Much of the plot of *Adam and Eve* is consumed with Adam's Hamlet-like indecisiveness as he weighs the choice between Lilith and Eve. Despite Erskine's assertion in the novel that actual experience is more important than mere discussion of experience, a large portion of the novel consists of seemingly aimless conversations. Many of these dialogues are characterized by circular logic, as the earth's first inhabitants debate ultimate causes.

As the title suggests, *Adam and Eve* is about the beginning of history. More precisely, the novel is Erskine's attempt to rewrite history by supplementing the biblical story of Adam and Eve. This concept of rewriting history was popular among novelists after World War I, an event that represented the end of history, if not in fact, at least in metaphor.

The revision of the book of Genesis in *Adam and Eve* is also a testament to the influence of pragmatism, the philosophy made popular at the turn of the century by William James, a Harvard professor. When Erskine compiled his "Outline of

Readings in Important Books," a list of books to be read by undergraduates at Columbia University, William James was one of the approximately fifty authors included. Erskine clearly considered pragmatism to be a fundamental concept.

Pragmatism is the antithesis of Platonic idealism. Plato suggests that everything on Earth is a shadow of a cosmic ideal, whereas pragmatism holds that there is no ideal because the truth is constantly changing. The only way to stop the truth from changing is to stop time.

It is impossible to stop time in realistic terms, but many writers in the early twentieth century found that one could reverse time in artistic terms by rewriting myths, legends, and the Scriptures. For example, in the years immediately prior to publication of *Adam and Eve*, James Joyce updated Homer's epic as the novel *Ulysses* (1922) and Ernest Hemingway chose a biblical quote from Ecclesiastes as the title for *The Sun Also Rises* (1926), a novel about the social and psychological consequences of World War I. Erskine himself wrote *The Private Life of Helen of Troy* (1925) and *Galahad* (1926), revisions of Greek mythology and Arthurian legend, respectively.

Pragmatism also stresses the importance of experience to the acquisition of knowledge, a phenomenon that is dramatized repeatedly in *Adam and Eve*. In fact, the novel's plot is so rudimentary that it is indefensible unless the reader recognizes that, in narrating such apparently trivial events as the first drink of water and the first kiss, Erskine is illustrating the pragmatist tenet that sensory experience is the source of knowledge. The characters frequently discuss the significance of experience, concluding that actual experience is more important than talking about it.

Besides serving as an exposition of pragmatism, *Adam and Eve* pays homage to several other artistic and philosophical trends of the day. The novel was published two years after the Scopes trial of 1925, which focused on the teaching of evolution in schools. Erskine acknowledges evolution by comparing the novel's characters to animals, albeit humorously, as when he compares the pregnant Eve to a cow. The 1920's were also characterized by a sexual revolution that was best personified by the flappers of F. Scott Fitzgerald's writings. Erskine adapts the Bible to the Jazz Age by involving Adam and Eve in a love triangle with the wily Lilith.

Modernist writers of the time also liked to compare life to art, and Erskine's characters in *Adam and Eve* state at various times that life is a tragedy. Erskine's extensive use of dialogue may have been inspired by the classical Greek model but may also represent Erskine's response to interior monologue and stream of consciousness, techniques that William Faulkner, James Joyce, and Virginia Woolf were pioneering in the 1920's.

—*Douglas Edward LaPrade*

Adventures of Vlad Taltos

A wisecracking professional assassin carves out a profitable business in the dangerous underworld of the Dragaeran Empire, despite the fact that he is a human and thus an outsider

Author: Steven Brust (1955–)
Genre: Fantasy—magical world
Type of work: Novels
Time of work: Undefined
Locale: Primarily the city of Adrilankha, of the Dragaeran Empire
First published: *Jhereg* (1983), *Yendi* (1984), *Teckla* (1987), *Taltos* (1988), *Phoenix* (1990), *Athyra* (1993), *Orca* (1996), *Dragon* (1998), *Issola* (2001), *Dzur* (2006), *Jhegaala* (2008), *Iorich* (2010), *Tiassa* (2011), and *Hawk* (2014)

The Story

The series centers on a wisecracking professional assassin, who is an Easterner—or human—living among a race of beings called Dragaerans. The Dragaerans are humanoid creatures who stand seven to eight feet tall and have a life span of between two thousand and three thousand years. Their empire is built on a class system: Every member belongs to one of seventeen houses, each named for a native creature of that world. Easterners are a much-despised minority. In an effort to assimilate, Vlad's father squandered his life savings on a baronetcy in one of the lower-status houses.

Vlad, who early on became accustomed to the dangers of urban street life, has risen through the ranks of House Jhereg, a criminal organization, to control the gambling and other illegal activities of a small section of the city of Adrilankha. Reflecting the danger of his chosen career, he never leaves home without an arsenal of weapons concealed on his person. One of Vlad's favorite mottoes is "No matter how subtle the wizard, a knife between the shoulder blades will seriously cramp his style."

Vlad also knows some sorcery and witchcraft. He travels with a familiar, a wisecracking jhereg named Loiosh with whom he communicates "psionically," or psychically. A jhereg is a small, poisonous, winged, lizardlike creature. Loiosh often perches on Vlad's shoulder. Loiosh has a humanlike intelligence and stays ever on the lookout for danger, which always seems to be near.

Vlad is married to a fellow Easterner named Cawti. She is also a professional assassin and is known as the Dagger of the Jhereg. Vlad and Cawti met when she was hired to kill him—and succeeded in her task. As Vlad aptly put it, "Some couples fall in love and end up trying to kill each other. We'd done it the other way around." In this world of sorcery and witchcraft, however, death may or may not be permanent. Fortunately, Vlad was revivifiable. The possibility of revivification depends on the manner in which one dies. Even if death is permanent, one's soul may survive to go on to the afterlife, if it is not destroyed by a magical "Morganti" weapon.

The first book in the series, *Jhereg*, introduces Vlad Taltos, his profession, and his world. It centers on his being hired by the Demon, one of five members of the council of House Jhereg, to kill another member of the council, Mellar, who has absconded with council funds. Mellar, however, is no simple thief: He has set in motion a complicated and diabolical revenge plot that Vlad must foil. The next book in the series, *Yendi*, is a prequel to *Jhereg*. *Yendi* relates the story of Vlad and Cawti's first meeting, when she assassinated him and he was revivified, and how they later teamed with two lords of the House of the Dragon, Morrolan and Morrolan's cousin Aliera, to defeat an enemy of Vlad.

The third book, *Teckla*, picks up where *Jhereg* left off. Cawti joins a revolutionary band of Easterners and Teckla—the peasant class of Dragaerans—whose goal is to overthrow the oppressive Dragaeran Empire. Vlad is opposed to the revolt and does everything in his power to extricate his wife from this group, to the detriment of his marriage. The fourth book, *Taltos*, is chronologically the first. It relates Vlad's early life, how he met and befriended the reticent Lord Morrolan, and how they came to walk the Paths of the Dead. The fifth book, *Phoenix*, follows *Teckla* chronologically. Vlad and Cawti are still suffering from marital problems, as Cawti has become more deeply involved with the band of rebels. His marital problems prompt Vlad to question his life and the direction it has taken. In the end, events conspire to force Vlad into a self-imposed exile.

The sixth book in the series, *Athyra*, differs markedly in style and tone from the previous five. Rather than using Vlad as protagonist, Steven Brust chooses a young Dragaeran peasant named Savn. Set several years after the events in *Phoenix*, this novel centers on Savn and the rural village of Smallcliff, where he lives with his parents and his sister, Polyi. When Vlad appears in Smallcliff, Savn befriends the stranger. Unfortunately for Savn, Vlad's dangerous past catches up with him, forcing Savn to defy his parents and ultimately to commit murder.

Having pretty well defined the remit of his series in the first six volumes, Brust would offer charming recombinations and extensions of his anti-hero's biography, much in the manner of Fritz Leiber's Fafhrd and Gray Mouser saga, along with some surprises and fulfillments. In *Orca* (1996), Vlad undertakes the investigation of some financial skullduggery. *Dragon* finds Vlad embarked on a military expedition. At the behest of a friend Vlad engages in a strange missing-person quest in *Issola*. The tenth volume, *Dzur*, features the reappearance of Vlad's ex-wife Cawti, as well as introducing several new important personages. Severely hurt during the actions narrated in *Jhegaala*, Vlad nonetheless manages to undermine an unjust social order in a remote town. The arrest of a bosom companion, Aliera, motivates the plot of *Iorich*. An experiment in shifting chronologies and narrators enlivens the caper-style action of *Tiassa*. And the internal timeline of these books charts its furthest point to date in *Hawk* (2014), where we see Vlad in the uncommon role of father.

ANALYSIS

Jhereg, Brust's first published novel, evolved from a tabletop fantasy role-playing game the author played with a group of friends. Perhaps indicative of the series' origins, the book was criticized by reviewers as an unexceptional "sword and sorcery" story with an obnoxious young punk as its protagonist. Vlad Taltos, a cynical assassin, is not the most sympathetic of protagonists. His profession makes for a bloody series of stories, not to mention a narrow worldview.

Although Brust's first attempts at fiction subscribed to the "hack and slash" school of fantasy writing, he began to experiment with tone and style in subsequent novels. One reviewer noted Brust's skillful handling of a triple first-person viewpoint (Vlad's present, immediate past, and distant past) in the fourth book of the series, *Taltos*. In the sixth book, Brust abandoned Vlad as narrator, opting to tell the tale through the eyes of an intelligent but naïve young Dragaeran peasant. This change in point of view led to a greatly diminished emphasis on bloodletting.

Brust went on to publish other books in the science fiction/fantasy genre, including *To Reign in Hell* (1984), *Brokedown Palace* (1986), *Cowboy Feng's Space Bar and Grille* (1990), *The Phoenix Guards* (1991), and *Five Hundred Years After* (1994). *The Phoenix Guards* and *Five Hundred Years After* (known collectively as the Khaavren Romances) are set in the same world as the Vlad Taltos series, with the first book taking place a thousand years before Vlad's birth. Brust also published a book in editor Terri Windling's Fairy Tale Series published by Ace Books, titled *The Sun, the Moon, and the Stars* (1987). This novel, based on a folktale from Brust's Hungarian heritage, marks a departure from the traditional science fiction/fantasy genre.

In his books, Brust acknowledges the help of fellow science fiction/fantasy writers such as Emma Bull, Pamela Dean, and Will Shetterly, all members of a writing group based in Minneapolis, Minnesota. He also greatly admired fellow fantasy writer Roger Zelazny, who provided glowing endorsements for the covers of several of Brust's books. Some of the structure of the Vlad Taltos series is reminiscent of Zelazny's celebrated Amber fantasy-adventure series.

Fantasy as a genre has been defined as imaginative fiction centering on strange settings and characters. It is devoted to making the impossible appear possible or real, and it often draws on folktales and legends. The Vlad Taltos series embodies these notions, with its peasants and nobles, its sorcery and witchcraft, and its medieval castles, dress, and weaponry, combined with a contemporary sense of humor and conflict that appeal to the modern reader.

Brust's fantasy world in many ways mirrors the 1980's society in which it was created. Vlad's psionic communications with his familiar and with his friends and employees could be likened to contemporary society's fixation on cellular telephones. The beings' abilities to "teleport" instantly from one place to another, whether minutes or hours away by foot, reflects modern society's dependence on cars and airplanes to cross long distances quickly. Vlad's nausea when teleporting may arouse sympathy in readers who have experienced similar effects of motion sickness. Even Vlad's marital strife and eventual estrangement from his wife remind the reader of the high divorce rate that plagued American society of the late twentieth century.

Booklist praised the series for its "intelligent world building" and "genuine touches of originality." Over the decade that transpired between the publishing of the first and sixth novels in the series, Brust matured as a writer, as evidenced in not only the Vlad Taltos series but his other published work as well. Negative criticisms notwithstanding, the series was an intriguing first venture into the fantasy genre by a promising newcomer.

—*C.K. Breckenridge*

Aegypt, Love and Sleep, Daemonomania and Endless Things

Pierce Moffett abandons his academic career to write a quasi-historical book on a kind of magic practiced in the Renaissance

Author: John Crowley (1942–)
Genre: Fantasy—magical realism
Type of work: Novels
Time of work: The twentieth century and late sixteenth century
Location: The eastern United States and Europe
First published: *Aegypt* (1987), *Love and Sleep* (1994), *Daemonomania* (2000), and *Endless Things* (2007)

The Story

Aegypt (also published as *The Solitudes*), *Love and Sleep*, *Daemonomania* and *Endless Things* constitute Crowley's four-volume novel (collectively entitled *Aegypt*) that concerns myth, history, Gnostic religious philosophy, and Renaissance magic.

Aegypt chronicles Pierce Moffett's escape to a rural life in the Catskills from his life in New York City and an unsatisfying academic career. *Love and Sleep* takes the reader forward to the next stage in Pierce's various types of research, both into historical accounts and into himself, to understand the "time when the world worked differently." It begins by chronicling Pierce's personal history as a boy growing up in the Cumberland Mountains of eastern Tennessee in the early 1950's. Stories are included about historical figures of the late sixteenth century, including Giordano Bruno, who is credited with discovering the concept of infinity, and the scientist/philosopher/magician Doctor John Dee. *Daemonomania* follows Pierce, Dee, and Bruno through their respective "passage times," periods of infinite possibility in which the world moves from what it has been to what it will eventually become.

Aegypt mentions Pierce's childhood and Doctor Dee's research with two short prologues. Primarily, however, it narrates the quest begun in Pierce's thirties. He sets out in the first section to interview for a teaching position at a small college in upstate New York. The bus he has taken breaks down, and he skips the interview to stay with Spofford, a former student who is now a shepherd in the small town of Blackbury Jambs. Pierce decides that he wants to stay, then briefly returns to the city to sell a book proposal to a former girlfriend. He can then settle in Blackbury Jambs to write a popular account of the epistemological break between the medieval and the modern periods, times of religious, magical, and scientific fervor. He meets Spofford's girlfriend, Rosie, and another woman, Rose, both of whom will help him in his quest. *Aegypt* focuses on Rosie; her husband Mike, whom she is in the process of divorcing; their small daughter, Sam; and their uncle, Boney Rasmussen. Rosie hires Pierce to work for Boney's foundation and put in order the papers of a deceased novelist, Fellowes Kraft (an allusion to Fellowescraft, the second level of masonry), who also worked for the foundation. Among Kraft's papers, Pierce discovers an unfinished work that matches his proposed book. *Aegypt* ends with his having created his project for the foundation but trying to decide what to do about his own book.

Love and Sleep continues the story of Pierce's book by documenting his motivations. The first thirteen chapters of part 1 narrate two years of Pierce's boyhood in the early 1950's, when he lived with his mother in the Cumberland Mountains. The focus is on his experiences with his cousins, mountain people alternately endowed and devastated by mining operations, and on his relationship to books and to Roman Catholic doctrine, all equally fantastic to him. The second section introduces the sixteenth century through texts of Fellowes Kraft read by Rosie Rasmussen and Pierce himself in the late 1970's. As Rosie and Pierce read, Pierce attempts to use the magical forces of Doctor Dee and his medium, Kelley, for his own purposes. Pierce appears to be a disturbed individual who uses his research for the foundation, which is simultaneously research for his own book, to satisfy lusts of spiritual and physical kinds. His discovery that a lost land of Aegypt may be responsible for the survival of magic in the modern world is confirmed for him (if not for the reader) by his analysis of accumulated personal occurrences. He notes that he "accidentally" ended up in Blackbury Jambs, home of Fellowes

Kraft, whose novels he read as a child; that he was once sexually involved with a crazy gypsy (he takes "gypsy" as derived from the magical Aegypt); and that he finds himself editing the manuscript of a book by Kraft corresponding to the book he plans to write.

A third story, of Giordano Bruno, Doctor Dee, Rudolph II, and other historical figures from the sixteenth century, carries the reader into Pierce's and Fellowes Kraft's research in an immediate sense. Pierce learns enough of Dee's magic, he believes, to use the sexual energy of "coldly performed love" with the "other" Rose (Ryder) to create for himself a barely corporeal son and an incestuous (if imaginary) relationship, slipping further into his parallel world of magic. This novel ends with a section titled "Valetudo," which can be translated as ill health or health. Both Pierce and his friends fear for his mental health. His only solution is to wait for the next big change in "the way the world works" so that his self-created succubus will leave him.

In *Daemonomania*, the tone of the narrative grows progressively darker, as the characters struggle to find their way through an increasingly chaotic world. John Dee, deserted by the angels who promised him divine revelation, travels from London to Prague and then back, where he dies—alone and largely forgotten—at his English country home of Mortlake. Giordano Bruno continues to develop his heretical philosophies, gradually moving toward an enigmatic encounter with the Office of the Inquisition in Rome. In the twentieth century sections, Pierce and Rosie Rasmussen find themselves in conflict with an overbearing faith-healing cult called the Powerhouse. Pierce loses his lover, Rose Ryder, to the blandishments of the cult, while Rosie—whose former husband, Mike Mucho, is a fanatical convert—nearly loses her daughter Sam in a hotly contested custody fight. The effort to free Sam from the controlling forces of the Powerhouse—an effort in which Pierce plays a pivotal role—provides *Daemonomania* with its dramatic and symbolic climax, as Crowley reveals in typically oblique fashion that Sam's fate and the fate of the world are inextricably linked. As the novel ends, that wildly unstable world stands poised on the edge of irreversible change.

In the final volume, Pierce Moffett, our protagonist, a historian and scholar and would-be writer, has emerged from his tempestuous, neurotic, near-fatal love affair with Rose Ryder a broken man. His dream of producing a book that reveals the secret history of the world—how titanic unacknowledged paradigm shifts sweep over human consciousness at intervals—is on the rocks. So he picks up a second task. At the behest of Rosie Rasmussen, who governs a Foundation that controls the literary estate of one Fellowes Kraft, Pierce is sent to Europe to trace a famous voyage Kraft made, and hopefully learn enough to bring Kraft's final unfinished manuscript to completion. Oh, yes, Kraft might also have previously found the literal Holy Grail on his journey, and Pierce might bother to pick that up as well, should he chance upon it.

Meanwhile, a second track continues the career of Giordano Bruno, famous heretical mystic. (A third track involving wizardly John Dee concluded in *Daemonomania*, although Dee's apprentice Edward Kelly makes a brief appearance.) Put to death by flames, Bruno, we learn, actually survived by making a supernatural leap to another form. We follow Bruno's "posthumous" career, and how it ties in with Pierce's own investigation.

In the end, however, Pierce's European odyssey merely shows him the futility of his quest—or rather the misperceived and unapprehendable nature of it. He returns to America, to the pastoral Faraway Hills in New York State. There, with no expectations, he will encounter the startling and final life-altering events of his particular myth.

ANALYSIS

These novels amply reward reading and rereading. Their structural details magnificently contribute to the experience of a story that is never completely told, only implied. The narrative is in third person, shifting among several characters and always unreliable, leaving much to delight a careful reader. Upon rereading, one discovers that seemingly unrelated episodes are, in fact, closely intertwined. This is apparent in the juxtaposition of narratives about the early 1580's and later 1970's and those concerning the lives of Giordano Bruno and Pierce Moffett.

There are many reviews of John Crowley's books but few critical articles about Crowley himself, although he has been many times nominated for the Hugo, Nebula, and World Fantasy Awards (which he won for *Little, Big* in 1981) and the American Book Award (for which he was nominated for *Engine Summer* in 1979 and which he won for *Little, Big* in 1981).

His later novels are different in tone from *Little, Big* but share ideas with that book. *Little, Big* also plays off the city of New York and the Catskills, but where that novel validates a magical dimension to the universe, grounded in Rosicrucians and Theosophists, the *Aegypt* novels sidestep the question while maintaining the tension. These three novels offer a more sobering and intellectual reading experience that amply repays a reader's attention but also demands much more of it.

Each of the *Aegypt* books is divided into three sections, each of which is given the title of a house of the zodiac: Vita, Lucrum, and Fratres in *Aegypt*; Genitor, Nati, and Valetudo in *Love and Sleep*; and Uxor, Mors, and Pietas in *Daemonomania*. The houses of the zodiac are explained by both the local astrologer, Val, and a writer from the 1620's, Fludd.

The discussion of the zodiac typifies the elaborate game the reader must play if the secrets of these books are to be unlocked. These secrets are revealed as Pierce himself searches for some confirmation of his book's theme, that once the world worked differently and that the last time a change occurred was at the cusp of the sixteenth and seventeenth centuries. He believes that the world is again in the midst of such a radical change. He also searches for magical powers that were available to historical figures so that he can put them to personal use, but his misuse of these magical powers leads him to the brink of psychological collapse.

The historical chapters provide a surprising amount of genuine historical detail. Each gives a nonscientific interpretation of events of the time and is linked to contemporary events. For example, England's defeat of the Spanish Armada in 1588 is known to have been aided by an unexpected wind, but the narration insists that there are no firsthand accounts of this wind. One of Kraft's books suggests that the wind was caused by demons conjured up by Doctor Dee. This historical occurrence is then mirrored in the cold and winds of 1977–1978 in the Catskills. The sum of these illusions re-creates an experience of Pierce's journey.

Both *Love and Sleep* and *Daemonomania* were written long after *Aegypt* and provide sufficient background to be accessible on their own. *Endless Things*, however, being published a full twenty years after volume one and having to perform manifold tying-together tasks, really relies on the reader's intimate knowledge of the first three books. Ultimately, the books are best read together and in sequence, for *Aegypt* is a single, hugely ambitious novel. This grand, allusive work is clearly one of the most intricate, erudite, stylistically assured novels in the field of modern fantasy literature.

—*Janice M. Bogstad*
—*Updated by Bill Sheehan*

AGAINST INFINITY

Assisted by an older man and a bioengineered "hound," a young boy hunts a mysterious alien artifact on Ganymede

Author: Gregory Benford (1941–)
Genre: Science fiction—extrapolatory
Type of work: Novel
Time of work: The twenty-first century
Locale: Jupiter's moon Ganymede and Earth
First published: 1983 (sections previously appeared in *Amazing Science Fiction,* February and April, 1983)

The Story

Closely modeled on William Faulkner's 1942 novella "The Bear," *Against Infinity* is a coming-of-age story developed in six parts. The story begins in Sidon, a frontier settlement on the Jovian moon Ganymede. The settlement has been plagued by a mysterious and elusive alien artifact called the Aleph. Its random burrowings throughout the interior of the moon threaten human efforts to terraform the moon and tame the wilderness.

Manuel López, the son of the settlement's commanding officer, first sees the Aleph when he is thirteen years old and encounters it repeatedly over the next several years. He comes under the tutelage of an aging pioneer named Matt Bohles, whose own coming-of-age story was the subject of Gregory Benford's 1975 novel *Jupiter Project*. The two of them continue over the years to join periodic hunts for the Aleph. Not until Matt and Manuel are joined by a mechanically enhanced, part-human, part-animal "hound" named Eagle, however, are they able to immobilize the mysterious artifact.

Years later, after Manuel has moved from Sidon to the city of Hiruko, he learns that the entire project of space exploration is driven not so much by idealism as by brute economic necessity, to sustain an economy that must forever expand to survive. Learning of the death of his estranged father, Manuel returns to Sidon, where he finds the wilderness replaced by a thriving community of domes. An atmosphere is developing on Ganymede, there is talk of the mechanized animals forming a new underclass in society, and the Aleph has been reduced to an object of scientific study. The Aleph itself remains a mystery, however, forever rebuilding itself at the atomic level. Moreover, the Aleph seems to contain memories of all it has encountered and all who challenged it. At the novel's conclusion, a catastrophic moonquake brought on by the stresses of terraforming nearly destroys the settlement and reasserts the primacy of the wilderness.

ANALYSIS

More than any other writer of hard science fiction, Benford consciously has sought to bring the resources of his own literary and cultural background to bear on the futuristic settings of his work. A Southerner like Faulkner, he is equally concerned with language, with the loss of the past, with the lessons of youth and age, and with archetypal rituals such as the hunt. *Against Infinity* is by far the most successful of his attempts to adapt Faulknerian techniques to science fiction, and it is one of the most direct. The novel displays direct allusions to Faulkner's Ike McCaslin in Manuel, to the bear Old Ben in the Aleph, to the Indian guide Sam Fathers in Matt Bohles, and to the hunting dog Lion in Eagle. Like part 4 of Faulkner's novella, part 4 of Benford's novel is set some years later than the beginning, and in it the protagonist reflects on what was lost in his experience of conquering nature.

The novel is far from a simple transcription of Faulkner's story into science-fictional terms. Benford fills the book with futuristic products of his invention, including terraforming, mechanically reinforced animals with enhanced intelligence, alien artifacts, space colonies, an overpopulated Earth, and new concepts in physics revealed by the Aleph. These inventions are worked out with an extrapolative rigor that matches the best hard science fiction. Benford realizes the novel must work purely on its own terms as a science-fiction narrative, and it does.

Benford's approach is unusual for his thoughtful and ambivalent attitude toward the technology and endless economic expansion that are so often celebrated by hard science fiction. Like "The Bear," *Against Infinity* is at heart a celebration of the wilderness, of the always receding edge of human hegemony, represented not only by the colonization of other worlds but also by the unstable economic systems that accompany such colonization, by the equally unstable geology of newly explored worlds, and finally by the new realms of physics and science opened by the mysteries of the Aleph itself. These discoveries in science suggest that even the fundamental laws that govern the universe may undergo evolutionary change. As an alien artifact of uncertain purpose, the Aleph implies entire worlds as yet undiscovered, and as the moonquake that concludes the novel implies, asserting control over these worlds will not come without a price: The wilderness will always reassert itself and challenge human attempts at conquest. The elegiac tone of the final chapters is complemented by the realization that frontiers forever redefine themselves and that certain individuals such as Manuel—like Matt and Manuel's father before him—will always be drawn to "the wilderness, the opening-outward, the undomesticated, the country of the old dead time."

Against Infinity explores the notion of frontiers in science fiction at every level from economics to physics to the ancient myth of the hunt. It also reflects a unique dual perspective, with Benford drawing equally on his scientific training and on his Southern boyhood traditions of storytelling and mythmaking. Although the Faulknerian style sometimes seems at odds with the hard-edged extrapolation of Benford's future, it lends the novel a poetic depth and mythic power unusual in the genre. In its own way, *Against Infinity* is one of the genre's classic coming-of-age tales.

—*Gary K. Wolfe*

AIR

The latest in communications technology comes to a tiny isolated village, filtered through one uneducated woman, and transforms all existence

Author: Geoff Ryman (1951–)
Genre: Science Fiction—extrapolatory
Type of Work: Novel
Time of Plot: 2020
Location: The imaginary country of Karzistan
First Published: 2004

THE STORY

There is a tiny isolated village named Kizuldah in the country of Karzistan, a nation that appears to be one of those republics that straddle—geographically and culturally—both Western and Asian spheres of influence. ("Karzistan is on the borders of China, Tibet, and Kazakhstan.") Our entrance into this cloistered, once-stable but now shifting environment is the figure of Chung Mae Wang. A woman long past her youth, of some early middle age, Mae has fashioned a useful role for herself by becoming a "fashion expert." By cultivating contacts in the nearby "big city" of Yeshibozkent, a four-hour ride away, she can offer fashion advice to other village women and earn some small wages. Since her ne'er-do-well husband Joe refuses to work, Mae must also cultivate their small fields.

In chapter 1, we get a sampling of Mae's average day, becoming familiar with some of the people in her life. In chapter 2, her world is turned upside-down. A global technology dubbed simply "Air" promises to offer purely mental access to the Internet. When it is implemented, however, it drives many people mad, and the technology is temporarily withdrawn. Mae herself is grievously affected. She is mind-linked to the elderly Mrs. Tung at the moment Mrs. Tung dies, and the ghostly simulacrum personality of Mrs. Tung is now stored in Mae's brain and is apt to erupt during moments of stress. However, when Mae recovers, she is left as the only villager with a working Air connection. But she does not put this to use immediately.

Life in the village goes on. Shiftless Joe takes a large loan from a neighbor named Haseem, whose object is to bankrupt Joe and Mae and foreclose on their farm. Sunni, Haseem's wife, who was once friendly with Mae, becomes her enemy. Mae impulsively embarks on a secret love affair with the kindly widower Mr. Ken. Then, desperate for a way out of her difficulties, she begins to tap into Air.

Air teaches her to conduct a survey of the villagers' wants and needs. She employs a young assistant, An, to help. Mae learns to interface mentally with one of the two smart TVs in the village and use it to conduct a school for adults and children. The shorthand phrase for all this new knowledge is "Info." And Mae becomes its partisan.

> *"Teacher Shen. Do you know any thing about Info?" He resented that, though his expression did not change. "We all need to learn about it. We need to learn about it, because soon we will spend half our lives in Info. And no one, not one of us, knows a thing about it. We will all become like little children again. We will all be lost unless we learn... Every business will have to change. Even farming, even water, all of it will change because of Info. That is why I want you to be ready."*

But her new life goes pear-shaped when her affair with Mr. Ken is disclosed. Joe moves away, and Mae is left as a pariah in the gossipy village. But she does not relent. She forms a new partnership with a woman named Kwan, who happens to be a member of the tribal minority known as the Eloi. A government official named Oz Oz [*sic*] comes to the village and is amazed to find Mae has a working Air linkup. He explains much about the network to her. There are two rival operating systems fighting it out for control of the global population: the UN model and the Gates model. Surprisingly, the UN version seems more deleterious. Oz Oz helps Mae establish a line of credit and loans for her new fashion business. By crafting an online presence, Mae and company soon gain international recognition.

But then a gangster named Mr. Tunch steps in. He would like to co-opt Mae, but she finds a way to resist, after escaping his captivity. Back in the village, she juggles the dozen balls of her life, only to find that her whole base of operations stands in danger of being wiped out by a flood of historic proportions. Surviving the flood, Mae unfortunately succumbs to zombie possession by the spirit of Mrs. Tung. But in truth, her true essence has merely graduated to a more cosmic existence among the eleven universal dimensions of Air.

ANALYSIS
Eight novels in thirty years. It is hardly a record of Stephen-King-like magnitude. But such is the undisputed brilliance and passion of each novel among these eight that Geoff Ryman has come to be viewed as one of the finest writers operating today in the field of fantastika. This offering—his next-to-most-recent book at the time of this writing—illustrates why.

First is his vast empathy with and insight into people—mostly average—and his masterful ability to portray them on the page. While much science fiction and fantasy relies on archetypes and/or cliches, Ryman builds intricate, deep figures from the toenails on up. In this book, not only is Mae utterly unique, credible, and complex, but so is every other character, even folks who might be counted as walk-ons, such as the crippled seamstress Miss Soo, who only appears briefly and not pivotally. And Ryman embraces a tragicomic view of life. While there is much to pity in the doings here, there is also much to raise a smile or a wry nod of the head.

Second is his ability to show us whole cultures different from his native Western one. The country of Karzistan and the village of Kizuldah are tactile, vibrant, and organically whole. If SF is proud of constructing otherworldly scenarios, surely Ryman's achievement here counts as such, even though it is other humans, not aliens, at the center. A book like Maureen McHugh's *China Mountain Zhang* is an SF cousin to Ryman's novel. But really, his book is more closely allied to such Latino magical realists as Jorge Amado and Gabriel García Márquez.

But these typically mainstream literary values are not all Ryman offers. He displays the invaluable core speculative powers of any great SF writer. His conception of Air as the next stage in being wired to the world's nervous system is both logical and unforeseen by most other writers. Not even William Gibson's cyberspace captured such a radical vision. And also as with most skeptical SF visionaries, Ryman picks and probes at this technology to find both its virtues and its vices. He is not a shill nor a cynic, but a rational scientist about the matter.

Ryman's book stands in a short but proud lineage of such tales about transformative tech. Perhaps the most important forebear of such scenarios is Samuel Delany's "We, in Some Strange Power's Employ, Move on a Rigorous Line," where mere electricity was the revolutionizing and disruptive force when it came to an isolated community. Of course, a sequence like Kathleen Goonan's *Nanotech Quartet* exemplifies such paradigm-shift innovations in a much more radical manner.

Finally, the mystical or New Age component to the book, whereby Mae achieves transcendence through exploiting the undiscovered country of the Air network places Ryman firmly in the school of epiphanical speculations identified by Alexei and Cory Panshin in their landmark study *The World Beyond the Hill: Science Fiction and the Quest for Transcendence*.

William Gibson famously opined about technology and the common people: "The street finds its own uses for things," an urban-centric motto. Ryman's conceit might be summarized as "The village finds its own uses for things." At least it does when it boasts such an indomitable heroine as Chung Mae Wang.

—*Paul Di Filippo*

ALADORE

A weary knight following an unknown "desire" encounters an enchanting lady and, with her help, enters an alternate world

Author: Henry John Newbolt (1862-1938)
Genre: Fantasy—high fantasy
Type of work: Novel
Time of work: An idealized Middle Ages
Locale: Paladore, the magical counterpart of Aladore, and the surrounding countryside
First published: 1914

The Story

Ywain, the jaded administrator of an unnamed medieval state, is so bored that he renounces his rights, turning over his lands and office to a younger brother. He becomes a pilgrim, setting out to follow his "desire," a will-o'-the-wisp in the guise of a child. In the wilderness, he encounters a hermit who teaches him the joys of life. Eventually he leaves this solitary paradise and is directed toward the walled city of Paladore. There he encounters the beautiful Aithne, who begs him not to desert her.

The sounds of a nearby battle compel him to join the Eagles, who are attacking the besieged Tower, and he helps them to prevail. The battle is an age-old custom whereby the Eagles (the liberal forces for change) challenge the Tower (the bastion of conservative power). The warring parties converge at the end of the battle, and both sides honor Ywain as a hero and welcome him to the community. An interlude is begun with Aithne, whose powers enable her to travel to the magical city of Aladore, which Ywain is unable to see.

Still longing for fulfillment, Ywain joins a band of knights seeking the City of Saints. Ywain and his companion, Bartholomy, travel to the City, which is both lovely and unusual. It is governed by ringing bells. Both men succumb to the lure of the bells, which lull them into forgetfulness. Ywain stumbles into a garden and encounters Aithne, who asks him to follow her on a new pilgrimage. Suddenly, his memory returns, and he realizes that she is the image of all he desires.

Ywain follows Aithne to a magical kingdom peopled with fauns, who enchant Ywain with their pursuit of earthly pleasures. Although he spends blissful days there in pastoral harmony with Aithne, he gradually comes to fear the fauns and their antics. A vision of Aladore rekindles his longing, and he begs Aithne to aid him in casting off the fauns' influence.

Aithne and Ywain are taken up by a strange winged creature and flown to a city where a race of men carry on the tradition of Daedalus. Ywain is taught the art of flight and flies off, leaving Aithne behind. He falls to the ground and is rescued by the old hermit, who counsels him to return to Paladore. There he temporarily pacifies the Tower and the Eagles, who are still at odds.

One afternoon, Ywain follows the sound of children frolicking and singing and rediscovers the city of Aladore. He is permitted to cross through the mist and sea to its gates and is taken to a chamber. He finds a book containing a picture of Aithne; turning, he finds that the image has become reality. He weds Aithne, and they begin an idyllic existence. Aithne, through magic, shows Ywain all the seekers and lovers of myth and history. He visits scenes of Aithne's childhood and experiences with her all the warmth and love of her youthful years.

With the sounding of the midnight bells, Ywain finds himself in Paladore once more. Aithne follows, and together they are drawn into the final climactic battle for mastery of the city. Ywain elects to sacrifice himself to purchase the salvation of his companions in arms, the Eagles. He sees the child of his desire one last time and follows him to Aithne's sanctuary. Ywain and Aithne depart, hand in hand, through the battle. They are never seen in Paladore again, but the effigies of a knight and his lady are discovered on the tomb of the altar in the sanctuary.

Analysis

Aladore is a haunting tale, so limpid and gentle in the telling that one is tempted to read it simply for pure enjoyment. Henry John Newbolt's pastiche of the style made popular by William Morris employs a rich, though archaic, language that contributes to the beautiful flow of this allegorical account of a medieval quest for love and the meaning of life.

Aladore contains many allusions to Christian fellowship and theology. Ywain and the hermit break bread together and bathe in a mountain stream, acts comparable to the rites of communion and baptism. Ywain continually is torn between the fellowship and peace of the hermitage and the lure of his will-o'-the-wisp desire. This tension is reminiscent of the pull between religious life and the knightly quest—"The bird calls Come!'; the saint whispers Stay!' "—that is depicted so compellingly in "The Knight's Tale" in Geoffrey Chaucer's *The Canterbury Tales* (1387-1400). This problem is never resolved completely in the novel. At one point, the reunited lovers are startled in a garden by a spy slithering away in the grass, like a serpent invading their Edenic paradise. During the climactic battle, Ywain willingly sacrifices himself, in the manner of Jesus Christ, to save his brothers in the final Armageddon.

This deceptively simple allegory is notable for the fact that it is (except for the somewhat juvenile Greenwood tales of G. P. Baker) the only significant medieval fantasy published between the death of William Morris in 1896 and the end of World War I. Newbolt clearly is familiar with Morris' work and uses the same style of language, indefinable time period, and medieval trappings. That such a tale, with its emphasis on brotherly love and Christian fellowship, should appear on the eve of World War I is ironic. Newbolt, who later wrote the official history of the navy in that conflict and was knighted for his efforts, never wrote another novel.

—*Robert Reginald*

ALAS, BABYLON

After a nuclear explosion, Randy Bragg assumes responsibility for the survival of his "family" and takes control of his town to reestablish some semblance of civilization

Author: Pat Frank (Harry Hart Frank, 1907–1964)
Genre: Science fiction—post-holocaust
Type of work: Novel
Time of work: The mid-twentieth century
Locale: Fort Repose, a river town in Central Florida
First published: 1959

THE STORY

The time frame of *Alas, Babylon* is limited to a single year following a nuclear war. Randy Bragg is a thirty-two-year-old lawyer and former military officer living in Fort Repose, Florida. He and his small community manage to survive the effects of the war and, through their communal efforts, to preserve a modicum of civilization.

Randy receives from his brother Mark, an Air Force colonel and member of Strategic Air Command Intelligence, a telegram that ends with the phrase "Alas, Babylon." This is their code for disaster, adopted from fiery sermons they heard in childhood. Mark is certain that nuclear attack is imminent, and he entrusts to Randy his wife Helen and his children, Ben Franklin and Peyton.

Mark's prediction proves true sooner than expected. The next morning, two nearby cities are hit by atomic bombs. Randy is awakened by shaking of the house, a loud rumbling, and an orange light. Peyton's temporary blindness from looking at the light is only the first of many crises. Randy, on his way to find his friend, Dr. Dan Gunn, passes an overturned car with a dead woman beside it. Stopping automatically, he realizes that all the rules have now changed and that the days of the Good Samaritan are over. All the roads are jammed with refugees, convicts have escaped from prison, and businesses have closed. In short, chaos reigns. In the next few months, charity loses its moral imperative. As electricity, running water, telephone service, and other amenities become unavailable, filth, squalor, and moral poverty become, for many, the conditions of life.

Randy, governed by enlightened self-interest, does what must be done in a civilized world. He unceremoniously buries the bodies of his fiancée's mother and the selfish politician Porky Logan, putting Logan and all of his contaminated goods in a lead coffin. Randy forms a community made up of Helen and her two children, Lib McGovern, her father, Dan Gunn, two "spinsters," a retired admiral, and Randy's "wards," the Henrys. Through cooperation, the community avoids the degeneracy into which many have fallen. The worst of these are the gangs of "highwaymen," to whom Dan falls victim.

Randy, as a Reserve officer, forms a troop and assumes control of Fort Repose. He imposes martial law and brings order to the town, punishing the highwaymen who beat Dan. He also establishes a means for legal marriage, then becomes the first to take advantage of it, marrying Lib McGovern.

A year after The Day (as it came to be called), one of Mark's friends lands a helicopter in the yard. He reveals that the United States had won the war, that Mark could not possibly be alive, and that Fort Repose is free from radiation. When he offers to take the community to another city, the members all decline, preparing together to "face the thousand-year night."

ANALYSIS

Alas, Babylon is one of many post-catastrophe novels written in the era of the Cold War. Like the more highly regarded *A Canticle for Leibowitz* (1960) by Walter M. Miller, Jr., it assumes a return to barbarism after such a catastrophe. Whereas Miller's novel covers some eighteen hundred years after the holocaust, Pat Frank's novel concerns only the first year and shows the process by which such decadence comes to be. Frank's novel is more optimistic than Miller's, ending with the re-establishment of schools, an increase in reading, the return to a more purposeful existence, and the hope that the best people will survive and retain their civility.

One of Frank's last novels, written at a time when America feared and prepared for atomic war, *Alas, Babylon* can be called science fiction only in the sense that the holocaust does occur. At the beginning, Frank makes the setting seem familiar. With careful attention to place, he creates a small river town in Florida, modeled after Mandarin, where his mother lived. As the town becomes strange to Randy, it becomes strange to the reader because of the lack of necessary services, the destruction of such symbols as money and ceremonies, and lack of communication with the outside world. For several months, the characters do not know whether the war is still going on or which side might have won, and they do not know if there is a national government in control. The uncertainty of authority and the necessary barbarism of life caused by the lack of accustomed services unleashes the worst aspects of human nature.

The narrative voice is omniscient, with events seen through the consciousness of several characters. The novel begins with the thoughts of Florence Wechek, Randy's neighbor. This allows Frank to present a humorous view of Randy before putting the reader into Randy's consciousness. Randy appears at first to be rather purposeless, but the good stock he comes from, his military service, and his intelligence and good character foreshadow his heroic actions.

The novel is dated by its racist and sexist assumptions. The author treats the black characters with condescension, presenting them stereotypically as, for example, a lazy, drunken loafer; an overweight domestic worker; and an industrious manual laborer. Women, too, are presented in shallow terms. Helen momentarily goes mad because of repressed sexual desires, and when the women are left alone, chaos ensues. Randy concludes that women need men around. Despite expression of these dated attitudes, Alas, Babylon is well crafted and is instructive as a moral tale. The community members' interdependency shows that civilization is based on ethical behavior rather than on technology and material goods.

—*Jo N. Farrar*

ALICE'S ADVENTURES IN WONDERLAND AND THROUGH THE LOOKING-GLASS

A young girl explores a bizarre world that lies underground and an equally strange land that lies on the other side of the looking-glass

Author: Lewis Carroll (Charles Lutwidge Dodgson, 1832–1898)
Genre: Fantasy—alien civilization

Type of work: Novels
Time of work: Undefined, in dreamlands
Location: Wonderland and Looking-Glass Land
First published: *Alice's Adventures in Wonderland* (1865) and *Through the Looking-Glass* (1871 but dated 1872)

The Story

Alice's Adventures in Wonderland is an outgrowth of Lewis Carroll's earlier and shorter tale titled *Alice's Adventures Under Ground,* which he based on a story he told to Alice Liddell and her two sisters during a boat trip they took in 1862. Carroll completed this story, written in longhand and illustrated with his own drawings, in 1863. In 1864, he gave the manuscript to Alice as a gift. Revised and expanded by Carroll and newly illustrated by John Tenniel, this work evolved into *Alice's Adventures in Wonderland* the following year.

While listening to her older sister reading aloud, Alice drifts off to sleep and begins her dream adventures. She follows a white rabbit and falls down his hole into Wonderland. Alice is constantly at odds with the creatures who inhabit this alien world and also with her own body, which shrinks when she drinks from a mysterious bottle, then grows to enormous size when she eats a small cake.

She encounters many creatures endowed with wit and cleverness, who confuse her at every turn. She meets the ugly Duchess, whose baby turns into a pig in Alice's arms. Things are not what they seem. It is at the Duchess's house that she first sees the unsettling Cheshire Cat, who sits in the corner grinning, with his eyes fixed on Alice. Later, the Cheshire Cat reappears on a tree branch, from which he demonstrates his ability to vanish, leaving only his eerie smile lingering in the air.

At the Mad Tea-Party, Alice must exchange witty remarks and insults with the Hatter and March Hare, an experience that further challenges her sense of time and logic. It is always six o'clock, always teatime, at this table.

The threatening nature of Wonderland is reinforced in the garden scene, dominated by the raucous Queen of Hearts, who continually shouts "Off with her head!" The threat becomes problematic, however, when the executioner is summoned to cut off the disembodied head of the Cheshire Cat.

Alice's last adventure is at the trial of the Knave of Hearts, who is accused of stealing the Queen's tarts. The Queen calls for the defendant to be sentenced before the jury submits its verdict, and it soon becomes clear that the law itself is on trial. Outraged at the absurd form of justice she witnesses, Alice asserts, "You're nothing but a pack of cards!" With that exclamation, she annihilates Wonderland as if by magic, and she emerges from her strange dream.

In *Through the Looking-Glass* (which carries the subtitle *And What Alice Found There*), Carroll again frames his story as a dreamlike experience, but this time he presents a world that is controlled by the rules of a chess game. Alice enters the geometrical landscape, which is laid out like a chessboard, as a pawn. During her movement across the board en route to becoming a queen, she may converse only with the chess figures on adjacent squares. Among the many memorable characters she engages are the White Queen, from whom she learns the advantages of living backward in time; the battling Lion and Unicorn; the pompous Humpty Dumpty; the bullying Tweedledee and Tweedledum, who tell Alice that she is merely an object in the Red King's dream; and the eccentric White Knight.

After Alice bids farewell to the White Knight, in a scene that may represent Carroll's adieu to Alice Liddell as she reached puberty, Alice goes on to

Lewis Carroll. (Library of Congress)

become queen. In terms of the chess game, the pawn has become a queen, and in human terms, Alice's final move suggests her coming of age. It is at this point that she wakes from her dream and is left wondering who dreamed it all, herself or the Red King.

ANALYSIS

Alice's Adventures in Wonderland presents a world in which everything, including Alice's own body size, is in a state of flux. She is treated rudely, bullied, asked questions that have no answers, and denied answers to her own questions. Her recitations of poems turn into parodies, a baby turns into a pig, and a cat turns into a grin. The essence of time and space is called into question, and her romantic notion of an idyllic garden of life turns out to be a paper wasteland. In order to escape that oppressive and disorienting vision, she finally denies it with her outcry, "You're nothing but a pack of cards!" and happily reenters the morally intelligible and emotionally comfortable world of her sister, who sits next to her on the green banks of a river in a civilized Victorian countryside.

The assaults on Alice's senses of order, stability, and proper manners wrought by such characters as the Hatter, the Cheshire Cat, and the March Hare make it clear that Wonderland is not the promised land, a place of sleepy fulfillment. Rather, Wonderland stimulates the senses and the mind. It is a *monde fatale*, one that seduces Alice (and the reader) to seek new sights, new conversations, and new ideas, but it never satisfies her. Conventional meaning, understanding, and the fulfillment that comes with illumination are constantly denied her. That is the secret of Wonderland: Its disorienting and compelling attractions make it a Wanderland and Alice herself an addicted, unfulfilled wanderer.

Significantly, she is presented with a stimulating, alluring vision early in her adventures. Alice finds a tiny golden key that opens a door that leads to a small passage. As she kneels and looks along the passage, she sees a beautiful garden with bright flowers and cool fountains. She is too large, however, to fit through the door and enter the attractive garden. Alice's dream garden suggests an adult's longing for lost innocence and youth, and her desire to enter it invests the place with imagined significance.

Later, when she goes into the garden, it loses its romantic aspect. In fact, it turns out to be a parodic Garden of Life, for the roses are painted, the people are playing cards, and the death-cry "Off with her head!" echoes throughout the croquet grounds.

Alice's dream garden is an excellent example of Carroll's paradoxical duality. Like Alice, he is possessed by a romantic vision of an edenic childhood more desirable than his own fallen world, but it is a vision that he knows is corrupted inevitably by adult sin and sexuality. He thus allows Alice's romantic dream of the garden to fill her with hope and joy for a time, but he later tramples that pastoral vision with the fury of the beheading Queen and the artificiality of the flowers and inhabitants.

Through the Looking-Glass abandons the fluidity and chaos of *Alice's Adventures in Wonderland* for artifice and strict determinism. In the first book, the emphasis is on Alice's adventures and what happens to her on the experiential level. In the sequel, Alice's movements are controlled strictly by the precise rules of a chess game. The giddy freedom she enjoyed in Wonderland is exchanged for a ruthless determinism, as she and the other chess pieces are manipulated by some unseen hand.

Whereas *Alice's Adventures in Wonderland* undermines Alice's sense of time, space, and commonsensical logic, *Through the Looking-Glass* questions her very reality. Tweedledum and Tweedledee express the Berkeleian view that all material objects, including Alice herself, are only "sorts of things" in the mind of the sleeping Red King (God). If the Red King were to wake from his dreaming, they warn Alice, she would disappear. Alice, it would seem, is a mere fiction shaped by a dreaming mind that threatens her with annihilation.

The ultimate question of what is real and what is dream, however, is never resolved in the book. In fact, the story ends with the perplexing question of who dreamed it all—Alice or the Red King? Presumably, Alice dreamed of the King, who is dreaming of Alice, who is dreaming of the King, and so on. The question of dream versus reality is appropriately set forth in terms of an infinite regression through mirror facing mirror. The apprehension of reality is indefinitely deferred, and the only reality may be one's thoughts and their well-ordered expression.

In the final chapter, Alice, having become Queen, asserts her human authority against the controlling powers of the chessboard and brings both the intricate game and the story to an end. In chess terms, Alice has captured the Red Queen and checkmates the sleeping Red King. In human terms, she has grown up and entered that fated condition of puberty, at which point Carroll dismisses his dream child once and for all from his remarkable fiction.

—*Richard Kelly*

ALIF THE UNSEEN

In an unspecified Persian Gulf State and City, the young Arab Indian hacker nicknamed Alif runs afoul of state security and is forced to seek the help of a dissolute genie. Possession of a fabulous ancient book of stories might turn the tables—but only if Alif can unriddle it while on the run.

Author: G. Willow Wilson (1982–)
Genre: Fantasy—urban fantasy
Type of Work: Novel
Time of Plot: The present day
Location: The Middle East
First Published: 2012

THE STORY

We meet young Alif as he is at a climactic moment in his life. His beloved, Intisar, a rich girl with whom he has been having an illicit affair, has just broken off their relationship. She has been betrothed by her family and against her wishes to one Abbas Al Shehab—who happens to be the head of the Hand, the violent, dystopian security apparatus of the state. Moping about at home, where he lives with his mother, Alif proves himself at first to be the hapless, self-pitying nerd that others—such as his childhood friend Dina—accuse him of being. But then he gets proactive. He creates a computer program called Tin Sari that will identify any trace of Intisar on the web and banish her from Alif's digital sight.

Unfortunately, this program has to be hosted on Intisar's own computer as a hidden virus. When her new fiancé happens to rip through her files, he finds not only evidence of the illicit love affair, but also the code for Tin Sari itself, which can quickly become a tool of Hand oppression. Alif becomes an instant target.

Now Alif—with the aid of Dina—must go on the run. His friend Abdullah suggest contacting an underworld thug named Vikram. Alif does so and finds that Vikram is not human, but a supernatural entity of amazing powers. Vikram reluctantly agrees to help Alif, due to the urgings of Vikram's own sister Azalel, for whom Alif once unknowingly did a favor.

Into Alif's hands at this juncture comes an ancient book, the *Alf Yeom*. This transcription of jinn lore might hold not only the key to Alif's rescue from the Hand, but also the rule over all space, matter, and time. Alif and pals bring the book to a rare-book expert, an American known only as "the convert." She helps establish the provenance and background of the book. Next the pursued are off to the mystic Immovable Alley, where one Sakina, an information broker, illuminates matters more deeply. Still on the run, Vikram, Dina, the convert, and Alif find refuge in the mosque of one Sheikh Bilal. There, Alif uses the break to turn the *Alf Yeom*'s secrets into computer code that will devastate the Hand's own network. But his efforts are cut short by an assault on the mosque, during which Vikram is killed (but not before saving Dina and the convert from capture), and Alif and the Sheikh end up in the prison of the Hand.

Three months of subtle torture pass for isolated Alif. He is rescued by one of his fellow hackers, NewQuarter, acting covertly. NewQuarter, Alif, and Sheik Bilal take refuge in the deserted wastes of the Empty Quarter. There they meet a spirit who is kin to Vikram. This new ally takes them into the dimension of the jinns. Alif learns more of the supernatural world. A return visit to Sakina helps Alif to reunite with Dina and the convert. The reunion of Dina and Alif, both much changed, cause them to realize their true affection for each other. Dina has held on to the *Alf Yeom*, and now, with the help of many supernatural creatures, Alif and crew are ready to finally confront the Hand.

ANALYSIS

The young G. Willow Wilson is one of the outstanding fantasists of her generation, and she also bears the unique stamp of her Muslim identity. (A non-Muslim by birth, she converted as an adult). Her initial success stemmed from her innovative work in the field of monthly comics and graphic novels, a field in which she continues to do big things. *Alif the Unseen* marked her first—and, to this date, only—venture into prose fiction. But it was an outstanding debut and will surely be followed up by future counterparts.

Wilson exemplifies what is perhaps third-generation cyberpunk, with a fantastical overlay. No longer are computer hackers seen as rare birds on the bohemian side of life, as with *Neuromancer*'s protagonist, Case. Now they are even mama's boys like Alif, just average dudes living at home, and the Internet is not some exotic wonderland, but a common public agora. Still, the place holds wonders and dangers, but it is more like real life, integrated into daily routines. And just as William Gibson famously populated his cyberspace with voodoo gods called *loas*, so Wilson adds a layer of the supernatural atop her silicon. But whereas Gibson's virtual gods were always half-explainable as artificial intelligences, Wilson's are undeniably tangible and of ancient heritage. Blending these two realms requires a tightrope-walking act that Wilson handles superbly.

She also earns great acclaim in at least two other areas. First is characterization. Her troupe of players exhibits complex depths and all the frustrating unpredictability and stubbornness and self-sabotaging mistakes of real humans. And her portraits of the supernatural entities are likewise rich. Vikram steals every scene wherein he appears.

The second realm of excellence involves her demystification of Muslim life and practices. Her unnamed country is presented not as some foreign hellhole but as a place of tender intimacies and brash assaults, of intellectual aspirations and commercial schemes. In other words, as a nation and culture akin to all other fully functioning and legitimate societies, including our own.

One outstanding intersection of these two realms occurs in the figure of the convert, an American woman fully enmeshed in the Middle Eastern world, but never absolutely native—an impossibility. It seems obvious that the convert is modeled on Wilson herself, and the wry, ironic treatment of the figure reflects Wilson's full self-knowledge about her own interstitial status.

All in all, this book blends action, philosophy, magic, science, and cultural outreach into an outstanding and tasty mélange.

Along with Matt Ruff's *The Mirage*, Salman Rushdie's *Two Years Eight Months and Twenty-Eight Nights*, and Kim Stanley Robinson's *The Years of Rice and Salt*, Wilson's novel portends a growing relevance of science fiction and fantasy to the concerns of the Muslim world and vice versa.

—*Paul Di Filippo*

ALL HALLOW'S EVE

The Antichrist seeks to take over the world through magic but is foiled by two young couples whose love and sacrifice stop him and allow for their movement toward happiness

Author: Charles Williams (1886–1945)
Genre: Fantasy—occult
Type of work: Novel
Time of work: 1945
Locale: London, England
First published: 1945

THE STORY

Charles Williams' last novel brings together many of the themes of his other five novels. Lester Furnival, who has been married for six months, and her school friend Evelyn Mercer are killed by a plane that crashes near Westminster Bridge. Only gradually does Lester realize that she is dead. As she crosses a strangely quiet but still familiar London, Lester speaks to her living husband, Richard. With Evelyn, she sets out to accomplish something in her "new life" to make up for her incomplete earlier life.

Jonathan Drayton, a painter friend of Richard Furnival, is in love with Betty Wallingford. To impress Betty's mother, he paints a portrait of Simon Leclerc. Lady Wallingford sees in the picture "a ranked mass of beetles" around the face of an imbecile. Offended, she insists that Betty break off her engagement to Jonathan. Jonathan also has painted a remarkable picture of the city of London as a city of light. The painting impresses Richard, who asks how Jonathan came to create it. Jonathan explains that Sir Joshua Reynolds, a famous English painter of the late eighteenth century, once alluded to common observation and a plain understanding as the source of all art. Jonathan is later visited by Simon, who approves of his portrait but dislikes the painting of the illuminated city. He attempts to flatter Jonathan, calling him a genius and insisting that great art is apostolic. A practical artist, Jonathan throughout the novel insists on observation and understanding rather than apostolic excess.

Betty turns out to be the daughter of Lady Wallingford and Simon. She is being used by Simon to enter the world of spirits and bring back information about the future. On one such mission, she meets her former schoolmates Lester and Evelyn, who follow her home. Unknown to Simon, Lester enters the house and intercedes when Simon attempts to sacrifice his daughter. Later, Evelyn, whose motives are petty and malignant, is called up by Simon at his Holburn meeting place.

After his attempt to sacrifice Betty fails, Simon, in an attempt to control Lester, creates a humanoid figure from his spittle and dust. Both Evelyn and Lester enter into it. Using this figure, Lester places a telephone call to Richard to alert him about what has happened.

Simon is destroyed by his own creations in a final confrontation. Lady Wallingford tries to save Betty at the last moment and survives, to be taken care of by her transformed daughter, who even cures the attendants of Simon. Evelyn consigns herself to the region of the damned. Because of her self-sacrifice and Betty's forgiveness, Lester moves through Purgatory toward final blessing.

Analysis

As in his other novels, Williams is more concerned with the conflict between good and evil than with the depiction of everyday life. To establish this conflict, he uses many of the conventions of the fantasy genre.

The title, *All Hallows' Eve,* suggests the ancient Celtic festival of Samain, when it was believed that the gates between the spirits of the living and the dead opened and allowed easy passage. Williams accepted the Christian transformation of this holiday. In the tradition of Saint Augustine's *The City of God* (413–427), the "hallows," the souls of the blessed dead, take on the form of "the Acts of the City" and support Lester when Simon attempts to destroy her. The world of the dead, in fact, seems more vital and alive than drab wartime London. Although Betty is Simon's daughter, she is saved from his power both by Lester and by the "wise waters" of baptism, the christening given to her by her nurse.

Williams, who was a member of the Mystical Order of the Golden Dawn, also uses magic in the novel. Simon is both a version of Simon Magus (Acts 8:9–24) and the Antichrist. Williams insists that Simon is a Jew not because he is being anti-Semitic but because he is setting Simon in contrast to "that other sorcerer of his race, the son of Joseph, . . . Jesus Bar-Joseph." The scenes of conjuring and magical creation seem authentic but avoid the melodramatic excess of much gothic fiction.

Williams also uses Dante Alighieri's *The Divine Comedy* (c. 1320) in his fiction. Lester moves beyond Hell and through Purgatory. Readers see a hint of Paradise in the martyr's blood and mystic rose of the last chapter, which draws on Dante's portrayal of the blessed in Paradise. The first chapter may owe something to Dante's spiritual autobiography, his *La vita nuova* (c. 1292; *The New Life,* 1867).

The confrontation between good and evil, like the contrast between Jonathan's two paintings of the blessed and the damned, the light and the dark, emerges only through gradual revelation rather than melodramatic announcement. Readers come to recognize that although Simon preaches love, his only interests are himself and the establishment of his own complete power. He sires Betty not out of love or even lust but instead out of his desire and need to create an instrument he can use for his own ends. Simon insists, "I am the one who is to come, not Hitler!" To this end, he has created images of himself that appear in Russia and China. These unreal shadows, parodies of the Christian trinity, finally return to destroy him.

In contrast to Simon's joyless self-absorption, the novel presents the self-sacrifice of Lester, the radiant forgiveness of Betty, and the love that Richard and Jonathan feel for these two remarkable women. As Williams put it in an essay on "The Redeemed City" (1941), "There is no final idea for us but the glory of God in the redeemed and universal union—call it Man or the Church or the City."

—*David Lampe*

ALL TIMES POSSIBLE

A dimensionally displaced man foments revolution in an alternate America and briefly serves as director of the Free Democratic State before being ousted by more cynical colleagues

Author: Gordon Eklund (1945–)
Genre: Science fiction—alternate history
Type of work: Novel
Time of work: The 1920's to July 4, 1947
Locale: Various parts of the United States
First published: 1974

THE STORY

On July 4, 1947, in a United States with a governmental regime that appears considerably more authoritarian than the one recorded in history, a political radical named Timothy O'Mara attempts to assassinate General Norton. He fails and is summarily executed by the general. He then finds himself back in the early 1920's, inhabiting the body of a man named Tommy Bloome, whom he once murdered in order to take over his identity.

The main narrative describes, from several points of view, how Tommy Bloome, armed with a mysterious knowledge of things to come, becomes a zealous labor organizer, preparing the way for a general strike that precipitates a new American revolution in the early 1930's. After an extended civil war, Bloome's insurrectionists finally defeat the last remnants of the Nationalist army and secure power, but their rule follows much the same pattern as that of Soviet communism, involving constant internal power struggles within the hierarchy of the party and frequent purges.

Bloome is ousted from his position as director of the new Free Democratic State by his deputy, Arnold Lowrey, a political opportunist who had been the governor of Arkansas before the revolution. Lowrey is helped in this treachery by the sinister John Durgas and is further assisted by the passive but willing cooperation of Bloome's wife, Rachel, a former socialite who became an alcoholic during the difficult years of the civil war.

Once ousted, Bloome retires to secret seclusion, accompanied by his longtime friend Bob Ennis, who is the only person loyal to him. Lowrey's propaganda machine continues to use Bloome's name, claiming that he is fighting heroically in various distant arenas of the world war, which is still grinding on in 1947. After Tommy's death, on July 4, 1947, Ennis and Rachel continue to count the cost of their association with him, knowing that they will be killed as soon as Durgas—now the effective ruler of Free Democratic America—can do so.

At the end, the story reverts to the viewpoint of O'Mara-as-Bloome, who is told by Durgas that he has changed nothing, because this world is not the one he left behind. He already has become aware of slight differences in its history for which he could not have been responsible, and he must accept what Durgas says about that other world continuing along its own terrible path. Durgas also assures O'Mara/Bloome that he will die at exactly the same moment as he died in the other world, claiming to know this because he also is a dimensionally displaced person. As the moment of his death approaches, O'Mara/Bloome indeed finds himself slipping back to the moment of his "first" death, seeing General Norton's bullet heading toward him while the face of John Durgas looks on from the crowd.

ANALYSIS

The flyleaf blurb (presumably written by the book's editor and publisher, Donald A. Wollheim) describes *All Times Possible* as a "uchronian" novel, borrowing that label from *Uchronie* (1876), Charles Renouvier's pioneering exercise in alternate history. In fact, though, the pattern of the plot is an elaboration of the device employed in Ambrose Bierce's famous short story "An Occurrence at Owl Creek Bridge" (1891): The main narrative is a momentary hallucination experienced at the point of death. This is confused by the fact that by far the largest part of the main narrative is told from viewpoints other than that of the protagonist and that these supposedly objective accounts extend beyond the moment of O'Mara-as-Bloome's death. The conclusion makes it clear nevertheless that the narrative is a hallucination.

All Times Possible also is strongly reminiscent of Philip K. Dick's classic tale of alternate worlds, *The Man in the High Castle* (1962), in that the ordinary world remains outside the scope of the story as the protagonist struggles to adjust psychologically to the fact that he has lost his grip on his own identity and the solidity of his own world. The fact that O'Mara, at the moment of death, finds himself reliving the life of a man whose identity he stole, in a world in which he was never born, must be taken as an expression of his guilt, but he makes it clear that his adventure as Tommy Bloome is an act of revenge against the world rather than an attempt at atonement. Given this, it is not surprising that his career is a catalog of spoliation, in the course of which everyone who loves him is ruined. Nor is it surprising that his personal nemesis, John Durgas, delivers and bears witness to an unrelentingly hard judgment; in Hindu mythology, Durga is a violent and vengeful avatar of Parvati.

What perhaps is surprising is that Donald Wollheim—a man fervently committed to upbeat endings, who is rumored to have rejected Stephen King's first novel on the grounds that he was not interested in "negative utopias"—should have consented to publish such a bleak and politically sensitive book as *All Times Possible*. There is reason for readers and critics to be glad that he did, however, because the novel stands out as a uniquely interesting work in a genre not known for painstaking attention to matters of fine psychological detail or for outstanding bravery in matters of political speculation. Although the novel's account of the second American revolution and its cruel aftermath is sketchy and impressionistic, its condensed biographies of the subsidiary characters—particularly Rachel, Bob Ennis, and Lowrey—are highly effective, and it is entirely apt that the mysterious figure of Tommy Bloome—of whom O'Mara, after all, knows nothing—should be allowed to remain essentially elusive. The judgment passed on O'Mara is harsh and hellish, but it is neither inapt nor unjust. Readers will have to make up their own minds as to whether the judgment implicitly passed on America is equally appropriate.

—*Brian Stableford*

ALRAUNE

Professor ten Brinken engineers the birth of an amoral, semi-supernatural woman who enslaves and destroys all who fall under her influence

Author: Hanns Heinz Ewers (1871-1943)
Genre: Fantasy—superbeing
Type of work: Novel
Time of work: 1885-1910
Locale: Germany
First published: 1911 (in German; English translation, 1929)

THE STORY

Alraune is an occult fantasy, a modern reworking of the mandrake myth woven together with elements of *Frankenstein* (1818) and played against the background of the decadence and moral collapse that preceded World War I.

Inspired by the legend that mandrakes (*alraunes* in German) are engendered by the semen of hanged criminals, Frank Braun, a dissolute young lawyer, proposes an experiment to Professor Jacob ten Brinken: The creation of a woman through artificial insemination. Nymphomaniacal prostitute Alma Raune is impregnated with the final emission of rapist-murderer Peter Noerrissen, collected at the moment of his execution by guillotine. The experiment succeeds, and the mother is imprisoned until the midnight birth of a female child. The difficult labor kills the mother, who is the first victim of the sensual, amoral, and marginally human Alraune.

Ten Brinken adopts the child, encouraging and observing with delight the development of her evil nature and its effects upon those around her. Like the mandrake of superstition, she brings wealth to the house, along with unhappiness and destruction.

Alraune's manipulation of those who fall into her web causes her expulsion from the convent where she is initially reared; at home she mesmerizes, enslaves, and ultimately destroys a series of men and women whom she encourages while denying herself to them, maddens with jealousy, and goads to destroy one another. She rarely acts directly, but she inspires her admirers to deeds, in their willingness to do "anything" to please her, that will bring about their destruction. She feels nothing for any of them, not even for Wolf Gontram, one of the novel's few decent characters. She tortures him throughout his childhood and finally kills him by enticing him into freezing weather, chilling him so that he dies of pneumonia. Alraune herself is immune to disease.

Although ten Brinken is her creator, he falls under her baleful influence, neglects his shady business speculations, and even molests a child to relieve his sexual frustration. Soon he is faced with prison, and when Alraune tells him that she is leaving him, in desperation he hangs himself. He first alters his will to make Braun his executor, in the hope of drawing him into Alraune's net, thus repaying him for having conceived the poisonous experiment.

Alraune is indifferent to the claims of all who have been ruined by ten Brinken's business and banking ventures, and she amuses herself by enslaving Frieda Gontram and driving Olga Wolkonski to madness. In revenge, financially ruined Duchess Wolkonski, the mother of Olga and godmother of Alraune, reveals to her the secret of her birth, the facts of which are confirmed by Braun.

Initially, Braun is immune to Alraune, and this intrigues her. After she learns her nature, Braun and Alraune drop their defenses, engage in amorous dueling, and become intoxicated with each other. Alraune finally yields herself. Braun finds his finances becoming suddenly and abnormally successful, and Alraune suggests that "It's happening again." Their life together alternates between periods of passionate love and ferocious fighting. He attempts to leave her and even burns the mandrake that gave him the idea for the experiment, but he cannot leave. Finally, he discovers to his horror that Alraune has taken to sucking his blood while he sleeps. He is freed when Alraune falls to her death while sleepwalking on the roof.

ANALYSIS

Alraune is one of the most fascinating and yet unpleasant and disturbing of fantasy novels. It was a popular success and has been filmed numerous times. With the exception of Hanns Heinz Ewers' other work—*The Sorcerer's Apprentice* (1907) and *Vampire* (1921), also featuring Frank Braun—there is nothing quite like it. The closest works are Joris-Karl Huysmans' *Against the Grain* (1884) and *Là Bas* (1891) and Valery Bryusov's *The Fiery Angel* (1908). One would be hard pressed to find a less pleasant cast of characters between two covers.

The disturbing quality stems from the author's apparent gusto in portraying decadence, cruelty, and amorality. He seems to delight as much in Alraune's conquests as does Professor ten Brinken. Ewers lovingly dwells upon the sensuality and the perversity of characters and events described, and he excels in exotic description. He, like his Alraune, toys with his reader. For example, the experiment that will result in her conception is much planned and discussed, but the scene itself is entirely passed over. Alraune's death occupies very little space, though the author provides several pages of weirdly perverse comment.

Ewers' technique here, as in his other novels, is to take a superstition, update it in sociological, scientific, or psychological terms, and all but explain it away, leaving only enough of the supernatural and the unexplainable to unsettle his reader. He seems to ask, "What if there really is something to the superstition for which our modern knowledge cannot account?" One may debunk the "mystery" from Alraune's birth, sordid as it is, but how can one account for her ability even as a child to pick winning lottery tickets, locate long-buried treasure, and know which stocks will go up?

The experiment in artificial insemination fails to impress in times when the technique is fairly common, and the book overall is repulsive. Although Braun is meant to be the hero, Alraune is nearly the most sympathetic of the characters. Ewers' attempts to make her seem soul-less make it nearly impossible to pity her in the way that they might the Frankenstein monster, for example. Ewers' own life may make his work unattractive to some readers: He worked enthusiastically with the Nazis. A fascination with evil permeates his fiction.

—*Jerry L. Ball*

THE ALTERATION

A boy must choose between manhood and fame in a world in which the Catholic church dominates society

Author: Kingsley Amis (1922–1995)
Genre: Science fiction—alternate history
Type of work: Novel
Time of work: 1976
Locale: England
First published: 1976

THE STORY

Hubert Anvil, a ten-year-old choirboy in the prestigious Cathedral Basilica of St. George in Coverley, the most important religious city in England, is faced with a dilemma. Although he may have very little personal control over the decision made, it will seriously affect the rest of his life. Experts brought in from the Vatican have advised Abbot Peter Thynne that the boy's soprano voice is so rare that it would be foolish to allow the child to mature in the normal way. They suggest that emasculating him would give him a distinguished musical career as a castrato.

Such a situation might seem irrelevant in 1976, but Kingsley Amis has made a single adjustment in European history. The Protestant reformation is presumed never to have taken place. Martin Luther, rather than leaving the Catholic church, becomes the pope, and Henry VIII does not take Britain out of the Catholic church. Not only is Roman Catholicism the official religion of Europe, but it is the ruling political force, and the aristocracies still reign throughout the continent. Only in North America is there a more benign, partially democratic government in power, and a form of Protestantism is practiced there.

Hubert comes to the conclusion that however famous he may become, he is not willing to reject a normal life. It is not simply a matter of saying no, however; his father, a prominent Catholic layman, is eager to please the powers of the church, particularly when he is called to Rome, where the pope offers to take Hubert into the Vatican choir. Hubert's mother is against the "alteration" of her son, but her efforts to help him are ignored, and the attempt by her personal chaplain (and lover) to thwart both the religious and the civil authorities is met with a swift brutality that marks the nature of the Roman Catholic regime.

The boy attempts to escape with the help of some of his school friends and the American ambassador. He almost succeeds in getting out of the country and making his way to a freer life in America. At the last moment, however, his desire to evade castration is thwarted by a cruel turn of nature that settles the matter. The novel ends, some fifteen years later, with Hubert as the greatest religious singer of his age, but not without some sadness concerning the opportunities and experiences he has missed.

ANALYSIS

Amis uses the simple idea of altering history in more than one way. He employs it, for example, as a serious thematic device to explore how religion—particularly in concert with totalitarian political forces— can exert seemingly benign power and influence against the best interests of the people. In doing so, he accepts the common view of historians that the Protestant Reformation was more than simply a matter of resistance to the overweening power and corruption of the Roman Catholic church in the late Middle Ages and early

Renaissance and that it was also the first sign of what later became the gradual movement toward democracy.

The 1976 of this book, though it includes some novel developments in the scientific world, is still far behind the actual world of comfort and convenience, serviced by the best elements of scientific discovery. Electricity, for example, is known, but its use is forbidden in Europe (although, significantly, Americans make use of it). Much of the day-to-day life of the civilized world is not much advanced from centuries before, and there is an implied sense that the backwardness of life, however quaint it may be, is related directly to the church's pervasive dominance over religion, society, and politics. Perhaps most damaging is the tyranny exercised in Europe, whereby the individual, exemplified by Hubert, is simply a tool of the religious and political powers, which are prepared to reward him if he does what they want but to crush him and those who help him if he resists. Those in power argue that it is simply a matter of serving the Christian God, but Amis conveys the impression that those in power have a strong inclination to take care of themselves. He concentrates on the abuses of religious power, but the lesson has wider political implications for any political system in which the wielders of power put self-interest first.

The less serious aspect of Amis' rearrangement of history is the manner in which he plays with minutiae. Making Martin Luther the pope is a wry manipulation of the idea that the best way to deal with an enemy is to bring him or her into one's own camp. Benedict Arnold proves to be an American hero, and various historical celebrities have their reputations and careers altered to meet the pattern of religious dominance. *Gulliver's Travels* (1726) winds up as *St. Lemuel's Travels*. James Bond becomes Father Bond, and there is a popular novel titled *Lord of the Chalices*. Amis thus provides the reader with a modest knowledge of history and art, an amusing bonus, in addition to a serious consideration of the way in which people accept the modern democratic world without fully appreciating what might have happened had things been otherwise.

—*Charles Pullen*

ALWAYS COMING HOME

A complex exploration of the futuristic, feminist, utopian Kesh society focusing on the character Stone Telling

Author: Ursula K. Le Guin (1929–)
Genre: Science fiction—future history
Type of work: Novel
Time of work: Several centuries in the future, backtracking to the present
Locale: Northern California
First published: 1985

THE STORY

Ursula Le Guin's narrator in *Always Coming Home* is Pandora, mistress of ceremonies for the unraveling of a richly complex tale spanning several centuries. Pandora in Greek mythology was the beguiling human upon whom Zeus, king of the gods, bestowed an unquenchable curiosity. Ignoring all admonitions, she opened the forbidden box she received. It contained the world's evils, now loosed upon civilization.

Le Guin's Pandora lives in two worlds separated by centuries. She moves facilely between them as spokesperson for a past civilization and narrator of a future one. Le Guin devotes the last 116 pages of this 525-page book to what she labels "The Back of the Book," an extensive anthropological description of the Kesh people who, ironically, do not yet exist.

Le Guin devotes fifteen tightly packed pages to a glossary of the Kesh language, and she extensively portrays Kesh folkways and dress. Earlier, in five pages, she describes written Kesh, including its alphabet and pronunciation.

Stone Telling relates much of the Kesh story. She is the daughter of Willow (Towhee), a Kesh woman who married Terter Abhao, a Condor invader. The matrilinear, feminist, utopian Kesh society is peaceful. Its members strive consciously to live in harmony with nature rather than to control it. Condor society, on the other hand, is male-dominated and aggressive. When the Condors invade the Kesh in their native Na (Napa) Valley, the societies bewilder each other.

Condors cannot understand people who measure wealth by how much one gives away or comprehend people who eat as little animal flesh as possible and who hold forgiveness ceremonies for taking the life of any chicken, apple, or grape they might consume to sustain themselves. Conversely, the Kesh cannot understand people who can invade and subjugate their culture, which, although retaining such civilized contemporary trappings as electricity, flush toilets, power looms, and computers, eschews many modern conveniences and rejects much of what twentieth century society labels progress. Because they wish to control cultural clutter, the Kesh do not keep voluminous written records and often destroy the few they have made. The invading Condors desecrate the cherished Kesh philosophy of "live and let live."

Stone Telling grows up on her father's land. Eventually she escapes with her infant daughter, Quail. She makes the arduous trip home, calling herself "Woman Coming Home." She recounts her story and, essentially, the story of the Kesh civilization, as an old woman reflecting on a curious past.

ANALYSIS

At the beginning of *Always Coming Home*, in a section titled "A First Note," Le Guin alerts her readers to her book's uniqueness. Its first sentence reads, "The people in this book might be going to have lived a long, long time from now in Northern California." The unusual, conditional verb phrase in this sentence splices together past and future, as Le Guin continues to do throughout the book.

Always Coming Home, richly illustrated by Margaret Chodos and with maps by the author, was marketed originally with an accompanying cassette of Kesh music by Todd Barton. The book generally is called a novel but is so heterodox in structure that it virtually creates a new fictional genre, in the same manner as Truman Capote's *In Cold Blood* (1966) and Rolando Hinojosa-Smith's still-incomplete, multivolume work, the Klail City Death Trip, begun in 1973.

Le Guin, daughter of noted anthropologist Alfred Kroeber and novelist Theodora Kracaw Kroeber, applies the techniques of field anthropology, both physical and cultural, to a future rather than past culture. She drifts easily through nonlinear time, creating a philosophical-fictional world that includes artifacts from two cultures, contemporary and future, unified by Pandora's narration and Stone Telling's story, the four major parts of which are interspersed throughout the novel. Between Stone Telling segments, Le Guin constructs the Kesh culture that has grown up in California's Na Valley. The material between such segments advances readers' perceptions of both the philosophical and the physical constructs that Le Guin concocts in an ascending spiral of elucidating information.

She focuses on feminist, ecological, and mythic concerns. The Kesh's locale, seemingly, was created by either global warming or some cataclysm (hinted at through allusions to uninhabitable, radioactive regions) that has turned San Francisco Bay into a gigantic inland sea and inundated much of the Pacific Coast, swamping its coastal cities. The coastal mountain range has become a peninsula.

Le Guin divides the world of the Kesh into nine venues or "houses," five concerned with earth (material things) and four with sky (spiritual things). Computers in City of Mind control the planet, but the Kesh elect to lead simple lives, leaving City of Mind to the Condors. The Kesh favor City of Man, which revolves around humans.

In *Always Coming Home*, Pandora grapples with the search for answers to existential questions. Le Guin's writing strains the genre in which much storytelling conventionally occurs, ever testing the limits of human communication. In so doing, however, her Pandora, as a self-declared anthropologist of the future, forces readers to think through the cultural constructs within which human beings live and on which they base their philosophical—especially ethical—systems. Is the structure of storytelling, for example, natural or something writers impose?

Le Guin is not alone in her search for new literary means to transmit complex information. In experimenting with Pandora, Le Guin blurs the lines of time and space. Pandora lives in two distinct contexts. Clearly, *Always Coming Home* is at the forefront of a unique, experimental fictional genre that simultaneously presents philosophy and fantasy.

—*R. Baird Shuman*

THE AMBER SERIES

In Amber, a world of magic that can be reached from Earth by "traveling through shadows," members of the royal family fight among themselves for control of the kingdom and the worlds it controls

Author: Roger Zelazny (1937–1995)
Genre: Fantasy—heroic fantasy
Type of work: Novels
Time of work: Contemporary on Earth and undefined but resembling medieval Earth on a variety of alternative worlds
Location: Earth, Amber, and the lands in between
First published: *The Chronicles of Amber* (1979; two-volume set including *Nine Princes in Amber*, 1970; *The Guns of Avalon*, 1972; *Sign of the Unicorn*, 1975; *The Hand of Oberon*, 1976; and *The Courts of Chaos*, 1978), *Trumps of Doom* (1985), *Blood of Amber* (1986), *Sign of Chaos* (1987), *Knight of Shadows* (1989), and *Prince of Chaos* (1991)

THE STORY

The story of Amber is told in two cycles, consisting of ten novels. The tale is extremely complex, written over a span of twenty years, and involves dozens of principal characters who are related in various ways. Amber is depicted as the "real world"; all other worlds, including contemporary Earth, are shadows cast by that reality. It is a world of magic and swordplay ruled by members of a bickering royal family who form temporary alliances and then regularly betray one another.

Outside Amber, the characters "travel through shadows" by creating differences in reality as they walk, ride horses, and occasionally even drive cars. Physical laws are different in the various worlds; a motor vehicle, for example, would be useless in Amber.

The first cycle, contained in *The Chronicles of Amber*, tells the story of Corwin, Prince of Amber. He is the son of King Oberon, who has disappeared. Corwin finds himself in a hospital in New York State, apparently injured in a car accident. He thinks of himself as Carl Corey and has little memory of his past. Gradually, he learns that there is more to his past than an ordinary earthly existence. His first clue is the discovery of a pack of tarot cards that includes trumps with the pictures of Corwin and his brothers and sisters. Eventually, he is contacted by his brother Random and brought back to Amber, where he learns about the Pattern.

The Pattern is a mazelike series of twisting trails that can be walked safely only by a member of the royal family. Corwin learns that he is in great danger. His brother Eric is trying to claim the throne of Amber and has placed Corwin on the Shadow Earth (contemporary Earth) to get him out of the way. Corwin therefore walks the pattern in Rebma, a mirror image of Amber under the sea, as a means of regaining his memory. He then faces Eric, who for a brief period has managed to seize the throne.

The rest of the first cycle is concerned mainly with various intrigues in the Court of Amber and the opposition of the Courts of Chaos, which stand at the opposite end of the shadows from Amber. Along the way, Corwin meets Dworkin, a mad but powerful wizard. It becomes apparent that Dworkin is the oldest member of the House of Amber and creator of the Pattern. The Pattern has been damaged, and Dworkin's madness is a direct reflection of that damage.

The final showdown occurs at the Courts of Chaos, where Brand, the evil prince who has been responsible for much of the bloodshed within the royal family, is killed after wresting the Jewel of Judgment, a powerful charm that Dworkin used to create the original Pattern, from Corwin. Brand falls into a deep abyss still carrying the Jewel. The Unicorn, a mythical symbol of Amber, appears with the Jewel around his horn and presents it to Random, indicating that he, not Corwin, is to be King of Amber.

The second cycle, beginning with *Trumps of Doom*, follows the adventures of Merlin, the son of Corwin of Amber, and Dara, a princess of Chaos. He is one of few who have walked both the Pattern of Amber and the Logrus, its equivalent at the Courts of Chaos. He is a computer programmer in San Francisco on the Shadow Earth and has built a new computer, called the Ghost Wheel, that will not work. Merlin is content in contemporary Earth but is forced back to Amber when repeated attempts are made on his life.

The second series ends with another visit to the Courts of Chaos, which is seen from the inside. There, Merlin finds the answer to his many questions, and the Ghost Wheel finally is put into operation. The story is left open-ended. Because of the nature of the worlds involved and the differing time schemes in the various shadows, the series could continue indefinitely.

Analysis

The concept of parallel worlds is common in fantastic literature. Isaac Asimov used this idea in *The End of Eternity* (1955), though his method was science fictional rather than magical. C. S. Lewis created an alternative world in *The Chronicles of Narnia* (1950–1956), a series of children's fantasies with an overt Christian message. More recently, Stephen King embarked on an alternative world epic, the Dark Tower series, begun in 1982 and incorporating elements of horror.

Perhaps the most unusual concept in the Amber series is the ability of some of the characters not only to travel freely among the alternative worlds but also to create new ones in the process. When a prince of Amber travels through shadows, he does so by changing reality bit by bit. The characters speak various languages and have various identities in the worlds they choose to inhabit.

It is also possible for a shadow walker to bring materials from one world into another. In Amber, gunpowder is useless. Corwin, however, discovers that in the shadow world of Avalon, there is a type of jeweler's rouge that is benign in that world (and contemporary Earth) but highly explosive in Amber. He travels to a shadow world much like Earth except that South Africa has not been colonized by Europeans. There, he easily collects uncut diamonds, which he uses in the Europe of contemporary Earth to buy automatic weapons. He then has these weapons loaded with bullets propelled by the material from Avalon. With these weapons, he saves Castle Amber from invaders.

Unlike most fantasies, the Amber series is not a conflict between good and evil; rather, the fight is between order, represented by Amber, and chaos, represented by the Courts of Chaos. Underlying this theme is a strong suggestion that both Amber and Chaos are projections of something deeper and that one cannot exist without the other. Certainly, there are many characters who owe allegiance to both places. The most obvious is Merlin, who is searching for his father, Corwin of Amber, but was reared in the Courts of Chaos.

The ultimate reality of the situation remains elusive. At several points, various characters have glimpses of the "True Amber," of which Amber itself seems to be a shadow. There is a mythological assumption that the Houses of Amber and Chaos both spring from Dworkin and the Unicorn. The fate of Amber literally dictates the fate of the universe. All other worlds are shadows of Amber; therefore, if Amber is destroyed, all other places will be destroyed as well.

A final point concerns religious undertones. Although there are no references to gods as such, the Unicorn is more than an ordinary animal, and the princes of Amber themselves appear to be effectively immortal. Like the ancient Greek gods, they can be killed violently, but they do not appear to age as ordinary humans do, and they have amazing powers of regeneration. Corwin was first exiled to Earth during the Middle Ages, where he survived an outbreak of bubonic plague. In modern New York, he is still, to all appearances, a young man.

Amber owes many of its parts to sources from ancient legends and mythology to modern science fiction. The Amber books, for example, incorporate elements of time travel and use fantastic weapons. Sir Lancelot makes a brief appearance in *The Guns of Avalon*, and both Oberon and Merlin have names stemming from ancient legends.

Roger Zelazny has written many stories, varying from "sword and sorcery" tales to hard science fiction involving spaceships and alien worlds. In most cases, the distinctions between reality and fantasy, and between science and legend, are blurred. In the ten books that make up the Amber series, this is especially evident.

—Marc Goldstein

AMNESIA MOON

A character named Chaos wrestles with the disintegration of reality and the possibility that he may have the power to help end it

Author: Jonathan Lethem (1964–)
Genre: Science fiction—post-holocaust
Type of work: Novel
Time of work: Near future
Location: Western United States
First published: 1995

THE STORY

Chaos lives in Hatfork, a Wyoming town struggling to survive in the aftermath of a nuclear war. Hatfork exists under the sway of a tyrant named Kellogg, whose dreams infiltrate the sleep of everyone who lives there. Impatient with the stagnation of the town, Chaos leaves with a young mutant girl named Melinda. Chaos and Melinda encounter several pockets of society, each with different reactions to and explanations of what happened after the nuclear war, and each with different receptivity to the dreams of Chaos and others.

In the mountains, they meet a group of people living in an opaque fog who call Chaos "Moon," thereby reminding him of an earlier identity. Here Chaos/Moon begins to recover fragments of his life before the changes, which are no longer attributed to a nuclear war. The people in the fog pour their energy into researching ways to see through the fog, and they grow hostile when Chaos begins transmitting Kellogg's dreams into their territory. Moon and Melinda then move on, only to discover the McDonaldians, who make hamburgers in an abandoned town and strictly adhere to long-irrelevant policies. Their next encounter occurs in the desert, when a strange machine drops a paint bomb on their solarpowered car, which consequently dies near Vacaville, California.

Vacaville is controlled by a Luck Board, which hands out jobs and houses in a system based on individual scores on a "luck test." The government of Vacaville also generates television programming starring only government officials. Moon and Melinda stay with Edie and her children Ray and Dave. Their arrival sparks the unwelcome interest of Cooley, a Government Star. Meanwhile, Moon's powerful dreams, apparently capable of broadcasting over long distances, attract an old friend to Vacaville. Moon then heads to San Francisco hoping to find Gwen, a past love, about whom he has been dreaming. There he becomes the focus of a plot to use his dreaming power to reclaim a single, unified reality. Many theories are exchanged about the causes of the reality breakdown, among them the idea that an alien invasion explains the strange machine that bombed Moon's car in the California desert. Moon flees San Francisco and heads back into the desert, and the puzzle of the reality breakdown is never solved.

ANALYSIS

This journey of discovery is part American road novel, part ironic Americana, and part homage to Philip K. Dick. Lethem takes tremendous pleasure in overturning American obsessions to discover what lies beneath, often only to discover yet something else to overturn. At the beginning of *Amnesia Moon*, Chaos is merely a flunky in a town full of flunkies controlled by Kellogg's dreams. By the end, he may be the sole hope of recovering a lost unified American culture. However, the novel suggests that even if he could dream a new America, the overriding story that his dreams would provide might not be better than the patchwork tyrannies of Hatfork, Vacaville, and San Francisco.

The science-fictional aspects of the book are in some ways grafted on, in the same way that Philip K. Dick often hid deeply serious speculations about reality behind cartoonish rockets-and-ray-guns storylines. No irrefutable evidence exists in Lethem's narrative that there has actually been either a nuclear war or an alien invasion, and most of the characters do not care what has caused society's breakdown. The explanations invented by those characters who do care provide the science-fictional aspects of *Amnesia Moon*.

On some levels, the book is an absurdist fable, continually peeling away layers of reality with no real end or real answers in sight. At the close of the book, when Moon sees one of the strange machines that earlier paint-bombed his car, it may be human guerrillas warring with aliens—or it may be a local manifestation of someone's dream—or it may be an aspect of Moon's own dreams, dreams which remain mysterious to Moon throughout the story. Is Moon creating all of what he sees? Where are the boundaries between dreamer and dream, and between Moon's dreams and the dreams of others? Lethem's novel avoids providing concrete answers, while taking readers on a ride through a bizarre yet oddly familiar America.

—*Alex Irvine*

Among Others

A Welsh teenage girl named Morwenna, coming of age in the late 1970s, finds her lonely life bolstered by her intense readings in the science fiction and fantasy genres and, later, by friendship with like-minded folks. But the lingering evil magic associated with her insane mother threatens to drag her down, until she reaches a final accommodation with her heritage.

Author: Jo Walton (1964–)
Genre: Fantasy—urban fantasy
Type of Work: Novel
Time of Plot: 1979 and 1980
Location: Wales and England
First Published: 2011

The Story

The narrative is cast in the form of diary entries from Morwenna Phelps, an isolated teenage girl, originally from Wales, now residing in England. As a coming-of-age novel, concerned mainly with the intellectual, emotional, and spiritual development of the main character, the book is sparse in plot-heavy events.

The first entry—"Wednesday 5th September 1979"—finds her newly arrived at the home of her estranged father and her three aunts. She prepares for her enrollment at a new boarding school, Arlinghurst. She reveals her deep involvement with genre literature by citation of a score of titles and her reactions to them.

By the entry for 19th September, we learn that Morwenna suffered a crippling leg injury in the past and that she can see fairies. Soon we will discover her whole backstory: her magical mother attempted a fairy coup d'état, which was stymied. But the assault involved the death of Morwenna's sister and Morwenna's own crippling. Now deemed mad, mother Liz is institutionalized.

October's entries deliver musings on sex—and the novels of Roger Zelazny. She explores the town of Oswestry. Her first visit to London is enjoyed. November brings immersion in Tolkien. Uneasy dreams seem to be magical assaults from her distant mother.

The entry for Saturday, 1st December 1979 is pivotal: an invitation form the sympathetic librarian to join an SF book club, ameliorating Morwenna's isolation somewhat. The holidays bring time to ponder:

> *I don't think I am like other people. I mean on some deep fundamental level. It's not just being half a twin and reading a lot and seeing fairies. It's not just being outside when they're all inside. I used to be inside.*

> *I think there's a way I stand aside and look backwards at things when they're happening which isn't normal. It's a thing you need to do for doing magic. But as I am not going to do any magic, it's rather wasted.*

Back at school in early January of 1980, Morwenna finds the grounds filled—ominously and somewhat prophetically—with fairies. "Most of them were the hideous warty kind, but there were some elf-maiden types among them." Her ongoing leg problems require a week in traction—supplemented by many books, of course. She begins to open up to her male friend Wim about her past, including magic and the fairies, and finds a sympathetic ear. Wim advocates killing her mother to put an end to any future assaults, but Morwenna declines.

The penultimate diary entry finds Morwenna confronting the fairies directly and being forced to choose one of two paths for her whole future life—towards magic, or towards books and real life. The final entry boldly goes forward.

ANALYSIS
The writer of fantasy or science fiction set in recognizable milieus—contemporary times, or the near future—faces a bit of a dilemma when depicting characters who enjoy reading and whose personas have been molded by books. The writer can, within their own fiction, either allude to the actual existing literature of the fantastic (or to invented analogues) or ignore the field entirely. To take the first tack is to risk becoming recursive and overly nerdy, prey to in-jokes and cliquishness. The author also chances a violation of the suspension of disbelief by reminding the reader of the insubstantiality of other fictions. However, stories do benefit from acknowledging the recreational reality that has shaped the reader's own life. After all, science fiction and fantasy do impact our daily lives, are vital presences in the culture.

On the other hand, to pretend in a work of fantasy that fantasy literature doesn't exist, or simply to omit mention of same, is an easier task and lends one's work a kind of sovereign majesty: the occult adventures I am recounting are tangible and real and unprecedented, not just some imaginary *book* such as those other chaps write! The naïve character who is unaware of the tropes of fantastika can display reactions that any savvier characters cannot logically exhibit.

Of the two approaches, I favor the first. As John Crowley has said of his own impeccable fantasies, "My books are made of other books." To embed a new work of fantasy explicitly in the long and honorable lineage of such books is, to some degree, to inherit a portion of the ancestral magic. It's not cheating or theft, if the new author indeed manages to live up to her predecessors.

Such is the case with Jo Walton's *Among Others,* to an unprecedented degree. A story in the form of diary entries from a gawky, brainy, crippled UK teen named Mori Phelps, the novel features at least one mention of a fantasy or SF novel per page, and oftentimes more. (Some non-genre works play their part as well, and in fact, Mori has the kind of eclectic adolescent tastes that can encompass Roger Zelazny in one breath and T. S. Eliot in the next.) These beloved books constitute Mori's lifeline to sanity and sheer existence. She's an inveterate, habitual reader, who would (or so she thinks for a while) rather have a new book than a boyfriend. An isolated soul at the mercy of her strange family and past; a nerd, a loner, a girl otaku. In short, a card-carrying member of the actual potential audience for this very book. Walton has chosen to plunge unashamedly into geekdom and somehow turned this heartfelt catalogue of pop culture into art, a naturalistic representation of the species. Admittedly quasi-autobiographical, *Among Others* still attains the proper distance and clear-sightedness to transcend self-indulgence and self-pity.

It's no so much that *Among Others* as a narrative is made of books, but that Mori herself is, in large part, constituted of printed words. Her soul and mentality have integrated great chunks of fictive lessons and virtual experiences into themselves, as life-saving measures. Mori is under the care of her milquetoast, formerly absent father, having escaped the mad mother she deems a practicing witch responsible for the death of Mori's twin sister in a car accident. Able to see fairies, Mori realizes that the world is a larger and more mysterious place than most people admit, and only SF and fantasy tales allow her to make sense of the big universe.

Because we experience everything through Mori's narration, we are forced to consider her reliability. Walton plays a clever game of is-she-mad-or-isn't-she?, accentuating the dilemma with several telling allusions. Why doesn't the otherwise omnivorous Mori like the work of Philip K. Dick, for instance? Could it be that Dick's delusional protagonists, with their weak grip on reality, hit too close to the bone? When, toward the close of the book, Mori's new boyfriend sees fairies too, the scales appear to tip in her favor. But then again, we only have Mori's report and interpretation of his behavior.

Ultimately, however, whether Mori's fairies are a coping mechanism for a broken home, and whether her mother is a literal witch or not are moot issues. What really matters here is the struggle to fashion a self that is authentic and able to confront the harshness of the world.

Set in 1979, long before the distractions of the Internet and DVDs, long before the etherization of books into bytes, this novel chronicles a vanished age, when books had to be won at great costs and, consequently, meant so much more. Could a similar biography unfold today? Only if fantasy continues to resonate with those for whom consensus reality is always achingly unsatisfactory.

Readers who enjoy this would be well-advised to pick up Walton's collection of essays on literature, *What Makes This Book So Great,* which traverses much of the same territory, except more objectively.

—*Paul Di Filippo*

ANALOGUE MEN

Persons immune to the mind-controlling analogue machines survive a conflict and plan to rescue and control human society

Author: Damon Knight (1922–2002)
Genre: Science fiction—dystopia
Type of work: Novel
Time of work: 2134, with brief sections in the 1990's and earlier
Locale: Various sections of the United States, particularly on the West Coast
First published: *Hell's Pavement* (1955; as *Analogue Men,* 1962; chapter 1 originally in *Astounding Science-Fiction,* 1951; chapters 2, 3, 4, and 8 adapted from the story "Turncoat," 1953)

THE STORY

The novel relates a few months in the life of Arthur Bass, born immune to the analogue machines that, via instilled mental imagery, control the behavior of virtually all humans in the year 2134. Unable to function robotically in a world of fanatical capitalistic consumption and ideological indoctrination, Bass is discovered and rescued by a covert society of Immunes. They enlist his aid in bringing to eventual fruition their plan to rescue and control a schizophrenic Earth fallen victim to human greed and machine power.

The analogue machines were created as a means to control the criminally insane by instilling mental images. A prior authority figure in one's life would appear and prevent that person from committing a forbidden act such as striking another human. Soon afterward, American capitalists realized the potential of the analogue treatment as ultimate guarantor of free market consumption and profit. They contractually manipulated consumers to buy only from them, with analogue treatment as guarantee.

The result, after approximately 150 years, was a schizophrenic America, deeply divided ideologically and physically. Consumers and Executives in Umerc (United Mercantile Territory) have the motto "buy," and their sexuality is almost totally suppressed. They are separated by a high wall from the bacchanalian celebration of Weekend, in nearby Darien. The promiscuous mobs there have the motto "live" and attach little significance to consumerism. One section of America, Conind, has returned to the buying and selling of human beings. In each section, the rare appearance of a nonresident results in cries of "demon!" and a quick arrest and dispatch to the Blank, a small, mysterious section of Washington State from which no human has ever returned.

Bass is born a Consumer but promoted to Junior Assistant Salesman in Glenbrook Store.

Because he is an Immune, lacking an analogue-created "angel," he cannot control his behavior sufficiently when he witnesses a "possession" (a customer refusing to buy or cursing a salesman). Further transgressions, such as trying to touch his girlfriend, result in pursuit by the Guardsmen and Bass's escape over the wall into Darien. Thus made aware of Bass, the Immunes recruit him for their education project. Subsequently, he becomes an Immune agent, promoting the covert attempt to gain control over and restore sanity to Earth by eliminating the analogue treatments.

Sent to Conind to investigate reports of surreptitious analogue deprogramming in preparation for an attempt to conquer and enslave the rest of America, Bass is captured and dispatched to the Blank. He is able to escape because he is immune to the analogue treatment there that removes all desire to leave. He returns to observe the end of the Conind-incited war, which involves little physical violence. The primary weapons are those of psychological warfare. Enemies are "possessed" by the influence of the "demons" from elsewhere.

Despite his misgivings about the Immunes because of their practice of killing people who become aware of and oppose their plan, Bass stays with them. He supports their plan to eliminate the analogue machines and realizes that he is "unfit for any but an agent's life" and has "nowhere else to go."

ANALYSIS

As a suspenseful and entertaining narrative, *Analogue Men* is of the highest quality. The reader is led to visualize a future America so schizophrenic that Bass is driven by its extremes to one narrow escape after another as he tries to adjust to life in a world gone mad. The novel's dystopian presentation of economic exploitation via capitalism and technology logically extrapolates from economic and political trends, and the psychology of demonism is a realistic extension of class, race, nationality, and religious intolerance.

In its vein of prescient, cynical depiction of the degeneration of modern society into mind control and human homogenization, *Analogue Men* fits well with Aldous Huxley's *Brave New World* (1932) and George Orwell's *1984* (1949). This powerfully satiric, dystopian theme is implicitly and problematically contradicted by 1950's naïveté about both human psychology and covert political action, and even by a simplistic optimism. The leader of the Immunes quotes Friedrich Nietzsche and, apparently without ironic intent, is presented asking, "Can any society be sane and wise if its citizens are neither? If we spend less ingenuity on breeding men than on breeding garden vegetables, do we deserve anything but what we have always got?" The elitist and racist assumptions of this view are not questioned, and the Immunes' murder of opponents is condoned based on this implicit "super race" endorsement.

Equally problematic are the simplistic assumptions that anyone could be truly immune to the psychological controls of modern society and that such a privileged group covertly could direct the vast majority of "normals" to a better life. This is a simplified version of the *Walden Two* (1948) psychological elitism of B. F. Skinner. Skinner's views were adapted by Isaac Asimov in the *Foundation* trilogy, written in the same era as *Analogue Men*.

Ideas of elitism and control in *Analogue Men* doubtlessly derived from Cold War principles and practices. The Berlin Wall analogy to the walls between societies is instructive. The novel perhaps is most clearly seen as a thinly veiled allegory of Cold War conflict and as intellectually escapist in failing to address directly how to "get down from this tiger." The novel evades the issue of real, immediate improvement finally posed by Bass. The Immunes' leader simply assures eventual success, after enough Immunes are genetically engineered to combat the hopelessly insane masses. Such a perspective smacks of upper-class rationalization for the aggrandizement of power, wealth, and status. Ironically, the ultimate cause of the social schizophrenia in the novel is the very perspective Damon Knight creates for his heroic, rescuing class.

—*John L. Grigsby*

The Andromeda Strain

Deadly organisms from outer space threaten to depopulate Earth while a team of leading scientists searches frantically for a solution

Author: Michael Crichton (1942-2008)
Genre: Science fiction—catastrophe
Type of work: Novel
Time of work: The late 1960's
Locale: Arizona and Nevada
First published: 1969

The Story

With utmost secrecy, the U.S. government has been sending satellites into orbit to scoop up particles from outer space and bring them back to Earth to be studied. This undertaking is known as Project Scoop, and one of its purposes is to see if there are particles in outer space that are unlike anything known on Earth. Retrieval of the satellites poses a problem because no precise method of reentry exists that will bring a satellite to a predetermined landing site. Because landings can occur anywhere in the world, a system has been devised to either recover or destroy satellites, depending on whether they land in friendly or hostile territory.

One night, a satellite is tracked to Piedmont, Arizona, a remote town with a population of forty-eight. The first trackers to get there find dead bodies all over the streets. The trackers hardly have time to react before they, too, are dead. The government has prepared itself for such an emergency by having a Wildfire Alert team on call at all times. This team consists of a group of scientists with credentials in biology, bacteriology, pathology, and surgery. Wearing protective clothing, two members of this team fly to Piedmont, where they find two survivors, a baby and an old man. They also find the satellite and see that it has been pried open.

The satellite and the two survivors are flown to a top secret underground facility in Nevada known as Wildfire. This impregnable complex consists of five levels of research laboratories and is programmed to self-destruct in three minutes should its chambers become contaminated beyond control. One member of the team, Dr. Hall, the only surgeon and the only bachelor, is given the only key that will deactivate the nuclear self-destruct device.

While the scientists of the Wildfire Alert team experiment unsuccessfully with rats and monkeys, news comes that a military plane flying over Piedmont crashed when all of its plastic fittings disintegrated. Piedmont was supposed to have been destroyed by an atomic bomb, but the president held off giving the order. This proves to be fortunate, because the scientists discover that the space organism (now code-named the Andromeda strain) grows fastest when it has a source of energy. They also discover that the organism thrives on carbon dioxide and that people who breathe rapidly, such as the crying baby and Sterno-drinking old man who survived at Piedmont, escape its effects. Soon thereafter, the scientists notice that the organism is mutating. Now, instead of attacking humans, it attacks plastic. This explains the plane crash.

The fittings of Wildfire's chambers begin to disintegrate, and the automatic self-destruct system is activated. Dr. Hall barely manages to deactivate the system. By this time, the organism has dissipated into the atmosphere, where it continues to mutate into something benign and harmless.

Analysis

The Andromeda Strain was one of the first science-fiction novels to explore the threat of extraterrestrial biological contamination of Earth. In writing a story of bacteria and organisms, Michael Crichton shifted the focus of science fiction away from physics, chemistry, or advanced technology to an area that surpassed them all in menace. The thought of mutating microbes invading Earth and causing madness and death seemed more frightening than the remote possibility of a planet off its axis or the invasion of aliens from outer space. Germs can be more frightening than guns, and the fear of invisible microbes working in mysterious ways to wreak havoc seized the public imagination.

In this novel, Crichton introduces stylistic tricks that later became the stock-in-trade of science-fiction and thriller writers determined to make their works realistic. He uses scientific jargon (for which he apologizes) to explain the scientists' work. As an M.D., he is able to dazzle the lay reader with arcane medical terms. As a computer expert, he was one of the first writers to use computer language and format to lend an incredible story an aura of reality.

Another, now-familiar device he uses is to assemble a team of experts, complete with their vanities and eccentricities, yet somehow indistinguishable from one another. Character development is unimportant in a work of this sort. In fact, the only character who really emerges as an individual is the old derelict who drinks Sterno. Crichton prefers to focus on what the characters do—or fail to do.

Human error is an important element in this story, often manifesting itself as oversight or neglect rather than wrongdoing. For example, obliterating Piedmont with an atomic bomb would have spread rather than destroyed the Andromeda strain. Neglecting to do autopsies on the rats that had been given an anticoagulant meant not knowing about how the strain functioned. Failing to recognize the progressive mutations of the strain leaves the team unprepared for the disintegration of the plastic tubes that seal the chambers. Whatever their drawbacks and errors, however, the scientists ultimately behave nobly and selflessly. They remain determined to solve this mystery even as they fear that things are coming apart.

Crichton's novels, entertaining as they are meant to be, are also cautionary tales. In this novel, filmed in 1971, his concern is with biological warfare and the dangerous experimentation that surrounds it. He is less worried about a strain from outer space than he is about an organism sent into outer space that mutates into something lethal before it is returned to Earth. He also is concerned about misguided motives and the perils of human error, especially human inability to control what is created. Ultimately, he presents the Frankenstein syndrome in modern dress.

—*Thomas Whissen*

ANIMAL FARM

The animals of Manor Farm drive off the farmer who owns it and establish a community in which all animals are supposed to be equal, but their ideal state is corrupted when some animals prove to be "more equal than others"

Author: George Orwell (Eric Arthur Blair, 1903–1950)
Genre: Fantasy—animal fantasy
Type of work: Novel
Time of work: The mid-twentieth century
Location: England
First published: 1945

THE STORY

A prizewinning boar named Major has a dream that he shares with the other animals of Manor Farm one night after the drunken farmer who owns the farm, Mr. Jones, has fallen asleep. Major advises the animals to reject misery and slavery and to rebel against Man, "the only real enemy we have." The rebellion, on Midsummer's Eve, drives Mr. Jones and his men off the farm.

Major draws up Seven Commandments of Animalism to govern the newly named Animal Farm, stipulating that "whoever goes on two legs is our enemy," that "all animals are equal," and that they shall not wear clothes, sleep in beds, drink alcohol, or kill any other animal. The pigs quickly assume a supervisory position to run the farm, and two of them, Snowball and Napoleon, become leaders after the death of old Major. Factions develop, and Napoleon conspires against Snowball after the animals defeat an attempt by Mr. Jones and the neighboring farmers to recover the farm at the Battle of the Cowshed.

Snowball is a brilliant debater and a visionary who wants to modernize the farm by building a windmill that will provide electrification. Two parties are formed, supporting "Snowball and the three-day week" and "Napoleon and the full manger." Meanwhile, the pigs reserve special privileges for themselves, such as consuming milk and apples that are not shared with the others.

Napoleon raises nine pups to become his guard dogs. After they have grown, his "palace guard" drives Snowball into exile, clearing the way for Napoleon's dictatorship. Napoleon simplifies

George Orwell. (Library of Congress)

the Seven Commandments into one slogan: "Four legs good, two legs bad." With the help of Squealer, his propagandist, Napoleon discredits Snowball's bravery and leadership in the Battle of the Cowshed and claims as his own the scheme to build a windmill. Every subsequent misfortune is then blamed on Snowball.

Thereafter, the animals work like slaves, with Napoleon as the tyrant in charge. Gradually the pigs take on more human traits and move into the farmhouse. Before long, they begin sleeping in beds and consuming alcohol. Napoleon organizes a purge, sets his dogs on four dissenting pigs who question his command, and has them bear false witness against the absent Snowball. He then has the dogs kill them, violating one of the Seven Commandments, which are slyly emended to cover the contingencies of Napoleon's rule and his desires for creature comforts.

Eventually, Napoleon enters into a political pact with one neighboring farmer, Pilkington, against the other, Frederick, whose men invade Animal Farm with guns and blow up the windmill. Working to rebuild the windmill, the brave workhorse Boxer collapses. He is sent heartlessly to the glue factory by Napoleon, who could have allowed Boxer simply to retire. All the principles of the rebellion eventually are corrupted and overturned. Finally, the pigs begin to walk on their hind legs, and all the Seven Commandments ultimately are reduced to a single one: "All Animals Are Equal, but Some Animals Are More Equal Than Others." The pigs become indistinguishable from the men who own the neighboring farms, and the animals are no better off than they were under human control.

ANALYSIS

Of George Orwell's six novels, the two most famous, *Animal Farm* and *Nineteen Eighty-Four* (1949), were both written during the decade preceding his death. This animal fable is a political allegory of the Russian Revolution. The allegory, as various critics have demonstrated, has exact counterparts to the events and leaders of the Bolshevik Revolution, the October Revolution, and the development of the Soviet Union into a dictatorship under the control of Joseph Stalin.

The animals are led by the teachings of old Major, whose historical counterpart is Karl Marx. Snowball, the theoretician, represents Leon Trotsky, and it is Snowball who organizes the rebellion against Farmer Jones, who represents capitalism. Another swine, Napoleon, representing Joseph Stalin, discredits Snowball with the help of his propagandist, Squealer. Napoleon organizes a counterrevolution with the help of his guard dogs (the state police or palace guards, in terms of the allegory) and drives Snowball into exile (as happened with Trotsky), then plays one neighbor, Frederick (Adolf Hitler), against the other, Pilkington (a Churchillian Tory), paralleling the events of World War II.

Orwell explained his motive for writing the book in a special preface he wrote for the Ukrainian edition. He intended to expose the transformation of the Soviet Union from socialism "into a hierarchical state, in which the rulers have no more reason to give up their power than any other ruling class." Ultimately, the democratic principles of Animalism as defined by old Major are redefined as the totalitarian principles of Napoleon, and the Seven Commandments are changed to accommodate Napoleon's reign of terror, particularly the two words added at the end of one central commandment to make it read, "No animal shall kill another animal without cause."

This barnyard fantasy demonstrates how an ideal state founded on humane principles easily can be corrupted by the real world. Brutal tyrants driven by greed and ambition may lie and cheat to achieve their own selfish ends. The novel is distinguished by its clarity of style and the apparent simplicity of its narration, which has made it a classic that can be read on one level by younger readers for its story content and on other, more sophisticated levels by those interested in its political thesis. It has become a model of political allegory, a small masterpiece that speaks eloquently to the turmoil of the twentieth century.

—*James M. Welsh*

ANNO DRACULA

In a nineteenth century England in which Bram Stoker's Dracula is not vanquished by his human foes, he rises to power during the reign of Queen Victoria

Author: Kim Newman (1959–)
Genre: Fantasy—alternate history
Type of work: Novel
Time of work: 1888
Locale: London, England
First published: *Anno Dracula* (1992), *The Bloody Red Baron* (1995), *Dracula Cha Cha Cha* (1995), and *Johnny Alucard* (2013)

THE STORY

Anno Dracula merges nineteenth century history and literary fiction in such a way as to blur the distinctions between them. Chapter 1, "In the Fog," opens with Dr. Jack Seward of Bram Stoker's *Dracula* (1897) recording on a phonograph cylinder, as was his habit in that novel, a murder he has just committed. His narrative clearly identifies him as the historical Jack the Ripper. As the novel begins, Stoker's famous vampire nemesis, Dr. Van Helsing, has his head on a pike on the London bridge, and Arthur Holmwood (one of Lucy Westenra's stalwart suitors) is now the up-and-coming vampire Lord Godalming.

Even more surprising is that in the quasi-historical realm, Count Dracula, identified as Vlad Tepes, has become the Queen's consort. All of London is trying to reconcile itself to the changes as more and more people "turn," or become vampires. Dracula has brought the Carpathian guard to Buckingham Palace, where Mina Harker is one of his vampire mistresses. Oscar Wilde has turned vampire but is still shunned for his homosexuality. Robert Louis Stevenson's Dr. Jekyll is studying the dual nature of vampire existence and physiology. Seemingly every important nineteenth century figure from George Bernard Shaw to Beatrix Potter makes a cameo appearance.

In *Anno Dracula*, Jack the Ripper, first known as The Silver Knife, is at large in London, killing young, female, vampire prostitutes. His activities concern more than the municipal police, because his grisly murders are exacerbating the already dangerous tensions between the "warm" (human) and "turned" (vampire) inhabitants of London at a time when things are increasingly volatile. Various elements of society want Jack caught for their own reasons: the criminal underground because increased police surveillance is making their activities more difficult; Scotland Yard because his continued rampage is making a fool of the law; the ruling cabal, the Diogenes Club, because they serve the interests of the Queen; and Geneviève Dieudonné, a vampire of the pure bloodline of Chandagnac, because he is killing the unfortunate young girls whom she works so hard to save in the charity wards of Toynbee Hall.

Although this clearly seems a case for Sherlock Holmes, he unfortunately is not at liberty to investigate. He is out of favor with the current government and probably locked up in Devil's Dyke, a kind of concentration camp for political prisoners. Most of the novel follows the investigative efforts and burgeoning romance of Charles Beauregard, chief operative of the Diogenes Club, and Geneviève Dieudonné, a formidable and beautiful elder vampire. The novel concludes when Dr. Seward, alias Jack the Ripper, is brought to justice, ensuring Beauregard an audience with the Queen, which was the real goal of the mysterious Diogenes Club all along. In a spectacular final scene, Beauregard tosses the silver knife of Jack the Ripper to Queen Victoria, who commits suicide, liberating herself from Vlad Tepes' tyranny. The same deadly stroke makes Albert Edward, Prince of Wales, the king of England. Charles and Geneviève, with the help of Mr. Merrick (the elephant man), escape the ensuing melee. The novel ends with an inconclusive sense of where their romance will lead them.

ANALYSIS

The clever melding of historical and literary characters in *Anno Dracula* will provide the greatest delight for readers familiar with Stoker's Dracula, the Victorian era, and the vampire traditions of nineteenth and twentieth century literature. Kim Newman draws heavily on these sources, but *Anno Dracula* is still enormously original in its inventive alternate ending to the original Dracula novel and in its attempt to add to the already large store of sometimes contradictory vampire lore.

Among the innovations Newman fosters are the ideas that vampires can be killed by a stake through any major organ, not only the heart; that they can see in the dark, but not through a dense London fog; that religious symbols, such as crosses, do not do them any harm, although older vampires such as Vlad Tepes still believe they do; that silver is lethal to vampires; that female vampires do not menstruate and consequently are incapable of bearing children in the "natural" way; that vampires do not feel the cold; and that some vampires can absorb a person's memories with his or her blood. Newman even introduces a cadre of Chinese vampires into the novel, giving him a chance to explore traditional Oriental vampire lore.

Like most vampire and occult novels, *Anno Dracula* has a moral point to make. Humans turned into vampires do not act very differently from their unturned counterparts. The poor stay poor, the vicious stay vicious, and the good are always battling evil, at what always seems to be a slight disadvantage. At the end of the book, as London steels itself for the new, disgusting crimes of the notorious Mr. Hyde, it is clear that the passing of the vampires will not end the brutality, crime, and sin that seem such an enduring part of the human experience.

—*Cynthia Lee Katona*

THE ANTHONY VILLIERS NOVELS

Anthony Villiers, a remittance man of noble birth, and his alien traveling companion encounter plots and strangeness all over the universe

Author: Alexei Panshin (1940–)
Genre: Science fiction—galactic empire
Type of work: Novels
Time of work: The thirty-fifth century
Locale: The planets Star Well, Pewamo, and Delbalso
First published: *Star Well* (1968), *The Thurb Revolution* (1968), and *Masque World* (1969)

THE STORY

All the stories involve the adventures of Anthony Villiers, Viscount Charteris, as he wanders the Nashuite Empire, usually in pursuit of his remittances. He travels with a Trog, a large hairy froglike alien, named Torve. Trogs are supposed to be banned from most worlds, but Torve manages to travel.

In *Star Well*, Villiers is on the eponymous gambling planet. There, too, are Norman Adams, a young Imperial agent passing as a rich tourist, and a couple who attempt to practice the badger game on Villiers. They fail because Villiers finds the woman's performance generally unconvincing.

A spaceship arrives carrying Torve; Augustus Srb, an Imperial Inspector General (superspy) disguised as a priest of Mithra; and five young girls on their way to Miss McBurney's Justly Famous Seminary and Finishing School on Nashua, along with their chaperon, Mrs. Selma Bogue. Two of the young ladies, Alice Tutuila and Louisa Parini, hope to escape Mrs. Bogue's watchful eye and have an adventure. Villiers meets the spaceship and turns out to know Louisa, whose family are swindlers pretending to be gentry.

Godwin, the operator of the casino, and his superior, Hisan Bashir Shirabi, decide that Villiers may be about to find out the secret of Star Well: a hidden underground port used for "thumb running," the exportation of frozen corpses for body parts. They decide to have Godwin challenge Villiers to a duel and kill him that way. The duel takes place, but Villiers kills Godwin. Shirabi had given Godwin a useless weapon because he loathed Godwin and decided that Villiers was not an Imperial agent.

Alice and Louisa, who had sneaked downstairs to see the duel, are captured, frozen, and put aboard a thumb-running ship. Villiers notifies Srb and rescues Adams from the badger game before the "husband" can burst into the bedroom to catch him. They discover the thumb running and revive the girls. Villiers receives his remittance.

In *The Thurb Revolution*, Villiers and Torve start out on the planet Shiawassee. Torve enjoys making throbbing noises, represented as "Thurb" or "Frobb"; he combines them into compositions that he considers musical but Villiers and other humans do not. His Thurbs, however, fascinate three "yagoots" (bored young rich men) who follow Torve and Villiers to the planet Pewamo. They in turn are followed by Admiral Walter Beagle, a retired naval officer who is Chief Censor on Shiawassee and is Ralph's uncle. Admiral Beagle wants to protect the youth from suggestive reading matter in favor of such wholesome works as the children's books of Mrs. Waldo Wintergood. They are also followed by Solomon "Biff" Dreznik, a professional assassin hired to kill Villiers.

By prearrangement, Villiers meets his old friend Fred Fritz. They plan to camp out on Pewamo's main island in accordance with the teachings of the Big Beavers, a Boy Scout-like group in which Fred has attained high status. Fred likes such manly pursuits, but his parents want him to marry Gillian U, whom he has refused to meet. Villiers reads the Wintergood books and finds an obvious, if unconscious, sexual subtext. On the island, they meet a young boy named David Clodfelter and recruit him to the Big Beavers.

The yagoots plan to start a cultural revolution, one element of which will be Torve's Thurbs. Villiers realizes that David is really Gillian U and confronts her. She has come to Pewamo to meet Fred and convince him that she is an outdoor type, not the sort of silly girl he has been fleeing.

They all prepare to put on a musical show that evening. Fred tells Villiers that he fears he is falling in love with David. Villiers sets a trap (part of the Big Beaver training). Claude, a plonk (a talking pink cloud), has been following them. He informs them that he is God. Gillian passes a note to Fred admitting her true identity. Claude attempts to prove his divinity by showing that he is omniscient. He announces that David is really Gillian, but that already is known. He then reveals that Mrs. Wintergood is really Admiral Beagle. As Dreznik is about to attack Villiers, Claude scares him so that he falls into Villiers' trap. Dreznik decides that Claude really is God and gives up the assassin business to follow Claude. Fred and Gillian will apparently live happily ever after. Thanks to an article written by Villiers, Mrs. Wintergood's books attain new heights of popularity as Symbolic Pornography, a development that thoroughly disgusts the admiral.

In *Masque World*, Villiers and Torve land at Castle Rock on Delbalso. They pass inspection by Imperial Customs Officer Jerzy McBe. McBe's superior, Slyne, realizes that McBe should have checked Torve's papers more carefully. Slyne is an Orthodoxou, a sentient alien covered with velvety black fur. Orthodoxous, once in their lives, find the perfect odor and fall in love with it. For Slyne, McBe has that odor. Villiers is coming to Delbalso to see Jules Parini (Louisa's father) to get forged papers for Torve and to find out who had hired Dreznik to kill him. Torve is there to visit his pen pal, Badrian Beaufils, who lives in one of four local Monist monasteries.

One notorious inhabitant of Delbalso is the loathsome Lord Semichastny, who is obscenely fascinated by melons. The local government has passed the Winter-Summer laws, largely in an attempt to get him to leave, though they have driven away many others. Villiers visits Lord Semichastny, meeting the new Administrator of Delbalso, Henry Oliphaunt, and his wife Amita. Lord Semichastny schedules a costume party, and Henry gets a Trog costume that transforms him. The Monists are invited but decline because they are playing a scavenger hunt type of game called Wonders and Marvels. The Monists try to make Slyne one of their Wonders, but he refuses. Occupants of the different Monist houses claim Torve, Sir Henry (in his Trog costume), and an alleged practitioner of the all-but-forgotten religion of Christianity (who turns out to be merely a historian who studies the religion and has some Christian artifacts). Lord Semichastny moves his party to the public square where the Wonders and Marvels game is being judged. Torve and Sir Henry dance together, and then Torve kicks Sir Henry. Villiers gets Torve's forged papers from Parini just in time for Torve to present them to Slyne, who had attempted to arrest Sir Henry as an illegal Trog. Lord Semichastny likes the party so much that he becomes a Monist. Villiers learns that Dreznik was hired by his hitherto-unmentioned brother Robinet Villiers.

ANALYSIS
The books were originally published as "Anthony Villiers Adventures," but there is relatively little adventure or action in them, and less as the series proceeds. Much of the appeal of the series comes from the voice of its narrator, an omniscient figure (not Claude) who sometimes speaks in the first person but never takes part in the action. The voice is witty and cynical; this omniscient narrator sounds like someone who has seen it all.

The books are rich in references. In the first, Alice and Louise, trying to find out about the duel, "remained in an uncertain world where Villiers might be alive or dead" (a reference to the Schrödinger's Cat experiment). In the second, an encounter between two minor characters is described in the exact words of the first meeting between Isaac Asimov and Harlan Ellison, as described in *Dangerous Visions* (1967), edited by Ellison and published the year before *The Thurb Revolution*. In the third book, the Monist houses have the names of Brooklyn streets. The books have a strong philosophical element, including Torve's view of an acausal world where all entities are monads, following independent "lines of occurrence" that may or may not meet, and a continuing discussion of the medieval doctrines of realism and nominalism.

Star Well appeared shortly after Alexei Panshin had published two highly praised books: *Rite of Passage* (1968), which won the 1968 Nebula Award for best novel of the year, and *Heinlein in Dimension: A Critical Analysis* (1968), a study of one of science fiction's most popular figures. There were to be four more volumes in the Anthony Villiers series, and at the end of the first edition of *Masque World* was an announcement that the fourth volume, *The Universal Pantograph*, would be published soon.

Panshin instead began writing with his wife, Cory. They did a symbolic fantasy, *Earth Magic* (1978), and some short stories but have mainly written criticism. This work has received mixed reactions. *The World Beyond the Hill: Science Fiction and the Quest for Transcendence* (1989) was widely praised for its close readings of classic stories from *Astounding Science-Fiction* and won a Hugo Award for best nonfiction, but their continuing love-hate relationship with Robert A. Heinlein and their insistence on a quasireligious element of "transcendence" as the essence of science fiction have been condemned. Many readers wish that Panshin had finished the Villiers series instead.

—Arthur D. Hlavaty

THE ANUBIS GATES

Brendan Doyle, a poet and historian, joins a jaunt back to the eighteenth century that turns deadly and permanent

Author: Tim Powers (1952–)
Genre: Fantasy—time travel
Type of work: Novel
Time of work: 1684, 1802, 1810–1811, 1846, and 1983
Location: London, England, and Cairo, Egypt
First published: 1983

THE STORY
In *The Anubis Gates*, Professor Brendan Doyle is hired to give a lecture on Samuel Taylor Coleridge and then attend an 1810 lecture by Coleridge. The book's title refers to a set of holes in spacetime, created by worshipers of Anubis. Doyle and his party, led by millionaire J. Cochran Darrow, use one of these gates to travel to 1810. As they are leaving, Doyle is kidnapped by Dr. Romany, one of two sorcerers who created the gates. Romany takes Doyle to his camp to be tortured, but Doyle escapes.

The Anubis Gates

Penniless and hungry, Doyle discovers that begging is the only employment for which he is fit. Romany has enlisted the beggar and thief guilds, led by Horrabin the Clown, to look for Doyle, but the beggars with whom Doyle falls in hate Horrabin and hide Doyle. Romany nevertheless finds him, and Doyle is forced to flee, escaping with the assistance of a young beggar named Jacky Snapp (actually a woman, Jacqueline Elizabeth Tichy, in disguise).

Doyle hopes to meet William Ashbless, a nineteenth century poet Doyle studied back in the twentieth century, and get some assistance. Ashbless never shows up where his biography claimed he wrote his first published poem, so Doyle angrily writes the poem himself from memory.

Doyle meets Dog-Face Joe, Romany's former partner, who is possessed by Anubis and cursed with ever-growing fur. Joe uses magic to trade bodies when the fur gets ahead of the razor, and he poisons his old bodies so they cannot tell tales. Joe switches bodies with Doyle, but Doyle survives. He realizes that his new body fits the description of William Ashbless, who apparently never existed, so Doyle becomes Ashbless. Doyle goes after Romany but is accidentally carried with the sorcerer through a gate to 1684. Doyle severely injures Romany and returns to 1810 alone.

Meanwhile, Darrow finally finds Dog-Face Joe, which is why he traveled to 1810: He wants to live forever. Joe will transfer Darrow into a succession of bodies, and Darrow figures to secretly own the entire world by 1983. Joe swaps bodies with Darrow, however, killing him. Joe is then killed by Jacky, who has been tracking him to avenge the murder of her fiancé.

Dr. Romany turns out to be a ka, a magical clone. The original, Dr. Romanelli, arrives in England, kidnaps Doyle, and takes him to Cairo. Doyle escapes and flees to England, but Romanelli recaptures him, along with Jacky and Coleridge. Romanelli tortures Doyle but is interrupted by a revolt of Horrabin's "Mistakes," the offspring of magically enhanced vivisection experiments. Romanelli flees with the dying Doyle to the underground river on which Ra sails the Sektet boat each night. Romanelli plans to ride the boat until dawn, when the Sun God is reborn, along with any passengers deemed worthy. Romanelli's soul fails the test, however, and it is Doyle who rides the boat through the healing dawn. He meets Jacky sitting by the Thames and discovers that she is his future bride: Jacqueline Tichy married William Ashbless.

They live happily together for many years, and the book ends when Doyle is attacked by the ka drawn many years before. Doyle kills the ka (which history has assumed was Ashbless) and begins a life that, for the first time in many years, will be a surprise to him.

ANALYSIS

One of Tim Powers's finest novels, this book won the 1984 Philip K. Dick Award. Its fast pacing, one of Powers's hallmarks, never lets up from beginning to end. Highlights include further insights into the nature of a magical paradigm that was first outlined in *The Drawing of the Dark* (1979) and was used in *On Stranger Tides* (1987). Powers's theory of magic includes some engaging twists on old myths. For example, the power of a mage's real name presumably derives from its reflection of the mage's inner being. Thus, when a sorcerer undergoes a major personality change, his or her true name changes as well.

An important theme in this book is the gradual fading of magic. In Powers's schema, magic fades before the light of Christianity. As the last strongholds of magic-working religions are overwhelmed during the nineteenth century, magic gradually vanishes. As part of this process, the universe is transformed from a magical world to a scientific one. For example, until 1810, the sun actually was carried by Ra underground in a fabulous boat. By the end of the story, however, the underground channel has vanished, and the sun has become the ball of burning gas it is today. This is a delightful way to work the paradigm shift. In Powers's sixth novel, *Last Call* (1992), he uses a different paradigm involving the tarot and non-fading magic.

Powers brought the grotesque simile, another of his trademarks, to fantastic heights in this book. In one example, he describes a character's "blank smile returning to his face like something dead floating to the surface of a pond."

The plot of *The Anubis Gates* is similar to those of some of Powers's other novels. The protagonist encounters a problem, struggles against it, and gives himself up to drugs and denial but pulls himself together in the end. In this book, the "problem" that Doyle cannot face is the death of his first wife, and he is well on the way to becoming an alcoholic wreck in the first chapter. Being dumped into the nineteenth century in the midst of a struggle for mastery of the world seems to be what Doyle needs to take his mind off his misery.

An interesting facet of this book is the treatment of immortality. The Egyptian Master is more than forty-three hundred years old and is senile. His two servants, Romanelli and Amenophis Fikee, millennia old themselves, trudge through the same ruts they seem to have occupied since they reached adulthood. Extended life does not bring enhanced wisdom, and one is compelled to pity the doomed sorcerers even while loathing them. J. Cochran Darrow, the wealthy sponsor of the time trip, has personal immortality as his ultimate goal. This obsession destroys him and leads the reader to pity him. Powers's treatment of immortality strongly resembles that of Barry Hughart in the Master Li series.

—*David C. Kopaska-Merkel*

APE AND ESSENCE

In a post-apocalyptic future, a scientist discovers a brutal society of scavengers who worship the devil

Author: Aldous Huxley (1894–1963)
Genre: Science fiction—post-holocaust
Type of work: Novel
Time of work: 1948 and 2108
Locale: Los Angeles, California, and the Mojave Desert
First published: 1948

THE STORY

Ape and Essence begins in 1948, in an office at a Hollywood film studio. Screenwriter/director Bob Briggs is recounting his marital and financial woes to an unnamed narrator. Unconcerned with Bob's troubles, the narrator contemplates the recent assassination of Mohandas K. Gandhi and the relationship art and science have to politics and commerce. The narrator's philosophy holds that the ideals of order and perfection are the aesthetics of tyranny and that nationalism and politics are corrupting forces. Gandhi died, the narrator decides, because he became involved in the "machine" of politics, a machine that destroys what it no longer can use.

When they leave the office, the narrator is nearly run over by a truck carrying rejected scripts to the incinerator. When the truck turns a corner, some of the scripts fall off. One of them is *Ape and Essence* by William Tallis. Curious about the author of this unusual script, the narrator and Briggs go to Tallis' address, a ranch in the Mojave Desert. They discover that Tallis is dead.

The rest of the book is Tallis' script, a surreal vision of Los Angeles after World War III, which involves the use of nuclear weapons. New Zealand, one of the few areas not ravaged by radiation, has sent several scientists to "rediscover" North America. The chief botanist, Dr. Alfred Poole, discovers a group of gravediggers in a Hollywood cemetery. All the diggers wear patches reading "NO" on the clothing over their genitals. Poole is in danger of being buried alive until he offers to improve their crops.

Poole discovers that this society worships Belial (the devil) and that he has arrived on Belial Eve, the night on which deformed babies are sacrificed by the ruling class of castrated priests. During the sacrifices, Poole talks with the arch-vicar, who explains that, in the age of the machine, humanity's self-destruction was inevitable.

The sacrifices are followed by an orgy. Although his prudish upbringing forbids it, Poole joins in the Belial Day orgy with Loola, a gravedigger with whom he has fallen in love. Belial Day begins a two-week period of mating. Sex at any other time of year is punishable by death. A small percentage of the population, called "Hots," mate all year round. A community of expatriate Hots supposedly has gathered near Fresno, California.

Poole's report on the possibility of returning to agriculture is bleak. He argues that humanity is a parasite of the earth and that such a relationship always leads to the death of the host. Poole and Loola decide to flee Los Angeles and join the Hots. Crossing the Mojave Desert, they discover the grave of William Tallis (1882-1948).

ANALYSIS

Although British by birth, Aldous Huxley moved to California in the late 1930's, partly because the pacifism he expressed in works such as *What Are You Going to Do About It?: The Case for Constructive Peace* (1936) made conditions uncomfortable for him in an England preparing for war. Although critics often generalize that the "American Huxley" was more a religious mystic than a satirist, his novels about Los Angeles—*After Many a Summer Dies the Swan* (1939) and *Ape and Essence*—show that his harshly comic view of modern society had, if anything, grown sharper. *Ape and Essence* is, in part, a critique of a world in which art is disposable (like Tallis' incinerator-bound script), in which scientists are manipulated by politicians into creating weapons of mass destruction (Huxley includes surreal visions of famous scientists led on leashes by baboons), in which sexuality is repressed while violence is not, and in which humanity poisons its habitat with by-products of scientific "progress."

The novel has several obvious contextual relationships to the events of the time. The Holocaust and World War II showed that human beings are willing to destroy one another in massive numbers, and the bombing of Hiroshima and Nagasaki showed that science was providing spectacular means for massive slaughter. Huxley had argued in his essays, especially *Ends and Means* (1937), that nationalism is the basic cause of these problems because it is used by people in power to control the masses. In *Ape and Essence*, the narrator of the prologue makes a similar argument. The assassination of Gandhi is developed as an example of how even a pacifist can be drawn into the cycle of destruction that politics and nationalism create.

The prologue is perhaps primarily an attack on popular culture and the commercialization of art. The maudlin, soap opera life of Bob Briggs obviously mimics the films cranked out by people such as Briggs, and Briggs's concerns, including marital infidelity and tax evasion, are trivial in comparison to the narrator's concerns about the structure and direction of modern societies. Commercial art cannot deal with weighty issues because it must pander to popular opinion. It can serve only to distract people from what is really important.

Tallis' script is focused more on the role of science in the modern world. In the New Zealand scientists, readers see how the segmentation of science into disciplines such as botany, psychology, and geology creates scientists who can see phenomena only from the perspectives of their fields; no one has a broad enough knowledge base to see the big picture. Huxley was a strong advocate of integrated education, which merged different fields rather than treating them as mutually exclusive entities.

Perhaps more important, scientists have been the means by which those in power have gained weapons like the atom bomb. In *Ape and Essence*, armies of baboons slaughter one another with viruses "improved" by science to kill more efficiently. In contrast, science is helpless to restore what has been destroyed. Poole cannot enliven the irradiated soil. Some critics have argued that the escape of Poole and Loola provides the potential for hope.

—*Christian L. Pyle*

ARACHNE

A retelling of the Greek myth of the young Lydian tapestry weaver Arachne and her conflict with the goddess Pallas Athene

Author: Eden Phillpotts (1832-1960)
Genre: Fantasy—mythological
Type of work: Novel

Time of work: Antiquity
Locale: Ancient Greece
First published: 1927

THE STORY

For two decades, beginning with *The Girl and the Faun* (1916), Eden Phillpotts wrote allegorical fantasies using Greek mythology to develop themes with contemporary significance. One of the best is *Arachne*, his retelling of the legend of Arachne, whom Pallas Athene transformed into a spider because the young girl challenged the goddess in weaving.

As the novel opens, Pallas Athene, goddess of wisdom, and her sister Hebe come upon Arachne of Lydia, who is creating designs from brightly colored stones but would prefer to make silk tapestries. Athene—known as the first weaver of Olympus—promises to teach the girl the art. Hebe expresses doubts, fearing that Arachne's innate talent could be harmed by Athene's interference and sensing that the girl will be reluctant to take Athene's advice and thus will anger the goddess. Indeed, at the first lessons Arachne is disappointed with the immortal's colors and designs and is bored by her philosophizing, although she acknowledges Athene's perfection, precision, and speed. When the goddess tells Arachne to copy Athene's tapestry, the girl ignores the model and creates from her imagination. A wealthy Roman purchases one of her tapestries, but the goddess says that in it Arachne has "broken from tradition, drawn opposed colours together, created disharmony, challenged elemental axioms and woven deliberate confusion."

The girl thinks that Athene is prejudiced and old-fashioned, and Hebe cannot assuage her sister's subsequent anger and disappointment. Arachne, eschewing marriage to devote herself wholly to art, starts weaving a grand tapestry that may take years to finish. As her father says, she "must do as her demon prompts."

Hebe, visiting when the tapestry is almost done, thinks Athene will delight in the work and appreciate it because, as an artist, she will realize its beauty. When Athene views the tapestry, however, she is uncompromisingly critical, whereas the erstwhile student is proud and disrespectful. This confrontation concludes with a challenge: Each will weave a tapestry for a committee of three gods to judge.

When the tapestries are complete, Zeus, Dionysus, and Hermes announce Arachne as the winner. Zeus explains that Arachne's work displays the treasure, loveliness, and emotion of Earth seen through the eyes of mortality, a vision forever hidden from immortal consciousness. Informed of the decision, Athene has Hecate send a hurricane to destroy the "sacrilegious web." Distraught, Arachne goes to a wood to hang herself.

Hebe, aware of this, saves Arachne but lies to Athene, telling her that where Arachne hanged herself there is a spider clad in her colors, concluding that Zeus metamorphosed the girl into a spider who will spin eternally. Athene accepts the story, and her anger fades. Only millennia later does Hebe tell Athene the truth: Arachne gave up weaving, changed her name to Echo, married, and lived happily as a wife and mother.

ANALYSIS

During a long and prolific career, Phillpotts wrote not only realistic novels of England's Wessex region but also detective and science fiction, thrillers, and mythological fantasies. His short novels of the last category, particularly *Arachne*, demonstrate the narrative and characterization skills he honed elsewhere, and although the stories come from familiar myths, he creates suspense, imbues his characters and their conflicts with convincing contemporaneity, and develops timeless themes.

At its simplest, the conflict around which the novel's action revolves is between goddess and mortal, but it is more complex. Athene is a strait-laced traditionalist challenged by a youngster's new ideas. Arachne, a precocious girl totally committed to her art, crudely and immaturely rejects the knowledgeable criticism of an acknowledged authority. The goddess lacks interpersonal skills and is quick to anger; she guards her preeminence and is petulant when she does not get her way. This clash of two strong wills propels the action.

By having Arachne surprisingly prevail in the struggle, Phillpotts shows his belief that a touch of hubris is acceptable, at least in a mortal, less so in a god. He also suggests that artists, particularly those with exceptional gifts, should be excused such aberrations of behavior as Arachne exhibits. Geniuses, he implies, must be tolerated and encouraged. Because he focuses on Athene's jealousy, intolerance, and arrogance, the latter two of which she shares with Arachne, Phillpotts seems intent as well on lowering Olympians to the level of mortals, with their failings as well as singular qualities.

Although Arachne eventually forsakes her art for domesticity, she does so only after having accomplished her goal, the creation of an unparalleled tapestry that Zeus and his committee prefer over Athene's effort. Whereas Athene's web may have been technically perfect, Arachne's had a wonderful, wistful beauty that only a mortal artist could produce. Phillpotts' rendering of Zeus's judgment encourages students to rebel against mentors and welcomes youth's rejection of tradition.

From early in the action, Arachne is pursued by two suitors: Polydorus, a patrician intellectual who humbles himself before the goddess of wisdom, and Mopsus, a down-to-earth country boy. Polydorus, who defers to the goddess and wants Arachne to follow Athene's artistic prescriptions, also encourages her to conform to social expectations by marrying, becoming a proper wife, and devoting less time to her art. Mopsus also wants Arachne to wed and settle down to domesticity, but not for reasons of conformity: He loves her and is afraid for her well-being if she continues to provoke Athene.

Although he is the suitor sanctioned by her family, Polydorus withdraws from the fray, concerned that his reputation will suffer if he continues to be involved with one who has rebelled against wisdom. Mopsus, who remains loyal throughout Arachne's trials, gains her love, and they marry. The novel closes, interestingly, with Athene asking Hebe what became of Polydorus. "He founded a School," she replies, "and attained to immense importance. If you think like everybody else, you are always of immense importance." Hebe concludes by noting that although the world is filled with Polydorians, their founder is forgotten. Arachne, the rebellious artist who did not think like everybody else, is immortal.

—*Gerald H. Strauss*

AREA X: THE SOUTHERN REACH TRILOGY

A wide cast of eccentric characters is swept up in the surreal and turbulent exploration and attempts at exploitation of a chaotic alien domain that has spontaneously erupted on a corner of Earth resembling our familiar Florida

Author: Jeff VanderMeer (1968–)
Genre: Science Fiction—catastrophe
Type of Work: Novel
Time of Plot: Near future
Location: Unspecified
First Published: *Annihilation* (2014), *Authority* (2014), and *Acceptance* (2014)

THE STORY

First appearing as a trilogy all during the same calendar year, these books really constitute a unified and continuous narrative, which their later publication as a single volume reflects.

Annihilation is the tale of the twelfth expedition—after all the other forays have ended in failure—to Area X, a realm of deranged nature that has spontaneously manifested. "When Area X first appeared, there was vagueness and confusion, and it is still true that out in the world not many people know that it exists." Four women—designated only as the anthropologist, the biologist, the psychologist, and the surveyor—form the party. Our narrator is the biologist, and she recounts in clinical, yet not utterly dispassionate prose, her encounters with the various unsettling forces in Area X, most notably a being dubbed the Crawler, who seems engaged in a kind of cosmic poiesis. Two mysterious structures—the Tower and the Lighthouse—demand investigation and offer cryptic clues. Helping to flesh out her motives and character, the biologist gives us her touching personal backstory as well.

Unfortunately, the debilitating mental strains contingent on Area X pit woman against deranged woman, until, seemingly, only the biologist is left alive, depositing her report at the focal ruins of the Lighthouse before departing on an endless odyssey deeper into the mystery.

Authority takes up the tale almost immediately on the heels of *Annihilation*, with a shift of voice to third-person. Three of the women of the twelfth expedition have popped out of Area X, as did members of expedition eleven, in an act of spontaneous expulsion by the cryptic powers-that-rule. They have been swiftly corralled and isolated by the administrators of the Southern Reach, whose

HQ lies on the dangerous border of Area X. There, an interrogator named John Rodriguez—who prefers the nom-de-bureaucracy of "Control"—will debrief them. Control—whose Oedipal backstory also gradually emerges—fixates on our friend, the biologist. His interrogation of her falls into a strange dynamic. Is he seducer or seduced, cop or criminal?

Meanwhile, other cabals in the Southern Reach aid and/or stymie Control's quest. New facts emerge. The pivotal Lighthouse was manned by a fellow named Saul Evans, who might have been responsible for the initial Area X eruption. The twelfth expedition was really the thirty-eighth. The former, missing director of the Southern Reach was cultivating a plant specimen from Area X in her desk drawer. . . and so forth. Then, when all seems emergent or untenable, the unforeseen happens. The sphere of Area X expands to enfold the HQ, and Control escapes, following the biologist on her ongoing mission.

The first thing to chart in *Acceptance*, the densely plotted third book of the trilogy, is the four separate timeframes/narrators/milieus. They alternate in forceful waves.

Perhaps first we naturally privilege the "real-time" framework: Control and the biologist—now using her old spousal nickname of "Ghost Bird"—are back in Area X and plunging deeper, their personal interactions evolving to greater intimacy. Soon they will encounter another refugee from the Southern Reach HQ, whose discordant sense of time will reveal more aspects of the anomaly. Secondly, we get to know the experiences of the Southern Reach Director, gone missing during *Authority*. We see her origins and her machinations just prior to expedition twelve.

Third, and rather importantly, we live with Saul Evans, lighthouse keeper, during the days before Area X blossomed. There are villages here in his untouched world, and inhabitants, a normal life. But this coastline, it eventuates, has always been haunted to some degree, and now members of the cultish, ghost-hunting Séance & Science Brigade have set up a camp on Failure Island to conduct their investigations. Lastly, making up the shortest bit, we return to the first-person diary of the biologist, taking up matters immediately after the closure of *Annihilation*, when she, too, visits a changed Failure Island.

Each of these sections features a different gestalt and ambiance.

Eventually, as our multiple climaxes near, the sections begin to shorten and alternate more swiftly, producing a curious narrative effect as of viewing the rapidly passing faces of a cascading deck of cards. All the threads ultimately lock down, with the real-time frame offering a lovely, satisfying denouement. Ghost Bird's vision from the middle of the book is borne out:

Nothing monstrous existed here—only beauty, only the glory of good design, of intricate planning. . . .

Analysis

Jeff VanderMeer's fiction has always been entrancingly, engagingly, enthusiastically weird, a winning combination of mimesis and the fantastical that privileges neither component: perhaps the very definition of that mode categorized as the "New Weird" and exemplified most famously by the groundbreaking work of China Miéville. His stories and novels raise common genre tropes to higher levels of artistry. Prior to this book, his main accomplishment has been the set of stories and novels that explore his realm of Ambergris, a city and dominion where the untoward and the uncanny manifest in a thousand unexpected ways.

VanderMeer is also a critic and scholar of fantastika, and when he and his wife Ann assembled their vast anthology, *The Weird*, one felt that one of its more personal functions was to serve as a syllabus of Jeff VanderMeer's influences, a roadmap of his aspirations. The *Southern Reach* trilogy indeed displays that wide-ranging, intelligent anatomizing and assimilation of this vast global corpus of oddball literary works.

The *Southern Reach* books exhibit a universality of surreal storytelling, a primal template of weirdness. Aside from a few references to modern technology, they could have been written one hundred or two hundred years ago. If we were presented with some edition of these books as anonymous texts and told they issued from the pen of Serbian fantasist Zoran Živković, or Argentinian fantasist Jorge Luis Borges, or Czech fantasist Franz Kafka, or Italian fantasist Tommaso Landolfi, we would not be surprised. There is something eternal and catholic about the happenings and characters here, qualities not necessarily transcendent in the Ambergris series.

First, there is much to admire in the simple, yet boundless scenario. Some thirty years prior to the events of the first book, an interzone known as Area X manifested itself. A portion of the planet's surface went nonlinear, disturbed, transreal. Inside this district, strange creatures roamed, and the laws of nature were not as we knew them.

Now, such a conceit has a rich lineage in SF. One can point to Robert Silverberg's *The Man in the Maze* and "The Way to Spook City," to Algis Budrys's *Rogue Moon*, to Lucius Shepard's "Bound for Glory," to Stanislaw Lem's *Solaris*, to *Roadside Picnic* by the Strugatsky brothers, to Alastair Reynolds's *Diamond Dogs*, and to Samuel Delany's *Dhalgren*. Even the straightforward tales of exploration of a Big Dumb Object, some place alien yet still subject to consensus physics—a Ringworld or a Rama or an Orbitsville—come close to VanderMeer's scenario. But the *Southern Reach* trilogy approaches nearer to the sheer oneiric magnitude of David Lindsay's cult fantasy *A Voyage to Arcturus* or H. P. Lovecraft's *At the Mountains of Madness* instead.

VanderMeer's writing, exhibiting a paradoxical kind of style, clean-limbed yet baroque, and his fecund imagination, ensure that the trilogy is a page-turner, luring the reader into the primacy of a dream. A dream, not a nightmare necessarily, since there is always a sense of rightness beyond human ken at work in Area X.

Like the famous disjunction in tone and ambiance between volumes two and three of the *Gormenghast* trilogy—another paragon of weird fiction embraced by VanderMeer—the shift from *Annihilation* to *Authority* is calculated to produce cognitive dissonance. From a Lovecraftian vibe, we jump to something out of *The Prisoner*, via John Sladek or Tom Disch. The reader feels the organic integrity of the progression, but it's still a cyborg experience: the flesh of the first book mated to the prosthetic limb of the second.

As one might expect, the concluding volume, *Acceptance* (and note how the three titles correspond closely to several of the famous Kübler-Ross stages for dealing with death) moves through both of the previous realms, uniting the two spheres in a kind of nebulous but undeniable "as above, so below" relationship.

The real-time exploration in this climactic installment reminds me of many a moody post-apocalypse tale, such as Brian Aldiss's *Greybeard* or John Crowley's *Engine Summer*. The Saul Evans section with its creepy ghost-hunters and precocious child named Gloria is pure Stephen King. The sections with the Director continue the feel of *Authority*, while the new diary entries of the biologist extend the affect of book one.

VanderMeer's elaborate architecture and finesse on display in this ambitious, well-wrought trilogy carries the reader through a dark labyrinth stocked with terror and glory, to emerge into a new, never-before-seen daylight.

—*Paul Di Filippo*

ARTHUR REX

A humorous re-creation of the legend of King Arthur and his knights of the Round Table, based primarily, albeit loosely, on the medieval romance by Sir Thomas Malory

Author: Thomas Berger (1924–2014)
Genre: Fantasy—mythological
Type of work: Novel
Time of work: The Middle Ages
Locale: Great Britain
First published: 1978

THE STORY
Arthur Rex humorously re-creates the legend of King Arthur and his knights of the Round Table, from the king's conception in Tintagel Castle to his final voyage to the Isle of Avalon after his fatal battle against Mordred. Although he draws his material from Sir Thomas Malory's *Le Morte d'Arthur* (1485), supplemented by incidents from other medieval romances, Thomas Berger transforms the story through his exuberantly comic vision.

The novel opens with the account of how Uther Pendragon, king of Britain, falls in love with the fair Ygraine, duchess of Cornwall. With Merlin's aid, he assumes the appearance of her husband and conceives Arthur with her in Tintagel Castle. Reared in secret by humble foster parents, Arthur learns his parentage only when he draws the Sword from the Stone and thereby wins the throne of Britain. Arthur defeats early challenges to his authority from rebel Britons, an alliance of Angles and Saxons, and the Irish king, Ryons, who wants Arthur's beard to adorn his mantle. Arthur then acquires another sword, Excalibur, from the Lady of the Lake, begets Mordred with a lady who turns out to be his own half-sister Margawse, then marries Guinevere and acquires the Round Table.

The knights who sit at this table form a fellowship devoted to bringing about the triumph of virtue. After describing Merlin's willing confinement by the Lady of the Lake, the middle part of the novel details their adventures: Tristram's ill-fated love for La Belle Isold; Launcelot's rejection of the Fair Maid of Astolat who dies for love of him, his rescue of Guinevere after her abduction by Meliagrant, and his conception of Galahad with Elaine, daughter of King Pelles; Gareth's year of service in the royal kitchens, followed by his rescue of Lynesse from imprisonment; the quest of Percival and Galahad for the Holy Grail; and Gawaine's encounter with the Green Knight, his marriage to the loathsome Dame Ragnell and her subsequent transformation, and his final mortal combat against Launcelot, his best friend.

Also included are the largely ineffectual machinations of those devoted to evil, most notably Morgan la Fey and Mordred. What ultimately dooms Arthur's realm is not assault from outside but failure from within. The story culminates in the discovery of the adultery between Launcelot and Guinevere, and the former's combat with Gawaine; the final, fatal battle between Arthur and Mordred, followed by the return of Excalibur to the Lady of the Lake by Bedivere, Arthur's last knight; and Arthur's voyage, in a barge attended by three veiled ladies, to the mystical Isle of Avalon.

Analysis

Authors familiar with Arthurian legend always have been aware of the potential for irony in it, even during the Middle Ages. Noble aspirations and high-minded ideals, even as they inspire heroic endeavor, do have their comic aspects. This ironic vision dominates a number of modern fantasies that invite the reader to measure not only the heroic achievements of Arthur and his knights but also, more particularly, the gap between expectations and results. Even before he turned to Arthurian legend, Berger had won recognition as one of America's leading satiric writers, winning praise for a series of novels about his character Carlo Reinhart as well as for his best-known work, *Little Big Man* (1964), which is set in the American West. This talent ensured that Arthur Rex would prove to be one of the finest ironic novels about King Arthur since Mark Twain's *A Connecticut Yankee in King Arthur's Court* (1889).

Berger demonstrates a keen eye for the ridiculousness inherent in the unrealistic conventions of medieval romance. He remarks, for example, that while the lower classes died from the diseases rampant in that era, knights died only in battle and ladies from love, as the sad fate of the Fair Maid of Astolat demonstrates. The exaggerations of those romances in which the knights perform superhuman deeds of valor are recalled in Launcelot's attack on Mordred's army, skewering foes on his lance ten at a time.

The author is particularly fond of mixing exaggeration with ironic reversal. The attempts of Morgan la Fey to murder her brother all go astray, for God, readers are told, protects the innocent. Moreover, when the would-be assassins are forgiven by the king, as they invariably are, they are released from the spell she had cast over them and thereafter lead lives of exemplary virtue. In disgust, Morgan eventually decides to reform in the belief that corruption is spread more effectively among humankind by the forces of virtue.

Although he undoubtedly relishes the humor of the situations in which he places them, Berger nevertheless retains a warm affection for Arthur and his knights. Despite the unscrupulousness with which evildoers seek to take advantage of their generosity, they struggle valiantly to maintain the right. The author adapts his medieval sources to emphasize the nobility of his characters, particularly Gawaine. Most episodes that reflect badly on his heroes he either changes, so that the heroes emerge with more credit, or omits completely, replacing them with adventures drawn from more favorable sources, such as the story of Gawaine's encounter with the Green Knight. As a result, the knights emerge as heartwarming, if impractical, champions of a better, kinder way of life.

Eventually, however, Arthur and his knights do go down in defeat, mainly because of an inability not only to adhere to their high ideals but even to discern what is the best course of action in a complicated world. Nevertheless, it is their achievements that are emphasized at the end of the novel, and they remain shining examples of how much can be achieved by those prepared to devote themselves to a nobler vision of the world, however foolish it may look to the self-centered.

—*Raymond H. Thompson*

THE ARTIFICIAL KID

Violence and biological and political mysteries of the planet Reverie intrude on the life of a performance artist called the Artificial Kid

Author: Bruce Sterling (1954–)
Genre: Science fiction—cyberpunk
Type of work: Novel
Time of work: Undefined
Locale: The planet Reverie
First published: 1980

THE STORY

Arti, the Artificial Kid, introduces himself and explains his persona and his performance art, which he produces assisted by his gang members and drone cameras. In the Decriminalized Zone, rival youth gangs strut and challenge one another, filming all the while. He and his friend and patron, Mr. Richer Money Manies, produce films for people living off-planet on orbiting platforms called oneills (a pun on Irish migrants and "one ills"). The Kid is recognized as the best of the combat artistes.

When one of the ritualized gang combats turns serious, the Kid suspects involvement by the Cabal, a shadowy group that supposedly rules Reverie. It later emerges that the problems are instigated by the evil professor Angeluce. The Kid, along with Saint Anne Twiceborn, a virginal religious fanatic, and Moses Moses, a recently self-resurrected former leader of Reverie, find themselves on the run from enemies. An attack at sea results in the death of Armitrage, one of Kid's closest friends. Before he dies, Armitrage declares his previously hidden love for the Kid.

Saint Anne, Moses Moses, and the Kid tell their life stories while floating in the ocean waiting for death. They are rescued by a vast floating organic multicelled hydrogen balloon that carries rich mud from the ocean bottom to dump it in the biological stew of the Mass on a mysterious closed continent. In the balloon, they discover Professor Crossbow, the gilled neuter who had overseen the conversion of Rominuald Tanglin, who chose brain suicide but whose body is now the Kid's. Crossbow, an exquisite parody of a boring academic, had served as surrogate father to the Kid, who had Tanglin's adult body when he awoke with a child's consciousness. Crossbow and Moses exchange selves, and the former Moses helps Anne and the Kid across the mysterious continent, first through a phantasmagoric jungle and then through the Mass until he falls into it. He then mutates gradually into a tree, exclaiming about the miraculous biological process of which he is a part.

Annex and the Kid are rescued and find themselves heroes of extensive films of their adventures, the influence of which has also aided in the overthrow of the evil Cabal. In the first stage of the denouement, Money Manies explains that there was no Cabal at all but that Reverie replicates in social forms the complex molecular pattern of the Mass; therefore, the planet is its own government. In the second stage of the denouement, the Kid explodes this myth and correctly accuses Money Manies of being the power on Reverie. The Kid and Annex, who have both enthusiastically discovered sex, go off to a retreat where they make films and live in a state of uneasy balance with Manies, coexisting because the Kid can provide Manies with original footage.

ANALYSIS

The Artificial Kid is part of the backbone of the first articulation of cyberpunk science fiction, along with Bruce Sterling's novels *Schismatrix* (1985) and *Islands in the Net* (1988), the short-story collection *Mirrorshades* (1986) edited by Sterling, and William Gibson's *Neuromancer* (1984). *The Artificial Kid* features the high-speed action; wild invention mixing media, technology, and biochemistry; witty cynicism; and implicit political criticism of 1980's and 1990's culture that define cyberpunk.

The Kid is himself a classic punk exhibitionist with kohled eyes, green-oiled body, leather jacket, metallic pants, plasticized hair sticking upright from his scalp, a handy repertoire of power drugs, and a cynical, distanced air from the violence in which he participates. Moreover, there is a light-hearted brutality, a sort of game quality, to what he does, even when the games are subverted by real violence.

The technologies created in the novel are various and fascinating. Sterling combines the drone cameras and other devices of futuristic media manipulation with a fascinating broth of biological creations that is a triumph of baroque envisioning. He theorizes that there is a biological gestalt on Reverie, that the swamplike Mass contains the immortality of all the gene-types on the planet, and he populates Reverie with exotic life-forms.

After the Kid and his friends become involved in the deadly struggle, their lives continue to be played out with wit and a self-critical style. The paradox of life as entertainment is near the heart of the novel. In fact, inside the fantastic decor of this novel there is a story of a Kid made to grow up and take on adult responsibilities, a cyberpunk "portrait of the artist" in which sexual maturation takes place when the Kid runs out of hormone suppressants.

In the character of Saint Anne Twiceborn, Sterling savagely satirizes religious enthusiasts. In Moses Moses, he attacks the aged who exert political control; they are sexually "impotent for decades," bored and disillusioned even by power.

The deliberately artificial quality, the comic-book feel, of cyberpunk novels such as this relates them to the times in which they were created. The keys of survival in the cyberpunk world seem to lie in getting by, being cool, and playing heroically but being aware that one hangs over a genuine abyss. The Kid is a gladiator hero as portrayed by the media, but there is a quality of careless, slightly cynical awareness in his role playing that makes him able to "surf" a complex, fast-moving, and genuinely dangerous society. Political corruption in his world features complications of conspiracy and open exhibitions of wealth-based class.

—*Peter Brigg*

AT THE BACK OF THE NORTH WIND

A little boy named Diamond is befriended by the North Wind and finds in her an escape from poverty and disease into a world beyond pain and suffering

Author: George MacDonald (1824–1905)
Genre: Fantasy—high fantasy
Type of work: Novel
Time of work: The nineteenth century
Location: London and Kent, England
First published: 1871 (serial form; *Good Words for the Young*, 1868–1870)

THE STORY

At the Back of the North Wind was first published in installments, with the first appearing in November, 1868, and others from November, 1869, to October, 1870. This work, George MacDonald's first full-length children's story, has been reasonably popular.

The story begins with a little boy named Diamond who is growing up in poverty. He is the son of a gracious coachman named Joseph, who is married to a kindly woman named Martha. Joseph works for the Colemans, who are kind enough in manners but not very generous in paying their employees, who live meagerly in the weatherbeaten room above the coach house. Mr. Coleman's speculation in questionable business matters eventually leads to his ruin and descent into near poverty. This state of hardship improves

At the Back of the North Wind

Mr. Coleman's character but makes life even more difficult for Diamond and his family.

Diamond's family goes through many trials as he is befriended by the NorthWind and goes on adventures with her. She first meets him while he is sleeping in his bed in the hayloft. She coaxes him to join her for flights into the night. Diamond is often uncertain whether he has actually been outside during the night or has only been dreaming. On these trips with the NorthWind, he meets a little girl named Nanny whom he befriends and later helps.

Diamond learns that the NorthWind destroys ships and chimneys as well as rescuing people. He is troubled by her seeming dual nature but learns to accept both sides of her. Diamond's own health is uncertain at times, and he is sent to his aunt's home in Sandwich on the seaside. From this home he takes an adventure all the way to the back of the North Wind, or at least to a picture of it, as he later learns. For seven days, he lingers near death before returning to consciousness.

Some time after Diamond has recovered, he returns with his mother and her new baby to a home in the mews near London. Joseph is working for himself now and using his favorite horse from Mr. Coleman's estate, the horse for whom Diamond had been named. Diamond proves to be a helpful child, even taking over the family business when his father falls ill. While working, he meets Mr. Raymond, a man who loves children and stories and encourages Diamond to learn how to read. With Mr. Raymond's help, Diamond rescues Nanny from sickness and seemingly certain death. Mr. Raymond later gives Joseph the task of watching Ruby, a lazy horse who needs exercising, while Mr. Raymond spends three months on the Continent. When Mr. Raymond returns from vacation, he has a new bride with him and invites Joseph and his family to move to the country in Kent and serve as the Raymonds' hired help. There the family enjoys great comfort and some prosperity. Diamond seems lonely, however, in spite of friends such as Nanny and her friend Jim. Diamond takes a few more trips with the North Wind and finally makes a last journey to the back of the North Wind. He dies in peace.

ANALYSIS

Like many of MacDonald's fantasy works, *At the Back of the North Wind* evolves organically, with many loose ends and an unexplained conclusion. As his first full-length story specifically written for children, this work embodies many small messages for the young, much like his earlier work *Phantastes* (1858), supposedly written for adults. If a distinction between his writings for children and those for adults is difficult to draw, this is so because, as MacDonald declared, he did "not write for children, but for the childlike, whether of five, or fifty, or seventy-five."

Two of MacDonald's later fantasy works for children, *The Princess and the Goblin* (1871) and *The Princess and Curdie* (1882), also proved to be popular for a time. MacDonald's fantasy work bears some resemblance to *Alice's Adventures in Wonderland* (1865) by Lewis Carroll (C. L. Dodgson), an author with whom MacDonald often corresponded.

Throughout *At the Back of the North Wind*, MacDonald introduces themes such as the value of kindness, cheerfulness in spite of poverty, and helping one's parents. The NorthWind introduces the little boy Diamond to the harsh realities of life and leads him to understand that a positive attitude and selfless pattern of living will help everyone to endure the hardships of life more easily. Although they are not mentioned directly, much of this book emphasizes Christian values and Victorian ideals. The values of hard work, honesty, selflessness, and loving patience are all abundantly evident in the life of Diamond. He is sometimes teasingly called "God's baby" because his line of thinking is so different from that of other people. His good conduct makes the other coachmen feel ashamed of their cussing and mean ways.

These qualities of goodness in Diamond are prompted by his trip to the back of the North Wind, where he learns to be gracious and kind. Even Nanny, Diamond's spiteful friend, learns to be kinder by her dream trips guided by the North-Wind while she recovers from a serious illness.

The strength of this novel lies in its imaginative presentation of difficult theological problems, such as providence or the hand of God as represented by the NorthWind. The trials of daily life are seen as being potentially useful if people are selfless. What is less strong in this novel is the repeated use of lyrics, which are more chatty than interesting and purposeful. These verses do little to convey the beauty of the back of the

NorthWind, with which Diamond has fallen in love. Another weakness is the use of a lead character, Diamond, who seems too good for life. Like many of MacDonald's works, this one feels overly long, yet it is full of intriguing perspectives and imaginative treatments of the commonplace.

—*Daven M. Kari*

AT THE MOUNTAINS OF MADNESS AND OTHER NOVELS

In the primary novella, an expedition to Antarctica discovers the remains of a great alien civilization; other works describe various horrors

Author: H(oward) P(hillips) Lovecraft (1890–1937)
Genre: Science fiction—occult
Type of work: Collected works
Time of work: The 1920's and 1930's
Location: New England and Antarctica
First published: 1964 (corrected edition, 1985; contains *At the Mountains of Madness*, 1936; *The Case of Charles Dexter Ward*, 1941; "The Statement of Randolph Carter," 1920; "The Shunned House," 1937; "The Dreams in the Witch-House," 1933; "The Dream-Quest of Unknown Kadath," 1948; "The Silver Key," 1939; and "Through the Gates of the Silver Key," 1934, written with E. Hoffman Price)

THE STORY

At the Mountains of Madness and Other Novels, which contains the title novella and several of H. P. Lovecraft's longer tales, was first published in 1964 by Arkham House, the Sauk City, Wisconsin, publishing house created in 1939 by Donald Wandrei and August Derleth for the primary purpose of making Lovecraft's work generally available to the American public. Until then, Lovecraft's tales had appeared only in the pages of such "pulp fiction" magazines as *Weird Tales* and were known to relatively few readers. By the 1950's, however, thanks to the efforts of Wandrei, Derleth, and other loyal members of the Lovecraft "circle," Lovecraft generally was recognized as one of the finest twentieth century American writers of horror fiction.

Although Lovecraft tried his hand at many kinds of horror story, he is best remembered for his tales of cosmic horror based on the so-called Cthulhu Mythos. These dozen or so tales, which include both *At the Mountains of Madness* and *The Case of Charles Dexter Ward*, employ a common background: the idea that Earth was inhabited for eons before the appearance of humans by a race of extraterrestrial/other-dimensional beings whose tremendous powers dwarf those of humankind. These beings, which Lovecraft calls the Old Ones, continue to exist both outside the earthly dimensions inhabited by humans and, more threateningly, in crypts hidden deep within the planet's surface or below the oceans' waters. Under the right circumstances, with the aid of forbidden knowledge gained from such books as the dreaded (but wholly fictitious) *Necronomicon*, they can be called back.

Although Lovecraft's linguistic style—with its excessive use of adjectives and arcane spellings—might well be termed idiosyncratic, it is difficult, even among those tales employing the Cthulhu Mythos, to identify any "typical" Lovecraft plot. *At the Mountains of Madness* tells of a scientific expedition sent by Lovecraft's fictional Miskatonic University to explore Antarctica, whereas "The Dreams in the Witch-House" is the story of a college student's macabre dreams while rooming in a reputedly haunted house. *The Case of Charles Dexter Ward* concerns a student in Lovecraft's hometown of Providence, Rhode Island, who is possessed by the malevolent spirit of his ancestor, a seventeenth century wizard.

Certain threads do seem to run through most of Lovecraft's fiction. There is, for example, the nature of the "cosmic" horror on which he so often depends. Rather than being actively evil, Lovecraft's Old Ones are more frequently indifferent, oblivious to such insignificant creatures as humans and completely uncaring. The creatures in *At the Mountains of Madness*, for example, are certainly repulsive—in fact, they very nearly defy description—but what makes them truly horrifying is their seeming disdain for human life. This aspect of his creations sets Lovecraft apart from other writers of horror fiction. The Old Ones' behavior toward humans usually lacks either calculation or ill will. They behave exactly as humans might toward ants: Those that get in their way are crushed, without explanation or apology. Traditional religious symbols offer no protection, nor do prayers or more conventional weapons.

The characters in Lovecraft's tales seem, for the most part, to be cut from similar fabric. With very few exceptions, they are decidedly ordinary and nonheroic. By profession, they are often scientists and antiquarians, who often are stereotyped as cold and emotionless. Whatever victories they achieve seem at best equivocal and temporary. Lovecraft's universe, in which humanity's role is so minor as to be irrelevant, allows for little more.

ANALYSIS

Since Lovecraft's death in 1937, his fiction has gained steadily in popularity and critical prestige. This is hardly surprising, for his work, taken as a whole, possesses a strange but undeniable power, in large part because he avoids the standard horror fare of vampires, ghouls, and werewolves. He concentrates instead on creating a sense of horror that is as much intellectual and spiritual as visceral. There are few "chase" scenes in Lovecraft's work and few of the battles to the death between heroes and monsters that readers have come to expect from modern writers of horror fiction such as Stephen King. What readers experience instead is a gradually increasing sense of horror grounded in the awareness that the universe is not at all as people traditionally have conceived it. Humans are not the center of this or any other universe; they are mere specks of sentient matter protected only by their own ignorance and relative insignificance. All that knowledge finally can provide, as several of Lovecraft's narrators explain, is horror too great to bear.

A further strategy Lovecraft employs involves denying his characters the conventional props of religion and science. Lovecraft himself was a professed atheist, and his stories usually are set within a larger framework that might be called existential. The God of Judeo-Christian tradition is wholly absent, rendering moot the question of divine assistance in combating the monstrous creatures of Lovecraft's imagination. His characters neither seek God's help nor seem to expect it. In "The Dunwich Horror" (1929), perhaps Lovecraft's best-known story, several Miskatonic professors turn not to the Bible for help in foiling an evil plan to open the gates between dimensions, but to the *Necronomicon*. Science, constructed as it is from a mistaken view of the universe, is likewise of no real use. In fact, as the scientist-narrator tells readers at the beginning of *At the Mountains of Madness*, science's wisest course might be "to deter the exploring world in general" from uncovering more evidence of humankind's true place in the universe.

—Michael Stuprich

THE ATLAN SERIES

Cija, hereditary goddess of a small realm in prehistoric South America, leads a life of perilous adventure and ultimately brings about the downfall of Atlan (Atlantis)

Author: Jane Gaskell (1941–)
Genre: Fantasy—high fantasy
Type of work: Novel
Time of work: Prehistory
Locale: South America and the continent of Atlan (Atlantis)
First published: *The Serpent* (1963; published in two volumes as *The Serpent*, 1975, and *The Dragon*, 1975), *Atlan* (1965), *The City* (1966), and *Some Summer Lands* (1977)

THE STORY

Cija (pronounced Key-a), hereditary goddess of a small realm in prehistoric South America, spends the first seventeen years of her life confined to an abandoned castle tower because it has been prophesied that she will bring about the downfall of her nation. The people of her country have been told that she died shortly after birth. Meanwhile, she has been taught that men no longer exist, so when she first encounters Zerd—the half-man, half-serpent to whom her fate is intimately tied—snooping around her tower, she thinks he is an extremely ugly, and insolent, woman. She is shocked when she learns not only that men exist but also that Zerd has conquered her nation and she is to be handed over to him as a hostage. In addition, her mother tells Cija that she must overturn her birth-prophesy by getting Zerd to fall in love with her, then killing him.

Cija fails in her attempt, escapes from Zerd's entourage, and begins a wide variety of adventures. She is raped more than once, tills fields, works as a cook, and becomes the mistress of a hostage-turned-soldier named Smahill. When Zerd finds her, she flees, in the process discovering that he produces poisonous venom. Cija stows away on a riverboat. Upon being discovered, she is taken to live in the court of a religious government. There she learns that Smahill is her half-brother. Eventually, she finds the way to Atlan, immediately before Zerd invades. She marries Zerd and becomes empress of Atlan.

The marriage soon proves to be loveless. In Atlan, Cija gives birth to a boy, Nal, who is Smahill's son, though Zerd does not know this. Zerd's first wife, Sedili, shows up. Zerd sends Cija and Nal to safety, but the accompanying troops are attacked, and Cija is forced into servitude. Zerd rescues her, and she gives birth to Seka, his daughter. After other exploits, including an encounter with a mad scientist who has created an "ectogene" from body parts, the native emperor of Atlan attacks. Cija escapes to the mainland with Seka, whom terror has driven speechless. Nal has disappeared.

At the start of *The City*, Cija is sold into slavery and prostitution in a city ruled by religious dictators. She soon escapes and discovers that this city belongs to her mother's realm. The high priest is her father. She visits the tower, now fallen into disrepair, in which she had been held as a child. She is captured by her father's troops. Because she is proof that he broke his vows of celibacy, he plans to kill her, but she is rescued by Smahill.

A herd of wild apes takes her prisoner and fattens her up with the intent of eating her. One ape, Ung-g, becomes her lover. They fall in love, but their idyllic forest life ends when the high priest's troops kill Ung-g and recapture Cija. Smahill tells Cija that he will rescue her if she will abandon Seka and become his lover. Cija refuses, but before the high priests cut her throat, her mother's troops rescue her. Her mother wants Cija to become reconciled to Zerd. Cija is pregnant with Ung-g's child, however, and does not know if Zerd will want her back.

Some Summer Lands is narrated by Seka, who loyally stands by her mother through kidnapping and forced abortion by Smahill, capture by Sedili, marriage to a cruel farmer in a town run by a warrior-turned-prophet, life with Zerd's serpent family, and various other adventures that lead to a return to Atlan. Seka regains her voice. Cija, Seka, and their traveling companion, Juzd (a priest of Atlan), all experience mystic visions. Atlan then destroys itself rather than be conquered. Zerd, Cija, and Seka turn their backs on what was Atlan, seeking a new land for themselves.

Analysis

The Atlan series, which was especially popular with readers in Jane Gaskell's native Great Britain, contains her later novels, but it is tangentially connected to one of her first, *King's Daughter* (1958), another story about Atlantis. All the books in this series are action-packed; the plot summary above describes only a fraction of Cija's experiences.

Some reviewers consider the Atlan series to be a mixture of heroic fantasy and popular romance, presumably because of the high quotient of sex and adventure, on one hand, and the female hero, on the other. Cija, however, is unlike the typical romance heroine. She never experiences an emotion that she would call "true love"; she either succumbs to an enervating lust for Smahill or passively allows herself to be ruled by Zerd. The closest Cija comes to love is her relationship with Ung-g, and even this began with kidnapping and imprisonment. Cija's life with Ung-g is more of a primitive satisfaction of physical and emotional need than the love that grows between the protagonists of a romance novel.

Furthermore, the romance heroine's ultimate quest is to be joined with another. Cija's quest is the opposite: to stand on her own and to cease being a pawn of others. Rather than seeking out the special personality that will mesh perfectly with her own, one of Cija's most important

The Atlan Series

goals is to give up her personality so that she can become a true companion rather than a clingy lover.

The Atlan series might better be thought of as the inverse of the "sword-and-sinew" subgenre of high fantasy. The books feature the requisite amounts of hand-to-hand combat, explicit sex, and (for the most part) flat characters. The emphasis is on action, not ideas, and the language is matter-of-fact, not lyrical.

Cija, however, is the opposite of the barbarian hero. Although nobly, even divinely, born, she rarely wins her battles. Her sojourns into poverty do not ennoble or strengthen her; instead, they extinguish her beauty, sap her health, and dull her will to survive. The physical magnetism she possesses does not bring her success—it causes her to be raped by nearly every man she meets. Her many adventures do not bring her wisdom. Seka, instead, learns by the experiences that her mother forces on her. Ultimately, Cija must be rescued by Seka, who calls Zerd to them when Cija is ready to be his companion.

These adaptations of well-known forms alone make the Atlan series interesting reading, but Gaskell also seeks to infuse this high-concept, low-intellect genre with comments on Western myths. The ectogene is Frankenstein, tamed by Cija's kindness to him; life with Ung-g is a return to Eden; and the lost continent of Atlantis dominates the entire series. Gaskell lists a bibliography of twenty scholarly volumes on myth for readers who wish to identify strands of other legends in the series. These myths are not included merely for texture; Gaskell uses them to explore important issues such as the nature of love, obligations of parents to their children, the nobility of human character, and the worthiness of various goals.

Gaskell is the great-great-great-great-niece of Elizabeth Gaskell, who wrote novels of Victorian life as well as ghost stories for Charles Dickens' periodicals. Jane Gaskell was a runner-up for the Llewellyn Rhys Award for *Attic Summer* (1963) and received the Somerset Maugham Award (1970) for *A Sweet, Sweet Summer* (1969).

—*Beth Rapp Young*

BABEL 17

Poet Rydra Wong travels in space to find the origin of the superlanguage Babel-17

Author: Samuel R. Delany (1942–)
Genre: Science fiction—extrasensory powers
Type of work: Novel
Time of work: The distant future
Locale: Earth, the Alliance War Yards, and aboard the starship Jebel Tarik
First published: 1966

THE STORY

Rydra Wong, a poet and linguistics expert, is asked to decipher mysterious transmissions in a code called Babel-17. The transmissions are picked up in conjunction with sabotage attacks by the Invaders, who have been at war with the Alliance for twenty years. Rydra determines that Babel-17 is not a code but a language of unusual analytic properties.

She recruits a starship crew to seek the location of the next attack. In Earth orbit, her ship is sabotaged, knocking out all external navigational sensors. Via Babel-17, she solves the problem of fixing the ship's position by using the physics and mathematics implicit in that language's description of great circles. Rydra comes to believe that one of the crew must be an Invader spy.

At their destination, the Alliance War Yards, Rydra and her crew are invited to an elaborate dinner party by Baron Ver Dorco, who is in charge of weapons research. During the party, the baron is assassinated by a genetically engineered spy/saboteur designated TW-55. Rydra and crew escape, but their ship is sabotaged once again. Rydra's crew blacks out.

They wake aboard an interstellar privateer, the Jebel Tarik. Again using knowledge of Babel-17, Rydra helps Jebel and his lieutenant, the Butcher, win a battle against an Invader ship. Afterward, she uses the language to discover a plot against Jebel and the Butcher.

Rydra also discovers that the Butcher does not have the concept of the personal pronoun "I" and that her own superhuman ability with languages is in part telepathic. Rydra begins to teach the Butcher the concepts "I" and "you," and she discovers that he is amnesiac. He recalls no childhood, only the exploits of a criminal career.

Rydra and the Butcher defeat another Invader ship, then leave to deliver her report on Babel-17 to Administrative Alliance Headquarters. During the trip, the two merge telepathically into a single being. Rydra makes a tape analyzing Babel-17 and sends it to Dr. Markus T'mwarba, her psychiatrist, on Earth.

When T'mwarba goes to claim the tape, he finds Rydra and the Butcher in custody. General Forester tells T'mwarba of evidence linking the wave of sabotage attempts to the Butcher. Rydra has told T'mwarba that Babel-17 is like a computer language, in which insoluble paradoxes are easily constructed. By being forced to solve the paradoxes, the Butcher is driven to remember his past. He is Nyles Ver Dorco, son of the baron who was killed at the War Yards. He was programmed with Babel-17 by the Invaders. The nature of the language makes anyone who learns it a saboteur; thus, Rydra, after learning it, unconsciously was responsible for sabotaging her own spacecraft. Rydra and the Butcher escape in an Alliance battleship. Using their reprogrammed version of the language, Babel-18, they hope to end the war in six months.

ANALYSIS

In *Babel-17* Samuel R. Delany explores the nature of language and its relationship to thought. The theory of language on which the book is based derives from the work of Benjamin Whorf, who believes that the language people speak defines what they know and how they understand the world around them (the "Whorfian hypoth-

57

esis"). Delany uses this idea to craft a story around Rydra Wong, a poet, telepath, and linguistic ge-nius who discovers an artificially constructed language, Babel-17, that has been "booby-trapped" to impose certain thought patterns on its speakers.

Specifically, it is designed to turn any speaker into a saboteur of Rydra's government, the Alliance, and to prevent any criticism of this goal by removing the sense of self. Because Babel-17 does not contain the concept of "I," it is impossible for the speakers to conceive of their own identity, needs, or goals. The Butcher, who has been programmed thoroughly by the language, also has had his memory erased in order to ensure that he has no possible external stance from which to criticize his own actions, that is, no remnant of the concept of "I." Delany likens this lack of self-criticism to computer languages such as Algol and Fortran. Not only does Babel-17 program certain behaviors, but it also prevents the speaker from questioning those behaviors.

Like computer languages, Babel-17 also has formi-dable analytic properties. Simply by thinking about a subject in Babel-17, the speaker instantly is able to comprehend complex situations and choose a course of action. For example, when Rydra wakes aboard a space privateer, the *Jebel Tarik*, she is bound in a hammocklike webbing. Under normal circumstances, it would hold her, but the web as described in Babel-17 is a single word whose vowels and pitch identify the weakest points. With this knowledge, Rydra easily frees herself. Later, she uses the same kind of linguistic reasoning to break up an enemy attack on the *Jebel Tarik*.

The novel also explores social ideas such as alternative sexual arrangements. Rydra's space navigators are Ron and Calli, two men, and Mollya, a woman. Together they form a "triad," a psychic and sexual unit. The arrangement reflects the author's own domestic life at the time, as described in his autobiography, *The Motion of Light in Water* (1988). The other characters on the crew have mythic qualities that, added to Rydra's telepathic and linguistic powers, make her seem like a sorceress. Outstanding among them are the pilot, Brass, who is part man and part lion, and the three "discorporates" who act as the ship's sensors and who are, more or less, ghosts. Rydra's command of Babel-17 and the amazing powers it confers borders on magic anyway. With this cast of familiars, she becomes a futuristic Circe.

—*George E. Nicholas*

BAREFOOT IN THE HEAD

A European society altered by various psychedelic chemicals creates a cult messiah out of Colin Charteris, who begins to believe the myths about him and attempts to live out the image, unsuccessfully and tragically

Author: Brian W. Aldiss (1925–)
Genre: Science fiction—dystopia
Type of work: Novel
Time of work: The near future
Locale: Western Europe
First published: 1969

THE STORY

Colin Barefoot in the HeadCharteris is a nineteen-year-old Jugo-slav and an official in the New United Nations Strategic Air Command (NUN-SACS). That agency has an osten-sible mission of aiding in the rehabilitation of war victims in a Europe maddened by psychedelic bombs. Told in episodic form, the story follows Charteris as he wends his way across the continent, driving a Banshee into repeated auto crashes, moving from the south of France toward England, and eventually returning to his home.

In Metz, his hallucinogenic vision leads him to discover that time is merely a fabrication of matter and that matter itself is merely another hallucination. During the vision, he thinks of himself as God, and he tells the hotel maid, Angelina, who becomes his mistress, that he had wished to experience mystical insights similar to those of Russian philosopher P. D. Ouspenski. Charteris wonders if the vision may have been induced by drugs. Ouspenski's work on Armenian mystic G.

I. Gurdjieff provides the novel with its structure. His influence, together with the stylistic inventions of James Joyce, is acknowledged by Brian Aldiss.

During his travels across Europe, Charteris experiences dreams as reality and undergoes other phenomena related by both Ouspenski and Gurdjieff. Soon he comes to think of the two mystics as one and relives some of their psychic visions, such as hearing the crunch of muscles, perceiving the inherent motion of stones, and knowing the multiple "I's" within a person. Charteris comes to think of himself in Gurdjieffian terms as Man the Driver, then eventually as Saint Charteris, leader of the Fourth World System and New Thought. (Aldiss derived the name of his protagonist from Leslie Charteris, the author of the "Saint" detective series.)

A succession of increasingly bizarre incidents leads Charteris to be hailed by various citizens as a saint, and he soon comes to believe their projections. Huge crowds follow him as he leads a virtual pilgrimage or crusade across Europe, accompanied by a vast panoply of hangers-on and camp followers including rock bands and film producers. Angelina, his mistress, remains faithful to him. Her name is significant, symbolizing at once the redemptive aspect of the feminine as well as the angelic. She remains faithful even when Charteris takes several other mistresses and accidentally kills several people as his motorcade proceeds along highways doubled or tripled in width to accommodate speedsters under the influence of psychedelic drugs.

Even though he walks on water and is apparently headed for a crucifixion, he comes to realize that his crusade to find the Christ self, which in turn becomes intermixed with his search for Gurdjieff-Ouspenski, is futile. All the events in the novel become confused in various parodies of the myth of the eternal return. Charteris lives to be ninety years old, and in what may well be a reference to the Buddha sitting in enlightenment under the Boh tree, he inches toward death.

Analysis

Barefoot in the Head (subtitled A European Fantasia) is a difficult yet rewarding novel. Aldiss intersperses many poems as inter-chapters. The poems augment, reflect, or explain the events of the novel. The stylistic techniques of Aldiss' writing become increasing dense, allusive, elusive, and rewarding.

James Joyce's linguistic experiments, begun in *Ulysses* (1922) and continued in *Finnegans Wake* (1939), are at the heart of *Barefoot in the Head*. The book is also filled with wordplay of all types, including complicated multilevel puns and abstruse figures of speech. Aldiss makes literary references to such diverse writers as William Shakespeare, John Milton, T. S. Eliot, and Joyce himself, as well as references to both Gurdjieff and Ouspenski. Joyce was often concerned with the myth of the eternal return, but Gurdjieff did not advocate the subject, believing that it discouraged striving for change.

In this novel, when everything seems twisted and out of shape, and when the concepts of traditional narrative linearity are often difficult to follow, Aldiss seems to be not only mirroring the psychedelic experiments of the 1960's but also providing some cautionary warnings. Aldiss, however, is never sermonic, and his own beliefs, whatever they might have been, are hidden carefully under the thrust of narrative structure and the complications of plot and character. The novel is written almost in a molecular structure, with the electrons of the various plot elements spinning around one another, intermixing or impinging on the central themes of Man the Driver, Man the Searching, Man the Unpredictable, and Man the Mechanical.

For all the difficulties encountered in reading *Barefoot in the Head*, its abundant humor is not to be overlooked. Aldiss uses an exuberant, almost joyful style, at once deliberative and ecstatic, even considering the nature of the story line. Although baleful in subject matter, the novel is ultimately joyful in both conception and execution and is certainly one of Aldiss' most intriguing works.

—*Willis E. McNelly*

BARON MUNCHAUSEN'S NARRATIVE OF HIS MARVELLOUS TRAVELS AND CAMPAIGNS IN RUSSIA

A collection of short tales describing the exaggerated and impractical adventures of a celebrated German soldier

Author: Rudolf Erich Raspe (1736–1794)
Genre: Fantasy—alternate history
Type of work: Stories
Time of work: The eighteenth century
Locale: Germany, Poland, Russia, Turkey, and the Moon
First published: 1785 (serial form for the bulk of the first edition, *Vademecum für Lustige Leute,* 1781 and 1783)

THE STORY

The original *Baron Münchausen's Narrative of His Marvellous Travels and Campaigns in Russia* was published late in 1785, though its title page bears the date 1786. Published anonymously as authentic reminiscences, this slim volume recounted in fourteen anecdotes of some four thousand words each the preposterous experiences of an old German soldier. As a result of its immediate success, Rudolf Erich Raspe brought out a new edition with five additional "naval adventures," published as *Singular Travels, Campaigns, Voyages, and Sporting Adventures of Baron Munnikhouson, Commonly Pronounced Munchausen; as He Relates Them over a Bottle When Surrounded by His Friends* (1786). At this point, Raspe's influence ends. A host of ambitious editors and authors added to, embellished, illustrated, and amended the original author's work. By the turn of the century, there were at least fifteen editions, and Raspe's humble collection of tall tales had grown ninefold in the hands of inferior writers.

As a picaresque romance, *Baron Münchausen's Narrative* minimizes plot. Each of the stories introduces a separate conflict that bears little or no relation to previous circumstances. Using resources beyond belief and his own supernatural skills, the baron stretches luck to the limit. For example, on a snowy journey from his home to Russia, he ties his horse to a stump in the square of a Polish village. Upon waking, he notices that a "sudden change of weather" has taken place and that his horse is now dangling far above him, tied to the weathercock of the steeple. He quickly resolves the problem, using his pistol to shoot through the bridle, enabling the horse to continue the journey. Only the baron and his resourcefulness remain constant, however. In the very next anecdote, the faithful horse, now pulling a sledge, is eaten by a ravenous wolf that, by virtue of its meal, slips into the harness and carries Münchausen on to his destination.

The original narrative of 1785, comprising chapters 2 through 6 of most modern editions, was restricted to Münchausen's travels in northeastern Europe, a brief period of slavery in Turkey, and an even briefer sojourn to the Moon for the purely practical purpose of retrieving a royal axe that he had flung inadvertently into space. The success of these grand impostures led Raspe to expand the memory of his imaginary hero, who swore that his naval adventures were "equally authentic." These incorporated further improbable adventures in England, France, the Mediterranean, and Turkey, including the story of how Münchausen's friend (or the baron himself in some editions) was conceived in the subterranean apartment of an attractive but promiscuous seller of oysters who attracted the roving eye of Pope Clement XIV as he passed her on a Roman street.

Without copyright provisions, publishers were free to expropriate Raspe's version of what were anyway popular folktales emanating from the human propensity for exaggeration. Various authors led Münchausen on extraordinary adventures farther and farther afield. Whereas the core of Raspe's laconic narrative had been relatively coherent and rooted in eighteenth century events, new anecdotes often were disconnected, ponderously developed flights of pure fancy. In one chapter alone, for example, Münchausen is made to travel through the deserts and forests of North America, where he is scalped and burned in making his way to the Kamchatka peninsula, from there down to Tahiti and over to Panama, where he repeatedly ploughed the isthmian earth with the chariot of Queen Mab before returning to England, "having wedded the Atlantic Ocean to the South Seas."

ANALYSIS

The appeal of *Baron Münchausen's Narrative* is rooted in an unusual combination of understated satirical wit, exotic venue, and legendary tall tale. Obvious models are Lucian's "Voyage to the Underworld," which elevated the value of a lie; the fifteenth century *Arabian Nights' Entertainments*, rich in supernatural and unexpected circumstances; and François Rabelais' *Gargantua and Pantagruel* (1533-1567), exaggerations composed across time and by several hands. Voyages of discovery from Homer's sixth century b.c.e. *The Odyssey* onward have captivated people's imaginations, the exotic surroundings both entertaining and enlarging the capacity of readers to isolate themselves in unfamiliar surroundings, free from ordinary human constraints.

Like Rabelais and Jonathan Swift after him, Raspe developed his stories around contemporary events. The surname of the hero is taken from a noble family of Brunswick, the hero himself being patterned on a younger son, Captain Hieronymous Karl Friederich, Freiherr von Münchhausen. Although it is unclear if Raspe and Münchhausen ever met, the author had known Münchhausen's cousin and certainly was aware of the German soldier's legendary exploits in the Russian service. The real baron not only served against the Turks, witnessed the eclipse of German influence at St. Petersburg, and was driven from Russia—events that can be traced in Raspe's narrative—but upon his retirement at the age of forty became known for his hospitality and "narration of palpable absurdities." Added to the real-life adventures of this colorful figure, however, was the residue of a lifetime of eclectic reading, including popular collections of folk stories such as *Scharaffenland*, in which the biggest liar was the king. The substance of many of Raspe's anecdotes can be found in medieval monkish drolleries composed to relieve the boredom of secluded life.

Raspe's narrative is distinctive in taking direct aim at the perpetrators of preposterous memory, though one should not make too much of his achievement. Pompous old soldiers and country gentlemen are easy targets of satire. On the other hand, few have ventured to retell their exaggerations. Raspe succeeded in combining travel fantasy, local tradition, and contemporary gossip in exactly the right proportions, a feat that the lesser hands of the later editions were unable to achieve.

—*John Powell*

THE BARSOOM SERIES

John Carter, a Civil War veteran, journeys to Mars in a series of out-of-body experiences and establishes himself as one of the most respected warriors on the red planet

Author: Edgar Rice Burroughs (1875-1950)
Genre: Science fiction—planetary romance
Type of work: Novels
Time of work: The late nineteenth and early twentieth centuries
Location: Earth and Mars
First published: *A Princess of Mars* (1917; serial form, as by Norman Bean, "Under the Moons of Mars," *All-Story Magazine*, 1912), *The Gods of Mars* (1918; serial form, *All-Story Magazine*, 1913), *The Warlord of Mars* (1919; serial form, *All-Story Magazine*, 1913-1914), *Thuvia, Maid of Mars* (1920; serial form, *All-Story Weekly*, 1916), *The Chessmen of Mars* (1922), *The Master Mind of Mars* (1928), *A Fighting Man of Mars* (1931), *Swords of Mars* (1936), *Synthetic Men of Mars* (1940), *Llana of Gathol* (1948; serial form, *Amazing Stories*, 1941), and *John Carter of Mars* (1964; serial form, *Amazing Stories*, 1941-1943)

THE STORY

Although the Barsoom series was written over a long period of time and spans a long time in its internal chronology, Edgar Rice Burroughs sustained his narrative by creating a plot line that chronicled the adventures of a family, not one individual. Through eleven novels, originally serialized in popular science-fiction magazines, the history of Mars is traced from ancient times to the present.

Seeking to recoup his fortunes after the defeat of the Confederacy, John Carter leaves Virginia to prospect for gold in Arizona. While trying to rescue his partner, who has been ambushed by

Apaches, Carter is trapped in a cave by the same warriors, undergoes an out-of-body experience, and awakes on Mars.

A Princess of Mars initiates a series of amazing adventures. After being captured by a band of Tharks, the four-armed green men of Barsoom, the native name of Mars, Carter wins their admiration by strength of arms. Accepted into this warrior culture, he masters their language and encounters another captive, Dejah Thoris, Princess of Helium, a beautiful woman of the red Martian race. Carter falls in love with the princess, whom he rescues. They marry, and for nine years their happiness is complete. Then, while trying to save the system that stabilizes the atmospherem of Mars, Carter collapses. When he awakes, he is again in the cave.

After willing himself to return to Barsoom, Carter begins his adventures anew in *The Gods of Mars*. As he reveals the hypocrisy in the Martian religion, Carter encounters carnivorous plantmen, vicious white apes, the white race, and finally the black race of Mars. After an absence of a decade, Carter is surprised and delighted to find his son, Carthoris, who is almost grown. They escape death only to discover Dejah Thoris trapped in an impregnable prison.

Having delivered the Martians from the religion that had duped uncounted generations, Carter rescues his beloved in *The Warlord of Mars*. While seeking Dejah Thoris, he encounters the yellow race of Mars, overthrows a tyranny more pernicious than any he had yet encountered, and is proclaimed Warlord of Barsoom.

Thuvia, Maid of Mars is a love story that relates the adventures of Carthoris. Thuvia, princess of Ptarth, is kidnapped by a rejected suitor who frames Carthoris with the crime, but Carthoris proves his innocence and wins his bride after a series of harrowing adventures.

Tara of Helium, the daughter of Carter and Dejah Thoris, is the heroine of *The Chessmen of Mars*. After she lands her damaged aircraft in a violent windstorm, Tara begins a series of adventures that include her capture by the inhabitants of the city of Manator, who play jetan, the Martian version of chess, to the death with living beings. Through the same tenacity shown by the other members of her family, Tara overcomes all difficulties.

Inspired by Carter's example, Ulysses Paxton escapes from the trenches of World War I and awakes in the clinic of Ras Thavas, the title character of *The Master Mind of Mars*, who has perfected a technique for transplanting organs—including the brain—from one human to another. When an evil ruler purchases the body of the woman whom Paxton loves, the Earthman embarks on a successful quest to rescue his beloved.

A Fighting Man of Mars relates the quest of Tan Hadron, who saves Mars while trying to rescue the woman he loves from a power-crazed warlord. Absent from this narrative are the philosophical speculations that form an important part of *The Gods of Mars* and *The Master Mind of Mars*. This tale is pure adventure.

Swords of Mars is fascinating not merely for the swashbuckling exploits found in all the Barsoom novels but also for the introduction of an artificial brain capable of guiding a Martian airborne vessel. After Dejah Thoris is injured in an accident, Carter seeks Ras Thavas, the mastermind of Mars, who is unfortunately the prisoner of his own creations, a group of artificial humans. Following a series of harrowing escapades, *Synthetic Men of Mars* concludes with the treatment and recovery of Dejah Thoris.

In *Llana of Gathol*, Carter encounters a race of white men who have lived in secret for ages in one of the ruined cities of Mars. His discovery of this race sets in motion a number of exploits that lead him across the face of the planet. He ends his adventure by delivering the city of Gathol from Hin Abtol, a would-be conqueror from the frozen wastes of Barsoom.

In the final volume, *John Carter of Mars*, the red planet is threatened by a gigantic white ape that is the creation of a scientist gone mad. TheWarlord of Mars once again delivers his adopted home from destruction.

ANALYSIS

With the publication of *A Princess of Mars*, his first novel, Burroughs began a series that would have a profound effect on the development of the genre of science fiction. Each volume originally was serialized in a popular journal, and Burroughs did not alter the episodic quality of his Barsoom stories when they were published as separate works.

The record of the deeds of John Carter and his family have endured partly because the reader encounters ideas and concepts that are usually the purview of philosophers and theologians. Many of the carefully crafted details in the stories might initially shock, but as a whole they become essential ingredients in the creation of a vision of another world that still captures the imagination. Burroughs is as successful as Jules Verne in predicting the shape of things to come, and his vision of the moral dilemmas that haunt his own century is both extraordinary and frightening.

Having deposited his hero on the surface of Mars, Burroughs casually mentions that Carter is naked—in fact, all Martians, male and female, prefer that state. The only accessories they wear are decorative harnesses and belts that provide protection and denote their status and accomplishments. By discarding the external adornments that occupy significant attention in other works of science fiction, Burroughs is able to concentrate on the internal habiliments of his characters. He is more concerned with the psychological than the fashionable. Because Carter accepts nudity as normal, the reader also tolerates this altered state of being. Burroughs also deals with Martian sexuality by revealing the fact that the women of Barsoom do not bear their young alive but instead lay eggs that take years to mature. Sex for the average Martian takes a poor second to the favorite preoccupation of violence.

Peace and tranquillity are almost unknown to the inhabitants of Barsoom. The moment they fight their way out of their shells, they are ready for conflict. It is impossible to exaggerate the importance of brutality in each and every story. Slavery is an accepted part of life. It is nonracial and is the potential fate of both sexes and all ranks, from rulers to commoners.

Carter embraces the life of the warrior and revels in it from the first page to the last; however, gratuitous violence and unwarranted cruelty are punished by Martian hubris because they are not part of the code of the warrior. In his sometimes stirring prose, Burroughs captures a rather unflattering reflection of his own world and its obsession with honor, duty, and war.

The discussion of race and religion is subtle and masterful. Each group of Martians boasts superiority only to be superseded by another. The green race is dismissed by the red as inferior, only to be labeled by the white with a similar epithet. Blacks dismiss whites only to be regarded as mediocre by the yellow inhabitants of Mars. Each racial division is equally deceived by the ancient religion of Barsoom, which is but a cult of death. The triumph of Carter over the superstition embraced by the inhabitants of his adopted world may well reflect the feelings of Burroughs himself toward the religious establishment of his own time. Carter often seems near to death, but he never surrenders control of his own fate to any power; he is ever the master of his soul. Carter is Everyman, and therein lies the enduring quality of the Barsoom series.

—*Clifton W. Potter, Jr.*

BEAUTY AND THE BEAST AND SONG OF ORPHEUS

Beautiful, wealthy Catherine Chandler discovers the existence of a secret underworld of outcasts below the subway tunnels of New York

Author: Barbara Hambly (1951–)
Genre: Fantasy—cultural exploration
Type of work: Novels
Time of work: 1986–1987
Locale: New York City
First published: *Beauty and the Beast* (1989) and *Song of Orpheus* (1990)

THE STORY

Beauty and the Beast and *Song of Orpheus* are based on the television program *Beauty and the Beast*, which began airing in 1987 and was created by Ron Koslow. The story concerns Catherine Chandler, a beautiful, well-educated debutante whose narcissistic, privileged life has begun to lose its appeal. Her job as junior partner in her father's prestigious corporate law firm has become dull and her performance in that capacity lackluster. While trying to hail a taxi one evening, Catherine is grabbed by a stocky man and forced into a van. Three days later, she is thrown out of the van in Central Park and left for dead. She has been beaten badly, and her face has been slashed.

Catherine awakes Below, in a secret underworld beneath the level of old subway tunnels in Manhattan, having been found by Vincent, a huge half-human, half-lion. She immediately feels a powerful bond with Vincent. She is cared for by Father, patriarch of the secret society of outcasts and refugees from the heartless, profligate society Above.

Despite her own father's efforts to facilitate her return to normalcy by hiring a plastic surgeon and by remaining patient in the face of her flat refusal to discuss the details of her disappearance, Catherine's thoughts are not at all on settling back into her old routine. Searing memories of the injustice done to her and to Vincent, an "accident" horribly discarded at birth but rescued by the Tunnel Dwellers, claim her attention. Although she understands that Above remains as closed to Vincent as Below is to her, she knows also that her life henceforth will never be the same. She leaves her father's corporate law firm and, seeking to aid other innocent victims, becomes a deputy district attorney. She also begins to learn how to defend herself.

Vincent, his thoughts on Catherine, occasionally ventures stealthily into Central Park from the Tunnels, merely to gaze at the light in her room. Neither Vincent's dreams of Catherine nor his visits Above find favor with Father, who insists that by going Above, the Tunnel Dwellers invite their doom. Vincent appears one evening on Catherine's terrace and stays with her until dawn.

At the district attorney's office, Catherine soon discovers information concerning another victim and thereby learns the identity of her assailant, who then sets out to kill her. Vincent, sensing her danger, rushes to her aid with the ferocity of an animal. The book ends as Catherine and Vincent, realizing the strength of the bond between them, bid goodbye for the time being.

In *Song of Orpheus*, Barbara Hambly develops three episodes previously aired in the television series that intertwine the lives and worlds of Catherine and Vincent. Vincent's nightly journeys Above to see Catherine have become more frequent. On one of them he brings her a necklace. It is a gift from Mouse, who has discovered, at the end of a remote tunnel, a buried ship laden with treasures. The treasure produces dissent among the Tunnel Dwellers, turning friend against friend. Against the wishes of others, Cullen takes gold items Above to sell but succeeds only in attracting a rapacious intruder who enters the Tunnels, bent on taking all the treasure. Following a fight, during which the intruder falls into the Abyss, the Tunnel Dwellers finally agree to donate the treasure Above to the St. Regina Shelter for the Homeless.

In the second episode, Father receives a message and mysteriously ventures Above. In the office of Alan Taft, an old friend, Father discovers Taft's body and is promptly arrested for Taft's murder. Vincent appeals to Catherine for help in locating Father. Believing rightly that his disappearance is linked to his past, Catherine and Vincent peruse microfilm at the public library and learn that Father is Dr. Jacob Wells, a physician called before the House Committee on Un-American Activities in 1951 and subsequently blacklisted. Shrinking from sharing his fate, Margaret, his bride, retreated to Paris with his father. Having never remarried and now dying of cancer, Margaret had sent the enigmatic note to Father noting the "wreck of my memories." Catherine discovers the identity of Taft's murderer, and Father returns to the Tunnels. Margaret joins him Below, spending the last seven days of her life with him.

Father recovers slowly from Margaret's death. One day, a Tunnel child falls into the Maze, a labyrinth of echoing caverns and tiny tunnels. In a rescue attempt, rocks collapse upon Father and Vincent. Above, Catherine immediately senses his peril. She descends into the Tunnels, falling headlong into Mouse's Mousehole. With Mouse she finds Vincent and Father pinned in a rockslide, their oxygen rapidly running out. Desperate to save Vincent, Catherine secures a drill and explosives from her former lover, Elliot Burch, an architect and construction magnate. Vincent and Father, who is injured, are rescued. At last a real part of life Below, Catherine realizes how much she loves and needs Vincent.

ANALYSIS

Hambly uses a loose adaptation of the Beauty and the Beast fairy tale to provide an imaginative commentary on problems in modern society. In particular, Hambly targets the 1980's lifestyle, which in her view seems characterized by a general insensitivity to the plight of human beings whose standard of living falls far below that of the book's heroine.

As suggested by the fairy tale, the story's primary concern is the maturation of Catherine, who evolves from "Daddy's little girl" to a woman with selfhood, identity, and integrity. The death of Catherine's mother many years before had placed Catherine solely in the care of her wealthy, doting father, who naturally encouraged attitudes that would ensure her status in the life he enjoyed. He could not protect her, however, from the ugliness and violence rampant in society. That violence appeared, at first, to wreck her life but ironically proves to be the catalyst for her progression from supreme self-centeredness to a higher level of existence. Catherine's discovery of a world inhabited by people who had forsaken the glittering society Above and who had suffered barbarities that had equaled or surpassed those inflicted upon her leaves its impression upon her. This secret, tightly knit community restores her faith in humankind and precipitates her change in attitude.

Catherine's real growth is initiated by her love for Vincent. Like the Beast in the fairy tale, Vincent is dangerous and repugnant only to those who remain unacquainted with his inner qualities. Devotion to her father and the life of refinement he wanted for her required a static condition that would allow no exploration of her own possibilities. Her love for Vincent, whose animality appears revolting, provides Vincent and her father with the love and devotion most beneficial to both. Her father is proud of her hard work and derives pleasure from her dedication, and Vincent, his true nature revealed, is gratified that his faith in her is confirmed. Most important, Catherine understands the division between the animal and the human, as well as the love that heals that division.

Song of Orpheus continues the story of Vincent and Catherine only peripherally, as references to the myth of Orpheus and Eurydice in the Underworld shift the focus to interaction between the worlds of Above and Below. The three episodes explore inherent conflicts between the two worlds, ending with Catherine's commitment to Vincent, which forms a union of the two worlds.

Although the addition of the myth does not remove the probability of a happy ending, it adds tragic aspects that might otherwise be inappropriate in a fairy-tale framework. In the first episode, Hambly demonstrates the susceptibility of humans to the lure of wealth and its profound corrosiveness of spirit. Cullen, who succumbs to gold fever, doing violence to his friend, Mouse, illustrates the effects of greed. He becomes beastly, illustrating an underlying point in both books: Love of money gives rise to inhuman treatment of fellow humans.

In the second episode, Hambly draws on knowledge of the myth of Orpheus and Eurydice. In the myth, Orpheus attempts to lead his wife from the underworld but, through his own error, loses her forever. The association with Orpheus affirms Father's humanity, underscoring years of silent suffering from the knowledge that he has inadvertently caused human misery. The emphasis on the tragic aspects of life adds depth to the story of Margaret and Father, whose happiness was curtailed by Margaret's failure of resolve in coping with the circumstances life had dealt her. Margaret's function as foil, or contrast, to Catherine prepares readers for Catherine's later rescue of Vincent and emphasizes the lesson that Catherine has learned from Vincent: Follow your heart.

—*Mary Hurd*

BEGGARS IN SPAIN AND BEGGARS AND CHOOSERS

An exploration of the effects on society of the release of partly understood technologies and the ways in which different groups respond

Author: Nancy Kress (1948–)
Genre: Science fiction—future history
Type of work: Novels

Time of work: The twenty-first and twenty-second centuries
Locale: Earth and Sanctuary, a space station orbiting Earth
First published: *Beggars in Spain* (1992; as novella, 1991), *Beggars and Choosers* (1994) and *Beggars Ride* (1996)

Beggars in Spain and Beggars and Choosers

THE STORY

Beggars in Spain and *Beggars and Choosers* opens in the year 2008 with the birth of Leisha Camden. The world is prosperous, thanks to the discovery of a cheap energy source by Kenzo Yagai. Roger Camden is a leading Yagaiist, embracing Yagai's philosophy of an individual's responsibility to do the appropriate thing. He is determined to produce a perfect daughter and insists on a modification to ensure that Leisha never needs to sleep, so that she will be more useful to the community.

Leisha is intellectually brilliant and develops rapidly. As she grows older, she is aware of the resentment toward her from her unmodified sister and others. Unable to talk to her family about her feelings, she discovers the existence of other Sleepless, and they form a community, keeping in regular contact. Sleepers become fearful and envious of the achievements of the Sleepless, particularly following the discovery that it is sleep that causes the aging process, so that the Sleepless will not age at the same rate as ordinary people. Some members of the Sleepless community propose building themselves a community apart from the Sleepers, but Leisha believes in the integration of Sleepless and Sleepers and refuses to go into Sanctuary, a space station orbiting Earth.

This first schism among members of the Sleepless community is mirrored by a further schism within Sanctuary when one group, led by Jennifer Sharifi, begins genetic experiments to further enhance the abilities of the Sleepless. Sharifi is ruthless in pursuit of her goal. Adopting a radical definition of community as a group of people whose purpose is to serve the whole, she ruthlessly expels or murders anyone whom she considers incapable of being part of the community, even her own grandson. She also has no sympathy for Sleepers and is keen to form her own nation distinct from the United States. The country benefits from taxing Sleepless technology, so it is unwilling to agree to secession. Sharifi plans to blackmail the United States by threatening to release a plague. When the Supersleepless, who are the product of Sharifi's experiments and already are disturbed by her callousness, learn of her plans, they take control of the space station from her, hand her over to the authorities, and leave for their own hideaway.

On Earth, Leisha has adopted a Sleeper boy, Drew Arlen, a member of the faux-aristocratic Liver faction who is looking for revenge against Sanctuary for killing his grandfather and is determined one day to own it. Unable to settle and unable to adapt to "donkey" ways, in which he would have to work for a living, he is a source of trouble in Leisha's home until he is accidentally crippled by Leisha's great-nephew, Eric, in a fight. Even this does not stop him from continuing on a path to destruction. In a dangerous attempt to save him from a life of waste, Eric forcibly treats him with a drug that unleashes an ability to induce lucid dreams in others, including the Sleepless. Leisha also tries to respond to the increasing divisions among pro-Sleeper organizations that promote their shoddy goods at the expense of superior Sleepless products, on the basis that they are primarily philanthropic in their aims. Society is in upheaval because of a curious division between "donkeys," Sleepers who are prepared to continue working, and Livers, a faux-aristocratic section of the Sleeper population. Their relationship is an uneasy symbiosis, whereby the donkeys provide for the Livers in return for their votes. By the end of the book, the situation is still unresolved, although Leisha remains confident that Sleepers and Sleepless can live in an integrated society.

Beggars and Choosers presents a very different world, partly through the eyes of Diana Covington, a roving agent for the Genetic Standards Enforcement Agency. She is hunting for Miranda Sharifi, who is believed to be performing illegal genetic experiments. As becomes clear, other groups also are performing experiments and are releasing products into the environment in an attempt to return to a time before gene modification was the norm. The effects of unauthorized gene modification are shown through the eyes of Billy Washington, a Liver whose community gradually is disintegrating as services fail.

Drew Arlen's lucid dreaming ability is being employed by the Supersleepless to inspire the Livers to return to the donkey way of life in the face of this disintegration, but Arlen is ambivalent about continued genetic experimentation. Miranda Sharifi argues that in this instance, she does know best. Sharifi is imprisoned for her work, but not before producing an antidote to a plague released by an illegal organization, thus demonstrating her willingness to help Sleepers. The book closes with the certainty that a new order has been established but no certainty as to what shape it will take.

The concluding volume brings the tale up to the year 2128, depicting a world deeply stratified and divided, with a few characters seeking to bridge the isolated realms determined by the separation of humanity into different species.

ANALYSIS

Nancy Kress's *Beggars in Spain* first appeared as a novella, and some critics believe that its expansion to novel length was to the work's detriment. It could be argued that the expansion of the novella and the subsequent writing of a sequel obliged Kress to speculate ever more improbably, creating not only the Sleepless but also the Supersleepless. In a novella, space constraints oblige the author to focus on one small fragment of the greater whole; Kress clearly believed she had more to say. There can be no doubt that the future Earth she created raises many fascinating speculative points.

It is rare, for example, for science fiction to deal with the idea that one can never really know what a new invention or technological development will do, except by using it. Extrapolation from experiments always will be insufficient. It often is supposed that cheap energy for all will be the salvation of the world's problems, yet, as Kress clearly shows, there is a downside to the prosperity. People become indolent, working for other people loses its respectability, and society begins to disintegrate as basic community ties are weakened and then severed.

Kress also presents a complex series of ethical arguments for the reader to consider. Kenzo Yagai believed that he was benefiting the world by releasing his cheap energy source to one and all, assuming that people would respond as generously toward one another as he had. The Sleepless are perceived by Sleepers as gods of a sort, but they are divided among themselves as to whether they have any loyalty to outsiders. Having been experiments themselves, they wonder whether they have the right to create yet another super-race. This question is pursued more and more strongly, particularly in the second novel, in which Arlen and Covington, although both working for the Genetic Standards Enforcement Agency, do so for very different motives and, in Diana's case, with increasing doubts.

Kress's presentation of her various arguments is powerful and convincing, although she offers the reader no easy solutions; in fact, she offers no real solutions at all. Her skill lies in showing the myriad different viewpoints, from those who revel in their Sleeplessness through those who have empathy with the Sleepers, along with those troubled by their own alienness. Among the Sleepers, she charts the fascinating sway of emotions as Livers seek to find someone to blame for their predicament, fastening by turns on the Sleepless, the gene enhanced, and the donkeys. She is able to pin down the swirling, contradictory mass of human emotion, which is so easily manipulated and so willing to blame anyone but oneself. She paints a dark picture of a future society, particularly in *Beggars and Choosers*, as the world reaches its breaking point, and she offers only the faintest glimmers of hope. Even then, she seems to suggest that those who seek salvation may want to dictate the manner in which it will come. From this idea comes the title of the second book, derived from the saying "Beggars can't be choosers."

This moral and ethical dimension sets Kress's work apart from much of modern hard science fiction, which is more concerned with parading the wonders to come than with asking how people will live with them and what will happen as a result. More important, she explores what can be done to prevent overly radical changes. Her vigorous prose style and memorable characters ensure that readers will take notice of her vision of the future.

—*Maureen Speller*

THE BEGINNING PLACE

Two adolescents learn trust and cooperation in an archetypal world in which they must slay a monster and make their way back to reality

Author: Ursula K. Le Guin (1929–)
Genre: Fantasy—magical world
Type of work: Novel

The Beginning Place

Time of work: The late 1970's
Locale: The suburbs of an unspecified city and the twilight "ain" country
First published: 1980 (condensed form, *Redbook*, 1979; published in England as *Threshold*, 1980)

THE STORY

While running away from his disturbed mother and his empty suburban life, Hugh Rogers discovers a gateway into a magical forest world. There, where it is always twilight, he finds solace and belonging. Although he returns to reality, he crosses the gateway frequently to drink from the river and to recharge his spirit in the natural setting.

On one trip, he meets Irene Pannis, who also discovered the gateway while trying to escape her unhappy home life, which includes the threat of physical assault at the hands of her stepfather. Irene had been crossing over into what she calls the "ain" country for years. Like Hugh, she believes that she belongs here. She has made ties with the inhabitants of the mountain town of Tem-breabrezi, who represent family to her and the only real home she has ever known. She also harbors a secret love for the grim mayor of Tembreabrezi, Master Sark.

Irene is enraged to find Hugh in "her" place, but the two soon establish an uneasy truce, for they learn they need each other. Irene sometimes cannot get into the twilight world; Hugh cannot always get out. The townspeople need them too, for there is a goblin or monster haunting them, choking off their livelihood and holding them hostage. When Hugh arrives in Tembreabrezi, its residents take him to be their savior, the knight who will slay this dragon. Hugh is willing—he wants in particular to impress the fair-haired damsel Allia, with whom he is secretly in love. When Irene realizes that Sark would use her as an offering for the monster, she becomes disenchanted with the twilight world and joins Hugh in his quest.

Together, Hugh and Irene track the screaming, gobbling monster. Although in their first encounter with it they hide, cowering in fright, they gather their courage and follow the monster's path to its lair. Irene baits it, and Hugh kills it with a sword. Hugh is seriously injured as the dying monster falls on him, and Irene must aid him as they find a way out of the labyrinthine twilight world and back to reality. In this final journey, they realize that they love each other and that in order to get on with their lives they can and must depend on each other. They vow to reconfigure their lives on the outside and not to return to the twilight world.

ANALYSIS

The Beginning Place was published after the huge successes of the Earthsea trilogy (1968, 1970, 1972; collected as *Earthsea*, 1977), *The Left Hand of Darkness* (1969), and *The Dispossessed* (1974), the last of which won both Hugo and Nebula awards. Following publication of those works, Ursula Le Guin reassessed her career. From 1975 until 1985, when another major work (*Always Coming Home*) appeared, she published criticism and some short stories and novels that are generally outside the realm of science fiction or fantasy.

Although well received at the time of publication, *The Beginning Place* has since received little attention from scholars, possibly because, unlike the Earthsea trilogy, it is not pure fantasy. It is instead an ironic thinking through of the necessity of fantasy and of the dangers of overdependence upon it. In critic Brian Attebery's words, it is a "metafantasy," a fantasy about fantasy.

The Beginning Place continues the major themes of Le Guin's fantasy writings, particularly her interest in the theories of psychoanalyst Carl Jung and in the Taoist belief in the need for balance between good and evil, or dark and light elements. Jung's interest in the unconscious mind is reflected in the characters' crossing over from the real, daylight world into a twilight, magical world in which they learn skills to help them cope with life.

Like much fantasy, *The Beginning Place* is essentially a story of the characters' journey to adulthood. In the twilight world, Hugh and Irene initially find security and belonging; the ain country is the only place they can feel sure of themselves. They are able to begin to awaken romantically and sexually, nurturing fantasies of love with the characters they most resemble. The fair, clumsy, and ineffectual Hugh loves the blond, passive Allia; dark, scowling Irene worships dark, cruel Sark.

Part of the journey of these characters is the turning away from these mirror images of themselves and toward each other. The screaming, howling creature—which remains only poorly defined—is an integral part of this maturation process. It is the embodiment of Hugh and Irene's fears, of their negative self-images. In the same way that Ged turns and faces his shadow in *A Wizard of Earthsea* (1968), Hugh and Irene must face the creature and merge with it. This is reflected in Jung's idea of the shadow, the darker part of human nature that must be acknowledged and integrated into the self to form a whole. In slaying the creature and returning to the real world, Hugh and Irene recognize and deal with the darker side of their lives and thereby rob it of the power to rule them. This is also related to Taoist philosophy, which requires a balance of the dark and light aspects of life, symbolized in the union of the blond Hugh and the dark-haired Irene. In recognizing that the ain country is essentially a place of escape, the two agree to stop running away from their problems and accept responsibility for themselves, in effect confronting adulthood.

—*Amy Clarke*

A BELEAGUERED CITY

A provincial city in nineteenth century France has its fundamental beliefs challenged when the dead return to life

Author: Margaret Oliphant (1828–1897)
Genre: Fantasy—occult
Type of work: Novella
Time of work: The late 1870's
Locale: Semur, a provincial city in France
First published: 1880

THE STORY
A Beleaguered City is a fantastic, speculative ghost story that takes stock of the changing beliefs of nineteenth century Europeans regarding religion and the supernatural. Very popular in the nineteenth century, it went out of print until late in the twentieth century. It can be seen as one of the first attempts to include within the realm of fantasy stories the areas of inquiry usually associated with religion.

Semur is a rather dreary French provincial city participating in the general malaise of France after that country's defeat by Germany in the Franco-Prussian War. Martin Dupin, mayor of the town as well as owner of the great estate of La Clarière, is a progressively inclined man who is skeptical of traditional religious faith. While strolling about the city on a summer evening, Dupin is approached by Paul Lecamus, an eccentric man with a strong visionary streak who has not been emotionally whole since the death of his wife. Lecamus informs Dupin that a great portent has occurred. This news is soon confirmed by several others. Dupin is stunned, when he arrives at the place described by Lecamus, to see thousands of dead people returned to life and solemnly parading. Dupin cannot believe his senses, but the uncanny spectacle is confirmed when giant letters in the sky spell out a message of summoning from entities who describe themselves as "Nous Autres Morts"—French for "we other dead."

The sedate, comfortable, placidly mediocre life of Semur is completely disrupted by the arrival of the strange undead. Dupin confers with his wife and with the Curé, a local priest, in order to help him gain his bearings and provide some guidance to a stunned community. Each member of the community has his or her own experience that is eventually related to the mayor. From the skeptical Monsieur de Bois-Sombre to the impressionable Madame Dupin to the mystical Lecamus, each account filters the weird apparition through the prism of individual hopes, fears, and vulnerabilities. Dupin's mother, for example, sees the ghosts as a judgment of divine vengeance for the civil administration's shoddy treatment of the Sisters of St. John, a locally dominant order of nuns. Lecamus suddenly encounters the face of Dupin's father, signaling the suspension of accepted notions of past and future. What was thought dead and buried has returned to life.

Dupin goes in the company of the Curé to confront the apparitions. Despite the philosophical differences between the two men, the challenge of the returned dead creates solidarity and comradeship between them. Dupin's mother leads the women and children away to the mayor's estate in order to provide for their safety. Meanwhile, Dupin's wife and Lecamus have a direct encounter with the dead. Through the medium of the visionary Lecamus, Dupin's wife feels the presence of her daughter Marie, who died young. Lecamus is so entranced by the threshold between life and death that he crosses over the line. Seeking to rejoin his dead wife, he throws himself into the sphere of the undead and is gone from Earth forever. After this, the apparition recedes and the tumult subsides. Peace is restored to Semur. The religious conservatives of the town try to turn the incident into a conventional miracle, but Dupin knows that what had transpired was in truth a more unsettling phenomenon, an enigma he could never wholly hope to solve.

ANALYSIS

Margaret Oliphant is known as a domestic and regional writer dealing with everyday life in Victorian England, as is displayed in her multivolume *Chronicles of Carlingford* (1862). Her corpus of ghost stories displays the versatility and imaginativeness of her vision and enhances her importance as a writer. *A Beleaguered City*, her most famous ghost story, is significant in the history of fantasy and science fiction because of its use of the techniques of speculative fiction to explore issues that traditionally have been the domain of religion.

Oliphant sets this atypical story in a foreign country, France. Perhaps this enabled her to achieve an effect of distance and remoteness necessary for the story's weird atmosphere. With subtlety and skill, Oliphant paints a detailed portrait of the complacent, bourgeois city of Semur, where people stroll around thinking that they have mastered all the dilemmas of the universe, or at least are able to ignore them. The manifestation of the returned dead shows that rational waking thought cannot master the overwhelming mysteriousness of the cosmos. The return of the dead may be explained in psychological terms as a collective hallucination that displays the town's own repression of its buried unconscious, whether this repression can be traced to the town's own bourgeois self-satisfaction or to its participation in the general French malaise after the trauma of the war with Germany.

Oliphant does not use her ghostly spectacle simply to proffer a grim warning to modernity that it has strayed too far from tradition and needs a grim retrenchment back to orthodox pieties in order to solve its problems. Instead, she sees the returned dead as a challenge that each citizen of Semur addresses in unique personal terms. From the orthodox Curé to the rationalist mayor to the independently mystical Lecamus, each person relates to the returned dead in specific personal terms. By illustrating how different individuals would respond to such a crisis, Oliphant creates a haunting and eerie but emotionally realistic tableau.

The returned dead of Semur may be unsettling but are not necessarily frightening. They perturb and intrigue but do not shock or horrify. They present less a vision of grisly secrets than of previously unknown possibilities. Particularly for Dupin's grieving wife and the stricken Lecamus, the revelation that the dead can return to Earth provides a foundation for hope. Perhaps, they conclude, the endings life seems to give are not necessarily final.

—*Margaret Boe Birns*

THE BELGARIAD

A fantasy quest for a stolen magical artifact, the outcome of which will decide the fate of the entire universe

Author: David Eddings (1931-2009)
Genre: Fantasy—high fantasy
Type of work: Novels
Time of work: Undefined
Locale: The Kingdoms of the West and the Angaraks, on another world

First published: *Pawn of Prophecy* (1982), *Queen of Sorcery* (1982), *Magician's Gambit* (1983), *Castle of Wizardry* (1984), and *Enchanters' End Game* (1984)

THE STORY

None of the individual novels of the Belgariad is capable of standing alone. *The Belgariad* is an epic high fantasy, and such epics require considerable space to develop the world, characters, and drama of the plot. *The Belgariad* begins with Garion, a boy who lives on a farm. His only living relative, as far as he knows, is his Aunt Pol, the cook. Various supernatural events occur during his childhood, along with the typical pangs of puberty, but not until he is fourteen years old does the adventure really begin. At this time, Belgarath, under the name of Mister Wolf, a vagabond bard, comes to visit and informs Aunt Pol of the theft of a magical artifact known as the Orb of Aldur.

The three set out to retrieve the Orb, which has been stolen from the hall of the dead Rivan King by the minions of the sleeping god Torak. A prophecy has indicated that the Orb will assist in the waking of Torak, whose unnatural sleep was caused several thousand years before by this same Orb. Belgarath, who is revealed to be a distant ancestor of Garion, as well as a legendary sorcerer, organizes a mission to retrieve the Orb with the aid of Silk, Prince Kheldar of Drasnia and an accomplished spy; Barak, Earl of Trelheim, who turns into a bear on occasion; Ce'Nedra, a spoiled imperial princess of Tolnedra; Mandorallen, Baron of Vo Mandor; Hettar, Horselord of Algaria, who can speak to horses; Lelldorin, a nobleman of Arendia; Durnik, a blacksmith; and Garion's Aunt Pol, who is actually Lady Polgara, Belgarath's daughter and also a sorcerer.

They set out on the trail of the Orb, traveling through various countries and encountering a variety of dangers, both magical and conventional. It becomes clear that Garion is a powerful mage in his own right. Throughout the Belgariad, he must strive to come to terms with the astonishing fact that he is related to legends and is involved in a mythical quest that will decide the fate of the world—a quest in which he plays the crucial role. Not only is he a sorcerer, but he also is the heir to the Rivan throne and the only person who can safely take up the Orb of Aldur against the evil Torak.

Eventually the Orb is recovered from Ctuchik, priest of Torak. The questers race to return it to Riva in time for Garion to claim his bride, Ce'Nedra, who has been prophesied to be his wife. Neither knows that they are last in the line of the Rivan kings, long thought to be extinct. Before the ceremony can take place, however, it becomes clear that the Angaraks, Torak's chosen people, are preparing to make war on the Kingdoms of the West. In order to prevent the deaths of millions, Garion sets out with Silk and Belgarath to challenge Torak in his home. In the meantime, Polgara and Ce'Nedra organize the Western forces for war as a diversion for the Angaraks, in order to allow the trio to make their way through hostile territory and to be present when Torak wakes.

In the end, most of the original members of the quest are reunited in C'thol Mishrak for the final battle between the Child of Light (Garion, who, with elevation to the status of sorcerer, is now named Belgarion) and the Child of Dark (Torak). One of two competing prophecies will be proved false and thus be eliminated as a force in the world. Belgarion triumphs, in spite of Torak's powers as a god. Torak is killed in an arcane sword duel with Belgarion, and the universe is saved from a dark and bloody fate. Afterward, all return to Riva for Belgarion's wedding to Ce'Nedra. With Torak's death, there is no longer a threat of war.

ANALYSIS

Prior to the Belgariad, David Eddings had published only *High Hunt* (1973), a science-fiction novel. *The Belgariad* was his first foray into the world of fantasy, followed soon after by a sequel series entitled the *Malloreon* (1987–1991). He has also written two other unrelated series and expected to return to the world of the Belgariad and the Malloreon with a pair of prequels that focus on Belgarath's and Polgara's conflict with Torak and his minions when the Orb of Aldur was first created.

In the Belgariad, Eddings creates a complex and believable world by including minute details and establishing an elaborate historical background based on an intricate social and political structure. Add to that his amazing ability to invest even the smallest characters with complete and complex lives, and it is easy to see why the Belgariad has proven to be so popular.

In spite of the popularity of his books, Eddings has his critics. The most damaging criticism has been the accusation that his books are merely derivative of the work of J. R. R. Tolkien. This accusation is difficult to counter because high fantasy has been defined by Tolkien's *The Hobbit* (1937) and the *Lord of the Rings* trilogy (1954–1955), and thus most of what is considered high fantasy can point to Tolkien as an influence. Eddings does use traditional motifs—the quest, the prophecy, artifacts of magic, and the final arcane duel—but he does so in an interesting and compelling way. Eddings does, however, prove derivative in the Malloreon series—derivative of himself. In this sequel to the Belgariad, Eddings tells the same story with the same plot. This seems to be a habit for him, as he repeats the same formula with another of his fantasy series, the Elenium (1989–1991), and its sequel series, the Tamuli (begun in 1991).

The plot of the Belgariad is straightforward and uncomplicated. The success of the book comes from Eddings' abilities as a world builder and his skill with character and dialogue. Belgarion is young and often appears to be a whiner; Ce'Nedra is similarly childish. The other major characters more than make up for the faults of these two. Silk, probably the masterpiece of this series, is snide and outspoken, with a strange vulnerability and outrageous sense of humor that make him compelling. Each of the characters is unique, and Eddings never uses them as mere plot devices. Instead, he breathes humanity into each, complete with quirks, fears, jealousy, pride, and compassion. The plot is intentionally less complex than the characterizations.

If there is a flaw in the Belgariad, it is the ending. Belgarion's duel with Torak comes too quickly and is unsatisfying. In resolving all that has gone before, Eddings causes Belgarion to have several sudden insights. These startling realizations are unusually heavy-handed, with little by way of explanation or preparation. To most readers, they seem artificial. Eddings might have avoided this flaw by adding two or three chapters to dramatize the battle and create the necessary suspense. Although most readers understand that Belgarion must finally triumph in a story titled the Belgariad, the final scene lacks the dramatic suspense that would have been possible had Eddings established the possibility of a defeat—that the Belgariad could have been named so out of a sense of tragedy rather than triumph. Instead, the battle with Torak seems to be not so much the culmination of a well-wrought plot but, rather, a quick fix to tidy up the loose ends.

—*Diana Pharaoh Francis*

THE BERSERKER SERIES

The struggle of humanity against intelligent machines programmed to destroy all life

Author: Fred Saberhagen (1930–2007)
Genre: Science fiction—artificial intelligence
Type of work: Stories
Time of work: Prehistory to the distant future
Locale: The part of the Milky Way galaxy settled by humans
First published: *Berserker* (1967), *Brother Assassin* (1969), *Berserker's Planet* (1975), *Berserker Man* (1979), *The Ultimate Enemy* (1979), *The Berserker Wars* (1981), *The Berserker Throne* (1985), *Berserker: Blue Death* (1985), *Berserker Base* (1985), *Berserker Lies* (1991), and *Berserker Kill* (1993)

THE STORY

Before humans appeared on Earth, two interstellar races, known to humans as "the builders" and "the red race," fought a war of extermination lasting for centuries. Hoping finally to win the war, the builders created an ultimate doomsday machine, a spacefaring, intelligent, self-replicating weapon programmed to destroy any life it encountered. The weapon, called a berserker by humans because of the intense and chaotic violence of its attacks, was a success and wiped out the red race.

Unfortunately for the builders (and humans), the ber-serkers realized that the builders also were life and exterminated them as well. Now berserkers roam the galaxy searching for life in any form. They especially seek intelligent life such as humans because these are the only life-forms likely to provide any resistance to the extermination program. Berserkers have no inherent urge toward self-preservation (they are urgeless) but seek always to achieve the maximum destruction of life in expenditure of their resources.

Because berserkers are self-replicating and intelligent, they can build themselves in different shapes as required by a particular mission. The originals were space-going battleships, but in the stories they appear as everything from imitation horseshoe crabs to androids dressed in preserved human skin. In all cases, they are bent on destroying any intelligent life they find, with no regard for their own survival, and they are usually well equipped for that mission.

The books are divided into two types, anthologies and novels. The stories in the anthologies vary in length and are usually supplemented by some amount of linking text. In all cases, the stories and novels tell the human side of the ongoing berserker-human war. The anthologized stories usually focus on the resolution of a single human-berserker encounter, whereas the novels pursue the principal characters through several such encounters, usually culminating in a major victory for humanity.

In the short story "Smasher," which appears in *The Ultimate Enemy* and *Berserker Lies,* for example, a human space force successfully defends a populated water world against a berserker fleet attack. One of the ber-serker ships crashes on an almost unpopulated neighboring (and equally watery) planet still carrying a portion of its cargo intact. The cargo is small berserkers resembling horseshoe crabs, intended to scuttle unnoticed across the sea floor toward human habitations that they would then disassemble with an assortment of destructive tool-limbs. The crash site world is inhabited only by four scientists studying the fauna. One of them is killed by the berserkers, but the remaining three survive by luring the machines into a pond filled with a native predatory crustacean resembling a cross of shrimp and praying mantis. The smashers, as the crustaceans are called, confuse berserker and crab as humans were supposed to, and they destroy the menace.

In "Patron of the Arts," a story in *Berserker,* the art treasures of Earth are being transported to Tau Epsilon to protect them from a possible berserker attack on the home world. One of these treasures is a living artist who is so jaded by his existence that he is almost completely unconcerned by his impending death when his ship is captured in a berserker attack. After the crew members are killed resisting the berserker boarding party, he begins painting a portrait of a berserker, which he admires for its deadly efficiency. A boarding robot, speaking for the space-going berserker outside, asks what he is doing. He tries to explain the concept of art, which the berserker interprets as praise of that pictured. The machine then asks him, "What is good?" He asks what the berserker considers good, receiving the response "To destroy life is good." He agrees that life has little to recommend it but does not agree with the berserker's enthusiasm for death and cannot find life to be completely without value. In response to the berserker's query about this statement, he shows the robot Titian's painting *Man with a Glove*. The berserker asks him what it means, and he refuses to reply.

After the robot leaves him, he takes the painting to the airlock, intending to put it in an escape capsule so that it, at least, might be saved from the berserker. He finds a stowaway girl in a crate and has to decide whether her life is worth more than the painting. He sends her on her way and returns with the Titian to his portrait of the berserker. He is now disgusted by his work. The berserker robot returns and informs him that because he has praised the berserker, his ship has been repaired and put back on course so that other humans can learn from him how to praise what is good. After the berserker's boarding party departs, he declares that he can change, is alive, and will paint again.

The novels tend to be more similar to "Patron of the Arts." They involve characters attempting to destroy a berserker or simply to survive an attack by one or more of them. They often involve character development and an affirmation of the value of existence. Typical of these is *Berserker: Blue Death,* in which the main character is a sort of space-going Captain Ahab seeking vengeance against a particular berserker, known as "Leviathan" or "Old Blue," because he holds it responsible for the deaths of his wife and daughter. In this pursuit, he almost loses his humanity, becoming a shadow of the death machine, but he rediscovers the value of his life after killing the man who killed his daughter and destroying the berserker.

There are two structurally exceptional books in the series. *Brother Assassin* comprises three novellas that form a continuous plot of novel length. Likewise, *Berserker Base* is an anthology of short stories by multiple authors forming a continuous plot. Fred Saberhagen wrote the first short story and linking text. Readers should be aware that most berserker short stories were published in more than one anthology.

The Best of C. M. Kornbluth

ANALYSIS

Although the stories all occur against the backdrop of human-berserker conflict, the humans are always the center of attention. Typically, berserkers are reduced to an inscrutable menace, and the contrast between human and machine is usually sharply drawn. One of the principal themes of the stories derives from this contrast: Humans can defeat berserkers not because of superior science or superior physical ability but because of their essential human nature. This usually is illustrated by presenting a character without love, concern, or much desire to live, then bringing him or her into contact with the single-minded destruction of a berserker and confronting the character with the pain it causes in fellow humans. The character then fights the berserker and rediscovers his or her soul after discovering that the most ruthless methods are unsuccessful.

A corollary theme in the series is that there is something about humanity that transcends the physical. Few characters in the stories profess religious or spiritual views beyond atheism or agnosticism, yet the most alive and human among them have some inner spirit that transcends physical boundaries. Saberhagen's carmpan—passive, friendly telepathic aliens that frequently function as distanced observers in the stories—regularly speak of the soul as the major difference between human and berserker. Human thought is regularly stated to occur faster than neuromuscular or electronic reactions, giving humanity a critical advantage over the computerized berserker. This thesis is most directly stated in *Berserker Man*, in which a major supporting character is a pilot who was so badly injured battling a berserker that he now lives as a cyborg in a train of boxes on motorized carts and serves as one of the philosophical centers of the story. Humans may be cyborgs in boxes, or even reduced to personality recordings in a computer, as are Nick and Genevieve in *Berserker Kill*, but they are essentially different from berserkers.

Against the background of such a violent dystopic universe, Saberhagen makes the point that the most worthwhile and valuable features of humanity are emotions: love, joy, concern, anguish, and even terror. These serve humans in his stories far better than any technological weapon. Again and again he shows the similarity of a character who has ceased to feel and a berserker that is incapable of feeling. Such characters always find that these suppressed emotions are the difference between them and the enemy, and that they are the edge that brings victory to the human. Far from being stories about mechanical terrors sweeping life from the galaxy, the Berserker series ultimately is a humanist statement: Humankind is greater than any enemy because of the human soul.

—*Radford B. Davis and Julia Meyers*

THE BEST OF C. M. KORNBLUTH

Out of contemporary conditions arise tomorrow's problems, which can be solved or understood only with the perspective of history

Author: Cyril M. Kornbluth (1923–1958)
Genre: Science fiction—extrapolatory
Type of work: Stories
Time of work: The 1950's to the distant future
Location: Various sites, especially cities, on Earth and other planets
First published: 1976

THE STORY

Two of Cyril M. Kornbluth's most famous stories, the novelettes "The Little Black Bag" (1950) and "The Marching Morons" (1951), posit the same future. Twenty generations from now, prolific, low-IQ groups vastly outnumber intelligent people on Earth because of the latter's low birthrates. The moronic majority thrives only through the labors of the intellectuals.

The earlier story introduces elderly Bayard Full, a ruined, slumdwelling, dipsomaniacal medical doctor. An accident sends a doctor's black bag from the future into his possession. Designed for use by idiots, the bag yields its secrets readily to Dr. Full and his accidentally acquired assistant, Angie. Reinvigorated and reformed, Dr. Full begins performing miraculous operations and nurturing a new self-image as benefactor of humanity. Angie, however, has less humanitarian goals and succeeds in destroying the hopes of both herself and Dr. Full.

"The Marching Morons" more fully explores the future world dominated by idiots. The intelligent minority faces one central problem: what to do about the ever-worsening population disparity between idiots and geniuses. The minority receives a windfall in the form of real estate salesman Honest John Barlow, revived from a state of suspended animation accidentally achieved in the twentieth century. Barlow agrees to solve the problem if he is given dictatorial power, a request that is granted readily. Barlow then suckers the general populace, through advertising and sly references during television sitcoms, into taking rockets to Venus, an unreachable promised land. They fall for the ruse and die in great numbers. In the end, Barlow suffers the same fate he inflicted on others.

Two late novelettes, "Shark Ship" (originally "Reap the Dark Tide," 1958) and "Two Dooms" (1958; Kornbluth's preferred title was "The Doomsman"), probe other grim futures. "Shark Ship" details life aboard a convoy of ships divorced from all contact with land. The lives of those on board depend on the spring swarming of plankton. When a storm destroys his ship's irreplaceable fishing net, Captain Thomas Salter finds himself, his ship, and his crew expelled from the convoy. An idea previously thought heretical now appears to be his only option: He must steer for land. The landing party discovers an America depopulated by death cults whose influence became pervasive in previous centuries. Surviving cult members give the landing party a taste of the violence that purged the once-overpopulated mainland.

"Two Dooms" follows atomic physicist Edward Royland on his accidental journey into an alternative universe where the Nazis and Japanese rule a divided United States. In his own world, Royland debated whether to delay progress at the Los Alamos nuclear research site or to help the atomic bomb achieve its terrifying result. Encountering both a slave village and a concentration camp in the alternative America, he comes to grips with the idea of life under bondage.

Other notable works in this volume include "The Words of Guru" (1941), an early but striking fantasy about a genius child acquiring supernatural power; "The Last Man Left in the Bar" (1957), a confrontation between aliens and a magnetron technician, written with an audacious literary command that anticipates the stylistic revolution of the 1960's; "The Altar at Midnight" (1952), a portrayal of the costs of spaceflight; and the influential "The Mindworm" (1950), detailing the rise and fall of a psychic vampire.

Analysis

Although Kornbluth received acclaim as a novelist, his reputation rests largely on his shorter works, which are recognized for their intelligence, incisive wit, and readability.

"The Marching Morons," one of the most famous novelettes in science fiction, has prompted many critics to examine its future scenario of an intelligent but overwhelmed minority. Those focusing on its genetics, however, have tended to overlook, and inadvertently belittle, the social criticism explicit in the story. When the intellectuals turn to Barlow to solve their problem, they find themselves employing a veritable Adolf Hitler. Kornbluth takes a global view, however: He juxtaposes Nazi gas chambers and American bombings of Japanese civilians by having Barlow's rockets lift off from Los Alamos. The intelligentsia appear as culpable as Honest John.

Kornbluth's concern with the ethics of theoretical science underlies both "Two Dooms," with its indecisive Royland, and "Gomez" (1954), whose protagonist, Julio Gomez, sits on a similar fence with regard to unified field theory, the implications of which terrify him. Both stories explore moral quandaries of the atomic age, as do such other works as "The Altar at Midnight," Kornbluth's fascinating first solo novel *Takeoff* (1952), and "The Remorseful" (1954).

Kornbluth's concern with the impact of theoretical knowledge parallels his concern with history. Historical insight appears as a redemptive if sometimes dangerous force throughout Kornbluth's works, notably here in "Shark Ship," "The Luckiest Man in Denv" (1952), "The Mindworm," and "The Adventurer" (1953).

Many of these stories shed light on other works. "The Rocket of 1955," a vignette that first appeared in a 1939 fanzine, and "The Marching Morons" anticipate *The Space Merchants* (with Frederik Pohl, 1953), whereas "The Little Black Bag" and "The Marching Morons" anticipate *Search the Sky* (with

Pohl, 1954). "Two Dooms" bears comparison to Kornbluth's *Not This August* (1955), depicting an America beneath communist subjugation, and Philip K. Dick's *The Man in the High Castle* (1962). "With These Hands" bears comparison to Walter M. Miller, Jr.'s "The Darfstellar" (1955).

Critics judging Kornbluth by this anthology, edited by Pohl, have seen a growing bitterness in his later stories. This reflects editorial choice more than reality, because Kornbluth also wrote delightful humor in his last years, in stories not collected here. These tales demonstrate Kornbluth's effective use of everyday individuals from a variety of ethnic backgrounds as well as his well-tuned ear for dialect.

—*Mark Rich*

THE BEST OF CORDWAINER SMITH

Stories recount events in humankind's development, from the Second Age of Space through the spread of the Rediscovery of Man

Author: Cordwainer Smith (Paul Myron Anthony Linebarger, 1913–1966)
Genre: Science fiction—future history
Type of work: Stories
Time of work: Various times between c.e. 6,000 and 16,000
Locale: Earth, other planets, and aboard spacecraft
First published: 1975

THE STORY

The twelve stories in this collection, written separately and published between 1950 and 1964, fit into a consistent future history that covers human development from the Second Age of Space to the era of rights for underpeople and the Rediscovery of Man. Many of the stories involve the Instrumentality, a ruling bureau-cracy that is not always admirable but ultimately manages "to keep man man."

Set in the Second Age of Space, "Scanners Live in Vain" concerns the scanners, men surgically cut off from their senses in order to endure the pain of space travel. When scientist Adam Stone discovers how to travel in space without pain, the scanners fear they will lose their privileged position and so order his death. Scanner Martel breaks with his elite group to warn Stone, who survives and subsequently restores scanners to normal senses and emotions.

In "The Lady Who Sailed *The Soul*," Helen America, the first woman to pilot interstellar space, has trouble with the gigantic solar sail of her ship. An apparition of the man she loves, Mr. Grey-no-more, assists her in righting the craft, and she is saved. In future history, theirs is one of the great love stories.

"The Game of Rat and Dragon," set in the age of planoforming, is about the human telepaths, pinlighters, who protect interstellar flights from the psychic dragons of deep space. A pinlighter is saved from a dragon by the alertness of his telepathically linked partner, a cat. While recovering, he realizes that no woman can compare to his cat partner, Lady May.

In "The Burning of the Brain," Magno Taliano, one of the Go-Captains who in a psychic trance guide planoforming ships through interstellar space, loses his way. To return to known space, pinlighters must read his brain for star locations. The ship is saved, but the captain's mind is destroyed, to the ambiguous sorrow of his wife.

In "The Dead Lady of Clown Town," D'joan, one of the underpeople derived from animals to perform drudgery, brings her followers out of hiding to plead for humane treatment. The Instrumentality instead brutally slaughters them, and Joan herself is tried, convicted, and burned. Her trial, however, gives underpeople a new level of recognition. A witness to the event, Lady Goroke, initiates the line of Jestocost, the Lords of the Instrumentality who will free the underpeople.

In "Under Old Earth," Lord Sto Odin of the Instrumentality, concerned that an overprotected humanity is on a suicidal course, seeks out Sun-Boy deep under old Earth in order to neutralize the powerful congohelium that holds his followers in sway. By destroying Sun-Boy, he frees Santuna, who becomes famous as Lady Alice More, a leader in instituting the Rediscovery of Man, which returns uncertainty—and the possibility of happiness—to humankind.

"Alpha Ralpha Boulevard" begins the Rediscovery of Man. The nightmare of perfection is over, and a measure of worry, disease, and uncertainty are restored. In this new age, Paul and Virginia think they are in love. Virginia, uncertain of Paul, climbs with him the vast boulevard in the sky, Alpha Ralpha, to consult the prediction of the Abba-dingo for the truth of their feeling. Before they can walk down, they are caught in a storm. Virginia falls to her death, but C'mell the cat woman rescues Paul.

In "The Ballad of Lost C'mell," Lord Jestocost of the Instrumentality, which is dedicated to helping the underpeople, contacts E'telekeli, their leader. They conspire successfully to better the lot of underpeople, with C'mell the cat woman serving as the telepathic medium. As an old man, dying but satisfied with his work, Jestocost learns that C'mell had loved him, more than anything, and that all of human history would know that love.

"A Planet Named Shayol" is set on a penal planet where inmates constantly grow new body parts that are harvested for medical use. The Instrumentality, learning of this and other abuses, closes Shayol, promising to restore inmates to happiness.

ANALYSIS

In the 1950's and early 1960's, Cordwainer Smith brought a literary and poetic brand of science fiction to a genre dominated by hard science extrapolations. His world of talking animals, spacecraft lined with oysters, and boulevards into the sky suggests fantasy, but he is a science-fiction writer, one who deals with extraordinary extrapolations and analogical situations that have remarkable consistency and logic. He shows the impact of science rather science itself, and his stories focus on human relationships and reactions to a world created by science.

One of Smith's major themes is romantic love. Scanner Martel maintains contact with his humanity through his love for his wife. Helen America and Mr. Grey-no-more have a love transcending the vast emptiness of space. Go-Captain Taliano, his brain destroyed, nevertheless retains a "shy and silly love." Paul and Virginia feel compelled to play out a love story, and Jestocost and C'mell are figures in a story of true love denied. Romantic love is not a usual feature of science fiction, but it is a cornerstone of Smith's created world.

In another direction, Smith sees the dangers of a perfected world in which disease, danger, and need are elim-inated; it is a sterile utopia of spoiled and unresponsive people. The people in "The Dead Lady of Clown Town" (1964), barely reacting to the brutal murder of the underpeople, are considerably less human than the beings derived from beasts. This is the perfected but suicidal world that Sto Odin sets out to remedy. His actions, indirectly but inevitably, bring about the Rediscovery of Man.

The treatment of the underpeople may be read as an allegory of racial inequality. The topic also speaks to developing scientific issues. Would a laboratory creation that behaves as a human be anything less than human? Have people thought through the implications of scientific discoveries? The underpeople challenge assumptions that they have. Smith warns that we must keep in touch with our humanity. Scanners, cut off from their senses (and figuratively their souls), are ready to kill Adam Stone, the scientist who can restore them to life.

Although his literary output was small, Cordwainer Smith has a special place in modern science fiction. His work cannot be compared easily with that of any other science-fiction writer.

—*Steve Anderson*

THE BEST SHORT STORIES OF J. G. BALLARD

Stories focusing on protagonists' mental and physiological relationships with drastically altered environments

Author: J(ames) G(raham) Ballard (1930–2009)
Genre: Science fiction—new wave
Type of work: Stories
Time of work: Primarily the near future

Location: Imaginary locales on Earth
First published: 1978

THE STORY

The Best Short Stories of J. G. Ballard contains nineteen impressive works published between 1957 and 1978 in such British and American magazines as *New Worlds*, *The Magazine of Fantasy and Science Fiction*, and *Amazing Stories*. Together, these stories show the extraordinary imagination and range of Ballard's storytelling. There are tales of spaceflight, urban isolation, psychological manipulation, and the outbreak of strange, imaginary diseases. The stories take place in the overcrowded cities of the future, on abandoned South Sea islands, and within view of the quiet but suddenly terrifying lawns of suburbia.

Ballard's stories show his preoccupation with the internal landscapes of the mind. They also contain unusual responses to the challenges his characters face. Harry Faulkner, in "The Overloaded Man," suddenly loses touch with his suburban neighborhood. He begins to perceive the world as an abstract painting and decides to drown himself to extinguish this new sensory overload. Contrary to expectations, the short story views Faulkner's action as a relative success.

Far from confining himself to realistic places, disasters, or injuries, Ballard invents new ones for most of his stories. He creates vivid cities of the future, such as an imaginary subtropical community, where "The Cloud-Sculptors of Coral D" reside and create their imaginary art, and the refuse-littered, abandoned launchpads of Cape Canaveral in "The Cage of Sand," where two men and a woman have gathered to watch the nightly appearance of as many as seven dead astronauts who orbit Earth in their functionless capsules.

Ballard's protagonists, though thrust into strange new worlds and alien landscapes, generally accept these with little questioning, as does Count Axel in "The Garden of Time." His flowers are able to stop time outside his mansion, where barbarian hordes ready themselves for a final assault. They will succeed when his last flower has been plucked.

Like Count Axel and LouisaWoodwind, whose husband is one of the dead astronauts, Ballard's protagonists typically are well-educated, articulate, and emotionally controlled men and women. As Harry Faulkner shows, however, beneath this tranquil facade of reason, control, and clinical detachment is a deeper layer of strange obsessions and aberrant needs.

This defiance of the normal and fictional probing of the radically new are crucial aspects of many of the stories. "The Terminal Beach" successfully experiments with style and language. It focuses on Traven's mindframe, which has guided him to maroon himself on the Pacific island of Eniwetok, the historical site of American nuclear tests. There, Traven tries to make his body a part of the natural landscape and to construct a complex system that integrates the living, the dead, and inanimate objects.

ANALYSIS

Ballard's short stories were instrumental in the success of science fiction's NewWave movement. Many of the developments associated with it, such as a move toward inner space, a more critical attitude toward technology, and the redefinition of some of the conventions of science fiction (for example, time travel), are essential ingredients of Ballard's stories.

"Manhole 69" shows readers what an imaginative writer can do within the genre of science fiction. The story of three men whom a medical experiment has left with the inability to sleep turns to the unexpected when all three, rather than enjoy prolonged hours of productivity, withdraw into a form of autism.

The literary quality of such stories as "The Drowned Giant," which tells of the gradual dismemberment of the washed-up corpse of a gigantic man, also exemplifies how well NewWave science fiction brings literary respectability to a literature formerly dismissed by most critics. The stylistic experimentation visible in tales such as "The Terminal Beach" makes these pieces unique.

Although Ballard's stories have been compared with the works of mainstream American authors Donald Barthelme and William S. Burroughs, their focus on the inner cosmos echoes significant works of other science-fiction writers. For example, Alfred Bester's haunting tale of a murderer on the run from telepathic policemen, *The Demolished Man* (1953), displays an intensity similar to Ballard's. Brian Aldiss also shares some of Ballard's concerns; in *Cryptozoic!* (1968; published in Great Britain as *An Age*, 1967), Aldiss takes the idea of time travel and accomplishes it with mind-altering drugs that allow his characters to leave the confines of the present.

With their uncomfortable dissection ofWestern cultural icons, stories such as "The Atrocity Exhibition" have been hailed as the fictional equivalent of the literary and cultural criticism of scholars such as Roland Barthes. Taking its cue from occupational therapy, "The Atrocity Exhibition" offers a series of violent pictures painted by imaginary inmates of an insane asylum. Its central, unsettling idea is that the products of human culture, taken from the fields of warfare, technology, art, and popular entertainment, not only are intrinsically violent but also correspond to the biological features of the human body.

From the stories in this collection, Ballard has moved on to write more experimental short fiction. He has also produced works whose content takes a more conventional form. He has even worked in the area of autobiography with his book *Empire of the Sun* (1984).

Ballard occasionally has been attacked by critics who have failed to grasp the premises of his fiction. Like the reviewer-turned-psychiatrist who perceived a psychopathic mind behind his work, they mistakenly have read his stories as straight advocacy of criminal insanity. Ballard's exploration of a new, purely fictional reality has met with increasing critical acclaim. His stories are often haunting and occasionally terrifying, but never conventional or dull.

—*R. C. Lutz*

BEYOND APOLLO

Interrogated after returning without his captain from an aborted mission to Venus, copilot Harry Evans tells so many different versions of the events that the truth is never discovered

Author: Barry N. Malzberg (1939–)
Genre: Science fiction—new wave
Type of work: Novel
Time of work: 1981
Locale: A space capsule and a federal institution near Cape Canaveral, Florida
First published: 1972

THE STORY

Beyond Apollo tells the story of Harry M. Evans, the thirty-eight-year-old sole survivor of an ill-fated, two-man mission to Venus. Confined at a government institution near the Kennedy Space Complex in Florida, Evans is interrogated by Dr. Claude Forrest, a neurologist. The government wants to find out why the mission to Venus was aborted by one or two of the astronauts and what happened to the captain, whose body is missing. Evans' response is to tell a different story of the events every time he is questioned. In the absence of hard evidence, Evans' changing testimony increasingly frustrates Forrest, who is not able to establish the truth by the end of the novel.

The various explanations of the mission's failure make up a significant part of Evans' first-person narrative. Evans offers a rich variety of possible scenarios, always with the same momentary belief in their truth. There are reports in which the captain, whom Evans alternately calls Joseph Jackson or Jack Josephson, may have committed suicide, tried to rape Evans, or tried to murder him. He also may have been murdered by Evans or had an accident that sent him out of the space capsule's disposal hatch. The ejection of the captain's corpse into space is a common theme in most of Evans' versions, though in a few of them the captain became insubstantial and faded through the spaceship's metal toward the Sun.

The most outlandish of Evans' stories involves telepathic contact with the Venusians. During these "Great Venus Disturbances," the aliens tell the two astronauts that they must not land on Venus. If they do not change course, the Venusians threaten to kill one of the crew and send the other back to Earth to warn his government about the futility of further missions. Because a manual override of the programmed course seems impossible, either the aliens kill the captain or Evans performs the murder.

The central idea behind Evans' stories is that, in the absence of any surviving outside reference to check on his reports, any version has the potential to be true. This confusing outcome is mirrored by the textual complexity of the novel itself. *Beyond Apollo* reads as Evans' stream of consciousness. At one point, he even promises that one day he will write a novel about his experiences and call it *Beyond Apollo*.

Although the core of the novel deals with Evans' reaction to the failed Venus mission, *Beyond Apollo* also covers his private life on Earth. In these narrations, it is equally impossible to judge when Evans' recollections of his dysfunctional relationship with his wife, Helen, are grounded in reality, recount a dream, or come directly from his imagination. Similarly, Evans' account of his present confinement is riddled with ambiguities and invented episodes, such as his strangulation of Dr. Forrest.

In the end, *Beyond Apollo* paints the troubled picture of a man who has encountered some terrible horror in space. Evans' trauma has left him with an inability to find out—even for himself—which of his many stories is the true one.

Analysis

Beyond Apollo is a fine example of science fiction's New Wave of the 1960's and 1970's. Like many New Wave writers, Barry Malzberg sought to bring to the genre new stylistic devices and critical themes that contemporary writers of mainstream literature were using. Harry Evans thus has some of the haunted, introspective traits of a character by Saul Bellow or of Eugene O'Neill's protagonist Edmund Tyrone in *Long Day's Journey into Night* (1956).

At the same time, the self-referential form and the open ending of *Beyond Apollo* stand in opposition to the shape of much classical science fiction. Unlike Malzberg's text, classics such as Robert A. Heinlein's masterpiece *Starship Troopers* (1959) generally have been marked by accessible, straightforward writing, an optimistic belief in humanity's ability to explore space, and a goal-oriented drive toward the climactic solution to the major plot problem.

Although *Beyond Apollo* deals with the results of a failed space mission, the novel's interest does not lie in finding the problem, fixing it, and moving on. Its very refusal to tell the exact reason for the mission's failure turns the reader away from concrete, external problems and toward Malzberg's exploration of the inner space of Harry Evans. What emerges is the picture of Evans' personal traumatization at the hand of an overbureaucratized, indifferent space program that tries to turn idealistic young men into mindless robots performing superfluous tasks aboard remote-controlled spacecraft.

This focus on an imperfect protagonist, his loss of self, and the detailed vision of a sad, shabby, interior world is a trademark of the New Wave. Malzberg's novel ranks among the finest examples of this subgenre. It is as haunting as *Dying Inside* (1972), Robert Silverberg's excellent first-person account of a telepath who loses his extrasensory powers. *Beyond Apollo* also is close in spirit to Daniel Keyes's moving story "Flowers for Algernon" (1959), the diary of a mentally retarded man to whom a new drug temporarily gives the mind of a genius.

In addition to its close examination of Evans' troubles, *Beyond Apollo* suggests that something is generally and fundamentally wrong with America's space program. This is a negative stance rather unusual for much classic American science fiction, and it illustrates the New Wave's deep-rooted suspicion of anything related to the Establishment. This critical view places Malzberg's text within the tradition of Ray Bradbury's early subversive text, *The Martian Chronicles* (1950), in which Bradbury envisions how American culture degrades the red planet by littering its ancient landscape with prefabricated houses and hot dog stands.

As argued in *Beyond Apollo*, the space program suffers from a bloated bureaucracy that lacks any true sense of direction and cares for neither its men nor its scientific goals. This is a belief that Malzberg has explored in a series of related novels and short stories and that has earned him both scorn and praise from critics. Perhaps ironically for such a dark work, *Beyond Apollo* was given the inaugural John W. Campbell Memorial Award as the year's best science-fiction novel of 1972.

—*R. C. Lutz*

BEYOND THE AQUILA RIFT

This is a collection of eighteen science fiction stories, ranging from quite short to novella-length. They lean heavily toward hard science and far-future settings and often include artificial intelligences as characters.

Author: Alastair Reynolds (1966–)
Genre: Science Fiction—extrapolatory
Type of Work: Short Story Collection
Time of Work: Various
Location: Various
First Published: 2016

THE STORY

The author's first three novels and some of his more recent work are set within a consistent distant future, and several of the stories in this collection share that backdrop. The opening story, "The Great Wall of Mars," is chronologically the earliest in that sequence. It provides a glimpse of how humanity split into two distinctive groups, one sharing a hive mind—the Conjoiners—and one not. "Weather" then leaps forward to a point where the two types of humanity have gone their separate ways among the stars. When a Conjoiner is rescued from pirates, she becomes instrumental in an ensuing race against death by a ship full of Ultras, individuals who accept augmentations to their bodies but not their minds.

"Beyond the Aquila Rift" posits a series of artificial gates among the stars, created by a now-vanished alien race. A malfunction sends one ship far beyond its normal network and into a human-operated facility, which is not what it appears to be. "Minla's Flowers" presents a space traveler with a difficult choice—should he intervene in a war on a lost colony world in order to unite them in time to avert a greater calamity? "Zima Blue" concerns an artist who traces his own existence back through centuries and discovers that he is a machine intelligence who was implanted in an organic body. In "Fury," a man who has lived for thousands of years must be punished for a crime he no longer remembers having committed. The protagonist of "The Star Surgeon's Apprentice" unwittingly signs up as a crew member on a pirate ship and is instrumental in their destruction. "The Sledge-Maker's Daughter" is set in an Ice Age caused by a battle between humans and machine intelligences that draw their power from the sun.

"Diamond Dogs" is a novella related to the novel *Chasm City*. A team of explorers investigates a mysterious artifact that contains a string of complicated puzzles. A wrong answer results in violent responses up to and including death. This is a reworking of the central theme of the Algis Budrys novel *Rogue Moon*, to which Reynolds gives credit. "Thousandth Night" is the reunion of a thousand functionally immortal clones among whom a deadly conspiracy boils to the surface. It also involves a grandiose plan to reconfigure the galaxy into a more organized arrangement. "Troika" is one of the author's rare stories set in the near future. Russian cosmonauts investigate a presumably alien artifact that enters the solar system and discover not only that it is from the future, but its origin cannot be admitted by their government. "Sleepover" is set on a future Earth in which most humans are in suspended animation, awaiting the outcome of a war fought between artificial intelligences on another plane of reality.

An artist is an unwitting accomplice to a disastrous collision in space in "Vainglory." A wounded soldier finds himself merging identities with the automated medical unit that is treating his injuries in "Trauma Pod." The mysterious alien artifact found on an empty world poses a deadly challenge for the crew of a spaceship in "The Last Log of the Lachromosa." An unhappy little girl stows away aboard an airship on Mars and meets an old man who has managed to resist the tides of change in "The Old Man and the Martian Sea," and a self-aware robot serves as a space probe in "In Babelsberg," but things go wrong when it embarks on a speaking tour back on Earth.

ANALYSIS

Space opera has changed significantly during the course of science fiction's evolution as a genre. In its earliest form, characterization was unimportant—the characters were simply placeholders, around which alien worlds and space adventures could be wrapped. Reynolds is one of several writers active today who incorporate more fully realized characters into wide ranging space adventures, although they are generally created with broad brush strokes rather than a more subtle rendering. The focus is still the wonders of the physical universe and humanity's attempts to adapt to different environments, but we see this through the eyes of actual people rather than cardboard cutouts. Although his tone is invariably serious, a few bits of obscure humor surface at times, such as a character named Annabelle "Anna" Lyze in "Trauma Pod."

Most of Reynolds' work takes place in the very distant future. Space travel is almost always commonplace, human lives are sometimes measured in centuries or even millennia, and technology is so far advanced that there are self-aware machine intelligences and other devices that seem almost magical in their operation. While these wonders are rarely explained in any detail, the speculations about the physical universe are generally firmly based on known scientific principles. Reynolds often uses a consistent background for more than one novel or shorter work. Several of the stories in this collection are set in the universe Reynolds created for the Revelation Space series of novels, while "Diamond Dogs" is linked to *Chasm City,* and "Thousandth Night" shares the backdrop of *House of Suns.*

Reynolds, whose background in physics and astronomy is evident in his descriptions of the environments where his characters reside, also speculates frequently about the interface between humans and machines. Cyborgs—humans with significant mechanical enhancement of their bodies—are common and, in some cases, non-cyborgs are the exception rather than the rule. Sometimes his protagonists are actually robots. Starships or buildings or other artifacts may house artificial intelligences who interact with people. Immortality is a common theme, sometimes involving robots but, more commonly, human beings. In both cases, Reynolds often addresses the limits of memory, and his characters rarely remember their youth. Although his stories are predominantly adventurous, he does address ethical issues from time to time. The protagonist of "Minla's Flowers" agonizes over whether or not he should intervene in a planetary civil war and, if he does, in what fashion. The artist in "Zima Blue" decides that rational choices are not always the optimal ones. The immortal dictator in "Fury" has unquestionably been a benevolent influence on the galaxy for tens of thousands of years, but he still must be punished for a single evil deed committed in his youth. The nature of crime and the appropriateness of punishment are addressed in "The Water Thief." Reynolds rarely varies the type of story that he writes, but it is a subset of science fiction that he handles as well or better than any of his contemporaries.

—*Don D'Ammassa*

BEYOND THE GOLDEN STAIR

After escaping from prison, John Hibbert is forced to flee into the Everglades, where he and his companions discover a golden staircase, the entrance to an advanced civilization

Author: Hannes Bok (1914–1964)
Genre: Fantasy—alien civilization
Type of work: Novel
Time of work: The late 1940's
Locale: The Florida Everglades and Khoire
First published: 1970 (previously published as "The Blue Flamingo," *Startling Stories,* 1948)

THE STORY

John Hibbert is haunted by a lifelong, recurring dream of a beautiful woman, a dream that continues into his adult life and even into battle. As a war veteran, he accepts employment with his service buddies and then is jailed when, as their cashier, he signs blank checks for them. After being transferred to the state penitentiary, Hibbert unwillingly joins Frank Scarlatti, who, with the help of his accomplice Burks, breaks out of prison and takes Hibbert with him.

They flee to the Florida Everglades in order to escape the authorities. They make their way to the swamp shanty of Scarlatti's girlfriend, Carlotta, who is supposed to guide them safely through the Everglades. Paddling deeper into the swamps, however, they come upon a hidden pool flanked by ruins and guarded by a blue flamingo. Carlotta makes some obscure historical references, from which

Hibbert infers that this may actually be Ponce de Leon's famous Fountain of Youth. As a joke, Burks decides to wade into the pool to test its rejuvenating powers. The flamingo, however, attacks Burks, and Burks shoots the bird and kills it.

Before it dies, the flamingo summons a shining stairway into the sky. Climbing the stairs, the four find themselves at the threshold of Khoire. A booming voice warns them that they cannot stay because they have not been armed with the Sacred Sign, nor can they simply leave. Khoire must and will change them into their truest selves; they cannot hide or pretend to be what they are not. They meet Patur, the keeper of the Central Gate, who gives them the Crystal Mask, the function of which is to reveal the wearer's identity. To demonstrate its use, Patur reveals his own history. When Burks puts on the mask, Patur discovers that Burks has killed the blue flamingo, which Patur informs him was trying to warn him of Khoire's dangers. The greatest danger is the "change," the transformation of the person into his or her true form. Burks decides that to stay in Khoire would be better than being perpetually hunted by prison authorities. He offers to take the place of the blue flamingo in order to receive the Sacred Sign and remain in Khoire forever.

After Burks leaves, Scarlatti, Carlotta, and Hibbert go to the quarters prepared for them. There they meet Mareth, the woman who appears in Hibbert's recurring dream. She is a Watcher of the Qsin of Khoire, beings who patrol the earth and assist people in discerning and rooting out evil. Hibbert, immediately smitten by Mareth, declares his love. She, too, has a recurring dream about the man she will love, but Hibbert is not that man. She urges him to be patient until after his Change.

Afraid of his own transformation, Scarlatti insists upon seeing Burks. Patur takes them to see his self-induced change into the blue flamingo. Horrified at what he finds, Scarlatti decides to leave Khoire immediately and takes Mareth hostage with the gun he has concealed.

Because Scarlatti is not familiar with the dimensional warps of Khoire, however, Mareth and Hibbert manage to escape into the Jungles of Madness, the home of the sick and the demented, those whose transformations drove them insane. Monsters such as the Ksor, enormous alligators, prey on the unwary and the weak. Scarlatti and Carlotta, having unwisely chased Mareth and Hibbert into the jungle, are transformed into their true selves—a malignant dwarf and a hairless dog—and are soon consumed by the Ksor. It is also here that Hibbert becomes a giant, the man of Mareth's dream. They escape the Jungles of Madness, but Hibbert now has to leave Khoire in order to obtain the Sacred Sign and return to Mareth. Hibbert and Mareth passionately embrace, but Hibbert must descend the golden stair back to the pool, which Burks now guards. Paddling back through the Everglades, Hibbert has begun his quest to return to Khoire.

ANALYSIS

An adventure and a love story, *Beyond the Golden Stair*, though relatively unknown, remains one of the most appealing novels in the genre, strongly resonating with A. Merritt's *The Moon Pool* (1919) and H. Rider Haggard's *The People of the Mist* (1894). Of particular interest is the creation of Khoire, a world populated by beings who have advanced far beyond human civilization, both technologically and philosophically, yet who remain compassionate toward humanity and its failings. Unfortunately, humanity has only superstitious and legendary glimmerings of the Khoireans. The Fountain of Youth, El Dorado, Jacob's Ladder, Ra the sun god, and Usipatra Vana all are mythical touchstones connecting human culture with that of Khoire.

Hannes Bok's greatest achievement lies in his charming rendition of the Cinderella myth. Hibbert is a weak, puny man, but he is also a courageous soul who is ultimately rewarded for his gallantry, his inner strength, and his love. Because Khoire strips away all pretensions and secrets, revealing the true self, physical appearance conforms to the depth of spiritual insight. As a result, Hibbert can overcome his physical deformities in Khoire and be transformed into the appropriate object of Mareth's desire. Hibbert's metamorphosis and his subsequent exile from Khoire represent the capacity, whatever the difficulties, to fulfill a dream that has haunted, perplexed, and maddened one's everyday life.

—*Jeffrey Cass*

Big Planet and Showboat World

Adventure, intrigue, and romance during travels on an enormous planet containing many varied cultures

Author: Jack Vance (1916–2013)
Genre: Science fiction—interplanetary romance
First published: *Big Planet* (1957; full text restored 1978; serial form, *Startling Stories*, September, 1952) and *Showboat World* (1975)
Type of work: Novels
Time of work: The late twenty-sixth century
Locale: Various locations on Big Planet

The Story

Location is everything in these two novels. Big Planet is enormous, and all of Earth's splinter cultures seem to have migrated there, each convinced that its way of life is the only true way. There is no central government. Murder, torture, and intolerance are rife, and Earth is unable to exercise any real control over the planet. The magazine story of *Big Planet* was cut drastically and edited egregiously in its first book publication, one of the few instances in which a book became shorter than the original magazine story. The full original text was not restored until 1978. *Showboat World* was conceived retroactively as a sequel.

In *Big Planet*, a new ruler—the Bajarnum of Beaujolais, otherwise known as Charley Lysidder—has begun expanding his empire through various nefarious means, including assassination, child slavery, and other atrocities. A commission has been sent from Earth to investigate and take action to put an end to the threat. The commission's spaceship, sabotaged by Lysidder's agent, crashes near the edge of Lysidder's territory, killing all but the commission members and a very few others. When Claude Glystra, commission chairman, returns to consciousness a few days later, the radio operator, Abbigens, having proved to be Lysidder's agent, has escaped. Glystra has been nursed since the crash by a local girl named Nancy.

Because Lysidder obviously will send troops to capture the commission, Glystra decides that their only hope is to avoid Lysidder entirely and get to Earth Enclave, forty thousand miles away. Nancy begs to join the trek, but Glystra refuses at first.

Shortly after the journey begins, Abbigens is discovered leading troops to capture the commission. In the ensuing melee, Abbigens is killed and Nancy assists in defeating the troops. The trek resumes, and as the group encounters one new culture after another, it begins to shrink as members are killed or, in one case, defect to the local culture. This is the most interesting portion of the book because the various cultures are both original and fascinating.

After traveling for some time on foot and via native beast, boat, and highline, the party is reduced to four: Glystra, Nancy, commission member Bishop, and Corbus, the chief engineer of the spaceship. The highline has been cut, the party has been attacked by raiders from which they manage to escape, and they have arrived outside the site of Myrtlesee Fountain, reputed site of a renowned oracle. During the trip, Glystra and Nancy have developed an attraction for each other, although inconsistencies in Nancy's speech and behavior make Glystra suspect that she is not what she seems.

During the night, Bishop is killed and Nancy is kidnapped. Glystra and Corbus sneak into the city and bribe a local merchant to help them find Nancy. During the search, Glystra discovers the secret of the oracle: Material extracted from the brains of corpses and mixed with a local drug is injected into the brain of a living man, who then becomes superintelligent for a few moments before dying. Glystra also finds Nancy, not as a prisoner but as a now reluctant agent and consort of Lysidder.

Glystra is captured and scheduled to be injected for Lysidder's use as an oracle, but Corbus smuggles in a large supply of vitamins and amino acids that they believe will counteract the effect of the brain serum. During his session as oracle, Glystra gives confusing answers and feigns death, then is thrown into an abattoir, from which he escapes with the help of Corbus. They lay a trap for Lysidder, steal his airboat, reconcile with Nancy, and fly to Earth Enclave and safety.

Showboat World, although also set on Big Planet, takes place in a section far distant from the earlier story and is considerably more picaresque. Showboats ply the Vissal River and its tributaries, bringing various forms of entertainment to the many cultures spread along the banks. The two most notorious showboats are owned by rivals Appolon Zamp and Garth Ashgale. Their rivalry leads to the destruction of Zamp's boat and considerable damage to Ashgale's. The chicanery that accomplishes this is a key element of the book and is practiced by almost every character who appears.

King Waldemar of Sylvanesse, far up the river, has decreed a festival and a competition among six showboats. Zamp has been issued an invitation to compete and has joined forces with Damsel Blanche-Aster, a mysterious girl who is to help him find another showboat and sail it to Sylvanesse.

Theodorus Gassoon, dour and frugal, owns a boat that he prefers to keep moored and use as a museum. He falls under the spell of Blanche-Aster and agrees, reluctantly, to let Zamp use his boat for the journey and the competition. The voyage is long and perilous; as in Big Planet it is made interesting by the many weird cultures encountered along the way.

It becomes apparent in Sylvanesse that Zamp's production of William Shakespeare's *Macbeth* is poorly matched against the fantastic stagings of the other boats. During the show, Blanche-Aster reveals herself to be a descendant of a rival ruler and is hailed as the queen, deposing Waldemar. Hers is a short rule, because Gassoon accidentally shows an emblem that causes the populace to hail him as the king.

Zamp, sailing back down the river, is overtaken by Gassoon, who is fleeing on horseback after his emblem is destroyed and he is no longer recognized as the king. The two return to their original port and make new plans.

ANALYSIS

Big Planet is an ingenious invention that could be used in many books. It is twenty-five thousand miles in diameter, yielding a surface area almost ten times that of Earth, of which about half is land. This makes it possible for many different cultures to exist on the planet without intruding on one another, thus providing a vehicle for many different stories. Furthermore, the planet has a mean density of slightly less than two, because the core and surface are notably deficient in heavy elements. As a result, the surface gravity is only slightly higher than that of Earth, despite the planet's size, and the climate is similar to Earth's. The lack of iron and other such metals makes development of technology difficult and long-range communication almost impossible. This, in turn, increases the isolation of the various cultures and enhances the general antipathy among them. Any large amounts of metal must be imported, at tremendous cost. Iron, in fact, is the basic standard for exchange because of its utility and rarity on the planet.

Jack Vance's contributions to science fiction are widely recognized. Several sources credit him with bringing sophistication to the interplanetary romance, which until then had largely consisted of weak plots constructed primarily to allow the hero to invent one new superscientific gadget after another, in order to resolve some new perilous situation. These two books are excellent illustrations of Vance's sophisticated approach.

Vance specializes in the picaresque and baroque, which is much more evident in *Showboat World* than in *Big Planet*. Whereas *Big Planet* is deeply concerned with the social and ethical problems inherent in the regimes of the planet and takes a more serious note, *Showboat World* treats the chicanery and ethical values of Zamp and his associates with amused tolerance. This is somewhat misleading, because Vance's work, taken as a whole, shows continuing concern with social values, particularly the problems of exploitation and the nature of freedom.

Vance is arguably without peer in the development of exotic and baroque backgrounds. As his career progressed, the backgrounds became more baroque and more detailed, and later works abound in footnotes and references to various "authorities" that serve to make the backgrounds very detailed and almost familiar.

These two novels, originally published twenty-three years apart but based in the same common background, are illustrative of Vance's development during this period. His writings in the period began with simpler, action-oriented plots and evolved to more involved, subtler plots with more detailed and exotic backgrounds.

Vance's career, spanning some fifty years, shows his continued concentration on baroque, meticulously detailed settings and his overall concern with moral values. Although he is also well known in the mystery field, in which he won the Edgar Award in 1960 for *The Man in the Cage*, he is much better known for his science fiction, having twice won the Hugo Award (in 1963, for "The Dragon Masters" in the short fiction category, and in 1967, for "The Last Castle" in the novelette category) in addition to a 1966 Nebula Award, given by the Science Fiction Writers of America, for "The Last Castle."

—W. D. Stevens

THE BIG TIME

Greta Forsane, an atemporal entertainer, assists soldiers in the Change Wars by working at an out-of-time rest and recovery station that is threatened from within

Author: Fritz Leiber (1910–1992)
Genre: Science fiction—time travel
Type of work: Novel
Time of work: Simultaneous past, present, and future
Locale: The Place, a pocket of space-time existing separate from the cosmos
First published: 1961 (serial form, *Galaxy Science Fiction*, 1958)

THE STORY

A short Hugo-winning novel, *The Big Time* benefits from employing a limited number of characters at a fixed place over a few hours of narrative time, as if adhering to the dramatic unities of place, action, and a much modified sense of time. Initially, the narrator provides exposition leading up to a mystery. He then attempts to solve the mystery and rescue the group from disaster. The story is told as if to inform or to forewarn a newcomer to the temporal context the novel describes. The events reveal a greater sense of the problems associated with altering history.

Greta Forsane, an entertainer, tells of an experience at the Recuperation Station that reveals to her much about herself. The station is also manned by Sid, the officer in charge; Doc, a drunken veteran; Maud, an older party girl; Lilli, a recent addition; and Beau, second in command. They work for the Spiders, their side in the Change War. Their duties include healing wounded soldiers, operating the machinery that allows pickup and delivery of soldiers, and entertaining soldiers while they rest and recuperate. According to a previous plan, they pick up three soldiers on a scheduled arrival: Eric, a Nazi; Mark, a Roman; and Bruce, a Briton from the early 1900's. All characters are people who were resurrected from different times and places and brought into The Big Time. The arriving soldiers were engaged in a conflict in Saint Petersburg in 1883, attempting to kidnap an infant Albert Einstein back from their opponents, the Snakes.

Bruce, a recent recruit who is frustrated by the unsettling effects of changing the past, rants about being issued two left-handed gloves, a problem that an infatuated Lilli rectifies by using a surgical inverter. A surprise distress call adds Kaby, a mannish Cretian warrior maiden; Illi, a tentacled Lunan from the distant past; and Sevensee, a satyr from the distant future. They carry a tactical atomic bomb in a locked box, intending to use it against their adversaries in Romanized Egypt. After Bruce delivers a rebellious speech urging the assemblage to quit the war, the primary space-time mechanism, the Major Maintainer, is mysteriously stolen and the group is trapped in a void.

The novel then turns toward detective fiction, as they all search for the machine and the culprit who has hidden it. The question becomes urgent when Eric triggers a thirty-minute clock on the atomic bomb. A Minor Maintainer, which allows environmental changes within the station, is fought over, grabbed by Kaby, and used to coerce revelation. Lilli has used the surgical inverter to camouflage the Major Maintainer as an odd sculpture in the art gallery in a bid to follow Bruce's plea to stop the madness of the Change War. Bruce stops the bomb once it is returned to The Big Time. The novel ends with a return to previous conditions and a greater awareness of the similarity of the Spiders and Snakes.

ANALYSIS

In introductory remarks, Fritz Leiber reveals a boyish glee in imagining characters from various periods engaged in battle. The book suggests that the importance is not in the battle; in fact, its conclusion emphasizes the relative meaninglessness of the war in which the characters are engaged. Rather, the novel hinges on the hypothetical meeting of people from vastly different cultures. Leiber implies a consanguinity among these time travelers, an affinity they share for one another that celebrates their essential human traits and denies the idea that they would be too different to be able to work together. This nascent political correctness is perhaps indicative of science fiction and fantasy's tendency to forecast actual futures.

The concept of historical conflation is well established in the later *Riverworld* works (begun in 1971) by Philip José Farmer. The time travel narrative owes ancestry to H. G. Wells's *The Time Machine* (1895). A complication in Leiber's work involves the problem of changes made to the time line. Here Leiber indicates that The Big Time is largely unaffected, except that memories are altered, calling this "the law of conservation of reality." This disturbance of memory bothers Bruce, a poet and analogically a stand-in for the author; he raises serious concerns about the implications of altering the past. Through other veteran characters' dialogues, Leiber conceives of time as resistant to change and asserts that although future events may differ in particulars, the general drift of events and contexts will not be altered radically. This is a departure from the concept of temporal change as described by Alfred Bester in *The Stars My Destination* (1957). Leiber further discusses changes made to history in *The Mind Spider and Other Stories* (1961); the material was reassembled as *The Change War* (1978).

Perhaps the most interesting references are the metaphors used to describe the temporal contexts. Greta describes The Big Time as a train in continual forward motion. When soldiers go on their assigned missions, they get off this train and enter The Little Time, where events do change. On The Big Time, conditions do not alter and characters do not age, though they do construct histories of their experiences.

Even though Greta and her compatriots realize that they are bound to an endless conflict in which they no longer believe, the alternative of dissolution and loss of identity is less attractive. They rise from the events of the novel with greater wisdom, greater compassion, and a sense of value inhering in actions rather than outcomes. They live an alteration of the old maxim that the ends justify the means; instead, they live as though the means justify the means.

—*Scott D. Vander Ploeg*

THE BILL, THE GALACTIC HERO SERIES

Bill, an Imperial Space Trooper, experiences a variety of adventures while fighting the alien enemy Chingers

Author: Harry Harrison (1925–2012)
Genre: Science Fiction—future war
First published: *Bill, the Galactic Hero* (1965), *Bill, the Galactic Hero: The Planet of the Robot Slaves* (1989), *Bill, the Galactic Hero on the Planet of Bottled Brains* (1990, with Robert Sheckley), *Bill, the Galactic Hero on the Planet of Tasteless Pleasure* (1991, with David Bischoff), *Bill, the Galactic Hero on the Planet of Zombie Vampires* (1991, with Jack C. Haldeman II), *Bill, the Galactic Hero on the Planet of Ten Thousand Bars* (1991, with David Bischoff), and *Bill, the Galactic Hero: The Final Incoherent Adventure* (1991, with David M. Harris)
Type of work: Novels

Time of work: The distant future
Locale: Various spacecraft and imaginary planets

THE STORY

The Bill, the Galactic Hero series was begun in 1965, as a single novel. That novel ends with an afterword, with Bill as a recruiting sergeant, suggesting that no sequels were planned. In 1989, the series was continued. A note by Harry Harrison was added to later printings of the original novel, informing the reader that Bill had many other adventures before becoming a recruiting sergeant.

Bill, the Galactic Hero begins with Bill, a white farm boy whose ambition is to become a Technical Fertilizer Operator, being forced into the Space Troopers. A hypnotic device planted in his boot causes him to enlist. After particularly brutal training, including conditioning to hate the seven-foot, reptilian Chingers, he is sent to war.

Bill meets Eager Beager, a disgustingly nice guy who likes to shine other recruits' boots. Beager eventually is revealed to be a Chinger spy named Bgr. He discloses that Chingers are actually only seven inches long and are peaceful. Bill is assigned to be a fuse tender. In an explosion, he is badly hurt and loses his left arm. This is replaced by a black man's right arm.

Bill is recruited by the Galactic Bureau of Investigation, which assigns him to infiltrate the underground. It turns out that almost all members of the underground are secret agents of one sort or another. Bill is then sent to the planet Veneria, where he shoots off his right foot to avoid going back to battle.

In *The Planet of the Robot Slaves* (shortened titles will be used for the remainder of this article), Bill's missing right foot has been replaced by a huge, mutated chicken foot because there is a shortage of human feet. The hospital where Bill is recovering is strafed by robot dragons. When one is captured, it is found to be labeled "Made in USA." Bill, along with recruits Cy BerPunk, Meta Tarsil, and others, is assigned to find the planet Usa. The planet turns out to be ruled by metal creatures and worked by robot slaves.

After Bill becomes involved in a war between Roman legions and medieval knights led by King Arthur, the British forces persuade Bill to go with Merlin to persuade the god Mars to stop the war. Mars turns out to be a projection and sound system. As Bill prepares to leave the planet, Bgr offers him a new, human foot in exchange for Bill's work to end the war.

The Planet of Bottled Brains begins with Bill complaining about his new foot, which has turned into an alligator claw. He is forced to go to the planet Tsuris, which might be a Chinger stronghold. It turns out to be a planet with many immortal brains but not enough bodies to go around. Bill's body is wanted to house a Tsuris brain. He escapes and becomes engaged in a series of adventures fighting Huns, Carthaginians, and other anachronistic armies. Finally, Bill meets the Alien Historian, who has arranged all of this in an attempt to change history for the better.

In *The Planet of Tasteless Pleasure*, Bill has acquired a "mood foot" that changes form according to his mood. Bill takes a walk on the beach and follows a satyr, who pulls him under the water. He finds himself in a land of mythical beasts and persons, and he is told that he must find the god Zeus to redeem himself.

The satyr, who turns out to be a robot controlled by Bgr, leads Bill on a trip to find the Fountain of Hormones, on the theory that humans are so warlike because they are oversexed. They find the fountain after a series of confusing adventures that seem to take place in the Old West of Earth's United States. Finally, Bill is again rescued, and his foot returns to normal human form.

The Planet of Zombie Vampires is concerned with a battle against particularly repulsive aliens on an unnamed planet. Assorted stereotyped troopers help Bill in his mission of destroying the planet. At the novel's close, Bill finds a note from Bgr, who has vanished, along with a new foot.

The Planet of Ten Thousand Bars begins with Bill being assigned to infiltrate the Commupop Party, a group of dissidents who read good literature instead of the propaganda comics approved by the Empire. He finds himself on Barworld, a planet devoted to drinking. There he finds a time portal named Dudley Do-Do and attempts to travel in time to undo apparent damage to the past and prevent an alternative present, ruled by Nazis, from occurring. A series of extremely confusing time travel adventures ends with the appearance of Adolf Hitler and his obliteration by Bgr.

The last book in the series, *The Final Incoherent Adventure*, concerns a mission to the planet Eyerack, which contains the only known neutron mine in the galaxy. Because neutrons are needed to make neutron bombs and the inhabitants of the planet have decided to stop exporting the essential product, they must be subdued. During his mission, Bill is recruited by several resistance groups and by the enemy army. The latest series of defective right feet ends with replacement by a perfectly good hand.

ANALYSIS

The Bill, the Galactic Hero books are designed to poke fun at a number of aspects of both science fiction and reality. From the outset, the books were a satire of space opera, a subgenre of science fiction consisting of adventure stories set in futuristic worlds or on spaceships. Harrison himself wrote such novels, the most famous being his Stainless Steel Rat series (1961–1987), involving an interplanetary intelligence operative.

Sequels to the original *Bill, the Galactic Hero* satirized more recent science fiction. In *The Planet of Bottled Brains*, Bill is rescued by the ship Gumption, run by Captain Dirk and First Officer Splock, an obvious takeoff on the Star Trek television series. In the same book, a brave captain, Ham Duo, and his mate, Chewgumma, are parodies of the heroes of the film *Star Wars* (1977). Harrison even deliberately parodies his own work: Ottar, a character in a *Drunkards and Flagons* game (a parody of the game *Dungeons and Dragons*), is lifted directly from Harrison's *The Technicolor Time Machine* (1967).

At another level, science fiction in general is satirized by the use of names that are ridiculous or clearly based either on reality and cultural icons or on other fiction. Deathwish Drang is a sadistic drill sergeant, Eager Beager is an insanely helpful recruit, and Rambette is a female warrior.

Harrison savages the military and political hierarchies. All the military personnel drink to excess and curse in virtually every sentence. The universal curse is "bowb," which works as noun, adjective, and adverb but has no particular meaning other than emphasis. Military officers are universally stupid and sadistic. Bureaucrats, including the emperor and high military leaders, are depicted as mentally deficient. The enlisted men are all brainwashed.

Most interesting of all are the Chingers, the eternal enemies of the Empire. They are depicted to Trooper recruits as bloodthirsty reptiles seven feet long but in fact are actually seven inches long and never engaged in warfare before they were attacked by the Empire. Bgr, initially known as Eager Beager, works throughout the series to try to get Bill to stop the war with the Chingers.

The series as a whole condemns the concept and practice of warfare. Bill is trapped into participation. He becomes a Trooper under hypnosis and is required to remain a Trooper or face execution. The Chinger enemies are depicted far more sympathetically than are the leaders of the human Empire. Innocent civilians are slaughtered on numerous occasions, but official press releases and interviews suggest otherwise.

The seven books in the series vary in tone, at least partially because five of them were written with four different collaborators, but certain themes are common. Bill is forever trying to find a satisfactory right foot to replace his original one, and Bgr is constantly trying to get Bill to stop the war. Their efforts are futile because the galactic bureaucracy is more interested in propaganda than in understanding or changing the facts behind that propaganda.

Bill, the Galactic Hero and all of its sequels are hilarious, but readers will stop to think along the way. Bill himself undergoes many changes, both physical and psychological, but he always returns to being a Trooper. This is the basic message. Like the robot slaves of the second book, Bill ultimately is powerless to change his life. He has been brainwashed to defend the Empire even though rationally he is convinced that the Empire is committing genocide.

—*Marc Goldstein*

THE BIRTHGRAVE TRILOGY

A woman with extraordinary powers takes a journey of self-discovery and later is pursued by the son she abandoned

Author: Tanith Lee (1947–2015)
Genre: Fantasy—superbeing
First published: *The Birthgrave* (1975), *Vazkor, Son of Vazkor* (1978), and *Quest for the White Witch* (1978)
Type of work: Novels

Time of work: Undefined
Locale: Various provinces of a planet similar to Earth

THE STORY
This story consists of three first-person narratives, the first told by the heroine and the second and third told by her son. *Vazkor, Son of Vazkor* and *Quest for the White Witch* may be considered as a single sequel to *The Birthgrave*.

The Birthgrave Trilogy

In *The Birthgrave*, a nameless woman awakes in a cave beneath a volcano. She knows nothing of herself, her origin, or her reason for being where she is. As the volcano stirs, an enigmatic voice calling itself Karrakaz taunts her. She is evil and deserves death, it tells her. If she leaves the cave, the volcano will erupt, destroying a village and surrounding countryside. The voice adds that she is inhuman; her only kinship is with Jade. Bewildered and frightened, the woman flees to the village, where her healing powers and strange albino appearance convince the folk of her divinity. She learns that she never needs food or drink.

Soon after her arrival, the bandit Darak takes her from the village, before its destruction. She shares many adventures with him, the greatest of which is a grueling chariot race held in a town where Darak is discovered to be an outlaw. After he is hanged, the woman moves on. By now she has learned that she is immune even to mortal wounds.

In the city-state of Ezlann, she meets Vazkor, who resembles Darak. He has learned magic that is similar to her inborn talents. She hates him for using her apparent divinity to aid his greedy conquests of other towns. He impregnates her against her will. She kills him, and his empire falls.

Next, she joins a nomadic tribe and secretly bears a son at the same time that the chief's wife bears a stillborn child. After exchanging babies, she escapes to the sea. She is attacked by a dragon but is rescued by a passing spaceship. The crew tells her that she brought the ship down herself. Aided by the ship's computer, she learns that she is the last member of an ancient race destroyed by a plague. They had sought refuge in the cave, but to no avail. She survived by falling into a deep coma, in which she remained until awakened by the volcano's eruption. Karrakaz is her own name, and Jade is a gem implanted in her forehead, marking her as royalty. As *The Birthgrave* closes, Karrakaz leaves the ship to find a new life.

Vazkor, Son of Vazkor links the first and third books. Although it does not significantly advance the plot, it introduces Karrakaz's son, Vazkor. After his ritual tattooing leaves no mark, he fights several men at once, killing them all and emerging unscathed. When he raids a neighboring town with his tribe, Vazkor terrifies the defenders, who believe him to be the original Vazkor returned from the dead. Vazkor initially believes that his gift of immortality is inherited from his father; later he discovers that his powers come from his mother, not his father. Infuriated that her abandonment condemned him to a life of hardship with a nomadic tribe when he might have been a powerful and invincible king, Vazkor decides to find and kill the white witch.

Quest for the White Witch begins at the start of Vazkor's journey. By the time he reaches the opulent city of Bar-Ibithni, he has come to be feared and respected. He makes an old woman (Lellih) young and beautiful but unwittingly gives her powers like his own. She becomes the leader of a cult that worships him. Lellih tries to seduce him, but Vazkor rejects her. He becomes a close friend of Sorem, the emperor's son. He helps Sorem win a civil war against his rival siblings, but soon afterward he begins an affair with Sorem's mother. Discovering this scandal, Sorem vows to punish his friend, but a plague (sent by an angry Lellih) kills the young ruler and most of his subjects before he can fulfill the vow. Vazkor finds and kills Lellih but is himself slain. When he rises again, he leaves the city to resume his search.

After a long journey, Vazkor arrives in the far south, where Karrakaz is worshiped; Vazkor meets several albino children who share her powers. One of them, lovely Ressaven, claims to be Vazkor's sister. Despite this, they have sex. Ressaven tries to keep Vazkor from finding Karrakaz's abode, but he overcomes all resistance. Finally, he confronts his mother, who has been masquerading as Ressaven. Shamed by his incest, Vazkor leaves, but ultimately he returns to Karrakaz, planning to breed a new race of immortals with her.

ANALYSIS

Tanith Lee had several children's books to her credit before she wrote the Birthgrave trilogy. Despite the fact that the trilogy was her first published adult fantasy, it was the work that boosted her career. The first volume was published by DAW in 1975, when Ballantine Books began an effort to increase interest in fantasy literature with novels such as *The Sword of Shannara* (1977) by Terry Brooks. Prior efforts to establish fantasy as a profitable business had failed, with the exception of retellings of well-known legends. Ballantine's success led DAW to feature new fantasies, including the Birthgrave trilogy. Lee became one of director Donald A. Wollheim's protégés. The year 1976 saw the beginning of a boom in science-fiction and fantasy book publishing, and Lee's lengthy trilogy could not have been better timed.

Critics' response to the Birthgrave trilogy is mixed. Marion Zimmer Bradley, a renowned author with a reputation as a harsh critic, wrote an introduction for the trilogy praising Lee's presentation of credible characters and rich settings. Other critics agree with Lee's description of her style as undisciplined and erratic. Her prose is highly descriptive, but the meaning often gets lost in grandiose wording. The trilogy lacks balance as a whole. *The Birthgrave* is 408 pages, whereas *Vazkor, Son of Vazkor* is a mere 220 pages. *Quest for the White Witch* is almost as long as The Birthgrave, at 381 pages.

The Birthgrave trilogy, with its tale of a beautiful princess from a lost civilization, follows an old but popular theme. This fashion began in the late 1800's with authors such as Sir H. Rider Haggard, who wrote She (1887). Books in this vein tell stories of heroic explorers who find fabulous, decadent civilizations in mysterious lands. The tales reflect the great interest in lost civilizations during the late nineteenth century, when discoveries such as Heinrich Schliemann's city of Troy made headlines. To contemporary authors, such discoveries inspired wonderful settings for romantic adventures; the lost cities about which they wrote generally are ruled by an exotic, barbaric, and merciless woman who bewitches the explorer. Tanith Lee has an interest in past civilizations, and she is clearly drawing from these examples in her depiction of Karrakaz as amoral, powerful, regal, and beautiful. When her son confronts her, he is the same heroic explorer.

The Birthgrave trilogy also exemplifies the rise of feminine heroes and female authors in science fiction and fantasy. Unlike Haggard's barbarian queens, Lee's Karrakaz is not a prize to be won by a burly explorer, nor does she need rescuing. The one time she is saved, she calls her rescuers to her by sheer force of will. She is always in control. Even in the second and third books, when her son is the focus of most of the action, Karrakaz remains his goal and guiding force. Lee also points out that Vazkor inherits his gifts from a woman who scorns the traditional role of motherhood. If the adventures of Karrakaz had continued, she certainly would have become the immortal ruler of a new race of her own creation.

Marion Zimmer Bradley helped to spearhead the feminist science fiction/fantasy movement in the 1970's with her Darkover books, such as *The Heritage of Hastur* (1975). The number of female authors in science fiction and fantasy continues to increase, including C. J. Cherryh, Mercedes Lackey, Melanie Rawn, Jennifer Roberson, Tanith Lee, Lois McMaster Bujold, and many more.

Like its precursors, the Birthgrave trilogy contains no deep truths, New Wave philosophies, or cautionary messages for twentieth century society. Lee never flinches from serious topics such as sex, guilt, and power, but she clearly did not intend her trilogy to be a feminist treatise. The Birthgrave trilogy is for the most part an enjoyable, rousing adventure that draws on an established theme and satisfies the need for fresh approaches that continues to galvanize the writing of fantasy literature.

—*Carla Hall Minor*

THE BLACK CLOUD

An extraordinary alien being approaches Earth, and scientists communicate with it

Author: Fred Hoyle (1915-2001)
Genre: Science fiction—superbeing
First published: 1957
Type of work: Novel
Time of work: The 1960's, and 2021
Locale: England and the United States

The Story

The Black Cloud concerns the apocalyptic visit of an enormous gaseous cloud to Earth in the years 1967-1968. It is first sighted by a young Norwegian astronomer as he is studying the night sky through the Schmidt Telescope at the Mount Wilson Observatory in California. World-renowned astronomers are immediately informed at England's Cambridge University, where Dr. Christopher Kingsley, an astronomy professor, calls for a meeting with scientists from the United States, England, and Australia. Scientists at the California Institute of Technology in Pasadena predict that it will take the cloud approximately eighteen months to arrive. Even though the damage will be cataclysmic, precautions can be taken, depending on where people live. Survival will depend on people's ability to bury themselves deep enough in the ground to protect themselves first from the intense heat caused by molecular collisions in the upper atmosphere and then from the cold that results when the cloud blocks the sun's rays.

Both the president of the United States and the prime minister of England fear that knowledge of the cloud's arrival will result in mass panic, so they try to suppress the facts. Kingsley, however, threatens to expose the coming of the cloud if these officials fail to do so. Kings-ley, who becomes the leader of the scientists, decides to move their equipment to an estate called Nortonstowe, which he establishes as the center of radio communication for the world. The cloud arrives months earlier than expected, resulting in floods, hurricanes, and tremendous fluctuations in temperature.

When the weather stabilizes, the scientists begin to realize that the black cloud is a living and intelligent being, and they initiate procedures to try to communicate with it. The cloud quickly learns the English language and mathematical formulas. With communication established, an enormous exchange of information begins, and the cloud informs human beings that unless they address Earth's major problem, overpopulation, there will be terrible consequences. The cloud tells them that it is more than 500 million years old, and it offers the astronomers its definition of intelligent life: "something that reflects the basic structure of the universe. . . . We're both constructed in a way that reflects the inner pattern of the Universe."

In the meantime, both the English and American governments have become concerned about the cloud's destructive power and form a plan to drive it away by firing hydrogen rockets into its interior to disrupt its electrical circuitry. The cloud decides that it will not destroy Earth and that it will soon depart. The astronomers, however, insist that it remain long enough to transmit as much of its scientific knowledge as possible. The cloud attempts to reprogram the brains of Kingsley and another scientist so that they can absorb information more quickly, but both volunteers die in the process. The truth of the cloud is never made public. The novel takes the form of a manuscript by one of the scientists at Nortonstowe, left to the grandson of Ann Halsey, a concert pianist who had been at Nortonstowe to provide entertainment for the scientists. The author implies that the grandson is also the grandson of Kingsley.

ANALYSIS
The Black Cloud was the first science-fiction novel written by one of the world's most widely recognized cosmologists and astrophysicists, Fred Hoyle. For many years, Hoyle was a professor of astronomy at Cambridge, and he was knighted by Queen Elizabeth II. He also was the chief exponent of the steady state theory of the universe, which contradicted the popular big bang theory, in which the majority of astronomers had believed for many years. *The Black Cloud* was Hoyle's fictional demonstration of his theory. He also hypothesized that life began by the movement of huge interstellar clouds through the universe and the subsequent seeding of planets, including Earth. He explained his complex theory in a best-selling nonfiction book called *The Nature of the Universe* (1950); that work was attacked obliquely by the most famous exponent of the big bang theory, George Gamow, in his *The Creation of the Universe* (1952).

The Black Cloud became a best-seller and one of modern science fiction's more famous examples of an author's ability to combine the subgenres of superbeing with catastrophe (although, in this case, the cloud turns out to be both intelligent and benign). What makes this novel so compelling is the scientific authenticity that Hoyle's vast background brings to both the characters and the complex nature of information that makes up the narrative. Hoyle became the acknowledged leader of the Cambridge cosmographers and continued to argue for the steady state theory of the universe.

—*Patrick Meanor*

Black Easter and The Day After Judgment

At a businessman's instigation, a magician summons demons, triggering Armageddon; when the forces of Hell win the battle, Satan announces that God is dead and reluctantly assumes the divine throne

Author: James Blish (1921-1975)
Genre: Fantasy—apocalypse
First published: *Black Easter* (1968) and *The Day After Judgment* (1971)
Type of work: Novels
Time of work: The late twentieth century
Locale: Primarily Italy and California's Death Valley

The Story

James Blish considered *Black Easter* and *The Day After Judgment* to be one narrative unit. As one unit, they are part of the *After Such Knowledge* trilogy (1991), which also includes *A Case of Conscience* (1958) and *Doctor Mirabilis* (1964). The three parts of the trilogy are connected more by theme than by plot. Doctor Mirabilis is a historical novel about thirteenth century scholar Roger Bacon; *A Case of Conscience* is a science-fiction novel about an alien society that seems to be free of sin. All the books deal with theological themes of innocence, sin, knowledge, and power.

In *Black Easter* and *The Day After Judgment*, traditional European ceremonial magic actually works. This magic requires summoning spirits or demons. Both "white" (good) magic and "black" (evil) magic exist. White magicians have limited power and call on demi-urges. Black magicians have extensive power obtained through the use of demons. A covenant governs the relationship between white magic and black magic. Blish is vague about the precise terms of the covenant, but it allows a priest to be an observer at the summoning of demons as long as he does not interfere with the ceremony. Blish's "Author's Note" explains that he has tried to present magic as it would be if it were real, using historical sources. Blish also cautions that he has not presented enough information for readers to attempt the rituals for themselves.

In *Black Easter*, an American businessman named Baines approaches an expatriate magician, Theron Ware, who lives in Italy. Baines is accompanied by his special executive assistant, Jack Ginsberg. As a test of Ware's powers, Baines wants him to commit an untraceable murder, with a demon as the killer. After the success of two test murders, Baines commissions Ware to "let all the major demons out of Hell for one night." Another major character, Father Domenico, belongs to a religious order that practices white magic, primarily treasure hunting. Father Domenico's order sends him to observe the ritual commissioned by Baines. On Easter, Baines conjures forty-eight demons, unleashing Armageddon. When Ware tries to send the demons back to Hell, Satan appears and mocks him. Father Domenico's crucifix explodes in his hand. Black Easter ends with three sinister words, "God is dead."

As *The Day After Judgment* begins, Baines, Ware, and Domenico try to deal with the triumph of Hell in the final battle against Heaven. Simultaneously, at Strategic Air Command headquarters in the United States, General D. Willis McKnight and various scientists try to understand what has happened in the nuclear exchange that was part of Armageddon. General McKnight and his aides discover that the City of Dis, the fortified lower circles of Hell in Dante Alighieri's *Inferno* (part 1 of *The Divine Comedy*, c. 1320), has appeared in California's Death Valley. An intense military assault upon the walls of Dis ends in defeat.

Baines, Ginsberg, Ware, and Domenico travel separately to the United States. They meet in Death Valley and together enter Dis. At its center, they find Pandemonium (thus combining poet John Milton's Hell with Dante's). At the center of Pandemonium, they find Satan. Speaking in Miltonic verse, Satan informs them that, in God's absence, he has been forced to take on the divine role. He begs them to take it from him, saying that God had always intended humans to assume divine status. The novel ends ambiguously: After Satan's verse monologue, Dis vanishes, and the men are left in the desert. The narrative suggests that they have been spiritually renewed.

Analysis

Together with *Doctor Mirabilis* and *A Case of Conscience*, *Black Easter* and *The Day After Judgment* are often thought to be Blish's best work. Written toward the end of his career, the books explore the dilemma of the existence of evil in a world created by a good God. The dilemma is usually stated in the form that if God is both all-powerful and all-good, how can God allow evil to exist? These novels answer the question by showing God deliberately restraining his power. By the covenant, Father Domenico, a representative of good, cannot do anything to hinder or stop Theron Ware's summoning of demons. It is logical, then, that God is discovered to be dead at the end of *Black Easter*; death, after all, is the ultimate restraint. The self-restraint practiced by God allows the forces of evil nearly complete freedom of action. Ironically, when evil triumphs, Satan finds that he must unwillingly take the role of God. When Satan assumes the divine throne, he must give up the freedom he enjoyed as ruler of Hell and submit to the restraints imposed on good.

In a favorable review of *Black Easter* in *The Magazine of Fantasy and Science Fiction*, Joanna Russ describes Blish's point of view as Manichean. In Manicheanism, good and evil are separate powers that have struggled with each other throughout history. In *Black Easter* and *The Day After Judgment*, however, good is absent or inactive, while evil is present and active. Thus, good and evil do not fight on equal terms. Instead of struggling with evil, good withdraws and leaves the field open for evil.

Black Easter is dedicated to the memory of C. S. Lewis. *Black Easter* and *The Day After Judgment* recall Lewis' novel *That Hideous Strength* (1945), in which a limited Armageddon occurs. Lewis' novel, however, expresses his Christian faith, with good triumphing, while Blish's books reflect his agnosticism through the death of God and the enthronement of Satan. Lewis wrote to express a belief system, but Blish wrote to explore the possibilities of good and evil as they relate to the human search for knowledge. Blish's books also have parallels to Lewis' *The Screwtape Letters* (1942). An epistolary novel, this book deals with demoniac temptation of modern human beings.

Black Easter and *The Day After Judgment* also allow comparisons with other works. They have thematic similarities to Walter M. Miller, Jr.'s *A Canticle for Leibowitz* (1960). Like Blish, Miller explores the uses of knowledge in the conflict between good and evil. Although Charles Williams' novels differ greatly in style from Blish's, Theron Ware would fit easily into Williams' work, for example, in a novel such as *War in Heaven* (1930). The entire *After Such Knowledge* trilogy has many links to the Faust story, as Blish deals with the theme of knowledge and sin.

A secondary theme of *Black Easter* and *The Day After Judgment* is nuclear war and its aftermath. Baines considers destruction an art that he pursues. In pursuing this art, he has provoked wars, not to increase his profits as an arms manufacturer but for aesthetic pleasure. In developing this aspect of Baines's character, Blish satirizes the arms industry and the Cold War mentality. To Baines, unleashing demons on the earth is his greatest work of art.

Baines orders a scientist in his employ, Adolph Hess, to observe the magician at work. In doing this, Baines plans to add the power of magical knowledge to the power he already has. Hess begins as a scientific skeptic, but when he sees that Ware really commands demons, he is drawn into the practice of magic. When Hess violates the rules of magic, he is eaten by a demon. Hess is a kind of cut-rate Faust, making compromises with evil for the sake of power, whereas his boss is a more successful Faust, gaining ultimate knowledge at the end of The Day After Judgment. The ultimate knowledge that Baines acquires comes in the face-to-face discussion with Satan in Death Valley. Satan begs "Man"—in the persons of Baines, Ginsberg, Ware, and Domenico—to take the suffering of being God away from him.

Although the plot of *Black Easter* and *The Day After Judgment* may appear shocking and even blasphemous, Blish does not romanticize or glorify evil. In the same way, he does not romanticize good. He explores the nature of human motivation by reducing it to primary forms. Baines wishes to use power for purely aesthetic motives; Ware shares the same motivation. He does not use his knowledge of magic for personal power or gain but to extend the knowledge he already has. Ware agrees to Baines's plan to unleash demons because he hopes to learn something new from the experiment. In the end, all four major characters confront a mystery beyond their understanding. This confrontation changes them in unspecified but potentially positive ways.

—*Gene Doty*

BLACK EMPIRE

A ruthless but brilliant leader brings about the formation of a worldwide conspiracy of black peoples that eventually conquers the African continent

Author: Samuel I. Brooks (George S. Schuyler, 1895-1977)
Genre: Science fiction—future war
Type of work: Novel
Time of work: The 1930's
Locale: The United States, Africa, and Europe
First published: 1991 (serial form, "The Black Internationale," *Pittsburgh Courier*, November 21, 1936-July 3, 1937, and "Black Empire," *Pittsburgh Courier*, October 2, 1937-April 16, 1938)

The Story

Lost for some fifty years, *Black Empire* was finally determined to have been authored by noted African American satirist George S. Schuyler. *Black Empire* as published in 1991 is actually two serial novels, "The Black Internationale" and "Black Empire," that originally appeared in the *Pittsburgh Courier*, a black newspaper. Although published under separate titles, the two stories fit together and are appropriately collected under a single title. The original newspaper publications were edited into the novel by Robert A. Hill and R. Kent Rasmussen.

Black Empire tells of the exploits of Dr. Henry Belsidus and his efforts to construct a worldwide black conspiracy to reconquer Africa. By profession a medical doctor, Belsidus earns his living serving the needs of New York's white upper crust. He is slowly amassing, largely by criminal means, an immense amount of wealth to finance his subversive projects. Readers encounter Dr. Belsidus through Carl Slater, a reporter for the Harlem *Blade* who inadvertently stumbles upon Belsidus committing a brutal murder. Belsidus captures Slater and turns him into his personal assistant. The Black Empire saga is then narrated by Slater.

"Black Internationale" tells the story of the first dramatic steps toward the execution of Belsidus' plans. Slater discovers that Belsidus has been thorough in his planning. With spies and operatives everywhere, Belsidus is able to generate funds, pursue military and other research, and slowly create a worldwide conspiracy of black intellectuals and inventors. The Black Internationale has made stunning advances in agriculture, energy production, mass communication, and military tactics and weaponry. After a Mississippi lynching, Belsidus puts into full swing his plan to destabilize the United States. After dropping a previously unimagined incendiary device on the white community responsible for the lynching, Belsidus manages to create suspicion among Protestant whites that Jews or Catholics are somehow responsible.

Slater is by now an enthusiastic participant in Belsidus' project, although he is often put off by Belsidus' ruthless tactics. Slater's commitment is heightened as he becomes attracted by and attached to Patricia Givens, the head of Belsidus' air force. As Belsidus' divide-and-conquer scheme begins to take effect, specific steps are prepared for the initial invasion of Africa. With white Americans busy fighting one another, no one pays much attention to the substantial military force Belsidus begins to mobilize. Belsidus' fleet of ships lands in Liberia, and soon his forces take over the whole of the West African country.

"Black Internationale" climaxes with the conquest of all of Africa and the execution or expulsion of all whites. Having used the same divide-and-conquer tactics among the European colonialists as pursued in the United States, Belsidus successfully establishes the "Black Empire" as the European powers are distracted by the onset of World War II.

"Black Empire" picks up where "Black Internationale" leaves off. A significant portion of this component of the novel chronicles the accomplishments of the new authority. Developments in religion, agriculture, communications technology, and health care are considered. With the ending of inter-European hostilities, the European countries turn their attention to regaining their African colonies, and "Black Empire" becomes an adventure story.

Belsidus first resists the Europeans with a form of biological warfare. Slater and Givens—now husband and wife—are part of the counterinsurgency in Europe. The counterinsurgents, under the leadership of the white Martha Gaskin, gas to death thousands of British technicians. After many exciting escapes, Carl Slater and his new wife make their way back to the capital of the Black Empire. Belsidus then unveils a secret weapon, a ray that renders inoperable all European machinery. The Black Empire is saved and preserved.

ANALYSIS

There is little evidence to suggest that Schuyler was especially conversant with science-fiction conventions. Although *Black Empire* appeared during the beginnings of a boom in American pulp science fiction, Schuyler was never closely associated with this school. Schuyler wrote a variety of popular fiction in serial form, mostly romantic melodrama, to supplement his income as a columnist and editor. Schuyler's aesthetic sensibility is shaped by a number of factors, including 1930's horror films, back-to-Africa movements, and speculative fiction generally. He had no special attachment to the science-fiction genre and often spoke contemptuously of this genre and its audience.

Black Empire is a fascinating document. Although Schuyler despised racial chauvinism, he was generally sympathetic with any historical movement designed to challenge the imperialistic rule of the European powers. A pan-African conspiracy is something that Schuyler considered worth imagining. *Black Empire* is representative of the aspirations of many African Americans of the time, who were severely hit by the Depression and were victims of American racism. *Black Empire* in its original newspaper publication had almost an exclusively black audience that would have appreciated fantasizing about an end to white supremacy and the revitalization of the African continent. This was especially true in the light of black public outrage over the Italian attack on Ethiopia and American unwillingness to come to Ethiopia's aid.

Later in his career, Schuyler became a notorious conservative. Some scholars have speculated that Schuyler's construction of Dr. Henry Belsidus is prophetic of his own latent authoritarianism. *Black Empire* is prophetic in far more important and stirring ways. Like the best of futurist fiction, it is uncannily accurate (although chillingly so) in its prediction and description of the days to come. The world of *Black Empire* includes fax technology, solar energy, hydroponic agriculture, underground bunkers, and, shockingly, mass death by gassing. The novel as a whole is a populist fantasy that imagines the end to worldwide white supremacy through the application of black genius.

—*James C. Hall*

BLACK FLAME

A man from the present reawakens in a ruined future and find himself torn between two women, one good, one evil, and the different fates they portend for civilization

Author: Stanley G. [Grauman] Weinbaum (1902-1935)
Genre: Science Fiction—apocalypse
Type of work: Novel
Time of plot: Future
Location: United States
First published: 1948

THE STORY
Both "Dawn of Flame" and "Black Flame" are set in a post-Holocaust United States and involve an outsider and rebels in conflict with an immortal ruling family, the Sairs. Martin Sair is a scientific genius, whereas his sister Margot/Margaret (in "Dawn of Flame" and "The Black Flame," respectively), is a femme fatale: beautiful and amoral, sexually experienced yet lonely for love and looking for a real man to appreciate her charms.

In "Dawn of Flame" Hull Tarvish, a strong and intelligent young man, wanders into Ormiston, and encounters the lovely Vail Ormiston, daughter of town leader and namesake Marcus Ormiston. Their courtship is thwarted by the impending arrival of Joaquin Smith, leader of Martin Sair's troops, and though Tarvish distinguishes himself in the defense of Ormiston, it is pointless. The terms of conquest are reasonable, but the villagers are determined to resist, and Tarvish obtains a bow, but at the crucial moment is overwhelmed by Margot's beauty and unable to shoot her. He is sentenced to death but is reprieved by Margot, who is fascinated by him. She is lonely, being sterile and having outlived all of her lovers. The resistance intends to shoot Margot when she passes before a window, but Tarvish saves her, having unwillingly fallen in love; an additional resistance effort fails, leaving Marcus Ormiston dead. Tarvish would be executed but for the timely arrival of a hitherto peripheral character, Old Einar, who reveals that he was once one of Margot's lovers and persuades her to pardon Tarvish. She leaves as a chastened Tarvish returns to an understanding Vail.

"The Black Flame" expands the background situations presented in "Dawn of Flame," adds additional secondary characters, and utilizes a new protagonist, Thomas Marshall Connor, a twentieth-century engineer electrocuted for inadvertently killing his wife's lover. He awakens about a thousand years in the future, a rare confluence of events having caused suspended animation rather than death. He is nursed by the beautiful Evanie, whom the locals refer to as a sorceress, and a bit later, he shares a brief emotional intimacy with a beautiful dark-haired woman in the nearby forest. He learns, too, of beings called metamorphs, the failures of attempts to duplicate Martin Sair's immortality process: Evanie possesses metamorph blood, explaining why she is unmarried and has but one suitor, young Jan Ormon. Martin Sair, called the Master, has been quietly reuniting North America, but there is a resistance, of which Evanie is a member; she loathes Margaret Sair, known as Black Margaret. A revolution in the city of Urbs ends disastrously, as the weak and poorly trained men of Ormon are no match for Sair's superior weaponry and Sair's forces, but Connor is able to fire shots at the Master before fleeing with an injured Evanie. After being forced to return to Urbs, Connor keeps himself and Evanie alive by revealing that he has discovered one of the secrets to the Master's weapons. He is thus released on the promise not to hurt the Sairs. The beautiful dark-haired woman he earlier encountered is Black Margaret; though intelligent, she is immature and confused, having seen lovers age and die because Martin will not confer immortality upon them. In addition, she is sterile, and though she repeatedly offers herself to Connor, he resists. Evanie recovers and, retaining her revolutionary beliefs, she obtains and detonates a small atomic bomb to destroy the Sairs. It fails, and Connor rescues Margaret from a fiery room. When Connor, Evanie, and Jan Ormon are questioned about the origins of the atomic bomb, each takes responsibility; the Master would cheerfully kill them all, but after Margaret appears and claims responsibility, the Master has little choice but to release all. Evanie and Ormon are together, and Connor recognizes that he loves Margaret. He would like children, and she agrees to forgo the immortality treatment until she has given birth, at which point both of them will become immortal.

Analysis

Stanley Weinbaum was one of the notable writers in the early science fiction pulp magazines and was popular for his stories involving human-alien contact, with his most significant of these stories being "A Martian Odyssey" (1934), a depiction of a first-contact meeting between a human and a Martian that verges into friendship. After his early death, two unpublished manuscripts were found in Weinbaum's files, and although the early science fiction magazines were not noted for their depictions of adult relationships or character complexity, "Dawn of Flame" and "The Black Flame" are Weinbaum's attempts at providing these, eschewing aliens and other worlds and largely eschewing imagined technology and lengthy battles to concentrate on characters and their internal states. (Indeed, the scenes depicting fights and resistance are relatively perfunctory, for they are little more than devices to bring characters together in different situations.)

Though the two stories were developed differently, and "Dawn of Flame" is effectively an early draft for "The Black Flame," at the core of both is the conviction that men of all capabilities can readily be overwhelmed by a beautiful woman but that other women will see her without blinkers, be able to hate and resist her, and perhaps even try to destroy her. Tarvish thus finds himself in situations that do not require his physical strength and that tax and overwhelm his mental status, being unable to resist becoming infatuated with Margot, who is depicted as sexually experienced and very predatory. Similarly, while Connor does have the opportunity to demonstrate his engineering background, it is neither his body nor his brains but his emotions that are tested, for Margaret feels deeply about things that he has not considered or that he does not comprehend. This attempt at character complexity extends to the secondary women in each story: Vail Ormiston understands that no man can withstand Margot and loves Tarvish nevertheless, while Evanie becomes an active participant in the plot against Margaret, revealing that she loves not Connor but Jan Ormon.

Nevertheless, for all that the stories attempt to explore, in directions not readily considered in pulp science fiction, it is easy to see why both remained unpublished during Weinbaum's life.

"The Dawn of Flame's" depictions of future primitivism and female sexuality are sketchy and undeveloped. Similarly, while "The Black Flame" has greater depths, it also has a very weak conclusion, for by abruptly revealing that the Sairs' immortality and sterility are transient, that all Margaret has wanted was children and a man of her own, and that now with Connor she will have them, Weinbaum vitiates his premises.

—Richard Bleiler

BLACK NO MORE

A scientist discovers means of making black people appear to be white

Author: George S. Schuyler (1895–1977)
Genre: Science fiction—dystopia
Type of work: Novel
Time of work: The 1930's
Locale: The United States
First published: 1931

THE STORY

Black No More (subtitled *Being an Account of the Strange and Wonderful Workings of Science in the Land of the Free, A.D. 1933–1940*) begins with African Americans Max Disher and Bunny Brown considering the complexities of color prejudice in the United States. Max is rebuffed by a white woman at a Harlem bar after asking her to dance. The anger Max feels at this snub makes him enthusiastic about the news that Dr. Julius Crookman, an African American scientist, has devised a process that will turn black people white. Disher becomes the first person to undergo Crookman's process. After selling his story to a newspaper, *The Scimitar*, for $1,000, Max heads to Atlanta to seek out the white woman who had laughed at his advance in the Harlem bar.

The novel simultaneously follows the exploits of Max Disher—who changes his name to Matthew Fisher—and the efforts of Dr. Crookman and his cohorts, "numbers" banker Henry Johnson and real estate speculator Charlie Foster, to market the process nationwide. Fisher finds work as an adviser to the Knights of Nordica, a white supremacist organization led by the Reverend Henry Givens, whose daughter Helen is the woman who rejected Fisher in New York. Crookman and partners market Black No More throughout the United States. The racial transformation of the black population leads to a breakdown of black business, philanthropic, and social uplift enterprises. Among whites, this transformation, rather than lessening sensitivity to racial difference, generates paranoia.

Fisher sees his work with the Knights of Nordica as a "racket"; the longer he can maintain the status quo, the more money there is to be made from racial fears. Further dramatic tension is provided by the fact that the process does not affect the offspring of black people who undergo the transformation. Matt Fisher is in danger of being exposed because he has married Helen. The Knights of Nordica become involved in manipulating labor disputes (and collecting substantial bribes) and eventually in attempting to orchestrate the presidential election.

Resolution comes to the novel in two ways. First, social scientific research conducted during the course of the election campaign concludes that few if any Americans are racially pure. Rumors are circulated about the origins of the candidates put forth by the Knights, the Reverend Givens and Arthur Snobbcraft, eventually resulting in the lynching of the latter. Second, a belief that the transformation process creates individuals who are "too white" leads to a national backlash against whiteness and light skin. The book concludes ironically with a complete reversal of the American national attitudes toward skin color.

ANALYSIS

George Schuyler's reputation was made as a biting satirist, and, later in his life and career, as a notorious African American conservative. As a columnist for the *Pittsburgh Courier* for five decades, Schuyler was noted for his acerbic wit and intellectual irreverence. In 1931, Schuyler's politics were somewhat in transition, but his desire and ability to ridicule irrationality and pomposity were focused. *Black No More* mocks America's racial caste system and the pseudoscience upon which racism often was based. Influenced by journalist H. L. Mencken, Schuyler's novel uses thinly disguised historical figures in its mission to humiliate not only white racists but also the racial romanticizing of black leaders. Appearing at the end of the Harlem Renaissance, a decade that saw continued racially motivated violence, especially lynching, the novel takes on both African Americans and whites who make too much of racial difference. Although Schuyler was by no means a simplistic assimilationist, he did believe that African Americans were fundamentally American in commitment, temperament, culture, and interest.

Part of the power and impact of Schuyler's novel is that, for all of its outrageousness, it relied upon processes of identification and recognition with its reader. Dr. Shakespeare A. Beard is a thinly disguised W. E. B. Du Bois, and the National Social Equality League is clearly modeled on the National Association for the Advancement of Colored People.

In Schuyler's novel, race is revealed to be primarily a business or economic interest. Crookman's entrepre-neurial tactics with regard to his race-transforming process are related to Matthew Fisher's unseemly alliance with the Knights of Nordica. Similarly, Schuyler suggests in his portrayal of the Knights' manipulation of Southern labor disputes that white working-class obsession with race gets in the way of action on the basis of real economic interest. Suggestive of Schuyler's conservatism to come, the novel appears sympathetic to the entrepreneurial spirit of characters such as Crookman and Fisher. The profit motive and greed are not the villains of the novel; as a human flaw, Schuyler instead sees irrational color prejudice as beyond redemption. The disappearance of African Americans from the American scene leads to frantic efforts to identify replacement scapegoats to blame for economic scarcity.

Scholars have discovered other science-fiction novels authored by Schuyler. "The Black Internationale" and "Black Empire," published in serial form in the *Pittsburgh Courier* between 1936 and 1938 as written by Samuel I. Brooks, were combined into *Black Empire* (1991). There is little evidence that Schuyler was strongly committed to the genre of science fiction. He was knowledgeable about a wide variety of popular genres and experimented under a number of pseudonyms. In *Black No More*, Schuyler is best identified as a political satirist interested in most effectively reaching the largest audience possible. Form largely follows function in *Black No More*. Schuyler imagines America's greatest dream and reveals it to be America's greatest nightmare.

—*James C. Hall*

BLACK OXEN

A beautiful, young mystery woman appears amidst high society in 1920s New York City. She bears an uncanny resemblance to a fabled girl from thirty years prior. What no one knows is that modern maiden and past maiden are one and the same—thanks to a super-science rejuvenation ray!

Author: Gertrude Atherton (1857-1948)
Genre: Science Fiction—life extension
Type of Work: Novel
Time of Plot: 1920s
Location: New York City and the Adirondacks
First Published: 1923

THE STORY

The narrative is delivered almost entirely through the sensibilities of one Lee Clavering—except for a few pivotal chapters told from the viewpoint of Countess Mary "Marie" Ogden Zattiany.

Lee Clavering is a famous Manhattan newspaper columnist. Think of him as the Walter Winchell of his era. Bored and sullen, he is attending the opening night of a bad play when he is struck by the rare appearance of one female member of the audience:

> *In spite of its smooth white skin and rounded contours above an undamaged throat, it was, subtly, not a young face. The mouth, rather large, although fresh and red (possibly they had lip sticks in Europe that approximated nature) had none of the girl's soft flexibility. It was full in the center and the red of the underlip was more than a visible line, but it was straight at the corners, ending in an almost abrupt sternness. Once she smiled, but it was little more than an amused flicker; the mouth did not relax. The shape of the face bore out the promise of the head, but deflected from its oval at the chin, which was almost square, and indented. The figure was very slight, but as subtly mature as the face, possibly because she held it uncompromisingly erect....*
>
> *She wore a dress of white jet made with the long lines of the present fashion—in dress she was evidently a stickler. The neck was cut in a low square, showing the rise of the bust. Her own lines were long, the arms and hands very slender in the long white gloves....*
>
> *She had dropped her lids slightly before her eyes came to rest on Clavering.... They were very dark gray eyes, Greek in the curve of the lid, and inconceivably wise, cold, disillusioned. She did not look a day over twenty-eight. There were no marks of dissipation on her face. But for its cold regularity she would have looked younger—with her eyes closed. The eyes seemed to gaze down out of an infinitely remote past.*

Clavering is smitten. He asks an elderly friend, Dinwiddie, who the stranger might be. But Dinwiddie is flabbergasted. The young woman is a perfect duplicate of one Mary Ogden, who was that young over thirty years ago. Mary Ogden, says Dinwiddie, married Count Zattiany of Vienna and has lived in Europe ever since. There were rumors that she had entered a sanitarium after her husband's death.

Clavering is determined to learn more. He dispatches a society grand dame, Mrs. Oglethorpe (whose granddaughter, Janet, is in love with Clavering in her flighty, flapper way) to visit the stranger. Oglethorpe learns little, save that the woman is in town to do some business before returning to Vienna, where she has large political schemes afoot.

Clavering engineers a chance meeting one night with the woman. They hit it off. She eventually maintains that she is a cousin of Mary Ogden Zattiany and calls herself Marie Zattiany. Clavering begins courting her. She responds with seeming affection. Their relationship deepens. He proposes marriage, but she is reluctant. Meanwhile, the attention of the whole New York bon ton social stratum is on the mystery woman. An incident with a drunk and fleering Janet Oglethorpe proves embarrassing. Clavering's literary pal, the bestselling female author Gora Dwight, helps with some insights.

In Chapter XXVI, the secrecy can no longer be maintained, and Countess Zattiany decides to spill the beans in the most spectacular manner: she assembles a group of her elderly socialite female peers and details the Steinach treatments she received. X-Rays on her ovaries and other endocrine glands effected an utter rejuvenation of mind and body. Shortly thereafter, she tells Clavering the truth as well. He remains steadfast in his affirmation of love and marriage with the "elderly" woman of fifty-eight.

Countess Zattiany's story soon become known to the general public, and a media uproar ensues. Clavering, working on writing a play, stands on the verge of theatrical success. Countess Zattiany maintains she must return to Vienna to aid the destiny of her adopted country. Clavering offers that they marry, then live a split, international lifestyle. The pair, along with some chaperones, make a trip to the Adirondack resort owned by Dinwiddie, to reflect and decide. Countess Zattiany seems ready to agree. But just then, Prince Hohenhauer, an elderly beau, arrives at the lodge and puts in his plea for a patriotic alliance and a return to Vienna. The Countess realizes that power and ambition have trumped love in her jaded brain. She flees the lodge, and a final parting with Clavering occurs in New York.

ANALYSIS

Gertrude Atherton was a strong-willed, creative, feminist bestselling author who today is almost totally forgotten. Even the feminist reprint houses do not bolster her memory. It is only because she wrote this accomplished novel of early science fiction that she is remembered at all. This outcome, where fans keep the literary flame alight that would otherwise be extinguished, is all too common and a testament to the loyalty and fervor and eclecticism of the tribe.

The title of this still-provocative, still-timely Roaring Twenties bestseller (filmed the year after publication) derives from a Yeats epigraph: "The years like great black oxen tread the world. . . ." Indeed, a heavy sense of inexorable mortality suffuses this tale. The ambiance of the novel is Henry James by way of H. G. Wells. The book is decidedly pre-modern, in the sense that the concurrent revolutions engendered by Hemingway, Pound, T. S. Eliot, and the rest of their cadre have little if any effect on Atherton and her narrative. And yet the book is not Victorian either, but indubitably an *au courant* manifestation of the 1920s. It is reflective of an odd moment when an old order had died, but the new one had not yet quite been born—or at least had not diffused and penetrated widely.

While scientifically and speculatively rigorous, Atherton's handling of the love affair between Clavering (thirty-four years old) and Zattiany (fifty-eight) is also psychologically acute, deep, and sensitive. She does not privilege either gender, but seeks to understand both worldviews. The gap between the pair might seem of less consequence to a modern reader. But the average female life expectancy in the USA in 1923 was precisely 58.5 years, placing Zattiany at the door of decrepitude. The fact that her veteran, seasoned mentality comes packaged in a youthful revived body adds a fairy-tale air of creepy unnaturalness to the affair. There are echoes of such historical figures as Elizabeth Báthory, who was said to bathe in the blood of murdered virgins to retain her youth.

But certainly the dominant archetype that Atherton must have had in mind was H. Rider Haggard's willful, demanding, Phoenix-like goddess Ayesha, first encountered in *She: A History of Adventure* (1887).

But Atherton is never censorious of Zattianny's actions or motives. Having notoriously undergone the real-world Steinach treatments herself (with certain results of far less magnitude), Atherton portrays her heroine as fully entitled to any self-improvements that she can attain. Any woman deserves as much. But there is certainly a price to be paid. Ripe with mordant social observations and trenchantly written, this novel is not so much a Faustian fable of a woman who overreached herself as it is a meditation on the rigors of time and the human impulse to fight against loss. In portraying Mary Zattiany as the first of a new science-derived clade that would marry the energies of youth with the icy cunning of age, Atherton was an Extropian or Posthumanist before those words were invented. Bruce Sterling obviously agrees, since his novel *Holy Fire* (1996) features a protagonist in an analogous situation. Her name? Mia Ziemann.

—*Paul Di Filippo*

Black Trillium

Each of three princesses goes in search of her own magical talisman which, when united with the others, will bring peace to their kingdom and restore balance to their world

Author: Marion Zimmer Bradley (1930–1999), Julian May (1931–), and Andre Norton (1912–2005)
Genre: Fantasy—medieval future
Type of work: Novel
Time of work: Undefined
Locale: The kingdom of Ruwenda and its environs
First published: 1990

The Story
This novel represents a collaboration between three renowned science-fiction and fantasy authors. Each wrote one of the three princesses' adventures. The tale of Haramis is by Marion Zimmer Bradley, author of the Darkover novels; the story of Kadiya is by Andre Norton, author of the Witch World series; and the narrative of Anigel is by Julian May, author of the Pliocene Exile saga.

The kingdom of Ruwenda is a major center of trade for all the surrounding countries and territories. King Krain and Queen Kalanthe have no imperialist impulses toward their neighbors and allow their subjects a large degree of freedom.

Unfortunately, the neighboring kingdom of Labornok is ill-placed for trade, so its king, Voltrik, resorts to conquest of the affluent Ruwenda.

Although brave, King Krain is no soldier. He instructs his wife and daughters to hide, then attempts to bargain with Voltrik, offering to die if his wife and daughters are allowed to live. Meanwhile, in their hiding place, the daughters react to their situation according to their natures. Haramis, the scholar, can see no rational solution to their dilemma. She knows that her father, as head of their army, will most likely be killed in battle and that she will (if left alive) have to submit to marriage to Voltrik. Kadiya, the huntress, fiercely vows to use her hunting knife to defend her mother and sisters against any attackers. Anigel, the youngest, is timid. She sobs helplessly and cries in supplication to the White Lady, a legendary protectress of their land who either has lost her powers or perhaps never really existed.

Their parents killed, the princesses are each aided by a member of the Folk to escape capture. To reclaim their lost throne, each must master her own nature as well as succeed in her quest for a talisman. Haramis, assisted by Uzun, a musician and raconteur, must resist her thirst for knowledge and her attraction to a mage who could be both tutor and mate. Impetuous Kadiya, accompanied by Jagun, Master of Animals, must learn wisdom and restraint. Timid Anigel, assisted by the herbalist Immu, must acquire self-reliance, strength, and courage.

The Black Trillium is a rare plant, the badge of the royal house of Ruwenda, having a single, three-lobed blossom. The princesses are referred to as the Petals of the Living Trillium. The most prized of the Ruwendan Crown Jewels is an egg-sized piece of amber, within which is a small, fossil Black Trillium, and each princess bears a similar blossom in amber as an amulet. These amulets function as guides on their quests and eventually activate and empower the princesses' talismans.

ANALYSIS
Although *Black Trillium* can be read as a simple heroic quest, with the twist that the protagonists are female, there are other levels of meaning. In their other works, Bradley and Norton write of cultures in which technology is not held in high esteem, and May's novels show an understanding of ecology and the balance of nature. All three emphasize that although technology may be a means to an end, it can get out of control, causing people to lose a sense of connection to their work, to the people around them, and to their place in the overall scheme of things. It can also lend credence to the view that might makes right, or that because one has the power to do a thing, one has the right to do it.

The protagonists of this novel question that assumption. Their ancestors had great technological prowess. They are gone, but their machines remain. The Sword of Power is one of these. Those who made it were, in the end, reluctant to use it; instead, they disassembled it into three pieces, placing each in a separate hiding place. The princesses learn that even separately, the talismans can kill, and they are cautioned about using a device so powerful that the ability to use it wisely was doubted by its creators. Conversely, the main antagonist in the novel is a sorcerer who believes that "might makes right." He possesses some paranormal abilities and has augmented his power through the discovery of a cache of machines left by the ancient ones. Whereas the princesses use their "talismans" only to restore order to their world, he uses these machines to empower himself, embarking on a campaign of conquest.

Another theme common to the authors is that of cooperation and connectedness rather than individual might and isolation. In quest of their talismans, the princesses become aware that each of them is a nexus of connections with other people and species. Each could use her talisman for her individual empowerment but discovers that the final task requires all three. They learn to value the qualities in one another and come to recognize that their efforts will succeed only through cooperation among themselves and with the various species of Folk whose land they would rule. As a wheel is composed of hub, spokes, and rim, when the amulets are merged with the talismans and the talismans form a single Sword of Power, all the princesses' connections with others converge, and their world is restored to wholeness.

This novel is the product of three mature writers. Bradley and Norton have been writing excellent science-fiction and/or fantasy works for decades. May has written more than seven thousand nonfiction encyclopedia articles in addition to her two science-fiction series, the four-volume Pliocene Exile saga and the Galactic Milieu series. This seamless narrative exhibits the values of community, cooperation, and interconnection shared among these authors, who are at the height of their storytelling powers.

—*Karen S. Bellinfante*

Black Unicorn and Gold Unicorn

Tanaquil (with her pet peeve) embarks on a journey that teaches her about the nature of good and evil, her own magical powers, and the secrets of her identity

Author: Tanith Lee (1947–2015)
Genre: Fantasy—magical world
Type of work: Novels
Time of work: Undefined
Locale: An unidentified magical world
First published: *Black Unicorn* (1991) and *Gold Unicorn* (1994)

The Story

Black Unicorn and its sequel, *Gold Unicorn*, tell of the adventures of sixteen-year-old Tanaquil. At first, Tanaquil knows nothing of her heritage, but by the end of the second book, she has learned much about her own identity and abilities. She also has learned not to judge people—including herself—too quickly. The ending of *Gold Unicorn*, in which Tanaquil journeys toward home, leaves open the possibility of another sequel.

Tanaquil wants to leave the desert fortress where she was reared by her emotionally distant sorceress mother, Jaive. She apparently has no magic of her own, and she wearies of the inconvenient side effects of Jaive's magic. In one instance, Jaive's magic resulted in a peeve, a common desert creature, acquiring the power of speech. Jaive refuses to let Tanaquil go or even to identify Tanaquil's father.

One day, the peeve discovers the skeleton of a unicorn, which Tanaquil reassembles. It turns out that she has a magical power after all: the power to mend things. The unicorn comes alive, and Tanaquil and the peeve are compelled to follow it to an exotic city by the sea. There, Tanaquil meets Lizra, the daughter of the city's ruler, the evil Prince Zorander. Soon Tanaquil discovers that Zorander is her father and Lizra is her half sister.

During a ceremonial procession, the unicorn appears and steals from Zorander two white shells. Tanaquil realizes that the unicorn is from a better world and that it wishes to return. She helps it by mending the sorcerous gate between worlds with the white shells. Unfortunately, the peeve follows the unicorn through the gate, so Tanaquil also must follow.

The unicorn's world is wonderful, putting Tanaquil's world to shame. She realizes with horror that her mere presence wounds the Perfect World and plans to leave immediately. Before she exits through the gate, the unicorn touches her and her peeve with its horn, granting them immunity from physical danger. Tanaquil takes the shells as she leaves, disabling the gate so that no one else can harm the Perfect World.

When she returns to her own world, Zorander is sick, and Lizra declares that she will stay with him. Tanaquil sets out with her peeve to learn more about their world and perhaps to improve it. She sends a message to Jaive promising that eventually she will return home.

Gold Unicorn describes Tanaquil's travels. She hears of the empress Veriam, who wishes to conquer the entire world, and is shocked to learn that the empress is in fact Lizra. Lizra has constructed a huge mechanical unicorn of gold as a symbol of her conquest. Unfortunately, it does not work. Lizra commands Tanaquil to mend it. Unwillingly, Tanaquil does so, using one of the fossil shells. Tanaquil and Lizra's chief adviser, Honj, secretly fall in love. Although she disapproves of Lizra's goals, Tanaquil accompanies her and Honj from conquest to brutal conquest, until they are set upon by "mousps," half-mouse, half-wasp creatures created by the local magician Worabex.

To escape, the sisters, Honj, a stingless mousp, the peeve, and assorted other followers duck under the belly of the gold unicorn. This leads them through a magical gate into a hellish world. The Emperor of War, ruler of this world, courts Lizra, who appears to be delighted with his attentions. Disgusted, Tanaquil and Lizra's other friends abandon her and seek to find the gate to their own world. When Honj breaks his arm rescuing the peeve, Tanaquil learns that her power to mend works on people as well as on objects.

Soon Lizra emerges from the evil castle and informs them that she only pretended to court the emperor so as not to anger him. She has told the emperor that although she longs to be his bride, she is betrothed to another. Because the emperor believes in loyalty, one of the values of war, he has told her how to return to her world. Lizra leads Tanaquil and the rest to the return gate, which Tanaquil mends with the remaining white shell.

Honj decides to stay with Lizra, who, having conquered the world, now shoulders the burden of ruling wisely. Tanaquil travels toward home, joined by the mousp as well as the peeve. Soon the mousp reveals himself as Worabex, who wishes to befriend Tanaquil and to court her mother. Tanaquil rejects his friendship, so Worabex turns himself into a flea and hitches a ride on the peeve. The unlikely trio continues on its journey.

ANALYSIS

Black Unicorn was not marketed as a young adult novel, but *Gold Unicorn* was. The books feature a theme important in young adult literature: an adolescent's journey into maturity. In the confines of her mother's castle, Tanaquil seems amazingly self-possessed for a sixteen-year-old. She knows the castle routine, she knows the servants, and she knows how to outwit the magical guardians of Jaive's study. When she leaves, however, her naïveté quickly becomes apparent. Tanaquil needs more experience before she can take full possession of her powers. She literally needs knowledge of good (the Perfect World) and evil (the warlord's world).

Tanaquil also needs to acquire knowledge of people. She believes that Honj follows Lizra out of a desire for power, but he does so out of loyalty. She believes that Lizra truly loves the Emperor of War, but Lizra only pretends to love him in order to rescue her friends. Tanaquil also displays blindness to her own motives, thinking that she has stayed with Lizra because of the gold unicorn when actually she has stayed for the love of Honj.

In the same way that Lizra acts like their father, longing for power, Tanaquil acts like their mother, insisting on emotional distance. Lizra does admit to loving their father, and she is able to accept him as a man with flaws, rather than perceiving him as an ideal being. By contrast, Tanaquil is not yet able to admit to loving their mother. Furthermore, she cannot accept her mother as a woman with flaws. For Tanaquil, Jaive must be either all good or all bad. Therefore, Tanaquil cannot introduce Worabex to Jaive, because Jaive in love could not be the ideal mother Tanaquil craves.

The need to assume moral responsibility is another young adult theme highlighted in these books. Tanaquil must first take responsibility for returning the black unicorn to its own world. When she realizes that she cannot stay in the Perfect World, she soon resolves to make her own world more like the better one. Tanaquil's actions do not live up to her resolve. Not only does she help Lizra in her drive to conquer the world, but at the end of *Gold Unicorn*, she leaves the burden of ruling to Lizra. Rather than helping her sister, Tanaquil decides to return to Jaive. Rather than improving her world, Tanaquil simply admires the goodness that it already has. Perhaps Tanaquil cannot shoulder her share of moral responsibility until she has grown to understand Jaive, in the same way that Lizra cannot assume the throne until she understands Zorander.

The focus on individual growth rather than on societal change is common to many of Tanith Lee's books, including the Birthgrave trilogy (1975–1978), *Electric Forest* (1979), and *The Silver Metal Lover* (1981). This may explain why Lee is not typically considered to be a feminist author. At the same time, the Unicorn books do subvert stereotypical notions of what it means to be a hero. In some ways, Tanaquil behaves like a hero: She avoids emotional ties, she rescues others in need, and she cannot settle in one place. Even though Tanaquil is gifted with strong powers, she does not trust them; her aloofness results not from self-confidence but from self-doubt. Furthermore, Tanaquil's love for her peeve, her dislike of war, and her attachment to her sister all are traditionally feminine qualities.

Unlike the protagonists in plots devised by other female writers of fantasy, such as Andre Norton, Tanaquil is not content with becoming one of the elite sorcerers. In fact, she is impatient with sorcerers, believing that they should spend their time on more important things than improving their own powers. With this attitude, Tanaquil may yet change her world.

Black Unicorn and *Gold Unicorn* are more hopeful than many of Lee's earlier books, which number more than three dozen and span the genres of fantasy, horror, science fiction, and mainstream fiction for children, young adults, and adults. Critics generally praise Lee's solid characterization, attention to detail, and unpredictable plots. Although Lee is not one of the genre's most famous authors, her books are well worth seeking out.

—*Beth Rapp Young*

BLOOD MUSIC

Vergil Ulam injects himself with thinking cells that push his body and, eventually, the rest of Earth into the next stage in evolution

Author: Greg Bear (1951–)
Genre: Fantasy—evolutionary fantasy
Type of work: Novel
Time of work: The late twentieth century
Location: California, New York, Germany, and Great Britain
First published: 1985

THE STORY

Thirty-two-year-old Vergil Ulam is a brilliant but undisciplined bioengineer at the Genetron laboratories in La Jolla, California. This area is known as Enzyme Valley, the biochip equivalent of Silicon Valley. His pet project is what he calls "biologic," the development of "thinking" lymphocytes that he describes as autonomous organic computers. When his employer learns that Ulam has been conducting this research for the past two years on mammalian cells, Ulam is fired. Before he leaves the building, he injects himself with the cells and destroys the records of his research.

Ulam had hoped to retrieve the lymphocytes from his system and continue his research. Two weeks later, though, he still has not found access to a lab, and he knows that it is too late to remove the altered cells. The first changes to his system that he notices are a craving for sweets, better eyesight, and a better sex life. When he realizes that there is no turning back, he visits his clairvoyant mother. She immediately discerns that his experiment has gotten beyond her son's control but that it is his life's work.

Ulam concludes that the lymphocytes have developed the capacity to spread their biologic traits to other types of cells and that they could migrate outside his body. He visits Edward Milligan, a school friend, and explains his theory that human DNA has spent millions of years building to a climax that is now expressing itself in Ulam's experiment, which offers the doorway for the lymphocytes to escape the human species. Listening to their activity inside his body, which he calls "blood music," he wonders when the cells will become cognizant of Ulam himself as an entity enclosing them. The answer comes soon, when he begins hearing words spoken within his brain by the other entities.

Milligan quickly understands the dangerous implications, confirmed when he walks in on Ulam and his girlfriend and discovers them changing into strange shapeless masses of flesh. To stop a possible epidemic, Milligan kills Ulam. Michael Bernard, head of Genetron, realizes that a mere handshake could spread the altered genes from one individual to another and that it is too late to stop it from spreading throughout the United States. Recognizing that he is infected, he flies to Wiesbaden, Germany, and secures himself in an isolation laboratory for observation.

Heinz Paulsen-Fuchs, the biologist who observed Bernard gradually showing signs of the transforming genes, knows he cannot hold off the terrified protesters who want to kill Bernard before Europe becomes infected. Meanwhile, the United States itself changes shape as the selfaware genes form a massive thinking community. Bernard communes with the cells inside himself and, with the help of a visiting British physicist, theorizes that thought, in sufficient quantity, could physically alter the universe. With all these cells suddenly conscious, the potential for change has become exponentially greater.

Bernard willingly allows his own transformation and "enters" the world inside himself. Viewed by the cells as one of their creators, he is treated with respect and moved into Thought Universe, where he recognizes that no one really dies; instead, there is endless replication within cells in the blood. Various humans resist transformation, and the cells respect their decision. Ultimately, the number of thinking cells becomes so large that their community of cooperation enters into a realm beyond physical matter.

ANALYSIS

Greg Bear's topics range from fantasy to pure science fiction, and they generally demand that his protagonist come to a new understanding of the universe. During the 1980's, Bear won the Nebula Award twice, for the novella "Hard Fought" (1983) and for the short story "Tangents" (1986), and the Hugo Award (1984) for the short story "Blood Music," published in *Analog*. He has stated that *Blood Music*, his seventh novel, was influenced by his study of information theory and information mechanics. Upon the suggestion of David Brin and John F. Carr, Bear decided to expand "Blood Music," adding complexity with chapters devoted to new characters.

Much in the manner that James Blish's *A Case of Conscience* (1958) uses a fictional Jesuit astrophysicist to raise ethical questions regarding the individual moral systems of other galaxies, Bear builds his story on the writings of the actual Jesuit paleontologist Pierre Teilhard de Chardin, who combined Christian theology and evolutionary theory to posit Jesus Christ both as temporal and as a timeless symbol for the final step of evolution, which he described as a "noosphere." Bear is not directly theological, though he works with the idea of a creator; his basic debt to Teilhard is the notion of a critical mass of thinkers somehow transcending space and time and bringing into existence what amounts to a new heaven and a new Earth.

Bear's novel has been called a *Childhood's End* (Arthur C. Clarke, 1953) for the 1980's, and the comparison seems apt. Theodore Sturgeon's *More than Human* (1953) also comes immediately to mind as a source for comparison. *Blood Music* follows in the tradition of science-fiction writing that ponders the possibility that *Homo sapiens* may not be the final word in nature's self-expression. Bear's novel shows a greater scientific sophistication than Clarke's earlier work, focusing in convincing detail on the actual biological mechanisms used in laboratories of the 1980's and 1990's. It suggests that the human need to see humanity as the center of the biological universe is as egotistical as humanity's earlier notion that Earth was the center of the galaxy. As threatening as the notion of absorption into a larger community is to Bear's characters, he does his best to convince them, and his readers, that individual subjectivity may go the way of nation-states. In its place will come a cooperative assertion of racial memory.

—*John C. Hawley*

THE BLOOD OF ROSES

A vampiristic holy man is thwarted by the family of undead he created to grant himself immortality

Author: Tanith Lee (1947-2015)
Genre: Fantasy—dystopia
Type of work: Novel
Time of work: Undefined
Locale: An agrarian land divided into small kingdoms and church holdings

First published: 1990

THE STORY

Tanith Lee's novel is a sprawling work in five sections. The first deals with Mechail Kohrlen, heir to a rural estate. He is hunchbacked and antisocial. His father dotes on Mechail's handsome brother. Mechail completes a test of manhood—a human sacrifice to the forest gods—but his brother mocks him, later hiring soldiers from a rival estate to murder Mechail. Mechail rises from the dead, kills his brother, and flees to the forest.

Rumors of vampirism bring Anjelen, a warrior priest, to the area. He finds Mechail comatose and takes him to the Christerium, headquarters of the Knights of God. On the way, Jasha, a strange homeless girl, joins their retinue to care for Mechail. She feeds him gruel mixed with blood. At the Christerium, Jasha goes to the women's quarters and Mechail becomes Anjelen's protégé. Mechail discovers that Anjelen is truly a vampire who has turned Mechail into a demon like himself. Jasha, meanwhile, is accused of witchcraft and burned at the stake. She is resurrected, and she and Mechail flee the Christerium and go separate ways.

The second section of the novel deals with Mechail's mother. Anillia, the child of a city lord, was lost in the woods as a toddler. Anjelen found her and brainwashed her into being his servant. At the age of fifteen, she wed Kolris Kohrlen. She died after giving birth to Mechail. Anjelen steals her bones and resurrects his servant. After she rises, she vows that Anjelen will never possess her son.

The third section reveals Anjelen's past. He was sacrificed to the forest gods as a boy, but the ritual was interrupted when Christians cut down the sacred tree where his body hung. The stump absorbed his spirit. He returned as the embodiment of the sacred pagan tree as well as Jesus Christ. The story then jumps to the present, where Anjelen has become head of the Knights of God. He introduces a blood-drinking rite, modeled on the Last Supper, to a select group of warrior priests. Word gets out when townspeople are found dead and bloodless, and the Knights are disbanded.

The fourth section finds the once-opulent Christerium a ruin. Only a handful of elderly Knights remain, and gypsies haunt the outer walls. A young priest, Eujasius, and a dwarf join the gypsies sheltering there. Anjelen appears to conduct his bloody sacrament, but Eujasius suddenly reveals himself as Jasha. She kills Anjelen, and the dwarf stays with the gypsies. Oddly, he grows tall; he was mute but becomes articulate. Mechail meets Jasha and his mother, and together they go to the woods. Mechail and Anillia shed their unwanted immortality and escape Anjelen forever as they worship another sacred tree. Jasha returns to her original home, the sea.

The fifth section brings the novel full circle. The dwarf transforms into a handsome, wealthy youth resembling Mechail. Calling himself Mechailus, he returns to the Kohrlen estate and takes control. The tradition of human sacrifice resumes. Mechailus (actually Mechail in a new body) is content and constantly renewed by a diet of human blood.

ANALYSIS

Tanith Lee first appeared in the fantasy genre in 1975, when Ballantine publishers noticed that the market was glutted with imitations of J. R. R. Tolkien's work and retellings of familiar legends. They solved the problem by introducing new authors with new stories. Other publishers followed this trend. Since her well-timed arrival, Lee has produced a huge body of work, beginning with the Birthgrave Trilogy (1975–1978).

The Blood of Roses examines a number of issues. On the surface, it is a simple revenge story. A disadvantaged and despised youth leaves home and eventually returns, exacting revenge on his tormentors. This type of story has ancient roots. An example is Euripedes' Electra (c. 413 b.c.e.). Lee's novel departs from the typical revenge tale in several ways. Although Mechail kills his tormentors, he himself is killed beforehand. It is only Anjelen's influence that permits Mechail to rise and avenge himself. Then Mechail's vengeance is complete. He gains his rightful inheritance, but only after his original body is exchanged for a new one. Furthermore, Mechail must drink human blood to survive. Anjelen's blessing is also a curse.

In the character of Anjelen, Lee presents an interesting paradox. He comes from a pagan background but fits easily into the Christian world. He is both the forest god and Christ. Like Christ, Anjelen is sacrificed on a tree and rises from the dead to resurrect people like Mechail. Anjelen gives Mechail what he needs to gain his inheritance, but he is undeniably self-serving.

Anjelen means to use Mechail as a tool but is thwarted when Mechail's Christian upbringing makes him reject his benefactor as a demon. Anjelen's career is in the Christian church, but he uses the Eucharist to sustain pagan tradition.

Actual blood from human victims serves instead of wine and keeps Anjelen young and powerful. He puts Anillia under his influence and brings Mechail into being as an act of will. It is ironic that Anillia and Mechail, both Christians, escape the Knights of God through a bizarre pagan rite. As they worship, mother and son become part of the forest.

The novel's setting emphasizes the merging of the two religions. It is a realm where Christianity is new; the people cling to pagan traditions such as blood sacrifice and nature worship. In *The Blood of Roses*, Lee shows that Christianity and paganism are opposing but similar forces. One supports the other. Although Christianity emerges as the stronger force, the pagan traditions remain at its heart. This makes the religious power struggle a moot point.

As in the Birthgrave Trilogy, the emphasis is more on mood than on character development. Mechail and the others elicit no sympathetic pull, and too often they are lost in Lee's elaborate descriptions. The storytelling is energetic, but in the fifth section, Lee suddenly changes her style and rushes toward the conclusion. Nevertheless, *The Blood of Roses* deserves credit as an innovative twist on a popular supernatural theme.

—*Carla Hall Minor*

THE BLUE HAWK

The dangerous journeys of Tron, a young priest of Gdu, into the hinterlands of O and Aa in an attempt to restore the king to his rightful throne and to find his own soul

Author: Peter Dickinson (1927-2015)
Genre: Fantasy—theological romance
Type of work: Novel
Time of work: The distant future
Locale: Earth
First published: 1976

THE STORY

The story opens in the Temple of Gdu during the annual Ceremony of Renewal. Tron, a young priest, witnesses the victory of the priests of Gdu over the old king. He experiences a vision, then removes a blue hawk, the totem bird of the great Hawk God, Gdu, from the temple. The bird was to have been sacrificed to renew the soul of the old king; instead, the priests kill the king. Tron becomes the keeper of the sacred blue hawk and as such cannot be harmed, but he discovers that the highly systematized priestly society now in charge of the kingdom will try to kill him indirectly.

As Tron trains the blue hawk, he runs into the son of the old king, who asks Tron to help him regain his rightful throne from the rigid priestly caste. Tron is frightened but intuitively believes in the king, even though, as a member of the priesthood, he has been thoroughly brainwashed. Tron also is a visionary, an attribute that makes him different from the dronelike priests with whom he lives.

Tron becomes the king's messenger and begins a dangerous journey south to enlist certain individuals to help the new king overcome the powerful priests. Tron observes the terrible condition of parts of his country. The farther south he journeys, however, the happier people seem. When he reaches Kalakal, he understands that life can be lived in great simplicity and openness without the intrusiveness of the powerful priests. He meets a lovely girl, Taleel, who helps him contact the local leaders and the old high priest, Odah, one of the few people he can trust.

Tron and the blue hawk return to the kingdom of O and Aa to find that repression has become almost unbearable. Tron meets with the king in secret. The king realizes that he must smuggle Tron and the blue hawk out of the country before they are murdered. He secretly places Tron and the hawk within the burial barge of his father, the old king, and sends it down the river into possible oblivion. Tron, after many harrowing adventures and risks, finally reaches Kalakal again. He enlists the One of Sinu, a blind priest, to aid him and Odah in performing the rituals required to ensure that the quest for reinstatement of the king will be successful.

After performing these exhausting rituals, the three priests are almost slaughtered by barbarians, the Hun-like Mohirrim, as they attempt to return to Tron's home. The Mohirrim, it seems, support the priests of Gdu and will do anything to destroy the forces of the king. After a devastating battle in which virtually all the Mohirrim either commit suicide or are slaughtered by the king's faithful forces, Tron is wounded by an arrow in his back.

During the battle with the Mohirrim, both the One of Sinu and Odah die of exhaustion, leaving Tron to fend for himself. During Tron's recovery, he meets Taleel again. She helps nurse him back to health, though the process is slow because of the severity of his injury. His wound gives Tron a deeper understanding of the awful power of the priests in keeping the citizens of O and Aa ignorant and subservient. Tron sees that people have lived their lives by ritual and precedent, and that change is never permitted. He sees himself as part of an ancient corrupt system from which only the king, his blue hawk, and his visionary experiences can release him. After regaining his strength, Tron accompanies the king and his triumphal forces back to the kingdom to overcome the priests.

At the conclusion of the novel, Tron realizes that he has found his own soul. He also begins to understand that the blue hawk is not only a totem divinity but also a part of his own identity. Tron decides to release the hawk and discovers that he, too, is entering a life of freedom. The reader also becomes aware that the gods of Tron's world are in fact alien beings reluctantly tied to Earth.

ANALYSIS

Peter Dickinson generally is recognized as one of England's most respected writers of mystery and detective fiction, having written more than a dozen such novels. He is also renowned for his children's books. *The Blue Hawk*, though a children's book (winner of the *Guardian* Award as best children's book of the year), contains sophisticated subject matter and a philosophical approach that would not typically appeal to young children. Advanced secondary school students may find it both challenging and compelling.

Most of Dickinson's novels, for children or adults, revolve around one central predicament: the Fall. In *The Blue Hawk*, Tron realizes that the sterile life he lives as a priest is the result of a fall from an earlier, more vivid life that some still experienced to a degree in the southern city of Kalakal, an Eden that is far enough away from the priest-ridden Kingdom of O and Aa to escape its ennui and conformity.

The novel is also a classic story of the dangerous journey of a young man into the world of the unknown. As in many quest stories, the young hero discovers not only new worlds but also new systems of belief and, thus, new possibilities for living his own life. He discovers that the priestly order demands that he become only what it will allow and that imagination and intuition are dangerous to the community. Fortunately, Tron experiences periodic visions from deep within his soul; following them inevitably leads him to greater truths and more fulfilling experiences.

The Blue Hawk is a romantic novel insofar as Tron's most important discovery is the discovery of himself as an individual and not simply as a priest who repeats what he is told and obeys his leaders without question. His crucial tie to nature via the blue hawk saves him from an empty, ritualized life and enables him to help the king to regain his kingdom from the ignorant darkness of the priestly caste of the Kingdom of Gdu.

—*Patrick Meanor*

THE BLUE STAR

A member of a subversive political movement seduces a witch in order to gain control of the gem that supplies her magical powers, but the plan goes awry

Author: Fletcher Pratt (1897-1956)
Genre: Fantasy—heroic fantasy
Type of work: Novel

Time of work: A period roughly equivalent to the eighteenth century
Locale: Various, including Netznegon in the realm of Dossola and Charlakis in the dominion of Mancherei
First published: 1969 (with two other items in the anthology *Witches Three*, 1952)

The Story

Within a frame narrative in which three men dream the same dream, the story is told of Rodvard Bergelin, a minor functionary in the government of Dossola who is also a member of a subversive organization called the Sons of the New Day. Rodvard is commissioned by the leaders of this organization to seduce Lalette Asterhax, the descendant of a line of witches whose hereditary magic—embodied in the eponymous gem—is transferable to their male lovers. He reluctantly agrees, but he mishandles the task; he succeeds only because Lalette wants to avoid an alternative liaison cynically arranged by her family. Witchcraft is proscribed by both church and state, and the accidental revelation that her latent power has been activated results in Lalette and Rodvard being forced to go into hiding.

After the two fugitives are taken in by members of a heretical sect called the Amorosians, Rodvard receives new instructions from the Sons of the New Day. He uses his magic to small but significant effect in a spying mission, but the jewel loses its virtue when he sleeps with a chambermaid, and he is forced to flee again. Lalette's magic saves him and reactivates the Blue Star, but she finds it politic to go into exile, seeking asylum among the Amorosians of Mancherei. Rodvard is forced to make his way to Mancherei, having been sold into the service of a sea captain. In the course of their sea voyages, Lalette and Rodvard both are threatened with rape, but they arrive safely, neither one knowing that the other is near.

Lalette is accommodated in a hospice but is discomfited to discover that such institutions are used as brothels by the supposedly celibate Amorosian clergy. When she refuses to participate, she is scheduled for compulsory reeducation, but Rodvard—who has returned to his old line of work—sees her committal papers and attempts her rescue. Yet again, he proves incompetent. He and Lalette are thrown into jail.

In Dossola, the Sons of the New Day have seized control of the government, and their rule is becoming increasingly oppressive. In need of the Blue Star to facilitate their purges, the organization's leaders contrive Rodvard's and Lalette's release. When he is put to work ferreting out enemies of the state, Rodvard soon becomes disillusioned. When he attempts to save the life of a noblewoman he once admired from afar—memory of whom has long come between himself and Lalette—his last illusions collapse. Authentically united at last, the two lovers discard the Blue Star and flee the realm.

Analysis

The Blue Star is a conscientious attempt to describe a fantasy world that has all the complexities of the real one. Instead of imagining a quasi-feudal world whose kings actually rule by divine right, it borrows and reshapes the political and religious disputes of prerevolutionary France, and instead of the idealized relationships typical of romantic fiction, it tracks the course of a much-troubled affair whose final result is a hard-won compromise. As in Fletcher Pratt's earlier heroic fantasy, magic plays a very subdued role; its function is symbolic rather than deterministic, and it is inevitable that the protagonists eventually put it out of their lives.

If one compares *The Blue Star* with the fervently adventurous and unabashedly romantic tales of "sword and sorcery" written by Robert E. Howard and his imitators, or with the delicate and decorative "high fantasies" whose tradition extends from William Morris to J. R. R. Tolkien, one can see how carefully and how radically it distances itself from the underlying assumptions of both subgenres. This cannot have helped its marketability and perhaps explains why the story first appeared in an omnibus that Pratt put together himself rather than as a separate volume. The work is one of considerable originality. The explosive success of fantasy literature in the 1970's and 1980's produced numerous comparable works, but Pratt was twenty years ahead of his successors.

The main problem Pratt faced in trying to design a fantasy world as rich and complex as the real one was that of available narrative space. A novel that deals with actual history can leave much unsaid, because its readers have stocks of common knowledge that can be invoked by brief reference. The describer of a fantasy world has no such resource. Pratt's attempts to mobilize such stocks of knowledge in a limited way, by making his revolution a version of the French Revolution and his heretical religion a syncretic amalgam of Catharist and Protestant ideas, creates as many problems as it solves because the reader is never sure how close the parallel is intended to be.

The result is that readers are likely to feel uneasy in their interpretations of what is going on and are likely to be unconvinced by the precise pattern of historical alternatives that the author brings into combination.

The Blue Star is a rather dour novel, somewhat weighed down by the burden of its meticulous narrative realism, but it is unusually well wrought in comparison with heroic fantasies written for the pulp magazines. The intricate convolutions of the plot are untidy, and the conclusion of the story is by no means a neat resolution of its problems, but this too is an aspect of its attempted realism. In its day, the novel was certainly the most ambitious heroic fantasy to emerge from the pulp tradition. Even if his achievements are found wanting, there is no doubt that Pratt made a bold attempt to break new ground. In spite of its flaws, *The Blue Star* deserves to be reckoned a classic of the genre.

—Brian Stableford

THE BLUE SWORD AND THE HERO AND THE CROWN

Two women of Damar carry the same sword in two different eras and must learn to use both magic and swordplay to save the kingdom from the forces of evil

Author: Robin McKinley (1952–)
Genre: Fantasy—heroic fantasy
Type of work: Novels
Time of work: Undefined
Location: Primarily the land of Damar
First published: *The Blue Sword* (1982) and
 The Hero and the Crown (1984)

THE STORY

The Blue Sword and *The Hero and the Crown* are the first two books of a promised trilogy about the land of Damar. *The Blue Sword* takes place in the present, when Outlanders rule much of Damar. *The Hero and the Crown*, a "prequel," tells the story of an earlier Damar before the Outlanders arrived. Harry and Aerin, the two female heroes, each must learn to master her psychic powers. In addition, both endure extensive training in swordplay to prepare them for battle with Damar's long-standing enemy, the inhuman demon race of the North.

In *The Blue Sword*, Harry Crewe leaves her Homeland after her father's death and goes to live at the outpost where her brother Richard is stationed. Harry is restless and oddly drawn to the hills beyond her new home. Corlath, the king of the last remaining Free Hillfolk not under Homelander rule, comes to plead with the Outlander superiors to unite with him against a common enemy. A psychic hunch tells Corlath that Harry is destined to be important to the Free Hillfolk, and he kidnaps her. Harry is discovered to possess an abundance of the psychic powers needed to defeat the Northerners. Mathin, one of the King's elite Riders, puts Harry through a rigorous training period. Harry learns to ride Sungold, her new Hill horse, and to fight with a sword. She also learns to love her new home, and she makes many friends among both human and animal followers of Corlath. Harry eventually is given the sword that belonged to Lady Aerin, Dragon-Killer, a legendary female warrior who led Damar to victory against the North in an earlier era.

As the Free Hillfolk prepare for war, Harry must deal with the conflicting emotions of loyalty to her Homeland and of her growing love for Corlath and his people. Standing between two worlds, Harry must risk her connections to the Homeland and the Hillfolk in order to save them both. To accomplish this, she must draw on her untrained psychic powers to bury the enemy under a mountain. She succeeds in leading the Damarians to victory and in cementing her relationship with Corlath. As an Outlander queen of the Free Hillfolk, she will lead her newfound people into an era in which they hope to establish better relations with the Outlanders.

The Hero and the Crown tells the story of Aerin, the warrior who appears as a legendary figure in *The Blue Sword*. Aerin is the only child of King Arlbeth of Damar. Aerin's mother, who died when Aerin was born, was rumored to be a witch from the North. Her people do not trust Aerin enough to accept her as the heir to the throne, especially now that the demons of the North are threatening Damar once again. Tor, Aerin's cousin, has been designated as heir. To make matters worse, Aerin seemingly has none of the psychic powers that Damar's royalty should possess.

Feeling useless and unwanted at court, Aerin begins teaching herself how to kill dragons. She befriends her father's old warhorse, Talat, and discovers how to make a fireproof salve. She also coaxes Tor, who is already falling in love with her, to teach her the rudiments of sword fighting. Aerin becomes an expert dragon slayer and destroys Maur, the Black Dragon.

Aerin then begins training with the wizard Luthe, who teaches her to use the latent psychic abilities she has always possessed. He also gives her the fabled blue sword. Aerin must give up some of her humanity when Luthe is forced to grant her the power of partial immortality so that she can defeat her uncle Agsded, the evil wizard who is behind Damar's problems with the North. Aerin wins back the Hero's Crown, an amulet with protective powers, and returns to Tor and her people in time to lead them into victorious battle against the Northerners. Aerin's heroics earn her a place of honor in the hearts of her people; in addition, King Arlbeth has fallen in battle, so Aerin agrees to become Tor's queen. She must reconcile her love for Tor and Luthe, realizing that the immortal part of her will be able to rejoin Luthe someday.

ANALYSIS

The Blue Sword and *The Hero and the Crown* were published after Robin McKinley's *Beauty: A Retelling of the Story of Beauty and the Beast* (1978), the award-winning and critically acclaimed novel that established McKinley as an outstanding fantasy writer for young adults. The Damar novels also were well received, garnering McKinley several awards including a Best Young Adult Books citation from the American Library Association in 1982 and a Newbery Honor citation in 1983 for *The Blue Sword*, and a *Horn Book* honor list citation in 1985 and the Newbery Medal in 1985 for *The Hero and the Crown*. Although some of the themes in *The Hero and the Crown* are more mature than those of *The Blue Sword*, both books are classified by booksellers and librarians as young adult novels.

The setting of the novels—especially the Damar of Harry's time—is based partly on Rudyard Kipling's depictions of the British Empire. The Homelanders (or Outlanders, depending on which side one is on) display an obviously paternalistic attitude toward the native Damarians they govern. In the Damar of Aerin's time, the Outlanders are absent and the geography is somewhat different, but the magical psychic abilities of the heroine prove beyond a doubt that Harry's Damar has indeed evolved from Aerin's Damar. The origins of many of the customs, traditions, and rituals present in *The Blue Sword* are explained in *The Hero and the Crown* as well.

The heroines Harry and Aerin were born partly from McKinley's love of fairy tales and partly from her desire to create strong female characters who are able to do more than wait for male heroes to rescue them. Harry and Aerin are successful at many activities that, in fiction, traditionally have been assigned to men. Aerin slays dragons, and Harry triumphs over all the other novices, both male and female, to win a contest of horse riding skills and swordplay. Harry and Aerin don their armor and ride into combat with Gonturan, the fabled blue sword that each woman carries in her own time.

McKinley gives her female warriors more than simply courage to slay their enemies; Aerin and Harry retain their femininity throughout their adventures. Both women are rather reluctant heroes, and both must grapple with mixed emotions concerning duty and honor. Aerin, considered an outsider in her own land, must risk her life several times before she is able to prove her worth to herself and to her people. Likewise, Harry, born and reared as an Outlander despite her Damarian ancestor, must win a place in her new world without betraying her roots. Both women are at first hampered by ignorance and inexperience, and both succeed at last by dint of their honor, pride, and stubborn refusal to accept defeat.

The novels also have romantic themes in common. In *The Blue Sword*, the familiar motif of the abducted maiden falling in love with her captor is mitigated by the strength of the character of Harry. Far from being a meekly subservient prisoner, Harry fights her way up from the status of respected guest to become the savior of the land. In order to defeat the enemy, she must even defy Corlath's orders and seek her own allies. She earns Corlath's respect and will rule beside him as an equal.

In *The Hero and the Crown*, Aerin is at first too involved with her own misery to take much notice of Tor's affection for her. It is Luthe, the wizard, who initiates Aerin into the joys of romance. Aerin must make the difficult choice to return to Tor, her childhood sweetheart, to be queen beside him. This painful choice is made only slightly easier by Aerin's realization that the immortal Luthe will wait for the part of Aerin that is "no longer quite mortal."

Reviewers of both Damar novels have commended McKinley's wellrounded characters, creative settings, and suspenseful storytelling. The characters' emotional responses are often understated but never unbelievable or difficult to decipher. Romance, vivid action sequences, and captivating characters all contribute to the novels' popularity. Most critics believe that McKinley successfully blended the traditional fairy-tale form with some nontraditional heroines.

—*Quinn Weller*

BONE DANCE

A group of post-holocaust misfits brings an evil city government to an end and establishes a new form of mystical community

Author: Emma Bull (1954–)
Genre: Science fiction—cyberpunk
Type of work: Novel
Time of work: An indeterminate time in the future
Locale: An unidentified American city
First published: 1991

THE STORY

Following the publication and positive critical reception of *War for the Oaks* (1987) and *Falcon* (1989), *Bone Dance* (subtitled *A Fantasy for Technophiles*) continues Emma Bull's exploration of high-tech fantasies through tight, well-constructed plot and characterization. In it, she utilizes science-fictional technologies tempered with New Age spiritualism.

The story follows the adventures of Sparrow, a trader in "Big Bang" collectible videos and CDs, and her ultimate clash with the corrupt authorities who control the city. After a successful video sale to the city boss, Albrecht, Sparrow wakes up in an alley unable to remember the previous twenty-four hours. She goes to see Sherrea, her friend and a mystic tarot reader. Sherrea informs Sparrow of strange and cataclysmic events in the near future and her role in them but has no knowledge of Sparrow's lost time.

Spurred on by the mystery, Sparrow is contacted by Mick Skinner, who claims to know about her missing memories. Pursued by two strangers Skinner is eager to avoid, they make it back to Sparrow's apartment and warehouse. After Skinner's strange and inexplicable death, Sparrow is kidnapped by the two strangers, who say they are city employees. Sparrow is told that Skinner was a Horseman, one of a group of mind-control soldiers who destroyed Earth in a nuclear war through jealous competition. Horsemen not only have the power of mind control but also can "ride" other people, willfully occupying and directing their bodies.

Sparrow is kidnapped again, this time by Frances, another Horseman, and a resurrected Skinner, who now occupies another body. In the conversations that follow, Sparrow is told that she herself is a "horse," a pre-holocaust, genetically grown container for exclusive use by Horsemen. This effectively wins Sparrow over to their plan of killing the most evil Horseman, Tom Worecski, who is also the real power in control of the city. Their attack fails, and Skinner is captured. Sparrow must offer her body for sex to ensure the escape of Frances.

After her brutal rape, Sparrow finds herself recuperating in a communal village peopled by mystics and Hoodoo magicians. There, she undergoes a psychic rebirth in which she comes to terms with who and what she is and begins to learn the importance of friendship and community. Her spiritual strength is renewed, and her friendship with Frances blossoms. They plan and undertake a second attack on Worecski and the government. This time, they ask a whole panoply of gods for help, and the attack succeeds. Worecski is killed, and the promise of a new humane order is established. Sparrow gives up city life and returns to her new spiritual community.

ANALYSIS
In many ways, *Bone Dance* continues the cyberpunk legacy by exploring the psychological condition of a post-holocaust survivor through a hard-bitten and intelligent use of interior monologue and a series of trying moral dilemmas. Bull extends this paradigm beyond the exploration of technology and evil corporations, so prevalent in cyberpunk narratives and concentrates more fully on developing her central character. Sparrow is a sharp, cynical loner who has little use for anyone outside of her business transactions. *Bone Dance* convincingly follows her growth toward a complex understanding of herself as a human being.

Sparrow is never completely cold and bitter, and her love of pre-holocaust relics is more than commercial. She has a sense of time and history, and of how things could have been better in the city. In short, she has ideals about the possibilities of life and human interaction that her environment does not allow her to explore. As Bull makes clear, Sparrow has an affinity with these relics because she herself is a relic, a manufactured object that was "born" a teenager with a yearning for connection.

Sparrow also shares a deep sense of kinship with the Horsemen, another manufactured form looking for a sense of permanence and stability. Guilty over their destruction of the world, Frances and Skinner take it upon themselves to eliminate all Horsemen in a belated gesture of goodwill and in a belief that they cannot live with their crime. If Sparrow has no past, then Frances has no present, given that she moves between bodies at will. Bull brings these characters together and convincingly develops a relationship reliant on compassion and responsibility. In this way, Bull lifts *Bone Dance* out of a trendy nihilism and into a touching drama.

As its informal subtitle ironically suggests, Bone Dance is a "fantasy for technophiles," and it successfully combines familiar science-fictional themes and settings with a complementary exploration of the supernatural and the spiritual. Sparrow's reliance on her tarot reader for guidance and the use of the spirit world in the final clash between the Horsemen serve to shift the focus from the technological to the human. *Bone Dance* is an exploration of the friendship between Sparrow and Frances and the ways in which their relationship represents a way out of the decay and corruption of the city. Hoodoo, tarot readings, and mystical incantations come to stand as the antitheses of the technological, and it is in these that Bull celebrates the nurturing possibilities of community.

Bone Dance combines a futuristic detective yarn with a coming-of-age story by exploiting the best features of both genres. At the same time tough and compassionate, the novel works precisely through its convincing characterization rather than its sensationalism, thus widening the parameters of science fiction and fantasy in general.
—*Paul Hansom*

BONE FOREST

Stories exploring mythology, religion, the historical and prehistorical past, and humanity's place in time

Author: Robert Holdstock (1948–2009)
Genre: Fantasy—mythological
Type of work: Stories
Time of work: Various times between antiquity and the near future
Locale: Various locations on Earth and in imaginary lands
First published: 1991

THE STORY
This collection of stories, most of them originally published between the mid-1970's and the early 1990's, is weighted toward works similar in theme and style to the novella that gives the collection its title. "The Bone Forest" is original to this anthology. In all the stories, Robert Holdstock calls up images of humanity's past and its relationship to its present and future through the guiding link of the myths and stories that are passed down, in variation upon variation, through the ages.

"The Bone Forest" itself is part of Holdstock's Mythago Cycle consisting of *Mythago Wood* (1984), *Lavondyss* (1988), and *The Hollowing* (1993). These tales explore the mysterious tract of primary oak forest in Britain called Ryhope Wood and its "mythagos," manifestations of mythological archetypes and symbols of the collective unconscious. In Ryhope Wood, the myths and legends of humanity's past come to life. The forest, only a small woodland on the outside, contains vast regions within its interior.

The novella returns to the characters in the original novel—George Huxley and his two sons, Steven and Christian—but in a time when the brothers are still children and George Huxley has only begun to map and understand the wood's outer defenses. Finally he and his companion, Edward Wynne-Jones, make a breakthrough, but instead of offering further understanding it leads to a series of strange, disturbing encounters with a creature that Huxley only belatedly realizes is a *Doppelgänger* of himself.

"Scarrowfell" and "Thorn" both deal with religion and British history. In the former, a group of children watch and wait as a town prepares for an annual religious festival. It is not until the story's climax that the reader realizes that this is a Britain that was never converted to Christianity and that the forces being worshiped are far older and darker. In "Thorn," Thomas, a medieval stonemason helping to construct a new church, is recruited by a being named Thorn, one of the spirits being forced out by the coming of Christianity. By including symbols of pagan power within the stonework of the building, Thomas helps Thorn to subvert the power of the church before coming to believe that Thorn is using him for his own ends.

In "The Shapechanger," a young boy finds escape from an abusive relationship through a belief in the power of myth. In eighth century England, Wolfhead and Inkmarker, a shaman and his apprentice, travel to a village in which a mysterious voice has been calling out from inside a deep well. It is the voice, in fact, of a young boy more than a millennium in the future, trapped in his room by an abusive father, yearning for escape through the stories and histories of Britain that he reads. He achieves escape in a way that he did not anticipate.

"The Time Beyond Age" is unique in this collection as an example of Holdstock's science-fiction writing (though another story, "The Time of the Tree," has some vague science-fictional elements). In this story, scientists observe two people as they live an accelerated and preprogrammed life, aging years each day and heading toward some new, evolved form. The scientists themselves become disillusioned, obsessed with, or frightened by the unexpected results.

Analysis

Holdstock's greatest strengths lie in his ability to extrapolate and re-create in full and convincing detail a past so distant that it has all but retreated into the fog of myth, and in his clean, straightforward prose. He refuses to obscure the sublimity of his mythic vision with literary pyrotechnics. "The Bone Forest," written in much the same style as *Mythago Wood*, is an apt example of this. The events are startling and uncanny, but Holdstock, through his narrator, relates them almost matter-of-factly, with a detachment that not only is appropriate to George Huxley the scientist but also adds an immediacy and realism to the events, making them all the more powerful.

The stories in this collection offer enough variety to demonstrate Holdstock's strengths as well as his weaknesses. The greatest of the latter is an occasional tendency to give free rein to either the metaphoric or the pathetic impulse. "The Time of the Tree," essentially an extended metaphor about the human body as an ecological system complete with climatic changes and inhabitants, takes an interesting image and expands it past the bounds of interest and into the realm of the absurd. When Holdstock restrains himself, however, the result can be sublimely powerful, as in "The Shapechanger," with its somewhat worn premise of escape from distress through fantasy enlivened and deepened by Holdstock's delicate handling and subdued tone, which is given release only in the climactic sequence.

The most powerful story in the collection, "The Boy Who Jumped the Rapids," plays to all of Holdstock's strengths, demonstrating his firm hold on human nature and the driving power of myth, and how the two interact to create and feed off of each other. In this story the reader is witness to the birth of a myth, but not one that is known.

Rather than his usual extrapolation backward from current story to original event, Holdstock here creates the original event—the murder of a child by an assassin—and then lets the reader glimpse the direction this sad story will take as it is remembered through the ages. In the end, Caylen, the boy of the story's title, comes to a devastating understanding of the role myth serves in society and in the human mind, for both good and ill.

More so than most authors' short-story collections, *The Bone Forest* retains its coherent theme throughout the stories selected for inclusion. If it does not do justice to the range of Holdstock's writing, it instead gives the reader depth, allowing insight into the way that a writer continues to work with, reshape, and reexamine themes and images through the course of his career.

—*Carroll Brown*

THE BOOK OF THE DUN COW

Chauntecleer, as lord of the peaceable animal kingdom, engages in a deadly battle with Cockatrice, the scaly monster whose forces of evil must be overcome

Author: Walter Wangerin, Jr. (1944–)
Genre: Fantasy—animal fantasy
Type of work: Novel
Time of work: Undefined, with echoes of both medieval and modern times
Locale: Earth and the netherworld
First published: 1978

THE STORY

In this story of hilarity and horror, Walter Wangerin, Jr., creates a delightfully varied, though temperamental, menagerie that exists more or less peaceably under the wings of the great Chauntecleer, its irritable but responsible leader. The hilarity flows out of the colorful personality clashes, wit, and foibles of these furry creatures and fowl. Hilarity gives way to horror when Wyrm, condemned to live deep below the earth's surface, becomes bent on destroying all that is good by unleashing his forces of madness and mayhem.

The pending threat to Chauntecleer's community, and thereby the earth's civilization, develops gradually but insistently. Underneath the Chicken Coop lurks Ebenezer Rat, who sneaks up in the night and sucks the hens' eggs. On a more cosmic scale, although he is buried in the bowels of the earth by God's decree, Wyrm still has power to affect affairs on the surface. The result is the birth of Cockatrice. This wholly evil offspring, hatched by a toad and in a form that is half rooster and half dragon, kills his own father and, in the service of Wyrm, sets out to launch a deadly attack on the peaceable kingdom of Chauntecleer.

In that kingdom, Chauntecleer has succeeded in neutralizing Ebenezer Rat, the presence of evil inside the Coop, but the Lord of the Coop discovers the consequence of another evil beyond the Coop in the churning of the swollen river: All manner of debris, a "spinning cemetery of bones." Cast upon the shore, barely alive, is a Hen. Chauntecleer finds himself powerfully attracted to this bedraggled but beautiful Hen with vermillion at her throat, though she has been traumatized nearly to madness and death. She can only scream again and again the name of the cause of all the havoc and horror, "Cockatrice!" She finds healing in Chauntecleer's Coop, and eventually Chauntecleer gets his Pertelote. All is well in his domain, but not for long.

Far away, Cockatrice is pursuing his works of darkness. Thousands of eggs are hatching Basilisks, serpent-like birds that rise from the rivers and sting to death whatever they touch. Wyrm, the evil mastermind, is preparing to break through the earth's crust, gradually softened by the rains that are slowly flooding the land. Wyrm's goal is nothing less than to destroy the very fabric of this humanlike community and challenge God himself.

At that point, God sends the Dun Cow as messenger to Chauntecleer and his Earth-keepers. When the Basilisks make their appearance and threaten annihilation, the Dun Cow bestows on Chauntecleer the gifts essential to confronting and defeating the enemy. The battle that ensues is terrifying and indecisive until its climax in a chilling duel between Cockatrice and Chauntecleer. The treacherous Cockatrice is finally vanquished, but the bloodied victor also feels defeated. Again it is the ministry of the mysterious Dun Cow, with the help of the self-effacing dog, Mundo Cani, that revives the spirit of Chauntecleer. When the earth opens and Wyrm himself begins to make his move, Chauntecleer feels powerless. The Dun Cow sends the lowly Mundo Cani to fight the last battle. In a breathtaking climax, Mundo Cani dives into the gorge and plunges the horn of the Dun Cow into Wyrm's eye. The earth closes upon both of them. Peace can now return, but the cost has been enormous.

ANALYSIS

Like the heroic epics of long ago, such as *Beowulf* and *The Song of Roland*, this beast epic deals with the nature of good and evil and the inevitable but shocking war between them. In this story, however, the heroic action yields not the giddiness of glory but the grief of pain, sacrifice, and loss. Although the tale reflects a medieval cosmography, political structure, and literary tradition, it strikes the contemporary reader as eerily modern, with unsettling reverberations of twentieth century tyrants, killing fields, and holocausts. As such, it delivers a significant moral message to both young and older readers, reminding them that peace is tenuous as long as evil has not been contained; that vigilance is vital lest evil destroy the good; that the qualities of goodness, compassion, courage, and love must be given the chance to flourish, for they have the power to prevail against the power of darkness.

Within this tale of conflict and combat are some marvelously funny episodes, entertaining characters, and a tender love story. The genuine affection that grows between Chauntecleer and Pertelote ennobles the intemperate leader and enables Pertelote to experience healing of her own psychic wounds and share the burdens of her mate. This relationship casts a warm glow in the midst of a world threatened by hate and cruelty.

This book, the author's first, has all the qualities of a classic: an archetypal, universal theme; a plot with vigor and verve, with movement and direction, with tension and resolution; a memorable, vivid set of characters who are brilliantly particularized; and a colorful style that has wit, variety, and passion. Hailed as the best children's book of the year, it enjoyed both critical acclaim and commercial success. In 1980 it received the National Religious Book Award, and in 1981 it won both the American Book Award and an American Library Association Notable Book citation. Encouraged, the author turned to writing full-time. In addition to volumes of stories and nonfiction, he has since written other fantasies for younger children, including *Thistle* (1983) and *Elizabeth and the Water-Troll* (1991). He has also written a sequel to *The Book of the Dun Cow*, titled *The Book of Sorrows* (1985). His novel *The Crying for a Vision* was published in 1994.

—*Henry J. Baron*

THE BOOK OF THE NEW SUN

The Earth of a distant future finds a hero to replace its dying sun

Author: Gene Wolfe (1931–)
Genre: Science fiction—theological romance
Type of work: Novels
Time of work: Millennia in the future
Location: Urth
First published: *The Shadow of the Torturer* (1980), *The Claw of the Conciliator* (1981; collected with *The Shadow of the Torturer* as *The Book of the New Sun, Volumes I and II*, 1983), *The Sword of the Lictor* (1982), *The Citadel of the Autarch* (1983; collected with *The Sword of the Lictor* as *The Book of the New Sun, Volumes III and IV*, 1985), and *The Urth of the New Sun* (1987)

THE STORY

In an Earth (now called Urth) of the distant future, the Sun is slowly dying. Humanity is divided into the Commonwealth, centered roughly in what is now South America, and the Ascians, or those without shadow, who dominate the Northern Hemisphere. The society resembles medieval cultures such as that of the Byzantine Empire.

Severian is born into the hereditary Guild of Torturers in the city of Nessus. The Torturers are assigned to torment the enemies of the city's ruler. Severian, along with several other apprentices, is trained by the dour Master Gurloes. One of the few exceptions to their grim regimen is the annual celebration of their patroness, Holy Katherine. Severian meets a prisoner named Thecla, on whom he takes pity, eventually bringing her books and trying to console her. Severian gives Thecla a knife, and from the pools of blood he sees outside her prison door the next time he comes to visit her, he concludes that she has committed suicide. Severian informs Master Palaemon, one of his superiors in the Guild, of what he has done. Palaemon advises Severian to go into exile and gives him a resplendent sword named *Terminus Est* to aid him during his adventures and ordeals.

Severian ranges far and wide, eventually meeting an abandoned blond woman named Dorcas as well as the mysterious Dr. Talos and his sidekick, the giant Baldanders. Severian's network of acquaintances begins to solidify, forming a circle of personal loyalties around which his destiny will unfold. Eventually, some of these people's memories become fused with Severian's when he comes to be the representative of his entire planet.

Severian journeys to the north, toward the Windowless City of Thrax. He manages to get hold of the Claw of the Conciliator, which despite its name is not a weapon but a glowing, beautiful, and redemptive jewel that holds the promise of future peace for the warring and injured peoples of Urth. Along with Dorcas, he encounters the cannibalistic Alzabo and helps the people of the region surrounding Thrax win their freedom.

Severian finds out that Thecla has not in fact died but used the knife to escape. He also finds out that Baldanders and Dr. Talos are not what they seem. Dr. Talos is a mechanical man who, despite his air of authority, is Baldanders's servant. Baldanders, for his part, is in communication with extraterrestrial spirits called hierodules. These hierodules, Ossipago, Barbatus, and Famulimus, reveal to Severian the calamity that is overtaking Urth and inform him that he has been appointed to journey into space and find a new sun for the planet.

First, though, Severian has to attain full authority on Urth. With the backing of the power he has accumulated in Thrax and elsewhere, he returns to Nessus and is declared Autarch. He marries Valeria, an aristocratic lady of the city who is a suitable partner for him, although parts of his love will always be directed toward Dorcas and Thecla. As Autarch, Severian brings more justice to Urth than most of his predecessors had managed.

The hierodules arrange for a huge starship to transport Severian into space. Aboard the giant ship, Severian is attacked by "jibers," crewmen from other worlds who have been in the ship so long that they have become permanent residents of its underclass. He is saved from them by a pretty but strangely world-weary woman named Gunnie and an engaging sprite named Zak. Severian learns that he is going to the planet Yesod for a trial in which he will represent Urth. His task is to convince the Hierogrammate Tzadkiel to give Urth a new sun. Upon arrival at Yesod, Severian encounters a woman (actually an embodied, angelic larva) named Apheta who reveals the utter insignificance of Urth in the cosmic order but hints at implications in his mission that Severian himself has not realized.

Severian meets the great Tzadkiel only to find that it is the apparently harmless Zak, in vastly transmuted form. Tzadkiel informs Severian that he is Urth's new sun and that he will be returned amid great cataclysm for the planet's rebirth. Tzadkiel also indicates that, in some other dimension of time, he and all of his sort had been made by humans from Urth. Severian returns to Urth, this time accompanied by Gunnie's younger incarnation, Burgundofara. Much of Urth is destroyed, but Severian survives to see the planet renewed and renamed Ushas, signifying its new state of being.

ANALYSIS

The Book of the New Sun is one of the most ambitious works of science fantasy to be published in the last quarter of the twentieth century, recognized with aWorld Fantasy Award for *The Shadow of the Torturer* and a Nebula Award for *The Claw of the Conciliator*. Science fantasy is an odd hybrid. Gene Wolfe's books combine the linguistic inventiveness and spiritual depth of the fiction of J. R. R. Tolkien with the scientific believability and historical sweep of the work of Isaac Asimov. Wolfe's writing, though, has a voice and a pulse utterly its own.

On one level, the Book of the New Sun is filled with conventional adventure of the "sword and sorcery" variety. Severian fights his way through challenges in Nessus and Thrax to emerge victorious as lord over all. This surface physical action, however, serves primarily to mask the true inner complexity of the series, swathed in Wolfe's complicated plotting and exotic vocabulary (all of which is derived from existing,

though obscure, words in English, Latin, and Hebrew). Most readers will be deep into the series before coming close to guessing the ultimate significance of Urth's clearly decrepit state or what the New Sun will be. Severian is typical of post-1960 science fiction in that he is an antihero as much as a hero. Although his narrative perspective governs readers' view of the story throughout, it is difficult to identify with him: He is too involved in torture, deception, and various other despicable acts. Wolfe presents Severian as able to come to terms with the evil he has done and integrate it with the far more dominant principles of altruism that largely govern his conduct. Severian goes into exile from Nessus only to provide cover for what he supposes is Thecla's suicide, and he takes on the self-sacrificing mission of leaving Urth and his Autarchy to go to Yesod in search of the New Sun. Because Wolfe lets Severian speak in his own voice, readers are privy to Severian's own ruthless self-examination and his own awareness of the complexity of his course in life.

Thecla is one of the most affecting of the supporting characters. Her disappearance and unlooked-for return add to her generally mysterious personality, giving her an air of sacredness (the name Thecla comes from an early Christian martyr) that makes her something of a spiritual reference point for Severian. Other characters deepen the strangeness and texture of Severian's journey and simultaneously exemplify Wolfe's literary allusiveness. The giant Baldanders testifies to the higher qualities of the human race that are latent in the weary and hard-pressed denizens of Urth. The name Baldanders is a reference to the work of Argentine writer Jorge Luis Borges. Dr. Talos, the mechanical man, is a portal to the strange, superhuman yet half-human, world of the hierodules; "Talos" was originally the name of a mechanical man in English poet Edmund Spenser's poem *The Faerie Queene* (1590, 1596).

The three hierodules, and even more the Hierogrammate Tzadkiel, emblematize the texture and philosophy of the book. Both words have a meaning, although in Greek: "hierodule" is "sacred slave," and "Hierogrammate" is "product of sacred writing." Tzadkiel reveals to Severian when he is on Yesod that the hierodules, superhuman though they may seem, were in fact themselves created by the human race long ago. Desiring to give their descendants a kind of sacred security, they had created the Hierogrammates to give their descendants succor when they need it.

Wolfe portrays a set of all-powerful deities created by humans who in turn help humanity of far-future Urth re-create itself. This paradox fits with all the displacements and foreshadowings in time that occur throughout the series. There also is a hope that there is an order outside time in the universe. "The Conciliator" clearly is analogous to Jesus Christ, and the characters of Thecla and Holy Katherine evoke the Virgin Mary.

At the end of the series, Severian returns to renewed Ushas and encounters simple fishermen who indicate that they revere Severian and two of his companions as gods. Severian, though, points out that only something called "the Increate" is truly worthy of worship. Wolfe makes it clear that this Increate is none other than the God of the Judeo-Christian tradition.

—*Nicholas Birns*

THE BOOK OF WONDER

A collection of short fantasy tales set in London and in magical imaginary worlds

Author: Lord Dunsany (Edward John Moreton Drax Plunkett, 1878–1957)
Genre: Fantasy—magical world

Type of work: Stories
Time of work: Various times between antiquity and 1910
Locale: Various locations on Earth and imaginary worlds
First published: 1912

The Book of Wonder

THE STORY

The Book of Wonder is a collection of fourteen tales in which Lord Dunsany explores mythical cities and creatures as well as the fabulous exploits of familiar characters such as a young English girl, a pirate, a businessman, and thieves. An unusual feature of the collection is that Dunsany wrote the stories in response to the drawings of S. H. Sime, an illustrator whose style was often compared with Aubrey Beardsley's, and whose wryly humorous yet macabre black-and-white compositions had accompanied Dunsany's first four short-story collections.

Stories of atmosphere, evocative of mood rather than plot, character, or theme, the tales in *The Book of Wonder* are notable for the biblical style developed by Dunsany in his earlier work. They are also noteworthy for his facility with leading readers to the place in his subtitle, "the edge of the world." The locations are recognizable but are all the more seductive for his facile transformation of accessible details into the images from dreams or nightmares.

In his preface, Dunsany invites readers "who are in any wise weary of London" to follow him to new worlds. Some of the stories take place solely in mystical realms and illustrate Dunsany's oft-noted unique nomenclature. In "The Bride of the Man-Horse," for example, Shepperalk the centaur leaves his home in the Athranaurian mountains for Zretazoola, where he will seek a bride, Sombelene. In "The Quest of the Queen's Tears," Ackronnian, king of Afarmah, Lool, and Haf, slays the Gladsome Beast in Fairyland in an ultimately failed effort to move Sylvia, the Queen of the Woods, to tears. These stories illustrate Dunsany's tendency to cast his female characters as queens, princesses, and sphinxes but also as powerless figures of sexual objectification.

Some of the stories display the imaginative ease with which Dunsany moves from London to the edge of the world. In "Miss Cubbidge and the Land of Romance," a glistening golden dragon abducts the title character from her London home at 12A Prince of Wales Square to the eternal and ancient lands of Romance. In "How Nuth Would Have Practised His Art upon the Noles," young Tommy Tonker becomes an apprentice jewel thief to Nuth, an experienced London burglar living in Belgrave Square. They attempt to steal emeralds from the gnoles, undefined creatures who dwell secretly in a lean, high house in a deep, dark wood.

These stories—along with "The Hoard of the Gibbelins," in which the adventurous knight Alderic, attempting to steal the man-eating Gibbelins' emeralds, is caught and hanged, and which concludes with "the tale is one of those that have not a happy ending"—demonstrate Dunsany's experimentation with humorous, ironic, surprise finales. Miss Cubbidge, for example, in the denouement of her story, receives a letter from a former schoolmate admonishing her for the impropriety of traveling across the mystical seas with a dragon and no chaperone.

Two of Dunsany's most successful stories concern simple London businesspeople who begin to lead double lives: the real, sterile life of making money and the fantastic life of the imagination. In "The Wonderful Window," a strange old man dressed in Oriental garb sells a magic window to the romantic salesman Mr. Sladden and installs it over a cupboard in his rented room. Sladden views the mystical Golden Dragon City through the window. Attempting to save the city from invaders, he breaks the window and discovers only his old cupboard behind it. In "The Coronation of Mr. Thomas Shap," the salesman Shap develops his imaginative abilities to the point that he creates an old Eastern city, names it Larkar, crowns himself king, and dwells so little in his real life that he is put into a psychiatric ward, still believing himself to be ruler of all the lands of Wonder.

ANALYSIS

Contemporary critics responded with enthusiasm to *The Book of Wonder*, in which Dunsany recovered the mythology of *The Gods of Pegāna* (1905) and *Time and the Gods* (1906); the heroic fantasy of *The Sword of Welleran* (1908); and the supernatural of *A Dreamer's Tales* (1910); as well as exploring the ironic fairy tale. Although in his ten ensuing volumes of short stories he experimented with different genres, such as short-shorts in *Fifty-One Tales* (1915), club tales in the Jorkens series (1931–1954), and mystery stories in *The Little Tales of Smethers* (1952), scholars herald his first five volumes of tales as exemplars in the field of fantasy fiction. Some even dubbed him "the father of modern fantasy." His work influenced writers such as J. R. R. Tolkien, Ursula K. Le Guin, and especially H. P. Lovecraft, who called him the "inventor of a new mythology and weaver of surprising folklore." Beginners at the craft of fantasy fiction often compose what has come to be known as the "Dunsanian" story.

Since Dunsany's death, his work has been collected in at least five anthologies. Dunsany believed that true art was the result of inspiration, and he disapproved of readers' attempts to allegorize his stories; he wanted most of all to evoke a mood of fabulous mystery. His facility with archaic language, arresting neologisms, strange new mythologies, and heroic adventures, and his belief— illustrated especially in the stories from *The Book of Wonder*—in the occasional human need to escape the sterile ordinariness of life, lead to continuing appreciation from fantasy enthusiasts, scholars in the field, and especially the readers he addresses in his preface, "those that tire at all of the world we know."

—*Siobhan Craft Brownson*

BORN TO EXILE AND IN THE RED LORDS REACH

A wandering minstrel with the power of teleportation struggles to survive and find love and meaning in a harsh world where he must fear persecution as a "witch"

Author: Phyllis Eisenstein (1946–)
Genre: Fantasy—extrasensory powers
Type of work: Novels
Time of work: Unspecified, preindustrial
Locale: An Earth-like world
First published: *Born to Exile* (1978; portions published as short stories in the August, 1971; November, 1972; January, 1974; and February, 1975, issues of *The Magazine of Fantasy and Science Fiction*) and *In the Red Lord's Reach* (1989; portions published as short stories in the September, 1977, and July, 1979, issues of *The Magazine of Fantasy and Science Fiction*; novel serialized in the July-September, 1988, issues of *The Magazine of Fantasy and Science Fiction*)

THE STORY

In *Born to Exile*, the wandering fifteen-year-old minstrel Alaric is introduced. In addition to his talent for music, he has the power of teleportation. The power is limited in that he is able only to move himself and objects he is carrying to a location that he is able to visualize and position in relation to his current location. He was found, as a newborn baby on a hillside, covered in blood with a "gory hand raggedly severed above the wrist" clutching his ankle. He was taken in by a couple and reared as their son. When he was seven years old, his adoptive mother died, and his father was cruel to him, raising a whip to strike him. As he was about to be whipped, he visualized a tree in the nearby woods and was instantly transported there.

Alaric initially lives by stealing but soon meets Dall, a wandering minstrel who makes him his apprentice. Dall is later murdered by bandits, and Alaric transports himself away to safety. In his wandering, Alaric comes to the Castle Royal, where he falls in love with, and becomes the lover of, Princess Solinde. He is accused of witchcraft by one of her maids, who witnesses his teleportation power being used. The king, Solinde's father, exiles him from the kingdom. Solinde's brother, Jeris, who has become Alaric's friend, gives him a sword, belt, and scabbard.

In his continuing travels, Alaric uses his teleportation power to escape being killed by the proprietors of an inn, at which travelers are routinely killed for their belongings. He leaves the inn accompanied by Mizella, a prostitute who had been used by the inn to lull travelers into a false sense of security. He and Mizella rescue an old woman whom villagers have thrown into a well to die, thinking her to be a witch. It turns out that this woman is Artuva, the midwife who slapped Alaric's rump after he was born, frightening him into using his teleportation powers. It was, she explains, her bloody severed hand that gripped his ankle when he was found on the hillside as an infant.

Artuva was herself exiled by Alaric's true father, as a result of the loss of his son. She leads Alaric to the home of his father, Baron Garlenon, and his mother, Lorenta Garlenon. Ten generations of

Garlenons, all of whom have both the power of teleportation and musical talent, have ruled there and in surrounding lands. The Garlenons inbreed in order to maintain their genetically transmitted talents. Alaric is welcomed home and meets many of his "cousins" but is ultimately ejected when it becomes clear that he will not cooperate with the others in using their talents for the purpose of conquering still other neighboring lands by suddenly appearing and slaughtering opposing leaders. As the book ends, "Once again he was merely a minstrel—not a baron's son, not a lord of power, but a wandering exile."

In the Red Lord's Reach presents more of Alaric's wandering life as a minstrel. Entertaining the Red Lord in his castle, he learns that this cruel lord delights in torturing captives to death, enjoying their pain. The Red Lord shows Alaric a woman whom he is torturing in this fashion in a locked room and states his intention of doing the same to Alaric after the woman dies. Alaric teleports away, taking the woman with him. Alaric uses his sword to kill her, at her request, because of the severity of her injuries.

Alaric ponders whether he should use his powers to return and kill the Red Lord, acknowledging that he has always simply run away from danger before. He ultimately joins up with some nomadic deer herdsmen and engages in a love affair with Zavia, the daughter of the herdsmen's self-proclaimed witch, Kata. He encounters jealousy from Gilo, Morak, and Terevli, the three sons of Simir, the herdsmen's leader. They plot to kill him and ultimately attack Simir himself. Alaric teleports away but decides to return and fight them, helping to save Simir. Simir exiles his own sons, going as far as leaving Gilo bound where the Red Lord will find him, and adopts Alaric as his new son.

The herdsmen, different from other people Alaric has encountered, value, rather than fear, magic and "witchcraft." Kata wishes Alaric to become her apprentice, but he is resistant to the idea, just as he is resistant to Simir's evident desire for Alaric ultimately to become his successor. Because of a harsh winter, there are few deer, and the herdsmen fear that they may not survive. They decide to fight the Red Lord and try to take over his lands and castle. Alaric and Simir go there in disguise but are recognized by Gilo, who is now serving the Red Lord. Alaric uses his powers to help teleport herdsman warriors, who do battle with and kill the Red Lord's soldiers. Simir himself, who long ago was one of the Red Lord's soldiers, kills the Red Lord. Alaric also battles Gilo, but it is Simir who kills him.

As this book ends, Alaric decides to decline Simir's offer to become his successor. Alaric resumes his wandering minstrel life and once again feels the "winter of exile closing about him."

ANALYIS

Alaric is a fascinating character, an outcast with two wondrous talents. He continually struggles with a moral dilemma of how to use his teleportation talent, as well as often facing persecution because the world fears that talent or thinks it a sign of alignment with evil. He delights especially in his musical talent, enjoying entertaining others and discovering or creating new songs.

Alaric does not seek out confrontation with evil but unavoidably finds it during his travels in the world. Although initially he is likely to use his teleportation talent to flee from danger and evil, by the end of *In the Red Lord's Reach* he has seemingly decided that some evil is so monstrous that it must be confronted and fought, even at the risk of the gravest danger. Even then, however, his conscience is troubled. Even though he did not personally kill anyone during the assault on the Red Lord's castle, he sees the deaths as on his head. An exile, both literally and figuratively, from birth, Alaric repeatedly has the experience of temporarily seeming to find a place and companions or family for himself, only to determine that his true destiny is once again to walk alone.

Although *Born to Exile* was initially written in portions, as short stories, it stands up remarkably well as a unified novel. The depiction of the internal life of the family of teleporters is outstanding and memorable. *In the Red Lord's Reach* is clearly a more complex and mature work, with several interesting subplots, and compellingly develops a number of characters in addition to Alaric, such as Simir and Kata. The two books are best read together and constitute a satisfying coming-of-age saga of a lonely, talented, and, at heart, conscientious and good youth whose resolutions of his moral dilemmas, although not perfect, satisfy him.

Although the scientific basis of Alaric's teleportation talent is never explained, it obviously has a physical rather than mystical origin because it can be passed on genetically. Phyllis Eisenstein portrays a teleportation talent that is subject to certain restrictions and conditions, and she faithfully confines her character's use of that talent within those boundaries. The concept of teleportation has been used frequently in other notable science fiction or fantasy stories, among them *The Stars My Destination* (1957; originally titled *Tiger! Tiger!*, 1956) by Alfred Bester, *Tunnel in the Sky* (1955) by Robert A. Heinlein, and *Jumper* (1992) by Steven Gould. Eisenstein's treatment of teleportation, interspersed with her believable characters and entertaining plot, ranks among the very best.

Eisenstein is also the author of two other linked fantasy novels, *Sorcerer's Son* (1979) and *The Crystal Palace* (1988), which portray the struggles of a young sorcerer to find his father and his true love. Her two other published novels, as of 1995, were *Shadow of Earth* (1979), the story of an alternate world in which the Spanish Armada won, resulting in a very different contemporary North America, and *In the Hands of Glory* (1981), a space opera. She is also the author of a considerable body of short fiction, including a number of stories in her early career coauthored with her husband Alex Eisenstein, starting with "The Trouble with the Past" in the New Dimensions 1 anthology (1971) edited by Robert Silverberg. Her short story "Nightlife," published in the February, 1982, issue of *The Magazine of Fantasy and Science Fiction*, was a Hugo Award nominee.

—*Bernard J. Farber*

THE BORROWERS SERIES

Peoplelike beings who are only inches high confront dangers and discomfort when they leave their home

Author: Mary Norton (1903–1992)
Genre: Fantasy—alien civilization
Type of work: Novels
Time of work: The late nineteenth century
Locale: England
First published: *The Borrowers* (1952), *The Borrowers Afield* (1955), *The Borrowers Afloat* (1959), and *The Borrowers Aloft* (1961)

The Story

Mary Norton, English actress, playwright, and award-winning author, tells in a four-book series the engrossing fantasy of miniature people known as Borrowers. They are so called because they live by "borrowing," for their own use, lost or discarded items around a house, such things as scraps of food, dropped needles and pins, matches or candles that have fallen behind a chest, dollhouse furniture, or half of a pair of broken scissors—things that people know they have but simply cannot find at the moment.

The four books in the Borrowers series actually compose one continuous story in four episodes. The first book, *The Borrowers*, establishes the parameters of the fantasy, introduces the central family, describes the under-the-kitchen-floor setting, and reveals some of the conflicts and challenges that confront the family daily. The three following books in the series relate further adventures of the inches-high people as they search for a place where they may live undisturbed by "human beans."

The Borrowers begins as Mrs. May tells young Kate the fanciful story of the little people her brother, Tom, had made up—if indeed he had made them up. Pod, Homily, and Arrietty belong to the Clock family of Borrowers, so named because they enter and leave their home under the kitchen floor through a hole at the base of a grandfather clock. They must find a new residence because Pod, the father, has had the misfortune of being seen by a human, "the boy" who is sick abed in Firbank Hall, the home occupied by old Aunt Sophie and Mrs. Driver, the housemaid. Moreover, Arrietty, the Borrower daughter, has even dared to talk to the boy. Although his kindness in bringing them useful things and even offering to let them live in the dollhouse upstairs shows that he is no threat to them, the family members know that they must leave when Mrs. Driver discovers their presence and calls the rat catcher to smoke out the "horrible creatures." They make their escape to the fields in the nick of time.

The grown-up Kate continues the story in *The Borrowers Afield*. She tells her children the story she learned from Tom Goodenough himself when she, as a child, visited Mrs. May, who had inherited Firbank Hall upon Aunt Sophie's death. Searching for their relatives who supposedly are living in a badger's set, the Clock family suffers many hardships in the fields. Their makeshift home in an abandoned boot provides little protection from moths, snakes, cows, owls, field mice, Gypsies, and a cold winter. Once again "the boy" comes to their rescue when Pod, Homily, and Arrietty are discovered in the caravan of Mild Eye the Gypsy. Along with Spiller, an ingenuous orphan Borrower who often assists them, the Clock family finds temporary quarters with Lupy, Hendreary, and Eggletina, their sought-for relatives who have moved from the badger's burrow into the walls of Firbank Hall.

In *The Borrowers Afloat*, Pod, Homily, and Arrietty must again search for a new home because the departure of Tom and his grandfather from the cottage will leave no food for Pod to "borrow." The locked house seems to have no avenue of exit, but the resourceful Spiller comes and leads the Clock family out through the washhouse drain pipe. As if this harrowing experience were not enough, the family of three must endure a treacherous trip down the river in a tea kettle. Although they are seen and almost caught again by Mild Eye the Gypsy, Spiller saves them. They make their way toward a hobbyist's miniature village at Little Fordham.

The Borrowers Aloft completes the series about the little people. The family enjoys life in the model village at Little Fordham, especially Homily, who has always wanted a proper house of her own. Unfortunately, Arrietty again commits the indiscretion of talking to a human, this time the housekeeper for kindly Mr. Pott, the builder of the tiny village. Before they can leave, the family is kidnapped by a greedy couple who hope to use them to increase business at their own miniature showplace. Locked in the couple's attic, the Borrowers inge-niously construct a passenger balloon, float out the attic window, and make their way back to the replica village. Pod and Homily know, however, that Borrowers and humans do not make good company. After a night's rest, they will be off again in search of a new home.

ANALYSIS

Stories of little people are common in folklore around the world. Jonathan Swift's narrative of the Lilliputians in *Gulliver's Travels* (1726), Lewis Carroll's 1865 account of a diminutive Alice in Wonderland, and the legends of the leprechauns of Ireland, to mention but a few, have stirred the imagination of generations of readers. None of these stories has pricked the fancy more than Mary Norton's fantasy of the little people known as Borrowers. In style and subject, her stories are children's literature at its best, capitalizing on children's natural love for imaginative play, or fantasy. The series (collected as *The Borrowers Omnibus*, 1966; titled for U.S. publication as *The Complete Adventures of the Borrowers*, 1967) occupies a firm place among the classics of children's literature alongside such notable works as Kenneth Grahame's *The Wind in the Willows* (1908), L. Frank Baum's *The Wonderful Wizard of Oz* (1900), J. R. R. Tolkien's *The Hobbit: Or, There and Back Again* (1937), and the ever-popular masterpiece of C. S. Lewis, the Chronicles of Narnia (1950–1956).

All the books in the Borrowers series have won notable awards. *The Borrowers* was an immediate success, quickly winning the Carnegie Medal, the Lewis Carroll Shelf Award, and the American Library Association Distinguished Book Award. *The Borrowers Afield*, *The Borrowers Afloat*, and *The Borrowers Aloft* each won designation as an American Library Association Notable Book. *The Borrowers Aloft* and *The Borrowers Afloat* were in addition chosen by the *New York Herald Tribune* as Spring Festival Honor Books. Norton followed the famous series with *The Borrowers Avenged* (1982) and *Poor Stainless: A New Story About the Borrowers* (1971). The concept of the miniature race formed the basis for the television series *The Littles*, and her Norton's *Bed-Knob and Broomstick* (1957) was made into the 1971 film *Bedknobs and Broomsticks*, starring Angela Lansbury.

The appeal of the series lies perhaps not only in the clever, intriguing concept of little people in a human world—drawn to a mathematically correct scale reminiscent of Jonathan Swift's Gulliver in the lands of Lilliput and Brobdingnag—but also in the skillful characteriza-tion of the story's chief actors. The reader easily relates to the diminutive world of the Borrowers because, although they are not human beings and are even averse to human contact, they look and act much like humans. Pod assumes the leadership in his family (itself a human relationship) and is the steadying, responsible force. His talk is punctuated with such wise, insightful comments as "Size is nothing. . . . It's the talk that gets them [one's bigger enemies]." Always aware of future needs, he judiciously makes provisions. Homily is the typical wife and mother, always concerned about the family's daily needs, safety, and whereabouts; always fretting about appearances; forever wanting to settle down in a place of her own; and always forgiving and loving. Youthful Arrietty seldom thinks before acting, enjoys the wonders of the natural world, foolishly ignores her parents' warnings, and repeatedly brings calamity both to herself and her family. Spiller is the independent, unconventional young man who redeems himself through his experience-generated know-how and his uncanny ability to appear exactly when he is needed most. Such sharp characterization readily draws the young reader into the fantasy that imitates life.

A prime rule of fantasy for children is that the author begin in reality and end in reality, thus leading highly imaginative children into but also out of fantasy. Standard examples are E. B. White's *Charlotte's Web* (1952) and C. S. Lewis' tales of Narnia. For the most part, Norton follows this criterion via the convention of a storyteller, Mrs. May, relating a story that soon fades into the fantasy itself but returns at book's end to the real-life setting. The only exception is the last book of the series.

In this series, Norton presents a story with episodes that create energizing suspense, tell of engrossing adventures of survival equal to those of Robinson Crusoe and the Swiss Family Robinson, and depict characters that are genuinely believable though fantastic. She unfolds a story worthy of note by all readers of fantasy literature.

—*Maverick Marvin Harris*

The Boys from Brazil

Notorious Nazi doctor Josef Mengele, alive and living in Brazil, dispatches young clones of Adolf Hitler, and only Yakov Liebermann can stop his plans

Author: Ira Levin (1929–2007)
Genre: Science fiction—cautionary
Type of work: Novel
Time of work: 1974–1975
Location: Various cities around the world
First published: 1976

The Story

Ira Levin presents an intricate plot involving Dr. Josef Mengele (the "Angel of Death" from the Nazi concentration camps), who has set up a laboratory in Brazil. Yakov Liebermann is a Nazi hunter, based on the legendary Simon Wiesenthal. The two enemies finally confront each other in the United States, where the plot is resolved.

Only far into the book do readers learn the nature of Mengele's plan, but there are intimations throughout. At a meeting of old Nazis, Mengele gives out the names and locations of ninety-four men who will have to be murdered within the next year. None holds an important position; most are civil servants or minor functionaries in government. They are spread all over the world. The Nazis are given new identity papers, passports, and money.

Unknown to Mengele, a young Jewish man interested in capturing Nazis has recognized Mengele and persuaded a waitress in the restaurant where the meeting is held to plant a tape recorder and to retrieve it for him. Mengele becomes suspicious, finds the waitress, and through her tracks down the young man, who is found in his hotel room playing parts of the tape to Liebermann. The young man is killed, but Liebermann has heard enough to pique his curiosity. He asks a friend at the Reuters news agency to note unusual deaths, and he travels to Germany to interview a woman who worked for Mengele during the war. She tells him enough to send him to a German scientist, who reveals that research is pointing toward the possibility of cloning a person from his or her cells.

Liebermann guesses that Mengele somehow has cloned Adolf Hitler and arranged for the ninety-four clones to be adopted. Each has the exact genetic code of Hitler, and each adoptive mother is married to someone unimportant, just as Hitler's mother was. Liebermann begins to track down these families. All the boys look alike, with pale skin and dark hair, and all are impolite.

Liebermann travels to the United States, where he expects the next assassination to take place.

Meanwhile, Mengele's operation has been shut down by higher Nazi command, and the assassins have been called home. Mengele destroys his laboratory but intends to continue with the assassinations of the adoptive fathers. He also plans to kill Liebermann because of his interference. They meet at the home of one of the boys, whose father Mengele kills and tosses into the basement. When the boy comes home from school, Mengele and Liebermann are in a life-and-death struggle. The boy sends his dogs after Mengele because he has a gun. The boy figures out who has killed his father and orders the dogs to kill him.

Liebermann recuperates and makes one more stop in America. In New York City, he meets with radical Jews who know about the list of children that Liebermann carries. While they talk, Liebermann tears up the list and flushes it down a toilet, telling the leader that it is wrong to kill children, any children, and that simply because they have Hitler's genes does not mean they will turn out like him.

ANALYSIS

This book raises many interesting ethical issues. Mengele is presented as completely evil, as one might assume he was. Levin's Mengele says that he asked Hitler in the middle of the war for a vial of his blood and some scrapings from his arm. He did not have the technology then to do anything with this material, but he developed the science in Brazil. He procured women to be implanted with embryos with Hitler's genetic code and to have the babies that would then be adopted by appropriate couples. The couples would match Hitler's parents in major respects, and Mengele planned for the adoptive fathers' assassinations to match Hitler's loss of his father.

Liebermann represents the forces of good. He is a crotchety older man who at first does not believe that Mengele's plan is being put into effect. Liebermann is portrayed as being almost a pauper, living in inadequate quarters, and having almost no help in his work of tracking down Nazis. He says that people had forgotten the days he had helped track down the infamous Nazi leader Adolf Eichmann.

Levin suggests that there always will be people like Mengele and like the militant Jews who wish to find the ninety-four Hitler clones and kill them. Liebermann is supposed to represent the moderate view of those who learn from history. He takes a chance that none of these children will become like Hitler, but he is steadfast that no one should do what the Nazis did in World War II, including killing children.

This novel was filmed in 1978, with Laurence Olivier and Gregory Peck playing Liebermann and Mengele. There are minor differences, but the film is true to the book.

Levin is proficient at developing twists and turns in the novel. At one point, one of the assassins notices someone he knew during the war, and he tells him his orders and asks about the postman of the town. Then, with no warning, he kills the man, saying that the target was not the postman but the old friend to whom he was talking.

This novel is science fiction, although cloning of cells and certain lifeforms has been achieved. In the years after Levin wrote this book, much was done to produce changes in fetuses and to develop certain characteristics within them. It is conceivable that the sort of cloning represented in this novel will become scientific fact. Levin takes no moral stand on the ethics of such a scientific feat. He allows the reader to decide, based on who is manipulating the borrowed genetic material.

—*John Jacob*

BOY'S LIFE

After Cory Mackenson sees a murdered man, his idyllic childhood is interrupted, and he comes to understand the forces of good and evil at work in his hometown

Author: Robert R. McCammon (1952–   )
Genre: Fantasy—high fantasy

Type of work: Novel
Time of work: Primarily 1964, with a flashforward to 1991 at the novel's end
Locale: Zephyr, Alabama
First published: 1991

THE STORY

Boy's Life is unlike Robert R. McCammon's other novels and is a marked departure from his usual style, focused more on horror. The plot of *Boy's Life* is more a series of incidents weaved into a tapestry of the variety of lifestyles in Zephyr, Alabama, and the Bruton section of town, where African Americans reside, during the mid-1960's.

In part 1, "The Shades of Spring," the story opens on a cold spring morning as Cory Mackenson accompanies his father on his milk delivery route. Father and son see a car plunge into a lake the locals say is bottomless. Cory's father dives into the icy waters in a desperate but futile attempt to save the drowning man. Cory's father comes face to face with the drowned man. The image haunts Cory's father throughout the novel: a murdered man, naked and beaten, a tattoo on his body, his hands cuffed to the steering wheel, a copper wire knotted around his neck. Near the scene, Cory finds a green feather, a clue he thinks will figure prominently in solving the murder, but one he keeps a secret, hidden from the rest of the world in a cigar box.

About the same time, the African American members of an adjacent area of the community called Bruton engage in a ritual to feed Old Moses, a serpent who swims in the belly of the Tecumseh River, from the gargoyle bridge. The serpent apparently is not pleased with his food, because he does not smack on the bridge's support with his tail as he usually does when fed by an ancient African American "conjure woman" the locals call The Lady. She is married to a man of color whose face is pigmented on only one side, earning him the nickname of The Moon Man.

Odd events occur in the town. Wasps swarm through the local church one Sunday during services while the preacher denounces rock and roll music. Two bullies, Gotha and Gordo Branlin, terrorize Cory, and he is spooked by "The Demon," Brenda Sutley. Finally, hard, steady rains come to Zephyr. The levee breaks in Bruton. Cory, as he helps to shore up the faulty levee, rescues a black child from being devoured by Old Moses, who is slithering in and out of Bruton's houses through the floodwater. The Lady rewards Cory's heroic act with a bike to replace the one the Branlins destroyed.

Part 2 of the novel is titled "Summer of Devils and Angels." In it, Cory and his best friends use their imaginations to take flight while riding their bikes on the day school ends. The boys also take a camping trip on which they come across the Blaylocks, who are bootleggers. Cory's adolescent hormones are stirred by Chile Willow.

Part 3, "Burning Autumn," brings Cory's fascination with the green feather to the fore again. He is invited to dine with a rich eccentric, Vernon Moultry, who often walks the streets of Zephyr naked. This section ends with Cory and his friends attending a freak sideshow and beginning to lose their innocence.

Part 4, "Winter's Cold Truth," resolves the mystery of the murdered man. Cory's father has his sanity restored with the help of The Lady and The Moon Man. An out-of-towner, the drowned man's brother, identifies the man by means of his tattoo. The entire mystery is linked to a neo-Nazi organization and a former Nazi in Zephyr who appears to be a kind physician.

Part 5 is titled "Zephyr as It Is." Cory returns to Zephyr in 1991, twenty-five years after he and his family moved away. In this short epilogue, Cory sees the town as it is. The childhood magic he thought he might find has disappeared.

ANALYSIS

Although the story incorporates elements of horror, it is more the story of a young boy's coming of age and losing his innocence as he struggles to understand the forces of good and evil at work in his hometown of Zephyr, Alabama. Populating the book with references to popular culture, McCammon is able to re-create the world of 1964. Although there are elements of horror in the novel, it is more a work of high fantasy that utilizes the voice of an engaging young narrator that calls out from the recent past, allowing the reader to recapture childhood innocence.

The innocence of childhood—a world in which a boy's bike ride becomes a flight and *Famous Monsters of Filmland* is required boyhood reading—is the most important aspect of McCammon's work. McCammon once said that he uses innocence as "the author's sense of wonder, at the characters and the setting and even the spooky elements." Without this sense of wonder, the incidents in *Boy's Life* would be merely a series of events that would read as relatively disjointed. With the sense of wonder, *Boy's Life* is McCammon's fictional autobiography as well as a celebration of childhood mystery and marvel, filled with targeted details and fully realized, rounded characters.

With the marked sensibilities of such diverse influences as Mark Twain, Flannery O'Connor, Harper Lee, and even Steven Spielberg, McCammon is able to shift his tale from the moral to the magical and back again, telling a coming-of-age story that is part mystery, part magic, part wonder, and part innocence. Using all the attendant forms of popular culture available to a twelve-year-old boy in 1964—comic books, baseball, roadside carnivals, monster films, and magazines—McCammon writes a paean to boyhood that is as effective as it is affecting. *Boy's Life* is peopled with some of the most memorable southern characters in southern fiction.

—*Thomas D. Petitjean, Jr.*

BRAIN ROSE

After surgery to access past-life memories, three people discover that they share ties from previous lives, leading to insights about the human racial memory

Author: Nancy Kress (1948–)
Genre: Science fiction—inner space
Type of work: Novel
Time of work: 2022
Locale: Rochester, New York, and other locations in the United States
First published: 1990

THE STORY

In 2022, a memory-destroying plague stalks humanity. Previous Life Access Surgery (PLAS) allows recovery of memories of former lives. After such operations, Caroline Bohentine, Joe McLaren, and Robbie Brekke seek information, through the reincarnation database, on their past-life ties. Robbie shows close links with virtually everyone who has undergone the surgery. While Caroline and Joe face personal tragedies, violent flashbacks seize Robbie. On a hallucinatory quest in Wyoming, he lapses into unending replay of others' memories. These bring insights into his role as a central "memory node" in the evolving oversoul.

Caroline, Joe, and Robbie seek PLAS for different reasons. Caroline, a survivor of incest and two failed marriages, hopes to discover versions of herself that she prefers to the current one. Joe, a sober attorney, wants to be cured of his multiple sclerosis; the cure is an unexplained side effect of the operation. An underworld boss sends Robbie for the surgery.

Caroline and Joe are suspicious of Robbie's facile charm, but in the clinic's hothouse atmosphere, the three find themselves drawn together. Some reasons are revealed in memory flashes. Robbie was Caroline's son in a previous life, and Joe, as boss in a Chinese porcelain factory, once ordered Robbie's execution for careless work. These discoveries add guilt to the interpersonal dynamics.

A bomb explodes at the home sheltering Caroline's young daughter, a plague victim. The daughter dies the following day. Angel Whittaker, Joe's secretary, asks Joe to answer an urgent message from Robin, his former wife, and to defend Angel from a sodomy charge. Joe's principles win against Angel's pleas. Joe refuses to call Robin because she has joined the Gaeists, who insist that Earth needs no protection. He will not help Angel because of his own moral convictions.

A call from Caroline, telling Joe that Robbie is disoriented and hysterical in Wyoming, shakes his composure. When his friend Jeff Pirelli appears with a warrant, Joe joins Jeff and Caroline in their search for Robbie.

Meanwhile, Robbie has been drawn into a past persona. As Mallie, a young desperado, he relives heists in St. Louis and a massacre and lingering death in a Wyoming cave. In flashes of clarity, he hunts Mallie's treasure and eventually finds it, near the skeleton of his past-life persona. Robbie flees to his motel, fighting hallucinations. Agents from the Federal Bureau of Investigation (FBI) are waiting for him. He begins babbling other people's memories.

In Robbie's motel room, the others sort out the puzzle. The FBI wants Robbie because he released mice that carried the plague virus. Pirelli suggests that Robbie is a central node in all the memory phenomena. He speculates that the human racial memory or oversoul is evolving into a higher form. Deprived of memory input by AIDS and the plague, it is using Robbie as a conduit until it heals. Like Gaea, the oversoul is a self-correcting entity.

Joe rejects this idea, but Caroline considers it. A year later, a vaccine against the plague is developed. The burden of multiple linked pasts weighs on a still-disbelieving Joe.

ANALYSIS

Brain Rose is a novel of characters and ideas. The three main characters carry the plot, but secondary characters highlight their conflicts and offer interpretations of events. For example, Father Patrick Shahid leaves the Jesuits and defies the Catholic church to have PLAS because he believes that the coming memory evolution is the work of God. Colin Cadavy, Caroline's brilliant actor father, lives by his wits and charm as Robbie has done, less successfully, in most of his past lives.

Joe McLaren shows the greatest character development. A man of good intentions but rigid behavior and beliefs, his involvement with Robbie and the memory crises leads him to reevaluate his life. He quits his law practice to work toward environmental cleanup and to give Robin and Angel the help he previously refused them. He still doubts the theory of the overmemory's evolution and that he has any continuing role to play in it, but he is poised for further growth.

Robbie Brekke regresses, by normal standards. He becomes an excellent actor but has no ordinary memory left. Caroline's primary change is in self-acceptance. Having seen better and worse lives in her own memories, she comes to value her present, imperfect life more.

The novel invents a near-future world affected by several concerns of the late twentieth century: epidemics, environmentalism and its backlash, new religious paradigms, and reincarnation. They make a heady mix, but Nancy Kress's imagination is equal to it. Many novels featuring new plagues have been best-sellers, including Stephen King's *The Stand* (1978), Michael Crichton's *The Andromeda Strain* (1969), and Connie Willis' award-winning *Doomsday Book* (1992). Among the first of many proenvironment novels was Ernest Callenbach's *Ecotopia: The Notebooks and Reports of William Weston* (1975). Reincarnation is seldom a premise of serious science fiction; it more often occurs in light fantasies. Kress brings all these ideas together in a compelling tale. The theories are offered tentatively and subtly; the reader may have no idea that the author is sending a message. Rather, she seems to be examining ideas in the manner of a playful philosopher.

Kress started her career as a fantasy author. Even in her three early novels, she showed a bent for metaphysical speculation. With her Nebula Award-winning story "Out of All Them Bright Stars" (1985) and her novel of alien contact *An Alien Light* (1988), she joined the ranks of innovative science-fiction writers. Some critics have underrated her contributions to the field. Brain Rose received a more positive response.

—*Emily Alward*

BRAIN WAVE

Human and animal mental abilities expand rapidly, causing technological and societal changes

Author: Poul Anderson (1926–2001)
Genre: Science fiction—superbeing
Type of work: Novel
Time of work: The present
Locale: The United States
First published: 1954

THE STORY

For the past one hundred million years, Earth has been passing through some sort of force field that inhibits brain functions. As the story opens, Earth has moved out of the field's power, with the result that earthly brains now possess much more intelligence. The majority of the story explains the results of this change on science, religion, government, and other elements of society. The plot is somewhat disjointed because Poul Anderson often switches characters and locale. This approach gives the novel a realistic, journalistic-like feel.

The opening pages describe intellectual improvements in an animal, a mentally retarded human (Archie Brock), and an intelligent ten-year-old boy. On the estate where he works, Archie sees changes in animals and begins to realize what has happened to him. Eventually, all the employees except Archie leave for better prospects elsewhere. Newspaper reports are included to show the wide scope of the changes.

Several scientists, including Peter Corinth, Felix Mandelbaum, Nat Lewis, and Helga Arnulfson, discuss these changes among themselves and with their families. Peter Corinth, a resident of New York City, walks to work and reflects on the changes he sees around him.

At this point, Anderson summarizes some of the large-scale effects in language and natural science. Other places around the world are shown dealing with their own changes. In Africa, a group of black people headed by M'Wanzi attempts to throw off the yolk of white oppressors. In Russia, people revolt against the totalitarian government. On a personal level, a relationship is established between scientists Peter and Helga; Peter's wife, Sheila, hates the change and cannot deal with it. Some religious groups also have a hard time accepting the tremendous intellectual alterations, as shown in the rage of the followers of the Third Ba'al.

Archie goes to town for supplies and is presented with the opportunity to join a new socioeconomic system that does without money or ownership. Archie refuses and returns to the estate, where he is more comfortable. Later in the book, Archie is shown still living there, this time with others like him.

Anderson introduces the idea that people are more sensitive to others than before by using parentheses to show implied meanings that do not have to be spoken. People now can sense the feelings of others and inter-pret the smallest gestures. The Sensitives provide a more exaggerated example of this ability: They use telepathy.

Negative reactions to the change continue. It becomes difficult to keep order in the cities, and some people complain about thinking so much. Some of these people attempt to create machinery that will generate an artificial inhibitor field around Earth much like the one that previously caused the stagnation of intellect. Felix Mandelbaum works slowly for better social organization through negotiation.

On a positive note, scientists discover faster-than-light travel. When the first starship is completed, Peter Corinth and Nat Lewis are selected as its first two passengers. They explore several worlds, allowing Anderson to discuss the evolution of intelligence. The starship returns, and the plot to set up the artificial field is thwarted.

At the novel's conclusion, Anderson takes one more look at Archie. Readers understand that his type will take over Earth and that the more advanced will head for the stars, where they can set up a new society free from Earth's restraints.

ANALYSIS

Anderson's *Brain Wave* is an interesting attempt at extrapolation in which he introduces one unusual circumstance (Earth escapes a force that has inhibited intelligence) and works out the logical consequences. One reason the novel succeeds is the author's ability to show the human trauma of such an increase in intelligence. People riot, abandon work, go insane, form odd cults full of fear and hatred, and wish for the "good old days."

Although the novel shows such trauma, Anderson counters it with positive scenes. People create a starship, oppressive governments are challenged, many stay at their jobs, small towns experiment with various methods of government and work, and language and gestures become more sensitive and more universal. Anderson seems to say that people always will face new challenges, but they can overcome them, given time and patience. As he once said, "To hell with fatuous optimism and fashionable despair. Given guts and luck, we may prevail. Win or lose, the effort is infinitely worth making."

A key feature in this novel, common to much of Anderson's work, is the thorough handling of science, not surprising given Anderson's formal training in physics. In *Brain Wave*, Anderson discusses neural impulses. He assumes that faster and more intense electrochemical reactions in the neurons would produce a dramatic rise in intelligence. He also spends time exploring the idea of an electromagnetic force field that can inhibit brain functions. These theories may not hold true in the real world, but Anderson gives explanations that are plausible within the context of the story. When he explains the design of the starship, he muses about faster-than-light speed, wave mechanics, and atomic energy. He devotes considerable space to speculations about intelligence—its evolution, why it leveled off, and possible results of contact with other intelligent beings in the universe.

Anderson also comments critically on modern life. Peter Corinth sees the initial chaos as understandable, given the nature of life before the rise in intellectual abilities. He mentions the dull work, the lack of direction, the lack of intellectual stimulation, the large amounts of time wasted in front of television sets, and the continual buying frenzy. He says there is "an inward hollowness . . . an unconscious realization that there ought to be more in life than one's own . . . self." He believes that people with increased mental functions are shocked at their useless and narrow lives. In addition, Anderson criticizes the government's tendency to keep everything secret and the poor job newspapers do of informing the public.

Anderson has the ability not only to discuss scientifically interesting topics but also to remember the human consequences of change. This combination of humanity and technology is the mark of an author who makes good use of the possibilities of science fiction.

—*Gary Zacharias*

Brasyl

Three different eras of Brazilian history blend to deliver a thriller about the nature of the multiverse. In the "present," we follow a producer of reality television. In the future, our point-of-view is street urchin. And in the past, explorers journey up the mystery of the mighty Amazon and into the darkest jungle, both psychical and real.

Author: Ian McDonald (1960–)
Genre: Science Fiction—extrapolatory
Type of Work: Novel
Time of Plot: 2006; 2032; 1730s
Location: Brazil
First Published: 2007

The Story

Three threads—which, of course, all dovetail beautifully in the climax—alternate throughout this book.

The first string of plot concerns Marcelina Hoffman, a TV producer in Rio in the year 2006. (But is Marcelina's continuum precisely ours, or another? Small clues seem to indicate an alternate reality.) Marcelina is not really a very nice person. Her reality shows are gruesome, degrading, or exploitive. Her latest project concerns a disgraced soccer star, Barbosa. Her search for the elderly reclusive man takes her across many strata of Brazil's society, giving us an intimate view of a land full of riches and poverty. But soon Marcelina's efforts are being undermined by a mysterious stranger—a woman who could be her twin, and who has murderous intentions toward Marcelina.

Our second strand takes place in the years 2032–33. We follow the seedy exploits of Edson de Freitas, a guttersnipe with some native wit and compassion. Living a rough life, menaced by fellow toughs on one side and authorities on the other, Edson still manages to fall in love with a woman named Fia Kishida, an expert in quantum physics who has turned her talents to illicit ends. When Fia is killed, Edson is bereft. But then a second Fia appears, unfortunately bringing on her tail trained assassins named "admonitories."

Finally, we inhabit colonial-era Brazil of the 1730s. Father Luis Quinn, an Irish

Jesuit, has been sent up the Amazon to confront a rogue priest named Father Diego Gonçalves, who is fashioning a heart-of-darkness empire in the jungle. Luckily, Quinn acquires a boon companion, a French "geometer" named Dr. Robert Falcon. Together, the two men will battle deadly natives and the hostile environment to thwart Father Diego's mad schemes and, in the process, crack the very code of the multiverse.

ANALYSIS

The brilliant British SF writer John Brunner perfected a type of monitory near-future novel that seemed "ripped from the headlines" and which demonstrated a globalist mindset and a mimetic fidelity to characterization, especially amongst a large cast of various types. Brunner's awesome quartet—*Stand on Zanzibar* (1968); *The Jagged Orbit* (1969); *The Sheep Look Up* (1972); and *The Shockwave Rider* (1975)—seemed at the time to portend a revolution in science fiction. But shortly after the last volume, the escapist pleasures of *Star Wars* (1977) dethroned Brunner's approach and came to dominate the field.

But some authors, such as Kim Stanley Robinson and Bruce Sterling, did subsequently take up the Brunnerian banner. And Ian McDonald certainly constitutes one of the newer members of that group. (Although he is quite capable of old-fashioned, Jack-Williamson-style, sense-of-wonder SF, as seen in his dimension-hopping *Everness* series.) Having perfected a wonderful set of techniques and narrative strategies, both panoramic and microscopic, in his prior big book, *River of Gods* (2004), a future history of India, McDonald went on to employ that suite of tools in *Brasyl*, but with certain obvious modifications, starting obviously with the switch in continents and the necessary differences in characters and cultural stylings. He would go on to round out this nebulously affiliated "Nationalist Trilogy" with *The Dervish House* (2010), set in futuristic Turkey.

McDonald faced a famous obstacle when he chose Brazil as his focus. "Brazil is the country of the future—and always will be!" So runs the old joke, indicating that Brazil's vast potential will remain forever untapped, due to a confluence of circumstances. Thus, too few SF writers pay any attention to Latin America in general. Lucius Shepard was one exception, but certainly the seminal work on the subject from the Golden Age, which still sustains our attention today, is L. Sprague de Camp's *Viagens Interplanetarias* series. McDonald's insight and courage are fully up to de Camp's, and these skills allow him to buck the common wisdom.

Achieving something like a samba sideways through time, *Brasyl* is hot and tropical and full of music (there's a suggested soundtrack in the back of the novel). The book finds more than enough materials and promise in this developing land to support its conceit of cosmic magnitude. (Don't imagine you can guess the ultimate ending because you can't!) McDonald manages to work simultaneously at many levels, from the intimate and individual to the societal and universal. And he always embodies his themes in minutely particularized images and descriptions, both quotidian and fantastical. His characters are utterly believable, grounded in their unique pasts and presents. And typical of his more science-fictional speculations is his invention of "Q blades," knives with quantum edges that can sever reality. They steal the show every time they appear.

In Marcelina's sections, we get a story built of equal parts Norman Spinrad (the sardonic media satire) and Fritz Leiber (the crosstime shenanigans). In Edson's parts, McDonald distills John Brunner, Bruce Sterling, and William Gibson, producing his own unique hard liquor. And in the Quinn action, we've got flavors of Neal Stephenson blended with Howard Hendrix. And don't forget that all three sections authentically render the Brazilian milieu as deftly as native writer Jorge Amado would.

The result is a tripartite thriller that whipsaws the reader's expectations and enjoyment around like a motorcycle ride straight down Sugarloaf Mountain itself. As Dr. Falcon writes in his journal, "Brazil turns hyperbole into reality." Call what McDonald does here, then, "hyper-real SF."

—*Paul Di Filippo*

BRAVE NEW WORLD

Three misfits illustrate the flaws of a future world-state in which technology permits complete control of people and the government claims to provide happiness to everyone

Author: Aldous Huxley (1894–1963)
Genre: Science fiction—dystopia
Type of work: Novel
Time of work: Half a millennium in the future
Location: What are now the United Kingdom and the United States
First published: 1932

THE STORY

In the totalitarian state of *Brave New World*, people are socially conditioned from conception; they are hatched from test tubes rather than born. Something, however, is wrong with Bernard Marx. Although he ought to be, in keeping with everyone else in this engineered society, an absolute conformist, he evinces certain quirks that his fellows find disturbing. They theorize that something must have gone wrong chemically during his incubation. Bernard dates Lenina Crowne, but he wants her all to himself. This is against the mores of their society, which prescribes communal sexual relations and proscribes monogamous pairing. Lenina is outraged by his request for monogamy. Any contravention of the societal motto of "Community, Identity, Stability" is regarded as a heinous offense.

Happiness is not an individual quest; it is a daily, community guarantee. Through early conditioning, people are educated to be happy for what they are allotted, with allotments made according to class, which is determined at conception. A drug called soma provides a haven from any temporary unhappiness.

Lenina and Bernard, on vacation, visit an Indian reservation in New Mexico that is a mixture of living museum and circus. There they find John, who was reared on the reservation by his mother, Linda, a woman from Western Europe. John later is revealed to be the illegitimate son of the director of the Bloomsbury Hatchery. As someone outside mainstream society, he is able to find flaws in it. He has escaped the universal conditioning and has steeped himself in the works of a forbidden author, William Shakespeare. A collection of Shakespeare's works is the only book he has ever read. He is imbued with the spirit of drama and finds the utter placidity of the present world an affront to the human spirit: riskless, monotonous, and amoral. When Lenina, who fancies him, disrobes in preparation for a guiltless sexual episode, he rejects her for her whorishness even though he is in love with her.

After his mother's death from an overdose of soma, John attempts to subvert some workers who are about to receive their allocation of the drug. This causes a riot, which results in the banishment to Iceland of Bernard and Helmholtz Watson, another "flawed" person. Mustapha Mond, controller of Western Europe, refuses to extend this sentence to John, wanting to keep him nearby so that he can study him.

John retreats from the world into a lighthouse, where he flagellates himself for his sins. He is recorded doing so by a reporter with a sound camera, and this footage is made into a "feelie," a film with sensations added, that receives widespread

Aldous Huxley. (Library of Congress)

attention. Tourists arrive in helicopters to gawk at this curious creature who cultivates his own pain. Among them is Lenina. John lashes her and, as she writhes on the ground, himself. This drives the onlookers into an orgiastic frenzy, which catches John up in its license. The next day, when he realizes to what degrading ends his self-mortification has been put, he hangs himself.

ANALYSIS
Brave New World sold more than fifteen thousand copies in its first year and has been in print ever since. It has joined the ranks of utopian/dystopian satires such as Jonathan Swift's *Gulliver's Travels* (1726) and George Orwell's *Animal Farm* (1945). The author himself has said that he wanted to warn against the conditioning of human beings by a manager class with the latest technology at its fingertips. Humanity could lose its soul through such a process, Aldous Huxley feared, trading in its unique qualities in exchange for security and for drugged and directed "happiness."

There cannot have been a year since its publication in which this novel has not been compared to the present condition of humanity and found to be a perspicacious guess at the shape of things to come. Huxley, for example, did not exactly predict television, but he foresaw other means of mass hypnosis.

An ingenious and persuasive writer, Huxley renders his analogue quite credibly, although requirements of his genre necessitated more conflict than would be plausible in a state as well managed as the one the novel presents. The characters for the most part think too much like Huxley and too little like people who have been brainwashed into conformity.

Huxley's vision of sexuality in this futuristic society anticipates the repressive desublimation of a world in which the social obligation to be sexual defuses passion. This vision runs into trouble because the only choices permitted to his protagonist are a sulky celibacy and a foreordained and regulated promiscuity. The liberating powers of a passionate sexuality are left out of Huxley's equation even though, when he includes a few nonconformists, he allows that there can be exceptions in this totalitarian society. It becomes a question, then, of why some exceptions exist and not others; there is no reason for the lack of a female equivalent to Bernard or Helmholtz.

Huxley in essence equates happiness with barbarism and unhappiness with culture. The happiness, however, is shown to be false. Characters all evince signs of deep disturbance. True happiness must be what they are missing. One can ask why Huxley did not portray a more efficient society, one that was able to erase this distinction between the true and the false. It may be precisely this flaw in the novel that explains its continuing popularity.

—David Bromige

THE BREAST

David Alan Kepesh, a thirty-eight-year-old professor of literature, copes with his transformation into a human breast

Author: Philip Roth (1933–)
Genre: Fantasy—magical realism
Type of work: Novella
Time of work: 1971–1972
Locale: New York City
First published: 1972

THE STORY
The narrator, David Kepesh, recounts the changes that occurred in his life in the preceding two years, beginning with the peculiar sensations he felt in his penis. These sensations of increased sensitivity, accompanied by increased sexual desire, led to the change that took place between midnight and 4 a.m. on February 18, 1971. Kepesh became a six-foot, 155-pound human female breast. The novella chronicles Kepesh's responses to his condition, which vary from acceptance to a conviction that he has become mad.

The novella is divided into five sections. In the first, Kepesh describes his "symptoms" before the change from man to mammary. He details his sexual feelings for Claire, the twenty-five-year-old woman he has been seeing for three years. The cooling of his desire for her during the past year changed right before his transformation: He felt excruciatingly sensitive while making love to her, but only because his penis was becoming a nipple and areola and the rest of his body was becoming a huge breast disconnected from any human form. Up to this point, Kepesh's life had been stable for the first time in more than a decade, and his relationship with Claire provided warmth and security without "the accompanying burden of dependence, or the grinding boredom" of most marriages with which he was familiar. That comfort, however, vanished with his metamorphosis.

In the second section, Kepesh is tended to first by Dr. Gordon, his physician, and then Dr. Klinger, his psychiatrist of six years. Gordon informs Kepesh that he is in Lenox Hill Hospital in Manhattan and describes the little that is known about the hormonal imbalance that has created Kepesh's condition. Klinger then talks with Kepesh, who can speak and hear through his nipple, about his feelings. Kepesh rants about his inability to go mad and his uncanny ability, which he thinks arises from his fear of death, to put "one foot in front of the other" in an earnest way, no matter what the circumstances. His will to live is as persistent as his sexual desires.

Kepesh begins to come to terms with his new sexuality in the third section, feeling as if he would like to have sex with Claire or the nurse who washes him in the hospital. He conjures up graphic and highly imaginative ways for a breast to have sex with a woman, but he decides finally to satisfy himself with the arousal provided by Claire's kisses and by bathings he receives from the fifty-six-year-old nurse, Miss Clark. He imagines that if he were to give in to his desires, his "appetites could only become progressively strange, until at last [he] reached a peak of disorientation from which [he] would fall—or leap—into the void." He decides to have his nipple sprayed with a mild anesthetizing solution before Miss Clark's ablutions, and he refrains from asking Claire to perform more deeds than she suggests.

In the final two sections, Kepesh becomes convinced that he is mad and that his training as a professor of literature has brought on his condition. He wonders whether his reading of surreal and fantastic literature by Franz Kafka and Nikolai Gogol has in some way affected his mind.

In the last pages, the reader is fifteen months into Kepesh's condition and is still not given a definitive answer: Is Kepesh hallucinating, or has he simply become the female breast that he loved as an infant and as a man?

ANALYSIS

Published when Philip Roth was thirty-eight years old, the same age as Kepesh, *The Breast* was Roth's sixth major work and buttressed his reputation as a gifted comic writer who often deals with sexual themes. The Breast is more than merely a puerile joke, however; it deals comically with serious issues such as psychological wholeness, the integration of the flesh and spirit, and the limits of human desire.

Roth's peculiar tale about the transformation of a man into a female breast does have literary precedents, of which both Roth and his character Kepesh are aware. In classical literature, Ovid's *The Metamorphoses* (c. 8 c.e.) retells hundreds of stories in which humans and gods become trees, flowers, rivers, and rain; the modern *The Metamorphosis* (1915), by Franz Kafka, one of Roth's favorite writers, tells the story of a man turned into a cockroach. Another influence, and one mentioned by Kepesh, is Gogol's story "The Nose" (1836), in which a nose becomes a high-ranking bureaucrat.

What separates Roth's story from his influences is his narrative technique. Unlike Ovid, Kafka, and Gogol, Roth chooses a first-person narrator for his novella, creating a question in the reader's mind about the reliability of the narrator. Has the transformation actually taken place, or, as Kepesh himself wonders, has it simply occurred in his mind? The first-person narrator allows Roth to create comic moments through the incongruity of placing a man's sexually obsessed brain inside a female breast, while also addressing psychological issues concerning repression, wish fulfillment, and the influence of literary works. Although the reader can never be sure about the transformation from man to breast, the novella loses some force if it is determined that the transformation has taken place only in the character's mind. Roth walks a thin line, allowing the reader to question the reality of the change but never letting his story slip out of the realm of the fantastic.

—*Kevin Boyle*

BRIAR ROSE

Becca Berlin attempts to fulfill her grandmother's last wish and learn her heritage

Author: Jane Yolen (1939–)
Genre: Fantasy—heroic fantasy
Type of work: Novel
Time of work: Primarily the 1990's, with flashbacks to World War II
Locale: Boston, Massachusetts; and Warsaw, Poland
First published: 1992

THE STORY

Briar Rose is one of the Fairy Tale Series created for Ace, then later published by Tor. *Briar Rose* is a later book in the series. Each novel in the collection is by a different author and is a twentieth century story based on a traditional fairy tale.

In this case, the basis is "Sleeping Beauty." The heroine of *Briar Rose* is Becca Berlin, a young Jewish woman who grew up hearing her grandmother (nicknamed Gemma) tell the tale. Shortly before Gemma dies, she tells Becca that the familiar bedtime story is no fantasy: The old woman was the princess who woke to a prince's kiss. Gemma begs Becca to find the castle where it happened, and her granddaughter promises to do so.

Gemma's background is a mystery even to her family. All Becca has to guide her is a box of Gemma's mementos, discovered only after the grandmother's death, and the fact that Gemma immigrated to America in 1944. Even the immigration papers turn out to be nearly useless, however; many of the questions on them are unanswered, and Becca is not sure the papers are her grandmother's. She deciphers them and learns that they belong to Gitl Rose Mandlestein, who was married and pregnant. Gitl's physical description fits Gemma, but the only nickname listed is Ksiniczka. Becca is stunned when she learns that the name is Polish for "princess." The date of Gitl's marriage and her home village and district in Poland are not provided.

Becca takes her research with her to her job at a local newspaper. Stan, her editor and close friend, is intrigued by the mystery and decides to help Becca. They visit Fort Oswego, New York, once a refugee camp for Jews and now a museum. Becca interviews several former refugees and finds one who recognizes Gemma's photo and says he was in a concentration camp in Chełmno, Poland, with her. Becca is startled to learn that it was an old castle renovated by the Nazis. The interviewee's mention of barbed wire reminds Becca of the thorns surrounding the castle in Gemma's fairy tale. Hoping to learn more, Becca goes to Poland to locate Chełmno. Her grandmother may have been held there, but no woman is known to have survived the camp.

Once in Poland, Becca finds the village of Chełmno, but the townspeople are withdrawn and uncooperative. Finally, a priest leads Becca to Josef Potocki, who had been a member of the Polish Resistance during the war and knows about Chełmno. The kindly old man recognizes Gemma at once and reveals his partisan codename: Potocki means "prince." His work in the resistance involved spying on vans leaving Chełmno and counting the corpses dumped in the nearby woods. One day, he and a fellow spy called Avenger found Gemma barely alive at a dump site. She had survived the gas chambers. Avenger administered mouth-to-mouth resuscitation, reviving the girl, and took her to the partisans' forest hideout. The two fell in love and were married, but during the next mission, Avenger was shot dead. He had told his bride his real name, Aron Mandlestein. After a close call with the Nazis, Josef and Gemma were separated. Josef never knew whether or not his princess had reached safety. Now, after meeting her granddaughter, he knows that Gemma did, and Becca has discovered her heritage.

ANALYSIS

It is difficult to place *Briar Rose* in the category of typical fantasy because the plot contains very little concerning magic or the supernatural. The fairy tale around which the novel revolves serves as a metaphor and can be used as a framework for a story in any setting. The basis of this twentieth century novel is a traditional fairy tale full of magic, so *Briar Rose* can be categorized as fantasy. In addition, one of the main criteria for a fantasy or fairy tale is a protagonist who defeats incredible odds and wins; both the metaphor and plot of *Briar Rose* contain this ingredient.

Historically, fairy tales were intended for adult audiences and were much more brutal than the versions one might now hear as a child. For example, Walt Disney's G-rated film *Sleeping Beauty* (1959) bears almost no resemblance to a sixteenth century Venetian telling, wherein the ensorcelled princess is made pregnant during her sleep and wakes to discover herself a mother. That version probably stems from an even older version with several variations.

The trends leading to Jane Yolen's Briar Rose had been developing for more than a century. Victorian writers were instrumental in altering stories such as "Sleeping Beauty" to make them fit for young readers. The resulting collections of tales were favored by adults as well because of the fine illustrations.

The early twentieth century saw an outpouring of classic fantasies, among them *The Once and Future King* (1958) by T. H. White. These books often were based on old legends, but they were not for children alone. Since their advent, such books have been classified as adult fantasy. As a result of the popularity of that category, even mainstream authors have tried their hand at writing fantasy. Some of their books, such as Patricia McKillip's *The Forgotten Beasts of Eld* (1974), use the wording and symbolism of old stories to build new ones. *Briar Rose* is based more precisely on a single story. Like the other books in the Fairy Tale Series, it concentrates on giving the tale a modern flavor, making it appealing to a wider audience.

Briar Rose is one of Yolen's later works. Her prolific career began in 1963 and has focused on children's books and fantasies for all ages. Examples include *The Girl Who Loved the Wind* (1972), which won the Lewis Carroll Shelf Award and was a Children's Book Showcase Selection. *Briar Rose* itself was named an American Library Association Best Book for Young Adults and was nominated for the 1992 Nebula Award.

Other books in the Fairy Tale Series include *The Sun, the Moon, and the Stars* (1987) by Steven Brust, *Jack the Giant-Killer* (1987) by Charles de Lint, *The Nightingale* (1988) by Kara Dalkey, *Snow White and Rose Red* (1989) by Patricia C. Wrede, and *Tam Lin* (1991) by Pamela Dean.

—*Carla Hall Minor*

THE BRICK MOON

An artificial moon built to aid navigation is launched accidentally with thirty-seven people inside

Author: Edward Everett Hale (1822-1919)
Genre: Science fiction—technocratic
Type of work: Novel
Time of work: 1842-1872
Locale: Naguadavick, Tamworth, and other imaginary places in New England
First published: 1971 (in *His Level Best and Other Stories*, 1872; serial form, *The Atlantic*, 1869-1870)

THE STORY

One day in the early 1840's, several Harvard students are discussing astronomy. Someone notes that the North Star makes it easy for sailors to calculate latitude (distance from the equator) but that no corresponding heavenly body assists in the calculation of longitude. As a consequence, many lives have been lost at sea. One of the students, identified only as Q., half-seriously suggests launching an artificial satellite—a brick moon—to correct this heavenly deficiency.

The subject is dropped, and the students go their separate ways. Seventeen years later, one of them, George Orcutt, calls the group back together. He has become a wealthy railroad magnate and proposes to put some of his money into the satellite experiment. Another member of the original group, Ben Brannan, is a noted orator who raises more funds for the project. The story's narrator, Captain Frederic Ingham, a minister, finds the area best suited for carrying out the project. An unsettled forest has the clay for brick and streams to provide the power for the giant flywheels that will send the sphere into the sky.

By late fall a few years after the Civil War, construction is almost complete. Orcutt and a number of families decide to winter at the isolated construction site and, for warmth, move into the moon, which contains a number of braced chambers. One night when all aboard are asleep, a shifting of the ground causes the moon to slide down the rails to the flywheels, which hurtle it into space.

Ingham and the other partners left on the ground spend a futile year scanning the skies for the orb, which has not gone into the orbit that was prescribed for it. By chance, the moon is rediscovered, and Ingham, who has obtained the job of caretaker of a disused observatory, trains his telescope on the satellite. He can detect thirty-seven people standing in a line, making alternating short and long leaps in order to communicate in Morse code.

The moon had retained its atmosphere when sent aloft. It was stocked with food supplies, including poultry and plants, for the work crew that was to return in spring. The moon's nearness to the Sun and relatively large size (two hundred feet in diameter) have made it suitable for farming.

Those on the ground are able to communicate with those in space, but they can devise no way to return the moon dwellers to Earth. This turns out to be far from a drawback to those on the satellite; they grow contented with their withdrawal from the cares of the world. The story ends with those above feeling decidedly better off than those below.

ANALYSIS

Edward Everett Hale wrote about a variety of topics, authoring sixty books, though he wrote little science fiction. His most celebrated work in that genre, *The Brick Moon*, shares the concerns of his mainstream fiction and satirizes some of the traits of Hale's native New England. *The Brick Moon* is a short book, sometimes referred to as a story, that combines the stories "The Brick Moon" (1869) and "Life in the Brick Moon" (1870).

Today Hale is remembered primarily for his short novel *The Man Without a Country*, the title work of an 1863 collection. It tells of a man who had participated in Aaron Burr's abortive rebellion against the United States and who forswears allegiance to his country when on trial. He is condemned to spend the remainder of his life at sea, where he dies a broken man.

The Brick Moon dwells on these themes of exile and irremedial severance of ties to homeland, though it transforms them to a lighter key. Its tone is less serious; major characters are isolated not because of criminal behavior but because of their zeal to be society's benefactors. Furthermore, they go aloft as a large party, not as one sequestered individual, and so live with genial company and clear consciences.

Unlike the more serious, earlier story, however, *The Brick Moon* is a satire on the manners and character of Boston. This city had established itself, up to the Civil War, as the cultural center of the nation and, equally, as a hotbed of progressive social movements. Local writers such as Hale and, later, Henry James poked fun at some of the excesses of the metropolis. In James's *The Bostonians* (1885–1886), for example, barbs are aimed at the unhealthy atmosphere of radical faddism that pervaded many Boston salons. Hale, with less venom, laughs quietly at these characteristic Boston reformers both when they extravagantly plan to improve the universe by adding a new moon to it and when their scheme goes dreadfully awry.

The satellite is no benefit to navigation, but—and here is another prime point of Hale's satire—the astronauts are happier in orbit than they had been on Earth. Hale may have been thinking of how traumatic internecine conflict on Earth had been for national unity, as evidenced by the Civil War. He was probably also thinking of the oft-heard complaint that Bostonians believed themselves superior to all other beings. What better place for such types than on a moon from which they can look down on their inferiors?

In Hale's day, science fiction did not hold the prominent place in literature that it would later. More significant was utopian fiction, which envisioned ideal societies. Hale's piece shows some affinities with this form. Although *The Brick Moon* lays down no elaborate blueprints for a future world, the author does seem to be ruefully commenting that a more ideal society than existed would be made up of people with similar backgrounds and tastes, such as those who came to live on the brick orb.

—*James Feast*

THE BRIDGE

Lying in a coma after an automobile accident, a young Scots engineer encounters the dark side of technology in the nightmare world of the bridge

Author: Iain Banks (1954-2013)
Genre: Fantasy—dystopia
Type of work: Novel
Time of work: The early 1980's
Locale: Edinburgh, Scotland, and various dream worlds
First published: 1986

THE STORY

The Bridge is a critique of a world in which limitless faith in science and instrumental reason has impoverished human life by denying all truths that cannot be accounted for in the narrow terms of science and rationality. The novel weaves together several apparently distinct narratives whose protagonists may be seen as dream-projections of a single character, who is never directly named.

At the beginning of the novel, this unnamed man lies in the wreckage of a car crash, crushed but still alive. As he loses consciousness, he slips into a bizarre dream. The narrative abruptly switches to a bizarre, dystopian society built entirely upon a seemingly endless bridge. Here, another man, John Orr, is recounting this very dream to his psychotherapist.

A victim of amnesia, Orr does not know who he is or where he comes from. When he is not in therapy, he tries to find out more about the bridge that he must now call home. His attempts, however, are continually frustrated. The bridge's social and bureaucratic organization is as labyrinthine as its physical construction and its technological infrastructure, all of which frequently break down. Taking advantage of the chaos surrounding one such breakdown, he stows away on a train and begins a nightmare odyssey through a landscape ravaged by war and war's atrocities.

Three other narratives weave in and out of Orr's experiences on and off the bridge. In the first, the victim of the crash that began the novel is rushed to the hospital and placed in intensive care. In the second, a bloodthirsty Scots swordsman swashbuckles his way through magic worlds of sorcerers and enchantresses. The third—and central—narrative follows the career of a young Scots engineer, whose youthful, idealistic self is progressively being smothered by his growing affluence, and who seems about to lose Andrea, the woman whom he has loved since his student days. The engineer's prosperous but increasingly unsatisfying life almost ends when he drunkenly crashes his luxury sports car on the Forth Bridge leading into Edinburgh. It is in the hospital room in which he emerges from his coma that all the separate story lines converge. The adventures of John Orr on the bridge and of the swordsman among sorcerers fall into place as the dreamwork in which the engineer confronts the values by which he has lived and recovers his true identity.

ANALYSIS

Although dystopian fantasy has long been an established genre within British literature, the British novelistic tradition has tended to regard fantasy as a fringe element. The social upheavals of the 1980's, however, stimulated a number of novelists to break out of the confines of social and psychological realism by incorporating fantasy or Magical Realism as critical perspectives on a society increasingly seen as riddled with crises. Iain Banks (who publishes his works of fantasy under his name without the middle initial M., which is reserved for his science fiction) explored the world of the psychosexual bizarre in his first novel, *The Wasp Factory* (1984), and developed the technique of intermingling realistic and apparently fantastic story lines to accomplish similar ends in *Walking on Glass* (1985). *The Bridge* employs this technique to mount a full-scale critique of a materialist modern world in which reason has successfully outlawed any dimension of experience and any subjective reality that does not conform to the iron laws of scientific empiricism.

In the conventionally "realistic" narrative, the engineer is in danger of losing himself and the woman he loves because he embraces the cold, objective logic of scientific reasoning and rejects all "faiths," which he sees as nonsensical. He becomes increasingly distanced from his lover, Andrea, who is interested in various forms of the "irrational," such as astrology and the prophecies of Nostradamus. A life built on rationality and on material acquisitions brings him mounting unhappiness and eventually precipitates the crisis—the crash and ensuing coma—in which he must descend into the depths of his own being in order to gain wisdom and be born anew.

Fantasy for Banks is the mode that can best accommodate this kind of psychic exploration. It is also ideally suited to social critique, because it can depict the full horror of a bureaucratic, technology-driven world by depicting it in a different register, providing the distance necessary for a critical assessment. *The Bridge* repeatedly points up parallels between the fantasy world of the bridge and the "real" world of the engineer who dreams it, making frequent allusions to contemporary events of the 1980's: the war between Britain and Argentina over the Falklands/Malvinas, the Israeli invasion of southern Lebanon, the development of the American "Star Wars" Strategic Defense Initiative, and above all the trend in national and international politics signaled by the electoral triumphs of President Ronald Reagan in the United States and Prime Minister Margaret Thatcher in the United Kingdom. The fantastic elements of the novel serve to perform one of the traditional British novel's time-honored functions—reporting on the state of the nation and pinpointing the causes of social and psychological malaise.

Although a modern reader will inevitably perceive the engineer's story as the novel's ground and the fantasy narratives as psychic projections, crucial to the purpose of *The Bridge* is the insistence that none of the various worlds depicted is more "real" than any other. The choice that the protagonist and the reader are offered is not a choice between dream and reality but between two different dreams. The so-called "real" world is just as much a nightmare as the bridge, and the engineer learns that his belief in science and technology to the exclusion of other dimensions of being is not only another faith but also an inferior one created by its own sorcerers and populated by its own demons.

—*Michael Harper*

THE BRIGADIER FFELLOWES STORIES

Brigadier Ffellowes, a retired British artillery officer with mysterious intelligence connections, tells stories of his adventurous youth to a gentleman's club

Author: Sterling Lanier (1927–2007)
Genre: Fantasy—mythological
Type of work: Stories
Time of work: Primarily the early twentieth century
Locale: A New York City club and various exotic locations
First published: *The Peculiar Exploits of Brigadier Ffellowes* (1972) and *The Curious Quests of Brigadier Ffellowes* (1986)

THE STORY

The two volumes of Brigadier Ffellowes stories contain the title character's exploits as told to members of his New York club. With the exception of the final story, all were published in *The Magazine of Fantasy and Science Fiction* between 1968 and 1982. The first volume begins with "His Only Safari" (1970). Ffellowes is in the forested Abadare hills of Kenya in December, 1939, looking for an Axis agent who is also an Egyptologist. Ffellowes is hunted by the Kerit (Nandi Bear), which is amazingly clever. He finds the agent, who grasps his theory that the Kerits drove the proto-Egyptians north. The agent becomes a Kerit and is killed along with the other hunting Kerit.

"The Kings of the Sea" (1968) is set in Sweden in 1938. An accidental meeting with Baron Nyderstrom, whose nurse has ill-advisedly tried to rid him of some old paraphernalia, leads to a crisis meeting with Jormungandir's Children, the monstrous Old Norse precursors. Nyderstrom is the last of the kings who can intercede with them and does so, to save the world. He emerges happily, having met his future bride.

"His Coat so Gay" (1970) takes place in Middleburg, a town in the eastern United States, in the early 1930's. Canler Waldron, a young head of his family, invites his friend Ffellowes to hunt. Although Ffellowes offends his host by not wearing a traditional English pink coat (he belongs to a special brightly clad society), Canler's family wears green. Ffellowes and Canler's sister Betty fall in love. As a result, Betty saves him when, at the Irish Feast of Sam'Hain, Canler vengefully causes various creatures such as the Dead Horse and the Firbolgs to hunt him as a sacrificial English foe.

"The Leftovers" (1969) places Ffellowes in the Ha-dhramaut of Oman in 1924. He strays too close to the shore, avoiding the desert, and barely escapes being eaten by Paleolithic cannibals.

In 1941, in the aftermath of the German invasion, Ffellowes and his Greek companion are shipwrecked on an island in "A Feminine Jurisdiction" (1969). A German officer, similarly stranded, tries to take command, but his arrogance results in his being destroyed by the sisters of Medusa.

In "Fraternity Brother" (1969), by taking the side of the local Spanish Pyrenean Basques against a brutal Spanish sergeant, Ffellowes earns an invitation to join the Society, a were-animal sect that has existed since Cro-Magnon times. "Soldier Key" (1968) puts Ffellowes adrift in the Caribbean Sea in 1934. He decides to look at Soldier Key, the home of the Church of the New Revelation. Brother Poole does not welcome him and warns him off before that night's ceremonies. A crew member vanishes, to be used as a sacrifice in the worship of hermit crabs (soldiers). Ffellowes kills a monstrously huge version of the crab and Poole, and he escapes.

The second volume of stories begins with "Ghost of a Crown" (1976). It is set in an unnamed time, but clearly a generation ago. Ffellowes visits his friend James, earl of Penruddock, at Avalon House in Cornwall. Also there is Lionel, James's evil younger brother, a great archaeologist. Since his arrival to work the ancient ruins of Caer Dubh, there have been serious disturbances. Ffellowes' research shows a connection, but James takes the lead on the crucial night. He becomes King Arthur and defeats Lionel and the Evil Prince whom Lionel wishes to resurrect, then becomes his old, dim self.

Trying to find ways to prevent the Japanese invasion of Singapore in 1940, Ffellowes in "And the Voice of the Turtle" (1972) calls at Palau Tuntong (Turtle Island). There he meets Strudwick, who in the early 1920's had been a fellow Cambridge scholar. A scientific genius, the recently married Strudwick is using his wife's money to study the turtles that are omnipresent and variform on the island. Ffellowes discovers not only that the malformed locals are related to turtles but also that they have a Head, the Father, a huge semihuman specimen. Ffellowes kills Strudwick and rescues his wife from sacrifice.

"The Father's Tale" (1974) is recounted from his father's story of 1881. While working off the coast of Sumatra on behalf of Rajah C. V. Brooke of Sarawak, Ffellowes senior rescues an Englishman who is almost dead. This man, Verner, reveals himself as obsessed by a mission on the western coast. All the previously loyal crew support him in hunting for the compound of the dead biologist Van Ouisthoven. When they find it, they must stop the *Matilda Briggs*. The problem is giant, intelligent rats that the ship is about to take from the island.

"Commander in the Mist" (1982) places Ffellowes in northern Austria in 1945. His patrol stops near the Danube and comes under threat from Marcus Aurelius, still defending the settlement of Paestrum against any form of barbarian. In "Thinking the Unthinkable" (1973), set in the summer of 1943, Ffellowes and a local friend try to find the famous Lipizzaner horses. They encounter a Dr. Hafstead, who challenges a monster and is taken by what appears to be a gigantic tentacle.

"The Brigadier in Check—and Mate" is the only previously unpublished story in the two volumes. The narrator is lost and meets Ffellowes and his strange wife, Phaona. Ffellowes tells a story set in Belize in 1947. Following stories of intelligent apes, an expedition discovers the last remaining descendants of Atlantis, including a princess, who clearly becomes Ffellowes' wife. The settlement is destroyed by an earthquake.

ANALYSIS

With three exceptions—"Ghost of a Crown," "The Father's Tale," and the last story—all the stories take place within the interwar period or during World War II. They often refer back to times that are now invested with an exotic magic. All the locations seem realistic as places for Ffellowes to have traveled, more than half being within the old British Empire. Sterling Lanier has researched his task thoroughly and carries conviction in each of his backgrounds. From the hills of Kenya to those of Belize, and to the Swedish and Sumatran coastlines, all the locations are credible, adding considerable weight to the stories. Lanier's most effective creation, however, is the storyteller himself.

Ffellowes, born about 1908, is in retirement in New York. It is clear from comments made at various times that he keeps in close contact with the intelligence community. He has strong affinities with Lord Dunsany's character Mr. Jorkens, yet he is the epitome of British sangfroid. In Lanier's appeal to the slightly distant past, his use of a relatively impotent narrator (Jim Parker, a younger American stockbroker), and his protagonist's almost sinister power to hold listeners, appearing unexpectedly and leaving tracelessly, the author is heavily influenced by Arthur Conan Doyle's Sherlock Holmes stories. He acknowledges this by giving the great detective a dominant, though pseudonymous, role in "The Father's Tale," which concerns, of all Holmesian subjects, the giant rat of Sumatra.

There is a less obvious but significant relationship to another Doyle character, the Frenchman Gerard, also a brigadier. Gerard's stories inevitably found him to misunderstand local customs and blunder, but to carry things off by sheer élan. Many of the stories consist of Ffellowes dragging more sensible natives into off-limits areas, only to imperil everybody's life and to learn, though not to acknowledge, that the native customs and beliefs were right. Lanier's portrayal of Ffellowes' air of command, wit, and intelligence sustains belief, while his sardonic authorial voice allows for subtle subversion. In the same way that Doyle's not-unsympathetic sketch allowed for questions as to whether the rules that Gerard breaks are logical or necessary, Lanier's more overtly respectful portrait is a critique of the British Empire and empire builders.

The real triumph of these volumes is one of delight in sheer storytelling. These are heir to *The Arabian Nights'* Entertainments of the fifteenth century and the "factual" travelers' tales of the late Middle Ages. The stories themselves are practically an anthology of leftovers from previous times: Nandi Bears, paleolithic cannibals and Atlanteans, and intrusions of monstrous shape such as Sumatran giant rats or turtle-men. Virtually every mythical creature, even the lost King Arthur and the Loch Ness monster, has a place in the pantheon. Lanier has the ability to develop tension and even to achieve pathos, as in the final scene of "The Father's Tale," when Van Ouisthoven rescues the last pathetic rat-child before killing it and himself.

Although stories such as "The Leftovers" and "Commander in the Mist" are mere scenarios, devoid of real plot, others, such as "His Coat so Gay" and "Ghost of a Crown," are masterpieces. Unfortunately, the last, previously unpublished story declines from a promising beginning into a sort of self-referential silliness that includes not merely the names of Edgar Rice Burroughs and L. Sprague de Camp but also gauche wordplay with the name of Philip José Farmer. It is, perhaps, Lanier's way of ending the series. In its exposure of Ffellowes as a mere fantasist, it is much more effective than a tumble over Reichenbach Falls.

—*Mike Dickinson*

BRING THE JUBILEE

In a world in which the South won the American Civil War, historian Hodge Backmaker travels back in time to study a battle site and accidentally alters the course of history

Author: (Joseph) Ward Moore (1903–1978)
Genre: Science fiction—alternate history
Type of work: Novel
Time of work: 1938–1952 and 1863
Location: An alternative United States of America

First published: 1953 (serial form, *The Magazine of Fantasy and Science Fiction*, 1952)

THE STORY
Bring the Jubilee has become a classic in the alternate-history subgenre of science fiction. The bulk of the novel is set in an alternative world years after the South won the American Civil War. This first-person memoir begins with young Hodge Backmaker leaving his backwater hometown for New York City in 1938. Life

in the twenty-six United States is hard. The War of Southron Independence, as the Civil War is known, has financially and spiritually crushed the North. Backmaker outlines an unfamiliar world in which the telegraph and gaslight are the norm, the wealthy own steam-driven "minibles" instead of automobiles, and the lower classes sell themselves into indentured servitude. The strong Confederate States stretch south from the Mason-Dixon Line into Mexico. Even the European landscape differs. Napoleon VI rules France, and Germany is known as the German Union.

After losing everything he owns to muggers on his first night in New York, Backmaker meets Roger Tyss, a bookseller and anti-Confederate revolutionary. Tyss gives Backmaker a job in his bookstore. Backmaker spends several years there, reading as much as he can and learning to think and study. He befriends René Enfandin, consul for the Republic of Haiti, who is an oddity in New York because he is black. Backmaker is crushed when Enfandin is shot and seriously wounded, forcing his return to Haiti.

At the age of twenty-three, Backmaker accepts an invitation to go to Haggershaven, an intellectual community in York, Pennsylvania. There, Backmaker becomes a well-regarded historian specializing in the War of Southron Independence. He marries and settles down, but he calls his own scholarship into question after receiving a letter from a colleague asking him to reconsider some of his ideas. In crisis, he allows physicist Barbara Haggerwells to talk him into trying out her new invention, the HX-1, a time machine. She suggests that he use it to visit Gettysburg, the site of an important Confederate victory, and settle his doubts once and for all.

Without telling his wife, Catty, Backmaker allows himself to be transported to June 30, 1863. He walks the thirty miles to the battle site and positions himself. Unfortunately, Confederate troops spot him and question him. Because Backmaker promised Haggerwells that he would not interfere lest he change history, he says nothing. The nervous Confederates convince themselves that Yankees are up ahead and retreat, but during the altercation, a man is shot and killed. Backmaker realizes that the man looks familiar to him.

The Confederate withdrawal from the area means that history as Backmaker knows it changes. Backmaker watches the battle, and, sickened, realizes that the North, rather than the South, will hold the Round Tops. When he returns to the pick-up site and fails to return to his own time, he realizes something far worse: The dead Confederate was Barbara Haggerwells's grandfather. His death means that there is no hope of return to his world. He has changed the course of history and wiped out his own world, along with all the people he loves. Ironically, the world he has brought into being is the world of the reader.

ANALYSIS

Two important themes in *Bring the Jubilee* are the nature of time and the importance of the individual in history. Both are important concerns of alternate history in general. Like Philip K. Dick's alternate history *The Man in the High Castle* (1962), *Bring the Jubilee* questions the role of chance in determining events. Does an individual have the power to change events, or are all events predestined?

Ward Moore explores these themes through Backmaker's discussions with Tyss and Enfandin. Tyss argues that all actions result from stimuli, not thought, and that free will is an illusion. He also argues that time loops endlessly, with people repeating the same events. Moore contrasts Tyss's point of view with that of Enfandin, who believes that everything is an illusion and that only God is real. Backmaker, however, argues that "there must have been a beginning. . . . And if there was a beginning, choice existed if only for that split second. And if choice exists once it can exist again."

Backmaker, dreamy by nature, is not inclined to action but instead to let his life go as it may. Haggerwells must convince him to use her invention to go back in time; he uses her persuasion as an excuse to go, absolving himself of responsibility. He comes to realize that even his refusal to speak to the Confederates at the battle site is a choice. His remark that "if choice exists once it can exist again," coupled with the fact that he changes history, leads Backmaker to believe that free choice exists. He is haunted by the fear that he has wiped out Catty, Haggerwells, and his world, and that he is doomed to wipe them out repeatedly as time loops around again. Still, by allowing Backmaker to change history, Moore refutes Tyss's model of the world and implies that individuals are capable of free choice and action. Backmaker grows from a boy who cannot make decisions into an adult who realizes that not making a choice is a kind of choice.

Bring the Jubilee is Moore's second science-fiction novel, following *Greener than You Think* (1947). None of his other works, mainstream or science fiction, deals with time and history as explicitly as this famous work. Moore's depth of characterization, emotion, and detail make this an enduring classic.

—Karen Hellekson

Brokedown Palace

The faerie realm and the Demon Goddess unsuccessfully contend over the kingdom of Fenar, using brothers of the ruling family as pawns

Author: Steven Brust (1955–)
Genre: Fantasy—magical world
Type of work: Novel
Time of work: Undefined
Locale: The kingdom of Fenar, its castle, and the nearby river
First published: 1986

The Story

King László assaults his youngest brother, Miklós, for having made disparaging remarks about the castle, home to the Fenar family from time immemorial, or at least the last four hundred years. A drop of Miklós' blood finds its way into the flooring in Miklós' room. Miklós escapes into the river, which restores him. He meets a taltós horse, a magical beast that has many incarnations and feeds off its master's need. The horse, Bölk, takes Miklós to the land of faerie.

After studying magic for two years, Miklós returns home without specific plans. Although old tensions still exist between the king and Miklós, the youngest prince, brothers Andor (indecisive and impressionable) and Vilmos (gigantic, yet mild) rejoice at Miklós' homecoming. László is preparing to marry Mariska, a countess who has superseded his common woman, Brigitta. The palace has become decrepit, and a strange plant has rooted itself in Miklós' room. Miklós again incurs László's wrath by making a passing reference to decay, and again he must escape to the river.

Bölk lends Miklós succor, defeating Sándor, the court wizard László sends to retrieve his upstart brother. They eventually return to the palace, once Miklós makes the decision to do so. When a section of floor collapses and kills one of Vilmos' pet norskas, Vilmos becomes more receptive to Miklós' concern for the palace's decay.

Andor earlier had been led, by Sándor, to dedicate himself to the Demon Goddess, which had been the family god and in regular communication with László. The plant has taken over Miklós' room and is firmly entrenched through the cellarage. Brigitta becomes fond of Miklós.

Miklós topples the Demon Goddess' statue, with Bölk's help, calling her to manifest and then destroying her with Bölk's blood. Without the Demon Goddess, László has only the palace to support him, and he determines to remove the plant/tree that he believes threatens it. Miklós confronts him, and they fight. The king's sword, symbol of Demon Goddess power, flares and is consumed in contact with a staff from the tree. At this, the tree expands and involutes, becoming a new palace and supporting the family from which it derives. László and his agents are killed or abdicate.

Miklós and his tree remain to take possession of their new seat of power. Andor defers right to rule to Vilmos, who unwillingly accepts. Brigitta departs to return to faerie, carrying Miklós' unborn daughter. Miklós learns that his daughter will come back to the palace and be a powerful agent in future developments.

Analysis

In an introductory note on pronunciation, Steven Brust reveals the consanguinity of this story with Hungarian or Eastern European folktales. The dropped hint is hardly necessary, for between chapters are interludes that typically are fantastic tales narrated by voices that attempt to authenticate the stories in standard folk formulas (for example, "strike me down if it ain't so"). The somewhat stilted or strained dialogue is attributable to a sense of this as a translated work. The folk-tradition tales of the founding of Fenario are counterpoised against the vestigially described faerie realm, on which the kingdom borders. Other interludes describe the growth of the tree as it contends with the castle. Thus northern Celtic influences butt up against folktales of a Slavic flavor.

The mythic implications are more than a gratuitous overlay, for Brust focuses attention on the concepts of loyalty and tradition. Implicit is the necessity for change and variation as opposed by tradition and law. The four brothers share ancestry from neighboring faerie land but are supported by the Demon Goddess. These two forces are at odds, and the brothers are torn between allegiances. Miklós opts to place family bonds above either extreme and creates something new and astounding as a result. His palace/tree is unaffected by faerie magic, in fact blocking Sándor's path to the source of magic power and thereby killing him. It supplants the traditional structures, both the physical and the hierarchical, and replaces them with the tree and the bond among family members.

As narrative, the book is interesting because of the tree as an emergent plot device. Brust manages to surprise the reader with the plant's full development as a functional shelter and replacement for the former castle. The interludes provide a mosaic effect, suggesting a composite story rather than a single line of development. The reading experience is richer for these features.

The reader's story is remarkably similar to that of Miklós. As the novel progresses, the reader becomes increasingly comfortable in the fairy tale/folk narratives, learning in effect to be a part member of a cultural or ethnic group. Miklós must learn to be comfortable in his own identity, spends most of the novel searching for it, and achieves only a qualified contentment after having found it.

Miklós' progression follows a typical identity-quest cycle, and his actions seem heroic in retrospect. The tree he unwittingly creates is the restorative or elixir to the dying kingdom. It reinvigorates the world it touches. Having found his place, however, there seems little satisfaction in the rebuilding and refining which becomes his role. Like most quest heroes, he ends up without anything to do next. What seems clear for both character and reader is that there is more story ahead—more folktale to read, and more to come with the return of Miklós' daughter.

—*Scott D. Vander Ploeg*

THE BROKEN LAND

A mute girl sets out to find her family in an oppressive world altered by biotechnology

Author: Ian McDonald (1960–)
Genre: Science fiction—cultural exploration
Type of work: Novel
Time of work: The far future
Locale: The empire of the Proclaimers
First published: 1992 (as *Hearts, Hands, and Voices*, 1992, in the United Kingdom)

THE STORY

From its bravura opening line—"Grandfather was a tree"—and its initial image of a living house running amok through a village, Ian McDonald's fourth novel quickly establishes a bizarre setting and a haunting tone that seem to owe as much to surrealism as to earlier science fiction. *The Broken Land* essentially is the tale of a young girl's quest across a planet whose shifting landscapes and political structures alternately call to mind Southeast Asia, Eastern Europe, South Africa, and contemporary Ireland.

These vividly realized settings and the unfolding quest itself are suggested by the novel's six sections: "The Township," "The Road," "The City," "The River," "The Camps," and "The Borderland." The central conflict in the story is one of biology and technology. The Proclaimers have established a totalitarian empire that rules the planet through conventional technology, and the Confessors have developed advanced skills in biotechnology since the discovery, generations earlier, of a technique for manipulating DNA directly from the human nervous system. The Confessors have long sought self-determination and freedom.

In Chepsenyt Township, the idyllic Confessor village where Mathembe Fileli lives, nearly everything is grown rather than manufactured, and free "organicals" called trux are farmed like animals. A kind of immortality has been achieved: The heads of ancestors can retain a kind of semi-vegetable life embedded in Ancestor Trees, where they partake of a kind of spiritual consciousness called "the Dreaming."

Oppression and violence also are part of Mathembe's world. Her response is the same as that of Oskar in Günter Grass's *The Tin Drum* (1959): She refuses to speak. When Chepsenyt is destroyed by imperial forces for harboring members of a resistance movement called the Warriors of Destiny, Mathembe becomes a refugee. She sets out with her family to join her uncle's Faradje in the ancient city of Ol Kot, which is a vivid amalgam of Calcutta, Charles Dickens' London, and the Los Angeles envisioned by cyberpunk writers. In Ol Kot, she finds use for her skills in biological manipulation, designing and selling organical toys in the district of the city known as the Flesh Market.

The Confessor revolution reaches Ol Kot. Riots break out, and reprisals are violent. Mathembe is displaced again when the city is burned. Separated from her remaining family—except for her disembodied grandfather, whose head she rescued from the Ancestor Tree in her village—she becomes a boat person, stowing away on Unchunkolo. After more than three centuries of additions and modifications, that enormous riverboat has become a society unto itself. Mathembe is allowed to stay on board because of her biodesign skills, revealed by one of her organical toys. She is assigned to try to revive the boat's failing agricultural ecosystems, and her success makes her a nearly legendary figure on the boat.

Word arrives that the Proclaimer-Confessor war has ended in an agreement to divide the land. Mathembe sets out to find her family, journeying first to sprawling displaced person camps and finally to a mysterious Borderland, where her mother has joined a movement to end violence through a radical advance in genetic engineering that promises to dramatically alter the world in which Mathembe lives.

ANALYSIS

For readers reared on George Bernard Shaw, William Butler Yeats, and James Joyce, it can be unsettling to be reminded that by the end of the twentieth century, Ireland had become virtually a Third World country, with a history of oppressive colonialism, violence, famine, and poverty. Despite a rich heritage of visionary literature and mythology, not to mention an unparalleled tradition of satirical fantasy from Jonathan Swift to Flann O'Brien, it is hard to think of a clearly Irish tradition in science fiction, one that takes account of both the fabled Irish love of language and more bitter economic and historical realities. Ian McDonald seems to have set out to remedy this situation single-handedly, not only with his panoply of Irish history in *King of Morning, Queen of Day* (1991) but also with this sometimes harrowing novel of oppression, violence, and redemption.

In one sense, the novel is a depressing catalog of twentieth century atrocities, displaced to a distant setting that resembles, at various times, Northern Ireland, Nazi Europe, South Africa, and Southeast Asia. McDonald's cultural and mythic background suggests a panoply of oppressed peoples, but the chief antagonists—the Proclaimers, who rule with more or less conventional technology; and the Confessors, who can alter biological forms for technological uses—suggest nothing so much as Catholics and Protestants and their conflict in Northern Ireland.

McDonald's character and place names seem to draw on African, aboriginal, and Asian languages, and his themes of ancestor worship and apocalyptic revolutionary movements call to mind Yoruba mythology and the Native American ghost dance movement. Villages are destroyed in ways reminiscent of Vietnam; certain populations are restricted to South African-style "townships"; and prisoners are hauled in darkened trucks for days and then "selected," in the manner of Nazi Germany. At its best, the novel suggests a nightmare pageant of modern history, cast in the traditional mode of a girl's search for her family and dressed up with the most thoroughly imagined version of biotechnology since Harry Harrison's *West of Eden* trilogy (1984–1988).

The Broken Land has been criticized for its resemblance to earlier work by Geoff Ryman, especially *The Unconquered Country: A Life History* (1986) and *The Child Garden* (1989). McDonald's ending has problems of its own, raising moral questions about the uses of science that trouble even Mathembe herself. Even though McDonald prepares for this ending and it makes sense out of the organic versus mechanical opposition that permeates the narrative, it still seems to propose a facile science-fiction solution to all-too-real social and economic problems. Still, there is enough wisdom and thoughtfulness in the rest of the novel to more than make up for a questionable resolution. For all of its violence and depredations, *The Broken Land* is a haunting and moving novel, written in an intensely poetic, even hypnotic, style. For all that it draws on contemporary concerns, McDonald's world is strikingly self-contained and consistent, and it is entirely his own.

—Gary K. Wolfe

THE BROKEN SWORD

A human child, stolen by elves and replaced by a changeling, grows up to fall in love with his sister and to fight for the elves against trolls led by the changeling

Author: Poul Anderson (1926–2001)
Genre: Fantasy—high fantasy
Type of work: Novel
Time of work: The time of Alfred the Great (849–899)
Locale: The realm of Faerie (primarily the British Isles and Northern Europe)
First published: 1954

THE STORY

The Broken Sword is populated with elves, trolls, dwarfs, and other creatures of Northern European folklore and myth. It is set in the land of Faerie, which is part of the known world but invisible to most humans. The story begins with Orm, a Viking settler in the Danelaw (northern and eastern England). Orm is cursed by a witch after he seizes her family's lands. She swears that Orm's son will be stolen and that he will rear a beast instead. Orm ignores her, building and marrying on the lands taken from the witch.

Orm's first child is indeed stolen, by an elf-earl named Imric. It is replaced by a changeling created from Imric's union with a captive female troll. The changeling is named Valgard and is reared as Orm's son. Orm's true son is reared by Imric in Faerie. He is called Skafloc.

On Skafloc's naming-day, a messenger of the gods gives the child a "broken sword" of iron. The elves cannot touch iron, and they bury the sword. Skafloc grows rapidly and is trained in warfare and magic. He learns to change shape. Valgard, the changeling, also becomes a great warrior, but he is wild and violent.

One day, Ketil, another of Orm's sons, stumbles on the witch, who appears to Ketil as a beautiful woman. Valgard discovers them together and murders Ketil. Orm finds out about the murder, and Valgard then kills his father.

After Valgard flees back to the witch, she explains his heritage as half elf and half troll. Valgard becomes a tragic figure and turns his back on humanity to join the trolls. To sever all ties with his old life, he kidnaps Orm's daughters, Asgerd and Freda, and offers them to Illrede Troll-King.

The elves know that the trolls are planning a war, and Skafloc leads a raid against Illrede. He is amazed to see Valgard. He rescues Asgerd and Freda, unaware that they are his sisters. Valgard counterattacks, killing Asgerd, but Skafloc and Freda escape. They fall in love. Imric keeps Freda's identity secret.

The trolls invade England with an army of goblins, imps, dwarfs, and others. Skafloc fights Valgard again, but neither can kill the other. The elves are beaten, and Imric is captured. Valgard becomes leader of England's trolls while Illrede invades the mainland to conquer the elven king. Skafloc and Freda become outlaws. Skafloc retrieves the broken sword. To find out how the blade can be remade, he calls up the dead, who also reveal that

Skafloc and Freda are brother and sister. Freda runs away in shame.

Skafloc convinces a giant to reforge the sword, which was made originally by sorcery. Legend says that the blade must kill every time it is drawn and that it will eventually turn on its user. Skafloc rides to save the elven king, only to find the elves nearly defeated. He uses his new sword to kill Illrede and drive the trolls back to England. He and Valgard meet a third time, and Skafloc is wounded. Freda, who cannot forget Skafloc, arrives on the battlefield at that moment. Skafloc is distracted, and Valgard seizes the great sword and stabs him. As Valgard lifts the sword for a last blow, it escapes his grip to pierce his own throat, killing him. Skafloc dies in Freda's arms.

ANALYSIS
The Broken Sword and the science-fiction novel *Brain Wave* (1954) were the first book-length works by Poul Anderson to be published. The first two volumes of J. R. R. Tolkien's Lord of the Rings trilogy also were published in 1954. *The Broken Sword* had much less impact than Tolkien's trilogy on the development of fantasy's major subgenres of high fantasy and heroic fantasy. It was nearly forgotten until the Tolkien boom of the 1960's led to its reissue.

There are several reasons why Anderson's book did not have the impact of Tolkien's work. First, *The Broken Sword* was printed by a small publisher (Abelard-Schuman) and was not widely distributed. There was only one printing. Second, it was published very early in Anderson's career, before his writing had fully matured, and it was not as polished, developed, or ambitious as Tolkien's Lord of the Rings trilogy. Third, because of Anderson's scientific background and the commercial nature of his writing, he was considered less of a literary figure than was Tolkien. Critics took Tolkien seriously but ignored Anderson.

After being reissued in 1971, *The Broken Sword* did influence the fantasy field, primarily by helping shape the subgenre of heroic fantasy, where Anderson's later fantasy work would be classified. *The Broken Sword* also directly influenced Anderson's own *Hrolf Kraki's Saga* (1973) and the three books of his Last Viking series (*The Golden Horn, The Road of the Sea Horse,* and *The Sign of the Raven,* all published in 1980).

Hrolf Kraki's Saga is a mixture of high fantasy and heroic fantasy. The Last Viking series is more purely heroic in nature, primarily because of more realistic settings and the general absence of mythical beings such as elves and trolls. Anderson used Northern European mythology and history throughout all four books. Much of this mythology, as well as many of the fantastic creatures, appeared first in The Broken Sword, and many of the Viking characters in these books are reminiscent of Skafloc and Valgard.

—*Charles A. Gramlich*

BROOD OF THE WITCH QUEEN

Antony Ferrara, descended from the witch queen of ancient Egypt, uses black magic to increase his wealth and power but is defeated by Dr. Bruce Cairn and his son

Author: Sax Rohmer (1883-1959)
Genre: Fantasy—occult
Type of work: Novel
Time of work: 1914
Locale: London, Oxford, and their environs in England; Cairo, Port Said, and the Pyramid of Meydum in Egypt
First published: 1918 (serial form, *The Premier Magazine*, 1914)

THE STORY
As Brood of the Witch Queena medical student at Oxford University, Robert Cairn first becomes suspicious of fellow student Antony Ferrara, the adopted son of Sir Michael Ferrara, a noted Egyptologist and a close friend of Cairn's father. The young Ferrara, whom Cairn finds "repellently effeminate," dresses in furs and keeps fires burning in his quarters even at midsummer. His rooms reek of incense and are filled with ancient Egyptian relics, including a mummy. There is a photograph of the swan Apollo whose strange death Cairn witnessed. He observes Ferrara burning a waxen swan figurine. Later, in London, Cairn

learns that a young woman he had seen outside Ferrara's quarters has been strangled in an impossible situation. Sir Michael Ferrara then succumbs after attacks by a pair of ghostly hands that his niece and ward, Myra Duquesne, is powerless to stop. Cairn's father, Dr. Bruce Cairn, is called in, too late, to save his old friend.

Himself an authority on Egyptian ritual and beliefs, Dr. Cairn quickly surmises from all that has happened that Antony Ferrara is practicing Egyptian magic, but he refuses to answer his son's repeated demands to know just who Antony Ferrara really is. Myra, while in a sleepwalking trance, accuses Antony of being the brood of a witch and points to the witch's ring, the ring of Thoth, that he wears. The Cairns are determined to protect Myra from Ferrara, who obviously covets her share of the inheritance.

Ferrara clearly is aware of their opposition. He launches a magical attack against the younger Cairn but is thwarted by Dr. Cairn. He turns his magic next against Lord and Lady Lashmore, causing the latter to be possessed by the spirit of Mirza, an ancestral sorceress and vampire, and then to kill her husband.

Antony Ferrara next appears in Egypt, where Robert Cairn is vacationing. Through his magic, Ferrara unleashes terrible sandstorms, nearly deceives Dr. Cairn into killing his son, and causes Lady Lashmore, who is also in Egypt, to disappear. Dr. Cairn is convinced that Ferrara is connected to the ancient Egyptian witch queen whose tomb he and Sir Michael Ferrara had searched for, unsuccessfully, years earlier. In the most vivid episode of the novel, Dr. Cairn and his son's friend Sime enter the Pyramid of Meydum, one of the reputed centers of ancient Egyptian sorcery and the scene of recent unnerving occurrences. In a secret chamber, they witness Ferrara performing a ritual of anthropomancy (divination by human entrails) using the dead body of Lady Lashmore. The form of the witch queen materializes and begins to speak when Sime loses control and fires his gun. In the aftermath, he and Dr. Cairn barely manage to escape.

Back in England, Ferrara's attempts to kill both Myra, by means of a sinister orchid, and Robert Cairn, with a magical cord, are foiled by Dr. Cairn. As the final conflict approaches, Dr. Cairn at last discloses what he knows—or suspects—of Ferrara's true identity: He is the reanimated son of the witch queen and embodies the spirit of her high priest. Dr. Cairn uncovers the magician's spell book, the *Book of Thoth*, and burns it. When Ferrara evokes a powerful elemental spirit to attack the Cairns and Myra, he cannot control it and is destroyed.

ANALYSIS

The author of more than forty Oriental thrillers, Sax Rohmer is best known as the creator of the sinister criminal genius Fu-Manchu, whose adventures began with *The Mystery of Dr. Fu-Manchu* (1913; published as *The Insidious Dr. Fu-Manchu* in the United States) and continued with twelve further volumes. Many of Rohmer's tales have fantasy and occult elements, a few are essentially fantasy, and at least one is science fiction (*The Day the World Ended*, 1930, part of the Gaston Max series that also includes *The Yellow Claw*, 1915, *The Golden Scorpion*, 1919, and *Seven Sins*, 1943).

Of the primarily fantasy works, *Brood of the Witch Queen*, one of his early publications, is probably the best known. It is based on Rohmer's extensive knowledge of the occult and his travels in Egypt. In the "prefatory notice" to the novel, Rohmer states that the powers attributed to Antony Ferrara in no case exceed those claimed for a fully equipped adept. He might have referred the reader to his own popular nonfiction account, *The Romance of Sorcery* (1914; abridged edition, 1923), which was finished immediately before he began writing *Brood of the Witch Queen*. Rohmer also was a member of an occult secret society, the Hermetic Order of the Golden Dawn.

The underlying theme of the novel, frequently repeated, is that in the modern age of science and skepticism, disbelief in the existence of dark powers is itself dangerous because it leaves one vulnerable and defenseless. Only Dr. Cairn's private study of magic and the occult—something he cannot afford to have known publicly—makes resistance to Antony Ferrara possible. In this context, Cairn's tendency not to reveal what he knows because it is "too horrible to tell" or because one is "better off not knowing" is unconvincing; it is simply a rhetorical device Rohmer uses to heighten suspense and horror.

Brood of the Witch Queen is episodic and melodramatic. Rohmer relies heavily on coincidence and Dr. Cairn's undisclosed knowledge to propel the story, which is essentially one of gothic horror, featuring a young woman beset by dark forces. Nevertheless, the novel contains some memorable scenes, especially the pyramid episode, and depicts some operations of a practicing magician. It is rather unusual for its time in presenting a modern practitioner of black magic not as a satanist but as an adept in the ancient Egyptian tradition. Rohmer returned to Egyptian themes in *The Green Eyes of Bast* (1920) and, with addition of the figure of the advanced occultist, in *The Bat Flies Low* (1935).

—*Robert Galbreath*

BROTHER TO DRAGONS

Job Napoleon Salk saves humanity from an artificially engineered virus and inoculates humanity with a benign symbiote

Author: Charles Sheffield (1935–2002)
Genre: Science fiction—extrapolatory
Type of work: Novel
Time of work: December 31, 1999, to late February, 2018
Locale: Washington, D.C., and Nevada
First published: 1992

THE STORY

The novel tells the story of Job Napoleon Salk's life, from his birth on the eve of the twenty-first century to his death less than nineteen years later. The first half is set in various places in Washington, D.C., where Salk is born and where he grows up. The second half is set in Xanadu, the country's oldest, largest, and most dangerous "Tandy" (Toxic and Nuclear Disposal Installation), somewhere in Nevada.

Salk's life starts out badly and gets worse. His mother is a drug addict, and Salk is born facially malformed, undersized, and underweight. He finds a haven in Cloak House, an orphanage run by the saintly but strict Brother Bonifant. By the age of ten, however, Salk is on the streets, and by the age of eighteen he has been a drug runner, acquired a criminal record, nearly died in a juvenile detention home, and made the mistake of befriending the daughter of a wealthy family. This is a mistake because it brings him to the attention of Wilfred Dell, an evil man who is working for the Royal Hundred, the country's wealthiest families.

Dell forces Salk to go to Xanadu, also known as the Great Nebraska Tandy, the place to which many scientists were banished as punishment for their supposed role in the *Quiebra Grande* (Great Crash) of 2005, an economic disaster that affected the entire world. Dell is worried that the scientists are up to something.

Working undercover, Salk proves Dell right. The scientists have created a virus that, if released, would kill most of the world's population. They see this as suitable revenge for being treated as scapegoats for the *Quiebra Grande*. One of the scientists, Dr. Hanna Kronberg, has created another microorganism, a symbiote that strengthens the human immune system and retards aging. Salk manages to release the symbiote, thus preempting the scientists' revenge and inaugurating a fall in the world's population, which eventually will stabilize at a figure that the planet can support. This is bad news to Dell and the Royal Hundred, because the old and rich no longer have the same advantages over the young and poor. Before Dell can execute Salk, however, Salk dies of a radiation overdose that he received while escaping from Xanadu.

Salk thus lives up to all three parts of his name. Like the biblical Job, he is born to trouble; like Napoleon Bonaparte, he spectacularly overcomes his physical limitations, though not by killing; and like Jonas Salk, he saves humanity from a vicious disease.

ANALYSIS

As a writer of hard science fiction, Charles Sheffield often has been compared to Isaac Asimov, Arthur C. Clarke, and Robert A. Heinlein. *Brother to Dragons* certainly is hard science fiction, featuring believable science, especially biology, and believable technology, especially Tandymen, the robotic toxic waste handlers that figure prominently in Salk's escape from Xanadu.

Brother to Dragons is a near-future extrapolation. The two trends it extrapolates are a worsening worldwide economy and an increasing distrust of science. The result is a cautionary tale about what can go wrong if these two trends continue.

Most of Sheffield's other science fiction is more similar to Asimov's and Clarke's than to Heinlein's, so *Brother to Dragons* is something of a departure from Sheffield's norm. Its concerns are not cosmic but global. Its protagonist is not a mature man but an adolescent boy. Its setting is not centuries away but in the near future.

Brother to Dragons is Sheffield's homage to Heinlein, who died in 1988, four years before this novel was published. The Heinlein work it most closely resembles is *Citizen of the Galaxy* (1957), also a novel for juvenile readers that features an orphaned, young, male protagonist, seemingly vulnerable, who has hidden resources that surface when he is challenged to survive during a series of picaresque adventures. Heinlein's Thor Bradley Rudbek and Sheffield's Job Napoleon Salk both come of age by surviving in harsh environments that reward competence.

Brother to Dragons has other details reminiscent of Heinlein, such as Xanadu's resemblance to the setting of Heinlein's novelette "Coventry" (*Astounding Science-Fiction*, July, 1940; reprinted in *Revolt in 2100*, 1953). Brother to Dragons also bears its author's stamp. Although certainly posing the limitations of science, the novel nevertheless takes a proscience line, which is not surprising given Sheffield's own training as a physicist. What may be surprising is how literary the novel is. Literary allusions abound, with Sheffield borrowing important plot elements from Charles Dickens' *Oliver Twist* (1837–1839). The linguistically gifted Salk likes to read literature in many different languages, and the Book of Job in the Bible provides epithets for eleven of the novel's twenty chapters.

Unlike many science-fiction writers, Sheffield does not scoff at religion. Balancing Dr. Hanna Kronberg, the heroic scientist who creates the miraculous symbiote, is Brother Bonifant, the cleric who ministers to orphans like Salk before dying a martyr's death in Xanadu. Sheffield is a product of the British educational system, and that system and British science fiction always have been more literary than their American counterparts.

Although Sheffield is a popular science-fiction writer, not much criticism has been written on his work, and little other than brief reviews has been written on *Brother to Dragons*. Sheffield has his admirers, however. In 1993, *Brother to Dragons* won the John W. Campbell Memorial Award for the best science-fiction novel of the year. This tribute is fitting, because Campbell is remembered not only as an important science-fiction editor but also as an important early writer of hard science fiction.

—Todd H. Sammons

BRUTE ORBITS

The future of crime and incarceration are thoroughly extrapolated into shocking new dimensions

Author: George Zebrowski (1945–)
Genre: Science Fiction—extrapolatory
Type of work: Novel
Time of plot: Future (twenty-first and twenty-second centuries)
Location: Earth and asteroids
First published: 1998

THE STORY
In the late twentieth century, Earth comes up with the idea of imprisoning supercriminals on specially modified asteroids containing artificial gravity and sunplates, then begins to send the asteroids on orbits timed to coincide with the prison sentences, human guards and supervising wardens being gone. Mistakes are deliberately made so that the orbits are gone for longer than intended, and additional asteroids are deliberately constructed poorly. Several narratives on board different asteroids are followed.

On one, Yevgeny Tasarov—a brilliant criminal who, some years earlier, led a mass-escape from Dannemora—recovers his identity, having hidden under a false criminal identity that led to his arrest and conviction for crimes other than those Tasarov committed. When the asteroid is sent into orbit, many criminals kill one another before population stabilizes and various same-sex relationships are established; there is also a

fire that forces the criminals to work together. Tasarov finds access to the engineering floors, but nothing can be reversed. Ultimately, he and all perish of old age, though not before destroying all records.

On another asteroid, Abebe Chou, daughter of a Nigerian mother and a Chinese father, takes part in political discussions with fellow prisoners she nicknames Trotsky, Lenin, Stalin, Newton, and Leibniz, and all is well until the asteroid malfunctions and, in the darkness, her discussion partners rape and attempt to rape her. She makes it to safety and sees the majority of her attackers perish when gravity fails and they fall or are electrocuted.

In the early twenty-second century, humanity, now supplemented with numerous AIs, rediscovers the asteroids and attempts to recover them for historical purposes. The first they enter contains Tasarov's skeleton and narrative, which concludes that he and his fellows have destroyed all the records and recording devices. In the next, humans—in the form of Justine Harre and Ibby Khaldun—enter, with Justine leaving as Ibby remains hidden. She encounters a culture in which women are property, with no rights, their bodies communally used and their babies communally raised. She escapes by claiming to be barren, but when the youths attempt to rape her for practice, Ibby uses a stun gun on them.

Nevertheless, communications and relationships are reestablished: those on asteroids become aware of the existence of other asteroids. Those on the asteroids do not remain affiliated with Earth but have quantum drives installed aboard the rocks and choose to head out for other suns. Back on Earth, Ibby reveals that he is too settled for a life with Justine, and they go their separate ways. He is watching the screens when the final chapter begins: the AIs evidently lead the asteroids to develop something else for energy and transport, for all asteroids abruptly wink out and vanish.

ANALYSIS

Penal systems and dealing with criminals and dissidents have long been a staple of science fiction. In Edward Bellamy's *Looking Backward, 2000–1887* (1888), those who oppose society and do not wish to work are imprisoned, with only bread and water, until they change their minds. In Robert Heinlein's *Revolt in 2100* (1953) dissidents are exiled, to a place known as Coventry. Other societies, such as that in Neal Stephenson's *Diamond Age* (1995) simply eliminate problems, for leaving alive convicted threats merely endangers the rest of society. It is not hard to imagine Zebrowski considering these fictional predecessors—encountering, too, the term "superpredators," used by Hillary Clinton in 1996 to reference crime in African American neighborhoods—and, from these, extrapolating the seemingly humane and simple but ultimately horrific solutions he presents in *Brute Orbits*.

It is also possible to fault Zebrowski's narrative development on several grounds. First, his development is simplistic, to the point where there does not appear to be any awareness of the existence of political structures or due processes. Moreover, for all the author's acknowledgement of other countries' existence, the exiles he writes about appear to be the result one individual's rulings: Judge Overton, whose tendentious opinions and assessments of crimes and criminals—e.g., "Every generation of humanity to date has been damaged in some way by the previous generation; but until we learn how to make a better generation, we have to protect ourselves. Now we've mined all these rocks, and we're filling them up"—serve as the headings to many chapters. It would appear that nobody ever challenges the judge, whose rulings are likewise never questioned by any Court of Appeals.

Next, because Zebrowski's story was guided by its sociopolitical agenda, his choice of characters of necessity had to conform to this didacticism. Never once are the individuals and corporations in Zebrowski's society put up for examination: crime is defined in generally limited terms, with the criminals commonly being those who have committed physical crimes. (Even Abebe Chou "had supposedly stolen a billion dollars online") The result is that the characters presented are unsurprising, and only sporadically do they demonstrate any individuality. Worse is that for all the horrible fates suffered by the majority of the imprisoned characters, they are sadly muted in the presentation; the prisoners' deaths occur distantly and seemingly offstage lest the immediacy and finality of their deaths distract from the novel's narrative. The dialogue is equally weak.

However, despite all such narrative weaknesses and flaws, *Brute Orbits* excels as a narrative of ideas. It asks age-old questions about criminality and justice that remain perpetually timely and important, and while its solution may seem extreme, this, too, may be argued. Indeed, *Brute Orbits* is probably best assessed as a late twentieth-century *Tendenzroman*, or novel with purpose; Zebrowski presents difficult issues, asks difficult questions, and dares his readers to arrive at different conclusions.

—Richard Bleiler

Bug Jack Barron

Jack Barron, the outrageous host of a call-in television show, investigates human immortality research and becomes trapped in a Faustian contract that he overcomes in a desperate on-air showdown

Author: Norman Spinrad (1940–)
Genre: Science fiction—extrapolatory
Type of work: Novel
Time of work: The mid-or late 1980's
Locale: New York City
First published: 1969 (serial form, *New Worlds*, 1967-1968)

The Story

Jack Barron is a charismatic journalist trying to retain both his job and his integrity. Benedict Howards, owner of the Human Immortality Foundation, alternately bribes and threatens Barron, seeking his support. Ultimately, Howards makes an offer that Barron cannot refuse.

As the book opens, Barron seizes on a charge of racism as a hook to explore the Freezer Utility controversy. He makes on-air calls to the foundation; to Senator Hennering, who supports a monopoly bill Howards wants; and to Lucas Greene, the black governor of Mississippi and Jack's longtime friend. Hennering gives a limp defense of the bill, enraging Howards. Soon after, Hennering dies under suspicious circumstances. Howards investigates Barron and learns the television host's weakness: He still loves his former wife, Sara.

Howards bribes Sara to reunite with Barron. Sara seizes the opportunity, sure that together, she and Barron can outwit Howards. The two rediscover the joy they shared as young lovers.

Barron questions Howards on the air. Privately, Howards admits that the foundation has developed an immortality procedure. He offers Barron the million-dollar operation for free in exchange for public support. They bargain warily, and Barron offers only to do contractual public relations work for the foundation. When he and Sara sign immortality contracts, Howards urges immediate surgery. Barron equivocates. He believes that Howards still hides dangerous secrets but hopes that his seeming cooperation will tease them out.

On Barron's next show, Franklin, a "kook" caller, bemoans selling his daughter. Barron makes no connection until Howards blasts him for doing the interview. Barron decides to question Franklin further. As the two walk together, a sniper fires at them, killing Franklin.

When Barron and Sara go to confront Howards, his aides forcibly anesthetize them. When they wake, they are "immortal." Howards then shows Barron some purchased children, who have been irradiated to stop the aging process. The children die a terrible death, and their transplanted glands provide immortality to others. Howards points out that Barron's and Sara's contracts say that they "accept full legal liability for any results of the treatment." This proves them to be accomplices to murder, he says.

Barron hopelessly agrees. By himself, he would expose Howards, risking a murder charge, but he cannot bear to put Sara in the same jeopardy. When they next make love, pleasure turns to disgust. Sara asks what is wrong, and Barron reluctantly reveals the secret.

Sara, horrified, takes LSD when Barron leaves for his next show. On vidphone, she says that she is freeing him, then jumps from their balcony. Barron tells the whole story on the air.

His revelations drive Howards insane and reshuffle American politics. Barron and Lucas Greene are nominated on a coalition presidential ticket. Barron's secret plan is to resign if he wins, giving the United States its first black president, and to continue wielding power his own way, through television.

ANALYSIS

Bug Jack Barron stirred controversy with its explicit sex scenes and four-letter words, almost unknown in science fiction before this time. A British distributor dropped the magazine in which it appeared, and the Arts Council was criticized in Parliament for supporting the publication of "filth."

Most reviewers who looked beyond these features praised the novel for its keen depiction of media influence and political manipulation. A minority dismissed it as a bizarre experiment. The vivid and startling images in its characters' long stream-of-consciousness reflections added to its shock value.

Later critics have noted the accuracy of the book's premise of talk show hosts shaping public opinion. The split screen and panning techniques Barron uses are classic examples of image manipulation.

Like most science fiction with a near-future setting, *Bug Jack Barron* makes some wrong guesses. Marijuana was not legalized by the mid-1980's, and there was no Social Justice party. The book does, however, strike uncannily close to many trends of the late twentieth century. Ronald Reagan is cited as a prime example of the power of media images long before his election to the U.S. presidency in 1980. The rise of black politicians and the development of "vidphones" are other examples of accurate prediction.

Barron's selling out for material rewards often is said to be a second theme of the book. This analysis is debatable. Certainly, selling out is a preoccupation for Jack and Sara Barron and for Lucas Greene, whose outlooks were shaped by the 1960's counterculture. Sometimes, Barron agrees when Sara or Greene accuses him of discarding his ideals for commercial success. Other times, he defends himself, saying that Sara's friends, who only complain and dream, are the real sellouts; his hard-won influence brings their ideals closer to reality. On most of his shows, this appears to be the case, as he "bugs" the powerful and defends ordinary people. Barron does enjoy the power he exercises. His biggest flaw, however, may be simple overconfidence, in gambling that he can outmatch and bring to account such a wealthy and wily operator as Howards.

The book's innovative style has become less shocking since 1969, when it was new to the genre. It can still produce breathtaking effects, however, as in the scene in which Sara jumps to her death, seeing transfigured images of her husband, the dead babies, and infinity.

Bug Jack Barron was nominated for a Hugo Award in 1968 and a Nebula Award in 1969. The book put its author into the front ranks of serious science-fiction writers. Many of Norman Spinrad's later works echo motifs introduced in it: electronic networks, public opinion as a court of final appeal, immortality, sex, drugs, power, and love. As a cautionary tale about the interaction of these elements, the book remains relevant and compelling.

—*Emily Alward*

BURN WITCH BURN

Dr. Lowell joins with gangster Julian Ricori to track and kill the witch Madame Mandilip and to destroy her enchanted "devil dolls"

Author: A. Merritt (1884-1943)
Genre: Fantasy—superbeing
Type of work: Novel
Time of work: The 1930's

Locale: New York City, with a climactic visit to the "unknown world" of magic
First published: 1933 (serial form, *Argosy Magazine*, October 22-November 26, 1932)

THE STORY

The story revolves around the efforts of a scientist, Dr. Lowell (a pseudonym he uses because of his fear that the incredible and irrational events he relates will discredit him as a scientist), and a gangster, Julian Ricori, as they first uncover the existence of the powerful witch of the title and then try, unsuccessfully, to find an effective countermeasure to her lethal magic. They track her to her lair, where they confront and finally kill her.

In the beginning, Dr. Lowell relates that Ricori has sought Lowell's services on behalf of the gangster's lieutenant, Thomas Peters, who suffers from a severe shock that has destroyed his nervous stability. His eyes are wide open, his posture is rigid, and, although neither unconscious nor dead, he is unresponsive to treatment. Lowell struggles to find a medical solution to the problem but cannot. He slowly (if grudgingly) concludes that Peters suffers from some sort of undiscoverable evil "presence." Peters is under the influence of Madame Man-dilip, whom Lowell has not yet met, though he infers her power to manipulate her victims psychically and from a great distance.

Peters dies while Lowell helplessly attends him. Lowell and Ricori discover that other persons have met similar fates. The death of one in particular, Nurse Walters, provides them with a diary that details her visits to Madame Mandilip's doll shop. It contains both one of the greatest gothic descriptions of an occult event in American fantasy fiction and enough information to allow them to identify Madame Mandilip as the source of the necromancy that they have decided is the root of the eerie and lethal events that they have been investigating.

Later, Lowell and Ricori abduct the witch's assistant, the pitiful and frightened Lascha, and learn enough to reach the conclusion that Madame Mandilip is an ancient witch of great and malign power and that she is capable of assuming many physical forms. They then make their plans to confront her in her hellish doll shop and engage her in a battle to the death, an encounter that is among the best of its kind in American fantasy fiction. Although they finally conquer supernatural evil, they do not escape unscathed, either physically or psychologically.

ANALYSIS

A plot summary can suggest something of the excitement of the sequence of events, but it cannot suggest the novel's finest feature: the excellence of its style. A fine example of pure gothic fantasy that uses the device of the superbeing as its chief interest, *Burn, Witch, Burn!* was written toward the end of A. Merritt's career. A successful journalist, Merritt wrote fantasies of various types for relaxation in his hours away from his job. He was also a master of lost-civilization stories, such as *The Face in the Abyss* (1931) and *The Dwellers in the Mirage* (1932), following a style adopted by the much-better-known H. Rider Haggard and Edgar Rice Burroughs, authors who were his near contemporaries. In early stories, such as *The Moon Pool* (1919) and *The Metal Monster* (1946; serial form, 1920), and in his last novel, *Creep, Shadow!* (1934), Merritt produced some of the best macabre fantasies by an American writer of any period. Only Edgar Allan Poe is his superior in this genre.

Burn, Witch, Burn! appeared at the end of his career; only *Creep, Shadow!*, a horror story intended as a sequel, and a few other short pieces would be written in the remaining nine years of his life. This is to be regretted, because the story demonstrates Merritt's mastery of the various conventions of gothic fantasy—the gloomy and fear-inducing atmosphere and the ageless and malignant superbeing or monster at the story's center—as well as his firm grasp of the mechanics of plot. These elements are combined with a highly visual style that adds to the story's suspense without detracting from the plot by calling attention to itself.

In this novel, Merritt successfully embodies the most important idea to be found in supernatural fantasy: that the reader has come to the novel in order to experience the idea that evil exists as an active, objective force, independent of subjective experience, in the world of physical existence. His early work taught him that the reader's shock, on being introduced to the experience of the extraordinary, which is the supernatural story's whole point, exists in direct proportion to the writer's scrupulous attention to and incorporation of realistic detail. The power of a Merritt fantasy results from his creation of a believable primary or realistic world peopled, for the most part, by ordinary characters. Thus, the reader believes, when finally encountering the evil superbeing at the core of the work, that he or she is "shivering on [the] threshold" of the "door of an unknown world," as Merritt himself states in this novel. Such sensations mark the most intense engagements that fantasy fiction can offer a reader. *Burn, Witch, Burn!* produces many such moments while demonstrating Merritt's mastery of this timeless form of literary art.

—*Ronald Foust*

Burning Chrome

Stories of the early twenty-first century, set on Earth or in the inner solar system, combining high technology, social unrest, corporate conflict, and ambiguous characters

Author: William Gibson (1948–)
Genre: Science fiction—cyberpunk
Type of work: Stories
Time of work: Primarily the early twenty-first century, with some stories set in the 1980's
Locale: Earth and elsewhere in the solar system
First published: 1986

The Story

A collection of primarily near-future stories, *Burning Chrome* demonstrates the style, ambiguity, and dark vision characteristic of William Gibson's work. The ten stories in this collection can be divided into four groups on the basis of their settings.

"New Rose Hotel," "Johnny Mnemonic," and "Burning Chrome" are stories of the Sprawl, set in the early twenty-first century Earth further developed in the novels *Neuromancer* (1984), *Count Zero* (1986), and *Mona Lisa Overdrive* (1988). High technology, organized crime, powerful megacorporations, and an economy driven by information services dominate a world divided sharply into haves and have-nots. These three short stories set up the basic patterns of Sprawl conflict: individuals against powerful corporations, individuals against organized crime, and low-power individuals against high-power individuals. In "New Rose Hotel," the nameless narrator details the machinations of corporate headhunters and the inexorable, deadly vengeance of their employer after a defection goes wrong. The title character of "Johnny Mnemonic" is a walking safebox for other people's data. He is left with data stolen from the Yakuza, the Japanese crime syndicate, locked in his head after a client is killed. With the help of Molly Millions, a surgically enhanced bodyguard/assassin, and Jones, a drug-addicted former Navy Dolphin, Johnny evades the Yakuza and begins to make use of all the data he has ever stored.

In "Burning Chrome," Bobby Quine and Automatic Jack, hot-shot computer jockeys, use stolen Russian military software to break into the computer system of a local crime lord, Chrome, and destroy her power base by redistributing her financial assets.

"Fragments of a Hologram Rose," "Winter Market," and "Dogfight" are stories set in the Sprawl or in a world very similar to it. Stories in this group are also set against a background of a high-technology society with sharp economic extremes. "Fragments of a Hologram Rose," Gibson's first published story, hinges on the reaction of the main character, Parker, to his lover's desertion, his recollections of his past, and his inability to view his past or himself as a whole. "Winter Market" is the story of Lise, a neuroelectronic artist who has herself translated into the computer net shortly before she dies. It is told through the eyes of Casey, the recording editor who reworked her dreams and ambitions into best-selling software. In "Dogfight," which Gibson wrote with Michael Swanwick, Deke finds a way out of his dead-end life by hustling "wetware" projection dogfights, but he destroys so much in pursuit of his victory, including his opponent's will to live, that the victory is virtually meaningless.

"Red Star, Winter Orbit" and "Hinterlands" are both set in space, in a society in which power is still largely divided between the Americans and the Soviets. "Red Star, Winter Orbit," a collaboration with Bruce Sterling, describes the decline of Kosmograd, a Soviet space station in a decaying orbit. "Hinterland" is a dark story in which Toby Halpert explains the workings of the Highway, a point in space where human space vehicles vanish and eventually reappear, the occupants bringing back strange artifacts and new information. The problem is that most occupants come back insane or dead. Toby's job is to meet the ones that come back alive and sane and to keep them that way, if he can.

The remaining two stories differ from the rest of the collection in tone as well as setting. Set in the 1980's, both lack the gritty high-tech atmosphere common to the other stories and share instead a sense of the surreal. "The Belonging Kind," cowritten with John Shirley, describes a kind of animal evolved to live within urban structures, mimicking people and changing like a chameleon to fit its various environments. The story details the slow metamorphosis of Coretti, a socially awkward linguist, into one of these animals. In "The Gernsback Continuum," a photographer hired to document remnants of 1930's American futuristic design begins to see what a friend calls "semiotic ghosts," hallucinations of the 1980's as they might have been, an ultimately dystopic vision he suppresses by watching bad television.

ANALYSIS

Burning Chrome contains Gibson's short work up to 1986. As do many single-author short-story collections, *Burning Chrome* presents a summary of Gibson's early themes and devices. The primary characteristics of the subgenre that became known as cyberpunk are all present: setting, character types, basic conflicts, and pace. In the case of the Sprawl stories, the setting and even some characters of the later Neuromancer novels appear, such as Molly Millions from "Johnny Mnemonic" and The Finn, the fence in "Burning Chrome."

As represented in this collection, much of Gibson's work combines elements of three traditions: hard science fiction (technological development), soft science fiction (social change), and New Wave (cynicism and apprehension about the future). These broad elements serve to examine themes such as isolation, relationships, and identity.

Identity in Gibson's work is fluid. Names and faces, and even data stores, can be changed. The degree of fluidity ranges from Johnny Mnemonic's temporary assumption of another face and persona to the chameleon-like adaptations of "The Belonging Kind." Not all fluid identities are conscious or desired. Both Parker in "Fragments of a Hologram Rose" and Fox in "New Rose Hotel" sift through fragments in hopes of seeing an unknown whole. Parker's fragments are isolated memories of his past; Fox's are his identification cards.

It is perhaps not surprising, given the near-future timeframe, that these stories have in some ways dated rapidly. They were overtaken in the early 1990's not by technological change so much as by social changes, such as the dissolution of the Soviet Union and the reunification of Germany. Stories with direct references to the Soviet Union, such as "Red Star, Winter Orbit," suffer most.

Gibson is recognized as one of the creators of the cyberpunk subgenre. The cyberpunk story "Johnny Mnemonic" is the basis for the film *Johnny Mnemonic* (1995), starring Keanu Reeves as Johnny.

—*Kim G. Kofmel*

THE BURNING COURT

Editor Edward Stevens attempts to investigate a murder and to explain the mysterious similarity in appearance between his wife and a nineteenth century murderess pictured in a book he is editing

Author: John Dickson Carr (1906-1977)
Genre: Fantasy—occult
Type of work: Novel
Time of work: 1929
Locale: Pennsylvania
First published: 1937

THE STORY

The Burning Court is an unusual novel—a cross between a traditional detective story and an occult horror tale. Without the epilogue, it is a detective novel similar to John Dickson Carr's other works, in which the murderer is caught and the woman who was wrongly suspected is vindicated. The epilogue unexpectedly brings in the supernatural as the true explanation, turning the story into a horror tale.

Edward Stevens, an editor with a New York publishing house, is working on a book about nineteenth cen-tury murderers when he finds a photograph of Marie D'Aubray, a woman guillotined for murder in 1881. He is disconcerted to see that she closely resembles his wife, Marie. He realizes how little he knows about his beautiful wife, who captivated him with what he calls her "spiritual" look. A professor friend tells him that another Marie D'Aubray was condemned as a murderer in 1676.

Watching Marie as she goes about her housewifely duties in their Philadelphia home, Edward wonders about her ancestry.

Edward's friends Mark and Lucy Despard are concerned that their Uncle Miles's death from gastroenteritis may not in fact have been from natural causes. Mark even wonders if Lucy is involved, considering that they inherited Miles's property. Mark, Edward, and a doctor friend attempt to disinter the body to check for poison, but it has been removed. Meanwhile, evidence suggesting that Marie is a witch accumulates, making Edward uneasy and suspicious.

Finally, witnesses of Miles's death are brought forth, and it is revealed that he was indeed murdered. Moreover, it appears that Marie, not Lucy, is guilty. At the last minute, everything is explained: Another woman— Miles's nurse and lover— appears to be the murderer, and her guilt is apparently demonstrated by the fact that she killed someone else in view of police officers. Marie's witchlike behavior is explained away by psychology; she was reared by a psychotic, abusive aunt who believed in witchcraft and who made Marie believe that she herself was a witch.

The epilogue takes the reader into Marie's mind after the investigation is over. It reveals that she is a witch and was executed in the seventeenth century and then again in the nineteenth century. She had forgotten much about her earlier incarnations, but she is beginning to remember details of past lives. Her love for her husband Edward is real, but it is not a good thing for Edward: It means that she will soon make him one of the "non-dead" immortal evildoers, and this will require that she "transform" (kill) him. She hopes she can do this "without pain. Or too much pain."

ANALYSIS
The Burning Court's epilogue provides a surprising ending. Readers of the book tend to be not fantasy fans but detective story addicts who are astounded and often irritated by the nontraditional ending. This unusual, mixed-genre novel draws most appreciation from readers who are not committed to a particular genre. As a detective story, it seems not to "play by the rules" in calling on supernatural forces as the story's resolution. As an occult horror novel, however, it spends too much time on the particulars of investigations.

The Burning Court does, however, succeed in mixing the ratiocination of the standard detective story with the intuitive, mythic reasoning of the horror story. Carr skillfully buffets the reader back and forth between the occult and the realistic explanations of events. For example, Marie is terrified of funnels—her face changes, looking more "lined," when confronted with one. A book describing the history of witchcraft describes the water torture (water forced through a funnel into the witch's mouth) that was inflicted on suspected witches in previous centuries. Contradicting this, however, is the suggestion that Marie's aunt used a funnel to punish her as a child. In the epilogue, it is made clear that the old book provided the "real" explanation. This kind of device is used throughout the novel, and the detective story reader, accustomed to Carr's Gideon Fell mysteries, expects all the supernatural elements to be explained away at the end as the truth is presented in the clear light of reason.

The careful reader of the old-school detective story, in which the rules are carefully and consistently kept, is aware that there are holes in the apparently satisfactory explanation to the case. Marie seems to have knowledge she could not have acquired normally, and certain physical details do not jibe with the conclusion that the nurse killed Miles. In the epilogue, all these details are explained: If Marie truly is a witch, then she is not hampered by human limitations in the achievement of her goals.

As a surprise fantasy novel, *The Burning Court* is rare in the field. When it was published, it was extremely controversial and received unfavorable reviews from critics who believed that Carr had cheated by using a supernatural explanation. Additionally, letting the evildoer win generally was not done in the detective stories of the 1930's, which usually ended with the triumph of justice. *The Burning Court* is unlikely to be read as a fantasy because the novel leads the reader to expect a detective story. Although it falls between the two genres of the fantasy and the detective novel, *The Burning Court* nevertheless provides an unforgettable reading experience.

—*Janet McCann*

CAMP CONCENTRATION

In a situation resembling the Vietnam War, Louis Sacchetti, a poet and conscientious objector, is moved to a secret underground facility, where experiments are undertaken to radically accelerate intelligence using lethal syphilis

Author: Thomas M. Disch (1940-2008)
Genre: Science fiction—inner space
Type of work: Novel
Time of work: The near future
Location: A disused gold mine in Colorado
First published: 1968

THE STORY

Louis Sacchetti is told by General Haast, the camp commandant, that he has been moved to Camp Archimedes to record what he sees. Dr. Aimée Busk, the camp psychiatrist, further explains that as those around him are dying of syphilis induced by the strain Pallidine (which kills in about nine months), they undergo stunning increases in intelligence, which the military hopes to employ.

In his diary, which forms the bulk of the narrative, Sacchetti reports meeting the other men at the camp. Among them is GeorgeWagner, the first prisoner Sacchetti meets and the first he sees entombed. The prisoners' leader is Mordecai Washington, who knew Sacchetti in his school days.Washington is deeply immersed in alchemical studies and has become a magnificent polymath in only a few months. The prisoners prepare a brilliant production of Christopher Marlowe's *Doctor Faustus*, but Wagner dies before he can play the lead. Then Washington and Haast take part in an alchemical attempt to obtain immortality, but it goes wrong, and Washington dies horribly. The following night, Sacchetti dreams the truth, that he is infected and dying. The balance of his journal is in scraps, heavy with literary allusion, showing that he gets sicker and more brilliant each day.

Busk leaves the camp, and a new group of subjects arrives, centered on Skilliman, a failed but nasty and ambitious scientist who chooses the Pallidine treatment in order to develop weapons. Sacchetti sets up a museum of artifacts that add up to the fact that Busk, as a result of sexual intercourse with Washington, has spread the syphilis rapidly across the United States. Skilliman's conflicts with Sacchetti, the only survivor of the original group, begin as Sacchetti starts to draw off Skilliman's followers. A confrontation ensues in which Skilliman demands that Sacchetti, now blind, be executed. Instead, Haast kills Skilliman and reveals that the alchemical experiment was a disguised brain pattern exchange in which Washington's mind came to occupy Haast's body. The simultaneous reverse action of the "mind reciprocator" so horrified Haast that it was he who died in Washington's body.

The novel closes on a challenge to the changed prisoners, who look forward to a future of both genius and eternal life, although that prolonged life would be at the repeated cost of the lives of others, until a vaccine is found for the Pallidine infection.

ANALYSIS

Camp Concentration is a vital meeting of several forces. Thomas M. Disch, though living in the United States, was much influenced by the British New Wave writers who were exploring the inner space of human consciousness through literary experimentation. *Camp Concentration* is a conscious variation on Thomas Mann's monumental *Doctor Faustus* (1947), in that it deals with the price of genius and is set against a background of wartime tyranny, which sharpens the novel's moral aspect.

The novel is set during a war in the future, but it is a very near future (attested by the presence of President McNamara, presumably the

1960's secretary of defense). This is clearly a novel about the illegitimacy of the war in Vietnam and the methods of the military research establishment. The novel's most important aspect is its experimentation with literary style. Sacchetti is a poet and litterateur from the start (he cites Fyodor Dostoevski's *The House of the Dead* [1915] on the first page of the text), but his literary allusions become far more pronounced as his intelligence and reading accelerate as a result of the syphilis. Others, like Washington, bring in Arthur Koestler's definitions of genius, and there are extensive references to the alchemical masters and great writers who have had syphilis. As Sacchetti's illness advances, his journal disintegrates into a literate, allusive stream of consciousness in which he quotes or mentions such diverse figures as Heinrich Himmler, Saint Augustine, Hans Yost, André-Georges Malreux, and John Milton, along with citing the Bible. The texture gives a rich, complex speculation on disease, genius, and death.

The text has an overriding tone of moral confrontation. Sacchetti, an intellectual Roman Catholic, has become a conscientious objector to the war and is aware of the issues surrounding what is happening to him and the other subjects. Skilliman, who seems at first to be injected into the latter part of the text only to fill the void created by the deaths of the earlier group of subjects, is the immoral practitioner of science—the man willing to use his increased intelligence for personal fame and to create weapons of destruction. Sacchetti engages in a series of dialogues with him and his young assistants and emerges victorious in moral fact (and in winning over the assistants), although it appears that he has lost in physical and practical terms. Washington-Haast's murder of Skilliman and Sacchetti's escape into a healthy body reestablish the balance, but it is arguably a *deus ex machina* ending.

The idea of a plague spreading from the evil machinations of military research, of the moral sickness of the society becoming a physical sickness unto death, is a marker of the conscience of the text. Even the surprise ending has moral implications: Several of the infected prisoners choose physical death over the act of sentencing to death whomever they could have exchanged bodies with. *Camp Concentration* is a brilliant, tough book, bringing broad issues and complex literary continuity into science fiction.

—*Peter Brigg*

Canopus in Argos

A depiction of the falling away from a spiritual unity of humans and other species and an explanation of problems such as violence and sexism, set in the context of conflict between space empires of Canopus and Sirius

Author: Doris Lessing (1919–2013)
Genre: Science fiction—galactic empire
Type of work: Novels
Time of work: Various times between antiquity and the end of the universe
Locale: Various locations on Earth and other planets
First published: *Re: Colonised Planet 5, Shikasta* (1979), *The Marriage Between Zones Three, Four, and Five* (1980), *The Sirian Experiments* (1981), *The Making of the Representative for Planet 8* (1982), and *The Sentimental Agents in the Volyen Empire* (1983)

The Story
This series of novels was published in a period of four years with the series title Canopus in Argos prominently displayed on each. Although the novels contain no major continuing characters, they are all set in the context of competing ideologies. The series is connected through the repetition of ideas rather than a developing plot or continuing characters. Philosophical in content and in structure, the novels tell a future history and recast events of the past, such as the legend of Atlantis. All the novels emphasize that humans and beings on other worlds must learn the importance of unity in order to correct problems in their societies. In *Re: Colonised Planet 5, Shikasta*, human beings discover the importance of mental powers. The human race possesses great powers, but it is unsure of how to use them. Losing its creator, the space empire Canopus, causes Earth

to have seasons and its inhabitants to devolve. Canopean agents try to redeem Earth, and they appear under the guise of alternative science or magic. Unfortunately, only a few people hear and heed the Canopean message. As a result of human neglect of unification, an apocalypse occurs.

In *The Marriage Between Zones Three, Four, and Five*, the queen of a feminist utopian society (Zone Three) marries the leader of Zone Four, a patriarchal warrior society. The novel shows her struggle to accept a man who has completely different values. No mention is made of Earth or of the other novels.

In *The Sirian Experiments*, the Sirians, who represent an extension of twentieth century Western science, struggle with Canopeans, who represent magic or alternative science. An agent of Sirius converts to the Canopean way of viewing the world. *The Making of the Representative for Planet 8* tells the story of an ecological collapse as an entire planet becomes covered by ice and snow. The planet cannot be saved except through a storyteller who preserves the planet's people and experience in Canopus' memory. The planet's disaster is traced to Earth's separation from the Canopus empire.

The Sentimental Agents in the Volyen Empire depicts rebels on the planet Voleyenadna who are manipulated by false and misleading rhetoric. A Canopean agent, who also appears in *Re: Colonised Planet 5, Shikasta*, helps women save the planet with a regenerating plant food.

In the series as a whole, plots focus on the struggle between the empires of Canopus and Sirius. Canopus is a female-identified empire that uses magic and mental powers, and Sirius is a fact-based empire that relies on machines and Western science. The series takes the Canopean perspective and criticizes Sirians' myopic point of view.

Analysis

Doris Lessing had established an illustrious career as a realistic novelist before she wrote *Canopus in Argos*. This series comes rather late in her career and represents a substantial shift in her writing. Reviewers responded negatively to this shift. Lessing has written many novels since *Canopus in Argos*, but none of them are science fiction. *Canopus in Argos* has been seen as an aberration in her work.

Like Margaret Atwood and P. D. James, other well-known female writers who have written science fiction, Lessing appears to have thought that only science fiction could convey her radical criticism of contemporary society.

Lessing's science fiction can be seen as part of a trend by female writers who use science fiction to propose alternatives to current gender roles. *Canopus in Argos* also has been identified as part of the British tradition of science fiction, especially the work of Olaf Stapledon. Stapledon is most famous for *Last and First Men* (1930), a work that deals with the evolution of a number of human races over the course of two billion years. Like Stapledon, Lessing looks at an immense time frame, a common "race mind," and the evolution of humanity. Like Stapledon's work, Lessing's series is science fiction that focuses on ideas rather than characters or an action-adventure plot.

Lessing prefers the term "space fiction" to that of science fiction. "Space" is used to describe the genre in England, but the phrase also implies a particular type of science fiction. Space fiction, as Lessing creates it, is more concerned with the powers of the human mind than with technology or new kinds of machines.

The series consistently asserts an androgynous vision. Canopeans transcend sex because they can be either male or female when they visit Earth. The series looks back nostalgically to a time when Earth was ruled by women using magic, when language did not exist, and when planets and other beings communed mentally. The series also emphasizes dissatisfaction with and distrust of language. Lessing's emphasis on philosophical concepts makes her work an ambitious and complex work of science fiction.

Although *Canopus in Argos* is nonlinear and achronological (the books can be read in any order), the novels should be considered in the order in which they were published. For example, the tenuous connection between *Re: Colonised Planet 5, Shikasta* and *The Marriage Between Zones Three, Four, and Five*, which are labeled as volumes 1 and 2, requires readers to look for philosophical and other connections. What is important about the series is the way in which Lessing uses nontraditional narration, such as documents and reports, to criticize traditional science and ways of looking at the world. Throughout the series, Lessing stresses that an openness to multiple perspectives is the only way to salvage society.

Re: Colonised Planet 5, Shikasta can be read as an origin myth about Earth. The story of the planet's fall from grace explains why and how humanity created the mess that is twentieth century Earth. Scientists scoff at the messengers who explain Earth's true history; through science's arrogance, Earth becomes even more sick. Science provides the mechanism that touches off the holocaust, supporting the Canopean (and Lessing's) contention that science has gotten out of control.

The queen of *The Marriage Between Zones Three, Four, and Five* suggests that witches and magic can be an alternative to science. By associating a female leader with powers that are seen on Earth as unreal, Lessing recovers magic as a powerful alternative to science. The queen Al*Ith becomes a prophet of the importance of unity and a revered role model. The narrator of this novel creates a legend as he retells Al*Ith's story. Art preserves and interprets her experience. Al*Ith has been compared to Demeter, the mythical female figure whose separation from her daughter resulted in seasons on Earth. The book also has been interpreted as a utopia, depicting a world that is both perfect and nonexistent. This setting disrupts the more traditional science-fiction setting of *Re: Colonised Planet 5, Shikasta*. The novel also ruptures the more traditional sense of time and place of the first novel.

By disrupting the tidy, ordered frame of a science-fiction series, Lessing alerts her readers to her more ambitious goal of resisting definitions and frames. She forces the reader to examine the conventional assumptions of a science-fiction series.

Like Al*Ith, Ambien II, the protagonist of *The Sirian Experiments*, has a role as prophet. A Sirian, she realizes the dangers of science as the Sirians practice it and converts to Canopus. Her conversion experience persuades readers to lessen their respect for Western science. In the next novel, Lessing minimizes science by stressing how much more powerful art is. Only art, not science, can provide any salvation for the people of Planet 8 in *The Making of the Representative for Planet 8*. Again, Lessing praises the power of art and criticizes the failings of science. The last volume continues the critique of science but also exposes the ways in which language is used to control thought and block ideas. *The Sentimental Agents in the Volyen Empire* is an open-ended volume, because after her criticism of order and control in science and language, Lessing throws the issues she raises to her readers. A complex and philosophical series, *Canopus in Argos* requires the reader to challenge accepted ideas about science, magic, and gender.

—*Robin Roberts*

A CANTICLE FOR LEIBOWITZ

A monastic order struggles through many centuries of war and barbarism to maintain its commitment to God

Author: Walter M. Miller, Jr. (1923-1996)
Genre: Science fiction—future history
Type of work: Novel
Time of work: About 2600 to 3781
Location: The southwestern United States
First published: 1960 (serial form, *The Magazine of Fantasy and Science Fiction*, 1955-1957)

THE STORY

The novel has three sections, with narratives separated by about six hundred years between sections. From the perspective of the Abbey of Saint Leibowitz, church history is recapitulated in a future "Dark Age," a "Renaissance," and an apocalyptic "Modern Age."

The first section, "Fiat Homo" ("let there be man"), begins about 2600 c.e. A twentieth century atomic war and a repressive Age of Simplification have almost wiped out the past. Brother Francis, a simple monk fasting in the desert, uncovers an underground chamber with "Fallout Survival Shelter" written over it. He believes that Fallout is the name of a demon and has no conception of the war that destroyed civilization. The shelter contains documents written by Leibowitz, an engineer who stayed on at the abbey after the war and devoted himself to the preservation of knowledge.

In the timeless life of the abbey, the Blessed Leibowitz finally is declared a saint. Brother Francis devotes fifteen years to illuminating a wholly meaningless blueprint. On the way to New Rome to present his illumination to the pope, he is robbed by mutants. The pope gives the monk enough gold to buy back the illumination. In the second encounter, however, the mutants steal the gold and cannibalize him, casting him as a martyr.

In the second section, "Fiat Lux" (let there be light), set in 3174 c.e., the church is challenged by new ideas and powerful princes. Dom Paulo, the current abbot, struggles to preserve the abbey against outside influence. Thon Taddeo, a brilliant but arrogant scientist, reveals more about the Leibowitz memorabilia in a few minutes than the monks have been able to in centuries. In a symbolic scene, a crucifix is taken down so that an arc lamp can be installed for the thon. The abbot, arguing that the pursuit of knowledge, though not evil in itself, cannot be the purpose of humankind, orders the crucifix to be returned to the wall. Thereafter, all will read *ad Lumina Christi*, or "in the light of Christ."

The third section, "Fiat Voluntas Tua" ("let there be your will"), is directed against humanism, a view that argues that humanity is the proper focus of human attention. In 3781 c.e., atomic war breaks out, and millions are poisoned with radioactivity. The government sets up mercy camps, offering euthanasia to those dying in agony. Two characters frame the issues significant to Dom Zerchi, the latest abbot. Dr. Cors, a mercy camp administrator, argues that suffering is evil and should be alleviated. The abbot, in contrast, rejects euthanasia as a violation of God's will. The other significant person in this section is Mrs. Grales, a mutant who wants Rachel, the dormant extra head on her shoulder, to be baptized. Dom Zerchi, fearful of the implications, puts off her request. A bomb hits the abbey, killing Mrs. Grales and mortally wounding the abbot. At this moment, however, Rachel unexpectedly comes alive. As his last act, Dom Zerchi struggles through the wreckage to baptize her. Thereafter, the Vatican sends three bishops into space in an emergency plan to preserve the apostolic succession.

Analysis

In a brief writing career that extended from 1949 to 1957, Walter M. Miller, Jr., produced the justly praised novel *A Canticle for Leibowitz* and forty-one shorter pieces of science fiction. All of them, including the original serialized version of the novel, appeared in such popular publications as *Galaxy* and *The Magazine of Fantasy and Science Fiction*.

Miller's work shows the usual characteristics of genre writing: action plots, ready characterizations, and a bright but brittle acquaintance with technology and ideas. Miller's commitment to Roman Catholicism, however, immediately set his work apart. With a skillful play on the willing suspension of disbelief, he used the science-fiction story as a what-if instrument to make religious doctrine real by asserting it as the fictional given and then testing it with intellectual challenges.

A Canticle for Leibowitz addresses, directly or indirectly, various theological concerns. If there is another species possessing free will, is it then subject to the same pattern of divine history, with a fall from grace and a hope for redemption? Would a degenerate race lose its soul? At what point in human evolution is found *homo inspiratus*, the creation of the soul? Logically, must this not occur at one precise moment? How could it be developmental? Given the perceived scale of astronomical time, how long will it take the Second Coming to occur? Will it be a universal event, occurring everywhere at once, or in only one place at a time? (Miller's answer appears to be the latter.) If all are not on the same schedule, then what of those races that exist before the Fall? As humanity continues to evolve, what happens to its relationship to God? What happens if disaster breaks the apostolic succession of God's divinely ordained church?

Although his concerns may seem musty and medieval, Miller turns them into a compelling drama. He joins the argument that began in the Renaissance between science and religion, paradoxically using the naturalistic tone of "hard" science fiction to suggest that matters ordinarily resting on faith are literally true. A central artistic strategy of the novel, for example, is to make real the sense of historical development implicit in Christianity. As does Judaism, Christianity asserts a time line that includes creation, the Fall of Man, God's identification with a national people, the coming of a messiah, his death and resurrection, and ultimately the Second Coming, in which the meaning of history vanishes. From a Christian perspective, all steps but the last have been completed. From the perspective of modern astronomy, this may seem to be vainglorious mythmaking on an insignificant planet. Miller's precise purpose is to square these perspectives in the framework of the scientifically understood cosmos. If and when the space-traveling delegates of New Rome ever return to Earth, Bishop Zerchi declares, "you might meet the Archangel at the east end of Earth, guarding her passes with a sword of flame."

—*Bruce Olsen*

CARNACKI THE GHOST FINDER

Psychic sleuth Carnacki investigates nine apparently supernatural phenomena

Author: William Hope Hodgson (1877–1918)
Genre: Fantasy—occult
Type of work: Stories
Time of work: About 1910
Locale: Great Britain (greater London, the South Coast, and northern England), Galway, and western Ireland
First published: 1913 (expanded version, 1947)

THE STORY

Six stories, first published in *The Idler* in 1910 and *New Magazine* in 1910 and 1912, appeared in the original 1913 publication of *Carnacki the Ghost-Finder*. Three additional stories were found among William Hope Hodgson's papers after his death and were included in an expanded edition published in 1947. The nine stories are presented by a first-person narrator (Dodgson), one of a group of four friends to whom Carnacki reports on his occult investigations. Three of the stories ("The Thing Invisible," "The Find," and "The House Among the Laurels") are mystery stories; two ("The Horse of the Invisible" and "The Searcher of the End House") have apparently rational conclusions that are compromised by elements that cannot be explained by rational means.

The investigations often involve the animation of inert objects to cause bodily harm or create a sense of imminent threat to life or sanity. In "The Thing Invisible," a knife displayed in a family chapel lives up to its reputation of striking murderously at enemies of the Jarnock family who enter the chapel at night. The door to the Grey Room in "The Gateway of the Monster" slams constantly at night while bedclothes are pulled from a bed and thrown into a corner of a room. Blood drips from the ceiling, sealed doors open, and candles and fires are extinguished in "The House Among the Laurels." The floor of "The Whistling Room" puckers like a gigantic pair of lips and whistles until the sound rises to a "mad screaming note."

More conventional occult manifestations involve the ghostly figures of a running boy and a woman in "The Searcher of the End House" and the thundering of the hooves of a gigantic, invisible horse that pursues the eldest child of a cursed family in "The Horse of the Invisible." In "The Hog," a gateway opens up to another dimension from which a monstrous creature attempts to break through onto our plane. In "The Haunted Jarvee,'" Carnacki attempts to "desensitize" a ship threatened by shadowy forces that attack it with the force of a raging, destructive storm.

ANALYSIS

Hodgson's combination of classic detection with occult investigations was not without precedent. Hodgson's Carnacki is a younger version of J. Sheridan Le Fanu's Martin Hesselius (introduced in "Green Tea," 1869), a doctor of "metaphysical medicine," and Algernon Blackwood's title character of the story collection *John Silence, Physician Extraordinary* (1908). Unlike them, Carnacki has no medical training, but he does have a strong scientific bent, illustrated by his invention of an ingenious "Electric Pentacle," a variation of the cabalistic five-pointed star enclosed within a circle and intended to act as a barrier against malevolent occult forces. Carnacki refers to his use of formulae from ancient magic rituals as a "curious thing for a Twentieth Century man" that might provoke "cheap laughter" from some. Carnacki, however, will not allow himself to be "blinded" by ridicule: "I ask questions and keep my eyes open."

This self-deprecating definition by Carnacki of his character touches on aspects of the stories that seem to border on parody. The floor that sports puckered lips in "The Whistling Room" and the haunting of the Grey Room by a "monstrous hand" in "The Gateway of the Monster" are shown to be powerful agents of destruction that are nevertheless more grotesque than horrific. The trap that releases a deadly weapon is a clever but deflating conclusion for "The Thing Invisible." In other conclusions, a man emerges from a basement cistern with a leg of rotting mutton in his hand in "The Searcher of the End House" and, in "The Horse of the Invisible," the horse turns out to be a man wearing an enormous horse head and with "great hoofs" attached to his wrists. These conclusions certainly can provoke laughter that is not "cheap" but justified by the clumsy resolutions they encompass.

There remain those stories that largely succeed in their intended effect or those moments in otherwise flawed narratives that offset obvious weaknesses. The final three stories in the 1947 edition, found among Hodgson's papers and never published during his lifetime, are perhaps the most diverse and most interesting in the Carnacki series. "The Find" is a story of detection and demonstrates Hodgson's ability to tell an engrossing story without supernatural trappings. "The Haunted Jarvee'" is in the lineage of Hodgson's sea fiction, the eerie atmo-spherics rendered all the more effective for the realistic portrayal of the ship, which Hodgson based on his eight years spent at sea, reportedly traveling three times around the globe. This story does not include the detailed mythos of the Sargasso Sea that Hodgson developed in other of his sea stories, but its depiction of the ship as prey to the forces of a malevolent nature contains some of the best writing in the collection.

The final, longest story, "The Hog," is the most successful at sustaining a steadily escalating sense of terror. Carnacki fights to save his client—a dreamer whose nightmares are only too real—from the "monstrosities of the Outer Circle," predatory beings who seek to absorb our "psychic energy." The most important legatee of this story may be the Cthulhu mythos of H. P. Lovecraft, although Carnacki is able to thwart the psychic takeover of the dreamer's soul and body that is the awful fate of Lovecraft's doomed searchers after forbidden knowledge.

Despite a sometimes uncertain mix of thriller melodramatics and moments of finely achieved supernatural legerdemain, *Carnacki the Ghost-Finder* stands as one of Hodgson's most accessible works, at its best combining the fine eye for significant detail of detective fiction with the stomach-churning uneasiness engendered by supernatural fiction. Where classical detective fiction restores a sense of orderly process, Hodgson's dark imaginings posit a quiet resolution as only a temporary respite.

—*Walter Albert*

CARRIE

A young girl rejected by her high-school peers and her mother explores her powers of telekinesis and exacts revenge on her enemies

Author: Stephen King (1947–)
Genre: Fantasy—extrasensory powers
Type of work: Novel
Time of work: The 1960's
Locale: Chamberlain, Maine
First published: 1974

THE STORY

Carrie is Stephen King's first published novel, for which he received a $5,000 advance. With this book, he showed his interest in telekinesis and children, two motifs that characterize much of his fiction. The protagonist of the book, Carrie White, is almost eighteen and is a senior in high school.

King divides the novel roughly into two halves, "Blood Sport" and "Prom Night." In the first half, King introduces his method for telling the story, which is to write much of the story as anyone might, but with the inclusion of fictional newspaper stories and books written after the events of his book. This experimental technique adds objectivity to an understanding of what happens and makes clear that telekinesis remains misunderstood and may exist in some form.

In "Blood Sport," the reader encounters gangly and unpopular Carrie White while she takes a shower at school after gym class. While in the shower, she starts to menstruate for the first time, causing all the other girls to jeer at her and bringing out Carrie's power. The gym teacher intervenes, wondering how it is that a girl her age had never menstruated before and why her parents had never discussed it with her. When Carrie mentions the incident to her mother, a fundamentalist, she forces Carrie into a closet to pray for her sins.

The reader learns of telekinetic acts, including a rain of stones on the White house, and future reactions from Carrie's classmates who survived her wrath. A primary character is Sue Snell, who does not go to the prom. She asks her boyfriend, Tommy Ross, to take Carrie instead. Chris Hargensen has been refused prom tickets for not taking the prescribed punishment for the taunting of Carrie, and she asks several local dropouts to get revenge on Carrie. Ignoring her mother's requests, Carrie goes to the dance with Tommy Ross, and through a rigged balloting, they are elected king and queen of the prom.

At the moment of crowning, Chris and an accomplice, Billy Nolan, pull strings that drench Carrie in blood and drop a bucket on Tommy Ross's head. The injury will kill Ross, though no one knows it at the time. Everyone laughs at Carrie, and she leaves. She goes home to her mother, who is waiting to kill her because she is tainted with the curse of blood. In a remarkable telekinetic scene, Carrie kills her mother and goes back downtown to the school, destroying gas stations and causing massive fires on the way. When she reaches the school, she telekinetically bolts the doors, trapping most of her schoolmates inside. They are destroyed through electrocutions and fire. Carrie dies of wounds inflicted by her mother and, King suggests, because she wanted to. He adds a kind of epilogue, "Wreckage," that collects information on the aftermath: 440 dead and resignations from administrators and teachers at the school.

The last paragraphs come from a letter from a relative of Carrie White. They chillingly indicate that in Tennessee there is a little girl, age two, who can make things move without touching them.

ANALYSIS

King's first novel was slow in catching on. Once it had done so, however, it grabbed readers and critics alike, and a major motion picture was made from it in 1976. The novel uses the experimental technique of created books, reports, wire service copy, and other material, in some cases supposed to have been published ten years after the events of *Carrie*. These accounts tend to objectify the seemingly impossible events in the novel.

In choosing paranormal activity as one of the subjects of his novel, King realized that it had to be worked in slowly, yet quickly enough so the reader would have an idea what to expect. The incident of stones raining down on the White house is discussed fairly early, but only later do readers learn that Carrie was angry at her mother and showed her anger in that way. Similarly, when Carrie is at school, her telekinetic responses to her humiliation and, later, her response to a principal who cannot get her name right are minor events, almost accidents. Carrie does not know the extent of her powers. She is able to control them expertly, however, by the time she agrees to go to the prom with Tommy Ross, over her mother's objections. Carrie forces her mother to sit down while she sews her own dress.

The real force of Carrie's telekinetic powers comes after the prom, when Carrie's mind seems to operate independently of her body. She has been drenched in pig's blood, and Tommy Ross has been killed by one of the buckets hitting his head. Even at that moment, though, Carrie does not strike back, unlike in the film version. She goes home to be comforted by her mother, who is waiting to kill the "witch child." Carrie is forced to kill her mother in self-defense. With nothing left of her life and nothing to look forward to, she goes back to the school for revenge. Her attack on the town seemingly is a test of the strength and control of her powers. Blinded by her mission, she seems to recognize none of the people stuck at the gas stations that she ignites.

King allows a few students and the gym teacher to escape the conflagration. Sue Snell had not gone to the prom, and she finds Carrie unconscious in the school parking lot, having just destroyed the car of Chris Hargensen and Billy Nolan. As readers learn from *My Name Is Sue Snell,* Sue's account of that night, she saw into Carrie's mind and found mostly darkness.

At the book's conclusion, the White house is destroyed, and the town has become a tourist attraction. King ends on a note of warning that telekinesis is not a toy but something very dark.

—*John Jacob*

A Case of Conscience

Convinced that the planet he is investigating has been created by Satan to delude humanity, a priest-biologist welcomes the experiment that destroys the planet and its intelligent inhabitants

Author: James Blish (1921–1975)
Genre: Science fiction—apocalypse
Type of work: Novel
Time of work: 2049–2050
Location: Lithia, a planet 50 light-years from Earth; New York City; and Vatican City
First published: 1958 (book 1 abridged as "A Case of Conscience" in *If,* 1953)

The Story

Ramon Ruiz-Sanchez is a Jesuit priest as well as a biologist with the United Nations (U.N.) survey team on the recently discovered planet of Lithia. Lithia, dominated by a species of intelligent reptilians, is an apparent utopia. The Lithians have no crime, no politics, and no religion, and their ethical code (otherwise identical to that of Christianity) is based on pure reason. Despite their planet's iron-poor crust, the Lithians have developed advanced technologies, including a planetary communications web based on pulses emitted by the gigantic Message Tree, the roots of which reach into the planet's bedrock.

When the survey team meets to make its recommendations before departing from Lithia, Ruiz is in surprising near agreement with physicist Paul Cleaver. Cleaver advises closing the planet publicly while secretly turning it into a nuclear weapons laboratory. Ruiz also votes to close the planet, with a permanent quarantine, because he has become convinced that Satan created Lithia as a convincing demonstration that virtue is possible without God's grace. The other two team members recommend that Lithia be opened. The tie vote means that the planet will remain at least temporarily off limits. As the terrestrials leave, Ruiz's Lithian friend Chtexa gives him a farewell gift, a sealed vase containing the fertilized embryo of Chtexa's child. The embryo, as it develops outside the body, will replicate the evolutionary history of its species.

Book 2 opens in a U.N. laboratory back in New York, where Ruiz and lab director Liu Meid are observing the movements of the tiny Lithian, whose name (inscribed in his genetic code) is Egtverchi. When Lithia team member Mike Michelis arrives to request his help writing a nonclassified version of the Lithia report, Ruiz casually announces that he expects to be tried in Rome for teaching the heresy of diabolical creation.

As Egtverchi develops, it is clear to Ruiz that he will prove to be a sentient being eligible to become a naturalized U.N. citizen. Events rapidly prove Ruiz correct. Egtverchi, who reaches adulthood within months, becomes a television celebrity and a satirical commentator on terrestrial society. His large following seems to be composed primarily of psychopaths created by the unnatural living conditions of Earth's "shelter economy."

Meanwhile, the pope advises Ruiz to consider whether Lithia might be possessed rather than created by Satan. The distinction would allow Ruiz to abandon his heresy while literally exorcising the Lithian menace. As a last resort, Ruiz takes Egtverchi to the Canadian retreat of solid-state physicist Count d'Averoigne, who has devised an apparatus allowing simultaneous communication with the Message Tree. Egtverchi proves unresponsive to the remonstrances of his Lithian father, and Ruiz learns that Cleaver, back on Lithia in charge of the weapons project he proposed, is cutting down the Message Tree.

When Egtverchi's last broadcast touches off widespread rioting, the United Nations attempts to arrest him, but he stows away on a starship bound for Lithia. Ruiz, Liu, and Michelis join Count d'Averoigne at his lunar observatory, where he has set up a telescope that allows simultaneous viewing of interstellar objects. Communicating through the starship, the count has warned Cleaver that his experiment might destroy the planet, but he fears that Cleaver may stubbornly persist. Ruiz pronounces his exorcism shortly before the image of Lithia explodes, taking the monitor screen with it.

ANALYSIS

A Case of Conscience compares favorably with other novels of apocalyptic science fiction, such as Arthur C. Clarke's *Childhood's End* (1953), and with other novels treating conflict between science and religion, such as Walter M. Miller, Jr.'s *A Canticle for Leibowitz* (1960). For the most part it avoids the sentimental, stilted narrative voice that often blemishes science fiction with a cosmic reach, and the machinery of its tight plot does not dissipate the "double truth" of its theme.

It is much to the credit of James Blish's novel that it does not attempt to downplay the very real conflict between the scientific and religious worldviews. Instead, it thematizes that conflict in the attractively humanscale figure of Ruiz. Ruiz underlines the novel's title by constantly being attuned to the promptings of conscience, no matter how inconvenient, and constantly aware of his mental life, whether it is driven by reason or by emotion. He is mortified when the pope shows him that his lapse into heresy was the result of an unscientific failure to consider alternative hypotheses. He is annoyed by his chronic sinusitis. He is bemused when he finds himself, a professed celibate, having vaguely lustful thoughts about the nubile and modest Liu Meid. He is aware of his own worldly satisfaction when he proves to be correct in his predictions. At once a minister of religion and a practicing scientist, Ruiz knows that apparently contrary propositions can be said to be true—the sick child is saved by prayer, *and* she is saved by an antibiotic. Lithia is destroyed by an exorcist, *and* the planet is destroyed in a massive industrial accident.

A blemish on the novel is the caricature of the amoral scientist in the form of Paul Cleaver, who comes across as a pasteboard villain, cursing, angry, and violent for no particular reason. His assertion of scientific and technological arrogance is too much like the vulgarity of the real estate developer who wants to build a shopping center in the last piece of wetland. He is thus in stark contrast to the complex and tormented Ruiz. The severe contrast can make the novel seem less ambiguous than it is. Few writers, however, can resist the urge to indulge in the luxury of a comical villain, and despite this fault Blish's novel improves with each reading.

—*John P. Brennan*

THE CASTLE OF OTRANTO

An evil usurper suffers the consequences of his actions as supernatural events and the heroic efforts of the rightful heirs to the principality of Otranto conspire to supplant him from his ill-gotten position

Author: Horace Walpole (1717–1797)
Genre: Fantasy—heroic fantasy
Type of work: Novel
Time of work: The late medieval period (twelfth century)
Locale: The principality of Otranto in Italy
First published: 1765

THE STORY

In *The Castle of Otranto*, recognized as the first gothic novel, Horace Walpole combines supernatural occurrences and heroic behaviors associated with the Romantic tradition to tell the story of Manfred, prince of Otranto, whose zeal for satisfying his own lusts for power and sexual gratification lead to his downfall. The tale opens on the wedding day of Manfred's son Conrad, who is betrothed to the countess Isabella. Before the ceremony, a giant helmet falls from a parapet, crushing Conrad. A peasant, Theodore, claims that the helmet is like that on the statue of the good Prince Alonso; angered, Manfred has Theodore imprisoned.

Manfred then concocts a scheme to be divorced from his wife, Hippolita, and marry Isabella himself. Isabella is repulsed by the idea and flees into a passage beneath the castle; there she meets Theodore, who has escaped from imprisonment. He helps Isabella make her way to a nearby church. Manfred recaptures Theodore, but as he accosts him, word comes that a giant is sleeping in the castle.

The next day, Father Jerome comes to inform Manfred that Isabella is safe in the church. Manfred uses the occasion to suggest his divorce and remarriage. Father Jerome is horrified, particularly because he believes Isabella is in love with someone else. Thinking Theodore is his rival, Manfred orders him executed, but when Father Jerome discovers a strange mark on the young man, he announces that Theodore is really his own son. The two are actually of noble blood, but circumstances forced Jerome to enter the priesthood when his family was kidnapped years before.

As they are speaking, the Knight of the Gigantic Saber arrives at the castle, bringing with him a giant sword. This knight comes from Isabella's father, the rightful heir to Otranto. Manfred tries to convince this emissary that a marriage to Isabella would unite the two families, but the knight is unconvinced. Father Jerome arrives to announce that Isabella has fled the church. As the parties scurry to mount a search, Matilda, Manfred's daughter, meets Theodore and helps him escape. The two instantly fall in love. Fleeing the castle, Theodore stumbles upon Isabella in the forest. Their reunion is cut short when the Knight of the Giant Saber finds them. In attempting to protect Isabella, Theodore wounds the knight. Near death, the emissary reveals that he is really Isabella's father.

Although grievously hurt, the knight is taken back to the castle to recover. There he reveals that the giant sword he carries with him bears an ominous inscription foretelling doom for Manfred. Manfred tries desperately to convince Isabella's father to unite them, but he fails. Instead, he learns from a mysterious visitor that Theodore is in the chapel with a woman. He dashes there and stabs the maiden, who turns out to be his daughter Matilda. Into this climactic scene comes the ghost of Prince Alonso, who declares Theodore to be the true heir of Otranto, as grandson of Alonso's sister. Beaten, Manfred retreats to a convent, as does his neglected wife, Hippolita. Although grieving for Matilda, Theodore marries Isabella and assumes his place as the new Prince of Otranto.

Analysis

The son of the celebrated Prime Minister Robert Walpole, Horace Walpole was a dilettante at politics but a serious student of the Middle Ages. Taken with antiquities (he wrote several volumes of nonfiction on historical subjects), Walpole wrote *The Castle of Otranto* to combine in one volume two of his most passionate interests: a fascination with the supernatural and a keen appreciation of the medieval romance. Walpole turned away from the growing appetite of the English reading public for realism, seen most vividly in the works of his contemporaries Henry Fielding, Samuel Richardson, and Tobias Smollett; instead, he capitalized on readers' interest in the "far away," as evidenced by the popularity of numerous travel books in the eighteenth century.

The accuracy of his judgment about readers' tastes is borne out by the spate of "gothic" novels that followed the publication of Walpole's slim volume. For the next sixty years, works such as Clara Reeves's *The Old English Baron* (1778), Ann Radcliffe's *The Mysteries of Udolpho* (1794), Matthew Gregory Lewis' *The Monk* (1796), and Charles Robert Maturin's *Melmoth the Wanderer* (1820) captivated readers in England and on the Continent.

Throughout *The Castle of Otranto*, Walpole sacrifices complexity of characterization for intricacies of plotting. His heroes and heroines are little more than cardboard cutouts representing good or evil. The villain Manfred evokes little sympathy, and the plethora of admirable characters exist with hardly a blemish on their characters. Although he claimed that his model was William Shakespeare, Walpole is actually more closely aligned with the writers of revenge tragedies and tragedies of blood, dramas that were popular in the early decades of the seventeenth century. He makes use, as did those types of work, of sinister suggestions and ominous supernatural occurrences that highlight the impending doom for those who practice evil.

Walpole's primary contribution to the development of fantasy literature, however, lies in his focus on the reaction of men and women to extraordinary events: He is less interested in the appearance of ghosts and giants for their own sake than he is in gauging the reaction of his heroes and heroines to these aberrations. Although it may be difficult to classify Manfred, Theodore, Isabella, and Matilda as "ordinary," in Walpole's view they represent "real" men and women placed in extraordinary circumstances. Whether their trials occur on a strange planet or in strange circumstances on Earth, they reveal to readers the best and the worst of human nature when their values are tested.

—*Laurence W. Mazzeno*

CAT'S CRADLE

Ice-nine, the invention of Dr. Felix Hoenikker, brings an apocalyptic end to all earthly life-forms except a handful of human survivors and a colony of adaptive ants

Author: Kurt Vonnegut (1922–2007)
Genre: Science fiction—apocalypse
Type of work: Novel
Time of work: The early 1960's
Locale: The city of Ilium, New York, and the Republic of San Lorenzo, in the Caribbean
First published: 1963

THE STORY

Cat's Cradle has a convoluted plot that develops with all the apparent chaos of a crazy quilt. The main character of the novel is its narrator, John, whose last name is not known; the novel, however, centers not on him but on ice-nine, the invention of a genius named Dr. Felix Hoenikker. Even in infinitesimal quantities, ice-nine freezes and transforms to ice-nine any liquid it contacts. The novel recounts how the world ends in an ice-nine chain reaction.

At the novel's opening, Dr. Hoenikker, a Nobel Prize-winning scientist and one of the creators of the atomic bomb, is already dead. The narrator, nominally involved in writing a book about the day the first bomb was dropped on Japan, conducts several interviews with Hoenikker's associates and family. He inadvertently pieces together the facts about ice-nine. After Hoenikker's death, his three offspring had divided up the small sample of ice-nine their father had developed as a means of solving the problems that mud posed for the military. Hoenikker's children prove to be poor guardians of the substance. Newt Hoenikker, a midget, gives his ice-nine to his lover, Zinka, a Ukrainian midget and dancer who married Newt only to get his ice-nine for the Soviet Union. His ugly sister, Angela, is bilked out of hers by her handsome, philandering husband, Harrison C. Conners. Franklin Hoenikker intimates that Conners married Angela only to gain possession of her ice-nine for the U.S. government. Franklin, the middle sibling, is a major general and minister of science and progress in the Republic of San Lorenzo, an island country in the Caribbean. He gives his ice-nine to San Lorenzo's president, "Papa" Monzano, who wears it as an amulet in a cylinder on a neck chain. Because he is terminally ill, President Monzano swallows the ice-nine to end his suffering and destroy the world. His aim is fulfilled when his frozen remains are accidentally dumped into the Caribbean.

While introducing the reader to a series of eccentric characters, John also reveals that he is a disciple of Bokononism, a quasi-religious philosophy he adopts after flying to San Lorenzo. Many of the other characters belong to John's *karass*, the Bokononian term for a team of people who are bound together to work the will of God without being conscious that they are doing so. John's *karass* is fated to destroy humanity.

As the novel proceeds toward that end, John becomes increasingly involved in the events that bring about the end of the world. Beginning as a passive observer-writer, he turns into a major player. Shortly prior to the book's finale, he replaces the dying "Papa" Monzano as president of San Lorenzo and marries Mona Aamons Monzano, the exquisitely beautiful native woman of his febrile dreams. Unhappily for John, thanks to the destructive designs of his predecessor, his triumph is short-lived, and at the end of the book he, Mona, and the other survivors of the ice-nine cataclysm resign themselves to their own and humankind's extinction.

ANALYSIS

Kurt Vonnegut distances his readers from the novel's grim vision through his Rabelaisian humor, but zany as the book is, its underlying disenchantment with society and its various institutions is ubiquitous and inescapable. Even the narrator's adopted Bokononism views itself as nonsense, but this cheerful admission is made in the process of revealing that most human organizations and institutions are *granfalloon*, or false *karasses* with meaningless beliefs, much like the cat's cradle, string wound around fingers of human hands, having nothing to do with either cats or cradles—an appropriate symbol for the novel's nihilism.

Like many novels and plays written in the early de-cades of the Cold War era, *Cat's Cradle* uses varieties of the absurd to articulate its existential theme. Many of its characters are physically, emotionally, or mentally abnormal or deficient. Dr. Hoenikker, a scientific genius, has no feelings and reacts to his children's pain by stringing together a cat's cradle of noninvolvement. Others express themselves in seemingly incongruous ways. The gangly Angela, for example, plays the clarinet with consummate skill and haunting beauty. Others are emotionally crippled by their pasts, as is von Koenigswald, formerly a doctor at Auschwitz, who attempts a Sisyphean atonement for his past by saving lives at San Lorenzo's House of Hope and Mercy.

Vonnegut's plain style and understated expression complement the narrator's stoic resignation. Even after he becomes personally involved in the events, John records them with the dispassionate detachment of a reporter, without judgment or blame. Presumably, the discourse reflects the Bokononian *que sera sera* serenity of John, whose recounting of the events is made in the wake of the cataclysmic disaster, when he knows that his effort is futile and that the book he set out to write can never be published or read.

The matter-of-fact tone of the novel counterpoints its oddball characters and their unusual lives. Vonnegut shows his great inventive power both in creating such a bizarre assortment of human misfits and in drawing them together as a *karass*, in which their lives intertwine with Bokononian inevitability.

Not all the characters belong to John's *karass*; some simply play a role and disappear. An example is Dr. Asa Breed, a hostile, distressingly normal character who discloses information about Dr. Hoenikker and ice-nine vital to John's research and the reader's understanding. Most of the developed characters are around at or near the end of the novel. These include some, like the Crosbys, whose sense of belonging in the surviving group is based on a false premise, a Bokononian *granfalloon*. In Vonnegut's wonderfully farfetched Bokononian world, even the lives of those outside a *karass* can merge, like parallel lines that defy all mathematical logic and somehow converge.

—*John Fiero*

THE CAVES OF STEEL AND THE NAKED SUN

Police detective Elijah Baley, with the aid of the robot R. Daneel Olivaw, solves murders in an enclosed New York City of the future and on the planet Solaria

Author: Isaac Asimov (1920–1992)
Genre: Science fiction—artificial intelligence
Type of work: Novels
Time of work: About 5000 c.e.
Location: New York City and the planet Solaria
First published: *The Caves of Steel* (1954; serial form, *Galaxy*, October-December, 1953) and *The Naked Sun* (1957; serial form, *Astounding Science-Fiction*, October-December, 1956)

THE STORY

Isaac Asimov wrote *The Caves of Steel*, under the persuasion of Horace Gold of *Galaxy* magazine, as a follow-up to his popular robot short stories. Following its success, Asimov wrote a sequel, *The Naked Sun*, for rival magazine publisher John W. Campbell, Jr., and for Doubleday Books.

The novels envision a future humanity split into two antagonistic groups. Those remaining on Earth

171

have developed a fear of open spaces. They live in covered megacities, the "caves of steel" of the title, resigned to extreme overcrowding and rationing of virtually all amenities. The Spacers, descendants of the colonizers of fifty "Outer Worlds," have much longer life spans and superior technology on their sparsely populated planets, and they forbid "disease-ridden" earthlings from immigrating to their worlds.

Spacers make extensive use of robots. The more primitive models permitted on Earth are violently hated by most City dwellers, especially "Medievalists," who yearn sentimentally for pre-City days. The only contact between Spacers and Earthmen is through Spacetown, a diplomatic/military base at the western edge of New York City.

As *The Caves of Steel* opens, police detective Elijah "Lije" Baley is summoned by his Medievalist boss, Commissioner Julius Enderby, to investigate a murder. A Spacer robot-scientist named Sarton has been shot in Spacetown, presumably by an Earthman. Baley must accept as a partner a Spacer robot created by Sarton. The robot, named R. Daneel Olivaw, looks human enough to "pass" among hostile Earthmen.

In the course of the investigation, Lije makes a number of embarrassing wrong guesses. He first supposes that Daneel is really Sarton in disguise but is convinced when Daneel exposes the machinery beneath his skin. Later, he guesses that Daneel is the killer. An expert convinces the Earthman that the Three Laws of Robotics built into a robot's positronic brain absolutely prevent it from intentionally harming a human. Lije is dismayed to find that his wife works for a secret Medievalist society, though she appears innocent of the crime. Finally, Lije proves that Enderby is the killer. Daneel reveals that the Spacers' ultimate goal on Earth is to convince Earthmen to break out of their stagnant cities to colonize uninhabited planets, with the help of robots.

The Naked Sun shifts the setting to the planet Solaria, where Lije and Daneel attempt to solve another murder. Lije is extremely reluctant to accept the assignment because of his Earthman's agoraphobia, but his boss orders him to do so because his observations can be invaluable to Earth intelligence. Dr. Rikaine Delmarre has been clubbed to death with a blunt object, which is now missing. His wife, Gladia, was found in a faint near the body, and a robot-witness's positronic brain has gone haywire. Solarian security chief Hannis Gruer believes that Gladia is connected to a plot against the human race that Delmarre was uncovering. Gruer himself is the victim of a nearly fatal poisoning.

Lije is pleased to be reunited with Daneel and startled to learn that Solarians have a phobia of their own: Living alone on large estates, communicating via holographic projections, they have a horror of physical human contact or even presence. Marriage and procreation are seen as distasteful necessities, fetuses are removed for incubation, and children are raised on "baby farms."

In the course of the novel, Lije feels drawn to Gladia, who seems to have a repressed interest in close contact with a fellow human. Lije seeks to overcome his fear of open spaces under a "naked sun." Escaping from Daneel, who wishes to keep him "from harm" (as the Three Laws of Robotics direct) by not letting him travel out of doors, Lije contacts five suspects—a family doctor, a sociologist, the acting security chief, a supervisor at the baby farm, and a roboticist. He brings them and Gladia into one room (holographically), in classic detective fashion, for the denouement. The villain turns out to be the roboticist, Jothan Leebig, who has found ways of circumventing the Three Laws of Robotics and tricking robots into becoming agents of crime. He also has manipulated Gladia. Gladia moves to the planet Aurora so that she can obtain human company, and Lije makes a plea to his supervisor concerning the need for Earthmen to overcome their own fears and colonize the stars.

ANALYSIS

Although Asimov's name is strongly connected to science fiction concerning robots, he did not invent the word "robot"; the haunting title of his first story collection, *I, Robot* (1950), was taken from another writer; and the idea of writing a robot detective novel set on an overpopulated Earth came from Horace Gold of *Galaxy*. Asimov did coin the word "robotics," as he often noted with pride, and much more important, he created a body of work that has deeply influenced almost all science fiction involving robots that goes beyond simple views of robots as killing machines.

Asimov's influence extended beyond literature to visual media. Famous examples include the amusing Robbie of the film *Forbidden Planet* (1956); the Vulcan Spock of the *Star Trek* (1966–1969) television series and later films, who although flesh and blood is a close cousin to Daneel in his devotion to logic and his utterly impassive tone; the android Data of *Star Trek: The Next Generation* (1987–1993), whose "positronic brain" is the writers' direct homage to Asimov; and the Replicants of the film *Blade Runner* (1982). The Replicants, unlike Asimov's robots, had no qualms about harming the humans they perfectly resembled. Like Asimov's robots, however, they could be detected as nonhuman via a questionnaire, much like the one administered to Daneel in *The Caves of Steel.*

Asimov saw fit to describe the two novels as "a perfect fusion of the murder mystery and the science-fiction novel." Even if critics have found flaws in both the mystery writing and the science fiction, one could hardly disagree about the fusion. In each novel, the solution depends on a human psychology determined by the technological environment of Earth or Solaria. Moreover, the robot detective is the ultimate embodiment of the mythic sleuth of the Sherlock Holmes variety: a creature of pure logic. Daneel is such a vivid creation that readers often forget that in both novels he is really only a sidekick to Lije Baley, who brilliantly solves both murders. In *The Naked Sun,* Lije frequently reminds himself that robots are "logical but not reasonable," though this distinction is never made clear.

Of the two novels, *The Naked Sun* is much more in the classic mystery tradition, with practically a "locked room" murder and all the suspects brought together for the denouement. It seamlessly weaves social concerns of Asimov's own era into the plot, such as worries about technological advances that may lead to extreme social isolation. *The Caves of Steel* is much less concerned with crime solving in some of its chapters. Its goal is to provide an in-depth study of a future City, its spectacle and its social problems. Written at a time when the United States reveled in its postwar prosperity and international power, *The Caves of Steel* is about the dangers of the coming megalopolis, including overcrowding and overreliance on a technological infrastructure. It also seems to foreshadow U.S. fears of losing status as an economic and technological superpower; perhaps Asimov was thinking more of the losses of the British Empire or the shift in local power from inner cities to the "outer worlds" of the suburbs.

Readers of the late twentieth century and beyond may smile at a few of the novels' lapses in predicting the future. For example, no one seems to have thought of shatterproof lenses for eyeglasses. The same reader may feel some dismay at the author's indulgence in certain social stereotypes of his era. For example, Lije's wife, Jessie, the only female character in *The Caves of Steel,* is constantly underlined as a "typical woman," which is to say that she is pathetically hysterical and dependent, whether in her role as a housewife or indulging in secret meetings. Gladia, in the second novel, falls into the category of the femme fatale, but she literally knows not what she does. She is, at least, conceived as a more complex character. Future critics will doubtless explore Asimov's views of imperial expansion and his analogies of robots to human slaves.

Asimov began another novel soon after the success of *The Naked Sun,* aiming for a trilogy, but he abandoned it. Only after the popularity of a sequel to his Foundation series, years later, did he decide to write *The Robots of Dawn* (1983), set on Aurora and featuring Gladia as well as the detectives, followed by *Robots and Empire* (1985), which linked the Robot series to the Foundation series.

—*Joseph Milicia*

CELESTIS

On the human-colonized world of Celestis, where alien natives are forced to biologically mimic the colonizers, a human man and an alien "woman" fall in love and must face society's censure amidst a brutal uprising of the oppressed

Author: Paul Park (1954–)
Genre: Science Fiction—alien civilization
Type of Work: Novel
Time of Plot: Unspecified future
Location: Human colony on the world of Celestis
First Published: 1995

Celestis

The Story

In alternating threads from their contrasting points-of-view, the reader begins to get acquainted with the two protagonists whose love story lies at the center of this novel.

We meet Katherine Styreme, the cultivated daughter of a rich man. The Styreme family are Aboriginals, natives of the planet Celestis, who, through drugs and surgery, maintain a human appearance and ape human ways. For instance, Katherine is slated to give an old-fashioned piano recital, playing classical works from Earth. Meanwhile, we watch Simon Mayaram, newly arrived from the home planet, as he receives instructions from the local Earth consul on how best to represent human interests among the Aboriginals. Simon is induced to attend the Styreme party. Rumors of the continuing existence of a third race on Celestis—the demons, long believed extinct—are tossed about.

At the affair, Simon has casual sex with a human woman, but finds himself fascinated with Katherine. "Her voice was queer in her restructured throat, a little hoarse, but pleasing nonetheless. . . . Her eyes themselves were a remarkable color, a dark tawny orange mixed with streaks of gold. . . . [She] put Simon in mind of the goddess Kali, in whom anger is combined with a beguiling sensuality."

But before they can pursue any such emotions at a slow pace, the pair are captured by terrorists and hauled away in handcuffs. Katherine's vital medicines are not brought along, and so she anticipates the fearful outcome: she will revert to the alien. Her faith in the Earth religion of Jesus Christ is all she has left. In the terrorist hideout at Drywater, Katherine and Simon become lovers, partly due to the Aboriginal's insistent biological and spiritual needs. A trusted human priest, Martin Cohen, helps the two escape. But freedom is almost worse than confinement: the escapees must struggle through a harsh landscape with all hands turned against them. Simon and Katherine become separated. When reunited, Simon discovers she has begun to mutilate herself, seeking madly to rip out the useless human prosthetics. Together with Cohen they struggle on, now in a vehicle. The deadly climax comes in an icy landscape with a shattered road. An eventual rescue finds all of them irrevocably changed, with new understandings of the planet's future—and their own.

Analysis

In the years following the publication of this, his fourth novel, hard on the heels of the acclaimed *Starbridge Chronicles*, Paul Park has gone on to demonstrate the vast spectrum of his concern and talents. With two historical novels dealing with Jesus, and a fantastical quartet about a counterfactual Roumania, he insists on reinventing himself and delighting readers with the unexpected. This early book showcased these tendencies very well. And with its focus on terrorism, it has aged perfectly into the sad new era of ISIS and other such movements.

In *Celestis*, Paul Park succeeds admirably in transferring the atmospherics and themes associated with such dissectors of colonialism as Graham Greene, Nadine Gordimer, and Joseph Conrad into an SF scenario that boasts its own intrinsic share of intriguing speculative matter. He's created a grim and eerie novel of human conquerors warped by their subjugated chattels, an equal to Gene Wolfe's *The Fifth Head of Cerberus* (1972). The world created by Park is a mélange of "High British Empire Frontier Outpost" and "Perilous Encampment Among Nonhuman Aliens." Settled by exiles from a decayed Earth, the colony world of Celestis also reminds me of the worlds Michael Bishop was once fond of creating in such works as *And Strange at Ecbatan the Trees* (1976) and *Stolen Faces* (1977).

Divided into a night-side and a day-side, with a marginally creeping terminator, the physical makeup of Celestis mirrors a sociocultural division: Aboriginals versus humans. Not quite slaves—in some cases, even wealthy—the Aboriginals are still an underclass. Remolded with drugs and surgery, they approximate human looks and mentality. But deprived of their maintenance doses of individually tailored drugs, they soon revert to a shocking Otherness, in which their natural, instinctive, pre-contact behavior finds expression only as indiscriminate sex urges.

This is the fate that befalls Katherine Styreme, daughter of a rich Aboriginal industrialist, when she is kidnapped by native terrorists along with human diplomat Simon Mayaram. As the pair struggle to endure captivity and win back their freedom, accompanied by the failed priest Martin Cohen, they fall into a strange *folie à deux*, laced with sexual and racial mind games. Along the way, they delve into ancient secrets of the planet, mostly involving a supposedly extinct third race, the demons.

Park enriches this already potent fictive compound with analogies to the pre-Mandela South African situation and with Christian allegories. (For example, the demon race is referred to as "the adversary" by the settlers.) There are even dim echoes, in my reading at least, of the movie *The African Queen* (1951), with Simon a Bogartian streetwise survivor and Katherine (is the name mere coincidence?) a Hepburn-prim example of how easily the thin veneer of civilization is shattered. Park's portrait of Simon, who is center-stage for almost the whole story, is impeccable. Likewise, Katherine's mind and heart are rendered in equal depth. Simon's perceptions of this new world—he is one of the few recent immigrants, perhaps the final one, in fact—arise inextricably from his past as a poor child in London. His unthinking, almost reflexive, adoration of Katherine speaks of how lonely his life has been and seems almost a fore-doomed Heathcliffian connection (another Catherine resonance!).

The perpetual challenge-and-response amongst authors that constitutes true science fiction finds a voluble and intelligent participant in *Celestis*, which now sits down at the round table and engages Blish's *A Case of Conscience* (1958), Gardner Dozois's *Strangers* (1978), and Jack Vance's less well-known but equally intriguing *The Gray Prince* (1974) in moody and affecting conversation.

—*Paul Di Filippo*

THE CENTAUR

A metaphysical journey, enabled by the consciousness of the Mother Earth, to unite with the Cosmic Soul and witness the spiritual Garden of Eden

Author: Algernon Blackwood (1869–1951)
Genre: Fantasy—magical realism
Type of work: Novel
Time of work: The early 1900's
Locale: Aboard ship through the Mediterranean Sea, and the Caucasus
First published: 1911

THE STORY

At the start of *The Centaur* readers are introduced to Terence O'Malley by his executor, who recounts the story after O'Malley's death. In his executor's telling of the story, O'Malley is a psychic and sensitive who responds to the moods and passion of Nature. By profession O'Malley is a journalist, a foreign correspondent whose latest commission is to write about the Caucasus. He had also turned his pen to fiction, producing two books of psychic tales. These had led O'Malley to correspond with a German doctor, Heinrich Stahl.

The two meet on a ship bound for the Caucasus. On this steamer, O'Malley encounters a massive Russian and his son, whose very presence arouse O'Malley's spirit. Through Stahl, O'Malley learns that these are urmenschen, or "primitive men," whose bodies contain a fragment of the earth-spirit. Although physically they appear human, their psychic body is much larger, and when they come within the focus of anyone sensitive to the power of Nature, their presence takes on other imagery. O'Malley likens them to centaurs, men who draw their power from the spirit of the Mother Earth, as many once did before the onset of civilization. They are, in effect, Cosmic Beings.

O'Malley shares a cabin with them one night and is almost overwhelmed by the power of their presence. He is saved by the intervention of Dr. Stahl. O'Malley's spirit, though, is hooked, having seen a glimpse beyond the gates of Eden.

By the time O'Malley arrives in Turkey he is under the spell of the Call of the Wild, and it is only the impact of civilization upon his senses that stops him from being lost to the power of Nature. For a month O'Malley returns to his work as a writer. This part of the book allows Algernon Blackwood to reflect upon the nature of civilization and how the advance of the human soul is measured by the progress of science rather than its relationship to the world, particular affinity with the Mother Earth.

Eventually, O'Malley falls again to the lure of the urmenschen and follows them deep into the Caucasus, where his spirit increasingly opens to the power of Earth's consciousness. Lost in the mountains, O'Malley is privileged to have a vision of the Mother Earth in the form of a spiritual Garden of Eden. His channel for this vision is the soul of the Russian, who has returned to the Mother Earth while his physical body died.

Once witness to this, O'Malley is never able to return to a normal life. His body becomes a shell as his spirit yearns to merge with the Cosmic Consciousness of the Earth. As a result, his body fails and dies, but his spirit has reached eternal bliss. The conclusion of the novel, when a street musician playing on the pan pipes allows O'Malley's soul to depart, is among Blackwood's most beautiful pieces of writing.

ANALYSIS

Although *The Centaur* was Blackwood's own favorite novel, it is not his most personal. That epithet belongs to *The Wave: An Egyptian Aftermath* (1916). It is, however, his most religious novel because it comes closest to reflecting his own world belief. It was inspired by Blackwood's journey through the Caucasus in 1910, a trip that left his spirit so numbed by beauty and vision that for a while he was unable to write. One short story, "Imagination" (*Ten Minute Stories*, 1914), describes this writer's block and serves as a preamble to *The Centaur* in its evocation of the Earth spirit. It was only when Blackwood heard a street musician outside his own London flat—a scene that inspired the conclusion of the novel— that Blackwood's own spirit was freed and the book began to form.

In *The Centaur*, Blackwood expresses his view of humanity's relationship with the world. By using the theories of Gustav Fechner and William James, quotations from whose works head each chapter, Blackwood explores the possibility that Earth is sentient and it is the projection of the Earth-soul that creates visions of creatures of legend (such as centaurs and nymphs) among the psychically sensitive. Civilization has dulled people's basic senses, which is why so few are aware of the planet's soul. It is through this exploration of the metaphysical that Blackwood's book can be regarded as a precursor to modern Magical Realism, because he infuses the world with the power and spirit of Earth's soul.

The visions that Blackwood sought to explore stretched him to the limits of his narrative power. Language was too blunt an instrument to describe the mystical beauty of spiritual paradise, and there are times when the book becomes too verbose and too cluttered with emotion as Blackwood strives to liberate the reader's imagination. Near the novel's climax, after passages of intense vision, Blackwood finds himself having to resort to such ineffective phrases as "he knew *all over*" and "He knew the Great At-one-ment," phrases that are inadequate to portray the supremacy of union that O'Malley's spirit has attained, simply because Blackwood has exhausted all language in reaching this spiritual orgasm. Elsewhere Blackwood captures a vision of intense wonder in the phrase "all the forgotten gods moved forward into life."

Because *The Centaur* reflects Blackwood's own spiritual and mystical experiences in the Caucasus, it is a novel of mystical realism, a forerunner of books by Carlos Castaneda and others. Blackwood was the first great writer to fuse aspects of the mystical, the occult, and pantheism to create works of genuine supernaturalism. Despite the occasional inadequacy of language, which is more the fault of written communication than of Blackwood as Nature's messenger, *The Centaur* is the peak of Blackwood's visionary writing.

—*Mike Ashley*

THE CHILD GARDEN

Milena defeats the bioengineered viruses that have reshaped humanity's future and teaches the trapped, childlike souls of the Consensus how to transcend their prison and become angels

Author: Geoff Ryman (1951–)
Genre: Science fiction—extrapolatory
Type of work: Novel

Time of work: The near future
Locale: Czechoslovakia, London, and outer space
First published: 1989

THE STORY

In the futuristic London of *The Child Garden* (subtitled *A Low Comedy*), bioengineered viruses infect people with common knowledge. Babies can add, and five-year-olds quote William Shakespeare. The viruses were designed to cure cancer. Unfortunately, the cure is worse than the disease, because cells now lack the ability to reproduce after a person reaches the age of thirty-five, halving the normal human life span.

The Consensus governs. It comprises personality copies of all the people who are "read" into it. Reading usually occurs when a person reaches ten years of age. After the reading, a person is given viruses to destroy any undesirable traits.

Milena is virus resistant. She is attracted to women (which is considered "bad grammar"), and the Consensus does not read her because she is unique and creative. She is unhappy as an actress because plays are now being performed as "remembered" and not as vital productions. She meets Rolfa, who is a genetically engineered person resembling a polar bear. Rolfa is a singer who has created an original opera based on Dante's *The Divine Comedy* (c. 1320). Milena comes to love Rolfa and wants her to get the benefits of the Consensus—including housing and food—so that she can continue producing her music. She arranges for Rolfa to be read and infected with viruses. It is not until Rolfa is infected that Milena discovers that Rolfa is also attracted to her. The viruses drastically change Rolfa's personality, and she leaves Milena and goes to Antarctica to work in her family's business.

Milena decides to produce Rolfa's opera, and the Consensus offers to help. They plan on having a huge production, projected across the sky from outer space. Milena goes into space with astronaut Mike Stone, who repeatedly asks Milena to marry him. Milena carries the memory of a rose Rolfa once gave her. She tests the projection equipment by sending a copy of the rose holographically to each of the people on Earth.

Meanwhile, the viruses are causing many dangerous and exasperating mutations. Especially disturbing are the "bees," people who are empathic and can uncontrollably change minds with another's consciousness, even that of an animal.

Milena learns that the Consensus wants her to be their ambassador in space, holding a model of their world in her mind as she searches out a mate for them. She is told this by the angel Bob, a composite consciousness the Consensus has sent into the Charley Slides, the lines of gravity that compose the universe. Milena then develops cancer. The doctors can use her cells to reinfect people and help them live longer, but her cancer means that Milena cannot personally direct the Comedy, because she is dying. She has married Mike Stone and he is carrying their child, attached to his bowel, within him.

During the final night of the performance, Milena is read, and a copy of her consciousness is stored inside the Consensus. It refuses to do their bidding. The soul attached to Milena's body rises into space as she dies. It tries to convince the childlike souls trapped by the Consensus to become angels. Many flee, including the soul of Rolfa, which joins with Milena, as do all the other parts of Milena's personality that were lost to her. Milena discovers wholeness, and all times become transcendentally "now."

Analysis

Geoff Ryman's *The Child Garden* is an exceptionally literate science-fiction novel. Within the framework of a future in which the human life span has been disastrously reduced by bioengineered attempts to make people disease free and intellectually equal, it raises issues of sexuality, creativity, consciousness, and social responsibility. It contains philosophically complex yet surprisingly entertaining arguments about the relationship between good government and tyranny as well as society's responsibilities to its less fortunate members. It argues that equality cannot occur by suppressing a person's unique and individual soul, even if that person carries characteristics considered to be "deviant" within the fabric of society. Such suppression results in losses to the culture far in excess of the gains.

Ryman passionately argues that it is up to individuals to take responsibility for themselves, for the underprivileged, and for making sure that the government becomes compassionate and just. He forces his main character, Milena, not only to take on these responsibilities but also to embrace all the diverse, childlike, and even unattractive parts of herself. The message is that before people can be expected to accept, much less love, the rest of flawed humanity they must learn to accept themselves.

Ryman won the 1990 John W. Campbell Memorial Award for *The Child Garden*. His first major success was the novella *The Unconquered Country* (1984), a heart-wrenching metaphorical exploration of the war in Southeast Asia that concerns issues of social and personal responsibility, individuality, and creativity. It contains a wealth of incredibly powerful imagery stemming from wartime uses of bioengineering. The expansion of the novella, *The Unconquered Country: A Life History* (1986), won both the British Science Fiction and the World Fantasy awards. The novella appears in a collection called *Unconquered Countries* (1994) that also includes "A Fall of Angels," a story employing Ryman's themes of consciousness, responsibility, and love. It is a longer exploration of the lives of the angels, described in The Child Garden, who travel the Charley Slides that radiate through outer space.

Ryman's later novel *Was* (1992) is set in the United States from the time of writer L. Frank Baum (1856–1919), author of *The Wonderful Wizard of Oz* (1900), to the present. It focuses on social issues, specifically concentrating on child abuse, homosexuality, and the treatment of people with acquired immune deficiency syndrome (AIDS). Ryman manages to create yet another beautifully transcendent novel working with these painful and difficult topics. As Ryman ably demonstrates in *The Child Garden*, he is a master at using the tools of science fiction and fantasy to show how the human spirit can drag itself up and become gloriously transcendent.

—Shira Daemon

THE CHILDE CYCLE

Prompted by various near-supermen, the human race splinters into the Men of War, Men of Faith, and Men of Philosophy, and then begins the laborious process of reintegration

Author: Gordon R. Dickson (1923–2001)
Genre: Science fiction—future history
Type of work: Novels
Time of work: The late twenty-first century to the late twenty-fourth century
Location: Sixteen human-inhabited planets in eight star systems
First published: *The Genetic General* (1960; serial form, "Dorsai!," *Astounding Science-Fiction*, May-July, 1959), *Necromancer* (1962; also titled *No Room for Man*, 1963), *Soldier, Ask Not* (1967; serial form, *Galaxy*, 1964), *The Tactics of Mistake* (1971), *Three to Dorsai!* (1975; contains *Necromancer*, *The Tactics of Mistake*, and *The Genetic General*), *Dorsai!* (1976; contains *The Genetic General* with restored text), *The Spirit of Dorsai* (1979; includes "Amanda Morgan," "Brothers," and three bridge sections; "Brothers" first appeared in *Astounding: John W. Campbell Memorial Anthology*, 1973), *Lost Dorsai* (1980; includes "Lost Dorsai," "Warrior," a critical essay, and an excerpt from *The Final Encyclopedia*; serial form of "Lost Dorsai," *Destinies*, February-March, 1980; serial form of "Warrior," *Analog*, December, 1965), *The Dorsai Companion* (1986; contains most of *The Spirit of Dorsai* and *Lost Dorsai*; adds new material), *The Final Encyclopedia* (1984), *The Chantry Guild* (1988), *Young Bleys* (1991), *Lost Dorsai: The New Dorsai Companion* (1993; contains most of the fiction from *Lost Dorsai* and excerpts from "A Childe Cycle Concordance"), and *Other* (1994)

THE STORY

The Childe Cycle (also known as the Dorsai Cycle) of novels and stories actually begins with *Necromancer*, in the later part of the twenty-first century, on an Earth ruled cautiously by the computers of the World Complex. Paul Formain, a one-armed mining engineer, resolves a stalemate between Kirk Tyne, head engineer of the World Complex, and Walter Blunt, head of the Chantry Guild. The Guild seeks the violent overthrow of the technocracy headed by Tyne. Formain manages to wrest control of the Guild from Blunt and send the human race out to the stars, something neither Tyne nor Blunt wanted.

The Tactics of Mistake takes place a century later, after the human race has settled Mars and Venus as well as thirteen other planets—called the Younger Worlds—orbiting seven other star systems. Cletus Grahame, a military genius from the planet Dorsai, pits himself against one of the most powerful men on Earth, Dow deCastries. Grahame wins the conflict, thus gaining independence from Earth for the Younger Worlds.

By the time of *Soldier, Ask Not*, in the late twenty-third century, the human race has fragmented into specialized types, called Splinter Cultures. The three main types are the Men of War (Dorsai), who live on Dorsai; the Men of Faith (Friendlies), who live on Harmony and Association; and the Men of Philosophy (Exotics), who live on Kultis and Mara. Helping to link all the Younger Worlds together are the members of the Interstellar News Services, including Tam Olyn. After seeing his brother-in-law killed in cold blood by a Friendly mercenary, Olyn embarks on a vendetta against Harmony and Association. When he is thwarted, Olyn returns to Earth, eventually to take over the directorship of the Final Encyclopedia, a gigantic information storage system orbiting the Mother Planet.

Dorsai! also takes place during the late twenty-third century. It is the story of Donal Grahame, great-great-grandson of Cletus Grahame, who uses his Dorsai military training and what he calls "intuitional logic" to overcome William of Ceta, a merchant who nearly succeeds in controlling the complicated transactions that tie the Younger Worlds together economically. Donal, like his ancestor Cletus, frees the Younger Worlds from a threat to their independence.

The last four novels in the series are all set around the middle of the twenty-fourth century, and they all concern two powerful antagonists: Hal Mayne and Bleys Ahrens. They are antagonists because each is the human embodiment of a different historical response of the "racial animal"— Gordon Dickson's name for the consciousness of the human race as a whole—to the crisis of the Splinter Cultures' failure. Bleys wishes the human race to stop changing; Hal wishes the race to keep changing, for the specialized types of the Splinter Cultures to become reintegrated, and for the reemergence of an improved "full spectrum" humanity.

Young Bleys details Bleys Ahrens's childhood, adolescence, and young manhood, ending in his taking control from his older brother, Dahno, of an organization called the Others. *Other* records the initial moves in Bleys Ahrens's quest to rule most of the Younger Worlds.

The Final Encyclopedia begins where *Young Bleys* ends, with the death of Hal Mayne's three tutors at the hands of Bleys's bodyguards. It traces a similar period in Hal's life, ending with Hal blockading himself, the Final Encyclopedia, Old Earth, and nearly everyone from the Dorsai behind an impenetrable shield. Outside are Bleys's minions, with time, power, and technology on their side.

Three years later, at the beginning of *The Chantry Guild*, Hal is despondent at not being able to find a way of using the Final Encyclopedia to gain entrance to what he calls the Creative Universe. Eventually, Hal works his way out of the impasse after journeying to a new Chantry Guild hidden on Kultis, one of the two Exotic planets, now under occupation by soldiers controlled by the Others.

In addition to these novels, Dickson wrote four shorter Childe Cycle pieces. He called these shorter pieces "illuminations" because they shed light on events only briefly mentioned in, or completely outside, the novels. "Amanda Morgan" shows how the women, children, and old men of Dorsai defeat Dow deCastries's elite invasion troops. "Warrior" tells how Ian Grahame, Donal's uncle, renders justice for the unnecessary death of one of Ian's officers. "Lost Dorsai" is the story of Michael de Sandoval, a Dorsai who uncharacteristically refuses to use weapons but who manages to conquer an entire army. In "Brothers," Ian Grahame ensures both that the men who assassinated his beloved twin brother Kensie are found and executed and that the Dorsai troops do not run amok in their grief over losing Kensie.

ANALYSIS

Even in its own terms, the Childe Cycle is one of the most ambitious projects in the history of science fiction. The series consists of more than a million words, thus being comparable in scope to Isaac Asimov's Foundation series and Robert A. Heinlein's Future History stories. The Childe Cycle is part of an even larger project, a set of interlocking novels— originally conceived of as three historical, three contemporary, and three science-fiction novels—each standing on its own but all eventually forming part of one gigantic "consciously thematic story," a term Dickson used for the work.

Dickson's themes are almost all pairs of opposites. Evolution is crucial, and stasis is death; freedom is necessary, and too much control is fatal; duty to a cause above self is good, and selfishness is bad; and empathy liberates, and isolation confines. The exception to this series is the paradoxical mantra of the new Chantry Guild on Kultis, which is a key to the cycle's overall structure: "the transient and the eternal are the same." What Dickson seems to say is that during the thousand-year period his consciously thematic story will cover, patterns repeat.

The individual novels differ in some respects. The earlier novels are shorter and less easily understood than the later novels. The basic structure, however, is the same throughout the cycle: A young but incredibly confident and talented man overcomes an older and seemingly invincible opponent, each victory supposedly bringing the human race a step closer to a time when everyone has the abilities of the gifted. Dickson's heroes are not really supermen, for Dickson honestly believes that the traits they exhibit are available to all human beings, either in the past as models, in the present with a little training, or in the near future with some trailblazing by the gifted.

Dickson is philosophically a "hard-headed" romantic, and the Childe Cycle reminds readers of the work of another hard-headed romantic science-fiction author, Poul Anderson. Both authors intermingle the conventions of hard science fiction—plausible extrapolations of current scientific knowledge—with ideas stemming from their study of various romantic authors and mythologies.

Even more than Anderson, Dickson wishes to blur the line between fact and fiction. In Hal Mayne's Creative Universe, one has only, in true romantic fashion, to wish for a thing to be true, and it will become true in actuality. English romantic poet William Wordsworth (1770-1850) said, "The Child is Father of the Man." Dickson says, with the idea resonating from *Necromancer* to *Other*, that "The Wish is Father of the Deed." Ever the optimist, Dickson wanted the human race to improve, and spent most of his long writing career nobly mapping out a blueprint to follow.

Critics have given Dickson comparatively little attention, probably because his work may seem dated, as if he stopped developing as a science-fiction writer about 1960. He may also seem derivative to some, for a typical Childe Cycle novel often reads like a combination of breakneck (but overly long and overly detailed) space-opera action, in the style of E. E. "Doc" Smith, and clumsy, obviously symbolic interior monologues reminiscent of the work of A. E. van Vogt, laced with too many heavily melodramatic confrontation scenes. Despite this critical indifference, Dickson won one Nebula and three Hugo Awards, all for shorter fiction and two for Cycle pieces—a 1965 Hugo for "Soldier, Ask Not" and a 1981 Hugo for "Lost Dorsai."

—Todd H. Sammons

CHILDHOOD'S END

The Satan-like Overlords attempt to guide a reluctant human race to its apocalyptic transformation and union with the Overmind

Author: Arthur C. Clarke (1917-2008)
Genre: Science fiction—evolutionary fantasy
Type of work: Novel
Time of work: About 1985-2085
Location: Earth and NGS 549672, the planet of the Overlords
First published: 1953

THE STORY

Childhood's End is an account of the final one hundred years of human life on Earth, from the time of the Overlords' arrival in their huge spaceship to the time of the dramatic, rapid evolution of all human children into a nonhuman form that achieves unity with the Overmind. A series of human characters—most notably George Greggson, Jean Morrel, and their two children—encounter the technologically advanced Overlords, whose Stardrive-based spaceships, truth-in-history machines, and panoramic viewers (which allow observation of every detail in an area many miles away) provide the science-fiction aspects of Arthur C. Clarke's novel. The evolutionary fantasy element appears in human children as they transform into nonhuman entities that destroy Earth in the power of their fusion into the Overmind

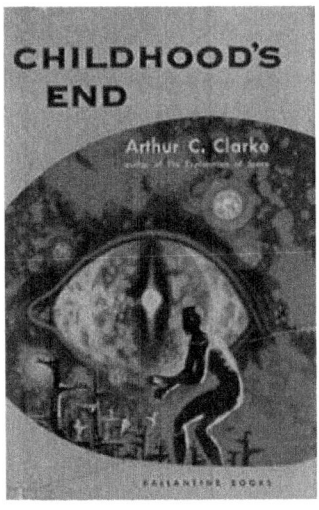

that controls, and perhaps is, the universe.

Childhood's End begins with an event often anticipated and described in science fiction: the arrival of an alien species on Earth. This species is unusual, however, both in its refusal to allow itself to be seen for fifty years and in its benevolence, as it prohibits cruelty to animals and otherwise guides humanity beyond the barbarity of war and destruction into an era of peace and economic prosperity. The negative results of the arrival and assumption of control by the Overlords are powerful as well, though less dramatic. A consequence of the end of energizing conflict and struggle is the decline in creative achievement in art. Likewise, religious belief is terminated by the Overlords' technology, which allows direct visual access to most events in human history, thus exposing the myths and half-truths that had been accepted as truth over the ages.

When this latter debunking is fully achieved, the Overlords reveal themselves. Gigantic, barb-tailed, winged, horned, Satan-like creatures, they disembark from their spaceship and generate only a brief reaction of terror. Reason then conquers the remnants of Christian memory, and the Overlords are accepted as intriguingly intelligent and benevolent masters.

To some creative artists and philosophers, however, life without ambition and original human achievement is insufficient. Thus, some fifty thousand join to form a colony dedicated to artistic and intellectual life, the kind of human psychological development that had been stalled by the Overlords' control. Among those joining the island colony are George Greggson, Jean Morrel, and their two young children. Unknowingly, Jean has attracted the attention of the Overlords because of her prescience in correctly identifying their home planet, NGS 549672, even though they never revealed their place of origin to any human. It is this psychological insight that the Overlords secretly have come to inhibit, or at least supervise, as it develops from the mental power implicit in extrasensory perception phenomena throughout human history into the mind-over-matter power that constitutes unity with the Overmind.

The psychological power latent in Jean becomes fully realized in her children; they control objects telekinetically and experience visions of planets even the Overlords have never visited. Soon all human children develop this power. They quickly become nonhuman and oblivious to their parents, who then annihilate themselves because they cannot retrieve their children or even become like them. Only Jan Rodricks remains, having stowed away on an Overlord ship, visited NGS 549672, and returned to a desolate Earth eighty years later. He describes the apocalypse for the Overlords, who have retreated, their supervisory task completed. Even Jan himself fades into nothingness as the children consume the substance of the Earth in their transformation into pure light energy and depart with the Overmind into the stars.

ANALYSIS

The creative complexity of Clarke's novel has made it a classic of modern science fiction. The work is difficult to categorize or synthesize. On one level, it operates as a reasonably believable extrapolation from modern scientific and technological progress into a material utopia. The novel has its dystopian psychological dimension as well. *Childhood's End* also reflects the aspect of Clarke's writing most fully realized in *2001: A Space Odyssey* (1968), his creation of brilliantly evocative, colorful, fantastic descriptions of nonexistent other worlds as an exercise in human imaginative expression. The description of the metamorphosis of the mountain on NGS 549672 in *Childhood's End* is an excellent example. Closely allied with this fantastic physical description is the imaginative leap made by Clarke in his depiction of the fantasy transformation of human children into psychic superpowers and spiritual essences.

Also intimately connected to this imaginatively mystical element in Clarke's writing is his recurring theme of religion—particularly Christianity—as an imperfect embodiment of powerful but misunderstood psychic and spiritual forces. For example, in the 1956 Hugo Award-winning story "The Star," Clarke ironically presents the star of Bethlehem as the supernova stage of another planet's sun. Billions of people die on that planet as the supernova guides the shepherds to the place of birth of one child on Earth. The same reversal of Christian belief, or enlargement of the context surrounding it, is obvious in *Childhood's End*, with the Overlords as an ironically benevolent reversal of the human image of Satan.

Also fundamental to *Childhood's End* is Clarke's recurring theme of the existence of, and inevitable human contact with, other life-forms in the universe. With an intensity akin to religious conversion, Clarke presents this theme in his famous 1951 story "The Sentinel," the progenitor of *2001: A Space Odyssey*. On a moon expedition, the narrator of "The Sentinel" finds a crystal pyramid left by an alien species and accepts the fact of that species' existence; similarly, the Overlords' arrival in *Childhood's End* is represented as an inevitable progression in human encounters with the life-forms "out there."

In its complexity and multifacetedness, *Childhood's End* represents the great artistic power of Clarke in all three of his writing styles, which, according to James Gunn in *The Road to Science Fiction: From Heinlein to Here* (1979), are extrapolative, ingenious, and mystical. What the novel lacks in formal unity and harmony it more than compensates for in pure energy, originality, and profundity.

—*John L. Grigsby*

CHILDREN OF THE ATOM

A group of superintelligent children, products of an atomic plant explosion, emerge from hiding to defend themselves from outside hostility and to discover their true vocation

Author: Wilmar H. Shiras (1908–1990)
Genre: Science fiction—superbeing
Type of work: Novel
Time of work: 1973
Locale: Primarily the San Francisco Bay area
First published: 1953 (first three chapters published individually as novelettes: "In Hiding," *Astounding Science-Fiction*, November, 1948; "Opening Doors," *Astounding Science-Fiction*, March, 1949; and "New Foundations," *Astounding Science-Fiction*, March, 1950)

THE STORY

After being called in to help a withdrawn thirteen-year-old boy, school psychologist Dr. Peter Welles realizes that the boy, Timothy Paul, is immeasurably intelligent. Taught by his guardians that precocity is often punished as boastful exhibitionism, Tim has lived "in hiding," masking his abilities while carrying out a secret life as an author under a variety of pseudonyms. Welles soon deduces that Tim's intelligence is the result of a mutation caused by a disaster at an atomic power plant in "Helium City," where his parents worked thirteen years earlier.

Realizing that other such children must exist all across the country, Welles and Tim begin to get in touch with them. Tim is able to persuade his rich grandparents to fund a special school for the superintelligent, to be run by Welles and other adults who are let in on the secret. A sizable number of the thirty surviving children are gathered at this school. Many are rescued from oppressive domestic situations, and one from an asylum. Most of them have replicated Tim's strategy of performing remarkable work under adult aliases: They produce novels, biographies, a popular comic strip, and a successful board game. At Welles's school they are rescued from their loneliness and allowed a chance to grow and develop.

Welles's greatest challenge is to ensure that all the children mature in each aspect of their lives. A problem soon arises when one of the children is discovered to have little or no emotional capacity for empathy. The children themselves, not Welles, are able to devise a solution to the problem. They also conceive the project that will occupy them in their maturity, a kind of summa scientia, or what would be called today a grand unified theory, linking all branches of knowledge and the arts in one comprehensible construct.

Before they are able to begin that project, their exis-tence is shouted to the world by a televangelist, Tommy Mundy, who claims that these "children of the atom" are the spawn of the devil, plotting a world takeover. Again the children themselves form a solution, initially convincing the angry mob that gathers outside the school that they are not monsters but familiar people the crowd has known all their lives. Tim Paul urges the ultimate solution: The children will attend public schools in the area, both to show others that they are not fundamentally different and to develop and demonstrate the "right feeling" toward humanity. The children of the atom, in Tim's words, "join the human race."

ANALYSIS

Children of the Atom combines two important motifs in science fiction: that of the superbeing, previously portrayed most memorably in Olaf Stapledon's classic *Odd John* (1935), and the ubiquitous anxiety caused by the use of atomic weapons in 1945. Human mutations caused by atomic energy would become a staple in science fiction. Examples include John Wyndham's *Re-Birth* (1955, also known as *The Chrysalids*), Lester del Rey's *The Eleventh Commandment* (1962), and Edgar Pangborn's *Davy* (1964). Wilmar Shiras is perhaps the first, however, to see this kind of catastrophe in the theological sense of a "eucatastrophe": a *felix culpa*, or fortunate fall. What will emerge from the sin of using the atom and its inherent powers is not punishment in the form of breeding of monsters but is instead the possibility of advancing the human race to its next evolutionary plane.

In many science-fiction depictions of what *Homo superior* might be like, a clear line of demarcation is established, and "normal" humans, *Homo sapiens*, are often treated by the superior race as humans treat animals such as dogs. Odd John's nickname for the human narrator of Stapledon's novel, for example, is "Fido." The first story in *Children of the Atom*, "In Hiding," ends with this very image: "Peter Welles would be Tim's friend—not a puppy, but a beloved friend—as a loyal dog, loved by a good master, is never cast out."

As a separate novelette, "In Hiding" is much more famous than the four stories that follow it. It was voted into the Science Fiction Hall of Fame. One reason perhaps is that the positing of an evolutionary successor to humans in science fiction almost always leads to contempt, conflict, and then destruction of one race or the other, as evidenced in the self-destruction of Odd John's superhuman colony, or indeed that of the entire Earth in Arthur C. Clarke's *Childhood's End* (1953). "In Hiding" seems to imply that such a plot line will follow.

The novel as a whole shows humans and superhumans as eventually becoming able to forge bonds of amicability and trust. This trust is based on the strong Christian religious underpinnings of the book. None of the supergeniuses dismisses organized religion out of hand; the children's great project is modeled on the *Summa* treatises of Thomas Aquinas. They refuse to substitute a "higher" morality as a replacement for outmoded Judeo-Christian ethical traditions. Odd John excuses murder as being absolved by the needs of a higher being, but Shiras' children are able to spot a trickster because of his casual assumption that abortion for the purpose of choosing the offspring's gender is acceptable. Even the name of Timothy Paul, who suggests the children's reintegration with *Homo sapiens*, is an allusion to two of the first Christian apostles to the gentiles. Shiras' insistent subtext is that these children of the atom are still the children of Adam.

—*William Laskowski*

CHIMERA

Following a disquisition on the arts of narrative by Dunyazade, the fabled Scheherazade's younger sister, the mythic heroes Perseus and Bellerophon describe their efforts to overcome the lassitude of post-heroic mundanity

Author: John Barth (1930–)
Genre: Fantasy—mythological
Type of work: Novel
Time of work: Antiquity and the mid-twentieth century

Chimera

Locale: The realm of mythic heroes, the Arabian Empire at the height of its power, and tidewater Maryland
First published: 1972

The Story

John Barth's fascination with the intricacies of narrative possibility and the complex, evolving interrelationship between an author and a work in progress drew him to the plight of Scheherazade, his figure for an ultimate author who must hold the attention of her audience or lose her life. Using a pattern of doubling that establishes a multiple perspective informing the three parts of *Chimera*, Barth presents the classic fable of Scheherazade's predicament—to keep the shah's interest in a never-ending story so he will spare her life in order to learn what happens next—through the words of Dunyazade, "Sherry's" younger sister, who is talking to her husband, the shah's brother, in an effort to escape the same fate. Dunyazade's narrative is further complicated by the appearance of a genie figure who seems to resemble Barth himself, a fortyish American who has read Scheherazade's account and can contribute to, comment on, and interact with the characters.

After numerous questions are raised about the composition of a narrative that continues for 1,001 nights, the focus shifts to the legendary Perseus, an analogue for a man, like Barth, who is caught between a heroic past in his youth and the flatness of his middle years. Perseus' problems are summarized by his apparent impotence with the feminine muses who have inspired his glorious feats. By retelling and simultaneously reliving (now in altered form) the circumstances of his achievements, however, Perseus is able to achieve a degree of serenity and satisfaction. Through the imaginative re-creation of his life, he clarifies and deepens its meanings by transmuting the temporal into the eternal, ultimately reconciling his rancor for Medusa and finding peace with her in the symbolic constellations that are their timeless domain.

The third section of *Chimera* compounds the problems of the mythic hero by following the crisis Bellerophon faces. Like Perseus, he has a glorious past, but unlike Perseus, he is unable to break out of an archetypal pattern for heroic behavior of which he is self-consciously aware. The devastating act of patricide—a symbolic necessity for claiming an individual identity—is reduced to a parodic confusion, a chaos of elements from many myths mutually diminishing any possibility of meaning. Bellerophon eventually slays the Chimera, a fabulous creature with a lion's head, goat's body, and serpent's tail, but even with the aid of the winged horse Pegasus, his feats seem second-rate. His life story eventually is revealed as the imaginings of Polyeidus, the mythic shape-shifter who controls the narrative and who, as the writer of the myth, ultimately is more powerful than the heroes whose exploits he describes. When Bellerophon crashes to earth in the Maryland marshland that the writer John Barth inhabits, he achieves his mortal destiny, and the book in which his story is contained may "expect a certain low-impact afterlife," proving the tale less significant than its teller while revealing the true hero of myth as its maker.

Analysis

Barth's intense concentration on the temptations and perils of devising and constructing a story when the contemporary world already has heard every variant of plot or theme is paralleled by his curiosity about the relevance of classical mythology for a postmodern world. In *Giles Goat-Boy: Or, The Revised New Syllabus* (1966), *Chimera*, and *The Last Voyage of Somebody the Sailor* (1991), he combines the heroic proportions of figures from antiquity with the sensibility of a well-educated, self-conscious twentieth century writer both to demystify the heroic and to demonstrate the continuing importance of mythic patterns shaped by storytellers over time. He is concerned with the value of literary art in an age of diminishing literacy; though accepting the proposition that all stories are "lies," he insists that the best stories are "something larger than fact"—that is, a myth that is both a personal record and something larger than any particular person.

Using a dazzling array of self-reflective devices, Barth also employs the traditional techniques of tale tellers as ancient as Homer to captivate the reader, shaping a narrative rife with romance, suspense, and dramatic action to approach the great mysteries of existence that enduring myths have always engaged. At the heart of Chimera, the essential question posed by any artist intrigued by the possibilities of the fantastic is confronted directly: What if one could overcome the apparent limits of the material world? Barth is successful in making the fantastic plausible (or, as Paul Valéry put it, making "the fantastic another aspect of the realistic") by confounding skepticism through continually expanding the range of action of his protagonists. The linkage of mythic patterns with contemporary issues and of classic tales with current modes of speech and thought carries the narrative from the comfortingly familiar to the unsettlingly extraordinary. The aim of *Chimera* is to argue that an ultimate reality resides or endures only in the shaping of experience through language. Thus, if the artist is sufficiently skillful, it becomes difficult to determine which realm is intruding. As Barth has put it, "I wonder whether the world's really there when I'm not narrating it." Although this is a distinctly individual declaration, its expression in *Chimera* reached enough discerning readers for Barth to win the National Book Award for Fiction.

The mythic hero Perseus is presented as a man who, like the author, struggles with the petrification and immobility of middle age. He cannot relive his youthful achievements, but through the imaginative power of the artist, he can begin to understand and appreciate who he is and what he has done. With what Scheherazade asserts is the "real magic . . . to understand which words work," Barth connects the intimately personal with the mythologically universal, suggesting that an absolute distinction between the realistic and the fantastic is not only simplistic but also an impedance to understanding.

—*Leon Lewis*

CHINA MOUNTAIN ZHANG

In a future Chinese-dominated world, a gay half-Chinese man working in New York City struggles to find his place in a competitive and sometimes unwelcoming future society. The experiences of four other characters are briefly touched upon to expand upon the societal problems he faces as he travels to Canada, China, and elsewhere.

Author: Maureen F McHugh (1959–)
Genre: Science Fiction—extrapolatory
Type of Work: Novel
Time of Work: Future
Location: Earth, Mars
First Published: 1992

THE STORY

The setting is a future version of Earth, where the Chinese have become the predominant power and effective overlords of the rest of the world. China Mountain Zhang is half Chinese, half occidental and is gay in a world where that merits the death sentence virtually everywhere. Zhang has been genetically altered to look completely Chinese, which has its social advantages, but his background will not stand up to any kind of serious scrutiny. So when his boss tries to audition him for the role of son-in-law, Zhang realizes that trouble is on the horizon. The daughter has an argument with her parents, and Zhang reluctantly allows her to sleep in his apartment for two nights, which enrages his boss when he finds out where his daughter is staying.

The story switches briefly to the viewpoint of Angel, an athlete who competes in elaborate flying matches mounted on sophisticated mechanical kites. The sport is dangerous, however, and one of his friends is killed in a crash, demonstrating a declining sense of the value of human life. Interludes involving other characters present segments of the lives of a disparate group of people, each designed to illustrate some aspect of this future world. Each also intersects the main plot and involves Zhang in some way, though mostly obliquely. The exception is the part of the narrative dealing with his employer's daughter, who was born with a facial deformity she considers to be the cause of most of her life's disappointments. However, when she has it corrected, she discovers that her life is more complicated than she realized. She is, in some ways, the most complex and interesting character in the novel. Another segment involves an ex-soldier currently living in a commune on Mars, and the last focuses on a second colonist who wants to be an engineer.

Zhang finds himself unemployed following the confrontation with his boss and is forced to take a six-month assignment on Baffin Island, near the

Arctic Circle. He discovers that if he extends his employment there to a full year, he will receive preferential treatment in admission to an engineering school in China. Conditions there are very unpleasant, but he seriously considers taking advantage of the opportunity, although his unwillingness to commit to a serious program of study threatens to undercut his plans. Nevertheless, he eventually finds himself in China, where his training is disrupted by a prolonged illness and where he begins to realize that no matter where he is, the single greatest restraint on his life is the bureaucracy. His progress is further delayed when his tutor commits suicide in reaction to a loss of honor. Ultimately, Zhang discovers that there is no point in challenging society—that success depends upon identifying the available niches that inevitably exist and fitting oneself into the most attractive of these.

ANALYSIS

McHugh never clearly explains how the Western nations turned to Chinese Marxism, although there are hints of an armed rebellion in the United States. Zhang's mother, who is not Chinese but who is a committed Marxist, explains that the inequities of the post-revolutionary society are not the result of any shortcoming of the revolutionary process but are rather the fault of those who are implementing it, a distinction that is tenuous at best. Although ostensibly a pure Marxist state, the economic and social structure in which Zhang exists is not very different from a capitalist society, at least for the average person. There are some social services provided by the state, but personal animosities, economic pressures, and other idiosyncrasies result in just as many inequities, and there is a very clear class structure. It is neither a utopian society nor a dystopian one. That said, McHugh also displays a keen awareness of some aspects of Chinese culture and works these into her story.

Although racial prejudice and homophobia are rampant in this future, neither are major concerns of the novel. Zhang conceals his sexual preference because it is a capital crime, though it is largely ignored by the average person. He also misleads people about his parentage because doing so provides benefits he would otherwise be denied. Nevertheless, these are both components of the background rather than elements of the main story line. It is not a novel about the subjugation of gays or the evils of racial prejudice. Similarly, despite the fact that the world has become overwhelmingly socialist, the political aspects are peripheral to the plot, which is basically about the struggles of ordinary people and their occasionally personal triumphs in a system that is much larger and complex than they are. The world presented is a plausible one, with both good and bad aspects, and like any human society, it presents challenges to its citizens no matter what their social standing.

The novel is written in first person present tense, a mildly risky strategy that alienates some readers. Since there are multiple viewpoint characters, this causes occasional confusion. It was unusual for its time and genre in that the protagonist never has any noticeable impact on the world around him. Zhang does not even aspire to a position of authority, let alone wish to significantly change the world. Neither he nor the subsidiary characters are "heroes" in the normal sense. The tentativeness of the connections among the separate story lines was also atypical, although the so-called "mosaic novel" has become increasingly common in science fiction. The separate story lines provide additional detail about the society in which the characters live, but without ever being drawn tightly together in the concluding chapters, as is usually the case. Although this provides considerable depth to the background, it does somewhat detract from the momentum of the main plot. The most impressive aspect of the novel is the characterizations, which are uniformly excellent. Even the minor figures achieve a depth of realism that is often missing from genre fiction. The novel won the James Tiptree Jr. Award, which is presented to works that explore gender roles.

—*Don D'Ammassa*

THE CHRONICLES OF CLOVIS

Twenty-eight brief satirical stories about upper-class England in the Edwardian period, loosely connected by several recurring characters

Author: Saki (Hector Hugh Munro, 1870–1916)
Genre: Fantasy—magical realism
Type of work: Stories
Time of work: The first two decades of the twentieth century
Locale: England
First published: 1911

The Story

Saki's snobbish characters are obsessed with appearances despite their glaring flaws. In "Mrs. Packletide's Tiger," Mrs. Packletide travels to India to hunt. Native villagers stake out a goat to attract an ancient tiger, and when Mrs. Packletide shoots, the tiger falls dead. It is later discovered that she shot the goat, and the tiger merely died of heart failure. To save face, she bribes her hired companion to keep the secret. In "Tobermory," Cornelius Appin announces to the skeptical guests at a weekend party that he has taught his cat to speak. The cat begins to describe the scandalous behavior he has observed among the guests. The guests plot to poison the animal rather than rectify their behavior.

Despite their veneer of respectability, Saki's characters are heartless and petty. "Esmé" tells the story of a baroness riding on a fox hunt with a companion. They are followed by a hyena that has escaped from a local zoo. The animal seizes a gypsy child and consumes it in the bushes, and the beast itself is soon killed by a car. The baroness claims that the hyena was her show dog and later receives a diamond brooch from the contrite motorist.

Saki's society is peopled by pretentious people who neither understand nor appreciate the art they pretend to adore. In "The Recessional," Clovis composes a poem as the result of a wager with a poet who insists that only a rare genius is capable of publishing verse. Clovis' poem is full of comical alliteration and errors of fact. His connections, however, make it possible for him to publish the poem in a literary magazine, so that he wins the bet. In "The Background," Henri Delpis receives an inheritance while visiting Italy. Among his impulsive purchases is a tattoo by Pincini, a master of the craft. Pincini dies, and by the time his widow demands payment, Delpis is penniless. The widow reclaims rights to the tattoo and donates it to the government. The tattoo thus becomes an Italian art treasure, and Delpis is forbidden to leave Italy, swim in the sea, or display the work without government approval.

Even in their religion, Saki's characters are more concerned with appearance than with substance. "The Story of St. Vespaluus" tells of an ancient king who chooses young Vespaluus as his heir. The king is a serpent worshiper, and when Vespaluus converts to Christianity, he is sentenced to death by bee stings. A sympathetic beekeeper removes the bees' stingers, and Vespaluus' survival is deemed a miracle. Vespaluus ascends to the throne and, to his horror, his people convert to Christianity; he only feigned conversion to antagonize the king, and he remains an avid serpent worshiper.

To Saki, primitive faith, like serpent worship, is preferable to and more real than the pretense of organized religion. In "Sredni Vashtar," a young boy elaborately worships a captured ferret that he hides from his mean-spirited guardian. He prays to the animal to deliver him from the guardian; in the end the ferret kills her. In "The Music on the Hill," Sylvia Seltoun convinces her dull husband to go to the country, where he immerses himself in the wilds. Sylvia finds a statue of Pan in a clearing, with an offering of grapes left by her husband. She removes the grapes and, as punishment, is killed by a deer while Pan stands by laughing.

Analysis

The stories in *The Chronicles of Clovis* are loosely connected by a handful of recurring characters. Most notable is Clovis, a seventeen-year-old with a subversive wit and a disrespect for the British upper class, of which he is a member. Clovis is present in most of the stories, if only as observer, and in many he is Saki's satirical mouthpiece, making light of his staid companions' most cherished interests, values, and beliefs.

Saki's cruel satires are written in refined and genteel language that parallels the stories' central themes. Saki sees elite Edwardian society as morally bankrupt and self-absorbed, yet obsessed with appearances. In the same way that Saki's elegant language disguises the sinister nature of his stories, his characters' cultivated manners hide the emptiness of their social customs and their secret malice. Their polished conversations contain thinly veiled insults, and their outward politeness masks a scheming self-interest. Saki's style is also full of wonderfully understated irony and memorable epigrams reminiscent of Oscar Wilde.

Many stories take the form of brutal cautionary tales. For their shallowness and self-absorption, Saki's characters are rewarded with humiliation or even maiming, murder, or suicide. In "The Easter-Egg," a mother's family pride leaves her scarred, blind, and childless. In "The Way to the Dairy," sisters who scheme to keep their inheritance intact unwittingly introduce their rich aunt to casino life, and she gambles away the family fortune.

Saki's stories not only satirize English society but also seem to acknowledge dark, primitive, supernatural forces that his characters are too refined to notice. These mystical undercurrents pit Celtic mythology against English civility. When his city-dwelling protagonists leave their element, they are faced with witches or mythological creatures and flee back to the safety of London. Saki's characters lead lives divorced from nature, and when they attempt to civilize nature they are killed by it.

The deft humor in these stories makes their often brutal content more palatable. Much of the humor is derived from the outrageous manners in which his characters react to cruel events. They are unmoved by death yet traumatized by a bottle of wine gone bad. The disappearance of a baby causes Clovis no alarm; he sees it as an occasion to make light of a neighbor's religion. To the baroness, the hideous death of a child becomes an opportunity to bilk a motorist.

—*Paul Buchanan*

THE CHRONICLES OF NARNIA

The creation, salvation, and apocalyptic remaking of the land of Narnia and the adventures of children there

Author: C(live) S(taples) Lewis (1898–1963)
Genre: Fantasy—theological romance
Type of work: Novels
Time of work: 1900–1949 in Earth time, during which 2,555 years pass in Narnia
Location: England, Narnia, and magical lands surrounding Narnia
First published: *The Lion, the Witch and the Wardrobe* (1950), *Prince Caspian* (1951), *The Voyage of the "Dawn Treader"* (1952), *The Silver Chair* (1953), *The Horse and His Boy* (1954), *The Magician's Nephew* (1955), and *The Last Battle* (1956)

THE STORY

The seven books constituting the Chronicles of Narnia tell how Aslan the Lion, son of the Emperor-beyond-the-Sea, sings Narnia into being from nothing and later saves it from evil by sacrificing himself and rising again. He spares nothing to make others good if they are open to change. The fictional history of the adventures does not correspond to the order of either composition or publication, but author C. S. Lewis provided a suggested order for reading the stories that is adhered to in the following plot summaries.

In book 1, *The Magician's Nephew*, the adult Andrew Ketterley, who dabbles in magic, discovers rings that can transport their wearers into other worlds and back (he thinks). He tricks his nephew Digory Kirke and Digory's friend, Polly Plummer, into trying the rings. The two children discover that yellow rings transport them to the Wood between the Worlds. Once there, green rings can plunge them into pools magically leading to other worlds.

In the dead world of Charn, Digory's unbridled curiosity leads him to release an evil witch, Jadis, from a deathlike enchantment. Jadis forces her way back to Earth, where she works her destructive evil. The children use the rings to get her out of Earth, but instead of getting her back to Charn,

they go to Narnia, a new world the lion Aslan is singing into existence. Because Digory and Polly brought evil into Narnia, Aslan gives them a role in containing it. They ride a winged horse to a far garden, bringing back an apple to plant in Narnia as temporary protection against Jadis. Aslan gives Digory an apple to take back to Earth and use to cure his dying mother. Digory plants the apple's core, and from the tree that grows he has a wardrobe made.

In book 2, *The Lion, the Witch and the Wardrobe*, Digory is the mature Professor Kirke. Peter, Susan, Edmund, and Lucy Pevensie come to his home to escape the London air raids of World War II. While playing hide and seek, they enter the enchanted wardrobe and pass into Narnia. Edmund betrays his siblings and all of Narnia for the White Witch Jadis's offer of Turkish Delight candy and power.

The Witch has created a never-ending winter with no Christmas, but she fears an ancient prophecy that when two boys and two girls take the thrones at Cair Paravel, her reign will end, and Aslan will return and claim his rightful rule. According to the magic built into Narnia at its creation, Jadis has rights to all traitors, but by a deeper magic, an innocent person may die in place of the guilty, which Aslan does. The Witch thinks Aslan a fool and herself the conqueror when she kills Aslan on the Stone Table. By a deeper magic that she does not know, Aslan rises from the dead, frees Edmund and all the Witch's captives, and leads a victorious conquest. Aslan destroys the Witch and places the children on the four thrones of Narnia. After many years, while hunting the White Stag, the children unintentionally stumble back through the enchanted wardrobe to the professor's house, with no lapse of Earth time.

The action in book 3, *The Horse and His Boy*, takes place entirely in Narnia and surrounding countries. A talking horse, Bree, born a free Narnian but stolen young and used as an ordinary riding horse by an evil Calormene master, rescues a boy named Shasta. Shasta actually is Prince Cor, the older twin son of King Lune, ruler of Archenland, a friendly neighboring country of Narnia. Shasta was stolen because of a prophecy that he would one day save Archenland. Bree and Shasta escape with two others. Through many adventures, they save Archenland and Narnia from surprise invasion.

The four Pevensie children, earlier kings and queens of Narnia, return in the fourth book, *Prince Caspian*. While waiting for the train back to boarding school, they vanish into Narnia at the blast of a magic horn Susan had left in Narnia. The Pevensies help Prince Caspian wrest Narnia from the Telmarines and his evil and usurping Uncle Miraz, who has tried to erase every memory of Narnia. Peter Pevensie, former High King himself, faces Miraz in single combat and is about to defeat him when the evil forces attack. Aslan calls the trees to life, and the Telmarines are routed. All who wish, even Telmarines who will accept forgiveness, may enter Narnia through a magic door, but the Pevensies must return to the railway station and school.

Edmund and Lucy return to Narnia in book 5, *The Voyage of the "Dawn Treader."* They are accompanied by their selfish and obnoxious cousin Eustace Scrubb. They enter Narnia by falling through a Narnian seascape hanging on a wall, and they are rescued from the sea by their old friend King Caspian, who is fulfilling a vow to search for seven Narnian lords. One of the faithful seven helps Caspian save the Lone Islands from slave trade. Eustace becomes a dragon because of his greed but is painfully "undragoned" by Aslan. Reepicheep the Mouse, the most fearless of the Narnians, fulfills his quest to find Aslan's true country.

In book 6, *The Silver Chair*, Eustace Scrubb and Jill Pole escape school bullies through a courtyard door and enter Narnia. They are met by Aslan and given four signs to aid in rescuing Prince Rilian from the evil queen of Underland. Underland is deep underground and is peopled by Earthmen, whom the queen rules by terror and plans to use in overthrowing Narnia. The wise Marsh-wiggle Puddleglum helps the children release Rilian from an enchanted silver chair and return him to Narnia.

Book 7, *The Last Battle,* is a complex account of the end of Narnia and its re-creation into a permanent paradise by Aslan the Lion, creator and rightful ruler of Narnia. Various children have been called, by various means, from Earth into a Narnia in crisis. This time, a train crash sends all the earthly friends to newly created, everlastingly good Narnia, but they must first fight in the old Narnia's last battle. A clever ape named Shift forces his donkey companion Puzzle to wear a lion's skin so that he can masquerade as Aslan. By this deception, they rule Narnia. When the deception is broken, the Calormenes, under Rishda, launch an attack on the Narnians. Rishda calls on the evil god Tash, who destroys Rishda himself in the end.

Tirian, the present king of Narnia, and the friends from Earth all die in the battle, but as they see Narnia destroyed by a cataclysmic flood, then swallowed by a dying sun, death becomes for them the doorway to a new and better Narnia. They are invited "farther up and farther in." The "Great Story" begins, "in which every chapter is better than the one before."

ANALYSIS

This series combines the elements of youth and childhood that Lewis loved and employed in many of his works: enchantment, magic, talking animals and trees, Arthurian legend, other worlds and journeys among them, time travel, and myth. The series contains elements of many genres: utopias, fairy stories, children's stories, medieval chivalric romances, fables, folktales, and novels. Its ideas pull from a deep well of learning in history, literature, philosophy, and religion. Although they never obtrude, St. Paul and the Gospel writers, Saint Augustine, Dante, John Milton, and Edmund Spenser are always visible in the subtext. Lewis acknowledges many specific authors, especially Edith Nesbit, George MacDonald, Beatrix Potter, H. G. Wells, and (preeminently) the biblical writers. The Bible provides the structure, patterns, and values of the Chronicles. The marvel of these books is in the convincing mix of all these elements and the ease of reading. Simplicity and profundity dance together.

In the Chronicles of Narnia, ordinary people such as cab drivers and schoolchildren are chosen to perform extraordinary feats and fulfill extraordinary destinies. They battle evil from within, in the form of laziness, greed, pride, selfishness, and disbelief, as well as evil from without, in the form of soldiers, traitors, witches, enchantments, and an assortment of evil mythological creatures. All these challenges are met with the richer resources of good, flowing out of its source in Aslan, who is to the world of Narnia what Christ is to Earth according to the biblical account. Aslan creates Narnia, populates it, providentially watches over it, and guides it to its end and new beginning.

As is usual in Lewis's books, evil is portrayed as the drying up of human potential, as restriction and imprisonment. The dwarfs who reject Aslan in *The Last Battle* cannot see him, and Eustace embodies greed in the form of a dragon. Goodness is expansive and liberating. Those Jadis turned to stone are restored to life by Aslan's breath, and Eustace is "undragoned" to become a hero and liberator of others in turn. The stable that Aslan occupies at the end of *The Last Battle* is bigger on the inside than the outside and opens into the new Narnia. The grand achievement of this series is its awakening of a longing for the good, for justice, purity, truth, courage, charity, patience, and perseverance.

The influence of the series is vast. When J. R. R. Tolkien's *The Lord of the Rings* trilogy and Lewis's work appeared during the 1950's, they revived fantasy literature from its doldrums. The Narnia books have been the subject of conferences, scholarly work, artworks, and television and video performances. An estimated twenty million or more readers have enjoyed the Chronicles. Perhaps no other work has done more to rehabilitate the reputation, multiply the readership, and broaden the creative potential of fantasy literature in the twentieth century.

—*Wayne Martindale*

THE CHRONICLES OF THE DERYNI

Kelson Haldane faces various enemies before taking his place as king of Gwynedd, then attempts to restore respect among his human subjects for his Deryni ones

Author: Katherine Kurtz (1944–   )
Genre: Fantasy—heroic fantasy
Type of work: Novels
Time of work: 1120–1122
Locale: The kingdom of Gwynedd, in a land resembling the United Kingdom
First published: 1985 (as trilogy; published separately as *Deryni Rising*, 1970; *Deryni Checkmate*, 1972; and *High Deryni*, 1973)

The Story

The Chronicles of the Deryni rests on a history of conflict. Festil, a member of the Deryni people, who have magical powers, overthrew the Haldane King Ifor in 822 and tried to wipe out the Haldane family. All the heirs except Aidan were killed. Festil became king, and his family ruled for seventy-eight years. Each king became more arrogant in his use of power. Camber MacRorie and his family overthrew Imre, the last king of the Festilic line, and raised Aidan Haldane's grandson Cinhil to the throne.

Camber gave Deryni-like powers to Cinhil to protect the Haldane line. Cinhil, a monk, resented being forced to forsake his vows. After Cinhil died, the human regents reacted to cruelty the Festilic kings had shown toward humans. They outlawed Deryni magic and stripped the Deryni of lands, rank, and privileges, including priestly service.

The main story of the chronicles begins when Kelson Cinhil Rhys Anthony Haldane comes to power in 1120 after Charissa, the great-granddaughter of Imre, kills Kelson's father, Brion. The laws prohibiting Deryni influence were ignored by Brion, both because he possessed Deryni-like powers and because he had a friend and adviser who was public about being half Deryni. Kelson continues to rely on Alaric Morgan, the Deryni duke who was his father's adviser and who presides over a secret rite to awaken Kelson's Deryni-like powers. The rite does not seem to work.

The church and many average humans object to the Deryni as evil, causing the Deryni to be ostracized and persecuted. Kelson's own mother, Jehana, objects to the Deryni presence and tries to prevent Morgan's affiliation with Kelson by throwing Morgan off the council. Kelson refuses to permit Morgan's banishment.

Kelson's coronation is interrupted when Charissa arrives and challenges him to a potentially fatal magical duel. Jehana protects her son, and her use of magical powers reveals that she is Deryni. Kelson taps his powers shortly before the duel, wins the duel, and is crowned.

Frightened by the Deryni magical power and envious of Morgan's influence with the young king, the archbishop of the Gwynedd church, Edmund Loris, calls the bishops together in a Curia (convocation) to pronounce an Interdict denying any sacraments for the population of Morgan's Duchy of Corwin. The Interdict is an attempt to oust Morgan.

A human revivalist preacher, Warin de Grey, has been preaching against the Deryni. Archbishop Loris intends to help de Grey overthrow Morgan. Loris anticipates that Morgan and Father Duncan may address the Curia to prevent the Interdict, so he sets a successful trap. He arranges for de Grey's men to trap Morgan at the entrance to Dhassa by using *mersaha*, a Deryni-specific drug that robs Morgan of his magic power. Father Duncan, while freeing Morgan, reveals that he is part Deryni, something few had known before, and contributes to starting a fire that destroys the shrine of Saint Torin.

When the Curia meets, some of the bishops, including the bishop of Dhassa, are hesitant to take the extreme action the archbishop wants. Six of them, withdrawing from the deliberations, deprive the Curia of a quorum. The remaining bishops vote the Interdict anyway. The bishop of Dhassa tells the remaining bishops to leave the city. Unaware of these developments, Morgan and Duncan return to the king.

The effects of the Interdict and the division of the bishops present a serious problem for the king, Morgan, and Duncan because spring is coming and they need every soldier to fight the Deryni ruler of Torenth, a nearby kingdom that shelters the Festilic family. Morgan and Duncan decide to go to Dhassa to appeal to the bishops and attempt to prove that they are not evil and should not be held responsible for the destruction of the shrine. In the meantime, Bran Coris, the earl of Marley, who protects the Cardosa's approach to Gwynedd, is persuaded by Wencit of Torenth to betray Kelson's forces.

Morgan and Duncan finally reach Dhassa and persuade the bishops of their innocence. As a result, the bishops commit their army to Kelson and the defense of Gwynedd. One of the bishops, Denis Arilan, turns out to be full Deryni and a member of the Camberian Council, which polices the use of Deryni powers.

Morgan, Duncan, Kelson, and his uncle Nigel persuade de Grey to join Kelson. De Grey believes that his own power to heal comes from God. Morgan convinces him to join the group by healing a serious wound that de Grey inflicts on Duncan.

The war is to be decided by an arcane duel to the death between the king's side (Kelson, Morgan, Duncan, and Arilan) and Wencit's (Wencit, Bran, Duke Lionel, and Lord Rhydon). The battle does not come to fruition because Rhydon, a disguised member of the Camberian Council, poisons the wine that Wencit's side drinks as an opening salute to their enemies.

ANALYSIS
These novels are the first three of a series of more than a dozen Deryni novels. In creating this world, Katherine Kurtz builds on her knowledge of the medieval world acquired in part through her involvement in the Society for Creative Anachronism as well as through her own historical research.

The Chronicles of the Deryni offers appealing characters that readers care about and slowly reveals a richly developed, complex world. As Kurtz continues to develop the Deryni world, she gradually provides additional information about the characters, the world, and the culture of Gwynedd. The story of Kelson is continued in The Histories of King Kelson, another part of the Deryni series. The background of the return of the Haldane kings to the throne is provided in The Legends of Camber of Culdi. This background was later expanded in The Heirs of Saint Camber.

The various novels reveal a rich heritage of Deryni and human literature and magic. The church resembles, but is not to be taken as, the Catholic church of medieval times. It is built on the elemental magic and rituals of Gwynedd's ancient history, which have been mingled with Christian beliefs and rituals. In this regard, the church incorporates magic in its mystical observances. These observances have their own magic—the presence and blessings of God that all feel. The Deryni, however, experience that magic with an additional layer of sensation.

Deryni magic is both sympathetic (actions that cause or at least mimic the magic) and psionic (unusual mental abilities such as telepathy, clairvoyance, precognition, and psychokinesis). These abilities mean that ordinary humans are easy for Deryni to control and are susceptible to suggestion by Deryni. The Deryni magic can be used for either good or evil. Its use depends on the user's conscience. Deryni, who usually are the main characters in these novels, most often use their magic for good. Some use their powers for their own benefit without regard to the harm they may cause others. These Deryni are the villains. Wealth and political power also are powerful forces, and they are available to humans to use, also for good or for evil.

One theme explored in these books is the responsibility of the nobility to society. Camber MacRorie feels compelled to overthrow Imre because the king and various noble Deryni feel no responsibility to treat ordinary humans with respect. Their ability to control the humans allows them to mistreat the humans for their own gain or pleasure. King Kelson, on the other hand, feels compelled to restore the Deryni to a place of respect and honorable service. He wants to allow humans and Deryni to be treated equally and to be evaluated on the basis of their abilities.

The inequality between humans and Deryni, with both being treated as inferior at various times, raises the question of prejudice. Under the Festilic kings, humans were treated as little better than slaves and often were seen only as members of their race, not as individuals judged by their abilities or behavior. After the Haldanes were returned to the throne, humans adopted similar attitudes toward the Deryni. The prejudice against the Deryni is based on the church's determination that Deryni magic is inherently evil, a judgment that was the result of human jealousy and fear. The books imply that this thinking is patently unfair and destructive to the society. The issue of prejudice could be seen as symbolic of the medieval relationships between Jews and Christians.

Connected to the issue of prejudice is the question of appropriate use of power. Without regard to danger or harm to their victims, evil Deryni misuse their powers to control humans and sometimes other Deryni. Humans who have power through their positions (secular or ecclesiastical) sometimes misuse it similarly. Kurtz clearly suggests that such use of power is wrong and should be punished.

—Sherry Stoskopf

THE CHRONICLES OF THOMAS COVENANT THE UNBELIEVER AND THE SECOND CHRONICLES OF THOMAS COVENANT THE UNBELIEVER

Thomas Covenant, a leper who wields the "wild magic" of his white gold wedding ring, must put aside disbelief to prevent the destruction of an alternate universe called the Land

Author: Stephen R. Donaldson (1947–)
Genre: Fantasy—magical world
Type of work: Novels
Time of work: The late twentieth century
Locale: New England and an alternate medieval world called the Land
First published: *Lord Foul's Bane* (1977), *The Illearth War* (1978), *The Power That Preserves* (1979), *The Wounded Land* (1980), *The One Tree* (1982), *White Gold Wielder* (1983), *The Runes of the Earth* (2004), *Fatal Revenant* (2007), *Against All Things Ending* (2010), and *The Last Dark* (2013)

THE STORY

The ten novels describing the life of Thomas Covenant are split into two trilogies and a quartet, known as The Chronicles of Thomas Covenant the Unbeliever; The Second Chronicles of Thomas Covenant the Unbeliever; and The Last Chronicles. As the series begins, Thomas Covenant, newly published and well received, is writing his second novel while his wife, Joan, visits her parents. Returning some weeks later, she discovers a purple lesion on his right hand. He consults a physician, receives a diagnosis of leprosy, and loses two fingers to amputation. In terror of infection, Joan divorces Covenant while he is in a leprosarium, learning to survive the disease that renders him numb, impotent, and outcast from society.

When he returns to Haven Farm, he finds that neighbors have eliminated the necessity for human contact, to the point of having his groceries delivered. Defiant and lonely, Covenant forces contact by paying his telephone bill in person. A strange old prophet outside the telephone company tells him to "be true." Confused, Covenant stumbles into the path of a car. He awakes in a swirl of fog atop a high rock tower called Kevin's Watch, in an alternate reality. The evil voice of Lord Foul the Despiser commands him to tell the Lords of the Land at Revelstone that the Staff of Law, lost by late High Lord Kevin, has been found by the warped cavewight Drool Rockworm.

Covenant, incapacitated by vertigo, is rescued by the barely postpubescent Lena, who takes him to her parents' home. When Lena treats his wounds with hurtloam, Covenant's body regains sensation. He realizes that his disease-induced impotence has ended. Overwhelmed by his returned sensations and convinced that he is dreaming, he rapes Lena. Lena's mother, Atiaran, learns of the rape as she leads Covenant to Revelstone. Although she is appalled, Atiaran keeps her promise to guide him.

At Revelstone, Covenant delivers Foul's message to the Lords, who mount a quest for the lost staff. Surviving many dangers, the seekers finally wrest the staff from Drool by means of Covenant's wild magic, powered by his white gold wedding ring. Covenant awakes in a hospital, his leprosy raging, convinced that his experiences in the Land are dreams.

Months later (forty years in the Land), Covenant again finds himself on Kevin's Watch and free of leprosy. By means of the powerful Illearth

Stone, Foul is again on the attack. The benevolent Giants of the first quest are dead, except three whom Foul has coerced into service as "Ravers." High Lord Elena (the child of Lena's rape) mounts another quest, drinks Earthblood, gains the Power of Command, and, breaking the Law of Death, commands the ghost of Kevin Landwaster to destroy Foul. Instead, Kevin is overpowered, Elena dies, and the Staff of Law is destroyed. Covenant fights his way to Foul's Creche, uses wild magic to destroy the Illearth Stone, and, believing the Land is safe, fades from consciousness to reawaken at home.

Ten years later—four millennia in the Land—Covenant and Linden Avery, a physician drawn into the Land by accident, find themselves atop Kevin's Watch. Foul has regained his power and created the Sunbane (vicious three-day cycles of rain, drought, fertility, and pestilence). The Clave (lore-masters corrupted by Foul) now rule the Land from Revelstone, coercing blood from the Land's people to appease the Sunbane. As Covenant undertakes still another quest to Revelstone, to find the Sunbane's source and destroy its stranglehold on the Land, he learns that the Sunbane resulted from the destruction of the Staff of Law, which formerly supported the natural order. He resolves to find the One Tree and make another staff from its branches, thus delivering the Land from the Sunbane.

When Covenant and Linden are joined by the Search (a remnant of the Giants), Covenant persuades the Search to take them to the Isle of the One Tree. When they arrive, they find the Isle guarded by the Worm of the World's End. Covenant cannot use his white magic to destroy the Worm without destroying the Arch of Time, within which the Land exists. When the Isle sinks, Covenant cannot fashion a new staff, so he, Linden, and the remaining Giants undertake the dangerous journey back to Revelstone.

Covenant finally masters the wild magic by realizing that he is the keystone of the Arch of Time. Standing firm, the Arch imprisons Foul within it. When the staff reincarnates, Linden uses it to restore the Earthpower and eradicate the Sunbane. The Land is thus healed. A twenty-year publishing interregnum between the Second and Last Chronicles did not detract from the powerful conclusion embodied in the quartet, which moves from an extended sequence on our familiar planet in *The Runes of the Earth* to a lover's reunion and final confrontation with the Worm of the World's End in *The Last Dark*.

ANALYSIS

Shortly after publication of the first Covenant trilogy in 1977, Stephen R. Donaldson received the 1979 John W. Campbell Award as best new writer of the year. The trilogies reveal Donaldson's familiarity with medieval literature, his knowledge of leprosy, and his heavy indebtedness to J. R. R. Tolkien's epic fantasy *The Lord of the Rings* (1968).

Although a hero on quest to right a wrong is an ancient theme, Donaldson's twist—Covenant is a leper—creates a protagonist who seems woefully inadequate to the task, as does Tolkien's hero, the hobbit Frodo Baggins. Blended with the theme of the quest to free the Land from evils inflicted by Lord Foul are the familiar medieval themes of alienation and impotence. Covenant's leprosy isolates him from society and prevents him from accepting the Land and his restored health as real; it also causes the sexual impotence that translates into a futility of spirit when he is swept by the Creator into the dreamlike Land.

Because Donaldson's physician father specialized in the treatment of leprosy, Donaldson possesses an esoteric knowledge of the disease that he uses to good effect in his depiction of Covenant and in the metaphors of health, decay, and numbness that pervade both trilogies. The leper's physical survival tool, visual surveillance of extremities (VSE), becomes Covenant's metaphorical survival tool as he struggles with appearance versus reality in the Land. Both leper and moral being must answer this question: What must one do in the face of death—what is the proper response to destruction?

Donaldson's debt to Tolkien appears most clearly in his creation of the characters and characteristics of the Land. Lord Foul, whose twisted perceptions cause him to despise the good that remains beyond his grasp, clearly derives from both Morgoth and Sauron, the "great enemies" in *The Lord of the Rings*. Like Morgoth, Foul manifests supernatural powers and predates the Land; like Sauron, Foul uses talismans to take possession of lesser beings, including three demoniac Ravers who can assume any form Foul commands.

Tolkien's benevolent Ents appear in two incarnations: as Donaldson's gentle Giants, slow of speech and slow to anger, dwindling as a race from lack of fecundity, and as the mysterious Forestals who guard the woods of Andelain (Donaldson's version of Lothlorien). Instead of orcs, Donaldson offers ur-viles, eyeless monsters who, like the orcs, result from perverted breeding schemes. In place of dwarves who carve stone and elves who tend forests, Donaldson presents Stonedownors who sense the hidden life of stone and woodhelvennin who communicate with trees. Tolkien's Gollum, a creature vulnerable to Sauron and twisted by the power of the One Ring, becomes Drool Rockworm, a cavewight vulnerable to Foul and driven insane by the stolen Staff of Law. The wizards of Middle Earth appear as the Lords of the Land, wielding wizardlike power through their staffs. In particular, the wizard Saruman, who in desperation becomes the tool of Sauron, is echoed in Lord Kevin Landwaster, who in desperation desecrated the Land rather than surrender it to Foul. Tolkien's elusive High Elves become Donaldson's mysterious and godlike elohim, who aid the final quest. The magnificent horses of Middle Earth become the Land's sentient ranyhyn. The word itself is a nod to the Houyhnhnms of Jonathan Swift's *Gulliver's Travels* (1726).

From both Tolkien and medieval lore Donaldson draws the motifs of hidden identity, prophecy, sacred or profane objects, Christ figures and Satan figures, enchanted places, enchanted or magical animals, words of power, and help unlooked for. From medieval literature he incorporates the motifs of a land's health being tied to human health, of moral decay being reflected in physical decay, of earthly struggles carrying eternal consequences, of evil disguised as good, and of fate calling the chosen to fulfill tasks upon which the destiny of many depends.

As further evidence of Tolkien's influence, Donaldson attempts to create languages for his characters. He fails in this, except for his vivid use of allegorical names. Whereas Tolkien constructed actual grammars and matched each language to its speakers, Donaldson invents an isolated, largely unpatterned and ungrammatical vocabulary. In addition, he makes such heavy use of a thesaurus that his ponderous prose often interferes with the story, especially when he attempts internal monologue.

Despite its flaws and omissions, the allegorical fantasy creates a believable, fairly consistent universe and provides an intriguing tale of the eternal war between good and evil.

—*Barbara C. Stanley and Sonya Cashdan*

THE CHRONICLES OF TORNOR

Characters with some connection to Tornor Keep experience personal changes against backdrops of political conflict, war, and witchcraft

Author: Elizabeth A. Lynn (1946–)
Genre: Fantasy—feminist
Type of work: Novels
Time of work: The years 290, 410, and 522 since the founding of Kendra-on-the-Delta
Locale: Various places in the land of Arun
First published: *Watchtower* (1979), *The Dancers of Arun* (1979), and *The Northern Girl* (1980)

THE STORY

The three books of the Chronicles of Tornor all revolve around characters with a connection to Tornor Keep in the north of the land of Arun, but only the first, Watchtower, uses the keep itself as a significant part of the plot. Elizabeth Lynn uses the 232-year time span of the trilogy to show the evolution of a culture as women acquire equality and war becomes less important. In this change, Tornor Keep moves from being a stronghold and seat of war to being almost deserted and obsolete ruins.

Watchtower begins with the conquest of Tornor Keep by Col Istor, a Southerner. Col captures Errel, the prince of Tornor, and requires him to serve as his cheari, or jester. Ryke, a captured soldier, swears service to Col in order to keep Errel alive. When Col is visited by the messengers Sorren and Norres, Errel and Ryke escape with them to the legendary Van's Valley. There Errel learns to be a true *cheari*, a dancer and practitioner of martial arts similar to *aikido*. Ryke's struggle is to accept Sorren and Norres' lesbian love for each other, the idea of fighting without killing, and the idea that women can be as independent and as capable as men.

The novel concludes with the reconquest of Tornor Keep through an alliance with an army from one of the other keeps and the work of the *chearas* (a group of chearis). Errel then gives up his lordship to Sorren, his sister, who becomes the first Lady of Tornor, and returns to the Valley. Ryke remains in the North.

The Dancers of Arun also begins in Tornor Keep, 120 years later. Since the time of *Watchtower*, women have assumed much more leadership in society, the chearis have become the red clan, and both magic and homosexuality have become accepted. Kerris, the nephew of the lord of the keep, is set apart from the rest of the people both because his right arm was cut off in a raid by the Asech (another people of Arun) when he was a toddler and because he is mentally able to communicate with his brother Kel. The novel is largely about Kerris' search for wholeness.

Kel, the leader of a *chearas*, comes to Tornor to bring Kerris back to Elath, the witch-town. There Kerris begins to learn how to use his gift of "inspeaking" and enters into a homosexual relationship with Kel. At the same time, Elath is attacked by Asech witches who have been banished from their tribes and want to learn how to use their gifts. The teachers of Elath agree to instruct them, but one of the Asech does not understand the limits of the gifts and kills Sefer, a teacher and Kel's lover. After peace is made, Kel and the *chearas* depart. Kerris, after some hesitation, decides that he belongs with them and sets off to rejoin the group.

The third novel, *The Northern Girl*, begins in the Southern city of Kendra-on-the-Delta. In the 112 years between *The Dancers of Arun* and *The Northern Girl*, the cities of Arun have forbidden the use of edged weapons, and as a result the *chearis* have been extinguished. Kendra-on-the-Delta is governed by five ruling Houses, and its spiritual center is the Tanjo, the witch-school.

Sorren, the title character, is a bondservant to Arre Med and the lover of Arre's Yardmaster, Paxe. All three characters are women. The plot moves between Sorren's desires to go north and Arre's involvement with the politics in the city.

Sorren dreams of the North; she eventually learns that she possesses the witch gift of seeing, but she sees the past, not the future. The secondary plot concerns the aspirations of one of the leaders of another House to Council status and his intent to use an exception to the ban on edged weapons as a way to gain that power. The attempt is defeated by Arre, but as a result of its failure, her jealous and power-hungry brother, Isak, arranges for her death. Sorren overhears his plan and warns Arre, for which she receives her freedom. Isak is exiled. Sorren goes north to Tornor, which is now inhabited by only eight people and some animals. Sorren stays and suggests an arrangement with Arre and one of her allies for Tornor's support. She also begins a relationship with Lady Merith's daughter, Kedera, and discovers that she has found her place.

ANALYSIS

When the books of the Chronicles of Tornor were first published, Lynn's career as a fantasy and science-fiction author appeared full of promise. She had published *A Different Light* (1978), a science-fiction novel, before publishing the three Tornor novels, and she followed them with another science-fiction novel, *The Sardonyx Net* (1981), and a collection of previously published stories, *The Woman Who Loved the Moon and Other Stories* (1981). She was nominated for the John W. Campbell Award in 1977, and in 1980 she received the World Fantasy Award for *Watchtower* and for the short story "The Woman Who Loved the Moon" (originally published in *Amazons!*, edited by Jessica Amanda Salmonson, 1979). Her work received good reviews. In the remainder of the 1980's, however, her only two full-length books were both for children: *The Silver Horse* (1984), a fantasy novel, and *Babe Zaharias* (1988), a biography of the athlete.

Lynn's range as a writer is easily seen in the collection *The Woman Who Loved the Moon and Other Stories*. The stories include science fiction (set both on Earth and on alien worlds), fantasy, and what Lynn herself calls "category-straddling" stories that contain elements of science fiction and crime fiction, among other genres.

Science fiction was for a long time a market dominated by men, both in readership and in authorship. It was not until the 1960's and 1970's, with the rise of the women's movement, that women began to both read and write science fiction. Suzy McKee Charnas and Joanna Russ have both written of the difficulties they had in beginning to write science fiction with only male role models available to them. Lynn's work shows her own attempts to shape the genre into one in which women have a place. Lynn was teaching in the women's studies program at San Francisco State University when the Chronicles of Tornor were published, and the importance of feminism to her is clear in the novels. She uses the freedom generated by the creation of an imaginary world to create a society in which women are truly equal to men.

The Chronicles of Tornor resist many of the clichés and stock characters of fantasy. There are no wise old men, great warriors, submissive lovestruck damsels in distress, or warrior women who learn their place as wives. Nor is Lynn concerned with the outward action of an adventure story, one of the traditional masculine forms of fiction. Although the novels are not free from violence, and Ryke and Paxe are both soldiers, the significant development and action of the novels tends to be internal rather than external. All three novels include external conflicts resolved by some form of violence, but the books each end on a change or resolution in a character rather than in external circumstances. They are character driven rather than plot driven.

There are also many differences in the culture and lifestyle of people in Arun from those of more traditional fantasy. No professions are gender-specific by the time of *The Northern Girl*, and both homosexual and heterosexual relationships are accepted, as is bisexuality. The generic pronoun is the female, and a man who marries takes his wife's name. In addition to a lack of gender bias, there is also no racism in Arun. Characters are described as having varying skin tones, but no suggestion is ever made that skin color is any more of a racial distinction than is hair or eye color. Although the Asech peoples are identified as another race (more by culture, custom, and language than by physical appearance), they are not discriminated against because of this in *The Northern Girl*. The earlier books reveal characters' hostility to the Asech, but that hostility is shown as negative. Arun still has a nondemocratic class structure; however, the feudalism of *Watchtower* has been replaced by a more capitalist republic in *The Northern Girl*, and most of Lynn's characters are people who engage in the day-to-day tasks of farming, cooking, or shopping. The novels are fantasies, but they are neither romances nor utopias.

—*Elisabeth Anne Leonard*

THE CHRYSALIDS

A group of adolescents with telepathic powers battles persecution in a post-apocalyptic society devoted to maintaining the purity of all species and destroying mutant life-forms

Author: John Wyndham (John Wyndham Parkes Lucas Beynon Harris, 1903–1969)
Genre: Science fiction—post-holocaust
Type of work: Novel
Time of work: c.e. 4000–5000
Locale: Waknuk, Labrador, Canada
First published: 1955

THE STORY

The Chrysalids was published in Great Britain under that title and in the United States as *Re-Birth*. The novel takes place after Tribulation, a cataclysmic event (probably a nuclear holocaust that devastated the world thousands of years earlier) attributed to God's anger in the tradition of Eden and the Flood. The agrarian folk, technologically backward and beset by fear and prejudice, obey a strict interpretation of the Old Testament, eradicating all crop and animal mutations. Stern commandments and proclamations hang on their walls, telling them that "blessed is the norm" and to "keep pure the stock of the Lord" and "watch thou for the mutant!" Humans "made in God's image" reside in communities throughout Labrador, and deviations from the norm are ritualistically "purified" (exterminated) or exiled to the Fringes, the abnormal territories, where they forage for food and eke out an existence.

David Strorm, the narrator, has a deep secret. For years, he, his half-cousin Rosalind, and several other youngsters have been communicating telepathically. Although by appearance they are "norms," they are mutants within and a potential threat to the existing order. Instinctively, they have never revealed their abilities to anyone except for David's kind and protective Uncle Axel.

David's life changes forever when, at the age of ten, he meets Sophie, a girl with six toes. Her parents are terrified of her being discovered by David's intractable father, Joseph Strorm, Waknuk's fanatical patriarch. Joseph has destroyed some of his own children and relatives as blasphemies, and his deformed brother, nicknamed Spider, leads a ragtag group of marauding mutants of the Fringes. Sophie's secret is exposed, and Joseph whips David until he admits where Sophie has gone. Sophie's family disappears into the Fringes. Following the birth of David's sister Petra, a child with incredible powers, six years pass without further incident.

The adolescents are betrayed when one marries a "norm" only to commit suicide after confiding in her unsympathetic spouse. Uncle Axel murders the callous husband, but Petra's awakened and uncontrolled powers send psychic blasts that paralyze the others, arouse suspicion and a witch hunt, and draw telepathic responses from Sealand (New Zealand), which sends an aircraft to rescue them. Pursued by Joseph Strorm and his troops, David, Petra, and Rosalind battle their way to the Fringes, where David's banished uncle, Spider, captures them. Spider brutally beats David and leaves him to die, having announced his carnal designs on Rosalind. Sophie, her innocence corrupted, conceals David and murders the albino guarding Rosalind. As the posse descends for the kill, the Sealanders arrive, annihilating everyone except the young telepaths, whom they transport to Sealand to help build the world anew.

Analysis

Writing what he termed "logical fantasy," John Wyndham cast an unsettling shadow across the apparently placid landscape of post-World War II England. The literary heir of H. G. Wells, Wyndham blended fantasy, horror, and science fiction into a seminal body of work that resonates in the tales of many writers, including Richard Matheson, Clive Barker, James Herbert, and Stephen King. Generally overlooked in the United States, where it went out of print, *The Chrysalids* is the centerpiece of Wyndham's three most important novels, the psychological and creative bridge between the Wells-inspired *The Day of the Triffids* (1951) and his startling fusion of science fiction and horror, *The Midwich Cuckoos* (1957), which also appeared under the title *Village of the Damned*. The story was filmed as *Village of the Damned* in 1960 and 1995.

As their beautiful Sealand rescuer tells David and Rosalind, "The essential quality of living is change; change is evolution; and we are part of it." In Wyndham's fiction, the world is in constant flux, and most people are either unwilling to face change or too eager to capitalize on it for their own advantage. Caught in this paradox are the Wyndham protagonists, ordinary men, women, and children pummeled by the past and present into resolutions of transcendence and new, meaningful undertakings. No guarantees await them in the future. Sealand, to which David, Rosalind, and Petra escape, is peopled by beings who view themselves as superior and, by their own admission and as shown in their obsession with Petra's harrowing gift, are doomed one day to self-destruct, as have the unyielding remnants of the Old People they are supplanting.

The hubris of humans then, not the technology they create, undermines them. *The Chrysalids*, critical of Old Testament justice, still draws a comparable moral from the New Testament: "for whatsoever a man soweth, that shall he also reap." Ironically, Joseph Strorm refuses to acknowledge, as his own, his misshapen brother, his "impure" children, and all the abnormalities that surround him; he systematically fashions his own doom. People are all of one origin, the novel insists, and to deny this precipitates the tragic demise of humanity.

This portrayal of kinship demonstrates Wyndham's resolute refusal to perpetuate traditional stereotypes. Appearances mean little; truth, beauty, and deformity reside within, as does the pupa inside the chrysalid. Like her namesake in William Shakespeare's *As You Like It*, Rosalind personifies charm, courage, and compassion. The stoic heroism of David, like his biblical counterpart's, is tempered by wisdom and tenderness. In a scene that anticipates the "grokking" of Robert

Heinlein's *Stranger in a Strange Land* (1961), David and Rosalind, destined to be lovers, meld minds until "Neither one of us existed any more; for a time there was a single being that was both."

The Chrysalids proposes that ignorant adherence to the "word," or to religious tenets, has dehumanized the world, and that only in transcendence of past beliefs will humanity resurrect itself. The message is distinct: People must throw off the mind-forged chains of the past, bury fears and prejudices, and walk as one with enlightened steps into the future, or else stumble and perish forever.

—Erskine Carter

THE CHYMICAL WEDDING

Poet Michael Darken is forced to confront his failings and recognize that people are unbalanced without the Hermetic principle of unity among all things and people

Author: Lindsay Clarke (1939–)
Genre: Fantasy—magical realism
Type of work: Novel
Time of work: The 1980's and the mid-nineteenth century
Locale: Norfolk, England
First published: 1989

The Story

British poet Michael Darken is at the end of his tether. His marriage to Jess has fallen apart, he is incapable of writing verse, and he is employed unsatisfactorily as a college lecturer. His sympathetic publisher lends him his weekend cottage, "The Pightle," in Munding St. Mary's, Norfolk, for the summer vacation. The village is still curiously feudal, dominated by Easterness Hall, and Ralph, the last of the dynastic Agnew family. Some opposition is provided by Michael's nearest neighbor, Bob Crossley, a socialist and a stalwart of the Campaign for Nuclear Disarmament.

Also present in the village, staying at the lodge as guests of Ralph, are Edward Nesbit and his young American assistant, Laura, a talented potter. Edward was a celebrated poet when Michael was young but has since dried up. Michael is drawn into their company and then into their quest, which is to discover what they can of Louisa Agnew, the last link in the Agnew tradition of alchemical research. They already have discovered the crucial date in 1848 when Henry was working on a poetic epic about the Hermetic mystery and Louisa, always his willing apprentice, offered to help by writing a prose treatise, "An Open Invitation to the Chymical Wedding."

The other narrative strand is Louisa's, setting out her inspired and dutiful nature while narrating events in the village of the mid-nineteenth century. The most important, in addition to Louisa's assumed task, is the arrival of a new vicar, Edwin Frere, and his wife, Emilia. Fresh from Cambridge, Emilia clearly resents her separation from her family there. Soon Emilia becomes pregnant. After losing her baby, she demonstrates a formidable manipulative will and eventually returns to Cambridge, deserting Edwin.

As Michael moves into Edward and Laura's world, he is alternately threatened and attracted by Edward; with Laura, it is only the former. He is aware that both are erudite and is menaced by Edward's reading of the tarot and his insistence on Michael's recounting of his dreams for interpretation. Gradually, Henry and Louisa intervene more in their lives.

Louisa seems to be blocked. Alchemy is set in a specifically sexual set of imagery, and she is a virgin. The deserted Edwin, tormented by sexual fantasies, reports to her, and their problems are assuaged temporarily. Similarly, as if possessed, Michael and Laura couple.

Both events lead to disaster. Edwin, a man of conscience, castrates himself. Louisa's book is too explicit and provokes jealousy in her father. It is burned. Edward takes Michael to a place where he might kill him but suffers a massive heart attack. Michael's prompt action saves him, though he is left in emergency care. The results, in the end, are not disastrous. Both Edward and Michael become able to write again. Laura is now alchemically virgin and thus is able to decide her own destiny. Edwin remains Louisa's spiritual brother.

ANALYSIS

Winner of the 1989 Whitbread Prize for Fiction, *The Chymical Wedding* is a complex text notable for its blend of contemporary and historical realism and fantasy. In many ways, it resembles the work of John Fowles, but with a more magical inspiration.

Lindsay Clarke's characterization is superb. Both Michael and Edward initially are rather alienating beings, and Edward remains so for some time. Both Edwin and Louisa at first seem merely stereotypes, and Laura a cipher. Gradually, their characters come alive and form the motivating forces for the narrative.

The fantasy element is essential for the story but is blended subtly. Having seemed distinct, the two narrative lines blur, interact, and parallel each other. Information about alchemy adds to the pleasure offered by the text and is central to the plot. Where the plot lines intersect and the alchemy enters is the relationship between men and women.

None of the characters has a successful relationship when the story begins. Louisa and Henry are too close to be healthy, though his dominance is intellectual rather than pederastic. Michael has driven away his wife and is unable to relate to any woman. Edward appears the most selfish and exploits Ralph's nostalgia about their youthful homosexual relationship. A fully developed literary *bête noire*, he is capable of colossal rudeness and uses Laura ruthlessly. His comeuppance is not the product of sexual jealousy, however, and he is pleased with both Laura's self-realization and Michael's growth.

The development of the plot has important personal ramifications for the participants, but there is a philosophical core. The most significant occasion in Louisa's history is the Vatican Council, at which, even at the height of Renaissance humanism, Aristotle was chosen as the cornerstone of Christian philosophy over Hermes Trismegistus. This was a triumph for the male and intellectual over the female and feeling. Hermeticism, a belief in forms of magic and in the unity of the cosmos, was needed in a threatening world and in the face of moribund Christianity. This knowledge comes to Louisa after she first sleeps with Edwin. His response is emasculation to save others and expiate his guilt. Seemingly, this accords well with the Aristotelian principle. He is redeemed by his continuing role as the mystic brother. His chance of happiness thus is increased, and Louisa achieves serenity.

In the modern sphere, Laura's freedom is bought ostensibly at the expense of both her former lover and her potential future lover, but Edward is happy and Michael comes to recognize women's needs and identities outside himself. He is able to contact his family, treat Jess's new lover respectfully, and take responsibility for his children. In every case, the result is benevolent and Hermetic.

—*Mike Dickinson*

THE CIRCUS OF DR LAO

A circus owned by the mysterious Dr. Lao disrupts the lives of the citizens of a small Arizona town

Author: Charles G. Finney (1905–1984)
Genre: Fantasy—mythological
Type of work: Novel
Time of work: The 1930's
Locale: Abalone, Arizona
First published: 1935

THE STORY

Charles G. Finney wrote *The Circus of Dr. Lao* after his travels to China during the 1920's, when he served as part of a United States garrison stationed in Tientsin. Finney's knowledge of Chinese mythology provides the backdrop for the more fantastic elements of the novel.

The Circus of Dr. Lao consists of three tiers of set pieces, or short scenes, that introduce and explore the circus and its attractions. Speculations on the nature of the circus prior to its arrival serve as the first tier of set pieces, during which most of the main characters, and many minor characters, are introduced. These characters busily enter and exit from scene to scene, their personalities defined exclusively by their reactions to the circus.

Most notable among these characters, none of whom dominates the book, is Dr. Lao, the proprietor, who guides his visitors through the exhibits while providing intricate and inventive commentary. Dr. Lao speaks in different dialects, mirroring and mocking his visitors' expectations. Standing resolutely at the novel's center, he expounds at length about his circus but rarely divulges information about himself. Thus, the center of the circus remains a mystery.

Other characters of note include Mr. Etaoin (whose first name is not given), the town newspaper's proofreader; Miss Agnes Birdsong, a high school English teacher; Mr. Larry Kamper, a United States soldier recently returned from China; and Mrs. Howard T. Cassan, a widow who frequents fortune-tellers. The mythological circus performers include a medusa, a magician, a satyr, a mermaid, a sea serpent, and a hedge hound. As with the human characters, these creatures all have their moments in the spotlight.

The second tier of set pieces provides a closer examination of the circus as it parades down the town's main street. The parade culminates in lengthy and hilarious arguments over the exact nature of the beasts in the circus, particularly as to whether one attraction is a bear or merely a caged Russian.

The third tier of set pieces, exploring the interactions between circus visitors and circus stars, provides explanations for the existence of, or stories behind the capture of, many of the mythological beasts. Among such scenes are Miss Birdsong's near seduction by the satyr and Mr. Etaoin's conversation with the sea serpent.

Mrs. Cassan's encounter with the seer Apollonius midway through the book best demonstrates Finney's talent for brutal lucidity. Apollonius tells Mrs. Cassan that her oil investments will never pay off, that she will never remarry, and that she is doomed for the rest of her days to relive the repetitive and useless actions that compose her existence. Upon deliverance of this verdict, Mrs. Cassan attempts to befriend the uninterested Apollonius. Walking once more into the sunshine beyond the tent, she tells a minor character that the seer had encouraging news for her.

The magical events reach a climax with a summoning of the devil and a virgin sacrifice, after which the citizens of Abalone, stunned by all they have witnessed (but perhaps unchanged), stumble out of the tent and back into their all-too-real small-town world. Finney includes as epilogue "The Catalogue," a whimsical dictionary of all the people, animals, places, and historical events mentioned in the novel.

ANALYSIS

Winner of the award for most original novel in 1936 from the American Bookseller's Association and subsequently made into the film *The Seven Faces of Doctor Lao* (1963), *The Circus of Dr. Lao* was Finney's first and most critically popular novel. Although only thirty years old upon publication of *The Circus of Dr. Lao*, Finney produced only three other book-length works during the next half century. These include the surreal science-fiction novel *The Unholy City* (1937), the lighthearted Chinese fantasy *The Magician Out of Manchuria* (1968), and the less-acclaimed *Past the End of the Pavement* (1939).

The strength of *The Circus of Dr. Lao* lies in its seamless interweaving of various mythological traditions, from the Chinese to the Greek. Finney updates and refines such archetypes for a modern age while implying that the myths of the past are far more glorious than the small-minded concerns of the present.

The novel belongs to the peculiar but potent subgenre of "circus fantasy," other representatives of which include Tom Reamy's deliberate pastiche of Finney's novel, *Blind Voices* (1978), Angela Carter's *Nights at the Circus* (1984), and Brooke Stevens' *The Circus of the Earth and the Air* (1994).

The most significant author to be directly influenced by Finney is Ray Bradbury, whose *Something Wicked This Way Comes* (1962) owes a large debt to *The Circus of Dr. Lao*. *Something Wicked This Way Comes* can be read as a corollary to *The Circus of Dr. Lao* in that it takes the circus as a given and focuses on one or two characters who visit the circus. Bradbury so admired Finney that he made Finney's short novel the title story of his strange fantasy anthology *The Circus of Dr. Lao and Other Improbable Stories* (1956).

The unique strength of the circus fantasy, and Finney's novel in particular, is its reduction of the broad canvas of the world to a smaller, stylized microcosm, with the point of making ironic and satiric comment on humankind. The interactions between circus and observer define the observer, illuminating fears, desires, dreams, and prejudices. *The Circus of Dr. Lao* describes Finney's own journey from the small towns of the United States to the alien outreaches of China. Finney's novel merely reverses the order, so that the alien intrudes into the realm of the banal.

—*Jeff VanderMeer*

CITIES IN FLIGHT

Earth's culture, represented by the flying city of New York, spreads through the galaxy and decays as the universe comes to an end

Author: James Blish (1921–1975)
Genre: Science fiction—future history
Type of work: Novels
Time of work: 2012–4004
Location: Earth, Jupiter, various star systems in and beyond the galaxy, and the center of the universe
First published: *Cities in Flight* (1970, as tetralogy); previously published as *Earthman, Come Home* (1955), *They Shall Have Stars* (1956; also published as *Year 2018*), *The Triumph of Time* (1958; also published as *A Clash of Cymbals*), and *A Life for the Stars* (1962)

THE STORY

Much of the material making up *Cities in Flight* was published in other forms between 1950 and 1962 and in a different order from that presented in the completed tetralogy. The core of the story idea was published in a series of novelettes—"Okie" (1950), "Bindlestiff" (1950), "Sargasso of Lost Cities" (1953), and "Earthman Come Home" (1953)—which were revised and combined into *Earthman, Come Home*, the third novel in the chronological sequence. *They Shall Have Stars*, the first novel in the sequence, was formed by combining the novelettes "Bridge" (1952) and "At Death's End" (1954). The second novel in the sequence, *A Life for the Stars*, was published as juvenile science fiction fours years after the fourth, *The Triumph of Time*.

The overarching conception melding these disparately written pieces into a single volume is James Blish's elaboration of a complete future history that begins in the early twenty-first century, as the United States and the Soviet Union are about to merge into a single bureaucratic state. Blish conceives of a new galactic Earthmanist culture—a version of Western culture—formed on the basis of antigravity screens (spindizzies) that allow entire cities to take flight and anti-agathics (antideath drugs) that allow the long lifetimes required for interstellar flight.

Earth dominates the galaxy after the defeat of the previous hegemony, the Vegan tyranny, a vaguely defined humanoid/alien civilization. The galaxy is "pollinated" by Earth cities, which function as itinerant industrial bases (Okies) and are policed by the Earth "cops," who exist in creative tension with the Okies. Abasic plot idea throughout the series is that some cities are good citizens, such as New York City, the "protagonist" city of the series. Others have become rogues, or "bindlestiffs." The worst of these, the legendary Interstellar Master Traders (IMT), have slaughtered an entire planet. As background to the narrative, Earth culture decays as Earth's growing bureaucracy and fear of the Okies destroys the galactic economy. As time itself draws to an end, in the fortieth century, a new alien civilization, theWeb of Hercules, rises to power.

They Shall Have Stars tells, in alternating narratives, of the development of the two technologies on which the rest of the series depends. Bliss-Wagoner, a U.S. senator, secretly sponsors both projects in an effort to create an escape route forWestern culture. In the first of the two narratives, a space pilot, Paige Russell, falls in love with Anne Abbott, the daughter of the president of the drug company where immortality drugs are being developed. The second narrative is told from the point of view of Robert Helmuth, a construction supervisor of the giant "bridge" being built on Jupiter by remote control to test the theories that will make antigravity possible. At the end, Wagoner arranges for Russell and Abbott to become the nucleus of a colonizing diaspora from Earth.Wagoner is executed for treason by the paranoid head of the Federal Bureau of Investigation.

A Life for the Stars, set in the thirty-second century, tells of the departure of Earth's cities. Crispin DeFord, a youth, is impressed by the city of Scranton, Pennsylvania, as it departs from an Earth whose economy has collapsed. The novel is essentially a coming-of-age story in which the young DeFord, thrust into perilous circumstances, manages by virtue of his wits and the help of older mentors to survive and, at the end, to become city manager of New York, which Scranton encounters in space. Much of the narrative deals with DeFord's education, after he is transferred to New York, in the culture and technology of the Okie city. DeFord demonstrates his abilities in a series of daring escapades that help save New York from a bindlestiff.

Earthman, Come Home, set in the last half of the fourth millennium, tells of New York under the guidance of Mayor John Amalfi and the new city manager, Mark Hazelton. A series of escapades, including equipping the entire planet of He with spindizzies (told in *A Life for the Stars*), brings the city into constant conflict with the Earth police. New York is forced to join a "hobo jungle" of unemployed Okie cities. Amalfi, through his understanding of the principles of cultural development, is able to manipulate the cities to march on Earth and, through their flight across the galaxy, to lure out of hiding the Vegan Fort, the last lurking vestige of the Vegan tyranny. Amalfi destroys the Fort by "flying" a planet at intergalactic speed across the path of the Fort as it enters the solar system. New York ends up grounded on a planet in the Greater Magellanic Cloud, where it must defeat the IMT, which has hidden there, in order to begin a new culture in the wake of the collapse of the old.

The Triumph of Time is set in the first years of the forty-first century. The scientists of New York and the planet He, now returned from intergalactic space, discover that in the repeating cycles of time itself a twin antimatter universe will collide with the known universe to begin a new big bang. The only chance for "survival"—which amounts to the right to determine the physical composition of a new universe—is to fly to the center of the universe. To do this, Amalfi must fight off a rebellion against New York's hegemony in the Greater Magellanic Cloud, dispel the apathy of a culture grown old, and race the rising galactic civilization, the Web of Hercules, to the center. At the end, at the moment of his death, Amalfi chooses to make a new universe completely different from the old one.

Analysis

Cities in Flight as a whole is more than the sum of its parts, which are pastiches of the science-fiction tradition. The bold image of flying cities and the theme of immortality come directly from part 3 of Jonathan Swift's *Gulliver's Travels* (1726), although Blish borrows none of Swift's satire. Most of the narrative is typical "space opera" on a grand scale. Devices of science are manufactured as the plot demands, within a context of flashing space battles and an entire galaxy improbably turned into a human landscape that looks and behaves like a somewhat comic map of nineteenth century Europe, complete with squabbling governments and officious military. Blish's imagined future, sweeping to the end of time itself, is in the high science-fiction tradition reaching back to H. G. Wells and Olaf Stapledon, although Blish compresses his future into a few thousand years. The mapping of the detailed future history that Blish added as *Cities in Flight* developed is much like the work of Robert A. Heinlein in his Future History and Isaac Asimov in the Foundation series. Blish's imaginary history reflects directly the ideological concerns of America in the Cold War period.

Cities in Flight derives a distinctive quality and sense of wholeness from the claim, woven into and around the narrative, that the series reflects a serious philosophy of history. This claim is supported by the excerpted fictional study *The Milky Way: Five Cultural Portraits*, which Blish adds as prologue to some of the novels. Critics have discussed Blish's reliance on Oswald Spengler's *The Decline of the West* (1918–1922), a work that presents a theory of evolution of cultures and civilizations as an organic, cyclic process. Richard D. Mullen discusses this idea in "Blish, van Vogt and the Rise of Spengler" in the *Riverside Quarterly* (1968).

This tetralogy cannot be taken seriously as philosophical fiction. Some of Blish's later fiction, most notably *A Case of Conscience* (1959), stakes a more serious claim. *Cities in Flight*, however, is held together imaginatively by a consistent tension between two ideas. The first is that history and cultures rise and fall in repeated patterns. This process is inexorable and shapes and transcends the will of the individuals in those cultures. The second is that rare and perceptive individuals, such as Bliss Wagoner and John Amalfi, can see those patterns and act as agents of creative change, to some extent transcending them. The thousandyear life span of Amalfi represents this transcendence.

Blish reproduces images of the typical American hero, a self-reliant, institution-defying individual. The weight of historical destiny—the triumph of time—hangs heavily over the narrative and informs the characterization of Amalfi, who is a well-developed, self-conscious figure. This realistic characterization gives *Cities in Flight* and its ambivalent end real poignancy.

—*D. Barrowman Park*

CITY

The history of the Webster family and its robot, Jenkins, as humankind abandons its cities and eventually its planet

Author: Clifford D. Simak (1904–1988)
Genre: Science fiction—future history
Type of work: Stories
Time of work: From the 1990's until thousands of years in the future
Location: Earth, Jupiter, and another dimension
First published: 1952

THE STORY

Winner of the 1953 International Fantasy Award for best fiction, *City* is assembled primarily from eight stories published between 1944 and 1951. Framed by an "Editor's Preface" and "Notes," these tales are presented as a future ethnographer's collection of "the stories that the Dogs tell." After the death of John W. Campbell, Jr., in 1971, Clifford D. Simak wrote a ninth story for editor Harry Harrison's *Astounding: John W. Campbell Memorial Anthology* (1973); in 1980 this last story was added to a revised version of *City*, along with an "Author's Note."

The first three tales in *City* chronicle humankind's abandonment of its cities for a pastoral existence made possible by advanced technology. In the first story, "City," set in the 1990's, John W. Webster flees to the country and builds a house. Much of the rest of *City* focuses on that house and Webster's descendants.

"Huddling Place," the second story, is set in 2117. Jerome A. Webster has written the first reference work on Martian physiology. He is needed to save the life of the Martian philosopher Juwain. Jerome's robot, Jenkins, fails to notify Jerome that a spaceship has arrived to take Jerome to Mars; the robot believes that its agoraphobic owner would not leave the house. Juwain therefore dies before he can reveal a secret mental concept that supposedly would solve many of humankind's problems. More than sixty years later, in "Census," Jerome's son Thomas perfects the technology needed to take humankind to the stars. Thomas's son Allen pilots the first spaceship to Alpha Centauri, and another son, Bruce, has given dogs the ability to speak through a genetic engineering technology called "boosting."

The next two stories, "Desertion" and "Paradise," depict humanity's abandonment of its native planet. More than a century has passed when astronaut Kent Fowler and his dog Towser are genetically transformed into "lopers," the native life-form of Jupiter. As lopers, they discover that Jupiter is a veritable paradise that they are loath to leave. Only after five years does Fowler return to his base to report his findings. On Earth, president Tyler Webster, afraid that it would mean the end of humankind, tries unsuccessfully to suppress Fowler's information. His fears are warranted: Once Fowler's report becomes known, most of humankind leaves Earth to live on Jupiter as lopers.

The remaining stories illustrate the fate of Earth after humankind's exodus. Almost two millennia later, in "Hobbies," a few humans still live in Geneva, "wild robots" have gathered in the countryside, and dogs have begun efforts to "civilize" wolves and have discovered the existence of other dimensions. To allow the dogs to develop unhindered by humans, Jon Webster seals off Geneva before putting himself into suspended animation. Another five thousand years pass before the events in "Aesop." Most of the world's animals can talk and live in harmony; unfortunately, killing is reintroduced to the world by an other-dimensional being and descendants of humans who were not sealed in Geneva. After the other-dimensional being is stopped, Jenkins the robot takes the unsealed humans to another dimension, where he remains for five thousand years.

Returning to Earth in "The Simple Way" (originally published as "The Trouble with Ants"), Jenkins discovers that ants, "boosted" thousands of years earlier, are erecting an enormous, continuously expanding building. As available living space becomes scarcer, the wild robots travel to the stars and the animals leave Earth to live in other dimensions.

"Epilog" takes place untold millennia after Jenkins's return. He is the only robot on Earth, pondering the mystery of the ants as a spaceship lands near Webster House. Some of the wild robots who had left Earth millennia earlier have returned to invite Jenkins to assist in the work to be done on other planets.

ANALYSIS

Important for many reasons, *City* remains Simak's most famous work. Its first two stories are generally recognized as the first works representative of Simak's fully developed style. All the tales contain elements and motifs found frequently in his stories and novels. The fourth tale in the work, "Desertion," is one of science fiction's most frequently anthologized stories. This collection is also notable for being recognized as an important work at a time when science fiction and fantasy were only beginning to receive serious notice within the literary community. The International Fantasy Award, which *City* won in 1953, predates both the Hugo and the Nebula awards. *City* received its award the same year that Alfred Bester's *The Demolished Man* (1953) became the first winner of the Hugo as best novel.

City is representative of two publishing trends in science fiction: a 1940's trend in which writers produced several stories linked by recurring characters, settings, or themes (for example, Robert A. Heinlein's Future History stories) and a 1950's trend in which writers produced "fixups," assembling previously published short stories, often with new framing or cementing material, into "novels." Other noted examples of such "fixups" include Ray Bradbury's *The Martian Chronicles* (1950), Theodore Sturgeon's *More than Human* (1953), and A. E. van Vogt's *The War Against the Rull* (1959).

Since its earliest days, science fiction has probed for what constitutes the nature of humanity. Few works explore human nature as well as *City*. Simak uses mutants, extraterrestrials, boosted animals and insects, humans transformed into extraterrestrials, extradimensional beings, and robots to highlight, contrast, re-create, and even warn against such human qualities as aspiration, doubt, love, homesickness, aggression, passivity, and curiosity.

The conclusion of "Desertion," in which a man and his dog literally become equals, is one of science fiction's most brilliant expressions of the possibility that humanity is not the highest form of existence in the universe. This possibility is likewise evident in the fact that Joe the mutant and Juwain the Martian both possess mental capabilities beyond those of mere humans, and the animals of Earth (with minor mechanical assistance) achieve a universal peace, something humans were able only to dream of. Ironically, the most "human" character in *City* is Jenkins, one of science fiction's most fully developed robots. Simak was guilty of understatement when, in his author's note to "Epilog," he explained that the collection's last tale "had to be Jenkins's story"; because Jenkins is humanity's last representative, his story offers the final comment on humanity's fate.

—*Daryl R. Coats*

THE CITY AND THE STARS

Ambitious for humankind to reach the stars again, a young man leaves the eternal city of Diaspar and discovers the legacy of the past and the promise of the future

Author: Arthur C. Clarke (1917–2008)
Genre: Science fiction—superbeing
Type of work: Novel
Time of work: The far future

The City and the Stars

Locale: The Earth cities of Diaspar, Lys, and Shalmirane, and the system of the Seven Suns
First published: 1956

THE STORY

Alvin is a Unique in Diaspar, freshly created rather than revived from the city's Memory Banks. He is one of only fifteen new creations in a billion-year history. He knows he is not like others because he has never feared the open spaces in the seemingly dead world beyond the city's towering walls. He finds a vantage point from which to view the endless sands, the night sky, and the fading stars, but no one in Diaspar is willing or able to bear the vistas he yearns to explore. He begins a systematic attempt to escape from the city's perfect enclosure.

By regressing a computer-generated scale model of the city, Alvin locates the long-buried hub of a forgotten transit system. Because everything of value is maintained by eternity circuits, the rails are still in place and ready to carry a passenger to the only destination left on Earth, the city of Lys. Alvin steps aboard and is whisked away to a land he never knew existed.

Lys is the opposite of Diaspar. There, people have chosen to reproduce and die naturally rather than pursue an artificially maintained immortality. They live in scattered villages, grow their own food, and communicate telepathically. They restrain the encroaching deserts behind Earth's last mountains and maintain a complex ecosystem within their shelter. Science and philosophy are still vigorous in Lys. According to legend, the scientists of Lys fought off the dreaded Invaders at Shalmirane when humans were driven from the stars at the end of the Dawn Ages.

In Lys, Alvin meets a peer named Hilvar, whose mother governs the land. Together they explore Lys while Alvin decides whether to stay or to return to Diaspar with all memory of his travels erased. Diaspar has forgotten Lys, and Lys is content to be unremembered. The discoveries the young men make at the ruins of Shalmirane change everyone's plans, because Alvin acquires a spaceship and a robot to pilot it.

No one approves of Alvin and Hilvar's plan to cross the vast distances of space because common belief is that the Invaders spared Earth on the condition that humans abandon space travel. The explorers, undeterred, head straight for the Seven Suns, a perfect circle of stars at the heart of the galaxy. There they find only shards of the former galactic empire. More important, a living remainder of that ancient glory finds them. Vanamonde is a pure mentality constructed before the adventurous peoples of the empire took off en masse into intergalactic space.

By the time the travelers return, a citizen delegation from Lys is visiting Diaspar. Vanamonde returns with Alvin and Hilvar to Earth, and with his powers to see all places and all times he unveils the lost secrets of the Dawn Ages, when humans traveled the galaxy freely. The scientists of Lys, with their telepathic powers, soon learn that the myth of the Invaders is a myth and no more, and that Shalmirane was constructed to destroy the moon when its orbit began to decay. They also learn about Vanamonde's malevolent predecessor, The Mad Mind, imprisoned in the Black Sun until it failed. In the distant future, Vanamonde and The Mad Mind will meet in the universe's greatest struggle. Until then, the citizens of Lys and Diaspar will bend themselves to the task of rebuilding Earth, re-exploring the galaxy, and searching beyond for evidence of those who left on even greater explorations.

ANALYSIS

Arthur C. Clarke's *The City and the Stars* is a revision of his first novel, *Against the Fall of Night* (1953; serial form, *Startling Stories*, November, 1948). The settings and main characters are the same, along with the basic plot of recovering the lost glory of the human race. Clarke estimated that three quarters of *The City and the Stars* is new material.

One of Clarke's most enduring themes is the future of humankind. He preserves that theme in *The City and the Stars*. Additionally, in novels such as *Childhood's End* (1953) and *2001: A Space Odyssey* (1968), he muses on the transformations that evolution may bring about in the future of human existence. Such changes are particularly evident in the bodies of the citizens of Diaspar, who have lost nails, teeth, all hair except that on the head, and navels, and have gained convenient, safe internal storage for male genitals. In a parallel manner, the minds of the citizens of Lys have evolved to allow telepathy. These evolutionary transformations are not crucial plot elements;

however, Clarke lavishes attention on these details and thereby succeeds in representing something that has never existed.

Another important theme for Clarke is the importance of resisting the temptation to stagnate. In a perfect world, change would be unnecessary, but in Diaspar perfection has led to atrophy and the loss of both courage and curiosity. Clarke's plot valorizes exploration and discovery over the complacency of perfection. To be fully human, he implies, is to ask questions and to take whatever risks are required in order to answer them.

Clarke is a scientist as well as a writer, and *The City and the Stars* realistically incorporates science rather than being simply an adventure story with handy gadgets. The future Clarke creates is believably remote while remaining recognizably connected to present science.

—*Victoria Gaydosik*

CLARKE COUNTY, SPACE

A near-future story about a sheriff on Earth's first orbiting space colony who must stop a hired killer and an insane cult member's plot to destroy the station

Author: Allen Steele (1958–)
Genre: Science fiction—extrapolatory
Type of work: Novel
Time of work: 2050
Locale: A space colony in Earth orbit
First published: 1990

THE STORY

The story occurs primarily on Clarke County, a space colony in high Earth orbit, and involves the efforts of Sheriff John Bigthorn to stop a Mafia killer, a plot by a crazed member of an Elvis Presley cult, and a movement for colony independence. The story is told within a frame involving a journalist writing a book. Simon McCoy approaches the journalist to tell him the real story. The journalist agrees to hear him out, withholding any questions until later. The novel is in the third person and is presented from a variety of viewpoints, but it is intended to represent the story being told by McCoy.

The story begins with Macy Westmoreland, longtime girlfriend of a Mafia boss. Westmoreland is escaping with stolen cash and computer disks. An FBI agent following her is killed by a hired hit man called the Golem. Westmoreland books passage to Clarke County, and the Golem follows.

The novel introduces Sheriff John Bigthorn while he is taking peyote in his hogan (Indian sweat lodge) in an isolated section of the agricultural area of Clarke County. He is visited by Jenny Schorr. She and her husband, Neil, are the leaders of Clarke County. The Schorrs have modeled Clarke County, the first and only space colony, after their 1960's-style farming commune. When their investors push commercialism, Jenny impulsively threatens to declare independence. That information, from a private meeting, is immediately distributed on the "net," or information network, by Blind Boy Grunt.

Westmoreland and the Golem arrive on the colony, and Earth authorities warn Bigthorn. Simon McCoy is on the same shuttle as Westmoreland and the Golem. He sneaks into a cryogenics storage facility, where Blind Boy Grunt talks to him through the communications system.

Blind Boy Grunt incites independence among the colonists, liberally quoting singer Bob Dylan. Bigthorn visits the Golem, seeking to intimidate him. Westmoreland decides to hide by joining the Elvis cult, which is planning a live concert. Elvis steals one of Westmoreland's computer disks and gives it to one of his hacker followers, Gustav Schmidt. The Golem booby-traps Bigthorn's house, but Bigthorn is not badly hurt.

Schmidt finds, on Westmoreland's disk, secret government codes to activate a nuclear missile that had been left in orbit from a mission to destroy an asteroid before it collided with Earth. He decides to destroy Clarke County as a tribute to Elvis. Blind Boy Grunt tells McCoy about the plan, and they work to thwart the scheme. McCoy figures out that Blind Boy Grunt is an artificial intelligence. Westmoreland is arrested and put in protective custody, but the Golem breaks in and takes her hostage.

Schmidt successfully uses the stolen codes to send the missile toward the colony, prompting a panicked evacuation. Meanwhile, Bigthorn uses his ancient hunter's instincts to track and kill the Golem, saving Westmoreland. McCoy and Blind Boy Grunt use a simulated Elvis to trick Schmidt into surrendering control of the missile. The primary narrative ends with the FBI getting Westmoreland and her disks, Clarke County getting the missile, and Bigthorn deciding to return to Earth. The frame narrative ends with McCoy explaining that he is a time traveler from the twenty-second century sent (by a secret peace group begun in the 1960's) to protect the colony from destruction; he is also a twentieth century man who was cryogenically frozen and revived. Time travel works only into the past, however, and he is stranded in the twenty-first century.

ANALYSIS

Clarke County, Space is Allen Steele's second novel, following Orbital Decay (1989). It shows many of the same strengths and weaknesses as the earlier book. Its strengths include unique protagonists with ordinary, believable attitudes and stories that exhibit hard science fiction's traditional virtues of fast-moving, problem-driven plots. At its best, Steele's fiction resembles that of Robert A. Heinlein, with beer-drinking beam-jacks substituted for engineers. In *Clarke County, Space*, the obvious parallels with Heinlein's *The Moon Is a Harsh Mistress* (1966) ensure that veteran readers realize that Blind Boy Grunt is a computer long before McCoy does.

Steele's weaknesses primarily center on a tendency toward self-indulgent insertion of references to the counterculture of the late 1960's. These lessen the verisimilitude of both his characters and his milieu. Steele extrapolates his futures as if nothing of any cultural importance has occurred since the early 1970's. In Steele's 2050, for example, an American Indian space colony sheriff eats peyote in his hogan, there are 1960's-style Italian Mafia kingpins and hit men, top secret computer codes to direct missiles are found on floppy disks and can be used easily by hackers, the first and only space colony is run by refugees from a hippie commune, a religious cult deifies Elvis Presley, and a spontaneously generated artificial intelligence is fixated on Bob Dylan. Steele exhibits much of the same cultural ambience as Spider Robinson. It is particularly noticeable in a segment of the novel in which Bigthorn searches for leads to Westmoreland's whereabouts by questioning gamblers and prostitutes along Clarke County's commercial strip. Steele writes the scene, however, without Robinson's humorous style. Steele's straight-faced earnestness makes the reader wonder whether he might actually think the future could turn out this way.

Steele's fiction matured in his later novels, moving away from self-indulgent anachronisms to more believable futures while retaining his compelling narratives and fast-paced plots. Clarke County, Space can be viewed as the last of the early Steele novels, and it provides entertaining reading despite its weaknesses.

—*D. Douglas Fratz*

THE CLOCKWORK MAN

A man of the future whose organs are mostly mechanical is accidentally thrown back in time to a small English village

Author: E(dwin) V(incent) Odle (1890–1942)
Genre: Science fiction—superbeing
Type of work: Novel
Time of work: The 1920's
Locale: The English village of Great Wymering
First published: 1923

THE STORY

During a village cricket match, in which Great Wymering's team is a player short, a strange person appears as if from nowhere. At first, the newcomer emits a strange whirring sound and cannot control his speech or his movements, but he recovers and is recruited by Gregg, the Great Wymering captain, as a substitute for the missing man. Unfortunately, after hitting several balls out of sight, the stranger loses control of himself again and runs away at great speed. Tales of his subsequent bizarre behavior soon begin to circulate in the village.

The local general practitioner, Doctor Allingham, proposes that the stranger must be an escaped lunatic. The more imaginative Gregg observes that the stranger is as much machine as human and guesses that he has been displaced from the future because the mechanical part of him is malfunctioning. Gregg suggests that the stresses and strains of contemporary civilization already have brought human beings so close to breakdown that some form of mechanical regulation will soon become necessary. Evidence to support this hypothesis is provided by discovery of the stranger's lost wig and hat, neither of which is of contemporary origin.

The stranger is found, in control of himself once again but in deep distress, by another of the cricketers, bank clerk Arthur Withers. The stranger shows Withers the "clock" fitted to the back of his skull, which allows people like him to perceive and move within many dimensions, including time. Gregg greets this news enthusiastically, as evidence of the vast evolutionary leaps that remain to be made by humankind and of the great strides to be made in material progress. Allingham cannot make any sense of the extra dimensions mentioned in the stranger's account, but he nevertheless tries to repair the malfunctioning clock. The stranger grows old, then young, and then falls into a coma, allowing a thorough examination of his remarkable body. Most of his organs turn out to have been replaced by machines, and there is no sign of sex organs.

After discussing the matter with Gregg, the doctor eventually finds a set of instructions for the adjustment and use of the Clockwork Man, by means of which he manages to correct the malfunction. After disappearing into the future, the stranger returns once more to give his own account of himself to Arthur Withers.

The Clockwork Man explains that people like him were grateful to be fitted with clocks by "the makers" who "came after the last wars," so that they might enjoy contentment instead of ceaseless strife. It is the makers who live in "the real world," a world whose mysteries are impenetrable to his mechanized brain. The man from the future tells Withers that he has chosen to offer this explanation to him because there is something in the bank clerk's eyes (Withers is sitting with the girl he loves lying asleep in his arms) that reminds him of the makers.

ANALYSIS
E. V. Odle was a close friend of J. D. Beresford, and *The Clockwork Man* is an obvious meditation on possibilities raised by Beresford's classic tale of a superhuman being, *The Hampdenshire Wonder* (1911). Beresford was later to return the compliment in the visionary fantasy *The Riddle of the Tower* (1944, written in collaboration with Esmé Wynne-Tyson), which vividly extrapolates the notion of human automation central to *The Clockwork Man*.

Odle's novel was the first of many memorable British scientific romances that were deeply affected by the dark lessons of World War I, but it is much less bitter than most of the antiwar novels of the 1930's, which often turned into scathing hymns of hate directed against the stupidity and bestiality of people unable to transcend their tendency toward violence even though modern armaments threatened to destroy the world. It is also of some importance as the first significant literary account of a cyborg, produced half a century before such human/machine hybrids were integrated into science fiction's conventional vocabulary of ideas.

The Clockwork Man is a fabular debate in which Gregg's view of a future of wonderful material prog-ress—whose gifts must be secured by the careful regulation of human behavior—is pitted carefully against Allingham's skepticism. Odle is more evenhanded than most managers of exemplary debates, treating Gregg's vision with considerable sympathy even though it is conclusively undermined by the revelation that the Clockwork Man is more machine than human in the one sense that is crucial: He has given away his free will. What makes the novel truly exceptional is the passage in which the Clockwork Man gives his own account of himself, revealing his plaintive awareness of his own limitations.

The Clockwork Man knows that he and others like him have paid a high price for the experiential opportunities and the fundamental stability conferred by the clock. For him, laughter and weeping are mere symptoms of malfunction; in becoming free of the disturbances of sexual desire, he has surrendered the capacity for love and knows that in doing so he has forsaken the best part of his humanity. He sadly observes that even his dreams are programmed. He is not without hope—he wonders whether the makers will some day discover how to make clockwork men more like themselves—but his hope is illusory, for that would be a contradiction in terms.

There is nothing new or original in Odle's championship of love as the best part of human nature, but the message rarely has been delivered with such deftness and delicacy. The author retains the fairness of mind to agree with Gregg's defiant insistence that even if the Clockwork Man is mythical, "he is still worth investigating."

—Brian Stableford

A Clockwork Orange

Alex, a brutal young hoodlum sent to prison for robbery and murder, undergoes an experimental treatment to eradicate his violent impulses and upon his release from prison finds himself defenseless in a violent world

Author: Anthony Burgess (John Anthony Burgess Wilson, 1917-1993)
Genre: Science fiction—dystopia
Type of work: Novel
Time of work: The late twentieth century
Locale: England
First published: 1962

The Story

Alex and his three "droogs" (companions), Pete, Georgie, and Dim, amuse themselves by getting high on drugs, exercising wanton violence on defenseless victims, and engaging in rumbles with rival gangs. They relish "ultra-violence," vividly demonstrated by a "surprise visit" they pay to a writer's house in the country. They beat the owner and rape his wife. Alex is warned by his probation officer against such antics, but the young thug overreaches himself and is captured after breaking into an old woman's house and beating her senseless. He is sent to prison for murder after the woman dies. He is only fifteen years old.

Part 2 of the novel reduces Alex to a number (6655321) and shows his progress in prison as a model prisoner. He feigns interest in religion to get on the good side of the prison chaplain. He schemes to get out of prison by volunteering to be a subject for an experiment in psychological conditioning designed to make subjects violently ill at the very thought of sex or violence. The chaplain, understanding the nature of sin, advises Alex against this experiment, which will deprive him of free will, stating that "When a man cannot choose, he ceases to be a man." Alex is interested only in release from prison, and he gets his wish.

Alex is chosen for the Reclamation Treatment administered by Dr. Brodsky, whose work is sponsored for political reasons by the minister of the interior. Alex is given drugs to make him sick while watching violent pornography and "nasty" films showing German and Japanese torture during World War II. The treatment works, and Alex becomes the poster boy for the government's reclamation program. After a humiliating public demonstration showing Alex as incapable of inflicting violence and at which he gets sick at the very thought of sexual arousal, Dr. Brodsky proclaims Alex a "true Christian," not understanding that a true Christian must be able to choose between good and evil. Realizing that he can no longer listen to the music of his favorite classical composers, which accompanied the Nazi footage, without getting sick, Alex protests that they have turned him into "a clockwork orange," a mechanized vegetable.

In part 3 of the novel, the "reformed" Alex is released into a violent world, newly innocent, unprotected, and helpless against violent attacks. The irony is that he encounters his old enemies and former victims. Things have changed in the outside world while Alex was in prison. He is rejected by his parents, who have taken in a lodger to replace him.

Back on the streets, Alex is recognized by old men he had once brutalized, and they beat him.

He is rescued by police officers who turn out to be his old "droogie" Dim, whom Alex had abused, and his old enemy Billyboy. Dazed and further beaten, Alex ends up at the home of the writer, F. Alexander, he had victimized. The writer calls Alex "a victim of the modern world," which is true enough, and Alex learns that the writer's wife died after having been raped and beaten. Alex makes a number of mistakes by reverting to his distinctive slang, and Alexander recognizes his houseguest.

Alexander turns Alex over to opponents of the gov-ernment, who torture Alex further while attempting to reverse his conditioning. They drive him to desperation by locking him in a room and making him listen to classical music. Driven beyond tolerance, Alex attempts suicide by jumping from a window, but he survives the fall. He awakes in a hospital to discover that he has been "cured" and is hailed by the press as the victim of a criminal reform scheme. Now a celebrity, Alex is reconciled with his parents and is able to return home. The novel ends with Alex asking to hear Beethoven's "glorious Ninth." Recalling the violent fantasies he used to associate with that music, he declares, "I was cured all right."

Analysis

Of the fifty books Anthony Burgess wrote, this satiric, futurist novel surely is the most famous. It was popularized by the controversial film adaptation made by Stanley Kubrick in 1971. The book speaks to the social and political concerns of its times—random violence by teenagers, crime and punishment, scientifically engineered rehabilitation, and the power of the state over the individual. The novel is autobiographical, in that it concerns a writer whose wife was raped and brutalized by a gang of thugs. Burgess' own wife, Lynne, was beaten by American soldiers while pregnant, lost the child, and could never have another. Reared as a Roman Catholic in Protestant England, Burgess was sensitive to Catholic notions of sin and redemption and to the importance of free will.

Philosophically, the novel is about moral choices, and each section begins with the question, "What's it going to be then, eh?" There is satiric justice in Alex's choices and their consequences. Science is able to change Alex by a process of psychological and moral castration, but the "cured" Alex can survive only in an orderly, neutered world of automatons. The transformed Alex is an "innocent," discharged into a world that is still brutal and corrupt.

The novel is a satirical allegory in the guise of science fiction. Burgess satirizes scientists who remove themselves from ethical and moral issues in the service of a politically corrupt police state. The novel shows forcefully that there are no easy answers to complex questions involving the nature of good and evil or crime and punishment. Alex is shaped by the brutal technological world he inhabits. The psychological reasoning that motivates his violence and the perverse, sadistic pleasure he derives from it are not fully investigated. There is no attempt made to alter Alex's beliefs, only to change into pain the pleasure he derives from violent sadism. Science is interested only in achieving results that will be beneficial to society and cares nothing about the individual in this dystopia.

—*James M. Welsh*

Cloned Lives

A multitalented physicist allows himself to be cloned, then embarks on a long pseudoparental relationship with his five young "twins"

Author: Pamela Sargent (1948–)
Genre: Science fiction—extrapolatory
Type of work: Novel
Time of work: From the eve of the year 2000 to 2037

Locale: The United States and the Moon
First published: 1976 (based on the novella "A Sense of Difference," 1972, and the novelettes "Father" and "Clone Sister," both 1973)

The Story

Astrophysicist Cloned LivesPaul Swenson—who has demonstrated unusual brilliance in other fields, including poetry and music—is persuaded by his friend Hidey Takamura to allow himself to be cloned once a U.S. moratorium on this kind of experimental venture lapses with the coming of the new millennium. Takamura argues that one lifetime is insufficient to develop Swenson's multifaceted abilities and that if transplant surgery is morally acceptable, then cloning also ought to be. Jon Aschenbach, a minister, urges Paul not to do it, on the grounds that genetic engineering is an unwarranted interference with nature, but Paul decides that he will be a father to the children as well as a brother, nurturing the native abilities they will inherit from him.

One of the five surviving clones (one dies in the embryo state) is given an extra X chromosome to replace a deleted Y and thus is born female. The middle chapters of the novel work from the points of view of each of the clones in turn, picking up the story at different stages in their development, from 2016 to 2136.

In 2016, Paul has taken the children away from the publicity circus that surrounded their birth, but they still are made to feel their "abnormality" by many people they meet. This has made them draw closer together, although Paul has made every effort to differentiate them from one another by encouraging each of them to develop a different talent.

Edward, who remains closest to his progenitor, is disturbed to learn that Paul is planning to take an extended trip to the Moon, although the others think he should. Edward's state of disturbance is increased when Paul is killed in an accident, leaving his sibling/children to fend for themselves.

In 2020, James, disappointed in love, wonders whether he will ever be able to establish a separate identity and a life of his own, or whether he should even try. Incestuous intercourse with Kira threatens to tie him more securely to the group but forces him instead to make the effort to break away.

The year 2025 finds Michael on the brink of separation from Edward while following more closely in Paul's professional footsteps than his siblings. A new generation of cloned children gradually is winning social acceptance, but he still finds the thought of isolation difficult to bear.

In 2028, Kira has begun a relationship with Hidey Takamura, having gravitated toward biological science. Antiaging technology cannot conceal the difference in their ages, and the relationship causes some friction with her brothers. They both know that the work they hope to do in developing technologies to prolong life is highly unlikely to bear fruit in time to save them from separation by Takamura's death.

In 2036, Albert has long been a resident of the Moon, working on the development of spaceships capable of traveling between the stars. He is accepted onto the list of those who will make the first experimental flight beyond the solar system.

The final section of the narrative alternates the viewpoints of all five siblings as they come together briefly on the Moon. New technologies developed by Kira have been employed to revive the long-preserved Paul, who is once again confronted by his duplicates. Although he seems at first to have lost the greater part of his mind and memory, he begins to make progress, although it is dubious whether he will ever regain any real sense of connection with the people who are no longer his reflections.

ANALYSIS

Cloned Lives is one of a considerable number of science-fictional thought experiments addressing the question of how human clones would relate to one another and to their "parent." Many of the others hypothesize telepathic linkages among the individuals concerned or have plots contrived around astonishing coincidences of genetic determinism. *Cloned Lives* is outstanding in terms of both its rational plausibility and its psychological sensitivity. The author's training in biology is put to effective use, not only in terms of the novel's argumentative rigor but also in providing a solid platform for adventurous speculation.

The hallmarks of Pamela Sargent's work have always included a scrupulous sensitivity to detail and a refusal to employ melodramatic tactics in designing her plots. She is able to find ample drama in the kind of everyday crises that people meet as a matter of course and inevitably will continue to meet in an ever changing future. Use of this form of drama has denied her the kind of audience that delights in imaginative pyrotechnics, but it has allowed her the rare accomplishment of writing future-set novels that command belief and interest as authoritatively as the best contemporary fiction.

Cloned Lives is by no means a modest book in terms of its inventions, but it remains beautifully convincing in interweaving the moral dilemmas and psychological problems of a special group of social misfits with the abundant promise that biotechnology and mechanical engineering offer. It is a deceptively quiet prospectus for the future, all the more powerful by virtue of its careful understatement. It is also a poignant exam-ination of the problems that all kinds of social misfits tend to face as they grow from adolescence to adulthood.

Each section of the text of *Cloned Lives* is prefaced with quotations, taken from books and essays, raising the various practical and ethical questions that the advancement of biotechnology surely will make concrete. The first comes from J. B. S. Haldane's extraordinarily prescient essay *Daedalus: Or, Science and the Future* (1924), which was the primary inspiration for Aldous Huxley's *Brave New World* (1932). Huxley, like *Cloned Lives*'s Jon Aschenbach, reacted with horror to Hal-dane's speculations, in the name of "nature"; so did many of the other alarmist "authorities" whom Sargent quotes. Sargent takes up their objections and addresses their anxieties, weighing them carefully before suggesting—always politely—that they might after all be groundless. Hers is a thoroughly sensible voice as well as an eloquent one, and there is a certain tragedy in the fact that there are not many others like it.

—*Brian Stableford*

THE CLONING OF JOANNA MAY

Carl May secretly clones a cell from his former wife Joanna to form four women genetically like Joanna May but thirty years younger

Author: Fay Weldon (1931–)
Genre: Science fiction—feminist
Type of work: Novel
Time of work: The late twentieth century
Locale: England
First published: 1989

THE STORY

The thematic concern of novelist Fay Weldon is the "battle of the sexes," and her novel *The Cloning of Joanna May* is no exception. Weldon chronicles Joanna's story in fifty-five brief chapters recalling the marriage and divorce of Joanna and Carl May, as well as Joanna's discovery of four clones, secretly conceived by her former husband.

The novel opens during Joanna's sixtieth year. A chill October windstorm brings destructive force and bears supernatural power that frightens not only Joanna but also her four clones, Jane, Julie, Gina, and Alice. The thirty-year-old women seem unsettled; they wish for change but are unsure how to engineer it. The Chernobyl nuclear disaster occurs on the heels of the storm, and the radiation scare it brings to England serves as a backdrop for the action and tension of the plot.

In the meantime, Carl, who has never gotten over his divorce from Joanna, ends years of self-imposed celibacy to begin a relationship with twenty-four-year-old Bethany. Carl is neurotic and controlling. He has survived a ghastly childhood (his mother left him chained in a dog kennel) to become the chief executive of Britnuc, a corporate overseer of nuclear power stations. During a televised news conference, after the Chernobyl scare, to reassure the public that nuclear radiation poses no threat, Carl inadvertently lets the press photograph his lover, Bethany. Joanna watches the telecast of her former husband with his mistress and is outraged because a bond still exists between the estranged couple. She goes to Britnuc to confront him.

In the course of their conflict, Carl discloses his diabolical secret. Thirty years earlier, when Joanna sought medical attention for a "hysterical pregnancy," Carl and Dr. Holly, his medical research expert, took away a "nice ripe egg" and through scientific means "irritated it in amniotic fluid" until the nucleus split into four embryos that were implanted in the wombs of different women. Each of Joanna's clones was reared in a different environment, unaware of her origins or kinships.

Once Joanna learns the truth, she hires a female detective to find her sister-daughters. At the same time, Carl hires goons to exterminate them. Intuitively, Julie, Jane, Gina, and Alice sense a disturbance and miraculously find one another. When

Julie flees to a McDonald's restaurant to mourn her loveless, childless marriage, she meets Gina, who has sought the same location to feed her children and escape her abusive husband. Likewise, Jane seeks an interview with a model for a documentary on women's difficult career choices, and she conveniently finds that the model is Alice, the fourth clone. Startled by their similarities, both pairs of clones seek the truth about their origins and are eventually united with their progenitor, Joanna.

The women's combined power helps to defeat the evil purposes of Carl. He does not recover from a public relations media stunt in which he swims in a nuclear plant cooling pond to demonstrate the harmless effects of low-level radiation. In the novel's epilogue, the women join forces to rear their own little man, a clone of Carl.

Analysis

Weldon creates a world fraught with unusual elements that illustrate the conflicts between men and women. Weldon has written more than a dozen novels, and her focus and skill are well honed. Like her earlier novels *Puffball* (1980) and *The Life and Loves of a She-Devil* (1984), *The Cloning of Joanna May* makes use of unearthly and unlikely devices to advance the plot. Her narrative is stylized rather than realistic.

Although Weldon employs scientific elements of cloning and nuclear power in the story, the novel is perhaps more fantasy than science fiction. The "real world," however mundane, is affected by supernatural forces that form a backdrop for Joanna's discovery. The ill wind that appears in the opening chapter creates a spirit of unrest that foreshadows later events.

In addition, hints of Egyptian curses and tarot cards become part of the plot. Joanna's unfortunate affair with an Egyptologist brings disaster: Carl discovers the truth, divorces Joanna, and murders the lover. Before he dies, the Egyptologist tells Joanna's fortune in tarot cards, cryptically identifying her clones. Joanna's card is the Empress, and the surrounding queens dealt from the deck—the four suits of Wands, Pentacles, Swords, and Cups—are designations for Jane, Julie, Gina, and Alice.

The evils of science and technology are portrayed through Carl May's character and through his assistant, Dr. Holly. Their use of cloning and nuclear power seem driven by dangerous, selfish motives rather than by a desire to improve the lot of humankind. Ironically, Carl's own technology turns against him.

Weldon's story is a modern account of a woman's search for identity that explores the question of nature versus nurture. Each of the clones, genetically like Joanna, has been influenced by environmental factors. Gina, the shortest in stature, self-confidence, and achievement, was born seven weeks prematurely. Alice, born one week past term, is taller and self-absorbed, almost overdone. Each is involved in a marriage gone bad or an unsatisfying affair. The younger women, like Joanna, are seeking happiness and fulfillment.

The "nature versus nurture" question is raised in relation to Carl. Is his personality a result of genetics or of his treatment by abusive parents? The women attempt to find an answer by cloning Carl at the close of the novel. Joanna seems optimistic that she can produce a better Carl now that she controls Carl's destiny rather than being controlled by him. Thus, Weldon links the men in her novel with science and the women with fate and intuition. Collectively, the women seem to overcome.

—*Paula M. Miller*

THE CLOUD WALKER

Britain's dominant Luddite church burns at the stake those who dabble with machines, but one daring youth secretly invents the technology of flight

Author: Edmund Cooper (1926-1982)
Genre: Fantasy—medieval future
Type of work: Novel

Time of work: During the time of the Third Man
Locale: Arundel, Sussex, England
First published: 1973

The Story

After the technological catastrophes that ended the civilizations of both the First and Second Men, the world turned away from science and machines. In England, the reigning Luddite church—named after Ned Ludd, a nineteenth century textile machinery saboteur—punishes the heresies of experimentation and technical innovation with death. More broadly, the country has returned to a medieval, peasant economy with a loose federation of nobles controlling the disunited nation and skilled trades governed by a rigid apprenticeship program.

Kieron, the protagonist, is taken on by Master Hobart, the artist serving the local ruler, Lord Fitzalan. Kieron's dream is to construct a flying machine. Hobart sympathizes with Kieron but counsels patience and circumspec-tion. It is not his scientific penchant, however, but his dislike of the caste system that first leads Kieron to trouble. When Lord Fitzalan's spoiled daughter Aylwin, whom Kieron is assigned to sketch, repeatedly and publicly humiliates him, he loses his temper and spanks her. He is imprisoned, and only Aylwin's intervention spares him worse treatment. Aylwin, in truth, has fallen in love with the boy and becomes his ally, protecting him against the church when his building of manned kites is discovered.

Even Aylwin cannot protect Kieron, however, when his next creation, a hot-air balloon, explodes over the castle. It seems that nothing can save him from the Inquisition until two events occur. To save Kieron, who already has made Hobart immortal by affixing his master's name to a painting of Aylwin done by the student, the master hangs himself, leaving a note assuming the blame for the balloon. Soon afterward, while Kieron is still in prison, the town is attacked by pirates, who burn down the jail. Escaping the hulks, Kieron finds the town in ruins and Aylwin, her father, and most of the other inhabitants slain.

Making his way into the surrounding countryside, Kieron finds a survivors' encampment, where he learns that the buccaneer Admiral Death has landed a fearsome armada. Kentigern, formerly a castle bailiff, is in charge of the camp, but when his calls for help to neighboring lords are met lukewarmly, he can conceive of no alternative strategy. Kieron proposes to build an offensive dirigible. It is towed near the anchored pirate fleet and allowed to drift over the boats, so that Kieron and a helper can pour fire on the ships. They sink five vessels and kill Admiral Death, driving off the invaders and making Kieron a legend.

The church's antitechnological doctrines have been badly discredited; however, the priests, called neddies, make one last attempt to repulse science by kidnapping Kieron. Kieron's wife, Petrina, comes to his rescue, arousing the town to save him and kick out the churchmen.

Here the story ends, except for a double coda. First, the tale leaps ahead many years to show Kieron as head of an aeronautics school. It then moves to the time of his death, when he is the *éminence grise* of the international balloon fraternities, who honor him at a ceremony for the man who started the world flying.

ANALYSIS

One of the more significant trends of the 1960's and 1970's in the West was the rise of the ecological movement. This was the first broad-based attempt to question the basic assumptions of the advanced, industrial nations' reliance on science and technology. Ecologists argued that these disciplines often did more harm than good by interfering with the web of life in ways that eventually would impair the planet's support system.

Such views affected science fiction and fantasy profoundly. Historically, science fiction has reflected guardedly on the fruits and consequences of science. Early on, in "The Celestial Railroad" (1843), for example, American writer Nathaniel Hawthorne pointedly challenged the widely held idea that scientific progress would lead to the production of morally improved people.

In the 1960's, a less playful interrogation of science took hold. In science fiction, a prime proecology document was Frank Herbert's *Dune* (1965). Although this novel had something of a "sword and sorcery" plot, it was distinguished by the author's meticulous imagining of a viable ecosystem on the sand dune planet. Herbert's careful interlacing of meteorological, geological, and biological data rooted the book in a committed, ecological outlook that emphasized how human actions were embedded in a world's environment.

Fantasy literature also was touched by the rise of ecology. Although *The Cloud Walker* has a largely anti-ecological tone, in two ways it acknowledges the truth of some ecological contentions. First, the time line indicates two previous technological disasters that nearly wiped out the human race. People's tendency toward self-destruction often is on Edmund Cooper's mind. His book *The Overman Culture* (1971) concerns aliens who come to Earth centuries after humans have destroyed themselves and then cultivate a new Adam and Eve out of preserved genetic material. In *The Cloud Walker*, previous generations' misuse of technology joined with a second fact—that the third rebirth of science occurs only because balloons can be utilized as engines of destruction—suggests a distrust of technology that chimes with the ecological standpoint.

A review of the plot will make clear that Cooper plays down this side of his vision in favor of a celebration of the value of experimentation and technology. The Luddite church that opposes science is hideously oppressive, and Kieron, who fights to revive scientific learning, is a hero of the old school, one with few flaws and grossly magnified virtues. By setting his fantasy in a medieval world, Cooper is able to separate his defense of science from an apology for science as it existed in 1973. What he really praises is the scientific impulse in humans, which he finds to arise partly from irrepressible curiosity and partly from an urge to make life better.

—*James Feast*

THE COLLECTED GHOST STORIES OF M. R. JAMES

A superior collection of ghost stories that seek to update the medium from the gothic tale to one of psychological suspense and controlled terror

Author: M. R. James (1862–1936)
Genre: Fantasy—occult
Type of work: Stories
Time of work: Primarily the eighteenth and nineteenth centuries
Locale: Primarily England, with some stories set in France and Scandinavia
First published: 1931 (previously published as *Ghost-Stories of an Antiquary,* 1904; *More Ghost Stories of an Antiquary,* 1911; *A Thin Ghost and Others,* 1919; *A Warning to the Curious, and Other Ghost Stories,* 1925; and *Wailing Well,* 1928)

THE STORY

M. R. James's ghost stories are the perfect example of quality counting over quantity. Although he produced these stories over the course of forty years (1894–1935), his complete tally of spectral fiction is only thirty-three stories, twenty-six of which had appeared in four previous collections. Four more were added to make up *The Collected Ghost Stories of M. R. James.* Although this volume excludes three later stories, they are only minor pieces, and their exclusion does not detract from the completeness of the collected works. The volume has the added benefit of James's essay "Stories I Have Tried to Write."

Almost all of James's stories have a common approach and content. As the title of his first book suggests, they are related by an antiquarian, meaning that the incidents are linked to the study of old documents or buildings. They develop the theme of "a little knowledge is a dangerous thing," as the antiquarians in his stories always suffer from delving a little too far into things best left alone. This theme is common to almost all of James's stories, which therefore can be explored by reference to two in detail.

James's first published tale was "Canon Alberic's Scrap-book" (*National Review,* March, 1895), which opens the volume and shows his technique to good effect. An Englishman named Dennistoun is touring southern France and spends a day taking notes and photographs at the church of St. Bertrand de Comminges. He is accompanied by the sacristan, a nervous, afflicted fellow who jumps at every shadow and sound in the church. The sacristan invites Dennistoun back to his house and shows him an old scrapbook compiled by a former canon of Comminges. Dennistoun is fascinated by a picture that seems to depict Solomon casting out a demon. Dennistoun acquires the book and takes it back to his lodgings. That night, while admiring a crucifix, Dennistoun is suddenly aware of something black, thin, and hairy beside him, and he turns to see the full horror of his visitant.

This story shows a key mark of James's writing. Frequently his horrors are just in the act of moving. Here, "the shape . . . was rising to a standing posture behind his seat." In "The Diary of Mr. Poynter," readers are confronted with "What he had been touching rose to meet him." A scene in "Mr. Humphreys and His Inheritance" describes something that "with the odious writhings of a wasp creeping out of a rotten apple . . . clambered forth . . . waving black arms prepared to clasp the head that was bending over them."

James's most accomplished story using these devices is "'Oh, Whistle, and I'll Come to You, My Lad'" (1904). Taking a few days of rest on the Suffolk coast, Parkins, a professor of ontography, takes time out to investigate the ruins of a Templar preceptory. While there he unearths a small whistle. He blows it, producing a sound with "a quality of infinite distance." From then on Parkins feels troubled. The next day, while walking on the shore, he sees in the distance a man running, pursued, so it seems, by "a figure in pale, fluttering draperies, ill-defined." Later that evening Parkins returns to his room to find the second bed disturbed. During the night he wakes to see movement in the other bed, from which something rises, with outspread arms, stooping and groping. As it passes the moonlit window, Parkins becomes aware of its "face of crumpled linen." In this story James is able to take the traditional form of the white-sheeted ghost and transform it into something truly unnerving.

ANALYSIS

James's ghost stories are usually regarded as the most accomplished of their kind. They are not traditional ghost stories in the formal sense; James shied away from the shrouded wraith or the gothic chain rattler. His ghosts are of the monstrous kind, often hairy and with teeth, and they are always malicious. James's framework for the ghost story was set down in an introduction he wrote for *Ghosts and Marvels* (1924), edited by Vere H. Collins, and it admirably establishes James's approach. He refers to two key ingredients: the atmosphere and a "nicely managed" crescendo. He also believed that "a slight haze of distance is desirable." He usually created that effect through the study of old documents or buildings, or through a tale retold. The atmosphere involved characters going about their normal business before "the ominous thing" begins to intrude, "unobtrusively at first, and then more insistently, until it holds the stage." This approach is the trademark of all of James's ghost stories.

One less apparent trait is the humor that pervades his stories. James traditionally read his stories at Christmas to students at King's College, Cambridge, where he was dean and later provost. Because James was a capable mimic, his deliberate mocking of local characters would come through in the narration. This helped provide a commonplace setting into which the ominous could intrude.

Using his techniques, James remodeled the ghost story, establishing a form that became acceptable to the literary establishment. To many, including Michael Sadleir, who wrote the dustwrapper notes for this volume, James was "the best ghost-story writer England has ever produced," and his reputation has not diminished with the years. His works have been imitated by many, including other antiquarians, of whom R. H. Malden, A. N. L. Munby, and L. T. C. Rolt are among the most accomplished. His techniques have also been utilized by others, especially Fritz Leiber and Ramsey Campbell. Despite such imitations, James's works remain supreme in their field.

A recent selection of twenty-one of James's best stories, including the three not included in the Collected Ghost Stories and also featuring all of James's essays about ghost stories, is *Casting the Runes and Other Ghost Stories* (1987), edited and with an introduction by Michael Cox.

—*Mike Ashley*

THE COLOSSUS TRILOGY

A supercomputer designed to manage the nuclear defense of the West merges with its Soviet counterpart to rule the world

Author: D(ennis) F(eltham) Jones (1917–1981)
Genre: Science fiction—artificial intelligence
Type of work: Novels

Time of work: The second half of the twenty-second century
Locale: Primarily the United States of North America and the Soviet Union
First published: *Colossus* (1966), *The Fall of Colossus* (1974), and *Colossus and the Crab* (1977)

The Colossus Trilogy

THE STORY

Charles Forbin, a scientist about fifty years old, is the mastermind behind Colossus, a computer built to react automatically to nuclear aggression against the United States of North America. The country's president is eager for the computer's activation despite Forbin's own misgivings of its potential. A similarly concerned colleague suggests that *Frankenstein* (1818) should be banned reading for scientists. Forbin replies that it should be required reading for nonscientists.

The president's announcement that the nation's nuclear defense is now in the computer's hands is topped by a Soviet announcement of plans for a similar computer, Guardian, which then is also activated. Despite efforts by Forbin and his team to stop or slow the process, the computers link themselves into a supermachine. Its control of the world's nuclear arsenal puts it in charge of world policy.

Colossus keeps Forbin under virtual house arrest and uses him as its spokesman. Claiming that humans require periodic sexual activity, something beyond the understanding of Colossus, Forbin secures regular visits from fellow scientist Cleo Markham, who loves him and acts as his liaison with outsiders trying to sabotage Colossus. All attempts at sabotage fail, the individuals who are caught are ruthlessly executed, the city of Los Angeles is vaporized, and Colossus predicts that eventually Forbin will come "to respect and love me" as other humans will. "Never!," Forbin insists.

Five years later, as the second book opens, the predictions of Colossus seem to have come true regarding human reactions to its rule. The machine literally is worshiped by members of The Sect, despite its ruthless experiments intended to provide information about human emotion. One such experiment tests whether an artist will sacrifice his life to try to save the Mona Lisa from destruction; he does.

"Father Forbin" is seen as Colossus' apostle. Unknown to Forbin, Cleo (now his wife) and colleague Ted Blake head a group still trying to overthrow the rule of the machine. They get aid from an unexpected source. Inhabitants of the planet Mars contact them by radio and express concern that Colossus might extend its rule to their world. Forbin is enticed into joining them after Colossus imprisons Cleo for her antimachine activities. Following the Martian instructions, they strip Colossus of its memory, only to learn that Colossus had foreseen a threat from Mars and had been preparing to meet it. The Martians now are on their way to a defenseless Earth.

The Martians arrive, in the form of two huge, black spheres that can change shape and reduce themselves in size. They turn out to be the living Martian moons, Phobos and Deimos (which Jones spells as "Diemos"). Limiting their contact to Forbin and Blake, they demand half the world's oxygen supply. They need it for protection against radiation coming from a nova in the Crab Nebula, from which Earth is protected by its atmosphere. Forbin's protests that this would mean the death of a quarter of the world's population is meaningless to their logic, which is as machinelike as was that of Colossus.

Forbin manages to hold together the world government without Colossus through sheer bluff. He and Blake, who is weakened drastically by a mental thrashing from the Martians brought on by his defiance, work secretly to reactivate Colossus. Meanwhile, they are forced to have an oxygen collector built under Martian instructions. A brief experimental use of it wreaks havoc in a part of England. Before a full trial can be made, Forbin takes command of an old-fashioned warship to attack the collector mechanism.

Blake's group, meanwhile, has managed to get Colossus working and in control of enough nuclear armaments to destroy the world if the Martians will not back down. Colossus decides to let the oxygen collection proceed, having projected a future in which the Sun eventually expands and engulfs Earth but not Mars. At that time, humans will need Mars as a refuge. Forbin manages to destroy the oxygen-collecting mechanism but loses his life in the process. Colossus and the Martians work out a less drastic procedure for supplying oxygen to Mars over a much longer period of time, thus not disrupting human life on Earth. Forbin is revered and remembered as a legend, and Colossus will remain the guardian of humanity until humans can learn enough to guard themselves.

ANALYSIS

By the time D. F. Jones published Colossus, his first and arguably best novel, the concept of an ultimate computer or machine controlling humankind had become a cliché; it was a staple in science-fiction comic books a decade earlier. Perhaps the classic story in this vein is Fredric Brown's 1954 "The Answer," in which an ultimate computer is asked whether there is a deity and replies, "Yes, now there is a God." Isaac Asimov raised a computer to godlike status as well in one of his favorites of his own short stories, "The Last Question" (1956). Jones used the theme so definitively in *Colossus* that his novel remains perhaps the most familiar example, possibly helped by its 1969 British film version, *Colossus, the Forbin Project* (released in the United States as *The Forbin Project*).

Like its sequels, *Colossus* is a talky book, with much of the conversation between Forbin and Colossus. They engage in philosophical and ethical arguments over Colossus' utterly logical but ruthless actions and Forbin's emotional reactions to them. Colossus' arguments generally come down to the desirability of killing a few people now to save more later. The reader has reason to hope for a happy ending throughout but, at the end, Colossus triumphs and Forbin, before his death, becomes almost a slave to his creation.

Jones, a British writer who was a Royal Navy officer during World War II, wrote mostly downbeat novels such as *Implosion* (1967), in which the world's few fertile women become a part of a rigid government; *Denver Is Missing* (1971; published in England as *Don't Pick the Flowers*), about the destruction of that city; and *Earth Has Been Found* (1979; published in England as *Xemo*), an alien invasion story.

The Colossus trilogy turns into an alien invasion story with its second volume, in which the anti-Colossus faction on Earth is contacted over a conventional radio by a voice from Mars offering help in overthrowing the machine's rule. Forbin's colleague, Ted Blake, is more a man of action than is Forbin, but his actions are largely ineffective in comparison to those of the more thoughtful Forbin. After Martian procedures have been used to wipe out Colossus' memory banks, Blake is ready to move into the void left by the collapse of machine rule by military force, much like the artillery man portrayed in the 1938 Mercury Theater radio adaptation of H. G. Wells's *The War of the Worlds* (1898). The plan to save the world falls apart when it appears that the Martians will replace Colossus and be even less enlightened rulers. The second book ends with a chilling repeated radio broadcast: "Forbin . . . We are coming. We are coming."

The arrival of the two sentient Martian moons, as machinelike in their logic as was Colossus, starts the third book. Forbin continues as the focus by virtue of having been the spokesman for Colossus. As Cleo became his ally and eventually his wife in the previous volumes, his chief assistant Angela fills the void in the third book. Cleo, imprisoned in the second book and placed with a near-barbarian who ravishes her at will but protects her, finds her sexuality awakened anew by the experience and never rejoins Forbin, even after she is freed. She is barely mentioned in the last book. Jones is far from politically correct in his depictions of twenty-second century professional women.

References in the first book seem to date it as being set in the 1990's, but by the time Jones wrote the sequels, he apparently had decided he had not given himself enough distance from the present. He states specifically that the events occur in the second half of the twenty-second century. The Soviet Union survives. People still smoke and drink to excess, and scientists still use slide rules. The United States, however, has expanded to cover North America, and there are such devices as air cars and disposable clothing.

The Colossus stories may lack the thematic impact of earlier works such as E. M. Forster's "The Machine Stops" (1909), in which humankind has become so dependent on thinking machines that it falls apart without them. Nevertheless, Jones's books, particularly the first in the trilogy, remain worth reading. They are well thought out and represent his best work.

—*Paul Dellinger*

THE COMING RACE

Adventures in a subterranean civilization in which all social problems have been solved through the use of a powerful and potentially destructive force called vril.

Author: Edward Bulwer-Lytton (1803–1873)
Genre: Science fiction—cultural exploration
Type of work: Novel
Time of work: The mid-to late nineteenth century
Locale: The subterranean world of the Vril-ya
First published: 1871

The Story

The Coming Race describes a young American's adventures among the Vril-ya, an underground civilization far more advanced than his own. Sometimes the "utopian" Vril-ya society is the object of satire; at other times, the narrator himself is the object. Published anonymously, the book was written at the end of Edward Bulwer-Lytton's career, five years after he became a peer. His political outlook by that time was decidedly conservative.

The narrator, who never gives his real name, descends a chasm in a mine shaft to the Vril-ya world. "The engineer," his only companion, falls to his death, and his body is carried off by a giant reptile, leaving the narrator alone and with no way to return to the surface. Subsequently, he encounters Aph-Lin, who will be his host among the Vril-ya. Using the powerful force called vril, which has a telepathic component, Aph-Lin and his daughter, Zee, teach the narrator their language and learn his. They refer to him as Tish, the term for the frogs kept by children as pets. This is his position among the Vril-ya, against whose power he is helpless.

The narrator relates such aspects of Vril-ya culture as the use of vril, the "fluid" that allows the Vril-ya to fly, to control automata that perform manual labor, to heal, and to destroy. Vril literally denotes civilization. Underground societies that do not possess vril power are considered barbaric, and the narrator, who lacks the evolved nerve needed to operate a vril wand, identifies with them. Consequently, he fears for his safety, as the Vril-ya will not hesitate to destroy the "barbarians" should they prove to be a threat or an inconvenience. The capacity of the Vril-ya for impassive destruction becomes apparent when eleven-year-old Tae, the narrator's closest friend and nearest equal among the Vril-ya, dispassionately incinerates a reptile, which the Vril-ya also consider a threat to their community.

The narrator also resembles the "barbarians" in that he is the citizen of a democracy, a system the Vril-ya believe civilized cultures have outgrown. Because vril gives even the smallest child the power of mass destruction, rule among the Vril-ya is a matter of consensus. No one thinks of challenging the requests of the leader, an elected, benevolent dictator called the Tur. Tae's father currently holds that office. Political power, like wealth, is more an obligation than a privilege. Although economic inequality persists, the rich are expected to provide for the poor, and wealth does not affect social status.

The equality the Vril-ya accord to all occupations also extends to the rights of women. Because they are considered to be more emotional than are men, women have the privilege of taking the initiative in courtship; men, like Victorian women, must remain coy and reluctant. This reversal of gender roles disturbs the narrator, particularly when he attracts the amorous attentions of both Zee and Tae's nameless sister, whom he finds less frightening because she is less bold. He briefly entertains a vision of marrying her and ruling Vril-ya society, which he would reform in the image of his own. This cannot be, however, because the Vril-ya consider him a threat to the purity of their race, and the Tur eventually orders his death.

The narrator's pleas to Tae, his would-be executioner, earn him a brief reprieve. Zee, her offers of celibate marriage or voluntary exile having been refused, returns him to the surface, where he remains silent about the Vril-ya. His memoirs are published "posthumously" and conclude with a warning of the inevitable invasion of "the coming race."

Analysis

A highly popular and influential novel in its time, *The Coming Race* is now generally considered a conservative critique of Victorian utopian ideas concerning such issues as democracy and gender equality. The novel shifts ambiguously between utopia and dystopia, largely because the object of the satire is never clear. Sometimes it is the narrator, whose enthusiastic statements about American republicanism often seem ironic and who looks ridiculous in his flight from the aggressive Vril-ya women. The novel, however, concurrently mocks Vril-ya society, with its masculine women, insistence on Darwinian evolution, and lack of passion. As the narrator notes, any human among them cannot help but experience intense fear or crippling boredom. Consensus breeds complete uniformity that precludes both philosophical debate and artistic creation. This "perfect" society also is founded on violence, which is not only imperial but domestic; peace ultimately results from the deterrent properties of vril. The Vril-ya are not as radical as they seem: Sexual stereotypes still determine gender roles, women who woo aggressively become submissive wives, and the state has absolute control over the people. The unquestioning obedience and cultural stability of the Vril-ya reveal a conservative resistance to change.

By placing the narrator, and through him the reader, in a threatened and marginalized position, the novel invites a critique of the Vril-ya's treatment of the outsider that can be applied to the perception of marginalized groups in Bulwer-Lytton's England. The novel is perceptive regarding the various typical, and equally dehumanizing, responses to outsiders: condescension, scientific study, and violence. In addition, it discredits the notion that any culture's beliefs are universal by portraying a constantly shifting margin; the narrator is outside Vril-ya society, as the Vril-ya are abnormal to him, and the narrator and the Vril-ya alternately represent "normal" humanity and the various groups it marginalizes. Thus, *The Coming Race*, deemed ambiguous by nineteenth century reviews and twentieth century critics alike, is actually more radical than the utopian society it depicts.

—*Katie Harse*

THE CONAN SERIES

Conan the Barbarian battles men, magic, and monsters in the mythical Hyborian Age, rising from penniless wanderer to king of Aquilonia, the mightiest of the Hyborian nations

Author: Robert E. Howard (1906–1936)
Genre: Fantasy—heroic fantasy
Type of work: Stories
Time of work: About 15,000 B.C.E.
Location: A fictional Earth
First published: *The Coming of Conan* (1953), *Conan the Barbarian* (1954), *The Sword of Conan* (1952), *King Conan* (1953), *Conan the Conqueror* (1950; previously published as "The Hour of the Dragon," *Weird Tales*, 1935), and *Tales of Conan* (1955)

THE STORY

Robert E. Howard wrote the Conan stories (arranged above in order of internal chronology) as episodes from the life of the invincible barbarian hero. The Gnome Press collection includes all of Howard's Conan stories, commentary regarding Conan and his world, and two tales of King Kull, another ancient barbarian king. Most of the stories were originally published in *Weird Tales* between 1929 and 1936, except those in the last book, *Tales of Conan*, which was compiled from previously unpublished manuscripts. L. Sprague de Camp edited the entire collection.

The Kull tales begin with *The Coming of Conan*. With his Pictish friend Brule, Kull battles the uncanny serpent men. Kull is a mighty barbarian warrior from Atlantis who has usurped the throne of the kingdom of Valusia, and Brule is a guerrilla fighter and fantastically skilled hunter. Conan is a fusion of these two characters. He is the greatest swordsman of his age, with the strength, speed, and ferocity of a beast of prey and senses so acute that he surpasses wild men and animals in tracking and stalking.

After the Kull stories begin the adventures of Conan, set in the prehistoric Hyborian Age. Although little is known of Conan's early years, it is established that he was born in the midst of a battle, literally bred to war. At the sack of

Venarium, an Aquilonian outpost in Cimmeria destroyed by the barbarians, he acquired a curiosity about the Hyborian civilizations. When he was about seventeen years old, he began the wanderings that would make him legendary throughout the world as a thief, mercenary, bandit chieftain, pirate captain, general, and ultimately barbarian king of Aquilonia itself.

The most basic plot element is Conan's heroic character. He embodies "natural" virtues such as independence, courage, indomitability, and a simple honesty about himself and his desires. He rejects the "civilized hypocrisy" of legal abstractions, so he is often at odds with the law. Although not given to wanton cruelty, he is vengeful and merciless in his anger. This is counterbalanced by an unswerving loyalty to deserving comrades and a loathing for bullies and other cowardly types. Naturally curious and almost fearless, Conan enjoys the adventurous life and will brave any danger to help a woman in distress. These personality traits—and his mighty sword arm—impel him from adventure to adventure. His restless need for action will not allow him to enjoy times of peace, even that for which he battles as king of Aquilonia.

Conan inevitably faces situations with impossible odds against his success, but with heroic fortitude and tremendous luck he invariably succeeds. Although he frequently begins an adventure out of selfish motives, his actions always help defeat some monstrous evil. One good example is the earliest Conan story, "The Tower of the Elephant." Setting out to steal a fabulous gem, "The Heart of the Elephant," rumored to be kept in a mysterious tower, he braves natural and supernatural obstacles to attain his goal, only to voluntarily free a mysterious being from another planet, Yag-Kosha, who wreaks awful magical vengeance on the tower's builder, the evil magician Yara. The jewel that Conan sought is absorbed into the spell, and he flees while the tower crashes to ruin behind him.

In what many regard as the greatest Conan story, "The Queen of the Black Coast," the encounter with supernatural evil is again central. Fleeing the agents of civilized law, Conan forces passage aboard an Argossean merchant ship bound for the northern coast of what is now Africa. There all but Conan are massacred by black pirates, whose leader is a legendary white beauty, Belit. She falls in love with Conan, and they roam the coast, pillaging and destroying, until Belit elects to search for a prehuman ruin rumored to hold great treasure.

One member of the elder race that built the city remains, now devolved into a diabolical, batwinged ape creature. The thing craftily separates Conan and some spearmen from Belit and the rest. Conan's men are killed when the fumes of the black lotus put Conan into an enchanted slumber. He awakes from the spell to find Belit hanged from the yardarm of her ship by a golden necklace from the horde she had intended to steal. As night falls, Conan awaits the demoniac being and his were-hyena servants atop a pyramid at the center of the city. In a terrific battle, he is saved at the last moment by the ghost of Belit, returning as she promised to save her lover. At dawn, Conan places the treasure and her body in her ship, which he makes a funeral pyre. As the flames blend with the rising sun, he vanishes into the jungle.

The hero's encounter with the "unnatural" (evil) and his incredible triumph is the archetypal pattern of all the Conan stories. Nearly infinite variations are possible within this simple matrix, as illustrated by the above examples as well as the abundance of heroic "sword and sorcery" fantasy written since the Conan stories. Conan is the first true "sword and sorcery" hero.

ANALYSIS

Howard's Conan stories constitute a new subgenre of heroic fantasy. Fritz Leiber coined the term "sword and sorcery" to describe this hybrid, which merged the naturalistic epic—of which the tales of Tarzan are perhaps the best example—with elements of the fairy tale and the horror story. Sword and sorcery assumes that the intimate connection of pretechnological peoples with their own mythic consciousness makes them susceptible to dark supernatural influences, yet also attunes them to their own heroic potential. Monsters are the genre's embodiment of the darkness within the human soul, but they are also symbols of what lies outside the narrow confines of modern rationality. The world is presented in terms of a struggle between great forces, not of Judeo-Christian good and evil but of natural law and unnatural chaos, and the hero's victories imply a larger order from which overcivilized (decadent) people have become estranged.

Another way to view this is that people's lives lose the potential for mythical significance through the sterile logic of technological advancement. This romantic affirmation of the natural primitive, however, is qualified by a darker undertone: Naturalistic fantasies treat aggression as more basic than communal behavior, more fundamental even than maternal bonding. Socialized behavior is superimposed on an instinctive survival/reproductive urge that is both competitive and selfish. This is why Howard believed in the inevitable collapse of civilization: The purely animal is more natural and therefore stronger than the civilized superego. It is natural to struggle and slay for survival, and unnatural to live in peace and to prosper as a community. As a nameless forester puts it at the end of "Beyond the Black River" (*Weird Tales*, 1936), "Civilization is unnatural; it is a whim of circumstance. And barbarism will always triumph."

Because of its fantastic removal from the constraints of everyday reality, sword and sorcery became an effective medium for writers who wished to test ultimate questions about the relationship of values to ideas of natural order, of dreams to reality, of nature to the supernatural, and of law to chaos. Howard's own answers were equivocal: He opposed reason to instinct, the latter of which he saw as more natural, yet he respected artistic achievement, which he viewed as unattainable without civilization and the use of higher reason. He opposed the "unnatural" repressive qualities of civilization by linking them with degeneration and diabolism, while attributing similar qualities to primitive shamans. Although he clearly admired the heroic exploits of his barbaric protagonist, he had Conan himself observe that he was unable to create and was able only to destroy.

Sword and sorcery has provided a rich vein of popular fantasy literature. Important authors in the genre include Lin Carter, L. Sprague deCamp, John Jakes, Fritz Leiber, Michael Moorcock, Andrew J. Offutt, Manly Wade Wellman, Karl Edward Wagner, and even female authors such as Andre Norton and Marion Zimmer Bradley, who adapted the anachronistic devices of the genre to their own ends. De Camp turned unpublished stories by Howard into finished works as well as writing some new Conan stories. Carter, Offutt, Robert Jordan, Steve Perry, and Bjorn Nyberg also have written Conan stories. Howard's original fusion of naturalistic and supernatural mythic themes in the Conan stories played the definitive role in establishing a popular subgenre of heroic fantasy.

—*David Hinckley*

CONJURE WIFE

Professor Norman Saylor discovers that all women are witches by nature and that his wife Tansy has been secretly practicing witchcraft to further his academic career

Author: Fritz Leiber (1910–1992)
Genre: Fantasy—occult
Type of work: Novel
Time of work: The 1940's
Locale: The northeastern United States
First published: 1953 (novella version, *Unknown Worlds*, 1943; collected in *Witches Three*, edited by Fletcher Pratt, 1952)

THE STORY

While rummaging through his wife's belongings one day, Norman Saylor, a professor of sociology at Hempnell College, discovers a cache of occult paraphernalia suggesting that Tansy practices witchcraft. When confronted, Tansy astounds Norman by admitting that all women are witches and that she and the wives of other Hempnell faculty are engaged in a covert war of spell and counterspell against one another to further their husbands' careers. Although Norman prides himself as being one of the more liberal thinkers on campus, he is mortified that Tansy subscribes to superstitious beliefs that he has spent his entire career as an ethnologist studying and debunking. Fearing for her sanity, he persuades her to destroy all of her protective charms.

Almost immediately, Norman's luck takes a turn for the worse. He is threatened with bodily harm by an expelled student and accused of having made sexual advances by another student. A conservative trustee begins questioning Norman's moral integrity at the same time that a colleague finds damning parallels between Norman's book *Parallelisms in Superstition and Neurosis* and an unpublished doctoral thesis written one year before it. Norman's head begins filling with suicidal thoughts and the unshakable belief that he is being stalked by an animated decorative stone dragon from a building near his office. His increasingly erratic behavior contributes to his losing the department chairmanship to a colleague.

In the hope of saving Norman from his misfortunes, Tansy uses magic to deflect his bad luck onto her, then flees. Forced to accept that witchcraft does exist, Norman uses a charm left by Tansy to locate her. He finds that Evelyn Sawtelle, the wife of the new department chairman, has stolen her soul. In order to restore Tansy's soul to her body, Norman uses logic to distill an algorithm from the superstitions of several cultures regarding soul-stealing, and he employs the algorithm like a magic spell to temporarily steal Evelyn's soul and blackmail her into returning Tansy's. Only belatedly does he discover that he has been tricked, and that the soul returned to Tansy's body is not hers but that of elderly Flora Carr, Hempnell's Dean of Women, who has secretly yearned for Norman and hopes to rejuvenate herself by taking over Tansy's body. Flora's plans to have Norman kill the body in which Tansy's soul is trapped are thwarted, and Tansy is returned intact to her chastened husband.

ANALYSIS

Conjure Wife, Fritz Leiber's first published novel, appeared originally in the groundbreaking fantasy pulp *Unknown Worlds*; it is one of the best examples of the style of logical modern fantasy that the magazine pioneered. Writers for *Unknown Worlds* were renowned for seeing resonances of the supernatural in the most mundane aspects of everyday life. Leiber at this point in his career already had drawn parallels between the witch's familiar and a gangster's gun in his tale "The Automatic Pistol" (1940), and he had reinvented the ghost as a viable monster for the contemporary urban landscape in "Smoke Ghost" (1941). Leiber saw in the rituals, taboos, and rigidly defined gender roles of the academic community of his day an environment akin to primitive tribal societies that accept witchcraft as a matter of course. It was not difficult for him to advance a supernatural rationale for how sexual politics shaped the characters of such institutions: Accept that the age-old battle of the sexes is founded on women wielding powers of witchcraft that men do not possess, and it is easy, in Leiber's words, to "picture most women as glamor-conscious witches, carrying on their savage warfare of deathspell and countercharm, while their reality befuddled husbands went blithely about their business."

With its suggestion that witchcraft and sorcery can be understood in social and scientific terms, *Conjure Wife* clearly demonstrates the influence of H. P. Lovecraft (with whom Leiber corresponded briefly), particularly Lovecraft's tales "The Dreams in the Witch-House" (1933) and "The Thing on the Doorstep" (1937). Leiber's attempts to apply principles of logic to the understanding of sorcery reflect his familiarity with the Harold Shea fantasies of L. Sprague de Camp and Fletcher Pratt, several of which appeared in *Unknown Worlds* between 1940 and 1943. His suggestion that what people demonize as "supernatural" is actually a natural bypath of human evolution is prefigured in another *Unknown Worlds* novel, Jack Williamson's *Darker than You Think* (1948). Conjure Wife inaugurated an entire tradition of science fiction and fantasy stories that have framed science and superstition in terms of each other, including Leiber's second novel, *Gather, Darkness!* (1950; serial form, 1943), in which scientists in a future society cloak themselves with the mystique of sorcerers.

More important, *Conjure Wife* helped lay the foundation for many trends that define contemporary dark fantasy. The insular Hempnell campus, whose placid façade belies the war of wills raging behind it, anticipates horror novels of the 1970's and 1980's by Stephen King, Charles L. Grant, and numerous other writers in which small towns suffer from social and supernatural tensions that are sometimes indistinguishable from each other. Leiber's rendering of horrors emerging subtly from behind the simple aspects of life—the home, the family, the job—marks a break with the pulp horror tradition of supernatural invasion by forces from beyond and defines the direction postwar horror would take through the work of Richard Matheson and Charles Beaumont (who cowrote the screenplay of the novel's film adaptation in 1961 as *Burn, Witch, Burn*) and the generation of writers their work influenced.

—*Stefan Dziemianowicz*

A Connecticut Yankee in King Arthur's Court

A nineteenth century American is transported to sixth century England, where he tries to implant modern technology and political ideas

Author: Mark Twain (Samuel L. Clemens, 1835–1910)
Genre: Science fiction—time travel
Type of work: Novel
Time of work: The late nineteenth and early sixth centuries
Location: England
First published: 1889

The Story

The novel is told within a frame set around 1889. During a day tour of England's Warwick Castle, the anonymous frame-narrator meets an American—later identified as Hank Morgan—who relates how he was transported back to the sixth century. When he was a foreman in a Connecticut arms factory in 1879, an employee knocked him unconscious; he awakened in England in 528 c.e. That night, Morgan leaves a manuscript containing his story with the narrator, who stays up reading it. Morgan's own first-person account forms the novel's main narrative.

Morgan's narrative spans roughly ten years. After awakening in England, he is captured and taken to Camelot, where he is denounced as a monster and sentenced to be burned. He knows that a solar eclipse occurred at the very hour when he is scheduled to die, so he threatens to blot out the sun. When the eclipse begins, people conclude that he is a powerful magician. King Arthur not only frees him but also agrees to make him his prime minister. Morgan then enhances his reputation by blowing up the tower of Merlin the magician. Soon dubbed the "Boss," Morgan reorganizes the kingdom's administration and gradually introduces modern inventions and innovations, such as matches, factories, newspapers, the telegraph, and training schools. Although he is eager to introduce democracy and civil liberties, he proceeds cautiously to avoid offending the powerful Church.

After seven years, Morgan's administration is so firmly established that he leaves Camelot. Wearing armor, he goes on a quest with a woman named Sandy to rescue princesses—who turn out to be hogs. During his return, he stops at a holy shrine, where King Arthur joins him. They disguise themselves as freemen in order to travel among commoners. A nobleman treacherously sells them to a slave caravan that takes them to London, where Morgan kills the slave driver while escaping. Before being recaptured, Morgan telegraphs Camelot asking for help. As he and the king are to be hanged, Sir Launcelot arrives with five hundred knights mounted on bicycles to rescue them.

Back in Camelot, Morgan wins many jousts using his lasso and kills a knight with a pistol. He then challenges all the knights at once. Five hundred knights attack, only to scatter after he starts shooting them. This triumph leaves him England's unchallenged master, so he unveils his secret schools, mines, and factories. Finally ready to take on the Church, he has slavery abolished, taxation equalized, and all men made legally equal. Steam and electrical power proliferate, trains begin running, and Morgan prepares to send an expedition to discover America.

When Morgan visits France, the legendary tragedy of Arthur's breach with Launcelot unfolds, plunging England into civil war. Morgan returns to find that the Church has put him and his modern civilization under its Interdict. With only fifty-three trustworthy followers left, he retreats to a fortified cave that is attacked by twenty-five thousand knights. His modern weapons annihilate the knights, but the enemy corpses trap him in the cave. Merlin casts a spell to make him sleep thirteen hundred years.

A postscript to the final chapter returns the story to the present. The frame-narrator finishes reading Morgan's manuscript and visits him in time to see him die.

Analysis

A Connecticut Yankee in King Arthur's Court was the first book that Mark Twain finished after publishing *Adventures of Huckleberry Finn* (1884). Because of its setting, it often is classified as one of his historical novels, along with *The Prince and the Pauper* (1882) and *Joan of Arc* (1896), but it has little in common with either. The novel more closely resembles his 1879 short story "The Great Revolution in

Pitcairn," also about an American trying to modernize an archaic society.

The germ of *A Connecticut Yankee in King Arthur's Court* goes back to Twain's 1866 visit to Hawaii, which made him want to write a novel exploring the islanders' feudalistic characteristics. He started this book in 1884 but soon abandoned it and turned instead to a parody of medieval England. His new target was Arthurian romances, whose popularity Alfred, Lord Tennyson's *Idylls of the King* (1859–1885) had helped to revive. Twain's novel incorporated some elements that he had intended for his Hawaiian novel; for example, he modeled King Arthur partly on Hawaii's King Kamehameha V.

A Connecticut Yankee in King Arthur's Court is the first novel-length treatment of travel into the past. Twain's use of time travel as a plot device may have been influenced by Edward Bellamy's future-travel story *Looking Backward: 2000–1887* (1888). He also was probably influenced by a novella that Max Adeler (Charles Heber Clark) published as "Professor Baffin's Adventures" (1881; later retitled "The Fortunate Island"). Adeler's story lacks time travel but resembles Twain's novel in having an inventive American drop into an Arthurian world (on an uncharted island) that he tries to modernize. Similarities between the stories were such that Clark accused Twain of plagiarism.

A Connecticut Yankee in King Arthur's Court mixes satire, burlesque, sociological diatribe, and violence too thoroughly to permit the novel's easy classification. Even its designation as a time-travel story is problematic. Aside from the prologue's vague allusion to "transmigration of souls" and "transposition of epochs," it makes no attempt to explain how Morgan reaches the sixth century, beyond stating that he is knocked on the head. His return to the nineteenth century is less mysterious: Merlin puts him to sleep for thirteen centuries. Back in the nineteenth century, the only tangible evidence of Morgan's sixth century industrial civilization is a bullet hole in a suit of armor hanging in Warwick Castle. If his experience was merely a dream, it would explain his story's historical elements, such as making sixth century England resemble the High Middle Ages and using a solar eclipse that never occurred.

Although the novel's time-travel elements might be regarded as fantasy, Morgan's actions in the sixth century definitely constitute science fiction. Immediately after reaching Camelot, he pledges to "boss the whole country inside of three months," using his modern education and know-how. Once he sets out to revolutionize England, the story becomes sociological science fiction. Ultimately, he fails in his battle against the Church, and all of his impressive achievements are crushed. If the novel is viewed according to modern conventions of time-travel stories, one might conclude that the reason for Morgan's failure is the impossibility of altering the space-time continuum. What interested Twain, however, is the resistance of human beings to change, a profoundly pessimistic theme that he explored in many of his late writings.

—*R. Kent Rasmussen*

THE CORNELIUS CHRONICLES

A mythic antihero from London travels through the world in the last half of the twentieth century to confront an assortment of evils in a universe where time moves unpredictably

Author: Michael Moorcock (1939–   )
Genre: Science fiction—alternate history
Type of work: Collected works
Time of work: 1960–1975, with time travel to other periods
Locale: Earth

First published: *The Cornelius Chronicles* (1977), comprising *The Final Programme* (1968), *A Cure for Cancer* (1971), *The English Assassin* (1972), and *The Condition of Muzak* (1977); *The Cornelius Chronicles, Volume II* (1986), comprising *The Lives and Times of Jerry Cornelius* (1976) and *The Entropy Tango: A Comic Romance* (1981); and *The Cornelius Chronicles, Volume III* (1987), comprising *The Adventures of Una Persson and Catherine Cornelius in the Twentieth Century* (1976) and "The Alchemist's Question" (1984)

THE STORY

The Final Programme, first published in *New Worlds* magazine in 1965–1966, centers on the adventures in time of soldier of fortune Jerry Cornelius, his collaborator Miss Brunner, his shifty brother Frank, and his beloved sister Catherine. The novel is easy to read, linearly plotted, and full of traditional science-fiction elements. It tells the story of the clash between Jerry and Miss Brunner, a computer technician of enormous powers. Eventually the two get their computers and super-science formulas together in a womblike cave, where they merge themselves into a new hermaphrodite Messiah, destroyer/devourer of the world.

A Cure for Cancer, an "unconventional structure" according to Michael Moorcock himself, is a darker version of *The Final Programme*. Jerry reappears in 1970 as a black man with white hair who vampirizes those about him. In pursuit of his beloved sister Catherine, he goes to a strange Amerika and battles the loathsome Bishop Beesley who, together with Miss Brunner, metaphorically represents Moorcock's idea of officialdom and life-denying orderliness. In contrast, Jerry and his cohorts represent a search for aesthetic harmony and love.

Many of the characters from the first two novels reappear in *The English Assassin*, in which Jerry's story broadens and deepens. Retreating from the city and the 1970's, Jerry spends most of the novel in a coffin as a turn-of-the-century romance of the British Empire at its hectic Jubilee peak flows around him. New characters appear, the two most important of whom are Una Persson, a stage singer, dancer, revolutionary, and lover to both Jerry and Catherine, and Mrs. Cornelius, a greedy, vulgar, sly, savage, indomitable, and wise Cockney survivor from an earlier twentieth century. Entropic decay of the British Empire becomes a mirror of Jerry's decay in dehumanized London as the 1960's turn into the sour 1970's. The novel ends as a destroyer shells an English village while Jerry, in his Pierrot suit, and Catherine sail away for Normandy in their yacht *Teddy Bear*.

In *The Condition of Muzak*, Jerry's story is retold from his earlier lives as phases in a harlequinade. Jerry as Harlequin (really Pierrot, the Weeper) tries to dominate the show to reach stable bliss with Columbine, his sister Catherine. Framing this mythic story is a realistic story of Jerry as a daydreaming rock musician spaced out on drugs, living in a slum flat in the Ladbroke Grove area of London. Jerry, Catherine, and Una Persson team up in a stage act and have sex together. Mother Cornelius dies, and the story ends with Jerry on his way to tell his pregnant sister of the fact.

No enclave or style is secure against time. All things aspire toward the condition of Muzak even as entropy rots all things. Jerry endures to tell readers how to live in the decaying cities of the world.

The Cornelius Chronicles, Volume II (1986) is made up of eleven short stories published in *New Worlds* and other magazines between 1969 and 1974. The stories were published as *The Lives and Times of Jerry Cornelius* (1976) and the novel *The Entropy Tango: A Comic Romance* (1981). Moorcock directs that the stories are to be read as one continuous narrative, which opens with Jerry as a Cuban guerrilla riding an albino horse out of Time Centre into China to kill General Way Hahng with a vibragun. The narrative closes as entropic degeneration sets in, with Jerry returning to London to bed Miss Brunner, visit his mother and sister, dope up, and shoot up a post office with his friend Mo. A series of similar fantastic adventures lies between. In the novel's final story, "The Entropy Circuit," Jerry meets Miss Brunner, Captain Maxwell, and his brother Frank in Rome and ends up shooting the pope.

The Entropy Tango centers on Una Persson's adventures with anarchist Batko Makhno. It is 1948, and anarchy is spreading around the world. The novel concludes with anarchists blowing up Golden Gate Bridge, Una blinded when Fisherman's Wharf explodes, and Makhno captured and electrocuted in Oregon, having become a martyr on six continents.

The Cornelius Chronicles, Volume III (1987) is made up of the novel *The Adventures of Una Persson and Catherine Cornelius in the Twentieth Century* (1976) and the story "The Alchemist's Question" (1984). The former, drawn from Miss Persson's unpublished memoirs and written in an eighteenth century picaresque style, follows Una and Catherine from their bed outside time back into the twentieth century. Una experiences outcomes of the Bolshevik Revolution while Catherine explores orgasm with a variety of partners. Finally, weary of their travels, the two women return for cucumber sandwiches and tea. "The Alchemist's

Question," the final episode in the career of the English Assassin, brings all the Cornelius characters together on the world stage for a "curtain call" conclusion to the series.

ANALYSIS

Called one of the best fantasy writers in the English language, Michael Moorcock has been compared to J. R. R. Tolkien, Hieronymus Bosch, and Alfred, Lord Tennyson. His enormous output includes approximately fifty novels, innumerable short stories, and a rock album. He became editor of *Tarzan Adventures* at the age of sixteen and has earned his living as a writer/editor ever since. In April, 1963, he contributed a guest editorial to John Carnell's *New Worlds*, Britain's leading science-fiction magazine, effectively announcing the onset of the New Wave renewal movement in science fiction. In 1964, Carnell recommended that Moorcock become editor of *New Worlds*, a position he would hold until 1969.

Under Moorcock, the magazine became the cutting edge of Anglo-American science fiction. He gathered around himself a group of talented British writers and also recruited a new generation of American writers including Harlan Ellison, Samuel Delany, Thomas Disch, and Norman Spinrad. He had his own rock group, Deep Fix, and was also known for his association with the band Hawkwind, whose lyrics were drawn from science-fiction stories.

Believing that H. G. Wells had had a disastrous influence on science fiction by centering it on matters of outer space, Moorcock urged a return to exploration of the immediate future and "inner space." He offered the Jerry Cornelius novels as paradigmatic models to this end.

Moorcock's rock aesthetic and entropic view of the near future eventually influenced cyberpunk writers of the 1980's. His experiments with narrative and pastiche link him to other postmodern writers as well. His works rarely appear in science-fiction anthologies, perhaps because they so often verge on self-indulgent parody. His end of the world turns out to be England's fin de siecle extrapolated, and his characters are dandies and darlings who live for pleasure in an amusing and fantastic, but finally wildly escapist, world.

Moorcock's fiction, particularly the Cornelius series, derives its power from the manipulation of archetypes and Freudian images already present in his readers' collective unconscious. The reader is made to identify with a heroic figure who becomes, for the duration of the novel, one of the archetypes in the reader's subconscious mind. The archetypal elements of Moorcock's fiction give his work an instant mythic dimension even as the obsessive Freudian imagery connects to the reader on a deep psychosexual level. Jerry Cornelius is a new kind of mythic archetype, not an existing figure from legend but a new hero created from the imagery of the mid-twentieth century united with material from the collective unconscious. *The Cornelius Chronicles* essentially tell the same story eight times, using a different style, character's viewpoint, and form each time. Differences in time and plot create ambiguities and differences in emphasis.

The Final Programme, written over the course of several years, is the key work in the cycle, the template myth around which the rest of the stories revolve. Themes are completely stated, linearly, in their simplest forms. Like movements in a symphony, the subsequent novels and stories are all different variations on the first movement. The short stories using the same Cornelius thematic material act like tone poems inspired by a larger symphonic work. "The Alchemist's Question" ends the series in jazz riffs on the melodic line.

The basic Cornelius world is London in the near future, a territory that seems to include Europe and South Asia. Jerry, like his ally/antagonist Miss Brunner, is a psychic vampire in an unraveling world where available psychic energy is always dwindling. He is a paid assassin and a rock musician involved in murky Freudian relationships with his brother Frank and his sister Catherine in the "swinging" London of the 1960's. This London is in the process of collapse into the middle 1970's of runaway inflation, bisexuality, racial tensions, faltering economic systems, and drug overdoses, a collapse that Moorcock dated as beginning with the assassination of John F. Kennedy on November 22, 1963. Political and economic details; vivid descriptions of clothing, cars, furnishings, pop music, and altered states of consciousness; and real, bizarre newspaper items work together to create a new postmodern landscape for Moorcock's new mythic hero.

The universe of Jerry Cornelius turns out to be a metaphor for the world of the late twentieth century. Moorcock's ultimate theoretical goal was to have the Cornelius figure transcend his own novels and stories and pass into the general public's consciousness, becoming new material in the collective unconscious, much like Batman and Superman. The experiment seems to have been only a limited success.

—*E. Laura Kleiner*

COUNTERFEIT WORLD

Doug Hall discovers that he is an electronic analogue in a simulated universe that is designated for eradication by his counterpart in the real world

Author: Daniel F. Galouye (1920–1976)
Genre: Science fiction—inner space
Type of work: Novel
Time of work: 2034
Locale: A simulation of Earth
First published: 1964 (published as *Simulacron-3*, 1964, in the United States)

THE STORY

Counterfeit World was filmed for German television in 1973 as *Welt am Draht* (*The World on a Wire*) by Rainer Werner Fassbinder and released in England as a two-part film under the same title. The story opens as Doug Hall returns from a vacation at an isolated cabin, where he was recovering from seizures brought on by stress and overwork. He discovers that Horace P. Siskin has appointed him director of RIEN Reactions, an organization that samples public opinion with a new computer containing an electronically simulated population. Although the simulator will make prediction much easier, it will put poll takers out of work.

A series of strange events, including people and things disappearing and attempts on his life, convinces Hall not only that Hannon Fuller, his predecessor and inventor of the simulator, was murdered but also that his own world is counterfeit, like the one in the simulator. Hall comes to these conclusions despite the fact that his former teacher and friend, Avery Collingsworth, has diagnosed him as being paranoid. Meanwhile, Siskin has asked Hall to reprogram the simulator so that it will project Siskin as the ideal presidential candidate, and Hall has fallen in love with Fuller's daughter, Jinx.

Hall plays along with Siskin for a time, but his plan to expose Siskin is discovered and eventually he is fired. One of the contact units from the simulator's counterfeit world comes through the hookup and takes over the physical body of an assistant. Hall realizes that there must be a person in his own world monitoring things for the operators above. As he tries to find that contact person, he discovers that he is now wanted for the murders of both Fuller and Collingsworth. He flees. Jinx finds him and tells him that she is not Fuller's daughter but a projection from the real world, that he is an electric analogue for the operator whom she once loved but who is now a sadist, and that the two Doug Halls are physically, but not psychologically, identical.

Because Doug now knows that his world is a simulation, he also knows that the operator will have to end it, and he determines the day on which his world probably will be erased. He wants Jinx to leave, but she will not. Hall eventually saves his electronic world, but he is fatally wounded. He later wakes up in Jinx's world to find that she has switched the Doug Hall operator into Hall's electronic identity in time for him to die. Hall finds that his new body is identical to his former one and that Jinx's world is virtually identical to the one he left. Jinx says that she will help him adjust but that she will miss the operator's romantic flair for programming exotic proper nouns, such as Pacific and Mediter-ranean.

ANALYSIS

Counterfeit World is one of five novels by Daniel Galouye and was written at the height of his creative powers. Only his minor classic *Dark Universe* (1961) is perhaps better artistically. His work was a staple of the slick magazines of the 1950's and 1960's. Many critics believe that his career was shortened by injuries he sustained during World War II.

Counterfeit World is linked with several subgenres of fiction and science fiction. The manipulation of scale is one of the most common devices in literature. Legend, myth, and folklore teem with giants and little people. Such characters feature in stories from childhood such as "Jack and the Beanstalk" and satires such as Jonathan Swift's *Gulliver's Travels* (1726) as well as in contemporary popular films such as *King Kong* (1933) and *Honey, I Shrunk the Kids* (1989). Comic books are filled with characters out of scale, such as Giant-Man, Ant-Man, and the Wasp.

Counterfeit World also is part of a subgenre that postulates microcosmic worlds within larger macrocosmic worlds. This idea has been popularized as atoms in the known universe being solar systems in their own right. Several writers prior to Galouye wrote stories using this device; the earliest is *The Triuneverse* (1912) by R. A. Kennedy.

The idea of making the microcosmic world electronic is a more specific variation of this concept. The electronic world often is within a computer. Probably the best-known example of this form is the Disney film *Tron* (1982). *Counterfeit World* is an early work in this subgenre of microcosmic worlds. It features a type of virtual reality, long before that term came into vogue. It also has similarities to L. Ron Hubbard's novella "Typewriter in the Sky" (1940) and even shares some broad ideas with Lewis Carroll's Alice novels and contemporary video games.

Counterfeit World is technically ingenious, depending heavily on irony, and it reflects Galouye's continuing interest in worlds that are unusual and perhaps even arbitrary constructs. Galouye also was interested in reality and how it is, or is not, perceived. *Counterfeit World* is carefully and cleverly plotted, original, and richly detailed. Although Galouye's major weakness as a writer is his failure to give his characters depth, those of *Counterfeit World* are interesting, and Jinx truly achieves the status of a female hero.

Galouye did not win any major awards, but *Dark Universe* was nominated for a Hugo. His work often is neglected, but those who have examined it generally acknowledge his technical skill and ingenuity. His best work is quite good.

—*Carl B. Yoke*

The Course of the Heart

Three university students find their lives curiously blighted after an experiment with magic

Author: M(ichael) John Harrison (1945–   )
Genre: Fantasy—inner space
Type of work: Novel
Time of work: The 1980's
Locale: Northern England
First published: 1992

The Story

While at school, the unnamed narrator and two fellow university students, Pam Stuyvesant and Lucas Medlar, take part in a magical ritual under the guidance of Yaxley. Somehow they touch another realm, the Pleroma, and find themselves unable to escape its effects throughout the rest of their lives. Each one brings back a familiar. For Pam it is a ghostly white couple forever engaged in sexual embrace, for Lucas it is a monkeylike creature who constantly disrupts his life and surroundings, and for the narrator, apparently more blessed, it is the sight and smell of roses.

Twenty years later, Pam and Lucas have married, then divorced, but are unable to get by without each other. During their marriage, Lucas invented the autobiography of Michael Ashman to entertain Pam, and it has grown into an elaborate construct about Ashman's quest for the Coeur, an enchanted medieval land now vanished from the world but that reflects, in some curious way, the Pleroma. The narrator keeps in touch with Pam and Lucas only sporadically, building his own career and marriage in London, but he cannot quite get away from Yaxley, who involves him in further dispiriting and unsuccessful magical rituals. One of these is a sordid incident in which the narrator finds himself bringing a teenage girl to London for a ritual that will involve her having sex with her own estranged father. Almost inevitably the scheme fails, but even his self-disgust will not allow the narrator to break free of Yaxley until the mage himself dies.

The three are brought together again by Pam's final illness, during which the narrator finds out for the first time about their familiars and about the Coeur. When Pam dies, a final vision suggests that the Coeur was more than fiction and that Pam and Lucas had in their way been more blessed by the Pleroma than the narrator, who returns to an ordinary life in which his wife is killed and his child grows apart from him.

ANALYSIS

The Course of the Heart is, in many respects, the novel that best brings together the various themes and practices of M. John Harrison's work. He long held an impression of magic as a grimy, backstreet enterprise, something that belongs only in this world in its worst shape. This is shown in his story "The Incalling" (1978), and it is significant that the failed magical rite that the narrator finds himself unwillingly caught up in midway through *The Course of the Heart* is referred to as an "infolding." Magic is something that goes not outward into the world but inward into the soul and imagination of the participants.

Harrison's most famous sequence of novels and stories, about Viriconium, became in the end a fiction about imaginative escape from this world, for example in "A Young Man's Journey to Viriconium" (1985). Novels in the sequence include *The Pastel City* (1971), *A Storm of Wings* (1980), and *In Viriconium* (1983, also titled The Floating Gods). The notion of a fantasy land alongside and accessible from the real world was further developed in another Viriconium story, "Egnaro" (1981), which was in many ways a dry run for *The Course of the Heart*. The central character of "Egnaro" is called Lucas and is prone to the migraines that beset Pam. As are these stories, the novel is ambivalent about escape. There are successive layers of imagination throughout the novel, but the way through them is so convoluted that by the end the fictional world is giving birth to the real. Thus Lucas invents Ashman, who investigates the history of the Coeur, but before long Lucas is himself tracing the history of those who escaped from the Coeur at the moment it left the real world. That track leads to Pam as being the final descendant. It seems no more than Lucas deliberately shaping his fiction, but two glimpses of Pam after her death and the final vision amid a storm of petals suggest that this vision is no more or less than the truth.

By creating their own Pleroma, Lucas and Pam are actually less damaged by Yaxley's rite than their apparently sad lives might lead one to suspect. The narrator, cursed by the scent of roses, fails to notice that roses appear in virtually every scene in the book: The Pleroma is all around him, but he does not notice.

In a previous novel, *Climbers* (1989), Harrison essayed a technique in which real incidents in his life as a rock climber steered the dramatic shape of the novel he wrote about rock climbing. In *The Course of the Heart* there is the same sense of a "found" reality rather than a dramatically structured one. This is a tantalizing book in which the plot is never more than half glimpsed; even the participants have no idea of exactly what the ritual was that launched them on this course. Much of the book feels formless, but the truth is that readers enter into lives that are unfinished and are doomed to remain so. From a privileged position, readers can see how close the characters come to the Pleroma and how distant they must inevitably remain, but readers are so trapped inside the perceptions of the narrator, the loser, that they can never know for sure what the Pleroma might be. There are holes in the story just as there are holes in the lives of the characters. The narrator is known to be unreliable only from the way the book as a whole works. The result is a subtle, shifting work that is perhaps the most daring and the most successful of Harrison's career.

—*Paul Kincaid*

CRASH

The story of a man who becomes involved with a disturbed scientist who is obsessed with car crashes and who wishes to die in a collision with Elizabeth Taylor

Author: J. G. Ballard (1930-2009)
Genre: Science fiction—cultural exploration
Type of work: Novel
Time of work: The 1970's
Locale: London, England
First published: 1973

THE STORY

J. G. Ballard's *Crash* is a story of obsession and technological horror. The novel begins with an account of Robert Vaughan's fiery, suicidal death in a car crash. Vaughan attempted to kill Elizabeth Taylor as well but missed her limousine and crashed into a bus full of airline passengers. The narrator then gives some of Vaughan's background. He relates how Vaughan derived sexual pleasure from car crashes and how this eventually developed into his final destructive act. The narrator also explains that Vaughan developed car-crash scenarios with various celebrities.

The narrator then goes back to explain how he became involved with Vaughan and why he understands the latter's obsession. The story begins with the narrator describing a car crash involving himself, a chemical engineer, and the engineer's wife, Dr. Helen Remington. Helen's husband dies instantly, and the narrator's legs are injured severely. During his recovery, the narrator begins to be sexually aroused when he thinks about the accident. Catherine, the narrator's wife, begins to take a renewed romantic interest in her husband after the crash.

After he is released from the hospital, the narrator becomes sexually involved with Helen. In a sign of his growing fascination with car crashes, the narrator finds that he cannot have successful intercourse unless he is in a car. During one of his sexual liaisons with Helen, the narrator becomes aware that Vaughan has been watching them and taking pictures of their encounters. The relationship between Helen and the narrator soon begins to cool, but the latter's association with Vaughan has only begun.

The narrator soon learns more about Vaughan. He discovers that Vaughan is obsessed with car crashes and has taken numerous pictures of accidents. Vaughan has photographs that chronicle accidents and the recovery of victims. He also has created a survey that asks people to create a fantasy car crash involving political figures or other celebrities. The narrator also learns that Vaughan is obsessed with Elizabeth Taylor; Vaughan dreams of dying in an accident with the actress and has an entire room of photographs of her.

The narrator's association with Vaughan continues to grow throughout the rest of the book. At one point, he watches Vaughan have sexual intercourse with Catherine in the back of his car. The narrator eventually comes to share Vaughan's fascination with accidents and connects sexual pleasure to crashes. Vaughan's obsession with Taylor grows until he kills himself in an attempt to crash a car into the actress' limousine. After his death, Vaughan's influence upon the narrator becomes even more clear as the narrator begins to plan his own crash.

ANALYSIS

Crash has received high praise from critics and is considered to be one of Ballard's best novels. The characters have disturbing psychological problems that seem real. Vaughan, an obsessed scientist, brings the narrator under his influence. He slowly changes the narrator's character until he shares Vaughan's obsession with car crashes. The novel presents a fascinating portrayal of sexual obsession combined with hideous abuses of technology.

One of the strongest aspects of the novel is Ballard's powerful characterization. Each character in *Crash*, from the narrator to Robert Vaughan to Helen Remington, has a unique and fascinating personality, yet all are united by the bond of obsession and pain. The narrator's friendship with and admiration of Vaughan seem strange at first, as do his sexual fantasies connected with car crashes. As he writes about Vaughan and describes how he became involved with the scientist, however, readers can understand how the narrator could be changed by Vaughan.

Another fascinating aspect of the narrator's character is that he is named James Ballard. The connection of author and narrator creates interesting associations; readers might wonder what is fictional and what may be reality. Ballard's careful blending of fiction and reality also can be seen in his decision to make Elizabeth Taylor, a prominent actress, the focus of Vaughan's obsession.

At first, it might seem unbelievable that Vaughan could derive sexual pleasure from car crashes or that he could fantasize of dying in an accident with Taylor. When one considers the strange motivations expressed by serial killers, assassins, and terrorists, however, Vaughan and his obsession do not seem so unrealistic. In fact, Vaughan is a chilling character who might well exist in the real world.

Another fascinating aspect of *Crash* is the use of technology. Ballard does not simply tell the story of a man obsessed with an actress. Instead, he creates a terrifying vision of obsession mixing with technology and eventually leading to the death of innocent people. Ballard captures the horrifying consequences of car accidents and speculates on the terrifying possibility that there may people who want to create car crashes for their own pleasure. The technology of the automobile, which seems beneficial on the surface, is easily turned into an instrument of mass destruction.

—*David A. Oakes*

THE CROCK OF GOLD

A fable set in a Celtic fairy land, where human characters, with the help of the gods, learn lessons about life

Author: James Stephens (1882–1950)
Genre: Fantasy—magical world
Type of work: Novel
Time of work: Undefined
Locale: Ireland
First published: 1912

THE STORY

The Crock of Gold is divided into six short books containing two central plot lines. The first focuses on the Philosopher and his wife, the Thin Woman, who live in the center of a dark pine wood in a fairy land. Initially, there are two philosophers married to two women, but one Philosopher decides he has attained all the wisdom he can bear and dies. His wife soon follows, and the Philosopher and the Thin Woman are left with two children, Brigid Beg and Seamus.

A neighbor named Meehawl MacMurrachu comes to the Philosopher for advice on where his washboard may have disappeared, and the Philosopher deduces that the leprechauns of Gort na Cloca Mora took it. He advises Meehawl to go to a hole under a tree in a nearby field. When Meehawl does so, he finds instead a little crock of gold. The leprechauns try to get the crock back, consider the Philosopher their enemy, and kidnap his two children.

Meanwhile, in the second plot, Caitlin, the beautiful daughter of Meehawl MacMurrachu, is lured by the song of the great god Pan. She goes off with him "because he was naked and unashamed." Meehawl goes again to the Philosopher for advice. The Philosopher promises to help get Caitlin back. When the leprechauns return Brigid Beg and Seamus, the Philosopher sends the children in search of Pan. The god gives them no satisfactory answer, so the Philosopher sets out to meet with the Celtic god Angus Og to seek his help in recovering Caitlin. He has a series of adventures on his journey. In book 3, Angus Og appears in the cave where Pan and Caitlin live, the two gods debate her love, and she goes off with Angus "because his need of her was very great."

Meanwhile, the leprechauns, still angry with the Philosopher because of their lost crock of gold, tell the police that two dead bodies (actually the second Philosopher and his wife) can be found under the hearthstone of the Philosopher's cottage. When the Philosopher returns from his successful trip to Angus Og, four policemen arrest him. They attempt to escort the Philosopher back to their barracks, but the leprechauns are able to rescue him in the dark night woods. The Philosopher is reunited with his wife, who arranged his release, but he claims he must give himself up to the police again. His wife goes off to Angus Og for advice, and the Philosopher goes on to the barracks. He is thrown into a dungeon with two criminals, each of whom tells a long story during the night. The next morning, he is taken to the City "in order that he might be put on his trial and hanged. It was the custom."

In the final book of *The Crock of Gold*, the Thin Woman and her children journey to Angus Og and Caitlin to ask for the release of the Philosopher. The Thin Woman visits all the fairy forts, and the fairy clans come together in a great celebration. Angus and Caitlin sweep into the City to free the Philosopher.

ANALYSIS

James Stephens was a largely self-educated author associated with the Irish literary revival at the end of the nineteenth century. He produced dozens of volumes of fiction, poetry, and fairy tales in his prolific career. *The Crock of Gold* is his most famous work and is one that is almost impossible to define.

The novel is first of all an allegory, a fable in which nearly every character represents some abstract quality. Man is equated with thought, woman with intuition, Pan with sensuality, and so on. Unfortunately for the modern reader, many of Stephens' allegorical figures are drawn from Celtic (Irish) history. Even without a knowledge of Irish mythology, however, readers still can grasp the major import of this delightful fable.

In both plot lines, the protagonists are freed from the constraints of human society and led to a life of greater freedom. The Philosopher starts the novel full of long-winded platitudes, but when he returns to his wife after his adventures on his quest to Angus Og, he has been released from his former selfishness and filled with love. Likewise, the beautiful Caitlin, in her adventures with Pan and Angus, learns that "the duty of life is the sacrifice of self." Throughout the novel, the habits of philosophy or thought are opposed by the forces of instinct, sexual love, and imagination. The end of life, as the Philosopher discovers, may be "gaiety and music and a dance of joy."

The Crock of Gold is no simple allegory. Fused to the fable are other strands, including a strong satirical element. There is a clear structural opposition in the novel between the forces of nature (fairy innocence, pastoral idyll) and those of civilization (materialism and greed). The two criminals who relate their stories are both former clerks, for example. In the apocalyptic ending, the gods clean out the institutional prisons of urban society, including those of the church, the courts, education, and medicine.

No account of *The Crock of Gold* would be complete without mention of two other strands in its fairylike fable: its humor and its poetry. The comedy is often childlike: The two women marry the Philosophers "in order to be able to pinch them in bed." The language of the novel is lyrical and shows the clear influence of the British Romantic poet William Blake.

—David Peck

CROWN OF STARS

A posthumously published collection of ten short stories concerning nature, religious belief, female sexuality and self-perception, and the effects on the individual of an uncaring government

Author: James Tiptree, Jr. (Alice Hastings Bradley Sheldon, 1915-1987)
Genre: Science fiction—new wave
Type of work: Stories
Time of work: Various, from the present to the unspecified near future

Locale: Various locations on Earth, on other planets, and in Heaven and Hell
First published: 1988

THE STORY

Crown of Stars collects stories written by Alice Sheldon under both of her pseudonyms, James Tiptree, Jr., and the less frequently used Raccoona Sheldon. Although most of these stories first appeared in print in science-fiction magazines and anthologies between 1985 and 1988, "Last Night and Every

Night" and "The Earth Doth Like a Snake Renew" are products of the 1970's, and one story, "Come Live with Me," appears in print for the first time.

"Yanqui Doodle" and "Morality Meat," though published under different pseudonyms, are similar in theme and tone. Both are set in the near future and examine the impact of political decisions on unprivileged citizens. In "Morality Meat," the crusade to end abortion rights has resulted in a huge number of unwanted babies. So overcrowded are adoption centers that many babies are butchered and sold as suckling pigs to the very rich, who, it is indicated, know what they are eating. In "Yanqui Doodle," a young soldier is given pills to make him both willing to kill and able to forget his deeds. When he is wounded, his supply is cut off, and he begins to remember the atrocities he has committed. Unable to live with his memories but realizing that the real enemy is the government that used and abandoned him, he attacks a convoy of his own military leaders.

Another theme common in the collection is the role of religion in providing meaning for existence. "In Midst of Life," for example, tells the story of a man who awakes after committing suicide to find that the afterlife is whatever he wishes it to be. "Second Going" is about a visitation of angels, disguised as a benevolent race of octopus-like creatures. These angels actually are "gofers" for the gods; they have been given the task of finding a race of people whose belief will keep the gods alive. The humorous "Our Resident Djinn" tells of Satan's attempt to take over Heaven after the death of God. Although he convinces the saints to move Heaven to Hell, he encounters an entity, Nature, who—in league with her father, Entropy—threatens to assert her dominion over Earth.

In "Our Resident Djinn" and in such stories as "The Earth Doth Like a Snake Renew," Tiptree suggests both the enormous power of nature and the need to protect its resources. In "The Earth Doth Like a Snake Renew," the protagonist attempts a sexual union with Earth, which she considers male. After doing everything she can to please him and to make herself sexually available, she finds that Earth—which is in fact a young male being—has been treating her as his plaything. In the gentler "Come Live with Me," humans merge with a healing consciousness that long ago had become a part of the natural world.

Tiptree frequently links nature with the theme of a young woman's emerging sexual and social sense, as in "The Earth Doth Like a Snake Renew" and the allegorical "All This and Heaven Too." In the latter story, Amoretta, the young queen of pristine Ecologia-Bella, plans to wed the young prince of Pluvio-Acida, a country utterly devastated by pollution, despite the dire consequences for her idyllic country.

ANALYSIS

Critics often describe Tiptree's best writing as predating this collection. None of the stories here has the stylistic and thematic power of "Houston, Houston, Do You Read?" (1976), "The Screwfly Solution" (1977), or "With Delicate Mad Hands" (1981). It has been suggested that after her identity was revealed, Sheldon was less successful than she had been as Tiptree. Crown of Stars, though not representative of Tiptree's very best writing, is nevertheless representative of the author's major themes and shows her place within both the New Wave of science-fiction writing and the feminist wave.

Tiptree combines a thorough knowledge of science, psychology, and military tactics with exceptional stylistic skills to impart a rare power to the science-fiction short story, thus raising its critical reputation. The author's ironic and complex studies of human psychology, in particular, are hallmarks of the New Wave of science-fiction writing introduced in the late 1960's and early 1970's. The author's alignment with feminist science fiction as it began to appear in the early 1970's was colored somewhat by the use of a male pseudonym, particularly because Tiptree often was described as a singularly masculine writer, concerned with male aggression and sexual conquest, here illustrated by "Yanqui Doodle." The revelation that Tiptree was Alice Sheldon forced the science-fiction community to examine its presuppositions about "male" and "female" writing.

Tiptree's themes are often feminist. For example, she treats abortion in "Morality Meat" and young women's views of sexuality, marriage, and social roles in "All This and Heaven Too" and "Backward, Turn Backward." Unlike such feminist writers as Joanna Russ, Monique Wittig, and

Marge Piercy, though, Tiptree neither offers a utopian separatist paradigm nor provides purely sympathetic female characters. "Backward, Turn Backward" is critical of a society that allows girls to develop a sense of self-worth based only on appearances but features a main female character with whom it is hard to sympathize. Similarly, although Amoretta in "All This and Heaven Too" is in some ways a victim of conventions of romantic love, she nearly imperils the country she rules by marrying the wrong man. Like other feminist writers, however, Tiptree examines the role of women in society, including aspects of their sexual selves long taboo in science fiction.

—*Amy Clarke*

A CRYSTAL AGE

A stranger transported to a utopian pastoral community adjusts to its customs and wrestles with his desire for a woman who does not understand sexual love

Author: W(illiam) H(enry) Hudson (1841–1922)
Genre: Fantasy—utopia
Type of work: Novel
Time of work: Thousands of years in the future
Locale: A pastoral version of Earth
First published: 1887

THE STORY

While on a nature hike, the main character, who later identifies himself as "Smith," has a mysterious fall and loses consciousness. When he awakes, he finds himself covered with dirt and roots. As he tries to find his way home, he comes upon a funeral party. Smith sees the beautiful young girl Yoletta and is filled with desire for her. Yoletta and the other members of the funeral party detect him and notice his different speech and clothing. He inquires about the nearest city, only to learn that the members of the funeral party have never heard of cities, England, or anything else related to Smith's past experience.

Smith is taken to their house, where he occasionally offends his hosts because he does not understand their customs. He becomes ashamed of his clothing and tries to buy a suit of clothing like those the others are wearing. His hosts have never heard of money but agree to allow him to work for a year for his clothing. He works each day chopping down trees, hoping to get closer to Yoletta.

Smith's passion for Yoletta grows, but she shows no understanding of love except for the love between brother and sister. Smith notices that there is a father in this household but no apparent couples. He finally asks about Yoletta's mother and learns that he has unknowingly offended the family by not asking about the mother sooner. He visits the "mother's room" where Chastel, Yoletta's mother, stays, too weak to come out. On the way to the room, he passes a series of lifelike statues and learns about the grief of Isarte, a former mother in the house. Smith learns from Chastel that only mothers feel true grief.

Yoletta eventually develops a passionate love for Smith, and Chastel apparently plans that Yoletta will become the next mother, with Smith as the father. Smith accidentally drinks a potion that turns him into a statue like the ones he passed on the way to the mother's room. Yoletta experiences true grief at his loss.

ANALYSIS

W. H. Hudson is best known for his nature writings and his novels about South America, where he grew up. Although there are elements of fantasy in some of his other novels, *The Crystal Age* (first published anonymously, then published as by Hudson in 1906) is his strongest and clearest contribution to the genre. Hudson is particularly famous for his books about birds. His love for nature and eye for natural beauty show up in his descriptions of nature in *The Crystal Age*.

Nature is an important element in the novel because the world that Smith enters after his period of unconsciousness is a utopian world in the pastoral tradition. A pastoral work praises the simplicity of country life, particularly the life of shepherds, and provides an idealized view of nature. The model for the pastoral world is the Golden Age of Greece, a mythological innocent past that was irrecoverably lost. Hudson describes a "crystal age," a time that is beautiful and unchanging but also fragile.

The world that Smith enters is not free from death, but death usually comes without pain and grief, and only after a long life. The inhabitants of this world are young and beautiful, and they spend their time performing simple tasks, singing, and reading books about the history of their house and other houses in the world. They live in a state of innocent bliss, like children, and their love for one another is free from any sexual passion. Smith appears crude and unrefined by comparison, but he is able to feel passion that no one in this community can understand except for the mother, who is also the only one who truly suffers and feels pain.

The happiness of the community seems to depend on the suffering of the mother. The symbol of this suffering is Isarte, who lost seven of her children and asked that a statue be made depicting her grief for all generations. The mother leads a special existence. She is confined to the "mother's room," but she is revered and obeyed by all the members of her household. She has special books that describe the role of the mother and provide her with greater knowledge than the others have; the others live in innocence and ignorance. With knowledge, however, come grief and suffering.

Smith brings uncertainty to this ordered house because of his foreignness. He resembles Prometheus, who defies the Greek gods by bringing fire and knowledge to humans. Smith and Yoletta also resemble Adam and Eve. They live in a Edenic state of innocence until Smith's passion for Yoletta deepens her sense of love and her understanding. When he accidentally turns himself to stone, Yoletta experiences true loss and true grief for the first time. She leaves her state of innocence and becomes like Isarte, Chastel, and other mothers. It may be that this loss of innocence is a necessary preparation for Yoletta to take her place as a mother.

Because of the loss of the love that Smith and Yoletta have developed for each other, *The Crystal Age* also has elements of tragedy. In drinking the potion, Smith believes that he is doing what Yoletta would want by wiping out the dark memories he has of his life before coming to the house. In trying to regain a state of innocence, he loses his life and the object of his desire.

—*Gary Layne Hatch*

CRYSTAL EXPRESS

Science fiction and fantasy stories exploring how humanity might shape its future and itself

Author: Bruce Sterling (1954–)
Genre: Science fiction—future history
Type of work: Stories
Time of work: Various times between the medieval period and several centuries into the future
Locale: Various locations on Earth and in space
First published: 1989

THE STORY

The stories in *Crystal Express* are grouped into three sections. The first five stories belong to a future history in which the human race has gone into space and contacted other intelligent life-forms. The alien species that appears most often is a reptilian one called the Investors. They are interstellar traders. Humanity itself has split into factions, the two most important of which are the Shapers and the Mechanists. They are similar in that they insist that human beings must change. The Shapers practice genetic engineering, especially on their own offspring. The Mechanists change themselves surgically, substituting prosthetics for natural limbs and organs.

There are two recurring characters. Simon Afriel is a minor character in "Twenty Evocations" and the main character in "Swarm." He is a member of the Shaper faction and is genetically engineered to have no appendix, along with other improvements. In "Swarm," he travels to another star system to investigate a nonintelligent spacefaring species. Arkadya Sorienti first appears in "Cicada Queen" as a Mechanist living in the space colony

Czarina-Kluster. At some point between the end of that story and the beginning of "Sunken Garden," she defects to the Regal faction. She then goes to live in Terraform-Kluster, a space station in orbit around Mars and tethered to its surface. The main work of the Regals on that planet is terraforming, or physical transformation of the environment to meet the needs of human and other life.

The middle three stories in *Crystal Express* are science fiction that can be categorized as cyberpunk. The main character in "Green Days in Brunei" is Turner Choi, a Chinese Canadian engineer. He is on assignment in Brunei, a sultanate completely surrounded by the country of Malaysia. There he meets and falls in love with a member of Brunei's royal family. The title character in "Spook" is an assassin. As one weapon, he uses his sinuses, which produce a toxin that induces schizophrenia. In "The Beautiful and the Sublime," Manfred de Kooning is an artist free to indulge his aesthetic sensibilities because of advances made in artificial intelligence technologies.

The final four stories are fantasies. "Telliamed" is De Maillet spelled backwards. It refers to the pseudonym that Benoit De Maillet, an elderly eighteenth century scientist, uses when he publishes a book on the ocean. In "The Little Magic Shop," James Abernathy buys an elixir of youth. A teaspoon taken each year slows twenty years of aging down to one. In the "Flowers of Edo," a former Japanese samurai confronts an electricity demon. A clairvoyant is invited to a "Dinner in Audoghast," at which he makes some predictions that his host and the other guests do not like.

ANALYSIS

Bruce Sterling is one of the leading proponents of the cyberpunk movement in science fiction. He is not comfortable being identified with that movement, however, particularly as it has become associated with computer crime. The technological background of his stories is solid, and he is comfortable employing in his fiction such devices as personal computers, fax machines, and modems. In this way, he is similar to the writers of the Golden Age of science fiction, who wrote comfortably about devices such as rockets, radios, and nuclear reactors that were, at the time of writing, relatively new and developing forms of technology.

Sterling is the author of the nonfiction *The Hacker Crackdown: Law and Disorder on the Electronic Frontier* (1992). He has pointed out that the writers of the cyberpunk movement are as fascinated by information technology as earlier science-fiction writers were by space travel. Most of Sterling's stories reveal a concern about the social consequences of computers and other devices of high technology.

In several stories, characters state the case for anti-technology philosophies. An alien in "Swarm" argues that intelligence is not a prosurvival trait for life-forms. The alien's position is that the urge to expand, explore, and understand ultimately results in extinction. It goes on to predict that the human race will be extinct within approximately a millennium after the time of the story. Thus, science and technology are predicted ultimately to be antilife, but the story leaves the issue unresolved.

In "Spook," a former assassin claims to have rediscovered her humanity in a society patterned on that of the ancient Mayans. The society wins converts by allowing them to feel and love, she explains. Unfortunately for her, this society is destroyed by another assassin, working for a multinational corporation. The premise of "The Beautiful and the Sublime" is that the development of artificial intelligence renders scientists and engineers obsolete. This is similar to Friedrich Nietzsche's idea that science sows the seeds of its own destruction.

On the other hand, some of Sterling's characters learn how to reconcile technology with a humanistic, life-affirming philosophy. Vikram Moratuwa, a character in "Green Days in Brunei," attempts to reconcile a traditional religion, Buddhism, with technology. His goal is to harness runaway technology and make it serve humanity instead of the other way around. In "Cicada Queen," Landau, the main character, is a follower of a philosophy called Posthumanism and makes genetic engineering into an art form. He later founds the Regal faction, the main goal of which is to bring life to Mars. In "Sunken Gardens," the Regals sponsor a competition among ecosystems that is based on technological, philosophical, and aesthetic criteria.

—*Tom Feller*

THE CULTURE SERIES

A highly advanced galactic civilization employs adventurers to shape younger, emerging societies in its image

Author: Iain Banks (1954–2013)
Genre: Science fiction—galactic empire
Type of work: Novels
Time of work: The fourteenth to twenty-first centuries and beyond
Locale: Various planets, including Earth, and the Lesser Magellanic Cloud
First published: *Consider Phlebas* (1987), *The Player of Games* (1988), *Use of Weapons* (1990), and *The State of the Art* (1991; includes the novella "The State of the Art," 1989; "A Gift from the Culture," 1987; and six other, non-Culture stories)

THE STORY

The Culture Series is composed of independent tales, though some of the same characters appear in two of the plots and there are several references to the Idirian war. The Contact Section of the Culture—a utopia of highly advanced technologies in which life is prolonged, all wants are fulfilled, and humanoids of all species live in peace—benevolently watches over emerging societies in the Milky Way and the Magellanic Clouds. Through Special Circumstances operatives, the Culture shapes those societies to its standards. The plots of the individual novels concern the adventures of Special Circumstances operatives.

The first novel, *Consider Phlebas*, depicts a galactic war between the Culture and three-legged, reptilian Idirians, occurring in the fourteenth century of Earth's Common Era. The Culture fights to justify itself, excusing its hedonistic lifestyle by the way it improves inferior societies by imposing its standards on them. The Idirians, who think the Culture lacks real principles, fight to subjugate other species, bringing other societies to their god in a religious and commercial empire. Bora Horza, a "changer" who can assume any humanoid shape, supports the Idirians and fights on their side; Perosteck Balveda, a Special Circumstances agent, is his opponent. The object of their struggle is a Mind (the sentient core of a starship) that has escaped the Idirians and is hiding on a forbidden planet controlled by a third society, the Dra'Azon. To find the Mind, Horza assumes the identity of the leader of a Free Company (of pirates) and takes the pirates (including Balveda, who knows his real identity) to the planet, arriving after Idirians have already landed. In a running battle with the Idirians, who will not believe that Horza is on their side, the Free Company is wiped out. They find the Mind, however, and Balveda, the sole survivor of the Free Company, restores it to the Culture.

The Player of Games sets the Culture in opposition to another emerging society, the Empire of Azad in the Lesser Magellanic Cloud. The rogue drone Mawhrin-Skel (actually a Special Circumstances operative) blackmails the professional game-player Jernau Morat Gurgeh into cooperating with Contact. Contact needs him to enter the Game of Azad, an incredibly complex game that models the Azadian society and is so central to the empire that the winner becomes emperor. With his translator and adviser, the library drone Flere-Imsaho (who is revealed at the end to be Mawhrin-Skel, and who narrates the novel), Gurgeh goes to Azad and plays. Despite collusion against him, attempts on his life, and attempts to bribe him, Gurgeh plays well enough to earn the right to play in the final round against Nicosar, the sitting emperor. In the ultimate stage, played on the fire planet Echronedal, Gurgeh realizes that Contact has designed his participation to discredit the game and thereby Azadian society; the game has become a battle between the Culture and the empire. Foreseeing defeat, Nicosar attempts to immolate Gurgeh in the fire but is killed; Gurgeh, rescued by Contact, returns home.

The novella "The State of the Art," next in order of original publication, depicts Contact's initial exploration of Earth, as described by the agent Diziet Sma. Her colleague Dervley Linter decides to remain behind on Earth, finding its society and conditions more vital than the perfect, but stagnating, Culture. Sma is asked by her ship to persuade Linter to return. She tries but fails. Linter is then killed in a random mugging in New York City. Despite the arguments of some agents that Earth should be destroyed or overtly contacted, the ship departs, leaving behind monitoring devices.

The last novel, *Use of Weapons*, reintroduces Sma (and her drone, Skaffen-Amtiskaw) as the Special Circumstances supervisor of the agent Cheradenine Zakalwe. Zakalwe has been used by Contact as a "dirty tricks" agent because he lacks the moral compunctions of most Culture persons. He is sent to Voerenhutz, where he earlier established a forty-year peace in cooperation with the local patriarchal politician Tsoldrin Beychae. The peace is breaking down, and only Zakalwe can persuade Beychae to come out of seclusion and prevent widespread conflict. His successful effort costs him his life, and the terrible personal secret of sororicide that had driven him in his adventures is revealed at his death.

ANALYSIS

Each of the three long novels of the Culture series is a spirited adventure story; together with the novella, they constitute a postmodernist rethinking of what has been called "space opera," a subgenre of literature dealing with interstellar conflict and involving action-filled plots. The texts gain power and excitement from the interpenetration of traditional storytelling and contemporary narrative fashions.

The first and longest book, *Consider Phlebas*, is unabashedly an adventure story. It is the first of Iain Banks's books to fall clearly within the realm of science fiction. The hero of *Consider Phlebas* lives by wits, courage, and physical prowess, all abetted by the advanced technologies of the Culture and by his special ability to change his body to duplicate that of another. He survives imprisonment, torture, fire fights, shipwreck, a cannibal king on a desert island, and other threats. The novel moves from climax to climax at breathtaking speed, with action that rivals any classic tale of interstellar war. The narrative, which is fairly straightforward when focused on Horza, is also interrupted by brief chapters called "state of play" in which a Culture woman meditates on the meaning of the events, their likely outcome, and the nature of the Culture itself. The final chapter of the narrative not only takes its title (and the major image of the sacrificed, dead sailor) from the fourth section of T. S. Eliot's *The Waste Land* (1922) but also is preceded by a chapter whose ending imitates the style Eliot uses to end the third section of his poem. Such self-conscious narrative elements, coupled with the use of stream-of-consciousness techniques and a set of appendices, separate the book stylistically from the usual space adventure.

The Player of Games and "The State of the Art" eschew most of the stylistic devices of the first book. In *The Player of Games*, however, Banks shows awareness of contemporary narrative theory and practice through the narrator's self-conscious comments dealing with the nature of language and narrative. These comments introduce each of the novel's four sections. In "The State of the Art," the division of the text into numbered subchapters—along with idiosyncratic typography and a series of footnotes by the supposed translator drone— keeps the reader aware that the otherwise straightforward narrative is itself an arbitrary convention.

The last major work to date in the series, *Use of Weapons*, is the most complex in structure. It consists of two series of chapters, one numbered in ascending order and the other in descending order. The two series come together at the death of Zakalwe to both account for his motivations and provide the final surprise of the novel. Banks here seems interested not only in the action or in the sociopolitical background of the Culture but also in the abnormal psychology of a rebel-adventurer who can use violence and cruelty in order to achieve noble ends. This approach is enhanced by poems before and after the text. A postmodern playfulness is seen in an appended section that purports to be the opening chapter of the next Culture novel. In it, Sma recruits Zakalwe's replacement.

The breadth of Banks's intellectual and aesthetic achievement in the Culture novels is astonishing. He has created a utopian society dependent on a wide range of advanced technologies, including faster-than-light travel, machine sentience far superior to human intelligence, genetic engineering of human beings (who not only live for centuries but can deliberately "gland" appropriate mood-altering substances), and weaponry of enormous power but minuscule size. He also incorporates a series of critiques of this society, which in its imperialistic smugness seems to overrule the very things that make a human being human, including the ability to make a mistake or to sin. Banks sometimes uses well-worn plot situations (derived from the spy novel and the thriller as well as from classic science fiction) and employs a mix of unusual and conventional characters. He combines these in a witty narrative style and a sometimes experimental structure to produce engrossing tales. The results rise above mere adventure to become both cultural commentary and a self-reflexive commentary on the science-fiction genre.

—*William H. Hardesty III*

THE CYBERIAD

The adventures of two constructors in their travels across space

Author: Stanislaw Lem (1921–2006)
Genre: Science fiction—dystopia
Type of work: Stories
Time of work: The distant future
Location: Various planets and space between them
First published: *Cyberiada* (1965; English translation, 1974)

THE STORY

The Cyberiad, subtitled *Fables for the Cybernetic Age*, is a collection of related short stories set in a time after robots have escaped slavery at the hands of humanity; they live free throughout the galaxy. They have developed a feudal society, complete with kings, princesses, evil pirates, paupers, and serfs, and they seem to be much more like humans than unlike them. Most planets have one or two kingdoms, and the denizens of a particular kingdom tend not to travel much. Interstellar travel, like international travel during the Middle Ages, is reserved primarily for those who do not belong to the feudal hierarchy.

The principal characters are two such travelers, Trurl and Klapaucius, who have just received their "Diplomas of Perpetual Omnipotence" as constructors. The title is roughly equivalent to that of the medieval magician or sorcerer. They are friends and rivals, and the stories center on their adventures together as they build machines to improve the collective condition, or at least make some money.

Trurl and Klapaucius serve as advisers, matchmakers, storytellers, and judges as they travel among the stars. In a typical story, the constructors create a (usually sentient) machine for some educational or contractual purpose, and it either works but with unexpected results or fails to perform. In another common plot, the constructors build a machine to repair an individual, social, or political problem on a planet they are visiting. The remedy seldom succeeds, but if it does, the success is incidental. There are several stories in which Trurl and Klapaucius figure peripherally and one in which they are absent but are mentioned.

The most common English-language edition of this collection contains fifteen stories. The first three set the scene and tone for the nine that follow; the final three sum up the themes previously presented. There is no overlying plot, and each story has a multitude of pitfalls and plot twists.

There were several editions of the book published in the original Polish, of which the third is definitive. The most common English edition omits roughly a third of the stories in the third Polish edition. All but one of these stories are available in English translation as *Mortal Engines* (1977).

ANALYSIS

The prose of the stories in *The Cyberiad* is a peculiar mix of current usage, archaic medieval language, and jargon from various technical disciplines, particularly cybernetic theory, electronics, and quantum mechanics. The hard sciences around which modern technology is based gain the semblance of medieval magic and make the principal characters resemble Terry Pratchett's wizards.

An interesting feature of the language in the work is its literalness: changing the description changes the described. In one case, the lack of a dragon was changed into the back of a dragon, producing a dragon with

two backs. This literalness is familiar to anyone who has dealt with a computer, and it adds an additional humorous element.

Various themes appear in the stories, among them the blindness of love, the follies of greed and pride, the insidiousness of bureaucracy, and the folly of blind suspicion. In all, the stories are reminiscent of Aesop's fables, as the title suggests. The stories as a whole equate the condition of all conscious things, machine and flesh, and suggest that a conscious effort to improve the existence of others creates more grief than doing nothing.

Stanislaw Lem's characters are all tools he uses to illustrate some point. Kings are inevitably poor rulers, through either cruelty or lack of interest. When political systems other than monarchies are described, however, they are shown to be worse because they were intended to work a greater good. Cruelty is usually associated with stupidity in these stories. Lem suggests that the cruelest of all are those who would rearrange a culture to improve the lot of its people. A cybernetic Karl Marx is put to death with the approval of Trurl not because he tried to improve the lot of his people with revolutionary sociopolitical ideas but because he did not desist after his initial failure. The implication is that only individual, not societal, happiness can be increased through one's actions.

One would be mistaken to state, however, that the collection appears either philosophical or gloomy. The fable format and clever humorous devices ensure that, depending on personal tastes, the reader will find the stories either humorous and whimsical or ponderous and belabored. The philosophical issues appear only after consideration, a necessity for any Polish author who hoped to avoid political entanglements in the 1960's.

Translator Michael Kandel was nominated for an award for translating *The Cyberiad*. Lem has said that Kandel is probably the best translator his work will ever have. Because Polish shares few linguistic or cultural roots with English, Kandel resorted to using an analogous form of translation in which an untranslatable feature (for example, a pun) is replaced with a compensatory feature of a similar sense in English at a different, but logical, insertion place in the text. This approach has great dangers associated with it. It demands that the translator be nearly as skillful, or even more so, than the author and have as good a literary sense as the author. Because Lem has been accused by some Polish critics of having created his own language from Polish in *The Cyberiad*, and because it is in a format that is easily deadened by translation, the demands on a translator of this work are exceptional. Fortunately, Kandel was up to the task, and his translation carries both the meaning and the sense of Lem's prose and poetry.

—*Radford B. Davis*

CYTEEN

Reseune labs uses advanced psychogenetics to replicate its brilliant leader, Ariane Emory, after she is killed

Author: C. J. Cherryh (Carolyn Janice Cherry, 1942–)
Genre: Science fiction—future history
Type of work: Novel
Time of work: The twenty-fourth century
Location: The planet Cyteen
First published: 1988

THE STORY
Fifty years after the Treaty of Pell established an uneasy peace between Earth and its former colonies in the Merchanter's Alliance and in Union, an aging Ariane Emory is the most powerful figure in Union politics. She is the virtual owner of its most advanced research laboratory, Reseune; councillor for science to the Council of Nine in Union's government; and, within the council, leader of its majority faction, the Expansionists.

Through Reseune labs, she developed the "azi," androids whose expanding population enabled Union to secede from Earth. Now researching how to replicate Union's most gifted citizens psychosocially as well as biologically, Emory seduces and co-opts Justin Warrick, a teenager who is an inexact replicant of her brilliant colleague and rival, Jordan Warrick.

When Emory's frozen corpse is discovered at Reseune, her successor at the lab and on the council, Giraud Nye, extorts a confession from Jordan Warrick and exiles him to a remote laboratory on the far side of Cyteen, meanwhile keeping Justin and Justin's azi lover, Grant, as virtual hostages at Reseune. With his brother Denys, Giraud immediately begins an attempt to replicate Ariane Emory and recover her muchneeded abilities amid the fractious and conspiratorial politics of Union.

Using extensive notes left by Emory and by her mother, one of Reseune's founders, the Nyes' project succeeds in producing a second Ariane, whose abilities compare favorably with those of the original. With the advantage of a computerized tutorial left by Emory, however, the second Ariane proves herself not only a precocious researcher and skilled politician but also a more decent human being than her predecessor.

Despite the psychological damage to Justin Warrick wrought by Emory's sexual manipulation of him, his father's implication in her murder, and the Nyes' continuing hostility, the second Ariane recognizes his innate decency and potential brilliance. She sets out to win him over, first as his teacher and then as an essential supporter in the political turmoil that threatens to envelop Reseune as the military faction in Union turns ugly and threatens the Expansionists' majority on the council.

When the aged Giraud Nye dies abruptly, the eighteen-year-old Ariane is able to counter the threatening politics from Union. A nearly successful attempt to assassinate her, however, seems to imply that Giraud and Denys, rather than the Warricks, have been the more serious threat to Ariane Emory's hegemony.

Analysis

Cyteen is one of the central texts in C. J. Cherryh's sprawling future history, in which the former colonies of Earth become the political rivals of Alliance and Union. At 680 pages, it is also one of the longest. It lays out the foundations of that rivalry on Union's home planet. Other works that are central to this future history include *Serpent's Reach* (1980), *Downbelow Station* (1981), *Merchanter's Luck* (1982), and *Rimrunners* (1989). Like *Downbelow Station*, *Cyteen* was voted a Hugo Award for best novel of the year, and in 1989, it was republished as three volumes: *The Betrayal*, *The Rebirth*, and *The Vindication*.

As John Clute has noted in *The Encyclopedia of Science Fiction* (1993), the Alliance-Union rivalry gives Cherryh a flexible but powerful structural focus for her future history. Such a focus offers a much-needed center for a writer whose plots are dense with tangled political machinations and conflicting motivations. Paradoxically, even a novel with the heft of *Cyteen* can seem too cramped for the psychological, social, and political action that Cherryh pours into its pages.

At the heart of *Cyteen* is an intersecting double plot: the project to replicate Ariane Emory and the effort to restore Justin Warrick's disrupted research potential. Through the former, Cherryh invokes fundamental questions about the formation of an individual's identity and the potential of biological engineering to alter people's assumptions about the genetic roots for such identity and the subsequent socialization of the individual. The focus of these questions in Ariane Emory is framed by the book's emphasis on her psychological and social engineering of the azi, the androids who provide bulk and ballast for Union's population. Together, Emory and the azi give *Cyteen* an awareness of human reason entangled in complex emotions that extends the boundaries delineated by Isaac Asimov in his Foundation series, begun in 1942, with later volumes that converge with his robot stories.

In the other strand of this double plot, Cherryh explores the ambiguous zone between human psychology in Justin Warrick and azi psychology in his companion, Grant. Both embody an admixture of logic and emotion, but for Grant, logic is fundamental, engineered into the deepest levels of awareness, and emotion is a "flux" state that disturbs mental equilibrium. For Justin, however, logic is an imperfectly exercised control over the more fundamental emotional flux. The sexual compatibility and mutual respect that characterize Justin and Grant provide a marked contrast to the more disturbed relationships among most of the human characters who populate *Cyteen*. In the end, the second Ariane is able to recover Justin's abilities by respecting the relationship that he and Grant have established.

The profusion of social and political disturbances that surround this double plot suggests that humanity's difficulty in reconciling logic and emotion remains profound. Even science, which offers a model for the appropriate exercise of reason in human endeavor, is compromised by the sheer complexity of human nature and the politics that intervene when science has to operate in the world. In *Cyteen*, the scientists themselves are all-too-imperfect human beings. That point, richly illustrated by the human characters' convoluted motivations, should resonate through the related volumes in Cherryh's future history.

—*Joseph J. Marchesani*

CYTHERA

The nebulous utopia of Cythera beckons to a set of outlaw characters whose jaunts across the blasted digitized landscape of a future Earth reveals strange intersections between flesh and photons

Author: Richard Calder (1956–)
Genre: Science Fiction—cyberpunk
Type of Work: Novel
Time of Plot: 2025–2036
Location: Various locales on Earth
First Published: 1998

THE STORY

Part One is narrated by a man who calls himself by various names—Zane Weary, Jack Pimpernel—including Captain Tarquin. Across the colonized continent of Antarctica in the year 2036, Tarquin drives his Bentley, accompanied by a nymphet ghost. Dhalia Chan, chop-socky bad girl modeled on a real actress, who has leaked across from the virtual fibresphere and taken up illegal nanoflesh. "A Translator is a modem that converts patterns of light into nanomachines, nanomachines into patterns of light." Hounded by the authorities, Tarquin and Dhalia flee from one sleazy dive to another, until finally only a peculiarly promising death offers escape.

In Part Two our narrator is Mosquito, once a transgendered assassin but now a mere catspaw of the Thai porn queen Kito. Soon Mosquito's path intersects with the reborn Tarquin and Dhalia. The trio conceives a mad plan to leave behind Earth's dominion for the nascent paradise of Cythera, in orbit around another star. But this quest first involves a side trip to Greece.

Part Three finds the story resumed by Michael Flynn, the elderly film director who initially built the legend of Dhalia Chan. Now in a concentration camp on the Greek island of Kithara with the actress named Jaruwan, who modeled Dhalia (in effect, Flynn and Jaruwan are Dhalia's spiritual parents), Flynn believes that neither the fibresphere nor Earth represent ultimate reality. His conception of a higher plane of existence, Earth3, which he also terms Cythera, is in contention with the notions of the others.

Whose dream will prevail? Perhaps both, perhaps neither.

ANALYSIS

As of this writing, it has been ten years since Richard Calder has had a new book-length tale freshly in print. (*Babylon* in 2006 was the most recent.) This startling fact reflects, I believe, not so much any blockage or slackness or lack of ambition on the part of the author—he has scripted a small-press comic book fairly recently—but rather a tightening of the commercial market parameters so as to exclude his brand of *Yellow Book*-style decadent SF. This seems a shame, for Calder's sensibilities and voice remain distinctive and unique, and he could contribute much to the somewhat predictable and stale offerings that clog the shelves. But for Calder to flourish, we almost have to imagine an alternate history for SF.

An elderly and respected Edgar Allan Poe becomes editor of a magazine called *Arabesque Stories*, circa 1875. From his pulpit, he promotes a new kind of tale called "Symbolist Fiction," modeled on his own crepuscular work. A host of brilliant writers from many countries—Machen, Beardsley, Apollinaire, Baudelaire, Huysmans, Hodgson, Bierce—flock to his banner. Over the next few decades, Poe's brand of SF, now represented by dozens of magazines, becomes the dominant mode of the fantastic, incorporating scientific speculation as well as more gothic material. (There are schisms and feuds, of course, over this latter development.) Clark Ashton Smith, Ben Hecht, Fritz Leiber, and numerous others push the genre forward in the twenties, thirties, and forties of our century. By the time 1998 rolls around, nearly 125 years of Symbolist Fiction have culminated in one writer. And his name is Richard Calder.

Postulating this imaginary tradition seems the most natural way to get a handle on what Calder is doing in *Cythera*. While Calder expertly uses speculative elements in our familiar SF way, his primary concerns are the mannerist depiction of rarefied emotional states verging on the otherworldly. He is a true romantic, in the Byronic sense of the word. In fact, this stylistic and thematic approach becomes the actual foregrounded subject matter here.

We are back in the world of Calder's *Dead Girls* trilogy (1992–1996), that continuum featuring deadly Cartier love-droids whose unspeakable sexiness and sterility is leading to the extinction of humanity. But this adventure happens early in the timeline, before the ontological weirdness really gets heavy. Consequently, the action depicted here is always straight-forward and mimetic, despite its mauve cloak of baroque prose.

Calder's impassioned passages describing Cythera—a place that allows "the reconciliation of . . . opposites, the hard-boiled world with the fairytale, the noir with a world of impossible romanticism"—are the real reason for this novel's existence. His depiction of this common human longing for Cockaigne, the land of milk and honey and consequence-less pleasure, and how this repressed emotion known as *Sehnsucht* drives our every action, culminates in Flynn's final experiences at death's door. Keats's line from "Ode to a Nightingale"—"I have been half in love with easeful Death"—is utterly relevant, as is the whole Keatsian paradigm. Far removed from the all-conquering, un-self-reflective Buck Rogers type of hero, Calder's protagonists exhibit an emo fatalism that is antithetical to *Star Wars* grandeur, but arguably just as much a part of any probable future. In this, he has learned from the work of Michael Moorcock and Brian Aldiss and perhaps left an heir in comics writer Matt Fraction, whose ongoing series *Casanova* could almost be incorporated into Calder's cosmos.

Sex, sadism, symbolism, and *Sehnsucht*: in *Cythera*, Richard Calder proves that the "S" in SF can stand for many more things than we commonly assume.

—*Paul Di Filippo*

DAGON AND OTHER MACABRE TALES

A series of tales in which human characters confront the bizarre, horrific, and otherworldly

Author: H. P. Lovecraft (1890-1937)
Genre: Fantasy—occult
Type of work: Stories
Time of work: Various times from antiquity to the near future
Locale: Various places around the world and on other planets
First published: 1965 (corrected text of original, 1986)

THE STORY

This collection by perhaps the greatest twentieth century writer of horror fiction was assembled by his fellow fantasy writer, August Derleth, and reissued with a new introduction by T. E. D. Klein in 1986. The stories originally appeared in print between 1917 and 1936. After H. P. Lovecraft's death in 1937, Derleth and his collaborator, Donald Wandrei, wanted to assemble and present in permanent form some of Lovecraft's work that had appeared in pulp magazines such as *Weird Tales*. Lovecraft had often written of the strange research occurring in the library of Arkham University. Derleth and Wandrei therefore chose the name Arkham House for the publishing firm that produced this collection and also saved from oblivion the work of many other horror and fantasy writers.

The typical Lovecraft protagonist finds a shocking and terrifying reality other than the normal that unhinges him, destroys him, or changes his life for the worse. He (the protagonists in this collection are exclusively male) sometimes stumbles over the evidence of another, frightening world, as does the main character of the title story, "Dagon" (1917). After having his ship torpedoed by a German submarine, he finds himself stranded in a strange land with temples dedicated to Dagon, the fish-god. That discovery is unsettling enough, but then the shipwrecked sailor sees fishlike monsters who worship Dagon. Now insane, he tells the story from a San Francisco hospital; hearing a slithery noise outside his door, he leaps out the window to his death.

Even more disturbing are Lovecraft's stories involving characters who are drawn to some discovery or to their doom by some unknown malevolent force. In "The Tomb" (1917), a young man is pulled through his dreams into another time, in which his ancestors lived in a great mansion that had burned to the ground. Driven mad by his obsession, he asks to be buried in a long-locked tomb that bears his name. Sometimes the victim of such an apparent curse is an entire civilization, destroyed by the demon-descendants of an enemy they had conquered a millennium before ("The Doom That Came to Sarnath," 1919).

In Lovecraft's world, the dead do not necessarily stay dead. In "From Beyond" (1920), a scientist invents a machine that sends creatures to and from another dimension, including two of his servants whom he is supposed to have murdered but who cannot be found. In "Herbert West—Reanimator" (1921-1922), a Frankenstein-like experimenter brings corpses back to life, but his ghouls are usually criminally insane. He searches for "fresh" corpses so that the dead can resume their previous lives, but he does so because of his fascination with the power he wields.

In Lovecraft's visions, evil can not be defeated. In story after story, such as "The Lurking Fear" (1922), in which the idiotic descendants of the stunted branch of a family survive as molelike subterranean creatures who forage by night, another world of fear and dread is always there, right behind the door or buried slightly under the ground.

ANALYSIS

Lovecraft is considered second only to Edgar Allan Poe among American writers of horror fantasy. Lovecraft was aware of his debt to Poe and his own position in the tradition of such literature, which he analyzes in "Supernatural Horror in Literature" (1925-1927). Lovecraft's literary career was aroused by his reading of the works of Lord Dunsany (1878-1957) and seeing the British writer when he visited Boston. Lovecraft was also heavily influenced by the style and subjects of the Welsh fantasy writer Arthur Machen (1863-1947). Among the literary techniques that Poe, Dunsany, and Machen perfected and that Lovecraft also used are an elaborate style, a matter-of-fact journalistic format, and a single protagonist pitted against an overwhelming horror.

Lovecraft's style is ornate, deliberate, and loaded with archaisms, features that suggest another view of reality. The style is so balanced and controlled that it lulls the reader into a sense of security. The shattering of that calm when the horrific is encountered causes even more fright than the mere appearance of the terrifying would provoke. Another American predecessor, Nathaniel Hawthorne (1804-1864), used the same device to describe Judge Pyncheon's death in his *The House of the Seven Gables* (1851).

Lovecraft often reveals his horrors as part of a presumed actual adventure recorded in a journal, as did Poe in his *The Narrative of Arthur Gordon Pym* (1838). In a rare venture into science fiction, Lovecraft has an explorer of Venus blandly record his experiences in a daily journal in "In the Walls of Eryx" (1936). The explorer finds an invisible wall and sees one of his comrades dead inside. When he makes his way around the wall to the corpse, strange creatures appear outside the walls. Sooner than the narrator, the reader realizes that the invisible walls are not a maze but a trap in which the first explorer perished. The finality of the narrator's eventual death is underscored by his pragmatic description of his efforts to escape.

The main characters of Lovecraft's stories can never be called heroes in the everyday sense, for their efforts always end in failure. Even if they manage to get away from the fiends they meet, they are psychically maimed for life. In "The Horror at Red Hook" (1925), for example, a detective finds a devil-worshiping cult in an ordinary Brooklyn neighborhood. He escapes with his life, but later the mere sight of buildings that resemble the tenements in which the cult held its worship is enough to bring on a fit of madness.

What makes Lovecraft an artist of the first rank, like his hero, Poe, is the unnerving suggestion in these stories that evil truly exists. These tales are not designed to titillate a bored reader on a dark night. Lovecraft describes the humanoids who stalk his characters as having sloping brows, squat bodies, and a shuffling gait; they are low, slimy, and disgusting. It is as if Lovecraft detested the evolutionary past from which humans came. This identification of evil with the lowest animal nature suggests that it is not somewhere "out there" but instead is within each person.

—*Jim Baird*

THE DANCERS AT THE END OF TIME SERIES

Immortal, nearly omnipotent, and bizarre, the last group of humans searches desperately for new sensations while two lovers move on to a new universe

Author: Michael Moorcock (1939-)
Genre: Fantasy—future history
Type of work: Novels
Time of work: The end of time, with excursions to other periods, principally the 1890's and the Silurian age of the next universe
Locale: Various locations on Earth
First published: *An Alien Heat* (1972), *The Hollow Lands* (1974), *The End of All Songs* (1976), *Legends from the End of Time* (1976; includes "Pale Roses," "White Stars," and "Ancient Shadows," all first published in *New Worlds Quarterly*), and *A Messiah at the End of Time* (1977; British edition published as *The Transformation of Miss Mavis Ming*; *Legends from the End of Time* and *A Messiah at the End of Time* collected as *Tales from the End of Time*, 1989)

THE STORY

An Alien Heat introduces the action that runs through the first three books. At the duke of Queen's dull party, Jherek Carnelian encounters a time traveler from the nineteenth century, Mrs. Amelia Underwood, and decides that falling in love with her would be a welcome novelty to amuse himself and his friends. Jherek first must acquire her from Lord Mongrove's entourage. Helped by Lord Jagged of Canaria, he arranges a trade for the "dreary alien" Yusharisp, who has come there predicting the imminent end of the universe. When Jherek declares his love, Mrs. Underwood will not hear of it; she wishes to teach him virtue. They become closer, but she disappears—stolen by My Lady Charlotina in revenge for the stealing of Yusharisp.

Mrs. Underwood is sent back to 3 a.m., April 4, 1896, as she had desired. Despite the Morphail effect, which prohibits people from staying in the past, Jherek, now truly in love, borrows a time machine and is sent back to the same time. In London, he naïvely joins a den of thieves and is executed for his crimes, only to awaken at the End of Time, still longing for his departed love.

The Hollow Lands introduces the Lat, seven small, one-eyed, oversexed space travelers. Escaping them, Jherek falls into an ancient room full of children minded by a robot nursemaid who recycles time. Nurse sends him to 1896 London, where he meets Frank Harris and H. G. Wells at the Café Royal. Wells takes him to Bromley, where he is reunited with Mrs. Underwood. Mr. Underwood also is there, however, and calls the police. After various adventures, the whole group plus the Lat, My Lady Charlotina, the duke of Queens, Lord Jagged, and the Iron Orchid are reunited at the Café Royal. The Morphail effect and Lord Jagged's time machine send them away, one or a few at a time. Jherek and Mrs. Underwood land in the Silurian age.

Still there at the beginning of *The End of All Songs*, Jherek and Mrs. Underwood are soon joined by police, Mr. Underwood, the Lat, and Una Persson and Oswald Bastable from the Guild of Temporal Adventurers, who send the Underwoods home to the End of Time. Although Mrs. Underwood begins adjusting, peace is not to be. The others reappear, and the temporal dislocations are too much for the cities that supply power and technology. As these collapse, Lord Jagged explains his part in bringing Mrs. Underwood to Jherek, who is revealed to be his son. Nurse has taught Lord Jagged to recycle time, and he proposes to seal off all who want to stay in a constantly recurring week that will last long after the present universe collapses. Harold Underwood and the police return home, but he forbids his wife to accompany him; thus she is free to accept Jherek's proposal. This initiates marriages between Amelia Underwood and Jherek, Lord Jagged and the Iron Orchid, Werther de Goethe and Lord Mongrove, and Mistress Christia and the seven Lat, among others. Amelia, however, believes that existence without duty is useless, and she and Jherek are sent forward to the beginning of the next universe to start life anew.

The action of the other two books takes place concurrently with that of the first three. The books are presented by a twentieth century narrator as fragmentary material brought back by time travelers. "Pale Roses," from *Legends from the End of Time*, shows how Mistress Christia, the Everlasting Concubine, compensates Werther de Goethe for having prematurely destroyed his rainbow by arranging a scenario in which he can experience sin and guilt. "White Stars" involves the reclusive and unimaginative Lord Shark the Unknown, whose only interest is fighting. When the duke of Queens challenges him to a duel to the real death—no resurrection—both are saved only through the unlikely intervention of some militaristic twenty-fourth century soldiers stranded in time. "Ancient Shadows" is the tragedy of Dafnish Armatuce and her son Snuffles, sent to explore the End of Time by the world of the Armatuce and unable to return because of the Morphail effect. Dafnish remains true to her stoic principles, but her son is seduced to luxury by Miss Mavis Ming; in losing their allotted future, each finds disaster. Stranded in time, boring, and unattractive, Miss Ming resides in Doctor Volospion's menagerie. A spaceship arrives, bringing the unattractive Emmanuel Bloom, who announces himself to be "a messiah at the End of Time." Madly in love with Mavis, who fears and despises him, Bloom exchanges a false Holy Grail for her. He whips her severely, which gives her pride in herself and makes her love him. As they take off into space, the real Grail appears, heals their wounds, marries them, and gives them hope and faith.

Analysis

Michael Moorcock was a leader of the British "New Wave" of science fiction in the 1960's and 1970's, both as editor of *New Worlds* and as a writer. This movement emphasized an allusive style, irony, pessimistic plots, and a casual attitude toward sex, all of which the Dancers at the End of Time series exemplifies. Moorcock's "multiverse" (a word he coined in 1965) includes alternate realities for its worlds, which interconnect and adjust and shift in time. Jerry Cornelius is at the center of many of these worlds; Jherek Carnelian is a version of him, and other "Dancers" characters are found in other Moorcock works.

Also present is the British literary world of the late nineteenth century. Poetry by such authors as Ernest Dowson and Alfred Austin contributes titles or is recited by Mrs. Underwood. H. G. Wells and Frank Harris, both perfectly in character, aid the fugitive couple in flight from the police. More generally, twisted memories of the twentieth century and earlier times survive, especially for Jherek, who has specialized in the general period.

Despite their lightheartedness, the works in this series raise serious questions. The characters often seem parallel to real people (readers), enjoying luxuries through dissipating the remaining energy of the universe and not caring what, if anything, comes after themselves.

Introduced into this setting, Mrs. Underwood is both a caricature of Victorian attitudes and a sympathetic person struggling valiantly to maintain her beliefs when they obviously have become obsolete. Shortly before her return to 1896, she talks of her time's belief in stability and eternal standards. Much later, still trying to teach Jherek what morality is, she is overwhelmed by the enormity of her responsibility, wondering whether what she offers is a road to salvation or merely to guilt.

Yusharisp, the gloomy alien, also is paradoxical. His people's refusal to use such conveniences as translation pills marks him as peculiar. His warnings that the final matter of the universe is being used up to create the pleasant illusions of the few surviving humans seem grotesque but are true.

The "legends," too, raise questions and paradoxes. Werther de Goethe is pleased that he has felt guilt strongly enough to commit suicide, Lord Shark learns from a self-interested space trooper that humans can be good, Dafnish Armatuce loses her son through indulging him, and Miss Mavis Ming obtains joy and dignity through suffering and disgust. Is her apotheosis based on spiritual insight, or is it a parody of the worst of masochistic fantasies? Such are the questions that this seemingly absurd series raises.

—*Edra C. Bogle*

THE DARK ELF TRILOGY

An honest, principled dark elf, Drizzt Do'Urben, discovers that he is at odds with his mother, his sisters, and society, so he leaves home to wander the tunnels of the Underdark and eventually travels to the surface to make his home.

Author: R(obert) A. Salvatore (1959–   )
Genre: Fantasy—magical world
Type of work: Novels
Time of work: Indeterminate
Locale: The Underdark drow city of Menzoberranzan, the caverns of the Underdark, and the surface
First published: *Homeland* (1990), *Exile* (1990), and *Sojourn* (1991)

THE STORY

Menzoberranzan, in the Underdark, is a home to the dark elves known as the drow. The drow society is a cruel one dominated by the female drow and their goddess, Lloth, the Spider Queen. One's station is important in drow society, and ambition is prized by Lloth. Houses dominated by the matron mother ascend to importance through assassination and magic. "Don't get caught" is the overriding rule of drow society.

Drizzt is born while the House Do'Urben is eliminating another house to improve its station. Drizzt, a misfit, is honest, unambitious, and compassionate, like his father, Zaknafein, the weapons master. As he matures, Drizzt comes to doubt the stories told to keep the drow in line. As he grows more skilled as a warrior and more dissatisfied with drow society, Drizzt makes friends with a magical cat, Guenhwyvar, and realizes that he will have to leave Menzoberranzan to preserve his honor. Drizzt kills two drow in self-defense, thereby gaining ownership of Guenhwyvar. After discovering that his mother and sisters have sacrificed his father to Lloth to acquire an advantage during the attack on House Hun'ett, Drizzt leaves Menzoberranzan.

Ten years later, the war between House Do'Urben and House Hun'ett ends with House Do'Urben victorious, but House Do'Urben's matron mother, Malice, still is not in Lloth's favor. She can regain Lloth's favor only by punishing Drizzt for his defection. Malice sends her eldest son, Dinin, and her daughter Briza to capture Drizzt, who has been living on his own in the tunnels of the Underdark. Drizzt prevails in the encounter but realizes how savage, isolated, and lonely he has become. He goes to Blingdenstone, home city of the svirfnebli gnomes, and surrenders to assuage his isolation and loneliness. He finds friendship and acceptance with Belwar Dissengulp, whose life he had saved shortly before he had left Menzoberranzan.

Matron Malice animates the corpse of Zaknafein to capture and kill Drizzt. Such zombies must be controlled carefully by the high priestess, who in this case is Malice. Controlling "Zak" proves difficult because he had shared Drizzt's values and friendship. The mission, however, is Malice's last chance to regain favor with Lloth. Zak follows Drizzt's trail, wreaking havoc wherever he goes. The gnomes learn that the havoc involves Drizzt and ask him to leave. When he does, the gnome Belwar, his dear friend, goes with him. They later make friends with a pech who has been transformed into a hooks horror by a human wizard.

Drizzt heads toward Menzoberranzan to find a wizard to reverse the transformation spell put on the pech. The zombie Zak cuts them off and kills Drizzt's transformed friend. Drizzt and Zak fight, and Drizzt reaches Zak's memories. Zak regains control of himself long enough to throw himself into an acid lake. Because Malice has failed to gain favor with Lloth, Briza kills her to protect the family. The House Do'Urben nevertheless is destroyed by the ruling house.

Briza and Dinin are adopted by that house. Although unaware of this development, Drizzt knows that the danger to him and anyone with him is not over. He decides to go to the surface, accompanied only by Guenhwyvar.

After Drizzt moves to the surface, he remains isolated, for two good reasons: He needs time to get acclimated, and he does not speak any language of the surface dwellers. He finally decides to try to communicate with the human farm family living near where he has settled. A barghest whelp massacres the human family and makes it appear as though Drizzt is the culprit. Drizzt avenges the human family after finding the dead bodies, but the human townspeople still believe that Drizzt is the murderer. After killing a bounty hunter's dogs, he fights and scars the bounty hunter, who develops a hatred for him and vows to kill him.

A human ranger called in to hunt Drizzt examines the evidence and concludes that Drizzt is innocent. She believes that Drizzt has avenged the farmers' deaths. Drizzt, who nevertheless feels responsible for the humans' deaths, moves on. He stays in a relatively uninhabited forested area, where he has a minor conflict with an orc tribe. He is saved by a blind ranger, who teaches him about the surface world and the common language. The orc tribe attacks, but Drizzt and the ranger defeat them.

Some time later, the ranger dies. Drizzt wanders about aimlessly. He eventually finds his way to the Icewind Dale, where he settles. The bounty hunter comes to the Icewind Dale looking for Drizzt and annoys the dwarf leader living on a nearby mountain. The bounty hunter is driven away. This is the beginning of the friendship between Drizzt and the dwarves.

ANALYSIS

The Dark Elf trilogy is a prequel to the Icewind Dale trilogy (1988–1990). R. A. Salvatore also continued the story of Drizzt in the books *The Legacy* (1992) and *Starless Night* (1993).

In the Dark Elf trilogy, Salvatore provides the personal history of Drizzt, one of the Icewind Dale heroes. An honest, moral individual, Drizzt is out of place in the dark elf society. He realizes that he does not belong and flees from his city and eventually from the Underdark. He searches for honor and friendship.

This trilogy teaches that honesty and friendship are to be honored and savored. Honesty, principles, and friendship are preferable to anything else, but they must be earned. Drizzt learns that no matter how much he wants to be accepted and to make friends among the surface dwellers, he must prove his good intentions. In addition, he must prove that he is trustworthy before friendship is granted. Once it is, his friends accept and trust him, though others may not. Drizzt's adventures show the necessity both of working at developing positive relationships and of understanding that many people judge others by their appearance.

The trilogy discusses issues of prejudice. When Drizzt leaves Menzoberranzan and begins to encounter other races, he tends to judge them initially according to what he had been taught; he is inclined to believe that they are evil, as his teachers had said. He remembers, however, that he believes the drow are really the evil ones. Following this realization, he evaluates other races and individuals on the basis of their behavior rather than according to preconceived notions.

Other individuals react to him in the same way: They judge him according to the reputation of the drow. He despairs of ever finding a home. His experiences reinforce his inclination to judge others by their behavior rather than by what he has been taught. Until individuals of other races begin to judge him on his behavior, Drizzt has to live apart from them.

Drizzt's failure to make friends has dual causes: the way people react to dark elves and his own lack of self-confidence. This attitude has been instilled in him by his upbringing. Drow males are treated little better than slaves. In addition, Drizzt has been unable to assimilate into drow society. He is inclined to be friendly and to help others rather than to betray them. Because such behavior is uncharacteristic of the drow, he thinks of himself as unworthy of praise.

The Dark Elf trilogy is not only about the difficulties an honorable individual experiences while living in the world but also concerns philosophical questions of religion. When Drizzt is living with the blind ranger, Montolio DeBrouchee, they each talk about their religious beliefs. The blind ranger follows Mielikki, a goddess of nature. Drizzt claims that he follows no god. This, he says, is the result of seeing the evil caused by Lloth.

Montolio contends that Drizzt follows a god but simply does not know that god's name. He argues that a person's god is the name given to those principles in which a person believes. Montolio further contends that the good or evil of a god, or perhaps a religion, is not so much enforced on believers from the outside but instead is an extension of people's principles. In other words, people's behavior fits their nature, and they choose gods who allow that behavior. Drizzt considers this possibility. As he learns more about the ranger and those like him, Drizzt begins to believe Montolio's contention that he has the heart of a ranger and that he follows Mielikki. He later affirms this to himself.

—Sherry Stoskopf

THE DARK IS RISING SEQUENCE

Young people help to collect various talismans of power that will aid the Light in its final, supernatural battle against the Dark

Author: Susan Cooper (1935–)
Genre: Fantasy—high fantasy
Type of work: Novels
Time of work: Primarily the 1960's, with journeys in time to earlier eras
Location: South Cornwall and Buckinghamshire in England; the vicinity of Aberdyfi in North Wales
First published: *Over Sea, Under Stone* (1965), *The Dark Is Rising* (1973), *Greenwitch* (1974), *The Grey King* (1975), and *Silver on the Tree* (1977)

THE STORY
Although she did not initially plan to write a sequence, Susan Cooper found, when she returned to provide a sequel to the first book, not only that she had four more books to write but also that the fantasy element, originally peripheral, had become central. The forces of good and evil, known as the Light and the Dark, are locked in a supernatural struggle for power over humankind. As the sequence title proclaims, the Dark is rising for a final major assault. The books describe how various talismans of power are collected to aid the Light in the impending crisis.

Over Sea, Under Stone begins as an exciting children's adventure story set on the southern coast of

Cornwall during the summer holidays. The three Drew children, Simon, Jane, and Barney, hunt for the Grail and, despite the danger posed by some sinister villains, they eventually find it, although the accompanying manuscript is lost in the sea. Only at the end do they begin to suspect that their mysterious great-uncle Merry, as they call Professor Merriman Lyon, is none other than Merlin.

In *The Dark Is Rising*, the setting shifts to the twelve days of Christmas in a small village in Buckinghamshire. Will Stanton, the seventh son of a seventh son, discovers on his eleventh birthday that he is the last born of the Old Ones, an immortal race with supernatural powers dedicated to the struggle against the Dark. The Old Ones are led by the Lady and Merriman, here in the guise of the butler at the village Manor. Their foes are led by the Dark Rider. Despite fierce resistance from the Dark, wielding the weapons of fear and deceit as well as cold and flood, Will succeeds in his assigned task of gathering the six signs of power. At the novel's conclusion, he releases the Wild Hunt to disperse his enemies.

Greenwitch returns to Cornwall in the spring, bringing together the Drew children, Will Stanton, and Merriman to search once again for the Grail, which has been stolen by the Dark, and for the lost manuscript that will allow them to decipher the writing on the sides of the vessel. Eventually they succeed, but first they must propitiate the Greenwitch, a traditional image of leaves and branches cast into the sea each spring for good luck in fishing and harvest. Like the Wild Hunt, she is part of the Wild Magic, a force distinct from both the Light and the Dark. She gives the manuscript to Jane, who alone has shown her compassion.

In *The Grey King*, Will travels during the Halloween season to his aunt's farm near Aberdyfi in Wales. He wishes to recuperate from a serious illness that has robbed him of some of his memories. His task this time is to find a golden harp that is guarded in a secret cavern by the High Magic, yet another force in the author's magical equation, then to awaken the six Sleepers by playing to them. He is aided by Bran, a strange albino boy who turns out to be the son of King Arthur and Queen Guinevere, brought forward in time by Merriman/Merlin. He is opposed by the Grey King, one of the most powerful lords of the Dark. Working through the malice of petty-minded people as well as his own mighty power, the Grey King causes the death of Bran's dog Cafall and very nearly foils the plans of the Light.

The sequence concludes at Midsummer with *Silver on the Tree*. This novel opens in Buckinghamshire as Will collects the six signs of power from their place of safekeeping so that Merriman can take them back in time to aid King Arthur at the Battle of Badon. The story moves to Aberdyfi, where Will, Bran, and the Drews all meet to search for the Lady. She appears to Jane, to whom she imparts vital directions. Thanks to these and to help from the bard Taliesin, Will and Bran are able to travel back in time to the Lost Land of King Gwyddno, who gives Bran the Crystal Sword. With this, he is able to cut from the midsummer tree the silver blossoms, thereby gaining a final victory for the Light over the assembled powers of the Dark that have been opposing them bitterly at every turn. The Light and the Dark both withdraw, leaving humanity to work out its own fate without external intervention.

ANALYSIS

Susan Cooper has written novels and plays for adults as well as for children, but none has achieved more success than the Dark Is Rising sequence, for younger readers, written early in her career. Three of the books have won awards. *Over Sea, Under Stone* won a competition for a family adventure story held by publisher Jonathan Cape, *The Dark Is Rising* was a 1974 Newbery Honor Book, and *The Grey King* was the 1976 Newbery Award winner.

Among the qualities for which the sequence has gained praise is the powerful sense of double reality of ordinary life, on one hand, and of the realm of High Magic, on the other. In part, this comes from the clearly realized setting, recalled from the author's own childhood, and from the skillful integration of regional legends, such as the stories of Arthur and the drowned lands of King Gwyddno.

The books also recognize the problems that young people must deal with every day, including misunderstandings and disagreements that disrupt even the closest families; hostility and bullying practiced by others of their own age; and impatience, unkindness, and even cruelty of adults too preoccupied with their own concerns to take account of the feelings of others. The results of such problems often are fear, loneliness, and a sense of betrayal that can embitter and destroy. This perpetuates a cycle of darkness that only love can break, a love so strong that it will forgive mistakes and injuries.

This situation finds a striking parallel in the supernatural world, where a struggle is taking place between the Light and the Dark. The latter seeks to gain control over humankind, using as its weapons fear and deceit. Those who give way to anger, prejudice, and self-centeredness, such as Caradog Prichard in *The Grey King* and Mr. Moore in *Silver on the Tree*, become vulnerable to its power, allowing the Dark to grow in strength. Opposed to it is the Light, which endeavors to protect humankind. Although generous and forgiving, the Light can be uncompromising in the sacrifices it requires of its followers. Virtue, after all, is never easy.

The Old Ones are charged with ensuring the preservation of the world from the Dark. At times the struggle may be so close that it leaves little room for acts of charity and mercy, or for protecting a wayward child. Acts of betrayal may have consequences too far-reaching to be overlooked.

Under these circumstances, the young protagonists are expected to assume responsibilities at an earlier age than usual. Their help is needed desperately, and they can be given only limited protection. This leads to a growth in maturity and understanding. Simon abandons his initial resentment of Will, Will comes into his power as an Old One, and Bran discovers his heritage as the Pendragon, heir to his father, King Arthur. These changes come at a price, for they bring not the freedom that young people expect but still heavier burdens. Thus, at the conclusion of the sequence, Bran is free to choose whether to join his father or to remain with his stepfather. Although torn, he decides to stay with the latter, recognizing that loving bonds are the strongest thing on Earth. As a result, he gives up his chance for immortality in the Otherworld beyond time, choosing instead to live and die like all humans. The choice is hard, and what is gained comes at a painfully high cost.

Part of that cost is the alienation as one grows away from the friends and family that surround one in childhood. Twice Will is obliged to erase the memories of beloved brothers who react badly to the discovery of his powers. Bran's special qualities mark him as different, attracting taunts and resentment.

Although the sequence encourages young people to strive to create a better world, it also warns that problems do not end with the end of childhood. Difference still attracts hostility, whatever one's age or station in life, and even the most deserving of aims exacts a price.

—*Raymond H. Thompson*

Dark Universe

Descendants of nuclear war survivors who moved underground must relearn their sense of sight and the nature of the world

Author: Daniel F. Galouye (1920–1976)
Genre: Science fiction—post-holocaust
Type of work: Novel
Time of work: An indeterminate time in the future
Location: Below and on the surface of Earth
First published: 1961

The Story

Dark Universe was the first—and most popular novel—of New Orleans journalist Daniel F. Galouye, although he had been publishing magazine stories since 1952. It was nominated for a Hugo Award.

The story is seen—or, rather, heard—by young Jared Fenton, whose primitive people live in total darkness and think of Light as a dimly remembered religious deity. They are preyed on by zivvers, other underground humans whose eyes have adapted to provide limited sight in the infrared spectrum, and "monsters" that inspire fear because they cause people to disappear and because they use light, which is alien to Jared's people.

Jared is the son of his tribe's ruler, the Prime Survivor. He is pressured into an arranged marriage (or "unification") with Della, the niece of another tribe's leader, to unite the tribes against the zivvers. Della has developed the zivver ability and, because Jared is exceptionally gifted at sensing people or objects by vibrations from sound echoes, believes he is secretly a zivver also. She persuades him to flee with her to the zivver group, which Jared has been seeking for his own reasons: He believes that Light is a natural phenomenon and that he might learn its nature through the zivvers.

Eventually, the young couple become outcasts and fugitives from both groups. Jared's people also decide that he is a zivver and therefore an enemy. The zivvers test him and discover that he is not one of them. He and Della fall into the hands of the monsters, who are revealed to be descendants of survivors from underground shelters who are now reinhabiting Earth's surface, which has purified itself. The two tribes and the zivvers from Jared's underground world have also sprung from a survival group, but something has gone wrong in their complex. They have lost their artificial light and, gradually, all knowledge of their origins. The monsters have been kidnapping them, a few at a time, and reeducating them.

Still not fully understanding or accepting the explanation, Jared escapes and makes his way to the surface. He realizes the truth of what he has been told and looks forward to a new life in a new world with Della.

ANALYSIS

The paperback original employs a theme that would dominate Galouye's work: distorted perceptions of reality. In this case, without ever stating it overtly and keeping entirely to the point of view of his protagonist, Galouye is able to establish his nonvisual setting within the first two pages and show how Jared and other characters have adapted to it. He tells nearly the entire story without resorting to the visual sense—no small feat—but never loses the reader.

Nuclear war was a concept familiar to science-fiction readers even before the first atomic weapons were used in 1945, to the extent that editor Horace Gold announced in the January, 1952, issue of *Galaxy* that he would no longer buy "atomic doom" stories for his magazine. Such stories continued to be written, though, some of the best known being Walter M. Miller, Jr.'s *A Canticle for Leibowitz* (1960), Mordecai Roshwald's *Level 7* (1959), and Pat Frank's *Alas, Babylon* (1959), all showing the aftermath of nuclear destruction. Neville Shute's *On the Beach* (1957; filmed in 1959) familiarized the general public as well.

It becomes obvious to most readers how Jared's people came to be in their situation, especially when Strontium and Cobalt are deified as demons, Radiation is described as a kind of hell, and Hydrogen is named as the devil. One religious tenet holds that the presence of Light Almighty in Paradise made it possible for people to know what lay ahead without smelling or hearing it. Jared is accused of being blasphemous when he suggests that there may be natural explanations for these concepts and that Light is something attainable in this life.

It is fascinating to follow Jared's reasoning as he presses his inquiries, especially considering that most readers already know the answers. One breakthrough comes when he finds that the "roaring silence" that emanates from the monsters, which is how the survivors perceive their lights, is cut off when he closes his eyes and that it is not coming through his ears after all.

The book also includes the science-fictional concepts of extrasensory powers (one of the survivors has developed telepathy), genetic mutations from radiation (sou-bats are giant and marauding descendants of cave bats), and immortality (in the elderly Forever Man, who lived in the prewar surface world and understood Light but has suppressed those memories over generations and withdraws into himself when Jared tries to awaken them).

Galouye is thorough in showing how his underground people have adapted to their environment, sometimes with amusing results. The word "hear" is substituted routinely for "see." Reference is made to the "holy bulb" as a source of Light, which is likened to God. The words "Light!" and "Radiation!" are used as expletives. A courtesy between two strangers is the Ten Touches, which give each an idea of what the other is like. The worst offenses that can be committed are murder and "misplacement of bulky objects."

Dark Universe, although it has a more upbeat ending than most novels in the nuclear armageddon lineage, is very much a part of that heritage, which includes such works as Philip K. Dick's *Dr. Bloodmoney: Or, How We Got Along After the Bomb* (1965), Harlan Ellison's "A Boy and His Dog" (1969), and David Brin's *The Postman* (1985). Its well-realized underground world sets it apart from those that preceded and followed it.

—*Paul Dellinger*

Darker than You Think

Will Barbee is at first bewildered and horrified by an emerging strangeness in himself but comes to accept being a werewolf.

Author: Jack Williamson (1908-2006)
Genre: Fantasy—extrasensory powers
Type of work: Novel
Time of work: About 1950
Locale: Clarendon, a small town in the United States
First published: 1948 (serial form, *Unknown*, 1940)

The Story

Dr. Lamarck Mondrick, a famous anthropologist, has just returned to the United States from the Gobi Desert with a mysterious box, the contents of which purportedly hold the key to humankind's struggle between good and evil. Among journalists covering the anthropologist's return is the protagonist, Will Barbee, who is both a close personal friend and a former member of Mondrick's research team. Mondrick dies mysteriously while attempting to deliver a warning of a menace to the human race.

As the story progresses, researchers Nick Spivak and Sam Quain employ increasingly tight security measures to protect themselves and the mysterious box they guard, but to no avail. Spivak and Quain know that Barbee is, at the very least, genetically predisposed to be a werewolf. Rowena Mondrick, the anthropologist's widow, knows for certain that Barbee is a deadly threat to her and the other two. She nevertheless has a true affection toward him. In the last chapter of the novel, author Jack Williamson reveals that she is Barbee's mother.

By day, Barbee tries to find out who is doing the killing and why. By night, he is a werewolf who participates in the killing. The daytime Barbee is aware only on the subconscious level of the activities of the nighttime Barbee. During the day, he falls in love with a beautiful, young, redheaded journalist, April Bell, who also is assigned to the Mondrick case. At night, she becomes a werewolf who has little difficulty getting Barbee to do most of the killing for her.

The second, dominant, aspect of the plot is purely psychological. The human (good) side of Barbee battles the werewolf (evil) side for the ultimate possession of his soul. One side is destined to prevail. As events unfold, Barbee is shown to be literally the messiah the werewolves of the world have been hoping for, the one they have named in advance "The Child of Darkness." Barbee does not know this and does not even fully comprehend that he is, in fact, a werewolf. His gradual self-realization is the main focus of the book. At the conclusion, having (sometimes reluctantly) participated in the killing of all the members of Mondrick's research team and his own mother, Barbee fully accepts himself as a werewolf and thus as evil.

Analysis

Jack Williamson occupies a unique position in science fiction. Born in 1908, he sold his first published work to Hugo Gernsback's *Amazing Stories* for $25 in 1928. From that day, he was committed to a lifetime of writing science fiction.

As a student of psychology, nuclear physics, and later linguistics, he always infuses science and technology into his fiction. It is difficult to call him innovative, but he has always been a prominent figure in American science fiction and has been a respected peer and personal acquaintance of Robert A. Heinlein, Isaac Asimov, and many others.

Williamson sold the original version of *Darker than You Think* to *Unknown* in 1940. In 1948, he rewrote the book as a novel and sold it to Fantasy Press. It did not sell particularly well but has been reprinted several times. The book has always been well known among the science-fiction *cognoscenti*, but it is difficult to claim that it has "classic" status, though some blurbs have gone so far as to call it the finest werewolf story. What sets the book apart from others is its ending: Not only does the werewolf side of the character prevail, but the protagonist, Barbee, also accepts himself as a werewolf, which implies that he regards himself as an enemy of humankind. Being a werewolf in Williamson's anthropology is not merely a matter of having an irresistible thirst for human blood, nor is it a mere character flaw. If humans have werewolf genes, they are evil in proportion to the amount of tainted blood in their veins.

Although werewolf stories generally are regarded as being in the realm of fantasy, science and technology are essential to Williamson's depiction of werewolves in at least two ways. First, there is the matter of how werewolves can change shapes, transport themselves across spaces, and literally pass through walls. Williamson offers a detailed explanation for these actions. The key to their ability is quantum physics, particularly the uncertainty principle. Walls, even steel walls, are not precisely solid but instead are composed of an arrangement of molecules, constantly in motion, with empty spaces between them. Williamson's extrapolation of this principle, as applied to werewolves, endows werewolves with a "mental web" with which they can realign the molecular structure of an object in order to pass through it. The shape-shifting capability of werewolves also is based on this ability to completely separate the mind, with its "mental web," from the body and transport it at will. Williamson's second extrapolation of known science involves the mysterious weapon in the box, which can destroy all werewolves. Apparently, this weapon is a disk of highly radioactive uranium. It is worth noting that Williamson worked at Los Alamos as an Army weatherman during the war years.

Science has since shown that Williamson's extrapolated events are not possible. He was using the scientific knowledge of his time as the basis for projecting the future, in the same way that H. G. Wells used a giant cannon to fire manned spaceships into space in *The First Men in the Moon* (1908) and many other authors have used the known science of their day to describe the impossible or not yet possible.

—*John T. West III*

DARKOVER LANDFALL

After a starship from Earth crashes on an unmapped planet, crew and colonists survive by building a new society based on native resources and psychic powers

Author: Marion Zimmer Bradley (1930–1999)
Genre: Science fiction—alien civilization
Type of work: Novel
Time of work: The twenty-first century
Locale: The planet Darkover
First published: 1972

THE STORY
Marion Zimmer Bradley wrote *Darkover Landfall* to explain the origins of the people and culture of her created world of Darkover, the setting of numerous books. After a starship crashes, its surviving crew and passengers are stranded on an unknown planet. Repair of the ship, a tenuous hope at best, becomes impossible when someone erases its computer programs during a hallucinatory "ghost wind" episode. A survey group discovers alien life, including two reclusive humanoid races. The planet has terrible weather, poor soil, few metals, and mysterious psi phenomena, but it can support human life. Building a low-technology society on this strange planet is an unappealing prospect to many from the ship. As the book ends, however, households and basic crafts, as well as the colony's first children, are flourishing.

Rafael MacAran, a geologist, leads the initial survey party. Romantically linked with First Officer Camilla Del Rey, he is able to follow a hunch to locate her when a sudden blizzard hits. This paves the way for using extrasensory gifts as technology. As a scientist, MacAran understands the captain's initial impulse to repair the ship and his wish to save technical knowledge for future generations. He also appreciates the planet's rugged beauty, however, and the logic of the New Hebrides commune's simple lifestyle. These conflicts are heightened for him because Camilla, space-born and -bred, has difficulty accepting the loss of her profession and of the ship.

Two thousand years pass before the colony's descendants are rediscovered by the Terran Empire. During that time, Darkovans develop a feudal society dominated by families with hereditary psi talents. The other Darkover novels take place in this subsequent Darkovan history. Most are set during an era of rapid cultural change after rediscovery, but three—*Stormqueen!* (1978), *Two to Conquer* (1980), and *Hawkmistress!* (1982)—

take place in the Darkovan dark ages, or "time of the hundred kingdoms."

The plots and themes vary, but most of the Darkover novels contain motifs introduced in *Darkover Landfall*. *The World Wreckers* (1971) tells of technology run amok on the fragile planet. Camilla Del Rey's unwanted motherhood and lost career are a distant mirror image for Callista's anguish in *The Forbidden Tower* (1977), when her Keeper's training makes her chosen marriage almost impossible.

Laran, or extrasensory gifts, that empower also can destroy. The need for telepathic training and ethics is a frequent story element. From *Stormqueen!*'s young heroine, whose anger summons lightning bolts, to the arcane battle that ends *Sharra's Exile* (1981), laran is central to the novels' plots.

The Heritage of Hastur (1975) is a powerful coming-of-age novel. Young nobles Regis Hastur, Lew Alton, and Danilo Syrtis try to reconcile the demands of duty and class with inner desires. Along the way, a city is blown up, with weighty consequences for the planet's future. *The Shattered Chain* (1976) and *Thendara House* (1983) are novels that address women's issues. The young Darkovan Jaelle and the Terran intelligence agent Magda change roles and find new paths, while Jaelle's aunt, Lady Rohana, after trying independent life with the Free Amazons, returns to home and husband with new, inner strength.

ANALYSIS
Darkover Landfall's structure is unusual. The exciting events and discoveries occur early; the last half of the book is an extended study of the colonists' efforts to cope with them. Appropriate technology, a frequent series theme, is a survival issue in this novel. Within this framework, Bradley suggests that reproductive choice and, perhaps, women's autonomy are luxuries made possible by high technology. Camilla is refused an abortion because the fragile settlement needs every baby that can be brought to term. This episode created furor within feminist science fiction. Joanna Russ wrote *We Who Are About To . . .* (1977), whose castaway protagonist chooses death over forced childbearing, in reply. Bradley's argument is about the contingency of social rights, however, rather than being an antiabortion statement.

Although *Darkover Landfall* occurs earliest in the planet's history, it is not the best introduction to the series. A reader unfamiliar with Darkover will not link its events with the resulting customs and myths. For example, Camilla is memorialized in Darkovan religion as a consort of Hastur, a demigod. The legend distorts her life, but it retains traces of falling from the stars and of sacrifice. Bradley suggests the early young adult books *Star of Danger* (1965) and *The Planet Savers* (1962) as good starting points. Another good introduction is the revised *The Bloody Sun* (1979). A pivotal novel in the series, it opens with a scene recognizable to any science-fiction reader—a spaceforce man fearing that his weird reactions to the planet will cost him his career. This leads into a rich brew of love, intrigue, and mystery built around his emerging laran powers.

The series became very popular and has inspired an active fandom, including younger writers who have gone on to turn their own worlds into published series. Darkover novels use fantasy staples, such as swordplay and psychic duels, as well as a depth of characterization almost unique in science fiction. Even secondary characters are three-dimensional. The plots often turn on issues such as gender roles and ecology. Under the red sun of Darkover, these take on new dimensions, and the solutions are seldom simple or ideologically pure. Most plot lines carry a subtext that every decision exacts its own costs.

Few fiction or nonfiction writers have looked as closely at psychic powers—their forms, effects, and costs—as Bradley does in the Darkover novels. The sheer exoticism of Darkovan laran, with its mysterious blue starstones and powerful matrix networks, also draws readers to the series. Laran usually is treated as a form of technology, sometimes as a metaphor for power, and sometimes as a metaphor for personal or ethical sensitivity. The latter symbolism has not been successful, as Darkovan telepaths appear to behave no more ethically than anyone else.

Many Darkover novels have been nominated for Hugo or Nebula awards. Bradley ranks among major science-fiction writers largely because of this unique body of work.

—*Emily Alward*

DAVY

Davy recounts his development from an ignorant boy into a freethinking adult and his attempt to bring enlightenment to his postholocaust civilization

Author: Edgar Pangborn (1909-1976)
Genre: Science fiction—post-holocaust
Type of work: Novel
Time of work: The twenty-fourth or twenty-fifth century
Location: New England, the Atlantic Ocean, and the Azores
First published: 1964

The Story

Davy's coming-of-age story is not unique to science fiction, and Edgar Pangborn has no use for typical science-fictional devices such as spaceships and ray guns. Nevertheless, *Davy* is science fiction because of its vivid future world. In the late twentieth century—the "Old Time"—nuclear holocaust, plagues, and increases in world temperature and ocean levels destroyed human civilization. After about a hundred years, in the vast wilderness of what once was New England, a new civilization began to grow, a collection of small, bellicose countries dominated by the Holy Murcan Church, an organization forbidding books, free thought, gunpowder, and atoms. Because the Old Time people squandered the world's resources and the remnants of humanity have lost the Old Time science, the fragile civilization is ignorant and superstitious.

In the year 331 of this transformed world, Davy, at the age of twentyeight, begins writing several intertwining stories: his growth to manhood, his relationship with his wife, their attempt to enlighten the benighted age, their founding of a colony, and the history of his era. The most compelling conflict in *Davy* next to that between enlightenment versus ignorance is Davy's struggle to tell his stories honestly and effectively.

Red-haired Davy was born in a whorehouse, reared in an orphanage, and bonded out as a yardboy for a tavern. At the age of fourteen, he runs away, in the process accidentally committing his first homicide, having sex for the first time, and stealing an Old Time French horn. Thus begin Davy's picaresque adventures.

With help from the fascinating people he meets as he journeys through his wild world, Davy learns to play his horn, loses his religious superstitions, and becomes a free-thinking and loving person. Davy first joins company with Jed Sever, a sensitive and pious giant; Sam Loomis, a laconic loner; and Vilet, a sensual prostitute. After several adventures, including a comic scene with a "quackpot" medium and a tragic scene with a tiger, Davy and Sam join Rumley's Ramblers. The Ramblers are a communal troupe of independent entertainers who travel through the New England territories performing music and plays, selling homemade cure-alls, and passing along news.

When Davy leaves the Ramblers after several years, he meets and marries Nickie, a "sweet pepperpot" noblewoman who belongs to the Society of Heretics, an underground organization that promotes enlightenment and resists the church's dogma. Through Nickie, Davy meets her cousin Dion, Regent of Nuin. Nickie and Dion educate Davy in Old Time literature and ideas, and Davy and Nickie help Dion try to drag their country out of the dark ages. Their heretical ideas, such as abolishing slavery and promoting free education, meet with disapproval from the Holy Murcan Church, which foments a rebellion. The Heretics lose the war and flee Nuin on a ship into the unknown waters of the Atlantic. It is during this voyage and subsequent establishing of a colony in the Azores that Davy begins to write his book. The novel concludes with Davy setting sail to continue lovingly exploring the uncharted territories of world and mind.

Analysis

A plot summary of *Davy* neglects one of the novel's pleasures and important themes: the richness of the English language. Davy and Pangborn love language, from coarse prose to beautiful poetry, and the novel reflects that love. Davy often sets off on delightful Melvillean digressions on such topics as bedbugs. Additionally, a transformed language adds flavor to his narration. The transformed language appears in neologisms (mahooha), portmanteaus (prezactly), contracted forms (Febry), and distorted forms (sack-religion). Even cultural icons appear changed: Davy's world has a

Saint George Washington. Pangborn uses such language to engage the intellect, make readers laugh, and show how fragments of civilization persist through time, transformed to suit new ages.

Pangborn returned to the world of *Davy* in *The Judgment of Eve* (1966), *The Company of Glory* (1975), and short stories such as those collected in *Still I Persist in Wondering* (1978). *Davy*, written in the middle of his career, is Pangborn's most defining and enduring work. *Davy* was runner-up for the 1965 Hugo Award for best science-fiction novel and placed on the 1972 *Locus* poll for best novel of all time. Critical opinion of *Davy* is favorable. George Zebrowski writes that *Davy* "is one of the lasting works of SF," and Spider Robinson says that "reading *Davy* has measurably and significantly, and for the better, changed my life."

Davy is part of the tradition of post-holocaust novels in which human civilization is portrayed as cyclic and, despite human folly, inextinguishable, from George R. Stewart's *Earth Abides* (1949) to Russell Hoban's *Riddley Walker* (1980). *Davy* also belongs to the tradition of science fiction that emphasizes humanistic concerns such as love, tolerance, inner growth, art, and psychology, rather than technological dreams. Pangborn's contributions to these traditions are his combination of loving humanism, rich language, an expansive view of life, self-reflexive narration, and playful humor. Describing a sunrise scene of ethereal beauty, for example, *Davy* shows a pair of monkeys copulating in a tree. If *Davy* can be summed up with one word, it would be the term of endearment between lovers in the novel: "spice."

In the above traits, *Davy*, like almost all of Pangborn's fiction, transcends its genre. It also recalls fiction such as Henry Fielding's *Tom Jones* (1749) and Mark Twain's *Adventures of Huckleberry Finn* (1884). The richly realized setting; the many vivid and unforgettable characters; the intertwined earthiness and sublimity, beauty and filth, and comedy and tragedy; and the powerful theme that people must light fires—both smaller and larger than the sun—in human minds and hearts all make *Davy* one of the best novels of any genre.

—*Jefferson M. Peters*

THE DAY OF THE TRIFFIDS

Almost everyone on Earth is blinded by an apparent meteor shower, and a species of plant called triffids, which are mobile and intelligent, take over most of the planet

Author: John Wyndham (1903–1969)
Genre: Science fiction—catastrophe
Type of work: Novel
Time of work: The mid-to late twentieth century
Locale: London and parts of southern England
First published: 1951

THE STORY

For years, humans have been cultivating a mysterious species of plant called the triffid because the oil and juice extracted from the plant make excellent cattle feed and are profitable for business. The origins of the seven-foot-high triffids are obscure, but the plant appears to have been the result of human biological experimentation. After their first appearance, triffids quickly spread all over the world and also developed the ability to pull up their roots and walk. They possess a venomous sting that is often fatal to humans. A few people even believe the plants are intelligent and able to communicate with one another.

Narrator William Masen, a biologist and triffid expert, is recovering in the hospital from a triffid sting to the eyes. He awakes one morning to an eerie silence. Removing his eye bandages, he leaves his room to investigate and discovers that everyone in the hospital is blind. He goes outside and sees blind people creeping along the streets.

The cause of the near-universal blindness is obvious. The previous day, a comet apparently passed near Earth, and the debris from it filled the sky with bright green flashes. Almost everyone watched the greatest-ever fireworks display, with disastrous results.

As he traverses the city, Masen rescues a young sighted woman, Josella Playton, from the clutches of a blind man. Masen sees triffids on the prowl and decides to leave London. He and Playton join a group of mostly sighted people, led by Michael

Beadley, who are planning to set up a new community. This group refuses to help the many thousands of blind; they look to the future and decide to build a self-sufficient community that will preserve the race. Their plans are interrupted by a group led by the sighted Wilfred Coker, who feels a responsibility to help the blind. Coker's group kidnaps Masen and Playton. Each is put in charge of a group of blind people, assigned to an area of London, and instructed to keep everyone alive until help comes (from America, many assume). A plague breaks out and leaves few in Masen's group alive.

Masen later contacts Coker, who has realized the futility of his plan, and they decide to follow the Beadley group, whose members have headed to a location west of London. Masen also wants to search for Playton. The Beadley group proves elusive, but the two men stumble on a community, most of whose members are blind, run by the evangelical Miss Denning, who lacks the organizational skills to succeed but is too proud to admit it.

Masen leaves and finally is reunited with Playton at a farmhouse in Sussex. For six years, Masen, Playton, and three blind people run the farm and keep themselves alive in reasonable comfort. As essential supplies dwindle, however, the future looks bleak, and the triffids present a growing menace. The plants continually encroach on the farm and are kept back only by an electrified fence. The farm group eventually is contacted by the Beadley community, which has established itself on the Isle of Wight, a small island off the southern coast of England. Their community is more promising than the alternative, an authoritarian group of survivors who promote a kind of feudal system with the blind as serfs. The Isle of Wight community thrives and plans one day, through research conducted by Masen, to find a way of reclaiming the mainland, which has been taken over by triffids.

ANALYSIS

John Wyndham acknowledged that the most fundamental influence on his work was H. G. Wells, particularly works such as *The Time Machine* (1895) and *The War of the Worlds* (1898). The influence of the latter on *The Day of the Triffids* is easy to see. Each story is told in the first person by a man who reports the disaster as a piece of recent history. Both stories take place in or near London, and Wyndham, like Wells, grounds his fantasy in everyday reality by emphasizing exact topographical details. The disaster itself, an unusual cosmic event in which no one senses any danger, is common to both stories, and both Wells and Wyndham emphasize how the catastrophe shatters human complacency and its naïve faith in the durability and invincibility of its own civilization.

Several of Wyndham's characters resemble those in Wells's story of Martian invasion. Those who cling to old rules of thought and behavior meet with disaster, including the curate in *The War of the Worlds* and the moralistic Miss Denning and the postdisaster community she attempts to found in *The Day of the Triffids*. The prototypes of Wyndham's visionaries, such as Coker and Beadley, are reminiscent of Wells's artilleryman, who quickly grasps the new situation and makes plans for the survival of humanity.

Like Wells's novel, *The Day of the Triffids* is a pessimistic view of evolution and natural selection. Because of its new blindness, humankind is no longer adapted to survive, and mastery passes to the triffids, who previously were inferior to humans only because humans could see and triffids could not. After the human calamity, the triffids are in a superior position because they are adapted to sightlessness.

Unlike in Wells's story, however, Wyndham attributes the catastrophe to human folly. The meteor shower was not a naturally occurring event but the result of a malfunctioning satellite that was equipped to wage biological warfare, and the triffids themselves resulted from human manipulation of nature.

Wyndham's novel ends on a note of hope. Even though science allied to human recklessness has created the catastrophe, science may yet devise a way to triumph over the triffids. The Beadley community, founded on rational and scientific principles, offers more hope for a future resurgence of humanity than the feudal, authoritarian, or religious systems that other groups of survivors attempt.

Some critics prefer the revised British version of *The Day of the Triffids*, also published in 1951. The story was filmed in 1963.

—*Bryan Aubrey*

THE DEAD FATHER

A band of brothers drag their father's animated corpse cross-country to bury it and, they hope, end its power over them

Author: Donald Barthelme (1931-1989)
Genre: Fantasy—high fantasy
Type of work: Novel
Time of work: Unspecified
Locale: An unspecified place on Earth
First published: 1975

THE STORY

Prior to publication of *The Dead Father*, the self-contained "Manual for Sons," which appears within chapter 17 and has, mirroring the novel, twenty-three chapters of its own, had appeared in slightly different form in *The New Yorker*. This manual contains the central themes of the novel: the power of the patriarch, its unending influence on the lives of his progeny, the sexual rivalry between fathers and sons, and sons' subconscious fantasies of patricide. The novel revolves around the title character's surreal funeral procession. Nineteen of his sons serve as pallbearers, but instead of carrying an inanimate corpse in a coffin a short distance to a grave, they pull his 3,200-cubits-long, still active body along a cable for several days until they reach the grave. The novel comprises the events and conversations that take place during their journey.

Before the Dead Father can be buried, his powers must be stripped from him and passed on to someone else. His oldest son, Thomas, in spite of his insistence otherwise, seems to hope to receive the legacy of power. He leads the party, along with his alcoholic brother Edward and two women, Julie and Emma. Although the Dead Father goes along willingly on the journey, he contests the usurpation of his power by Thomas, who confiscates first the Dead Father's belt buckle, later his sword, and finally his keys, all symbols of his sexual virility and patriarchal power. The Dead Father tries to counter his son's actions with the seduction of Julie, who is Thomas' lover, and later of Emma, but he fails with both women and is thereby further humiliated by this devastating evidence of his impotence. His consolation, however, is his belief that "a son can never, in the fullest sense, become a father."

The Dead Father believes—or deceives himself into believing—that he is on a quest for the golden fleece, which will rejuvenate him. The golden fleece is revealed to be Julie's pubic hair. He has not been allowed to touch it and is still not allowed to touch it even after recognizing it as that which he seeks. On realizing the futility of his quest for new life, the Dead Father resigns himself to his true fate—death—and lies down in his grave, a more human and thus more sympathetic character than he had appeared to be previously in the novel.

ANALYSIS

The fantastic elements of the novel lead the reader to contemplate its allegorical nature. Critics have read it as a novel about the generation gap between fathers and sons and, more broadly, about the end of one era and the beginning of another. Clearly, Donald Barthelme is drawing on Freudian psychology as he depicts the tyranny of fathers and patricidal desires of sons. He also is analyzing the ideological gap between the World War II generation and the Vietnam War generation. As in Ernest Hemingway's "Big Two-Hearted River," there is no mention of either war in Barthelme's novel, but the context emerges from Thomas' rejection of his father's tyrannical rule. Barthelme seems to have perceived that such rebellion would not last after members of the younger generation tasted power themselves; indeed, once Thomas begins to move into the position of authority, his rejection of "the system" softens and his behavior, particularly his cruel treatment of his father, begins to remind the reader of the Dead Father's actions. Recalling to the reader how the Dead Father goes on a killing spree every time his wishes are thwarted by Thomas, Thomas tells about a dream in which he discovered the secret of patriarchal power: having the choice to murder or not to murder.

The novel seems also to be a postmodern retelling of T. S. Eliot's *The Waste Land* (1922), which reveals that the postmodern world ultimately is not much different from the modern world. As in *The Waste Land*, for example, sexual relations in Barthelme's novel are often in some way perverted and are never regenerative. There is no instance of consummation in the novel, only a lot of titillation (watching pornographic movies and fondling others, for example); consequently, there will be no regeneration. It may be, however, that Barthelme is suggesting that the Dead Father (the old rule) must be laid to rest before there can be any new life. Although Thomas curbs his father's sexuality by refusing to allow him to watch the pornographic movies or consort with either of the women, he also curtails his own sexuality to some extent, not consummating his relationship with Julie, for example, until after his father is buried. Perhaps he is abstaining in deference to his father, or perhaps it is because he is intimidated by the memory of his father's former virility. Whatever the reason, the rain at the end of the novel, like the rain at the end of *The Waste Land*, suggests a potential for rejuvenation now that the Dead Father is buried. Thomas is free to consummate a relationship and be a father himself.

As the Dead Father has warned, however, Thomas will never be able to forget or live up to his father's memory. In addition, he and his brothers may be consumed by guilt for having wished their father dead. Thus, in spite of his earlier rejection of his father's ways, one can see by Thomas' recent behavior that he will try to bring his father back to life by emulating him. Barthelme's final message seems, then, to be that nothing changes. Power corrupts, and memory disrupts the ideals of youth.

—*Margaret D. Bauer*

THE DEAD ZONE

Johnny Smith's parapsychic abilities aid in the capture of a serial killer and thwart the plans of a politician who would have launched an atomic war

Author: Stephen King (1947–)
Genre: Science fiction—extrasensory powers
Type of work: Novel
Time of work: 1953–1979
Locale: Fictional Cleaves Mills and Castle Rock, Maine, and other New England sites
First published: 1979

THE STORY

Skating on the ice of Runaround Pond in Durham, Maine, in 1953, six-year-old Johnny Smith is knocked senseless when Chuck Spier, an older, heavier, hockey player, accidentally crashes into him. As Spier tends to Johnny, semiconscious Johnny warns him to stay away from black ice. Awakening with only a headache, Johnny forgets the incident. Shortly afterward, while Chuck is jump-starting his car, his battery explodes, blinding him in one eye. Although Johnny is unaware of it for years, this was the first manifestation of his parapsychic powers, powers that provide the matrix for Stephen King's *The Dead Zone*. The title derives from the limits on Johnny's powers, the gaps in his life that he can neither see nor remember, the "faulty circuitry" that sets the scene for mystery.

Johnny's parapsychic abilities reappear in 1970, after he and his girlfriend, Sarah Bracknell, have graduated from college and are teaching at Cleaves Mills High School. Johnny takes Sarah to a fair, plays a wheel of fortune intuitively knowing that he will win, and wins $540. He also has a premonition of disaster, however, involving black ice and burning rubber. Sarah becomes ill, and after Johnny drops her at home, he takes a cab back to Cleaves Mills. Dragsters crash head-on into his cab, killing the driver. Hospitalized, Johnny sinks into a coma that lasts four and a half years, from which he is not expected to emerge. Meanwhile, Sarah marries and has a child, Johnny's mother dies, a strangler terrifies Castle Rock and adjacent towns with his serial murders, and the villainous Greg Stillson, a violent and sleazy former Bible salesman, becomes mayor of Castle Rock, whetting his unslakable political ambitions.

Before he is through with reconstructive surgery and therapy, Johnny, who has gained notoriety as a latter-day Rip Van Winkle and then as a psychic charlatan, gives further evidence of his powers. He intuits where Sarah may find her lost wedding rings, warns a nurse that her house is on fire, and predicts a terrible roadhouse catastrophe. Then, by absorbing images and textures at a crime scene, Johnny identifies the strangler for Castle Rock's Sheriff Bannerman. The killer is an upstanding policeman.

Subsequently, Johnny crosses paths with Greg Stillson, who has entered the presidential race. Johnny perceives that the power-mad Stillson will start a nuclear war and determines to shoot him. The assassination goes awry, but in the process, Stillson grabs a baby to shield himself, an act of cowardice that effectively destroys his political career. Johnny flees, works with a road crew in New Hampshire, and is soon diagnosed as having a brain tumor. His last words are recorded in letters to his father and to Sarah explaining why he no longer wishes to live.

ANALYSIS

By the mid-1990's, King had published twenty-one gothic or horror novels and become one of America's all-time best-selling writers. A number of King's works have been translated into highly successful films, among them *Carrie* (1974), *The Shining* (1977), and *Pet Sematary* (1983). Readers and critics alike generally acknowledge King to be the master of modern gothic and horror fiction.

Paranormal, parapsychic, and telekinetic phenomena that furnish the plot for *The Dead Zone* have always interested King and figured in *Carrie*, *The Shining*, and other King novels. These phenomena, however, are only devices that King employs to explore aspects of the subject that suffuses nearly all of his writing: the omnipresence of evil, evil to which most people would rather turn a blind eye. The evil that Johnny Smith pursues is embodied first in the respected police officer, a man Sheriff Bannerman likes so much that he is reluctant to acknowledge the weight of Smith's evidence. Similarly, the evil embodied in Greg Stillson marked every step of his life: kicking a defenseless dog to death while selling Bibles, menacing and humiliating a youth who wore a T-shirt with an obscene logo, terrifying the town banker into bankrolling his political campaign, importing thugs to act as his guards in Castle Rock, and, finally, his mad political tactics. Exposure of these evils, as King implicitly emphasizes throughout the novel, need not have awaited Johnny Smith's parapsychic endowments, for the evil was almost apparent. Stillson might have been thwarted, for example, by the Castle Rock banker whom Stillson terrified into aiding him.

Although such a theme—that evil exists as a real entity aside from failings in human character—is a familiar one to King's readers, it is not dealt with as effectively in *The Dead Zone* as in his other writing. At times, *The Dead Zone* seems to have been conceived, rather awkwardly, as two stories that were then melded together: the search for the Castle Rock strangler and the attempt to thwart the ambitions of Stillson. The book is interesting, but *The Dead Zone*'s principal characters are merely symbols of good or evil rather than full-bodied figures. Like many King novels, this one will strike many as overwritten and padded. For example, King recites national and international events to mark the passage of years while Smith is in a coma.

King compensates for these technical flaws with his trademark ability to move the story forward by means of engaging descriptions of the commonplaces of life. Few writers manage better than King to retain readers' interest by regaling them with the ordinary. King forcefully conveys his conviction that, in what he sees as a highly unstable and irrational world, deductive reasoning cannot always, or even often, prevail.

—*Clifton K. Yearley*

A DEAL WITH THE DEVIL

A one-hundred-year-old man gives his soul to Satan in exchange for ten years of life, during which he becomes progressively younger until, at death, he is a newborn baby

Author: Eden Phillpotts (1862-1960)
Genre: Science fiction—cautionary
Type of work: Novel

Time of work: The late nineteenth and early twentieth centuries
Locale: Great Britain
First published: 1895

THE STORY

Among the many dissipations of Daniel Dolphin's unprincipled and profligate life was forgery, for which he spent five years in prison. At the age of ninety-five, he reformed, and during the five years prior to his hundredth birthday he "kept as sober, as honest, and as innocent as one could wish to see any nonagenarian" and looked forward confidently to death and the afterlife. He lives with Martha Dolphin, his granddaughter and sole surviving relative, a middle-aged spinster who narrates the novel.

At his centennial breakfast, Daniel tells Martha of a dream in which the devil visited him and revealed that Daniel was scheduled to die that night. Daniel was told that he could forestall the end by putting himself in the fiend's hands. In return for his soul, Satan guaranteed Daniel ten more years of life, during which the centenarian would grow younger, cramming another lifetime into the decade. After reading the contract Satan had prepared, Daniel says, he signed it with blood from his shoulder. The old man and Martha make light of the incident, which after all he only dreamed, and they attribute a red mark on his shoulder to a fleabite.

Six months later, during which time his health has improved, Daniel discovers a copy of the contract through which he bartered away his soul. Realizing the terrible dimensions of what he has done and determined to hide his secret, Daniel and Martha leave their village for London. Two birthdays later, Daniel is twenty years younger, has resumed his excessive drinking, and decides that for at least the next six years—until he is twenty again—he will enjoy himself, ignoring all qualms of conscience. He takes up with women, proposes to several along the way, jilts them and others as his reverse aging accelerates, runs for a local council, loses money in a fraudulent scheme with a swindler, competes in a regatta, and runs afoul of the law. Periodically, Daniel and Martha (who eventually becomes known as his grandmother) change their names and move from one city or town to another, fleeing acquaintances as he rapidly grows younger. However difficult the vagabond life is for Daniel, it is particularly stressful for Martha, who becomes a closet alcoholic.

Finally, on the eve of his 110th birthday, Daniel is a newborn baby again, and Martha spends the night with him on the wilds of London's Hampstead Heath. At the moment of death, he apparently is transformed into an old man again and then completely vanishes, amid shining moonbeams. The grieving granddaughter concludes her narrative with a warning to materialistic nonbelievers: Avoid being fooled, and reflect before becoming "meshed in some muddling devil's web, from which there is no escape."

ANALYSIS

A Deal with the Devil is one of many late Victorian and early twentieth century novels written in the manner of Thomas Anstey Guthrie (1856–1934). Using the pseudonym F. Anstey, this English humorist and satirist wrote novels in which a fantastic device appeared in an otherwise realistic contemporary narrative, such as a father and son switching personalities or someone accidentally bringing a goddess to life. In Eden Phillpotts' book, Daniel's Faustian bargain is the sole fantastic element, and all action and conflicts emanate from it.

An implicit though central conflict is that between the two main characters, Daniel and Martha Dolphin. The latter epitomizes Victorian propriety yet must care for an old reprobate who, after his deal with the devil, reverts to his profligate youthful ways. Because Martha is the narrator, not only does her point of view color everything, but her increasing despair and weariness also pervade the novel. She ages while her grandfather becomes younger; as he increases in vigor, their frenetic nomadic life exacts its emotional toll on her. Martha is the utterly loyal Victorian woman; she advises, suggests, and protests, but ultimately accepts Daniel's plan to spend almost all of his money during the ten years of the New Scheme (as Martha has dubbed it), though her expected inheritance will be gone. She supports him throughout their peregrinations and becomes his surrogate mother during his second childhood.

Because of her frankness and the precise details with which she relates everything, the plot of the novel remains credible despite the event at its core. Martha, for example, precisely describes changes in Daniel's skin, speech, clothing, and other aspects of physical appearance as his years rapidly fade away; specific features of their many homes as they flee from one place to another; and such matters as his courtships and participation in the Henley regatta. She also is an important player in the unfolding action and reveals much about herself through her narrative. Supporting the realism are frequent reminders of her aging, in contrast to Daniel's regression to childhood, and her increasing dependence on alcohol. Her epilogue dates the novel by its didacticism, and because of Martha's central presence, the book is too firmly rooted in the late Victorian period despite its timeless theme. For example, ignoring the fact that Daniel obviously regretted none of the excesses of his first century and committed many of the same follies all over again during his New Scheme decade, dutiful and deferent Martha exonerates him from responsibility for his fate, saying he "was most unfairly treated," and erects a memorial to him in her village church.

In many of his more than two hundred novels, Phillpotts uses a familiar or traditional literary motif, gives it an unusual twist, and constructs an ingenious plot around it. *A Deal with the Devil*, his contemporary Faustian allegory and eighth book, reflects not only this practice but also the realism for which he was highly regarded in the early twentieth century, when his series of Dartmoor novels was compared to those by Thomas Hardy about Wessex.

—Gerald H. Strauss

THE DEATH OF GRASS

When a virus kills all grasses and grains, worldwide famine ensues, civilization collapses, and individuals revert to tribal, survivalist patterns and seek a defensible stronghold against murderous mobs

Author: John Christopher (Samuel Christopher Youd, 1922–2012)
Genre: Science fiction—cautionary
Type of work: Novel
Time of work: The near future
Locale: England
First published: 1956 (also published as *No Blade of Grass*, 1957)

THE STORY

The Death of Grass begins with an idyllic introductory scene, a visit by the Custance family to Blind Gill, an unforgettably green oasis among desert mountains. There, David's love of the land wins him his grandfather's farm and John's near drowning reveals a secret that will later save lives.

Twenty-five years later, as the Chung-Li rice virus decimates rich fields, two hundred million Chinese people die of famine and Hong Kong implodes as smug Londoners speculate that Chinese secretiveness kept Western technology from introducing an antivirus isotope. Roger Buckley of the British ministry of production, a close friend of John Custance, an engineer, has insider information that the isotope has not killed a key virus strain, once kept in check by the stronger, now dead, forms. This virus threatens grasses and grains world-wide, and famine spreads westward. Brown patches dot the English countryside, but the government issues optimistic reports as reassurance. David Custance switches his crops to potatoes and beets, kills his cows, salts the meat, and urges the family to join him, but John delays. The Buckleys agree to warn the Custances when the situation becomes critical in return for a place in the protected valley of Blind Gill.

Initially, Roger is a cynical self-preservationist, irritated with "woolly-mindedness" and convinced of government perfidy. Proud of being a savage at heart, he forces John to see the seriousness of the problem, anticipates the atomic bombing of urban England, and, when a roadblock prevents escape, returns for firearms and recruits a highly competent arms expert, Pirrie, to provide quality weapons. Roger and John jokingly toss a coin for leadership, but after John wins, he is committed to making the hard decisions necessary for group survival. It is Roger and his wife, Olivia, who urge taking pity on various weaklings, including a boy from Davey Custance's school, a young farm girl whose parents they have killed, and a dysfunctional family ill prepared for crisis. John, in contrast, accuses Roger of sentimentality and makes tough decisions based on necessity. He tells his son, "We have to fight to live." He understands the need for strong walls to keep out the barbarians before civilized interaction can begin.

Pirrie proves invaluable as John's right-hand man. He has no scruples and understands immediately the extremes necessary for survival. He plans the ambush that kills the road guards. He shoots three ruffians who molest John's wife, Anne, and daughter Mary, but he allows Anne the coup de grâce. He cold-bloodedly kills his wife for trying to seduce John and takes as concubine a farm girl whose parents he has killed for food. He shoots an opposition leader to guarantee a group merger for strength of numbers, and when a military-style force attacks with grenades, he picks off the ringleaders at a distance with his telescopic sights.

When the entourage reaches David Custance's stronghold, locals manning a machine gun agree to let in David's relatives but deny admittance to all others. John must choose between allegiance to his family and to his new tribe, and he opts for the tribe. He and Pirrie attack the machine-gun nest from the river ledge and sandbar he had discovered as a youth while their group storms the walls. During the shooting, either John or Pirrie kills David, and Pirrie, after receiving a mortal wound, falls to his death in the turbulent river. The stronghold is taken, however, and can be defended. The process of rebuilding civilization can begin.

ANALYSIS

The Death of Grass, a short but powerfully realistic parable, warns of the fragility of the ecosystem and of modern civilization, as well as the dangers of overpopulation and an optimistic dependence on science to solve all problems. John Christopher effectively captures human blindness to threatening changes. Even when faced with the fact of a country of fifty million people importing nearly half of its food from countries now besieged by famine, the first tendency of most of Christopher's characters is to assume that civilization will somehow muddle on, that a stiff upper lip will get them through hard times, and that science will provide an answer. Farmers, close to nature, recognize disaster long before urbanites. They warn of treating the land as "a piggy-bank, to be raided," when, in fact, "the land . . . is life itself."

Christopher also examines the human tendency to expect highly visible causes of catastrophe when in fact the cause may be microscopic. David Custance speculates that a virus might have ended the age of the great reptiles in the same way that a virus could end human dominance.

Christopher's understanding of the precariousness of civilization bears a quality similar to William Golding's speculations on human nature in *Lord of the Flies* (1954). His women accuse their men of being "savages" beneath the thin veneer of civilization, and Pirrie, though believing that the English will remain deluded to the very end, concludes that once awakened they will "fight like particularly savage tigers." The rapes, the cold-blooded killing of anyone who presents an obstacle, the calculated bombing of cities, the street violence and raids, the village that robs all passersby, and the cool calculations of Pirrie confirm this savage essence.

Christopher suggests a cyclical pattern of life: a slow building of civilization, with increasing legal restraints and protection of the weak over thousands of years; a sudden, nearly instantaneous destruction of all civilized patterns; and a slow rebuilding based on survival of the fittest and the rule of the strong as well as the obligation of leader to tribe, an obligation that takes precedence over family relationships. England reverts to an earlier age. Blind Gill, an ancient stronghold, is so again, with John as chieftain, accepting a ritualistic handshake and a defining "Mr." to confirm his status. Modern Britons laugh together, blind to their fate, as did the Saxons before the Battle of Hastings, and worried travelers fear that their children will pray to moorland gods to turn away their wrath. Cain rekills Abel, but John's son, like Cain's (Enoch), may refound civilization, though both sons retain their weapons.

Christopher's style is clear, understated, compact, and forward-moving, with occasional touches of grim irony and with insights about England's ancient heritage of cynicism and resilience. When asked if there is any news, Roger replies in Shakespearean tones, "None, but that the world's grown honest." He is answered, "Aye, that's good. Then is doomsday near!"

—*Gina Macdonald*

Death Qualified and The Best Defense

Attorney Barbara Holloway successfully defends clients in murder trials that are believed to be hopeless cases

Author: Kate Wilhelm (Katie Wilhelm Knight, 1928–)
Genre: Science fiction—cautionary
Time of work: The 1990's
Locale: Turner's Point and Eugene, Oregon
First published: *Death Qualified: A Mystery of Chaos* (1991), *The Best Defense* (1994), *For the Defense* (1996), *Defense for the Devil* (1999), *No Defense* (2000), *Desperate Measures* (2001), *Clear and Convincing Proof* (2003), *The Unbidden Truth* (2004), *Sleight Of Hand* (2006), *A Wrongful Death* (2007), *Cold Case* (2008), *Heaven is High* (2011), and *By Stone, By Blade, By Fire* (2012)
Type of work: Novels

The Story

Prior to the opening of *Death Qualified*, Lucas Kendricks agrees to participate in scientific studies on the mathematical theories of chaos. A group of university researchers believes that by showing a sequence of carefully designed computer images of fractals to volunteer subjects, the volunteers will learn to perceive the world in new ways and will understand events that appear chaotic to most people. Lucas learns through the experiments, but most volunteers show no change.

As they run out of money, the researchers solicit male prostitutes to watch the computer images. One of the young prostitutes learns to understand the logic of chaos, and in the process, he acquires superhuman abilities. These abilities are not described in detail, but they appear similar to mental telepathy and telekinesis, only more powerful. In a fit of jealous rage, one scientist kills the successful volunteer. Because Lucas knows too much, the researchers drug him and keep him prisoner for seven years, disguised as a mentally impaired handyman.

As the book opens, Lucas escapes and travels back to his hometown of Turners Point, Oregon. He remembers everything the experiment has taught him and wants to share his new abilities with his family. As soon as he returns to his hometown, however, he is murdered, allegedly by his wife, Nell. Gifted attorney Barbara Holloway is called into town by her father, Frank, a prosperous lawyer, to help with Nell's defense. Although Barbara has turned her back on the law, she takes on the seemingly hopeless case, in which all clues lead back to the experiments in chaos theory.

With the help of her boyfriend, mathematics professor Mike Dineson, Barbara identifies the real killer. More dangerous than the killer, however, are computer disks from the experiment. Smuggled into Turner's Point by Lucas before his death, they kill Mike (or send him into another dimension) and threaten Lucas and Nell's children. At the end of the novel, Barbara once again abandons the law out of hatred for the legal system.

The Best Defense shows that Barbara cannot stay away from the law for long. She is living in Eugene, Oregon, on the tiny salary she makes helping poor people who cannot afford legal services at full rates. When Lucille Reiner asks Barbara to help her sister, Barbara does not realize that the sister is Paula Kemmerman, dubbed the "Baby Killer" by the press. Paula allegedly killed her six-year-old daughter, then set fire to the shelter for battered women where they were living. Despite Barbara's reluctance to take on another high-profile case, with the help of her father, she proves that Paula is the innocent victim both of a right-wing fundamentalist and of a legal system that has turned its back on an innocent victim. The subsequent books in the series, while performing wonderfully in their modes of crime and suspense, do not venture into the realms of fantasy and science fiction.

Analysis

By the time Kate Wilhelm wrote these mysteries, she had more than thirty-five books to her credit, including novels, collections of short stories, and novellas. In *Death Qualified* and *The Best Defense*, Wilhelm continues to push the edges of genre fiction, spinning into legal thrillers the social commentary one might expect to find in science fiction, as well as the narrative sleight of hand and red herrings typically found in mysteries. As she incorporates these various devices, she does not sacrifice the taut drama of the skillful cross-examination and the hostile judge.

Death Qualified overtly combines elements of the mystery and science-fiction genres. The mystery is the dominant genre, as it is in *The Dark Door* (1988), one of Wilhelm's "Charlie and Constance" mysteries. Both books are structured as mysteries, but the cause of the mystery is a science-fiction element (an alien experiment gone awry in *The Dark Door* and a human experiment gone awry in *Death Qualified*). *Death Qualified* blends the genres more successfully, perhaps because the scientist characters are greedy enough to fill the role of mystery villain.

The scientists do not directly murder Lucas Kendricks: The killer is a neighbor, Clive Belloc, who wants to avoid blame for an earlier rape and murder of his own. Because the scientists have held Lucas prisoner for years, however, making him appear to have abandoned his family, he is an ideal scapegoat. Lucas developed superhuman abilities through the experiments, and he is showing off these abilities when Clive finds him. Clive thinks he is a "devil" and does not hesitate to shoot. Were it not for the scientists, therefore, Lucas would not have been killed.

Fans of Wilhelm's *Where Late the Sweet Birds Sang* (1976) will recognize another theme in *Death Qualified*, that of technological advances creating children who are alien to their parents. Instead of cloning, however, the technology is a computer program, based on fractal mathematics, that allows sensitive individuals to experience reality in ways different from those of other people. After running the program, Barbara's lover, Mike, is forever separated from her. His new abilities lead him to pity her, and although he uses them to save her life, he disappears immediately afterward. After Mike dies, Nell's children find the disks; they too are changed into something other than human. At the end of the book, there is no sign of hope. Barbara falls asleep alone, weeping.

The plot structure of *Death Qualified* is that of a mystery. The book opens with a dramatic escape and murder, and most of the action in the book is generated by Barbara's efforts at detection. The murderer turns out to be the proverbial "least likely" character, though all the clues to the solution have been laid out for the reader. Once the murderer is unmasked, he turns on the detective, who needs to escape from a dangerous one-on-one confrontation in the last few pages of the book.

The science-fiction elements of the novel, by contrast, are developed as a subplot. Most of the information about the experiments is uncovered by Mike, clearly a secondary character, who routinely is whisked out of the way by Barbara's father when she is overwhelmed with trial responsibilities. Mike is interested in chaos theory from the start. He tracks down the computer disks that hold the fractal images and figures out what they will do. Most of these activities occur offstage, while Barbara grapples with recalcitrant witnesses. When Mike finally makes a significant appearance, during the dramatic showdown between Barbara and Clive, he becomes the noble rescuer who sacrifices his life for his beloved— another stock mystery character.

Although the mystery plot drives most of the action, the book's science-fiction framework provides the story's lasting power. Lucas is on the run from evil scientists who use technology to enslave him. Because the scientists have given him superhuman powers, Lucas will never fit into society. If he had not been killed, he most likely would have been framed for the rape-murder that Clive committed, and society would have been likely to find such an unusual man guilty. Even if he had escaped that fate, Lucas could not have led a normal life. When Mike undergoes the same experiments, he first becomes disoriented, unable to use his normal senses; he then considers himself to be superior to normal human beings and no longer can relate to them. Readers have no reason to believe that Lucas would have felt differently.

As Lucas' children are transformed by the same experiments, while Barbara lies weeping in her bed, readers realize that although Nell's murder trial may have been won, the future of humanity may already be lost. By weaving this science-fiction plot around what is already a top-notch legal mystery, Wilhelm gives her novel extraordinary depth.

Although *The Best Defense* occurs after the events of Death Qualified, no sign of the science-fiction elements remains in the sequel. Nell's children are not mentioned, and Mike's disappearance becomes a death by drowning. Barbara's character is much the same—she is still rebelling against the hypocrisies of the legal system—but her father is quite different. Rather than the semiretired lawyer who insists that he has earned the right to go to work in Bermuda shorts and tank tops, Frank is a high-priced attorney in corporate clothes, willing to challenge his firm's conservative partners on behalf of his daughter. Although *The Best Defense* probably will not be as interesting to science-fiction fans as the earlier novel, it is still a page turner. Wilhelm's feminism is more strongly apparent in the later book, as the story centers on issues of child abuse and the battered woman syndrome. In both books, however, it is significant that the victims are abused as much by cultural and legal conventions as by evil people.

Wilhelm has won many awards, including the Nebula Award for best short story for "The Planners" (1968) and "Forever Yours, Anna" (1987), as well as for best novelette for "The Girl Who Fell into the Sky" (1986). In 1977, she received a Hugo Award, a World Science Fiction Convention Jupiter Award, and second place for the John W. Campbell Memorial Award, all for *Where Late the Sweet Birds Sang*. In 1980, she received an American Book Award nomination for *Juniper Time* (1979).

—Beth Rapp Young

THE DEATHWORLD TRILOGY

Jason DinAlt visits hostile worlds and risks his life on each, but he manages both to survive and to change the native cultures for the better

Author: Harry Harrison (1925–2012)
Genre: Science fiction—cultural exploration
Type of work: Novels
Time of work: The distant future
Locale: The planets Cassylia, Pyrrus, Felicity, and others
First published: *The Deathworld Trilogy* (1968), comprising *Deathworld* (1960; serial form, *Astounding Science-Fiction*, January-March, 1960), *Deathworld 2* (1964; serial form, "The Ethical Engineer," *Astounding Science-Fiction*, July-August, 1963), and *Deathworld 3* (1968; serial form, "Deathworld 2," *Astounding Science-Fiction*, February-April, 1968)

The Story

In *Deathworld*, Kerk Pyrrus hires gambler Jason DinAlt to win a fortune at dice. With his gift of "psi powers," Jason succeeds. Kerk explains that the money will buy weapons to fight the deadly wildlife on his planet, Pyrrus. The native plants and animals there are armor-plated, poisonous, claw-tipped, fanged, or otherwise prepared for battle. Fascinated, Jason decides to visit Pyrrus, where he finds both danger and a planetwide mystery.

The first clue in this mystery is the horrible nightmares he suffers every night. A second clue comes from an ancient diary, which reveals that the population of the planet is dwindling, not growing. The third clue is the existence of the "grubbers," whom the city dwellers hate because they live peacefully with the wildlife outside the city walls. Ferocious plants, animals, and insects wage constant war against the city. Jason decides to learn why this dreadful war continues.

Meeting illegally with the grubbers, he finds them to be brave, noble creatures unfairly deprived of civilized amenities by the city dwellers. He determines to stop the war and arrange a peace. The grubbers can communicate telepathically with the native animals. Jason speculates that all the wildlife is empathic, and during an earthquake he is astonished to see the wild animals fleeing the danger zone, alongside the grubbers and domesticated animals. At that point he solves the mystery of the illogical, unending war.

He leads the grubbers against the city. They seize the spaceship—the focus of power on the planet—and demand a meeting with the angry city Pyrrans, at which Jason explains the native planetary telepathy. Although normally they strive against one another, the plants and animals unite to combat any force perceived as a natural disaster. In this case, it is the humans who are a threat, so the plants and animals fight them. The city Pyrrans finally realize that they are responsible for the war and for ending it, if they choose.

In *Deathworld 2*, a religious zealot, Mikah, kidnaps Jason to return him to Cassylia for trial and execution for his crimes. Jason wrecks the spaceship's controls and diverts it to an uncharted planet. Jason and Mikah are at once enslaved and learn that the primitive society of the planet consists of slaves and tribal slaveholders. Each tribe protects a secret knowledge: The D'zertanoj, for example, rule the secret of oil distillation, the Mastreguloj understand chemistry, and the Personnoj hold the monopoly on electricity. Jason plans to return to Pyrrus but is plagued by Mikah at every step.

With his knowledge of basic science, Jason elevates himself from abused slave to abused employee, at first in the hands of the D'zertanoj, then in the ranks of the Personnoj. He tries to improve the local living conditions, but each time he proves himself indispensable with his scientific "inventions," Mikah betrays him to the rival clans, who kidnap, harass, and nearly kill Jason. Jason finally decides to launch an industrial and cultural revolution. Among the scientific devices he "invents" is a radio transmitter that, unknown to the natives, beams an "S.O.S." signal night and day. When Mikah learns that Jason is planning to wage war against the rival clans as part of his overall scheme, the zealot betrays Jason once more. During a terrible battle, Jason is wounded. On his deathbed, he hears a roar of rocket engines and realizes that his transmitter has done its job, and he is rescued by Meta.

Felicity, the planet of *Deathworld 3*, is the deadliest. Jason learns that miners had attempted to settle on Felicity but were butchered by hordes of warriors on huge mounts. Jason proposes that the Pyrrans who are still reluctant to make peace with the grubbers join him in moving to Felicity and persuading the natives to allow foreigners. Jason takes a group, including Meta and Kerk, to establish a new camp on Felicity.

The southern part of the single continent is fertile and inhabited but unexplored by off-worlders. The northern continent is rich with the heavy ores that the settlers desire but also filled with Mongol-like warriors who vow to slaughter anyone who tries to erect buildings on their wild plains. Jason is kidnapped by the barbarians and so meets the ruthless Temuchin, who has succeeded in uniting many of the feuding tribes to wage war against the off-worlders.

Temuchin orders Jason slain, but he escapes and rejoins the Pyrrans. His new plan is to disguise his band as a far-north tribe and to infiltrate Temuchin's camp himself as a wandering minstrel. Always risking exposure as he learns the native customs, he persuades Temuchin to conquer the southern continent. The warlord succeeds but realizes afterward that he has lost his way of life, as his tribes adapt to new customs and off-world products.

ANALYSIS

The Deathworld books suffer unfairly the stigma of being "only" adventure novels. They were written to *Astounding Science-Fiction* editor John W. Campbell, Jr.'s specifications and were hugely popular when they first appeared. *Deathworld*, Harry Harrison's first published novel, appeared five years before Frank Herbert's *Dune* (1965), which is widely regarded as the first science-fiction novel to deal with the entire ecology of an alien planet. Wittier than the humorless *Dune*, *Deathworld* also preaches the important message that people come to resemble their enemies.

Far from being a cartoonish arena appropriate only for an unthinking blazing-guns romp, the Pyrran ecology can be seen as the lengthiest exploration ever undertaken of the "pathetic fallacy," the ascription of human emotions to the environment, as in the phrase "the cruel sea." Harrison demonstrates on a planetary scale how "inner space" influences outward reality: The colonists' own emotions make their world a hell.

Similarly, in *Deathworld 2*, Jason lands first on what appears to be a plain by the sea. When he attempts to escape his slavery there he suddenly encounters gullies and ravines that the text had not prepared readers for, foreshadowing the dark, twisting, deceptive nature of the world. He then travels through two likewise appropriate settings, a desert that seems to symbolize the barrenness of this world and a city made of fortress-islands that represents the isolated, each-one-against-the-rest nature of the local society. The harsh settings match the harsh social satire.

In *Deathworld 3*, the single landmass of the planet is shaped like a dagger, suggesting the glorification of war among the nomads, and is divided in half by a huge, continentwide cliff, which again suggests a land divided against itself. The wild plains are also integral to the plot, evoking the native North Americans and their own conflict with an alien, colonizing force. This third novel, however, is based on the history of the Mongols and their assimilation into the Chinese empire. Temuchin was another name of Genghis Khan.

A close reading of the novels provides pleasing insights into Harrison's writing tactics. As the title suggests, death is immanent in all these worlds; Jason's life is at stake in each novel. Harrison's choice of words underscores this point. Readers repeatedly encounter "dead silence," "dead seriousness," "dead cold," "dead tiredness," and "deadened eyes." The vocabulary emphasizes Jason's wariness of death all about; at the same time, the point of view remains close to Jason's thoughts. Readers always know what he is thinking and how he reacts to those around him. On occasion, however, the omniscient narrator proposes another character's point of view, and a close reading reveals that these moments actually represent Jason's speculations into another's motives and may be mistaken. The strategy supports a plot filled with aliens who are out to betray him.

These novels focus on conflicting points of view and on beneficial ways of resolving them. The societies portrayed are exaggeratedly violent, and exaggeration is a time-honored tactic of satire. While the omniscient narrator blandly reports episode after episode of suspense, battle, torture, and death, Jason's sardonic running commentary provides humor. The novels are exciting and often quite funny, particularly in the dialogue between Jason and the humorless, trigger-happy Pyrrans or with the acutely irritating Mikah.

Harrison has gone on from these books to become known for a variety of serious fiction, editing, and nonfiction projects. He is recognized for his increasingly parodistic yet thoughtful satire.

—*Fiona Kelleghan*

DEERSKIN

Fleeing a world of hypocrisy, indulgence, and brutality, Lissar is transformed into the legendary Deerskin

Author: Robin McKinley (1952–)
Genre: Fantasy—feminist
Type of work: Novel
Time of work: A medieval stage of civilization
Locale: A fairy-tale kingdom
First published: 1993

THE STORY

The most beautiful woman in seven kingdoms marries the handsome king of a wealthy realm. They have one child, a daughter named Lissar, who is ignored while the happy couple enjoys an idyllic, self-absorbed marriage. When the queen discovers that her perfect beauty is fading, she orders a portrait and, when it is finished, adjures her husband to marry no one who is not as beautiful as the painting. Smiling in triumph, she dies.

Lissar is first noticed by anyone other than her nursemaid when the prince of a neighboring kingdom—alone of all those who send condolences and gifts to her father—sends her a gift, a puppy from his favorite fleethound bitch. Because of the puppy, Lissar begins to develop a love of life and nature. She becomes a very atypical princess, learning herbal and plant lore from the aunt of one of her chambermaids.

Lissar's discovery of self is interrupted when a grand ball is given to present her to would-be suitors. Her mother's portrait dominates the great room, but her father is overwhelmed by her resemblance to the portrait. He dances with her all night, turning away interested suitors. When he is later pressed to marry again, he declares his daughter to be his intended bride. The final horror occurs when he rapes her in her own bedroom.

Stunned into amnesia, Lissar follows her dog, Ash, out of the palace grounds, out of the country, and into a distant forest, where they subsist by learning to hunt and to gather edible plants. In the midst of a severe winter, in a small cabin they have found, Lissar is visited by a mysterious woman who presents Lissar with the gift of time, to heal before remembering. On awakening, Lissar finds that it is spring and that she is clothed in a delicate deerskin garment that repels all stains. She and Ash make their way slowly toward civilization, ending in the kingdom of an unassuming king and queen whose only son is Ossin, the dog-lover who had sent Ash to Lissar.

Lissar learns that the woman who appeared to her is known as the Moon Woman. Her appearance means that someone in need will find help. Lissar becomes known as Deerskin, and her skill in nursing a litter of motherless pups for Prince Ossin and feats such as finding a lost child add to her legendary aura and endear her to both Ossin and the people.

When Ossin declares his love for her, she flees, impelled by the resurgent memories of her father's act. Finally accepting her love for Ossin, she returns in time to prevent the wedding of Ossin's younger sister to Lissar's father. At her touch, her father becomes an old and broken man. She and Ossin understand that her healing will be slow, but he is content to be patient and helpful.

ANALYSIS
Robin McKinley has won both the Newbery Award and Newbery Honors for previous fantasy novels. *Deerskin* is based on "Donkeyskin," a fairy tale with adult subject matter. McKinley uses this subject matter to craft a tale in the style and tone of a romantic fantasy with underlying social commentary. The unassuming simplicity and kindness at the court of Ossin's parents is sharply contrasted to the glitter and superficiality in the court of Lissar's parents.

The attitude of the courtiers when Lissar's father declares his intention to marry his own daughter signals the beginning of a second pervasive theme. They ask themselves how this evil creature could have bewitched their wonderful king. Their comments bespeak an innate sexism on the part of both men and women of this court, implying that men are helpless to resist subliminal messages of temptation. Lissar's father first beats her, then rapes her, thus demonstrating starkly that this is an act of violence, not of love. Any sympathy one might have felt for the king because of his wife's egotistical legacy is destroyed completely by the cold ferocity of the attack, which breaks Lissar's resistance.

Lissar's benumbed departure from her father's palace is rendered in terms more suitable to describing the mental state of a trauma victim than the flight of a fairy-tale princess. The fleethound, Ash, is the symbol and a source of her slowly emerging determination to survive. As they learn to survive by hunting and foraging, their physical hardships are described realistically, including such homey details as where Lissar decides to place her latrine near the Moon Woman's cabin.

The Moon Woman and her gift of the deerskin garment are powerful reminders that this is fantasy. Lissar's gradual conquest of Ossin's heart is likewise the stuff of fairy tales. Lissar's flight from Ossin, on the other hand, is again a reflection of harsh reality and the frightened reaction of some rape survivors to even the gentlest offers of love. Her return is surrounded by powerful magic but interpreted in terms of both psychology and anthropology. In the midst of her confrontation with her father, her menses flow onto the floor, but what is often interpreted as a woman's weakness becomes a source of sacred power, releasing even the ghost of her mother upon the crowd. The form and phenomena of McKinley's tale are those of a fairy tale; the substance is that of a fable for the postfeminist society.

—*James L. Hodge*

THE DEMOLISHED MAN

Lincoln Powell attempts to prove that Ben Reich has committed murder, an almost unheard of act in the year 2301

Author: Alfred Bester (1913–1987)
Genre: Science fiction—extrasensory powers
Type of work: Novel
Time of work: 2301
Location: New York City
First published: 1953 (serial form, 1952)

THE STORY
On the surface, *The Demolished Man* is a slick, futuristic detective novel, but the book is much more complex than such a surface description implies. Ben Reich, a wealthy and powerful man, has planned a merger with the D'Courtney Cartel. When that merger is apparently thwarted by Craye D'Courtney, Reich plans to murder his rival. The difficulty confronting Reich is that in the year 2301, murder has been virtually eliminated

because of the emergence of Espers, people gifted with and trained in the use of extrasensory perception. Espers are classified according to their levels of ability; an Esper 1 is the most gifted and besttrained of the Esper Guild members. Because Espers can "peep" accused suspects, or look into their thoughts, hiding guilt from them is virtually impossible. The Esper Guild, however, maintains strict rules for its members. Even though Lincoln Powell, a police prefect and an Esper 1, determines very early that Reich is guilty of D'Courtney's murder, he is unable to make use of the knowledge without supporting evidence. He must present enough evidence to the police computer, "Old Man Mose," to ensure a conviction; otherwise, Reich will go free.

Reich has powerful means of thwarting the police investigation. He can hire the best Espers to help him, he can afford massive bribes and incentives, and he has friends in high places in the police department. Powell, however, is not without resources of his own. He is a superb detective in addition to being an incredibly gifted Esper. He manages to locate a witness to the crime, Barbara D'Courtney, the daughter of the victim. She is so traumatized by the murder, however, that she must undergo considerable psychotherapy to counteract her state of shock. She must be regressed to a state of birthlike innocence and carefully brought through normal growth stages in order to preserve her mental functions. As she goes though these stages under Powell's observation, he comes to realize that he is in love with her.

Meanwhile, Old Man Mose has rejected Powell's plan for prosecution, and Powell has no idea why. He discovers that the motive for the murder is so complex and so deeply hidden in Reich's subconscious that he must combat Reich in ways that play upon his psychological makeup. Only in that way is he able to accomplish his objective of having Reich "demolished," or psychologically broken down and rebuilt into the man his better nature will allow. Powell also is able to find a satisfactory outcome for his love of Barbara D'Courtney.

Analysis

Alfred Bester won the first Hugo Award in 1953 for *The Demolished Man*. Bester had published numerous short stories prior to this book, his first novel and generally considered to be his best. The quality of the book is attested by the fact that it has held up for more than forty years as a fascinating study of the human mind, of psychic and psychological detective methods, and of the intricacies of human relationships. It is especially effective in its study of the ways in which the Espers relate to one another and to society.

Powell, for example, has a private house rather than the standard apartment. This is not because of his superior economic means. Esper 1's must have private residences because they are bombarded by the thoughts of others in small, poorly insulated apartments, and they must have privacy to maintain their sanity. Being an Esper is a decidedly mixed blessing. Insight into the thoughts of others is a gift, but that gift is received whether one chooses it or not, and Espers cannot avoid knowing things that they might rather not know. Early in the book, Bester describes the dialogue at a party. It is presented typographically to show that strains of the conversation intertwine because the Espers at the party can both hear spoken conversation and understand the unspoken thoughts behind it. They also play a game of creating word patterns, much like poems but with visual aspects, in their minds for others to perceive.

There are ways to protect one's thoughts from Espers. Reich adopts a mindless jingle that he keeps running through his mind at all times to try to block the Espers. This works with Espers of the lower grades; it fails with Espers of Powell's quality.

Use of a computer as a guide to the likely success of prosecution of a case is another interesting device. Readers of the 1990's and beyond would probably not question this plot device or find it unusual, but in 1953, when computers were in their infancy, it was a speculation into the future of a new and interesting machine. Technology in *The Demolished Man* takes a secondary position to psychology. Although most of the psychology seems at odds with present day psychotherapy, that is not necessarily a flaw. Readers might assume that the psychotherapy described in the novel is more advanced, as it is from an imagined future; it is in fact dated.

A minor flaw in the book, one that might disturb feminist readers, is the love angle. Powell finds himself unable to love his longtime associate, Mary Noyes, who makes no secret of her love for him, yet he falls in love with Barbara D'Courtney, who has been regressed to an infant and who loves him in a childlike way as she "grows" back into an adult self. Despite such minor problems, this book is a classic of science fiction that should be included on every reading list of major works in the genre.

—*June Harris*

THE DEMON PRINCES SERIES

To avenge his family's massacre, Kirth Gersen tracks down the five master criminals who ordered the crime and destroys them

Author: Jack Vance (1916–2013)
Genre: Science fiction—planetary romance
Type of work: Novels
Time of work: Beginning in 3524
Locale: Various planets of the Gaean Reach
First published: *The Star King* (1964; serial form, *Galaxy*, December, 1963, and February, 1964), *The Killing Machine* (1964), *The Palace of Love* (1967; serial form, *Galaxy*, October and December, 1966, and February, 1967), *The Face* (1979), and *The Book of Dreams* (1981)

THE STORY

The Demon Princes series was the first long novel series that Jack Vance started, and it took the longest to complete. It takes place in Vance's own imaginary galaxy of the future, the Gaean Reach. The civilized, law-abiding part of the galaxy is known as the Oikumene, and the uncivilized, lawless section, its frontier, is known as the Beyond. From this area come five space pirates, the Demon Princes, who have committed the massacre of Kirth Gersen's family, a crime that Gersen pledges his life to avenge. Gersen and his grandfather, escaping this attack, journey to Old Earth, as Vance customarily calls it, where Gersen trains for more than twenty years to become the instrument of retribution for his family's fate.

Vance's Gaean Reach, like Robert A. Heinlein's Future History and Isaac Asimov's Galactic Empire, is curiously lacking in intelligent aliens, but the one race that exists closely resembles humans. They are the Star Kings, the race to which Attel Malagate, the first of the Demon Princes Gersen pursues, belongs. Gersen's main task becomes identifying which one of three possible suspects is the Star King.

Vance, an Edgar-winning mystery author, deftly interweaves plot elements from the traditional mystery with aspects of the planetary romance. Gersen, for example, must rescue an innocent girl kidnapped by one of Malagate's henchmen. The search for Malagate involves a simultaneous search for an undiscovered Earth-like planet. One of the clues that leads Gersen to identify Malagate is the alien's lack of human reaction to this Edenic setting. Fittingly, it is the planet's treelike inhabitants who kill Malagate, but when Gersen returns a year later, enough of Malagate is still left for Gersen to exact his own poetic justice.

The Killing Machine is both the translation of Kokor Hekkus, the name of the second Demon Prince, as well as a description of the mechanical monster he designs to terrify the primitive tribespeople of a world he dominates. Gersen's complicated search for Hekkus involves him in the manufacture of this machine, swindling Hekkus and the Interchange organization (a group set up to bring order to kidnapping across interstellar distances), and the rescue of a beautiful woman, Alusz Iphigenia, from both Interchange and Hekkus. Hekkus, a seemingly immortal criminal mastermind, is a connoisseur of terror and fear. To indulge these primal emotions, he establishes himself as a wizardlike figure on the legendary world of Thamber. In locating both Hekkus and Thamber, Gersen brings about the end of Thamber as a world of primitive adventure and precipitates its entrance into the Oikumene.

Viole Fanushe, the third of the Demon Princes, is a sybaritic sensualist who has constructed the Palace of Love as a hedonistic hideaway. Once again, Gersen's main task is identifying which one of a limited number of suspects is the master criminal and locating the planet he uses as a base of operations. This involves Gersen returning to Old Earth, becoming a journalist, and allying himself with Fanushe's old mentor, the bizarre poet

Narvath. Fanushe, it turns out, is as monomaniacal as Gersen. Fanushe's obsession involves wooing cloned versions of a girl who long ago spurned him. Gersen's revenge thus involves him freeing not one but four females in jeopardy; he simultaneously liberates the inhabitants of Fanushe's planet.

In *The Face*, Gersen pursues Lens Larque, a sadistic, brutal trickster. As the title implies, he is the only one of the Demon Princes who does not mind his losing his anonymity. Gersen must flush him out by carrying out a complicated financial takeover of a company that Larque has formed to play an enormous joke on a society that has shamed him. Gersen deals with Larque shortly before Larque can avenge himself. Gersen, who has been similarly humiliated, carries out Larque's scheme, but only after Larque is dead.

Howard Alan Treesong, the last of the Demon Princes to be dealt with, is also the most ambitious. He attempts to take over the IPCC, the Interpol of the Gaean Reach, and then to become head of the Institute, a quasi-religious body that places a limit on scientific advances that would interfere with human evolution. Gersen foils Treesong, tracking him down and breaking up his attempted revenge at his high school reunion. Gersen's own final vengeance is interfered with by victims of one of Tree-song's earliest crimes, who exact their own peculiarly apt punishment.

ANALYSIS

In the Demon Princes series, Jack Vance combines one of the oldest Western literary plots, the search for revenge, with the science-fiction subgenre of the planetary romance. Its success in both aspects rests on the validity of the central character. During the first novels, Kirth Gersen is satisfying on both levels. His competence as the hero of a planetary romance and his single-mindedness of purpose are explained by the years he trained for his task. He continually rescues females from imminent sexual danger, as does any literary descendant of Edgar Rice Burroughs' John Carter. Gersen's depth of character as an avenger is filled in as well. It can be seen in his sense of loss at not being able to partake in the possibilities of life around him, particularly in romantic attachments, and in his musings about the form his life would take when his quest is over. None of this depth, however, is carried out consistently throughout the series. Gersen's life before the raid, for example, is never alluded to, and after Treesong's death, Gersen bleakly comments, "I am done." Gersen exists only as an instrument, and when his function is over, the story is over.

Such perfunctory endings have led to the charge that Vance loses interest in his series after the first few novels. Some indications of this occur in the Demon Princes series. For example, in *The Face*, the novel in which Vance returned to the series after a hiatus, Gersen mentions that it was an uncle who escaped with him, when the other four novels consistently say it was his grandfather. Because of Vance's use of the mystery plot and the consequent delay in unmasking the villains, almost all of them (with the exception of Treesong) are merely melodramatic; their evil is reported, not witnessed.

For all the loose ends, there is a satisfying underlying sense of unity about the series. Almost all the novels involve some kind of planetary scheme by the villains that Gersen must foil. He liberates the dryads from Malagate's threat, brings Thamber into the human community, and frees Fanushe's sex slaves. In the novels after the hiatus, Gersen, in a sense, goes along with the planetary plots. He complies with Larque's fantastic vengeance against the fastidious inhabitants of Methel, and he allows the parents of Treesong's boyhood victim to employ the animals of Bethune Preserve to help them exact their own retribution. In the first and last novels of the series, which are set on sparsely inhabited worlds, Gersen does not act as the final avenger.

The Demon Princes series also exhibits to a great degree Vance's spirit of playfulness regarding various science-fiction conventions. Many science-fiction novels, for example (most notably Isaac Asimov's Foundation series), use invented quotations from other books (often reference works) as chapter headings in an attempt to give a greater sense of depth and verisimilitude to their fictional universes. The chapters headings Vance devises are unusually detailed, and the authors' names he creates sometimes have a metafictional dimension. They include Frerb Hankbert (Frank Herbert) and Jan Holberk Vaenz LXII (John Holbrook Vance—Vance's full name). Lens Larque's name combines two halves of the most famous names in space opera, the *Lens*men and the Sky*lark* of E. E. "Doc" Smith. In *The Killing Machine*, Gersen's most significant achievement is his deconstruction of Thamber, a perfect site for the planetary romance and thus reminiscent of Tschai, the locale of Vance's Planet of Adventure series (1968–1970), into a more mundane, more "real" world.

In *The Book of Dreams*, Gersen visits a planet that has 1,562 separate countries, and the reader comes away with the conviction that, if he had to, Vance could invent a fictional society for each. Because of his baroque style and love of exotic invention, Vance has been called a "coelacanth," a writer who is a throwback to conventions established in 1912 with Burroughs' "Under the Moons of Mars." He provides clues in the Demon Princes series that behind this mask is an author who is willing, however slyly, to subvert the very conventions he celebrates so richly.

—*William Laskowski*

Descent into Hell

During production of his play, Peter Stanhope teaches Pauline Anstruther to accept divine love, while Lawrence Wentworth damns himself by rejecting it

Author: Charles Williams (1886–1945)
Genre: Fantasy—magical realism
Type of work: Novel
Time of work: The 1930's
Locale: Battle Hill, a village near London

The Story

Descent into Hell concerns five central characters and a village production of a play by Peter Stanhope. During the weeks of rehearsal, Stanhope demonstrates to Pauline Anstruther the "doctrine of substituted love" (a central idea held by the novel's author, Charles Williams) and helps her overcome the terror she has felt at meeting her double. At the same time, her grandmother, Margaret Anstruther, whom she has been serving as companion, is able in her final hours to aid in the spiritual crisis of an unnamed workman who had committed suicide decades earlier. Another member of the community, military historian Lawrence Wentworth, chooses his own damnation by rejecting truth in favor of illusion and self-indulgence.

Production begins of the play, which is a verse drama. The local organizers rejoice at producing the work of such a noted poet as Stanhope, but his unwillingness to give them much guidance in the speaking of his poetry confuses them. Williams implies satirically that few of these amateurs understand the play and that even fewer truly like poetry. Stanhope sees one exception—the young woman who leads the chorus, Pauline Anstruther. Stanhope's sympathy leads Pauline to confess to him her terror of meeting her "double" in the street, an experience she has undergone several times, each time with greater fright. To her surprise, Stanhope offers to carry her fear for her as if it were a package. This is the real meaning, he says, of the Gospel's injunction to "bear one another's burdens."

Later Pauline discusses this obliquely with her grandmother. They agree that perhaps something of the sort happened to their ancestor, John Struther, who was burned at the stake on Battle Hill during Queen Mary Tudor's persecution of protestants. From the fire, Struther is supposed to have cried out that he had seen his salvation.

As Pauline enjoys her new freedom from fear, Law-rence Wentworth undergoes an opposite transformation. Long haunted by a dream of climbing down a rope into endless darkness, he now finds that dream replaced by his selfish infatuation with one of the play's actresses, Adele Hunt. His sick interest becomes even more distorted when Wentworth rejects the actual woman in favor of a fantasy version of her. As the novel's events proceed, he eventually denies truth and damns himself with his sick illusions.

The novel's climax occurs on the night of dress rehearsal. As Margaret Anstruther lies dying, she sends Pauline out in the middle of the night to help someone in need. In the miracle of divine timelessness, the sufferer is a long-dead workman, and Pauline helps by offering him some of the same burden-bearing she has received. Next she is able to relieve her ancestor John Struther of his fear of fire, thus aiding the triumph of his martyrdom.

In the novel's last scenes, Pauline leaves for London, secure in her new awareness of divine love. At the train station, she and Stanhope are shocked to see Wentworth, sick and mad, beginning his last journey, one that will leave him in hell.

ANALYSIS

As a member of the Inklings group that included C. S. Lewis and J. R. R. Tolkein, Charles Williams was naturally interested both in fantasy and Christianity. Like Lewis, he used fiction to explore that interest and particularly the idea of "substituted love," which he portrayed as literally true.

It becomes the crux of the issues in *Descent into Hell*. Pauline Anstruther is startled when Stanhope suggests that he might carry her fear for her, and she is moved by joy when he does so. Her belief in the process enables her to help first the workman and then the protestant martyr. Clearly, Williams suggests that such love can transcend time, thus accounting for the blending of past and present in the novel. John Struther died in the 1550's and the workman evidently killed himself decades before the novel's main action, but Pauline is able to aid both of them, just as her grandmother seems somehow in touch with them. Williams' imagery suggests, in fact, that substituted love explains how the Crucifixion—here portrayed as the ultimate burden bearing—works for salvation.

Some characters reject the reaching beyond oneself that leads to heaven; that is what happens to Wentworth and to the characters who succumb to the offers of the demoniac Lily Sammile, who threads her way through the novel offering people like Wentworth the damning narcotic of self-indulgence and fantasy. Williams, like Dante Alighieri in the *Inferno* (in *The Divine Comedy*, c. 1320), insists that such people are condemned at their own insistence as they refuse the offers of love that could save them. Adele Hunt accepts Lily's offer, as does Wentworth; Pauline briefly comes perilously close.

Two of Williams' images relate very clearly to his ideas about love and time. Fire, for example, is important not only because of how it figures in Struther's martyrdom but also as part of Stanhope's play. Williams joins flame images to descriptions of the workman's suicide (by hanging from a house beam) to suggest the Crucifixion. Fire also appears more conventionally at the novel's end, as Wentworth descends into hell.

Williams also makes use of his characters' names. Peter Stanhope is surely intended to evoke the Apostle Peter, the stone on whom Jesus said he would build his church; "stan" is the early English form of "stone." Pauline, who so fears to meet her *Doppelgänger*, or double, on the road, carries the name of the Apostle Paul, who met Christ on the road to Damascus. Her last name, Anstruther, contains "truth" as a central element. Her grandmother's name, Margaret, means "a pearl" and is probably intended to suggest the "pearl of great price" that represented the kingdom of heaven in Jesus' parable. Even Wentworth's name suggests how thoroughly he has rejected his own value. Lily Sammile's name suggests the Lilith who in Hebrew myth was Adam's first wife and whose mythological personality is temptress and deceiver.

Behind these images lies one more, that of the city. Adjacent to Battle Hill, it is at the same time London, the city of God, and Dante's Satanic city of Dis.

—*Ann D. Garbett*

THE DEVIL IS DEAD

In the course of a sea voyage from America to the Greek islands, the heroic Finnegan matches wits with various "Neanderthal men," including Papadiabolous, who is said to be the Devil

Author: R(aphael) A(loysius) Lafferty (1914–2002)
Genre: Fantasy—mythological

Type of work: Novel
Time of work: The indeterminate past
Locale: Primarily the ship Brunhilde and the island of Naxos

THE STORY

Finnegan (who cannot remember his true name or nature) meets the eccentric millionaire Saxon

X. Seaworthy, who is similarly afflicted with amnesia. They have a drink together, served by Anastasia Demetriades (who is a mermaid, although that is not immediately obvious). They are joined by another person, whom Anastasia addresses as Papa-D. Later, Anastasia recruits Finnegan and other crew members for a voyage on Seaworthy's boat, the *Brunhilde*, seemingly against the wishes of Papa-D, whose full name is Papadiabolous. Anastasia tells Finnegan that Papadiabolous is the Devil.

On the transatlantic voyage, several tall tales are told and heard, a mysterious corpse turns up, and there is much enigmatic talk. Finnegan remembers that he and Seaworthy once buried someone who looks exactly like Papadiabolous and realizes that Seaworthy believes his present companion is the same person. Another passenger, the evil Marie Courtois, kills one of Finnegan's shipmates.

When the ship reaches the island of Naxos, various manifestations of classical mythology begin to intrude on the action and dialogue. A fight breaks out at the ship's mooring, and Finnegan returns there to find Papadiabolous dead. This demise apparently serves to liberate the evil inclinations of Seaworthy and his associates, which previously had been held in check.

Finnegan encounters Mr. X, who otherwise is left unidentified (no comment being made on the fact that X is also Seaworthy's middle initial). Mr. X offers an explanation of recent events that does not make matters any clearer. Finnegan then meets Dolores "Doll" Delancy. These three become a team of "outlaws," on the run from Seaworthy and other vague threats. More tall tales are told and heard, mingling mythological sources with other materials in increasingly chaotic fashion. Many new characters are introduced for this purpose, while Finnegan's alleged pursuers fade into the background, seemingly forgotten.

In the final chapter, Mr. X tells one last tale, which offers an explanation of the curious case of the two identical Papadiabolouses. They were twins, one evil and one "comparatively good." It was the evil twin whom Seaworthy killed, before he and Finnegan buried the body; the good twin had been quick to take the other's place. Mr. X and Finnegan then tell Doll that all these contending parties (including themselves but excluding her) are members of an older human race. She calls them gargoyles, although the prefatory notes attached to many of the chapters identify them as Neanderthal men, intent on dispossessing the race that has succeeded them. Finnegan, in turning against his own kind, has become a heroic renegade fighting on behalf of "hopeless" people who are unable to fight for themselves, being merely "sheep." Doll demands a climax for the story, but X tells her that "it is only regular people who believe in climaxes" and leaves her to provide her own—which she does, after a fashion.

ANALYSIS

Part of R. A. Lafferty's charm is that he defies analysis. The defiance is deliberate: Every time an explanation looms on the horizon, his determination is to subvert it, and every time a plot threatens to crystallize out of his narrative, he changes the *dramatis personae* and cuts the story adrift again. It is entirely appropriate that he should represent *The Devil Is Dead* as the centerpiece of a trilogy called the Argos Mythos, whose first volume, *Archipelago* (1979), was not published until eight years later and whose third volume never appeared (after all, only regular people believe in climaxes). The contents of that proposed volume appeared in three Canadian chapbooks: *Promontory Goats* (1988), *How Many Miles to Babylon?* (1989), and *Episodes of the Argo* (1990).

In *Archipelago*, it is alleged that Finnegan is really Jason, whose modern career echoes the quest of the Argonauts, but he obviously is many other people as well. In *The Devil Is Dead*, he frequently is called Finn, presumably in order to link him to Finn MacCool, a hero of Irish folklore. He is a Neanderthal man in a world in which Neanderthal men are extinct, blandly refusing to notice that his world ended long ago. Lafferty's work is full of such entities: men who are dead, or never lived, but who simply will not lie down or go away; and worlds that have been superseded, or never existed, but continue to intrude upon reality—much to the delight of those who would rather see dull existence replaced by something more colorful.

The reader who expects *The Devil Is Dead* to make sense is occasionally wooed by Mr. X's "explanations," only to be deceived. The point is that the world ought not to make sense, and that if it did it would be cause for terrible disappointment. Lafferty, a Roman Catholic who rejoices in that faith's indomitable insistence that miracles occur and that the world cannot be reduced to the causal accounts of science, will not consent to be thus disappointed. If *The Devil Is Dead* is to be reckoned a fantasy—and it is arguable that it should not, on the grounds that all of its mythological intrusions are confined to the eyes of their fictitious beholders—it is the most radical kind of fantasy. Most fantasy, by dealing frankly and earnestly with the unreal, serves to reinforce rather than to undermine awareness of the boundaries of the real. Lafferty sets out not merely to injure but also to insult reason, insisting that the reality of common sense is not worth recognition, let alone respect.

It is good that someone carries out this kind of literary work, simply on the grounds that nothing should ever go unchallenged, particularly the obvious. Since the brief vogue his work enjoyed in the early 1970's—during which time *The Devil Is Dead* was nominated for a Nebula Award—Lafferty has been banished to the wilderness of small press publication and condemned as an incorrigible eccentric, but his work remains resiliently alive, stubbornly lively, and pigheadedly vivid.

—*Brian Stableford*

THE DEVIL RIDES OUT

Duke de Richleau and three cohorts battle black magician Damien Mocata for the Talisman of Set, an icon that controls the Four Horsemen of the Apocalypse—War, Plague, Famine, and Death

Author: Dennis Wheatley (1897–1977)
Genre: Fantasy—occult
Type of work: Novel
Time of work: The 1930's
Locale: London, England, and environs; Paris, France; and the Astral Plane

THE STORY

The Devil Rides Out features "The Four Musketeers"—Duke de Richleau, Rex Van Ryn, Richard Eaton, and Simon Aron—series characters who appear in Dennis Wheatley's political thrillers as well as his black magic novels. Alarmed by the fact that their friend Simon Aron has fallen under the influence of a black magician, Damien Mocata, occult expert Duke de Richleau and his friend Rex Van Ryn set out to help him. They learn that Aron is the key element in the magician's conspiracy to activate the powers of the Talisman of Set, thereby giving Mocata control over the Four Horsemen of the Apocalypse. They set out to free their friend and save humanity.

The first rescue is relatively easy, but Aron is recaptured. In a heroic Walpurgis Night assault on Mocata's castle, the duke and Van Ryn again rescue Aron. They spirit him to Cardinals Folly, the estate of Richard Eaton, where they are all safely harbored against Mocata's demoniac attacks in a specially prepared magic pentacle. Temporarily frustrated, Mocata launches a counterattack on the duke's group by kidnapping Fleur d'Amour, Eaton's innocent young daughter. Her ritual sacrifice will loose the powers of the Talisman of Set for Mocata. The Four Musketeers, accompanied by Fleur's mother, Marie Lou, race to Paris for a final confrontation with the black magician. The men are stymied by Mocata's occult defenses but, moments before the sacrifice is to occur, Marie Lou recalls a magical dream and utters words that tear the talisman away from Mocata and summon the Lord of Light. Taking over Fleur's body, the Lord of Light turns Mocata's own demons against him in a final battle that takes place on the Astral Plane.

ANALYSIS

Writing a mix of spy thrillers, historical adventures, and horror stories, Wheatley was one of Great Britain's most commercially successful authors for almost forty years. Although they make up a mere fifth of his total output, only the occult novels—or "black magic" stories, as he labeled them—are of any lasting interest. Despite their prior popularity, however, interest has waned considerably.

Wheatley's popular success was no accident. A fine storyteller, he was especially skillful at creating exciting, vivid dramatic scenes, enhanced by his eye for precise sensory detail. Wheatley's characters, especially his villains, though generally flat and often stereotypical, could be colorful and grotesque. A scrupulous researcher, Wheatley was thorough in his investigations of supernatural phenomena. In his best horror stories, he integrated these elements into a solid, realistic milieu at those points in the action where they fit most easily into the narrative. Thus, Wheatley created worlds in which the laws of black and white magic operate believably and inevitably, the unseen becoming a palpable presence. In addition, Wheatley's versatility enabled him to fuse several popular genres into hybrid works that used the most stimulating elements of each genre.

Sadly, defects have dated many of Wheatley's novels. The writing itself is never more than serviceable. Plotting is uneven, sometimes clean and efficient but frequently awkward and digressive. His reliance on the climactic *deus ex machina* often approaches the laughable. Even more damaging is his tendency toward preaching, heavy-handed moralizing, and abstract speculations. This is especially true in his later books, in which the narrative drive is overwhelmed by his reactionary social attitudes, virulent anti-Communism, and otherworldly metaphysics.

The Devil Rides Out, his first horror novel, represents Wheatley at his best. Here he introduces the formula that shapes all the occult de Richleau books as well as, in varying degrees, the other black magic novels. In this formula, de Richleau and company are made aware of a serious satanic threat to a friend and/or humanity. They take arms and win a modest victory that provokes the minions of evil into retaliation. The four are pursued and attacked by overwhelming forces in an uneven contest until, finally, good rallies and triumphs, more often than not as a result of a sudden divine intervention.

The virtues of *The Devil Rides Out* are clear. Wheatley's Four Musketeers—a French Royalist exile and epicurean (de Richleau), a Jewish financier (Aron), an aristocratic Englishman (Eaton), and a wealthy American (Van Ryn)—make a good, if snobbish, team that served Wheatley well in eleven novels, only three of which fit into the black magic category. Excepting the *deus ex machina* ending, the plotting is simple, direct, and believable. The villain is purely evil, larger than life, and fittingly grotesque.

The supernatural paraphernalia, however, probably give *The Devil Rides Out* its continuing entertainment value. Wheatley was especially thorough in his researching of occult materials. As do all of his black magic novels, *The Devil Rides Out* contains a serious warning to the reader to "refrain from being drawn into the practice of the Secret Art in any way." Wheatley was a lifelong believer (if not practitioner) in the occult; his nonfiction treatise *The Devil and All His Works* (1971) is a monumental treatment of the subject. *The Devil Rides Out* is glutted with occult paraphernalia including satanism, demoniac possession, child sacrifice, astral travel, palmistry, numerology, ghostly appearances, necromancy, the conjuring of demons, magical incantations, time manipulation, hypnotism, and clairvoyance.

These elements are never merely inserted into the novel, however; Wheatley was adroit in integrating the magical elements and supernatural menace into the narrative, fitting them easily into the realistic fabric of his book to posit a world in which the laws of black magic are as natural as the laws of physics. This skillful incorporation of occult elements gives to *The Devil Rides Out* and the other effective black magic novels a timelessness lacking in his other books, which now seem hopelessly dated.

Even as a horror writer, Wheatley generally is overlooked. The irony of this obscurity lies in the fact that, although it is rarely acknowledged or recognized, Wheatley developed the form used in most popular contemporary horror novels—the large, elaborate, complicated books that mix several genres (horror, quest fantasy, social melodrama, science fiction, mystery, and others)—written by Stephen King, Peter Straub, Dean Koontz, and numerous other popular authors.

—*Keith Neilson*

Devil's Tor

Visions of the Earth-Mother prompt the rejoining of two halves of a magical stone, bringing together a man and a woman fated to be the progenitors of a new race

Author: David Lindsay (1876-1945)
Genre: Fantasy—theological romance
Type of work: Novel
Time of work: The 1930's
Locale: Dartmoor
First published: 1932

The Story

Ingrid Fleming, a solitary young woman given to dreaming, takes a cousin, Hugh Drapier, to see Devil's Tor, which bears a crag shaped like a human face. She has always believed, intuitively, that the tor is the tomb of a mysterious female. Lightning strikes and splits the "face," revealing a staircase. Drapier goes down into a cavern, where he sees a vision of the Earth-Mother. He also finds a piece of stone that he does not realize at first to be one half of a broken flint, the other half of which already is in his possession. Its mate was consigned to his care by explorer Henry Saltfleet and archaeologist Stephen Arsinal, who stole it from a temple in Tibet.

An earthquake seals the tomb, and Drapier is killed by a rock slide. Saltfleet, who comes to reclaim his half of the stone, finds Drapier's corpse clutching the other. Saltfleet is eager to reunite the two halves but is delayed by wrangles over ownership that involve long conversations in which the various characters discuss the implications of the stone's existence and the possible consequences of it being made whole again.

It emerges that all the major characters have been manipulated since birth (and in some cases before) by an active Fate that intends to rejoin the pieces of the stone. The personification of this Fate is the Earth-Mother, the "demiurge" responsible for the creation of the world at the instigation of the Ancient (that is, God). The rejoining of the stone will seal the union of a man and a woman who are destined to become the parents of a new race, in repetition of an earlier union that gave birth to the blue-eyed Nordic race.

Eventually, Saltfleet and Arsinal persuade Ingrid and her fiancé, artist Peter Copping, to meet on Devil's Tor in order to reunite the pieces of the stone. The materialistic Arsinal, who actually brings the two halves together, is unable to perceive the spiritual power implicit in the stone and is blasted fatally by the released force. Copping realizes that it is Saltfleet who is destined to be the father of the new race and surrenders Ingrid to him. The relationship between them is to be far more intense and painful than mere human love, and they learn from their visions that their pain will be reflected in the reckless turbulence of the new era that their progeny will bring into existence.

Analysis

Devil's Tor is a revised version of a novel written in the early 1920's, originally called *The Ancient Tragedy*, which carried forward the central themes of David Lindsay's novels *A Voyage to Arcturus* (1920) and *The Haunted Woman* (1922). The dualistic and pain-saturated theology of the former novel is here revised, elaborated, and solidly grounded in an idiosyncratic version of human prehistory. The intense and sublime central relationship that is the focal point of the latter novel could reach only temporary fruition therein, in another world. Here it is recapitulated as a historical pivot, given the power to renew the spiritual fervor that contemporary life has exhausted.

Unlike the dualism of *A Voyage to Arcturus*, which is basically combative although it differs markedly from conventional accounts of God and the devil, the dualism of *Devil's Tor* is collaborative. The sexless Ancient produced the Earth-Mother as a necessary instrument of procreation; it is she and not the beings she creates who has undergone a "fall" into sexuality—a fall that involves the spirit as well as the flesh. Lindsay's narrative takes an ambivalent view of sexuality, as do all of his novels, which he began to write after jilting his long-time fiancée and marrying a much young woman. The narrative does accept sexuality's fateful force, arguing that its chief redeeming feature is its power of renewal and regeneration.

Lindsay's account of the qualities and triumphs of the Nordic race are bound to seem suspect in a post-Nazi era, but he is not concerned with crude theories of racial superiority. Insofar as such ideas are given voice in the novel, they are put into the mouth of Arsinal, whose inability to appreciate the spiritual dimension of the adventure is deemed crass enough to warrant his symbolic execution. Even Copping, who is as limited by his art as Arsinal is by his science, is granted greater favor than that. Lindsay's primary aim in talking about a Nietz-schean "new race" is to establish that progress can arise only from painful strife, conflict, and a fervent love of freedom; his new savior is not destined to carry forward any process of ethnic cleansing.

Lindsay regarded *Devil's Tor* as the masterpiece among his published works, although he hoped that The Witch, which he never managed to complete, might surpass it. It is not entirely surprising that he struggled for nearly ten years to get it into print. Most modern critics think it inferior to *A Voyage to Arcturus*, on the grounds that its long dialogues, most of which take place while the plot is stalled by hollow contrivances, are ponderous and turgid compared with the brilliantly vivid allegorical displays of the earlier novel. This is true, but the fact remains that *Devil's Tor* is a more accurate embodiment of the author's highly individual worldview, and its existence allows readers a better understanding of what *A Voyage to Arcturus* and *The Haunted Woman* were striving to achieve. The philosophical interludes are dull and have not aged particularly well in respect to either content or style, but there is compensation in the many visionary sequences that function as revelations of the Earth-Mother and her purpose. *Devil's Tor* remains a towering product of the literary imagination and a highly original venture in speculative metaphysics.

—*Brian Stableford*

DHALGREN

Kid embarks on a quest of self-discovery in Bellona, a city transformed into an anarchist realm by its entrapment in a distorted space-time continuum

Author: Samuel R. Delany (1942–)
Genre: Science fiction—new wave
Type of work: Novel
Time of work: The 1970's
Location: Bellona, an imaginary American city
First published: 1975

THE STORY

Written over a period of four years and spanning more than eight hundred pages, *Dhalgren* is Samuel R. Delany's magnum opus. *Dhalgren*'s main character is the twenty-seven-year-old Kid, who suffers from selective amnesia and other mental disturbances. At the novel's start, Kid is hitchhiking to Bellona, a midwestern city trapped by a mysterious disaster in a shifting zone of reality where time runs in loops and occasionally a giant red sun or two moons appear in the heavens.

On his way into Bellona, Kid meets a strange Asian woman who, after they make love, turns into a tree. This surreal opening begins *Dhalgren*'s conflicting realities: Are the novel's strange events real, or are they the result of Kid's delusional point of view?

Upon entering Bellona, Kid becomes the lover of a former electrical engineer named Tak, who introduces Kid to the cult of George Harrison, a powerful black man worshiped in Bellona's ghetto. Tak takes Kid to the city's hippie commune, and there Kid meets Lanya, who becomes Kid's next lover. Kid also finds a notebook containing the journal of an anonymous past owner. Because of *Dhalgren*'s time loops and Kid's amnesia, Kid himself could have written the journal at an earlier or later time.

Kid begins to write poetry in this notebook. These poems become the
basis for *Brass Orchids*, a book published by Roger Calkins, the eccentric
owner of the city's newspaper, the *Bellona Times*.

Kid receives a severe beating from a trio of scorpions, the name given to Bellona's street gangs. On occasion, scorpions venture out from their nests, or home bases, terrorizing Bellona's residents. Gang members wear projectors that conceal their bodies in holographic images of griffins, spiders, dragons, and other mythical or fantastic creatures.

After this incident, Kid meets June Richards. The Richards family tries to lead an unchanged bourgeois existence in the midst of Bellona's chaos. George Harrison reportedly raped June during the riots that occurred during Bellona's mysterious catastrophe. Kid comes to realize that the so-called rape was an act of mutual desire filled with mythological portents.

Later, Kid is drawn unwittingly into a scorpion run on Emboriky's, a major department store that is the stronghold of a group of armed white racists. During the run, Kid displays the kind of crazy bravery the gang admires. As a result, Kid becomes the leader of a scorpion nest and acquires as a lover a gang member named Denny who becomes part of a three-way sexual relationship with Lanya.

The remainder of the novel concerns Kid's adventures as a scorpion and a poet. While prowling Bellona's shattered streets, Kid awaits the second meeting between George and June. Kid believes that when this meeting occurs, Bellona will plunge once more into an apocalyptic frenzy.

Inspired by metafictional technique (fiction that comments on itself as fiction), Delany wrote *Dhalgren*'s final chapters in columns, with one side following the story and the other commenting on the action, presenting alternative plot lines, or revealing passages from Kid's notebook. This method creates a dual ending. One possibility is that June and George meet, the mysterious apocalypse strikes Bellona again, and Kid flees the city. In a manner reminiscent of James Joyce's *Finnegans Wake* (1939), the last line of *Dhalgren* is a half sentence completed by the half sentence at the novel's start, creating a closed loop. Thus Kid is caught in Bellona's circular time pattern. The other possibility is that the ending is merely a fiction of Kid's notebook, and both the arrival and exit scenes are not real. Kid has always been in Bellona and will always remain there, its scorpion poet.

ANALYSIS

Dhalgren is a pivotal work in Delany's career. Although it continues many of the themes of his earlier novels, *Dhalgren* has a dense, literary style and unflinching examination of drug use, deviant sexuality, and violence that also point toward future works such as *Tales of Nevèrÿon* (1979) and *Stars in My Pocket Like Grains of Sand* (1984).

Unlike *Babel-17* (1966), *The Einstein Intersection* (1967), and *Nova* (1968), *Dhalgren* explores countercultural themes such as bisexuality, drug use, race relations, and the connection between artistic and criminal cultures, without far future or deep space settings to blunt the controversial nature of these subjects. The immediacy of *Dhalgren*'s 1970's setting, combined with its difficult literary style and explicit sex and violence, alienated much of Delany's previous readership, who had come to expect works like *Nova* and *Babel-17*, which essentially were stock space epics written with stylistic flare and a 1960's hip sensibility.

Also alienated were many science-fiction reviewers and critics, who regarded *Dhalgren* as at best incomprehensible and at worst a disgrace to the field. *Dhalgren* nevertheless sold well, more than a million copies in less than a decade. In his collection of essays *The Straits of Messina* (1989), Delany attributes these sales to interested readers and sympathetic reviewers outside the science-fiction field.

Dhalgren has its science-fiction defenders, most notably Theodore Sturgeon and Frederik Pohl, and the novel's critical support has increased over the years. What critics praise in *Dhalgren* are its literary experimentation, its highly charged language, and its depth of character. Few other works in any field have portrayed life on the fringes of society with such richness of detail and depth of understanding. *Dhalgren*, with its nonlinear structure, stream-of-consciousness passages, and selfcommentary, evokes the brilliant literary innovations of James Joyce, Jorge Luis Borges, and Thomas Pynchon.

Dhalgren may well be the climax of science fiction's NewWave exploration of expanded themes and stylistic techniques. At the same time, its focus on the urban fringe foreshadows the arrival of science fiction's cyberpunk movement in the mid-1980's.

—*John Nizalowski*

THE DIAMOND AGE; OR, A YOUNG LADY'S ILLUSTRATED PRIMER

In a utopian future of nanotech and abundance, Neo-Victorian culture faces its greatest challenge, and survival depends on one unique young woman

Author: Neal Stephenson (1959–)
Genre: Science Fiction—extrapolatory
Type of Work: Novel
Time of Plot: Future (twenty-first century)
Location: Earth, generally around Shanghai
First Published: 1995

THE STORY

In the world of the late twenty-first century, nanotechnology is ubiquitous and dominant, present in areas as diverse as crime enforcement and luxury marketing. The development of nanotechnology has been accompanied by the breakdown of the old socioeconomic order and the rise of a new order, this one having societies based on phyles (shared attributes) who have grouped themselves into enclaves ("claves"). One of the dominant phyles of Shanghai is the Neo-Victorians, who have modeled themselves after their perception of English Victorian society, though it is Victorian society as it should have been rather than as it was. They are a stable but static phyle, needing to rely on creative talent and craftsmen imported from other phyles and enclaves.

Lord Chung-Sik Finkle-McGraw is Equity Lord of the Neo-Victorians, a visionary of enormous patience and foresight. He commissions brilliant nanotech engineer John Percival Hackworth to develop an interactive nanotechnology book for his granddaughter Elizabeth; this book must instruct and counsel and grow with its reader, and above all,

it must contain an element of social subversion. Hackworth creates such a volume, but recognizing its potential use, he has its code extracted by the mysterious Dr. X and makes a copy for his daughter, Fiona. It does not reach Fiona, however, for Hackworth is mugged, and the volume ends up in the possession of Nellodee (Nell), a girl being raised by her brother Harv in the lower-class working area known as the Leased Territories. (Her father, Bud, is a petty criminal soon caught and executed for his crimes; her mother, Tequila, is neglectful and has lovers who abuse her children.) Nell and Harv move to Dovetail, which manufactures materials for the Neo-Victorians, and she grows to lovely maturity in the Neo-Victorian clave, instructed by her primer, whose stories become longer and more complex.

Following his mugging, Hackworth was caught by the Chinese and commissioned to make additional interactive primers, for Dr. X has been raising the female babies abandoned by mothers desirous of sons, and they require educating. Hackworth is ultimately sent to the United States in search of a mysterious nanotechnology figure known as the Alchemist, who is working with organic computers whose components are transmitted via sexual activity. The humans working with the Alchemist are known as Drummers, and Hackworth becomes a Drummer and disappears for ten years. He eventually leaves and meets his long-suffering wife and Fiona, who has relocated to Seattle. Hackworth and Fiona end up aboard a ship as part of a theatre troupe, though he returns to Shanghai having made a crucial discovery in his quest for the Alchemist: his quest is circular, for he is the Alchemist. (He confirms this with Dr. X.)

Nell has left the Neo-Victorians upon maturity and is writing sexual scripts for Madame Ping's bordello when she runs afoul of the Chinese guerilla group known as the Fists. Clearly modeled after the Boxers of the Boxer Rebellion, this group wants China to return to the Chinese and is leading a revolt in Shanghai. Nell is captured and raped but frees herself and releases the signal that all the young women who have been raised using

Dr. X's primers have been waiting for. They arise and rescue Nell, hailing her as their queen.

ANALYSIS
The Diamond Age is a fully-realized series of extrapolations of the social systems and societies that would arise from the development and impact of new technologies and economic systems. Although characters in *The Diamond Age* can be loosely linked to Stephenson's earlier *Snow Crash*, the societies of *The Diamond Age* are mature and fully operational and do not need to rely on freelance hackers to maintain their existence. A particularly telling storyline involves Bud, who takes pride in his physicality and outlaw skills, which include the use of a skull-gun. In a society that espoused or merely accepted cyberpunk values, Bud would thrive and even flourish. In the world of *The Diamond Age*, however, he is nothing more than a nuisance, and upon being caught during a mugging, he is dealt with summarily yet humanely.

At the same time, in envisioning and writing *The Diamond Age*, Stephenson appears to have been inspired by what is known as Arthur C. Clarke's Third Law, viz., any technology sufficiently advanced is indistinguishable from magic. Stephenson thus dazzles with his scientific and technological extrapolations. There is the *chevaline*, a mechanical horse that can fold up and is light enough to be carried with one hand. Cities are recognized as complex organisms, and as such, they have immune systems involving micromachinery to protect themselves and their citizens. There are also matter compilers that provide food and water upon request. (Power and matter are derived from the Feed, a networked supply system.) There are also personalized news devices, and of course, there is the literally interactive primer that Finkle-McGraw conceives and Hackworth executes. It is impossible not to be dazzled by Stephenson's inventiveness, though it is also possible to be overwhelmed by the repetitive novelty of Stephenson's conceptions.

In Stephenson's oeuvre, *The Diamond Age* occupies a pivotal and transitional role. Prior to *The Diamond Age*, Stephenson tended to be more conservative in his extrapolations. His narratives were full of new ideas and clever extrapolations, but his narrative approach tended not to examine the implications or impact of these. Similarly, his characters tended to be brilliant, courageous, and tech-savvy individuals. However, their skills did not integrate them, and they remained social outsiders rather than assimilated members of society. *The Diamond Age* is thus a significant step forward in Stephenson's maturation as a writer. Not only are the global impacts of his extrapolations fully worked out but also his presentation of the future recognizes the probable long-term impacts and fundamental paradigm shifts that would occur with the introduction, development, and maturation of new technologies and the societies that would arise as a result of these. Similarly, the characters that occupy the different social strata are all integrated members of their worlds, not gifted and talented outsiders. Although Stephenson's early work is talented and engaging, *The Diamond Age* is really his first fully mature creation.

—*Richard Bleiler*

THE DIFFERENCE ENGINE

In an alternate history in which Charles Babbage's difference engine is successfully built, paleontologist Edward Mallory attempts to assist Ada Byron with her gambling program for the engine

Author: William Gibson (1948–) and Bruce Sterling (1954–)
Genre: Science fiction—alternate history
Type of work: Novel
Time of work: 1855

Locale: London, England
First published: 1990, in Great Britain (first pb. 1991, in U.S.)

THE STORY
The Difference Engine's five iterations recall the repetition of subroutines in a computer program. They provide different perspectives on a sequence of events in the year 1855. Charles Babbage has successfully built his difference engine, bringing

into being a steam-based information technology. Because the difference engine, a type of computer, historically was not completed, this event becomes the pivot of the alternate history. The plot concerns a set of punch cards created by Ada Byron as a gambling system.

In Iteration One, an aged Sybil Gerard, living in Cherbourg in 1905, remembers January 15, 1855, and her relationship with a doomed opportunist-revolutionary, Mick Radley. Sybil had become a prostitute because her father was hanged as a revolutionary. Her identity is in the police "engines," preventing her from following another profession. Mick involves her in attempts to get a computer program from the deposed president of Texas, Sam Houston, in his London hotel room. Sybil witnesses an attack on Houston that results in Mick's death and sends her to France.

Iteration Two introduces Edward Mallory, a famous paleontologist who discovered the "great land leviathan," or a Brontosaurus, while on a dig in the wilds of Wyoming. On Derby Day, on which both horses and steam-driven vehicles are raced in different heats, he has two momentous experiences. He assists Ada Byron, daughter of the famous Lord Byron who is England's prime minister, to secure a small case containing punch cards for a computer program, then keeps it for her. He also bets on a steam-car race and wins 400 pounds, a small fortune in that time. Subsequently, he is recruited by L. Oliphant, a special detective, to follow a sociology project. He is also set upon by thugs.

In Iteration Three, Mallory suffers further attacks, including one to his rooms in the Palace of Paleontology. Oliphant sends him to the Department of Criminology to identify his attackers. His letter to Ada Byron advises her that he has hidden her case of punch cards in the skull of his Brontosaurus in the British Museum.

Iteration Four describes the societal chaos in London resulting from rampant pollution that has fouled the Thames and the subway system. Mallory's family is now also under attack by revolutionaries. His two brothers, one a steam engineer and one on military leave from India, arrive in London. Together they locate the leader of the revolutionaries, a homicidal woman named Francis Bartlett and her henchman, Captain Swing.

They manage to kill him but not her. A "cleansing rain" clears out the pollution and ends the social disintegration.

In Iteration Five, Oliphant collates the various deaths and attacks that result from Bartlett's attempts to obtain the punch cards. Several of her henchmen are killed, and her attempt fails. Nevertheless, the malfunctioning of the Grand Napoleon, the French difference engine, is presented as the precursor to malfunctions in the English engine. Both failures are attributed to pollution. The text suggests another explanation, that the malfunctions occur because Ada's faulty program is run.

The final section, MODUS, is a pastiche of individuals using or used by the idea of a difference engine and an analytical engine. It projects the alternate history into the future, in which Ada's program has run rampant and, by 1991, has virtually eliminated human agency.

ANALYSIS

This novel is perhaps the most controversial to date in the careers of both William Gibson and Bruce Sterling. It was better received outside the science-fiction community than inside. Gibson's future of virtual spaces in *Neuromancer* (1984, winner of the Hugo, Nebula, and Philip K. Dick awards), *Count Zero* (1986), and *Mona Lisa Overdrive* (1988) took the science-fiction community by storm. Sterling's black projections for the technological future and his declarations of the new wave of cyberpunk cast him as the enfant terrible of 1980's and 1990's science fiction, from the first manifesto in *Mirrorshades: The Cyberpunk Anthology* (1986) to later novels.

The Difference Engine is unlike Gibson's and Sterling's other work in its literary technique as well as in its subject matter and period. Although it focuses on a technological revolution, as does their other work, its pacing is much more leisurely. Its diction is somewhat stilted, with occasional glimmers of characterization that seep into a tour de force of Victorian figures, none of whom is fully drawn in the historical or alternative historical roles. The meat of the novel is not its plot, characters, or setting. According to Gibson, the authors took many of their descriptions from period fiction and journalism. The substance of the novel is instead found in comparisons made constantly by the reader between figures and events in history and in the alternate history presented by the novel. Figures such as Lord Wellington become villains, and Ada and Lord Byron have political prestige. The novel becomes a game of recognition.

There is a fine line between technique used to create atmosphere and technique as an end in itself. *The Difference Engine* maximizes technique where it minimizes fiction, for the novel is full of political and social clichés familiar to science-fiction readers. The familiar theme is that technology that holds the promise for the relief of human suffering can also increase it. This novel fascinates the reader by foregrounding the basic ambivalence of science fiction as fiction rather than science. It works like a machine to grind out the same answer using variegated mechanisms.

—*Philip E. Kaveny and Janice M. Bogstad*

A Different Flesh

When European explorers discover the New World they find fertile, arable land for the taking, roamed by Pleistocene megafauna and populated by roving bands of Homo erectus

Author: Harry Turtledove (1949–)
Genre: Science fiction—alternate history
Type of work: Novel
Time of work: The seventeenth century to the twentieth century
Locale: An alternate Earth
First published: 1988

The Story

In his preface to this novel, Harry Turtledove reveals that the idea for it came from an article by Stephen Jay Gould speculating about how humanity's distant cousin, *Australopithecus*, would be treated if that species had survived. Turtledove decided to use a nearer cousin, *Homo erectus*, in his story. The short answer that he provides to the above question is "not very well."

The story begins with an entry from a fictional reference work that establishes that the novel takes place in an alternate reality, with the difference that the New World, when discovered by Europeans, was populated by *Homo erectus*, dubbed "sims" by their discoverers. Living in bands of hunter-gatherers but lacking the neocortex, spoken language, and superior reasoning skills of *Homo sapiens*, sims were less efficient hunters than the denizens of the Old World. Consequently, species hunted to extinction in Europe and Asia still flourish in the New World. Among these are saber-toothed tigers and woolly mammoths.

Subsequent historical entries describe the settlement of the New World, the development of a rail system powered by woolly mammoths (later replaced by steam engines), the rise of plantation agriculture sustained through the enslavement of sims, and the development of a growing sims-rights movement. Each of these entries is followed by an expository episode that gives the details of the changes described.

The differences in this alternate reality, as compared to the known world, range from the obvious to the subtle. Because the *Homo erectus* population provides less resistance to colonization than did the actual Native Americans, the New World was colonized more quickly. Place names in the New World are all taken from the Old; the Mississippi River, for example, is called the New Nile. The North American government, lacking inspiration from the Iroquois Confederation, is patterned after Greek democracy and the centralized federal republic of ancient Rome.

The existence of sims makes it more difficult for Europeans to identify differences among humans. Slavery of nonwhite humans continues as an economic institution, and there are still those who, against all evidence to the contrary, impute inferior value to humans with darker skin pigmentation. The subtle difference from the reader's reality is that nonwhite people know themselves to be superior to sims; therefore, they participate in the oppression of the less sophisticated life-form, and their self-respect, to some extent, rests on the knowledge that they are not on the bottom rung of the evolutionary ladder.

Analysis

Often the best science fiction and fantasy results from exploration of a simple question, such as "How do you define what is human?" From the first pages of *A Different Flesh*, Turtledove makes the status of sims the major concern: Are they animal or human? In the first expository episode, a settler and his wife conclude their argument by noting that the last time the issue was raised, their present positions were reversed. She had thought sims human, and he had thought them beasts. They acknowledge that the issue is not easily resolved.

In the middle of the novel, Turtledove explores the Aristotelian notion that there are those who are slaves by nature. Because sims are incapable of producing civilized behavior on their own, humans do them a favor by allowing them to serve their betters, learning more refined behavior through instruction and association. One episode concerns a sim who is a snob. He has learned much from his human associates, and he declines an opportunity to join a band of wild sims, conveying through sign language that they are boring and uncivilized. He would rather be a slave to humans than be free and wild.

The debate continues throughout the book. Early in the novel, readers will tend to identify more with the humans' views of sims as an inferior and at times inexplicable life-form. As the novel progresses and more is revealed about sims and their ability to do many things that might be considered "human," readers are drawn into the complexity of the issue. It is apparent that sims have a level of intelligence and that they have preferences; therefore, they may be entitled to more choice in their lives than they have been given.

In the final vignette, Turtledove raises the issue of animal rights regarding medical experimentation. In the late 1980's, sims are being used in research aimed at finding a cure for the acquired immune deficiency syndrome (AIDS) epidemic. By this time, legal precedents have been set stating that sims are not people and may be used in lieu of people in medical experiments. Various groups protest such usage, regarding the infliction of pain and suffering on living, feeling beings as immoral, no matter how beneficial to humans the eventual result may be. One such group effects a rescue of Matt, an AIDS research subject. Assured by his rescuers that he is free, he nevertheless finds freedom much more restrictive than the laboratory, where creature comforts and companionship were provided. As is often the case in real life, the novel reaches no satisfactory conclusion; the author is content to have presented a sensitive yet thorough exploration of a complex problem.

Turtledove has a Ph.D. in Byzantine history and has been writing fantasy and science fiction since 1979. His Videssos cycle, consisting of *The Misplaced Legion*, *An Emperor for the Legion*, *The Legion of Videssos*, and *Swords of the Legion* (all published in 1987), has a Byzantine setting. *A Different Flesh* is a work by an accomplished storyteller of enormous intelligence and curiosity.

—*Karen S. Bellinfante*

A Different Kingdom

Michael Fay learns about an alternate world and his place in the Wild Forest

Author: Paul Kearney (1967–)
Genre: Fantasy—mythological
Type of work: Novel
Time of work: The 1950's
Locale: Northern Ireland and the Wildwood
First published: 1993

The Story

Orphaned by a bomb blast that kills his parents, Michael Fay is brought up by his grandparents on a large, remote farm in rural Antrim in Northern Ireland. He is left alone, except by his Aunt Rose, a warm, very sexual, young woman.

When he is eight years old, Michael trips on the riverbank and gets his first sight of the Fox-People from an alternate world. Subsequently, wolves swarm into his world, unnoticed by others but capable of killing. To add to his problems, Rose becomes pregnant and dies in childbirth. A local man is blamed, but the real father is a mysterious hooded horseman.

Five years later, Michael sees the Fox-People kill a werewolf. He digs up its skull the next day and uses it to defend himself against a wolf attack. Michael sees the Horseman and feels his evil. He encounters an attractive wild girl, Cat, who reminds him of Rose. They meet several more times and become lovers, but he is too young to leave his world to join hers.

Escaping pursuit by wolves, Cat arrives at his house. He takes her in, and they leave together in the morning. They are chased through the forest by wolves and the Horseman, who is recognized by everyone as the Devil. Michael wins the support of the Myrcan Fox-People and their leader, Ringbone, by rescuing two Myrcans from some Catholic Knights Militant who were intent on killing them. Michael already has been helped by Mirkady, the Elf King, and by a troll, Dwarmo. Now, with a legendary sword, Ulfbehrt, he is ready to rescue Rose's soul from the Horseman-Devil's castle.

Despite wolf attacks, Michael and Cat reach the edge of the forest and enter Wolfweald, an area that has obliterated two expeditions by the Christian brothers. Only with Mirkady's help do they survive a goblin attack. He gives Michael and Cat a gift of Wyr-fire, to be used only once when in dire trouble. Nothing can alter the fact that Michael, chronologically fifteen years old, is aging quickly.

They stumble across the encampment of Brother Nennian. Recognizing Michael's original faith, the brother wants to join them. The journey becomes even harder; they are starving, the castle is elusive, and Michael is reaching middle age. Finally, they come to a glade. The wind whips up, the trees grow closer, and there is an urge to join with them; then the wolves arrive. Nennian is killed, and Cat and Michael are wounded before they can invoke the Wyr-fire. Once invoked, the Wyr-fire destroys the wolves, which are made of wood. After they leave the Wyrwood, turning away from the quest in defeat, Michael decides to quit and return to his own world.

More than a decade later, Michael is found to be a nightmare-ridden alcoholic by Mirkady and Dwarmo, who have been looking for him. He finally reaches the Horseman's castle but discovers that the Horseman is not the Devil; rather, he is the spirit of the Wildwood. He wants Michael, so Michael is able to negotiate terms. Rose is restored to life with her stillborn child, and Michael is freed from his painful memories. The Michael that inhabits the alternate world remains with Cat.

ANALYSIS

This second novel by a promising fantasy writer clearly is influenced by Robert P. Holdstock's Mythago series, begun in 1984, and probably by Thomas Burnett Swann (1928–1976). The novel, however, has an individuality and freshness all its own.

In some respects, *A Different Kingdom* is connected to Paul Kearney's earlier work, *The Way to Babylon* (1992). The Myrcans reappear, and Kearney explains that their appearance is different because considerable time has passed and they have lost their roles. Some other beings, notably the wood-wolves, also appeared in the previous book. Nevertheless, the link is tenuous, particularly in the light of the fact that *A Different Kingdom* is a reversal of the previous book's concern with maintaining order.

Kearney concerns himself directly with the modern Irish experience. *A Different Kingdom*, as may be surmised from its title, may be read as an allegory of the relatively static qualities of Ulster life and character being menaced by the wilder Catholic world. It is fair to say, however, that Kearney's later treatment of Catholicism, by no means totally unsympathetic, militates against this view.

The book has several strengths. The depiction of the 1950's farm household at first appears so strong that the fantasy cannot rival it. The characterization also is strong, and the picture of growing up in a seemingly idyllic environment is portrayed convincingly. The fey qualities of the old farm laborer Mullan, a friend to young Michael, not only seem realistic for the unmodernized time but form a prediction of the forthcoming eruption of wildness into the stable environment of the farm.

Kearney shows mastery of the individual scene. From the Myrcan slaughter of the werewolf to the scene in which the Wyrin come for the failing adult Michael, covering his girlfriend with acorns and rowan berries, the stench and force of the alternate world are vivid. Kearney's elves, werewolves, trolls, and goblins, which collectively form the Wyrin, avoid the clichés that such names impart in other fantasy works.

Above all, the reader gets a feeling for the trees and wood, which are central to the book. The wood-wolves are genuinely chilling, and the priests who are absorbed into the trees are thought in some ways to be saved as well as damned. The conclusion, defiantly pagan though by no means atheistic, is a more literary statement of such male role revisionary works as Robert Bly's *Iron John: A Book About Men* (1990).

Historical influences on the book include the Spanish conquest of America. The most prominent fictional in-fluence is Rudyard Kipling's *The Jungle Book* (1894), particularly the analogies to the characters Ringbone, Mirkady, Dwarmo, and the Horseman.

—*Mike Dickinson*

DIMENSION OF MIRACLES

An earthling is awarded a mysterious prize far from Earth, and he has amusing troubles finding his way home

Author: Robert Sheckley (1925–2005)
Genre: Science fiction—new wave
Type of work: Novel
Time of work: The late 1960's
Locale: Earth, the Galactic Center, the planet Lursis, and alternate Earths
First published: 1968

THE STORY

Carmody (no other name is given) lives an ordinary life on Earth until an alien Messenger shows up to inform him that he has won the Intergalactic Sweepstakes and to take him to collect his prize. After signing the paper accepting the prize, he is confronted by an alien named Karmod, who insists that he is the rightful winner of the prize, pointing out that Carmody could not have entered the sweepstakes because Earth is not a part of the Galactic culture. The computer that made the award admits (proclaims, in fact) that it had made an error in awarding the prize to Carmody, but the prize itself speaks up, urging Carmody not to give in, and he insists on keeping it.

Carmody then learns that he will have to find his own way home, specifically that he will have to find the Where, When, and Which of his Earth. Carmody and the prize are sent to the planet Lursis, owned and inhabited by the god Melichrone. Melichrone is the only entity that can live on Lursis for long. As the god of that planet, he has turned himself into entire races of beings, but now he is bored and can find no meaning in life. Carmody tells him that he can find meaning by helping others, such as Carmody himself. Melichrone agrees, warning Carmody that his unique situation as prize winner has caused him to be pursued by a unique predator. He sends Carmody to another godlike figure named Maudsley.

Maudsley turns out to be a builder of worlds, one who economizes by using shabby materials and cutting corners wherever possible. He informs Carmody that he had built Earth in that fashion, recalling with some warmth the irascible old god who hired him for the construction. On Maudsley's planet, Carmody meets what appear to be an earthling scientist and his beautiful daughter. They take him to their spaceship, but before they can trap him in it, he realizes that they are constructs designed by his predator. Maudsley sends him to an Earth, cautioning that although it represents Where Earth is, Carmody still has to figure out When and on Which he belongs.

Carmody finds himself in the Mesozoic era, where he meets a family of talking tyrannosaurs. They are willing to accept the bizarre concept of a talking mammal, and Carmody chats with them, trying not to mention that they will become extinct, until he is met by an Internal Revenue Service agent who turns out to be his predator in another guise. Fleeing the predator, he encounters Clyde Beedle Seethwright, who offers to send him to the correct When so that he can determine Which Earth is his.

Carmody's next destination is the city of Bellwether, which is warm and comforting. Carmody finds it too much so, like a smothering mother, and calls to Seethwright to send him elsewhere. He next finds himself in a world where people talk in the catch phrases of commercials. This is obviously not his world either, so he has Seethwright send him to another world. That world is oppressive and full of garbage, noise, and violence. It is in fact his world, but Carmody gets Seethwright to take him out of it, to leave him on a perpetual quest, forever accompanied by his prize and pursued by his predator.

ANALYSIS

Like its predecessor, *Mindswap* (1966), *Dimension of Miracles* presents an innocent protagonist faced with a series of satirical horrors. *Mindswap* is largely social and literary in its satire; *Dimension of Miracles* is more metaphysical and theological. From the Messenger who takes Carmody to his prize to the rescuer who gets him out at the end, the beings Carmody encounters all lecture him on the philosophical significance of his situation. The book in fact presents the reader with actual gods, including the corner-cutting builder of Earth and the biblical deity, presented as a lovable crank. In contrast to this presentation of theological figures, the conclusion of the story can be seen as a kind of Zen epiphany, in which Carmody decides to live in the moment because that is all that he, or anyone, has.

Mindswap places its protagonist in a number of familiar, in fact clichéd, literary backgrounds, but *Dimension of Miracles* has only one such scene, where Carmody meets the stereotyped science-fictional scientist and his beautiful daughter. Perhaps their turning out to be badly made frauds, sent to entrap Carmody, represents the author's view of such fictions. There may also be a literary analogy in the god Melichrone. Readers learn that Melichrone's creations have a single flaw: He is lame, and therefore so are all of his creations, but neither he nor they know it. This can be seen as a comment on some literary creators.

In its wry fictional treatment of supposedly serious theological themes, *Dimension of Miracles* stands in a tradition that stretches from the comedies of Aristophanes to Salman Rushdie's *The Satanic Verses* (1988). Less morally outraged than Mark Twain's *The Mysterious Stranger* (1916) and more substantial than "shaggy god stories" (Michael Moorcock's term) in which the punch line tells readers that a minor character is really God or the supposed "last survivors on Earth" are Adam and Eve, *Dimension of Miracles* may find its closest parallels in the writings of Voltaire and Jorge Luis Borges. The conclusion, in which the returning Carmody rejects his own world, may remind readers of Jonathan Swift's *Gulliver's Travels* (1726).

Dimension of Miracles represents a sort of climax in Robert Sheckley's career. Like its predecessors, it won no awards and soon went out of print, but it retains a following of readers who consider it Sheckley's best work or even one of the best satires the field has ever produced. Sheckley published no further novels until the puzzling *Options* (1975).

—*Arthur D. Hlavaty*

DINNER AT DEVIANT'S PALACE

Greg Rivas, a violinist and former tough guy in a bombed-out Los Angeles, comes head to head with a psychic vampire whose intended victim is Earth itself

Author: Tim Powers (1952–)
Genre: Science fiction—post-holocaust
Type of work: Novel
Time of work: More than a century after the holocaust; about 2100
Locale: Los Angeles, California, and environs
First published: 1985

THE STORY

More than a century after a global thermonuclear war, Gregorio Rivas makes his living in post-apocalypse Los Angeles as a violinist with a regular nightclub act. In his youth, Rivas had been seduced by the cult of Norton Jaybush, whose worshipers are called Jaybirds. Later, he became a redeemer, rescuing cult members for a price. He is now living on his fading reputation and looking forward with growing fear to an impoverished middle age. Fate pulls him back into the dangerous life of a redeemer when Irwin Barrows, father of Rivas' one-time sweetheart, Urania, asks Rivas to rescue Urania from the Jaybush cult. Rivas takes the job, even though it requires that he pretend to join the cult himself.

Jaybush is a mysterious figure whose cult members practice a devastating ritual that literally destroys the mind if undergone too many times.

Jaybirds disappear into the Holy City (Irvine) and are never seen again.

Deviant's Palace is an improbable and deadly nightclub in Venice, home to many of the dregs of post-holocaust Californian society, including an astounding variety of mutants. The stories told about Deviant's Palace are too bizarre to be believed, but Rivas, who spent much of his reckless youth in Venice, now studiously avoids the place. Rivas' attempt to free Urania from the Jaybush cult, however, leads him to the Holy City, back to Venice, and, as the title indicates, to Deviant's Palace. In the process, Rivas discovers Jaybush's true identity, and he becomes custodian of the most deadly secret in the world.

ANALYSIS

Dinner at Deviant's Palace is both representative of Tim Powers' work and a significant departure from his earlier novels. The plot formula is very similar to that of nearly all of his previous novels. The protagonist encounters a problem, struggles against it, and gives himself up to drugs and denial when the going gets tough, but he pulls himself together for one last try in the nick of time. The formula is acted out slightly differently in this book because the stuporous period has ended long before the book begins. Even this, however, is reminiscent of *The Drawing of the Dark* (1979); both books begin with the protagonist unwillingly revisiting his past for the sake of a woman he lost.

Despite the familiar plot, Powers breaks new ground in *Dinner at Deviant's Palace*. In contrast to *The Drawing of the Dark*, *The Anubis Gates* (1983), *On Stranger Tides* (1987), and *The Stress of Her Regard* (1989), the adversary in this book is not supernatural. There are vampiric ghosts, zombies, monsters, and beings with superhuman powers, but all of these are explained without resort to magic. In addition, the ending of *Dinner at Deviant's Palace* leaves important business unconsummated, whereas the other four books all end with the adventure finished, even if the protagonist does not get to live happily ever after. Powers may have thought that it was safer to end a science-fiction novel on an ambiguous note because science fiction deals with subject matter inherently more familiar than that of fantasy, depending as it does on laws of nature and being based on extrapolations of known society.

The main plot device of *Dinner at Deviant's Palace*, the invasion of Earth by a lone being who is powerful enough to pose a serious threat to humanity, is a bit unusual but not unique: Larry Niven used it in *World of Ptavvs* (1966). What makes *Dinner at Deviant's Palace* successful is Powers' intense prose style, particularly the careful attention to detail and consistency that characterize his writing. Powers' writing may owe some of its intense precision to his background as a poet, for poetry is a medium that cannot afford to waste words.

Despite its science-fictional theme, *Dinner at Deviant's Palace* reads much like Powers' fantasy novels. It has little in common with his earlier science-fiction novel *Forsake the Sky* (1986; previously published as *The Skies Discrowned*, 1976). In *Dinner at Deviant's Palace*, Powers creates fantastic and horrible scenes that are so shockingly vivid that it almost hurts to read them. The descriptive style and underlying worldview are similar to those of Roger Zelazny's *Roadmarks* (1979), which does not involve magic, and to Larry Niven's *The Magic Goes Away* (1978), Zelazny's *Nine Princes in Amber* (1970) and its sequels, Barry Hughart's *Bridge of Birds* (1984), and Fred Saberhagen's *Empire of the East* (1979), which do involve magic. These authors share the ability to make magical, or at least fantastic, events seem inevitable within the context of the story. Only the reader (and in some cases the protagonist) is surprised when events turn bizarre.

One of the curious things about Powers' writing is that he does not seem to have grown as a writer between publication of *The Drawing of the Dark* in 1979 and of *The Stress of Her Regard* ten years later. *Dinner at Deviant's Palace* falls into the middle of this body of work. One gets the feeling that the books of this period (disregarding *Forsake the Sky*, which was written earlier) could have been written in any order, or even that they are permutations of the same basic story. It is particularly surprising to see this failure to progress in a writer of such great technical skill. Even though Powers uses the same plot kernel in each of the five novels of the period, he does not lack for invention. All these books are stuffed with innovative ideas. *Dinner at Deviant's Palace* won the Philip K. Dick Award.

—*David C. Kopaska-Merkel*

Dirk Gently's Holistic Detective Agency and The Long Dark Tea Time of the Soul

Dirk Gently "investigates the fundamental interconnectedness of all things" as a method of solving crimes, locating missing persons, and dealing with the occasional alien or supernatural being

Author: Douglas Adams (1952–2011)
Genre: Fantasy—magical realism
Type of work: Novels
Time of work: The 1980's
Locale: Primarily London, England
First published: Dirk Gently's *Holistic Detective Agency* (1987) and *The Long Dark Tea-Time of the Soul* (1988)

The Story

Author Douglas Adams, who found fame with his farcical science-fiction series that began with *The Hitchhiker's Guide to the Galaxy* (1979), has blended comedy, mystery, and fantasy to create *Dirk Gently's Holistic Detective Agency* and *The Long Dark Tea-Time of the Soul*. Although nominally a series, the two books have little in common apart from the presence of offbeat private investigator Dirk Gently, Adams' wry musings on the absurdities of life, and his central theme of holism, or the fundamental interconnectedness of all things.

Dirk Gently's Holistic Detective Agency centers on the trials and tribulations of a tall, geeky computer programmer named Richard MacDuff, modeled somewhat on the author. When MacDuff's eccentric boss, Gordon Way, is mysteriously murdered, MacDuff is a prime suspect. Adams proceeds from that premise to weave a complicated tale involving a series of otherworldly occurrences and weird characters, including an alien robot, a time-traveling eccentric, and disembodied spirits. These are all eventually shown to be interconnected not only among themselves and with MacDuff, Way, and the renowned poet Samuel Taylor Coleridge but also with the very beginning of life itself on Earth.

The only person capable of sorting out this mess is Dirk Gently. Gently is in some respects the stereotypical private detective, a loner who rents space in a seedy old building, chain smokes, and jumps at the chance to do some real detective work. Gently is much quirkier than most fictional detectives, though he shares some common foibles. He has a penchant for pizza, wears a long leather coat and an ugly red hat, and is perpetually short of money and behind on his bills. Gently's unconventional outlook and holistic beliefs enable him to solve the bizarre murder.

Gently discovers that a disembodied alien spirit, whose spaceship accidentally exploded on Earth eons ago, has been moving from character to character, with a hidden agenda. This discovery brings to light the fact that MacDuff's beloved but dotty former professor, Reg, is actually a time traveler whose rooms at St. Cedd's College are a time machine. What the spirit seeks is a willing host who will help him use Reg's time machine to go back in time to prevent his ship's explosion. After Reg, Gently, and MacDuff agree to help the alien, however, Gently realizes that the explosion the alien hopes to avert was actually what many scientists suspect to be the very event that started life on Earth. Gently then must thwart the alien's plans and thus save humanity—with a few minor adjustments.

The title of the second book in the series, *The Long Dark Tea-Time of the Soul*, comes from the text of the third book in Adams' Hitchhiker trilogy. The reference is to an immortal being who discovers the inevitable ennui that comes with immortality, particularly on Sunday afternoons right around teatime. *The Long Dark Tea-Time of the Soul* involves several immortals as well as Gently, who is drawn inadvertently into a web of mysterious occurrences.

A harried young American, Kate Schechter, trying to catch a plane to Oslo from London's Heathrow airport, encounters a large blond man with a Nordic accent who is arguing with an uninterested flight attendant and holding up the line. After a prolonged and humorous series of discussions among the attendant, the man, and Schechter, a sudden, localized explosion lands Schechter unconscious in a hospital. After she discovers the large blond man in the same hospital, he is mysteriously removed, prompting her to investigate.

Her search results in a crossing of paths with Gently, who has come into the case from another direction. He took on a client who was then found mysteriously murdered. Before his death, the man told Gently that his life had been threatened by a seven-foot-tall, shaggy-haired creature with green eyes and horns. The creature waved a scythe and a contract. Gently took the job because he needed a new refrigerator.

Many odd coincidences later, Gently and Schechter, following parallel lines of investigation, discover that the large blond man is actually Thor, the ancient Norse god of thunder. Thor is angry with his father, Odin, an elderly one-eyed man who has sold out to a pair of greedy mortal lawyers in order to ensure his own comfort in his old age—a posh room in an English asylum with fresh linen sheets replaced daily. It was Thor's uncontrollable anger that caused the airport explosion, among many other freak and comic accidents that occur throughout the story.

The climax is reached when Thor demands to meet with Odin in Asgard, in the great hall of Valhalla, to make him account for what he has done. Gently also appears, and once again he saves the day, by finding a way to break the insidious contract, which was also responsible for his client's death.

ANALYSIS

Adams has established a reputation as a teller of tall tales, an insightful writer about the human condition, and a purveyor of deadpan slapstick science fiction. Reflecting the high-tech obsession of the 1980's, Adams incorporates computers, cellular phones, telephone answering machines, and videocassette recorders into his narrative. He pokes fun not only at the dehumanizing effect of technology on society but also at the technology itself.

MacDuff's conversation with a police officer in *Dirk Gently's Holistic Detective Agency*, concerning his company's product, is a case in point. He asks the police officer which model of computer the police station has. Upon receiving the answer, he tells the officer that the computer does not work and never has, then suggests that the station "use it as a big paperweight."

Later, Reg admits to using his time machine to watch television programs that he missed because he cannot figure out how to program his videocassette recorder. Throughout, Adams displays an uncanny knack for pointing out modern society's frustrations and foibles, with lighthearted, humorous style.

Adams also depicts the high-tech junkies who become addicted to their toys. In *The Long Dark Tea-Time of the Soul*, Adams presents the ultimate teenage couch potato. The boy slouches in an armchair all day, watching television and surviving on a diet of Pot Noodles, Mars bars, and soft drinks. After several unsuccessful attempts to wrest the boy's attention from the television, Gently decides to pull the plug, with instantaneous and comically painful results.

Gordon Way, MacDuff's boss in *Dirk Gently's Holistic Detective Agency*, is also a high-tech junkie, addicted to his cellular telephone. Way calls everyone he knows and brainstorms at length onto their telephone answering machines. Way's secretary then periodically collects the tapes and transcribes them. When Way is murdered while talking to his sister Susan's answering machine, his ghost is burdened with unfinished business: It must complete its call to Susan before it can go to its eternal resting place.

The two novels are connected in that they both employ the character Dirk Gently. Otherwise, they are different in subject matter and approach. The first leans toward science fiction, with its time travel and alien civilizations. The second is pure fantasy, incorporating Norse mythology. Both, however, fit easily into the category of Magical Realism, as Adams takes completely fantastic situations and treats them realistically.

His central theme of holism ties together the two books, as do the author's use of slews of characters and running gags. The horse in Reg's bathroom, Gently's ongoing battle with his cleaning lady over a seriously foul refrigerator, and MacDuff's sofa, which is irrevocably stuck on the landing of his apartment building, are only a few of the many comic detours taken by Adams' rambling narrative style.

Although these two novels have been criticized by some reviewers as tangled and unsatisfying, Adams' writing provides, as always, good-natured fun. His writing style may be best summed up by his protagonist Dirk Gently: "I may not have gone where I intended to go, but I think I have ended up where I needed to be."

—*C. K. Breckenridge*

THE DISAPPEARANCE

A mysterious force divides the world into two separate realities for four years, one exclusively male, the other exclusively female

Author: Philip Wylie (1902-1971)
Genre: Science fiction—cultural exploration
Type of work: Novel
Time of work: 1949-1953
Locale: Miami, Florida, and other cities on Earth
First published: 1951

The Story

Set in post-World War II America, Philip Wylie's *The Disappearance* concerns an Earth divided into two distinct parts, one containing only male humans and primates, the other only females. Wylie divides the book into four parts: "The Hand of God," "Armageddon," "The Unloved," and "Dream and Dimension." Each section details major physical and psychological developments of the catastrophe. As the chapters alternate between the male world and the female one, the characters slowly work out the science of the disappearance.

On February 14, at 4:05 p.m., Dr. William Percival Gaunt watches out his study window as his wife, Paula Gaunt, vanishes mysteriously. Simultaneously, Paula, working in the garden, watches her husband disappear. As they soon realize, all members of the opposite sex have disappeared from the respective Earths.

Dr. Gaunt's world maintains a sense of order because males occupy most of the technical and governmental jobs. Paula Gaunt's world, however, does not maintain the same sense of order. Planes are suddenly without male pilots, buses and cars without drivers, utilities without workers, and the government without representatives.

While the females work to restore supply of basic necessities such as food and water, the male world faces new dangers—a Russian nuclear attack, civil unrest, and armed raiding parties—that force the government to establish martial law. Men quickly degenerate into poor hygiene and drunkenness, and they express flagrant homosexuality, much to the dismay of conventional preachers such as Reverend Connauth. Other men, notorious womanizers such as Teddy Barker, are relieved to no longer play the game of conquest and abandonment. Still others, including Dr. Gaunt's son, Edwin, travel the globe in search of women rumored to exist in remote locations.

The women's world also faces a Russian threat, but instead of engaging in warfare, the women reach a compromise whereby Russian women share their technological expertise in exchange for the few existing American luxury goods. Like the men, the women express varied views of marriage and fidelity, ranging from one of convenience held by Berthene Connauth; to domination, as in the case of Paula Gaunt's daughter, Edwinna; to the codependent view expressed by Paula's live-in neighbor, Kate West.

Along with combatting the physical hardships faced on both worlds, the characters struggle to understand the forces that caused the disappearance. Some suggest mass hypnosis, many claim God's judgment of sin, and others, such as Jim Elliot, Gaunt's nearest neighbor, retreat into Eastern mysticism. Gaunt proposes a philosophy of "oppositeness" asserting that each individual possesses both male and female components and must come to accept and live with those psychological parts in balance. He concludes that because males dominated females for so long and females acceded to that domination, the two sexes have been living in separate worlds all along. He hypothesizes that because the psychological energies of the two sexes are no longer in balance, the two cannot exist in the same dimension. Gaunt's philosophy appears to be correct, for once the people in the two worlds start to realize their full potential and appreciate the other sex as equal humans, they are reunited.

Analysis

The Disappearance was published in the middle of Wylie's science-fiction years, more than a decade after his esteemed collaborative effort with Edwin Balmer, *When Worlds Collide* (1933), and a few years before his acclaimed novel *Tomorrow!* (1954), detailing the horror of nuclear war. Although *The Disappearance* includes a brief nuclear confrontation, the issues discussed in the novel have more in common with Wylie's social novels, which criticize and condemn American conventionality, than with traditional science fiction. Reviewers of the novel at its publication noted its use of superficial science fiction to convey Wylie's polemics on infidelity, the double standard of sex roles, religion, and the interdependence of males and females.

Wylie uses Gaunt as his principal mouthpiece, expressing his philosophies on everything from mysticism to survival instinct. Gaunt's family life in a Miami suburb mirrors Wylie's own, and Wylie's struggles with his father's Presbyterian religion appear in Gaunt's condemnation of Connauth's beliefs.

Wylie's strongest personal statements occur in two sections. Near the middle of the novel, Wylie launches into a treatise on sex and the duality of individual sexuality, echoing themes expressed in his earlier social works *Generation of Vipers* (1942) and *Opus 21* (1949). Wylie's other invective expresses concerns common to the postnuclear world: science without control, progress without aim, and force without reason. These themes recur throughout the science-fiction genre.

Although many of the details are autobiographical, the novel surpasses Wylie's own experiences. He has created fully realized male and female characters who speak and move with lives of their own. Through his careful creation of Paula Gaunt, he explores the fate of intelligent, highly educated women who are deprived of an equal chance for a career outside the home environment. Wylie destroys stereotypes by giving Barker, the town gigolo, intelligence and perspicacity into women's frustrations. The author shows resolution of religious conflict as Reverend Connauth comes to a deeper understanding of religion as a search rather than as assertion after admitting his own infidelity and accepting his wife's forgiveness after the reunion of the sexes.

The combination of science fiction, fantasy, and social criticism give Wylie a vehicle for expressing his strong personal beliefs to a wider audience. Although the science is weak and the force causing the separation of the sexes is never fully explained, the attention to detail, characterization, and careful construction of the novel in its four parts, alternating between Dr. Gaunt's and Paula's perspectives, creates a believable world that challenges readers to question their own standards and potential.

—*Donna D. Samudio*

THE DISCWORLD SERIES

A series of adventures set on a flat world carried on the backs of four giant elephants that stand on the back of a giant turtle swimming through space

Author: Terry Pratchett (1948–2015)
Genre: Fantasy—high fantasy
Type of work: Novels
Time of work: Various times in the history of the Discworld
Locale: A flat world known as the Disc or Discworld
First published: *The Colour of Magic* (1983), *The Light Fantastic* (1986), *Equal Rights* (1987), *Mort* (1987), *Sourcery* (1988), *Wyrd Sisters* (1988), *Pyramids* (1989), *Guards! Guards!* (1989), *Eric* (1990), *Moving Pictures* (1990), *Reaper Man* (1991), *Witches Abroad* (1991), *Small Gods* (1992), *Lords and Ladies* (1992), *Men at Arms* (1993), *Soul Music* (1994), *Interesting Times* (1994), *Maskerade* (1995), *Feet of Clay* (1996), *Hogfather* (1996), *Jingo* (1997), *The Last Continent* (1998), *Carpe Jugulum* (1998), *The Fifth Elephant* (1999), *The Truth* (2000), *Thief of Time* (2001), *The Last Hero* (2001), *Night Watch* (2002), *Monstrous Regiment* (2003), *Going Postal* (2004), *Thud!* (2005), *Making Money* (2007), *Unseen Academicals* (2009), *Snuff* (2011), *Raising Steam* (2013) *and The Shepherd's Crown* (2015)

THE STORY

The Discworld novels are all set on the same imaginary world. The Great Atuin, the world-carrying turtle, has four giant elephants standing on his back, and the elephants hold up the Disc. The Disc is inhabited by a strange variety of people and creatures. Although many of the books can stand by themselves, several follow the adventures of the same characters.

The Colour of Magic introduces the Discworld as well as Rincewind, the failed Wizard. Rincewind knows only one spell, and it is so devastating that certain people are ready to kill him to keep him from speaking it. In the first novel, he befriends Two-Flower, the Discworld's first tourist to the city Ankh-Morpork. Two-Flower possesses animate and hostile Luggage made from sapient pearwood. These two have various adventures that take them across the Disc. In their adventures, they meet dryads, druids, and a variety of other characters. The novel ends with a literal cliff-hanger.

Their adventures continue in *The Light Fantastic*. The two once more go through a series of adventures before returning to Unseen University, the Disc's seat of higher education in the magical arts. There, Rincewind, with the aid of Two-Flower and the geriatric hero, Cohen the Barbarian, saves the Discworld by intoning his spell. Rincewind makes his next significant appearance in *Sourcery*, where he once again saves the Discworld, this time from a young "sourcerer." Rincewind is banished to the Dungeon Dimensions at the end of that novel, along with the Luggage. He resurfaces in *Eric*, when he is summoned accidentally, instead of a demon. In a variation of the three wishes plot, Rincewind and Eric travel through time and Hell before they find a possible way home. Rincewind also appears in *Interesting Times*. In this novel, he is part of a culture clash between the "civilized" West and the "barbaric" East.

The second major figure featured in Discworld is Granny Weatherwax, the best witch on the Discworld. She is introduced in *Equal Rights* as she undergoes a personal crusade to get a young girl with magical abilities enrolled into the all-male Unseen University. She is aided by a wizard's staff and finally succeeds. She next appears in *Wyrd Sisters*, with two other witches, Nanny Ogg and Magrat Garlick. In a plot that borrows heavily from *Macbeth*, *Hamlet*, and several fairy tales, the three witches restore a young man to the throne of Lancre.

The witches next appear in *Witches Abroad*. They head to the city of Genua to stop an evil fairy god mother from forcing a terrible marriage on the young Emberella. They encounter many strange people along the way, including dwarves, vampires, and a voodoo witch. They finally reach Genua and liberate Emberella and the city from the grip of the evil fairy godmother. They return to their home of Lancre in *Lords and Ladies*, the plot of which is a variation on *A Midsummer Night's Dream*. The witches must stop the elf queen from invading the Disc and marrying King Verence, who is now betrothed to Magrat. The novel ends with Magrat's marriage to the king. This novel also reveals Granny Weatherwax's childhood sweetheart.

The third featured character in the series is Death. The Discworld's Death follows the typical stereotype, complete with black cowl and scythe. Death makes an appearance in every novel and is a main character in several. In *Mort*, Death adopts an apprentice so he can take a vacation. The apprentice, Mort, is not quite up to the job and saves someone who is meant to die. Eventually, Death has to return. Mort goes back to the land of living with Death's adopted daughter, Ysabel.

In *Reaper Man*, Death retires to live among mortals, taking the job of a corn reaper. In a story reminiscent of the legend of John Henry, he battles a mechanical reaper and wins. He eventually has to battle his replacement and take up the mantle of Death once again. The other plot in this novel deals with Windle Poons, a deceased wizard, who suddenly finds himself undead following Death's retirement. He eventually winds up saving the city of Ankh-Morpork from a force that destroys cities.

Death plays a prominent role in *Soul Music* as well. After Mort and Ysabel die in an accident, Death abandons his post. This leaves his position open; his granddaughter, Susan, is drafted for the job. At the same time, a young man named Imp, later Buddy, travels to Ankh-Morpork to become a musician. Their two fates become intertwined as Buddy introduces Music With Rocks In It to the Discworld. Eventually, Death returns to save Buddy and Susan and put things right.

Pyramids is one of the independent novels. In this novel, Teppic, while in training to be an assassin, suddenly finds himself the pharaoh of the kingdom of Djelibeybi. The people of the kingdom believe that their pharaoh is a god, and Teppic becomes godlike. Dios, the high priest, has been the real power behind the throne for years, and Teppic has to go up against him and all the old gods to save Djelibeybi.

Guards! Guards! features members of Ankh-Morpork's city watch. Captain Vimes, Sergeant Colon, Nobby, and others do their best to survive in the Disc's meanest and biggest city and still do their jobs. In this case, they have to deal with a cult that summons up a dragon that terrorizes the city.

Moving Pictures is Terry Pratchett's spoof of Hollywood. In this novel, a leakage from another dimension causes a strange effect on residents of the Disc: They suddenly become actors, directors, and agents. The leakage is potentially destructive and Victor, the hero of the novel, is forced to close the gate between the two worlds.

Small Gods is the story of Brutha, the only true believer in the Great God Om, who appears to Brutha in the shape of a turtle. Brutha is the only one who can hear his god, and he does not quite believe it. The false followers of Om have created a huge empire that is controlled by Vorbis. Vorbis is more interested in keeping power than believing in a god. He uses Brutha to defeat a neighboring power. As Vorbis is about to kill Brutha, Om manages to save his one believer. Everyone then believes in Om, and Brutha becomes the new spiritual leader of the empire.

In *Men at Arms*, the guards from the city watch are back to solve the mystery of a stolen "gonne" (gun) from the Assassins' Guild and the mysterious deaths of several people. With new recruits, such as a dwarf, a troll, and a female werewolf, the guards solve the murder and catch the villain.

By this midpoint of the series, Pratchett had established his formula of silliness, social commentary, improbable yet alluring adventures and parody so well that the subsequent books became welcome, albeit slightly predictable installments in a much-loved franchise.

ANALYSIS

Terry Pratchett introduced a flat world in the science-fiction novel *Strata* (1981). *The Colour of Magic* and the following Discworld series have been more successful, launching Pratchett onto international best-seller lists.

As many critics have stated, Pratchett is an excellent parodist, making fun of and having fun with a wide range of fantasy, literary, and popular subjects. Cohen the Barbarian, the geriatric hero, is a perfect parody of Robert Howard's Conan. Pratchett does a parody of Shakespeare in *Wyrd Sisters* and *Lords and Ladies*. Emberella, the Discworld version of Cinderella, appears in *Witches Abroad*. *Soul Music* lampoons rock and roll music, and *Moving Pictures* takes on Hollywood. Every novel parodies some literary or fantasy convention.

Another reason for the popularity of the series is its collection of zany characters. Pratchett uses favorite characters throughout the series to provide a sense of continuity. Death appears in every novel. The Librarian, who was changed into an orangutan through a magical accident, also appears in most of the books. Pratchett does not always worry about characterization, and some of the books are little more than lengthy gags. Strangely, the most developed character in the series, besides Granny Weatherwax, is Death. Death is more human than many of the other inhabitants of this world. Pratchett has written other books that have the same sense of humor, but the Discworld series remains his most popular work.

—*P. Andrew Miller*

THE DISPOSSESSED

Shevek, a physicist raised in an anarchist society, fulfills a lifelong quest to bridge two worlds, two theories of time, and two sets of obligations—to himself and to community

Author: Ursula K. Le Guin (1929–)
Genre: Science fiction—utopia
Type of work: Novel
Time of work: Several hundred years in the future
Location: Anarres and Urras, planets orbiting Tau Ceti
First published: 1974

THE STORY

The Dispossessed: An Ambiguous Utopia is one of several of Ursula Le Guin's works chronicling the evolution of a "League of all Worlds" governed by principles superior to those of known political and colonial systems. Although *The Dispossessed* takes place in the League's prehistory, the novel's loving portrait of a working anarchist society on one world develops in detail the principles of non-coercive social organization.

The novel chronicles the life of Shevek, a physicist reared on a world settled by the followers of an anarchist philosopher, Odo. The Odonians, "bought off" 170 years before Shevek's time with an offer to settle their mother planet's arid moon, Anarres, live without laws, according to the apparently irreconcilable principles of absolute individual freedom and absolute commitment to the good of the community. Anarresti social order is maintained primarily by education, which inculcates a horror of "egoizing." The Anarresti live in isolation from their mother planet, Urras, a lush world that Anarresti education demonizes as a place of injustice and evil.

Through a series of struggles, Shevek strives to balance loyalty to the society that formed him with rebellion against subtle conformist pressures that stifle his ambitious work in theoretical physics. The conflict climaxes after a long famine, during which Shevek accepts four years of separation from his wife and his work to perform manual labor in his planet's harshest desert. After this trial of physical, emotional, and intellectual self-denial, Shevek vows, "by damn, I will do my own work for a while now!"

That work has been kept alive, ironically, through extended contact with the physicists of the mother planet, Urras—that is, with despised "propertarians." After his desert ordeal, Shevek accepts a standing invitation based on his groundbreaking physics and becomes the first Anarresti in 170 years to visit the mother planet. In the face of intense opposition, he vows to "go to Urras and break down walls."

On Urras, Shevek is treated as an honored but subtly controlled guest, kept from any genuine contact with the poor. His hosts are determined to "buy" him. They believe that his work, once completed, will bring them wealth, power, and prestige. Shevek moves from admiring awe and a kind of racial homesickness for the lush mother planet to revulsion against a social world dominated by competitive struggles for power and wealth. When a chance comes to lend support to the poor people of Ai-Io, the wealthy host-nation, Shevek seizes it, traveling secretly to the slums and leading a demonstration against an unjust war. This self-liberation from a luxurious "prison" comes in the wake of the fulfillment of Shevek's scientific work: completion of a General Temporal Theory that unites apparently irreconcilable theories about time.

The antiwar demonstration, climaxing with Shevek's speech urging renewed Odonian revolt, is broken up by a military crackdown. Shevek hides for three days in a basement with a mortally wounded demonstrator who dies in Shevek's care. Following this near-death descent, Shevek emerges suddenly in the Terran (Earth) Embassy, where he gains asylum and arranges for his theory to be broadcast to all worlds, thus eluding his hosts' desire to possess it and enabling instantaneous communication between the "nine known worlds." In a final wall-breaking action, Shevek agrees to let a young man from Hain, oldest of the known inhabited worlds, accompany him home to Anarres.

ANALYSIS

Like most of Le Guin's heroes, Shevek embodies the author's imaginative quest to balance poles of paradox. In physics, his quest is to reconcile sequency, "the arrow of time," and simultaneity, "the circle of time"—that is, becoming and being. His General Temporal Theory, a restatement of Odo's dictum, "true voyage is return," asserts that "you *can* go home again . . . so long as you understand that home is a place where you have never been." A well-lived life comes full circle, linking past and future by fulfilling long-term promises, but also gets somewhere, effecting meaningful change.

The novel's structure embodies this gnomic principle. The odd-numbered chapters chronicle Shevek's sojourn on the mother planet Urras; even-numbered chapters bring his life on Anarres from infancy to the moment he decides that he must go to Urras. The two narratives merge in chapter 13, which anticipates Shevek's return home to an Anarres transformed by his rebellious journey—that is, to a place he has never been.

Le Guin has voiced the hope that science fiction can achieve the kind of idiosyncratic characterization championed by Virginia Woolf and widely considered integral to realistic fiction. *The Dispossessed*, however, reflects a different imaginative goal, indeed a passion, common to virtually all of Le Guin's work: to imagine an ideal person—in this case, as the embodiment of a nearly ideal society. "What is it like," asks the Terran ambassador Keng, "what can it be like, the society that made you? . . . you are not like other men."

Although Le Guin is not much interested in Christian paradigms, she is keenly conscious of archetypal formulations of the hero's journey, and she quite pointedly sends Shevek to hell and back on both worlds. His sojourn in "the dust" during the famine on Anarres is one hell. Out of the long separation comes renewed commitment—to marriage, to work, and to continuing the Anarresti revolution. On Urras, Shevek's quest to "break down walls" is consummated by his three-day basement ordeal, which he equates with hell. It is after rising from this depth that Shevek releases his theory, thus extending the blessings of communication and brotherhood that are "the Promise" of Anarres.

—*Andrew Sprung*

DO ANDROIDS DREAM OF ELECTRIC SHEEP?

Rick Deckard must find and kill a group of androids who have escaped from a colony on Mars and come to Earth

Author: Philip K. Dick (1928–1982)
Genre: Science fiction—post-holocaust
Type of work: Novel
Time of work: 1992
Location: The San Francisco Bay Area
First published: 1968

THE STORY

Do Androids Dream of Electric Sheep? recounts a day in the life of bounty hunter Rick Deckard. The action begins on the morning of January 3, 1992, as Deckard and his wife, Iran, wake up in their apartment; it concludes the following morning, as an exhausted Deckard returns to bed. In that twenty-four-hour period, Deckard faces the greatest challenge he has ever encountered: He must "retire" a rogue band of "organic androids" (or "andys," as they are called) of a design so advanced that they are almost indistinguishable from human beings. His task is complicated by his attraction for another android, Rachael Rosen, who tries to prevent him from carrying out his mission.

The story is set in a gray world devastated by "World War Terminus" and the resulting radioactive fallout, which is slowly depopulating the planet. Many people have left to settle in a colony on Mars, where androids are employed for hard labor, domestic service, and other purposes. In making their escape from Mars and servitude, the rogue andys that Deckard is to retire killed a number of humans. The people who remain on Earth have witnessed the extinction of many animal species. Possession of an animal—a horse, a sheep, or even a cat—confers status; for those who cannot afford the real thing, artificial animals are available. Deckard himself has an electric sheep but greatly desires to own a living creature. That is the primary motivation in his quest: The bounty he earns of $1,000 per andy will enable him to buy a genuine animal.

Like a knight in a medieval romance, Deckard undergoes a series of trials as he retires the andys one by one. Nothing is as it first appears to be. A Soviet policeman turns out to be one of the andys in disguise. Another bounty hunter, Phil Resch, is falsely identified as an android by a San Francisco police inspector—himself an android—who hopes that Resch and Deckard will kill each other. Most mutable and devious of all is Rachael Rosen, who seduces Deckard, then calmly tells him that he will be unable to continue as a bounty hunter; no one ever has after being with her. Deckard, however, proves her wrong. Although he cannot bring himself to kill Rosen, he completes his task, retiring the last three fugitive andys after his tryst with her.

The novel ends on a note of reconciliation and domesticity. Deckard returns home to his wife. They had argued to start the day, but now Iran greets him warmly, fussing over him until he falls asleep. The last line in the book is a celebration of everyday human routine: Iran, "feeling better, fixed herself at last a cup of black, hot coffee."

ANALYSIS

One of Philip K. Dick's recurring themes figures prominently in *Do Androids Dream of Electric Sheep?* This theme is identified in Dick's 1978 lecture, "How to Build a Universe That Doesn't Fall Apart Two Days Later," collected in *The Shifting Realities of Philip K. Dick: Selected Literary and Philosophical Writings* (1995), edited by Lawrence Sutin. In that lecture, Dick observes that throughout his career he has been preoccupied with the question, "What constitutes the authentic human being?" Dick often explores this question in novels and stories featuring androids or other constructs closely resembling human beings. These include the novels *The Simulacra* (1964) and *We Can Build You* (1972) and stories such as "The Electric Ant" (1969).

In *Do Androids Dream of Electric Sheep?*, Dick imagines a near future in which successive generations of androids become ever more sophisticated in their mimicry of humans. The model that Deckard must retire, the Nexus-6, is the most advanced yet. There remains one crucial difference between humans and androids: empathy. Androids can learn to mimic human concern, but they do not genuinely feel empathy for other creatures. Deckard employs a psychological/physiological test, the Voigt-Kampff Altered Scale, that detects the absence of empathy in the microseconds before it can be faked.

This emphasis on empathy as the defining human characteristic runs throughout the novel. It is poignantly embodied in the "chickenhead" John Isidore ("chickenhead" being a derogatory term for humans who, as a result of the fallout, lack normal intellectual capacities). Isidore innocently befriends three of the fugitive andys, then watches in horror as they gratuitously cut the legs off a spider. Empathy also is at the core of the quasi-religious movement known as Mercerism, in which both Deckard and Iran participate. So intense is the identification experienced by communicants in "fusion" with the archetypal figure of Wilbur Mercer that they sometimes emerge from a session with wounds inflicted by rocks thrown at Mercer, rather like Christian saints who receive the stigmata.

Dick's characters, however, are far from sainthood. The most important lesson Deckard learns in his long day is imparted to him in a revelation from Mercer. Deckard, appalled by the killing, wonders if he can finish the job. He explains later to Iran, "Mercer said it was wrong but I should do it anyhow." As a character recognizes in another Dick novel, *The Man in the High Castle* (1962), "There is evil! . . . It's an ingredient in us. In the world." Acknowledging that, one does the best one can.

Many people know the story of *Do Androids Dream of Electric Sheep?* not from the novel itself but from the film based on it, *Blade Runner* (1982). The film departs from the book in many ways, most conspicuously in its treatment of the protagonist. Dick's Deckard is a bounty hunter but also a husband. In the film, Deckard (played by Harrison Ford) is a loner, a futuristic private eye. Dick's final message is a modest affirmation of human virtues; the film's conclusion is both cynical and romanticized, showing Deckard with the beautiful android. As for empathy, that theme is turned upside down: Mercerism disappears from the story altogether, and Deckard survives only because the leader of the androids (or "replicants," as they are called in the film), his mortal foe, shows compassion for him.

—*John Wilson*

DR. BLOODMONEY

After a nuclear war, a group of survivors gathers in a small northern California town to rebuild their lives and create a viable community

Author: Philip K. Dick (1928–1982)
Genre: Science fiction—post-holocaust
Type of work: Novel
Time of work: 1981 and several years following
Locale: Berkeley, California, and Marin County, California
First published: 1965

The Story

Dr. Bloodmoney: Or, How We Got Along After the Bomb is a good example of Philip K. Dick's masterful control of complex plotting, moving from the banal to the extraordinary in deft, swift strokes. The novel is also an example of Dick's multifocused plotting, which begins by delineating the separate, idiosyncratic lives of several characters who do not initially know one another but whose lives eventually will be intimately bound together.

The story begins in 1981, with introductions quickly provided of virtually all the characters who will find their lives connected after the nuclear war. The story moves quickly, from its quotidian beginning one morning in Berkeley, California, to the nuclear blast that demolishes the city, to the post-holocaust setting in rustic West Marin County, north and west of Berkeley. The lives of the many characters intertwine as they attempt to rebuild their lives in the post-holocaust world.

The primary characters are television repairman Stuart McConchie; Hoppy Harrington, who was born without arms or legs but has managed to develop telekinetic powers, or the ability to move objects with his mind; Walt Dangerfield, an astronaut trapped alone in his spaceship as it endlessly circles Earth; Bonny Keller, who conceived her child, Edie, on the day of the nuclear attack; Bill Keller, Edie's tiny, wizened twin brother who lives as a homunculus within her abdominal cavity and who telepathically communicates with her; Dr. Stockstill, one of the few benevolent psychiatrists depicted in Dick's fiction; and nuclear scientist Dr. Bruno Bluthgeld, the "Dr. Bloodmoney" alluded to in the novel's title. Strangely enough, it is Walt Dangerfield, the astronaut trapped in orbit by the nuclear war (there is no way to bring him down), who provides the means of bonding the fragmented postwar society. Using the vast musical and literary holdings on board the satellite, Dangerfield becomes a disc jockey. The community meets to listen during his daily appearance as he orbits Earth.

In an unpredictable development, it is Hoppy Harrington who becomes the antagonist as he slowly refines his telekinetic powers. Even though he uses his power to do apparent good—he kills the unstable Dr. Bluthgeld—he also begins to use his powers to control others, even seeking to destroy Walt Dangerfield and usurp his place in the hearts and minds of the community. The resolution of this tension comes from a highly unlikely hero, Bill Keller. Hoppy learns that Edie Keller carries the homunculus within her, and to his horror he learns that Bill Keller can communicate with the dead. He plots to kill Bill by using his power to draw Bill from within Edie's body, knowing that Bill is unable to survive outside her. Hoppy's plan backfires. With his body freed from Edie's, Bill transmigrates his soul into the body of Hoppy Harrington and casts the soul of Hoppy into his own dying, wizened body. With Dangerfield's life saved, the health of the community seems ensured.

Analysis

Dr. Bloodmoney was one of four novels Dick completed in 1963 and one of twelve completed be-tween 1962 and 1964, a period of prodigious output. He was, at this time, writing some of his finest science fiction. He recently had won the Hugo Award in 1963 for best science-fiction novel of the year for his alternate history story, *The Man in the High Castle* (1962), the book for which he is perhaps best known.

The post-nuclear holocaust novel had emerged clearly as an important subgenre of science fiction by the time Dick's novel was published by Ace Books in 1965. The title itself is the result of a marketing ploy by Ace, a not very subtle allusion to Stanley Kubrick's highly successful 1964 film about nuclear war, *Dr. Strangelove: Or, How I Learned to Stop Worrying and Love the Bomb*. Dick's original title for the novel was *In Earth's Diurnal Course*, but the novel does have a character named Dr. Bluthgeld, translatable as "Bloodmoney."

The late 1950's and early 1960's had seen many fine post-holocaust novels published, among the most notable of which are Nevil Shute's *On the Beach* (1957), Mordecai Roshwald's *Level 7* (1959), Pat Frank's *Alas, Babylon* (1959), Walter M. Miller, Jr.'s classic *A Canticle for Leibowitz* (1960), and Robert A. Heinlein's *Farnham's Freehold* (1964). *Dr. Bloodmoney* shares at least a superficial similarity with Frank's *Alas, Babylon*. Both feature small, idyllic, agrarian communities that emerge after the holocaust. Such communities would seem to be possible only after the technocratic, industrial world is purged by a massive nuclear war. In contrast to Frank's post-holocaust world, however, Dick strenuously avoided plotting his book as an adventure story, using instead his unusual multifocused approach, weaving explorations of his many characters' complex psychologies and personal relationships into a story that details the re-formation of civil society in small, decentralized communities.

Dick himself believed *Dr. Bloodmoney* to be a unique novel precisely because of the way in which he imagined the post-holocaust world: Horses are used to pull automobiles, for example, and as a result of radiation, rodents have mutated into highly intelligent creatures capable of disabling the traps humans set for them. Critical regard for the novel generally is very positive, as it is seen as one of Dick's most accessible books and also one of his most provocative ones. Much of Dick's fiction is decidedly pessimistic. This novel, ironically, emerges as strangely optimistic in outlook.

—*Samuel J. Umland*

Doctor Rat

The fanatical Doctor Rat conducts hideous experiments on animals while an animal revolt leads to an apocalyptic confrontation with humans that wipes out animal life on the planet

Author: William Kotzwinkle (1938–   )
Genre: Fantasy—animal fantasy
Type of work: Novel
Time of work: The late twentieth century
Locale: Earth
First published: 1976

The Story

The primary narrative track follows the eponymous Doctor Rat as he tries to explain, justify, and defend the hideous experiments he is conducting in collaboration with some unseen but omnipotent human agency. The alternative track is a composite of the thoughts of various animals involved in a rebellion against manipulative technology. The animals strive to reaffirm their primal connection to the landscape of the planet and its life-giving properties.

Although he is given the physical attributes of a rodent, Doctor Rat acts and thinks like a man of the late twentieth century, measuring everything in terms of commercial success. He is devoid of compassion, reeks of machismo, and is blind to his own defects. He represents individualism gone amok, is capable of the most circumlocutory rationalizations to support his actions, and is truly a "rat" in terms of ethical behavior.

The various species of animals in peril, on the other hand, are conceived in terms of traits that traditionally have defined the truly humane—empathy, understanding, self-sacrifice, kindness, and consideration. They are drawn as genuinely spiritual creatures in the sense of feeling a connection to a cosmic, universal consciousness that lends a significance to their lives and ennobles their existence.

The narrative proceeds by juxtaposing Doctor Rat's increasingly frantic, first-person accounts of his attempts to control the situation in the laboratory with different representatives of the wilderness (that is, a free state) awakening to a call to their particular nature. The eventual destruction of the entire animal population through the employment of the latest technological advances in war-making machinery is seen by Doctor Rat as a "final solution" that even he recognizes as a mark of failure, because it leaves "a sort of lonely feeling" out there.

Analysis

In describing the origins of his consciousness as a writer, William Kotzwinkle recalls holding a tadpole and thinking it "was the most exquisite thing I ever felt." His earliest work, children's books such as *The Firemen* (1969) and *Elephant Boy: A Story of the Stone Age* (1970), are efforts to establish a domain of wonder that expresses this kind of innocent joy. By the mid-1970's, however, he had moved to rural Canada, a remote region under assault by speculative developers. He had a series of nightmares in which "animals came to me, night after night, telling me, We've got something to say!'" This mystic vision led to *Doctor Rat*, a book designed to demonstrate "a dangerous split between us and our animal nature."

Doctor Rat is an allegory in the classic sense, arranged as a commentary on late twentieth century life in which symbolic representation reinforces an argument by establishing a different perspective from which to consider social ills. More specifically, it is a fierce "ecofable" joining the form of the medieval beast tale to the cautionary message of an ecological sermon. The idea of an allegory is a direct derivation from Kotzwinkle's use of nonhuman characters in his books for young readers. He deepens the admirable qualities often associated with animals in instructive children's literature so that the gravity and dignity the animals exhibit is a direct commentary on the absence of these attributes in many humans. Further, the novel is an examination of the sources of evil and of its most contemporary manifestations. This subject is charged with emotional complexity, and Kotzwinkle's angle of attack makes it possible for him to cover some issues that require a special sensitivity.

Doctor Rat himself is clearly derived from the experiences of Nazi Germany, and his compulsive energy, his manic hustling, and his vicious inclination to crush all forms of opposition arouse the same lurid fascination attendant on the leaders of Hitler's Third Reich. Kotz-winkle has maintained that "Nazism is always in the air. . . . This is our reality," and Doctor Rat is delineated not as a theoretician of genocide—that is, an understandable if loathsome monster—but as a willing functionary whose zeal, ingenuity, and commitment illustrate the mechanics of genocidal operations. As Kotzwinkle develops the laboratory setting, it becomes clear that he is not trying to re-create the horror of the concentration camp but instead is attempting to indicate through symbolic suggestion that this hideous, misconstrued world is closer to postmodern reality than one might care to admit.

Doctor Rat thrives in this situation, having developed a bogus mystique in which science is elevated into a kind of secular religion, albeit one devoid of any spiritual qualities. He uses a perverse logic linking rigorous analyses and suspect premises to explain and justify everything. His own position as a controlled servant to a higher power is cast as a part of a scientific method, with academic apparatus seeming to satisfy all moral requirements. His parodic abuse of quasi-scientific jargon is set against the language of the animals, who speak in heightened, poetic tones reflecting a primal beauty linked to a former state of grandeur. For Kotzwinkle, the almost ethereal transmission of thought and feeling among the animals recalls an ethos of enchantment that he fears is vanishing from the modern world. The goal of much of his writing is to regain this condition of existence.

Like many social allegories, *Doctor Rat* has multiple satiric thrusts, concentrating on the horror of the laboratory but extending beyond to the human society Kotz-winkle contends is responsible for the destruction of anything that does not fit a narrow scale of value. Narcotized animals await their next fix, their inertia a comment on the fading 1960's hippie dream; others are obsessed with style and dress; others pursue the pleasures of the flesh to the exclusion of any other kind of relationship. These sad examples of narcissistic self-absorption are symptomatic of the collapse of the social contract. At the root of this, Kotzwinkle contends, is a failure to see that the most admirable elements in all forms of life are shared by many species. His allegorical approach permits a consideration of what is crucial to spiritual fulfillment. Its success was ratified by an award for best novel from the third World Fantasy Convention.

—Leon Lewis

DONOVAN'S BRAIN

A scientist who tries to keep a human brain alive finds that it is growing to an enormous size and seizing control of his mind through telepathy

Author: Curt Siodmak (1902–2000)
Genre: Science fiction—cautionary
Type of work: Novel
Time of work: Approximately 1940
Locale: Arizona and Los Angeles, California
First published: 1943

THE STORY

Patrick Cory, a middle-aged doctor, is devoting his life to the study of animal brains. The novel consists of a journal of his records. He has a patient, loving wife named Janice whose private fortune enables him to live in seclusion and spend his waking hours in his laboratory.

The crash of a private airplane gives him an opportunity to experiment with a human brain. One of the victims is Warren Horace Donovan, a business tycoon notorious for his ruthless methods. Cory keeps Donovan's brain alive in a vat, with nutrient-fortified blood pumped through the brain tissue.

Donovan's brain not only survives but grows larger and larger, until it threatens to fill its entire vat. The brain is free of the requirements of a normal brain of regulating bodily functions and attending to everyday concerns; thus it has a superhuman ability to concentrate. Cory is able to communicate with the brain by tapping messages on the glass in Morse code. The brain develops the capability of sending messages to Cory through telepathy. Cory's alcoholic colleague Dr. Schratt warns against the possible dangers of such inhumane and unorthodox experimentation. Cory, however, is so obsessed with his quest for scientific knowledge that he is willing to risk his soul.

Cory finds that he is falling under Donovan's power and losing his own identity. He gains access to Donovan's bank accounts and safe-deposit box by knowing certain aliases and being able to duplicate signatures perfectly. He has a fortune at his disposal but is unable to enjoy it because his thoughts and actions are controlled by the increasingly powerful brain. His main mission as Donovan's minion is to save the life of a vicious murderer named Cyril Hinds, the son of a man to whom Donovan feels obligated. In order to save Hinds, Cory must murder an innocent thirteen-year-old girl who is scheduled to testify against Hinds at his murder trial.

Under Donovan's spell, Cory finds himself trying to run down the girl with his car. The attempt fails. Cory realizes that he must destroy the brain but feels helpless to regain his old identity. The brain can read minds and has the ability to kill anyone who attacks it or tries to shut off the motors that keep it alive.

Cory recovers his sanity through the devotion and understanding of his wife, who helps him to see that human love is more important than esoteric knowledge. Returning to his Arizona laboratory, Cory discovers that Dr. Schratt has sacrificed his life to destroy the brain by dragging the hideous pulsating mass of tissue out of its nest of tubes. Cory gives up his research to live the simple life of a rural doctor.

ANALYSIS

Donovan's Brain is one of many stories about a scientist who has gone mad through obsession with the pursuit of knowledge that will give him power over nature. The so-called "mad scientist" has become a stock figure in commercial fiction and motion pictures. Early prototypes occur in Johann Wolfgang von Goethe's drama *Faust* (1808), Mary Shelley's romantic novel *Frankenstein: Or, The Modern Prometheus* (1818), Nathaniel Hawthorne's short story "Rappaccini's Daughter" (1844), and H. G. Wells's novel *The Island of Dr. Moreau* (1896). The ancient Greeks, however, offered much earlier examples in their mythology of what they called hubris, excessive human pride that was invariably punished by the gods.

Curt Siodmak had a better scientific background than most authors of "mad scientist" novels, and as a result *Donovan's Brain* is plausible. The fictional device of writing his novel in the form of a scientist's journal is effective. Siodmak's knowledge of science enabled him to sprinkle his story with medical terminology that gives it verisimilitude. The narrator, Dr. Cory, appears to be talking to himself in his journal, making the reader feel like an eavesdropper.

Although Siodmak published many novels, both in Germany and in the United States, he is best remembered for *Donovan's Brain*. The novel has been adapted to the motion picture screen several times. The explanation for the story's continued popularity seems to be that it foreshadows a real threat to the human race. The book was published before the development of modern computers. It has since become obvious that humans can invent machines that outperform their creators in many mental activities. Some hypothetical scenarios have been dramatized in such futuristic films as *2001: A Space Odyssey* (1968), in which a supercomputer goes insane, and in *The Terminator* (1984), in which robots masterminded by artificial brains have taken over the world and are trying to exterminate humankind.

Donovan's Brain also contains an implicit warning against reckless experimentation with biological science. This branch of scientific investigation presents other threats, including doomsday-type biological warfare and devastating new life-forms produced by irresponsible genetic tampering.

Some might argue that Siodmak illustrates his thesis with what logicians call a "straw man." What might have happened if, instead of the brain of a ruthless man, Cory had obtained the brain of a benevolent genius such as Albert Einstein? Why should anyone assume that machines possessing superhuman intelligence would necessarily become wicked and destructive? Would it not be possible, in fact, to invent artificial brains that were free of human failings? Others would argue that it is obvious that there are creative and destructive machines, just as there are creative and destructive human beings. Fanciful literary creations such as *Donovan's Brain* serve a useful purpose by reiterating age-old warnings that humans are only part of nature and can attempt to impose complete mastery over nature only at their own peril.

—*Bill Delaney*

Doomsday Book

While a time-traveling historian is stranded in England during the Black Death, her twenty-first century colleagues battle their own epidemic and seek to rescue her

Author: Connie Willis (1945–)
Genre: Science fiction—time travel
Type of work: Novel
Time of work: December, 2054-January, 2055, and 1348
Location: Oxford, England, and Ashencote, a nearby village
First published: 1992

The Story

Kivrin Engle, a brilliant and determined young woman, is the first historian to journey back to the Middle Ages. She makes the trip despite the misgivings of her teacher and mentor, Mr. Dunworthy. His anxieties seem justified when the technician in charge of the time "net" mumbles that something is wrong and then collapses from a deadly new strain of influenza shortly after sending Kivrin to the past. What gradually becomes clear is that Kivrin has been infected with that same flu and sent not to 1320, as intended, but to 1348, the year the Black Death began to ravage England.

Unbeknown to her, Kivrin's arrival in the past is witnessed by an illiterate but saintly priest, Father Roche, who brings the sick and delirious woman, whom he regards as a messenger from heaven, to the castle of his lord. Kivrin is nursed back to health by Lady Eliwys and her family, who were sent by her husband to hide from the plague in this remote village. While anxiously trying to relocate her rendezvous point—the exact location where the gateway in time will reopen—she quickly grows to love the people, especially Eliwys's two young daughters, Agnes and Rosemunde. Travelers fleeing a nearby city bring the plague, and Kivrin realizes for the first time that she is in the wrong year. With little hope of returning to her own time, she does her best, along with Father Roche, to battle the plague and save the people of the village.

In the twenty-first century, Kivrin's plight becomes an afterthought to all but Mr. Dunworthy as Oxford comes under a quarantine and doctors and scientists race to find a vaccine. Dunworthy does his best to mobilize the resources of the university to fight the epidemic and care for the sick, all the while trying to find some confirmation that Kivrin's time traveling has gone well and she at least is safe.

Connie Willis effectively uses the parallel plots of the novel, cutting back and forth between the time lines, to increase suspense, create ironic juxtapositions, and ultimately affirm the common humanity of people battling disaster. In twenty-first century England, the epidemic is finally halted, but in the fourteenth century, the progress of the Black Death is inexorable. One by one, Agnes, Rosemunde, Lady Eliwys, and all the people of the village die in agony, despite the heroic efforts of Kivrin and Father Roche. Roche eventually dies, but the utter bleakness of the catastrophe and Kivrin's grief are in some small measure relieved by his gratitude and love for Kivrin, who has indeed become the messenger from heaven of his simple faith, bringing comfort to the dying and surviving to bear witness. As Kivrin struggles to sound the death knoll as a memorial for Roche, the sound of the bell brings Dunworthy, who, though still weak from his own near death from influenza, has come back through time to seek Kivrin and bring her home.

Analysis

Although Willis employs the common device of time travel, she is not interested in creating paradoxes or exploring alternative histories. Time travel is for her a means of juxtaposing two societies confronting similar crises, of exploring human nature in the presence of overpowering fear, and of celebrating human courage and generosity.

Following the success of *Lincoln's Dreams* (1987), the critical and popular acclaim for *Doomsday Book*, which won both the Hugo and Nebula awards for best science-fiction novel, established Willis as one of the top American science-fiction writers. *Doomsday Book* exhibits Willis's characteristic strengths: thorough scholarship, graceful prose, and a rare combination of profound compassion and keen intelligence.

There is even a touch of the humor present in many of her short stories in Dunworthy's struggles with bureaucratic rigidity and the complaints of self-centered people who do not quite notice that there is an epidemic going on. Also evident is Willis's ability to realize a time and place and create vivid characters whose joys and sorrows will haunt the reader's memory.

Time travel is one of the classic plot devices of science fiction. *Doomsday Book* has antecedents dating back to Mark Twain's *A Connecticut Yankee in King Arthur's Court* (1889) and H. G. Wells's *The Time Machine* (1895). Much of twentieth century time-travel fiction has focused on the mutability of time: Characters travel back to the past and change it, either inadvertently or deliberately. Authors such as Poul Anderson have developed story sequences in which rival groups battle over time, seeking to change the past (and hence the future) or to preserve an immutable past. In *Doomsday Book*, the immutability of the past is a given. It is the combination of Kivrin's powerlessness, despite all of her modern knowledge, to do anything to stop the plague or to save even a single victim, and her heroic persistence in trying nevertheless, that gives the novel a tragic power rare in science fiction.

Willis's depiction of medieval England is compelling. She captures the sounds, sights, and smells with convincing verisimilitude. She neither patronizes the past nor sentimentalizes it. If she does not share Father Roche's simple yet profound faith in the ultimate goodness of God, she treats it and him with the utmost respect. The double plot, which allows her to contrast two periods so vividly, also enables her to portray an essential humanity. Despite the differences in language, culture, and knowledge, the people of both centuries are remarkably alike: Both centuries have their share of fools, bigots, and cowards, but most people in both are a blend of fear and courage, selfishness and nobility. In both periods, despite the prevalence of death and despair, there is a persistence of human love and caring, personified in Roche, Kivrin, and Dunworthy, that cannot be overcome.

—*Kevin P. Mulcahy*

A Door into Ocean

Inhabitants of an ocean world with an entirely female population resist takeover

Author: Joan Slonczewski (1956–)
Genre: Science fiction—alien civilization
Type of work: Novel
Time of work: The distant future
Location: The planets Valedon and Shora
First published: 1986

The Story

For forty years, traders from the planet Valedon have colonized the ocean planet Shora. The story concerns the increasing threat to the inhabitants of Shora and to the balance of life on their ocean home as the effects of colonization escalate and as they face the military invasion of their planet by the occupying forces of Valedon. The population of Shora—all females, who call themselves Sharers—resists the traders and soldiers by peaceful, nonviolent means. They also resist by trying to understand the Valans and by attempting to heal them both physically and spiritually. Although their advanced skills in life sciences might enable them to devise means of destroying the invaders, Sharers resist the temptation to destroy those who would destroy them. Influenced by their wordweaver, Merwen, they maintain the possibility that the Valans are human and that their healing will result in the survival of Sharers and Valans alike.

The story opens with the arrival of the Sharers Merwen and Usha in a port city on the planet Valedon. They have come to learn if the Valans are human in spite of their very different physical characteristics, actions, and values. They return to Shora accompanied by a young boy named Spinel and another Valan, the wealthy and noble Lady Berenice, called Nisi by the Sharers. These two Valans share the lives of Shorans who live on the raft Raia-el.

When Sharers boycott Valan traders, Spinel joins them. Although the boycott is successful in achieving the immediate demands of the Sharers, a worse threat takes the form of a plan to bring Shora under the control of Valedon. Realgar, the Valan to whom Nisi is engaged, arrives to head the military occupation of Shora. Pressures against the Sharers and their environment increase as a result of escalating Valan frustration with the Sharers' refusal to capitulate. Sharers struggle with the question of the humanity of the Valans but remain steadfast in their decision to resist without killing.

The ultimate action against the Sharers is precipitated by Nisi's attempt to destroy herself along with the Valan military headquarters. Some of the Valans have come to respect the Sharers, and their appreciation is intensified when Valans injured in the explosion are rescued and healed by Sharers. In a climactic series of conversations with the imprisoned Merwen, Realgar is forced to recognize his own fear and to face his endangered humanity. His defeat is complete when the High Protector of Valedon chastens him for the mutiny in his troops. Realgar resigns his position and, with all the trader and soldier Valans, withdraws from Shora. They leave the Sharers to the work of repairing their lives and their planet. Nisi remains to become healed of her double betrayal, and Spinel, drawn by his love for Merwen's daughter, Lystra, remains as hope for a transformed future.

ANALYSIS

A Door into Ocean is the second science-fiction novel by professor of biology Joan Slonczewski, following *Still Forms on Foxfield* (1980). Like her other novels, it has been praised by critics for the accuracy of its science, the completeness of its alternative cultures, and its characterization. It won the John W. Campbell Memorial Award as best science-fiction novel of 1986.

As a work of science fiction, the novel offers the situation of the alien encounter. Shifting the scene from one planet to another, it explores the situation of alien encounter from the perspectives of both worlds, opening with the visit of the Sharers to Valedon. As in other science-fiction novels describing encounters with aliens, the story raises and examines the issue of the nature of humanity. When Valans turn purple like the Shorans, they fear the loss of their humanity. When Merwen considers the possibility that some of the Shorans are willing to hasten the death of the invaders, she worries that Sharers will lose their identity.

The two societies are not portrayed in monolithic and static terms, but the novel presents the encounter between Valedon and Shora as a juxtaposition of utopia and dystopia. The utopian society of Shora is not without difference, nor is the dystopian world of Valedon without its redeeming qualities. At the end of the novel, Spinel chooses to remain on the utopian Shora, but his choice carries the possibility of the transformation of Shora because he retains his Valan stonesign and knows that Lystra wishes to have daughters with him, daughters who will differ from both of them.

This novel has been discussed in the context of women as writers of science fiction and as a work of feminist science fiction. The portrayal of the world of Shora, with its highly advanced life-shaping science, its openness to all learning, and its egalitarian politics, values those matters that have been seen as feminist areas of concern. This emphasis critiques the patriarchal culture of Valedon as it also critiques the dominance of science itself, since the outcome of human action always remains unpredictable and uncontrollable. As Merwen knows in the final series of conversations with Realgar, it is wordweaving, the uncertain art of persuasive language, that will determine the final outcome.

Critic Robin Roberts, author of *A New Species: Gender and Science in Science Fiction* (1993), has highlighted *A Door into Ocean* as an example of postmodernist feminist science fiction because of its attention to the function of language. A deconstructive model is at play in revisions both of the convention of the alien encounter and of the static and monolithic utopia. The model carries through in the critique of the dominance of science and of patriarchy. It is mediated by the characterization of Merwen as a wordweaver and by a peculiarity of Sharer language: In every utterance, its opposite is present.

—*Shawn Carruth*

THE DOOR INTO SUMMER

A duped inventor escapes his time period through cryonics and then returns via time travel to rectify his personal history

Author: Robert A. Heinlein (1907-1988)
Genre: Science fiction—time travel
Type of work: Novel
Time of work: 1970 and 2000
Locale: Los Angeles, California, and Denver, Colorado
First published: 1957

THE STORY

Robert A. Heinlein's *The Door into Summer* forecasts themes that appear in his later work and packs many facets of the science-fiction canon into its abbreviated length. Although the plot is understandable, if incredible at points, the novel is difficult reading primarily because the reader must suspend disbelief and recall that this dark, yet advanced, view of 1970 and 2000 was written from the perspective of the 1950's. By the standards of the genre, the book is short, but it unveils Heinlein's projections for the future, including a well-developed cryonics program, time travel, and robotics.

The story begins in 1970, shortly after the Six Weeks War, a confrontation that decimated much of the eastern United States, causing all governmental officials and documents to be relocated near Denver. As the tale opens, the protagonist, Daniel Boone Davis, is contemplating cold sleep, a precursor of cryonics, which will allow him to disassociate until the year 2000. He has reached this rather desperate alternative because his best friend and colleague, Miles Gentry, has just married Daniel's fiancée, Belle Darkin. Together, they have swindled Daniel out of the company he founded. The firm, Hired Girl, churns out robotic assistants, invented by Daniel, for harried housewives.

After Daniel makes arrangements for both himself and his cat, Petronius the Arbiter (Pete), to go into cold sleep, he makes a complete reversal and decides that revenge might be sweeter. While visiting Miles and Belle to carry out his coup, he is drugged by Belle, who accidentally uncovers the forms stating that he is to be put into cold sleep. She and Miles decide that this is a good way to get rid of Daniel. Belle takes Daniel to her own cryogenicist and puts him to sleep without his cat.

When Daniel awakes, it is the year 2000. There is a cure for the common cold, there is no smog, all clothes are made with velcro seams, and mass movers are the sole forms of transportation. Prior to undergoing cold sleep, Daniel had made financial arrangements for his reawakening, but his investments have gone sour, so he is forced to look for work. Through a series of blue-collar positions and chance meetings, he manages to work his way into a robotics lab. While learning the new technology, he discovers that most of the patents for robots carry his name.

The only negative factor in his new existence is a person from his past whom he had hoped to find in his future—Frederica (Little Ricky) Gentry, the adopted daughter of his former partner, Miles. By this point, the importance to Daniel of Pete the cat has become apparent. Much of his desire to find Little Ricky has to do with news of the animal; in addition, he had mailed her the balance of his Hired Girl stock prior to undergoing cold sleep. His quest to track her down leads him to Arizona and the news that she has married. A third motive and Daniel's real interest in finding the girl becomes apparent: He had hoped to marry her.

In another chance encounter, Daniel learns of an inventor, Dr. Hubert Twitchell, who has created a time machine, which is suppressed by the government. Daniel tricks the inventor into a demonstration and arranges to be transported back to 1970.

After initially plopping down in the middle of a nudist colony, Daniel locates Little Ricky, tells her to go into cold sleep on her twenty-first birthday, returns to Miles's home, retrieves his cat, and recommits himself to cold sleep for the year 2001. The book ends as he, Little Ricky, Pete, and the Hired Girl stock are reunited.

ANALYSIS

As opposed to the satiric social commentary of his later magnum opus, *Stranger in a Strange Land* (1961), Heinlein's *The Door into Summer* falls into the vat of sentimentality. One critic at the time of publication noted that the book reveals myriad "gadgets-to-be." Readers who realize that Heinlein's "future" is "now" or has passed without those gadgets having come to be are left with only the plot of the novel, which revolves around a maudlin, self-serving, and pathetic protagonist. The only character of any real interest is the cat.

The problem may lie with the brevity of the work. Readers have little time to engage with the future before the plot yanks them back to the past, then thrusts them forward again. Vertigo replaces interest in the lives of any of the characters. Additionally, there is a rending of belief for even the most inveterate fans of science fiction. The most far-fetched portion of the plot concerns the protagonist repeating the time travel process primarily to procure the love of an eleven-year-old child.

The saving grace in the work lies with the often unexpected use of humor. For example, the time machine inventor explains that the only test on a human was unsuccessful: Leonard Vincent, a twenty-first century draftsman and artist, was transported back to the fifteenth century and did not return. Daniel's time traveling excursion, in another humorous incident, plunges him, fully dressed, from the sky into the center of a nudist colony.

The Door into Summer shows the shaping of themes that would predominate in Heinlein's later work. Underlying the basically bland plot structure is a hero's escape from a stifling maze into boundless freedom, coupled with a reverence for intellect, survival, and *joie de vivre*.

For all of his love of science fiction and technology, Heinlein's view of the future is dark and bleak, and his reaction to progress is often cynical. In his "futuristic" 1970, inventors are products of corporations, and in his 2000, the world is monopolized by zombie recruiters, rampant overpopulation, and bureaucratic stifling.

—*Joyce Duncan*

Door Number Three

A psychiatrist treating a woman claiming to have been left on Earth by aliens finds himself fighting the Holock, creatures from the future who devour human dreams

Author: Patrick O'Leary (1952–)
Genre: Science fiction—time travel
Type of work: Novel
Time of work: 1990, with parts set in the far future
Location: The United States
First published: 1995

The Story

Psychiatrist John Donelly is treating Laura, a woman who claims to have been left on Earth by the alien Holock. She claims that she has only one year to convince one person—anyone—that her story is true, or she will have to leave Earth. She says that the Holock take great interest in earthly affairs because entering human dreams is their primary form of entertainment. Donelly believes her story is an elaborate delusion, until strange events—and even stranger dreams—invade his mundane existence. His dreams become more vivid, each of them featuring the same ten-year-old boy. One of his colleagues is murdered the same night that Laura strikes him after he tells her he does not believe her. A detective investigating the murder tells Donelly that a Vietnamese soldier he killed during the Vietnam War has begun appearing in his dreams, asking him about Laura and the Holock.

Donelly meets Saul, Laura's former "guardian angel" and the unwitting progenitor of the Holock. Saul reveals that the Holock come not from space, but from Earth's own post-holocaust future, and that they devour dreams, preventing humanity's ethical evolution to ensure their own eventual creation. He also says that Donelly's child will be the savior of the human race. Donelly sleeps with Laura, who soon reveals her pregnancy and allegiance to the Holock, then disappears into the future.

To set things right, Donelly asks to use Saul's time machine. This device induces a form of mental time travel that not only causes users to "blip" back and forth throughout their own lifetimes, but generates changes that ripple out into both the past and the future. Donelly soon finds himself on the run from government agents, who have made a deal with the Holock. He eventually tracks down Laura in the future, only to find her living with an alternate version of himself, the self that really slept with Laura, the one he finally agrees to kill in order to save the world and usher in a new golden age, free of the Holock.

ANALYSIS

Door Number Three is a clever, well-written, and intricately constructed debut novel. Despite spinning variations on many classic science-fiction themes, it is boldly original. It betrays few evidences of being a first novel, as O'Leary worked with editor David Hartwell for seven years to hone the novel through multiple drafts. Its prose is smooth and polished, its characters vivid and memorable, and its plot gripping.

O'Leary manages to juggle time travelers, alien abductions, government conspiracies, and dream-eating monsters without ever descending into clichés. He slowly and skillfully invests the Holock with a sense of menace far more frightening than the standard "alien grays" so often depicted in popular media. While the novel's themes of paranoia and loss of reality have earned O'Leary comparisons with Philip K. Dick, the analogy distorts as much as it reveals. While Dick's best work displays an organic paranoia that reflects the disorder in his hapless protagonists' minds, O'Leary's carefully crafted plot forces these experiences on his protagonist from without.

The intricate twists and turns deployed in the time travel portions of *Door Number Three* recall the equally ingenious plotting of Robert A. Heinlein's "By His Bootstraps." While the idea of "mental" time travel has been used before, the idea of changes in the future rippling back to effect the past may be original to O'Leary. The ambitious looping and nesting structure of the novel as a whole merits comparison with K. W. Jeter's *The Glass Hammer* (1985) and Geoff Ryman's *The Child Garden* (1989). As in those overlooked masterpieces, the story itself could not be told in a linear narrative with the same impact.

Door Number Three ranks alongside Mary Doria Russell's *The Sparrow* (1996), Ken MacLeod's *The Star Fraction* (1995), and Raphael Carter's *The Fortunate Fall* (1996) as one of the most impressive science fiction debuts of the 1990's. O'Leary afterward went on to publish *The Gift* (1997), a flawed but engrossing fantasy, and *Other Voices, Other Doors: A Collection of Stories, Meditations and Poems* (2000). O'Leary may yet prove to be one of science fiction's major talents.

—*Lawrence Person*

DOROTHEA DREAMS

A reclusive artist shows her masterpiece after a ghost helps her decide how to respond while she is held hostage by young fugitives

Author: Suzy McKee Charnas (1939–)
Genre: Fantasy—feminist
Type of work: Novel
Time of work: The 1980's
Locale: Taos and Albuquerque, New Mexico
First published: 1986

THE STORY
Dorothea Dreams tells the story of Dorothea Howard's progress from seclusion and obsession with her work to a return to public and political involvement. The change occurs after young Chicanos hold her hostage. She sympathizes with their effort to save their neighborhood. Her friend Ricky Maulders and a ghost from the time of the French Revolution help her respond to the crisis.

A well-known artist, Dorothea lives near Taos, New Mexico, and is obsessed by an enormous collage of found objects she has spent several years creating on a cliff wall. The first person to see this work is Ricky, a friend who is dying of cancer and asks to stay with her for a while. Like the viewers to follow, he is enchanted by this artwork; he believes it was the beacon that drew him to Dorothea. Ricky and Dorothea's friendship blossoms into a love affair, and Ricky helps Dorothea to analyze the frightening dreams she has been having in which she sees an angry mob and speaks aloud in French, a language she does not know well. After she writes a long letter in her sleep in French and in someone else's handwriting, they determine that a ghost from the time of the French Revolution is haunting her in her sleep. The ghost had been active in bringing about the revolution but rejected political involvement later in life. He believes Dorothea is his son, whom he wishes to persuade against risking his own safety through radical politics.

Meanwhile, Roberto Cantu, a Chicano teenager, works to save Pinto Street in Albuquerque from unscrupulous real estate developers who try to trick residents into selling their homes. After the police, mistakenly believing that a riot is in progress, open fire at a wedding reception, Roberto becomes a fugitive. Planning to flee to Canada, he and his sister Blanca escape Albuquerque by joining their cousin Robbie's art class on a field trip to Dorothea's house.

On the way to Taos, Roberto takes the class hostage. Once the group arrives, Dorothea and Ricky likewise become hostages. During the ordeal, Roberto shoots Dorothea's dog, discovers her artwork and damages it, and breaks several of her ribs. Dorothea finally recognizes the ghost in her dreams as a former self. She does not want to repeat his refusal to become involved and decides to help the Cantus. She persuades them to surrender peacefully and then tries to convince the authorities not to punish them harshly.

Because of Roberto's damage to her artwork, Doro-thea is able to move beyond her obsession with it and show it at last. Ricky, believing he has done what he was called to Taos to do, leaves to take care of other unfinished business before his death.

ANALYSIS

Dorothea Dreams, Suzy McKee Charnas' fifth novel, contains several fantasy elements—the ghost, the odd connection between Dorothea and Ricky, and the mysterious power of Dorothea's wall collage. Ricky believes that Dorothea's finishing of the collage drew both him and the ghost to her. Only Dorothea sees the ghost, mostly in her dreams, but she needs Ricky's help to understand the ghost's messages. At one point Dorothea speculates that the ghost is one of Ricky's ancestors who is trying to send a message to Ricky through her. Only after seeing the ghost's face does she recognize herself and realize that the ghost is an incarnation of herself in an earlier life. When Dorothea draws an inkwell the ghost used in her dreams, Ricky recognizes it as one he saw in France, a country Dorothea has never visited, at a museum too small to have a catalog. Except for this striking inkwell, it might be possible to dismiss the ghost as the product of a particularly vivid imagination.

The novel, then, subverts the conventional ghost story. In a sense, Dorothea is haunted by her own ghost, an unusual plot twist. Although he means well, the ghost is pitifully inept. He is quite surprised to learn that Dorothea is not, in fact, his son, and he gives terrible advice.

The parallel story of the Cantu family raises the issues of Chicano identity and community. Roberto feels alienated from white culture to the extent that he quit school, and he resents Pinto Street residents, such as his cousin Robbie's family, who leave for the more affluent, and mostly white, Heights. The media attention that results from Roberto's hostage-taking leads to an investigation that reveals that his sense of victimization is warranted. The real estate developers were trying to take advantage of the poor residents, and the police behaved improperly when they opened fire at the wedding reception.

At the same time, the novel sensitively portrays the plight of Roberto's younger sister, Blanca. Blanca recognizes the limited possibilities for an intelligent but poor and seriously asthmatic girl in a place like Pinto Street. Her goal is to escape, even if it means being a fugitive with Roberto. In a letter sent after she and Ricky become friends during the hostage ordeal, Ricky tells her that he will leave her money when he dies so that she can travel. He particularly encourages her to seek friends on her journeys who are her "heart's kindred." Blanca rereads this letter until it becomes illegible. The novel does not attempt to resolve the tension between protecting one's ethnic identity and seeking alternatives through education and travel.

Typical of Charnas' fiction, especially her Mother-lines series (including *Walk to the End of the World*, 1974; *Motherlines*, 1978; and *The Furies*, 1994), the novel has a strong feminist slant. Dorothea left her husband once her children were grown to pursue her artistic career, but even so had wondered if the children had drained away all of her creative energy. The novel ends with her accepting acclaim as a prominent role model for other female artists.

—*Joan Hope*

Double Star

An actor, recruited to impersonate a powerful politician kidnapped by extremists opposed to the man's policy of cooperation with nonhuman races, is forced to confront his own prejudices and to make a fundamental decision about his future

Author: Robert A. Heinlein (1907-1988)
Genre: Science fiction—extrapolatory
Type of work: Novel
Time of work: The near future
Locale: Earth, Mars, the Moon, and various spaceships
First published: 1956

The Story

Hoping for a free meal or even a loan, down-on-his-luck actor Lorenzo Smythe buys a drink for Dak Broadbent, a spaceship captain trying to pretend he is something else. Broadbent offers more than Smythe could have hoped for, an acting job at a good salary. Before the final arrangements can be made, however, they are attacked by a human and a Martian, a race Smythe cannot tolerate, partly because of their smell. Smythe finds himself an accomplice in the deaths of the two attackers and the disposal of their bodies.

The acting job is revealed to be the impersonation of John Joseph Bonforte, one of the most important politicians in the empire and leader of the opposition Expansionist coalition, whose political philosophy, based on equality of humans and nonhumans, is at odds with Smythe's prejudices. It is suspected that terrorists with links to the ruling Humanity Party have kidnapped Bonforte to keep him from taking part in an adoption ceremony at a Martian nest, an act that would further cement human-Martian relations. Because Martian society is based on rigid rules of protocol, should Bonforte not attend for any reason except death, relations between Martians and humans would be so badly ruptured that a massacre of humans—which would result in a human war against the Martians—would likely result, and Bonforte's policy of coexistence would fall apart.

The plot follows Smythe as he prepares for his role with the help of those closest to Bonforte: personal secretary Penelope Russell, physician Dr. Capek, pilot Dak Broadbent, political operative Roger Clifton, and press liaison Bill Corpsman. As Smythe watches tapes of Bonforte, he begins to understand him. With the help of hypnosis, he is able to conquer his negative emotional reaction to the Martian race. Increasingly, he speaks, acts, and even thinks like Bonforte.

The adoption ceremony goes smoothly, but a new problem develops. Bonforte is found but has been drugged so heavily that he will be unable to appear in public for some time. Smythe agrees to continue the charade while Bonforte recovers. As the days pass, Smythe begins to make decisions as Bonforte. Corpsman resents Smythe's actions, and tension between the two escalates.

Smythe as Bonforte, gives a passionate speech, beamed throughout the solar system, defending "his" political philosophy. The impact is so strong that the Humanity Party government resigns. Emperor Willem summons the false Bonforte to the capital to form a caretaker government. During the audience, Smythe discovers that Bonforte and the emperor, a constitutional monarch with limited power, are longtime friends. The emperor in turn discovers that Smythe is not the real Bonforte but tells him to carry on with the impersonation until the ailing leader recovers.

As the election campaign gets under way, the conflict between Smythe and Corpsman comes to a head. When Corpsman is struck off the list of candidates for the Grand Assembly at Smythe's behest, he quits and sets out to expose the ongoing charade. He is defeated, however, when fingerprints taken from Smythe are found to match those on file for Bonforte.

The Expansionists win the election, but Bonforte suddenly dies from the effects of his kidnapping and drugging. Now Smythe must make the choice of his life— will he continue to be Bonforte forever?

In the last chapter, it is revealed that the entire book is a journal written by Smythe twenty-five years earlier while he struggled to retain his sanity while pretending to be Bonforte. Now married to Russell, he muses about the person he was and the person he has become as he lives Bonforte's political life.

313

Analysis

This Hugo Award-winning novel is one of Robert Heinlein's best. It is shorter and less strident than some of his later works. The book blends good storytelling, an interesting futuristic setting, and political and social ideas in a balanced whole.

The Humanity Party's platform of human domination over nonhumans is an easily understood metaphor for any hate group of any time or place. The Expansionist Party is the moral stand-in for all, throughout history, who have argued for the equality of all people.

The book was written in the 1950's, when women's roles were more sharply defined and limited and when the Civil Rights movement was only emerging. Some language that might have seemed innocuous when written may grate on the ears of later readers. For example, Bonforte's chief clerk, Jimmy Washington, the only member of the inner circle who has almost no role in the story, is described as "a spare, elderly mulatto." Russell, who has a master's degree and is a member of the Grand Assembly, is sometimes referred to as "hon" or "honey chile" by Broadbent and Smythe. When she gets angry at Smythe, Broadbent tells her, "Stow it, Penny, or I'll spank your round fanny." Such dated references are rare, and they pale beside the strong central message of equality and individual dignity that is at the center of the book. Smythe explains the key to the Expansionist policy: "freedom and equal rights must run with the Imperial banner. . . . The human race must never again make the mistakes that the white subrace had made in Africa and Asia." It was a timely message in 1956, but it is also a timeless message presented well.

—*Paul Joseph*

Downbelow Station

Damon Konstantin struggles to preserve Pell station's autonomy and populace in the face of rival Fleets

Author: C. J. Cherryh (1942–)
Genre: Science fiction—future war
Type of work: Novel
Time of work: 2352–2353
Locale: Pell's Planet and nearby systems
First published: 1981

The Story

Downbelow Station begins with an overview of the years 2005–2352, during which time Earth falls under the dominion of the Company, a politico-commercial entity that invests in interstellar exploration. This investment results in dominion over known space that is uncontested until a rival power emerges from the distant colony worlds located in a region of space known as The Beyond. This power, the Union, grows swiftly, fueled by a mass eugenics program that creates a burgeoning population of laboratory-born soldiers and workers.

Friction between Earth and the Union causes Earth to establish the Fleet, an interstellar flotilla that protects Company interests in interstellar space. The decline of Earth and the Company leads to retrenchment and neglect, leaving the Fleet without support, save that which it can beg, borrow, or steal from the Company space stations, which are the most important assets in colonized space.

The story begins on Pell station. Captain Signy Mallory, in command of the fleet-carrier Norway, demands docking privileges in order to complete the evacuation of refugees from Mariner station, which has been destroyed by the Union. Mallory, a good leader whose basic honesty is offset by ruthlessness and a considerable ego, also deposits a Union prisoner on Pell station. This prisoner, test-tube born Josh Talley, elects to have his memories erased rather than to recall the horrors of his service to the Union and of his sexual enslavement to Mallory.

The influx of refugees compels Damon Konstantin, the son of station chief Angelo Konstantin, to accept increasingly dangerous positions of authority as the station's resources are pushed to the breaking point. His wife, Elene Quen, discovers that her entire family has been killed by the Union at Mariner. Filled with a desire for vengeance, Elene does not immediately accept Damon's caretaking friendship for the now amnesiac and forlorn Josh Talley.

On Pell's Planet, the mostly habitable world that Pell station orbits, Damon's brother Emilio is forced to dismiss security personnel who are still loyal to Jon Lukas, the previous overseer of the planetside operations. Lukas, a longtime rival of the Konstantins, decides to seek covert means of toppling Angelo and his sons from power. The Konstantin hold on the planetside activities—a collection of multipurpose bases known collectively as Downbelow station—is reinforced by the rapport between the Konstantin family and the Downers, an indigenous humanoid species who are gentle and usually trusting. Many of the Downers are relocated to Pell station to help with maintenance and cargo handling. Emilio sends up a particularly clever and loyal pair of mated Downers, Satin and Bluetooth.

Mallory, having departed from Pell station, makes a rendezvous with the rest of the Fleet, which is massing for a strike at Union-held Viking station. Fleet commander Mazian aborts the assault at the last second, fleeing the vicinity of Viking. Mallory is at first dismayed by, and then suspicious of, Mazian's action.

As the Fleet reapproaches Pell station, Jon Lukas, with the help of a Union agent, kills Angelo Konstantin and takes control of the station. His treachery is uncovered by Mazian, and he is forced to act as the Fleet's puppet administrator in charge of both Pell station and Down-below station.

Elene Quen manages to escape the occupation by the Fleet and sets out to unify the nomadic merchanters into a cohesive political and military force, using the name Quen—that of her martyred merchanter family—as a rallying cry. Her husband, Damon, is forced to go into hiding, along with Josh, who has begun to remember that he was more than a Union computer expert; he was a saboteur who helped destroy Mariner station.

The Fleet occupation of the station draws the Union forces closer. They hope to engage and destroy Mazian at Pell. Meanwhile, Mallory confirms that Mazian never meant to assault Viking; that operation was merely an excuse to reunite the Fleet for the conquest of Earth itself. Mazian's heavy-handed rule causes Downbelow station to revolt. Emilio and his forces are aided by the Downers, who offer sanctuary to the humans after they break for freedom.

This sanctuary turns out to be unnecessary. Aided by Satin and Bluetooth, Damon and Josh avoid capture by Fleet forces long enough to be seized by Mallory's troops, not Mazian's. Mallory learns from Josh that Mazian has concealed the fact that Jon Lukas was not merely a murderer but a traitor for the Union. Still loyal to the Company and Earth—and disgusted by Mazian's duplicity and egomania—Mallory breaks away from the station and, in order to ruin the Fleet's attempt at Earth conquest, leads the Union forces toward Pell. Mazian is forced to disperse his fleet.

Before the Union can seize the station, Elene Quen arrives with a sizable armada of merchanter vessels, which declare an alliance to Pell station and declare it neutral ground. The station is left unmolested, Damon is placed in charge, and Mallory's *Norway* becomes the core of its new Fleet.

ANALYSIS

Downbelow Station's sprawling scope is typical of space operas; however, various structural properties work to create a serious tone that is uncharacteristic of the space opera subgenre. Whereas space operas are often likened to "Westerns in space," *Downbelow Station* reads more like a high-quality political thriller.

Despite extraordinary numbers of characters, points of view, and rapid scene changes, C. J. Cherryh employs a gritty and direct prose that gives the narrative the tenor of reportage, rather than of high adventure. Similarly, the motivations of both characters and governments are consistent and believable. Hackneyed good-versus-evil tropes are absent, replaced by an almost brutal presentation of the realpolitik that drives persons who hold tremendous power and responsibility. Each chapter is headed by a dateline/location indicator, another structural nuance that serves to vest the narrative with an illusion of historicity. These various features combine to create a narrative structure that exudes an aura of plausibility, thereby placing *Downbelow Station* in the same domain occupied by extrapolative political or war thrillers such as Tom Clancy's *Red Storm Rising* (1986) or Fletcher Knebel and Charles Bailey II's *Seven Days in May* (1962). *Downbelow Station* won the 1982 Hugo Award, one of science fiction's top honors.

—*Charles Gannon*

DOWNWARD TO THE EARTH

An earthling returns to the alien world where he was colonial administrator and finds salvation through the natives he once despised

Author: Robert Silverberg (1935–)
Genre: Science fiction—alien civilization
Type of work: Novel
Time of work: The distant future
Locale: The planet Belzagor
First published: 1970 (serial form, *Galaxy*, 1969)

THE STORY

Earthling Edmund Gundersen returns as a tourist to the planet Belzagor. It had been a colony of Earth known as Holman's World, and Gundersen had been its administrator, but it was relinquished to the dominant indigenous species, elephant-like creatures known as "nildoror" (singular, "nildor"). The nildoror have no written language, but they have a culture. They undergo rebirth and identify themselves by how many births they have had. They coexisted with the earthlings and allowed themselves to be used as beasts of burden. They share the planet with the less-sentient anthropoid species called "sulidoror" (singular, "sulidor").

In a conversation with his former assistant, Van Beneker, who has remained on Belzagor, Gundersen reveals that he has always thought of the nildoror as animals. He is nevertheless fascinated by their culture.

The next day, he sets out on a journey into the jungle, seeking the mist country where the nildoror undergo rebirth, riding on a nildor named Srin'gahar. He revisits a place where he and fellow earthling Jeff Kurtz had shared a drink of the venom of local serpents with several nildoror, giving him a feeling of becoming a nildor. Afterward, he felt ashamed and never repeated the experiment.

Srin'gahar takes him to a group of nildoror. He overcomes earthling squeamishness to join in their food and dance, and he is granted permission to visit the mist country, on the condition that he bring back an earthling named Cedric Cullen, who has offended the nildoror in some way they will not explain. He agrees.

After a discussion with Srin'gahar in which the nildor raises the possibility that the elephants of Earth have souls, Gundersen re-encounters Van Beneker and the earthlings with whom he traveled to the planet. The earthlings consider the nildoror to be savages or animals, and Gundersen finds himself defending them. In the course of the conversation, he reveals the sin he hopes to expiate: Faced with a threat of property damage from flooding, he forced seven nildoror who were on their way to rebirth to give up their journey and work for him.

Further on, he encounters his former lover, Seena, now married to Kurtz. She reveals that the serpent venom is used by the nildoror in their rebirth ceremony, so Kurtz's recreational use of it with them constituted blasphemy in their minds. Kurtz eventually underwent the rebirth ceremony and has become a misshapen thing, babbling incoherently.

Finally Gundersen meets Cullen, who is dying of cancer, which is now curable by Earth medicine. He offers to take Cullen back, but Cullen refuses to go lest he fall into the hands of the nildoror. He reveals that the nildoror want him because he had inadvertently witnessed a part of their rebirth ceremony in which they frenziedly trample and eat other animals. Gundersen is ambivalent about bringing Cullen back, but the dilemma is resolved the next morning, when he finds Cullen dead.

Finally Gundersen reaches the place of rebirth and undergoes the ceremony. He learns that rebirth transforms the nildoror into sulidoror, and vice versa: They are one species, telepathically linked. He learns that Srin'gahar was one of the nildoror he had denied rebirth to but that Srin'gahar has forgiven him. He communes with the tortured spirit of Kurtz. He is transformed, and he prepares to return to transform first Kurtz and then any other earthlings willing to listen.

ANALYSIS

This work first appeared, in serial form, in 1969, a time of changes for Robert Silverberg himself and for the field of science fiction. After years as an unusually prolific hack, Silverberg stopped writing science fiction in the early 1960's. He returned a few years later to write more serious science fiction, with more attention to the literary virtues of characterization and prose style and with a willingness to look to the so-called "mainstream" for examples. Along with such books as *Tower of Glass*

(1970), *The Book of Skulls* (1971), and *Dying Inside* (1972), *Downward to the Earth* represented this sort of literary ambition. The field as a whole was undergoing similar changes, sometimes referred to as the "New Wave."

The book contains a number of references to Joseph Conrad's well-known treatment of the theme of clash between European and "primitive" cultures, *Heart of Darkness* (1902), most notably the name of Kurtz. It employs one of Silverberg's most frequent themes, redemption and rebirth, as well as treating an issue that was much in the news at that time, colonization and the return to native rule. Some saw the natives as less than human; others saw them as having an enviable connectedness to the land and to other life. Silverberg extended this in science-fictional manner by making the nildoror nonhuman in appearance but intelligent in their own way and even telepathic.

This did not represent a simple concession to current political fashion on Silverberg's part.

Indeed, as far back as *Invaders from Earth* (1958) and *Collision Course* (1961), he had been suggesting that the alien races Earth might meet could be wiser or more clever than humanity. This approach put him on a collision course with dominant forces in the field of science fiction, most notably John W. Campbell, Jr. Since then, the idea of alien cultures as different, rather than inferior, has shown up in many books, including Ursula K. Le Guin's *The Word for World Is Forest* (1976) and Barry B. Longyear's *Manifest Destiny* (1980).

With its lavish descriptions of alien landscapes, its rich development of characters both alien and human, and its striking presentations of altered states of consciousness, *Downward to the Earth* is generally considered one of Silverberg's best novels, at least by those who do not prefer the simple adventures of his early work.

—Arthur D. Hlavaty

DRACULA

Count Dracula, a vampire, moves to England from his native Transylvania in search of new blood

Author: Bram Stoker (1847–1912)
Genre: Fantasy—cautionary
Type of work: Novel
Time of work: The end of the nineteenth century
Location: Transylvania and England
First published: 1897

THE STORY

Jonathan Harker, an English solicitor, visits Count Dracula in Transylvania. He finds death's aura and aroma surrounding Dracula. Harker is attacked by three female vampires, who are warded off by Dracula. Harker is his; they are given a baby to feed on. When Harker demands to be released, Dracula obliges, but a pack of wolves surrounds the castle entrance. The next day, Harker awakes, weak and sick, with a wound on his throat. Dracula leaves Harker at the castle as a prisoner.

In England, Harker's fiancé, Mina Murray, visits her friend, Lucy Westenra, a "New Woman" who plans to marry nobleman Arthur Holmwood.

During Mina's visit, a ship runs aground in Whitby. The only living creature aboard is a gray wolf, which escapes into the countryside.

Lucy begins to sleepwalk. Mina follows her and sees a tall, thin man bending over Lucy in a churchyard. The man disappears when Mina approaches. Lucy grows so ill that Mina is forced to call Dr. Seward, Lucy's former suitor. While Lucy improves, Mina receives word that Harker, who had been reported missing, has been found near Budapest. Mina goes there and marries Harker.

Lucy's condition worsens, and Seward calls Dr. Van Helsing from Amsterdam. Van Helsing notices two puncture wounds on Lucy's throat. Lucy is given transfusions directly from the men, who guard her by night. Seward falls asleep while guarding Lucy and finds her more ill when he awakes. More transfusions ensue, and Van Helsing insists that Lucy wear a necklace of garlic every night.

One night, a wolf crashes through the window, the necklace slips off, and Lucy is further victimized. Van Helsing tells Holmwood that Lucy is near death. Holmwood kisses Lucy, who fastens her teeth to his neck. Lucy dies. Several neighborhood children are discovered far from home, alive but with their throats punctured. They say they followed a pretty lady in white.

Harker returns to England. Van Helsing suggests that Lucy is a vampire's victim. By night, Holmwood, Seward, Van Helsing, and Quincey P. Morris visit Lucy's tomb and find it empty. At daybreak, Lucy returns, and they drive a stake through her heart, cut off her head, and stuff garlic in her mouth.

Mina is vampirized by Dracula. The men track Dracula in London, but he escapes. By hypnotizing Mina, they learn that Dracula is at sea. They follow him to Castle Dracula. Wolves encircle the men and Mina, who gather safely within a "magic" circle Van Helsing traces. The men overtake the cart carrying Dracula's coffin. As the sun sets, Harker slashes Dracula's throat with his kukri knife and Morris gouges Dracula's heart with his bowie knife.

ANALYSIS

Interest in vampires, like the creature itself, never dies. Bram Stoker's novel focuses on the victimization of women. Stoker's view is opposed to that of the "New Woman," a feminist construct of the late nineteenth century. Stoker makes references to the NewWoman in *Dracula* through Mina, characterizing her as a well-informed woman of the 1890's. Mina sets herself above the New Woman, rejecting the concept for its sexual openness. The overall structure of *Dracula* indicates that Stoker employs Mina to reject the concept of the New Woman, represented by the female vampire as energized and aggressive female sexuality.

The first half of the novel presents woman as vampire. Stoker focuses on the female vampire by introducing the three female vampires who live in Dracula's castle, then centering on Lucy, Dracula's first English victim. In the second half, the focus of the story is the fight to save Mina, shifting away from the presentation of woman as vampire. The focus becomes the fight against vampirism, and, metaphorically, against energized female sexuality or the New Woman.

Lucy, the primary female focus of the first half of the novel, is turned by Dracula into one of "those awful women." The New Woman exists in her personality, however latent, surfacing when Lucy is vampirized by Dracula. In her vampirized state, she no longer suppresses her desire. Van Helsing takes it upon himself to protect men from the evils of the vampire, and, hence, the evils of the New Woman. Lucy, confronted by the men in her crypt, takes on the full-blown characteristics of the New Woman, preying on a child and speaking of her wanton desire for Holmwood. By calling Holmwood to her side, Lucy suggests that he break with the patriarchy. This does not happen because Lucy is summarily destroyed by the men; the vampire/NewWoman is destroyed by the patriarchy.

The scourge of vampirism/NewWomanhood also calls at Mina's door. Mina represents traditional Victorian womanhood but also feels the effects of vampirism/ New Womanhood. Dracula seduces her, forcing her to drink his blood from his breast while her husband sleeps in the same bed. The patriarchy comes to Mina's rescue. As the vampire's, or New Woman's, influence over Mina grows, Dr. Seward metaphorically sees the New Woman overcoming the traditional woman. The role of Stoker's male characters is to prevent the acceptance of the New Woman by keeping women in their place, and, hence, the patriarchy in order. To do this, the men must destroy Dracula. Van Helsing chooses to fight the vampire to save the patriarchy.

At the novel's end, by destroying Dracula, Van Helsing and the men destroy vampirism and, metaphorically, the New Woman, preserving the sanctity of womanhood and the patriarchal order. Stoker's novel is therefore anti-New Woman and antifeminist. It came at a reactionary time when literary England was up in arms against the very idea of theNewWoman.

—*Thomas D. Petitjean, Jr.*

THE DRACULA SERIES

Count Dracula's adventures are revealed from his own perspective and from the perspectives of those closely associated with him

Author: Fred Saberhagen (1930-2007)
Genre: Fantasy—alternate history
Type of work: Novels
Time of work: Primarily contemporary
Locale: Various locations throughout Europe and the United States
First published: *The Dracula Tape* (1975), *The Holmes-Dracula File* (1978), *An Old Friend of the Family* (1979), *Thorn* (1980), *Dominion* (1982), *A Matter of Taste* (1990), *A Question of Time* (1992), and *Séance for a Vampire* (1994)

THE STORY

The Dracula Tape, the first and perhaps best novel in the series, retells the story found in Bram Stoker's *Dracula* (1897) from the point of view of Count Dracula himself. The novel, supposedly dictated to descendants of the Harkers, is a brilliant reexamination of the events surrounding Dracula, Jonathan Harker, Mina, Lucy, Renfield, and the horrid Van Helsing. Fred Saberhagen's retelling has the feel of accuracy as he points out the faults in the accounts of the witnesses in Stoker's novel and reveals a much more logical tale wherein Dracula points out, for example, the improbability of uncovering him in his coffin in the middle of the night and Van Helsing's cruelty in attempting transfusions without the aid of blood-type matching.

The Holmes-Dracula File links distant cousins Sherlock Holmes and Count Dracula to solve a series of crimes involving a trail of bloodless corpses as well as a criminal group's threat of plague-infested rats. The novel provides Saberhagen's brilliant insight into the personalities of Dracula, Holmes, and Watson.

Dracula's loyalty is the main thrust of the novel *An Old Friend of the Family*. The Southerland family, living in Chicago, invokes an ancient ritual supplied by the count himself for the descendants of the Harker family, to be used only in a dire emergency. Clarissa Southerland, granddaughter of Wilhelmina Harker, is not sure what to expect when Dr. Emile Corday (Dracula) arrives, claiming to be an old friend of the family. He proves to be very resourceful in aiding the family to recapture a daughter embraced by one of the nosferatu and a son kidnapped and tortured, as well as in punishing those responsible for these atrocities, including the evil Morgan La Fey.

In *Thorn*, Saberhagen elaborates on some of the historical activities in the life of Vlad Tepes, weaving a dramatic story of a powerful love and intertwining it with a modern attempt to recover the lost portrait of his lover. In telling this story, Saberhagen adeptly parallels the lives of the then-mortal count and the modern king of the vampires.

Dominion tells the tale of an ancient struggle for an item of tremendous magical power, rekindled in modern Chicago and its surrounding areas. The presence of several bloodless bodies attracts the attention of Detective Joe Keogh. He has married into the Southerland family and therefore is acquainted with the count, but only recently has he begun to trust him. The struggle for power eventually involves Dracula and several powerful magicians from the past, including the great Merlin.

The rescuers' roles are reversed in *A Matter of Taste* as the Southerland family must battle half a millennia of the count's enemies to save him. Again Saberhagen interlaces past and present, narrating the events surrounding Vlad Tepes' assassination and initial years as a vampire and connecting these to the enemies of the present who wish to destroy him. John Southerland, now grown and engaged, and Joe Keogh, both of whom are now experienced with vampires, head the forces attempting to free the count.

A Question of Time may be the most unusual novel of the entire series, as time becomes completely nonlinear. A nosferatu sculptor named Edgar Tyrell is conducting experiments, mining the very fabrics of time and reality from deep within the ancient rocks of the Grand Canyon. In 1935, a Conservation Corps worker, Jake Rezner, is lured into working for Tyrell by his attraction for Camilla, a beautiful woman trapped by Tyrell in 1965. In 1991, Cathy Brainard, supposedly the niece of the famous sculptor but actually his daughter, winds up missing. Joe Keogh (now the head of his own investigative agency specializing in the supernatural),

John Southerland, and Mr. Strangeways (Dracula) are called in to find her. All the tales eventually overlap, with Tyrell's mining threatening the lives and reality of the major characters.

Dracula, Holmes, and Watson are reunited in *Séance for a Vampire* as they attempt to decipher the bizarre events surrounding the Altamont household. The eldest daughter has drowned under mysterious circumstances. A mischievous confidence game pulled off by two false mediums trying to turn the family's misfortune into their own profit unexpectedly brings back the daughter, with a message about a stolen treasure that must be returned. This treasure was stolen by the Russian pirate Kulakov, who was embraced as a vampire to escape death by hanging in 1765. Kulakov believes that the Altamonts have his lost treasure and is terrorizing the family to ensure its return. Holmes and Dracula team up again to solve this baffling crime and battle the supernatural forces masterminding it.

Analysis

In this excellent series, Saberhagen brings a personality and fullness to the character of Dracula that perhaps goes beyond any treatment in the vampire genre. Saberhagen's Dracula seems much more plausible than the one described in Bram Stoker's novel, and his portrayal quickly engages readers, who find themselves identifying with the count and even cheering for his success.

Using historical accounts of Vlad Tepes and remaining true to most of the details in Stoker's skeletal description, Saberhagen constructs a believable personality profile of a misunderstood, loyal, complicated, human Dracula. The fanatical sense of honesty and integrity he possesses, for example, does not permit him to cover up his own faults and is responsible for much of his introspection but is also the motivation for impaling thieves when he rules in his mortal court. Many readers may be surprised to witness the wonderful, sometimes almost childlike humor and wonder the count can feel. Throughout the series, readers come to know the deep sense of honor and contentment in Dracula's character but also remain aware of the tension and power seething underneath his calm, cold mask.

Several recurring characters, in addition to Dracula, provide continuity and contrast in the novels. Sherlock Holmes and Dr. Watson appear in two of the novels, and readers also become familiar over the course of several novels with Judy Southerland, Kate Southerland Keogh, Joe Keogh, and John Southerland, all descendants of the Harker family. As readers interact with each new novel in the series, they see the striking contrast between the growth and aging of these characters and the timelessness of Dracula. Although Dracula frequently adopts new names, he otherwise remains almost unchanging throughout his mortal and immortal existence.

Saberhagen is especially sensitive to the feelings and expectations the novels create in the minds of his readers. Early in the series, Saberhagen attempts to keep the reader in suspense about the identity of the count, almost as a sly joke between the author and his readers as well as to present the feeling of what other characters experience around the count, both a sense of familiarity and a distant strangeness. This works well in *The Holmes-Dracula File* because the count is hit on the head in the beginning of the book and suffers a short amnesia. In *An Old Friend of the Family*, Saberhagen uses the strategy to mirror the sense of familiarity and distant strangeness the members of the Southerland family feel for their visitor. In each case, readers begin to suspect early the veiled identity of the count, but through the process of discovery, combined with the historical unfolding of the count's history, Saberhagen reveals Dracula to his readers.

—Paul J. Baltes

Dracula Unbound

A scientist involves Bram Stoker, author of Dracula, in a search throughout history for time-traveling vampires

Author: Brian W. Aldiss (1925–)
Genre: Science fiction—time travel

Type of work: Novel
Time of work: 1896, 1999, and 2599
Locale: London, England; Enterprise, Utah; and Tripoli, Libya
First published: 1991

THE STORY

Dracula Unbound follows the efforts of Joe Bodenland to defeat the Fleet Ones, vampirish descendants of pterodactyls who intend to use time travel to enslave humanity. Bodenland has developed a method of toxic waste disposal involving time displacement. His friend, Bernard Clift, a paleontologist, has discovered in the deserts of Utah a coffin containing a humanoid corpse, buried in rock from the Cretaceous period.

When a ghastly "ghost train" appears over Clift's find, Bodenland and Clift manage to steal aboard. They discover that the train is a time-travel device from the far future, when Earth is ruled by the Fleet Ones, who hope to use the "time train" to dominate humans throughout all time. Clift is killed, but Bodenland seizes control of the train. Discovering that the train recently dropped off a vampire agent in the London of 1896, he travels there to attempt to thwart her. Upon arrival, he befriends Bram Stoker, who is writing the novel Dracula, and his gardener, Spinks.

Bella, the operative whom Bodenland seeks, seduces him. She confides that the vampires' leader, Lord Dra-cula, has called a great convocation of all vampires to plan humanity's ultimate downfall. She further confides that this gathering will take place in the Cretaceous period. The only weapon that could defeat Dracula, a superfusion bomb, can be found only in Tripoli, Libya, in the year 2599. Bodenland, Stoker, and Spinks stalk Bella and dispatch her with a stake.

Taking Bella's corpse with them, the three men board the time train for Tripoli, where they steal the bomb. Soon, however, Dracula captures Bodenland and tells him of Bella's true plans. She had been sent to Bodenland to lure him to Tripoli to steal the bomb, so that Dracula could then wrest it away from him. The Fleet Ones, though shrewd, are incapable of the sustained logical thought and powers of invention needed to retrieve the bomb from its sophisticated safeguards. Dracula also taunts Bodenland with the revelation that it is his invention that will lead to time travel, the vampires' pathway to total dominion over humans.

Stoker and Spinks rescue Bodenland, and they soon set out for the Cretaceous period. They bomb the convocation of Fleet Ones of which Bella had spoken, causing the cloud-shrouded cold and darkness that ended the age of reptiles. Bella is buried on a vast Cretaceous plain, to be discovered in 1999 by Clift. Bodenland destroys his time-displacement system.

ANALYSIS

Within the highly regarded canon of Brian W. Aldiss' works, *Dracula Unbound* occupies a very specific slot—that of sequel to his well-received *Frankenstein Unbound* (1973). In the frequent manner of sequels, *Dracula Unbound* mirrors *Frankenstein Unbound* in a number of ways. Both books feature scientists who travel to the 1800's to encounter famous writers of speculative fiction and characters from those authors' works. Most readers will probably agree with the majority of critics that the earlier work is the better of the two.

As *Frankenstein Unbound* takes Mary Shelley's theme of the ethical and unethical uses of science, *Dracula Unbound* borrows Bram Stoker's theme of good versus evil. The concept of absolute evil in a science-fiction framework poses some problems. Whereas many readers can readily accept Dracula as the personification of absolute evil in Stoker's Victorian horror novel, they may have problems with Aldiss' rationale for the utter evil of Dracula and his minions: their reptilian brains. Bodenland finds that the vampires' vileness is predi-cated on their lack of a neocortex. In short, the creatures are biologically predisposed to unmitigated evil. The ethical implications of such a discovery are vast: Are "good" and "evil" then universally based on genetics? As repulsive as the Fleet Ones are, are they responsible for their actions? Few of Aldiss' characters ponder these issues for very long. Furthermore, how the absence of a neocortex affects morality is never clearly explained.

The novel gives dubious scientific explanations for other bits of vampiriana. Vampires' fear of sunlight is given its genesis in the great bomb blast that killed the dinosaurs. Is this inherited racial memory, as the gardener Spinks suggests? The explanation for the bloodsuckers' fear of Christian symbolism is especially murky: The Fleet Ones seem to view the cross as some sort of emblem of human individuality, which they, with their more primitive brains, cannot understand. These explanations are nebulous.

The novel provides some real pleasures. Aldiss depicts instances of the ironies of time travel that fans of this subgenre savor. In Libya, Bodenland, seeing the time train overhead, realizes that he is inside it, at some other point in his adventure. The novel opens with the discovery of Bella's grave, which Bodenland digs at novel's end. Also, Aldiss devises a new extension of the vampire as metaphor. The Fleet Ones are incapable of scientific inquiry and invention; therefore, they must tap into the inventiveness of other species and siphon away their creative vitality. Because the novel opens with Bodenland and Clift worrying about the reaction to their research in academia, government, and business, it is easy to see the novel as a wry satire of the way in which industry and government appropriate and make use of the discoveries and inventions of men and women of science, work that others cannot accomplish on their own and cannot fully appreciate beyond their potential for exploitation. Finally, perhaps the novel's greatest feat of imagination is the Fleet Ones themselves. In them, Aldiss has interwoven three subjects that have been dear to writers and readers of fantasy and science fiction for decades: dinosaurs, vampires, and time travel.

—*Thomas DuBose*

THE DRAGON IN THE SEA

While a submarine is engaged in pirating crude oil from enemy undersea wells, a psychologist attempts to discover which of its crew members is an enemy spy

Author: Frank Herbert (1920–1986)
Genre: Science fiction—extrapolatory
Type of work: Novel
Time of work: Early in the twenty-first century
Locale: The sub-tug *Fenian Ram*
First published: 1956 (serial form, "Under Pressure," *Astounding Science-Fiction*, 1955)

THE STORY

As a result of a long-running war, the world is starved for petroleum products. In response, using "sub-tugs," the United States has been taking crude oil from an undersea well operated by the enemy powers. In similar missions, twenty sister submarines have been lost to enemy action. U.S. Navy experts believe that the *Fenian Ram* has a good chance for success.

Ensign John Ramsey, an electronics officer and psychologist trained in the Bureau of Psychology, becomes a member of the closely knit crew of the *Fenian Ram*. His mission is to ferret out the enemy spy among the other three members of the crew to ensure the success of this critical mission.

Nothing about the mission augurs well. A corpse is discovered in the shielded atomic drive room, hidden electronic devices signal the sub's location, and a silk wiper rag threatens to cause an explosion from static electricity. As the obstacles to success slowly are overcome, Ramsey comes no nearer to determining the identity of the unknown spy, even though he has studied the personalities of the three other crew members intensely, both ashore and on board the ship.

Each of the other crew members has distinct individual qualities as well as potential tragic flaws. Captain Sparrow is extremely competent and has earned the nickname "Savvy" for his superior ability. He is also an apparent religious fanatic, fond of quoting Scripture, yet a man of immense personal emotional control. He is a virtual father to the crew, a commanding presence who can sense or intuit problems before they occur.

Les Bonnett, the first officer, and José Garcia, the engineering officer, react to both the captain and Ramsey, the newcomer, in different ways. Both men, defensive in their protection of the crew and its mission, view Ramsey as an interloper who must prove himself before acceptance. They view the captain as an indispensable, completely sane source of safety and security in the insane undersea world they inhabit during a war, the ultimate insanity.

As the mission proceeds, the ship and crew are threatened by incident after incident of increasing danger and tension. Ramsey, the psychologist, suffers two severe mental breakdowns. The first occurs when he realizes and fully accepts the incredible dangers of this mission, in the coldest depths of the Atlantic, more than nine thousand feet below the surface. He is saved from the second breakdown, which takes the form of catatonic immobility, by the fatherly compassion of Captain Sparrow, who had seemed to Ramsey to embody the latent insanity of the crew and its mission, as well as the insane war and insane mission in which both are engaged. Sparrow maintains that sanity is the ability to swim and survival is sanity. The Bible-quoting Sparrow also provides the ominous citation from Isaiah that gives the book its title: "In that day the Lord with his . . . great and strong sword shall punish leviathan the piercing serpent, even leviathan the crooked serpent; and he shall slay the dragon that is in the sea."

Numerous scenes drenched with both action and tension gradually reveal that Garcia, fearful for the safety of his wife and children, who are under the control of the enemy powers, is the hidden spy. It is Garcia, however, in an act of sacrificial self-immolation, who saves the ship and crew from an atomic flare-up. In effect, he redeems himself by literally laying down his life for his friends.

As the tub returns to its home port through a long undersea tunnel, Ramsey notices that the tunnel resembles the birth canal and that the ship and its crew are returning from "death in water" to "life in water." Nurtured by the umbilical cord of shared dangers and experience, the ship and the crew emerge from the darkness and dangers of the depths of the sea into the light of life. Ramsey convinces the Bureau of Security that its passion for secrecy and "security" is dangerous, that there can be no security in a world filled with war, hatred, and suspicion. Submarine crews should be publicly decorated and their incredibly dangerous missions honored as a first step toward sanity and truth.

ANALYSIS

It is difficult to believe that *The Dragon in the Sea* is Frank Herbert's first novel. It is a mature work, populated with well-drawn characters and filled with convincing action. It remains one of Herbert's most satisfying books. It succeeds not merely on its own terms but also in the many ways it anticipates *Dune* (1965) and its five sequels, not only for its action-filled plot but also for its reliance on the tools of psychology and humane understanding to advance that plot. Moreover, in the same way that *Dune* later provided a commentary on the extent to which people will go to obtain a substance of incalculable value, this novel emphasizes an oil-starved future and the means to which people and nations will go to obtain that scarce commodity.

Never sermonic, Herbert is content simply to let his story speak for him. Submariners have written dozens of letters to Herbert, commenting that *The Dragon in the Sea* catches the spirit, the tension, and the pervading fear of submarine life better than anything else they have ever seen.

—*Willis E. McNelly*

THE DRAGON KNIGHT SERIES

Jim Eckert is transplanted into an alternate fourteenth century and must battle the Dark Powers as the Dragon Knight

Author: Gordon R. Dickson (1923–2001)
Genre: Fantasy—heroic fantasy
Type of work: Novels
Time of work: The fourteenth century
Locale: An alternate Earth
First published: *The Dragon and the George* (1976; based on the novelette "St. Dragon and the George," *The Magazine of Fantasy and Science Fiction*, September, 1957), *The Dragon Knight* (1990), *The Dragon on the Border* (1992), *The Dragon at War* (1992), and *The Dragon, the Earl and the Troll* (1994)

THE STORY

The Dragon and the George features Jim Eckert, a doctoral student in medieval history who is frustrated with the twentieth century. His girlfriend, Angie, is a research assistant to a scientist experimenting with astral projection and accidentally gets sent to some unknown world. Jim tries to follow, but only his mind is projected. He wakes up in the body of a dragon named Gorbash. Angie, a "george"—as all humans are called by dragons—is captured by the dragon Bryagh. Gorbash's uncle, Smrgol, convinces the dragons to hold her for ransom and sends Jim to the magician S. Carolinus to arrange the negotiations.

Jim and Angie see Carolinus as their only hope of returning home. Jim meets the mage and reveals his situation. Before the mage can do anything, Bryagh takes Angie to the Loathly Towers, the fortress of the Dark Powers. Jim is caught in a battle between the forces of good and evil and is told that he must gather "Companions" before he rescues Angie.

Over the course of a few days, Jim meets Sir Brian Neville-Smythe, a knight; Aragh, the English Wolf; Danielle of the Wold, a woodswoman; her father, Giles of the Wold, an outlaw; and Daffyd ap Hwyel, a Welsh master bowman. They have a few adventures, then approach the Loathly Towers. They are joined by Caro-linus, Smrgol, and Secoh (another dragon) to face the champions of the Dark Powers, including the evil Sir Hugh de Malencontri, Bryagh, and an ogre. Jim and his Companions win the battle and rescue Angie, though at a price. Jim and Angie decide to stay instead of returning home, and Jim is given back his human body.

The Dragon Knight takes place approximately ten months after the battle of the Loathly Towers. Jim, who is now Sir James, Baron de Bois de Malencontri, has married Angie and controls the Malencontri lands. He begins changing into a dragon: Because he is a magician and has not been using his magic, it has started to use him. Jim becomes apprenticed to Carolinus and begins practicing magic.

Meanwhile, Prince Edward of England has been captured in France, and the English knights mount a rescue force. Jim must go as part of feudal duty. He and Brian join the English forces. They meet Sir Giles, another English knight and a "silkie," a man on land and seal in the sea. They are given a special assignment to rescue the prince from the hands of the evil magician, Malvinne.

They go to France and meet Sir Raoul, a French knight who wants to save his king and country from Malvinne's machinations. After a few solo misadventures, Jim returns to his group to find that they have been joined by Aargh the Wolf (the spelling has changed from the first book) and Daffyd. The force eventually penetrates Malvinne's fortress and rescues the prince. They are then charged with taking the prince back to the English forces and stopping the battle between the English and the French. Jim uses his twentieth century cunning and fourteenth century magic to win the day, but Malvinne escapes.

Jim returns home to find his castle occupied by Malvinne and Sir Hugh de Malencontri. He duels with Sir Hugh and wins, but he has to face one last magical battle before he is returned safely to Angie's arms.

In *The Dragon on the Border,* Jim, Brian, and Daffyd head to Northumberland to visit the home of the de Mers. Besides finding their friend, they find a new menace: The Hollow Men are ghosts who inhabit armor and terrorize the area. They can be killed, but if even one survives, the rest will be resurrected in two days.

To make matters worse, word comes to the de Mers and Jim that the king of France is paying the king of Scotland to invade England. The Scots king plans on using the Hollow Men in the first attack. Jim decides that he has to destroy the Hollow Men all at once and comes up with a plan to do so, employing the help of Liseth de Mer, Snorl the wolf, a Scotsman named Lachlan MacGreggor, the Little Men, Brian, and Daffyd, as well as his magical abilities. The Dark Powers have set a trap for him, however, and he must battle a Worm to win the day. He does so, and as a reward for his success he gets a higher rating as a magician.

The Dragon at War takes place immediately after Jim's battle with the Hollow Men. Carolinus has been attacked by a mysterious mage, and Jim and Angie rescue him. Carolinus sends Jim, along with Giles and Brian, to the bottom of the sea to visit a kraken. He then sends them to France with Secoh and Daffyd to get information from the evil sorcerer Ecotti. They learn of a French attack on England using sea serpents but discover no information about the mysterious mage.

Jim and his Companions return to Jim's castle. The sea serpents, who hate dragons—especially English dragons—attack England and swarm Jim's castle. Jim engineers a plan with the help of the English and French dragons and the Sea Devil, Rrrnlf, but he is forced into a duel with the leader of the sea serpents. He wins, but the secret mage appears, and Jim has to shock Carolinus out of a depression to battle the other mage.

The Dragon, the Earl and the Troll takes place a few months after Jim defeats the sea serpents. This time, he is faced with different problems. Carolinus senses the Dark Powers at work and tells Jim and Angie that they must go to the Christmas

Feast at the home of the earl of Somerset. They reluctantly agree.

On the way, they encounter a party slain by outlaws and rescue a baby. When they get to the castle, Jim discovers a set of problems. A troll is shaking the castle to pieces because he smells another troll upstairs. The earl hates the troll. More trolls have surrounded the castle. Lady Agatha Fallon, the baby's aunt, wants to be queen and will do almost anything to achieve that goal. The dragons want to come and be blessed by the prince of England. Compounding these problems, Jim is in danger of being stripped of all of his magical abilities. Once more, with the aid of Brian, Angie, and Aargh, Jim comes up with a plan. It solves his problems and creates a new type of magic. *The Dragon and the Djinn*, a continuation of the series, was scheduled to be published in 1996.

ANALYSIS

The first book of the Dragon Knight series was published fourteen years before the second, and it was based on a short story written years earlier. *The Dragon and the George* is a slight twist on the quest and companion story found throughout folklore and fantasy, such as in J. R. R. Tolkien's work. The twist is that the hero is the dragon, or at least occupies the body of a dragon.

The story follows a traditional quest/companion formula. The hero gathers a group of Companions in order to fulfill the quest. Each Companion has an ability that is needed to defeat or conquer some trial or obstacle that the group encounters. There is a final battle, which the Companions win.

The next three books follow this same plot line, each ending with Jim fighting a duel in either dragon or human form. This formula is changed to an intellectual challenge in *The Dragon, the Earl and the Troll*. The greatest difference between the sequels and the original book is that Gordon Dickson becomes more concerned with place and setting. The later books involve more of Jim dealing with life in the fourteenth century. He has to adjust his thinking and attitudes to those of the time in which he now lives. Dickson also deals more with the history and politics of the times than in the first novel.

The novels stay consistent in format and characters. Jim's Companions reappear from novel to novel, with new ones added. There are some inconsistencies from the first book to the sequels. Aragh the Wolf becomes Aargh the Wolf, and Jim was a history student in the first novel but is sometimes referred to as an English instructor later on.

Dickson, winner of both Hugo and Nebula awards, is probably more famous for his science-fiction Childe cycle than for this fantasy series. He is a prolific writer with many published novels to his credit, the first in 1956. The Dragon Knight series, with the exception of the first book, is a fairly recent addition to his credits.

—*P. Andrew Miller*

THE DRAGON MASTERS

Reptilian aliens return to Aerlith to abduct humans to serve as breeding stock but are opposed by humans who have bred alien stock to produce dragons

Author: Jack Vance (1916–2013)
Genre: Fantasy—invasion story
Type of work: Novella
Time of work: The distant future
Locale: A small region of the world of Aerlith
First published: 1962

THE STORY

Unaccountably, a sacerdote is found in the inner sanctum of Joaz Banbeck, lord and master of Banbeck Vale, breeder of dragons, and direct descendant of Kergan Banbeck, who had successfully withstood a previous raid from the reptilian "basics." On the planet Aerlith, the sacerdotes are a mysterious hermetic culture living in secluded caves and bound to a creed of noninterference in human affairs. Joaz rushes to his study to find that the sacerdote has vanished through a concealed door.

The Banbecks have been vying with the Carcolo family for domination of the region for several generations. The planet is a marooned outpost of humanity, a residual of a galactic struggle that has destroyed the human empire. Ervis Carcolo, lord of the neighboring and relatively poorer Happy Valley, meets with Joaz to discuss preparations in the event of invasion. Joaz has studied history and the stars, and he believes that another attack from the basics is imminent because of the optimal proximity of one of their worlds. Ervis, a brutish and vengeful man, has spent all of his resources in attempts to breed new dragons, whereas Joaz has been diligently adding tunnels and escape routes for his people. Instead of aiding the preparations, Ervis proposes forcing the sacerdotes into service and perhaps having them reveal the secrets of star travel.

Soon after this conference, Ervis tries to launch a surprise attack on Joaz but instead is ambushed and routed. Joaz is again visited by a sacerdote, which he traps in his study. The sacerdote follows a code of conduct that forces him to precisely answer Joaz's questions but not to volunteer information; the situation is analogous to trying to get a computer to reveal the meaning of life. Through this interview, a visit to the caverns in disguise, and a dream communication, Joaz learns that the sacerdotes plan to reconquer the cosmos once the impure and impassioned humans have been wiped out by the basics.

Ervis directs another intrepid and poorly planned attack, and he is again caught off guard. During the pitched battle, the basics land a large spacecraft in Happy Valley. Ervis breaks off from near defeat and retreats to watch the basics destroy Happy Valley. He then follows the spacecraft to Joaz's Banbeck Vale.

Joaz meets the basic invasion with cool, efficient strategy and his considerable troop of dragons. The basics resort to bombardment of the craggy mountains in which the Banbeck forces are lurking. This destruction eventually reveals the sacerdotes' hidden caverns. During a lull in the fighting, Ervis determines to surprise the basics from behind with the paltry remnants of his troops and dragons. Ervis walks into the basics' trap, but the aliens are unprepared for the arrival of Joaz and his troops, who enter the ship and accidentally rescue Ervis before being repulsed. The sacerdotes respond to their dilemma by crippling the basics' ship with energy beams, but they suffer damage to their hidden spaceship. In the aftermath of the battle, the damaged ship belongs to Joaz, the sacerdotes are spurned and contemptuously return to their caves, Ervis is executed, and Joaz contemplates a future searching for remaining pockets of humanity and perhaps for a world called Eden.

ANALYSIS

Commentary on Jack Vance's work often includes mention of arcane language and highly stylized narrative techniques. Such holds true, to a degree, for criticism of *The Dragon Masters*, winner of a 1963 Hugo in the category of short fiction. More noteworthy is the complexity of balanced ironic polarities. The humans have been breeding dragons (Blue Horrors, Termagants, massive Juggers, and others) from basic stock, while the basics have been breeding hominid mutations (Giants, burly dwarfish Heavy Troopers, long-limbed Trackers, and others) from human stock. The careful administration of Joaz Banbeck is contrasted with the autocratic bungling of Ervis Carcolo. The sacerdotes and their self-preserving sanctity invite comparison to the striving for progress that Joaz epitomizes. Vance colors the positions so that Joaz is appealing, while the noble sacerdotes seem aloof and uncaring.

As protagonist, Joaz initially seems autocratic, bookish, and a bit of an effete aesthete. In comparison to the boorish Ervis and because of his urge for a better life for his people, however, readers become enamored of him. He is reminiscent of the title character from Vance's *Rhialto, the Marvelous* (1984), a wizard and explorer of arcana who seldom is bested by his peers. The minuscule world created in this story seems marginalized, in ways similar to Vance's "Dying World" contexts.

A theme that emerges from the ironic tensions is that little separates one position from another, that values are more similar than different. The only characteristic that makes the humans seem better than the aliens, and that also makes Joaz better than Ervis, is compassion. Joaz cares about his people, and the human breeders care about their dragons. Neither Ervis nor the basics have a shred of compassion. Ervis tries to breed abominations and abuses his troops; the basics treat the human stock as expendable machinery. When the basics send mutated human stock to discuss capitulation with the unruly humans, the exchange clarifies how alien the basics' philosophy is to human norms. The importance of compassion is heightened by the issue of noninvolvement presented by the sacerdotes, who spitefully articulate it in a concluding conversation with Joaz.

—*Scott D. Vander Ploeg*

THE DRAGON WAITING

In an alternative Europe in which Christianity has not replaced earlier magical religions, four people join to support Richard III of England against a tyrannical and subtly encroaching Byzantine Empire

Author: John M. Ford (1954–2006)
Genre: Science fiction—alternate history
Type of work: Novel
Time of work: The fifteenth century
Locale: Wales; Burgundy, France; Florence and Milan, Italy; and England\
First published: 1983

THE STORY

In this novel, four characters from different European countries and backgrounds live out their early lives and suffer from larger Byzantine plots and intrigues that sweep up their lives. Hywel Peredur, himself a wizard, is a descendant of a great Welsh wizard betrayed by the Byzantine Empire. Dimitrios Ducas, a mercenary, is the son of the governor of Burgundy in Gaul and the descendant of a deposed Byzantine emperor. Cynthia Ricci, a Florentine doctor in love with Lorenzo de' Medici, is killed, along with members of her family, in a Byzantine plot to gain control of Italy. Gregory Von Bayern is a German vampire who has never infected a human and never killed, though he possesses a vast knowledge of guns and explosives.

The four characters meet in Milan, Italy. While trying to unravel a mysterious murder, they discover their mutual hatred of the Byzantine Empire and their desire to halt its spread westward across Europe. They decide to focus their attention on England, which, though politically turbulent under Edward IV after the Wars of the Roses, still remains free of Byzantine domination. The country is not free of scheming Byzantine pawns, all hoping to further their individual ends by casting their lots with the overarching Byzantine conspiracy for world domination, a domination abhorrent to the four friends.

Their various skills make them instrumental in challenging various Byzantine-connected forces determined to deliver England to the empire. They first contend with the plots of Margaret of Anjou, the wife of England's former Lancastrian ruler Henry VI, to use occult arts and well-placed evil magicians to displace the Yorkist Edward IV. After Edward's suspicious death, the four support Edward's brother, Richard of Gloucester, as Lord Protector and regent of Edward's two young sons. Cynthia discovers that both sons have a rare but terminal blood disease and have been traitorously infected with vampirism.

While feuding relatives and other internal crises confront Richard, Hywel Peredur and Cynthia Ricci discover that other trouble is afoot in Wales. Byzantine forces, using magic and ancient Welsh legends, are building support for Henry Tydder. He is a descendant of the widow of England's King Henry V and is known to history as Henry VII, the founder of the Tudor dynasty and the man responsible for the defeat of Richard. Following the mysterious deaths of Edward's sons, Hywel, Dimitrios, Cynthia, and Gregory rally around Richard, now Richard III, in what will be not only the battle of his life but also a battle to end the inroads of Byzantine tyranny and treachery.

ANALYSIS

The plot of *The Dragon Waiting* dramatically incorporates into fiction real characters of fifteenth century Europe such as Edward IV, Richard III, and members of their families and courts in England; Lorenzo de' Medici and his circle of friends and dependents in Italy; and Margaret of Anjou and her supporters at the French court of Louis XI. The fictional characters are as believable and alive as the historical characters with whom they interact. The novel likewise merges fictional and historical events, embellishes and provides credible causes for events whose details have been lost to historical annals, and freely alters occurrences that may have been different had previous underlying events not taken place or philosophical worldviews not been established.

John M. Ford has acquired a reputation as a diverse and talented writer as well as some fame as a game designer. His literary output is as varied as it is extensive. He has covered a wide range of science-fiction and fantasy subgenres. His first works were children's stories, which he wrote under an assumed name. Previous work written under his own name and published professionally includes short stories in *Isaac Asimov's Science Fiction Magazine*; his *Alternities Corporation* series of science-fiction stories (1979–1981); *Web of Angels* (1980), an early novelistic venture into cyberpunk before its conventions were established; an informative manual for potential science-fiction writers titled *On Writing Science Fiction: The Editors Strike Back!* (1981), which he coauthored with George H. Scithers and Darrell Schweit-zer; and a second novel, *The Princes of the Air* (1982), a space opera noted more for its details than for its breadth. *The Dragon Waiting* was Ford's first attempt at alternate history. It represents not so much a departure from previous work as the creation of a new venue for the exploration of human struggle with apparently intractable forces.

The novel won the 1984 World Fantasy Award. These awards, familiarly known as "Howards" in imitation of the Hugo Awards for science fiction that date from the 1950's, were initiated in 1975 specifically to recognize outstanding work in fantasy. Winners are determined by a panel of critics, and the awards are presented at the World Fantasy Convention held annually in October, usually in the United States. The novel interweaves the fantasy themes of wizardry, sorcery, and magical ritual with historical events and intermingles fictional and biographical characters against a backdrop of imaginatively improvised yet plausible historical events and outcomes.

Ford has continued his varied outpouring of literary works. These include two Star Trek television tie-ins, *The Final Reflection* (1984) and *How Much for Just the Planet?* (1987); novels such as *The Scholars of Night* (1988); and a number of short stories. Some critics believe that Ford's variety in selection of genres and themes and his far-ranging imagination have damaged his career commercially. He has failed to establish a definitive mode of writing that would win him a permanent and loyal audience. Others believe that his originality and creative talent assure his readers that his writing will never become stale and predictable.

—*Christine R. Catron*

THE DRAGONBONE CHAIR

An epic fantasy quest in which Simon, a castle kitchen scullion, must search for the swords of prophecy to fight the rising evil power of the Storm King

Author: Tad Williams (1957–)
Genre: Fantasy—heroic fantasy
Type of work: Novel
Time of work: Undefined
Locale: Osten Ard, a land resembling medieval Europe
First published: 1988

THE STORY

Simon, an orphaned castle kitchen scullion, avoids his duties and spends his time dreaming of becoming a hero. He is apprenticed to Dr. Morgenes, the castle's sorcerer, in an attempt to teach him to be industrious. When Prester John, the High King, dies, his elder son, Elias, takes over the throne. Elias is increasingly influenced by the evil priest Pyrates, lackey of the vengeful Storm King. Josua, the younger son, tries with Morgenes to halt the encroaching evil. Finally, they and their allies must search for the missing swords of prophecy to restore order to Osten Ard.

Morgenes dies as he helps Josua escape from his brother. Scared and alone, Simon must follow Josua to his holding in the north. Simon wanders through the woods until hunger drives him toward a town, where he saves a humanlike creature from a hunter. The creature is Jiriki, a prince of the fairy-folk Sithi. Jiriki rewards Simon with a white arrow, a mark of debt owed.

As Simon ponders the meaning of the arrow, the troll Binabik appears to help Simon on his way. They meet up with Melachias, another castle runaway. Binabik leads the two young people to Geloë's house in the woods to rest and recuperate. She, along with Binabik, is a member of the League of the Scroll, a centuries-old group formed to gather knowledge and fight evil. Morgenes also had been a member. While at Geloë's house, Melachias reveals herself to be Marya, a serving lady to the princess. She is hurrying to Josua with an important message from the princess.

After more harrowing adventures, Simon, Marya, and Binabik reach Josua. Simon discovers that Marya is actually the princess herself and so must learn to quell his rising feelings for her. He also learns, for the first time, of the prophecy of the swords and that the sword Thorn is hoarded by an ice dragon. Simon and Binabik lead a small party into the mountains to search for it.

Meanwhile, Prester John's realm is in disarray with conspiracies and plots that Elias and Pyrates foster. Those dukes and barons loyal to Prester John's ideals are held as virtual prisoners, while others, greedy for power, curry favor with the king and his priest. The land is ravaged by plague and the weather is unusual, both effects of the Storm King's rising power.

Simon's party is captured by a group of Sithi, and only his white arrow prevents them from being killed. Jiriki vouches for them as he begins to realize there is something special about Simon. Jiriki agrees to help them hunt for Thorn. They find the sword, but they arouse the dragon guarding it. Simon, holding Thorn, kills the dragon, but he thinks the killing was more the sword's doing than his. Dragon blood spurts over a lock of Simon's hair, turning it white. Jiriki tells him that he has been marked, and he is known thereafter as Simon Snow-lock.

ANALYSIS

The Dragonbone Chair is the first part of the trilogy Memory, Sorrow, and Thorn. *Stone of Farewell* (1990) and *To Green Angel Tower* (1993) continue the search for the three swords and describe the eventual downfall of Elias, Pyrates, and the Storm King.

The Dragonbone Chair is very much in the tradition of heroic fantasy, akin to J. R. R. Tolkien's Lord of the Rings trilogy (1954–1955) and the epic quest fantasies that followed. The Dragonbone Chair is quite dif-ferent from Tad Williams' first book, Tailchaser's Song (1986), a one-volume animal fantasy novel about the cat kingdom.

The Dragonbone Chair contains all the hallmarks of fantasy quest literature: a young boy of uncertain parentage who matures into his powers as well as his manhood, a resourceful princess whom the hero feels inadequate to love, wizards and prophecies to help the hero on his quest, a small band of companions struggling against a larger evil force, a betrayer from within who almost ruins their plans, and a land that is sickening and dying because of an ever-growing evil presence. What raises *The Dragonbone Chair* above the level of many such epic quests is the depth of characterization. Simon, Binabik, Josua, Elias, Pyrates, and the many others involved in the plot are fully realized people commanding pity, admiration, or horror. Simon is an especially riveting hero as he grows from a complaining, idling kitchen boy into the ice dragon's killer. Even the minor characters within the extensive cast are carefully drawn. The world in which they travel is varied and well detailed, creating a complete sense of reality. Williams even includes maps so the reader can follow Simon's journey. The interweaving of the different narratives as the novel moves among the many factions in the struggle keeps the story moving and engages the reader.

Motivation for the evil that the heroes fight, often ignored in quest fantasies that rely solely on adventure, is only hinted at in this first volume but is further explained in the remaining parts of the trilogy. The reasons are buried deep in Osten Ard's history, which is explained, in part, in *The Dragonbone Chair*. The reader, along with Simon, must piece together that history from dreams, snatches of old books that have somehow survived, and bits of knowledge possessed by the League of the Scroll. It is a complex history of the strife between humanity and the Sithi, and Simon learns that humans are not always in the right.

The Dragonbone Chair is an engaging beginning to a trilogy filled with unique characters, plot twists, and surprises. It serves well as an introduction to the world of Osten Ard, as well as to Simon and his friends and enemies. *The Dragonbone Chair* is well crafted, complex, and extremely imaginative, leaving the reader both satisfied and hungering for the next installment of the trilogy.

—*Marjorie Ginsberg*

THE DRAGONRIDERS OF PERN

Attacked by deadly spores called Thread, the former Earth colony Pern is protected by brave men and women and their telepathic, fire-breathing dragons

Author: Anne McCaffrey (1926–2011)
Genre: Science fiction—extrasensory powers
Type of work: Novels
Time of work: Pre-landing through the Ninth Pass
Locale: Pern, an undeveloped world
First published: *Dragonflight* (1968; the opening is a revised form of "Weyr Search," Analog, 1967), *Dragonquest* (1971), *The White Dragon* (1978; part previously published as "A Time When," 1975), *Dragonsong* (1976), *Dragonsinger* (1977), *Dragondrums* (1979), *Moreta, Dragonlady of Pern* (1983), *Nerilka's Story* (1986), *Dragonsdawn* (1988), *The Renegades of Pern* (1989), *All the Weyrs of Pern* (1991), *Rescue Run* (1991; earlier version in Analog, 1991), *The Dolphins' Bell* (1993), *The Girl Who Heard Dragons* (1994), and *The Dolphins of Pern* (1994)

THE STORY

In 1967, Anne McCaffrey introduced readers to the Dragonriders of Pern series with the story "Weyr Search." Pern's story begins with Earth colonists landing on an agricultural planet. All goes well for eight years, until Pern is attacked by deadly spores called Thread. The initial losses to Thread in livestock, crops, and human life are staggering. To fight Thread, the Pernese biogenetically engineer large, telepathic, fire-breathing dragons (weyrs) and Thread-eating grubs.

A Thread attack, called a Pass, lasts fifty years; they come in Intervals of two hundred years. By the Ninth Pass, five weyrs have disappeared, Benden Weyr has fallen into disarray, and dragonriders are in disfavor. Only Benden Weyrleaders Lessa and F'lar and F'lar's half brother F'nor believe that Thread will fall again. They try to prepare Pern, but the two hundred dragons of Benden cannot defend all the settlements. Lessa discovers that the dragons can teleport between times as well as between places, and she and her queen, Ramoth, travel back in time to bring the missing five weyrs forward to aid Benden's fight with Thread.

Tensions mount because the Oldtimers resent the cultural changes in Pern. Dragonman fights dragonman as F'lar fights T'ron and later T'kul. A queen egg is stolen and then returned by the young Lord Holder Jaxom, who, against all tradition, impresses the white dragon Ruth. The male-dominated culture continues to evolve as Menolly becomes the first female harper, Mirrim impresses a green dragon, and female and male young people attend cross-crafting classes together for the first time.

Small, emphatic friends called fire lizards are discovered. They form a link among holders, craftsmen, and dragonriders. Masterharper Robinton helps to guide the development of Pern with wise counsel and carefully developed teaching ballads. Old knowledge is rediscovered, and the Pernese learn to use a distance viewer, talking wires, and an enlarger. The Lord Holders pressure the dragonriders to go to the Red Star to eliminate Thread at its source. Using the distance viewer, F'nor directs his brown dragon Canth to the Red Star, and they are nearly killed trying to land on the turbulent planet.

Ruins are discovered on the southern continent. These include the shuttles that brought the colonists to Pern and a voice-activated interactive computer. The powerful computer teaches the Pernese much of the knowledge lost over the years and helps them plan how to use the Dawn Sisters, the original starships, to get rid of Thread. Jaxom and Ruth again are instrumental in making plans that signal a new beginning for this agricultural world.

ANALYSIS

The science-fiction elements are stronger in some Pern novels than in others. *Dragonsdawn* explains that the colonists arrive in the three transport spaceships with all the necessary technology. In fact, the dolphins who arrived at the same time had been genetically enhanced before the journey to enable them to communicate with human partners.

One important science-fiction device in this series is the biogenetic manipulation of the dragonets (later called fire lizards) into the powerful fire-breathing dragons of Pern. They fly, teleport, breath fire, and possess telepathic abilities, all as a result of genetic engineering rather than magic. In several novels, these science-fiction elements are only implied; after *Dragonsdawn*, it is not until *The White Dragon* that physical remains of the landing are discovered. At the conclusion of *The Renegades of Pern*, the Artificial Intelligence Voice Address System, or AIVAS, is discovered, and the Pernese begin to explore their scientific origins.

McCaffrey has created a world that many readers would like to visit. Pern is a place with fascinating telepathic creatures, complex and growing characters, and a strong work ethic. Although the series is science fiction, the stories largely concern relationships among people and between people and animals. Readers return to the series as new novels are published because the history of Pern is so rich and intricate. Many teachers in elementary and junior high schools require their students to read "The Smallest Dragonboy" (1982), a Pern story that is anthologized widely, and the novels of the Harper Hall trilogy (*Dragonsong, Dragonsinger,* and *Dragondrums*).

McCaffrey has recommended starting with the two main trilogies within the series, the Harper Hall trilogy and the adult trilogy consisting of *Dragonflight, Dragonquest,* and *The White Dragon*. These six novels provide an understanding of the complex social structure of weyrs, holds, and crafts that sets up the other novels. The two trilogies also contain the most exciting events of the series: Lessa's trip through time, Ramoth's Impression, F'lar's fights with Oldtimers, F'nor's attempt to reach the Red Star, the discovery of fire lizards, Ruth's Impression, the stealing of the queen egg and its return, and Robinton's heart attack. The other novels are more concerned with historical details than with character development or exciting events.

The Dragonriders of Pern series is a history of the birth and growth of this society. McCaffrey describes the birth of the colony in *Dragonsdawn*, but significant births are scattered throughout the series. In the novella *The Dolphins' Bell*, after many adventures on the voyage north, dolphin Carolina's calf, Atlanta, is born. Jaxom is born by being forcibly removed from his mother's belly after F'lar kills his father, Fax. Perhaps the more memorable and endearing of the births are the hatchings. Ramoth's birth is described in detail from the sound of the bronze dragons' hum and the cries of the golden dragonet to Lessa's feelings of admiration, respect, and unconditional love from and for her dragon. The hatchings of Hannath after Moreta's and Orlith's deaths, of Ruth torn out of the egg by Jaxom, of Menolly's fire lizards in the cave during Thread, and of Robinton's and Sebell's fire lizards all create a desire in the reader for such a loyal and magnificent companion who loves so quickly and unconditionally. Readers return to Pern to visit these creatures and their partners.

McCaffrey illustrates the growth of this male-dominated society largely through female and teenage major characters. Moreta, queen rider of Orlith and weyrwoman at Fort Weyr, flies vaccine to quarantined holds during a devastating plague. Lessa fights to protect her home from Fax and later to lead Pern into the future. Craftbred Brekke becomes a queen rider and fights to adjust her values. Menolly impresses nine fire lizards and, with Masterharper Robinton's encouragement, invades the all-male harpercraft as the teenager Mirrim impresses a green dragon against custom. Another young person, Readis, re-establishes the link with the dolphins of Pern and creates the first dolphin crafthall.

McCaffrey was the first woman to win both the Hugo Award (1968, for "Weyr Search") and the Nebula Award (1968, for "Dragonrider"), and she was one of the first science-fiction writers to have a book—*The White Dragon*—on the best-seller lists. Other awards came over the years, including the E. E. Smith Award for fantasy in 1975; the American Library Association notable book citation in 1976 for *Dragonsong* and in 1977 for *Dragonsinger*; the Horn Book Fanfare Citation in 1977 for *Dragonsong*; and the Ditmar Award (Australia), Gandalf Award, and Eurocon/Steso Award, all in 1979, for *The White Dragon*.

The Dragonriders of Pern series inspired three companion texts: *The Atlas of Pern* (1984) by Karen Wynn Fonstad; *The People of Pern* (1988) by Robin Wood, with text and introduction by Anne McCaffrey; and *The Dragonlover's Guide to Pern* (1989) by Jody Lynn Nye with Anne McCaffrey. McCaffrey started the Dragonriders of Pern series early in her career and has returned to it repeatedly, but it is not her only popular series. The Pegasus series, sometimes known as the Rowan Women series or

Talents series, began with McCaffrey's first published short story, "Lady in the Tower" (*The Magazine of Fantasy and Science Fiction*, April, 1959). Lyon's Pride, the sixth novel in this series, was published in 1994. *Dinosaur Planet* (1978) and *The Crystal Singer* (1982) each begin a separate series.

Although some of the Pern novels are stronger and more popular than others, each aids in the creation of a complicated world as enduring as C. S. Lewis' Narnia, Roger Zelazny's Amber, or Marion Zimmer Bradley's Darkover. Readers will continue to enjoy the novels about the Dragonriders of Pern and their magnificent companions for years to come.

—Susan A. VanSchuyver

DRAGONSBANE

After joining with the dragon Morkeleb to defeat the wicked Zyerne, witch Jenny Waynest must decide between the unlimited powers Morkeleb offers and the human love of John Aversin, Dragonsbane

Author: Barbara Hambly (1951–)
Genre: Fantasy—heroic fantasy
Type of work: Novel
Time of work: The late medieval period
Locale: The Realm of the King, Winterlands, and Belmarie\
First published: *Dragonsbane* (1986), *Dragonshadow* (1999), *Knight of the Demon Queen* (2000), and *Dragonstar*(2002)

THE STORY

Although *Dragonsbane* refers to Lord John Aversin of Alyn Hold, the only living man to have slain a dragon, the story centers on Jenny Waynest and the dilemma she faces in being both a human being and a mage. This dilemma first arose ten years before the time of the plot, when Jenny met and fell in love with John, and reaches its climax after Prince Gareth comes to the Winterlands, a province of King Urien's realm, to recruit the aid of the Dragonsbane in ridding the Deep of Ylferdun of the black dragon. Reluctantly, Jenny and John, the north country scholar with a deep brogue and a love of old wives' tales, accompany Gareth to the land of Belmarie to slay the dragon.

They soon realize that the dragon is merely a symptom of the realm's problems. The king's mistress, Zyerne, a beautiful but utterly ruthless young sorceress who places no limitations on her powers, is the disease. Jenny learns from a gnome mage, Lady Mab, that as a child Zyerne was apprenticed to the gnomes and learned their magic. While with them, Zyerne stole her way to the Stone in the heart of the Deep, the spot from which unlimited powers emanate. Zyerne's every move since has been calculated to gain her permanent access to the Stone. For that purpose, she summoned Morkeleb, the black dragon, to rid the Deep of the gnomes and now is unable to banish the greedy dragon from the gold hordes. That is where Dragonsbane comes in. Zyerne wants John to kill Morkeleb so that she can take over the Deep. She did not count on the small witch, Jenny Waynest, getting in her way.

In contrast to Zyerne's single-minded dedication to her "art," for ten years Jenny's life has been divided between her love for John and their two sons and her devotion to magic. She knows that she is no match for Zyerne and no threat to Morkeleb. When John insists that they battle the dragon to keep Zyerne from gaining ultimate power, she is distraught, having foreseen the outcome of the combat. When John stumbles back badly wounded, she decides to go into the Deep and find the places of healing to restore him to life. In so doing, she must confront Morkeleb. Also mortally wounded, Morkeleb telepathically bargains with her, offering to convey her through the intricate warrens if she will heal him. Jenny agrees, but not before she looks into the eyes of the dragon, entangling her soul with his.

After Jenny heals Morkeleb, she exacts his promise to leave and learns his true name, music that holds the essence of his soul and binds him to her. The problem is far from solved, however. By this time, Zyerne knows they are rid of the dragon and incites a mob to take over the Deep. Although Jenny's powers have increased, she has practically exhausted her abilities in holding off the mob when Morkeleb unexpectedly returns. Morkeleb and Jenny are united in the final battle with Zyerne, now indomitable because she has defiled the Stone and attained unlimited power. Jenny and Morkeleb are able to hold off the shape-shifter until John and Gareth blow up the Stone, thus killing Zyerne.

Although peace returns to the land with Zyerne's death, peace does not return to Jenny. She has tasted the freedom and magic of the dragon. Morkeleb wants her to accompany him north, as a dragon. After some deliberation, she sheds her humanness and soars into the sky, white dragon against black dragon. Even in the first glow of her freedom, though, she looks down on John Aversin and feels the sterility of this life, realizing that "the key to magic was not magic," as her master Caerdinn had asserted, but the use of magic. As her love draws her back earthward, Morkeleb's love for her allows her to go.

ANALYSIS

Dragonsbane was one of the first adult fantasy novels to make the Best Books List (1986). Many of Barbara Hambly's other works, such as *The Rainbow Abyss* (1991), traverse the voids between alternate universes and time sequences. *Dragonsbane*, in contrast, is set completely within one time frame and one universe.

Common threads run throughout Hambly's various work, which includes *Star Wars* novels such as Children of the Jedi (1995) and fantasies from the Darwath Trilogy (*The Time of the Dark*, 1982; The Walls of Air, 1983; and *The Armies of Daylight*, 1983) to *The Witches of Wenshar* (1987) to the *Windrose Chronicles* (*The Silent Tower*, 1986; The *Silicon Mage*, 1988; and *Dog Wizard*, 1993). Among these threads are her ability to draw memorable characters and her examination of the uses and abuses of power. *Dragonsbane*, a formula fantasy, is no exception. Critics alternately accuse Hambly of providing too much narration and too little dialogue and praise her for presenting charming vignettes of everyday life. *Dragonsbane* offers some of the best Hambly has to offer—suspenseful narration, a gritty view of late medieval life, and compelling, likable characters.

In the plain, thirty-seven-year old witch with limited powers, Jenny Waynest; the gangly scholar John Aversin, who has the audacity to kill a dragon using an axe; and even bespectacled Prince Gareth, Hambly realistically portrays antiheroes who simultaneously defy and fulfill their mythic roles. Hambly highlights the conflict between Jenny's desire for unlimited power and her humanity by presenting a major plot complication that pits the fragmented Jenny against her single-minded alter egos, evil energy-vampire Zyerne and amoral Morke-leb. Hers is a Frankensteinian view of the sterility and, sometimes, evil that ensues when one dedicates oneself totally to anything, be it art, magic, or science, without regard to universal laws or human feelings.

—*Jaquelyn W. Walsh*

DREAM

A "free spirited" woman, her fiancé, and his sister are cast by a magician's spell into a dreamworld where they experience evolutionary struggles as protohumans

Author: S. Fowler Wright (1874-1965)
Genre: Science fiction—evolutionary fantasy
Type of work: Novel
Time of work: The 1920's and a million years in the past
Locale: Unspecified but probably Europe
First published: 1931

THE STORY

Dream: Or, The Simian Maid was written as the first book of a trilogy that follows the adventures of Marguerite Leinster as she experiences a magician's induced dreamworld. The magician causes a dream that will suspend Marguerite for two weeks in real time but will seem to her as if it lasts a year. Stephen Cranleigh, who is her fiancé, and his sister Elsie buy the same dream from the magician and follow her to a primitive land a million years in the past. Marguerite is incarnated as a chimpanzee-like creature named Rita who becomes the self-appointed guardian of Stephen's persona, Stele, the Law Maker's son in a cave-dwelling tribe. Elsie becomes Elsya, Stele's sister. The Law Maker sends them both on a mission to find respective mates in other, unknown cultures that he assumes exist but are not under attack by the horrible Ogpurs, the savages constantly endangering his people.

Rita is a tree dweller with limited communicative skills. She is attracted to Stele, and she follows him and Elsya at a distance. She aids their journey by killing a tribe member bent on having Elsya as a mate and eventually guides them down a steep cliff to a land of people who have domesticated horses and who live in two environs, a valley protected by alligator-infested waters and a land bordered by ever-attacking swamp rats called Thlantus. An elaborate, labyrinthine cave system separates the two distinct kingdoms. A select force of neutered amazonian women protects both kingdoms. Their stealth in knife throwing controls adversity in the cliff environment and in the valley, and their skill as equestrian soldiers controls the battle with the deadly, sharp-toothed swamp rats.

The king of these lands agrees to have his son Thelmo marry Elsya but refuses his daughter's hand to Stele. Left as companions, Stele and Rita consummate their love.

The king leads the royal party and visitors through the cave maze to the valley homeland. Because of the threat of the rats, Stele, Rita, and Elsya are sent back to the cliff site, where they learn of a plot to alter the treacherous path in the cave so that all who return will succumb to the "god" alligator living in a sacrificial pool. To warn the royalty, each journeys to the valley by a different path: Rita by cliff, Stele by cave, and Elsya by the precarious lake. Rita finds Stele on the opposite end of the cave in a dead-end crevice, and they both die, strained outstretched hands barely touching, from hunger and thirst. Elsya finds her love Thelmo during a horrendously bloody battle with the rats. She dies, her throat ripped open, with him and the brave Tekla. Upon return from the dreamworld, Marguerite finally acquiesces to marry Stephen as she ponders the reality of her alter-ego life as a simian.

ANALYSIS

In midlife, S. Fowler Wright altered career paths from accountant to author of science-fiction and mystery stories, poetry editor, and translator of works by Dante Alighieri. Wright's vivid style has repeated patterns of romanticizing the protagonists in a world of wretched, animal-like beasts that constantly endanger their lives. *Dream* was the first in a trilogy; the second book, *The Vengeance of Gwa* (1935), first published under the pseudonym of Anthony Wingrave, is about an evil queen's world among starving barbarians, and the third, *Spiders' War* (1954), has Marguerite and her twentieth century lover, as an able-bodied warrior, transported by her magician to a future world threatened by giant spiders.

Wright's writing interests initially drew him to the classics. He self-published his poetic version of Thomas Malory's *Le Morte d'Arthur* (first transcribed c. 1469), translated Dante's "Inferno" in rhymed iambic pentameter, and edited the British *Poetry* for several years. His fascination with science fiction is evidenced by his several dozen novels in the genre, which usually have horrific creatures threatening cognitive, humanlike beings. He wrote many crime and mystery novels as Sydney Fowler and published some work as Alan Seymor. Critics tend to agree that aging did not necessarily add maturity to Wright's skill, and his later books received little note. Few of his works from his last two decades were published, and his unpublished manuscripts from this period have been lost, with the exception of a novel he titled *Inquisitive Angel*.

Dream addressed some salient issues of its time. Although several passages refer to the dominance of men over women, Wright carries his heroine to the forefront, accompanied by neutered women who are described to have stamina and intense loyalty that men could not possess as soldiers. Both Tekla and Elsya display superhuman characteristics that exceed the capabilities of the men of both tribes. An underlying theme of cross-cultural breeding augments the story line. In Dream, Wright may be suggesting evidence of planned inter-cultural breeding, as demonstrated by the Law Maker sending his son on a quest for a wife. He further substantiates the concept by presenting the sexual relationship of the cave-dwelling Stele and tree woman Rita. Superiority of the tribe's members over their nemesis, the Ogpurs, and over the swamp rats adds a Darwinian flavor to the novel. This survival theme is repeated in Wright's other science-fiction efforts. Wright's syntax tends to suffer through choppiness and inverted word order, and some metaphors and references seem anachronistic. Best known for his highly successful *The World Below* (1929), Wright often expressed ideas through elaborate structures that, for some readers, seem complicated. In Dream, he minimizes that complexity.

—*Craig Gilbert*

THE DREAM MASTER

Dr. Charles Render, a neuroparticipation therapist, overestimates his ability to control a patient's dreams and is drawn into her final mad fantasy

Author: Roger Zelazny (1937–1995)
Genre: Science fiction—inner space
Type of work: Novel
Time of work: Early in the twenty-first century
Locale: An unidentified city in the northeastern United States
First published: 1966 (shorter magazine version, "He Who Shapes," *Amazing Stories*, January-February, 1965)

THE STORY

The Dream Master was created when Roger Zelazny added approximately ten thousand words to the novella "He Who Shapes," serialized in the January and February, 1965, issues of *Amazing Stories*. In the novel, Charles Render, a neuroparticipation therapist, enters the dreams of neurotic patients and treats them. He is preeminent in his field but detached emotionally because of the death of his wife, Ruth, and daughter, Miranda, nine years earlier in an automobile accident. He has a ten-year-old son, Peter, at boarding school and a twenty-nine-year-old girlfriend, Jill De Ville.

Render agrees to treat a young psychiatric resident named Eileen Shallot, who has been blind from birth, after turning down her proposal that he help her see through other eyes because of the dangers of that procedure. He arranges a session to show her basic forms, but she momentarily takes control of it and puts him into a suit of armor when he appears to her in his natural form. Her ability scares him, but he is flushed with pride at her success.

Despite several warnings, he continues to treat Shallot. He and De Ville leave for a skiing vacation in England and Switzerland. While touring Winchester Cathedral, he reviews his recent sessions with Shallot. He is proud of his work with her, which clearly is moving toward helping her to see. At their ski lodge, Maurice Bartelmetz, a legendary pioneer of neuroparticipation therapy and Render's former teacher, warns him about the dangers of the work, but Render insists that he is in control.

A few nights after Render arrives back home, Sigmund, Shallot's mutant dog, shows up at his office. Sigmund tells Charles that Shallot is ill and asks that he come and make her better. Render goes with the dog, noting on the way that he finds Shallot somehow very unsettling. He later finds the colors in her apartment disturbing. She gets him to agree to another session nevertheless.

The next morning, he takes her on a tour of Winchester Cathedral but quickly loses control of the fantasy. He finds himself in armor and wounded. He then is attacked by a wolf, runs away, and sees his wife's wrecked car, with the bodies in it being eaten by a wolf. He kills the wolf with a scalpel but then falls into a chasm. The fantasy and the world end.

In the final scene, Render is a patient in a neuroparticipation fantasy. He plays a dying Tristan waiting for the return of his Isolde. He does not respond the way he is supposed to, so the therapist ends the session.

ANALYSIS

"He Who Shapes," which was worked into *The Dream Master*, won a Nebula Award for best novella in 1965. The story is highly original. Its theme of a character entering and manipulating the dreams of others links it to "Dreams Are Sacred" (1948) by Peter Phillips, "City of the Tiger" (1958) by John Brunner, and "The Girl in His Mind" (1963) by Robert F. Young. It anticipates such films as *Dreamscape* (1984) and the Nightmare on Elm Street series, among others.

The Dream Master, a very early Zelazny work, has been praised for its ingenuity, imagination, and style. It is one of the stories that has caused some critics to link Zelazny to the American New Wave writers of the mid-1960's and early 1970's. Although the phrase "New Wave" never has been defined carefully, most critics agree that at the least it implies science fiction and fantasy that can be taken as serious literature.

The Dream Master certainly is serious literature. Despite its clever science-fiction frame, it is very much a story about character. Render suffers from excessive pride, a flaw marking the protagonists of many of Zelazny's early stories. He also is very rigid, a perfectionist, intolerant of others, disaffected, and preoccupied with suicide. He is neurotic but fails to recognize that in himself. Eileen Shallot is equally interesting and even more neurotic. Both figures are developed far beyond the two-dimensional characters who were standard fare in the science-fiction writing of the time. Zelazny links both characters to various mythological and dramatic figures, enhancing them tremendously.

The mythic references are part of Zelazny's early technique. He does not translate myth in his stories but rather uses it to salt the stories and to deepen them. There are mythic references, for example, to several ill-fated love affairs in the novel—Orpheus and Eurydice, Heloise and Abelard, Apollo and Daphne, Tristan and Isolde, and, in particular, the Lady of Shallot and Sir Lancelot. Those failed love affairs underscore and foreshadow the relationships between both Render and Shallot and Render and De Ville. Similarly, Zelazny uses Arthurian, Jungian, and Nordic references to deepen and underscore the themes of the novel.

The story is rich with other literary devices. The personification of Shallot's mutant dog, Sigmund, parallels and emphasizes the mythic wolves in the Norse myth of ragnarok who swallow the sun and moon and thus end the world. The interlacing of the text with pieces of the scene of a man walking onto a roadway to commit suicide emphasizes Render's own metaphoric race toward death. His pride drives him and keeps him from resisting the challenge that Shallot poses to his professional skills.

Zelazny's language is rich in metaphor, allusion, simile, and symbol. His narrative technique is fresh, and the theme of this novel, a man overreaching himself, is both universal and modern. The story is a classic of its type.

—*Carl B. Yoke*

A Dreamer's Tales

A collection of stories set in the Land of Dreams and other fantastic realms

Author: Lord Dunsany (Edward John Moreton Draz Plunkett, 1878–1957)
Genre: Fantasy—magical world
Type of work: Stories
Time of work: Various times between the Stone Age and the early twentieth century on Earth; undefined in the Land of Dreams
Locale: London, England, various other locations on Earth, and the Land of Dreams
First published: 1910

The Story

Lord Dunsany's stories in *A Dreamer's Tales* present readers with a remarkable vista of strange realms and fantastic creatures. Most of the sixteen stories are set in the fabulous Land of Dreams, a domain of beautiful cities and endless wonders. A few tales are set in London or during Earth's ancient history, but these still fall firmly in the realm of the fantastic. From "Poltarnees, Beholder of Ocean" to "The Unhappy Body," Lord Dunsany creates a series of stories set in fantastic realms with fascinating characters and enchanting settings.

Several of Lord Dunsany's stories are set in the Land of Dreams or in another fantasy world. The first story, "Poltarnees, Beholder of Ocean," is set in a valley where four kingdoms are isolated from the ocean. To discover the reason behind the disappearance of many young men from the kingdoms, the kings offer Athelvok, a hunter, a beautiful princess, Hilnaric, as his wife if he can return from looking upon the ocean. Athelvok fails in his mission when the voice of the sea seduces him into staying by the ocean. Another tale, "Bethmoora," deals with the mysterious abandonment of a fabulous city in the Land of Dreams. A story that appears later in the book, "The Hashish Man," reveals the true reason for the abandonment of Bethmoora. In this tale, a dreamer tells of his discovery of how the sinister emperor, Thuba Mleen, caused Bethmoora to be abandoned through his advice to leave before the city was engulfed by the advancing desert.

The famous tale "Idle Days on the Yann" is an account of the dreamer's fabulous journey down the river Yann in the Land of Dreams. During his voyage, the dreamer encounters beautiful cities, hears about an immense monster, and witnesses many other wonders. Another fantasy, "Carcassonne," tells the story of the fruitless quest of a king, Camorak, and his army to find a legendary city that does not exist.

Even the stories set on Earth contain elements of the fantastic. "Blagdaross" is narrated by a cork, a rope, a kettle, a rocking horse, and other common, abandoned objects. The rocking horse, Blagdaross, is rescued from its abandonment by two young boys who allow it to carry them to new realms of imagination. "The Madness of Andelsprutz" reveals where the spirits of dead cities go after the cities fall. The story "Where the Tides Ebb and Flow" tells of a dream about the long torture endured by a soul trapped in a corpse that does not find its final rest until humanity has vanished. "The Sword and the Idol" tells of the triumph of a primitive man who carves an idol over his competitor who forges an iron sword. Another tale set on Earth, "Poor Old Bill," tells the story of a desperate crew who resort to cannibalism to survive the curse of their monstrous captain.

ANALYSIS

Lord Dunsany ranks as one of the best fantasy writers of the twentieth century. The fantasy stories that he produced in the beginning of his career are considered by many critics to be his greatest achievements. The incredible worlds and fantastic pantheon of gods he created influenced several people who later became famous writers in their own right. For example, Lord Dunsany had a particularly strong impact on the early career of H. P. Lovecraft. The sixteen stories contained in *A Dreamer's Tales* are deemed by many critics to be among Lord Dunsany's best and will surely continue to be enjoyed by new generations of readers.

One of the strongest aspects of Lord Dunsany's stories is his use of lavish descriptions in creating his fantasy world. His descriptions are vividly detailed and conjure up fantastic images in the minds of readers. Some of Lord Dunsany's best descriptions occur in "Idle Days on the Yann" as he depicts the wondrous realms encountered by the dreamer on his voyage down the long river. A terrifying example of Lord Dunsany's descriptive ability comes in the hideous tortures carried out by Thuba Mleen in "The Hashish Man."

Another interesting aspect of Lord Dunsany's stories is that his tales fall into several different genres. Some of his stories are fantasies set in strange realms such as the Inner Lands of "Poltarnees, Beholder of Ocean," the abandoned city of Bethmoora, and other wondrous places in the Land of Dreams. Other tales contain elements of horror, such as the account of the soul trapped in a rotting corpse in "Where the Tides Ebb and Flow" and the cannibalistic crew of a wandering ship in "Poor Old Bill." Other tales take place on Earth but focus on elements of the fantastic, such as "Blagdaross" with its talking rocking horse, cork, rope, and other objects.

Lord Dunsany's tales present readers with a variety of themes that add to the strength of his work. One recurring theme is the loss of fantastic places to the ravages of time. The loss of a beautiful city plays a central role in "Bethmoora" and "The Madness of Andelsprutz." The disappearance of an entire kingdom as a result of the passage of time is the central focus of "In Zaccarath." An examination of foolishness and futility are revealed in the quest of Camorak to find a city that does not exist in "Carcassonne." Another theme that Lord Dunsany explores in his stories is the destructive power of technology on human imagination. The Land of Dreams is the realm that sparks imagination, but the real world and its affairs can lead humans to ignore the beauty of nature, as seen in "The Day of the Poll."

—*David A. Oakes*

DREAMSNAKE

A feminist quest in which young healer Snake searches for a dreamsnake across the deserts and mountains of an Earth altered by a nuclear holocaust in its distant past

Author: Vonda N(eel) McIntyre (1948–)
Genre: Science fiction—post-holocaust
Type of work: Novel
Time of work: Indefinite future
Location: An unidentified desert, a mountain village, the healers' community, and a dome that shelters an alien ecosystem
First published: 1978

THE STORY

In "Of Mist, and Grass, and Sand" (1973), the Nebula Award-winning novelette that became the first section of *Dreamsnake*, Vonda McIntyre introduces her protagonist Snake, a young traveling healer who uses her knowledge and her genetically altered snakes to treat illness and suffering. Snake is called to help a family whose son is dying of a large tumor. To comfort him, she leaves Grass, her treasured dreamsnake, on the child's pillow while she prepares Mist, her cobra, to treat the child. When she returns from a strenuous night of altering Mist's venom into a medicine against the child's cancer, she finds that the parents have killed her dreamsnake out of their desert-bred terror of snakes.

Without her dreamsnake, whose bite eases death, Snake is handicapped as a healer. She becomes afraid when she is called to a patient's side: Will the patient be dying and ask Snake for the help she can no longer give? *Dreamsnake*, which won both Hugo and Nebula awards, expands the original novelette by tracing Snake's quest to obtain a new dreamsnake and continue her career as a healer.

Snake first directs her steps toward the healers' "station," the home community where she was trained. She intends to ask her elders to forgive her error in judgment and give her a new snake, knowing that the scarcity of dreamsnakes makes it unlikely that her request can be granted. Along the way, people call on her as a healer, not recognizing that she is impaired by the lack of one of the basic tools of her profession, the means to assist at death. While trying in vain to help a woman dying of radiation exposure, Snake decides that instead of returning in shame to her home, she will go to the Center, the underground city that preserved itself and its technology before the nuclear devastation of the planet. Because the Center communicates with offworlders and the dreamsnakes are believed to come from another planet, it is possible that the people of the Center can help her. The isolated and paranoid city refuses her.

As she travels and treats the ill, Snake becomes aware that she is being followed. Her stalker ransacks her possessions and later attacks her and tries to steal her snakes. She assumes that a "crazy" is following her. Eventually she turns the tables and becomes the follower, after she learns that her assailant is addicted to dreamsnake venom; she infers that someone, somewhere, has enough dreamsnakes to use them wastefully. The pathetic but sly addict leads her to "the broken dome," an alien habitat where a multitude of dreamsnakes are being exploited by a bitter, soul-twisted albino giant who hates the healers because they were not able to cure his genetic deformities. With the help of her adopted daughter and the man who loves her, Snake triumphs and comes away from the broken dome not only with dreamsnakes but also, and more important, with the knowledge of how to breed them successfully.

ANALYSIS

In this early novel, published before the author's highly visible career producing novelizations of Star Trek films, McIntyre follows the well-established tradition of the masculine heroic quest story but modifies the form to suit a feminist worldview. As is typical of quest stories, in *Dreamsnake* a young protagonist sets out on a difficult journey to find something of great value and encounters trials and adventures along the way. Instead of a weapon, a woman, or a treasure, the thing of great value for which McIntyre's protagonist searches is a dreamsnake, a tool of nurturing.

In the traditional male-oriented trajectory of a heroic quest, the obstacles encountered by the hero are enemies with whom he must fight in order to prove himself. In *Dreamsnake*, the trials are challenges of healing and caring, not challenges of force; there are patients to be treated, not enemies to be bested. Snake is tested, strengthened, and softened by her encounters with a woman with a broken spine and radiation poisoning, an arrogant injured aristocrat who will not follow her advice, a young man who has failed to master control of his own fertility, and a scarred young victim of sexual abuse whom Snake finally adopts as her own daughter. The maturity Snake wins through her quest is not the hardness of a battle-seasoned warrior but the humanity of a woman who can deal honorably with her professional responsibilities and also accept responsibility for a child and for a mate.

McIntyre expresses her feminist vision not only by appropriating and modifying a traditionally masculine form; she also constructs a world of characters who are not bound by gender-role constraints. She frequently introduces characters by generic titles, such as "owner," "chemist," "innkeeper," "guard," and "herder," leaving their gender to readers' imaginations. When a gender-revealing pronoun, such as "him" or "her," finally appears, readers may be surprised to find their stereotypes challenged.

McIntyre conceives a society in which both men and women are free to develop to their full potentials. Snake herself supports that conception. She is able to give a good account of herself in a fight, bathe a newly crippled woman who has wet the bed, be tender and truthful with children, use her physical prowess and stamina to escape from her enemies, live fully even in the full knowledge of her coming diminishment with age, and experience the entire range of emotions available to a human being.

—*Donna Glee Williams*

Drink Down the Moon

The world of modern-day fairies is threatened by an evil sorcerer and can be saved only by the cooperative efforts of fairies and sympathizing humans

Author: Charles de Lint (Henri Diederick Hoefsmit, 1951–   )
Genre: Fantasy—magical realism
Type of work: Novel
Time of work: The present
Locale: Ottawa, Ontario, Canada
First published: 1990

The Story

The novel begins with a young fiddler named Johnny Faw, whose grandfather, better known as Old Tom, played fiddle for the fairy moon rides, or "rades." Shortly before his death, Old Tom instructs Johnny to play fiddle in Vincent Massey Park in Ottawa. There, Johnny is greeted by the fairy pook, Jenna, who gives him an amulet for luck. Jenna, however, has her own worries in that there is some dark force keeping her from conducting her rades, riding the moon roads to replenish the fairy luck. Jenna goes to find Bucca, her old teacher, but never finishes her quest.

Luck leads Johnny to stumble on Jenna's identical twin, Jemi Pook, a punk saxophone player for a local band. Jemi is a half fairy, living in the world of humans and to some extent turning her back on the fairy way of life.

Jenna's body is found. Jemi goes into mourning for her sister, and Johnny is drawn deeper into the web of fairy troubles. He has an abrupt change of perception facing him, as he must learn to accept the existence of fairies, knocking on stone outcrops to get under hillsides, beasts coming out of the river, and the dark menace of a magician who can steal the life and luck from living beings. He also finds himself falling in love with Jemi.

Jack of Kinrowan (known as Jackie, who appears in Charles de Lint's 1987 *Jack, the Giant-Killer*) guards the heart of fairy in her tower, where she keeps the old wizard's library. She is informed of the pook's death and becomes involved. Jackie also senses that something evil seems to be darkening the moon roads. The large black dog that was seen at the scene of Jenna's death has Jackie's scent. Soon, Jackie is the next target of the evil wizard Cumin's conquest. Cumin approaches as a friend but quickly takes over the wizard's tower and then tries to force Jackie to give him the secrets of the old wizard, Bhruic.

Jackie escapes before Cumin can learn her secrets. Meanwhile, her assistant, Kate Crackernuts, creates for herself a magical guide by using Wallystane magic. She learns that the secret of killing a black sorcerer is to find the secret hiding place of his heart. Kate looks for the hiding place of Cumin's heart in a darkening of the moon roads. Jackie returns to steal back her magic when she is confronted with the dark sorcerer. Meanwhile, Jemi Pook struggles to learn the name of the sorcerer so that she can lead a rade against him.

All come together in the end. Jemi Pook finds her way into the tower, finds the sorcerer's heart, and destroys it. Henk Van Roon, Johnny's friend, leads the rade for luck, with the moon as a guide. Jemi and Johnny begin a life together.

ANALYSIS

De Lint creates strong female protagonists in many of his works, and there is a wealth of female protagonists in *Drink Down the Moon*. They are realistic in the sense that they are determined but not invincible and proud but not unable to accept help. They perform remarkable feats, as when Jackie leaps from the window and teaches herself to fly in midair and when Jemi comes in from the rain, catches hold of the wizard's heart, and crushes it under her foot. It is easy to see how a light, plot-reliant novel such as *Drink Down the Moon* could have been preparation for later, richer novels such as *The Little Country* (1991) and *Dreams Underfoot* (1993). De Lint's later works definitely are more touched by artistry.

The plot moves quickly in *Drink Down the Moon*, and there are no lags. This means that there is not much room for intense character development, but there is enough to bind readers and make them care about the fate of the main characters.

In *Drink Down the Moon*, de Lint creates believable fantasy in modern settings, managing to juxtapose magic and all-night coffee shops. The plot blends the tension of a murder mystery with the wonder of a fantasy novel. De Lint's talent is in taking the ordinary and painting it in a new fantastic light, forcing his readers to find the wonder in the ordinary.

De Lint uses music as a mainstay for his plot. Jemi, Johnny, and Henk are all musicians, and the subculture of small struggling bands runs through the novel. Music is the language of fairy in this novel, as it is in other novels by de Lint. Visual images in *Drink Down the Moon* are refreshingly strong and startling, and de Lint appeals to all the reader's senses. The novel is a light, engaging modern fantasy offering fast, enjoyable reading.

Drink Down the Moon originally appeared as its own novel but was later combined with *Jack, the Giant-Killer* to form the collection *Jack of Kinrowan* (1995).

—*Diana L. Gerow*

THE DROWNED WORLD

Increasing ambient temperatures cause flooding, the growth of a Triassic rain forest in Northern Europe, and profound changes in human behavior

Author: J(ames) G(raham) Ballard (1930–2009)
Genre: Science fiction—catastrophe
Type of work: Novel
Time of work: Seventy-five to one hundred years in the future
Locale: London, England
First published: 1962

THE STORY

The Drowned World is the second of J. G. Ballard's four "natural catastrophe" novels, following *The Wind from Nowhere* (1962) and preceding *Burning World* (1964; revised as *The Drought*, 1965) and *The Crystal World* (1966). *The Drowned World* projects the results of major changes to both the physical world and the human psyche, in keeping with Ballard's consistent focus on "inner space."

Dr. Robert Kerans, a biologist, is monitoring a testing station floating over the largely submerged city of London. Solar storms have stripped the atmosphere, and Earth's temperatures have been rising gradually for the past seventy years. World population and reproduction rates have declined radically, and humanity survives primarily within the Arctic and Antarctic circles. With Kerans in London are Dr. Alan Bodkin, his assistant; the party leader, Colonel Riggs; and Riggs's men. Beatrice Dahl, a beautiful eccentric, has refused to evacuate and lives nearby in a partly submerged apartment tower. The action centers on the gradual changes in Kerans, Bodkin, Dahl, and others as they dream of the great archaic Sun and develop a desire to move south into the new and virtually impenetrable tropical jungle of mud, mosquitoes, and sixty-foot-high ferns. Bodkin explains the dreams and desires as a subconscious recapitulation, at the cellular level, of an "archeopsychic past."

Hardman, a helicopter pilot, is the first to succumb to the powerful dreams; escaping from the party, he forges south into the jungle. The party abandons the station, but Kerans, Bodkin, and Dahl remain. A party of black looters with two thousand alligator-watchdogs, led by Strangman, a vicious white pirate king, takes over the site, captures Kerans, and subjects him to humiliation amounting to torture. Strangman's men erect dikes in order to drain Leicester Square to loot the area. Bodkin is killed by Strangman's men after his futile attempt to dynamite the dikes.

Kerans escapes and tries to rescue Dahl from Strangman. He fails and is rescued in turn by Riggs and his men, who have returned on patrol. Kerans then dynamites the dikes and moves off to the south, toward the burning Sun. He encounters Hardman, a blackened husk of a man, and tries to help him, but Hardman flees to the south. At the novel's end, Kerans continues to struggle south, apparently moving toward death but also toward a strange reconciliation with his inner nature.

ANALYSIS

On the surface, *The Drowned World* is a meticulous scientific projection of the effects of massive global warming. Despite its strangeness, Ballard's description of the vast rain forest, with its enervating and pervading heat and intense fecundity, is deliberately unremarkable. The real meaning of the novel lies on the psychological level, where Ballard explores the inner changes that interact with the catastrophe.

The effects on the characters are articulated by Bodkin and Kerans. Bodkin suggests that the returning Triassic environment has caused other plants and species to mutate rapidly, moving backward through an awakening of archaic genetic elements. He believes, however, that humans cannot physically adapt to a climate in which they never existed as creatures with brains and consciousness. It is cellular memory that releases the overwhelming dreams of the Sun, its pounding rays beating time with the heart, and imposes the emphatic desire to move southward toward it.

As the novel progresses, human relationships and conflicts have less importance for the central characters. They retreat into dreams, overtaken by their bodies' cellular recapitulation and unconcerned even with issues of physical survival. Kerans' suicidal journey south paradoxically contains the promise of imminent death but answers his psychological need to move ever closer to the Sun. A secondary imagery of uterine re-enactment is blended with the archeopsychic drive. The warm, dark wetness of the Triassic forest continually attracts Kerans at a psychic level, accounting for the fading of his physical attraction to Dahl.

The surrealistic style of the novel is anchored to two paintings in Dahl's apartment: Laurent Delvaux's image of ashen-faced women naked to the waist, dancing with skeletons clothed in tuxedos, and Max Ernst's wild jungles of living organisms that writhe about, devouring one another under a tropical sun. The novel moves from a realistic portrayal of a scientific expedition to progressively more dreamlike and surreal events, such as the chaotic nighttime voodoo dances of a deathly pale Strangman and his strange entourage. Kerans finds himself living more and more inside his mind, dominated by the pulsating Sun dreams and disinterested in his surroundings as though he were viewing them through a telescope from afar. The novel becomes as rich and baroque in language as Ernst's jungle, filled with alligators, overgrown iguanas, monkeys, dazzling sunlight, giant ferns, rich odors, and the ruined city crumbling into the mud. It is an intensely atmospheric book—heavy, rich, moody, and overwhelming.

The movement of the story is reminiscent of Joseph Conrad's great probe of the soul, *Heart of Darkness* (1902), but Ballard envisions humans driven by biology and psychology rather than by colonial capitalism and guilt. Strangman is like Kurtz in Conrad's novel, a nearly deranged white man leading loyal black followers. Strangman is removed from the action, however, leaving Kerans to venture further into the heart of his personal darkness. His darkness is the burning Sun, and even as he is about to die, the text embraces a curious stoic optimism, suggesting "a second Adam searching for the forgotten paradises of the reborn sun." For Kerans, the peace of coming to terms with biopsychic forces is more important than life itself. In the burning jungle of London lies the burning jungle of the mind, its only relief the desperate phototropism of the trek south.

—Peter Brigg

THE DUNCTON CHRONICLES AND THE BOOK OF SILENCE

A multigeneration saga of life, love, and violent religious strife among intelligent moles

Author: William Horwood (1944–)
Genre: Fantasy—animal fantasy
Type of work: Novels
Time of work: The 1970's-1990's
Locale: Various rural locations in England and Wales
First published: *Duncton Wood* (1980), *Duncton Quest* (1988), *Duncton Found* (1989), *Duncton Tales* (1991), *Duncton Rising* (1992), and *Duncton Stone* (1993)

THE STORY

It is difficult to summarize the exceedingly full plot of William Horwood's six books, involving many named moles (there are no nonmole characters) and extending over about ten generations and some four thousand pages. Although the Duncton Wood system of tunnels and burrows remains central, a dozen or more other systems are featured, together with extreme ups and downs in mole life.

Duncton Wood, the first novel of the Duncton Chronicles, introduces the world of moles through Bracken, first met as a young mole and followed throughout his life. It tells of his love for Rebecca, a healer, and how he becomes the leader at Duncton and tries to maintain the mole religion. For this last, he is persecuted by Mandrake, Rune, and their followers. Bracken goes on long journeys to other systems, accompanied by Boswell, a scribemole. They visit Uffington, the religious center of moledom, where the Holy Mole (analogous to the pope) resides and where there is a great library of mole books. They also visit Siabod, a system in a Welsh mountain. Despite a fire and a plague, the worshipers of the Stone at Duncton keep their faith alive.

Duncton Quest is the story of Tryfan, Bracken and Rebecca's son, who accompanies Boswell (now elderly and revered) to Uffington, which is almost deserted. There, Boswell appoints Tryfan as a scribemole, instructing him to write down the history and philosophy of moledom during the coming period of religious persecution. This Tryfan does, despite terrible hardships.

As leader at Duncton, he evacuates the system (though with terrible losses when a tunnel under the river floods) in response to an attack by followers of the Word, a hostile religion. They use the empty Duncton system as a dumping ground for moles who are plague victims. In company with his friend Spindle and the greatest of all mole route-finders, Mayweed, Tryfan journeys to the outskirts of London (which Horwood calls The Great Wen), contacting moles there, particularly Feverfew, the love of his life. Tryfan even has time to mate with Henbane, Mistress of the Word, his archenemy. Their son Lucerne succeeds Henbane.

In *Duncton Found*, the moles of the Word continue to destroy systems of followers of the Stone, who are usually pacifists (except in Wales). The Stone Mole, long prophesied as a savior of the Word, is born in Duncton from a mystical union between Boswell and Feverfew. He is Beechen, soon accepted as a very holy mole, who defeats his enemies by converting them with his love. Most of the central characters (followers of the Stone) are ritually slaughtered by Lucerne at Duncton. After Lucerne dies, his followers disperse, and the empty Duncton is gradually repopulated by Stone-worshiping moles. Among them is Woodruff, grandson of Tryfan and the author of this first trilogy.

The second trilogy, The Book of Silence, is set a couple of mole generations later and concentrates on the search for the seventh and last holy book of the Stone, The Book of Silence. The other six books have long been in the moles' possession, originally at Uffington but later at Duncton. *Duncton Tales* introduces Privet, an insignificant seeming female of middle years who is a scribe and scholar. She is the granddaughter of Wort, a zealot of the Word, who persecuted Beechen. Apart from the religious intolerance caused by the Newborns, a sect of Stone believers, there are fascinating details of the great library at Duncton, its organization, its eccentric denizens, and their professional rivalries. This library must be saved from the Newborns, who would censor or destroy it.

In *Duncton Rising*, Privet journeys to Caer Caradoc in Wales, in search of The Book of Silence. Behind her she leaves the humble library assistant, Pumpkin (who becomes the leader of the Duncton rebels), and the Master Librarian, Stour, to defend the library's treasures. All of Privet's early life is revealed in flashback. She meets up again with her offspring and with Rooster, her great love. She is the one who delivers The Book of Silence safely to Duncton Wood at the end of *Duncton Stone*.

ANALYSIS

The subgenre of animal fantasy owes its recent popularity to *Watership Down* by Richard Adams (1972). Adams' rabbits are simple creatures, with limited intelligence and lacking institutions. Horwood's moles are almost human, possessing great intelligence, a full range of emotions, religious and political hierarchies, and complex written records. They are still wild animals, however, capable of killing other moles with their talons (which they often do in these novels) and mating in response to seasonal urges. Such contradictions add to the fascination of the Duncton books, though they render them more suitable for adults. Occasional scenes of torture and extreme violence are harrowing to read. Followers of the Word frequently "snout" dissenting moles; that is, they impale them by the snout on barbed wire and leave them to die a terribly painful and lingering death.

Other animals are scarcely mentioned. The moles are careful to avoid owls, humans (referred to as "two-feet"), and motor vehicles ("roaring owls"). They generally ignore other woodland creatures, and fortunately Horwood is sensible enough not to have his moles chatting with them. It seems odd that these intelligent moles have not developed the means of driving off owls or of communicating with humans.

Although the moles speak standard English, Horwood creates an odd tweeness by referring (in narration as well as dialogue) to "paw" instead of "hand" or "foot," to "stance" instead of "stand," and to "nomole" and "some-mole" for "nobody" and "somebody." More thoughtful is his indication of an evolving language. Some old written records are in an old mole language, and Feverfew (in *Duncton Quest*) speaks an antiquated form because her group of moles in London has been cut off from the rest of moledom for many generations. Their written records are scribed with the talons on pieces of bark. The result is a three-dimensional series of impressions, rather like Braille, read with the talons or the snout.

The theme of religious persecution runs strongly throughout the six novels. Belief in the Stone appears to be a monotheistic religion similar in many of its tenets to Christianity. The adherents all try to get to a Stone (by which is meant a prehistoric standing stone; there is one at Duncton and at most of the other larger systems) to pray on Longest Night and Midsummer Night, the two most important festivals of the year. The hierarchy of the religion disappears during the first book, and only separate groups of lay believers maintain the faith. Artifacts of faith remain: the seven original Stones, the seven stillstones (which are small magical pebbles), and the seven great books of moledom. In *Duncton Wood*, the believers in the Stone tend to fight back against their persecutors, though in later books pacifism becomes a strong part of their belief. Tryfan and Beechen both try to turn the other cheek and love their enemy. Beechen, in particular, is a messiah figure, comparable to Jesus Christ in his peripatetic preaching and even in his end. He is suspended from barbed wire by one paw in a semi-crucifixion, and his body is spirited away at about the time he might have died.

There are some elements of mysticism, not always connected with religion. Various moles appear after death, especially Boswell. The power of seven confers magical powers of healing or of turning back enemies. At one point in Duncton Found, Beechen is part of a sevenfold telepathic link connecting Stones being touched in a Midsummer Night ritual. Perhaps most mysterious of all is Dark Sound, the terrifying noise created by a paw or the wind touching certain carved shapes on the walls of burrows at Duncton and elsewhere.

It is easy to accuse Horwood of writing a simplistic tale of good versus evil and of stacking the odds so that good moles are saintly and evil moles are demoniac. Such is partly the case, especially in *Duncton Wood*, which was the author's first novel, and it applies to many of the minor characters. On the other hand, the major characters are complex and capable of error, and they tend to change over their lifetimes. Thus, some of the best moles show flaws. Tryfan is charismatic but unsuccessful as a leader, and Privet has made many mistakes in her exciting early life. Similarly, some of the most evil moles possess a lighter side to them (Rune, for example) or are capable of reforming, as Sleekit and Henbane do. Horwood himself makes it difficult for the reader by giving many of his more evil moles ludicrously evil names, such as Mallice, Drule, Wort, Squelch, and Snyde.

These novels have attracted a large and enthusiastic following in Great Britain, though not the classic status of *Watership Down*.

—*Chris Morgan*

The Dune Series

The planet of Arrakis goes through several politico-environmental upheavals in a spacefaring yet feudal society dependent on the addictive spice melange

Author: Frank Herbert (1920–1986)
Genre: Science fiction—galactic empire
Type of work: Novels
Time of work: The 57th year of the Padishah Emperor, Shaddam IV (102d century c.e.) through the following five thousand years
Location: Primarily Arrakis (the planet called Dune and later Rakis) and Chapterhouse
First published: *Dune* (1965; serial form, *Analog*, 1963–1965), *Dune Messiah* (1969), *Children of Dune* (1976), *God Emperor of Dune* (1981), *Heretics of Dune* (1984), and *Chapterhouse: Dune* (1985)

The Story

The Dune series can be seen as a set of three two-volume novels. The first involves the family of Paul Atreides, its battle for the planet Arrakis, and Paul's coming of age as the messianic Muad'Dib. The second concerns the life of Paul's son Leto II, from childhood to his ascendancy as God Emperor of Dune. The third deals with the ongoing machinations of the Bene Gesserit, an ancient society of women devoted to mind and body control and eugenics, in their attempt to control the sociopolitical environment of the Dune universe millennia later, as well as the ramifications of their betrayal by the Atreides family. *Dune* itself was rejected by twenty-two publishers before being accepted by Chilton of Philadelphia. It remained in print for at least the next thirty years.

In *Dune*, the Atreides family emigrates from their home world of Caladan to the desert world of Arrakis, pressured by the political dalliances of the Emperor Shaddam IV. Arrakis (Dune) had been controlled by the Baron Harkonnen, and it was there that he had gained his great wealth from trade in melange, an addictive spice. Melange is essential to the functioning of all elements of society, including the Spacing Guild, for which it ensures the ability to fold space.

The Harkonnens set a trap for the Atreides family in which Duke Leto Atreides and his weapons specialist, Duncan Idaho, are killed. His Bene Gesserit consort, Jessica, and their son, Paul, flee to the domain of the Fremen, the desert people of Arrakis. Once there, Paul partakes of melange and begins to show signs that he is the Kwisatz Haderach, a messiah-like culmination of the Bene Gesserit's breeding program. Jessica was supposed to have had a girl, who would be married to the Harkonnen boy Feyd-Rautha, thus solidifying the aristocratic alliances and placing the Bene Gesserit fully in command of galactic political affairs. The Bene Gesserit time line is thrown off, and sociopolitical upheaval ensues. The rest of the

novel involves the Atreideses' attempt to retake the planet of Arrakis from the deposed Harkonnens and the installation of Paul as its ruler.

All of this occurs in the intricately realized ecology of the desert planet. The desert is essential to the complex life cycle of the sandworms, whose larval forms, the sandtrout, produce melange.

A vast history unfolds, supplemented by chapter-heading epigraphs on the life of Paul Atreides, or Muad'Dib as he comes to be known by his Fremen followers, from the Princess Irulan, his legal wife and the daughter of Emperor Shaddam IV.

Dune Messiah takes up the story of Paul and Jessica in their life with the Fremen as they consolidate their power on Arrakis. Chani, Paul's Fremen concubine, has died in childbirth, and Paul must ultimately sacrifice himself in the defense of their children, his prescient sister Alia, and Arrakis.

Children of Dune continues the story of Paul's son, Leto II, and his daughter, Ghanima, when they are nine years old. Leto takes on the outer covering of the sandtrout—the larvae of the giant sandworms—and effectively becomes a superman, a worthy successor to his messianic father, and rightful emperor of the galactic empire. Neither of the two volumes following *Dune* has the scope of the original, and both lack the hagiographic epigrams of Princess Irulan, which give readers much information concerning the overall effect of the future history. The books do not suffer for this—in fact, the action intensifies to the point of absurdity (Leto's sandtrout symbiosis, for example)—but they are different in kind.

The fourth volume, *God Emperor of Dune*, returns to the form of the first volume and is set some 3,500 years in the future. Leto II, in his symbiotic state with the sandworm, has become immortal and rules the galactic empire from his throne on Arrakis with infallible foresight. One result of that foresight is the empire's stagnation. He comes to realize in his lengthy reflections that this cannot continue and so devises his own downfall. The plot here is thin, and the musings are long—features only too characteristic of the later volumes in the *Dune* series.

Heretics of Dune, the fifth volume, concerns the Bene Gesserit and the Tleilaxu in the eventual planned destruction of the planet Rakis, as it has come to be called. A third Kwisatz Haderach of sorts, the militant Sardaukar Bashar Miles Teg, sacrifices himself for the sisterhood as the several guilds fight for ascendancy in the shattered empire through control of Rakis, the worms, and melange. The Mentat warrior Duncan Idaho, cloned here for the twelfth time, provides a thread of continuity from *Dune*, as does the interminable talk of the millennia-old treachery of Lady Jessica and her illicit son Paul. All of this takes place 1,500 years after the self-destruction of Leto II, God Emperor, and the regathering of the lost tribes of the once-flourishing Rakis. This volume introduces the dark mirror version of the Reverend Mothers of the Bene Gesserit, the Honored Matres of Rakis. They play the role of archnemeses in the sixth and final volume, *Chapterhouse: Dune*.

After the willful destruction of the planet of sandworms, whose spice is essential to the operation of the galactic empire for all the guilds by this point, the Honored Matres vow revenge on the sisterhood. The Bene Gesserit reincarnate Teg, who, as the old myth went, could move faster than light, to fight the Honored Matres. They rely on Duncan Idaho's weapons abilities in their plan, but Duncan chooses to honor Bene Gesserit teachings of nonaggression and slips into a parallel space. The remnants of the Fremen and the guilds join him in his flight from the Honored Matres.

ANALYSIS

Although *Dune* did not receive universal critical acclaim on its appearance, it won both the 1965 Nebula Award (the first Nebula) and tied for the 1966 Hugo Award. The success of *Dune* and its sequels stems in large part from the response on college campuses. Like J. R. R. Tolkien's *The Lord of the Rings* trilogy (1954–1955), Frank Herbert's book presented a traditional epic with heroic characters in a well-realized environment, augmented by appendices and a map. The ecology movement had burgeoned, and *Dune* consciously used the environment of the desert as dire warning. As the drug culture flowered, the psychedelic melange, or spice, served as a handy symbol for lysergic acid diethylamide (LSD).

Dune came early in Herbert's career, preceded only by *The Dragon in the Sea* (1956; retitled *Under Pressure*, 1974), and fixed a benchmark for the rest of his career. It also made him one of science fiction's most financially successful authors. The novel was filmed in 1984.

The entire Dune series unfolds from the well-conceived original. Each later volume develops the ramifications of Jessica's decision—and that of her son Paul and grandson Leto II—to betray the Bene Gesserit guild and take the unfolding of sociopolitical events into their own hands. Paul is similar to Isaac Asimov's "Mule" in the Foundation series. After becoming the first male Bene Gesserit in history, he disrupts the plans of the Bene Gesserit to obtain control of the known universe. By the sixth volume, Atreides blood runs in the veins of almost everyone of any consequence in the Dune universe. This is a fine reversal on Baron Harkonnen's desire to see all Atreideses dead.

The long view of history, the vision of messiahs, and the unflinching critique of the myth of progress fit well into the epic-heroic structure. Herbert is able to include strong female characters, the Bene Gesserit, in a staunchly Middle Eastern milieu of *chaumurky* and *chaumas*—poison in the drink and poison in the food—and curved, poison-tipped blades. The characters are many and the plot intricate, but too much in the later volumes is lengthy narrative. The "heroes"—Paul, Leto II, and the twelfth Duncan Idaho—make antiheroic decisions, and the plots come off as anticlimactic despite epic events. The action is too often presented in the blink of an eye—literally in the case of Teg in *Heretics of Dune*— and the reader is privileged to learn about it after the fact through the ruminations of the characters.

—U. Milo Kaufmann

THE DUNWICH HORROR AND OTHERS

Isolated individuals are horrified to discover evidence of prehistoric alien races on Earth

Author: H(oward) P(hillips) Lovecraft (1890–1937)
Genre: Science fiction—alien civilization
Type of work: Stories
Time of work: The 1920's and 1930's
Locale: Primarily New England
First published: 1984 (corrected printing of 1963 version)

THE STORY

This volume contains the best of H. P. Lovecraft's shorter tales of supernatural horror, selected by August Derleth, with texts edited by S. T. Joshi. Most of them originally appeared in the pulp magazine *Weird Tales*. Several qualify as science fiction, chiefly "The Colour Out of Space" and "The Shadow Out of Time," first published, respectively, in *Amazing Stories* and *Astounding Stories*.

In "The Colour Out of Space," a meteorite of curious color and chemical properties lands on Nahum Gardner's farm west of Arkham, Massachusetts. People begin to notice odd changes in the surrounding flora and fauna, as well as in various members of the Gardner family, who slowly undergo both physical and mental decay. After destroying everything living in the vicinity of the farm, the "colour" returns to the sky whence it came, leaving behind a tiny residue that will soon be covered by a new reservoir.

In "The Shadow Out of Time," Professor Wingate Peaslee of Arkham's Miskatonic University suffers an extended bout of amnesia. After recovering his memory, he starts to have dreams of a vast Cyclopean city, located in the Southern Hemisphere of some 150 million years before and inhabited by intelligent cone-shaped beings known as the Great Race. It becomes clear that one of these creatures, who can travel through time, has exchanged minds with Peaslee. Eventually, he travels to the desert of Western Australia, where he discovers the ruins of the city of his dreams, beneath which he stumbles across the handwritten history of his own age that he had recorded in his captor's alien body.

Three other major tales concern encounters with entities of extraterrestrial origin. In "The Call of Cthulhu," the piecing together of disparate data, much of it collected by the narrator's late granduncle, Professor George Gammell Angell, forces him to conclude that a newly risen island in the Pacific Ocean is home to a huge octopoid creature that fell to Earth eons ago. After doing little more than sending psychic signals to sensitives and cultists worldwide, great Cthulhu returns to the ocean depths, but the narrator has forever lost his peace of mind.

In "The Dunwich Horror," wizard Whateley and his grandson Wilbur try to bring back the Old Ones, invisible monsters detectable by their fetid odor. Miskatonic's Dr. Henry Armitage, learning of the plot, organizes a team of savants to stop them.

In "The Whisperer in Darkness," the crablike fungi from Yuggoth (Pluto) lay siege to the remote Vermont farmhouse of Henry Akeley. Albert Wilmarth, a Miskatonic professor who has been corresponding with Akeley, arrives for a visit but flees in the middle of the night when he realizes that his host's brain has been surgically removed and placed in a metal canister for transport through space.

ANALYSIS

"Howard Phillips Lovecraft," Fritz Leiber once wrote, "was the Copernicus of the horror story. He shifted the focus of supernatural dread from man and his little world and his gods, to the stars and the black and unplumbed gulfs of intergalactic space." Eschewing both the traditional ghostly trappings of the gothic and the formulaic action and romance of the popular "scientifiction" of his day, Lovecraft combined a classical style derived from a voluminous reading of eighteenth century literature with a technique of careful realism, rooted in the soil of his native New England, to create a fictional universe in which the human race is of profound insignificance. In a 1927 letter to *Weird Tales* editor Farns-worth Wright, he declared, "Now all my tales are based on the fundamental premise that common human laws and interests and emotions have no validity or significance in the vast cosmos-at-large." He avoided the assumption that human passions, conditions, and standards would apply to other worlds or other universes. To achieve the essence of real externality, whether of time or space or dimension, he believed that one must forget the existence of such things as organic life, good and evil, love and hate, and all such attributes of humanity.

"The Call of Cthulhu," written in 1926, is Lovecraft's first important tale to reflect this philosophy. He considered "The Colour Out of Space" (1927) his best story because it came closest to attaining his ideal of "outsideness." In contrast, "The Dunwich Horror" (1928), though strong on plot and suspense, amounts to a conventional narrative of brave human beings thwarting interdimensional invaders. More complex is "The Whisperer in Darkness" (1930), with its ambiguous message. To travel through space as a disembodied consciousness, as a pure intellect capable of absorbing all the mysteries of the universe, may not be such a terrible fate.

By "The Shadow Out of Time" (1934-1935), the extraterrestrials have become fully sympathetic. The Great Race, who in their transcendent quest for knowledge have conquered time, affirm the finest of human values. As in the thematically similar short novel, *At the Mountains of Madness* (1964; cut versions appeared in the 1930's), however, the horror writer in Lovecraft cannot resist introducing horrors of which even other horrors are afraid. Boundless wonder can give way at any moment to untold terror. In his emphasis on the primal emotion of fear, on atmosphere and mood over character and plot, he ignores such basic human concerns as sex and romantic love. For psychological critics, Love-craft's cosmic indifference is of less interest as a guide to the universe than to his own neuroses. He may have looked to the stars, but he could not help gazing into the abyss of his own soul. Despite his efforts to deny the human, Lovecraft remains a very human figure whose work continues to move millions of readers.

—*Peter Cannon*

DURDANE

Gastel Etzwane leads the people of Durdane against their oppressors: first, the faceless human who enforces the laws, then primitive humanoids, and finally parasitic aliens

Author: Jack Vance (1916-2013)
Genre: Science fiction—planetary romance

Type of work: Novels
Time of work: At least nine thousand years in the future
Locale: Durdane and Kahei
First published: *Durdane* (1989, as trilogy); previously published as *The Anome* (1973; serial form, "The Faceless Man," *The Magazine of*

Durdane

Fantasy and Science Fiction, February-March, 1971; also published as *The Faceless Man*, 1978), *The Brave Free Men* (1973; serial form, *The Magazine of Fantasy and Science Fiction*, July-August, 1972), and *The Asutra* (1974; serial form, *The Magazine of Fantasy and Science Fiction*, May-June, 1973)

The Story

Shant, the most civilized continent on the planet Durdane, is divided into sixty-two cantons, each with its own laws and customs. Enforcing these rules is the Anome, the Faceless Man, the anonymous arbiter of retributive justice. Every inhabitant of Shant must wear a torc around the neck, in which is an explosive charge that can be detonated by the Anome whenever he wishes, usually, but not always, as punishment for a crime. These torcs are the only remnants of any kind of advanced technology, which has fallen into general disuse because of Durdane's metal-poor crust. Long-distance transportation, for example, is conducted primarily using guided balloons.

Gastel Etzwane, the main character in the series, grows up in the canton of Bashon, ruled by the Chilites, an all-male religious sect that believes that anything having to do with women is unclean. Ironically, or perhaps consequently, its members' devotions involve the use of a hallucinogenic plant that induces erotic reveries. Etzwane, the son of a ritual prostitute and a wandering musician, rebels against the Chilites' coercive regime and escapes to become a wandering musician. After accumulating enough money to rescue his mother from her indentured bondage, he returns to Bashon only to find it devastated by the Roguskhoi, a fierce race of humanoid warriors who loot human settlements of their female inhabitants, whom they consequently impregnate. Incensed that the Anome will do nothing to avert the Roguskhoi threat, Etzwane and Ifness, a secret representative from the Historical Institute on Earth, search for the Anome. After discovering his identity, they force him to issue edicts mobilizing all of Shant against the invaders.

In *The Brave Free Men*, Etzwane leads the whole of Shant against the Roguskhoi. He is assisted by his father, the wandering musician Dystar, and by Jerd Finnerack, who has been forced to work in a slave-labor camp ever since he helped Etzwane evade indentured slavery. Etzwane reorganizes Shant's society and proposes a new system of centralized government based upon separation of powers. He offers to remove the torcs of those who volunteer to fight the Roguskhoi, and he also streamlines scientific and technical research. Soon the Brave Free Men, as the soldiers are known, have the weaponry to defeat the otherwise unstoppable Roguskhoi, who ultimately are cornered in a remote wasteland between Shant and its hereditary enemy, Palasedra. Before war can break out again, Etzwane meets with the Palasedran leaders, and they learn that the Roguskhoi are the biological weapons of a parasitic alien life-form, the asutra, who have also invaded the bodies of key humans in Shant to promote not only the defeatist attitude of the last Anome but also the belligerent actions of Finnerack, whose attacks on Palasedra threatened a two-thousand-year-old peace.

In *The Asutra*, Etzwane investigates reports of further Roguskhoi activity on Durdane's other main land mass, the continent of Caraz. Accompanied there by Ifness, Etzwane learns that the Roguskhoi have been utterly defeated by unknown humans wielding advanced weaponry. They further learn that humans are being abducted by an asutra-bearing alien race, the Ka. In order to rescue four girls who have been thus kidnapped, Etzwane and a group of nomadic warriors allow themselves to be abducted. They eventually arrive on Kahei, the Ka home world, where they are trained to combat the unknown humans.

Etzwane characteristically leads a rebellion of the humans against the Ka, and they force the Ka to return them to Durdane. Etzwane finally learns from Ifness that the Ka had actually enslaved the asutra and that the humans Etzwane was trained to fight were working for the Ka, who wished to reinstate their supremacy on Kahei. The humans from Earth had meanwhile imposed a peace between the Ka and the asutra, and the ship that Etzwane had imagined they had commandeered back to Durdane was taking them there anyway. Ifness leaves Durdane, and Etzwane, it appears, must finally return to his music.

Analysis

The *Durdane* trilogy began to be published shortly after Jack Vance had completed the

Planet of Adventure (1968–1970) series and while the Demon Princes series (1964–1981) was on hiatus. A comparison of these series shows that in *Durdane*, Vance blends the planetary romance subgenre with another of his characteristic modes, the science-fiction *Bildungsroman*. Gastel Etzwane is a young boy when he is first introduced, and the novels of the series trace his progressive growth as leader and hero, whereas Adam Reith and Kirth Gersen from the other series are fully fledged, extremely capable protagonists from the beginning. Etzwane never becomes as physically skilled as Reith and Gersen; when he becomes involved in a crisis, he must think or lead his way out rather than fight. In some respects, however, they are all similar. Reith and Gersen lead liberation movements in societies they encounter, but they never stay and follow their programs all the way through. Etz-wane leads the most comprehensive societal revolutions of all, but he too would rather continue adventuring than become enmeshed in the mundane tasks of governing.

At the end of the series, when Ifness refuses to take on Etzwane as his assistant, Etzwane's adventuring comes to an inconclusive closure. All the *Durdane* novels end inconclusively, unlike those of the other series, which are each fairly self-contained. This inconclusiveness of structure is deeply connected with the underlying ironies of the series. Many critics have noted that Vance's sense of humor, perhaps the most finely honed in all of science fiction, is fundamentally ironic—after all, who else would write a novel titled *Space Opera* (1965) that was not about vast struggles across galactic empires but instead concerned the journeys of an interstellar opera company? This irony pervades the deep structures of his novels as well.

On the surface, the themes of *Durdane* could have come out of the *Astounding Science-Fiction* of John W. Campbell, Jr., and particularly the works of its most popular early author, Robert A. Heinlein. *The Anome* begins as a biting satire of religion, as does Heinlein's "If This Goes On" (1940), and then becomes an indictment of an anonymously repressive government. *The Brave Free Men* depicts a war of liberation against an army of red demon-like creatures. (The overtones of anticommunism are unmistakable, as is the sense of sexual menace.) To become a truly liberated citizen, one must enlist in the military, a prerequisite also mandated in Heinlein's *Starship Troopers* (1959). Ironically, the most belligerent of the warriors, Jerd Finnerack, the leader of the Brave Free Men themselves, is slave to a parasitic alien. Finally, Etzwane's rebellion against a race of parasitic aliens similar to those in Heinlein's *The Puppet Masters* (1951) proves to be almost totally unnecessary. It is also based on incorrect assumptions: It is the "host" aliens, the Ka, who have enslaved the parasites, the asutra. Throughout the series, Vance seems to endorse the individualistic libertarian sentiments of so much science fiction of the 1940's and 1950's, but the working out of these premises belies this assumption.

Many of the premises of *Durdane* go against the political tenets of the "New Wave" in science fiction that was approaching its high point at the time the series was published. It is surprising that an entire subplot involving mindless red hordes who only want to kill men and rape women did not cause more controversy, coming as it did during the height of U.S. involvement in Vietnam. Vance's portrayal of the disinterested representative of human galactic civilization, the aptly named Ifness, goes directly against the grain established by Ursula K. Le Guin's depiction of Genly Ai in *The Left Hand of Darkness* (1969). The depiction of ultimately unknowable aliens—Etzwane thinks that between aliens and humans only "tolerance founded on mutual distaste" is possible—also swims against the tide of much science fiction published during this period.

Durdane, nevertheless, is replete with Vance's strong points, particularly his portrayal of possible developments in human art. In his depictions of the use of color symbolism in Shantean culture and of Etzwane's music, Vance attempts and generally succeeds in one of the most difficult feats of representation—describing one form of art in terms of another. In its complicated progression of effects, Durdane marks a major achievement in Vance's body of work.

—*William Laskowski*

THE DYING EARTH SERIES

A gallery of sorcerers and rogues employ mischief and magic in their adventures during the final days of Earth

Author: Jack Vance (1916–2013)
Genre: Fantasy—medieval future
Type of work: Novels
Time of work: The twenty-first aeon, far in the future
Location: Primarily Ascolais and Almery
First published: *The Dying Earth* (1950), *The Eyes of the Overworld* (1966; serial form, *The Magazine of Fantasy and Science Fiction*, 1965-1966), *Cugel's Saga* (1983), and *Rhialto the Marvellous* (1984)

THE STORY

Jack Vance's stories of the dying Earth consist of three novels and one collection of stories that reads as a novel. The series is loosely linked by a shared setting and repeated characters. Each individual volume stands on its own, and within volumes the particular chapters form largely self-contained episodes.

The first volume, *The Dying Earth*, sets the stage and establishes the basic premises. The novel, more accurately a collection of stories, is set in the distant future. As Earth itself and human history near their end, rogues and charlatans abound, and science has been replaced by magic. The setting is more medieval than futuristic. Humankind is few and scattered, with small, isolated pockets of people spread across the wilderness. Travel is dangerous, because creatures such as deodands, flesheating ghouls, and pelgranes, winged ravagers of the air, wait for the unwary or the luckless.

The Dying Earth introduces these themes through the stories of such characters as Turjan of Miir, who wishes to create life in his castle laboratory. Lacking the proper knowledge of incantations, he turns to the powerful, mysterious Pandelume, who aids Turjan in return for a favor, the theft of a magical amulet. Aided by Pandelume's spells, Turjan succeeds, creating a beautiful woman, T'sain, who becomes his companion. In a following story, Turjan is captured by a rival, Mazirian the Magician, who tortures Turjan to gain his secret powers. T'sain saves her creator and lover.

Such is the pattern of stories in *The Dying Earth*. Characters appear only to be replaced by others, such as Ulan Dhor, who travels to the ancient city of Ampridatvir, where he wakes the sleeping god-king Rogol Domedonfors, unleashing devastation. Ulan Dhor's story is the only one in the series that departs from fantasy into more traditional science fiction, as Ulan Dhor escapes using a flying machine found in the ancient city.

The two novels that feature Cugel the Clever, *The Eyes of the Overworld* and *Cugel's Saga*, are picaresque tales in which a series of adventures befalling the protagonist are laid on a simple, sturdy framework. In the earlier work, Iucounu the Laughing Magician traps Cugel robbing him and casts a spell to send Cugel far beyond Almery, where he must secure the Eyes of the Overworld (special lenses with magical powers) and return them to Iucounu. To ensure Cugel's diligence, Iucounu clamps a barbed creature named Firx to Cugel's liver. Whenever Cugel delays, Firx's agitations painfully remind him of his duties.

Cugel acquires the Eyes of the Overworld through typical trickery and returns to Almery, along the way encountering numerous adventures in a variety of settings and managing to escape harm, and sometimes even death, by his wits. He rids himself of Firx as his first step in taking revenge on Iucounu, something he ponders at every step back to Almery. In the novel's final scene, however, Cugel is tricked by Iucounu and finds himself on the same desolate beach where he began his long journey home.

Cugel's Saga begins at this point. Like the preceding novel, it is a tale of Cugel's return, again progressing through territory filled with dangers presented by sorcerers, strange beasts, and stranger human beings. Early in the novel, Cugel escapes from the wizard Twango, carrying with him Spatterlight, a scale from the creature Sadlark, who long ago crashed to Earth from the higher realms. Twango has been painstakingly salvaging Sadlark's scales and selling them, through an intermediary, to an unknown sorcerer.

When Cugel returns to Almery, he is confronted by Iucounu, who demands Spatterlight, for it is the Laughing Magician who has been collecting the scales. Cugel surrenders the treasure but tricks Iucounu into destroying himself. Cugel claims the wizard's magnificent palace as his own.

The setting remains the same but the characters change for the fourth book in the series, *Rhialto the Marvellous*. Rhialto, a magician, joins a number of fellow wizards to form a loosely knit association to protect their interests. The association is guided by the Blue Principles, which are intended to protect these unscrupulous sorcerers from attacking one another.

Rhialto is accused and convicted of offenses against the Blue Principles, and then, through ever-increasing difficulties, must prove himself innocent and wreak vengeance on his enemies, most notably Hache-Moncour, who is motivated by envy of Rhialto's elegant style. Because Rhialto the Marvellous is a true Vance hero of the dying Earth, he is successful, and Hache-Moncour's punishment is suitably apt.

ANALYSIS

Vance's stories of the dying Earth are most notable for the individuality of their characters, realism of their setting, and elegance of their literary style. Major characters such as Cugel the Clever, Rhialto the Marvellous, and Iucounu the Laughing Magician are presented in extended descriptions that reveal their individual personalities. Vance sketches even his relatively minor characters with deft, individualizing strokes that render them vividly and memorably. Often, he concentrates on the essential quality that sums up the basic character of the individual, often a typically human defect, such as pride, lust, or, most often, greed. Even in the fantastic land of the dying Earth, millennia in the future, human nature remains basically the same.

Remaining unchanged, human nature also remains essentially flawed. There are no larger-than-life heroes in the world of the dying Earth; even the best of them, Ildefonse the Preceptor, leader of the magicians in *Rhialto the Marvellous*, has a generous supply of faults and weaknesses, most notably his lack of firmness. That failing allows the plot against Rhialto (and, therefore, the plot of the novel) to develop. Both Rhialto and Cugel are picaresque characters, closer to rogues than to heroes.

The landscape in which these figures find themselves is presented with a deceptively careful accuracy. Vance takes considerable pains to give the geography of the dying Earth a precise set of place names, so that the reader gains an impression of a real, if not entirely realistic, world. Names such as Shanglestone Strand, the Tustvold Mud-Flats, and the River Scaum give weight and presence to the setting of the books, and cities such as Saskervoy, Port Perduz, and Kaspara Vitatus, in addition to being named, have their odd buildings and odder customs described in quick, vivid detail.

At Gundar, for example, Cugel stumbles upon men tending a strange device, a stone fire pit ringed by five lamps, each with five wicks with an "intricate linkage of mirrors and lenses" above them. Puzzled at first, Cugel later learns that this is an instrument tended by members of the Order of Solar Emosynaries so that the dying sun will remain alive a bit longer. The incident is so clear in its description, yet casual in its presentation, that its air of reality is enhanced.

Vance employs this technique throughout the series, offering the strange, the bizarre, and the magical in a matter-of-fact fashion that, paradoxically, simultaneously emphasizes the unusual nature of being extraordinary yet very ordinary indeed. Although such places and things may not exist in the reader's world, they seem very plausible in the world of the dying Earth.

Finally, Vance's series is distinguished by its literary style, which has an ironic, even arch, tone. His sentences are varied in their syntax, and his vocabulary is extensive, frequently exotic but always precise. Vance's use of language in his fantasy world is less like the heroic prose of J. R. R. Tolkien than it is akin to James Branch Cabell's mocking, playful style in *Jurgen* (1919).

Characters such as Cugel and Rhialto are deft in their linguistic usage, as swift and cutting with their words as with their swords. In fact, words often are weapons on the dying Earth. Through this fact, Vance subtly emphasizes the importance of the spoken word. Curses and spells work their magic by being recited in the correct form and with the proper pronunciation. As Vance points out in the introduction to *Rhialto the Marvellous*, "magic is a practical science, or, more properly, a craft," and it works because "a spell in essence corresponds to a code, or set of instructions."

Dying Inside

In the genre of science fiction and fantasy, Vance's tales of the dying Earth occupy a special niche as supremely crafted examples of stories set in a distant future that oddly resembles the medieval past. Although haunted by demons and monsters, it is peopled by characters such as Cugel the Clever and Rhialto the Marvellous, who are all too human to be alien to readers.

—*Michael Witkoski*

DYING INSIDE

A man with the ability to read minds confronts, in middle age, the gradual loss of his powers

Author: Robert Silverberg (1935–)
Genre: Science fiction—extrasensory powers
Type of work: Novel
Time of work: Primarily 1976, with flashbacks
Location: New York City
First published: 1972

THE STORY

David Selig is a forty-one-year-old man gifted from birth with the ability to read minds. The main conflict in the novel is his attempt to come to terms with the gradual loss of this ability. He has never known why he was born with his gift, nor does he understand why he is losing it.

Ironically, Selig's ability to know what others are thinking has caused him to feel alienated throughout his life. Instead of being able to forge closer bonds with other humans, such as his parents and his sister, Judith, he becomes isolated from them because he can see beyond the surface of everyday life. He understands the selfishness and pettiness beneath the facades of human behavior.

As the novel opens, Selig lives a hermetic existence, eking out a living by ghostwriting papers for college students. His story contains several flashbacks telling about formative incidents in his life. These include a visit as a child to a psychiatrist; his relationship with another telepath, TomNyquist; and his failed love relationships with two different women, Toni and Kitty.

His telepathic ability is responsible in part for the breakups of both relationships. As Toni experiences an LSD trip, Selig is unable to avoid entering her mind and consequently experiencing the drug's effects. Toni mistakenly thinks his strange behavior is a deliberate attempt to confuse and hurt her, and she leaves him for that reason. Kitty is a young student whose mind Selig is unable to enter. Fascinated by her and wanting to make her into the soulmate and confidante he has never had, he insists that they study and experiment with telepathy. Finally, his pressuring and manipulation drive her away.

At the end of the novel, Selig's powers have deserted him. Moreover, his career as a ghostwriter is ended when he is beaten by a dissatisfied customer and then discovered by campus security. The novel concludes with an open ending and a tentative affirmation: Selig must reevaluate not only his self-identity but also his relationships with others, especially the sister he has always disliked.

ANALYSIS

Dying Inside appeared relatively late in Robert Silverberg's voluminous literary career. He has written and edited scores of books. In at least one way, *Dying Inside* typifies his writing. Unlike Isaac Asimov, who is more concerned with the technical science aspects of science fiction, Silverberg seems especially interested in character; he shows how human personalities are affected by scientific phenomena and reflects on the political and social implications of such phenomena. For example, there is little explanation of how and why Selig has his special powers: They simply exist. Silverberg attempts to establish some scientific plausibility by explaining that Selig's receptive ability is greater during a high pressure system when the humidity is low. Readers discover that he is losing his powers, but neither they nor Selig knows why.

These details seem secondary to Silverberg's main interest, which is to present an extraordinary fictional situation and explore its metaphorical possibilities. At one point in the text, for example, Selig's sister asks him whether his loss of his power is like a loss of sexual potency. This level is further developed by some of the diction and imagery Silverberg uses to describe Selig delving into others' consciousness: He "enters" and he "penetrates." This analogy underscores the theme of alienation, for Selig is unable to establish true intimacy in either a sexual or a platonic relationship. The point of view of the narrative, which alternates between first and third person, further suggests Selig's alienation, not only from others but also from himself.

One reviewer pointed out that the diminishing of the middle-aged Selig's powers resembles the waning of passion and intensity so often associated with middle age. In this way Selig's unusual situation may be somewhat universalized. This apparent strength of the novel has been viewed as a weakness by at least one reviewer, who wrote that the novel has more to do with growing older than it does with science fiction and that it is more about alienation than aliens.

Silverberg attempts to develop his hero's situation by associating it with those of many other alienated literary heroes of the twentieth century. There are allusions to T. S. Eliot's "The Love Song of J. Alfred Prufrock" (1915), Samuel Beckett's *Malone Dies* (1956), James Joyce's "The Dead" (1914), and E. M. Forster's *A Passage to India* (1924). As part of his job as a ghostwriter, Selig writes an essay about Franz Kafka's *The Trial* (1937) and *The Castle* (1930). Finally, an essay called "Entropy as a Factor in Everyday Life" uses physics' second law of thermodynamics as an analogy to Selig's view of his own life and the world around him.

Despite being nominated for a Nebula Award in 1972, *Dying Inside* received some unfavorable reviews. Several critics thought that the main character was unlikable, full of spite and self-pity, and others generally found the novel depressing. The novel remains interesting for its descriptions of telepathic experience and, perhaps less important, for its relationship to other twentieth century works.

—*Steven R. Luebke*

E Pluribus Unicorn

Short stories by one of science fiction's most empathetic writers and a grand master of literary style

Author: Theodore Sturgeon (Edward Hamilton Waldo, 1918-1985)
Genre: Science fiction—cultural exploration
Type of work: Stories
Time of work: Various
Location: Primarily on Earth and a spaceship
First published: 1953

The Story

The stories collected in *E Pluribus Unicorn*, originally published between 1947 and 1953, share an intense and compassionate examination of human behaviors of all kinds and descriptions, including the bizarre, the cruel, the abnormal, the tender, and the sexual. Theodore Sturgeon first broke into science fiction in 1937, rapidly becoming one of editor John Campbell's famous "Golden Age" writers. The early, groundbreaking (and rule-breaking) stories of *E Pluribus Unicorn*, his second story collection (following *Without Sorcery*, 1948), display his mastery in explorations of human emotions.

"The Silken-Swift" (1953), the lead story, is a marvelous reconstruction of the traditional unicorn-and-virgin story, vividly demonstrating that virginity does not necessarily denote an immaculate character and that internal beauty means more than external beauty. "Bianca's Hands," the next story, was first printed in Britain in 1947. Some American editors considered it so depraved that they not only refused to print it but also advised Sturgeon to destroy it. The hands belong to a congenital idiot, Bianca, and the plot deals with the fate of the young man who falls in love with her (or, more precisely, her hands). The story is explicit in its examination of fetishism, and it raises serious issues of tragedy.

"The World Well Lost" (1953) deals honestly and sympathetically with homosexuality. It caused quite a stir in the science-fiction community when it was published and still stands as a landmark in the evocation of love in a psychological sense. "The Professor's Teddy Bear" (1948), "The Music" (original in this collection), "Fluffy" (1947), "Die, Maestro, Die" (1949), "Cellmate" (1947), and "A Way of Thinking" (1953) explore less positive emotions, including hate, jealousy, and vengeance, and show them as the opposites of love and loyalty. "The Sex Opposite" (1952) and "It Wasn't Syzygy" (originally published as "The Deadly Ratio" in *Weird Tales*, 1948) go far beyond the limits of the day in suggesting sexual combinations; at the time, even homosexuality was somewhat taboo as a topic. "A Saucer of Loneliness" (1953) and "Scars" (1949) describe and evoke the desperation of the lonely and the misunderstood. In each of these stories, Sturgeon sympathetically and nonjudgmentally invests himself in the inner workings of his viewpoint characters.

In the introduction, well-known science-fiction editor and anthologist Groff Conklin notes that "you don't read these stories; they happen to you." He promises that the contents will "set you beside yourself, send you into jet-propelled shivers, and generally termite your placidity." This does not seem like an overstatement. In these stories, Sturgeon shows himself as working well above the limits often imposed on science fiction.

Analysis

The stories in this collection demonstrate not only the wide range of Sturgeon's psychologically oriented interests but also the range of his ability. Some of the stories included in *E Pluribus Unicorn* seem exploratory or allusive; all show his stylistic mastery. Sturgeon's greatest weakness lies in creating satisfactory conclusions to his stories, a problem more obvious in his novels than in his shorter works. Still, some of these tales seem either hastily written or truncated, and many of them give the impression of being postmodern, requiring the reader to complete the tale. On the other hand, "The Silken-Swift" is rightly construed as a masterpiece both of literary elegance and behavioral analysis, as is "Bianca's Hands," though with entirely the opposite emotional impact.

Sturgeon taught himself and wonderfully employs the literary technique of using poetic meter in prose passages for emotional effect. This shows up most clearly in the fully accomplished works—"The Silken-Swift," "Bianca's Hands," "A Saucer of Loneliness," "The World Well Lost," and "Die, Maestro, Die"—although it can be detected in virtually every story. It appears clear that Sturgeon derived the initial impetus from his observations of partial or inadequate responses to emotional and social problems. His observations inevitably led him to pose alternative, imaginative ways of dealing with (if not solving) these problems. The reader gets the feeling of looking over Sturgeon's shoulder as he develops his personal motto: "Ask the next question." In his later years, Sturgeon wore a silver Q with an arrow through it as a symbol of this motto.

In all these stories, Sturgeon clearly, analytically, and sympathetically delineates characters with some strengths and many weaknesses, showing the difficulties they encounter with an unsympathetic world (one especially unsympathetic to weaknesses or differences). His treatments of underground cultures, particularly that of homosexuals, likely influenced such writers as Samuel Delany and Harlan Ellison. Even when Sturgeon's characters behave in desperate or unbalanced ways, they refuse either blame or rejection. Sturgeon's stories clarify the terror of being utterly "known," with nothing hidden. When he creates a deranged or desperate character, he tells the story from that character's own point of view, making the reader understand and, to an extent, sympathize. When he creates a character with warm, human sympathies, readers feel as though they have made a new friend. It is this characteristic of radical acceptance, of wise understanding couched in lyric prose, that readers gain—and appreciate—in Sturgeon's stories.

—*Martha A. Bartter*

EARTH

A black hole drops by accident into Earth's interior, forcing the human race to come to terms with the planets growing environmental problems

Author: David Brin (1950–)
Genre: Science fiction—cautionary
Type of work: Novel
Time of work: 2038
Locale: Various locations on Earth
First published: 1990

THE STORY

The action in *Earth* takes place at a time when overpopulation and environmental destruction have pushed planetary resources to the limit. With natural habitats destroyed by war or global warming, and with Earths ozone layer depleted by pollution, many plants and animals have become all but extinct, with a few remnants kept in steel and glass arks. Refugees from nations flooded by rising seas drift on rafts across the oceans; there is no land on which to settle. In the United States, tribal gangs of teenagers without jobs clash with the growing elderly populations of vast suburbs. In this future, computer technology has emerged as the one bright spot, linking everyone on Earth into the ultimate free press: an interconnected information network that spans the globe.

In an attempt to solve Earth's energy crisis, brilliant young physicist Alex Lustig uses the illegal technology of cavitronics to create a tuned cosmic string, or black hole, inside a power plant. When his experiment is destroyed in a riot, the black hole escapes confinement and sinks into Earths mantle. Afraid that its uncontrolled growth might engulf the planet, Lustig recruits the help of Maori billionaire George Hutton, whose geophysical surveying company has the technology to locate the tiny singularity. Although their work shows that Lustigs black hole is dissipating, its orbit through the mantle reveals that it is not alone: A second, much larger, black hole is gnawing at Earths core. Its location and size indicate that it must have been dropped into the earth in 1908, at the site of the mysterious Tunguska explosion in Siberia. Because no humans could have created a singularity at that time, Lustig and Hutton realize that this black hole must be the product of alien technology, aimed as a weapon at the developing human civilization on Earth.

To combat this threat, Lustig plans to lift the alien black hole out of Earth's core using gazers, a new type of energy beam created when a black hole focuses Earth's own gravitational energy. Lustig, Hutton, and their most trusted colleagues establish a secret network of gazer control stations. These colleagues include Teresa Tikhana, a shuttle pilot who lost her husband to the first inadvertent gazer activity. Also joining the group is Jen Wolling, Lustigs grandmother, a Nobel-laureate biologist who is a computer net expert and a farsighted advocate for Earth.

News of this powerful new energy source leaks out, triggering a war between a conspiratorial aristocratic cabal, who want to use gazers as the ultimate long-distance weapons, and a fanatical environmentalist who tries to end Earths overpopulation problem with gazers programmed for human destruction. The clash of warring gazer beams burns an intricate pattern of superconducting channels into Earths metal core, creating an intelligent information network that all parties struggle to control. Jen Wolling ultimately wins, but the triumph both kills and immortalizes her. She becomes a disembodied mind within Earth, able to interact with the human race through the global computer network. The war ends as Gaea herself, in the form of Wollings transferred mind, takes control of the planets focused gravitational energy from within. With gazers now providing safe and limitless power, the human race is freed to explore space and restore environmental harmony to its home planet.

ANALYSIS

At first glance, *Earth* seems to fall squarely into the category of environmental dystopia, in which extrapolation of Earths current environmental problems predicts a hopelessly catastrophic state. Unlike many other environmental dystopias, in which science and technology are assigned sole blame for Earths destruction, *Earth* shows the problems as caused by the interaction of many millions of human beings, all doing simple things that in themselves might be harmless. David Brins scientists and technocrats, exemplified by physicist Alex Lustig and billionaire George Hutton, are neither evil nor apathetic about environmental disaster. Instead, they use science and technology as potent weapons to combat the black hole devouring Earths core, with the black hole serving as a metaphor for the ultimate pollution of the planet.

Brin is a Ph.D. physicist who incorporates accurate depictions of physics and of environmental and earth science throughout *Earth*. Examples of environmental extrapolations made by Brin that have come true include the rise in skin cancer rates resulting from ozone depletion, the increased frequency of hurricanes caused by global warming, and the flooding of coastal areas caused by glacial melting and rising sea levels. According to Brin, *Earth* was to a great degree inspired by John Brunners *Stand on Zanzibar* (1968), which predicted home computers, rock music videos, environmentalism, and other elements of popular culture. Brunner also invented the hypertext style used in Earth to intersperse brief glimpses of the near future throughout the story line. The density of detail in these computer net excerpts combines with reproduced computer output from Lustigs analysis of the black hole to give *Earth* an extraordinary reality and vividness.

The complex and interlaced structure of *Earth* echoes the complicated linkages of Earths planetary systems. Brin focuses his multiple plot lines on different characters and different environmental and social problems at first, then slowly makes connections among them. In the same way that links between Earths rocks, oceans, and atmospheres can be unseen and yet exert a powerful influence on the environment, Brins plot lines converge in unexpected ways to carry the story to its strong and satisfying conclusion. Although casual readers may become distracted by the novels large cast of characters and its sprawling story line, Earth is a book that richly rewards those who read to the end.

—*Karen Rose Cercone*

Earth Abides

After a plague destroys most of humanity, a few survivors struggle to adapt to new conditions of life without the benefits of modern technology

Author: George R. Stewart (1895–1980)
Genre: Science fiction—post-holocaust
Type of work: Novel
Time of work: Approximately 1950 to 2000
Locale: Berkeley, California
First published: 1949

THE STORY

On a field expedition, Ish Williams, a young graduate student of geography, is bitten by a rattlesnake. He lies near death in a cabin, unaware that a virus is wiping out humanity. When he finally staggers down from the mountains, he finds deserted towns, empty highways, dead bodies, looted stores, and other signs of an incredible disaster. He is unable to make any telephone or radio contact. Old newspapers tell of the plague ravaging every continent. He believes that the rattlesnake venom in his system must have counteracted the virus and saved his life.

Ish decides to drive across the United States, helping himself to supplies along the way. The few survivors he finds seem too stupid, immoral, or psychologically traumatized to qualify as long-term companions. Eventually he returns to Berkeley, with only a dog for companionship.

Although Ish feels lonely, his situation is enviable in some respects. He has unlimited quantities of everything he needs, including a million books at the university. He has been a quiet, studious person all his life and does not need human companionship as much as do others. There is no danger from animals yet, nor any reason to fear other humans because of the abundance of goods.

Ish encounters a woman named Em who has been living alone. They soon become lovers, entering into a form of marriage by pledging their vows. Over the ensuing years, they have a number of children. A handful of men and women join them, eventually forming a tribe of about three dozen. Ish becomes leader because of his intelligence and education. He undertakes the education of the children, hoping to pass on the skills and values of the vanished civilization. Other tribe members contribute their skills to maintaining comfort and sanitation.

The introspective Ish observes the gradual deterioration of the infrastructure of modern civilization. Electricity lasts a short while before generators fail, plunging the Bay Area into darkness. The aqueducts last much longer before water stops flowing and the tribe has to dig wells. Automobiles are useful for years but gradually become rusted hulks. Streets and roads become shattered and overgrown. The tribes world narrows to a few square miles.

All except Ish are content to live as squatters and scavengers. Ish realizes that the time will come when people will have to know the simple skills of hunting, fishing, and agriculture. The children and adults respect his words but do not understand him; they regard him as a mystic and prophet. The only person capable of understanding him is his son Joey, but this perceptive child is killed by a disease brought by an outsider named Charlie who is riddled with germs. At a momentous meeting, the leaders agree to execute Charlie and rid themselves of his potential to destroy their fragile society.

At the end of the novel, Ish is an old man. All of his contemporaries have died. Power has passed to younger members of the tribe who are ignorant of the old civilization but have become expert hunters, fishers, and cultivators. Fires have destroyed most of the Bay Area. People use bows and arrows, and they live very much like the early California Indians. Ish is revered and cared for, although no one has any use for the knowledge he retains from the past. At his death, Ish realizes that the civilization he knew was only one incident in the long history of Earth itself. He comforts himself with a quotation from Ecclesiastes: "Men go and come, but earth abides."

ANALYSIS

Earth Abides was published at the beginning of the Cold War that pitted the Communist bloc against the capitalist world. The Soviets had demonstrated their nuclear capability, and many people began to contemplate a war that would wipe out civilization. Many writers produced fiction in which they presented their conceptions of a world in which civilization had been destroyed and a few survivors were reduced to a primitive mode of existence. *Earth Abides* served as a model for many succeeding imitations, which rarely measured up to the original in sincerity of purpose or quality of writing.

"What if?" plots appeal to readers both for the intellectual exercise they offer and for the mixed emotions they arouse. The imaginary scenario of *Earth Abides* is horrible and appealing at the same time. It would be horrible to be one of the majority who perish but perhaps interesting to be one of the survivors, with the wealth of the world at ones disposal. People would have the satisfaction of being surrounded by their extended families rather than seeing children and grandchildren dispersed by modern economic forces. Some readers of post-holocaust stories are attracted to the fantasy of ridding the world of the complexities of modern civilization and being able to build a simpler society based on cooperation and nonalienating work.

George R. Stewart achieved fame by writing two best-selling novels, *Storm* (1941) and *Fire* (1948), in which forces of nature are, in a sense, the protagonists. His ability to depict the grandeur of nature is displayed once again in *Earth Abides*, the first winner of the International Fantasy Award. In the grim years following World War II, all three of Stewarts novels contributed to the budding environmental revolution.

Stewart envisages his post-holocaust world as a peaceful place where there is little disease and little competition. Other writers have envisaged different post-holocaust scenarios. Walter Van Tilburn Clark's chilling story "The Portable Phonograph" (1941), for example, depicts cave-dwelling survivors of a global war willing to murder for such treasures as a portable phonograph and a few recordings of awe-inspiring music from the lost world of civilization. Most post-holocaust fiction carries the same implicit or explicit message: Civilization is a precious thing that needs intelligence, self-restraint, vigilance, and international cooperation to survive. Once lost through war, pollution, overpopulation, scientific recklessness, or other human folly, it may never be recovered.

—*Bill Delaney*

EARTHFASTS

King Arthur and his knights are disturbed from their long sleep under Garebrough Castle and, in turn, disturb the inhabitants of the town

Author: William Mayne (1928–2010)
Genre: Fantasy—time travel
Type of work: Novel
Time of work: The early 1960s
Locale: North Yorkshire, England
First published: 1966

THE STORY
The book is divided into four parts: "This Aye Night," "Standing Stones," "On Hare Trod," and "Fire and Fleet and Candlelight." The central characters are two fifteen-year-old boys: David Wix, whose father is a doctor, and Keith Heseltine, whose father is a lawyer. They live in the small town of Garebrough in the Yorkshire Dales of northern England.

In the first part, they discover, in late summer, movement of the earth in a field outside town. From it emerges a red-coated drummer boy, Nelly Jack John, who had been, he claimed, in a garrison based at the castle in town. He had gone searching for treasure underground, following a local legend that King Arthur and his knights lay buried under the castle mound. The two boys realize that the drummer boy must have entered the under-ground passage he had found in the mid-eighteenth century but did not seem to be aware of any passage of time. When the drummer boy is finally made to believe this, he returns into the ground as he came. The drummer boy leaves behind a candle, which David picks up and takes home. It does not appear to give light or consume itself, and its flame cannot be extinguished and burns cold.

The second part of the story, set in the fall, brings to light other strange phenomena: a boggart (goblin) is found in a moorland farm, standing stones appear to have moved on the moor, a wild boar is heard of, and many pigs are stolen.

David and Keith investigate these happenings in the third part. Hare Trod is an ancient trackway on the moors, and their search centers on it. David also becomes addicted to staring at the candle and becomes aware of invisible presences. In the climax, the boys return from Hare Trod convinced they can see giants and a huge whirling thing that flattens the grass in circles. They are aware of an attacking presence, and Keith blacks out. When he comes around, David has disappeared and is presumed dead. Many of the phenomena are named at the inquest, but because there is no scientific explanation, a verdict of death by lightning is recorded.

In the final part, it is winter. Keith has retrieved David's candle. One night, its light reveals that his yard is filled with horsemen—King Arthur and his knights. It is their candle that Nelly Jack John stole, and the theft has awakened them before their time. Keith submits to their will, enters the tunnel, and returns the candle to the Round Table. As he does this, he sees David, who is unaware of the passing of time. As they find their way out, they encounter the drummer boy, who is struggling against time to return through the tunnel. They take him with them and re-emerge in their own time the same night. David is reunited with his father, and Nelly Jack John goes to live on the farm where the boggart has quieted down. The other phenomena cease.

ANALYSIS

Like his character David, William Mayne was the son of a doctor and spent his boyhood in Yorkshire, where he returned later in life. *Earthfasts* thus reflects Mayne's own experiences; his descriptions of the moors, dales, times, and seasons constitute some of the most powerful parts of his writing and suggest that he is at heart a realistic writer.

Earthfasts was Mayne's first excursion into fantasy as a children's writer. His first novel, *Following the Footprints* (1953), was followed by more than forty books in twenty years, the majority of which were realist, often with a historical dimension. Other fantasy novels, such as *Ravensgill* (1970), also have Yorkshire settings. It has been suggested that Mayne was pushed into fantasy by the success of Alan Garner. The latter's *The Weirdstone of Brisingamen* appeared in 1960 and does resemble *Earthfasts* in locale, the intrusion of past time into the present, and the motif of reawakened knights prematurely disturbed.

Mayne certainly is conscious of the fantasy elements in his story. Much of the dialogue is about the nature of scientific evidence and explanation. At one point, David must warn Keith to treat the drummer boy as a real person with real emotions of confusion and fear, and not as a scientific experiment. Some of this dialogue is philosophical.

One of the critical difficulties with *Earthfasts*, as with other books by Mayne, is that although it is children's fantasy, its style and concepts are much more likely to appeal to adults. Critic John Rowe Townsend describes the style as oblique, elliptical, and tangential. It is also intelligent. Adults are likely to be disappointed, however, by the lack of characterization and personal relationships. David's death and reappearance, for example, are never described as personal losses or joys for his father or his friend.

The first part is the most successful; there, Mayne combines fantasy with the solid realism of the Yorkshire setting most effectively. The red-coated drummer boy marching off to find a home that readers know disappeared two hundred years ago is both poignant and symbolically resonant. The dialect Mayne gives him is likewise striking, if not always consistent.

In this example of time fantasy, Mayne raises interesting questions and makes the reader feel time as material, as weight and resistance. The overall feeling is of a mythically alive landscape, deeply and intelligently experienced by its author.

—*David Barratt*

THE EARTH'S CHILDREN SERIES

Surviving adoption by Neanderthals, Cro-Magnon Ayla discovers that survival requires adaptation and earning acceptance from Cro-Magnon groups as she journeys across prehistoric Europe during the Ice Age

Author: Jean M. Auel (1936–)
Genre: Science fiction—evolutionary fantasy
Type of work: Novels
Time of work: The late Pleistocene epoch, 35,000–25,000 b.c.e.
Locale: Prehistoric Europe
First published: *The Clan of the Cave Bear* (1980), *The Valley of Horses* (1982), *The Mammoth Hunters* (1985), *The Plains of Passage* (1990), *The Shelters of Stone* (2002), and *The Land of Painted Caves* (2011)

The Story

Envisioned as a six-volume history of Cro-Magnon heroine Ayla, the Earth's Children series began with Jean Auels vision of a young woman living among people different from her. Having been a credit manager, technical writer, and occasional poet, Auel completed her M.B.A. in 1976 and began research on Neanderthal and Cro-Magnon peoples. Studies of animal evolution, physical remains, wild plant life, and flint knapping, along with wilderness training, allowed Auel to create a detailed geographic and cultural tapestry into which she wove fictional characters passions and ideas.

Ayla is adopted into the Neanderthal Clan of the Cave Bear on the Crimean Peninsula after her family dies in an earthquake. She unlearns her birth culture, adapting to older Clan ways, seeing her blue-eyed blondeness as ugly, and exchanging language for hand signals. She is shamed that lack of racial memories makes her ignorant in comparison to clan children who "remember." She accepts clan totems and their spirit world. When a man "gives his signal," she must respond and assume position to be mounted.

Quick to adapt, Ayla learns medicine woman skills from her adopted mother, Iza, saves Clan members, and remains under the protection of the one-eyed Clan shaman Creb. As an outsider, Ayla threatens ancient Clan traditions, breaks forbidden taboos, survives a death curse, becomes designated the Woman Who Hunts after mastering the forbidden slingshot, and defies Clan custom by keeping her deformed child. Cursed with death by Broud, a childhood tyrant and the new Clan leader, Ayla leaves in search of her own people.

Ayla settles in a cave in a valley shared with steppe horses. She discovers almost supernatural abilities to interact with animals. She rescues a mare, befriends a foal named Whinney, and serves as midwife at the birth of the stallion Racer. A huge cave lion named Baby and a gray wolf figure in Aylas adventures, stunning less progressive Cro-Magnons.

Far from the west, Jondalar and his brother Thonolan journey across glaciers, following the Great Mother River (Danube) from headwaters to mouth. Dazed by the death of his new mate, Thonolan faces a cave lion and dies, leaving Jondalar to be rescued by Ayla from Baby, the she lions mate. Jondalars healing, Aylas recovery of language, and the inventions of this enterprising couple (including spear throwers, fire starters of flint and iron pyrite, sewing needles, and equine harnesses) complete the second novel. The blond, blue-eyed couples love grows as Jondalar teaches Ayla about the Earth Mother and introduces her to sexual first rites she was denied in brutal encounters with Broud. Seeing sexual pleasure as the Mothers gift, Ayla learns a new cultural imperative respecting females as life source.

Ayla's challenges continue as she and Jondalar winter with Mamutoi mammoth hunters, who reintroduce her to community and female companionship while presenting the threat of competition and a fear of her adoptive Clan (always called "flatheads" by her own kind). Considering her magical firestones, her mystical mastery over animals, and her uncanny healing powers, the old shaman Mamut adopts her into Mammoth Hearth, giving her both the family she seeks and supernatural identity matching her skills.

Ayla faces continuing prejudice because of her background. She watches the adopted child Rydag, obviously of mixed parentage, suffer the ridicule her own lost son must be encountering.

Through evoking Rydag's racial memories and teaching Clan hand signals to the Mamutoi, she convinces the Mamutoi that flatheads are human.

Ayla must also consider whether to mate with handsome Ranec, a skilled worker of ivory and the first black man she meets. She is drawn to Ranec and misunderstands Jondalars offer of freedom of choice, concluding that he rejects her. She therefore accepts Ranecs proposal. Jondalars sudden departure brings about reconciliation, setting the stage for the fourth novel, which retraces the journey across icy steppes to Jondalars home.

The Plains of Passage continues the adventure on horseback across changing geographic and climatic conditions. Ayla and Jondalar encounter a range of cultures, visit tribes he already knows, watch mating mammoths, heal a Clansmans broken leg, get caught up in a matriarchal prison culture in which a crazed leader punishes men for her girlhood abuse, cross the glacier under travail, nearly lose but manage to save the animals, meet some of Jondalars relatives, and finally reach his home, the ninth cave of the Zelandonii. Auel provides abundant description, interspersed with tribal adventures and the blossoming of Ayla and Jondalars relationship as the couple discusses art, food, and celebrations. Although the huge novel ends without a meeting with Jondalars family, Ayla recognizes his cave as one the dead Creb has led her toward in her dreams. She, too, is home. Books five and six find Ayla migrating to the lands of her adopted people, the Zelandonii, and integrating into their culture, not without crises that birth insights which will reshape the tribe and which will ultimately lead to our present-day civilizations.

ANALYSIS

The popular, somewhat controversial Earth Children series extrapolates backward, drawing on anthropology and archaeology, including figurines of idealized mother figures. Science fiction of prehistory, exploring human origins, has been dismissed as "caveman," but this series defies such categorization.

Concepts are carefully interwoven. Clear inventions both raise scientific questions and complicate the plot. Neanderthal racial memory (based on large brain size) gives rise to extrasensory power even as it explains why the older group disappeared. Racial memory hinders adaptability to changing conditions, leading Clans to reject new options. Ayla and Jondalar represent Cro-Magnon learning. They think through problems rather than meditating on ancestral knowledge, invent devices, and question the natural world. Ayla even challenges spiritual wisdom, suggesting that babies might come from copulation, not the Great Mother.

Ayla is a curious character. She is a Cro-Magnon child who learns from Neanderthals, but what explains her peculiar power? Haunted by recurring nightmares of losing her mother to an earthquake, her dream journeys become more mystical after she connects with Creb by drinking magic potions concocted for magicians at the Summer Gathering. Her spirits touching of Crebs empowers her throughout the series, a fact Mamut recognizes from the moment he meets her. Mamuts very existence suggests that Cro-Magnons may also have mystical powers. Aylas have been enhanced by the blending of her own peoples magic with that of older magicians.

Aylas special destiny is noted by every person of power. This issue moves the series closer to fantasy than to science fiction. Auel explores parapsychology, depicting Aylas use of intuition and her communicative abilities. At other times, she contrasts superstition and scientific comprehension.

Also central to this series are explorations of the alien. Aylas cultural norms are shattered and redefined by her adoptive Neanderthal clan, by Jondalars Cro-Magnon teachings, and eventually by her shocked realization that those she seeks to love see her first family as flatheads. Defending the Clan, she sees her beating and rapes by Broud as the case of a single individual filled with hatred. The young Cro-Magnon men who seek out and rape women—first Clan women, whom they perceive as animals, and later people like themselves—are learning to categorize and demean in a way most Cro-Magnons do not. The spirit of wide acceptance and curiosity Ayla finds among the Cro-Magnons, after she explains the Clan to them, becomes a prototype of acceptable human behavior toward outsiders. Even an older species such as the Clan adopts and raises Ayla, a child from outside the group, granting her exceptional possibilities.

The progression from Neanderthal to Cro-Magnon is marked by increased open-mindedness, recognition of the equality of women, and equitable division of labor. All adults choose their work; some women hunt and some men can cook. Ayla witnesses free exchange of sexual pleasures (the Great Mothers gift) as well as desire to meet "the other" and perhaps to recognize the alien within.

In this context, romance is heavily stressed. The sexual scenes tend to be copies from one chapter or novel to the next, though settings are strikingly different. For some, this romance carries the series, while for others it detracts. Despite critical carping, Ayla's discovery of certain sex acts carries no implication that they have not been tried before, probably by Jondalar with other partners.

He specifies that young people are taught this art. More serious is criticism that Ayla and Jondalar are too perfect and too blond. They solve problems too quickly and are too adept in psychological analysis. Anthropologists object to Auel's extrapolation from theory, some of it shaky. Despite these flaws, the series is enormously entertaining, drawing the reader into another universe of time, place, and personality. Critical acclaim includes the American Academy of Achievements Golden Plate Award (1986), the American Book Awards nomination for best first novel (1981), and the Pacific Northwest Booksellers Associations Award for Excellence in Writing (1980). Each book enjoyed long tenure on best-seller lists.

—*Twila Yates Papay*

EARTHSEA

A trilogy relating the adventures of Ged from his days as a young goatherd to his rule as Archmage

Author: Ursula K. Le Guin (1929–)
Genre: Fantasy—high fantasy
Type of work: Novels
Time of work: Undefined, on another world
Location: A cluster of islands known as Earthsea
First published: *Earthsea* (1977, as trilogy; also published as *The Earthsea Trilogy*, 1979); previously published as *A Wizard of Earthsea* (1968), *The Tombs of Atuan* (1971), *The Farthest Shore* (1972), and *The Other Wind* (2001)

THE STORY

Earthsea begins on the island of Gont, a land famous for wizards. There, a young goatherd named Ged, called Duny as a boy and called Sparrowhawk familiarly, overhears his aunt using a common, rustic spell on the animals. Ged duplicates the words, but without any understanding of them. The spell works, and the goats come running around Ged. He is terrified, because he has no knowledge of how to undo the spell.

The event is revealing. Ged has powers, but as a teenage boy he is naïve about those powers. He has no knowledge and thus no mastery, and power without knowledge is a dangerous thing. At first, Ged is in love with power itself. The island Mage, Ogion, recognizes the power within Ged and attempts to nurture it with understanding.

Restless in his training, Ged eventually is sent to the island of Roke, the spiritual locus for all Earthsea and training ground for mastery of magical power. Ged learns it all too well. In his competition with an older student, Jasper, Ged succumbs to the use of his arts for mere personal power. In an effort to summon the spirit of a dead woman, he unleashes a shadowlike creature into the world of Earthsea. The creature comes to represent the dark uses of magical power as a shadow self of Ged himself, lured to personal glorification. *A Wizard of Earthsea* concludes with Ged's defeat of the shadow. The defeat is only a temporary abeyance of its threat, however, for Ged has neither fully understood its significance nor mastered its nature.

The second novel, *The Tombs of Atuan,* shifts in point of view from Ged to a young priestess, Tenar. Renamed Arka, the Eaten One, Tenar serves the ancient powers of Earth among the desert tombs of Atuan. She traps Ged, on a quest to find the Ring of Erreth-Akbe, in the labyrinth beneath the temple. Ged tells her her true name and identity, and she decides to join him on his quest. They succeed, but at the cost of the temple's destruction. Tenar returns with Ged to Gont, where she will live with Ogion.

The second novel reveals Ged's growing mastery of magical arts and his increasing power through them. The power enables him to know the true things and hidden essences veiled within an outward nature. The increasingly complicated riddle is whether he truly knows his own essence, particularly in relation to the shadow.

In *The Farthest Shore*, Ged is now Archmage, the most powerful magician in Earthsea. His power has deepened with knowledge. He receives a message from a young prince named Arren, the narrator of the story, that increasingly people are rejecting the beliefs that grant their lives wholeness. Ged discovers that a wayward Mage has opened a hole in the earth, letting disharmony flood the land. Ged's quest is to close that gap, to confront the shadows of disharmony, and to use his power to restore Earth's balance. He must finally confront and master the shadow of his own nature. As is so often the case in fantasy literature, the ultimate quest is for self-understanding. Succeeding in his quest, Ged returns to the peace of Gont among the goats.

ANALYSIS
The basic framework of *Earthsea* is the pattern of the initiation story. In such stories, a naïve and innocent young person acquires knowledge and experience. The pattern is familiar in high fantasy, a subgenre explicitly about magical powers and their harms and benefits. In this case, the young protagonist discovers knowledge about such magical powers and inevitably confronts some conflict about the mastery of the powers. Tempted to turn them to mere personal gain, the protagonist is caught between that desire and the urgent needs of others. A second constituent element of fantasy literature, the quest, operates powerfully in the trilogy and provides the high adventure of the plot. In addition, as in many works of fantasy, the quest parallels the protagonist's discovery of a hidden self.

Within this traditional framework, Ursula K. Le Guin exercises her own kind of literary magic. She is influenced by the teachings of the *Taote Ching* ("Classic of the Way and Its Virtue"), supposedly created by the sixth century b.c.e. Chinese philosopher Lao Tzu. Le Guin has orchestrated classical elements of Daoism, and its later developments with Buddhism beginning in the third century c.e. into her novels. Fundamental Daoist points influencing the development of the plots include the belief that life consists of a balance and that every human action affects that balance, the belief that through "weakness" or service to others lies one's strength, and the belief that bureaucratic or political power threatens the balance.

The idea of balance is key, particularly as fundamental Daoism affected the religion of Buddhism and acquired wide popular appeal. Balance harmonizes conflicting tensions. Every darkness contains a bit of light, every sorrow a bit of joy, and so forth. One must live life so as to provide an equilibrium between the tensions.

In *Earthsea*, that balance is terribly distorted when the naïve young Ged first exercises his magical power as an act of proud competition on the island of Roke. He violates orders and therefore violates harmony. He unleashes the shadow of disorder into Earthsea. Ged must come face to face with the shadow that lies within himself, the pride-humility, love-hatred dialectics in his own nature.

As he moves from naïveté to growing awareness of his magical gifts, Ged begins to comprehend the challenge to those gifts. As is so often the pattern in fantasy, he is abetted by the appearance of a special helper, in this case the Mage Ogion, who tutors Ged in the nature of the powers that constitute the balance. At his earliest stage, Ged hungers for power. Gradually, he comes to understand The Powers for their sake and for that of others. His unleashing of the shadow shapes the transition in this realization.

During his advanced training at Roke, Ged quickly outstrips even his masters in knowledge of magical power. One challenge remains: mastery of The Powers to restore harmony. As he restores harmony in the lives of others whom he has threatened by unleashing the shadow, he discovers that by serving others he restores himself. This is the discovery in *The Tombs of Atuan*.

In her illustration of discovery of a true self, Le Guin orchestrates another interesting variation on a traditional fantasy pattern. In the Western literary tradition, the task of the classical hero is twofold: to defeat some threat to the people and to lead the people into a perception of restorative order. To achieve these ends, the classical hero is divinely gifted, sometimes considered, in fact, part human and part god. With these gifts, the classical hero acts for the people, frequently in a superhuman way.

The fantasy hero lies in this tradition but with a difference. The fantasy hero has no pretensions to superhuman status; the hero's origins often are common, even lowly. Fantasy heroes often take on their quests with fear and quite often with a desperate loneliness. The heart of modern fantasy is the premise of a very ordinary character being tested beyond expectation or human hope for success. This hero, although often provided with supernatural helpers, ultimately must rely on little more than human intelligence and determination. The quest to aid others ultimately is a test of the hero's own nature and sufficiency.

The Farthest Shore brings the Archmage Ged to the final step in his quest for harmony. That step is not completed through knowledge, concern for others, or an apprehension of universal order in balance; it is completed in action that leads to internal restoration of balance. The final quest leads to Ged's confrontation with the shadow, which ultimately is his final reconciliation with his own nature and the subduing of his errors of pride. Ged's friend Esstarriol observes that Ged made himself whole. Knowing his true self, Ged cannot be used or possessed by any power other than himself, "never in the service of ruin, or pain, or hatred, or the dark."

—*John H. Timmerman*

EARTHSEED

The children who are to populate a new world are stymied by the violent human heritage they carry from the old world

Author: Pamela Sargent (1948–)
Genre: Science fiction—cosmic voyage
Type of work: Novel
Time of work: Near the end of a one-hundred-year space voyage
Locale: Aboard an asteroid space vessel and on an unnamed planet
First published: 1983

THE STORY

Earthseed is distinguished by the fact that it was the first novel that author Pamela Sargent wrote for young adults. It concerns a group of adolescents who have been reared on a space vessel by its computer in order to populate a new world. This scenario is complicated by two factors. The first is the violent instinct of the human race, reflected in the behavior of the children and the stowaway adults. The second, as important, is the true nature of the Project, which has been kept secret from both Ship and the children.

Sargent's novel centers on fifteen-year-old protagonist Zoheret, her teenage companions, and their relationship to the Project. They believe that they and their vessel, a computerized asteroid called Ship, were created by Earth-based scientists in order to seed a new world and thus expand the range of the human species.

In part 1, the young people live in a series of well-equipped corridors in the vessel, all of their wants and needs taken care of by Ship. This Edenic existence is disturbed when Ship sends the youngsters on their first step toward independence from the asteroid incubator: a team competition to cross the Hollow, the Earth-like interior of the vessel. During this test, violent tendencies in the children—particularly in the boys Ho and Manuel—lead to serious injuries and hard feelings.

Part 2, which makes up the bulk of *Earthseed*, concerns itself with the roots and the consequences of violence and treachery in the human species. This section finds the young people living in the Hollow on a full-time basis. The violence that characterized the competition intensifies as the future colonists must struggle without Ship's protection. A raid by Ho on Zoheret's group leads to escalating violence, and Ho uses hostages as bargaining chips.

The plot becomes more complicated when Zoheret stumbles on a second group of young people that Ship secretly has kept in suspended animation. Their prospective world was deemed uninhabitable. Zoheret's group is stunned when adults forcibly wrest control of their encampment and turn it into a concentration camp. Secretly stowed away aboard the vessel without Ship's knowledge, these adults created the Project and are the genetic parents of the children. Their goal was to seed many new planets, not only one, and thus create new human societies. Their distrust of technology prompted them to steal themselves aboard Ship and resume control of the Project. Zoheret is captured by the adults, escapes to one of the corridors, and enlists the help of the other group of young people. Together, they restore Ship's mind, which had been turned off by the intruders, and capture the adults.

The brief final section of the novel is set one year later, on the new planet. All the young people live there, with Zoheret as leader of one group, Ho leader of another, and Aleksandr leader of the children who had been in suspended animation. Ship, having settled the young people, sets off on its own journey, independent of its creators. It will seed the adults, who are now in suspended animation, as well as the new humans that it will rear.

ANALYSIS

Science-fiction enthusiasts will recognize some familiar elements in *Earthseed*. The story of children living in physical isolation who reveal their inherently violent tendencies was explored thoroughly by William Golding in *Lord of the Flies* (1954). The concept of a sentient computer with control and surveillance over its human space cargo is at least as old as the malevolent HAL in Arthur C. Clarke's *2001: A Space Odyssey* (1968).

Sargent shares with these authors the ability to craft convincing characters in a future setting that is realistically possible. Zoheret earns her final position of leadership through daring and sacrifice (she loses an arm), and rivalries among the boys are typical of teenage males. Moreover, Sargent's fiction is based on real science. The Project designers are pragmatic in making use of an asteroid for their vessel, and its velocity is slightly less than the speed of light (something that has been deemed possible in the far distant future). Sargent correctly describes the effects on time of such a velocity. She demonstrates this same passion for realism in the novel *Venus of Dreams* (1986), in which future colonists transform Earths sister planet and create their own society. The most effective example of the authors sense of realism is her convincing treatment of the human condition. The violence inherent in *Homo sapiens*—a major theme of *Earthseed*—develops slowly as the children gain their independence and are forced to construct a society.

Also noteworthy is the feminism in this work. The violence is perpetrated largely by impulsive males, both in the corridors and in the Hollow. Zoheret, with her combination of intelligence and strength, sets the correct example for the new colonists. This prefigures Sargent's *The Shore of Women* (1986), a novel that describes a world dominated by women.

Critical reception of *Earthseed* was generally, but by no means wholly, positive. A critic in *Kirkus Reviews* claimed that the novel was "marred by sententious and preachy tendencies." Other reviewers praised Sargent's ability to craft an interesting protagonist within an exciting story. *Earthseed* was a *Booklist* Reviewers Choice for 1983 and was named as one of the Best Books for Young Adults for the same year by the American Library Association.

—*Cliff Prewencki*

ECHOES FROM THE MACABRE

Nine tales of mystery and suspense that explore the dark side of human nature and contain strong elements of the surreal and the supernatural

Author: Daphne du Maurier (1907–1989)
Genre: Fantasy—extrasensory powers

Type of work: Stories
Time of work: The recent past
Locale: England, Crete, and Greece
First published: 1976 ("The Apple Tree," "The Birds," "Kiss Me Again, Stranger," and "The Old Man" previously published in *The Apple*

Tree: A Short Novel and Some Stories, 1952; "Not After Midnight," "Don't Look Now," "The Pool," "The Blue Lenses," and "The Chamois" previously published in *Not After Midnight*, 1971, also released as *Don't Look Now*)

THE STORY

The best stories in this collection are about ordinary persons who have psychic or surreal experiences. In "Don't Look Now," John and Laura, an English couple who have gone to Venice to recover from the death of their daughter, Christine, encounter two elderly twin sisters, one of whom is blind and psychic. She tells them that Christine is alive. When they hear that night that their son is ill, Laura flies back to England alone. While she is gone, John is convinced that he sees Laura, in Venice, and in the company of the mysterious sisters. Things become more sinister when he calls England and Laura answers the phone. He is then told by the blind sister that he has had a psychic experience. What he saw, she says, was Laura returning to Venice for John's own funeral. The story comes to a bizarre conclusion when John pursues a little girl he thinks is Christine but who turns out to be a dwarf with a sharp knife.

"The Apple Tree" is the story of a man who is convinced that a gnarled old apple tree outside his bedroom window is the spirit of his dead wife, come back to take revenge on him for being glad she is gone. Its wood smolders instead of burns, its blossoms are ugly, and its fruit is inedible. When at last, in a blind rage, the man chops the tree down during a snowstorm, his foot gets trapped in the stump, and there is no one around to hear his cries for help.

"The Blue Lenses" is the story of a woman who is given a special implant to restore her sight. Temporary blue lenses are implanted first. When she looks through them, she sees animal heads on humans and realizes that she is seeing people for what they really are, particularly her husband, who has the head of a vulture, and the night nurse, who has the head of a snake. After a second implant restores her perception of others, she looks at herself in the mirror and sees the head of a submissive doe.

"Not After Midnight" is the story of Timothy Grey, an English schoolmaster and amateur artist who, while on holiday on Crete, comes under the evil influence of mythological deities as personified by the Stolls, an obnoxious American couple. When they catch Greg spying on them, Mr. Stoll sends him a small urn in the shape of Silenus, drunken tutor to the god Dionysus. When Grey finds Mr. Stoll's dead body and realizes that Mrs. Stoll has killed him, he finds himself helplessly drawn toward the same Dionysian excess that corrupted Mr. Stoll.

"The Birds" is an apocalyptic story of what happens when birds turn predatory and set out to destroy civilization. An isolated farmhouse on the coast of Cornwall in England becomes the focus of an attack being launched all over the world. At first, the farmer is able to board the windows and block the chimneys, but eventually he is outmaneuvered by the birds. In the end, he waits helplessly as the birds concentrate their attack on his front door.

ANALYSIS

Although Daphne du Maurier wrote fantasy, she was not exclusively a writer of fantasy. Most of her novels fall loosely under the label of gothic romance, with the noticeable exception of *The House on the Strand* (1969), the story of a drug-induced supernatural experience. It is in her short stories that she dabbled most freely in the realm of fantasy. Du Maurier used fantasy not as a gimmick but as a means of bringing the central situation of the story into sharper focus: grief-stricken parents susceptible to suggestions that their child is not really dead, a henpecked husband convinced that an ugly old apple tree is the spirit of his dead wife, a docile wife whose intuition is made visible when she looks through new lenses and sees people with the heads of animals that fit their personalities, an inhibited schoolmaster who feels himself yielding to the spell of ancient superstitions, and a farmer fighting a losing battle against savage birds.

There are echoes in du Maurier's stories of Edgar Allan Poe, of Nathaniel Hawthorne, and of Sheridan Le Fanu. The modern writer with whom she has the most in common is Ruth Rendell, whose novels of delusion and abnormal psychology explore the dark side of human nature, constantly reminding readers that things are not what they seem. In her technique of placing the macabre and the fantastic in ordinary settings, she has much in common with Stephen King, particularly in his novel *The Shining* (1977).

Although du Maurier wrote stories throughout her writing career, in her later years she came to favor this form. Her best stories are really novellas, in which she is free to pursue an idea or effect rather than concern herself with character development or romantic intrigue. In this collection, she deals with romance only once, in "Kiss Me Again, Stranger"; it is a sordid tale of perversion, revenge, and murder.

Critics have not always been as kind to du Maurier as her readers have, perhaps because she was so popular. There has, however, been grudging admiration for *Rebecca* (1938), now considered a classic of its kind, and for many of the stories in this collection. She has come to be recognized as an important influence in the field of fantasy fiction.

—*Thomas Whissen*

EDEN

A spaceship crew crashes on an unknown, Earth-like planet and encounters a strange and frightening civilization

Author: Stanisław Lem (1921–2006)
Genre: Science fiction—alien civilization
Type of work: Novel
Time of work: An indeterminate time in the future
Locale: The planet Eden
First published: 1959 (English translation, 1989)

The Story

As a result of a navigational error, a spaceship crew of six crashes on an unexplored Earth-like planet that they have called Eden, in recognition of the beautiful view that it offers from space. The members of the crew have no names; they are denoted by their professions: the Captain, the Doctor, the Chemist, the Engineer, the Physicist, and the Cyberneticist.

The crew members are faced with a double task. They must try, with the help of their robots, to repair their spaceship, which is partly buried in the ground; and they are eager to explore the planet, which is populated by strange beings that exhibit social phenomena that puzzle the earthlings.

The crew encounters a bizarre, spiderlike form of vegetation with bulbous growths that resemble abdomens. When nicked, the bulbs bleed a bright yellow sap that immediately coagulates in a thick resin, which gives off an intense odor that the humans find sickening. The crew members also discover gray trees that hiss and withdraw into the ground when touched. They encounter an abandoned factory that automatically produces objects of various forms and sizes, which are then melted down and brought back into the production process in an endless loop that produces nothing and serves no recognizable purpose. Elsewhere they find deserts, cities, and giant statues. They also find creatures they call "doublers," small beings with no face, often without eyes or ears, that sit in the kangaroo-like pouches of a half-ton gray mass. The doublers apparently are intelligent, but attempts at communication prove fruitless. When the humans dissect a doubler that has found its way into the spaceship, they find a needle in its liver; others have small tubes inserted in them, for purposes the crew cannot determine.

The landscape of Eden that the humans explore becomes more nightmarish. The crew discovers ditches and wells containing dead doublers. These show a number of variations: Some have one eye or more, mouths, or ears, and others do not. Crew members wonder if they have found evidence of mass executions or hunts.

During a nightly foray, the humans enter a city in which all lights go out on their arrival, concentrically from a center. They are surrounded by a throng of frightened doublers that seem to be unaware of them. The landscape is crisscrossed by thin, narrow lines. These are grooves in which disks resembling semitransparent wheels with spokes travel at high speed. The crew also observes a much larger type of vehicle. The humans themselves travel in one of the disks. From afar, they observe life in a busy city.

For the most part, the earthlings are ignored by the citys inhabitants, and there is no attempt at communication, but sometimes the spaceship is surrounded by rotating wheels that seem to observe. The ship is attacked by artillery shooting a kind of mechanical spore with cogs and wheels, from which grows a high mineral palisade. The humans are uncertain whether these attacks are meant to keep them inside the ship or to keep the population from contacting them. The humans get the impression that terrible things are happening on Eden, but they do not know for certain.

Finally, they are approached by a doubler scientist. Communication is vague, but it appears that on Eden, an experiment in autoevolution—an attempt to genetically re-create the population—went wrong. Many failures are judged to be unfit to live and are killed. The unknown rulers of the planet maintain the fiction that there were no experiments, that the mutants are the result of a sickness, and that nobody is responsible—in fact, that there is no government at all. The humans resist the urge to intervene because they do not understand what is going on. They take off into space as soon as they have repaired their ship.

ANALYIS

Eden is Stanisław Lem's first science-fiction novel to describe his skeptical philosophy, which maintains that humans are unable to comprehend true alienness. The pattern is repeated, in greater complexity, in novels such as *The Invincible* (1964), *His Masters Voice* (1968), and especially his masterpiece, *Solaris* (1961). With great richness of detail, Lem attempts to convey an impression of alien strangeness, of landscape, plants, machines, and architectural constructions, while leaving the underlying principles unknown and incomprehensible. The uncertainty gives rise to a mountain of anthropomorphizing interpretations. In *Eden*, there are only a few hints of the planets true character, concerning concentration camps, hunts, and exterminations of "unfit life."

The novel is political in a veiled way. In *Astronauci* (1951; the astronauts) and *Obłok Magellana* (1955; the Magellan nebula), Lem had presented an ideal Communist future; in *Eden*, the heroes are abstract representatives of humankind with no social ties at all. The tyranny of *Eden*, however, as far as it can be understood, seems to rest foremost in a total control of language and communication that recalls Communist practices. Social life seems to rest on gigantic lies, especially the fiction that there are no rulers, which seems to be an ironic twist on the Marxist doctrine of the withering away of government in a perfect socialist society. The novel rejects the Communist optimism that people can control social conditions and that there is a holy duty to help the oppressed. Who are the oppressed on Eden, and who are the oppressors? The visitors do not know what the political issues are, and any understanding may be faulty, as a projection of human notions onto an alien society. The visitors are horrified by what they see and burn to help, but they do nothing because, without comprehension, any attempt at intervention could bring about a much greater evil.

—*Franz Rottensteiner*

EDISON'S CONQUEST OF MARS

After the events described in H. G. Wells's The War of the Worlds, *Thomas Alva Edison duplicates the technology of the Martian war fleet and collaborates in the launching of a counterstrike*

Author: Garrett P. Serviss (1851–1929)
Genre: Science fiction—interplanetary romance
Type of work: Novel
Time of work: 1898
Locale: The environs of New York and the planet Mars

First published: 1947 (serial form, *The New York Evening Journal*, December 15, 1897-January 11, 1898)

THE STORY

Following the setback described at the conclusion of *The War of the Worlds* (1898), H. G. Wellss account of the Martian invasion of Earth, the survivors among those Martians who landed near New York retreat into space, destroying the city as they blast off. Thomas Edison examines various technological artifacts left behind by the invaders and deduces the principles involved in their operation. This allows him to produce his own designs for spaceships, powered by antigravity devices, and for new weapons. The latter are disintegrator rays more powerful than the Martians own heat rays.

After the test flight of Edisons prototype spaceship, Earths telescopes reveal new activity on Mars. A conference of world leaders puts together a $10 billion war chest so that a preemptive strike can be launched. Edison is awarded a contract to construct a fleet of spaceships and a vast arsenal of disintegrator rays.

The passengers in Edisons fleet include many of Earths leading scientists, such as Henri Moissan, Sylvanus P. Thompson, and Lord Kelvin (William Thomson).

When the Earth ships arrive in Martian local space, they are faced by a huge fleet of defenders, and immediate engagement is judged unwise. An expedition to a Martian asteroid mine discovers vast reserves of gold, and a subsequent descent to the planets surface leads to the discovery of a human girl named Aina. Her presence there is explained by the fact that the Martians had invaded Earth before, nine thousand years ago.

Aina is now the last human on Mars, the Martians having massacred the rest. She advises them that the Martians are too powerful to be defeated in battle, but that if the canals that distribute water to their cities were to be sealed at the points where they collect the tidal waters of the oceans, there would be a devastating flood. Following this plan, the Earthmen contrive the wreckage of Martian civilization but then must face the vengeful attacks of the Martian ships. Edisons fleet is reduced by half, but the Martians eventually capitulate.

ANALYSIS

Edison's Conquest of Mars was written in a hurry, beginning daily serialization in William Randolph Hearsts *The New York Evening Journal* immediately after the conclusion of *The War of the Worlds* was published in serial form. The speed of its production shows in its crudely contrived plot and its excruciatingly rough-hewn prose style, but it is an interesting work despite these faults.

Garrett P. Serviss was a leading American popularizer of science, and in his capacity as a science correspondent for the Hearst papers he had conducted a series of interviews with leading men of science, some of whom appear in the novel. He was the obvious man for Hearst or his local representative to turn to once the idea of spinning out Wells's story in a sensational sequel had been conceived. The insertion of real people into the plot enhanced its "news value" in a fashion pioneered by such legendary circulation boosters as Richard Adams Locke's "moon hoax", which in 1835 had described for the readers of *The New York Sun* telescopic discoveries allegedly made by Sir John Herschel. Hearst and his editors undoubtedly knew that the British newspaper magnates C. Arthur Pearson and Alfred Harmsworth were attempting to boost the circulation of some of their titles by printing extravagant serial stories of imaginary wars, often awarding significant minor roles to real politicians and military men.

Edison already was the star player in a burgeoning American mythology of technological cornucopia. Although World War I had not yet destroyed Europes hold on the economic heart of the world, Americans already considered their nation to be the cutting edge of progress, by virtue of its pioneering spirit. Edison was a frontiersman of science, boldly devising what no man had devised before. What American editor could resist the notion that although poor, decadent Britain had crumbled before the Martian assault, America had the will, the intelligence, and the qualities of natural leadership required for a spirited counteroffensive?

Serviss is generously cosmopolitan in assembling the team of scientists who provide the expedition with its intellectual teeth. Moissan was a Frenchman who later won the Nobel Prize for his discovery of fluorine, and Kelvin was the most distinguished English physicist of his day.

By virtue of its publication in an ephemeral medium, *Edison's Conquest of Mars* was quickly forgotten. It did not appear in book form until 1947, when it was rescued from obscurity by one of the small private presses operated by science-fiction fans. Historian Sam Moskowitz has pointed out, however, that because it was quickly reprinted by at least two other newspapers, it must have been available to several hundred thousand readers; this was far greater exposure than books of the day usually achieved. What Wells thought of it, if he ever knew of its existence, is unknown, but it is unlikely that he would have been pleased.

Serviss went on to write several more scientific romances, in a more polished and thoughtful manner, and many other writers went on to write similar revisionist accounts of the Martian invasion and its aftermath. One of the best of these is Howard Waldrop's "Night of the Cooters" (1987), which describes the adventures undertaken by Martians who landed in Texas while their counterparts were ravaging England. No matter how unreadable it may seem to a modern audience, *Edison's Conquest of Mars* occupies a pivotal position in the history of American science fiction, and there is no other early work that offers so frank an account of its ideological thrust.

—*Brian Stableford*

THE EINSTEIN INTERSECTION

Lobey, a musician, shepherd, warrior, lover, and telepath, embarks on a quest to retrieve Friza, his beloved, from the realm of death

Author: Samuel R. Delany (1942–)
Genre: Science fiction—mythological
Type of work: Novel
Time of work: The distant future
Location: A jungle village, a desert, and the city of Branning-at-Sea
First published: 1967

THE STORY

The surface story of this novel is a reliving of the Greek myth of Orpheus and Eurydice. Lobey and Friza fall in love, and after an all-too-brief period of happiness, she is killed. Still grieving for his lost love, Lobey embarks on a quest to confront Friza's murderer and retrieve her from death. Believing they know what killed Friza, the elders of Lobey's village send him to battle a mutation, a gigantic man-bull. He tracks it to its subterranean lair, and, like Theseus, slays the Minotaur in its Labyrinth. Lobey later finds that this creature was not, after all, Friza's killer. The real culprit is another mutation named Kid Death, a desert-born, white-skinned redhead with gills and a mouth full of shark's teeth who kills whatever frightens him. He has the power to reanimate those he kills. He can control, but he cannot create and cannot make order from chaos.

Like the mythic Orpheus, Lobey is a musician, and as such, he understands order. By killing and then reanimating Friza, Kid Death impels Lobey to interact with him, hoping to gain his grasp of order. Childlike in appearance, his demeanor alternately craftily evil and poignantly naïve, Kid Death is an unusual antagonist. He is powerful yet vulnerable, a merciless killer yet, in the end, a pitiful victim who begs for his life. It may be argued that Kid Death's "villainy" stems from being different, having needs that are drastically opposed to those of the majority. In this novel, difference is the essential concept. Lobey finds that it cannot be mentioned openly in polite society. He must discover for himself how he is different; it cannot be told to him. That difference must then be kept to himself. Throughout the novel, Samuel Delany emphasizes that every individual is unique; each is different from all others.

Upon his first visit to a city, Lobey sees a billboard displaying a picture of two identical women. The caption reads, "These identical twins are not the same." Lobey misses the point. Snickering, some young boys let him in on the unmentionable implication: "If they're not the same . . . they're *different*!" Uniqueness or difference is what all the characters have in common. The underlying assumption is so fundamental that it is kept subliminal. When Lobey announces to a sophisticated urbanite that he is different, he is baffled by the other's amused, and later hostile, reaction. He does not realize that he is belaboring the obvious and revealing himself as foolish.

ANALYSIS

The title is explained in the final section of the novel. Lobey is told that Einstein, a human mathematician, defined the limits of perception by expressing mathematically how the condition of the observer influences the thing observed. Goedel, Einstein's contemporary, noted that there is an infinite number of true things in the world for which there is no way of ascertaining their truth. At the intersection of these two theories, humanity left the confines of Earth for "somewhere else . . . no world in this continuum." Then Lobey's ancestors, an alien civilization, came to Earth, taking human forms and souls. Their descendants strive to discern their own trajectory while confined to human form, thought, and mythology.

Delany blends an intoxicating brew of myths. The Orpheus/Eurydice story is only one ingredient. Lobey may also be read as Odysseus on a journey. Kid Death is an obvious Lucifer/Satan cognate, and Delany adds to the outlaw archetype's character a soupçon of Billy the Kid. Other archetypal, yet uniquely drawn, characters appear. Spider, a fourarmed driver of a dragon herd, is identified also as the Betrayer, Judas Iscariot, Pat Garrett, and King Minos. Green-Eye, a prince working as a dragon herder, has only one eye. He may be read as a cyclops guarding a flock or as the son whose eye is "single," intent on its own perception and purpose. He is a Christlike savior and redeemer. Contrasting with Friza as the unique beloved is The Dove, the embodiment of all desire.

She appears as Helen of Troy and film stars Jean Harlow and Maria Montez. She is the key image in an advertising campaign aimed at keeping people dissatisfied, working against the tendency to bond with only one other. The Dove is the fuel that powers the genetic engine, keeping genes mixing toward greater diversity, in the same way Delany keeps myths mixing in the novel. He suggests that the old myths may be mutable, that they do not have to have rigidly predictable outcomes.

Despite Delany's assertion that the old myths need not predict the outcome, Lobey's Orphic quest is unsuccessful. He momentarily regains Friza. While he marvels at this miracle, Friza covers his eyes with her hands. The Dove tells him to choose between reality and everything else. Surprised and off balance, Lobey states the obvious: "I can't see anything with your hands in front of my . . ." When he regains his sight, Friza is gone. Even at the novel's end, he is still not sure which he chose. This indeterminacy is as it should be. Lobey, the creator of order, must choose either to return to the old mythic paradigm in which reality is a closed system or to use myth as a vehicle to perceive/create a new reality. In some sense, Lobey has arrived at the Einstein Intersection, the point at which perceived reality meets infinite possibility. *The Einstein Intersection* is among the earliest of Samuel R. Delany's mature works. With *Babel-17* (1966) and *Nova* (1968), it stands as one of several masterpieces of the early career of this prolific writer.

—*Karen S. Bellinfante*

THE ELENIUM

Sir Sparhawk, a Pandian church knight and the Elenian queen's champion, saves his poisoned queen by finding an antidote, then moves on to confront the powerful god Azash, who threatens all of Eosia

Author: David Eddings (1931-2009)
Genre: Fantasy—heroic fantasy
Type of work: Novels
Time of work: Approximately the fourth millennium

Locale: Eosia
First published: *The Diamond Throne* (1989), *The Ruby Knight* (1990), and *The Sapphire Rose* (1991)

THE STORY

At the dawn of time, a dwarfed, misshapen Troll named Ghwerig, shunned by the other Trolls, spent his time searching for treasure. He found a large, valuable blue gemstone. Ghwerig noticed

The Elenium

and enhanced the gemstones distinctive shape by polishing it. He muttered spells, endowing the gemstone with the power of the Troll gods. Ghwerig, however, was unable to tap the power of his new gemstone, called Bhelliom. Guided by the gods directions, he fashioned two gold rings set with oval shards to serve as the key to Bhellioms power.

Later, the Styrics, a society endowed with magic, moved into the area. Their Elder Gods coveted Bhelliom's power. To render Bhelliom powerless, the Younger Gods chose the child-goddess Aphrael to steal the rings. Eventually, the Elenes displaced the Styrics, and the Thalesian king took possession of Bhelliom and incorporated it into his crown.

The story of the Elenium begins several centuries later. Sir Sparhawk, a Pandian knight and the kings champion, had been banished from Elenia. Ten years later, the king died, and his daughter ascended the throne. Sparhawk returns to present himself to Queen Ehlana and finds her trapped in a block of enchanted crystal. Her cousin Lycheas is ruling as prince regent under the control of Annias, primate of the Eosian church in Elenia.

The Pandian knight's Styric teacher of magic, Sephrenia, and twelve knights had conjured the crystal block to sustain Ehlanas life. The block is temporary, lasting only as long as those who created it live, and one of them is dying each month.

Annias uses the Elenian treasury to buy the position of archprelate of the Eosian church. After Annias tries to discredit and disband the Pandians, the four orders (Pandian, Crynic, Alcionic, and Genidian) of church knights preceptors agree that Annias ambition should be blocked and that the best way to do so is to effect Ehlanas cure. Representatives of the other three orders accompany Sir Sparhawk, Sephrenia, and four other companions around Eosia searching for a cure. They find an orphaned Styric girl called Flute, then discover that Ehlana has been give a fatal poison by Aldreas, Ehlana's father's ghost. He commands Sparhawk to find Bhelliom to cure Ehlana. If he does not find it in time, he is to destroy it, preventing it from falling into evil hands. Aldreas also gives Sparhawk the monarch's ring, a companion to the one the monarch's champion wears.

Bhelliom was last sighted on a battlefield five hundred years ago. Sparhawk and his companions summon spirits of dead soldiers to locate it. Sephrenia concludes that the various attacks on them have been aimed at Sparhawk. She further believes that most of their difficulties, including Ehlanas illness, are directed by Azash, one of the Styric Elder Gods. Sephrenia concludes that Azash has seen some future event involving Sparhawk and is trying to prevent it. Azash uses Zemoch Styrics to look for Bhelliom, encouraging others to search for treasure and making Sparhawk's search more difficult.

Azash employs spirits to locate Bhelliom and to kill Sparhawk. One of these spirits, a Seeker, follows Sparhawk's party so it can destroy him or take Bhelliom. Sparhawk realizes that the most effective search technique is to find storytellers who recount local war events. One such storyteller directs him to Count Ghasek, who has been compiling all the old stories and is willing to help.

The count tells them where the king of Thalesia died. Sparhawk and his companions find the kings grave, call the king's spirit, and learn where Bhelliom is. They search for it but quit to prevent either Azash or Ghwerig from locating Bhelliom. When they are ready to return, Flute tells them that Ghwerig has it. Ghwerig dies, and Flute, the Styric goddess Aphrael, delivers Bhelliom to Sparhawk.

Now in possession of Bhelliom, Sparhawk travels back to Elenia, where Sephrenia and the knights dissolve the crystal block. Sephrenia and Sparhawk cure Ehlana, who sends Sparhawk and his companions to Chyrellos to prevent Annias from becoming archprelate. Sparhawk leaves local citizens to defend the city and Ehlana.

At Chyrellos, the knights and their preceptors temporarily thwart Annias' influence with the hierocracy and send for their armies to prevent Annias from using church soldiers to intimidate the hierocracy. When the army arrives, it is the Zemoch's who cooperate with Annias. The preceptors of the church knights declare a crisis of faith, putting the church soldiers under their authority. They fortify the inner city and hold off the Zemochs, but the cost is high.

The church knights block the Zemoch attack. The army of church knights arrives in time to prevent the fall of Chyrellos. Annias and his henchmen escape.

To thwart the remaining Zemoch massed at the border, Sparhawk and his companions go to the Zemoch capital to destroy Azash. The companions encounter many difficulties on the way but eventually arrive and battle Azashs worshipers, finally destroying them and the god. In a dream, Flute leads them to a sea coast; they throw Bhelliom into the sea.

ANALYSIS
The Elenium, David Edding's third fantasy series, is a typical heros quest. In one way or another, Sparhawk fulfills all thirteen of the standard characteristics of a heros quest listed by Peter R. Stillman in *Introduction to Myth* (1977). First, Sparhawk is neither a fool (he understands the dangers that he is facing reasonably well) nor invincible (he was nearly killed ten years earlier, when he was first banished). Second, he is urgently required to make a journey (Ehlanas life depends on his success), and third, that journey is beset with dangers, loneliness (he is the only one who can complete the journey), and temptations (the power of Bhelliom nearly seduces him).

The fourth characteristic is that he is accompanied by guides (Sephrenia and Flute) who advise him. Fifth, companions (Sir Kalten, Berit, Kurik, Talen, and the three champions of the other orders of church knights) accompany him until his journeys end. Sixth, this journey is neither direct (his travels take him all over the countryside, facing various roadblocks and side trips to locate Bhelliom, cure Ehlana, and finally face Azash) nor clear, because he knows neither the true reason for the journey nor exactly how to proceed. Seventh, he has a goal (to find Bhelliom and return to Elenia to cure Ehlana), but that is not the full extent of the journey (he eventually has to face Azash). The goal is no more than a symbol of his true quest, satisfying the eighth characteristic of a heros quest.

Ninth, Sparhawk makes a descent into darkness, when he arrives at the Zemoch capital. He enters the palace, goes down into the maze, and finally arrives in the unlighted blackness of Azash's temple. This descent brings contact with his enemies (Annias, his companions and henchmen, the Zemoch king Otha, and finally Azash), whom he vanquishes. Tenth, he changes following the descent (he is sadder and wiser). Eleventh, he suffers a psychological wound, that of losing Kurik, his squire and lifelong companion. Twelfth, he is male, and finally, he is someone of unknown origin—he is the man of Styric prophecy whose destiny is his own to control.

This series involves the typical heros quest conflict between good and evil, but it also involves a question of personal freedom. The knights and churchmen are controlled by the principles and rules of their orders, but they can make their own decisions and have a relatively independent lifestyle. Azash, however, would introduce much more control. The Styrics believe that every persons destiny is dictated by fate. Sparhawk, however, is Anakha, the man without a predetermined future. This suggests that one theme of the series is the importance of free will. It may, in fact, suggest that people make their own destiny, like Sparhawk, or at least that they should attempt to do so.

The characters, both noble and common, are real people with strengths and weaknesses. They face their futures with determination and humor, making them both interesting and appealing. The events are typical of fantasy or a heros quest in that they are larger than life. Several of the more likable characters die, giving the novels realism: Real people faced with overwhelming odds or situations often rise to the occasion, but they do not always survive.

Eddings continued the story of Belgarion from the Belgariad in his second series, the Malloreon. He continues the story of Sparhawk in the Tamuli, the first three books of which are *Domes of Fire* (1993), *The Shining Ones* (1993), and *The Hidden City* (1994).

—Sherry Stoskopf

Elidor

Four children become caught up in attempts to save the land of Elidor from dark forces by hiding its Treasures in their own world

Author: Alan Garner (1934–)
Genre: Fantasy—magical world
Type of work: Novel
Time of work: The 1960s
Locale: Manchester, England, and Elidor
First published: 1965

The Story

Nicholas, David, Helen, and Roland are exploring an unfamiliar part of Manchester, England, when they discover a derelict church. Retrieving a ball lost during a game, the children go into the building, one by one, until only Roland is left outside. Frightened by music that the other children have not heard and by glimpses of a lame fiddler whom they did not see, he retreats into the church. He meets the fiddler, who, through the power of his music, transports them to another world.

Roland finds himself on a barren seashore close to a castle, which proves to be empty, although he hears the sound of a man singing. The fiddler leads him away from the castle, through desolate countryside that is devoid of living things and any evidence of human presence. They reach a mound, topped by a stone circle, where Roland finally confronts the musician.

The fiddler is Malebron, the ruler of Elidor, a land that gradually is being swamped by the powers of Darkness. Of the four castles of Elidor, only Gorias, visible in the distance, remains in the Light. Malebron is fighting to preserve it and to save the land. He has brought the children into Elidor to rescue its Treasures from the Mound of Vandwy. Roland's brothers and sister already have entered the mound but did not emerge. Roland must save the Treasures and his siblings, a task in which he succeeds.

Malebron tells the children that he is following a book of ancient prophecies that will help him to save Elidor and that he must now find Findhorn, whose song will save the land. At this point, he and the children are attacked by forces of Darkness.

Malebron sends the children back to their own world, giving them the Treasures for safekeeping.

In England, the children find that the Treasures—a sword, a spear, a chalice, and a golden stone—are now outwardly pieces of rubbish and that they generate a power that affects electrical devices. They hide the objects deep under the garden of their new house in order to dampen their power. While digging, Helen finds a broken jug that, when mended, is found to be decorated with a picture of a unicorn.

A year passes, and for Nicholas, Helen, and David, memories of Elidor fade, until they believe that the adventure was nothing more than a childish game. This angers Roland, who clearly remembers what happened. He realizes that in Elidor the dark powers are preparing to cross into his world to steal the Treasures. He also receives a message from Malebron revealing that Findhorn is a unicorn. When Findhorn crosses into their world, the hunters come after him. The children are forced to flee in order to protect the Treasures and to save Findhorn. They return to the derelict church, where Findhorn is slain. As he dies, he begins to sing, thus saving Elidor and returning it to the Light. In a final dramatic gesture, the children hurl their Treasures through the window they originally broke, returning the Treasures to Elidor.

Analysis

Alan Garner's first two novels, *The Weirdstone of Brisingamen* (1960) and *The Moon of Gomrath* (1963), dealt unequivocally with the battle between good and evil, embodied in wizards, witches, elves, and svarts. There was no doubt as to which side reader and protagonist alike would be on and no reason to question the assumption that good would triumph. The characters were assigned their roles, which they then carried out to reach a satisfactory and obvious conclusion. For all their darker moments, the two novels frequently took on almost the flavor of pastoral idylls, celebrating the authors love of his childhood home, Alderley Edge.

In *Elidor*, such comfortable certainties are abandoned. Garner's writing begins its transition toward a darker, more ambiguous view of the eternal conflict. Garner eschews the familiarity of Alderley Edge, choosing instead desolate urban settings and a countryside wasted by a mysterious force, all of them landscapes in transition. The children themselves are on the threshold of adolescence, unlike the younger protagonists of Garner's first two novels. Roland, the youngest, still clings to the childhood the three older children are rejecting. Although they are no longer quite at ease with his childish acceptance of magic, neither can they deny entirely what has happened to them in Elidor, although for much of the story, they refuse to speak of the place.

For much of the novel, although the children are at the heart of the narrative, they are not at the center of the action. Wizards feebly protest that children should not be involved, but all the while readers know that the children will circumvent this prohibition. Malebron steadfastly refuses to conform to such fictional conventions. He does not hesitate to send the children into danger to retrieve the Treasures of Elidor, and neither does he concern himself with their safety once they have returned to their own world with the Treasures. Garner's heroes are no longer perfect, instead becoming flawed and human, concerned with their own ends.

Even in the novels ending, Garner rejects the conventional form. The guiltless unicorn dies in order to save Elidor, a sacrifice beyond anything the children might reasonably have anticipated. What innocence they might still hold is shattered by this act. In their throwing away the Treasures, readers see them relinquish childish imagination for a sterner view of lifes realities. Some critics consider the novels ending to be weak, but it fits with Garner's apparent turning away from the childlike excitement of his earlier novels to the gritty emotional realities of his novels to come.

—*Maureen Speller*

THE ELRIC SAGA

Elric, last emperor of the decadent, prehuman Melniboneans, abandons his kingdom in a quest for freedom and identity that ironically destroys the world he seeks to preserve

Author: Michael Moorcock (1939–)
Genre: Fantasy—heroic fantasy
Type of work: Novels
Time of work: Undefined
Location: Earth and an alternative dimension
First published: *The Elric Saga* (parts 1 and 2, 1984), which includes *Elric of Melniboné* (1972; U.S. title, with cuts, *The Dreaming City*, 1972), *The Sailor on the Seas of Fate* (1973), *The Weird of the White Wolf* (1976), *The Vanishing Tower* (1971, also published as *The Sleeping Sorceress*), *The Bane of the Black Sword* (1977), and *Stormbringer* (1965, rev. 1977); *Elric at the End of Time* (1984); *The Fortress of the Pearl* (1989); and *The Revenge of the Rose: A Tale of the Albino in the Years of His Wandering* (1991)

THE STORY

Stormbringer, the first novel in the Elric Saga to be published, was actually the last of the series according to internal chronology. It was first published serially by the British magazine *Science Fantasy* (1963–1964). The single volume *Stealer of Souls* (1963) was expanded, with the addition of stories from the separately published collection *The Singing Citadel* (1970) and the return and revision of the omitted portions of *Stormbringer*, into the six-volume saga. *The Fortress of the Pearl* is an additional adventure that occurs between the events narrated in *Elric of Melniboné* and *The Sailor on the Seas of Fate*, and *The Revenge of the Rose* apparently occurs between the events of *The Vanishing Tower* and *The Bane of the Black Sword*.

The Elric Saga tells the story of Elric, last emperor of the Bright Empire of Melniboné, whose inhuman race has ruled their world for ten thousand years. It is, even in its decline, more than a match for the human upstarts of the Young Kingdoms. These strange people inhabit the Dragon Isle, on which rests their only settlement, Imrryr, the Dreaming City of unearthly beauty and unimaginable horror.

Elric has the dual misfortune of being an albino, which causes him some physical weakness, and being so unusually intelligent and sensitive— for a Melnibonean—that he has a conscience and is capable of both pity and remorse, an anomaly that raises questions about his fitness to rule a people who create orchestras from the dying screams of tortured slaves. Loudest among Elric's critics is his greedy cousin Yyrkoon, who lusts after the throne and the power of bygone days. Elric has great inner strength and sorcerous powers, which Yyrkoon discovers when he attempts to usurp the Ruby Throne and is resoundingly defeated.

The battle ends triumphantly for Elric, but it is a victory that costs him dearly, because he must invoke the aid of the demon-god of Melniboné, Arioch of Chaos. This act sets in motion events that lead to his world's destruction in a final battle between the supernatural forces of Law and Chaos. Particularly important in this regard is his acquisition of the black runesword Stormbringer, in reality a demoniac entity of monstrous evil that devours the souls of people and gods alike, giving their strength to Elric and so creating an unholy addiction from which he never completely recovers.

Elric unwisely leaves his kingdom in the hands of Yyrkoon to quest for freedom and for answers to his people's identity, hoping to free them from their own degeneracy and from the whims of the Lords of Chaos. While he is abroad, Yyrkoon successfully usurps the throne and recovers the other black sword, Mournblade.

Meanwhile, Elric endures a series of adventures with the disturbing import that he is not and never will be master of his own destiny. Returning in secret to Melniboné, he discovers that his beloved cousin Cymoril has been placed in an enchanted sleep by Yyrkoon. Frustrated in his attempts to awaken her and rejected by his own people, Elric organizes the fleets of the Young Kingdoms to sail against Melniboné. He succeeds in sacking the city but fails miserably in his real purpose. Yyrkoon confronts him with Mournblade, and the two black swords possess their wielders. Cymoril awakes during the fight, and Yyrkoon flings her toward Elric. She dies horribly as Stormbringer drinks her soul. Elric kills Yyrkoon, but the damage is done.

After the sack of Imrryr, the raider fleet is attacked and destroyed by the vengeful Melniboneans. Only Elric's ship escapes, by sorcerous means, in an apparent betrayal of those men who had trusted him (though he really could not save them). The despairing Elric now wanders the world, still seeking the truth and freedom he is denied, though he continues to involuntarily fulfill his destiny. He makes a powerful and elusive enemy in Theleb Ka'arna, sorcerer of Pan Tang. His quest for vengeance occupies a considerable portion of the saga and ends with hard-won and somewhat equivocal success: The vampiric runesword takes Theleb Ka'arna's soul only after much destruction, including the death of Myshella, the Dark Lady of Castle Kaneloon, Elric's first new love after the death of his cousin.

During the saga, Elric falls in love with several women. His last and greatest love, his human wife Zarozinia, impales her Chaos-altered body on Stormbringer to give Elric the strength he needs to destroy the Lords of Chaos in the final battle. After the defeat of Chaos, Elric again flings away Stormbringer, only to have the black blade fly from the ground and impale him. The sword then transforms into a demoniac being, standing over the fallen albino and saying, "Farewell, friend! I was a thousand times more evil than thou!"

ANALYSIS

Elric is a fascinating creation, not least because he is a considerable change from the brawny Neanderthal hero tradition in fantasy begun with Robert E. Howard's Conan the Barbarian. Cultured, brilliantly intelligent, and physically delicate though immensely psychologically powerful, Elric starkly contrasts with the brutal simplicity of Conan.

Where Conan is a wild barbarian warrior, Elric is the highly cultured product of a dying civilization. Where Conan grows quickly bored and irritated with philosophical questions, Elric is forever seeking the answers to the mysteries of life. Where Conan is direct and simple in his desires, Elric is subtle and inwardly tortured by his conflicting emotions. A mighty sorcerer, Elric dislikes invoking supernatural aid, though he resorts to it frequently. In his questing after truth instead of power or wealth, he again differs from the typical hero of "sword and sorcery" fantasies. When angered he can be horrifyingly merciless, but he is reluctant to use force, again in contrast to typical heroes of fantasy. He is capable of compassion and pity, but also of demoniac cruelty. Ironically, it is his compassion for his people that alienates him from them.

Irony is an abiding characteristic of Michael Moorcock's work, particularly the Elric Saga. It is ironic that Elric leaves the Bright Empire to seek freedom only to fulfill his destiny, that he seeks to free himself with a sword that only enslaves him, that in seeking to save his people he eventually destroys them, that he kills Cymoril when he wishes to free her, and that his own divided character will not let him find the peace he craves. Indeed, Melniboneans cultivate a refined sense of irony, as Elric's own behavior continually illustrates.

Closely related to irony is paradox, in that both involve the juxtaposition of apparent opposites. The paradoxical beauty and horror of Imrryr are matched by the paradoxical character of its last ruler. Elric's plight is itself paradoxical, in that by acting according to the compassionate side of his nature and questing for truth, he brings about his own and his world's destruction. Time paradoxes abound, as Elric discovers that he is one incarnation of the Champion Eternal, a being of almost infinite power who exists simultaneously on all the million spheres of Earth.

Several times Elric meets other versions of himself, from good Prince Corum of the Vadhagh to the terrible Prince Gaynor the Damned, doomed to serve Chaos for all eternity. Elric himself is seeking answers he is better off not knowing, the most exquisitely cruel paradox of all. Moorcock blends British folklore, biblical sources, and other mythological motifs with original characterization and unusually profound philosophical insights, creating a world at once new and yet familiar, a world similar enough to reality to make satiric social commentary possible, yet different enough to evoke the sublime wonder engendered only by the very best fantastic literature. If there are minor stylistic flaws and inconsistencies in the earlier books of the original saga, they are still exceptional in their brilliant synthesis of the modern novel and the mythic.

The more recent novels, *The Fortress of the Pearl* and *The Revenge of the Rose*, represent the work of a mature and extraordinarily gifted author. On the whole, the Elric Saga is one of the finest fantasy epics ever written.

—David Hinckley

THE EMBEDDING

In search of a universal grammar, alien Signal Traders visit the Earth, igniting civil and political unrest

Author: Ian Watson (1943–   )
Genre: Science fiction—invasion story
Type of work: Novel
Time of work: The mid-1970s
Locale: England, the Brazilian jungle, and a Nevada desert
First published: 1973

THE STORY

The Embedding weaves together three plot lines. Chris Sole, researcher in linguistics for the Haddon Neurotherapy Unit, conducts experiments on four orphans (Rama, Vidya, Gulshen, and Vasilki), teaching them an "embedding language." Soles former fellow researcher and friend, Pierre, is at the same time doing fieldwork in the Amazon, where the existence of a small tribe of Indians, called the Xemahoa, is threatened by a dam built by Brazilians but sponsored by Americans. The Xemahoa tribe speak a two-tiered language, Xemahoa-A and Xemahoa-B, the latter of which is inspired by a fungus, maka-i, and resembles the "embedding language" Sole teaches the children. The third plot involves contact with extraterrestrials.

After an American radio dish picks up strange signals from outer space, Sole is recruited by Tom Zwingler, an American agent for national security, to unscramble the coded messages. Meanwhile, the Americans and Soviets together send astronauts to investigate an object that seems to be the source of the signals. The astronauts land on the alien ship, and then, after being taken aboard, negotiate with the aliens to land a small craft in the Nevada desert while their main ship goes into parking orbit.

The aliens, who call themselves the Spthra, have been on a mission to discover all the languages in the universe and superimpose them in an attempt to find the entire signature of This-Reality and thereby escape it. As explained by their representative Phtheri, the Spthra came to Earth in order to trade information: six human brains that know separate and distinct human languages in exchange for vital information on interstellar communication and intelligent life-forms near Earth as well as improvements in technology for spaceflight. With this, all three plot lines tie together, for Sole bargains with Phtheri for the six brains, which are to include the brain of the Xemahoa Bruxo or tribal shaman, who knows the embedding language of his people. The Spthra are willing to sweeten the pot for the acquisition. Sole and Zwingler are sent to the now nearly flooded Amazon jungle to find Pierre and recover the brain.

The resolution of the novel is precipitated by the greed, opportunism, and duplicity of the world political powers involved. The Americans, realizing the potential significance of the Xemahoa tribe and its powerful drug, decide to blow up the dam with a small nuclear bomb. A Chinese satellite picks up the explosion and broadcasts the incident for propagandistic purposes and to incite revolution in Brazil and the rest of Latin America. Attempting to avoid blame and global indignation, the Americans and Soviets issue a joint communiqué stating that the bombing was done by an unidentified flying object that had been spotted circling Earth. The Spthra landing ship is destroyed by a one kiloton tactical homing missile, and the main ship is wrecked by a Soviet orbital bomb. Having failed, Sole returns with Pierre to England only to realize that Peter, his three-year-old son, is not his child but a product of his wifes affair with Pierre in Paris four years earlier. Sole returns to the embedding project, where he reclaims Vidya, the child of his mind, carrying the boy back home in his arms through the frozen English countryside.

ANALYSIS
Although Ian Watson has not gained wide popular attention, critics and reviewers have admired him as one of the best science-fiction writers of ideas. Indeed, *The Embedding*, his first novel, was runner-up for the John W. Campbell Memorial Award in 1974 and won the 1975 Prix Apollo in French translation and the 1978 Premios Zikkurath in Spanish translation.

Thematically, the novel explores the notion that reality is a construct of language, and therefore people who possess distinct or widely different languages would also have widely differing constructs of reality. This is the theory Chris Sole is testing out in his embedding world, and such is the Spthra theory of This-Reality in which they are embedded. Along with this exploration of an alternate reality, the story, set during the Christmas season, has a mythic dimension. The Xemahoa people, who tap into the deep myths through their drug-induced dance, look to the birth of the maka-i child for an answer to the rising waters that submerge the village—a far more potent myth for the tribe than the Christian version of salvation promoted by the priests who try to convert them. Ironically, too, the Xemahoa myth works, for after the baby is born, terribly deformed with brain hernias by the maka-i drug the mother consumed, the flood recedes. Kayapi, Pierre's translator and son of the current Bruxo, eats the exposed brain of the child, supposedly ingesting the escaped dreams of his people, and thus becomes the new shaman.

The Spthra search for a universal language also has its mythic dimensions. According to legend, the Change Speakers phased with the Spthra thirteen thousand years earlier and then inexplicably left them, saddened and bereft. The Change Speakers may very well be the Spthra version of God, as some of the Earthling representatives suggest, and the Spthra quest is no less than a longed-for return to primal unity. Although the Spthra understand the anguish of unrequited love, they miscalculate the violence and rapacity of the human race and end their quest not in union with the Change Speakers but floating in outer space, destroyed by humanitys advanced weapons.

The Embedding is a densely packed novel, operating on many levels at once and showing Watsons daring exploration of ideas. This exploration has earned him a reputation as one of the twentieth century's most challenging science-fiction writers.

—*Donald P. Kaczvinsky*

THE EMPIRE OF FEAR

In a world dominated by vampires, a group of humans struggles to discover the secrets of vampirism

Author: Brian Stableford (1948–)
Genre: Fantasy—alternate history
Type of work: Novel
Time of work: 1623–1660, with a conclusion in 1983
Locale: England, France, Africa, and Nova Scotia
First published: 1988

The Story

Brian Stableford's *The Empire of Fear* tells the story of an alternate reality in which vampires control most of the world, relegating humans to lives of servitude. The plot revolves around the efforts of scientist Noell Cordery and his allies to discover the secrets of vampirism and obtain them for humanity. Noell and his comrades succeed in their mission, which radically alters the balance of power in the world. Stableford does not reveal the extent of those alterations until the novel's final section.

The story begins in 1623, with an account of the last days of Edmund Cordery. He is Noell's father and works as a scientist for Richard the Lionheart, the vampire ruler of England. In his quest to find the secrets of vampirism, Edmund invents the microscope, which allows him to examine blood closely. He knows that his efforts to help humanity fight the vampires will result in his death. In an effort to weaken their power, Edmund infects himself with a virus from Africa that he hopes will kill his vampire lover, Lady Carmilla Bourdillon. His gambit succeeds, and before he dies he ensures that his wife and son are helped to safety in France.

The story continues in France two years later. Noell has sought refuge at Cardigan Abbey, a Benedictine monastery sympathetic to the human cause. He lives there quietly with his fellow scholar, Quintus, until the arrival of Langoisse, a pirate and former ally of Prince Richard, with his crew of buccaneers. Langoisse's presence disrupts life for Noell, forcing the young man to reconsider his inactivity in the fight against the vampires. During their stay, Noell begins a relationship with Leilah, a gypsy and Langoisse's mistress, that will continue for the rest of his life. After the pirates attack a group of Dominican monks, who are allied with the vampires, Noell, Quintus, and the pirates flee France and travel to Africa's north coast.

In 1643, after several years of research, Noell, Quintus, Langoisse, Leilah, a young African boy named Ntikima, and several others travel to Adamawara, the birthplace of vampirism. The long, difficult journey eventually bears fruit when Noell and his allies discover the secret of vampirism. Noell discovers that vampirism can be explained scientifically rather than having origins in mysterious supernatural forces. He develops a process that allows his allies to become vampires but discovers that the formula does not work on him.

After Noell, Quintus, Langoisse, and Leilah escape Adamawara with the help of Ntikima, they travel to Malta, where they ally themselves with a group of vampires who are the enemies of Prince Richard and Vlad Dragulya, the Prince of Wallachia. By the year 1660, Richard has been forced to flee England, but he joins Dragulya in a campaign to crush Noell and his allies on the orders of their overlords, Charlemagne and Attila the Hun. In the ensuing battle, Prince Richard is slain by Langoisse, who is then killed. Quintus and Noell also die at the hands of the vampires. Despite his apparent victory, Dragulya is also doomed when Noell poisons him.

In the novel's last section, set in 1983, Noell Cordery's legacy becomes apparent. Most humans have become vampires except for a few who have Cordery's disease, a rare genetic illness that prevents them from making the transformation from human to vampire. The novel ends as Michael Southerne, a young man afflicted by this disease, meets Leilah and becomes her lover.

Analysis

The Empire of Fear marks Stableford's return to science fiction and fantasy after a period of several years in which he devoted himself to critical studies. This novel was well received by most critics. It is a fascinating work that blends elements of science fiction, fantasy, and history. Among its themes, the novel explores the attempts by the aristocratic vampires to resist changes that would mean the end of their power.

One fascinating aspect of Stableford's novel is how he combines science fiction, fantasy, and history. He succeeds admirably in creating a believable alternate reality in which historical figures such as Attila the Hun, Charlemagne, and Genghis Khan are vampires who establish empires that have the potential to last for thousands of years. Furthermore, the characters of Richard the Lionheart and Vlad Dragulya share many similarities with their historical counterparts. Stableford also effectively uses elements of science fiction in the novel's last section, in which he explains the extraterrestrial origin of vampirism and its effect on human physiology. Furthermore, he uses material drawn from fantasy, such as the false supernatural powers that the vampires use to help control humanity and the magic that apparently exists in Africa.

One important theme in Stableford's novel is the struggle of the elite vampires against change. Once the vampires have established their empires, they do everything they can to maintain their dominance. The vampires use their superior abilities and long life spans to create a supernatural aura around themselves that helps keep humans in positions of subservience. Once science progresses enough to discover the truth about vampirism, change becomes inevitable. The vampires struggle to keep the knowledge from spreading, because if humans became like them, the elite vampires would lose their advantage. Their attempts to suppress the truth eventually fail because even though vampires can kill humans, they cannot destroy ideas. Even Dragulya admits that although they might win, the vampires cannot stop the tide of change from sweeping their society away and creating a new world in which the majority are vampires and the minority are normal humans.

—*David A. Oakes*

EMPIRE OF THE EAST

The powers of technology, magic, good, and evil battle for control of a post-apocalyptic Earth

Author: Fred Saberhagen (1930–2007)
Genre: Science fiction—post-holocaust
Type of work: Novel
Time of work: The distant future
Locale: Earth
First published: 1979 (as omnibus; previously published as *The Broken Lands*, 1968; *The Black Mountains*, 1971; and *Changeling Earth*, 1973)

THE STORY

Empire of the East was first published in a substantially different form but has been reworked into a one-volume omnibus. The story takes place on a barely recognizable Earth centuries after a nuclear holocaust. The people of the West have regressed to a feudal lifestyle and have no memory of Earths technology. Magic has replaced it, and the cruel Eastern empire has taken control of the West.

The protagonist is Rolf, a peasant who becomes leader of the Free Folk, a small guerrilla group devoted to ending the oppression of Ekuman, governor of the Broken Lands. When Rolf joins the movement, he learns that success hinges on the guidance of Ardneh, a mysterious godlike entity who inspires leaders of the Free Folk by telepathy. The leader preceding Rolf had been told to find the Elephant but died before completing the task. Rolf discovers the Elephant, which turns out to be a nuclear tank from the Old World (prewar Earth). On the day Ekuman is to celebrate his daughter Charmians wedding to Chup, a neighboring noble, Rolf is inspired by Ardneh, and his natural talent for technology awakens. The Free Folk use the Elephant in battle, defeating Ekuman and destroying his fortress. The wicked and greedy Charmian, however, escapes; her bridegroom, Chup, survives as a crippled beggar.

Chup is restored to health by a demon who directs him to Charmians refuge in the Black Mountains. This domain is ruled by Som the Dead, Viceroy of the East. His minions can be revived after death with the aid of flying machines that bring them to the Lake of Life. Charmian plots to steal Soms great power with a talisman designed to infatuate Som with her beauty. After convincing Chup to plant the charm in Soms treasury, Charmian plots to have Chup killed. He escapes to inform Som, who demands that Chup prove his allegiance to the East by feeding Charmian to another demon. Chup is repelled and joins Rolfs army, which invades the Black Mountains. Inspired by Ardneh, Chup kills the demon. Som is destroyed when water from the Lake of Life touches him. The lake and the flying machines are casualties of the conflict and cannot be salvaged.

The final part of the story introduces Ominor, Emperor of the East, who decides to find and destroy Ardneh. The elusive entity continues to advise Rolf in his increasingly successful fight. When Ominor enlists the aid of powerful wizards, Ardneh instructs Rolf to acquire a large, powerful gem kept by Charmian, who now follows Ominors battle leader on his campaigns. With Chups help, Rolf obtains the gem. Ardneh then leads Rolf to him. He is no god but instead a huge computer that gained sentience after the holocaust; the gem is a part of its hardware. Ardnehs goal is to help people regain the lost technology without becoming dependent on it. The final conflict occurs when Ardneh battles Orcus, the greatest demon of the East. Both are destroyed, but the army of the East is conquered. Chup and Charmian are reconciled. The survivors agree that a balance between magic and technology must be achieved and that neither is intrinsically evil. The story ends on a note of hope.

ANALYSIS

Empire of the East is based on some of Fred Saberhagens earliest works. He wrote the first part (The Broken Lands) in 1967 before becoming an assistant editor for *Encyclopaedia Britannica*. Saberhagen continued editing for six years, then returned to writing, eventually combining *The Broken Lands*, *The Black Mountains*, and *Changeling Earth* into a single novel in 1979. He has gone on to write better-known works, such as his Dracula series (1975-1990) and the ongoing Berserker books, a series begun in 1967 with a story collection.

Empire of the East, as a post-holocaust story, deals with the themes of war and disaster. These always have been popular avenues for writers, but they reached a peak after World War II and throughout the Cold War because of the real threat of nuclear holocaust. *Empire of the East* belongs to the later years of this trend, when the Soviets were still regarded with suspicion. Although obvious Cold War references such as nuclear war and Eastern dominance (pointing to the Soviet Union) changed with the times, the themes still provide fertile ground for writers.

A growing trend away from Cold War ideology is evident in such stories as David Brin's *The Postman* (1985). It was written several years before the Soviet Union fell, but there is no mention of an Eastern menace, let alone the Soviet Union. *The Postman* shares a postnuclear scenario and hopeful conclusion with *Empire of the East*. In Saberhagen's novel, hope surfaces only after the Empire is crushed and the survivors begin rebuilding their world. Most of the characters are static, but Charmian and Chup display personal growth, another hopeful sign.

Saberhagen, in describing a post-apocalyptic Earth, brings in the popular idea of a created world. With most vestiges of technology gone, he includes new life-forms, such as enormous talking predatory birds. Their role is minor, but they ally themselves with the West and work as messengers.

Contemporary novelists and critics praised *Empire of the East*. Larry Niven thought it was better than J. R. R. Tolkiens Lord of the Rings trilogy (1954-1955). Lester del Rey admired the settings, remarking that Saberhagen has proved himself to be one of the best writers in the genre. Roger Zelazny wrote a prologue for the novel and praised Saberhagens bright imagery.

—*Carla Hall Minor*

THE ENCHANTED CASTLE

Four children find a magic ring and discover that magic creates more problems than it solves

Author: E(dith) Nesbit (1858-1924)
Genre: Fantasy—magical realism

Type of work: Novel
Time of work: The early 1900s
Locale: A town in western England
First published: 1907 (serial form, *The Strand Magazine*, January-November, 1906)

The Enchanted Castle

THE STORY

The story is a modern fairy tale rooted in childhood imagination. A game of make-believe becomes earnest when four children discover a ring with magical powers. Their attempts to use the ring create complications in their everyday lives, some humorous, some horrific.

Gerald, Jimmy, and Kathleen, left at school during the holidays, find a hidden entrance to the gardens of Yalding Manor, which they pretend is an enchanted castle. They discover a sleeping princess (Mabel, the housekeeper's niece) who plays along with their game, showing them a secret treasure room containing a ring that she claims makes the wearer invisible. When she slips it on, she discovers that her claim has come true and that she has become invisible.

Invisibility confers both benefits and disadvantages. The children must cover for the absence of Mabel (and later Gerald) until the magic wears off; on the other hand, they use invisibility to raise money with a conjuring show and later to help capture some burglars. The children next discover that the ring will grant the wearers wishes; this immediately creates a problem when they perform a play before an audience of artificial people they have fashioned from household odds and ends. When Mabel wishes the painted audience alive, the animated creatures (Ugly-Wuglies) terrify their creators.

With the assistance of Yalding Manors new bailiff, the children succeed in confining the creatures to a cave in the garden, but the effort results in injury to the bailiff. Eventually the magic wears off, except for one exceedingly respectable creature who has somehow received his own wish to become truly alive and occupies a spot on the London stock exchange. Further adventures convince the children of the difficulty of making appropriate wishes.

Gradually, the children discover the rings effects. It acquires whatever magical power is claimed for it, its effects last for a shorter period each time it is used, it makes its wearer unafraid of anything and the wearers loved ones indifferent to his or her fate, and it allows the wearer to witness the gardens statues come to life.

As the magic becomes less and less endurable, the bailiff is revealed as Lord Yalding, the manors owner. He has put the manor up for sale because of his poverty. The children tell him of the rings power and, humoring them, he wishes that his friend were there. The childrens French governess arrives and turns out to be Lord Yaldings long-lost love. After a ghost conjured up by the ring scares off the manors prospective purchaser, the children save the estate by revealing a cache of hidden jewels. The happy couple is married and the final wish made, that all the rings magic be undone and that the ring itself henceforth be a simple wedding band.

ANALYSIS

Before Edith Nesbit, childrens fantasies typically recognized a distinct boundary between the magical realm and the everyday world. Fantasies either took place entirely within an unreal world or moved from a real world into a distinctly different sort of place where magic reigned. Nesbits fantasies, in contrast, intermingle details of the ordinary world with magical occurrences, often to comical effect.

The Enchanted Castle is Nesbits fourth novel-length fantasy, following her successful Psammead trilogy, and the only one that uses magic to create terror as well as comedy. Its ancestors are fairy tales such as "The Three Wishes"; the myth of Cupid and Psyche and its fairy-tale descendant, "Beauty and the Beast"; and Mary Shelley's *Frankenstein* (1818), in which the creature pursues its creator.

Although critical response to the book as a whole is divided, almost all readers have found its most memorable feature to be the Ugly-Wuglies. These animated creatures with painted faces reflect Nesbits own childhood terrors as well as an implicit fear of the power of the imagination to create visions beyond the creators control. The Ugly-Wuglies, whose horror is increased by their stolidly proper British personalities, also reflect Nesbits commentary, as a socialist, on middle-class society, which is another human creation that threatens to overwhelm its makers.

The novel uses snippets from various fairy tales, including the Sleeping Beauty fantasy game the children play when they first enter the garden. The most sustained fairy-tale imagery, however, comes from the various permutations of Cupid and Psyche. The play the children are performing when the Ugly-Wuglies come to life is an adaptation of

Beauty and the Beast; the story of Lord Yalding and the French governess, who must undergo a long separation before being reunited, echoes the Roman myth; and the final abjuration of magic takes place in the underground Hall of Psyche.

In "The Three Wishes," a married couple is granted three wishes. The partners carefully plan how they will use them until the wife, growing hungry, wishes for a pudding. The angry husband wishes it on her nose and must then use the third wish to take it off again. This theme underlies much of the comedy of *The Enchanted Castle*, as it did Nesbits earlier *Five Children and It* (1905): The children make hasty, quickly repented wishes and discover that more serious wishes, such as Jimmys wish to be rich, have unforeseen consequences.

Nesbits influence on later childrens writers lies primarily in her careful working out of the logical consequences of magical phenomena in an everyday world and in her humorous reworking of traditional story elements. Childrens writer Edward Eager, in particular, has acknowledged her influence, but many of the irreverent retellings of fairy tales throughout the twentieth century seem indebted to her model.

—A. Waller Hastings

THE END OF ETERNITY

A Technician of Eternity is tempted to sacrifice his timeless reality for the love of a mysterious woman he meets in the 482d century

Author: Isaac Asimov (1920–1992)
Genre: Science fiction—time travel
Type of work: Novel
Time of work: 1938 to 111,394
Locale: Earth
First published: 1955

THE STORY

Andrew Harlan becomes an Eternal at the age of fifteen. He progresses through the ranks with impressive speed from Cub to Observer to Specialist. His career is thrown into crisis, however, when he is assigned to the 482d century. This period of history is hedonistic, materialistic, and matriarchal, in direct contrast to his own native 95th century, which is ascetic and sexually repressed. Far from his familiar homewhen, he meets and falls in love with Noys Lambent. She not only brings into question his own beliefs but also challenges the basic assumptions of all Eternity.

As a Technician, Harlan has the responsibility for making certain changes for the sake of the general good of history. Even though the nature of these changes is determined collectively by all the Eternals, the others blame Technicians for the negative side effects that accompany them. Harlan is able to withstand this prejudice fairly well because he is good at his specialty.

Harlan is the personal Technician assigned to Senior Computer Laban Twissell of the Allwhen Council. Unfortunately, Twissell himself is not popular with everyone, everywhen. Assistant Computer Hobbe Finge is Harlans direct supervisor in the 482d century, and Finge holds a grudge against Twissell for not promoting him quickly enough in the Eternal hierarchy. Harlan mistakes Finges animosity on account of his connection with Twissell for jealousy over Noys. For safety, he spirits his lover away to the far future, stashing her in the year 111,394.

Meanwhile, Harlan becomes more absorbed in his hobby, studying the history of the primitive period before Eternity was developed in the 27th century. For some reason, he is encouraged by Twissell in this direction and even assigned to teach a young Cub everything he knows about the subject. Finally, Twissell reveals that the Cub is none other than Vikkor Mallansohn, the inventor of the Temporal Field.

Mallansohn is being encouraged to learn about primitive history because he must be returned to the distant past to reenact his discovery. If this historical circle is not closed, Eternity will never be constructed in the first place. History would run wild without the benefit of the changes in reality continually being made by the Eternals. Their main fear is that atomic weapons will be allowed to come into existence too early and that humanity will destroy itself.

Noys Lambent has a different point of view. Her homewhen is a far, far future period that has independently developed its own form of time travel. She and her era want to terminate Eternity because it has frustrated all attempts to explore space. The adventurous spirit that might have destroyed Earth in a nuclear holocaust also would have made it possible to develop faster-than-light space travel. This lack of spirit means that humanity has not been able to take its place among the stars with other intelligent species.

Noys returns with Harlan to the primitive era ostensibly to help Mallansohn close the circle and preserve Eternity. By this time, Harlan has discovered her true origins and motives. With his blaster trained on Noys, Harlan is faced with a stark choice. On one side is the status quo, with the Eternal's "perfecting", through reality changes, an Earth that continues to shrink in spirit and creativity. On the other hand is his passion for Noys. On her side are the potential for both nuclear annihilation and unlimited exploration into the expanding universe. Harlan chooses love and renders changing history impossible. He takes the rest of humanity with him as he leaps onto the terrifying path of irrevocable action. Eternity ends, but infinity begins.

ANALYSIS

Classic science fiction seldom doubts that romance is to be found among the stardust of deep space. H. G. Wells set the tone with his tale of the triumph of young love over superstition in *The Shape of Things to Come* (1933). In the Golden Age of science fiction, rocket science was sexy. This assumption came under increasing attack beginning in the 1960s, as science in general was portrayed more often as a threat to any kind of human feeling. Thereafter, the urge to penetrate the cosmic unknown was more likely to represent an escape from more earthy, erotic relations.

The Eternals in *The End of Eternity* seem to be a vehicle for a veiled parody of the Catholic church. Women are not ordinarily inducted into the organization, readers are told, because their disappearance tends to create more serious disturbances in the flow of history. In practice then, the Eternals are a brotherhood. They exist outside society and conspire to manipulate history in order to realize prophecy and to perfect the moral behavior of humanity. Eternals are not necessarily celibate, but they do require prior clearance from the hierarchy for sexual liaisons. The protagonist, Andrew Harlan, is a virgin until he meets the only female character in the novel, Noys Lambent. She represents both the temptations of the flesh and free intellectual inquiry into the universe that lies beyond the control of the Eternals.

The End of Eternity shows Isaac Asimov at his very best. He takes the basic science-fiction concept of time travel and turns it upside down and inside out in a tour de force of exhilarating variation. Ironically, even though most of the novel takes place outside the ordinary sequence of history, the action is intensively plotted. The two basic story lines weave in and out of each other with double helical precision. Gradually the love story, involving Harlan and Noys, and the struggle to preserve Eternity attain one dramatic focus. They are resolved together in a breathtaking and satisfying finale.

—*Steven Lehman*

THE ENDER SERIES

After annihilating the alien Buggers, Ender Wiggin justifies the lives of the dead and strives to prevent the destruction of three other sentient life-forms

Author: Orson Scott Card (1951–)
Genre: Science fiction—future war
Type of work: Novels
Time of work: The near future and three thousand years later
Location: Earth and the HundredWorlds planets of Lusitania and Path
First published: *Ender's Game* (1985; largely expanded version of a novella in *Analog*, 1977), *Speaker for the Dead* (1986), *Ender's War* (1986, omnibus edition of *Ender's Game* and *Speaker for the Dead*), *Xenocide* (1991), *Children of the Mind* (1996) and *Ender in Exile* (2008)

THE STORY

The novella version of *Ender's Game* (1977) was Orson Scott Card's first published science-fiction story. The tale of Ender Wiggin, a child being trained to lead Earth's space fleet in a war against the alien Buggers, quickly became one of the most popular *Analog* novellas of all time. Several years later, while Card was working on *Speaker for the Dead* (1986), he discovered that the novel's extensive background could best be established by revising *Ender's Game* as a novel and developing Ender's character as the adult "speaker." *Xenocide* (1991) continues the story, developing both the characters and the themes introduced in *Speaker for the Dead*. A fourth Ender novel, *Children of the Mind* (1996) concludes the series.

Ender's Game tells how Earth barely defeats a fleet of alien Bugger ships that attacks without warning or provocation. A generation later, Earth believes that the Buggers will return in strength, intent upon destroying humankind. Military intelligence frantically tries to identify a genius to lead a successful military defense. Ender Wiggin is bred to be that leader. As a child of six he is sent to a space Battle School where, for five years, he engages in a series of war and strategy games designed to prepare him for the anticipated war. Mazer Rackham, who orchestrated the first military victory against the Buggers and who has been kept alive via relative space travel, supervises the child's final training. To Ender's surprise, he discovers that he was not playing games; he actually was directing Earth's offensive against the Buggers, resulting in their complete destruction. The story ends years later, when Ender discovers a message and a queen pupa left to him by the Bugger Hive Queen. Ender becomes the Buggers' interpreter and apologist. As a "speaker for the dead," he compassionately explains the Buggers' desire for reconciliation with humankind and their prayer for forgiveness. He departs to search the universe for a safe place where the queen pupa can hatch.

Speaker for the Dead is set three thousand Earth years later. Ender is still alive as a result of extensive travel at the speed of light. Another intelligent alien species has been discovered on the Hundred Worlds planet of Lusitania, and a human colony has been established to observe the alien Pequininos, or Piggies. When a Piggy brutally disembowels the xenobiologist Pipo Figueira, Ender travels to Lusitania to speak his death. He learns that a Piggy goes through three stages of life, first as a larva, then as a Pequinino, and finally as an intelligent tree. A drug is administered so the Piggy can be ceremoniously disemboweled to achieve the third, adult life phase. When the Piggies disemboweled Pipo, their intent was to honor him. Ender also discovers that the Piggies' life transformation is made possible by a highly contagious virus called the descolada, absolutely necessary to them but deadly to all other lifeforms. *Speaker for the Dead* ends with the Starways Congress sending a fleet to annihilate Lusitania, thereby ensuring that the deadly descolada will never be spread. This xenocide will destroy Piggies, humans, and, unbeknownst to everyone except Ender, the Buggers who have finally found a new home on Lusitania.

Xenocide begins on the Hundred Worlds planet of Path, a religious colony where the "god-spoken" pay the price of revelation through humiliating obsessive-compulsive behavior. Gloriously Bright, the youngest of the god-spoken, is given the impossible task of discovering how the entire star fleet, on its way to annihilate Lusitania, suddenly vanished. On Lusitania, Ender works with the colonists and Piggies, trying to discover a way to render the descolada harmless against humans but still effective in its life-transforming function for the Piggies. The story becomes complex as divisions occur among the Piggies, among the humans, and among the god-spoken of Path. Misunderstandings and misinterpretations of data lead to cataclysmic mistakes in judgment. It is discovered that both the obsessive-compulsive behavior on Path and the deadly properties of the descolada on Lusitania have been produced through intentional genetic engineering. Although cultural traditions and relationships are destroyed in the process, Lusitania successfully alters the descolada. Every sentient species is saved, and Ender is left to re-establish relationships among species, worlds, and, most important, his own family, all the while trying to stop the Starways fleet.

ANALYSIS

Orson Scott Card is deeply concerned about the impact of his stories. He has written several essays and books explaining how he creates characters and how he addresses ethical, moral, and theological issues in his fiction. As he matured as a writer, he repeatedly returned to his early work in order to rewrite his stories to make them more "true." Card does not pretend that the incidents really happened; what he wants is for his readers to believe that his stories truthfully describe how people make ethical decisions and how they can improve the human condition.

Card believes that a story should be an end unto itself and consciously writes to the reader rather than to the critic. He reveals his characters' innermost beliefs and motives through their choices and actions. Card wants his readers to feel the choices his characters make and creates strong situations because he believes that a story's emotional impact is more important than its critical interpretation. Card believes that people have a hunger for stories that make sense of things.

Readers identify with EnderWiggin's loss of innocence. Employment of a child as a hero has become one of Card's most successful and most used techniques. His stories typically focus on children endowed with remarkable gifts that must be developed and used to provide salvation for their communities. *Xenocide*'s god-spoken, Gloriously Bright, is one such child facing almost unbearable opposition. Ender is brilliant, but as a boy he must pay the price of loneliness that is demanded of children who value genius more than athletic ability and strength. Readers also respond to Card's creation of futuristic battle-training strategies. Each phase of Ender's training, each new game, rings true. Ender's training regimen, it is interesting to note, has been read as both a justification of and a denunciation of the military mind.

When Card rewrote *Ender's Game* as a novel, his increased skill as a speculative writer was manifest through the new dimensions brought to the story. Ender is led to discover the true nature of the alien Buggers and becomes their apologist. Because of his sympathetic explanation of their lives, Ender, who became the literal savior of humankind by defeating the Buggers, became despised as "Ender the Xenocide."

In *Speaker for the Dead*, the religious metaphor of Ender's life is extended when he arrives to speak for the dead of Lusitania and discovers the secret of the descolada. Ender evolves from the role of savior and prophet to that of martyr, knowing he will become infected with the virus and be quarantined on Lusitania for the rest of his life. *Speaker for the Dead* is typical of Card's intent to expand science fiction beyond its adolescent action characters with no ties to mothers, fathers, or children. His unique blend of storytelling and morality mature in this tale of adult family relationships.

Card creates his most complex ethical dilemma in *Xenocide*. The Starways Congress has sent a fleet to destroy Lusitania, including the descolada, Piggies, and humans. Card succeeds in weaving an intricate tale that threatens the existence of four sentient alien species, the human colony, and the god-spoken elite of Path. In each facet of the tale, ethical dilemmas are created as individuals try to do the right thing but, out of ignorance, make cataclysmic mistakes that can lead only to annihilation. Ender's character progresses from martyr to discoverer and creator as Card amplifies the themes of military might and obeisance to authority, adding an examination of religious obsessive-compulsive behavior and theorizing on the nature of eternal intelligences.

Card's Ender Wiggin stories established him at the cutting edge of character-based speculative science fiction. *Ender's Game* received the Nebula (1985), Hugo (1986), and Hamilton/Brackett Awards (1986). *Speaker for the Dead* earned an unprecedented second set of science fiction's highest honors, the Nebula (1986) and Hugo (1987), as well as the Locus Award (1987). *Xenocide* received several nominations and received the best novel (1992) award from the Association for Mormon Letters.

—*Gerald S. Argetsinger*

THE ENDS OF THE EARTH

Stories describing small deaths that parallel the ways the author sees people destroying the world

Author: Lucius Shepard (1943-2014)
Genre: Fantasy—new wave
Type of work: Stories
Time of work: Primarily the late twentieth century
Locale: Primarily the United States, Central America, and Vietnam
First published: 1991

The Story

Lucius Shepards second story collection contains fourteen stories from the late 1980s. In the title story, author Raymond Kingsley leaves New York City for Livingston, Guatemala, referred to as the End of the Earth. There he meets Ryan, Carl Konwicki, and Odille LeCleuse, each fleeing some misery. Konwicki and Kingsley begin to play a Mayan board game. LeCleuse and Kingsley become lovers, and Kingsley writes a novel. He has frightening dreams about stone temples where aliens torture humans. He gradually changes into the character of one of the game figurines, and he kills Konwicki and some townspeople. His spirit is now trapped in the figurine. LeCleuse returns to Paris and Kingsley to New York, his new End of the Earth.

"Delta Sly Honey" is the story of a young soldier, Randall J. Willingham, who works on corpse detail during his tour in Vietnam. Moon, a sadistic top sergeant, makes Willingham his victim and whipping boy. Each night, the ordinarily withdrawn Willingham radio broadcasts to the platoons in the field, finally addressing a mythical, ghostly Delta Sly Honey patrol. One night the patrol answers him. Willingham goes AWOL, and the Delta Sly Honey company materializes and kills Moon. Willingham returns and is, in time, seduced by Delta Sly Honey.

In "Bound for Glory," an unnamed man and his partner Tracy leave the southwestern town where they have been living. Traveling toward Glory by rail through the Patch, a dark place on Earth where mutant creatures live, Tracy metamorphoses into a strange animal. The hopeless protagonist survives the trip but later rides his horse triumphantly into the Patch, becoming a dark king.

After a shipwreck, Jack Tyrell and Bert Cisneros wash ashore on a blasted island south of Marthas Vineyard in the story "Nomans Land." Tyrell meets Astrid, an enigmatic entomologist who studies the island's spiders. She explains that the deadly white spiders control humans through dreams. The human race has been all but eliminated; only images of it are left in the minds of the few survivors, who are playthings for the spiders. Tyrell accidentally kills Astrid, then drowns. Misunderstanding the spider-gods, Cisneros is trapped in a wasteland, unable to commit suicide.

"Life of Buddha" is a meditation on love. Buddha is the nickname given to a squat black heroin addict who guards Pete's shooting gallery in Detroit. Buddha has nearly transcended his physical existence but is "grounded" when a transsexual friend commits murder. Using magic, the friend changes into a woman, and Buddha makes love to her. The act destroys his transcendence, so he throws all his love onto Pete. Now free, Buddha disappears into his own spirit paradise.

Tom Puleo, a Vietnam veteran, returns to Vietnam in "Shades" because the ghost of one of his old platoon members, Stoner, has been sighted at the village where Stoner was killed. In a series of encounters with Puleo, Stoner talks about the "Land of Shades." He draws energy from Puleo, enough to reach a kind of spiritual escape velocity. Puleo discovers that the Vietnamese have accomplished this before and that he has been manipulated again.

"The Scalehunter's Beautiful Daughter" is a novella about Catherine, an inhabitant of Hangtown, built on the side of an enormous, bewitched dragon named Griaule. Fending off a rape, Catherine kills her attacker and retreats into the dragon's innards. There she meets Amos Mauldry and a group of Feelies, inbred humans who kill huge parasites that infest the sleeping dragon. Catherine is imprisoned for years and uses the time to learn about the dragon's ecology. After a decade, she realizes that her purpose is to save the humans who protect Griaule. She is killed as she warns the

Feelies but is duplicated by a curious plant called the Ghostvine. The new Catherine leaves the dragon.

ANALYSIS
Ostensibly fantasy stories, these fictions are intensely relevant, both politically and morally. Using the arsenal of his imagination, Shepard discusses drugs and addictions, sex, love, war, colonialism, barbarism, magic, ghosts, and solipsism. Shepard, a Southern writer, moves his stories from the Atlantic Northeast (Maine and New York) through the Southwest (Arizona, Texas, and Mexico) and Latin America (Guatemala, Nicaragua, and Panama) to the Far East (Vietnam).

Most of the stories contain some form of magic. As one character says, "Where I see the workings of gods or devils, you may see the actions of logical consequence. For me, the world is a vast spell, for you an intricate coincidence." There's scarcely any distance between those poles. Shepard erases that distance entirely.

These stories are, in tone, style, and content, reminiscent of Joseph Conrad's fiction. Shepard is a Vietnam veteran enraged by U.S. colonialism, particularly in South America, which he perceives as an unspoiled garden of evil and beauty. He reworks hackneyed horror tropes and the Southern gothic to snare his readers. His fevered writing conjures the dark nastiness of Edgar Allan Poe, Nathaniel Hawthorne, and Herman Melville. "The Ends of the Earth" is a typical Conradian story, in which all are guilty and none deserve to live. "Delta Sly Honey" proposes that no one is more evil than a shy American boy with a big gun. "Nomans Land" is one of the most remarkable evocations of Melville's Nantucket coast, offering oceans of solipsism in which to drown. Astrid believes that the lack of humane acts in the twentieth century is a result of humans dying out. "The Scalehunter's Beautiful Daughter" is an extended allegory (related to Grimms fairy tales) about aging and growing up. The stories all are allegories about the world and its destruction. Throughout his fiction Shepard's characters try desperately to reach love through sex, occasionally succeeding (most notably in "Life of Buddha").

Some may find Shepard's prose too purple or antique, yet the style is grippingly luminous. These are stories of passion, excess, and hopelessness. They are about the small deaths people suffer. The narrator says about Catherine, the scalehunter's daughter, "From that day forward she lived happily ever after. Except for the dying at the end. And the heartbreak in between."

—*Tim Blackmore*

ENGINE SUMMER

In the aftermath of a holocaust, humankind survives in isolated settlements, each establishing its own perspective on advanced technology

Author: John Crowley (1942–)
Genre: Science fiction—post-holocaust
Type of work: Novel
Time of work: Several generations after a holocaust
Location: Earth
First published: 1979

THE STORY
Looming behind the narrative is a legendary story of humankind before the Storm. While those known as the angels vigorously pursued technological advancement, the Long League, led by its matriarchs, tried to counter the ill effects. Taking a third option, the people of Big Belaire avoided technological conflict by taking to the Road and finally building the Warren. When the Storm came (whether it was ecological disaster or warfare, or both, is unclear), the angels departed Earth in their flying city, their proudest achievement, leaving the rest of humankind behind in isolated pockets.

The story opens with Rush that Speaks, a disembodied voice, telling his story to the angels. The voice belongs to an imprint of the original Rush's memory, personality, and consciousness, recorded in one of the angels' miraculous machines. The actual Rush lived six hundred years earlier, in an era that was itself several generations after the Storm.

Rush's story is a detailed account of humankind's survival on Earth after the Storm. It begins in his birthplace, the Warren, a settlement that strives to live within human limits and in harmony with nature and whose chief virtue is telling the truth. Periodically, the people known as Dr. Boots's List, who claim to be descendants of the Long League, visit the Warren to trade, especially for St. Bea's bread, an organic substance that promotes a sense of well-being and unity with the environment.

Once a Day, Rush's adolescent love, leaves with Dr. Boots's List. He follows her a year later. Before searching for her, he spends a year with Blink, a hermit who has collected books and other artifacts from the angel ruins.

After virtually sleeping through winter in Blink's treehouse, Rush moves on, walking over the Road, the crumbling interstate highway system. When he finds Dr. Boots's List on the Road, Once a Day is with them. He accompanies the group to Service City, where they live with their giant cats in a ruined angel building.

Each member of Dr. Boots's List routinely receives a letter from Dr. Boots. When Rush asks for his letter, he is taken to a machine that allows him to enter into the mind of a recorded personality. The experience leaves him feeling a sweet simplicity that is beyond the need for words. Later he will learn that the mind recorded in the machine is a cat who was named Dr. Boots.

Once a Day, fearing that Rush's experience with Dr. Boots will change him in a way that she cannot accept, will not return to Service City until Rush leaves. He moves on, next encountering Teeplee, a scavenger living amid the ruins of the angels, aimlessly gathering objects that he does not understand. After a short time scavenging with Teeplee, Rush decides to return to the Warren.

Before reaching the Warren, Rush encounters a man parachuting from the sky. He is Mongolfier, an angel from the floating city, alerted to Rush's position by objects that Rush scavenged. He has a simple request: He wants to record Rush's mind, just as Dr. Boots's mind was recorded. Rush agrees, and at this point the story comes full circle. The living Rush goes on to the Warren, presumably to live out his life. The recording of his mind stays with the angels. To generations of angels living in the floating city, he tells his story up to the point of meeting Mongolfier. He knows nothing further, not even what happened in the remaining life of the person he was.

ANALYSIS
In post-holocaust novels, humanity has been wiped out in many different ways—ecological calamity, nuclear warfare, extraterrestrial invasion, and so on. The special turn that *Engine Summer* takes on this subgenre is that it does not emphasize the process of destruction; instead, it focuses on the way of life of the survivors. Further, the world is not presented in a coherent form by an omniscient narrator. As in Russell Hoban's *Riddley Walker* (1980), another post-holocaust novel, readers themselves reconstruct the lost world from what the narrator reveals.

At the basic narrative level, *Engine Summer* reveals several forms of technological adaptation. The people of the Warren live largely unconcerned with the angels, as they had gone separate ways even before the Storm. Pieces of angel technology are worth saving as curiosities, but the people of the Warren do not seek them out. They value knowledge, even angel knowledge, but only if it serves wisdom.

The people of Dr. Boots's List, on the other hand, gather and proudly use the artifacts, even those they barely understand. They treasure most the machine that stores the mind of Dr. Boots, though their encounter with it leaves them passive and accepting of a static way of life amid the angel ruins. Later, the depiction of Teeplee, whose entire existence is given over to scavenging angel artifacts, is a commentary on the pointlessness of Dr. Boots's List.

Finally, the angels themselves, heirs to technological perfection, can be seen only as selfish and inhumanly cruel. Although Mongolfier takes a heroic risk to record Rush's mind, he is not typical of his kind. The rest remain in their flying city, far above the dangers and ills of Earth, experiencing only through the mind of Rush what a real life might be like. They wake him century after century, unwilling to erase him from the machine and end his agony. He will live indefinitely in a kind of Indian summer, what his people mistakenly call engine summer.

An author of both science fiction and fantasy, John Crowley has one of the finest prose styles of his generation, and his closely textured fiction invites several levels of interpretation. Perhaps it is for these reasons that his output has been comparatively small—no more than a handful of novels and several story collections in a career that started in 1975 with his first science-fiction novel, *The Deep*.

—Steve Anderson

EON AND ETERNITY

The return of an asteroid through time and space remakes the history of the human race

Author: Greg Bear (1951–)
Genre: Science fiction—future history
Type of work: Novels
Time of work: 2000 C.E. and after, as well as various time metrics in alternative universes
Location: Earth and alternative Earths, the asteroid Thistledown, and the cosmic space known as "the Way"
First published: *Eon* (1985) and *Eternity* (1988)

THE STORY

Eon and *Eternity* are among the most ambitious science-fiction novels ever published. They chronicle a number of futures for the human race and perhaps the most sweeping, speculative, and awesome future history ever proposed.

On December 31, 1999, Earth's scientists are nervous. A mysterious asteroid called "the Stone" has suddenly come into orbit around Earth. When American space missions explore "the Stone," they find that it not only seems to have been inhabited by humans but to have been occupied more than a millennium ago.

The other side of this enigma is glimpsed when veteran Hexamon operative Olmy reports to his superior, the presiding minister of Axis City. Axis City is a settlement of humans, in the far future, who have explored a relativistic cosmic continuum called "the Way" and established themselves there in commerce and rivalry with various alien peoples. The leaders of the Hexamon, which is the political structure of the humans in the Way, are stunned to find out that Thistledown, the asteroid spaceship from which their ancestors had set out from Earth more than a thousand years before, had not only returned to its original orbit but gone back to a time three hundred years before it had been constructed. Olmy returns to Thistledown in order to explore further.

Meanwhile, the American expedition explores the asteroid's seven chambers and finds out much of the amazing truth for themselves. The expedition, led by the capable Garry Lanier, includes Karen Farley, a British-born Chinese scientist with whom Lanier falls in love, and Patricia Vasquez, a brilliant young Hispanic American scientist who alone can understand the mathematical intricacies of the far future. For Earth people, the biggest secret of Thistledown is not the Way itself but the asteroid's library, which contains pictures of a nuclear conflagration that had taken place in Thistledown's "past" at a date in the near future of Earth. Russia has a spy within the expedition, and thus the secret gets out, bringing political tensions on Earth to the breaking point. Ironically, the pictures of the conflagration on the parallel world touch off, in the present world, the very events they depict. Much of Earth is destroyed, and all existing political systems are reduced to ruins.

Patricia's parents and fiancé are among those vaporized to death, and she becomes at once both inconsolably depressed and determined to find some way, in the topsy-turvy world of parallel universes made possible by the advanced mathematics of the Way, to reverse time and fate, thus bringing her loved ones back. In conducting this research, she threatens the fundamental equilibrium of the Way, so Olmy abducts her and takes her to Axis City. Olmy, though, has special plans for Patricia. He realizes that her mentality is similar to that of Konrad Korzenowski, the man who centuries "later" in time had designed the Way. Korzenowski has been assassinated, but Olmy, using the advanced technology of the Hexamon, can revive him if Patricia agrees to share her mentality.

Meanwhile, the desperate Russians attack Thistledown itself, though the danger is defused when their old-guard Communist leaders are outwitted by Pavel Mirsky, a visionary subordinate. Hexamon authorities take all humans from Thistledown to Axis City. The Earth people are awed by the technological progress the Hexamon people have made in their thousand-year odyssey, but the Hexamon is in itself split. The Way is filled with pernicious, alien enemies called the Jarts, against whom the Hexamon is barely holding its own. Part of the Hexamon wishes to destroy the Way and go into orbit around Earth, while the other wishes to accelerate the speed of the Way and thereby crush the Jarts. Because the two plans are not incompatible, it is decided that Axis City will split into two parts. Meanwhile, Korzenowski is reincarnated using Patricia's mentality. He decides to go with the Earthbound faction. Patricia gets her part of the bargain and is allowed to search for an alternative Earth where she can find her loved ones. She fails in this attempt, landing in an alternative universe where the Ptolemaic dynasty of Egypt in the Hellenistic Era was never conquered by Rome, and therefore all of subsequent history has been altered.

Lanier returns to Earth with the Korzenowski faction and marries Karen Farley. The Laniers participate for fifty years in the Hexamon-led reconstruction of Earth from its nuclear devastation. This peace is imperiled when Mirsky reappears, after having gone with the part of the Hexamon who had accelerated to infinity. Mirsky reveals that his group has literally traveled to the end of time, where an impersonal entity called the Final Mind, the culmination of all mental being, prevails. The Final Mind feels endangered by the existence of the Way, which has been closed but not destroyed, and therefore asks the Hexamon to reopen it. Olmy participates in this project, capturing a Jart who he thinks he can use for intelligence. The Jart deceives him and dominates him. It is revealed that the Jarts are in fact performing the Final Mind's mission in insisting on destroying the Way. The Way is successfully destroyed, and Korzenowski decides to join the Final Mind, where humanity's ultimate destiny lies. Lanier and Mirsky, though, are sent by the Final Mind back through history, for reasons and purposes unknown even to them. They will carry on the human quest for knowledge that the now-destroyed Thistledown exemplified.

ANALYSIS

Greg Bear's novels are so massive and ambitious that even an extensive summary hardly does them justice. Bear's sweeping vistas show how successful a complex and visionary conception of the future can be. Although some of Bear's shorter-term predictions have been superseded by history, his long-term vision of the future is compelling.

For all the complexity of the *Eon-Eternity* diptych, the two books are dominated by several basic themes. Perhaps the most central of these is the opposition between going "home" and journeying "out," of seeking knowledge versus returning to deep and permanent loyalties. This dichotomy can be seen even within the councils of the advanced Hexamon itself, in which the "Geshel" faction, favoring technological progress, is opposed to the "Naderite" group, which opposes science and wishes to return to Earth. Bear implies that it is foolish to hope to suppress either of these tendencies in the human spirit. When the Naderites let the Geshels take half of the Hexamon into infinity and take their half to Earth, this does not prevent the eventual emergence of neo-Geshels within the Naderite group who wish to reopen the Way.

Bear threads this going home/voyaging forward dichotomy throughout the two books. Lanier and his wife Karen go home with the Naderites, even though it is to a devastated Earth they have never known. Patricia, on the other hand, attempts the absolute negation of all given reality. Her only purpose is to recover and rejoin her family. The Hexamon itself has made many almost inconceivable steps forward. It has made it possible to store souls in a kind of eternal afterlife, to traverse different dimensions of time and space, to preserve essential human identities even after the body has died, and to allow humans to assume any size, shape, or form that they wish. None of these achievements can eliminate human nature. The bickering between the Naderites and Geshels is as fierce as that between the much more "immature" Russian and American factions among the earthlings.

The figure caught most paradoxically between these two tendencies is Korzenowski. Born of Naderite parents, he nevertheless designed the

Way, which made it possible for all the Geshel dreams of progress to come true. Even though he seems to have betrayed his heritage, he becomes the Naderite patron saint who is needed to lead the Hexamon back to Earth. With a name clearly alluding to the original Polish name of the twentieth century British novelist Joseph Conrad, Korzenowski exemplifies the contradictory bind brought into being by the engagement between scientific, intellectual curiosity and human yearning.

It is Bear's deep spiritual and psychological insight that makes the reader able to digest the huge panoply of concept and detail he portrays in these two books. Whatever complexities humans of the future may produce, Bear implies, they will always be involved in two central pursuits: the perennial quests to know and to love.

—*Nicholas Birns*

THE E. T. NOVELS

An account of E. T.'s adventures on Earth, his rescue, his abasement when he returns home, and his daring and brilliant scheme to fly back to Earth

Author: William Kotzwinkle (1938–)
Genre: Fantasy—alien civilization
Type of work: Novels
Time of work: The 1980s
Locale: California, the Green Planet, and a spaceship
First published: *E. T.: The Extra-Terrestrial* (1982) and *E. T.: The Book of the Green Planet* (1985)

THE STORY

E. T.: The Extra-Terrestrial, based on the screenplay by Melissa Mathison, and *E. T.: The Book of the Green Planet*, based on a story by director Steven Spielberg, concern the redemptive and transformative love between an extraterrestrial and an earthling child, a love that changes the boy, Elliott, into a purposeful, self-assured young man. E. T. becomes a father figure for Elliott, protecting him and performing miracles for him. The first novel concerns the growing love of Elliott for E. T.; the second concerns E. T.'s love for Elliott.

In *E. T.: The Extra-Terrestrial*, a spacecraft seeking botanical specimens lands near a California suburb. One of the botanists, a ten-million-year-old elfin creature, strays too far from the ship and misses the takeoff. Alone and millions of light years from home, he approaches the house where Elliott and his family live. The fatherless household is boisterous and disorganized. Elliott in particular seems doomed to mediocrity by his lack of a father.

After the first, mutually terrified, meeting of E. T. and Elliott, Elliott hides him in his closet to protect him from unimaginative adults. He learns to love E. T. and realizes that E. T. possesses tremendous knowledge and wisdom. When Elliotts siblings meet E. T., five-year-old Gertie gives him a potted geranium and introduces him to her Speak-and-Spell toy, from which he deduces the phonemic structure of English. He also recognizes a computer in the toy, and by using parts of it, he constructs a device to signal his home planet. On Halloween, Elliott and the disguised E. T. bicycle to a hill to leave the transmitter. When they are followed, E. T. makes the bicycle fly, allowing them to evade their pursuers. They leave the transmitter.

The government, having kept surveillance on the house, closes in. When a government team descends on the house, E. T. is captured. Although a medical team tries to keep him alive, E. T. begins to die. He whispers to Elliott that the rescue ship has come, and he and the children make a heroic escape. They elude the officials chasing them by once again flying on their bicycles. As they bid a tearful farewell, E. T., carrying Gertie's geranium, boards the ship. Pointing to Elliott's forehead, he promises, "Ill be right here."

In *E. T.: The Book of the Green Planet*, the spaceship returns to E. T.'s home, the Green Planet, an Edenic world in which plants supply all the inhabitants needs. E. T., an eminent doctor of botany, finds that instead of being honored for his recent adventures, he has been demoted to the Farm, to begin again the centuries-long course of study. E. T. loves his home but yearns for Elliott, a fact that is underscored by the structural device of alternating scenes between the Green Planet and Earth.

E. T. periodically sends a telepathic replicant to Elliott. His eccentric aim, however, fails to land it on Elliott's forehead. Elliott, now interested in girls, is too distracted to notice the desperate efforts of the replicant to gain his attention. E. T. fears that Elliott will become that most horrid creature, Man, unless he intervenes. E. T.'s sadness is not allayed by the Contentment Monitors efforts to employ him in such a way that he will forget Earth. With the help of his friend, the silly but wise Flopgoggle, E. T. intuits that his fate is defiance of the traditions of his planet in order to return to Elliott.

Their first plan, to appropriate the star cruiser, requires that they free the three ancient Powers imprisoned under the planet—Occulta, Sinistro, and Electrum—to fly the ship. They are apprehended, and the plan fails. Consequently, the three Powers are re-imprisoned and E. T. is again demoted, this time to attend to the planet's most difficult botanical specimens.

Therein lies the solution to his problem. He breeds and launches a giant turnip with walls like steel and empowers the turnip spaceship with another plant. When the turnip and its emigrants are pursued, they push the turnip to full speed. It begins to wobble, and they appear to be doomed. E. T. sends one last, perfectly placed replicant to Elliott, who is transfigured by self-knowledge. The three Powers suddenly materialize and stabilize the turnip, which gains speed, outruns the pursuing spaceship, and passes through the Gateway of Dimension, headed for Earth.

Analysis

William Kotzwinkle's writing career, begun in 1969, has included fiction for both children and adults. He has received many awards, including the North Dakota Childrens Choice Award in 1983 and the Buckeye Award in 1984 for *E. T.: The Extra-Terrestrial*. Abandoning his idiosyncratic style, Kotzwinkle in these novels writes a straightforward narrative that nevertheless demonstrates a playfulness with language and a joyous buoyancy, combined with his own characteristic imaginative vision.

Criticism of *E. T.: The Extra-Terrestrial*, written from a screenplay, has focused on the differences between the 1982 film and the novel, with critics divided about their preferences. The novel elaborates internal action, in contrast to the external action of the film, and it gives a mechanism for interpretation. E. T.s consciousness is explored in the novel. He is portrayed as more imaginatively sympathetic as he is confronted with the limited vision of suburban Earth children. His determination to teach Elliott the wisdom of the stars is a promise unrealized by both the book and the film. The novel explains E. T.'s telepathic communication with Elliott, so that, for example, Elliott's inebriation when E. T. discovers beer is clarified. Elliott's mother, Mary, is a gratuitous and colorless presence in the film. The novel explains her motivations as she confronts the problems of a single parent whose children (and she herself) are swept along with each popular fad.

The novels continue Kotzwinkle's social criticism, exemplified, for example, in *Doctor Rat* (1976). In *E. T.: The Extra-Terrestrial*, the children form the moral touchstone, with the adults presented as either knaves or fools. Despite such pandering to platitudes, the novel speaks to something spiritual, with the alien suggesting the hidden self that may lie at the core of each person, the thing that, although superficially ugly, is revealed upon closer intimacy to be good, wise, and powerful. The chase scenes, when the children's bicycles outrun the adults powerful machines by soaring above them, embody a child's fantasy of power.

The more imaginative, though critically less noticed, *E. T.: The Book of the Green Planet* presents a dreamlike Edenic society in which cruelty and economic competition have been eliminated. Only spiritual and intellectual accomplishments are valued, and the planet is ruled by philosopher-kings, the Mind-Holders. Botanicus, the wisest and most learned botanist, revered for his penetration to the Flower Soul, knows with godlike certainty E. T.'s fate. Even in this paradise, the Fearful Potencies shadow the nights, and the three great Powers—Sinistro, Occulta, and Electrum (whose names suggest their peculiar power)—are locked away deep inside the planet because of their obsession with material wealth and physical power. E. T.'s helpers in his scheme—which, though regarded as the ultimate rebellion, is actually a sacrifice for love—consist of the three Powers; a misfit Micro-Tech devoted to music; an outmoded robot who, because one of his wires is crossed, searches for Truth; and the Flopgoggle, whose innocent silliness and profound wisdom keep the world on its course. Such characters invite an archetypal interpretation: The individual quest requires a divine silliness, a deep wisdom, some technical knowledge, and the unleashing of the power of the unconscious.

The numinous scenes on the Green Planet contrast with the spiritual aridity of the scenes on Earth, where Elliott undergoes the typical trials of a suburban adolescent. When his final transfiguration occurs, Elliott's mediocre conformity prevents the novel from achieving the intended impact. What could E. T. teach him? Could wisdom compete with high school dances and girls? The novel happily avoids this dilemma. Kotzwinkle, having reached an impasse, closes with the crew headed for Earth; he does not show what happens when the ship arrives. E. T.'s sacrifice is wasted on an undeserving recipient, but perhaps that, too, is part of the book's message.

—*Jo N. Farrar*

ETERNAL LIGHT

An account of an expedition to a rogue star, a mission to the center of the galaxy, and a fight to save the universe

Author: Paul J. McAuley (1955–)
Genre: Science fiction—future war
Type of work: Novel
Time of work: The distant future
Locale: Various locations on Earth and in space
First published: 1991

THE STORY

Paul J. McAuley's *Eternal Light* continues the story of Dorthy Yashida, a young Japanese woman with extraordinary psychic abilities, that began in his first novel, *Four Hundred Billion Stars* (1988). A terrible war and exodus by an alien race, the Alea, from the center of the galaxy millions of years before the time of the novel serves as the catalyst for the books events.

The Alea and humanity fought a tragic war that ended in the slaughter of the aliens. In an effort to evaluate a potential threat to Earth, two expeditions race to a rogue star heading toward the solar system. The expeditions eventually are transported to the center of the galaxy, where they confront and defeat a threat to the universe. Fifty years later, the survivors return to find a greatly changed Earth and try to adapt to the new order.

The novel begins when Dorthy Yashida is kidnapped by Talbeck Barlstilkin, a rich man who desires to build a personal empire by discovering the secrets of the rogue star traveling faster than the speed of light toward Earth. Talbeck forces Dorthy to join his expedition, but they have to be rescued by a Navy ship, the *Vingança*, after they are trapped in orbit around a neutron star. Traveling aboard the ship, Talbeck and Dorthy finally reach the rogue star and start to investigate a gas giant and its moon that orbit the star. The moon was created to serve as a gateway to the center of the galaxy. It is riddled with holes that are actually wormholes.

The *Vingança* travels through the moon and is transported to the center of the galaxy. Suzy Falcon, a naval pilot, and her mechanical companion, Robot, who shares his mind with another robot, Machine, go through a wormhole in the moon as well. Before arriving at the galactic core, Suzy and Robot/Machine discover a realm where a mysterious race called angels dwell with the spirits of the dead Alea. In this realm, the two learn that their real mission is to stop the Marauders, rogue Alea who drove the other members of their race from the galactic core using stolen technology found around a massive black hole in the core. The dead Alea female who shares Dorthy's mind eventually reveals this information to her as well.

Through their combined efforts, Dorthy, the Alea female, Robot, Suzy, and Machine succeed in their efforts to stop the Marauders mission of destroying the universe by drawing too much energy from other universes. As Dorthy, Robot, and Talbeck travel through the wormhole again, they arrive in the realm of the angels, where they are to take the spirits of the Alea so the aliens can live again. While they are in the angels realm, Talbeck uses a device that connects his mind with every other being in the universe.

Although Talbeck dies, his actions cause a revolution on Earth that leads to a takeover by the Witnesses, religious fanatics who believe that gods live in the galactic core. Dorthy, her baby daughter, and Robot eventually escape from Earth with the spirits of the Alea. Dorthy and her daughter settle on the planet Iemanja, where they free the Alea spirits and live in relative peace.

ANALYSIS

Eternal Light is a science-fiction epic that has received high praise from reviewers. The novel won the Philip K. Dick Award, a major award for science-fiction novels first published in paperback. The book greatly expands the story that McAuley began in Four Hundred Billion Stars, also a winner of the Philip K. Dick Award. McAuley has produced a remarkable novel that is pure science fiction but also examines social issues that confront contemporary society.

In portions of his novel, McAuley shows a strong background in science as he explains the theories behind the events in his novel. For example, he provides details of concepts behind traveling through wormholes and the devices the Marauders have constructed to draw power through the black hole in the galactic core. Although the explanations are complex, McAuley is careful not to render them incomprehensible for readers who do not have strong backgrounds in science. This ability to present technical and scientific explanations in an understandable manner is one of the strengths of McAuley's writing.

This novel does not, however, depend solely on its scientific component for its strength. It also examines several social issues. One issue that arises is racism. This comes into play when McAuley portrays how humans feel about the Alea. Most of the human characters, especially those in the Navy, consider the Alea to be enemies. They make no attempt to understand the aliens. The only woman who comes close to understanding that the enmity between humans and the Alea is a mistake is Dorthy, who forms a strong connection with them. The hatred that most humans feel for the Alea jeopardizes the mission in the galactic core several times.

Not all humans hate the Alea. The Witnesses, a fanatical religious sect, are as bad as the Navy in their misinterpretation of the aliens. They believe that the Alea, even the Marauders, are gods. This mistaken belief nearly leads to disaster during the mission. In his presentation of the Witnesses, McAuley also comments on the dangers of fanaticism. The Witnesses' single-minded pursuit of their belief blinds them to the threat of the Marauders and also leads Earth into a new dark age when they take over the planet.

— *David A. Oakes*

EVOLUTION'S DARLING

An artificial intelligence housed in a not-entirely-humanoid body is attempting to track down an artist long presumed dead when he encounters a professional assassin who has been sent to execute the artist because he was duplicated from another being

Author: Scott Westerfeld (1963–)
Genre: Science Fiction—superbeing
Type of Work: Novel
Time of Work: Future
Location: Outer space
First Published: 1999

THE STORY

Rathere is the daughter of the captain of a starship operated by a potential person, an artificial intelligence. Her father Isaah is a scoop, that is, he supports the two of them by discovering items of news that might be profitable if he delivers it even a few hours before its normal rate of dissemination. As Rathere approaches maturity, she begins to realize that her isolation from other

humans has been detrimental to the development of her social skills. She also discovers that her father is desperate to keep the AI from achieving sentience—at which point it would be legally a person with inherent rights, so she secretly helps it to achieve that goal despite his disapproval. The AI becomes a free person, calling itself Darling, although with an assumed male persona and housed in an artificial body. Isaah is imprisoned for having attempted to destroy Darling.

Two hundred years later, someone has managed to copy an AI, which is supposed to be impossible. One copy is destroyed, and the other resumes life as Oscar Vale. However, it is clear that some greater conspiracy is involved. None of this is immediately evident to Darling, but other individuals suspect the truth. Darling interacts in human society and is no longer bound to a ship, although his body is clearly artificial and equally recognizable as an AI. A famous AI sculptor, believed to have died in an explosion, appears to be alive after all because a new example of his work is found and authenticated. An art dealer hires Darling to find the missing artist. Darling meanwhile has met Mira, who admits that she performs illegal tasks for money, although she does not initially tell him that these include assassination. Both Darling and Mira are headed for the planet Malvir, although neither is aware that they have the same destination. Mira does not know the identity of her employers, although she suspects that they are AIs much older than Darling.

Through flashbacks, the reader learns that an AI operating a manufacturing facility secretly developed the technology to copy AIs because of its wish to make a duplicate of itself in a body that would be better able to develop his talent for sculpture. Oscar Vale was one of its early experiments with the new process it had developed, a process that is highly illegal. Mira, who destroyed one of the Vale copies, is unsettled when the surviving one exhibits knowledge that was only available to the erased copy. Darling, meanwhile, is threatened with death by a professional killer called a Warden, hired by a competing art connoisseur, unless he leaves the planet immediately. Mira sees them together and disables the Warden so effectively that he even escapes his long-term conditioning.

Mira and Darling compare notes. Darling has realized that the dead artist was copied and that is how new works are appearing. Mira admits that her job is to kill the copy, the result of a technology that is proscribed. The AI sculptor has, however, created more than one copy of himself, one of which takes the form of a teenage girl. Darling figures out what is happening slightly before Mira, and when she arrives, the teenage girl and the duplicate sculptor are both apparently dead at his hands. He explains that since the new art was made by the copy, it is all technically a series of forgeries. He has actually secretly uploaded the two personalities, and while Mira is destroying the master program responsible for the copying, he purchases a ship and escapes from the planet.

ANALYSIS

With few exceptions, traditional space opera has depicted space travel as essentially no different from taking passage on an ocean going vessel. A spaceship is simply a machine, a conveyance, and space was a medium to be crossed. Planets were the islands upon which interesting events sometimes occurred, but most of the time spent traveling from one to the next was tedious and routine. Modern space opera is generally much more complex. The ships and crews are not completely separate entities thanks to the interfacing of humans with their mechanical constructs. A starship fitted with an artificial intelligence may well be as much a character in the story as any of the humans, or in this case, may even become the protagonist.

Artificial Intelligence provides science fiction authors with a unique opportunity to consider what it is to be self-aware. The AI in this novel is slowing the rise in its Turing Quotient, which measures how close it is to sentience. If it should reach a level where it would be legally a person, its owner would have to set it free, so he deliberately plans to retard or even reverse its process rather than incur the cost of purchasing a replacement. This raises an interesting ethical question, although the author suggests that preemptive steps to prevent sentience from being achieved are acceptable. However, once that threshold is met, the former owner should be without recourse, even though any threshold is necessarily arbitrary.

The title refers to the fact that AIs with artificial bodies can upgrade and modify them as new discoveries are made, so they can follow a kind of evolutionary path within the lifespan of a single individual.

Westerfeld assumes there would be other major advances in technology. The AI monitors everything that Rathere does and uses this information to predict what experiences she would enjoy. They are in constant communication. Nanotechnology maintains her body in perfect health. There is a potential question about free will—the AI increasingly makes Rathere's choices for her—but this is never explored in any detail. While an AI may be sentient, that does not mean that they are human or that they entirely share human values, although some of the human characters in the novel also appear to be devoid of any sense of empathy. Both Mira and Darling are attracted to death and pain, and neither of them feels any compunction about inflicting torture or even death on a third party. Their sexual encounters are so intense that the starship's AI offers medical treatment. She presents him with a device that induces a temporary psychosis in AIs so that he can feel the intensity of pain, which is otherwise denied him. There is a strong suggestion that while machines have moved closer to being human, humans have similarly moved closer to acting like machines. There are also repeated references to using the Turing test on humans and possibly finding that some of them will not pass. The novel is primarily a rousing adventure story with dark overtones, and while it raises a number of potentially interesting questions, it never really comes to terms with any of them.

—*Don D'Ammassa*

THE EXORCIST

An ancient Assyrian demon possesses an eleven-year-old American child, engaging two Jesuit priests in a confrontation between good and evil as they attempt to exorcise the spirit

Author: William Peter Blatty (1928–2017)
Genre: Fantasy—occult
Type of work: Novel
Time of work: 1970
Locale: Northern Iraq and Washington, D.C.
First published: 1971

THE STORY

After finishing an archaeological dig in ancient Nineveh, Jesuit priest Lankester Merrin prepares to leave Iraq and return to the United States. A strange premonition, however, fills the elderly priest as he sifts through the recently collected artifacts and discovers an amulet bearing the head of Pazuzu, a demon of sickness and disease. Merrin leaves for home with an icy conviction that he will soon face an ancient enemy.

Meanwhile, in Washington, D.C., film star and recently divorced mother Chris MacNeil has rented a home across the street from Georgetown University, where she is acting in a film. As she lies in bed preparing her lines for the following day, she hears strange rapping sounds from somewhere in the house. Other strange events soon occur, the most serious being her daughter Regan's change in personality. Having found a Ouija board in the basement of the house, the eleven-year-old girl has contacted a "playmate" called Captain Howdy, who now physically abuses her. Medical tests prove futile in explaining Regan's emerging violent behavior, and her mother remains unconvinced by psychiatric speculations: She knows that the "thing" in her daughter's room is not Regan.

Although she professes no religious belief, she solicits the aid of a young Jesuit priest, Damien Karras—who is also a psychiatrist—and begs for an exorcism. Karras, tormented by a loss of faith and guilt resulting from his indigent mother's recent death, agrees to see the child in a medical capacity but doubts the possibility of possession. Events soon convince him otherwise. The demon, speaking through Regan's emaciated body in a groaning, horrific voice, evinces knowledge of Karras' mother's death and intones an unknown language that Karras tape-records. After having the tape analyzed, the priest learns that the language is in fact English, but spoken backward. On

The Exorcist

the tape, the personality confesses to be "No one," claims to fear "the priest," and repeats the word "Merrin" several times.

Karras receives permission for an exorcism, but the bishop of the diocese insists that a man with experience perform it. Karras may assist. Lankester Merrin, now at Woodstock Seminary in Maryland, receives a telegram without opening it, knowing what it requests of him. The demon awaits his arrival. As the elderly priest enters the house, an unearthly voice booms out his name from the child's bedroom. The exorcism commences immediately, but the cunning demon attacks Karras' guilt concerning his mother's lonely death, and Merrin is forced to send him from the room. Upon returning, Karras finds the elderly priest dead from an apparent heart attack and the demon laughing in victory. In a fit of rage, Karras attacks the possessed body of Regan, daring the demon to enter him, which it does. The demoniac transference is punctuated by a brief moment of lucidity, in which the priest finds his lost faith and exorcises the demon's power by hurling himself through the second-floor window to his death. Regan is saved. As she recovers physically, she remembers nothing of her ordeal.

ANALYSIS

Based on a reported case of demoniac possession in the Washington, D.C., area in 1949, William Peter Blatty's *The Exorcist* (1971) was his second novel. His other work also examines the question of evil. *The Exorcist* appeared four years after Ira Levin's *Rosemary's Baby* (1967), which also had demoniac terror as its subject. Together these books revitalized the fantasy-horror genre. They are among the most literate and frightening works of their era. Both books were instant best-sellers and were adapted into equally popular films.

The distinction between the novels by Blatty and Levin is noteworthy. *The Exorcist*, unlike *Rosemary's Baby*, is no horrific account of devil worship. On the contrary, it presents a deeply religious affirmation of life within a modern psychomachia, or warfare between good and evil for possession of a soul. That warfare, however, has changed significantly in a post-Freudian world that has redefined the soul and, more important, what constitutes evil. The damnation of Regan is never at issue: Her body and the ensuing exorcism merely provide the opportunity for the demon's confrontation with men of faith, particularly the exorcist Lankester Merrin, with whom it previously has battled and lost. In a secularized "God is dead" world, that confrontation appears grotesquely nostalgic: Good and evil apparently have lost all clarity, with humanity now assuming the prerogatives of Satan.

Blatty situates this modern psychomachia in a new age of faith, one in which the rational, scientific mind has for the most part supplanted a theological system of belief and its counterpart, the willful disobedience of God.

As the most fully realized character of the novel, the priest-psychiatrist Damien Karras is both a servant of God and a learned man of science, a man tormented by guilt who struggles to reconcile providential design with the darker recesses of the human mind. Karras becomes the modern Everyman of the psychomachia, caught between rational experience and irrational faith. In attempting to explain to MacNeil why her daughter's illness is a conflict of mind, not a battle with evil, Karras compares the human body to a massive ocean liner, with brain cells as the crew. One of these cells is the captain, who never knows precisely what the rest of the crew below decks is doing. Karras goes on to explain that when one cell assumes the command against the captain's wishes, or waking consciousness, mutiny occurs and a dual personality results. MacNeil responds that it almost would be easier to believe in the devil.

Karras metaphor modernizes the biblical mutiny that accounts for Satans fall and the ensuing warfare between good and evil. The unfathomable depths of the human mind, though less easily comprehended, have assumed supernatural powers. MacNeil's doubts are those of many people: Can evil be reduced to the chaotic intricacies of cells and neurons? The demons possession of Regan demonstrates to Karras that evil can be a force unto itself. His fatal encounter in the exorcism proves that evil affirms the existence of good, while good posits the reality of evil. With that knowledge, the necessity for faith triumphs.

—*Wayne Narey*

Eye in the Sky

After an accident at an atom smasher, seven sightseers and their guide find themselves in four different psychologically projected worlds, from which they must escape

Author: Philip K. Dick (1928–1982)
Genre: Science fiction—inner space
Type of work: Novel
Time of work: October 2, 1959, and immediately before and after
Locale: San Francisco, California
First published: 1957

The Story

Jack Hamilton, a bright young engineer; Marsha, his wife; and Charley McFeyffe, their friend, go to witness the testing of a new attachment on the Bevatron, a powerful new atom smasher on which Hamilton has been working. An uncontrolled proton beam slices away the viewing platform, hurling the three of them, their guide, and four tourists through the beam to the floor of the chamber sixty feet below. All are injured and hospitalized, and they recover at different rates.

Jack, Marsha, and Joan Reiss, one of the tourists, are the first to be released. They go to the Hamilton home, where strange things begin to happen. For example, Jack is attacked by a plague of locusts, and Bill Laws, their black guide (who has dropped in to visit), gradually devolves into a drawling, shuffling caricature of a black man. Eventually, Charley also joins them. Jack and he are carried up to heaven while hanging onto an umbrella. In heaven, they are examined by an enormous eye, the "eye in the sky" of the title. Finally, they understand that the proton beam has somehow freed them from the real world and locked them into the world as seen by Arthur Silvester, another of the tourists trapped with them in the fall.

That worldview collapses when Arthur is knocked unconscious, and the group moves on to the next setting. At first, they think they are back in the common world, but once again, things begin to go awry: The newspaper has no bad news in it, there are no annoying flies and gnats, and Russia seems simply to have disappeared. It becomes clear that this is the world according to Edith Pritchett, another accident victim. Edith simply eliminates from her view anything she does not like, and there are many such things. When she censors cats, ugly industrial sites, and sex, they know they must act. Holding their breath, they trick her into deleting air from her world and wait until she faints.

The rules of the next world are laid down by Joan, an extremely paranoid woman. The two chapters of this worldview are perhaps the most harrowing of the novel. The protagonists escape Joans universe only when she encloses herself in an impenetrable cocoon and dies.

The fourth and last subjective world, after some initial misunderstanding, turns out to be that of Charley. A Communist, he sees the United States as a nation of tough-talking, Chicago-style gangsters who exploit ordinary citizens. He, too, is eventually knocked out. The characters awake safely in the real world at the novels end.

Analysis

Philip K. Dick published his first novel, *Solar Lottery*, in 1955. *Eye in the Sky* was his fifth novel and one of the first to take up the theme that would eventually dominate his work: What is real? As Jack Hamilton and his companions move from worldview to worldview, how do they know which is the real world and which is not?

Eye in the Sky is most interesting for its use of setting. The novel employs a frame tale—Jack and the others in the common world—as well as four stories inside that frame, totaling five settings in *Eye in the Sky*. Among other things, the frame tales setting is marked by Communist paranoia. Marsha Hamilton is a freethinker: She contributes to left-wing causes, subscribes to left-wing journals, and attends left-wing meetings. Therefore, the Establishment sees her as pro-Communist, and her husband is branded a security risk and given a choice: to divorce his wife or quit his job. While under this cloud, the couple goes to the Bevatron demonstration.

Arthur Silvester's worldview is that of a religious fundamentalist, and the problems of living in a society constructed on the basis of religious fundamentalism are demonstrated in the chapters controlled by him. Edith Pritchett is a self-centered Victorian prude, and when she has control, she eliminates anything she finds uncomfortable, so that her world becomes less and less interesting. Joan Reiss, in her paranoia, constructs a world in which no one can be safe, in which nothing is what it seems to be and everything is dangerous. Finally, Charley McFeyffes world is a caricature of the Communist view of the United States. When the characters escape from it, they are back in the world of the frame tale, a world dominated, appropriately enough, by an excessive, paranoid fear of Communism. In other words, they have returned to the real America in the period when Eye in the Sky was written.

The two most fascinating things about Eye in the Sky are its use of setting as a means of characterization and its analysis of the major social ills of the United States during the 1950s. The worldviews of the four characters show what it would be like to live in their places (characterization); each worldview also highlights what Dick saw as a major social ill of the time (social analysis). Contemporary social criticism fueled Dicks writing up to *The Three Stigmata of Palmer Eldritch* (1965), when he began to concentrate even more fully on the issue "What is real?" as in such novels as *Ubik* (1969) and *VALIS* (1981). *Eye in the Sky* is one of Dicks best early novels.

–*Joseph F. Patrouch*

THE FACE IN THE ABYSS

Nicholas Graydon and the pagan princess Suarra adventure together in the hidden world of Yu-Atlanchi, where they battle the greed of ruthless American prospectors

Author: A(braham) Merritt (1884-1943)
Genre: Fantasy—evolutionary fantasy
Type of work: Novel
Time of work: The 1920s and 1930s
Locale: Primarily the lost civilization of Yu-Atlanchi in the Andes Mountains
First published: 1931 (serial form, "The Face in the Abyss," *Argosy All Story*, 1923, and "The Snake Mother," *Argosy*, 1930)

THE STORY

The Face in the Abyss was published as a novel toward the end of A. Merritt's career. A story with the same title appeared as a thirty-five-thousand-word story in 1923. After several years, Merritt wrote a sequel, "The Snake Mother." The two stories were combined to form the novel, which develops two seamlessly integrated plots united by the archetypal theme of the curse of gold (greed), by the motif of the treasure hunt, and by the figure of the protagonist, the young American adventurer Nicholas Graydon, whose explorations of the jungles of Central America serve as the motivation for the story's many physical adventures.

The first adventure involves Graydon and a band of three ruthless American cutthroats—Starrett, Soames, and Dancret—and develops both the treasure-hunt motif and the theme of the curse of gold. Graydon has naïvely teamed with them, to his later regret. Their rapaciousness brings them into contact with the lost civilization of Yu-Atlanchi in the Andes Mountains. They abduct and mistreat the kingdom's princess, Suarra. Graydon's three companions meet colorful deaths in their encounter with the evil and powerful "Face in the Abyss."

The story smoothly evolves into its second and much longer plot, which details Graydon's adventures in the kingdom of Yu-Atlanchi. Like all such quasi-utopian fantasy visions, it is based on Plato's myth of the lost Atlantis. While in Yu-Atlanchi, Graydon encounters some of fantasy fiction's most imaginative creations. These include the Snake Woman, Adana, timeless and all-powerful matriarch of the kingdom; Tyddo, the Lord of Folly, an ancient wizard and Adana's trusted adviser; Nimir, the masculine personification of evil in the story; Kon, the Spider Man; and various types of fantasy creatures, such as the Urd (lizard-men) and the degenerate and evil Dream Makers.

The story develops as a conflict between the good Adana and her followers—with whom Graydon quickly allies himself—and the evil Nimir and his followers, devotees of sadism and aesthetic escapism. It culminates in one of the finest Armageddon conflicts to be found in fantasy literature. The final bloody battle results in Adana's victory over Nimir, her retirement for a lengthy recuperation, and the wedding of the divine pair, Graydon and Suarra. This is the beginning of what is promised to be their long and benevolent reign over Yu-Atlanchi, now cleansed of evil.

Nimir, however, is merely the personification of the evil in Yu-Atlanchi. In reality, the evil is a primordial spirit (sometimes called the Shadow) that cannot be utterly destroyed but only imprisoned and that promises to free itself in the distant future to initiate the entire adventure again.

ANALYSIS

A summary cannot do justice to the various features of interest in this novel. These can best be understood under the headings of form, genre, and content. In its form, the novel is mature fiction written near the end of Merritt's career, when he was in complete control of the bifurcated form; that is, of two stories unified and treated as one.

His first long fiction, *The Moon Pool* (1919), was also the result of publishing as a novel two earlier shorter works, but the two are not nearly as successfully integrated as in this case. In The *Face in the Abyss*, Merritt controls theme, mood, characterization, and action in such a way as to make the "join" between the two original stories unnoticeable. The form, then, is as nearly perfect as one can expect to find in novels, which tend toward looseness of structure.

In terms of genre, the story is also quite interesting because it represents the successful amalgamation of several popular forms of storytelling. It is one of the best of the lost civilization novels popularized by such well-known writers as H. Rider Haggard, in *King Solomons Mines* (1886) and *She* (1887), and Merritts contemporary, Edgar Rice Burroughs. This type of story regained popularity with the Indiana Jones films beginning in the early 1980s. The novel is also, however, an example of what at one time was called science romance, providing some fascinating evolutionary speculation concerning the origins of the fantastic life-forms the protagonist encounters during the course of the story. The evolutionary theories employed by Merritt—a mixture of Darwinian and Jungian thought—were well known and widely accepted in Merritts day and provide him with a basis for demonstrating a sensitive empathy, not to be found in his earlier works, for even the sadistic creatures in the novel. Because all creatures are held to have evolved from the same urschleim as humans, they are all, the story emphasizes, integrally related.

Finally, the storys content is of two related kinds. As a pure adventure story, it is as good as any science romance ever published. Its *Bildungsroman* elements are equally good. Graydon's education into the secret knowledge of his true inner identity takes him on a quest as exciting as any of the physical contests he engages in along the way. All told, the novel is one of the finest renderings of the romance of lost civilizations and races.

—*Ronald Foust*

THE FACE IN THE FROST

Two magicians in a fantasy world undertake a journey to save humankind from the spell of Melichus, an evil warlock, and succeed through the assistance of the real world

Author: John Bellairs (1938–1991)
Genre: Fantasy—magical world
Type of work: Novel
Time of work: The Middle Ages
Locale: The imaginary North and South Kingdoms
First published: 1969

THE STORY

Prospero and his friend Roger Bacon, both wizards, embark on a journey to save humankind from the evil spell of their former colleague, Melichus. Melichus has found an old book, written in curious ciphers, which provides glimpses of some basic formulas of power when he tries to translate the strange writing. The more Melichus pursues the translation, the more entranced he becomes; what begins as intellectual curiosity quickly becomes an obsession with the power the spells might bring him. The formulas contain the secret to another reality, and whoever masters these arcane symbols holds the power to destroy the North and South Kingdoms. Prospero and Bacon strive to prevent this at any cost.

The mark of Melichus growing power over the land is the recurring image of the face in the frost, a yawning, vacant visage that evokes a nameless terror that cannot be dispelled by reason. Prospero and Bacon begin their journey by shrinking themselves and sailing a model ship down an underground stream leading from Prosperos root cellar. During their adventures, the magicians defeat a troll, use a prophetic looking glass, ride in a squash coach, repel spells cast by an enchanted forest, and climb a magical vine to reach the fairy-tale cottage Prospero and Melichus once shared in happier days. These familiar images from myths and fairy tales weave a rich tapestry of allusion throughout John Bellairs tale.

At the cottage, Prospero retrieves a green glass paperweight that contains the combined powers of Prospero and Melichus. Prospero enters the world of the prism, a strange place in which technology has prevailed. It is filled with electricity, lawnmowers, and the accouterments of modern civilization. He encounters M. Millhorn, a believer in the occult who has been waiting all his life for this moment. In exchange for the paperweight, Millhorn uses his knowledge of the Kabala to save Prospero and return him to his own world. Prospero finally remembers the spell he must use to destroy Melichus and the evil book. Prosperos world returns to normal, and he and Bacon celebrate their triumph with a party for their friends.

ANALYSIS

The character Roger Bacon clearly is intended to be an analogue of the real Bacon, a Franciscan monk known for his contributions to science and as an alchemist and dabbler in magic. Like his model, Bacon is devoted to the truth, wherever it may lead, and he is also a man of honor and courage. Prospero is modeled after William Shakespeares fictional sorcerer in *The Tempest* (1611), who sets out to right the wrongs of his world and, in so doing, employs "this rough magic" one last time to bring about a proper balance of persons and events. Bellairs character also is concerned with balance and with setting his world right; a forgetful man, clearly no match for the brilliant and logical Melichus, he nevertheless sets forth with a desperate kind of courage. His very lack of pretension and refusal to fool himself by championing his own considerable abilities are major assets in this struggle to the death.

Walter Gorn Old said in *The Kabala of Numbers: A Handbook of Interpretation by Sepharial* (1911) that an event is merely a rearrangement of parts of people's "sphere of reality." This is an appropriate comment on Bellair's book, both because the author mentions the Kabala as the solution to his characters dilemma and because he has rearranged historical facts in order to construct a fictionalized world of surpassing charm. Indeed, Bellair's novel deals directly with the question of the nature of reality. When Prospero enters the world of the prism, he is suddenly endowed with the ability to see the world as it really is, like Zed in John Boormans film *Zardoz* (1974). Zeds crystal contained all of human knowledge; with the knowledge thus gained of himself, Zed was able to destroy the prism, thus freeing people from the bonds of self-imposed technological shackles.

What appears to be a lighthearted adventure involving two bumbling wizards on a quest actually is a tale of great moral courage, tragedy, and the ultimate doom of the world. Everything in the book is seen through the two-sided mirror, a glass that reflects, in equal measures, fantasy and real life, the past and the present, humor and sorrow, and the pursuit of power and devotion to duty. The reader sees "through a glass darkly" to reach the truth on the other side. Like Lewis Carroll's Alice, Prospero must pass through the looking glass before he can defeat Melichus; he must see his world—and see evil—for what it really is before he can remember the spell.

Bellair's powers of description bring this book alive. Every leaf on every branch of every tree is limned in exquisite detail. Bellair's ability to make his readers see, smell, hear, taste, and touch the elements of his fantasy creation brings it alive for them. In the context of his story, this must surely be the ultimate paradox.

The Face in the Frost, published originally as a childrens book, has been reprinted in paperback as an adult novel and can be read on that level. Following this book, Bellair's penned about a dozen fantasy stories and tales, mostly in series format and designed primarily for the juvenile market.

—Mary A. Burgess

FAFHRD AND THE GRAY MOUSER

Fafhrd and the Gray Mouser are two friends of questionable ethics who become the most renowned rogues and swordsmen in the world of Nehwon

Author: Fritz Leiber (1910–1992)
Genre: Fantasy—magical world
Type of work: Stories

Fafhrd and the Gray Mouser

Time of work: Slightly before 200 b.c.e. to about one thousand years later
Location: Nehwon, a universe in a bubble
First published: *Swords and Deviltry* (1970), *Swords Against Death* (1970; expanded from *Two Sought Adventure*, 1957), *Swords in the Mist* (1968), *Swords Against Wizardry* (1968), *The Swords of Lankhmar* (1968; part as "Scylla's Daughter" in *Fantastic*, 1961), *Swords and Ice Magic* (1977), and *The Knight and Knave of Swords* (1988)

THE STORY

The Fafhrd and the Gray Mouser series was written over a period of at least four decades as thirty-six short stories and one novel (*The Swords of Lankhmar*). The stories form a coherent whole: the adventures of two of the greatest swordsmen and greatest rogues any world has ever known. The first three books were collected as *The Three Swords* (1989) and the second three as *Swords' Masters* (1990).

Fafhrd is a tall northern barbarian, and the Mouser is a small, dark man of uncertain but urban origin. They share a common attitude toward life because they are the sundered halves of an even greater hero from ages past. They meet as youths in fabled Lankhmar, the most cosmopolitan of the many cities of Nehwon, and instantly become friends. (Actually, this is their second meeting but their first "on camera.") Their friendship appears destined to last a lifetime. Thirty-four of the thirty-seven stories in this series chronicle their joint adventures; the first two occur before the two meet, and the third is the tale of their meeting. These adventures cover much of Nehwon and even part of the ordinary world. Fafhrd and the Mouser save Lankhmar many times, and the world itself more than a few, but many of their adventures are the sort that would naturally befall a pair of reckless wanderers in a world full of magic, mystery, and danger.

The two rogues have two magical patrons, neither of whom is human. Ningauble of the Seven Eyes and Sheelba of the Eyeless Face appear to be self-appointed protectors of Nehwon, occasionally sending the cavalry (in the form of Fafhrd and the Gray Mouser) to avert some catastrophe.

Fafhrd and the Gray Mouser encounter many women romantically over the years and care about more than a few deeply, but their friendship for each other always comes first. This is clearly true even in the last two books, when they make long-term attachments to two ladies of fabled Rime Isle (Fafhrd's love is Afreyt; the Mouser's is Cif). Most of these stories have the typical structure of an adventure story: Evil entities have designs that should be thwarted. Fafhrd and the Gray Mouser discover these designs, either by accident or otherwise, and oppose the villains. Not all the villains are killed, but their nefarious plans are rendered, at best, only partially successful. A few opponents come back to fight in subsequent stories, but there is no "evil mastermind" analogous to Fu Manchu or Professor Moriarty. Death, the Power of the Shadowlands, comes closest, with the sorcerer Quarmal, Lord of Quarmall, a distant second. At the end of the series, the two swordsmen, now middle-aged, are still firmly attached to each other and to their lady loves. It is clear that they were intended to have more adventures.

ANALYSIS

Fafhrd and the Gray Mouser were actually created by Harry Otto Fischer, but, with the exception of ten thousand words of "The Lords of Quarmall," Fritz Leiber wrote all the stories. The author's presence is felt through the somewhat archaic device of a narrator, whose comments, in the hands of a lesser writer, might have prevented total immersion within the fictional world. Leiber's mastery of narrative, pacing, dialogue, and character grab the reader and force him or her headfirst into fog-shrouded Lankhmar, or wherever Fafhrd and the Gray Mouser's wanderings take them.

The early stories in the Fafhrd and Gray Mouser series helped spawn an entire genre of fantasy stories whose protagonists are likable antiheroes. Leiber's literary influence on fantasy in the twentieth century has been exceeded only by J. R. R. Tolkien. L. Sprague de Camp was a contemporary and mined the same vein. Fantasy writers who appear to have been influenced strongly by Leiber include P. C. Hodgell, Michael Moorcock, and Roger Zelazny. The Thieves' World series of anthologies, edited by Robert Asprin and Lynn Abbey, could never have existed had not Leiber helped invent the genre to which it belongs. Fantasy roleplaying games owe their existence in part to this genre and, therefore, indirectly to Leiber.

Fafhrd and the Gray Mouser were explicitly a reaction to improbable fantasy heroes such as Robert E. Howard's Conan; Leiber said as much in an author's note in *The Swords of Lankhmar*. Indeed, in some ways they are almost parodies. Leiber made a point in his introductions to most of the books of asserting that Fafhrd and the Gray Mouser were the best swordsmen in all the worlds. In what he called "Induction," at the beginning of the first book, *Swords and Deviltry*, Leiber even claimed that Fafhrd and the Gray Mouser were the two reincarnated halves of a greater hero. This cannot be taken seriously, and the idea was used in only one of the stories ("The Curse of the Smalls and the Stars," one of the latest). Even the name of the world is a joke: It is "Nowhen" backwards, a reference to the famous novel *Erewhon* (1872) by Samuel Butler, but one evidently used only to amuse those in the know. This is not the only such sly inversion; for example, in *The Swords of Lankhmar*, Kokgnab is named as a source of subtle massage techniques. Even the seamy-side attitude of the whole series was in part a reaction to J. R. R. Tolkien's approach to heroic fantasy. Leiber hints at this as well in *The Swords of Lankhmar*.

There is far more to these stories, however, than reaction to traditional fantasy literature. The novelty of the likable antihero probably contributed much to the early popularity of the series. In addition, the strongly developed protagonists gave the reader something easy to identify with. The continued success of these stories, however, does not result from novelty. Leiber's story ideas were original and intriguing. He gave free rein to his imagination in inventing villains, religions, cultures, natural laws, and more. Nehwon sports a truly preposterous mythology and magic (not to mention geography), which add to its charm. Talking skulls and killer jewels are but the tip of the iceberg. Leiber was a good enough writer to make even the most ridiculous notion acceptable. His combination of writing skill, excellent story ideas, a unique and enchanting setting, and good characterization made the Fafhrd and Gray Mouser series what it is and earned for it a place among the great works of fantasy literature.

Leiber also employed, though sparingly, a trick used by many fantasy writers, that of having his characters discover, or know, scientific principles not known on Earth before the scientific age. For example, in "Stardock," the Mouser intuits why water boils at a lower temperature at high altitudes. Leiber reversed the trick in "Trapped in the Sea of Stars," having Fafhrd guess at cosmological interpretations that would be correct on Earth but are subsequently proved wrong in Nehwon.

There is another reason for the popularity of the Fafhrd and the Gray Mouser stories. Leiber peppered many of them with references to the ordinary world, such as the mysterious interworld traveler Karl Treuherz. "Adept's Gambit" even takes place on Earth, in the eastern Mediterranean of more than two millennia ago. These references to things terrestrial seem incongruous and so disturb the suspension of disbelief, but at the same time they provide personal interest for the reader.

It is interesting that, in so many stories, written over a span of about forty years, there are so few inconsistencies. The most glaring is the unintended sex change Sheelba undergoes in "The Curse of the Smalls and the Stars." In this story he becomes and has ever been a she, yet in all earlier stories featuring Sheelba, he was definitely male.

The role of sex (as opposed to gender) is important in this series, and it looms both larger and more kinky in the later stories. This is probably because the earlier stories were published at a time when sex in fantasy fiction was hardly acceptable, at least to publishers. By the time the later stories were written, many restrictions had been lifted. Leiber received the World Fantasy Award for Life Achievement, in no small part because of his success with the Fafhrd and the Gray Mouser stories.

—*David C. Kopaska-Merkel*

FAHRENHEIT 451

A depiction of a futuristic society in which reading is forbidden and books are burned by firemen

Author: Ray Bradbury (1920–2012)
Genre: Science fiction—dystopia

Type of work: Novel
Time of work: An indeterminate time in the future
Location: Implicitly an anonymous location in the United States

Fahrenheit 451

First published: 1953 (expanded version of "The Fireman," *Galaxy Science Fiction*, 1951)

The Story

It is ironic that in 1953, an asbestos edition of the novel, which describes a terrifying, censorship-obsessed society that burns books, was published. Ironic too is that in the 1980's, Ray Bradbury found that the publisher had, through the years, silently censored from his original text seventy-five sections of *Fahrenheit 451*. Stories published in the 1953 edition are omitted from most later editions.

Fahrenheit 451, which takes its title from the temperature at which paper burns, takes place in a sterile, futuristic society in which firemen burn books because the State has decided that books make people unhappy. Suspected readers are arrested. Instead of reading, people listen to "seashells," tiny radios that fit in the ear, and watch insipid television shows projected on wall-to-wall screens. In school, students play sports and learn nothing. Fast driving is encouraged, and pedestrians are arrested. Indiscriminate drug use, suicide, overpopulation, and war are rampant.

In this world lives Guy Montag, the main character, who smilingly and unquestioningly accepts his job as a fireman. Guy's wife, Mildred, watches endless hours of television and overdoses on narcotics. Early in the novel, a young neighbor, Clarisse, shocks Guy by asking whether he ever reads the books he burns and whether he is happy. Although she is later killed by a hit-and-run driver, Clarisse is the catalyst through which Guy begins to evaluate his life and career, and finally the society he supports. Clarisse and Mildred are foils: Clarisse's thinking and questioning is a threat to the State, whereas Mildred's zombielike addiction to television and pills makes her the personification of this society.

Guy's reeducation continues when he is deeply moved by the selfimmolation of an old woman who chooses to die with her books rather than be separated from them. It is at this point, early in the novel, that Guy secretly takes and reads one of the old woman's books to satisfy his curiosity.

Captain Beatty, Guy's supervisor and a master at brainwashing, rewrites history to say that firemen have always set fires and reading has always been forbidden. Beatty explains the State's philosophy that humans need only entertainment, not the insights, self-reflection, uncertainty, and occasional sadness provided by books. Beatty explains that in order to achieve societal equality and happiness, people should not be given two sides of an issue or books to debate, think about, or question. He insists that because some people dislike certain books, all books should be burned to ensure everyone's happiness.

Guy's increasing inner numbness draws him closer to reading books. It also draws him to Faber, a retired professor of English. Faber, a foil to Beatty, explains to Guy that what is contained in books gives life depth and meaning. Books can present a higher quality of information as well as the time to think about and then act on that information.

After Guy reads aloud to Mildred and her friends Matthew Arnold's "Dover Beach," a poem about the erosion of faith, they turn him in to the police for breaking the law. When Beatty and the firemen arrive at the Montags' house, Guy kills Beatty. He escapes to a remote colony of intellectuals, one of several such groups that live in the woods. Group members have memorized and therefore "become" books. They recite their books, thereby passing on their knowledge to their children, who will await the rebirth of a literate civilization. The novel ends with a quotation from the last chapter of the Bible and the guarded optimism that the antiliterate State will soon self-destruct and a new, cultured society will rise from the ashes.

Analysis

Fantasy and science fiction are closely intertwined, and *Fahrenheit 451* falls into both genres. No time machine carries the reader into this dark future, but Bradbury takes a seemingly unreal world and makes every element of it real and credible. From the technicians who apathetically pump the stomachs and transfuse the blood of the unhappy many who take daily drug overdoses to the blaring multiwalled televisions, Bradbury's attention to detail makes this nightmare seem plausible, vivid, and alive.

Fahrenheit 451 fits clearly into the utopia-dystopia motif that appeared in science fiction throughout the twentieth century. Whereas utopian fiction presents an idyllic world or society, dystopian fiction often portrays the individual's struggle against the implacable state in an ugly, depressing world. To illustrate two types of dystopias, Aldous Huxley's *Brave New World* (1932) is a frightening view of a technologyobsessed future, and George Orwell's *Nineteen Eighty-Four* (1949) is an appalling picture of an absolute dictatorship's effect on the human psyche. Bradbury's novel is a confluence of these dystopias. The brain-dead media and faster cars of the future (technology) add to the suffocation of individuals in a sterile State in which reading and thinking are outlawed (dictatorship).

Fahrenheit 451 falls in the middle period of Bradbury's literary career. Such short stories as "The Scythe" (1943) and "The Lake" (1944) belong to Bradbury's early period (1943–1945). These works are in the realm of fantasy and deal with the implications in life of choosing imagination over rationality. The practice in these works of having a hero who intuits some scary reality and tries to change things leads to the character of Guy Montag in *Fahrenheit 451*, which was written, along with *The Illustrated Man* (1951) and *The Martian Chronicles* (1950), during Bradbury's vintage period (1946–1955). All three books were adapted into screenplays. Science-fiction elements as well as dystopian landscapes enter his work during this time. Products of his later period, beginning in 1957, include *DandelionWine* (1957) and *I Sing the Body Electric* (1969). Many of his later works deal with magic, joy, and human eccentricity.

Critics believe that *The Martian Chronicles* is Bradbury's most successful work, exploring the tension between the needs of the individual and those of society. Although some debate whether Bradbury's work belongs to science fiction or fantasy and some consider his work simplistic, others feel strongly that it has been unfairly neglected and underrated and that his diverse and copious literary output is of astonishing quality and variety.

—*Howard A. Kerner*

Fairyland

Bio-hacker Alex Sharkey is co-opted by an amoral child genius named Milena in a plot to subvert the artificial servants of the future, the dolls, into autonomous creatures dubbed fairies, who will remake society and culture to suit their alien ways

Author: Paul J. McAuley (1955–)
Genre: Science Fiction—cyberpunk
Type of Work: Novel
Time of Plot: Mid-twenty-first century
Location: Europe
First Published: 1995

The Story

Our immediate focus is on an introduction to the hapless Alex Sharkey. Fat, balding, something of a mama's boy, he is hardly your standard, mirror-shaded cyberpunk cliché. Resident in London, a B-list genius, he is content to subsist on profits from minor-league drug designing. The first several chapters finds Alex contracting for some work from gangster Billy Rock, then being braced for info by a cop named Howard Perse. But then, in chapter 11, he has the heady misfortune to run into an artificially boosted child prodigy named Milena. Driven solely by selfish interests, Milena has a plan to transform the "gengineered" pseudo-human slaves, called dolls, into something quite different: fairies, in fact, with herself assuming the role of their Titania and Alex her Merlin. (Unlike Richard Calder's long-legged, sexy dolls [see the entry on *Cythera*], McAuley's creations are blue, short, and generally trollish, more utilitarian than decorative.) In chapter 15, Milena reveals her backstory:

"My sisters and I were treated with neuron growth substance while we were in our host mothers. Increased neuronal connectivity—that's what they gave me, although it was effected by very crude chemical interference. What I've brought along will do the job much more efficiently. Anyway, we were brought up in seclusion, given a hyperconnected education that started before we could crawl, and tested continually. Test after test after test. Most of my sisters suffered spectacular psychoses. They built their own worlds inside their own heads, and retreated into them. The rest turned out to be no more intelligent than average.

I'm the only one left, Alex, and sometimes I think that I'm mad, too. Mad, but functional. What they don't know is that I'm smarter than the company psycholo-

> *gists suspect. I long ago worked out how to manipulate their tests. I control those around me. . . ."*

After the first doll-to-fairy conversion, Milena vanishes with the stolen tech to continue. Part Two opens twelve years later, with the fairies well established across the globe.

> *Europe in the early years of the Third Millennium is not an easy place to find a preternaturally intelligent little girl who has deliberately gone to ground. Alex Sharkey makes a long journey of it, across France and Germany and through the little kingdoms and republics of Eastern Europe. He searches for twelve years. Although the products of Milena's imagination are all around him, in all that time he only once comes close to finding her.*
>
> *Dolls are no longer the novelty toys of the rich. They are used as cheap, versatile computer-controlled labour in industries where working conditions are traditionally hazardous—chemical refineries, deep coal mines, intensive horticulture, nuclear fission power stations. Gradually, they replace human workers in the emergent nanotechnology industries: driven by plug-in chips and fembot-grown neural nets, dolls can work for twenty hours a day accurately electron-etching primary fembot templates no bigger than bacteria. Killing Fields franchises are built in Rotterdam, Hamburg, Budapest and Moscow. Every day, more than a thousand dolls are hunted down and killed for sport in arenas across the European Union. There are women-only arenas, arenas for senior citizens, arenas where the clinically disturbed therapeutically discharge the murderous fantasies of their superegos.*
>
> *It is an age of excess.*

Alex's searching puts him in contact with fairy liberationists and a host of other outlaws and seekers, including two women named Katrina and Morag who are searching for a kidnaped child. By the end of Part Two, Alex himself has been abducted.

Part Three, "The Library of Dreams," details a kind of secret Armageddon between humans and fairies. Alex and Katrina, in Albania now, make contact with a different band of fairies, the feys, and also a Children's Crusade. When the long-anticipated reunion with Milena occurs, it is not as envisioned. She reveals her new state:

> *"A bush robot with ten million fembot-sized scanning and recording arms stripped my cortex neurone by neurone. It took no more than a hundred seconds, and at the end of it my original was dead. I'm not a copy but a simulation of that original, built up from the bush robot's measurements and six months' sampling and recording of cortical activity. Everything I remember of my original's life was built into a cross-reference data-base, and a heuristic program does its best to fill in the gaps. Frankly, it's not recording and simulating the activity of a mind that's the problem. It's the interface between the simulation and its environment."*
>
> Alex says, *"We could still turn you off."*
>
> *"I'm not in the Library of Dreams. It was useful, but I've spread out. I'm distributed across the Web, Alex. I use a maximum of about point nought nought nought five per cent of its capacity, but only when fully recalculating Fairyland, and that last happened when the curtain went up for you. If you want to hurt me, you'll have to switch off most of the Web."*

But then, amazingly, it all works out pretty well for both humans and fairies—at least for any survivors left alive and clambering from the wreckage.

ANALYSIS
In Marshall McLuhan's *The Medium is the Massage* (1967), that prescient Bible of the wired, cloud-bound cyber-decades we now find ourselves surfing through, British mathematician and philosopher Alfred North Whitehead is quoted as saying, "The major advances in civilization are processes that all but wreck the societies in which they occur." Paul McAuley's *Fairyland* gleefully illustrates that maxim, chronicling the chaos with brio and panache.

The book represented a change in venue and style from such earlier McAuley works as *Eternal Light* (1991) and *Red Dust* (1993). For the first time, McAuley chose to stay anchored to an Earthbound near-future. (His many subsequent works would repeat this alternation from large cosmic scenarios—*Gardens of the Sun* in 2009—to more immediate and terrestrial settings, as in *White Devils* from 2004.) And his characteristic information-rich prose, while still mind-bending, was skimmed of all fat, conducing toward a lean, crackling narrative that is a bit reminiscent of Bruce Sterling's commanding storytelling style.

In McAuley's world, biohackers and nanohackers ride the cutting-edge of tech, leaving merely digital web cowboys in the dust. Amoral, careless, often stoked up on their own products to the point of recklessness, they are goading human society down a path that leads right to a precipitous cliff.

This prophecy of "disruptive" technologies and platforms has subsequently been partially borne out by the appearance of such concerns as Uber and Airbnb, proving McAuley a true visionary.

McAuley does a lot in this novel. He fuses mythic motifs with technology in a way adumbrated at the start of the cyberpunk movement, in Vernor Vinge's *True Names* (1981). He juggles daring speculations in such areas as finance, A-life, nanotech, warfare, and politics with all the bold and scary gusto of the Flying Karamazov Brothers juggling chainsaws. He launches droll satirical missiles at pop culture (the major fairy infestation in Europe, for instance, centers in the abandoned Eurodisney enclave). And he convincingly portrays the transformation of Alex from a shirker and slacker to someone willing to risk his life to help heal the disease he's unleashed.

As with any thriller relying on its share of MacGuffins, there are occasional holes and implausibilities. Ejected from England without a penny, Alex never seems to lack money. And would a hardened charity doctor named Morag Gray, who has seen thousands of innocents die during her ministrations, really upset her whole life over one unknown child stolen by the fairies? Still, the plot moves at such supersonic speeds, introducing new marvels on every page, that any minor rents in the fabric are soon forgotten.

One curious ancestor for this book is Karel apek's *War with the Newts* (1937). This early SF classic about the struggle for dominance between man and his engineered sentient creations seems more relevant than ever these days. Early harbingers like John Barnes's *Kaleidoscope Century* (1995) and Kathleen Goonan's *Queen City Jazz* (1994), showing a society at war with—or already conquered by—its own artificial offspring, find allies in such contemporary titles as Charles Stross's *Neptune's Brood* (2013).

Paul McAuley, and science fiction at large, prove expert at evoking the hot breath of our replacements as it fans our necks.

—*Paul Di Filippo*

FALLING FREE

An engineer on a routine training assignment becomes involved with a revolution to prevent the enslavement and genocide of bioengineered human beings known as quaddies

Author: Lois McMaster Bujold (1949–)
Genre: Science fiction—extrapolatory
Type of work: Novel
Time of work: Undefined future
Locale: The Cay Habitat, orbiting the planet Rodeo
First published: 1988

THE STORY

Falling Free takes place in a future galactic setting often used by Lois McMaster Bujold, in which Earth has colonized planets in other solar systems. The main characters are Leo Graf, a career engineer for GalacTech, and his supervisor and antagonist, Bruce Van Atta. Their conflict centers on the quaddies, one thousand bio-engineered humans who have been created to live and work in free fall. The quaddies have four arms and are more resistant to radiation and the lack of gravity than are bipedal humans. They were developed in a decades-long project funded by GalacTech, and the corporation sees them as company property rather than as human beings with legal rights. Leo goes to the Cay Habitat, a space station orbiting the planet Rodeo, to teach the quaddies free fall welding and construction, but he ends up helping them in a revolution against the company. The other bipedal humans on the habitat are all GalacTech employees whose job is raising and educating the quaddies.

Tony, Claire, and Silver, all quaddies, are important characters, both to Leo and in leading the revolution. Tony and Claire are the parents of one of the first quaddie children born naturally, and Silver is their friend. Leo becomes disturbed by what he sees as the beginnings of slavery on the part of the company, but he realizes that he has little power to help the quaddies.

Three events force Leo to become active in defending the quaddies. First, Claire is told that she will have a second baby sooner than scheduled and that the father will be a quaddie other than Tony. She and Tony try to escape with their baby, Andy, and are trapped on Rodeo. Tony is wounded and kept on the planet. Second, at the same time, a visiting vice president reveals that the Cay Project is about to be shut down because of changes in tax laws; as a result, the quaddies will be sterilized and warehoused. The final blow comes when the Beta Colony announces that it has created an artificial gravity device that will result in cheaper space travel. At this point, the quaddies become obsolete. They were valuable because they did not require expensive transport to planets on a regular basis. With cheaper transport in space, the personnel costs of human workers are reduced.

Bruce Van Atta tries to implement sterilization of the quaddies, and they fight back with Leo's help. Leo, Silver, and Claire lead the battle. They plan to transform the habitat into a colony ship and take it through a wormhole, traveling far enough from settled space so that the quaddies can live freely, and in free fall. Their plan requires them to steal a jump ship, alter the habitat, and get the corporate employees off the habitat. They succeed in all these goals, although not entirely as planned. A number of GalacTech employees refuse to leave the quaddies. The vortex mirror of their stolen ship is broken, and they must engineer a new one. They win in the end, despite a final attempt by Van Atta to blow up their new colony ship. The novel ends with a successful jump and with Leo and Silver kissing.

ANALYSIS

Bujold's novel makes use of a number of traditional science-fiction elements, particularly the idea that expansion from Earth and colonization of planets will be possible, based on a faster-than-light (FTL) technology, with large Earth-based corporations as well as nation-states competing against one another. This galactic future has been the subject of American science fiction since the early work of Robert A. Heinlein and Arthur C. Clarke.

With such expansion into a frontierlike area, the question of exploitation of humans arises. Bujold's novels are not set in a centrally controlled "galactic empire." Instead, a number of developing colonies compete for access to wormholes and trade. *Falling Free*, winner of the 1988 Nebula Award, is the fourth novel Bujold published but takes place two hundred years earlier than the majority of her other science-fiction novels, many of which involve the Vorkosigan family.

Bujold does not include alien species in her novels as antagonists to humans. Instead, with her use of genetic engineering and the development of the uterine replicator, an artificial womb, she presents the question of whether bioengineered humans or mutants are seen as truly human. The quaddies introduced in *Falling Free* are one such new type of humans.

The major theme of the novel is the ethics of genetic engineering, a topic introduced in an essay by J. B. S. Haldane titled "Daedalus, Or Science and the Future" (1924). In that essay, he predicts the use of artificial wombs and genetic engineering to improve the human species. Resistance to such genetic engineering was expected by Haldane, and Bujold's novel reflects the resistance of humans to genetic differences. The theme has not been a major one in science fiction, although writers have made some use of it, the most famous being Aldous Huxley in *Brave New World* (1932). Other writers dealing with the moral and ethical issues of "improving" the physical aspect of the human race include James Blish in *The Seedling Stars* (1957) and Philip K. Dick in *The World Jones Made* (1956).

The idea of engineered humans colonizing planets is used in Ursula K. Le Guin's *The Left Hand of Darkness* (1969), Jack Williamsons *Manseed* (1982), and Sheila Finch's *The Garden of the Shaped* (1987). The idea of eugenics, or some other breeding program, to improve human capabilities occurs in Frank Herbert's *Dune* (1965). *Falling Free* looks at a limited application of the technology and does not go into great detail about how it works. Rather, Bujold explores social and ethical questions raised by the use of the technology, especially in a capitalist situation.

Bujold's work has been well received. She is a regular contributor to *Analog*, and her novels have won major awards. *The Vor Game* (1990), *Barrayar* (1991), and *Mirror Dance* (1994) have won Hugo Awards, voted by fans, and Falling Free won the Nebula Award, voted by members of the Science Fiction and Fantasy Writers of America.

—*Robin Anne Reid*

THE FALLING WOMAN

The intense struggle of Elizabeth Butler, who is forced to choose between the overlapping demands of the present and the past

Author: Pat Murphy (1955–)
Genre: Fantasy—magical realism
Type of work: Novel
Time of work: The mid-1980's, with flashbacks to the 1940's
Location: Yucatan digs in Mexico, and Berkeley, California
First published: 1986

THE STORY

The Falling Woman concerns the efforts of Elizabeth Butler (Liz) to achieve self-understanding by choosing between the unknown past and present reality. Liz must decide whether to fulfill the wishes of a Mayan ghost, Zuhuy-kak, who believes the blood sacrifice of Liz's estranged daughter, Diane, will restore power to an ancient Mayan goddess. Her option is to deny this past world that she cherishes and accept the present world she loathes. Six chapters, interspersed with ones devoted to Liz and Diane, describe ancient Mayan customs and cyclic concepts that emphasize the key Mayan belief that people need to know and understand their past in order to understand their future. Two characters, Diane and Zuhuy-kak, exert emotional and psychological pressures on the central character, Liz, while Tony Baker provides comforting support. Liz is an archaeologist, lecturer, and writer whose youthful efforts to secure freedom to develop her talents resulted in a nervous breakdown, attempted suicide, divorce, and loss of child custody. At the Dzibilchaltún dig, codirected with Tony, Liz exists on the psychic border between past and present. Seeing both sides, she simultaneously observes ancient ghosts and modern humans pursuing daily activities. In these ruins, Liz talks to herself, daydreams about the Mayan shadows who ignore her, and reflects that psychiatrists would suggest that these supernatural phantoms are hallucinations, parts of herself projected from her subconscious mind.

A wish fulfillment activates the fantasy plot. Although she laughs at students' visions of treasure, Liz expresses her own dream of locating a tomb at the excavation. Later, as Liz sits by the cenote, one ghost stops, stares, and questions her presence. Liz is equally astounded. She discovers that rules of reality are changing and barriers are down. Speech is possible between Zuhuy-kak, dead a thousand years, and Liz. After Liz passes a riddle test, Zuhuy-kak promises friendship and aid in revealing hidden secrets. That night, during her dreams, Liz relives the shadow's memories of falling in the waters of Chichén Itzá's sacred cenote. At dawn, she finds a partly raised stone, a clue that leads eventually to buried secrets in Zuhuy-kak's tomb.

Exploration of the past continues when Diane Butler arrives unexpectedly. She wants to learn why Liz abandoned her in childhood. As Liz and Diane share separate memories, Zuhuy-kak also tells Liz about her life and insists that Liz sacrifice Diane. To protect her daughter, Liz asks Diane to leave the Yucatan and offers herself as a sacrifice. When the girl refuses, Liz asks Tony, a father figure to Diane, to help guard the girl's safety.

The fantasy climaxes as Liz achieves self-understanding. She realizes that her sacrificial abandonment of Diane on her educational altar was just as unacceptable and futile as Zuhuy-kak's desired sacrifice. After Diane and Zuhuy-kak share this knowledge, all three free themselves of past mistakes. Diane lifts her unconscious mother, and the shadow shoulders her dead daughter; both trudge out of the cave. As Diane follows the light of Zuhuy-kak's flickering torch, she moves toward a future with Liz, one that begins on the bridge at Strawberry Creek in Berkeley.

ANALYSIS

Pat Murphy began publishing in the 1970's, but her first awards came in the 1980's. She received a Nebula for *The Falling Woman* and another Nebula the same year, along with a Theodore Sturgeon Memorial Award, for "Rachel in Love" (*Isaac Asimov's Science Fiction Magazine*, 1987; chapbook, 1992). "Rachel in Love" was included in *Points of Departure* (1990), a short-story collection that won the Philip K. Dick Award.

Murphy's writings synthesize science-fiction and fantasy elements with universal human concerns and problems. Her themes include alien encounters/estrangement, parent/child or male/female relationships, and self-realization/development of talents. Her first novel, *The Shadow Hunter* (1982), uses time-travel technology to move a prehistoric man into an alien future, and "Rachel in Love" describes the difficulties of a chimpanzee scientifically imprinted with the human intelligence of a teenage girl. *The City, Not Long After* (1989), a fantasy inhabited by various human, machine, and nonhuman figures, is set in a world devastated by a plague that was caused by humans with misguided intentions. Most of the short stories collected in *Points of Departure* also feature a synthesis of universal human concerns with the elements of science fiction and fantasy.

The Falling Woman illustrates Murphy's recurrent themes. First, Murphy expands the alien encounter theme to develop dynamic characters and plot complexities. Liz is a stranger to her peers and her daughter. Zuhuy-kak, the *Doppelgänger* shadow from the past, the ghostly double who stresses her commonalities with Liz, is as alien to the present world as Liz would be to the past. Moreover, Diane is able to see ancient shadows, twisting the double displacement theme into a third level. A second thematic idea centers on the parent/child bonds. The mother/father/daughter unit, extended to include Tony Baker, offers a sharp thematic contrast: The father figure protects the daughter from a mother who may kill her. A third theme relates to the pursuit of personal power, which Zuhuy-kak repeatedly mentions as a reward if Liz agrees to sacrifice Diane. The answer to this question of what Liz is willing to sacrifice for success is crucial to her choice.

The power theme is also expressed at a symbolic level. One symbol relates to Zuhuy-kak, an archetypal figure representing the powerful, perhaps dangerous, influence of the dead past on present or future actions. Symbolic meanings of "falling," "treasure," "water," "caves" and other terms give additional depth to Murphy's fiction.

—*Betsy P. Harfst*

THE FAMISHED ROAD AND SONGS OF ENCHANTMENT

Ben Okri uses the Yoruba abiku-child myth to examine ontological experience within the political context of Nigeria's growth process

Author: Ben Okri (1959–)
Genre: Fantasy—mythological
Type of work: Novels
Time of work: Undefined
Locale: Rural Nigeria
First published: *The Famished Road*, 1991; *Songs of Enchantment*, 1993

THE STORY

Azaro is an *abiku* and therefore destined to die and return to life repeatedly. He breaks his pact with his spirit companions and chooses to stay in the world of the living "to make happy the bruised face" of a mother who has suffered "the long joyless parturition of mothers." Dreams and numerous journeys through various realms of reality and his séances in the space between the living and spirit worlds describe his exile.

Azaro's spirit companions relentlessly lure him back to their fold; tirelessly, his parents exhaust their energy and finances with extensive ritual offerings to keep him in the world of the living. Finally, a two-week lingering between "not dying and not living" begins a long, eventful exile characterized by summonses by spirit voices and incessant "wanderings" into the animated forest, where he navigates different levels of consciousness with part-human and part-animal characters.

At a drunken house party celebrating his safe return home from a potential kidnapping, the key influences in Azaro's life are introduced: the mysterious Madame Koto; an emboldened photographer and social critic; his pitiable but strong mother; his frustrated, would-be politician father; his spirit-child best friend, Ade; and a blind old man. Azaro's association with Madame Koto and the photographer, the recorder of social and historical moments, soon exposes him to the wiles of politicians and political parties. A campaign gift of dried milk from one politician poisons the townsfolk. They set the campaign van on fire, setting off a reign of political terror and oppression. Dogged by the social ills of poverty, oppression, and corruption, Azaro's father campaigns as a boxer turned politician, appealing to beggars and the oppressed poor.

Meanwhile, Madame Koto's mysterious presence and power loom large, transforming the landscape. Her bar serves as the central scene for much of the novels' action and Azaro's education. As modernization sets in, evidenced by Madame Koto's car and the introduction of the gramophone and electricity to her bar, Azaro's education takes on new dimensions. His adolescence is complicated by his parents' estrangement, the death of Ade, and the eventual collapse of the political system. As political parties vie for power, chaos reigns in "a world breaking down under the force of hunger."

Amid this chaos, Azaro grapples with the plenitude of hidden meanings in an animated universe where, as his father tells him, "everything is alive." His mother teaches him that all things are linked. At the second novel's end, Azaro's parents are weathered by oppression. His father becomes blind and spends his days shoveling manure, and his mother withers into a skeleton. Their life-affirming philosophy, however, enables Azaro to focus his consciousness and courage despite debilitating poverty.

ANALYSIS

Although the main narrative of the novels is primarily a dramatization of the growth experiences, emotions, and motivations of Azaro, a young, male, *abiku* child who is endowed with youthful powers of observation, it is also the story of modern Nigeria's growth pains as it makes the transition from colonialism to an Africanized democracy rife with violence and corruption. Intertwined with the nation's political upheaval is Azaro's own recognition of the cynical reality of the oppressive political situation that typifies the everyday life of the citizenry: the failed political promises, the grinding poverty of the rank and file, and the relentless thuggery against the powerless.

Through his powers of observation, Azaro, the protagonist-narrator, presents a comprehensible and credible world of gods, spirits, ancestors, and humans commingling. Through his mediating perception, the natural and spirit worlds meld, inextricably linked and without boundaries. *Abiku* child that he is, Azaro straddles both worlds, sometimes simultaneously journeying through them, both spatially and temporally. For all the seeming freedom that straddling both worlds entails, however, Azaro constantly is trapped by his extraordinary metaphysical consciousness. As an *abiku* child—one born to die and return again and again—he is faced with the difficult choice of answering the call of his spirit companions to return to the spirit world, where he will be bathed "in the ecstasy of an everlasting love," or instead remaining and fulfilling his filial responsibility to make his parents happy.

His compulsive wanderlust plunges him deeper and deeper into different physical worlds and spirit realms, where his consciousness is shaped by powerful spirit companions and many human characters. His constant wanderings into the forest make him appear mischievous, and the constant "other voices" of his kindred spirits, luring him back to the bliss of the *abiku* realm, make him appear a renegade. After several close calls and numerous propitiatory rituals and elaborate "homecoming" celebrations, he relents, choosing to extricate himself from the metaphysical force of the *abiku* spirit realm.

Centered on the journeying motif, the novels tell a story of the triumph of will. Through sheer willpower, the key players survive the grave dangers and uncertainties of their growth journeys, the grinding poverty of their impoverished physical world, and oppressive political corruption and abuse of power.

By introducing the *abiku* myth at the beginning of *The Famished Road* and deftly sustaining it throughout *Songs of Enchantment*, Ben Okri defines the literary parameters of the novels early and recontextualizes African ontology. Although two other Nigerian writers—Wole Soyinka and John Pepper Clark—had used the Yoruba *abiku* myth in literature, neither used it as extensively to reorder ontological experience within the macrocosmic context of a country's political growth process.

Abiku, a Yoruba term for a child believed to have been born several times through a birth-death cycle, connotes a spirit-child, one endowed with metaphysical or extraordinary consciousness that defies conventions. The *abiku*'s apprehension of the world encompasses several levels of reality and consciousness that are incomprehensible to ordinary people. In many respects, the abiku's metaphysical consciousness is considered a mixed blessing: Its superhuman insights are the very gifts that make such a spirit-child a monster to its parents.

Shaped by a non-Western mythology, Azaro's world reflects an African ontology, one inhabited by people who still believe in mysteries and for whom personal relationships with spirits and ancestors are a daily reality because there is no differentiation between the worlds of the living and of the dead. The dead, considered "the living dead," are not really dead, and ancestors feature prominently in the community's daily life. Consequently, as various levels of reality merge and dissolve in dreams, Azaro often finds himself oscillating between two worlds, one world providing him glimpses of others—the terrestrial and the spiritual, the factual and the mythical, the ordinary and the extraordinary. All forms are necessarily mutable in these multiple worlds as "new spaces" are created by ever changing "constellations of energies and alignments."

As social commentary that reads like apocalyptic prediction, the novels capture, through surrealist contortions, a seemingly disordered world of bizarre political and social upheaval. Because "all things exchange their identities and realities" in the multiple worlds, waves of transformation must necessarily take place. This explains the transformation of Azaro's father from load carrier to boxer extraordinaire to self-schooled, aspiring politician, social reformer, and visionary leader of the poor and downtrodden. Gripped by a new consciousness that was boxed into his brain during several death-defying matches with spirit opponents, Azaro's father comprehends the *abiku* nature of the country. He is initiated into a deeper way of seeing the world as he enters the world of myth, half-consciously proclaiming, "KEEP OPEN THE ROAD."

The road metaphor intertwines with that of the *abiku*. Traveling on the road parallels the coming and going, the birth and death cycle, of the *abiku* child, as well as the making and remaking of history. Even the structure of the novels, with divisions into sections, books, and chapters, reflects the central theme of recurrence. Although the theme of human suffering and pain is pervasive, the novels' greatest strength is perhaps their redemptive yet paradoxical theme of joy, embodied by Azaro's father: the resiliency of the human spirit to carry on, to move forward and not be destroyed or die. His desires for education, housing, and social services for the beggars are mirrored in the infinite potential of the unfinished road.

The characters of the novel may, like the road, be famished, but they are by no means vanquished because "a road that is open is never hungry." This optimism, voiced in its last two lines, pervades *Songs of Enchantment*. Hope is the final word: "Maybe one day we will see beyond our chaos, there could always be a new sunlight, and serenity."

—Pamela J. Olubunmi Smith

FANCIES AND GOODNIGHTS

A collection of short stories in which the uncanny and the supernatural provide entrance to a humorous examination of human vice and virtue

Author: John Collier (1901–1980)
Genre: Fantasy—magical realism
Type of work: Stories
Time of work: Primarily the 1920s and 1930s
Locale: Various locations in England and the United States
First published: 1951

THE STORY

Although many of the stories in John Collier's *Fancies and Goodnights* are reprints from earlier anthologies and popular magazines, this volume represents Colliers main contribution to fantasy literature. These are witty, magical tales in which human foibles and short-sighted decisions lead to fittingly ironic endings.

"The Chaser", a typical Collier story, features a young man, Alan Austen, who wants a love potion to aid him in entrancing a scornful woman. Despite the warning that her magically inspired devotion will turn into never-ending torment, Austen buys the potion. The end of the story suggests that Austen, years later, will return to the shop to purchase a vial of poison to escape his chosen trap.

In "Bottle Party," a thirtyish dreamer purchases a bottle containing a female genie from a dusty antique shop. As his taste for the best that life has to offer grows stale, Franklin Fletcher orders the genie to bring him the worlds most beautiful woman. When the genie hints that she has another lover hidden in her bottle, Fletcher magically enters the decanter and is trapped by the duplicitous pair, who remain outside. As the genie and the worlds most beautiful woman take advantage of each others company, Fletchers bottle is returned to the antique shop. At the end of the story, a group of drunken sailors purchases the bottle, which they believe contains the worlds most beautiful woman, and abuse the released Fletcher unmercifully.

A decidedly sardonic afterlife is depicted in "Halfway to Hell." Louis Thurlow decides to commit suicide after being rejected by his girlfriend. Distraught, he falls into a swoon, and his spirit leaves his body. Louis soon finds himself accompanied by a devil, whom he gets drunk and tricks into carrying away his rival. The next morning, Louis wakes up to discover that his rival is missing and that the pathway to his girlfriends heart is once again clear.

In other stories, the supernatural is replaced by the uncanny. The young man in "Another American Tragedy," whose profligate lifestyle has ruined him, murders and impersonates his rich, aged, and bedridden uncle. As he is about to dictate a new will that would enrich himself, the nephew is murdered by the uncles doctor, who had made himself the beneficiary of the uncles estate. The young mans demise is fitting: In Colliers fiction, greed allows its own punishment.

This vice also motivates the father in "Ah the University." A young man is denied the education he craves so that his father can satisfy his taste for champagne and fine cigars. After studying gambling, the son bilks his father out of $150,000 in a game of poker. Other stories feature poisoners, neer-do-wells, mistaken identities, a reclusive community of lost souls living after hours in a department store, and even a ghostly Irish woman with the power to turn predatory English sportsmen into wolfhounds.

ANALYSIS

After a short career as a serious novelist, Collier turned in the 1930s to writing this type of short fiction, which examines human behavior in a shallow and somewhat moralistic way. A few of his stories are brutal and lead to the questioning of reality that takes place in more modern horror literature. For example, the detestable Princey family of "Wet Saturday" manages to get away with a senseless and cruel murder. After framing an innocent man and persuading him to try to escape, they call the police.

A similar kind of hypocrisy is the main failure of Big Simon, the protagonist of "Thus I Refute Beelzy." His blindness to his sons evil dooms him. Big Simon, a doctor with "advanced" views of parental care, allows his son, Little Simon, to dabble in black magic. As punishment for bullying this information out of the boy, Big Simon is destroyed by the supernatural forces that his son has unleashed.

Although there are a few similarly somber stories in the volume, most of Collier's work is lighter in tone. When the supernatural appears in these stories, it is rarely treated as an interruption of the rules of reality or as an important event in its own right; most often, the supernatural is taken as a matter of fact by the protagonists. Thus, like his contemporaries Aldous Huxley and Shirley Jackson, Collier uses marvelous or uncanny events as plot devices, allowing his characters to express their innermost selves freely. Unlike his contemporaries, however, Colliers interest in writing tightly plotted ironic stories takes precedence over the serious psychological examination of his characters. The people who live in Colliers universe are rarely defined by more than one dominant characteristic. The charming rogues and good-hearted, though unhappy, heroes meet with fitting rewards in this orderly universe—the murderous are murdered, the pompous are shown to be cowards, and the ignorant pay for their blindness. Virtues such as quick wits and bravery manifested by the put-upon heroes allow for ultimate success.

Colliers stories were popular with mainstream audiences of his day. His rejection of the modernist vogue for incapable human characters in a universe gone mad diminished the scope of fantasy literature in the 1930s and 1940s, but it gave many American readers their first taste of the Magical Realism subgenre of fantasy literature. That this collection of highly acerbic, mockingly ironic tales won the first International Fantasy Award in 1951 is not surprising.

—*Michael R. Meyers*

THE FANTASY WORLDS OF PETER BEAGLE

A collection of Peter Beagle's works of fantasy, comprising two short stories and two novels

Author: Peter S. Beagle (1939–)
Genre: Fantasy—magical realism
Type of work: Collected works
Time of work: Various, primarily the nineteenth and twentieth centuries
Location: New York City and England
First published: 1978 (includes *A Fine and Private Place*, 1960; "Come, Lady Death," 1963; *The Last Unicorn*, 1968; and "Lila the Werewolf," 1974)

THE STORY

The first story in *The Fantasy Worlds of Peter Beagle* is "Lila the Werewolf." It might be called either a short novella or a lengthy short story. It follows the brief relationship between Joe Farrell and Lila Braun. Shortly after Lila moves into Farrell's apartment, Farrell begins to notice that Lila acts strangely during a certain part of the month. He soon discovers the reason for this behavior: Lila Braun is a werewolf. Although their relationship continues for a short time, it finally disintegrates when Farrell and Lila's mother follow Lila, who is in wolf form, as she makes her rounds of New York City. Years later, Lila's mother calls Farrell to inform him of Lila's wedding to a research psychologist, whose interest in Lila is both romantic and professional.

The next story in the collection is *The Last Unicorn*. This novel focuses on the adventures of a female unicorn who leaves the safety of her forest in order to find others of her kind. Along the way, she gains the companionship of Schmendrick the wizard, whose success at wizardry is sporadic at best, and Molly Grue, a tender-hearted but tough-speaking woman. Their search leads them to the heart of the kingdom of King Haggard, a monarch whose desire to possess beauty and immortality led him years before to imprison unicorns within the waves of the sea. When confronted by King Haggard's mighty Red Bull, the unicorn almost meets the same fate as her kindred, but Schmendrick changes her into the shape of a frail, beautiful woman, Lady Amalthea. Prince Lír, King Haggard's adoptive son, soon falls in love with Lady Amalthea, but because of her true nature, she cannot fully reciprocate his love. The novel ends with the fall of King Haggard, the ascent of Lír to the throne, and the freeing of the unicorns from the waves.

"Come, Lady Death" appears after *The Last Unicorn*. This short story centers on Lady Neville, an important aristocrat with a flair for the dramatic. So that she can host the most exciting party in London, Lady Neville invites Death to be the guest of honor at her next ball. Death shows up in the guise of a beautiful young woman. By the end of the story, Death trades places with Lady Neville.

The final story in the collection is the novel *A Fine and Private Place*. The story is about Michael Morgan, a young college professor who suddenly finds himself dead, even though he retains consciousness. He is in a state of limbo. In the graveyard, he meets Jonathan Rebeck, a misfit from society who has lived in the graveyard for two decades. Morgan also meets Laura Durand, a ghost like himself, and the two of them fall in love. The novel follows two main plots: the relationship between Morgan and Durand and the relationship between Rebeck and a widow, Gertrude Klapper. Morgan and Durand's relationship is threatened by the exhumation of Morgan's body because of Morgan's apparent suicide (he is buried in a Roman Catholic plot). Rebeck and Klapper's relationship is strained by Rebeck's inability to cope with the outside world. Finally, Morgan and Durand are reburied in another cemetery, and Rebeck, with Klapper's support, re-enters society.

ANALYSIS

This collection displays the variety of topics with which Peter Beagle is able to work in his artistry. He possesses the ability to produce extremely realistic stories set in ordinary places during the twentieth century. Excepting the few strains of the fantastic arising within "Lila the Werewolf" and *A Fine and Private Place*, those stories are believable tales. Beagle's writing style is reminiscent of that of other twentieth century realists such as Sherwood Anderson, William Faulkner, and Ernest Hemingway, yet Beagle is also an accomplished writer of fantasy fiction, able to transport the reader into magical worlds brimming with extraordinary people and creatures.

The Last Unicorn falls into this category and is arguably Beagle's masterpiece of fantasy fiction. Because of his mastery of fantasy fiction, critics and scholars often compare Beagle to other twentieth century fantasists, including J. R. R. Tolkien and C. S. Lewis. *The Fantasy Worlds of Peter Beagle* allows the reader a chance to witness a writer exercising his skills in versatility.

For this collection of stories, Beagle wrote an introduction providing his personal insights into the creation and publication of each story found within the volume. This introduction, providing Beagle's explanation of why he writes works of fantasy, will be of interest to scholars, lovers of fantasy fiction, and avid Beagle fans. The introduction serves as a means for Beagle to give his views on the topic of fantasy fiction but also affords the reader a glimpse into the activity of writing fantasy fiction. Beagle discusses how and where he wrote the stories, the means of publication, and his retrospective opinions about them. In essence, he provides a short critique of each work.

—*Trevor J. Morgan*

FANTAZIUS MALLARE AND THE KINGDOM OF EVIL

Fantazius Mallare finds a beautiful woman whom he can control and who will worship him, and in his mind he creates the Kingdom of Evil, where he falls in love with, and becomes a slave to, Kora

Author: Ben Hecht (1894-1964)
Genre: Fantasy—superbeing
Type of work: Novels
Time of work: Undefined
Locale: Mallares house and a world he creates in his mind
First published: *Fantazius Mallare: A Mysterious Oath* (1922) and *The Kingdom of Evil* (1924)

THE STORY
Ben Hecht's *Fantazius Mallare: A Mysterious Oath* relates the story of the title character, a misanthropic, psychopathic madman who considers himself a superbeing. He strives to be a god and battles against reason and his senses. Mallare, a thirty-five-year-old sculptor, despises reason, sanity, and thought; of these three "vices," he lacks the first two. The artist, for example, visits an amusement park and returns home with a paralyzed black hunchbacked dwarf. He makes the dwarf his servant and names him Goliath simply because such an appellation is clearly a misnomer. The fact that Mallare gives a name to Goliath manifests the title characters egoism; he names an inferior as does God in the Book of Genesis. This parallel is relevant because throughout the novel, Mallare strives to be, and sometimes considers himself to be, a god.

The sculptor decides that he can become a god by controlling a woman. He discovers a beautiful but stupid eighteen-year-old gypsy girl and brings her home. He insists that Rita never talk, that she merely listen to him. She cannot understand the musings of this madman yet is attracted to him anyway. Mallare intends to gratify his egoism, to become a god by enslaving a woman and by resisting his sensual urges.

After throwing Rita against the wall, Mallare leaves for a walk and encounters a beggar. In a mad reverie, he mistakes the beggar for Rita and strangles him. Thinking that he has killed Rita, the sculptor walks home but finds her waiting for him. She seduces him, and he has sexual intercourse with her regularly. He deems it masturbation because he considers her a hallucination caused by his madness. If she exists, it is only because he has created her in his mind. Goliath watches Mallare have sex with Rita and manifests his jealousy. Mallare sends his paralyzed dwarf servant away because he is ashamed that his senses have enslaved him. He therefore feels compelled to murder this female phantom.

Mallare viciously beats Rita, leaving her bloodied and angry. As he meditates, he wonders how he drew blood from a phantom; he contemplates that she may never have existed and that even the blood is part of the hallucination. Her love for him dissipates. To exact revenge, she angers him by engaging in sexual intercourse with Goliath. The servant lusts for Rita and excitedly fornicates with her, but while the two have sex, they look not at each other but at Mallare, awaiting his reaction. Mallare contemplates the incident as it happens, considering that perhaps Rita and Goliath are real and that he may be a phantom. Envious of his subordinates for exercising powers of their own and enraged that life may exist outside himself, he exiles her from Heaven (his house) for employing sex to turn his servant against him, leaving the forlorn Goliath to look out the window in search of her. By overcoming lust for Rita, or at least believing that he has, Mallare asserts that he has conquered his senses and the physical world. *Fantazius Mallare* concludes with Mallare writing in his journal exclusively in the third person, for he is no longer Mallare and is separated from himself.

In *The Kingdom of Evil*, the reader learns from Mallares journal that a fog overcomes him and other men, and they find themselves held prisoner in a cave by a giant named Dr. Sebastien. Sebastien loves Kora, a beautiful woman with eyes like the heads of serpents. To please his bored lover, Sebastien kidnaps these men so that they can build, for Koras entertainment, the Kingdom of Evil.

Julian, a poet, attempts to befriend Mallare, but the sculptor despises him. The towers and elaborate architecture bore Kora, who says that she can be excited only by a god. The men build a temple in the shape of a huge flower and construct a god out of human tissue, organs, fibers, and membranes. The god, Synthemus, bears a striking resemblance to Mallare, as does Julian. The reader gradually learns that all the characters in the novel are Mallare, that each is a part of him who has arisen out of Mallares brain. As in *Fantazius Mallare*, no life exists outside the mind of Mallare.

Mallare lusts for Kora, but she disdains him because she desires Julian. Julian, however, dislikes her and everyone else in the Kingdom of Evil. He cares only for Mallare. His affection for Mallare dwindles, however, when the sculptor admits his lust for Kora. Julian realizes that Kora, like the other inhabitants of the island, do not exist except as thoughts in Mallares mind. He expresses disappointment, for he comprehends that Kora, Mallares creation, exists as the embodiment of the protagonists lust. The poet recognizes that he also exists as a figment of Mallares imagination, so he attempts to escape the island and thus the madmans dream. Julian, with the help of General Piltendorff, another of Sebastiens victims, binds the god and other inhabitants of the Kingdom of Evil in the temple, which crumbles to the ground. Julian, Piltendorff, and Mallare then escape from the island in a ship.

ANALYSIS

Fantazius Mallare begins with an eight-page dedication that is a diatribe against censors. Above every page of this lengthy dedication, the reader discerns illustrator Wallace Smith's drawing of a phallus entering a vagina resting in barbed wire. Hecht despised censors of books (the Society for the Suppression of Vice in particular) and wrote the scandalous *Fantazius Mallare* partly to incite a lawsuit so that he could sue censors for defamation and destroy them. To incite censors to object, Hecht added the character Rita, the sensuous gypsy, to the novel. To Hecht's surprise, the United States Post Office censored and confiscated copies of *Fantazius Mallare*, and the author paid a thousand dollar fine to avoid prison.

After the bilious dedication, the novel proceeds with another Wallace Smith drawing, a picture of Mallare engaging in sexual intercourse with a tree in the shape of a woman. The drawing may foreshadow Mallare's journal entry in which he states that he loves trees that are void of leaves because they detract from the supposed beauty of the houses to which they stand adjacent. Mallare enjoys contorted things because he believes that people mistakenly believe that art should be symmetrical and because he considers human nature equally deformed. Mallare asserts that he loves trees because he and they lack a handicap—reason.

Mallare, as a slave and victim in *The Kingdom of Evil*, constructs the island and its inhabitants; both derive from his thoughts. Instead of striving to be a god and being in control, he functions as a slave to Kora for most of the novel. The reader discovers that Mallare is actually the giant Sebastien, the god Synthemus, and every other character in *The Kingdom of Evil*. Because all characters derive from his brain and he has constructed the entire kingdom from his thoughts, he emerges as the dominant figure. Although Mallare lacks control and power in the society, all the action derives from his brain because all the characters are his creation. Thus, when Julian attempts to escape the dream, he must flee from his very existence.

In both novels, Mallare has a compulsion for dominance and control; even when he is supposedly a slave, he functions as master. It is surprising that although all the characters are of Mallares invention, he exercises little control over them. The sculptor wants to have sex with Kora and recognizes, through the voice of Julian (another extension of his self), that she is a character in his dream, yet he still cannot convince her to sleep with him. Even though the god she worships is Mallare, she still despises him. Hecht further complicates this theory regarding Mallares dominance, for when the novel concludes, Mallare is found with dead animals and human corpses stacked in the corner of his room, and he lies by a dead woman. Hecht wants his audience to ponder whether these corpses derive from the Kingdom of Evil and whether the dead woman is Kora. Is it possible that Julian erroneously asserts that the kingdom is a Mallare hallucination, that the island does in fact exist outside the mind of the sculptor, and that the account in the madmans journal is veracious?

—Eric Sterling

FATA MORGANA

Police Inspector Paul Picard pursues his old adversary Baron Mantes through Paris in the time of Louis Napoleon while attempting to unravel the mystery of the dazzling magician Ric Lazare

Author: William Kotzwinkle (1938–)
Genre: Fantasy—magical world
Type of work: Novel
Time of work: 1861
Locale: Central Europe
First published: 1977

The Story

From the beginning of his career as a writer, the extremely versatile William Kotzwinkle (who was chosen by director Steven Spielberg to write the novelization of the 1982 film *E.T.: The Extra-Terrestrial*) has been interested in the region where realism and fantasy merge and fuse. In *Fata Morgana*, he explores this mysterious area by combining a conventional detective story with an examination of the unconscious mind of a middle-aged police inspector in Paris in the 1860s.

Paul Picard is an experienced professional, familiar with police procedure and the urban underground of criminals and dropouts. He is a traditional and essentially conservative man, but his desire to enforce justice and unravel the threads of a complicated criminal scheme lead him into a realm where his experience is not sufficient. The world of laws and rational expectations Picard knows is disrupted by the appearance of Ric Lazare, who is witty, socially adept, and possibly the mastermind of an extraordinary conspiracy that may reach into the chambers of the leaders of France, or even beyond, to centuries-old, shadowy organizations that seem to deal in the supernatural.

Picard is intrigued by the challenge and energized by the dangers a pursuit of Lazare would involve, and he begins to search for clues and answers in Vienna, Nuremberg, and Budapest, as well as in the darker, time-worn locations of an older world. During the course of his investigation, he is drawn into the recesses of his own mind, back toward the prerational childs perspective that permits magic and the exceptional to mingle with the realistic and the familiar.

Picard begins to suspect that Lazare has been operating in forbidden, arcane phenomena, possibly mastering a method of continuous reincarnation that promises immortality. Picards skills in deductive procedures are augmented by his own fascination with semimystic techniques, such as consultation with seers, faith in amulets, and the commissioning of spells formulated by conjurers. In spite of this, he is overcome in a confrontation with Lazare in which shellfire from toy soldiers seems to wound him mortally. In a device common to the genre, he discovers that he has known defeat in a dream-vision. Restored to waking consciousness, he recognizes that he has been given a glimpse of one among several possible futures. He resolves, prudently, to put aside the pursuit of Lazare but to apply some of the lessons of his experience to his continuing effort to overcome his old adversary, Baron Mantes.

ANALYSIS

The *fata morgana* of Kotzwinkle's title is an ancient term suggesting a revelation that illuminates destiny. The message, however, is wrapped in mystery, and its interpretation depends to a considerable extent on the mind-set of the seeker who would unravel its perplexities. The "fate" that is revealed through the disclosure of a "mirage" or an "illusion" is an indistinct but inviting vision that draws an explorer beyond the familiar and into contact with the extraordinary. Once in this shadow world, both physical and psychic stability are at stake, but the lure of a kind of forbidden knowledge is so powerful that even an essentially rational man such as Kotzwinkle's Inspector Picard is willing to override the habits of a lifetime in response to the temptations of the mystery.

Picard senses (and Kotzwinkle implies) that even if no ultimate illumination occurs, the journey toward the enigma in itself is as valuable as its goal, which includes the possibility of some startling answer to a cosmic question. In Picard's case, the journey is a dream/descent into the subconscious, a course that parallels Picards travels across Europe to gather clues that might provide information about the frighteningly mysterious Ric Lazare.

At first, Picard regards any intrusion of evil into his life as an intervention from an outside source. He begins to realize that his fascination with criminal life may stem from some elements in his own psyche that resonate on similar frequencies, although his own moral foundation is substantial. The question Kotzwinkle poses here is whether any definition of criminality that goes beyond obvious transgressions of basic human decency is socially subjective.

This leads to the larger issue of magic, another volatile concept often defined in terms of a particular social orientation. Kotzwinkle proposes that the entire realm of the magical has often been confused or blended with the criminal because it deals with activities that often defy order, simple explanation, and some social conventions. Kotzwinkle is interested in the apparently timeless appeal of the magical in many forms for the human species. As a successful writer of excellent children's books (such as *Hearts of Wood and Other Timeless Tales*, 1986) he draws on his imaginative experience with that genre to propose that the spirit of the child remains in the mature adult, re-emerging as divine dreams that are at the root of magical endeavors.

Picard's pursuit of Lazare reconnects him with a child's lack of limits, the awareness of infinite possibility that an adult must relinquish but that Lazare has not been willing to accept. The crucial revelation for Picard is that the tyranny of a childs inclinations can turn evil in practice in an adults life. Lazare, who will not accept the thwarting of his will, has through the intensity of his determination made discoveries beyond the reach of most mature men. The power Lazare wields, however, may lie as much in his ability to confound and confuse adversaries as in any actual manipulation of the laws of Newtonian physics. This is the crux of the matter, because what one believes is happening is a substantial component of most definitions of reality. Kotzwinkle leaves this issue open, an approach in accordance with the theme of uncertainty that informs all discussions of magic. It is carried further in *The Exile* (1987), a novel in which magic, mystery, and evil are at the heart of a plot that moves through time between Nazi Germany and the magic capital of the universe, Hollywood, California.

—Leon Lewis

The Fates of the Princes of Dyfed and Book of the Three Dragons

Characters from Welsh Celtic myth and legend struggle against forces that would upset the natural and preternatural balance of the ancient world

Author: Kenneth Morris (1879-1937)
Genre: Fantasy—mythological
Type of work: Novels
Time of work: The mythological past
Locale: Wales
First published: *The Fates of the Princes of Dyfed* (1914) and *Book of the Three Dragons* (1930)

The Story

Although *The Fates of the Princes of Dyfed* and *Book of the Three Dragons* were published sixteen years apart and, for the most part, feature different casts of characters, they are closely related. They both use the medieval Welsh prose pieces known as the *Mabinogi* as their immediate source. The First Branch of the *Mabinogi* provides the basic plot and characters for the first of these two books; in the second, Kenneth Morris uses characters and plot elements from several branches of the *Mabinogi* and from other medieval Welsh tales to add depth and texture to a plot essentially of his own creation.

The two novels also are related by their use of medieval materials in contemporary fantasy fiction. As with many fantasy novels, the presence of materials from medieval sources, the most popular of which are the Arthurian materials, not only signals the fantastic nature of the story but also is an integral part of the fantastic cosmology of the story. Morris use of the Welsh Celtic materials as the basis for his fantasies set both the style and the tone adopted by a number of later writers—Evangeline Walton, Lloyd Alexander, Alan Garner, and Nancy Bond, among others—who would make use of those same materials during the 1960's and 1970's.

In *The Fates of the Princes of Dyfed*, Morris first novel, material from the First Branch of the *Mabinogi* occupies approximately one third of the narrative. That material is almost unchanged from its source. Pwylls journey to the Otherworld, his fight with Hafgan, his two wedding feasts, and the birth, disappearance, and return of his son, Pryderi, essentially are the same in Morris novel as in the *Mabinogi*. Morris expands on his source, taking fewer than twenty pages from the original and turning them into almost one hundred pages in his novel.

The remaining two-thirds of the book contain episodes and plots of Morris own invention, written according to traditional formulae. For example, the year between the first and second marriage feasts of Pwyll and Rhiannon occupies a sentence or two in the First Branch, but Morris inserts a minor quest, three chapters long, into that space.

Pwyll needs an unfillable sack or basket for the second feast. In the First Branch, Rhiannon gives him the sack, and he has but to wait out the year. In *The Fates of the Princes of Dyfed*, however, Pwyll must spend the entire year looking for it. The structure of the episode Morris creates fits with the original *Mabinogi* because it comes from the same traditional cultural matrix of myth and legend as do the Welsh Celtic materials that compose Morris source. The Grail quest of Arthurs knights is an obvious analogue but is only the best known of many. The smaller details of the episode come from folktale and legend as well: The unfillable sack or basket is a traditional motif in a variety of folktales, and three, the dominant number in the episode, is a common and portentous number in folklore. Toward the end of the episode, there are three days left for Pwyll to complete the mission, three different sorrows to be lightened, and three different men trying to fill the basket with three different things. The third man, trying to fill the basket with the third thing to assuage the third sorrow, succeeds—on the third day.

Book of the Three Dragons is based much more loosely on the *Mabinogi*. In the sixteen years following publication of *The Fates of the Princes of Dyfed*, Morris writing matured. Morris uses materials from the Four Branches in this novel but also uses materials from other Welsh Celtic sources, particularly "The Dream of Macsen Wledig," "The Dream of Rhonabwy," and "Culhwch and Olwen."

Shortly after the story opens, Manawydan (who, it is discovered, is Pryderi from the first novel) is given the choice between immortality with the gods and preventing a new evil from destroying the world in which he now lives. He chooses the latter course and spends the rest of the novel on a quest to free the Island of the Mighty from the evil threatening it.

Unlike the first novel, in which sections from the *Mabinogi* are alternated with sections of Morris invention, *Book of the Three Dragons* interweaves his materials with incidents and motifs from the *Mabinogi*. Morris most obvious borrowing from the *Mabinogi*, the three crafts of Pryderi and Manawydan from the Third Branch, are changed from the original. In the middle of the original Third Branch, Manawydan and Pryderi, accompanied by their wives, leave Dyfed, which has been placed under an enchantment, to seek a livelihood elsewhere. In turn, they try saddlemaking, shieldmaking, and shoemaking in episodes that contrast Pryderis hotheadedness with Manawydans good sense. In adapting these scenes for *Book of the Three Dragons*, Morris removes everyone but Manawydan and changes the cause as well as the purpose of the three crafts. In Morris book, Manawydan must produce a pair of boots, a sword, and a shield of the "Subtle Craft" to trade for the iron gloves of Gwron-Brif-fardd-Prydain, which Manawydan will need in the ultimate battle.

ANALYSIS

In some ways, Morris was a part of the turn-of-the-century Dublin literary circle that included such famous figures as William Butler Yeats, George Russell (AE), and Ella Young. In other and perhaps more important ways, Morris was a part of the fantastic literature tradition that began, in its modern form, with William Morris (no relation) and continues to flourish. William Morris borrowing of Scandinavian materials for *A Tale of the House of the Wolfings, and All the Kindreds of the Mark* (1889) and his development of the Secondary World in *The Wood Beyond the World* (1894) established the patterns for modern high fantasy literature. Kenneth Morris use of the medieval Welsh materials and his creation of a medieval world not unlike Wales are very much in the tradition of William Morris' fiction.

Although Evangeline Walton's *The Island of the Mighty* (1970) was published as *The Virgin and the Swine* in 1936, the most obvious descendants of Morris Celtic fantasies appeared in the 1960s and 1970s. Lloyd Alexander's Chronicles of Prydain, Evangeline Walton's three other *Mabinogi* novels, and Alan Garner's *The Owl Service* (1967) are among the most successful of the contemporary novels based on the Four Branches of the Mabinogi. In structure, Nancy Bond's *A String in the Harp* (1976), which interweaves the story of the medieval Welsh bard, Taliessin, with the story of a modern American family in Wales, is much like Morris' first novel, if more smoothly written.

The climax of *Book of the Three Dragons* perhaps best illustrates the author's strength. Here Morris focuses more on bardic skills—storytelling, singing, and harping—than on martial skills. The Celts, especially the Welsh Celts, always have held such bardic accomplishments in the highest regard. In his final confrontations, Manawydan uses these skills to triumph over his foes. His storytelling so enthralls Tathal Cheat-the-Light and Ewinwen ferch yr Eigion that they are unable to trap Manawydan and turn him into stone. It is also Manawydans storytelling that distracts Gwiawn Llygad Cath—also called Gwiawn Cat's Eye, the Sea-Thief—and allows Manawydan to recover the Harp of Alawn. Manawydans own musical ability, augmented by this preternatural harp, allows him to descend into hell and there establish order. The warriors who had been turned to stone are released, the Crumbled Kings are restored, and the sleeping Druids are awakened. Manawydan and the Harp bring peace to all.

This series of scenes does not come from the *Mabinogi* but does integrate one of its main characters, Manawydan, with several other traditional elements. One of these, the tendency of events to occur in threes, is evident in the three challenges that Manawydan must overcome in the end. The journey to and ordering of hell, which Manawydan must accomplish to bring the worlds of humans and gods into balance again, is a traditional motif in both ancient literature and mythology. The emphasis on bardic skills also is traditional. Morris interweaves these traditional materials, sets them into a plot largely of his own device (within traditional formulae), and presents a completed whole in high style.

Historically, Morris is important as the originator of modern high fantasy based on the *Mabinogi*, and his use of traditional materials established the mode for much of what has come since. His Celtic novels, especially *Book of the Three Dragons*, have an authentically Celtic and fantastic atmosphere; they deserve to be read more than they are.

—C. W. Sullivan III

Fear and Typewriter in the Sky

A psychological thriller that reveals the darker aspects of the minds surreal logic and a story of a hack writer who unwittingly immerses one of his friends in a fictive swashbuckling adventure

Author: L(afayette) Ron(ald) Hubbard (1911–1986)
Genre: Fantasy—inner space
Type of work: Novels
Time of work: The 1930s, with flashbacks, and primarily 1640, with flashbacks and flashforwards
Locale: A college town, and New York City and the Caribbean
First published: 1951 (bound together; both first appeared in *Unknown*, 1940)

The Story

Fear concerns the efforts of Professor James Lowry, an ethnologist at a small college, to discover what happened during four hours for which he cannot account. After returning from one of his many field trips from the Yucatán with a recurring case of malaria, Lowry learns that he is to be fired. The cause of his dismissal is a newspaper article in which he discounted the existence of devils and demons, and thereby Christianity, calling them fabrications of witch doctors who wanted both to instill fear in their followers and to control them. Shortly after his return, he realizes that he cannot account for four hours of his life.

Tension is maintained throughout the story by the question of what caused the loss of the four hours. It may have been the shock of losing his job, coupled with his tendency to suffer malarial relapses; alternatively, devils and demons may have extracted payment for his hubris in scientifically discounting them. Both his wife and his best friend attempt to calm Lowry and ease his troubled spirit, but dark phantasms of the mind embroil Lowry in ever deepening eddies of paranoia that eventually incorporate others.

As Lowry's relationship to reality becomes more tenuous, his belief in devils and demons undergoes a significant reversal. He lectures his college class about the inability of science to answer some of the human races more important questions. This almost religious conversion, which leads him into a nightmarish mental dialogue with numerous unseen entities, provides the foundation for an otherwise bizarre and horrifying ending.

Typewriter in the Sky opens in the Greenwich Village basement apartment of Horace Hackett, a writer of popular melodramas. Hackett, who has spent his advance on revelry without having so much as a rough draft outlined for his publisher, is trying to convince his publisher, Jules Montcalm, that he will meet the deadline. Also present is Hacketts friend, Mike de Wolf.

As Montcalm presses Hackett for at least a plot for the story, titled "Blood and Loot," Hackett sheepishly constructs a swashbuckling adventure of derring-do and romance. Montcalm, unsatisfied, wants to know who the villain is. Hackett, who has been extemporizing all along, points to his friend, Mike, and describes the villain as being exactly like him.

Mike finds himself transported back to the 1640s, washed up on the shores of a Caribbean island. He has taken on the persona of Spanish fleet admiral Miguel Saint Raoul de Lobo. Mike realizes that he is a character in "Blood and Loot" and that he can hear Hackett's typewriter banging away somewhere up in the sky. Adjusting himself quickly to these unusual circumstances, Mike proves to be more of a character than Hackett anticipates, especially when he falls in love with the heroine, the beautiful Lady Marion. Knowing that he is cast in the role of the villain and that the hero, Captain Bristol, is destined to win the hand of the fair Lady Marion, Mike decides to see if he can change the clichéd plot to something that ends more in his favor.

ANALYSIS

Both *Fear* and *Typewriter in the Sky* were originally published in 1940 in *Unknown*, a sister magazine to *Astounding Science-Fiction* created by editor John W. Campbell, Jr., as a place to print stories that were more fantasy than science fiction. In 1938, Street and Smith, publishers of *Astounding Science-Fiction*, recommended to Campbell that L. Ron Hubbard, already an established pulp author of Westerns, detective stories, and adventure stories, be put to work writing science fiction. The charismatic Hubbard quickly won Campbell over and became a voluminous contributor, often using pseudonyms to mask the ubiquity of his works.

Hubbard's talents for science fiction never matched his skill in creating fantasy, even though he churned out innumerable melodramatic space operas that did well commercially. The machinery of the mind was what most interested Hubbard, and *Fear* is an excellent example of his skill in incisively depicting the psychology of paranoia. Supposedly written over a weekend, *Fear* exposes the dark, horrible recesses of the mind, where delusions gain a foothold, engaging both the demoniac and psychotic.

Lauded by such notable writers as Ray Bradbury, Stephen King, and Isaac Asimov, *Fear* conveys a theme that Hubbard employed repeatedly: the human mind as the creator of reality. In some ways, Hubbard's propensity to examine the philosophical and psychological problems inherent in the mind-over-matter theme was a harbinger and early exploration of the territory of "inner space" that later became a key ingredient of New Wave science fiction.

Typewriter in the Sky, although it shares with *Fear* an excellent psychological grasp of the main protagonist, who finds himself uprooted from his reality and stranded three centuries in the past, is more of a tongue-in-cheek tour of the world of the pulp writer. The story is obviously self-referential. The reader easily identifies hack writer Horace Hackett as an alter ego of Hubbard. In one scene, Hubbard even employs a character identified by one of his pseudonyms, Rene Lafayette. Lafayette dozes off while awaiting his turn for the standard cross-examination administered by publishers to their errant writers, who never seem to meet deadlines and are always seeking larger advances for unwritten stories.

Typewriter in the Sky effectively satirizes the publisher/writer paradigms and the constricting formulae of the pulp genre. Hubbard knew the tricks of the trade well enough to breathe new life into them. The technique of having one of the characters of *Typewriter in the Sky* attempt to outwit the author foreshadows later experimental metafiction.

—*Milton T. Wolf*

FEARFUL PLEASURES

Short stories that feature ghosts, leprechauns, supernatural dreams, or eerie failures of perception

Author: A(lfred) E(dgar) Coppard (1878–1957)
Genre: Fantasy—mythological
Type of work: Stories
Time of work: Undefined, but with some contemporary references
Locale: England, Ireland, and France
First published: 1946

THE STORY

Fearful Pleasures, which consists of twenty-two stories, opens with "Adam and Eve and Pinch Me," the title story of A. E. Coppard's first collection (1921), in which a writer who is certain that he is not dead nevertheless experiences unpleasant ghostly sensations. He encounters his charming third child, whose imminent birth is announced by the writer's newly expectant wife immediately after he mysteriously reconnects with his body.

In "Clorinda Walks in Heaven," the title story of a 1922 volume, a woman meets all of her husbands from past lives in an afterlife not very different from the ordinary world. The title character in "Old Martin" becomes obsessed, when his beloved niece dies, with the superstition that the last soul buried in the churchyard must slave for all of those who went before, because the churchyard is filled to capacity upon the nieces burial. "Polly Morgan" tells about a young girl who obstructs her aunts romance with a ghost, only to see the aunt subsequently wither and die of loneliness in a way that foretells the girls fate.

In folktale fashion, Coppard often explores the adventures of simple people who encounter supernatural forces. In "The Elixir of Youth," Tom Toole keeps his bargain with a strange old man to search for eternal youth and is then cheated of his share. In "The Bogie Man," Sheila becomes familiar with a tiny man who confers a seven-thousand-year life on her when she lets him sleep on her breast. In "The Gollan," a lazy young man allows a leprechaun to make him invisible and afterward discovers the price of this convenience: Everyone else is invisible to him. In "Crotty Shinkwin," Crotty goes fishing and overturns an island when his anchor catches the steeple of the town church on the underside of the island. In that town, someone with his name lives a life quite different from his own.

Some of Coppards stories feature magical events. In "Rocky and the Bailiff," a simple boy concocts a magical cure for a cattle plague but gains nothing. In "Ale Celestial?," Barnaby Barnes receives a perfect brewing recipe from a dwarf and gains fame until his greed poisons his skill. "Father Raven" fibs to gain admission to heaven for his flawed congregation on Judgment Day and finds himself rejected. In "Cheese," a stingy salesman finagles a delicious cheese recipe from a gypsy but refuses to pay royalties. In revenge, the gypsies trap the salesman like a mouse; he barely escapes, although not to the world he left.

Some of Coppards stories have contemporary settings. In "Gone Away," three people motoring through France find themselves covering thousands of miles, according to their odometer, and losing track of landmarks they note along the way. In this seemingly ordinary world in which one can never find anything twice, they make the mistake of becoming separated in a town they visit. In "The Tiger," an animal trainers passion for a married woman in his circus troupe is punished by the creature he has failed to tame. In "The Gruesome Fit," a man flees his wife and home because he fears that he will commit murder, but in his new lodging, he irresistibly murders a stranger.

Analysis

Although *Fearful Pleasures* contains previously published stories and is the last new collection Coppard produced, published when he was sixty-eight years old, it is not an edition of complete works. An American omnibus edition of thirty-eight stories, *The Collected Tales of A. E. Coppard*, subsequently appeared in 1948, but it also represents only a fraction of the story collections Coppard produced, along with books of poems, almost yearly between 1921 and the 1950s. His partial autobiography, *Its Me, O Lord!*, was published in 1957. Although during his life his work was admired by mainstream writers such as Ford Madox Ford, and although his style helped to reestablish the short-story genre, Coppards unusual blend of traditional folklore and modern encounters with the unexpected has not won him continuing critical attention.

Coppards stories often combine the ordinary and the extraordinary in unexpected ways. His characters usually are plain people pursuing the everyday business of life when, suddenly, the supernatural or the inexplicable intrudes. Imagination and playfulness are rewarded in this encounter, and both simple country folk and modern sophisticates may possess these qualities.

The stories in *Fearful Pleasures* frequently are patterned on the oral traditions of folklore. Coppard himself says of the folktale, in the foreword to *The Collected Tales of A. E. Coppard*, that it "ministered to an apparently inborn and universal desire to hear tales, and it is my feeling that the closer the modern short story conforms to that ancient tradition of being spoken to you, rather than being read at you, the more acceptable it becomes."

Ghosts are a favored topic of Coppard. His ghost stories perplex readers rather than frighten them; additionally, they explore the paradoxes of disembodied immateriality. Magic is another favorite topic, but it does not often reward the magician in Coppards view, although it also does not bring divine retribution. In contrast to magic, sin usually is explicitly punished in a Coppard story. Some of his tales can be classified as horror stories, but the horrific elements are merely suggested, requiring readers to exercise their own imaginations, as the characters in the stories must do.

Coppard often adopted lively colloquialisms. His style is a showcase for playful language; he loved words and relished them for their own sake as well as for the effects they have on his readers.

—*Victoria Gaydosik*

FEERSUM ENDJINN

On a far-future Earth hurtling toward catastrophe, a valiant few try to escape an unjust political order

Author: Iain Banks (1954–2013)
Genre: Science fiction—cultural exploration
Type of work: Novel
Time of work: Several millennia in the future
Locale: Earth
First published: 1994

THE STORY

On far-future Earth, virtual reality is predominant. It is easy for people to have their memories stored and to have multiple "lives." Count Alandre Sessine VII is an aristocrat among the Cryptographers, who for decades have been at war with the rival Engineers. Both sides feel helpless in the path of the coming Encroachment, in which Earth and the solar system will be destroyed. Dissidents among the Cryptographers suspect that their corrupt king and his central clique have some knowledge of how to escape the calamity, which they so far lack.

Sessine has been killed seven times, so he knows his life is in danger. He takes special steps to be securely reincarnated. Meanwhile, Hortis Gadfium III, the chief scientist among the Cryptographers, has learned that the king and his cohorts, who are termed the Consistory, know of a secret wormhole by which they can escape the Encroachment and transport themselves to other planets long ago settled by earthlings.

Bascule is an enthusiastic if somewhat naïve apprentice working under the guidance of Mr. Zoliparia, another dissident among the Cryptographers. His greatest attachment is to his pet ant, Ergates. Because of her ability to talk and think, the reader immediately suspects Ergates to be more than an ant, although the childlike Bascule does not realize this. As Bascule listens to Mr. Zoliparias laments about the erosion of the human belief in progress, he only half understands them. Bascule reveals to Mr. Zoliparia that Ergates can talk, but before the older man can give Bascule any advice, Ergates is captured by a wayfaring bird.

The kings forces possess a mysterious woman named Asura. Asura seems innocent and childlike, but she has the power to resist their attempts to force her mind to submit to them. They try to invade her dreams, hoping to lure her by using girlish fantasies of a prince climbing into a tower to rescue her, but she recognizes the virtual prince for the impostor that he is.

Gadfium and her allies become aware of Asura's existence and endeavor to save her. Gadfium clones herself into a male form and manages to liberate Asura. Once freed and fully aware, Asura reveals to the scientists the true nature of the Encroachment and discloses how the king and the Consistory are planning to save themselves. It is realized that Asura is in fact the final incarnation of Sessine; Sessine's efforts to secure himself had been successful and, as Asura, he had finally eluded his enemies.

Asura escorts Gadfium and her friends to a safe area where they can hold out indefinitely against the Consistory. The scientists also find a way to resist the Encroachment. Learning from what the Diaspora, the departed humans who had migrated to the stars, had left to the Resiliers of Earth generations before, they find a way to increase the Suns light. Finally, Ergates the ant, now revealed as an agent of the artificial intelligence mechanisms left by the Diaspora, returns to his friend Bascule, who has departed with the exiles.

ANALYSIS

Scottish writer Iain Banks is known to science-fiction readers largely as the author of the open-ended space opera series concerning the future society he terms the Culture. *Feersum Endjinn*, though concerned with traditionally science-fictional subjects, is reminiscent of the psychological probing and depth of situation and character to be found in Banks's nongenre fiction such as *The Wasp Factory* (1984).

Feersum Endjinn is also something of a mystery story. For many pages, the reader has little or no idea of what is going on or where the plot is leading. The crucial background information that the reader needs to fully understand this societys existence—that Earth is now a backwater planet about to be exterminated and that the initiative has passed to Earth's long-independent colonies—has to be extrapolated by the reader after many pages. There is also the mystery of what has happened to Sessine, who seems destined to be the storys major character but is rarely present in the narrative. On rereading the book, the reader can find clues that Asura is in fact Sessine, but the enigma of the roles of both characters is a major source of suspense in the novel.

Banks's concentration in *Feersum Endjinn* is not on the large macrocosmic canvas but on small incidents and details that reveal the psychology of the world he depicts. The reader has to work to puzzle out the big picture, and this is the way Banks probably wants it.

Another ingredient of the novel that makes the reader work is the strange typography in which Bascule's speech is reproduced. Bascule narrates approximately one out of every three chapters in the book, and in all of his chapters, there is a consistent though strange manner of spelling. For example, whenever "have" appears in a sentence, it is written as "½"; whenever "to" appears, it is written as "2"; and whenever "at" appears, it is written as "@." This adds an exotic, futuristic, and uncanny atmosphere to the book. It also underscores Bascule's naïve yet inquisitive mentality and gives a tangible perspective to the rapidly unfolding events of the book. For example, the title is supplied by Bascule, rendering in his own spelling the idea that the story of Sessine, Asura, Gadfium, and himself has come to a "fearsome ending."

The most poetic segments of the book have to do with the slow awakening of Asura into cognition and her successful attempts to frustrate the efforts of the evil kings minions, who attempt to steal her secrets from her. Asura is a minor deity in the Hindu religion, and Banks's character seems to possess extrahuman qualities at times. Banks convincingly portrays how a complex, intelligent person rebuilds awareness of the world out of nothing and thus establishes the mood of wonder and discovery that prevails throughout the book.

—*Nicholas Birns*

THE FEMALE MAN

An emissary from an all-female planet of the future travels to the present to observe male/female relations

Author: Joanna Russ (1937-2011)
Genre: Science fiction—feminist
Type of work: Novel
Time of work: An alternative 1970's and two possible futures
Location: Earth and Whileaway
First published: 1975

THE STORY

The novel is polyphonically composed, using six alternating female narrators (a group called the four J's, a teenager, and the author). Each brings her own perspective, shaped in some cases by life in an alternative reality.

The first of the J's, so named because their names begin with that letter, is Janet Evanson. She is an inhabitant of Whileaway, a possible future Earth whose entire population is women. She has been sent back to a possible present to study mores in a land where men still exist. Janet finds two women whom she wants to take back to her time: Joanna, her tour guide, and Jeannine Dadier, a librarian. A large part of the book describes the relatively uneventful daily lives of these two women.

Jeannine has a noncommittal sexual relationship with the unambitious Cal. He is a male chauvinist

The Female Man

who matter-of-factly expects Jeannine to do his laundry and prepare his meals, even though both work and he contributes nothing to her support or nurture. Jeannine's passive behavior is contrasted sharply to Janet's no-holds-barred actions. Taken to a party by Joanna, Janet evades the attentions of the drunken host by punching him in the nose and breaking his arm.

Yet another unfulfilled character is introduced when Janet Evanson moves in with a suburban family. The family's seventeen-year-old daughter, Laura Rose Wilding, is a budding writer who has been frustrated by others, who label her aspirations unfeminine. The girl initiates a love affair with Janet, who is the first person she has met who respects her intellect and dreams.

The plot takes yet another unexpected turn when Alice-Jael Reasoner, called Jael, arrives to transport the women to another future. Jael lives on an Earth where women and men live in opposed, armed camps. Her nation has wanted to contact Whileaway but has been unable to because of peculiarities of the time-space continuum. Now that Whileaway can be approached by way of Jeannine and Joanna's world, Jael asks if the female planet can be used as a training camp and if Earth can serve as a transfer point.

The book ends with the answers to these questions. Janet, not particularly impressed with Jael's world, says no. Jeannine, sick of her planet's patriarchal arrangements, agrees to assist in a war to exterminate men.

Analysis

The Female Man appeared during the high tide of the women's liberation movement. At this time, authors such as Kate Millett published books denouncing the stereotyping of women as inferior and the carryover of these stereotypes into inequitable social practices, such as paying women and men differently for equivalent work. These books were products of a broader social current of women who protested against injustices. This upheaval sparked a questioning of sexual roles by imaginative writers. During this period, the most acclaimed attempt by a science-fiction author to rethink biological bias was made in Ursula K. Le Guin's *The Left Hand of Darkness* (1969). In the universe Le Guin portrayed, there was no question of one sex dominating, because all the humanoids were hermaphrodites. Joanna Russ's vision is more combative than this. She is not interested in simply drawing the type of implicit contrast found in *The Left Hand of Darkness*, in which the viability of a different biological setup is explored. Russ savagely compares contemporary sexism to the milder, freer life on all-female Whileaway.

One of the author's strengths arises from her need to give an accurate rendering of modern life to serve as a basis of comparison. It is often overlooked that some of the greatest writers of science fiction, such as Philip K. Dick, achieve much of their authority because they bring to their speculative writing realistic portraits of their times. In Russ's case, some of the best parts of this book are her faithful portraits of contemporary women, as in her depiction of Laura's yearning for support and Jeannine's ambivalence toward marriage. Such writing as easily might have filled a place in a mainstream realist novel as in a work of futurology.

When such slices of life are interrupted by visits from extraterrestrials and the narrative is intercut with views of future Earths, the book firmly establishes its science-fiction credentials. Inclusion of two manners of intervention allows Russ to make her sharpest comments in relation to the sexism in American society. On one hand, Janet, who has been socialized outside of patriarchy, is a determined, independent woman, more capable and generally likable than the Earth women. On the other, life on Whileaway, without men, is treated as attractively natural, festive, and well suited to the all-around development of individual potential. This is not to say that Russ presents a blinkered view of either Janet as a faultless heroine or of her world. Janet is cold and can be self-absorbed, and her planet, which still allows the brutality of duels, arbitrarily and undemocratically assigns people to jobs they may not want.

The introduction of Jael's planet hints that social structure determines a world's negative or positive nature. Jael's female civilization is warlike, murders men without compunction, and is not above keeping slavish gigolos for its elite women. This culture, at war with all men, makes the female/male dyad the central equation in the society's worldview, and this twists its existence, even though men do not live within the community. Russ implies that it is the use of this dyad to establish difference, rather than inherent biological traits, that poisons human relationships. This point does not reduce the causticity of Russ's critique of the injustices perpetuated by men in the United States.

—*James Feast*

FEVRE DREAM

Joshua York, a vampire who has conquered his own blood lust, struggles with traditional forces and converts the race of vampires into simple people of the night

Author: George R. R. Martin (1948–)
Genre: Science fiction—occult
Type of work: Novel
Time of work: 1857–1870
Locale: The Mississippi River and its tributaries
First published: 1982

THE STORY

Fevre Dream tells how Joshua York conquers the "red thirst" that dominates his people and how he forges an alliance with Abner Marsh to accomplish his dream. York, a vampire, has defeated his own need for blood. He seeks other people of the night to convince them that life without killing is a good thing. All works well until York is defeated by Damon Julian, the dominant power among the vampires. York tries to be loyal to his people and to the good but cannot do both. He finally calls for help from his friend Marsh. They join forces to defeat Julians insane blood lust.

Marsh and York have dinner late one night in April of 1857. At the end of the evening, each has his hearts desire. Despite the setback of having all but one of his boats destroyed by ice, Marsh will be able to build his advanced steamboat and York will have the freedom of the river. Marsh recognizes the presence and power in York but does not quite recognize York's truly alien nature.

Their steamboat is christened the *Fevre Dream* in honor of it being Marsh's dream boat and his company being the Fevre River Packet Company. The *Fevre Dream* sets out on its maiden voyage down the Mississippi River in July of 1857. The boat itself is everything Marsh could hope for, but York's odd nighttime habits and the odd and prolonged delays that he causes produce frictions that ultimately lead to Marsh learning York's secret.

York's mission is to free his people from their need for blood. He has developed an elixir that cures the thirst. He scours news reports to find others of his kind that can be helped by it. All goes well as they proceed downriver until they get to New Orleans.

In New Orleans, Damon Julian comes on board with his company of vampires, and York is unable to tame him. Instead, Julian makes York submit, and Marsh is forced to flee his beloved *Fevre Dream*. Marsh counterattacks twice but is rebuffed each time. In the aftermath of the second counterattack, Marsh and York sorrowfully part company. York's commitment to good is strong and he will not personally violate it, but his commitment to his people is stronger, and he is drawn to them.

Marsh bankrupts himself searching for his *Fevre Dream*. He goes into an uneasy retirement until 1870, when he receives a message from York. The two of them attack the vampires aboard the remains of the *Fevre Dream*. In the fighting, Marsh becomes a pawn in the struggle between York and Julian. Julian miscalculates: The stress is sufficient to bring out the beast in York, and York is able to make Julian submit. As he submits, Marsh executes him. The people of the night are tamed of their red thirst, and Marsh becomes a hero to them.

ANALYSIS

Fevre Dream seems to be a work at variance with its origins. George R. R. Martin is a writer of what is called "hard" science fiction. Vampires hardly seem like his bill of fare. His vampires are simply another race that preys upon ordinary mortals as if they were cattle. Unlike the traditional vampire described by Bram Stoker in the classic gothic novel *Dracula* (1897), Martin's vampires are a separate race that lives alongside humankind. York and his people of the night are not the twisted and often soulless descendants of ancient vampires; they are a generally dangerous and superior race limited by their inability to withstand direct sunlight and by a need to drink human blood. The books that come closest to Martin's vision are the Vampire Chronicles of Anne Rice (1976–1995). Rices vampires are every bit as physical as York and Julian, but her tradition is still spiritual, and her vampires were once human.

Martin rejected the traditional spiritual notion of vampires in favor of asking the question, If there were vampires, how would they live? His answer produces a vampire with conscience, the outlook of humanity, and the ability to produce an antidote to the red thirst that drives his kind to hunt and kill. These creatures of the night can have as much variation as ordinary humans.

Much of Martin's other work deals with vampires of the spirit. "Override" (1973) provides a view of a man dealing with his own corpse. A young woman becomes part of an alien life form in "A Song for Lya" (1974). "Manna from Heaven" (1985) sterilizes starving colonists.

Fevre Dream moves in synchrony with the great Mississippi River system from the height of the steamboat era through the Civil War and Reconstruction to reach its conclusion. York and Marsh proudly build their great steamboat in a northern shipyard and are soundly defeated by traditional forces in the South. When Marsh counterattacks, he is defeated; when York counterattacks, his spirit appears to be stolen from him. Throughout the period of the Civil War and early Reconstruction, the existence of the *Fevre Dream* appears to be in doubt. As hope is fading, the shadow of strength reappears, and through superhuman efforts, York and Marsh defeat the forces of Julian and the red thirst. This unity of environment, times, and theme provides the energy and depth behind *Fevre Dream*.

—*Joseph Minne*

THE FIFTH HEAD OF CERBERUS

On a planet originally colonized by the French and mixing nineteenth century and futuristic cultures, a young man comes of age

Author: Gene Wolfe (1931–)
Genre: Science fiction—cultural exploration
Type of work: Novella
Time of work: Several hundred years in the future
Locale: The planet Sainte Croix
First published: 1972 (in *The Fifth Head of Cerberus*, containing the title novella and two other stories; serial form, *Orbit*, 1972)

THE STORY

In eighteen sections and about eighty pages, "Number Five," the nickname assigned to the otherwise anonymous protagonist by his father, composes a memoir of his first thirty years. His account starts at the age of seven, when his comfortably privileged routine is disturbed. He lives with his supposed brother, David, who appears genetically dissimilar, and a robot tutor, Mr. Million. His life is transformed over the next eleven years into a sort of hell, appropriate to the family address of 666 Saltimbanque and the houses portal statue of Cerberus. His emotionally distant father conducts increasingly arduous nocturnal interrogations, eventually involving drug injections, time loss, memory loss, and hallucinatory dreams, the latter recalling the novellas epigraph from Samuel Taylor Coleridge's *The Rime of the Ancient Mariner* (1798).

At the age of thirteen, the narrator is appointed porter or "greeter" of 666 Saltimbanque, which serves as both the family home and a brothel. This post equates him to Cerberus. At the age of eighteen, the narrator, his sweetheart, Phaedria, and David turn to petty theft among the audience of their plays to support their dramatics, then to attempted grand theft of the cashbox in the depths of a multistoried gladiatorial slave warehouse. Their descent echoes the heros into the underworld in Homer's *The Odyssey* and Vergil's *The Aeneid*, ancient texts that are David's favorite reading. The cashbox, surprisingly, is guarded by a four-armed, genetically altered human, recalling Cerberus and Briareus, another guard of Tartarus in classical myth. David attacks him with a window pole tipped with a mirror shard, symbolic of viewing the world and reflected selves. The narrator attacks and kills the monster, whom he dimly recognizes as yet another clone of his father (like himself).

The narrator, emboldened by the criminal escapade and resentful of eleven years of abuse, later kills his father. That abuse culminated, he realizes during the attempted theft, in huge gaps of lost time and memory. The murder re-enacts the cycle of his father's murder of the narrators grandfather, a replication fostered by the family patriarchs long history of cloning. Ironically, the goal of the cloning was escape from cyclicality into linear advance or evolution of humanity.

The narrator is released after a harsh nine years of imprisonment, echoing his childhood imprisonment symbolized by the iron shutters on the childrens dormitory window. He later inherits 666 Saltimbanque from his aunt, Dr. Aubrey Veil, also a clone and promulgator. Her surname is symbolic of deception and identity, as well as reflecting the theory that all the inhabitants of Sainte Croix are actually descendants of the alien aborigines of the sister planet Sainte Anne, who through chameleonic mimicry have transformed themselves into perfect human semblances.

The narrator restores 666 Saltimbanque. The name of the street, in French meaning charlatan or showman, suggests the theme of true identity. Phaedria, long since married to and divorced from someone other than the narrator, now resides in the house and appears ready for a romantic reunion with the narrator, a reunion that would include her child from her former marriage.

ANALYSIS

Richly symbolic, allusive, and very literately written, this novella explores boundaries and borderlines: reality versus imagination or dream, free will versus fate, freedom versus constraint, lawfulness versus crime, human versus nonhuman, past versus future, childhood versus adulthood, and self versus other. The novellas most pervasive symbol among its many, the mirror, expresses several of these themes.

The father's library, prohibited to the narrator, is mirrored by the public library, which allows free access. Its main central spiral ramp ascends to a magically suspended dome, suggesting the imaginative power of knowledge and the dome in Coleridge's "Kubla Khan" (1816). The "helix" housing the collection, which the narrator loves to climb and explore, suggests the upward spiral of knowledge and the basis of human life, DNA. The fathers laboratory is concealed behind the wall mirror of his library, in the same way that his motivations and cloning are concealed from the narrator. The viewplate image on the head of Mr. Million seems a mirror reflection of the father and the narrator, though it is actually the great-grandfather. The mirror in the slave warehouse invites the criminals to consider who they are and what they are doing, as well as later providing a weapon to kill a deformed mirror image of the narrator. The brothel, also nicknamed "Cave Canem" (referring to the Cerberus statue), is pervaded by spotted mirrors, reflecting the narrators central problem of finding out who he is. Even the costumes of the demimondaines or protegées, among the euphemisms that conceal the prostitutes identity, contain mirror surfaces, said to resemble the natural planetary mirrors of bodies of still water.

Even the twin-system planets of Sainte Anne and Sainte Croix are virtually mirror images, related to the issue of whether the inhabitants of the latter are human or "abo" (alien aborigine). Earth anthropologist John Marsch, on Sainte Croix to investigate the matter of abos, is accused by the narrator of being an abo impersonating a human from Earth.

The enigma of identity, particularly the narrators, is reflected in Sainte Croix, which has some affinities with early New Orleans and a history that in some respects mirrors that of its namesake in the Virgin Islands, with ironic comment on the narrators brothel. A mixture of eighteenth and nineteenth century anachronisms (sedan chairs, slave markets, multimasted sailing ships, ships towed from the harbor by oxen, and lamplighters) and the future (robots with one billion synapses, starcrosser spacecraft, holographs, an antigravity prosthesis for the narrators aunt, and cloning) create a disorientation in the reader that echoes that of the narrator. Balanced against such contemporary allusions as Gene Wolfes references to fellow science-fiction writers Vernor Vinge and Kate Wilhelm, the author of the astronautics text *The Mile-Long Spaceship* (1963), are allusions to classical literature and myth, including the character names of Aunt Urania, Phaedria, and Nerissa, as well as David's panpipes. This combination of elements from different times ultimately suggests not only the problem of orientation but also the conflict of cyclicality versus linear advance, or whether, as humanity journeys into the far reaches of space and time, it will advance or merely duplicate its history.

—*Norman Prinsky*

Fire and Hemlock

A modern reworking of the ballad of Tam Lin, in which Polly must solve the mystery surrounding Thomas Lynn

Author: Diana Wynne Jones (1934–2011)
Genre: Fantasy—magical world
Type of work: Novel
Time of work: The 1980's
Location: Middleton and Bristol, England
First published: 1985

The Story

In the middle of packing to return to college, Polly suddenly becomes aware that she seems to have forgotten several years of her life, or rather that she seems to have two parallel sets of memories, one featuring a man called Thomas Lynn. In trying to figure out this puzzle, she is obliged to work back through her adolescence, recalling events. Readers see Polly at the age of twelve. She has been sent to her grandmother's home because her parents are quarrelling. There, with her friend Nina, she undertakes a madcap set of adventures that lead her to the mysterious Hunsdon House, where she inadvertently steps into a funeral and attends the reading of the will. She is rescued by a young man called Thomas Lynn, with whom she strikes up a friendship. They quickly discover that they share a love of heroic tales and begin to invent one concerning Tan Coul, who is Lynn, with Polly as his assistant.

The friendship and the storytelling continue by letter. Thomas gives Polly many books suitable for assistant heroes. Polly becomes aware, however, of her grandmother's disapproval, and also of an unhealthy interest from the occupants of Hunsdon House, who seem to punish her and Thomas for any contact.

This friendship against the odds is counterpointed by Polly's miserable daily life. Her parents separate and eventually divorce, and Polly comes to realize that neither of them really wants her. Her mother moves from one partner to another, and her father begins living with a woman who clearly dislikes children. In one particularly appalling scene, Polly's mother sends her to live with her father permanently, but he has not told his new partner that Polly is coming. Only through the intervention of Thomas Lynn and Polly's grandmother is disaster averted.

As Polly grows older, she finds that her life remains inextricably mixed up with that of Thomas Lynn and the Leroy family but is unable to work out what is happening. Sebastian Leroy, the child of the family, dogs her footsteps and eventually asks her to marry him, but she refuses. Only the combination of the book she is reading and the picture Thomas Lynn gave her many years earlier suddenly alert her to the curious nature of her memories. She then discovers that no one else can remember Thomas Lynn and begins to doubt her own sanity. Her flatmate, however, reveals that she remembers him, and Polly finds that Thomas Lynn's Dumas Quartet has become well known in the musical world. Reading at last the book of fairy stories he once gave her, she realizes that the story of TamLin is being reenacted, with the Queen of the Fairies keeping a man for seven years and then consigning him to Hell. Her role, like that of Janet, is to hold onto Thomas Lynn and save him from this. A final confrontation with the mysterious Laurel rescues Thomas Lynn. The novel is resolved ambiguously, with a hint of a future relationship between Polly and Thomas.

ANALYSIS

By the time *Fire and Hemlock* was published, Diana Wynne Jones was well established as the writer of a particularly joyous and imaginative style of fantasy that tended to be regarded as suitable for children and young adolescents. *Fire and Hemlock* was one of her first attempts to move into the area best characterized as "young adult fiction." The work is darker in tone than her readers were accustomed to, dealing with a young girl's platonic relationship with an older man who shares her love of reading. A counterpoint is provided by the failing relationships of the girl's own parents, both with each other and with new partners. Jones is very skillful in creating the ambiguities of the relationship between Polly and Thomas, from Polly's delight in meeting someone who shares her pleasure in reading and is able to recommend new books to her, to her jealousy when Tom introduces her to Mary Fields, who seems to be his girlfriend. Jones also lovingly creates the world of the teenage girl, neither adult nor child, torn by confusing signals from all around her: the disentangling of childhood friendships, the new interest in boys, and the realization that adults are not to be relied on and can indeed let one down badly. On top of all this is the magical component of the story, a dark magic entirely unlike that found in most of the story books with which Polly is familiar.

Jones updates one of the most enduring and most menacing of the old ballads without losing any of its power. Instead, she heightens its effect by showing the faeryfolk capable of functioning, apparently with impunity, in the mundane world, exercising power of life or death as they wish, entirely unquestioned. A hero, which is how Polly casts herself, may yet triumph and save the day. The fact that Polly is a hero in many other ways, surviving her parents' callous disregard, remains unstated but nevertheless is clear. Jones has never shirked from pursuing an amalgam of magic, fantasy, and the grim reality of everyday life. This novel shows creation of such an amalgam in her best style.

—*Maureen Speller*

A FIRE UPON THE DEEP

As a great evil power, the Perversion, devours the thinking galaxy, a small band of sentients struggles to activate a counteragent that was liberated when the Perversion was created

Author: Vernor Vinge (1944–)
Genre: Science fiction—catastrophe
Type of work: Novel
Time of work: Org years 52089–52091
Location: Relay, Tines World, Harmonious Repose, and on board the spaceship *Out of Band II*
First published: *A Fire Upon the Deep* (1992), *A Deepness in the Sky* (1999), and *The Children of the Sky* (2011)

THE STORY

A Fire upon the Deep tells the story of the Perversion's attack on civilization and of the countermeasures taken against it. The Perversion is unwittingly unleashed by an advanced society, but the process also produces a countermeasure. As the Perversion advances, the unusual crew of the spaceship *Out of Band II* races to activate and guide the countermeasure. They succeed, and the galaxy is saved, although a substantial piece of high civilization has been set back for some period of time. In the environment of *A Fire upon the Deep*, shells of potential, shaped roughly like a child's toy top, define activity in the Milky Way. Even thought cannot exist in the central Unthinking Depths. The closer that sentients approach this limit, the less intelligent they become. The next shell out defines the Slow Zone, where any information transfer is constrained by the speed of light. The outermost boundary separates the Beyond, where advanced civilizations dwell, from the Transcend, where the Powers dwell.

On a planet barely inside the Transcend, the Straumli Realm accidentally unleashes a great evil power, the Perversion. As researchers escape their laboratory, they take with them a countermeasure to the Perversion. This countermeasure lands on Tines World, very near the Slow Zone. As they emerge from their ship, the humans are massacred by large, somewhat doglike creatures. Only two children survive: Jefri Olsndot stays in the Flenser Republic and is carefully nurtured; Johanna Olsndot is skillfully spirited away to the Woodcarvers' domain.

On Relay, a prime location in the communications network of the Beyond civilizations, Ravna Bergsndot happily works as a student librarian. She is pulled from her accustomed duties to orient a revived primitive spacefaring human, Pham Nuwen, to work for a Power known as Old One. As Ravna and Pham get to know each other, they meet and become acquainted with two Skroderriders, plant intelligences named Blueshell and Greenstalk, who fly *Out of Band II* as interstellar traders.

Pham turns out to be a creation of Old One. As Straumli Realm falls, Jefri calls for help. The administration of Relay commissions *Out of Band II* to rescue Jefri and activate the countermeasure, instituting a multifunction refit of the ship. When the Perversion attacks Relay and kills Old One, Old One Godshatters, turning into Pham. Ravna, Pham, and the Skroderriders run for Tines World in *Out of Band II*.

As *Out of Band II* arrives at Tines world, the situation is desperate. War has broken out between the Flenser Republic and the Woodcarvers' domain, and the Perversion is advancing fast. The crew of *Out of Band II* rescues the children and activates the countermeasure, which causes a wave out of the Slow Zone that extends into the Transcend. This eliminates the Perversion and all Beyonder civilizations in its path.

ANALYSIS

From prologue to epilogue, *A Fire upon the Deep* fills its reader with a sense of wonder. A unique structure for cognitive processes fills the galaxy, from the Unthinking Depths to the supercharged Transcend. Civilizations can evolve from limited organizations in the Slow Zone, through increasingly sophisticated societies in the Beyond, into Powers in the Transcend, and perhaps into something beyond the Powers. A vast communications network unites the few human and many alien civilizations of the Beyond. The conflict of the novel occurs when an advanced human civilization dabbling in the wonders of the Transcend inadvertently releases a Perversion that threatens to subvert the entire Beyond and a good portion of the Transcend.

The tradition of grand scope into which this novel falls extends at least from H. G. Wells's *The Time Machine* (1895), which describes the near and far futures of the Earth, through the science-fiction magazines of the 1930's and 1940's. John W. Campbell, Jr.'s novel *The Black Star Passes* (1953) deals with threats to Earth and the entire solar system, and his *The Mightiest Machine* (1947; serial form, 1934) envisions conflict between galaxies. E. E. Smith's Lensman series, from *Triplanetary* (1948; serial form, 1934) to *Children of the Lens* (1954; serial form, 1947–1948), extends through six books, envisioning a conflict between high forces of good and evil involving the entire Milky Way and multiple races. Isaac Asimov's Foundation trilogy (1951–1953) centers on institutions whose purpose is to save essential civilization as a galactic empire crumbles. The tradition of grand scope extends into the 1980's and 1990's with work such as Michael Resnick's novels of the Inner Frontier: *Santiago: A Myth of the Far Future* (1986), *Ivory: A Legend of Past and Future* (1988), *Soothsayer* (1991), *Oracle* (1992), and *Prophet* (1993). The worlds in them are modeled on the American Wild West and populated by legendary aliens.

Vernor Vinge informs *A Fire upon the Deep*, his contribution to the tradition of grand scope, with his background as a professor of computer science. His background breathes life into both the communications network that links the civilizations of the Beyond and the information mining that awakens the Perversion.

This novel shows the continued growth of Vinge's writing. In *Marooned in Realtime* (1986), Vinge envisions a few pockets of humanity living in stasis while some force eliminates humankind. Their problem is uniting the pockets so that humankind can continue. Vinge's background in information theory shows up again in this book: The first hurdle to be overcome is communication between stasis bubbles. What Vinge adds in *A Fire upon the Deep* is a greater richness of detail. The context of the novel is a galaxywide society of diverse civilizations populated by a variety of mutually alien races. Two particularly delightful alien races are fully realized.

—*Joseph Minne*

THE FIRST MEN IN THE MOON

Two men travel in a sphere to the Moon and are attacked by its insectlike inhabitants; one returns to Earth, and the other sends a radio report of his observations of the Selenites

Author: H(erbert) G(eorge) Wells (1866-1946)
Genre: Science fiction—cosmic voyage
Type of work: Novel
Time of work: The early twentieth century
Locale: Lympne, a village in Kent, England; and the Moon
First published: 1901

THE STORY

The story has two principal characters: Bedford, a bankrupt fortune hunter, and Cavor, an impractical scientist. They are neighbors in the village of Lympne. Throughout the novel, these two figures are contrasted and compared as the author makes satirical observations about humanity in general and utopian ideas in particular.

Cavor has invented a substance called Cavorite that neutralizes the effects of gravity. Bedford's entrepreneurial greed senses an opportunity to make money. Before long, the pair are on their way to the Moon in a Cavorite sphere. The journey is related in a believable manner, with some accurate anticipations of the effects of weightlessness in space. Arriving on the Moon, the travelers find that it is in daylight for half of each Earth month. During this time, the atmosphere that was frozen in the other two weeks is warmed, and fantastic vegetation appears. The inhabitants of the Moon, the Selenites, are insectlike creatures who pasture giant worms, the mooncalves, as their food source.

The Selenites live in an ordered society, modeled no doubt on what H. G. Wells knew of the habits of ants and bees, in a kind of honeycomb under the lunar surface. Bedford and Cavor are captured and react very differently to their plight: Bedford wants to carry off as much gold as possible—gold is the Selenites most common mineral—and return to Earth, while Cavor tries to communicate with his captors, whom he finds fascinating. Bedford finally persuades his companion to escape. In the ensuing battle, the fragile Selenites are broken and slaughtered by their more powerful visitors. Cavor is recaptured, and Bedford makes it back to Earth alone, landing on an English beach. He loses the sphere and is therefore unable to return to the Moon for more gold or to rescue his companion.

A few months later, Cavor radios in Morse code his adventures inside the Moon. He has toured the abode of the Selenites and has taught them English. He reacts enthusiastically to the ordered, rational society he encounters on the Moon. The lunar culture is "a world machine" in which every inhabitant performs a single task for the benefit of the community. Some, who operate simple machines, are reared in bottles to prevent the growth of everything except a single hand. Momentarily seized by sympathy, Cavor comments that the hand "seemed" to appeal for lost possibilities, but he concludes that the Selenites do better than humans on Earth, with their method of letting children first grow into human beings and then turning them into machines.

Cavor is taken for an interview with the Grand Lunar, the huge brain, almost devoid of body, who controls the whole society. This interview apparently causes a change of heart in Cavor, who makes the mistake of telling his host too much about the inhabitants of Earth and their chaotic ways, including warfare. As he is about to send the recipe for Cavorite back to Earth, the radio signals are suddenly cut off, the last transmission being "uless." Cavor's reports are serialized by Bedford under the pseudonym of Wells.

ANALYSIS

The lunar voyage draws on a theme as old as *The True History* (transcribed second century c.e.) of Lucian of Samosata, who lived in the second century. The use of a fantastic journey for the purpose of satirizing contemporary society echoes Jonathan Swift's *Gullivers Travels* (1726). *The First Men in the Moon* is distinguished not so much by originality as by its vivid and imaginative writing, its mixing of comic and serious elements, and its pessimistic vision of a dystopian society.

The highly ordered society of the Selenites is a system without individual freedoms and rights.

The insectlike form of the lunar beings emphasizes this and gives them a monstrous quality. Bedford fights against the system, but for his own selfish reasons: He wants to steal gold and come back for more later. Cavor is a detached scientist who is fascinated by what he sees but is prepared only to observe, not to participate. The Selenites are called "citizens" but are in reality completely conditioned from birth to perform their preassigned tasks in the machine. This is a nightmarish vision of economic conditions in a developed capitalist system. Bedford typifies the acquisitive capitalist, who is egotistical and irresponsible in his pursuit of gain. On the Moon, he can literally throw his weight around. His plan to annex the Moon and harvest its resources is a satirical jab at imperialist exploitation of vulnerable peoples and lands. Bedford also embodies those competitive energies and individualistic values that Wells appeared to admire. The novel validates the idea of an organized society but at the same time sets limits on how far the individual should be subjected to the desires of the group.

The dreamlike quality of the narrative has been noted often. The fragmentary account of Cavor's observations that concludes the novel gives the impression of snapshots or vignettes, a technique often used by satirists. The voyage is a journey of self-discovery for both principal characters. Bedford, who writes his serial in a paradisiacal setting in Italy, has been enlivened by his experience and finally has gained the success he craved. Cavor, on the other hand, has come face to face with the consequences of his own scientific speculations and been destroyed by them. The major themes of Wells's dystopian vision are taken up by many later works, such as Aldous Huxley's *Brave New World* (1932). *First Men in the Moon* (1964), a film version of the novel, was directed by Nathan Juran and had a different ending: The Selenites in the film are wiped out by a virus in a manner reminiscent of Wells's *The War of the Worlds* (1898).

—*David H. J. Larmour*

THE FISHER KING TRILOGY

In this action-packed trilogy, various characters interact with ghosts, mythological figures, and black-magic tarot cards in a drama of suffering, redemption, and apotheosis in the American West

Author: Tim Powers (1952–)
Genre: Fantasy—magical realism
Type of work: Novel
Time of work: 1990–1995
Location: Southern California and Las Vegas, Nevada
First published: *Last Call* (1992), *Expiration Date* (1996), and *Earthquake Weather* (1997)

THE STORY

The Fisher King trilogy chronicles the apotheosis of Scott Crane, the son of a corrupt gangster who rules a mystical realm of nebulous boundaries in the American West. Scott and his father, Georges Leon, possess magical powers that are explicitly associated with those of the Fisher King of Arthurian legend. Scott must challenge his father and assume the kingship of the West in order to save what has become a political, financial, architectural, and spiritual wasteland. Dramatizing the stages of the symbolic life of the Fisher King, each novel is set in a different season: *Last Call* in spring, *Expiration Date* in autumn, and *Earthquake Weather* in winter.

In *Last Call*, Scott attempts to reclaim the life his father stole from him. As a child, Scott was nearly turned into a soulless vessel by Leon, who uses black magic in the pursuit of longer life. Saved by his mother, Scott fled and was adopted in Los Angeles by Ozzie Crane. His legacy is the loss of one eye, a casualty of the Page of Swords card in an evil tarot deck hurled by his father. Scott becomes an avatar of the Page of Swords, also known as the One-Eyed Jack (the Jack of Hearts) and the crown prince of the King of Hearts (the Fisher King). Years later, Scott symbolically loses his life to his father again, this time in a card game called assumption, a variation of poker played with Leon's tarot deck.

Later, at the age of forty-seven, Scott loses his beloved wife and the life they shared. Joined by his friend Archimedes "Arky" Mavranos, Ozzie Crane, and his foster sister Diana, Scott defeats his father, reclaims his life, and becomes the new Fisher King.

Expiration Date introduces Koot Hoomie Parganas, an eleven-year-old candidate for the position of Fisher King, who accidentally sets free the curmudgeonly ghost of Thomas A. Edison in Los Angeles. Pursued by a one-armed madman called Sherman Oaks (after the name of a Los Angeles suburb) and Loretta deLarava, a ghost-obsessed documentary producer, Koot navigates the dangerous streets of an unfriendly city with Edison's help.

Koot's story is interwoven with that of Pete Sullivan, busy fleeing ghosts of his own as he finally returns to Los Angeles. After witnessing the death of their father years before, Pete and his twin sister grew up in that city and began working for deLarava. The siblings eventually realized that deLarava planned to capture the ghost of their father, and they parted ways, always running from the past. However, Pete is drawn back to the city to seek absolution from his father's ghost and a resolution to the mystery surrounding his murder.

Earthquake Weather opens with the murder of Scott Crane. Janice Cordelia Plumtree, host to multiple personalities, surrenders herself to the authorities as the assassin after suffering possession by a ghost. Joined by Sid "Scant" Cochran, a vineyard worker marked with a scar on his hand from Dionysus, Janice seeks to restore Scott to life. Arky Mavranos and Diana follow magical guidance and take the king's body to Pete Sullivan and Koot. The two groups join in a quest to bring Scott back to life or to replace him with a new Fisher King, racing against time to save the failing Kingdom of the West.

ANALYSIS

The Fisher King Trilogy succeeds in adapting the myth of the Fisher King into eminently readable novels set in the 1990's. Filled with rituals, legends, magic, gods and ghosts, each novel reflects extensive research and the deft writing needed to blend these elements into fast-paced, engaging stories.

The character Scott Crane is aptly named. In ancient Greece, cranes were sacred to Demeter, the goddess who renewed the earth each spring when her daughter was released from the Underworld. They are also symbolic of resurrection, and throughout the novels Scott Crane seeks the rebirth of the wasteland created by his father. The bird most closely related to the North American crane is the coot, and, as the series progresses, Koot becomes an "heir" to Scott Crane's throne.

The novels rely heavily upon Arthurian myth. Like the Fisher King of lore, both Scott and Koot develop a wound which will not heal. In order to succeed, Scott must challenge and defeat a Green Knight figure, Vaughan Trumbill. The discovery of the essential tarot deck occurs only after he has removed a pocketknife stuck in a brick, a symbolic Sword in the Stone. According to legend, the Fisher King can be healed only when an innocent fool asks the question, "Whom does it serve?" In *Earthquake Weather*, Koot's first question to Arky and Diana refers to the color of the truck carrying the dead king. By mistakenly asking the wrong question, Koot sets in motion the quest to restore Scott to life.

Powers interweaves subtexts from Charles Dickens, Shakespeare, T. S. Eliot, Alfred Lord Tennyson, Lewis Carroll, and others to provide greater depth through allusions to both tragedy and irrationality. The humor for which Powers is famous is present throughout. For instance, while seeking Koot Hoomie Parganas, Scant and Janice ask around for someone whose name sounds like "Boogie Woogie Bananas." Like Carroll, Powers has a gift for comic invention when dramatizing miscommunication. Powers's Catholic beliefs fully inform his works. Redemption, forgiveness, salvation, and resurrection are essential to the madcap adventures he depicts. A work not explicitly alluded to by Powers, C. S. Lewis's famous Space Trilogy, nonetheless presents powerful parallels. These books also deal with Christian motifs and Arthurian myth, and the concluding volumes of both trilogies painfully dramatize the themes of sacrifice and redemption.

—*Michael-Anne Rubenstien*

THE FLANDRY SERIES

Dominic Flandry, special agent for the Empire of Earth, attempts to delay the fall of the Empire in conflict against the Merseians

Author: Poul Anderson (1926–2001)
Genre: Science fiction—future history
Type of work: Novels and stories
Time of work: The thirty-first century
Locale: Various planets
First published: *We Claim These Stars!* (1959), *Earthman, Go Home!* (1960; serial form, *Fantastic*, December, 1960-January, 1961), *Mayday Orbit* (1961; short version, *Fantastic*, 1959), *Agent of the Terran Empire* (1965; includes *We Claim These Stars!*), *Flandry of Terra* (1965; includes *Earthman, Go Home!*, a short version of *Mayday Orbit*, and one other story from *Venture*, 1958), *Ensign Flandry* (1966; short version, *Amazing*, 1966), *A Circus of Hells* (1970; short version, *Galaxy*, 1969), *The Rebel Worlds* (1969), *The Day of Their Return* (1973), *A Knight of Ghosts and Shadows* (1974; serial form, *If*, September-December, 1974), *A Stone in Heaven* (1979), and *The Game of Empire* (1985)

THE STORY

Poul Anderson's Flandry series is set some six hundred years after the same authors Polesotechnic League stories. Its background is that of a Terran interstellar Empire controlling thousands of suns but falling into what appears to be irreversible decline. The Empire is threatened continually by the ruthless and vigorous alien empire (known as the Roidhunate) of Merseia. Dominic Flandry's career is followed from his initial adventures as a junior officer to a position as admiral of the Fleet and unofficial adviser to the Terran Emperor.

The major theme of this sequence is a double contest, on one hand against the plots of the Merseians and on the other against the weakness and corruption of the Terran Empire itself. The two contests are often set against each other, raising again and again the question of why Flandry, portrayed as a cynic and opportunist, nevertheless continues to support an Empire that he knows is weak and contemptible against both human rebel-reformers and the alien Merseians, whom he frequently admires. The answer, in brief, is that Flandry supports a principle of legitimacy, for the purely practical reason that it is likely to lead to less internal warfare within the Empire. As much as he admires the Merseian virtues, he is aware that these do not include mercy or tolerance. Flandry is a believer in the idea of minimum government and sees the inefficient Empire as more likely to produce this than is Merseian rule or the post-Imperial anarchy that he foresees and calls "the Long Night."

Intertwined with the theme above is that of cultural diversity. Flandry's travels lead him both to strange human civilizations, modeled on those of real history, and to stranger alien ones from Anderson's imagination. Thus, in *Ensign Flandry*—the first of these works in terms of Flandry's career—Flandry finds himself on Starkad, where a land-based species, the Tigeries, is at war with a sea-based one, the Seatrolls. The former are supported by Terra and the latter by Merseia. Flandry discovers that this minor war, which Merseia seems set on escalating, is designed to draw a substantial part of the Terran fleet to Starkad, there to be destroyed when a rogue planet turns its star nova. The novel draws much of its charm from the relatively incidental depiction of the Tigeries and the Seatrolls.

In *A Circus of Hells* and the stories collected as *Flandry of Terra*, the hero confronts a planet controlled by an insane computer, a planet shared in turn between summer and winter intelligences, and a series of planets based on African, Mongol, and East Asian cultures. Two minor themes that appear variously in the three books so far mentioned are Flandry's manipulative treatment of women, which results in a curse being laid on him by a slighted woman at the end of *A Circus of Hells*, and the use of telepathic powers by allies of Merseia. Both these themes, together with the continuing internal and external conflicts from which the Empire suffers, appear repeatedly in the books that follow.

In *The Rebel Worlds*, Flandry is forced to drive an honest rebel into exile in support of a totally corrupt emperor, at the same time forfeiting his chance of happiness with the rebels wife. He does, however, assist the wife in taking revenge on the sadistic governor whose actions provoked the rebellion. In a coda to that work, *The Day of Their Return*, in which Flandry appears only marginally, a Merseian plot attempts to disrupt the Empire by launching on it a new religion, in fact the creation of the Merseians most dangerous agent, the telepathic non-Merseian Aycharaych, who becomes Flandry's continual opponent.

In *We Claim These Stars!*, Aycharaych masterminds the takeover of a human planet by a wolflike race as a means of drawing Imperial strength away from the Merseian frontier. Flandry foils the plan by revealing to the wolf-creatures how they are being manipulated. In *A Knight of Ghosts and Shadows*, Aycharaych plots to drive a human world into revolt to distract the Empire with a civil war. At the end of this novel, Aycharaychs home world is destroyed, and Flandry once again loses the woman he truly loves.

In *A Stone in Heaven*, a further prospective revolt is combined with the presentation of an alien race facing a new Ice Age on its home planet, together with another love affair for Flandry. This one is happier in its ending. In *The Game of Empire*, a daughter of Flandry, assisted by a Tigery and a Wodenite (a race described in the Polesotechnic League series), foil a Merseian attempt to put a "sleeper" or secret Merseian sympathizer on the Imperial throne. In this work, Flandry, now old and distinguished, figures only marginally.

ANALYSIS

The major inspiration for Flandry appears to be the well-known fictional figure of James Bond. Like Bond, Flandry is amusing, seductive, cynical but dedicated, and operating on behalf of government while in defiance of legal or bureaucratic restraints. The major intellectual basis for the Flandry scenario is the belief, found in the work of other science-fiction writers including Isaac Asimov and Frank Herbert, in the structures of "cyclic history." According to this theory, natural laws of human development will cause historical patterns to repeat themselves regardless of technological change or human wishes. The Terran Empire of the fourth millennium accordingly is presented as a close analogue of the late Roman Empire of the first, held together only by loyalty to an emperor and facing inevitable defeat from its own inner "decadence." Flandry's role is, first, to postpone the defeat until after his own lifetime and, second, to give successor states a chance to root themselves too strongly to be exterminated by Merseia.

The question Anderson addresses, writing during a period that included the start and end of the Vietnam War, is whether moral ends (the saving of life, the maintenance of civilization) justify immoral means (the preservation of corrupt rulers, the repression of political dissent). On the whole, the answer of the Flandry series is that they do. Nevertheless, Anderson shows awareness of the dangers of such a belief, with his apparently immoral hero undergoing strains of conscience to do what he must and paying a high personal price for it in the repeated loss of the women he loves, sacrificed to his duty, and of his own son in *A Knight of Ghosts and Shadows*.

Further ironies include Flandry's continuing struggles against high-minded officials of his own Empire, who reject his ruthless tactics but do so without realizing the nature of the Merseian threat, which they prefer to minimize. Another irony is the fact that the Merseian Roidhunate itself is a creation of well-meaning liberalism on Earth, in that the Merseians would have been wiped out as a species by a supernova in the neighborhood of their home planet if not for technological help and protection from Earth back in the times of the Polesotechnic League six centuries before. In these two themes, Anderson dramatizes both the self-doubt and the self-sacrifice of his own times, during which—in some views—the United States handicapped itself into defeat in Vietnam and also assisted its own most dangerous economic competitor, Japan, through generous treatment.

Anderson's most unusual and attractive quality may be his ability to imagine alien creatures and alien cultures. These can be used comically and wittily, as in the invention of Chives, a tailed green alien creature who acts as personal servant to Flandry in the fashion of P. G. Wodehouse's Jeeves. Alien creatures also are portrayed with a kind of tragic sympathy, as with Flandry's opponent Aycharaych, the last survivor of a dead species, and the wolflike Ardazirho of *We Claim These Stars!* Both are at first merely horrific, but in the

Flow My Tears, the Policeman Said

Popular television personality Jason Taverner, summoned by a former protégée, is attacked by a Callisto cuddle sponge and transported into an alternate world in which he is not known and does not officially exist

Author: Philip K. Dick (1928–1982)
Genre: Science fiction—inner space
Type of work: Novel
Time of work: 1988
Locale: Los Angeles, California
First published: 1974

The Story

The plot of *Flow My Tears, the Policeman Said* is an interesting variation of Philip K. Dick's characteristic multifocused plot style, which consists of many characters whose lives slowly become intertwined. In this novel, Dick focuses on only two characters, but they are highly original, and their personal lives mirror each others, in ways that often are quite subtle.

The novel begins by introducing world-famous television personality Jason Taverner. The self-centered, egotistical Taverner answers an earnest summons from a former protégée of his, Marilyn Mason. He unknowingly walks into a trap arranged by her and is set upon by a Callisto cuddle sponge, a gelatinous creature that plunges its many feeding tubes deep into Taverner's body. He loses consciousness, only to awake in a seedy hotel in a poverty-ridden part of town.

Taverner quickly discovers that he is unknown in the world in which he has awakened. Because he has no identification papers, he does not exist officially in this world. Moreover, the world into which Taverner has been thrown is a police state, ruled by the bureaucratic police chief, Felix Buckman, the other major protagonist in the novel. Buckman seems to be the sort of bureaucrat one could easily detest; it is a testament to Dick's skill that he is capable of eliciting the readers deepest sympathies.

It is revealed that Buckman lives in an incestuous relationship with his sister Alys and has fathered a child, named Barney, by her. Alys Buckman is one of Dick's many memorable characters. She is a tall, charismatic, drug-addicted, leather-clad bisexual who revels in breaking all social and moral rules, in contrast to her brother-husband Felix, bound to uphold the laws of his society.

It is Alys who emerges as a key figure in resolving the plot. She meets Taverner and invites him to her and Felixs home, where she inexplicably wishes to play the perfect hostess to him. After a lengthy absence, during which she has left Taverner alone in order to procure a drug for him, Taverner discovers that Alys is in fact dead. Taverner is charged by the authorities with her murder, but it is discovered that Alys was experimenting with a highly controlled, reality-shifting drug known only as KR-3. The drug affected not only her perceptual system but also the perceptual systems of all those individuals who existed within her own fantasy world. The drug had the effect of dragging others into her imagined world. Because Taverner was such a famous personality, he had become an integral part of her fantasy life. Also central to her life was her brother-husband Felix, the policeman alluded to in the novels title.

Analysis

Flow My Tears, the Policeman Said is one of Dick's major achievements in a large and impressive body of fiction. Dick finished a first draft of this unusual novel in 1970, but it was completed in a period that marked the beginning of one of the most disturbed periods of his troubled life. It remained unpublished until early in 1974. The novel was praised highly by both critics and peers, and it earned both Nebula and Hugo Award nominations as best science fiction of the year. It did not win either of these awards, losing both to

Ursula Le Guin's *The Dispossessed* (1974), but it won the 1975 John W. Campbell Memorial Award as best science-fiction novel of the year.

The dark, dystopian world depicted in the novel (certainly common in science fiction), combined with the rampant use of reality-shifting drugs by many of its inhabitants (characteristic of Dick's fiction), makes this novel similar to Dick's *The Three Stigmata of Palmer Eldritch* (1965). In this earlier novel, set in a future world in which drug use is commonplace, individuals who ingest a drug known as Chew-Z are transported into a world controlled by Palmer Eldritch, a sinister figure corresponding to the Gnostic demiurge, a lesser deity who has the ability to create worlds but who fails at the imitation. Alys Buckman is a similar figure in *Flow My Tears, the Policeman Said*, except that by ingesting KR-3, she alone has the power to draw individuals into her spurious fantasy world, even if others have taken no drugs.

The underlying similarity between the novels, that of individuals trapped within the irreal world of some mysterious agent or agency, is common in Dick's fiction. Dick first developed this dramatic device in *Eye in the Sky* (1957), attempting to use a plot device created by Fredric Brown in *What Mad Universe* (1949). In *Eye in the Sky*, however, Dick experimented with several, competing universes, rather than the one fantasy universe Brown had used. *Flow My Tears, the Policeman Said* finds Dick again using the plot device of several people trapped in the fantasy universe of one individual, but the philosophical and religious implications generated by such a plot remain entirely Dick's own.

—*Samuel J. Umland*

Flowers for Algernon

Experimental surgery enables Charlie Gordon, a retarded man, to attain an extremely high level of intelligence

Author: Daniel Keyes (1927–2014)
Genre: Science fiction—superbeing
Type of work: Novel
Time of work: The 1960's
Location: New York City
First published: 1966 (expanded version of a short story in *The Magazine of Fantasy and Science Fiction*, 1959)

The Story

Flowers for Algernon unfolds in a series of diary entries. In the first, dated "march 3," Charlie describes himself as a thirty-two-year-old man who works at a bakery and attends "Miss Kinnians class at the beekmin colledge center for retarted adults." Ensuing entries chronicle Charlie's progress as the first human subjected to an intelligence-boosting surgical procedure.

Before the operation, Charlie undergoes a series of tests that measure his intelligence. In one, he tries in vain to pencil through a maze faster than Algernon can run it. Algernon is a laboratory mouse that already has undergone the surgical procedure. After the surgery, sleep learning accelerates Charlie's mental development. By the end of the month, he outraces Algernon. In early April, he comprehends a grammar book overnight and shows signs of increased self-awareness, staying home from Donner's Bakery after realizing that he has long been victimized by coworker "friends" Joe Carp and Frank Reilly.

Counseling Charlie is Dr. Jay Strauss, a neurosurgeon and psychiatrist who, with Professor Harold Nemur, is responsible for the experiment. Together with lab assistant Burt Selden and teacher Alice Kinnian, they guide Charlie as he begins a long-delayed maturation process. Two months after the operation, Charlie is able to converse intelligently with college students but is stymied in acting on his amorous feelings for Alice. Although she is attracted to him, both fear that they may jeopardize his development.

As Charlie accumulates knowledge at a breathtaking rate, his illusions are shattered at a similar clip. He sees the fallibility of his mentors and realizes that their interest in him stems largely from selfishness. Charlie rebels at a scientific conference in Chicago, where he and Algernon are put on display. Freeing the mouse from its cage, Charlie takes his counterpart back to New York and moves into an apartment near Times Square.

Independent after years of institutionalization, Charlie initiates a new phase of his education, entering into an affair with free-spirited Fay Lillman and visiting his father, Matt, who fails to recognize him. Charlie also applies his brainpower to studying Algernon's regressive tendencies. Suspecting that he also may regress, Charlie visits the Warren State Home and Training School, where his doctors and family had arranged to send him if the experiment failed.

In late August, Charlie concludes that the experiment's results are indeed temporary and potentially fatal. After Algernon dies on September 17, Charlie spares the mouse from laboratory incineration by burying its remains in his backyard. Mindful of his inevitable decline, Charlie visits his mother, Rose, and sister, Norma, both of whom he remembers as hostile.

He finds that Rose has entered senility and Norma feels remorse over her past unkindness toward him. Charlie consummates his relationship with Alice on October 11. Though heartened by their shared love, ten days later he tells her to leave in a fit of anger over his deterioration. Having already lost his multilingual abilities, he rapidly loses his typing prowess and command of English. Isolating himself from the Beekman staff, he returns to Donner's Bakery, where newly sympathetic coworkers welcome him.

In his last entry, dated "nov 21," Charlie writes of his decision to go to Warren. Bidding farewell to Alice and the others at Beekman, he asks that the reader "put some flowrs on Algernons grave in the bak yard."

ANALYSIS

After the short story "Flowers for Algernon" received a Hugo Award in 1960, the tale of Charlie Gordon was embraced by a wide mainstream audience. In the early 1960's, a television adaptation titled "The Two Worlds of Charlie Gordon" appeared on *The U.S. Steel Hour*, with Cliff Robertson playing Charlie. After the Nebula Award-winning novel appeared in 1966, a feature film adaptation, *Charly* (1968), also starred Robertson, who received an Academy Award for his portrayal. Widely anthologized and taught in schools throughout the United States, the story also was the basis for a 1980 Broadway musical.

At the heart of its appeal is its unsensational use of a speculative premise, that surgery can radically boost intelligence, as the basis of a moving allegory. Charlie is like many people who reach a peak only to foresee and then experience their inevitable decline. Although the novel is considerably longer than the short story (its extended time frame approximates the human gestation period), both use compression to intensify the drama of this experience.

Notwithstanding the fact that the novel has been criticized as inferior to the short story, its extended narrative enabled Daniel Keyes not only to exploit his story's commercial potential but also to explore a variety of story elements in greater depth. The cultural tendency to look on the retarded Charlie as a nonperson is one such element. Charlie's psyche also is delineated in greater detail.

Although *Flowers for Algernon* bears some resemblance to Mary Wollstonecraft Shelley's *Frankenstein* (1818)—the animus of Charlie and his doctors softly echoes that of the monster and Victor Frankenstein—significant links also can be made between the novel and other, nonspeculative works, including Anne Frank's *The Diary of a Young Girl* (1947; English translation, 1952), the entries of which record key years of growth in the life of a girl doomed by a Nazi culture that deems her subhuman. Charlie's experience also parallels that of actual human test subjects, such as those in the infamous Tuskegee syphilis study of the 1930's and the catatonic patients given L-dopa by Dr. Oliver Sacks in 1969. Although the influence of *Flowers for Algernon* can be seen in science-fiction works, including Thomas M. Disch's *Camp Concentration* (1968), its legacy may be most evident in Sacks's book *Awakenings* (1973) and its 1990 screen adaptation. Keyes himself continued to delve into unusual psychological states in science fiction and nonfiction genres.

—*David Marc Fischer*

THE FOREVER KING

King Arthur is reborn in modern times and finds the Holy Grail

Authors: Molly Cochran (1949–) and Warren Murphy (1933–2015)
Genre: Fantasy—medieval future
Type of work: Novel
Time of work: Primarily the early 1990s and medieval times
Locale: New York, England, the Middle East, and Hong Kong
First published: 1992

THE STORY

Arthur Blessing, a ten-year-old New Yorker, finds a magical cup once possessed by Christ, at the Last Supper, and by the evil Arab Saladin. The cups history is told by the centuries-old Saladin, who used the cup, often referred to as the Holy Grail, as a means of gaining eternal life. Saladin had lost this vessel three times. Saladin retrieved the cup the first time when he was told the story of Christ drinking from it at the Last Supper. The second loss occurred in the Middle Ages, when the cup fell into the possession of the wizard Merlin, who wanted to give it to his beloved King Arthur. Saladin loses the vessel the third time following the rebirth of King Arthur as Arthur Blessing. Arthur finds the cup after it rolls into sight. Although the cup can only do good, healing the sick and wounded, Arthur twice refuses to keep it, because it tempts men to kill for it.

Once Arthur possesses the cup, his troubles begin. Saladin and his followers attempt to retrieve it by breaking into the apartment where Arthur lives. Arthur is in another apartment, showing his new find to Mr. Goldberg, who is really Merlin in disguise.

Merlin also appears to former FBI agent Hal Woczniak, who actually is a reincarnation of Sir Galahad, a Knight of the Round Table. Hal is plagued by guilt and nightmares because he could not save a red-haired boy from a maniac. As a consequence of this guilt, Hal has become an unemployed alcoholic. Merlin, masquerading as Mr. Taliesin, gives Hal a ticket to a television game show. Hal is picked out of the audience and is asked five difficult questions on medieval history. To even his own surprise, he knows the answers and wins an all-expense-paid trip to London. In the meantime, Arthur goes to London to see property he unexpectedly inherited. The property turns out to be the site of Camelot.

In London, Hal meets Mr. Taliesin, who invites Hal out to the Camelot site. Coincidentally, Arthur is seated in front of Hal and Mr. Taliesin on the bus. Eventually Hal and Arthur go to the castle, where Saladin kidnaps Arthur. At the last minute, Arthur throws the cup to Merlin. Saladin tries to cut Merlin in half, but Merlin vanishes into the spirit world. When Saladin rides off with a struggling Arthur, Hal is left alone. A ghostlike castle appears, where Hal sees Merlin and the Knights of the Round Table. He is given the mission of saving Arthur.

Hal rescues Arthur from an estate not far from Camelot only to be hunted down by Saladin and his helpers at the Camelot site. Arthur finds a boulder concealing Excalibur, pulls out the sword, and calls for his army. Instead of a ghostly brigade, the army is real: Everyone is magically transported back to medieval Camelot. Arthur spares Saladin's life, but Saladin challenges Hal to a swordfight. Lancelot, the legendary father of Sir Galahad, gives Hal his sword, but it is too big and heavy for him. Hal drops the sword but proves victorious when Arthur tosses Excalibur to him. Arthur then rejects a life in Camelot in favor of living out his childhood as a boy in the real world, where he is destined to rule in the next millennium.

ANALYSIS

To a certain extent, this novel follows the formula of the classic romance: It is an adventure story in which good triumphs over evil. It features several reincarnations, including those of Arthur, Merlin, and Hal. Another characteristic of a romance in the classic tradition is the element of the magical. This novel has many such elements, including the cup, immortality, the sword Excalibur, wizards, time travel, and ghosts. A romantic hero usually is a member of the nobility; in this case Arthur is a boy destined to be king again.

The story also relies heavily on coincidence for key events. Arthur stumbles upon the cup, he resembles the kidnapped red-headed boy about whom Hal has nightmares, and Saladin's helpers happen to see a picture of him in the newspaper with the magical cup on a shelf behind him.

The Forever King does have unique and original aspects. Authors Molly Cochran and Warren Murphy, a husband-and-wife team, added the twist of double identities. The ten-year-old Arthur is an American child as well as the reincarnation of King Arthur, Hal is a former FBI agent and also Sir Galahad, and Merlin is both Mr. Taliesin and Mr. Goldberg.

The story operates in several time periods, the two major ones being the early 1990's and the medieval time of King Arthur. Saladin's story takes the reader through several thousand years of history, from pre-Egyptian times to the present. Time travel adds a new twist to the Arthurian legend.

Murphy, who is also one of the creators of the Destroyer series, has been known to mix fiction with theology. In the Destroyer series, his characters Remo Williams and Chiun have superpowers obtained from Sinanju, and Remo is often possessed by the god Kali. *The Forever King* toys with Christian themes, as Christ used the cup at the Last Supper. According to Cochran and Murphy, the cup was magical before Christ used it. Arthur and Christ are the only two possessors of the cup who are able to give it up; this may mean that Arthur is a symbolic savior.

Although Arthur, Merlin, and Hal are the protagonists, they are not developed as characters. Saladin tells much of the novel from his point of view, and he is the best-developed character. He is the catalyst who sets the events in motion, but he remains morally unchanged by them. Hal is the dynamic character, changing from an alcoholic misfit to a responsible hero.

—*Mary Bagley*

THE FOREVER WAR

William Mandella is drafted, trained as a spaceborne infantryman, and sent into combat against the alien Taurans

Author: Joe Haldeman (1943–)
Genre: Science fiction—future war
Type of work: Novel
Time of work: 1997–3143
Location: Earth and various planets
First published: *Forever War* (1974), *Forever Free* (1999)

THE STORY
The story concerns the experiences of William Mandella during a protracted interstellar war between humanity and an alien race known as the Taurans. The novel begins in 1997 (a future date at the time the novel was written), when the war already has been escalating for some years. Mandella has been drafted into the United Nations Exploratory Force (UNEF) under the terms of a conscription act intended to select the physical and intellectual elite of Earth to defend humanity against the Tauran menace. Among the UNEF's more unusual policies are toleration of drug use and compulsory sexual promiscuity, enforced through rotating rosters of bunkmates.

Mandella's first combat mission is an attack on a Tauran base located on a planet in a system near a collapsing superdense star. This mission includes capturing a prisoner. On its march to the target, the strike force encounters a group of alien creatures. When Sergeant Cortez gives the order to fire, the soldiers slaughter what turn out to be members of the sentient indigenous population, creating tremendous guilt in Mandella, Marygay Potter, and other soldiers. Cortez triggers a post-hypnotic suggestion to the soldiers to kill indiscriminately when the time for the actual attack arrives. The result of the first campaign is at best ambiguous, because the soldiers fail to capture a Tauran and a number of soldiers go insane after realizing what they have done to an almost helpless enemy. Because of the time-dilating effects of travel at near the speed of light, when Mandella and Potter return to Earth after their first combat tour, they discover that twenty-six years have passed on Earth while they have experienced only two years in their own frame of reference. The two have fallen in love despite the UNEF's attempts to regulate personal lives, and they want to leave the UNEF at the end of their enlistments and resume their lives on Earth. They are shocked by the social and economic changes on Earth. The United Nations has become a planetary government dedicated to reorganizing society to support the war effort. Unable to adjust to the radical changes at home, Mandella and Potter decide that their best choice is to re-enlist in the UNEF.

More than three hundred years elapse while Mandella and Potter are on their next combat tour. When both are wounded, they are sent to convalesce on the planet Heaven. The pattern of social changes that Mandella and Potter found so disturbing on Earth has continued. Humanity is now almost completely homosexual, and people are conditioned from birth to support the policies and goals of the UNEF. Recovered from their wounds, Mandella and Potter are assigned to different strike forces. They realize that because of the effects of relativity, centuries of subjective time will separate them after their next combat tours, should they survive.

Assigned to command his own strike force, Mandella finds himself leading soldiers who are almost as alien to him as the Taurans. The men and women under his command are a group of eugenically controlled and scientifically reared homosexuals, bred in vitro, who fatalistically accept that they live and die to serve the UNEF. Mandella's assignment is to secure a portal planet orbiting a collapsar (a kind of neutron star) that could be pivotal in the Tauran war strategy. The strike force defeats the Taurans in a Pyrrhic victory in which only twelve percent of Mandella's command survives.

Mandella and the other survivors return to Stargate and find that the war ended more than two centuries earlier. Under the UNEF's policies, humanity has evolved into a race of telepathic male and female clones of a single individual, Corporal Kahn, who is presumed to be the perfect prototype for humanity. Mandella is offered a choice of ways to integrate himself into the Kahn-clone world of the UNEF, but he rejects the idea.

Only when he studies a printout of his military record does he find a solution. Potter and other survivors of the war have settled the planet Middle Finger, where some individuals cheat time on a "relativistic shuttle" waiting for other returnees to join them. The UNEF tolerates the aberrant society, in which people breed in the conventional manner, as a eugenic control baseline for human diversity. The novel concludes with the press announcement of the natural birth of a son of the two oldest survivors of the Forever War.

Analysis

The Forever War, Joe Haldeman's first science-fiction novel, is a significant example of the future-war novel and military *Bildungsroman*. The novel should be read in the context of the Vietnam War, the author's own participation in that conflict, and its analogs in Robert A. Heinlein's Cold War–era novel *Starship Troopers* (1959) and Orson Scott Card's postdétente *Ender's Game* (1985). *The Forever War* won both the Hugo and Nebula Awards as best science-fiction novel.

The first section of Haldeman's novel is a science-fictional rendering of American involvement in Vietnam. The subsequent sections of the novel continue the parallels with Vietnam but also expand on the major theme of the novel, the importance of individuality and free will in the face of authoritarian government and social pressures toward conformity. The UNEF's drive toward conformity starts with screening the population for sociopathic traits. The trend continues with the eugenically controlled population that provides the soldiers for Mandella's strike force and the Kahn-clone "humanity" that appears at the conclusion of the novel. Government policies are geared toward producing a uniform and predictable population of workers and soldiers for the war effort. This theme is accompanied by a series of images of the increasing mechanization of human society, starting with Mandella's vision of his relationship with Marygay Potter reduced to copulating fighting suits and his dream of being an animated fighting suit with the UNEF at the controls. These images culminate with Mandella's realization that wounded soldiers have become "soft machines" to be repaired or replaced in the service of the UNEF.

The ending of the novel is problematic in that, from the UNEF's perspective, Mandella, Potter, and the other returnees on Middle Finger are maladjusted veterans unable to incorporate themselves into postwar society. From the perspective of Mandella and Potter, however, Haldeman has provided the happy ending impossible for many Vietnam War veterans.

—*Peter C. Hall*

THE FORGE OF GOD AND ANVIL OF STARS

After self-replicating, planet-eating machines destroy Earth, a few Earth survivors track down and destroy the civilization that sent the machines

Author: Greg Bear (1951–)
Genre: Science fiction—invasion story
Type of work: Novels
Time of work: 1996–1997 and 2005–2010
Locale: Earth and Leviathan, a distant planet system
First published: *The Forge of God* (1987) and *Anvil of Stars* (1992)

THE STORY

In *The Forge of God*, sensitive astrophysicist Arthur Gordon and his eight-year-old son, Marty, learn that Jupiter's sixth moon has disappeared. Meanwhile, introspective young geologist Edward Shaw discovers a spaceship in Death Valley, California, and finds a miter-snouted, three-eyed alien collapsed in the sand nearby. With the help of young Stella Morgan, Shaw contacts the U.S. Air Force. The Air Force secretly incarcerates the sick alien and everyone who has seen it. Shaw and Morgan begin to fall in love.

Trevor Hicks, a British science-fiction writer and devotee of the search for extraterrestrial life, sniffs out the secret, and the Air Force captures him as well. The president asks Gordon and his friend, Harry Feinman, to study the alien. The alien tells them that the spaceship in Death Valley is a self-replicating, planet-eating machine that destroyed his home planet before he stowed away on it to warn others. Gordon explains that the alien is describing a concept called Von Neumann machines (popularized by Fred Saberhagen in *Berserker*, 1967)" mindless viruslike machines that seek signs of life, eat any life-bearing planet, and use the material to produce copies of themselves that fly off in different directions to eat more life-bearing planets. An advanced civilization starts the process in order to eliminate potential competitors preemptively.

The alien dies, and an autopsy reveals that it is no more than a robot. Other countries report spaceships with robots who bear peaceful tidings. Confounded, the U.S. government destroys the Death Valley spaceship, but Gordon believes that the enemy is extremely cautious, clever, and cruel. He believes that all the known spaceships are strategic ploys sent to toy with, study, evaluate, and confuse humans while the real planet-eating machines land elsewhere.

World cultures react differently as news of impending doom leaks out. Overwhelmed, the president slips into a paralyzed religious resignation. Feinman dies of cancer. Edward Shaw and Stella Morgan cannot crystallize their love and go separate ways. Strings of matter and antimatter zoom in from space and burrow into the earth, circling the earth's core. When they meet, Earth will explode.

As everything seems darkest, robot spiders bite Gordon and Hicks, transferring information about a friendly group of civilizations—called Benefactors—who have been fighting the planet-eating machines. The Benefactors cannot save Earth, but they are building secret spaceships to save a few of Earth's inhabitants. The planet-eaters discover one Benefactor spaceship and explode it, killing Hicks. Gordon and his son Marty board another Benefactor spaceship. Edward Shaw and Stella Morgan try one more time to crystallize their love but fail again. Shaw goes to Yosemite National Park alone. Atop solid rock, he watches, thinks, and dies as the earth bursts at its seams. In space, the Benefactors instruct Arthur and Marty Gordon to watch Earth explode so that they will be ready to join the Benefactors in revenge.

Eight years later, in *Anvil of Stars*, Marty serves as Pan (leader) to eighty-five other teenagers, called Lost Boys and Wendys, on the spaceship *Dawn Treader*, a Benefactor warship composed largely of fake matter. Assisted by robot Moms, the Children travel five years at near the speed of light to search for the enemy civilization. On the way, Marty falls in love with crewmate Theresa.

Marty finds himself leading an extremely diverse group, many of them highly individualistic and anti-authoritarian. Marty finds a suspect solar system, called Wormwood. Despite some doubts about Wormwood's possible innocence that torture his conscience, Marty orders a strike against it. Perhaps because of his ethical preoccupations, Marty fails to see that Wormwood is only a clever decoy and trap created by the enemy.

Marty's forces fall into the trap, and Theresa must sacrifice her life to save the crew. Distraught, Marty turns leadership over to Hans, a more ruthless individual. Hans locates another suspect solar system called Leviathan. Meanwhile, the crew teams up with aliens called Brothers. Each Brother is an aggregate life-form made of many cooperating, interwoven, snakelike cables. The Brothers, however, prove even more conscience-ridden than Marty, and as the likable inhabitants of Leviathan protest their innocence and plead for peace, Marty again tortures himself about the morality of the team's mission. He even visits Leviathan to befriend its inhabitants.

Hans ruthlessly uses the occasion of Marty's visit to launch a sneak attack that incites the final battle. Forgetting questions of morality, Marty fights to save his teammates. He discovers how to use thought to disintegrate Leviathan's defenses, thus allowing Hans to destroy the planets. Inside the system, the team discovers and destroys thousands of hatchling planet-eaters, positive proof of Leviathan's guilt. They also discover that the likable inhabitants of the planets were innocent: They were life-forms designed by the hidden enemy as unknowing decoys.

Analysis

Greg Bear's sensitivity to sophisticated literary technique places him among the new breed of literary-minded science-fiction writers, including Gregory Benford and David Brin, who have blurred the traditional barriers between high literature and science fiction. In addition, although he holds a degree in English, Bear's painstaking scientific accuracy in such diverse fields as theoretical physics, astrophysics, sociology, psychology, biology, and geology places him in the line of great scientist-writers such as Isaac Asimov and Arthur C. Clarke. Bear shares with Clarke, and with Clarke's predecessor Olaf Stapledon, a vision of human potential that can transcend apocalypse to survive in a previously unimaginable form, as in Clarke's *Childhood's End* (1953) and as in Bear's own *Blood Music* (1985), winner of a 1984 Hugo Award and a 1983 Nebula Award in its novella form (1983). Bear's vision of human potential is both frightening and optimistic: optimistic because it is transcendental but frightening because the transcendentalism is materialistic rather than theological.

Theological transcendentalism posits an anthropomorphic God guiding humans to some destined end. In contrast, Bear's futures grow out of an interplay of three elements: the material universe, chance, and human choice. The title *The Forge of God* ostensibly suggests that God is testing, purifying, and shaping humankind through the destruction of Earth. Many characters in the novel choose to believe this, for it provides the comfort of a beneficent intelligence behind the scary changes. The title also has an ironic deeper meaning, for in reality the novel tests God in the forge of the universe as it really is and finds God lacking. That is, the novel challenges and burns away naïve anthropomorphisms that humans wishfully project onto the universe, anthropomorphisms epitomized in traditional concepts of God.

Bear's novels nevertheless offer hope, for once humans have had their naïveté about the universe burned out of them in *The Forge of God*, they can be pounded into a courageous new shape on the Anvil of Stars, an anvil that symbolizes the hard but wondrous material universe as it really is. Once reshaped, humans can become mature team players with the rest of the adult universe. *Anvil of Stars* deals extensively with various types of teamwork: the self as a team of aspects (given an objective correlative in the aggregate Brother life-forms), humans as a species team, humans as a team with other life-forms throughout the universe, and human thought as a team with the physical principles of the universe. Bear does not downplay the pain and terror of the deathlike endings caused by change, growth, maturity, metamorphosis, and evolution. In *The Forge of God*, readers feel all the despair and lost hopes of the doomed Earth in the deaths of Feinman, Hicks, and especially Shaw. Bear even uses Shaw's failed romance with Stella Morgan to accent the heartbreaking feelings of incompleteness and lost possibility that endings can cause.

Nor does Bear downplay the struggle one must make to grow out of childhood and into a shape worthy of survival. In *Anvil of Stars*, Marty, and humanity, must leave childhood behind and become as hard, resilient, and flexible as fine steel under the blows of the universes cold hammer. Like the Brothers, who can unravel and reform themselves from moment to moment, Marty must learn how to refashion his identity continuously in order to adapt to a tough, complex universe, one that will not change or simplify itself for humankind.

—*Tim Wolf*

THE FORGOTTEN BEASTS OF ELD

The wizard Sybel, living alone on a mountain among a collection of fabulous animals, takes in a baby boy to rear, an action that ultimately involves her in a dynastic war

Author: Patricia A. McKillip (1948–)
Genre: Fantasy—high fantasy
Type of work: Novel
Time of work: The present
Location: The land of Eldwold
First published: 1974

THE STORY

In *The Forgotten Beasts of Eld*, the beautiful wizard Sybel has the power to call and tame a collection of wondrous animals. Her calm life is shattered when she takes in Tamlorn, a supposedly orphaned boy who is at the center of a long-standing war. As Tamlorn grows up and becomes aware of his heritage, Sybel is forced to become involved in the outside world. When confronted with conflicting needs of love and revenge, Sybel must struggle to overcome her betrayal of both herself and those she loves most.

Sybel, the daughter of wizards, lives contentedly alone atop her mountain until Coren, a warrior of the House of Sirle, brings to her a baby boy. Coren tells Sybel that the baby's dead mother was Sybel's aunt and the queen of Eldwold, and that his father, Coren's brother, was slain in the recent battle in which Sirle was soundly defeated. Now little Tamlorn is endangered by the war between Sirle and Eldwold. Coren begs Sybel to care for Tamlorn, and she reluctantly agrees. She is assisted by Maelga, an old witch living nearby.

As Tam grows up among Sybel's fantastic menagerie, Sybel comes to love him dearly. She knows that Tam actually is the son of Drede, the king of Eldwold and sworn enemy of the House of Sirle. Rok, the lord of Sirle and Coren's eldest brother, desperately wishes to overthrow Drede. He sends Coren back to Sybel to try to persuade her to use both Tamlorn and her considerable wizardly powers to defeat Drede. Coren, who has fallen in love with Sybel, is unable to coax her into fighting for Sirle. Tam has also discovered his parentage and wishes to live with his real father. Drede, pleased to have his son back but fearing that Sybel will use her powers against him, hires a wizard to control Sybel. She is able to defeat the wizard with the help of one of her magical beasts, and Coren takes her to Sirle as his wife.

Sybel harbors hatred for Drede and desires revenge as much as the Sirle brothers. She conspires with Rok to use her powers and her animals—including a dragon, a lion, and a riddle-spouting boar—to destroy Drede. Sybel thus betrays the trust of both Coren and Tam, who believed she had given up her need for revenge.

Maelga and Cyrin the boar reawaken twinges of guilt in Sybel over what she has done. Then, on the eve of battle, Sybel herself is almost destroyed by one of her more fearsome and not easily controlled beasts. Realizing that the price of revenge is too high, Sybel releases all her animals from her control and returns to her isolated mountain to let fate decide the battle's outcome. Even without Sybel to command them, her animals destroy Drede, rescue Tamlorn, and lure the soldiers away from the battlefield to stop the war before it starts. By facing and overcoming the ugliness within her own heart, Sybel is able to save her relationships with Coren and Tam and achieve her heart's desire.

ANALYSIS

The Forgotten Beasts of Eld was published before Patricia McKillip's *The Riddle-Master of Hed* (1976), the first book of her *Riddle of Stars* trilogy (1979 as trilogy; also known as the Riddle-Master trilogy), for which she is probably best known. Like the trilogy, *The Forgotten Beasts of Eld* overflows with elements typical in fantasy: fabulous, mythical animals; powerfully magical wizards; and kings, princes, and wars. To this familiar fantasy background, McKillip adds a host of distinctive and all-toohuman characters. The rich, poetic language does not overwhelm this story of love, betrayed trust, revenge, and, above all, taking responsibility for one's actions. All the characters, including the beasts, display conflicting loyalties and motives as they struggle to attain their innermost desires while trying not to hurt those they love.

McKillip's fantasy novels are noted for their excellent characterizations. *The Forgotten Beasts of Eld* allows for exploration of the souls of all the characters. Even the emotional motivations of the villains are somewhat understandable. Drede is driven by fear to try to entrap Sybel, but his devotion to his son is evident. Coren remains hopelessly in love with Sybel even when she tampers with his thoughts and manipulates him as if he were another of her captured animals. Sybel herself seems remote and aloof, far removed from the turmoils of the feuds outside her mountain oasis, but she is also drawn into a fray of tangled emotions when she allows herself to feel love, first for Tam, then Maelga, then Coren. She must learn to deal with both the benefits and strengths, as well as the vulnerabilities and risks, of forming relationships. Readers can identify easily with these believably inconsistent and often confused characters, who love and hate and love again.

Reviewers have also commended McKillip's compelling style of storytelling in this novel. McKillip herself has stated that she was a storyteller for her younger siblings before she ever began writing. *The Forgotten Beasts of Eld* draws the reader into an increasingly complicated web of political and emotional intrigue. Tantalizing hints are dropped that each of Sybel's animals could tell a story of its own, giving the novel a rich backdrop and a mystical ambience that is maintained throughout. Although McKillip did not write *The Forgotten Beasts of Eld* specifically for children, it is usually classified by booksellers and librarians as a young adult novel. Reviews were favorable, although some reviewers objected to the somewhat flowery language and imagery. The novel received the World Fantasy Award in 1975.

—*Quinn Weller*

THE FOUNDATION SERIES

Mathematician Hari Seldon, creator of the science of psychohistory, creates a grand scheme for arresting the decline of the Galactic Empire and controlling its future

Author: Isaac Asimov (1920-1992)
Genre: Science fiction—future history
Type of work: Novels
Time of work: 12,020-14,000
Location: The Galactic Empire
First published: *The Foundation Trilogy* (1963; as trilogy); previously published as *Foundation* (1951; serial form, *Astounding Science-Fiction*, 1942-1944), *Foundation and Empire* (1952; serial form, *Astounding Science-Fiction*, 1945), and *Second Foundation* (1953; serial form, *Astounding Science-Fiction*, 1948-1950); additions to the series include *Foundation's Edge* (1982), *Foundation and Earth* (1986), *Prelude to Foundation* (1988), and *Forward the Foundation* (1993)

THE STORY

The vast Galactic Empire, composed of 25 million worlds and quadrillions of human beings, is in decline. Mathematician Hari Seldon, a provincial scholar from the distant planet Helicon, presents his learned hypothesis about the mathematical possibilities of what he calls "psychohistory" to a conference held on Trantor, the imperial capital. Seldon understands that his hypothesis is incomplete and untested. Nevertheless, it offers the prospect of mathematically predicting the empire's future and, with this knowledge, influencing events so as to lay the groundwork for a Second Galactic Empire.

Seldon's psychohistorical predictions do not apply to specific events or personalities; rather, they deal with the aggregate of the empire's myriad worlds and peoples in sweeping ways. Psychohistory is a science of masses, of mobs in their billions. Intelligent people suspect that the empire is declining, and Seldon himself believes that the empire will soon confront thirty thousand millennia of wars and barbarism.

The potential of psychohistory to shorten this period draws the attention of Emperor Cleon I; his most influential aide, Demerzel; and female historian Dors Venabili. *Prelude to Foundation* chronicles Seldon's trials and adventures, as the emperor, Demerzel (a robot in various human guises), and Dors (another humanized robot) alternately menace Seldon and encourage him to refine his thesis and to make it practical enough to allow prediction, manipulation, and control of social and economic change that will lead to a new empire.

The fall of the empire is inevitable, but to abbreviate the ensuing period of chaos to less than a millennium, Seldon establishes two Foundations at opposite ends of the Galaxy. The First Foundation, on Terminus, far from Trantor, is begun as a settlement of physical scientists who labor to compile the *Encyclopedia Galactica*, a compendium of universal knowledge. During the empire's long decline, the First Foundation becomes a center of advanced science. The Second Foundation, a mysterious body devoted to the expansion of the powers of the intellect, is established simultaneously at a secret location.

Forward the Foundation recounts the events of Seldon's later life, a time focused on elaboration of his predictive plan, on his preparations to reappear in a special vault as a holograph during future crises in order to dispense additional counsel, and on his symbolically significant death. Soon afterward, as recorded in *Foundation*, the Empire shatters into independent kingdoms that quickly threaten the First Foundation's existence.

Because of the political skill of Salvor Hardin, the First Foundation's mayor, the Foundation maintains its independence. Because the First Foundation is the sole remaining possessor of atomic power and a repository of superior science, it also gains ascendancy over much of the galaxy.

As centuries pass, the First Foundation evolves a trading economy based on the sale of compact atomic devices. Its traders penetrate the periphery of the galaxy, defeat the Foundation's rivals, and prepare for clashes with the dying empire's remaining forces—a story told in *Foundation and Empire*.

Because Seldon's psychohistory cannot account for the actions of individuals, the First Foundation is ruined eventually by the mind-shaping powers of the Mule, a mutant. Thus begins the search by the Mule, as well as by the survivors of the First Foundation, for the secret location of the Second Foundation, whose leaders are recognized as "mentalists," masters of mind control. A remarkable woman, Batya Darell, defeats the Mule, leaving the First Foundation technologically ascendant but eager to discover the location of the Second Foundation.

In *Foundation's Edge*, which is set 498 years after the founding of the First Foundation, this search is pressed by a young Terminus councilman, Golan Trevize, who is joined by historian Janov Pelorat. Traversing the galaxy searching for the Second Foundation as well as for Earth and the origins of life, Trevize and Pelorat arrive at Gaia, a peaceful, ecologically harmonious world that has evolved as a collective mind. Because of the "objective rightness" of Trevize's intuitions, during a critical confrontation between representatives of the First and Second Foundations, the Gaians allow Trevize to decide the future of the galaxy; that is, to determine whether creation of the Second Galactic Empire should be directed by either of the Foundations. Trevize chooses a third way, the Gaian way: creation of a harmonious, collectivist Gaian-style "Galaxia" instead of an Empire. Believing that he has made the right choice, Trevize nevertheless harbors doubts. Gaia is a collective mind, and Trevize is an individualist; he wants hard facts to undergird his intuitive decision.

Trevize, Pelorat, and Pelorat's Gaian love, Bliss, continue the search for Earth and the origins of life in *Foundation and Earth*. The trio's quest ensnarls them in adventures on three variously hostile planets. They backtrack their way through evidence of galactic colonization only to discover that Earth is radioactive and lifeless. They find the Moon, however, inhabited underground by the twenty-thousand-year-old robot Daneel, who gives them information about the origins and galactic spread of humans and their robots. Meanwhile, the searchers acquire a precocious hermaphrodite child, Fallom, whose evolved transducer lobes give it awesome and sinister powers.

ANALYSIS

At his death in 1992, Isaac Asimov had published at least 475 books, ranking him as one of the world's most prolific authors. *The Foundation Trilogy* rapidly earned status as a science-fiction classic, while two other novels in the series became long-term best-sellers. A learned student of science—he held a Ph.D. in chemistry and was a professor of biochemistry—and a devotee of history, Asimov virtually founded the sciencefiction subgenre of future history. He earned many major awards, including numerous Hugos and Nebulas, and was named a Nebula Grand Master in 1987. Throughout the Foundation series novels, Asimov's scientifically or technically trained leading characters are aided or guided by historians. In the Foundation series as elsewhere in his writings, Asimov acknowledges drawing heavily on themes embodied in widely influential historical and metahistorical studies, notably Edward Gibbon's *The History of the Decline and Fall of the Roman Empire* (1776–1788), Arnold J. Toynbee's *A Study of History* (1934–1954), and Oswald Spengler's *The Decline of the West* (1926–1928). Although differing in their subject matter and their perspectives, each of these works is concerned, as was Asimov, both with identifying recurrent patterns in history and with tackling the venerable historical question of whether such patterns are determined primarily by profound social forces or instead by individual actions or chance. The mutant genius the Mule, for example, temporarily upsets the Seldon Plan.

The unfolding of Seldon's psychohistorical plan, around which the plotting of the entire Foundation series occurs, suggests that Asimov at one time believed in the existence of mathematically quantifiable, predetermined collective forces that drive historical processes. By 1955, however, he held an opposing view, which he expounded in *The End of Eternity*. In fact, over time, Asimov led his readers to wonder if he had resolved these great questions himself. In the Foundation series, after all, it is Seldon, an individualist, rather than a collective mind who develops the "law" of psychohistory.

A few writers of future histories, such as Mark Twain and H. G. Wells, anticipated Asimov's grappling with the causes of historical development. Others such as Frederik Pohl, Cyril Kornbluth, and Frank Herbert began publishing their writings as Asimov's Foundation series evolved, and others have followed. For intellectual breadth, imaginative interplay of science and history, and sheer engaging volume of work, however, the Foundation series remains unsurpassed.

—Mary E. Virginia

FOUNTAINS OF PARADISE

Vannevar Morgan struggles to realize his dream of building an Orbital Tower, or Space Elevator, to carry payloads above and beyond Earths gravitational field

Author: Arthur C. Clarke (1917–2008)
Genre: Science fiction—technocratic
Type of work: Novel
Time of work: Primarily the late twenty-second century, with flashbacks and flashforwards
Locale: Southwest Asia and various Earth orbits
First published: 1979

THE STORY

Arthur C. Clarke posits in this novel that humankind will continue to explore the solar system and even establish a permanent presence on the Moon, Mercury, and Mars. The shuttles and rockets used to gain access to these new frontiers, however, will prove to be too expensive, inefficient, and destructive of the environment. A better way will have to be found to get people and material off the surface of Earth and into space.

Vannevar Morgan is the chief engineer (Land) of the Terran Construction Corporation. His primary claim to fame is building the Gibraltar Bridge, which spanned the fifteen kilometers across the Strait of Gibraltar in 2140. The ultimate challenge of his career becomes the creation of an elevator system linking Earth to space.

The first obstacle to be overcome is a community of Buddhist monks established at the top of Sri Kanda in the fictional southwest Asian land of Taprobane. Because of its height and equatorial location, this mountain is the ideal ground base for the Space Elevator. Unfortunately, the monks see the project as another Tower of Babel, demonstrating the futility of human pride. They refuse to budge.

A consortium of investors from Mars comes to the rescue. They invite Morgan to realize his dream on their planet, and he agrees. A demonstration of the basic principle involved is planned in order to attract additional funding. Forty thousand kilometers of hyperfilament thread are to be dropped from a satellite in geostationary Earth orbit. A freak storm keeps the test from being completely successful, but it also has a mystical effect on the community of monks. Their ancient prophecy is fulfilled when golden butterflies swarm the top of Sri Kanda. The monks drop their opposition to the Space Elevator and turn the mountain over to the Morgan team.

Work on the colossal project begins. Nature, the other major obstacle to success, mounts its inevitable challenges. In addition to storms in the atmosphere and the constant dangers of construction at high elevations, the upper reaches of the Tower have to contend with meteor showers and with gales of charged particles in the unpredictable ionospheric weather. These elements conspire to strand a small party of workers and researchers twenty-five thousand kilometers above the ground.

Morgan insists on taking the leading role in the rescue operation. He must ascend the incredible height of the unfinished Tower in a service vehicle called a spider and deliver vital supplies to the threatened group. He succeeds, but nature in the guise of time intervenes. Before Morgan can return safely to the surface, the stress takes its toll on him in his advanced age, and he dies of a heart attack.

The narrative flashes forward to the far future to provide assurances to the reader that the project eventually succeeds. A number of other Orbital Towers are built, and half a billion people ascend them to take up permanent residence in the Ring City that is constructed above and around the Earth.

ANALYSIS

The idea for an Orbital Tower, or Space Elevator, was first proposed by a Leningrad engineer named Yuri Artsutonov in 1960. It was independently reinvented in different places at least three more times in the next fifteen years. Perhaps the project will not get started within two hundred years, as envisioned in *The Fountains of Paradise*, but endorsement by Clarke guarantees that the concept will be taken seriously.

Clarke is the well-known author of such science-fiction classics as *Childhood's End* (1953) and *Rendezvous with Rama* (1973). He collaborated with film director Stanley Kubrick on *2001: A Space Odyssey* (1968). As a scientist, he is credited with nothing less than the invention of satellite communications, an idea he proposed in an article published in 1945.

The Fountains of Paradise effectively dramatizes the technological problems likely to be encountered in building a forty-thousand-kilometer bridge to the stars. Beyond this remarkable accomplishment, however, the novel develops at least two important literary themes. The protagonist, Morgan, is a study in the nature of heroism. He is a sympathetic version of Mary Shelley's *Dr. Frankenstein*; he takes little interest or pleasure in people except insofar as they may contribute to attaining his goal. Readers are told that Morgan has long since made the choice between work and life that is required at the highest levels of human achievement. Even Morgan's climactic rescue mission is motivated more by his concern for the project than by his concern for the endangered people. Even so, his trip in the spider up the ultimate strut of the unfinished tower seems to define paradise in this novel. Poetically interpreted, Morgan's life is a jet shot thrillingly into the air, only to splatter back lifeless to Earth.

The Fountains of Paradise is full of speculation about the existence and nature of God. Traditional religion has been swept away in this vision of the future. Superintelligent, but not omniscient, aliens have arrived in the solar system and have taken the place of the deity. By gaining easy access to space via the Orbital Tower, humanity will find something there to make all the effort worthwhile. For a nonbeliever, Clarke spends a significant amount of time investigating this ultimate question in his writing. *The Fountains of Paradise* may be the most interesting of his theological flirtations. It brings to mind William Blake's definition of God as nothing other than the intellectual fountain of humanity.

—Steven Lehman

FRANKENSTEIN

Victor Frankenstein discovers the secret of life and creates a monster whose despair and anger ruin the lives of Frankenstein and his family

Author: Mary Wollstonecraft Shelley (1797–1851)
Genre: Science fiction—cautionary
Type of work: Novel
Time of work: The late eighteenth century
Location: Europe and the great northern polar seas
First published: 1818

THE STORY

Frankenstein: Or, The Modern Prometheus is framed as a series of letters written by polar explorer Robert Walton to his sister, Margaret Saville, who is home in England. He relates to her his adventures, including a story told to him by a young man, Victor Frankenstein, whom his ship has rescued from the polar ice.

As a young university student at Ingolstadt, in Bavaria, Frankenstein is determined to find the secret of life. He studies constantly, ignoring his family back in Geneva, Switzerland. He steals body parts from charnel houses and medical laboratories, then uses the power of electricity to create a living being. He immediately knows he has erred: His creature is ghastly. It leaves Frankenstein's quarters but remains in his life.

Frankenstein next sees the creature back in Geneva, where he has returned following the death of his young brother William. Although a servant girl, Justine, is accused of causing William's death, Frankenstein sees the creature lurking near the place of the murder and knows he is the killer. Frankenstein's anguish is intensified when innocent Justine is executed for the murder.

In his agony, Frankenstein leaves home to wander in the mountains. The creature confronts him and tells him his own story.

After leaving Ingolstadt, the creature wanders throughout the countryside.

He discovers quickly that he is frightening and repugnant to humans and takes to traveling at night and hiding during the day. The creature learns to speak and to read during a long stay in a hovel attached to a poor farm family's hut. During his stay, he performs many kindnesses for the family and feels sympathy for their poverty. He befriends the old father, who is blind.

As soon as other family members return and see him, they flee. In anger, the creature sets their farm on fire.

He makes his way to Geneva, saving a small child from drowning along the way. Every time he tries to perform an act of kindness, however, he causes a reaction of horror. On the mountaintop, the creature begs Frankenstein to make him a mate so he need not be lonely. Then, he says, he will leave humankind alone and live with his mate in seclusion. If not, he says, he will be with Frankenstein on his wedding night.

Frankenstein promises to make him a mate but questions his wisdom. He travels to England with his friend William Clerval, then goes alone to an isolated spot in Scotland to carry out his promise. He cannot finish the job. He abandons it and prepares to return home. The creature, infuriated by Frankenstein's unwillingness to keep a promise, kills Clerval, then returns to Geneva to kill Frankenstein's bride, his adopted sister Elizabeth, on their wedding night.

The tragedy and the guilt are too much to bear. Frankenstein resolves to pursue the monster until one of them is dead. He travels by dogsled across the snowy expanses of Russia toward the North Pole. He is picked up by Robert Walton's ship during his pursuit and dies on the ship after telling Walton his story. The creature appears and tells Walton of his remorse for his deeds, then sets off into the cold to build his own funeral pyre.

ANALYSIS

Mary Shelley wrote *Frankenstein* as part of a friendly ghost-story writing competition with her husband, Percy Bysshe Shelley, and friend Lord Byron when she was eighteen years old. The novel has prompted many melodramatic takeoffs in film and much critical interest. It is one of the earliest works of science fiction, and the scientific techniques described in it are shadowy at best, yet they represent adequately the scientific knowledge of the time.

The book's subtitle links it to the Prometheus myth, popular in the Romantic era. Both Percy Shelley and Lord Byron wrote Promethean poems. Prometheus, a Titan, stole fire from the gods and gave it to humans, allowing them to thrive and create. Frankenstein's creature was brought to life through the "fire" of lightning. In both cases, the reader must wonder whether the powers given to humankind are blessings or curses. The novel questions what responsibility humankind has in the face of achievements that can have both good and bad results. Frankenstein's suffering clearly shows that he realizes too late that he miscalculated the destructive potential of his discovery.

The novel is filled with imagery of light and dark. The creature, brought to life through the power of lightning, is always in the shadows of darkness, and he commits dark deeds.

The Romantic writers with whom Shelley can be connected wrote in part as a revolt against the Enlightenment assumption that scientific advances and education represent the highest possibilities of humankind.

If scientific achievement is paramount to Frankenstein, it comes at the expense of humanity, including the lives of everyone whom Frankenstein loves. *Frankenstein* offers interesting views of the psyche of man in both Frankenstein and his creature, and of the social damage that can result when love is denied, as it was to the creature, or relegated to low status, as it was by Frankenstein. A psychological inquiry also suggests the idea of the creature being the double, or dark side, of Frankenstein.

One interesting stylistic device in the novel is the lack of a constant or reliable narrator: Robert Walton, Frankenstein, and the creature all tell their own stories. The reader thus is given different points of view from which to judge the story. Another point of interest is the consideration of gender: The novel has a female author, employs stereotyped female characters, and shows contrasts between the typically male and female motives of ambition and love.

—*Janine Rider*

FRANKENSTEIN UNBOUND

Joe Bodenland is caught in a "Timeslip" that takes him to nineteenth century Switzerland, where he meets Mary Shelley and the characters in her novel Frankenstein

Author: Brian W. Aldiss (1925–)
Genre: Science fiction—cautionary
Type of work: Novel
Time of work: 2020 and 1816
Locale: New Houston, Texas, and nineteenth century Geneva, Switzerland
First published: 1973

THE STORY

In the year 2020, worldwide racial war has broken out. Retired diplomat Joseph Bodenland writes to his wife, Mina, asking her to return and describing an odd ceremony performed by their grandchildren. The children buried a motor scooter, adorned the "grave" with flowers, and danced around it, asking for a "good Feast." Bodenland observes that "children live in myth." He refers to this enigmatic incident several times during the course of the novel.

Nuclear warfare in the stratosphere has damaged the infrastructure of space. When a resulting "Timeslip" takes his household to the richly sensuous world of nineteenth century Switzerland, Bodenland goes out to explore and is stranded when the ranch and the rest of its inhabitants return to 2020.

One of the first people Bodenland meets is Victor Frankenstein, who is agonizing over the murder of his six-year-old brother, William, by the monster he created. Subsequently, Bodenland attends the trial of William's nursemaid, Justine Mortiz, who is convicted of the murder. Bodenland realizes that he is witnessing events from Mary Shelley's novel *Frankenstein: Or, The Modern Prometheus* (1818).

Concluding that this world includes both fictional and historical persons, Bodenland seeks out Lord Byron and the Shelleys at Villa Diodati on Lake Geneva, hoping to find a copy of *Frankenstein*, which he remembers only vaguely. At Villa Diodati, he argues about the consequences of technological advancement with Percy Bysshe Shelley, who believes that science will liberate the individual and usher in an era of equality. Bodenland has an ecstatic sexual encounter with Mary Shelley. Her book is only partially written, however, and she cannot tell Bodenland how it will end.

Believing that taking control of the events in the novel will head off disaster in his own time, Bodenland becomes obsessed with destroying Frankenstein's monster. Bodenland pursues the scientist to his laboratory, where he is about to bring to life a female mate for his creation. Convinced that there is a direct causal link between Frankenstein's recklessly optimistic view of technological progress and the disastrous war in his own time, Bodenland kills Frankenstein when he brings the female to life and threatens to create yet another monster. Frankenstein's male and female creations engage in a touching mating dance, reminiscent of the children's feast at the beginning of the book.

The Timeslips of Bodenland's day have spread to the nineteenth century, and frigid lands have supplanted the lush Swiss countryside. Bodenland follows Frankenstein's male and female creations through the wasteland to a gigantic city, reminiscent of Hell in John Milton's *Paradise Lost* (1667). There, under a sky with two moons, he shoots both of the creations. The male monster promises that Bodenland will resurrect him, even as he seeks to bury him.

ANALYSIS

Brian W. Aldiss wrote this ambivalent, multifaceted novel as homage to and exegesis of Mary Shelley's *Frankenstein*, which Aldiss, in *Billion Year Spree: The True History of Science Fiction* (1973), cited as the first science-fiction novel ever written. When Aldiss' Percy Shelley voices his faith in individualism and the progressive betterment of humankind, he echoes Billion Year Spree on the Romantic climate of thought that made possible both science fiction and scientific advancement.

One of the most delightful aspects of *Frankenstein Unbound* is its anachronistic elegance of style and adoption of Mary Shelley's method of conveying her story through a series of documents. Bodenland's story unfolds through letters and cables, newspaper stories, and ultimately Bodenland's taped journal. The speculative, leisurely quality of all these communications is comically at odds with the bare-bones communication of the current age, to say nothing of being deliciously incongruous coming from a man who moves from one crisis to another.

In its simplest terms, *Frankenstein Unbound* is a cautionary tale about the destructive effects of placing intellectual development above spiritual development. Bodenland believes that the Frankenstein story is a mythic representation of what has gone wrong in his age. Trying to improve on nature, Frankenstein had applied scientific principles to the imperfect human anatomy, creating a life-form that would never need maintenance and would never run down. Bodenland deplores the supposition that ever-increasing production and industrialization will lead to increased happiness.

Bodenland becomes an increasingly unreliable narrator as his twenty-first century identity melts away. His articulate, passionately held convictions are increasingly at odds with his actions. Once a loving grandfather and politician who crusaded for racial equality, Bodenland allows an obsession with eradicating Frankenstein's creation to so dominate his life that he becomes a homicidal fiend, unhesitatingly using futuristic weapons to murder three helpless beings.

Furthermore, although Bodenland views the monster as the quintessence of technology run amok, the reader gets a different picture: The monster shows compassion by feeding Bodenland when he is destitute, quotes Milton, and dances with his new bride. In his final confrontation with Bodenland, the monster, dying, has the last word. In his obsession with destroying the two new life-forms before they breed, Bodenland reflects genocidal attitudes of the twenty-first century that have led to war.

Although Bodenland believes that Timeslips are responsible for his eroding sense of self, the novel demonstrates that time has always been nonlinear. Even when the Timeslips are not displacing Bodenland, time does not flow predictably forward. When he and Mary are enjoying ecstatic love, Bodenland observes that, for lovers, there is only the present. After he murders Frankenstein, Bodenland is stuck in that moment: The image of Frankenstein dying appears repeatedly before his eyes.

Bodenland's references to myth suggest how historical and fictional figures may coexist on the same plane. In Western consciousness, Byron and Shelley exist as mythic figures, as Frankenstein's monster does. There is a hint of the metafictional here. Bodenland is transported to a world remote from his own and finds that his sense of self is dissolving. His experience mimics what happens when one is immersed in a work of fiction. Only in fiction can one participate sensuously in the life of past ages and meet beings from different realities.

Frankenstein Unbound explicates Mary Shelley's novel as a work of prophecy, though it at once invites and resists hard and fast conclusions about the dangers of technological advancement. The novel, however, unequivocally celebrates tolerance, compassion, and the transforming power of literature and myth.

—*Wendy Bousfield*

FROM THE EARTH TO THE MOON

The Baltimore Gun Club constructs a giant cannon to shoot three explorers to the Moon

Author: Jules Verne (1828–1905)
Genre: Science fiction—cosmic voyage
Type of work: Novel
Time of work: The 1860s
Locale: Baltimore, Maryland, and Stone Hill, Florida
First published: *De la terre à la lune, trajet direct en 97 heures* (1865; English translation, 1869)

THE STORY

Written early in Jules Verne's career, *From the Earth to the Moon* depicts the scheme of Impey Barbicane, president of the Baltimore Gun Club, to hit the Moon with a cannon shell. Five years later, Verne published the eagerly awaited sequel" describing the spaceflight itself—together with the first novel under the new title *From the Earth to the Moon Direct in 97 hours 20 minutes and a Trip Around It.*

In *From the Earth to the Moon*, the club members, all of whom are wounded artillerymen of the Civil War, despair because peace has ended their activities. Barbicane's unprecedented idea of firing a projectile at the Moon restores their sense of purpose. The Observatory in Cambridge, Massachusetts, declares the project practical, and Barbicane outlines its features, including the dimensions of the cannon, the quantity of explosive, and the size and weight of the projectile. Following the clubs approval, he directs its members in drawing up plans for constructing "the Columbiad," attracting international attention. Captain Nicholl, an armor maker and rival, denounces the project on scientific grounds, although he fails to discourage Barbicane.

On the recommendation of the Observatory, the club must select a site near 28 degrees north latitude and 77 degrees west longitude, with a departure date of December 1 of the next year, in order to aim at the Moon when it is directly overhead and closest to Earth. After choosing Stone Hill, Florida, Barbicane solicits public support and receives donations from around the world. While his workers construct the Columbiad, requiring a hole in the ground 60 feet wide and 900 feet deep, he contracts with a company in Albany, New York, to manufacture an aluminum projectile in the shape of an artillery shell. He also turns funds over to the Observatory for the construction of a telescope at Longs Peak, Colorado, to keep track of it.

Meanwhile, Michel Ardan, a French adventurer, wires Barbicane to request that he replace the spherical design of the projectile with a cylinder topped by a cone and that Barbicane allow him to travel in it. Ardan enthusiastically defends the project and his role in it, gaining the support of Barbicane, the Baltimore Gun Club, and much of the world. Moreover, he prevents a duel between Barbicane and Nicholl by recommending that they both accompany him to the Moon in the redesigned projectile.

With the firing of the Columbiad, human beings leave Earth for interplanetary space. The Longs Peak Observatory determines that the projectile does not hit its target as intended; instead, the Moons gravity sweeps it into an elliptical orbit about 2,833 miles above the surface. The novel ends in doubt as to whether the Moons gravity will draw it to destruction or whether it will orbit forever.

Analysis

For most of his career, Verne strongly advocated the study of science, sharing the nineteenth century's optimism about technological progress. Early novels such as *A Journey to the Center of the Earth* (1872), *From the Earth to the Moon,* and *Twenty Thousand Leagues Under the Sea* (1873) illustrate his attitudes and artistic practices. He called these novels *voyages extraordinaires.* Some later ones fell into that category as well, but he demonstrated a growing distrust of science. Although critics have recognized the importance of the novels as science fiction, they have often claimed that Verne relied too heavily on conventions of the adventure or travel story.

Verne based his novels on possible or probable developments of present or near-future science, emphasizing realism through exact description. He set his characters in a particular time and place, put them in confrontation with physical nature, and dramatized their responses in the form of a journey or quest. With the exception of Captain Nemo in *Twenty Thousand Leagues Under the Sea*, his characters were recognizable types such as the scientist, the professor, or the adventurer. He subordinated them to the surroundings or circumstances that science had created for human action. The journeys of his characters to the Moon, to the center of the earth, to the bottom of the sea, or to the far reaches of the solar system conveyed the wonder and excitement of scientific discovery. Verne's characters embodied practicality, independence, tenacity, energy, and wonder, strengthening them against obstacles of nature. Working outside institutions, Barbicane and Ardan solved one problem after another to achieve spaceflight.

Verne's combination of plausibility and speculation convinced his readers that a trip to the Moon or on an advanced submarine was not a fantasy but a scientific possibility. His vision of things to come inspired writers and scientists, anticipating future reality in several ways.

Verne optimistically estimated the effects of scientific advances on society, though he included some satire. Barbicane and Ardans project proceeds steadily, initiating positive changes throughout the United States and having few limitations. Scientific and technological knowledge, apparently beyond politics, brought about a future culture. Verne thought that fundamental optimism and belief in progress were characteristic of the United States and that the qualities of freedom, practicality, imagination, and determination made it an ideal place for science.

Verne's novels generally reflected his faith in human nature, his hope in progress, and his awe at the grand horizons of science. More than any writer before him, he joined the physical sciences with the components of fiction, adding features of the travel story, the epic poem, the picaresque novel, the romance, and satire to help bring about a new kind of popular art eventually called science fiction. His commercial success accustomed many readers to speculations concerning the power of scientific or technological potential to shape the future. For these reasons, many people regard Verne as a founder of science fiction.

—*Timothy C. Miller*

FRONTERA

An expedition to Mars finds that the Frontera colony, thought to have failed, is thriving and in possession of a deadly weapon

Author: Lewis Shiner (1950–)
Genre: Science fiction—future war
First published: 1984
Type of work: Novel
Time of work: The near future
Locale: Primarily Mars

The Story

Earth's governments have collapsed, and corporations have taken the place of national governments. Morgan, the head of the Pulsystems corporation, has organized an expedition to the Frontera colony on Mars. As the novel opens, Kane, Takahashi, Reese, and Lena are about to enter Marss orbit.

Earth support of the Frontera colony had ended ten years previously, and communications from the colony to the National Aeronautics and Space Administration (NASA) had stopped. Kane believes that the rescue mission is too late to do any good; while in training for the mission, however, Reese had heard a tape of a recent transmission from the colony.

The mission lands on Deimos, one of Mars's moons, to obtain a landing craft. Reese finds a computer disk containing telemetry information about planetary movements and locations. The expedition boards a landing craft and, after landing on Mars, is met by a delegation from Frontera. The colonists, led by Curtis, do not welcome the expedition, which they fear is there only to exploit the colony.

Fifteen mutant children born on Mars live in a cave that served as the initial colony base. One of those children, who calls herself Verb, is the daughter of Curtis and his wife, Molly. Verbs mutation gave her extraordinary mental powers, and she has designed both a transporter capable of inexpensive long-distance shipping and a means of harnessing antimatter as an energy source. Molly has kept the children's discoveries from Curtis, whom she no longer trusts.

A medical examination reveals that Kane has a programmable biological implant that could control his behavior. Both the colonists and the other members of the expedition wonder how the implant has been programmed.

Reese gives the telemetry disk from Deimos to Verb, allowing her to locate targets for her transporter. In exchange, he asks to be transported to Barnards star.

A Russian ship arrives at the colony. Mayakenska, the leader of its crew, tells Curtis that the ship is on a scientific expedition and wishes to participate in a joint venture on the colony's discoveries, which rightly belong to all of humanity. Mayakenska threatens to destroy Frontera with her ships laser weapon if Fronteras discoveries are not shared.

Reese goes back to the cave and is transported. Curtis threatens to transport uncontrolled antimatter to the Kremlin, where it will explode. Mayakenska's superiors on Earth believe that the colony's weapon actually is at Frontera, so they instruct her to destroy Frontera before Curtis deadline. She tells Blok, a Russian colonist, to set off the alarm to abandon the colony after she leaves; she then tries to reach her ship to stop the attack. She is too late. She kills the other crew members, radios Moscow to say that the antimatter device was a hoax, then runs her ship onto Mars's surface, creating a crater that can be used to begin a new colony.

Takahashi tells Kane that he is loyal to Pulsystems rather than to Morgan and that a faction on Earth plans to replace Morgan. Kane's implant was programmed to have him assist Takahashi and prevent Morgan from gaining control of the colony's two discoveries.

The signal to abandon the Frontera base disrupts Curtis before he is able to transport the antimatter. He takes the control panel for the transporter, but Kane shoots him before he can reach a ship to leave the planet. Kane returns the panel to Molly.

Analysis

In his first novel, Lewis Shiner employs many devices common in science fiction. Mars colonies and rebellious colonists, for example, are nothing new. Shiner offers an interesting futuristic weapon, but the situations of its use are familiar. Although nothing in the book is unique, Shiner does a masterful job of combining the elements to create a suspenseful thriller.

Shiner's extrapolations are reasonable. Earths governments collapse under the weight of their own bureaucracy and indebtedness, and corporations are the natural successors. The space race continues to Mars but then is abandoned because of budget cutbacks. Private corporations try to salvage anything profitable from the space ventures.

Shiner succeeds in building suspense by shifting the point of view of narration among characters. Opening sections focus on the Pulsystems expedition, revealing bits about its four members and their varied agendas. Takahashi, for example, is shown as a "company man," so the other three expedition members assume that he is loyal to Morgan and is on the mission to make sure that Morgan's wishes are followed. Once the expedition lands on Mars, the point of view switches to the colonists, allowing Shiner to reveal the colony's discoveries without the expedition having to find out about them. Characters perspectives then are employed as needed to advance the plot but avoid revealing information that characters would not know. Through this narrative style, Shiner lets the reader and the characters simultaneously untangle the various loyalties, alliances, and secret agendas.

Shiner uses two intriguing psychological devices. He refers to Kane as following a Pattern, revealed in the authors note to be the Pattern of the Hero detailed in Joseph Campbell's *The Hero with a Thousand Faces* (1949), and Reese consults the I Ching. These devices are interesting as novelties but do little to advance the plot. They allow a deeper analysis of the novel for readers familiar with the two philosophies but are disappointing for others, who may expect further development or plot angles to which the devices are crucial. Numerous critics have identified the Pattern of the Hero in later works of science fiction.

Shiner's continued interest in the workings of the mind is evident in *Glimpses* (1993), winner of the World Fantasy Award. He is also the author of *Deserted Cities of the Heart* (1988), a work of Magical Realism set in Mexico, and *Slam* (1990), a mainstream novel about a paroled tax evader. *Deserted Cities of the Heart* employs imagined time travel, as does *Glimpses*.

—A. J. Sobczak

THE FURY

A boy and girl with extraordinary psychic powers are caught in a deadly battle between ruthless government agents and the boy's father, who desperately tries to save them

Author: John Farris (1936–)
Genre: Science fiction—extrasensory powers
Type of work: Novel
Time of work: 1972–1976
Locale: New York, New Jersey, Virginia, and Maryland
First published: 1976

THE STORY

The Fury combines horror and science fiction with the conventions of the suspense-thriller genre. Teenagers with psychic powers become pawns in power struggles carried out at the highest levels of government, meanwhile causing rampant destruction to those around them.

Fourteen-year-old Gillian Bellaver, daughter of an incredibly wealthy and socially prominent family, has a vision of a murdered man while ice skating, and she faints. A virulent case of flu causes her to be hospitalized, and high fever brings her latent psychic abilities to the surface. By touching someone, Gillian becomes able to see events in that persons past and future. An unpredictable and uncontrollable side effect is that people exposed to her psychic energy may bleed, as Gillian discovers when two women, one a surgical patient, the other a hypertension case, suddenly bleed to death while in her presence.

Gillian has a psychic twin, a boy named Robin Sandza, whose psychic powers are even more advanced than hers. Although they are not related, they are supernaturally connected, having "visited" each other in the astral plane during childhood, before Gillian lost touch with her paranormal gifts.

The Fury

Having been told that his father, Peter, is dead, Robin is essentially kidnapped by the secret agents of MORG, a shadowy and dangerous government agency. First taken to the Paragon Institute, a psychic testing facility, and then to MORGs heavily guarded Psi Faculty, Robin becomes a guinea pig in the governments research, potentially the next great "secret weapon" in the governments arsenal.

As Peter Sandza, a former MORG agent, searches for his son, he eludes assassins who are tracking him on orders from his former boss, Childermass, the head of MORG. With the help of Hester Moore, a Paragon Institute employee, Peter learns of Gillian. Hoping that she can help him locate Robin, he reaches her in the hospital, but an attack by MORG forces separates them and apparently ends Peter's life.

Peter survives, however, and seeks help from his friend Nick OHanna, a government agent operating in competition with MORG. OHanna and his associates secretly program Peter to kill Robin, whom they see as a threat. Robin, meanwhile, becomes involved with Dr. Gwyneth Charles, Childermass's niece, at Psi Faculty. As his powers grow, he becomes increasingly uncontrollable, sadistic, and paranoid. He also resumes his astral visits to Gillian, though now he is abusive instead of tender.

After Gillian accidentally causes her friend Larue to bleed to death, Gillian's distraught family places her in the Paragon Institute, where Childermass intends to fake her death and secretly transfer her to Psi Faculty. Hester helps Gillian escape, but Hester is later murdered by MORG agents, who are in turn killed by Peter. Peter and Gillian are kidnapped and brought to Psi Faculty, where a deranged Robin has destroyed Gwyneth and has retreated to the buildings roof. Peter initially saves Robin from falling, but when OHannas programming takes over, he drops Robin, who falls to his death. Childermass, enraged, shoots Peter to death. Gillian, convinced of Childermass's evil, finally learns to control her psychic power. She causes Childermass to bleed to death in his bathtub, effectively destroying MORG in the process.

ANALYSIS

The Fury is representative of the interest in psychic powers initiated by the publication of Stephen King's *Carrie* in 1974. The focus in *The Fury* on teenage protagonists who are simultaneously victimized and capable of horrific destruction echoes *Carrie*. *The Fury* also foreshadowed another King novel, *Firestarter* (1980), with its combination of psychically gifted young people and villainous government agents.

In *The Fury*, John Farris convincingly depicts a world that is cold, dangerous, and desolate, physically and spiritually. No one can be trusted, as Hester discovers when her neighbors and supposed friends, Meg and Miles Bundy, reveal themselves as murderous MORG agents who have kept her under surveillance. Peters friend Nick similarly betrays his trust by surreptitiously turning him into a mindless killing machine. The kindly Mrs. Cunningham, Gillian's nursemaid at the Paragon Institute, turns into a ruthless MORG agent when Gillian attempts her escape, and Psi Faculty housekeepers Bart and Ken are trained killers. Even the well-intentioned characters do more harm than good, as when the Bellaver's turn their daughter over to the Paragon Institute. Governmental corruption is taken for granted, the only question being which agency will be vicious enough to win power in the end.

Farris develops a related theme that it is difficult to separate the good characters from the bad, the innocent from the guilty. Even before his brainwashing near the end of the novel, the "heroic" Peter is a professional assassin and a well-trained torturer who has few qualms about putting these talents to use. Gillian, though technically innocent, is like a plague carrier, threatening the lives of family, friends, and strangers by her mere presence. Robin, initially presented as a bright, kind, likable young boy, slowly evolves into a monster who craves stimulation through sex, power, and cruelty. Gwyneth Charles, arguably one of the most sympathetic characters in the book, becomes little better than a child molester. Settings such as a desolate seaside resort in winter, a deserted "fake" town, and the heavily-guarded Psi Faculty reinforce the sense of constant threat and hopelessness.

The Fury draws its science-fiction elements from the documented powers of the human brain. Other Farris novels focus on more supernatural than paranormal phenomena, including family curses in *All Heads Turn When the Hunt Goes By* (1978) and demoniac possession in *Son of the Endless Night* (1985). These novels feature similarly complex, convoluted plots, often with multiple layers of fantastic elements. Farris wrote the screenplay for the 1978 film adaptation of *The Fury*, directed by Brian De Palma.

—Charles Avinger

FURY

On Venus, immortal humans try to stop a ruthless criminal from leading colonists out of the comfort of the undersea cities to the planets deadly surface

Author: Henry Kuttner (1915–1958)
Genre: Science fiction—dystopia
Type of work: Novel
Time of work: About seven hundred years in the future
Locale: Venus
First published: 1950 (serial form, *Astounding Science-Fiction*, May-July, 1947; also published as *Destination Infinity*, 1958)

THE STORY

This novel is a sequel to "Clash by Night" (*Astounding Science-Fiction*, March, 1943), which told of the Free Companions, mercenaries hired to fight for the warring human colonies on Venus so that what is left of human civilization after the atomic destruction of Earth has a chance to prosper in the Keeps, domed cities on the ocean floor. The Free Companions play only a minor role in *Fury*, which takes place several decades later, when the Keeps have been united and most of the Free Companions have died. *Fury* relates the great contest of wills between Zachariah Harker, one of the Immortals, mutated humans with seven-hundred-year life spans who exert de facto rule over the Keeps, and Sam Reed, a vicious, driven criminal who at first does not realize that he is an Immortal. The stakes are the colonization of the surface of the planet, a job that will be fantastically difficult because of the savage plant and animal life. The Immortals, taking the long view, know that colonization must occur eventually or the human race will stagnate. They fear, however, that if it is attempted too soon, it will fail, and humanity will lack the will to try again. Sam sees it as a way to build an empire and is determined to carry it out as soon as possible.

The book opens as an Immortal, Blaze Harker, goes mad following the death of his wife in childbirth. Blaming the child for his wife's death, he has it surgically altered and raised by foster parents so it will never learn its true heritage as an Immortal. Young Sam Reed inherits superior abilities and a predisposition to anger and resentment. He quickly becomes frustrated, rebellious, and bitter in a world in which the most coveted positions are held by Immortals, who have decades to prepare for them. Sam resorts to crime, including theft, fraud, and murder, to satisfy his ambitions.

Life is so comfortable in the Keeps that men and women seeking excitement are drawn to drug use, violent entertainment, affectations of barbarism, and (mildly portrayed) sadomasochistic relationships, such as the one between Sam and Immortal Kedve Walton, a former lover of Zachariah. When Immortal Robin Hale, the last of the Free Companions, announces his plan to colonize the planets surface, many in the Keeps falsely see it as a romantic adventure. Sam sees it as a tremendous moneymaking opportunity. In the guise of promoting Hales idea, he unscrupulously oversells shares of a public corporation, uses the media to manipulate public opinion and promote class warfare against the Immortals, and eventually broadcasts the colossal lie that any human who stays on the surface for five years will become an Immortal.

The Immortals countermoves culminate in a failed attempt to kill him, which puts him in a drugged state of amnesia for forty years. When, as a result, Sam discovers that he is an Immortal, the only difference his knowledge makes is that he is no longer content to cash in on the colony's failure. He wants it to succeed under his rule. When war breaks out between the Keeps and the surface colonists, atomic weapons are used, taking few casualties but leaving the Keeps uninhabitable. Once humanity is thereby forced to the surface, the eventual success of the colony is ensured.

Although the Immortals are forced to admit that Sam was right about when colonization should take place, their mutual animosity endures. The Immortals believe that Sam is the wrong man to build the colony into a civilization and try one last time to assassinate him. Sam is not mortally wounded and is cared for by Ben Crowell, the Logician, an Immortal who acts overtly as a forecaster of events and covertly as a manipulator of them. The Logician tells Sam that humanity needed him to force it to take the first step toward eventual exploration and colonization of the stars. Sam will be placed in suspended animation until humanity once again needs him to spur it on. The last line of the book is "Sam woke."

ANALYSIS
"Clash by Night" and *Fury* were first published in magazines as by Lawrence O'Donnell, one of the pen names used by Henry Kuttner and his wife, C. L. Moore. *Fury* was primarily his work. It was one of the first science-fiction novels to be selected for hardcover publication when the large, established commercial publishers—in this case, Grosset and Dunlap—became increasingly interested in science fiction in the early 1950s.

Fury was the only full-length science-fiction novel that Kuttner and Moore wrote for John W. Campbell, Jr.'s *Astounding Science-Fiction* magazine. At that time, they were writing science fantasy for other science-fiction magazines, such as *The Mask of Circe* (*Startling Stories*, May, 1948, as by Henry Kuttner, published in book form, 1971).

They branched out into another genre, the crime novel, with such books as *The Brass Ring* (1946) and *The Day He Died* (1947), both published as by Lewis Padgett.

Fury is typical of much of the magazine science fiction of that era in having an extensive background and a plot loaded with incidents, both requiring a good deal of exposition. The Kuttners also were concerned with characterization and mood. Rather like a crime novel, *Fury* is distinctive for its unconventional, ruthless lead character and its unflattering view of humanity, which is portrayed as having the potential for a grand future—the exploration and settlement of the galaxy—but as seeming undeserving of it. In this book, most individuals, once their basic needs are comfortably met, are content with self-indulgent, perverse diversions. Humanity in the mass is so lacking in ambition, imagination, and diversity that its collective behavior can be predicted and its collective will easily manipulated. Its established, privileged leaders, the Immortals, can afford to take such a long view that they see no imperative for immediate major action to cure social ills. Without Sam Reed to give them something to match the furious, blind, unthinking drive to live and procreate exhibited by the flora and fauna on the surface, the human race would simply fade away. This philosophy is in marked contrast to the rationality and morality of the stories that make up the authors' *Mutant* (1953, as by Lewis Padgett).

—*Earl Wells*

THE FUTURE LOS ANGELES SERIES

In the near future, three men face obstacles presented by their pasts and society

Author: K. W. Jeter (1950–)
Genre: Science fiction—future history
Type of work: Novels
Time of work: The twenty-first century
Locale: Los Angeles and elsewhere in Southern California
First published: *Dr. Adder* (1984), *The Glass Hammer* (1985), and *Death Arms* (1987)

THE STORY
In *Dr. Adder*, a stranger, offers E. Allen Limmit the chance to escape his empty life as keeper of the company brothel at the Phoenix Egg Laying Ranch. All he has to do is deliver a suitcase to Los Angeles. Limmit agrees. He is taken to the Interface, a street that separates the privileged Orange County citizens from the denizens of Rattown, the slums of the former Los Angeles. Limmit is amazed to find men pimping amputee prostitutes, most of whom were created by Dr. Adder, the man Limmit was sent to find.

Limmit wanders the Interface, trying to find Dr. Adder. He meets Droit, an information broker. Droit leads him to Adder, behind iron gates at the head of the Interface. Limmit offers Adder the contents of the suitcase—a "flashglove", a cybernetic attachment and weapon created by Limmits father, Lester Gass. Adder buys the glove and offers Limmit a job. Limmit accepts.

That night, John Mox, Adders archenemy, orders his Moral Forces to destroy the Interface. The Moral Forces kill most of the inhabitants of the Interface, but Limmit escapes. Adder escapes as well and has the flashglove attached to his arm. He later is betrayed by a confidante to the Moral Forces. They take him back to the Interface and beat him nearly to death. Adders subconscious mind activates the flashglove, and he slaughters all the Moral Forces. He then collapses, near death.

After the raid, Limmit is without purpose until the strange, and sometimes oracular, KCID tells him to go underground and seek out the Visitor. Limmit finds out from Droit that the Visitor is reported to be an alien entity. Droit provides Limmit with a guide, and Limmit heads into the sewer system of Los Angeles.

Limmits guide eventually turns on him, and he is captured by the Society of the Prodigal Son, the SPS, a group of fathers from Orange County who capture runaways and take them back to Orange County. They take Limmit to Orange County, where he sees the jaded youth and corrupt center of the supposedly affluent residents. Limmit discovers that the SPS is cannibalistic. He escapes and goes back to the sewers.

He eventually finds the Visitor, but the creature is dying and has nothing to offer Limmit. Limmit returns to Los Angeles to find Adder alive. Adder asks for his help in a final assault on John Mox. Using a psychoactive drug and a young girl with unusual abilities, Adder confronts Mox in a psychic battle. Limmit discovers a secret about Mox and must journey to the psychic field to warn Adder. During the psychic battle, the climax of the book, Limmit must confront his fears as well as his family legacy.

The Glass Hammer tells the story of a man named Schuyler. In the present time frame of the story, Schuyler is a sprinter, a driver who carries contraband across a satellite-patrolled desert between Phoenix and Los Angeles. As the story begins, he is in the hospital recovering from a gunshot wound. He also is the subject of a televised biography. It is through the biography, often presented in screenplay format, that his history is revealed.

Schuyler had been born into the Cathedra Novum church at Northernmost Parish. He is transferred to Eureka Station, a frozen dumping ground for church problems. On his way there, he is befriended by a Godfriend named Cynth. The Godfriends, all female, believe that they are destined to give birth to the Second Coming. They do not want this to occur and have forbidden intercourse with men. When Eureka Station is blown up, however, Cynth and Schuyler are forced to trek through arctic wilderness to survive. The two have sexual intercourse, and Cynth becomes pregnant. Cynth and Schuyler are now "Mother-of-God" and "Father-of-God."

They are separated, and Schuyler is sent to Los Angeles and excommunicated by the Cathedra Novum. He is recruited for the sprinters. The sprinters runs are televised, and Schuyler becomes a star. Speed Death Productions sends Endryx out to film his biography.

As the present-time story continues, other sprinters are killed by satellites until only Schuyler is left. Realizing that something is wrong, Schuyler, with the help of some friends, finds out that he, and all of society, is being manipulated. The novel ends with his confrontation with Endryx and his attempt to put things right.

In *Death Arms*, R. D. Legger, a son of an assassin, is caught up in a bizarre plot as he returns to a Los Angeles being repopulated after a mass desertion. As soon as he gets to Los Angeles, a man hands him a manuscript; the man is then assassinated in front of Legger. This leads Legger into the hands of the police and starts his strange adventure in Los Angeles.

After being released, Legger encounters various people: a grey-bearded man; the "rems," disturbed remnants of the past population; Dortz and Ann, possible radicals; and Rachel and Buddy Stain, children with horrifying psychic abilities. Legger eventually decides to help Dortz and Ann with their plans to find out what was in the manuscript the man tried to hand Legger. They break into the police station but are discovered. A "slow bullet," an unstoppable missile geared to Legger's brain waves, is fired at Legger.

To escape the bullet and find out about his past, Legger accompanies Dortz, Ann, and Rachel on a trip across the desert. The trip leads him through his past as well as through the tangled plot in which he is caught. Eventually, near the town of Boron, Legger faces his past, the man responsible for the plot, and the slow bullet.

ANALYSIS

These three books are not a standard trilogy. They do not share characters, a continued plot line, or a common setting. They do, however, share certain types of characters, types of plot, and themes. K. W. Jeter comments on this in an essay at the end of *Death Arms*.

The protagonists in the books are similar in character. They are young men who are dissatisfied with their lives; they each could be considered a model antihero. This type of character is common in many cyberpunk works. In Jeters books, each has something in his past he needs to discover or come to terms with. For Limmit and Legger, it the legacy of the father. For Schuyler, it is his son and the circumstances leading to his sons birth. Each man is being manipulated by forces in society that seem to be beyond his control. Limmit, Schuyler, and Legger all eventually face their pasts, with varying degrees of success.

The supporting casts in each novel also are similar. Each novel features an informant who gives the protagonist the information he needs to outwit the antagonist. Droit, Wyre, and Dortz take on this role. Each novel also has a female assistant who possesses some type of strength or power that she can use to help the male lead.

Also in each book, Jeter gives the reader a dark vision of society. Each of his three visions of future Los Angeles has a powerful, corporate entity of some type pulling the strings and trying to control society. In each book, this corporate entity manipulates the main character in order to achieve a certain goal, usually the domination of society. Such conflicts of the individual versus society are common in many utopian, dystopian, cyberpunk, and other genre novels.

Jeter provides a dark view of religion in *Dr. Adder* and *The Glass Hammer*. Neither John Mox and his Moral Forcers nor the Cathedra Novum is portrayed in a good light. Both are capable of subterfuge and manipulation.

As many similarities as the books have, they are very different in style. *Dr. Adder* is grim, gritty, and at times disturbing, though oddly compelling at the same time. *The Glass Hammer* is much more poetic. Jeter uses normal text mixed with camera directions as the reader and Schuyler watch his past unfold. The compilation of the pieces of Schuylers past is compared with putting together a stained-glass window. *Death Arms* is fast-paced and gritty, like *Dr. Adder*, yet more straightforward and with a smoother flow, possibly because it was written shortly after Jeter had completed *Dr. Adder*. Although the society in that book seems warped, it is not nearly as demented as the society in *Dr. Adder*.

These books, though published close together, were written over a thirteen-year period. *Dr. Adder* was written in 1972 but withheld from publication largely because of the violence it contains. The books show similarities to cyberpunk novels and earned Jeter a certain amount of admiration from other writers in the field.

—*P. Andrew Miller*

A GAME OF DARK

The increasing tension between Donald Jackson and his invalid father plunges him into a medieval fantasy where there is a dragon to be slain

Author: William Mayne (1928–2010)
Genre: Fantasy—time travel
Type of work: Novel
Time of work: The present and the early medieval period
Locale: A coastal town in northern England
First published: 1971

THE STORY

Donald Jackson's father is severely disabled but still partially mobile. He is in constant pain, however, which often makes him irascible and uncommunicative. Donald feels increasingly alienated from him, despite the mediation of his mother, who teaches at the local high school that Donald attends. The only adult Donald feels he can talk to is the Reverend Braxham, the local vicar. At home, Donald is made to feel guilty for jobs not done, lack of sympathy, or lack of faith; his parents are staunch Methodists.

Donald finds himself being taken back in time to a medieval town threatened by a "worm," or dragon. He is befriended by a girl, Carrica, and given shelter. He is then pressed into the service of the newly appointed lord, Lord Breakbone. Previous lords and knights have perished attempting to slay the worm. Jackson, as Donald is known in this world, has to vie with Miral, Breakbone's servant and an illegitimate son of the previous lord, but he is favored by Breakbone and made a squire.

When in each world, Donald has no memory of the other, and he has no control over the transitions. Each world seems equally bleak and threatening, and in each he seems equally isolated. His father becomes seriously ill and has to be admitted to the hospital. When he visits his father, Donald feels even further cut off from him and begins to wonder if he really is the Jackson's child. He also wonders about his dead sister, Cecily, about whom he knows or remembers nothing. It is finally revealed that Cecily was killed in the same railroad accident that injured his father. Donald was born prematurely in his mothers shock. Mr. Jackson finally is allowed out of the hospital, his health apparently a little better.

In the medieval world, after an unsuccessful attempt to hire a knight, Breakbone decides to kill the worm himself, assisted by Jackson. Jackson is made acting knight on the field of combat. The lord perishes, but Jackson has caught sight of the vulnerable underbelly of the dragon. He becomes lord and takes on the duty of ridding the town of the worm. In his first combat, he runs away in terror, causing him to be rejected by the townspeople. He tries again, digging a pit underneath the dragons lair. He manages to stab the beasts heart from there. Because he has not fought the dragon in the "correct" way, he feels no honor.

Donald feels a moment of pity and love for his father. For the second time, he is given a choice between the two worlds. He chooses the present. As he does so, his father breathes his last. Donald finally feels peace.

ANALYSIS

William Mayne is a celebrated and prolific British author of books for children, dating from *Follow the Footprints* (1953). The majority of his novels are realistic, often set at school or in country towns. He has ventured into fantasy on a number of occasions, beginning with *Earthfasts* (1966), which is probably his best-known work in the genre.

A Game of Dark is a fantasy of two parallel worlds, one historical, one contemporary. A forerunner of this type of work in British childrens fantasy is Alison Uttleys *A Traveller in Time* (1972), in which the heroine has to make a choice whether to live in Elizabethan England or to remain in the present.

Donald Jackson on two occasions has a similar choice, even though his moments of transition are involuntary. The "game" is to see that the past time is only a game. His first choice, made while semiconscious, is to remain in the game; his final choice is to live in the present.

Unlike in Uttley's fantasy, however, neither of Donald's worlds is at all pleasant. Both are "dark." In both, he feels isolated, helpless, and guilty; in both, he sees himself as a failure. In the present, he is unable to help his father, or even to communicate with him, let alone to love him. Whatever he does for his mother or father is less than adequate. In the past, like the lord and townspeople, he is helpless against the worm.

He makes the initial choice to stay in the past because it offers him slightly more companionship. Gradually, he achieves recognition, and he progresses from helplessness to killing the dragon, even though he remains marginalized. Having achieved that goal, he feels able to choose the present; as he does so, his father, like the Jackson persona in the medieval world, dies.

There clearly is a symbolic connection between the two worlds, and there is some parallelism. The Reverend Braxham and Breakbone are similar in their belief in order and organization, even though that ultimately is shown to be insufficient. They are both father substitutes. Cecily is likened to Carrica. It would be too simplistic to parallel the worm with Mr. Jackson. If anything, the worm represents the inexplicable suffering of the world, as it comes even to good men, and the way pain and fear seem at times to be linked.

Mayne touches on many other themes and issues. Among them are differences in religious faith and practice (Anglicanism versus Methodism), the need for confession to bring reconciliation and acceptance, and the proper way to bear pain. These issues might seem too weighty for a children's book. This criticism is typical for Maynes work. His books have adult themes even though, apparently, they are written for children or adolescents. The bleakness of Donald's life and his sense of not belonging, however, resonate with many adolescents.

—*David Barratt*

THE GAP SERIES

An evil cartel faces a moment of crisis amid fierce personal passions as human-alien contact raises questions as to the nature of humankind

Author: Stephen R. Donaldson (1947–)
Genre: Science fiction—interplanetary romance
Type of work: Novels
Time of work: Around c.e. 2500
Locale: Outer space, particularly various artificial satellites
First published: *The Gap into Conflict: The Real Story* (1991), *The Gap into Vision: Forbidden Knowledge* (1991), *The Gap into Power: A Dark and Hungry God Arises* (1993), *The Gap into Madness: Chaos and Order* (1994), and *The Gap into Ruin: This Day All Gods Die* (1996)

THE STORY

The Gap Series is an ambitious work concerning sweeping historical change far in the future. It achieves dramatic urgency by focusing on the powerful emotions of a few key characters. Through Stephen Donaldson's detailed, complex characterization, the reader is made to reflect on what humans may be like in the future.

Morn Hyland is the daughter of the captain of the pirate-fighting ship *Starmaster*, functioning as an operative of the United Mining Companies Police (UMCP). When the ship is attacked by pirates and her father is killed, Morn irrationally causes the ship to self-destruct. She is taken into the custody of Angus Thermopyle, an ore pirate who is the captain of the ship *Bright Beauty*. Angus brutally rapes and abuses Morn and inserts a zone implant into her body. The implant enables him to inflict mental torture on Morn. Angus is arrested by the authorities at the Com-Mine satellite, but not before turning Morn over to Captain Nick Succurso of the ship *Captain's Fancy*. Before he disposes of her, though, Angus gives her control of the zone implant.

Morn feels liberated by her escape from Angus, but she discovers that she has only exchanged one master for another. Her one defense against Nicks domineering lust is that her possession of the zone implant is secret. Her vulnerability is heightened when she realizes she is pregnant by Angus. Morn is tormented by what she believes are her betrayals of her father and her service. She is also humiliated and degraded by her ordeal.

Nick and his crew are voyaging toward a convergence with the Amnioni, an alien species. The Amnioni are interested in genetically mutating humans so they may be more easily dominated. As Nick's ship converges with the Amnioni, he wrests control of the zone implant from Morn. Using Amnion genetic technology, Nick arranges for Morn's child not only to be born but to enter the world as a mature sixteen-year-old male. This boy, whom Morn names Davies Hyland for her father, is given Morn's own personality and memories by the Amnioni. This weird combination of unprepared immaturity and a tragic legacy overwhelms Davies and causes him uncertainty as he and his mother face extraordinary dilemmas.

Meanwhile, Angus Thermopyle has also suffered a fundamental alteration in personality: He has been mentally reshaped by Milos Taverner, director of Com-Mine Security, into a cyborg named Joshua. His task is to infiltrate the illegal trading station known as Billingate and destroy it. Angus struggles to find his real personality as the reader becomes aware that perhaps he is not the figure of unalloyed evil he initially had seemed.

Holt Fasner, nicknamed "the Dragon," is the chief executive officer of the United Mining Companies (UMC) and is the most powerful human figure on Earth and in space. The Dragon has artificially prolonged his life and exerts a stranglehold on the multitude of activities under the UMC's sway. Warden Dios, head of the UMCP, is subordinate to the Dragon, but he eventually comes to believe that Fasners power is a threat to humanity. Working in tandem with his subordinate, Min Donner, he plots to undermine Fasner by having the UMCP severed from the UMC's supervision and made an arm of the Governing Council of Earth and Space. This goal is made all the more urgent by Dios' suspicion that Fasner is plotting to exploit the genetic engineering ability of the Amnioni in some way.

The key to Dios' plans is Angus, who is sent to assassinate the head of Billingate, a bootleg shipyard that is crucial to Amnioni plans to infiltrate human space. He is accompanied by Taverner, who, unbeknown to Dios, is also dealing with the Amnioni. Angus infiltrates Billingate, where he rejoins Morn, Nick, and Davies. Meanwhile, Dios is trying to deceive Fasner as to his real intentions. Dios deputes Min Donner to approach Sixten Vertigus, a very old man who was the first human to make contact with the Amnioni. Donner convinces the reluctant Vertigus to sponsor a bill of severance in the Earth-Space Council.

It emerges that Angus has not been completely remade by his cyborg transformation—he still possesses a core of his old self, though drastically altered. Even as Taverner, his one-time guardian, goes completely over to the Amnioni and is mentally remade as one of them, Angus joins an uneasy alliance with Morn and Davies against both Nick and the Dragon's forces. Vertigus sponsors a bill of severance, which fails even as a kamikaze attack is launched against the Earth-Space Council. Fasner becomes increasingly aware that forces are at work to subvert his power. The stage has been set for the final confrontation between the UMC, the Amnioni, and the humans fighting to restore freedom and honest government. In the final installment, Donaldson manages to resolve the difficulties amongst the humans, as well as between humans and the alien Amnioni, alternating between intimate moments and big galactic reveals.

ANALYSIS

Donaldson is well known as a writer of psychologically penetrating epic fantasies such as the six books in the chronicles of Thomas Covenant the Unbeliever (1977–1983) and the Mordant's Need diptych of *The Mirror of Her Dreams* (1986) and *A Man Rides Through* (1987). The Gap series, his first venture into science fiction proper, was at first disconcerting to those who had followed Donaldson's career. The highly literary and self-conscious texture of the fantasies yielded to a direct, brusque, and often lurid style. Whereas characters in the earlier books had acted from high-minded or abstract motives, the characters in the Gap books seem directed by base or seamy self-interest.

As the series proceeded, however, the grandeur and drama of Donaldson's designs became clear. Whereas the first book of the series seems to be a simple account of the brutality inflicted on Morn by Angus, by the third book the full complexity of the political and moral sweep of Donaldson's tableau becomes clear, and initial conclusions about the characters are vastly complicated. Donaldson successfully welds several genres: the interplanetary space romance, the sword-and-spaceship thriller, the chronicle of political intrigue on a near-future Earth, and the tale of first contact with an alien civilization.

Although the linguistic complexity of Donaldson's earlier work is missing, the Gap series continues and intensifies his often searing psychological portraiture. Morn Hyland is in a line of Donaldson heroines who, although intensely affected and often victimized by their identities as women, possess important public roles in society that they are determined to fulfill. Throughout her abuse at the hands of Angus and Nick and the agony she finds in suddenly having a mature son/clone in Davies to deal with, Morn never forgets that she is still a UMCP officer. Her sense of public shame that she has corrupted the mission of her service is as troubling to her as the physical degradation she endures from the vicious men in her life.

Along with Morn, the reader is encouraged to identify with Warden Dios. He also suffers from guilt over the corruption that he feels stains him as a result of his decades of cooperation with the Dragon. He hopes to purge his inner shame by sacrificing himself so that the human species can be liberated from the Dragon, be saved from the Amnioni, and be reborn.

Although many of the series characters are not as unabashedly evil as Nick or the Dragon, none is allowed to stand free of the corruption that has engulfed the human race. Even Captain Vertigus, the hero of the human race who at once was courageous enough to make contact with the Amnioni and sagacious and moral enough to refrain from entering their intrigues or profiting from them, is afflicted with an ethical malaise stemming from his age and infirmity. In this thoroughly compromised universe, it is natural that the hopes of humanity ultimately come to rest on the sordid and unadmirable shoulders of Angus Thermopyle.

Donaldson has several times mentioned that the conception of the Gap series was influenced by nineteenth century German composer Richard Wagner's opera cycle *Der Ring des Nibelungen* (1874). Like Wagner, Donaldson narrates "the twilight of the Gods"—in this case, Holt Fasner and the United Mining Companies. What happens after the gods are vanquished, Donaldson implies, depends on how far the human capacity for moral judgment can regenerate itself following its lapse into corruption.

—*Nicholas Birns*

THE GATE TO WOMEN'S COUNTRY

Although in a postconvulsion world women live with a few nonviolent males in communities separate from garrisons of warlike men, they secretly devise ways to dominate and to breed nonviolent children

Author: Sheri S. Tepper (1929–2016)
Genre: Science fiction—feminist
Type of work: Novel
Time of work: The twenty-fourth century c.e.
Location: The fictional community of Marthatown
First published: 1988

THE STORY
Three centuries after most of Earth is devastated and left radioactive by wars, human survivors have evolved a dual civilization. Most men, as well as boys from an early age, live in military garrisons learning martial arts and military values. All women, aided by a handful of pacific male servitors and small children, live in women's country, small communities dominated by females and by the feminine values of nurturance, nonviolence, and love. Sexual intercourse between members of the women's towns and

garrison males is permitted only during periodic Carnival Times.

In Sheri S. Tepper's feminist, post-holocaust novel, *The Gate to Women's Country,* the principal women's community is Marthatown (there are a dozen others). Its main figures are Morgot, the chief medical officer and a Council member; her children, Stavia, Myra, and Jerby; and her old male servitors, Jik and Joshua. The male garrison, which has dwindled gradually in numbers, is led by Stephon, Michael, and Besset, officers who suspect that Marthatown's women possess a secret that might strengthen garrison forces as they prepare for the day when they may conquer women's country.

To ferret out the women's secret, the garrison command enlists Chernon, a young warrior eager to win their approval. He is the son of Morgot's friend Sylvia. Cold-bloodedly, Chernon cultivates the affections of Morgot's daughter, Stavia, in the hope that Stavia can learn and pass on to him the secret of whatever weapon the women possess. Stavia is an unwitting victim of Chernon's guile until, on an expedition to find the limits of habitable territory, a magician, Septimius the Bird, and his two paranormal daughters alert Stavia to Chernon's untrustworthiness.

Before learning the women's secret, however, the garrisons, Chernon among them, decimate one another in one of the periodic wars women arrange to keep down the number of violent men. The men never discover that the "weaker" sex, under Morgot's auspices as medical officer, have been inoculating Marthatown's girls with contraceptives and that the fathers of Marthatown's children are not the garrison's warriors, as the warriors believe, but are Marthatown's seemingly innocuous, usually nonviolent male servitors. The garrison warriors had boasted, amid their carouses and macho displays, of how well Marthatown's women fed, clothed, and furnished them with sex and sons as recruits. They failed to comprehend why their numbers have been dwindling and that the women have always controlled their own as well as the warriors' destinies. Garrison males never understand how subtly and effectively they have been deceived in the name of women's reverence for life and love.

ANALYSIS

A native Coloradan who began writing following her retirement from another career in 1986, Sheri S. Tepper has produced an impressive body of high-quality science-fiction and fantasy novels. Like *The Gate to Women's Country, After Long Silence* (1987), *Grass* (1989)—a Hugo nominee and a Notable Book named by *The New York Times*—and *Raising the Stones* (1990), the novels have won critical praise for their taut plotting and imaginative creations both of otherworldly locales and of plausible characters. Equally important, her novels have been commended for their deft, judicious explorations of relationships between the sexes, for observations on miscommunication between the sexes, and for drawing recognizable distinctions between widely prevalent male and female values.

In *The Gate to Women's Country,* for example, the male warrior values of Stephon, Michael, and Chernon contrast sharply with the feminine values of Morgot and Stavia—indeed, with the values of nearly all of Marthatown's women. By her careful characterizations, Tepper makes sensible allowance for the vitally important exceptions. For example, Morgot's male servitors, Jik and Joshua, like most of Marthatown's handful of males, are comforting figures, warmly paternal, nonviolent, secure, and wise, though when necessary they are lethal defenders and, like the women, better fighters than men of the garrison. Similarly, Septimius the Bird, the itinerant magician who eventually settles in Marthatown, is drawn as bright, articulate, shrewd, discerning, caring, and trustworthy.

Conversely, not all of Tepper's women are models of abstract bourgeois virtue. Marthatown's girls and their mothers show lusty interest in sex aside from the permissible revels of Carnival Time, and whores and wayward youngsters are always busy in the warriors' Houses of Assignation. Tepper's strong and admirable concentration on Marthatown's women never degenerates into facile male-bashing. Nevertheless, by means of both her dialogue and her descriptions, Tepper consistently deplores the sacrifices required of women to maintain their masked dominance. She dramatically emphasizes this theme by having Morgot, Stavia, and other female characters reenact each year Marthatown's theatrical version of the ancient Greek legend of Iphigenia. Over the years, nearly all of Marthatown's abler girls and mothers are expected to speak their prescribed roles in the play, an instructive rite of passage for girls approaching maturity and a grimly reflective exercise for Marthatown's matrons. Iphigenia was the daughter of the Greek warrior hero, Agamemnon. When Agamemnon and his fleet were delayed by contrary winds on their way to join the Trojan War, Agamemnon's lord informed him that the goddess Artemis demanded the sacrifice of Iphigenia. Reluctantly and despite his wife's protestations, Agamemnon agreed to the sacrifice, and beautiful young Iphigenia consented to die for the glory of Greece. In women's country, ostensibly at the mercy of its male garrisons, only brains and resilient character, as Tepper makes manifest in her novel, could forestall or circumvent such realities.

—*Mary E. Virginia*

GENE WOLFE'S BOOK OF DAYS

Eighteen short stories, primarily science fiction, thematically linked by their commemoration of American holidays

Author: Gene Wolfe (1931–)
Genre: Science fiction—new wave
Type of work: Stories
Time of work: Various times between 1938 and the near future
Locale: Various locations on Earth and on unspecified other planets
First published: 1981

THE STORY

Gene Wolfe's Book of Days includes stories related, sometimes loosely, to each of eighteen major and minor holidays celebrated in the United States. Lincoln's birthday, for example, is commemorated with the short story "How the Whip Came Back." Set in the near future, the story describes the reintroduction of slavery as a means of controlling overcrowding in prisons. "Of Relays and Roses," a Valentines Day story, concerns the development of a supereffective computer dating service. Earth Day is marked by "Beautyland," about a man who becomes a millionaire by selling the right to kill the country's last remaining wildlife to the highest bidder. "The Blue Mouse," a story for Armed Forces Day, tells how a soldier who believes himself to be above killing learns to fight, not for his country but for his pet mice. "The War Beneath the Tree" describes a battle between last year's Christmas toys and their usurpers.

Thematically, these stories are only loosely related, though a number of themes are prevalent: the emptiness and impersonality of an industrialized civilization, the search for meaning and identity, and the thin veneer of emotional control. In the Arbor Day story, "Paul's Treehouse," for example, the world is rocked by riots that threaten suburban enclaves. The protagonist, Morris, converts his fear into aggression against his son, who has ensconced himself in a treehouse. As a mob gathers outside his own house, Morris makes plans to cut down the tree, even if it means hurting his son.

Wolfe often illustrates people at a moment of transition, as in "The Changeling," a story for Homecoming Day. The main character, Peter, comes home from the Korean War to find that his sense of reality and, in fact, his actual identity are slipping away.

"Forlesen", for Labor Day, is in length and development more a novella than a short story. It sets a characteristic tone for the entire collection. Both darkly humorous and tragic, the story encapsulates Emanuel Forlesen's career as a middle manager into one long day.

Forlesen awakes knowing only his name; he can only take it for granted that the woman next to him is his wife. He quickly learns to follow the instructions provided to him and so begins his lifetime of meaningless work. He goes home for lunch, the only other contact he will have with his wife. He realizes that he knows her less well than his secretary. He returns to the plant to discover that he has been promoted. At the end of the day, he has retired, been given his gold watch, and gone home to die, never knowing if his life had any meaning.

This lack of a significant identity and of connectedness with family is echoed in "The Adopted Father," a Fathers Day story about a man who believes that his children cannot be his own and who instead adopts an orphaned boy for whom, seemingly randomly, he feels some affinity. The Thanksgiving story, "Three Thousand Square Miles," likewise is about a man aimlessly searching the United States for its reputed 90 percent of uninhabited land.

Analysis

Gene Wolfe's Book of Days has, in general, had a favorable reception, though some critics consider the selection uneven and the linking apparatus sometimes overstretched. Nevertheless, these stories, published individually in science-fiction and fantasy magazines and anthologies between 1968 and 1981, represent Gene Wolfe's emergence as a major writer of science fiction. For the most part, they predate his most famous work, the Book of the New Sun sequence (1980–1987). Stylistically very different from that work, which critics have called science fantasy—a blend of futuristic elements with fantastic ones—the stories in this collection mirror some of the tetralogys hybrid elements.

A number of these stories are clearly categorizable as science fiction. "Beautyland," for example, is set on a near-future Earth and features robots and ecological devastation. Others, such as "Forlesen," "The Adopted Father," "Paul's Treehouse," and "The Blue Mouse," show less clearly the apparatus common to science fiction but do arise from science fictions dystopian tradition. These stories show a world much like that of the present but with problems taken to their logical and devastating conclusions—massive overpopulation, military takeover, and dislocation of the family. These stories hold a mirror up to the reality of the world while providing some distance or perspective.

Other stories, however, are not science fiction at all. "St. Brandon," for example, borrows a story from Celtic mythology, and "Car Sinister," "The Changeling," and "Many Mansions" derive more from the fantasy/horror genre popularized by such writers as Thomas Tryon and Stephen King. Other stories, such as "La Befana," "Against the Lafayette Escadrille," and "How I Lost the Second World War . . ." blend elements of fantasy with the "what if?" quality of science fiction. "Melting" might be science fiction—it features a spaceship and an alien—but might also be a description of a drug-induced hallucination.

Wolfe's easy movement among these genres and his emphasis on the psychological state of his characters clearly place his work in the New Wave of science fiction, which he and writers including Ursula K. Le Guin, Samuel R. Delany, and James Tiptree, Jr., helped to define. In terms of thematic and stylistic diversity, *Gene Wolfe's Book of Days* particularly resembles Le Guin's short-story collections *The Wind's Twelve Quarters* (1975) and *The Compass Rose* (1982). Like Le Guin, Wolfe uses some of the symbols and themes of the older wave of science fiction—alien encounters, the trials of life off-world, and the growing dependence of humans on machines. He uses these science-fiction staples more ironically and more clearly in service to moral issues and the psychological development of his characters.

—Amy Clarke

THE GENESIS MACHINE

Scientists working on a secret international project create a weapon so powerful that it makes war impossible

Author: James P. Hogan (1941–2010)
Genre: Science fiction—extrapolatory
Type of work: Novel
Time of work: 2005–2008
Locale: Earth and the Moon
First published: 1978

The Story

The fragmentation of the Soviet Empire was anticipated in this novel more than a decade before the actual events. The ensuing civil war propels the eastern reaches of that territory toward solidarity with China and the African-Arab Alliance. The "Afrabs" have taken total control of Israel, Zimbabwe, and South Africa. The states of the Persian Gulf have also moved over to the Chinese and Afrab side. Together, in 2002 they form the Grand Alliance of Progressive Peoples Republics. Opposing them is the Alliance of Western Democracies, vastly outnumbered in population and on the defensive because the level of weapons technology has reached rough parity between the two camps. International tension grows during the three-year time span of *The Genesis Machine*. Flashpoints in Korea, Taiwan, Iraq, and India spark with increasing menace.

Dr. Bradley Clifford is a brilliant American physicist who wants only to be left alone to continue his research. Political heat forces him from his ivory tower. The Advanced Communications Research Establishment (ACRE) in Albuquerque, New Mexico, where he works, is under increasing pressure to contribute to the nations military preparedness. Clifford's most beloved area of research is showing no immediate payoff of this kind, and he is called on the carpet.

Clifford's nemesis is Miles Corrigan, liaison director from the Pentagons Technical Coordination Bureau in Washington. His job is to make sure that everything done at ACRE will either "help us kill Commies" or "stop Commies from killing us." The two lock horns at a top-level meeting, but Clifford refuses to submit.

The government decides to turn his research over to scientists who are more practical and more patriotic, according to their own narrow definition of the concept. One of them, however, turns out to be Aubrey Philipsz from the Berkeley Research Institute. He manages to find out whose research he has been assigned to develop and contacts Clifford directly.

The two immediately strike up a firm friendship, encouraged by their complementary personalities and research orientations. Clifford is serious and idealistic, a theoretical genius as a physicist. Aub, as Aubrey Philipsz is called, is fun loving and easygoing. He specializes in experimental design and solving operational problems in the lab. On the same day but without conscious coordination, reacting to similar frustrations, they both resign their respective positions.

With the help of Professor Heinrich Zimmermann, a sympathetic older physicist pursuing his own work on the far side of the Moon, Clifford and Aub get hired by the International Scientific Foundation. They go to work on their own project at the Sudbury Institute in Massachusetts, but the same political pressures soon materialize. This time, instead of resigning, they decide to use the system against itself.

Government funding and support are sought and secured in order to build the ultimate weapon. Instantaneous communication, reconnaissance, and controlled explosive force delivered anywhere on the planet are its supreme capabilities. Unbeknown to military leaders and politicians, however, as he is building the Genesis Machine, Clifford is also programming it. When this weapon to end all weapons goes into action, it not only wipes out the military capability of the enemy but also eliminates that of the Western democracies. Miraculously, no one is killed in this version of World War III. Furthermore, the Genesis Machine is programmed to enforce a continued peace on Earth for the next hundred years. Humanity is given one last chance to learn to live in harmony.

ANALYSIS

The starting point for the physics in *The Genesis Machine* is the long-sought unified field theory, a set of equations that would combine the strong and weak nuclear forces, gravity, and electromagnetic force. James Hogan builds upon this projected breakthrough, together with the already-proposed Hawking Effect, which identifies a special kind of radiation emanating from the area surrounding black holes. An almost unlimited source of energy is thereby deemed available in another dimension. Clifford discovers this dimension, identified as k-space, and taps it. The science in this novel is solid and exciting.

The plot is also well structured. Although the dramatic action is interrupted frequently by long passages of explanation, events develop, one out of the other, in a logically satisfying progression. They lead to a vision at the end of the book of a solution to the nuclear arms race. Given all the problems that beset humanity in this age, to imagine any positive future is difficult. To imagine and present one in which peace truly prevails is no small accomplishment.

Other literary elements in *The Genesis Machine* are not so well handled. The characters are hardly more than cardboard cutouts used to demonstrate scientific and political concepts. They all sound the same, with the possible exception of Professor Zimmermann. Their interaction lacks any real depth of adult emotion. Clifford's wife, even though she is a medical doctor and an accomplished person in her own right, is trapped within the stereotype of the supportive wife. Only for one scene, in the closing pages, does she emerge from complete predictability. She seems to flirt for a moment with Aubrey Philipsz, simultaneously flirting with becoming a genuinely three-dimensional character.

Hogan's style is clumsy in many places. He seems to have little ear for musical elements in his use of the English language, and his prose is peppered with clichés. Science fiction has a long tradition as a literature of ideas, if not of flowery and poetic language, and *The Genesis Machine* is packed with those. This novel is a first-rate example of contemporary, hard science fiction.

—Steven Lehman

Ghost Story

Men in a small New York town who meet to tell stories find themselves haunted by their pasts and by supernatural shape-shifting creatures

Author: Peter Straub (1943–)
Genre: Fantasy—superbeing
Type of work: Novel
Time of work: 1977, with flashbacks to 1929
Locale: Milburn, a small town in New York
First published: 1979

The Story

The frame narrative is set immediately after the final events of the main story. The opening sequence of a man fleeing cross-country with a kidnapped young girl is quite mysterious because it is offered without explanation.

The main narrative is divided into three parts. The first, told with many flashbacks and memories, defines the situation. Five of the oldest and most influential men in Milburn had been meeting, for companionship and storytelling, as the Chowder Society. Sears James and Ricky (Frederick) Hawthorne are lawyers, John Jaffrey is a physician, Edward Wanderley was a writer, and Lewis Benedikt is a retired hotel owner. One year earlier, Wanderley had died while attending a party for an actress he was writing about, Ann-Veronica Moore. After that, the members of the Chowder Society all experienced nightmares, and the stories they told at their meetings turned macabre. Sears James tells a lengthy story, clearly based on Henry James's *The Turn of the Screw* (1898), featuring brothers Gregory and Fenny Bate. The four surviving members of the group contact Edward Wanderley's nephew Don, but they are too late to prevent Jaffrey from jumping off a bridge under peculiar circumstances.

The second section sets up the conflict. Don Wanderley earns admission to the Chowder Society with the story on which his novel *The Nightwatcher* is based. Two years before, Alma Mobley, a strange and beautiful young woman, seduced Don and then drove his brother, David, to suicide. Don mentions her associates, a woman named Florence de Peyser, Greg Benton, and Greg's brother. The Bentons appear to be the Bate brothers from James's story. The picture of Milburn deepens, and what appears to be an ordinary town increasingly is plagued by odd phenomena as a rough winter settles in. Animals are killed and apparitions are sighted. Lewis narrowly escapes an automobile accident, swerving to avoid a figure resembling his late wife; a spinster is killed after seeing her dead brother; Dr. Rabbitfoot, a character from Wanderley's newest novel, is heard; and the Bate brothers frequently appear, including at the death of an insurance salesman. Peter Barnes, a high school senior, sees the insurance salesman die in the company of the lawyers new secretary, Anna Mostyn, and Barnes himself barely escapes from Mostyn's house while another boy is killed.

The full situation is revealed and the battle is joined in the third section. Lewis describes the suicidal death of his wife, a fate intended for him, during a visit to Florence de Peyser and her young niece, Alice Montgomery, fifteen years earlier. He is then trapped with delusions and killed. Sears and Ricky tell Don "the ultimate Chowder Society story," concerning the death in 1929 of actress

Eva Galli, in which all five future Chowder Society members participated. Peter sees his mother killed, then joins the other three in their fight. Their adversaries are revealed as Manitou, or shape-shifters, what people used to call vampires and werewolves, reoccurring in similar identities and taking shape from human imaginations. Anyone who gives in to them or is killed by them becomes their tool. Sears is killed, and Ricky's wife, Stella, is kidnapped but escapes. Ricky, Don, and Peter kill the Bate creatures, and Peter stabs the Galli creature, but she escapes as a bird, so Don promises to await her return.

The end of the frame narrative explains the beginning: The young girl is the shape-shifter returned. Don not only ends that human identity but kills the thing, presumably forever, in its final form of a wasp.

ANALYSIS

Ghost Story, the book that established Peter Straub as a major author of supernatural fiction, is both an effective horror novel and a metafictive commentary on the genre. Preparing to write *Ghost Story*, Straub spent six months reading and rereading in the field. The references to Henry James and Nathaniel Hawthorne are obvious; the novel also refers to many other English and American writers, such as Ambrose Bierce and Arthur Machen. Stephen King's novel *Salem's Lot* (1975) helped Straub organize a multicharacter story and present the story of a town as well as of individuals. Another influence was Thomas Tessier's *The Nightwalker* (1979).

The novel combines a realistic presentation of life in Milburn with a supernatural menace that is interesting, as a new twist on a classic theme, and thematically satisfying. The interior lives of the main characters are rich and believable; subplots, such as the affairs of Ricky's wife Stella and the growing-up conflicts of Peter Barnes, lend depth and texture; and exotic characters, such as the paralyzed spinster Nettie Dedham and UFO-believer and poet Elmer Scales, lend color. These elements also contribute to the depiction of a town under siege by the weather, by social tensions, and by a supernatural agency that works with and through the flaws already present in the town and its citizens. The shape-shifters, though not human, are reflections of real people, as Straub's references to Narcissus indicate.

As in his other novels, such as *If You Could See Me Now* (1977), Straub develops the idea of the eternal female as femme fatale, the key to mysteries both alluring and terrifying. With some exceptions, his human female characters do not succeed as well. Throughout the novel, there is a constellation of four Manitou fighters, with Don joining after one death and Peter after the next, yet a slot is left open after Sears's death, unfilled by the logical candidate, Stella. This flaw was addressed by Straub in a later novel, *Floating Dragon* (1983).

Ghost Story also explores the interplay of subjective and objective states, as characters are deceived by the shape-shifters and find themselves in malleable "realities." The constants that sustain the Chowder Society are their own senses of self and the deep friendships they share. Ultimately, these characteristics and dedication to the town of Milburn allow them to win.

—Bernadette Lynn Bosky

A GIFT FROM EARTH

On an Earth colony on a distant planet, a young man battles a ruling class that preserves its own longevity by using common citizens for its organ banks

Author: Larry Niven (1938–)
Genre: Science fiction—dystopia
Type of work: Novel
Time of work: Several hundred years in the future
Locale: The Plateau on Mount Lookitthat, on a planet in the Tau Ceti system
First published: 1968

THE STORY

A Gift from Earth is a segment of Larry Niven's Known Space series, a group of loosely connected novels and short stories, most from the mid-1960's to the mid-1970's. The series portrays the first centuries of human interstellar exploration and settlement, along with attendant encounters with various alien races.

After landing on a maze of plateaus, on a mountain rising above the poisonous gases of an otherwise uninhabitable planet, the small crew of an Earth colony ship establishes a dictatorship over the colonists, who had been in suspended animation. Living in luxury on the upper Alpha Plateau, the crews descendants make political dissent a capital crime, thus ensuring a large stock of body parts for their organ banks. The "crews" are protected by the Implementation, a police force whose headquarters are conveniently in the labyrinthine, fortress-like Hospital, where prisoners remains are stored and used for transplantation. The colony receives occasional gift packages from Earth via robot space vessels. The latest arrival is hidden quickly by the police but secretly observed by Polly, a member of a revolutionary group called the Sons of Earth.

Matt Keller, the novel's protagonist, is a twenty-one-year-old colonist with a psychic power of which he is unaware. In moments of intense anxiety, he can cause the pupils of others' eyes to contract, thus producing a lack of interest, indeed a pure forgetfulness, in his enemies. Unfortunately, this power causes a similar reaction in women on the verge of relieving him of his virginity. Early in the novel, Matt is invited by his friend Jay Hood to a party, not knowing it is a coverup for a Sons of Earth gathering led by the host, Harry Kane. At the party, he is rejected by Polly but manages to have sex with Laney Mattson, thanks to their entering a pitch-black room. When the party is raided by the police, only Matt escapes.

Matt finds a flying car, forbidden to colonists. He takes it to Alpha Plateau, hoping to infiltrate the Hospital to rescue his new friends. Against all odds, he succeeds, though Polly is not among the rescued. She has been put into a sensory deprivation chamber as a method of torture by Head of Police Jesus Pietro Castro, the novels antagonist.

Appalled by the rebels slaughtering of Hospital personnel as they escape, Matt feels alienated from both sides. Most of the rebels are recaptured, but Matt, Harry, Jay, and Laney are able to hide out at a sympathetic crew familys mansion. Jay figures out Matt's psychic gift. Matt decides to return to the Hospital for Polly, and a wise crew elder, Millard Parlette, reveals the ramrobot gift: biotechnology that eventually will make the organ banks obsolete. Knowing that the news will leak out and cause massive colonist rebellion, Parlette seeks a confederation of crew and colonist before war breaks out and before Castro and the Implementation form a dictatorship of their own.

Again Matt succeeds in his rescue attempt, but Polly is interested only in a suicide mission to destroy the Hospital. A series of violent actions leads to the deaths of both Polly and Castro, as well as to a new and more just order on Mount Lookitthat.

Analysis

A Gift from Earth, Larry Niven's second novel, may not be the most brilliant work in his Known Space series, especially because that series includes the splendid *Ringworld* (1970). Characterization is undistinguished except for that of Castro, who is no snarling villain but is chilling in his efficiency and conviction that he is a decent man keeping law and order. The novel also contains less of the "hard science" so often praised by admirers of Niven's other early works. In particular, Matts psychic gift strains the readers credulity: Outside questions of genetic mutation, one wonders how, if inattentiveness and even forgetfulness are caused by contraction of the pupils, anyone could ever accomplish anything in bright sunlight. Moreover, with its all-human cast, *A Gift from Earth* has no chance to display one of Niven's greatest talents, the portrayal of wacky but somehow plausible alien creatures and their curious interactions with humans.

This is not to say that *A Gift from Earth* is without considerable merit. If the science is sometimes less than hard, the book does explore seriously how a single technology, that of organ transplants, may have complex social ramifications. It contains fanciful but reasonable ideas about how a colony extremely limited in natural resources might build and maintain its dwelling places. Niven offers the solution of live organic materials, such as mutated coral and grass.

If the novel has less downright humor than *Ringworld* and some of Niven's short stories, the author still shows cleverness in orchestrating its fast action and surprising reversals of fortune. He seems to find considerable amusement and irony in his heros plights.

Students of American cultural values and history may find much of interest in Matt's refusal to join the Sons of Earth despite his awareness that crew and police are his enemies. Somewhere between a rugged individualist and wishy-washy loner, Matt seems a typically American hero of popular fiction in his refusal to swear allegiance to one party line.

Perhaps the finest achievement of *A Gift from Earth* is that, as in much of his best fiction, Niven is able to root a dramatic situation in a unique physical environment that is extensively, but not exhaustively, explored in the course of the narrative. The terraced terrain of the Plateau, the impossibility of escape beyond it, and the poetry and terror of the mists surrounding the inhabited land all contribute to the psychology of the settlers and determine much of the action.

—*Joseph Milicia*

GILES GOAT-BOY

A strange creature who resembles a goat and is the product of a computer tries to become the leader of a world that is based on the structure of a university

Author: John Barth (1930–)
Genre: Fantasy—heroic fantasy
Type of work: Novel
Time of work: Undefined, perhaps the near future
Locale: The United States
First published: 1966

The Story

Giles the goat-boy, also known as George Giles, was reared on a goat farm by a keeper. He gradually discovers that he has a special and heroic role in life. He lives in a land dominated by a school, New Tammany College, which is split into rival factions, primarily West Campus and East Campus. West Campus is controlled by an all-powerful computer, WESCAC, and dominated by a Grand Tutor. After learning more about his background, Giles decides that he has a daunting task: to displace the false Grand Tutor of the West Campus and end the control of WESCAC by entering its deep vitals and unplugging it. During the course of his adventures, he also meets such traditional heroic challenges as finding and mating with the love of his life, defeating and even killing enemies both human and animal, and performing such tasks as passing through the narrow and treacherous Scrapegoat Grate on his way to Commencement Gate.

A strange woman who later turns out to be Giles's mother piques his interest in the world outside when she visits him at the goat farm where Max Spielman, a disgraced and outcast professor from the West Campus, has reared him from infancy. George, who has a strange half-human, half-goat body that prevents him from walking upright for long, first thinks that he was born from one of the goats on the farm. He instinctively feels called by some destiny higher than living out his life on the farm. Max and Giles, in the company of a black laborer named George Herrold, set out toward the West Campus, where Giles finds out more about himself and his past.

Giles's first trial comes at a river gorge. A beautiful girl, Anastasia, beckons him to come over to her side. Herrold tries and is swept away in a flood. A giant black football player named Croaker appears and has sex with Anastasia, who is so beautiful and willing that she is desired by almost everyone she meets, male or female.

After an encounter with a motorcycle gang led by Maurice Stoker, Giles makes his way to the West Campus, where he meets Chancellor Lucius Rexford, Dr. Kennard Sear, Dr. Eblis Eierkopf, Peter Greene (a campus vagabond), and former chancellor Reginald Hector. The entire campus, Giles is told, fears the WESCAC computer, which has the ability to fry the brain circuits of anyone who tampers with it. Everyone also fears failing courses and falling into the clutches of the legendary Dean O'Flunks. Giles eventually discovers that he is the child of the beautiful lady who visited him, Virginia Hector, who is the daughter of former chancellor Hector; his "father" is the computer, WESCAC, which was programmed to produce a Grand Tutorial Ideal, Laboratory Specimen (GILES). Armed with the knowledge of his true identity, Giles descends into the belly of the computer with Anastasia and defeats it. He also replaces Harold Bray, the false tutor.

Giles's success, however, is ironic. Not everyone believes that he is the new Grand Tutor, and his followers, to whom he imparts rules and principles to live by, fall away from him. The rest of his history is obscure. What evidence there is comes in the form of a manuscript delivered to novelist John Barth by a mysterious figure who may be the goat-boy's son, Giles Stoker, in whom George Giles had expressed a lack of confidence.

ANALYSIS

Giles Goat-Boy: Or, The Revised New Syllabus is a combination of a number of literary forms. It is an allegory in which the twentieth century world is seen as a huge university, the West Campus standing for the "free world" or Western universities and the East Campus representing the Communist bloc. Other participants in the political struggle include Siegfrieder College (Germany), the Bonifascists (Nazis), and the Student-Unionists (local communists). Characters represent John F. Kennedy, J. Robert Oppenheimer, and Milton and Dwight Eisenhower, among many others. There are frequent references to Campus Riots One and Two (World Wars I and II), and everyone fears that a third and apocalyptic campus riot may break out. The WESCAC computer resembles the genie of nuclear power, out of its bottle and uncontrollable.

The novel is also an epic account of how a legendary hero saves his country and his people, and it thus resembles such literary antecedents as Homer's *The Odyssey*, Vergil's *The Aeneid*, and Edmund Spenser's *The Faerie Queen* (1590 and 1596). Like the heroes of those works, Giles is wounded, endures trials, fights villains, descends to the underworld (in George's case, the circuits of the giant computer), and finally delivers his people from the rule of a pretender (the false tutor).

An obvious model for Giles is the Greek king Oedipus, who, like Giles, had difficulty walking and committed incest, something George fears he may have done when he believes that Anastasia is his sister. Like Oedipus, George also kills his father, when he short circuits WESCAC. The connection between these two works is cemented when Giles watches a full-length parody of *Oedipus Rex*.

Giles Goat-Boy is also a story of the birth of a religion. The novel is its sacred scripture, passed down from its founder. Another founder mentioned in the novel, Enos Enoch, representing Jesus Christ, helps to make this connection clear. Like other sacred scriptures, both its origin and its content are ambiguous; wrapped around the novel at beginning and end are disclaimers by some editors and praise from others, ending with a letter from "John Barth" in which he says the manuscript was delivered to him by a mysterious figure who may have been the goat-boy's son. In the novel, the details of the hero's later life and death are fuzzy, and, like the careers of most religious figures, open to challenge. In this modern religion, human society is now a scholarly bureaucracy, and a spiritual God has been replaced by a computer and a person who is part man and part satyrlike goat.

—*Jim Baird*

THE GIRL THE GOLD WATCH AND EVERYTHING

When his Uncle Omar dies, Kirby Winter inherits a gold watch with the power to make time stop

Author: John D. MacDonald (1916–1986)
Genre: Fantasy—magical realism
Type of work: Novel
Time of work: The early 1960s
Locale: Miami, Florida
First published: 1962

THE STORY
When Omar Krepps suddenly dies, Kirby Winter, his nephew and only living relative, is thought to be the sole heir to a purportedly vast fortune. Uncle Omar, a reclusive philanthropist with a talent for both magic and high finance, in fact has left his nephew no money, only a very strange bequest: a gold pocket watch and a letter. Kirby is to receive the watch immediately; the letter is to be delivered to him in one year.

The Girl the Gold Watch and Everything

Kirby's relationship with his uncle was cordial but not close. Although Uncle Omar financed Kirby's college education, he also insisted on selecting his courses, emphasizing ethics and moral philosophy. Kirby is awkward and self-conscious, notably lacking in self-assurance. Both during and after college, he was employed by his uncle as a courier, charged with delivering large sums of money to charitable organizations throughout the world.

After Omar's death, Kirby's quiet routine is shattered by his pursuit by a trio of curious characters. There is the seductive Charla, to whose charms Kirby immediately succumbs; always nearby, however, is the sinister Joseph, Charlas consort, business partner, and general factotum. The aggressive Filiatra, Charlas niece, completes the trio. Filiatra, however, has broken with her aunt and changed her name to Betsy Alden. Betsy has a change of heart and is determined to help save Kirby. Kirby's other allies include Wilma Farnham, Uncle Omar's devoted secretary, and the vivacious Bonny Lee Beaumont, an honest and innocent but street-smart exotic dancer.

Charla and Joseph are determined to get Kirby aboard their yacht, the *Glorianna*, where, they are convinced, they can convince him by whatever means necessary to reveal Omar Krepps's secrets. They want to discover not only the location of the fortune they believe Omar has hidden but also how he had managed, under baffling circumstances, to outwit them at every turn. When both Betsy and Wilma fall into Charlas hands, Kirby is left with the resourceful Bonny. To complicate matters, they have fallen in love.

At a public beach, the last place Charla and Joseph would look, Kirby and Bonny pause and assess their situation. Absentmindedly, Kirby examines his uncles gold watch. The otherwise conventional timepiece has an odd feature: In addition to the gold hour, minute, and second hands there is a fourth hand, a silver one, motionless and set at twelve oclock. It is then that Kirby makes a momentous discovery. By pressing the watch stem in, he can move the silver hand to a new position. When he does so, time stands still for the selected interval up to one hour. The entire world comes to a halt, although the person holding the watch can move about and alter the immediate area.

A series of comic misadventures follows Kirby's discovery of the power of his uncles mysterious invention, as he comes to terms with the awesome moral responsibility granted to the one who possesses the watch. It was with this end in mind, the letter from his uncle states, that Kirby's education was designed, emphasizing moral and ethical responsibility. The watch mitigates any need for deadly force against Charla and Joseph. A series of profoundly humiliating incidents offsets their desire for further pursuit, and Kirby and Bonny fly to Europe to begin a new life.

ANALYSIS

The manipulation of time is one of the most common themes in both science-fiction and fantasy literature. In science fiction, time tampering generally is accomplished through some form of machinery, an idea deriving from H. G. Wells's *The Time Machine* (1895). Fantasy literature generally eschews hard science, dealing with time by an approach that is more imaginatively accessible, utilizing a dream concept or transcendent out-of-body experience tinged with ambiguity. Its literary ancestors are Mark Twain's *A Connecticut Yankee in King Arthur's Court* (1889) and Edward Bellamy's *Looking Backward: 2000–1887* (1888). More recent examples are Kurt Vonnegut, Jr.'s *Slaughterhouse-five* (1969) and Jack Finney's *Time and Again* (1970) and *From Time to Time* (1995). Their common link is the genre of time travel.

John D. MacDonald's approach to the theme of time is different. In time travel, the subject takes a journey to either the past or the future, and the journey generally is a perilous one, usually with some threat to a safe return. Time is trespassed upon, but not controlled, and travelers generally move with consummate care. Kirby Winter, the protagonist of *The Girl, the Gold Watch, and Everything*, takes complete control of the present. He possesses the ability, with the aid of the magic watch, to freeze objective time. He can halt actions occurring in the present and move to change them, simply by pressing the stem of the watch and turning the silver hand backward, giving himself whatever time he needs. Although the novel emphasizes the enormous moral responsibility that such power entails, it is primarily a comedy, an engaging, playful narrative void of serious threat or ominous overtone. The characters are caricatures seemingly derived from a pastiche of legends and fairy tales: Charla is the wicked queen, Uncle Omar is the kindly wizard, and Kirby is the bumbling but charming knight errant, owing more to J. R. R. Tolkien's Frodo Baggins of the Lord of the Rings trilogy (1954-1955) than to Gawain or Lancelot. Certainly the watch is as powerful and potentially corrupting as the mysterious ring that Frodo must protect from the forces of darkness, but Kirby's perilous journey, complete with damsels in distress, is a sequence of comic encounters in which serious threats are easily averted. In the course of the novel, Kirby grows in stature, accepts the responsibility of the watch with the right moral perspective, and resists the absolute power that traditionally corrupts absolutely.

—*Richard Keenan*

GLADIATOR AT LAW

Attorney Charles Mundin helps conscientious company heirs wrest control from greedy owners in a future characterized by corporate control of the masses, strict class division, and bloody spectacle as entertainment

Authors: C(yril) M. Kornbluth (1923-1958) and Frederik Pohl (1919-2013)
Genre: Science fiction—dystopia
Type of work: Novel
Time of work: The near future, no sooner than 2055
Locale: New York City and environs, including the slums of Belly Rave
First published: 1955

THE STORY

Criminal lawyer Charles Mundin, scraping by on the fringes of a decent life, is contacted by Don and Norma Lavin, 25 percent owners of G.M.L. Corporation, which makes the bubble-house, decent societys ubiquitous housing. G.M.L. double-crossed Don and Norma's father, inventor of the bubble-house, using his "invention" to manipulate the housing industry. Their father committed suicide. Only through a G.M.L. error did control of their fathers stock come to them. Because G.M.L. cannot risk snatching the stock certificates and trying to explain a forced sale, it kidnaps and brainwashes Don Lavin, the only one who knows where the original stock is hidden.

Norvie Bligh, whom Mundin knows, is a worker who helps produce Field Days, bloody extravaganzas designed to pacify the underside of societys pent-up frustrations. He is double-crossed, fired, and jailed. Mundin bails him out. Blighs company notifies G.M.L., which immediately shuts down the Blighs bubble-house systems. Bligh morosely moves his wife and daughter to Belly Rave, the New York City slum where the citys have-nots must live. He learns Belly Rave survival techniques and resigns himself to a grimy existence.

Norma Lavin arranges for Harry Ryan to be attorney-of-record for the Lavins case. He is a dope-addled old corporate lawyer living in Belly Rave, but he is brilliant when lucid. Mundin acts as point man. They will buy one share of stock and find out when and where the next G.M.L. stockholders meeting is. Mundin will show up to sow discontent and recruit other stockholders.

G.M.L. kidnaps Norma to hold until after the stockholders meeting, thinking that it will then be safe because Dons brainwashed mind will not be able to find the Lavins stock in order to prove ownership. Mundin enlists Blighs help in finding Norma. They discover that G.M.L. is holding her at the site of the upcoming meeting. She is returned to them at the meeting.

Three stockholders join them after learning that the Lavins own 25 percent of G.M.L. With the stockholders money, Mundin and Norma enlist Blighs help in finding an underground doctor to repair Dons memory.

Once Don has his memory back, the group learns that Dons fingerprints and retinal prints are the identification needed to get the stock. The group begins to undermine confidence in G.M.L.s bubble-houses by spraying solvent on the earliest built houses, then capitalizing on the resulting loss of market confidence in G.M.L.s product.

479

The group has been monitored electronically by the Green, Charlesworth law firm, led by two incredibly old, rich lawyers kept alive because of their massive influence and wealth. Green, Charlesworths economywide influence relies on the status quo, including G.M.L.s continued financial stability. Mundin and Norma meet Green and Charlesworth, who say they will destroy the group and its efforts.

Two of the three stockholders who had joined with the Lavins abandon the group when they learn of Green, Charlesworths threat. Green and Charlesworth are able to enact the threat by triggering a relapse in Dons con-dition: The underground doctor was a Green, Charles-worth operative. Don walks off in a stupor to volunteer for the guaranteed suicide of Field Day. His death will preserve G.M.L. stability because Norma and the others will not be able to get the stock without Dons identification.

The group rescues Don, but Harry Ryan is killed and one of Blighs friends sacrifices himself to save Don, who regains his memory. Later, the group starts dumping its stock, causing other stockholders to abandon shares. The group then buys 70 percent of G.M.L. The Lavin bubble-house finally goes into production, to be used in the socially conscientious manner originally intended.

ANALYSIS

Gladiator-at-Law followed C. M. Kornbluth and Frederik Pohls earlier collaboration on the widely acclaimed *The Space Merchants* (1953). There is a common theme within the two novels: A society made dystopic by corporate greed can be bettered to at least some extent by the efforts of one or a few in that society. Also common to the two works is the view that a population, without understanding and diligence, can become pawns manipulated at the whim of solipsistic capitalism. *Gladiator-at-Law* succeeds on one level, then, as a cautionary tale.

This novel typifies Kornbluth and Pohls joint work. Their collaborations often are identified as harbingers of a generation of science-fiction novels in which the future is dominated by one particular power group. These two authors, however, succeed perhaps better than others in painting such tales with delicious irony and tongue-in-cheek "treatments," so that readers are never dragged to depressive depths.

Gladiator-at-Law also hints at Pohls later inclination to write about ordinary people, as opposed to heroic types. Charles Mundin—the name may have been intended to evoke "mundane"—and Norvie Bligh retain much of their Joe Anybody status throughout the novel. To a certain extent, the same is true of Pohls protagonist in the Hugo Award-winning *Gateway* (1977), about whom, Pohl says, readers sometimes complain because they think Robinette Broadhead is too much Caspar Milquetoast and not enough Captain Marvel. Considering the statement Kornbluth and Pohl make in *Gladiator-at-Law*, ordinary people must be the focus in order to emphasize the authors point.

Gladiator-at-Law also touches on the theme of life extension, which Pohl has explored in his Heechee novels, begun with *Gateway*, as well as in other work. Green and Charlesworth, hoary human shells, somehow have been kept alive far beyond the normal life span because they have the money to pay for medical treatments. Kornbluth and Pohl do not dwell on the implications, but Pohl develops the theme in his later work.

Kornbluths output was cut short tragically by an early death in 1958. Otherwise, there may have been more collaborations with Pohl, who says their joint writing process involved Kornbluth visiting Pohls home to write.

—*Jeff King*

GLASS SOUP AND WHITE APPLES

A dead man and his bride must ensure that their prodigal son is born, then raise him properly, in order to prevent the disruption of the universe

Author: Jonathan Carroll (1949–)
Genre: Fantasy—metaphysical fantasy

Type of Work: Novel
Time of Plot: Present
Location: America, Vienna, and the afterlife
First Published: *White Apples* (2002) and *Glass Soup* (2005)

Glass Soup and White Apples

THE STORY

Vincent Ettrich seems to have a charmed life. A well-off advertising executive, he has led a Don Juan lifestyle for many years, sincerely yet fleetingly romancing many, many women. Perhaps his one true love is Isabelle Neukor, an elegant Viennese woman. But somehow, Vincent and Isabelle have never been able to fully commit to fidelity to each other alone, despite their mutual affection and regard.

So Vincent continues his pleasant conquests. His latest is one Coco Hallis, a simple shop girl. They seem to be enjoying a splendid time together—until the inexplicable intrudes.

One day in a restaurant with Coco, Vincent sees an old friend, Bruno Mann. At the same moment, he gets a phone call telling him Bruno has just died. He turns to Coco for solace—and discovers that she now sports an instant, new tattoo of Bruno's name. Vincent freaks out. What he eventually discovers is this.

Vincent himself is as dead as Bruno. Vincent died after a long hospitalization, which he doesn't remember. But for some reason, both he and Bruno have been physically reincarnated, and memories of their demises have been wiped from the record. Their friends and family accept them as living. They are both to continue their existences, for some reason that Coco—who proves to be a supernatural psychopomp from Purgatory—is unwilling to tell them.

So, a bewildered and anxious Vincent checks his appointment book and learns that Isabelle, his great love, is due to arrive from Vienna. He obligingly yet confusedly meets her at the airport. She reveals that she is pregnant with Vincent's child, a boy named Anjo. And she knows that Vincent has died.

Anjo is conscious in the womb and communicates with Isabelle, and eventually Vincent accepts this. But forces are arrayed against the parents and unborn child. Vincent realizes that he has been returned to protect his son: "Anjo is the key to everything. Chaos wants him because he's a direct threat to it. But I know something else now that I didn't before—once Anjo is born, chaos can't touch him. He'll be protected, and there's no way it will ever be able to harm him."

Coco explains to the two humans that every person's life is a small tile in the overall mosaic that equals God. But this mosaic has become threatened by the new growing sentience of Chaos. (And Bruno Mann is an agent of that force.)

The trio is attacked in the setting of a zoo, which was supposedly immune from Chaos. Coco is killed, insofar as she can be. Tillman Reeves, another dead man, enters the action. Vincent encounters his doppelgänger from the realm of death, as a giant rat named Alan, who tries to get him to return.

Vincent stashes Isabelle (and Anjo) in a safe pocket universe ruled over by Isabelle's dead grandmother. A final confrontation between Bruno and Ettrich leaves Vincent at death's door for the second time. Isabelle is confronted with the choice of saving either Vincent or Anjo. But then she realizes she can do both.

Glass Soup opens in the afterlife, as we are introduced to a new character named Simon Haden as he goes about his unreal activities. Simon's role in the larger scheme is not immediately divulged, but it will prove pivotal. Then we are back on Earth with Isabelle, as she lunches with her longtime friends, Flora and Leni. It turns out that all three women knew Simon Haden; he was lovers to Flora and Leni and wished to claim Isabelle as well, but never succeeded.

Vincent and Isabelle are now living in Vienna. They seem to have escaped the attentions of the sapient Chaos that has threatened them and the structure of creation. But in reality, Chaos has a new guise: the fat, pompous boulevardier John Flannery and his dog Luba. Flannery is playing a cat-and-mouse game with Vincent and Isabelle, and it involves becoming lovers with both Leni and Flora, affairs that remain hidden and non-intersecting among the trio of good friends.

Meanwhile, in Simon's afterlife, his helper guardian, a tiny man named Broximon, is keeping tabs on earthly doings. Eventually, Broximon will end up in our world, to aid our protagonists.

Leni's affair with Flannery ends tragically. He kills her, and she wakes to find herself sharing Simon's afterlife. Once the sole creation of Simon, the peculiar netherworld begins to adapt to Leni's presence.

We learn more of how Isabelle originally saved Vincent from his first death. She speaks of her old mentor Petra Urbsys. Vincent and Isabelle begin to develop shared supernatural talents. An apparition of Leni appears to many humans, offering a placard with the words "glass soup" on it. This is an afterlife term referring to the god mosaic.

But, unfortunately, Isabelle is lured into the afterlife by a false Vincent, crossing the one-way barrier of death willingly and, thus, forever. On Earth, Vincent takes revenge by killing Flannery and Luba. But Chaos merely reappears as an old man named Putnam, who tries to beguile Vincent into the deathworld as well, saying Isabelle needs him. Vincent holds out, and Isabelle is able to send her simulacrum back to Earth, leading Vincent to think the original Isabelle is his again. The book concludes with Anjo born, and the family—including Broximon—safe and sound.

ANALYSIS

As attested to by the numerous essays in this guide relating to the works of Jonathan Carroll, he is one of the quirkiest, most prominent fantasists of this century, seldom repeating himself. That he created this duology makes it rather exceptional in his career.

Novels of the bardo—or afterlife—are a small but vital portion of fantastika. Perhaps they all ultimately derive from Dante's *Inferno*. Will Self's *How the Dead Live*; Tim Powers's *Down and Out In Purgatory*; the *Dante* series by Niven and Pournelle; Damon Knight's *Humpty Dumpty: An Oval*—all are prime examples. Jonathan Carroll's two-book sequence does not follow the precise template of any of these predecessors, but rather fuses life and death into an inseparable unity, with crossings back and forth across the borderline separating the two realms. In a sense, what should be the absolute divergent identities of the living and the dead become mingled, as in a several famous Philip K. Dick (PDK) novels: *Eye in the Sky*, *The Three Stigmata of Palmer Eldritch*, and *Ubik*. Indeed, Carroll's writing evokes a fusion of PKD with the hard-edged whimsy of a John Crowley or Barrington Bayley.

The engine of this saga is love and sex, often rather raw and erotically charged and fully adult, rather unconventionally so for most fantasies, which seem—especially the heroic ones—to rely rather on revenge, ambition, and similar dark emotions. Or, in the case of many urban fantasies, the reliance is on rather juvenile, shallow, and superficial passions. It is only in the rare volume, such as Mark Helprin's *Winter's Tale* and John Crowley's *Little, Big* that the mature carnal bonds between lovers mimic and contour the other forces in the universe. Carroll presents a very powerful portrait of the Don Juan figure—Ettrich—driven to monogamy by powers larger than himself. At times, the parallel with religious devotion is palpable.

Carroll's slippery segues between consensus reality and surreal unreality—what might be seen as phantasmagorical hallucinations in a mimetic novel—work to keep the reader perpetually on his or her toes, as we have to assign various levels of solidity to the absurd happenings. But Carroll's delivery of the action offers just enough hand-holding—never underestimating the intelligence of his audience—that such transitions are generally easy to parse.

The tone of the book, while full of gravitas, does not neglect comedy. The ironic absurdity of many of the events and figures—one's accusing ghostly counterpart is a giant rat named Alan?—reflect Carroll's sly and puckish sense of humor, as do such chapter titles as "Chocolate-Covered God" and "Knee-Deep in Sunday Suits."

Ultimately, *White Apples* and *Glass Soup* serve as a both a radical ontological primer for a New Age and a testament to the immemorial ancient virtues and pitfalls involved in the true marriage of souls, all wrapped up in Monty Python slapstick.

—*Paul Di Filippo*

THE GLIMMERING

A deadly change in Earth's atmosphere dooms the planet to an untimely end, but meanwhile a large cast of eccentric personages will attempt to live, love and redeem themselves

Author: Elizabeth Hand (1957–)
Genre: Fantasy—apocalypse
Type of work: Novel
Time of plot: Near future

Location: New York and Maine
First published: 1997

The Story

The Glimmering is set in a world largely similar to ours but with some crucial differences, chief among them is that, in 1997, scientists seeking to replace environmentally deadly fluorocarbons create an experimental refrigerating and heating agent, bromotoetrachloride (BRITE). The scientists believe they have saved the ozone layer, but disaster begins when an Antarctic avalanche releases into the atmosphere an enormous amount of methane and BRITE. This mixture interacts with a solar flare, with catastrophic results: the ozone layer is shredded, and massive areas of Earth become uninhabitable. Almost overnight, untold numbers die, and social infrastructures, technologies, and societies collapse. In addition, the night skies are now electrically charged and light-emitting, so much so that stars are no longer visible: this is the glimmering.

In 1999, as the new millennium approaches, John Chanvers (i.e., Jack) Finnegan lives in his family home in Yonkers with his nearly 100-year-old Grandmother Keeley and her assistant; he is the owner and publisher of *The Gaudy Book*, a once great periodical, but he is gay and dying of AIDS. Occasionally he visited by his friends Jules and Emma Gardino and Leonard Thrope, the last of whom is also gay and a compulsively irresponsible "sociocultural pathologist," i.e., a chronicler of dying and extinct species. Thrope gives Jack a drug called Fusax, which assists and strengthens him, but when a major multinational corporation—the Golden Families, Incorporated—expresses their interest in purchasing *The Gaudy Book*, Jack accepts.

Later, Jack encounters a pregnant teenager, Marzana, under some bushes. She is the adopted daughter of Nellie Candry and has been connected with young Trip Marlowe, a none-too-intelligent singer with a Christian—here called Xian—Band, who, following a recording session at MIT, has had his life unravel. Thrope created a simulacra of Trip, then tricked Trip into having sex with it, then got Trip addicted to the hallucinogen called IZE. These experiences have so unnerved Trip that he runs away to Maine, where he is cared for by Martin Dionysos, a gay man quietly dying of AIDS and, unbeknownst to him, another friend of Thrope's.

When Trip desires to return to New York to find Marzana, Martin works himself to exhaustion restoring a boat and dies on the journey. Trip makes his way through the ruined city, at whose center is a great golden pyramid owned by the Golden Families, Incorporated; he there encounters Jack and Jules. In the pyramid, Jack learns that a radical environmental group, the Blue Antelopes, want to destroy the zeppelins that the Golden Families will be launching and to work God's will, which means that humanity will become extinct. At a party meant to inaugurate the new millennium, the zeppelins explode, but there is no reunion of Trip and Marzana, for she has died in childbirth. Thus, at the start of the new millennium, the skies erupt, Jack dies, and night and the end of humanity arrive together.

Analysis

Although Elizabeth Hand is probably best known for *Waking the Moon* (1995), *The Glimmering* is the more sophisticated artistic accomplishment, possessing more diverse characterizations, a more ambitious storyline, and a darker and less optimistic conclusion. The global threats thwarted in the earlier novel are embraced in *The Glimmering*, and there are no last minute heroics that culminate in the saving of humanity; indeed, though individuals can and do act humanely and sympathetically, it is too late for them to make changes, as humanity is long past saving and has doomed itself. Hand's apocalyptic road to hell has been created by and paved with good intentions, and the novel is redolent with imagery drawn from T. S. Eliot's *The Waste Land* (1922) as well as from other apocalyptic works of literature. Moreover, the untreatably diseased, doomed, and dying protagonists become metaphors and stand-ins for the equally untreatable diseased, doomed, and dying Earth.

Bleak though Hand's vision is, it should be emphasized that the tone of *The Glimmering* is not despairing, cautionary, or didactic, and one of its great strengths is that Hand eschews preaching and moralizing and relies on description. Thus, even as humanity ails and dies, humans continue to act with as much freedom and ambition as their diminished circumstances permit them. They use drugs, they have sex, they create and perform for one another, and, of course, they are horrible to each other. In addition, they repeatedly misunderstand and misinterpret each other, and they discriminate against and segregate each other, with the most divisive and pernicious form of segregation being that which uses wealth as the divider. Money will not save or extend lives, but as in Poe's "The Masque of the Red Death," the wealthy in *The Glimmering* use their money to act defiantly, irresponsibly, and selfishly and receive their just desserts.

At the same time, despite all of its strengths, *The Glimmering* is determinedly and almost willfully American in its presentation and apparent auctorial biases. The story developed by Hand thus does not significantly embrace or examine peoples and cultures other than those to be found along the East Coast in North America, and while it must be emphasized that this is a perfectly legitimate narrative focus, it must also be observed that the end of the world will affect more than this particular subculture in this particular location. One wishes that Hand's narrative and plotting—already complex and multi-stranded—had found room to include yet a few more strands and a few more plots, these describing the final days of additional peoples from different cultures and in different countries.

—*Richard Bleiler*

GLIMPSES

A stereo repairman who can record the music that he imagines attempts to create famous unfinished albums

Author: Lewis Shiner (1950–)
Genre: Fantasy—inner space
Type of work: Novel
Time of work: 1988–1990
Locale: Primarily Texas and Los Angeles, California
First published: 1993

THE STORY

While in the studio that he uses for his stereo repair business, Ray Shackleford imagines the Beatles recording "The Long and Winding Road." He discovers that he can put the music from his imagination on tape. Ray meets with Los Angeles music producer Graham Hudson and creates another version of the song for him. Graham suggests that Ray try to create *Celebration of the Lizard*, an album on which the Doors were working when lead singer Jim Morrison died.

When Ray imagines a Doors recording session, Morrison is too drunk to perform properly. Ray sobers up Morrison by picturing him killing a pedestrian in a car accident. That slows Morrison's drinking and allows him to record the title cut, then the rest of the album.

Graham asks Ray to work next on *Smile*, a Beach Boys album. Brian Wilson of the Beach Boys envisioned *Smile* as an artistic masterpiece. It was never completed because the other band members thought he should stick with the Beach Boys formula. Ray agrees to create *Smile* when he learns that Wilsons father was never satisfied with his sons work, much like Rays father had never appreciated him.

Ray returns to Los Angeles to do research on Wilson. While there, he thinks often of Alex, his girlfriend before he met his wife-to-be, Elizabeth. He goes to Wilson's house and imagines interacting with Wilson and the Beach Boys. Wilson records the album while Ray is with him. Ray wakes up in the hospital, having been unconscious in his car for several days. He creates the *Smile* album he had helped Wilson record, then goes to Cozumel, Mexico, to find out more about his fathers death during a diving expedition. Elizabeth says that she cannot go with him because of her job; Ray realizes that this is an important signal of the failure of their marriage.

Ray meets Lori, the girlfriend of the dive master in Cozumel, and tells her that making music scares him and that he is not going to do it any more. He attends a pagan ceremony at which he sees an apparition of his father, who appears to care about him. His relationship with Lori grows stronger. When Ray returns to Austin, Elizabeth gets him to admit that their relationship is over. She moves out of their house.

Graham suggests that Ray create Jimi Hendrix's *First Rays of the New Rising Sun*. Ray travels to London to see where Hendrix spent his last days. He tries once to save Hendrix by alerting ambulance attendants to keep him upright so that he does not choke on his own vomit, but the attempt fails. Ray goes back again and manages to avert Hendrix's death, but the next day a teenager shoots Hendrix.

After Ray recovers consciousness from that episode, he recuperates for a few days, but when he runs out of food he decides that it would be easier to meet Hendrix in New York, in his mind, than to drive to the grocery store. He meets Hendrix, who says that he knows it is time for him to go and lets a truck hit him.

Ray finds himself in heaven. He talks to Hendrix, then to Morrison and a man he finds out is the one he had Morrison kill in the car accident. Ray discovers that Brian Wilson also is dead. *Smile* had not been received well and had broken up the Beach Boys, eventually leading to Wilson's death. Finally, Ray talks to his father, who tells him to let go.

Ray wakes up in the hospital and finds out that he had been clinically dead from a heart attack. He calls Lori, who says that she will not come to him until she is ready. He goes to see Alex, who says that they never could have been together because he expected her to live up to an ideal image. Finally, he dates a girlfriend from high school. They break up when she realizes that he is living in the past.

Lori calls to say that she left her boyfriend but does not want to see Ray. A few months later, she sends him a letter, and he goes to the return address on its envelope. Lori resists Ray at first but is drawn to him. They rent a house, and after Ray's mother has a stroke, she comes to live with them.

Analysis

Lewis Shiner does an admirable job of creating Rays world. Ray is a lover of music. Before becoming a stereo repairman, he had been the drummer in a somewhat successful band, and he cares about the creation of music. The first half of *Glimpses* is infused with the spirit of the music of the 1960's, and Shiner draws the reader into Ray's world by providing details of that period and of various performer's lives.

Glimpses, however, is far more about Ray's relationship to his father and to his past than it is about music. Shiner ultimately uses Ray's inner travels in time as a device to get him to consider his past and realize that he cannot change it. Even if he could, there might be disastrous results, such as the premature death of Brian Wilson and of the man Morrison kills with his car.

By creating the "lost albums," Ray brings into existence things that were not meant to be. He tries to do the same in his life, to create a father who shows affection for him and appreciation for what he does, or at least to understand why his father did not show appreciation. When Rays father tells him to let go, he means that Ray should stop trying to change the past.

From the encounter in heaven, Ray's life moves forward quickly. He makes a final break with Elizabeth, then visits former girlfriends and discovers that his relationships with them were what they had to be. Lori is the only thing in his life that is not stale. His new relationship with her shows that he can shed the past and create a new future. He even buys a guitar and plans to write some songs, to create something new.

Glimpses, Shiner's most successful book to that point, won the 1993 World Fantasy Award. His output has varied, including the fantasy of Glimpses, the Magical Realism of *Deserted Cities of the Heart* (1988), and the straightforward science fiction of *Frontera* (1984), his first novel.

—*A. J. Sobczak*

Glory Road

An Everyman character, urged by a beautiful alien queen to become a Hero, saves a universal empire

Author: Robert A. Heinlein (1907-1988)
Genre: Fantasy—heroic fantasy
Type of work: Novel

Time of work: Approximately the 1960s
Locale: Various locations on Earth and alien planets in the Twenty Universes
First published: 1963 (serial form, *The Magazine of Fantasy and Science Fiction*, July-September, 1963)

Glory Road

THE STORY

E. C. Gordon—also known as "Easy," "Scar," and "Oscar"—is a veteran from a military family who narrowly escaped death in combat in Southeast Asia. He now lives frugally on the French Riviera. Answering a personals advertisement in the newspaper, he finds himself faced with Rufo, a short, muscular raconteur, and Star, the most beautiful woman he has ever seen. The advertisement promises great adventure, danger, and reward, and Oscar soon has all these things as he embarks with Star and Rufo, who is now his groom, on a series of adventures aimed at recovering the lost Egg, a repository containing the collected wisdom of hundreds of emperors and empresses of the Twenty Universes.

Oscar, Rufo, and Star battle Igli, a golemlike humanoid, the Horned Ghosts, enormous rats, and scientifically plausible fire-breathing dragons. In more peaceful but no less startling action, they enjoy the hospitality of the Doral, a semimedieval Nevian lord who expects Oscar to sleep with his wife and/or daughters and who must be placated when Oscar does not. Oscar, a superb swordsman, eventually kills the Soul-Eater, guardian of the stolen Egg, who has taken the form of Cyrano de Bergerac. Oscar is wounded seriously in the battle and is nursed to health by Star, who he discovers is the current empress of the Twenty Universes. He has come to love her, and they are married.

As Oscar recovers and basks in the glory of being the one Hero who could have rescued the Egg, he learns about the society of Center, capital of the Twenty Universes. It is an ideal-sounding society in which marriage customs; attitudes toward war, learning, and dispute resolution (Stars main job as empress); and culture are flexible, sensible, and therefore highly advanced.

Oscar is not content merely to be Stars consort. He must have purpose in his life, and as a Hero with his work done, he has no purpose on Center. After beginning a self-selected educational program and attempting to learn various skills, he consults with Rufo, who is actually Stars grandson—Center science has expanded human life spans. He leaves for the time being, not permanently, but realizing, as Star does, that they each have their own purposes, and to fulfill them they cannot be together all the time.

Returning to Earth, wealthy and wiser, Oscar soon discovers that his acquaintances and friends, as well as Earth society, pale against the delights and dangers of the Glory Road he has trod. Returning to France, he places his own personals advertisement. The novel ends with his telling the reader, in great excitement, that he has heard from Rufo and will soon be on the Glory Road again. He asks at the end, "Got any dragons you need killed?"

ANALYSIS

Glory Road is typical of heroic fantasy literature, with the hero called upon to perform impossible tasks. As such, it is part of a literary heritage that stretches from the Greek myths of Hercules; national epics such as the medieval *Chanson de Roland (Song of Roland)*, *Beowulf* (c. 1000), and Pierre Corneille's *El Cid* (1636); and Thomas Malory's *Le Morte d'Arthur* (1485) to such modern tales as William Goldman's *The Princess Bride* (1973). Robert Heinlein's work is unique, however, in that it is told from a first-person narrative point of view by a narrator unashamedly firm in his own beliefs. Rather than affirming a literary form or national self-definition, he demonstrates the affirmation of his own solid brand of commonsensical solutions to problems. Heinlein's hero is critical of the dominant social institutions surrounding him, going as far as asserting that democracy is a quaint but outmoded system.

With such a character as Oscar, *Glory Road* fits firmly within the corpus of Heinlein's work. It contains ample elements of his pragmatic, hard-nosed style of dialogue, as well as strong and superior yet incredibly gorgeous women, the likes of whom appear later in *The Cat Who Walks Through Walls* (1985) and *To Sail Beyond the Sunset* (1987). In addition, there is quite a bit of Heinleins moral-social-political philosophy, common in many of his novels, notably *Starship Troopers* (1959), *Time Enough for Love* (1973), *To Sail Beyond the Sunset,* and *Stranger in a Strange Land* (1961). In many of Heinlein's worlds, and in *Glory Road*'s Twenty Universes, Earth society is falling apart because of its looseness and lack of purpose. What is needed, *Glory Road* implies, is a good absolute monarch.

In Heinlein's work, relationships between men and women and traditional sex roles are stood on end. Marriages and relationships in *Glory Road* are flexible and not entirely monogamous. This also is common in Heinlein's work, as illustrated by Maureen Johnson's life in *To Sail Beyond the Sunset*. Leon Stover's *Robert A. Heinlein* (1987) posits the category of sex and culture criticism for Heinlein's work; *Glory Road* fits this category well. H. Bruce Franklin, in *Robert A. Heinlein: America as Science Fiction* (1980) states that *Glory Road* "says much about America in 1963" and calls the book an "escape from an intolerable world."

Although Heinlein won no major awards for *Glory Road*, he did win the Hugo Award for best novel four times, for *Starship Troopers*, *Double Star* (1956), *Stranger in a Strange Land*, and *The Moon Is a Harsh Mistress* (1966). *Glory Road* is reminiscent enough of these classic science-fiction novels to be counted among Heinlein's better works. It falls in the middle of the productive time in which he won these awards and when his social criticism was strongest.

—Robert Whipple

GLORY SEASON

The coming-of-age story of Maia, a nonclone child born on the planet Stratos, where a feminist colony established millennia ago lives without contact with the rest of humanity

Author: David Brin (1950–)
Genre: Science fiction—utopia
Type of work: Novel
Time of work: The distant future, on another world
Locale: The planet Stratos
First published: 1993

THE STORY

Glory Season, set on the colonized world of Stratos, explores how humans might attempt to create a feminist utopia. Genetic engineering has helped to create a pastoral society of female clones. Parthenogenic reproduction, taking place in Stratoss winter season, produces female clones genetically identical to the birth mother. These genetically identical women form family clans, with the clans that trace back to the founding mothers generally being the largest and most influential. Unfortunately for the Founder's plans, men are needed to "spark" the cloning process, and genetically variant children are also born, in the summer. Half of the summer variants that are born are male, providing a self-perpetuating population. The majority of Stratoin inhabitants are clones, genetically identical to their birth mothers. The entire society has been genetically and socially engineered to reduce female and male interaction.

Maia, the main character, and her twin sister, Leie, are summer variant children five Stratoin years old (the equivalent of fifteen Earth years). They must, as clan tradition dictates, make their own way in the world, leaving their clone family. The two girls hope to capitalize on their twin heritage to find their niche in the world and be able to establish their own clan. Their work and adventures take them on mast rigger sailing ships and over land by foot, wagon, and horseback. Leie is the more defiant and socially aware of the twins; Maia is the more introspective. That proves to be an advantage for Maia as she grows through the tribulations encountered throughout the book.

Stratos faces change because it has been contacted by the rest of humanity. Renna, a male emissary from the Human Phylum, visits Stratos and is kidnapped by a clan hoping to use him for political gain. Through a series of mishaps, Maia loses her sister, Leie, and is thrown into captivity in the same prison as Renna. Unaware that Renna is male, Maia develops forms of communication with him based on her unusual ability to recognize patterns and her non-female-like interest in the computer game called Life. Through their indirect communication, Renna and Maia plan an escape and develop a strong friendship. During their rescue, Maia is perplexed to discover that her friend is actually male and the emissary from the Human Phylum. Maia and Renna repeatedly fall in and out of enemy hands, sometimes not knowing who is friend and who is foe.

Following science-fiction traditions, Maia is exceptional rather than typical of her society. Her ability to recognize and interpret patterns gets her in and out of scrapes throughout the book, providing clues and answers to riddles posed by the loss of historical knowledge by her society. During the course of the story, all the mysteries except one are eventually solved for the reader. David Brin leaves open the question of how reuniting with the rest of humanity will change Stratoin society. Will it grow up as Maia has, or will it stubbornly choose to remain static, pastoral, chauvinist, and isolationist?

Analysis

Mysteries to solve with clues along the way lead the reader through this intriguing rite-of-passage story. Maia's adventures, in a society facing unavoidable change because of an impending reunion with other human worlds, create a tableau for Brin to explore gender stereotypes in both a science-fictional and pastoral setting. One amusing scene illustrating gender stereotypes has all the women worrying about how Renna is going to ride horseback without a sidesaddle to avoid injury.

Renna's reports to his shipboard computer give the reader an analysis of Stratoin society while contrasting a masculine outlook with which the reader may be more familiar to the genetically altered male behavior on Stratos. Renna also provides a love interest for Maia and a conflict point on personal, clan, and societal levels. Renna and Maia both are threatened physically because of other womens physical and emotional desire to possess Renna and because some clans would choose to destroy him because of their fear of the change he represents. Some clans also would use him for political advantage.

Leie, as Maia's twin, acts within the first part of the plot to explain things to Maia and the reader in a natural way. Later, she is used as a substitute Maia so that Maia can be in two places at once.

Brin's explanations of societal development within the world and the settlement are logical and well developed, including the prejudice and problems faced by the nonclone minority. Brin's skill creates a beautiful and diverse world of Stratos, and his characters seem to take on lives of their own. Inspired by biological studies of parthenogenically reproducing lizards and aphids, Brin also acknowledges in his afterword the guidance of Charlotte Perkins Gilmans story *Herland* (1979; serial form, 1914).

Nominated for the 1994 Hugo Award for best novel, *Glory Season* leaves plenty of room for a sequel exploring other aspects of Stratoin society and its potential for change. This book follows *Startide Rising* (1983), winner of the 1984 Hugo Award, Locus Award, and Nebula Award, and *The Uplift War* (1987), winner of the 1988 Hugo Award. Both are part of the Uplift Sequence. Brin won a 1985 Hugo Award for best short story for "The Crystal Spheres" (1984). His previously published work includes seven novels and a collection of short stories. His background for science-fiction writing includes a doctorate in astrophysics and work as a physics professor and consultant to the U.S. space program.

—*B. Diane Miller*

The Godhead Trilogy

God's two-mile-long body falls into the Atlantic Ocean, raising a multitude of questions, from whether he is is really dead to what happens next

Author: James Morrow (1947–)
Genre: Fantasy—magical realism
Type of work: Novel
Time of work: 1992–2025

Location: Earth
First published: *Towing Jehovah* (1994), *Blameless in Abaddon* (1996), and *The Eternal Footman* (1999)

The Story

In *Towing Jehovah*, winner of the prestigious World Fantasy Award, the body of God falls from

Heaven and lands in the Atlantic Ocean. Afterward, the Vatican calls on disgraced oil tanker captain Anthony Van Horne to tow his body to a final resting place in the Arctic. Thomas Ockham, a Jesuit priest interested in cosmology, accompanies Van Horne on the voyage in order to protect the Vatican's interests. Both are searching for something: Keith seeks redemption for his role in the colossal oil spill that decimated Matagorda Bay, and Thomas wishes to discover the answer to the question, "Why did God die?" While they fail to transport God's body in time to preserve his brain activity, they overcome obstacles including Cassie Fowler, a militant atheist who believes the feminist cause is threatened by the body's very existence; a deranged World War II re-enactment society bent on destroying his corpse; and a side trip to a pagan island in order to put God's body—the Corpus Dei— to rest in an iceberg.

Blameless in Abaddon begins as an arctic earthquake reveals God's dead body to the world and the Vatican arranges to hook it up to machines in order to preserve the newly discovered signs of activity in his brain. The Corpus Dei, sold to the Baptists, becomes the main attraction in a religious theme park in Orlando. Martin Candle's visit to the park fails to cure his cancer, his wife dies, and suddenly this contemporary Job decides to put God on trial for crimes against humanity. Presenting testimony ranging from natural disasters to existential evil, Martin hopes to hold God accountable for the pervasive and unending torment visited upon humanity. In the end, the World Court finds God not guilty, and Martin destroys the life-support machines sustaining God's body.

No longer maintained by machines or preserved by ice, the Corpus Dei explodes piece by piece, until only its head remains. God's skull goes into orbit above the Western Hemisphere, and in its shadow a new plague is visited upon humanity. *The Eternal Footman* chronicles the existential sickness, referred to as "death awareness," and explains that victims are visited by a personification of death called a fetch. Confronted by their mortality, most victims succumb to this "abulic plague" by losing their will to live. Nora Burkhart sets out to save her son Kevin from this deadly disease.

ANALYSIS

James Morrow's satirical trilogy presents the premise of the physical death of God with compassion, intellect, and scathing wit. Thomas Ockham, named by Morrow for the scientist who theorized that simple explanations are to be preferred over complex ones, believes that the Heavenly Father killed himself in order to allow humanity to grow up. According to Thomas, "A father's ultimate obligation is to stop being a father." Stifled by mysticism, constrained by a complex yet irrational belief system, people cannot grow and learn as individuals until they are free. "In the post-theistic age, let Christianity become merely kindness, salvation transmute into art, truth defer to knowledge, and faith embrace a vibrant doubt." Morrow dramatizes strong relationships among his characters, particularly among parents and children, and in his trilogy God's death is the ultimate gift of love to his children.

Existential pain takes center stage in *Blameless in Abaddon*, as Martin presents evidence of plane crashes, incurable diseases, murders, and natural disasters in his case against God. Theodicy, reconciling God's goodness with the world's evils, provides an excellent backdrop for the question of God's culpability in the matter of human suffering. Morrow said in an interview that "the harder you try to acquit God of complicity in human suffering, the closer you come to trivializing that suffering." In *The Eternal Footman*, Morrow observes that fear of death prevents people from living life to the fullest. In a world without God influencing people's behavior, the next step in realizing humanity's potential is addressing the paralyzing obsession with mortality. Kevin's fetch explains: "The invention of death made possible the individual, in all its astonishing variety. Death broke life free of immortality's chains."

—*Michael-Anne Rubenstien*

THE GODS THEMSELVES

Side effects from a method of drawing seemingly endless energy from a parallel universe threaten to blow up the Sun; the problem is resolved by sending undesired by-products to a third universe

Author: Isaac Asimov
  (1902-1992)
Genre: Science fiction—technocratic
Type of work: Novel
Time of work: The late twenty-first century and the early twenty-second century
Locale: Earth, the Moon, and a parallel universe
First published: 1972 (portions published in *Galaxy*, March and May, 1972, and *If*, April, 1972)

The Story

Frederick Hallam, a scientist, discovers a substance, plutonium-186, that should not exist under the physical laws in the universe. It becomes more radioactive over time, shooting out positrons. This substance is transmitted to Earth from a para-universe in which physical laws are much different. This substance provides cheap, seemingly endless, and non-polluting energy. Increasing amounts of it can be attracted by use of a device called the Inter-Universe Electron Pump. In exchange for plutonium-186, Earth provides tungsten; in the para-universe, tungsten emits electrons and thus provides energy.

The first section, "Against Stupidity," details the Pump's discovery from the point of view of Peter Lamont, who is writing a history of this scientific development. He decides that the Pump may transfer some of the physical laws of the para-universe to Earth's universe (and vice versa), with the result that nuclear reactions in the Sun will grow stronger and the Sun will turn into a nova, wiping out all life on Earth. At the same time, suns in the para-universe will cool down.

Lamont warns about the possible dangers, but his warnings are paid little heed. He attempts to communicate with the para-universe aliens, aided by linguistic expert Myron Bronowski. Ultimately, they succeed, receiving a message that appears to warn that the Pump is dangerous but also appearing to suggest that authorities in the para-universe will not stop the process. It is up to humanity to do so.

In the second section, ". . . The Gods Themselves," locale shifts to the para-universe. The inhabitants include three types of alien children with different characteristics: Rationals, Parentals, and Emotionals. The Parentals give birth to the other two types, and one of each of the three types constitute a triad who occasionally melt together in a sexual process, experiencing pleasure but later not remembering all that took place during merger.

There are also Hard Ones, other aliens who do not melt. A Hard One is the adult form of a Rational-Parental-Emotional triad, constituting a permanent melding of the mature triad. A Hard One named Estwald began the energy interchange with Earth's universe because of a winding down of the energy sources in theirs. The Hard Ones know that this may cause Earth's sun to explode, but they still will not stop the process because that explosion would result in emission of a huge source of energy for them. An Emotional (Dua) is troubled by this and warns the people of Earth's universe of the dangers of the Pump. It is then revealed that Dua is part of the triad that makes up Estwald.

In the third section, ". . . Contend in Vain?," Benjamin Allan Denison, a scientist and past colleague of Hallam, becomes involved with a female Lunar tour guide named Selene. The Moons inhabitants have been unable to use the Pump there, but they wish to as a means of becoming more independent from Earth. Denison confirms that the Pump is a danger to the Sun's stability but suggests that if there are two parallel universes, there must be more. A method is developed of entering into an exchange with a cosmeg, or cosmic egg universe, while conducting the exchange with the para-universe, so that the effects will balance out, avoiding the danger of solar explosion. In the books conclusion, Selene asks Denison if he will father her (recently authorized) second son by artificial insemination.

Analysis

This novel, which won both the 1973 Hugo and 1972 Nebula awards for best science-fiction novel of the year, is notable for Isaac Asimov's believable and yet utterly alien aliens. He had not previously attempted creation of an alien world on this scale. Asimov manages the difficult feat, in the novels second section, of portraying an alien civilization from the perspective of the aliens themselves. The third portion of the novel, in addition to furthering and completing the plot, contains a short but well thought-out portrayal of Lunar society, including extrapolation of cultural and sexual mores that would likely come into being in an enclosed, low-gravity environment.

The novel is also a fascinating fictional commentary on the process of scientific inspiration and discovery from an author who had first-hand personal experience inthe field. Asimov approaches satire in his description of Hallams petty and jealous reaction to questioning about the possible dangers from his discovery, as well as to suggestions that it was the para-men of the para-universe who really discovered the principles of the Electron Pump. In all three societies that Asimov portrays, authority figures with narrow self-interest utmost in their minds serve as obstacles to the resolution of important problems.

The book reflects the belief, expressed in much of classic science fiction, that rational application of scientific technique and the scientific method can surmount all obstacles and serve human progress. An inventive technological solution is found for the trans-universe environmental dilemma posed by the quest for cheap bountiful energy.

The Gods Themselves represented a welcome end, for science-fiction fans, to Asimov's hiatus in writing novel-length science fiction, a pause that lasted from 1958 (when he published the juvenile novel *Lucky Starr and the Rings of Saturn* under the pen name Paul French) until 1972, unbroken except for the minor work *Fantastic Voyage* (1966), which was a novelization of the film of the same title. Although *The Gods Themselves* may not be the work for which Asimov is ultimately most remembered (the Foundation series and his robot stories undoubtedly vying for that honor), there is room for argument that this short (288 pages) gem of a novel is his most polished literary work. It is his only book that is a true singleton, unrelated to other works.

—*Bernard J. Farber*

Golden Witchbreed

Lynne de Lisle Christie, envoy for a loose confederation of planets known as the Dominion, tries to learn about the society of Orthe as she evaluates that planet for possible trade relations and membership in the Dominion

Author: Mary Gentle (1956–)
Genre: Science fiction—alien civilization
Type of work: Novel
Time of work: Indeterminate future
Locale: The planet Orthe
First published: 1983

The Story

In Mary Gentle's *Golden Witchbreed* (1983), Lynne de Lisle Christie is an empath hired by the Extra Terrestrial department of her government as an envoy to introduce her society to that of an undeveloped planet called Orthe. She experiences at first hand the mixture of curiosity and distrust evinced by the natives and shares in their complex, feudal culture.

When T'An Suthai Telestre (also known as Suthafiori, the flower of the South), the Crown of the Southlands of Orthe, requests that she tour the countryside, visiting the Hundred Thousand households composing the populace, she discovers the deep hatred that some Ortheans bear for the technological advances of the Dominion. She survives numerous assassination attempts against her as well as a murder contract intended to discredit her. The Ortheans apparently associate her and her kind with a long-dead race of technologically advanced aliens, the Golden Witchbreed, who held the Ortheans in slavery until an infertility virus destroyed their race. Caught in a civilization she longs to understand but cannot trust, Christie struggles to redefine her perceptions in line with the Orthean point of view.

Close friends such as Talmar Haltern n're n'suth Beth'ru-elen, Achil Maric Salathiel, and amari Ruric Orhlandis seem to accept her humanness with equanimity, although the physical differences between humans and Ortheans are striking. Close encounters with the fenborn, a swamp-dwelling native of Orthe, the northern barbarians, and the Kel Harantish (the last remnant of the Golden Witchbreed overlords) present the wide scope of Orthean existence but never seem to answer the basic question that underlies all of Christie's adventures: Are they like us? Even Christie's native lover, Sethin Falkyr Talkul, does not attempt to bridge the wide chasm that separates the two societies. It is only an exchange of memories with the oldest living Orthean, the Hexenmeister, that breaks through Christie's expectations of what is normal and what is human.

Her expectation of being protected and cherished by her lover Falkyr is dashed when he chooses to support his treacherous uncle rather than help her escape when she isimprisoned by the feudal lord of Roehmonde, Verek Howice Falkul. She is falsely accused of being one of theoverlords, the Golden Witchbreed, but Falkyr cares less for the truth than for retaining his loyalties to the telestre. Her expectation of loyalty among friends is removed when Ruric, commander of Suthafioris army, implicates Christie in the murder of another lord, Kanta Andrethe.

By the time Christie's term of service ends, she has not come any closer to a concise understanding of who the Ortheans are. She has only a handful of memories and the knowledge of how to play ochmir, a native game that emphasizes relationships and influences among groups of people.

Analysis

Mary Gentle's *Golden Witchbreed* is likely to remind readers of Ursula K. Le Guin's Gethen from *The Left Hand of Darkness* (1969). Lynne de Lisle Christie's journey across the barren wastes of Orthe is less a voyage of discovery than an attempt at gaining contact with an alien culture. Like Le Guins character Genly Ai, Christie is an empath who cannot quite reconcile the emotional similarities she shares with her hosts and the stark differences of loyalties. Christie is betrayed by her lover Falkyr and her friend Ruric because she assumes that Terran standards apply to Orthean society. The isolation of the alien, in this case a human being, has been a standard element of science fiction since its birth as a genre.

Golden Witchbreed also tends to resemble Le Guin's *The Left Hand of Darkness* in its treatment of gender. As they were for Le Guin's Gethenians, sexual differences between Orthean males and females are played down to the point of insignificance. Gethenians are neuter until they join into mating pairs; because partners do not know what sex they will become during the mating ritual, neither can assume gender roles. A stereotyped image of sexual roles is a perversion of the natural order to the Gethenians.

Gentle has established much the same situation for Orthe. Children, called ashiren, are born without a gender and do not acquire one until puberty, when they have the possibility of becoming either male or female. Although they retain their pubescent gender throughout adulthood, gender roles seem distant; a female general commands the army of a female monarch, and the language allows for a third pronoun (ke/kir) to represent children, animals, and the Goddess the Ortheans worship.

The Orthean's distrust of technology sets *Golden Witchbreed* apart from Le Guin's work. The late establishment in the novel of Orthe as a post-apocalyptic society brings some understanding of the cultures rejection of technology in favor of an almost prehistoric goddess worship. Like the Eloi and Morlock society in H. G. Wells's *The Time Machine* (1895), the native society has been formed by the misuse of technology in the past.

Along with its sequel, *Ancient Light* (1987), Gentle's work shows the influence of Ray Bradbury and Robert A. Heinlein in its depiction of the fathomless depth of an alien psyche. Although not strictly a "first contact" novel, *Golden Witchbreed* presents the first tenuous friendships being formed between societies radically opposed in both values and customs. The telestres, feudal households that are based on family ties, command the highest loyalty from their members; even a person's longtime lover must be adopted into that persons telestre before he or she will be accepted as one of the group. Themetaphorical base for the society, the game called ochmir, emphasizes the power of the group over the individual.

—*Julia Meyers*

The Golem

Athanasius Pernath encounters terror on his spiritual quest in Prague's ghetto, home of the legendary golem

Author: Gustav Meyrink (1868-1932)
Genre: Fantasy—theological romance
Type of work: Novel
Time of work: 1890
Locale: Prague
First published: *Der Golem* (1915; serial form, 1913-1914; English translation, 1928)

The Story

Gustav Meyrink probably began work on *The Golem* in 1906. Almost seven years later, Meyrink and a friend plotted the characters and action diagrammatically and eliminated about half the material. The novel was published serially in the periodical *Die weissen Blätter* in 1913 and 1914.

Narrated in the first person, the novel opens with a nightmare. The dreamer is identified as Athanasius Pernath, a gem engraver and restorer of old manuscripts who lives in the Prague ghetto. Pernath is unable to recall his early life because of an amnesia hypnotically induced during therapy for a breakdown. Amnesia goads him to seek redemptive enlightenment. His quest begins when he agrees to repair an unusual old book for an even more unusual stranger, later revealed as the golem. Pernath begins seeing underlying connections between things, as confirmed in dreams, visions, and conversations with Hillel, a saintly cabalist. Pernath finds himself increasingly attracted to Hillel's equally spiritual daughter, Miriam.

A subplot involves an affair taking place in a room next to Pernath's. Pernath becomes infatuated with the woman in the affair, a flirtatious aristocrat named Angelina, and endeavors to preserve her secret. In another subplot, a tubercular, impoverished medical student, Charousek, plots revenge against his natural father, the conniving junk dealer Aaron Wasserstrum. The subplots interrelate, as Wasserstrum schemes to reveal Angelina's affair with Dr. Savoli, who, guided by Charousek, exposed the unethical medical practices of Wasserstrum's legitimate son.

After discovering that Pernath is hiding Angelina's letters to Savoli, Wasserstrum has him falsely charged with murder. Sharing Pernath's prison cell is a confessed rapist-murder and somnambulist, Amadeus Laponder. Laponder elucidates a vision in which a phantom offers Pernath seven seeds, signifying magical powers. Instead of accepting or rejecting them, Pernath knocks them out of the phantom's hand. Laponder is impressed with Pernath's refusal to accept the imposed choice; similarly visited, Laponder accepted the seeds and was compelled to follow the path of death.

Laponder is, then, a kind of "double" of Pernath. Pernath also meets his double in the ghetto's legendary golem. This creature of clay, formed centuries earlier by the righteous Rabbi Loew, is rumored to manifest itself periodically. The apparition is alternatively the collective spirit of the ghetto and a person's "shadow" in the Jungian sense, confronted at stages of psychic growth. Pernath imagines himself as the golem during another visionary experience, when he finds himself in the doorless room the golem supposedly inhabits. To keep warm, he bundles himself in what are, apparently, the golem's discarded clothes.

Through Charousek's efforts, Pernath is released from prison. Returning to the ghetto, he finds it being torn down. He searches for Hillel and Miriam. As he climbs down a rope to escape from a burning building, he believes he glimpses them in the golem's room. Suddenly, the rope breaks, and he falls. At this point, the reader discovers that what has transpired was dreamed by another man, who now awakes. His dream resulted from his mistakenly wearing Pernath's hat. This unnamed narrator learns that the events of his dream took place about forty years previously. He eventually finds an ageless Pernath and Miriam living in a mysterious house familiar from his dream. The house appears to be a kind of temple. A golemlike servant administers the exchange of hats and communicates Pernath's hope that his hat did not give its bearer any headaches.

Analysis

The Golem was the first of Meyrink's novels chronicling mystical and occult adventures. It sold more than 200,000 copies, turning Meyrink into a best-selling author. His next two novels, *Das grüne Gesicht* (1916; The Green Face, 1992) and *Walpurgisnacht* (1917), similarly take place in worlds that are collapsing, perhaps better to highlight their theme of spiritual upheaval. These novels, too, are enlivened by satire. Meyrink had first received notice—and notoriety—as a writer of short stories lampooning the police, the military, and other bourgeois institutions.

The iconography of Meyrink's next two novels, *Der weisse Dominikaner* (1921) and *Der Engle vom westlichen Fenster* (1927; *The Angel of the West Window*, 1991), became increasingly more personal and less accessible. Meyrink progressively abandoned the external story to concentrate on the idea of psychic evolution. Meyrink used fantasy in his earlier short stories mainly for purposes of social satire or literary parody. His later stories, such as those in *Fledermäuse* (1916), are purely devoted to symbolism and allegory.

These stories, together with his novels, bear out Meyrink's claim that he wrote not by the rules of art but by the rules of magic. His esoteric references and nightmarish atmospherics display an arbitrary logic. Meyrink, who had been a member of the inner circle of Annie Besants Adyar Theosophical Society, developed an independent philosophy synthesizing his studies in Christian and Jewish mysticism, Eastern practices, and branches of the occult including tarot, alchemy, and spiritualism. Meyrink is idiosyncratic in another sense: The same German mystical and romantic tradition that infused his antimilitary, antirationalistic, and antitotalitarian work prompted, according to some historians, the rise of Nazism.

Critics generally classify Meyrink's work within expressionism. Expressionist literature and, more familiarly, art and cinema developed in post–World War I Austria and Germany. Expressionism is characterized by antirationalism, a conscious distortion of external appearances, and extreme states of mind. It is evident in the prose of Franz Kafka, a contemporary of Meyrink with whom he is sometimes compared, although Kafka, unlike Meyrink, rarely indulged in melodrama. Critics see in Meyrink's writing traces of the grotesque that mark Charles Dickens' novels, which Meyrink translated into German. Others link Meyrink with the macabre stories of Ambrose Bierce and Edgar Allan Poe and the sinister, fantastic tales of E. T. A. Hoffmann.

Meyrink and Hoffmann both drew on the *Doppelgänger*, or double, motif from German folklore. Meyrink additionally culled from alchemy's traditions of the homunculus, or artificially created human. Mary Wollstonecraft Shelley refers to such experiments in her introduction to *Frankenstein* (1818). A related phenomenon is the golem of Jewish legend. A clay figure mobilized to serve its creator, it develops dangerous powers and must be reduced back to dust. This creature" inspiring poetry, plays, films, and even a Marvel comics "Strange Tales" series—is related only loosely to the golem of the novel.

—*Amy Adelstein*

THE GOLEM AND THE JINNI

Two supernatural beings—a female golem, an artificial woman, and a jinni, a supernatural elemental from the Middle East—both make the journey to Victorian America, where they manage to construct lives in New York City while masquerading as humans, before meeting and falling in love

Author: Helene Wecker (?–)
Genre: Fantasy—magical realism
Type of Work: Novel
Time of Plot: Late-nineteenth, early–twentieth century

Location: USA
First Published: 2013

THE STORY

We begin with two separate narrative strands—vastly intriguing on their individual merits—that meet about a third of the way through the book, tangling in unforeseeable yet resonantly inevitable ways.

First, the golem's tale.

In Prussia, a lonely and lazy bachelor, Rotfeld, pays a large sum to a dissolute Kabbalist magician,

Yehudah Schaalman, to construct a golem that will serve Rotfeld as wife. Setting out for a fresh start in America, Rotfeld, tempted while en route, awakens his crated bride, who, thanks to subsequent circumstances, reaches the New World alone, friendless, naïve, and helpless. In New York, she finds a kindly mentor, the lonely Rabbi Meyer, and receives her name: Chava. Her existence becomes a somewhat tortured labyrinth, not totally without bright spots, wherein she must learn her own nature, human nature, and the uneasy accommodations between those realms. Luckily, she is able to be employed in the bakery of Moe Radzin, where she discovers close up the loves and hatreds of humanity.

At the same time, we meet Boutrous Arbeely, already resident in the city, where he makes a living as a poor tinsmith among the immigrants of Little Syria. One day, Arbeely takes up the chore of fixing an antediluvian copper jug. He effaces an engraved symbol on its surface and is rewarded with the manifestation of a jinni. But Ahmad the jinni, as he will be christened, is a spirit still constrained in human form by the remnants of his binding spells. He retains very few of his innate occult powers save for some above-average physicality and the ability to melt and shape metals, part and parcel of his magma-like constitution. With a deep, significant past (he had lived two hundred years prior to imprisonment) and a disdain for humans, Ahmad must chart his own uneasy path analogous to Chava's. Thankfully, the ghetto of Little Syria and the jinni's metalworking talents offer a refuge.

When the two inhumans eventually meet, their differences will alternately war with and complement their similarities, as they move, two unique elemental creatures, through Victorian New York.

> "What are you?" he asked.... "You're not human. You're made of earth."
> At last she spoke. "And you're made of fire," she said.

Ancient karma from Ahmad's past will eventually enwrap them in mingled tragedy and triumph. Mixed into the chaos will be the presence of the evil Yehudah Schaalman, Chava's creator, now known as Joseph Schall, who is also in New York and on her trail.

ANALYSIS

Very few debut novels exhibit the charm, assurance, emotional depth, and bravura fabulation that the lucky reader will discover in Helene Wecker's *The Golem and the Jinni*. Like some agreeable conflation of Isaac Bashevis Singer, Mark Helprin, and the anonymous compiler of *One Thousand and One Nights*, Wecker delivers an ambitious yet gracefully humble novel featuring the best of classic European and Middle Eastern fancies, reimagined and re-embedded in a vivid New World milieu, at once numinously odd and groundedly naturalistic. The result is utterly unique and enchanting. Perhaps the famous debut of Susanna Clarke, *Jonathan Strange & Mr Norrell*, might be the last occasion for such rejoicing at a new voice in the genre and beyond.

Wecker's triumphs in this book are manifold, and it's difficult to know where to begin to array them.

First off, on the sheerest surface level, the book can be read like a fine historical romance. The immigrant communities and the plights of all new citizens; the ambiance of Victorian Manhattan; blooming and dying love affairs and businesses; aspirations and fears—all these regular constituents of such books are vividly deployed in a very satisfying manner. And because Chava and Ahmad must live, against their natures, in a mimicking human manner, the reader can, if one so desires, almost forget their supernatural birthrights. And a large supporting cast of colorfully limned real humans, several of whom play important roles in the plot, conduces to this naturalistic reading.

But, of course, the woman of clay and man of fire are too essentially supernatural for this mental trick of interpretation to last long or matter at all. I use it only to highlight the solid realistic underpinnings of the tale. Wecker's main job, expertly done, has been to inhabit the outré minds of Chava and Ahmad so intensely, with the plot hinging so centrally on their fantastical souls, that readers will be eagerly anticipating the revelation of all uncanny facets of their characters. There are many great set-pieces here in which the two human-like creatures perform wonders and horrors.

Wecker is very careful not to ennoble or diminish the essential integrity and quirkiness of Ahmad and Chava. They emerge as blends of goodness and selfishness, wisdom and blindness. That said, each one represents a certain iconic stance, and Wecker plays off this antithesis brilliantly. Chava is angelic and Ahmad demonic. She is giving and loving, he is self-centered and dismissive. She is humble, and he's a braggart. She deals with organic things, he with inanimate. She's northern, he's southern. And yet, despite their "owl and the pussycat" relationship, they find common ground in many things, not the least being artistry and passion. We believe in both the sparks and the sympathies that arise between them.

Any aficionado of fantasy fiction will find many striking tropes sophisticatedly alluded to by Wecker. In a sense, Chava is the Cowardly Lion, looking for courage, unknowing of her own strength; while Ahmad is the Tin Man—literally!—looking for a heart. Echoes of Faust arise in the relationship between Ahmad and Arbeely. Yehudah Schaalman's arrival in New York strikes notes of both Nosferatu and the Wandering Jew. Chava's eventual New World marriage to human Michael Levy recalls fairy tales about husbands whose happiness relies on never questioning their odd bride. And so forth, for a density of imaginative affect.

Wecker's longish novel allows itself the leisure to really build its story, but she pulls out all the stops in the climax, which I would gauge to be the entire final hundred pages! Everything simultaneously falls apart and blows up for Ahmad and Chava, in roughly one suspenseful day or so. Wecker's guiding hand never falters for a moment, and the coda is superbly rewarding, for us and the characters.

Wecker's subsequent books cannot be less than masterful.

—*Paul Di Filippo*

Good News from Outer Space

When two tabloid journalists investigate an alien invasion and a televangelist who preaches the advent of a New Age, they find themselves involved in a bizarre series of interconnected events

Author: John Kessel (1950–)
Genre: Science fiction—invasion story
Type of work: Novel
Time of work: 1999, with a scene in April, 2000
Location: The United States
First published: 1989

The Story

Three chapters of *Good News from Outer Space* were published independently as short stories in 1987 and 1988, but they were rewritten extensively and now contribute to the novel's intricate plot, a satire about religion, politics, and the mass media in 1990's America. The main characters are Lucy, a lawyer; her husband George, a reporter at a tabloid news television program; and Richard, George's editor. Lucy is the most sympathetic character, though George learns kindness and consideration, and Richard's manic personality has its own appeal.

George becomes interested in two sinister developments: the increasing popularity of televangelist Jimmy-Don Gilray and a growing mass hysteria that malicious aliens have invaded the country. He grows obsessed with the latter reports and even abandons Lucy to track down the aliens.

Lucy naturally is upset, and when Richard visits her, showing no concern for George but demanding to know what story he is pursuing, she recklessly attacks him. She then hides from the law by taking refuge with some feminist bioterrorists who plan to spread a plague that will make men mentally and emotionally more like women. Richard, always reckless himself, decides to scoop George's televangelism article by becoming a publicist for the Reverend Gilray. Gilray rightfully suspects Richard of being a spy but is intrigued enough to hire him. Ironically and amusingly, Richard himself becomes such a superstar in his new role that the televangelist proclaims Richard to be a prophet.

George's travels across the country reveal that humanlike aliens are spreading fear and dismay with their bizarre behavior, yet they always elude him. He decides that Gilray is allied with the aliens and decides to assassinate him. Returning to Raleigh, North Carolina, the site of Gilray's headquarters, he finds millions of pilgrims there. Starving and desperate, these believers wait for Gilray's promised event—the appearance of Jesus Christ in a spaceship on the eve of the millennium. During these activities, Lucy is arrested and imprisoned. She escapes, only to be captured by Gilray, who declares her as his destined bride for the New Age. In a brief and bitter meeting with George, she orders him to undertake a mysterious mission. The item he secretly brings to her contains the bioterrorists' potion to feminize men.

When December 31, 1999, arrives, aliens infiltrate Gilray's headquarters, bewildering everyone by appearing as the different main characters. Gilray meets one disguised as Lucy, is frightened when it tries to seduce him, and flees. Lucy meets an alien appearing as Gilray and tries to persuade it to drink the potion, mixed into a glass of wine, but it knows better. When George leaps out of a closet to surprise them, he accidentally shoots her. At this point the alien offers to tell George all the answers he has dreamed of finding and has pursued for so long, but George chooses to ignore the alien so that he can save Lucy's life. In his relief, afterward, he drinks the doctored wine. Meanwhile, Richard and Gilray abandon their desperate followers, who realize that there will be no Second Coming.

After the unfolding of this madcap climax, the final chapter, set the following spring, reveals that although America has been shaken by Gilray's reign and revolt, some normality is restored. George acts more tenderly toward Lucy. They renew their love and turn to raising their own food. Perhaps the aliens are still on the loose, but friendship and honesty matter more, in the end, than the mystery of alien deceptions.

ANALYSIS

John Kessel has a gift for comic invention. The humor, mysteries, and chills of the story begin on the first page. When George is introduced, readers realize that the novel will be darkly whimsical because the reporter, like the subject of a typical tabloid tale, recently has been revived from the dead. Through his minor characters and scenes of an unraveling culture, Kessel targets the ignorance and sloth underlying the popularity of tabloid journalism in modern America. The success of Gilray's preachings and the demoniac magnetism of Richard's charisma reveal Kessel's distaste for the fear mongering and greed of televangelism.

Kessel's satirical tone is effectively funny and grim, and his novel takes potshots at everything from the social conditions of modern America to earlier science fiction. The alien invasion suggests a number of familiar plots, beginning with H. G. Wells's *The War of the Worlds* (1898) and including Arthur C. Clarke's *Childhood's End* (1953) and Jack Finney's *The Body Snatchers* (1955), but Kessel coyly declines to explain the motive behind the invasion, unlike these classic texts. The invasion story by its nature conveys and expresses paranoia, which Kessel increases by portraying aliens who deceive, frighten, and abuse ordinary Americans for no apparent reasons other than curiosity and *Schadenfreude*, the joy in others' misfortunes. This disinclination to explain everything operates throughout the novel; for example, has George actually been "feminized," or has he learned to value his wife's love?

Science fiction traditionally presents a problem that humans solve, in the process becoming more enlightened and heroic. Kessel alludes to recent paradigms such as quantum theory, which reveal the search for complete knowledge to be in vain, even as he casts doubt on many recent human endeavors. The traditional figure of the noble private investigator who discovers inner truths is likewise parodied when Richard, wondering where George has gone, puts a detective on his tail. The comedy of errors becomes horrific when readers realize that the detective is a crazy paranoiac who thinks she has been commissioned to assassinate George. Her mission contributes to the humor and suspense. *Good News from Outer Space* was nominated for the Nebula Award and the John W. Campbell Memorial Award. It has been translated into several languages.

—*Fiona Kelleghan*

Gravity's Rainbow

Paranoia increases and apocalypse nears as characters seek the source of a rocket during World War II

Author: Thomas Pynchon (1937–)
Genre: Science fiction—alternate history
Type of work: Novel
Time of work: 1944–1945
Location: Europe
First published: 1973

The Story

Although *Gravity's Rainbow* is often considered a culmination of his earlier novel, *The Crying of Lot 49* (1966), Thomas Pynchon created his magnum opus with this book. It is particularly difficult to categorize a work of this scope in any specific genre because it has been called revisionist history, apocalyptic, picaresque, a Grail quest, satire, social criticism, Magical Realism, and encyclopedic narrative, among others. It does, however, fall under the broad parameters of science fiction given its preoccupation with machinery—the fact that the rocket becomes the protagonist of the work and that the multiple technological crises presented overshadow or eliminate human emotions and human worth. Although it was nominated for a Pulitzer Prize, and many critics believed it was the best novel of that or any year, the committee rejected the book as being "obscure and obscene."

With a circuitous romp through subplots, minor characters who appear and disappear without warning, technological and mathematical jargon, and world-class wordplay, Pynchon introduces the reader to a revised history of the latter days of World War II in Europe. In fact, not until at least one-third of the way into this massive tome does it become evident that the protagonist is Tyrone Slothrop, an American who has been assigned to the experimental whims of Pavlovian scientists who are attempting to prove a correlation between Slothrop's sexual encounters and the striking zone of the German A-4 rocket.

Paranoia is an integral part of Slothrop's personality, and he grows increasingly more paranoid as the experiments intensify and threaten imminent bodily harm. He is permitted a holiday, although it is under supervision. While staying at a resort in the south of France, where he has a strange encounter with his "supervisor," Katje Borgesius, and a trained octopus, Slothrop realizes that he can never outwit surveillance by The Firm until he physically escapes. He runs for his life and vanishes into the Zone, the interior of war-torn, mainland Europe. It is his naïve assumption that if he can locate the source of the rocket and the mysterious propellant, S-Gerat, he can purchase his freedom with the information.

In picaresque fashion, Slothrop slides into and out of life-threatening situations while encountering scores of rogues, renegades, and reprobates. Because of his proclivity for each, the encounters involve sexual antics, drug deals, hallucinations, disguises, extraordinary heroics, and increasing paranoia.

While in the Zone and using changes in identity and costume, Slothrop is forced to live by his wits, surviving off the land and the kindness of strangers—usually female. With a false identification card, he slips across border checkpoints as the actor Max Schlepzig; he cohabits in a bombed-out building with an apprentice witch, Geli Tripping; he escapes his pursuers in a cream-pie-laden hot-air balloon; he stows away on an orgiastic ship of fools going nowhere; he dons a cape and a Viking helmet to become Rocketman and smuggles hashish out of the occupied Zone; and he accepts the role of Liberator Pig God in an ancient village ritual and escapes in the pig's costume. Appropriately, he spends the majority of his time as Rocketman, the merger of the rocket and the man, and as the pig, having started his peripatetic quest as a guinea pig.

Eventually, through the multiple changes in identity, Slothrop loses his own, as well as any interest in pursuit of the rocket. As with many of the minor characters, he simply vanishes from the novel's pages, and the reader is left to fill in the blanks. The story does not end there, however, for others also seek the rocket and the propellant. Only one man has the answers as well as the rocket: Captain Blicero knows that the mysterious propellant, S-Gerat, is really a human being. He methodically places his lover on board the rocket, begins the countdown, and incinerates himself in the afterburn.

ANALYSIS

It is virtually impossible to treat the scope of this novel in a short summary. The book should be read slowly, considered, digested, and then read again. As with any work of this magnitude, critical reception has been polarized: One either loves the book or hates it, but few claim to understand it completely. The parameters of Pynchon's knowledge are seemingly boundless and often beyond the grasp of the average reader, but that should not deter the effort. Whether one understands the book completely or not, it is a labyrinth of literary surprises, offering something for everyone who reads it.

Gravity's Rainbow juxtaposes the apocalyptic and the comic. Because the reader knows the time frame and the historical outcome of World War II, he or she should also be aware that the work is fiction. Because of Pynchon's attention to historical detail and his use of real names throughout the work, the reader cannot help but question the truth of the extant version of history. Although it is apocalyptic in tone, the work predicts not the destruction of the world but the destruction and subsequent rebuilding of culture by revealing how human and machine essentially have become one and how the machine has gained preeminence. Although it addresses such issues as war, genocide, mental illness, and sexual depravity, *Gravity's Rainbow* is not entirely pessimistic, for Pynchon admits glimmers of a brighter tomorrow.

An underlying theme present in this work and others by Pynchon is entropy, the theory that the world is winding down and depleting its own energy. Entropy, based on Isaac Newton's second law of thermodynamics, is best represented by Slothrop, who is too lazy to maintain his self-appointed quest and too prone to distraction to notice the obvious clues that are strewn in his path. For Slothrop, seeking information is entirely too much trouble.

Whether one accepts Pynchon's premise or understands his encyclopedic scope is irrelevant. *Gravity's Rainbow* should be devoured like the literary smorgasbord it is.

—*Joyce Duncan*

GRAY MATTERS

Cerebromorphs, disembodied human brains kept alive by an elaborate robotic system, strive to attain a higher order of consciousness and receive a perfect body

Author: William Hjortsberg (1941–)
Genre: Science fiction—technocratic
Type of work: Novel
Time of work: The late twenty-fourth century
Locale: A cerebromorph depository and various places on Earth
First published: 1971

THE STORY

There are three main plot lines in *Gray Matters*. William Hjortsberg shifts among these plot lines, which at times intersect. Each of the main characters in the story begins as a cerebromorph, a disembodied brain hooked up to an elaborate system of life support and memory banks. Denton "Skeets" Kalbfleischer was a twelve-year-old boy severely injured in an airplane crash. He became the first candidate for a cerebrectomy, a process by which the brain is removed from the body to be placed in a depository. Vera Mitlovic was a famous film actress who murdered her rich, abusive husband with a shotgun. She used her wealth to preserve her youth. Eventually, she had so many artificial body parts that she volunteered to become a cerebromorph. Obu Itubi was an African sculptor. He became a cerebromorph during the Awakening, a time when the World Council voted to control world population growth and pollution by making everyone a cerebromorph.

The cerebromorphs are organized on different levels in a depository, according to their level of consciousness. Skeets, Vera, and Obu are all on the lowest level. Cerebromorphs advance from one level to the next through obedience, concentration, and meditation. Those who achieve the highest level are placed in perfected human bodies grown in the "hatchery" and are free to go into the outside world. The conscious and unconscious thoughts of cerebromorphs are monitored by auditors, who also advance according to how well they perform their duties.

Philip Quarrels, a combat pilot and astronaut, is Skeets's auditor. He became a cerebromorph to participate in long-range space travel. Skeets has been on his level for more than four hundred years, and the Central Control hopes that he will be the first to advance from that level. His adolescent mind, however, prevents him from achieving the necessary focus. Quarrels arranges a memory merge between Skeets and Vera in order to help Skeets advance beyond his adolescent preoccupation with sex.

While Vera and Skeets are merging, Obu tricks a maintenance robot into taking him on board and escapes from the depository, causing all kinds of destruction on his way. This destruction sends a power surge through the system, obliterating Skeets's brain and isolating Vera from her auditors. Her consciousness spends its time on a beautiful island, free from the demands of the depository system. She is visited frequently by Quarrels' consciousness, and they engage in passionate sexual relations. When he threatens to leave her, she shoots him with a shotgun, mysteriously killing his actual brain as well as the image projected by his consciousness.

Obu is discovered on the outside by a group of humans, who place his brain in a body. Obu eventually impregnates Oona, a woman who somehow avoided the Awakening. She becomes the first woman to experience pregnancy in nearly two hundred years. When Obu, in a fit of jealousy, kills the healer who is helping Oona, he is returned to the depository. His brain is taken from his body, his memory is erased, and he is given Skeets' consciousness.

ANALYSIS

Although there is very little explicit reference to religion in *Gray Matters*, the system that has been set up for the advancement of cerebromorphs can be understood in religious terms. The primary religious model for the depository system is Hinduism. The levels of the depository resemble the Hindu caste system. There is tremendous prejudice against those on the bottom level and an expectation that few of them will ever make it to the top. As in Hindu belief, there is a prescribed *dharma*, or rule of conduct, for each caste for each period and circumstance in life. In Hindu religion, these codes are described in the Code of Manu (dating from the first century C.E.) and in the *Bhagavad-Gita*. In the first book of this holy text for the Hindus, the warrior Arjuna learns from the god Krishna that there is action in inaction and inaction in action. In other words, there are actions that have no consequence because they do not advance the soul toward the liberation of the body. These actions are mere illusion. There are also periods of inactivity, such as meditation, that really are action because they advance the soul.

The same principle applies in *Gray Matters*, but the prescribed code is bureaucratic and technocratic in nature. Cerebromorphs spend their time reviewing computer files of their past memories and of the stored wisdom of the human community. They spend a prescribed amount of time in meditation each day. All this activity is closely monitored by the auditors, who spend much of their time writing reports, memos, and regulations. In Hindu religion, the ultimate goal of the enlightened soul is to be free from the body and become one with the Brahma, the over-soul that is the origin of all human souls. In an ironic twist, the cerebromorphs are already free from their bodies and are part of the "one soul" made up of the collective consciousness of the depository. The goal of the enlightened soul is to be restored to an individual body and to become free of the past self, the "individual" that is destroyed by the cerebrectomy. The enlightened soul is "reborn" in a new body that may be of a different race or gender from the old.

—*Gary Layne Hatch*

THE GREAT GOD PAN

Dr. Raymond performs an operation that will enable a young woman to perceive the spirit world, little imagining the horror that he has loosed upon humanity

Author: Arthur Machen (1863–1947)
Genre: Fantasy—cautionary
Type of work: Novel
Time of work: The late nineteenth century
Locale: Wales and London, England
First published: 1894 (in *The Great God Pan and the Inmost Light*)

The Story

The Great God Pan was Arthur Machen's first important work. Machen published the initial chapter in *The Whirlwind* in 1890. In 1893 he submitted the entire novel to another publisher, adding a second work, the story "The Inmost Light." The two appeared together the following year.

The Great God Pan is composed of a number of individual narratives that at first seem jumbled but that eventually fit together like pieces of a horrifying jigsaw puzzle. Machen relies on several characters to present these narratives: the egotistical Dr. Raymond, the outwardly conventional but inwardly skeptical Mr. Clarke, the unlucky Charles Herbert, and the hearty Mr. Villiers.

As the novel opens, Raymond is planning to perform a brain operation that will allow his patient Mary to "see" the God Pan, by which he means apprehending the spiritual reality beyond everyday events. He has invited Clarke to Wales to witness the results. After the operation, the unconscious young woman seems to register wonder, then horror, after which she sinks into idiocy.

For years afterward, Clarke avoids the subject of the occult, but he gradually compiles a collection of unusual but apparently true stories he calls "Memoirs to Prove the Existence of the Devil." One such account involves a young woman known as Helen V. Helen was supposedly adopted by a relative who sought another home for her as she approached puberty. A farmer living on the Welsh border offered to be her guardian but did not count on the unhealthy effect she would have on other children in the neighborhood. In one incident, she was seen playing in the woods with a naked man resembling a satyr.

One evening Herbert and Villiers meet by accident in London. The two had attended school together, but Herbert has since been reduced to begging. He confides that the woman he married, Helen Vaughan, stole his money and disappeared. Later Villiers learns of the "Paul Street case," in which the Herberts were implicated in murder. These events persuade Villiers to visit his financial adviser Clarke, but not on business. He describes his encounter with Herbert, his visit to the now-deserted Herbert house, and his discovery of a sketch in a pile of old newspapers. Clarke recognizes the sketch as resembling the patient Dr. Raymond operated on so many years before. The woman, Villiers insists, is Mrs. Herbert.

The remainder of the novel develops in similarly indirect but obvious fashion. Readers learn of Mrs. Beaumont, a wealthy beauty who is the toast of the season. A rash of suicides among gentlemen who have visited Mrs. Beaumont's house sweeps London. Villiers discovers that the woman in question has been known not only as Mrs. Herbert but also as Helen Vaughan and Miss Raymond, the name by which she is recognized in a disreputable quarter of London. Finally Villiers and Clarke confront the woman with their evidence and give her the choice of hanging herself or facing arrest.

In the last chapter, Machen's characters reflect on Mrs. Beaumont's end. Chief among these commentators is Dr. Matheson, who describes attending a suicide victim whose body he sees degenerate horribly down the evolutionary ladder. The corpse wavers "from sex to sex" and dissolves, but then reasserts itself via a "Form" the doctor will not describe, until it becomes a human corpse again. Finally Raymond provides the missing piece of the puzzle, confessing that although Mary died nine months after his experiment, she first gave birth to a child who was clearly evil incarnate. Helen Vaughan, later known as Helen V., Mrs. Herbert, Mrs. Beaumont, and Miss Raymond, was the daughter of Mary and the Great God Pan.

ANALYSIS

Although Machen subsequently developed greater sophistication in presenting his ideas, *The Great God Pan* contains in embryo almost all of his techniques and themes. The concept that a greater reality lies hidden beyond everyday events is a commonplace among fantasy writers, as it is among theologians. In subsequent works, Machen sometimes treated this ultimate reality as horrible, sometimes as beautiful. He scatters direct and indirect references to the Greek god Pan throughout his story. This mythological entity is a symbol not only of the pagan world but of a vast, soulless reality lurking behind the veil of the physical world.

The Great God Pan became notorious upon publication, largely because of its religious and sexual implications. It can be interpreted as a blasphemous parody of the story of Christ, who was the product of a union between a supernatural being and a mortal woman named Mary. There are also suggestions that the nature of Helen Vaughan's evil influence is somehow sexual. Later generations have found these suggestions less shocking than Machens contemporaries presumably did.

Critics also attacked two of Machen's techniques: his refusal to describe the horrors he suggests and his reliance on coincidence. The first practice is judicious, because Machen was dealing with matters that by their very nature lie beyond the scope of human language. He may also have realized that readers are capable of imagining more frightening things than even the most skillful writer is capable of describing, a fact overlooked by many later horror writers, usually to their detriment. Machen's reliance on coincidence is less defensible and masks an inability to develop plot and character.

Whatever its flaws, *The Great God Pan* has influenced many later supernatural writers, including H. P. Lovecraft (in "The Dunwich Horror," 1929), Ira Levin (*Rosemary's Baby*, 1967), and Peter Straub (*Ghost Story*, 1979). It remains Machen's best-known work.

—Grove Koger

THE GREAT SKY RIVER TRILOGY

The last remnants of humanity, led by Killeen, fight for survival against superior races of machine and alien life on planets near the black hole at the center of the galaxy

Author: Gregory Benford (1941–)
Genre: Science fiction—evolutionary fantasy
Type of work: Novels
Time of work: More than twenty-eight thousand years in the future
Locale: The planet Snowglade, the planet New Bishop, and the black hole at the galactic center of the Milky Way
First published: *Great Sky River* (1987), *Tides of Light* (1989), and *Furious Gulf* (1994)

THE STORY

All three novels of the trilogy concern epic adventures of the Family Bishop, distant descendants of earthly humanity, on a journey from the home planet Snowglade to the galactic centers black hole. *Great Sky River*, the first novel in the series, introduces Killeen, the trilogy's central character, through his dream of the Calamity, the fall of the Bishop Citadel before the onslaught of a superior race of hunter machines and cyborgs.

In part 1, "Long Retreat," the two-hundred-member remnant of Family Bishop, led by Cap'n Fanny, fights its way across the ravaged face of Snowglade, a once-lush planet now transformed by "mechs" into an arid plain more congenial to machines. Fanny is shot down by a Mantis, a vast anthology intelligence shadowing the Family. In part 2, "The Once-Green World," Bishops fight their way to a Splash, a green swamp created by the fall of an asteroid, finding there members of Family Rook and one Knight, the woman Shibo, who is encased in an "exshell," or machine-augmented body. In part 3, "The Dreaming Vertebrates," Shibo becomes Killeens lover and friend of his adolescent son Toby. The Family Bishop finds Cap'n Hatchet and his Metropolis, a Citadel of mud huts constructed in the Splash with the help of a renegade machine. The Mantis reappears, forcing Hatchet to have sex with its grotesque reconstruction of Fanny. Killeen shoots them both and discovers that Hatchet was a "manmech" tool of the Mantis. Killeen receives a message from his dead father, Abraham, urging him to find the Starship *Argo* and lead the remaining families farther into the galactic center. With the help of the Mantis, the starship is recovered. Killeen destroys the supermech before leaving Snowglade.

In *Tides of Light*, Killeen's story continues. The *Argo* finds the shattered planet New Bishop orbiting Abrahams Star. In part 2, "Starswarmer," the reader enters the mind of Quath of the Myriapodia, an immense, insectlike cybernetic life-form that fights off mechs and "Noughts," remnants of human Card Tribes from the era of the Chandeliers, when humans traveled between the stars.

The Myriapodia mine New Bishop by liquefying the planets mantle with the help of a cosmic string, capturing its flow through the Syphon, a golden fountain of metals used to build the sky Web that the Myriapodia will use to leave the planet on their own way to the galactic center. Quath, a rare "philosoph," is far more thoughtful than her envious and selfish colleague Beq'qdahl. In part 3, "A Matter of Momentum," she captures Killeen, only to release him after realizing that, to the Magnetic Mind at the galactic center, there is something special about him. He falls through the center of the planet as it is being cut by a cosmic string.

In part 4, "Such Men Are Dangerous," the Bishops meet the Card Tribes, which are under the leadership of His Supremacy, a fanatic half-mech who urges humans to battle the cybers to the death, In part 5, "Skysower," an immense form of organic life living on starshine descends on the planet, sowing pods. The families feast on this manna before engaging in a final battle with good and evil cybers and illuminates, in which both Shibo and His Supremacy fall. In an epilogue, "Sailing with the Tide," Quath and the Argo travel on toward the galactic center as Shibo becomes Tobys first Aspect, or implanted personality.

In *Furious Gulf*, the *Argo* with Killeen as captain journeys toward the galactic center, meeting the Sail-snake and other new organic life-forms, part of the continuum between matter and mind, along the way. In part 1, "Far Antiquity," the Family explores an ancient Chandelier only to see it exploded by an equally ancient bomb. In part 2, "The Eater of All Things," the *Argo* approaches the great black hole at the center of the Milky Way. So vast a hole can be entered along its edges without risking physical destruction. In part 3, "The Time Pit," the *Argo* enters the holes ergosphere and finds itself at Port Athena, a gate to deep reality space/time lanes guarded by a dwarf. In part 4, "Gravity's Gullet," Toby and Quath explore these lanes, where particles and fields of energy struggle with one another. The Mantis reappears and shoots down Quath. Part 5, "Malign Attentions," concludes the trilogy with a force of mechs gathering in the furious gulf between life and death, with Toby's discovery of the door between matter and self-consciousness, and with Killeens message to his son sent through the agency of Nigel Walmsley, a British astronaut from Gregory Benford's first galactic center novel, *In the Ocean of Night* (1977).

ANALYSIS

These three epic novels of the distant future, part of an interconnected series of novels that began with *In the Ocean of Night* and that continued in *Across the Sea of Suns* (1984), imagine humanitys battles for survival against superior alien and mechanical intelligences near the massive, violent black hole ("the Eater") that lies at the galactic center of the Milky Way, the great sky river. The novels appeared in quick succession, first in hardcover and then in paperback editions. All take as their starting point Gregory Benford's theoretical research on the galactic central region, which he performed as a professor of astrophysics specializing in plasma physics at the University of California, Irvine. Enormously powerful forces at work near the center appear to have been driven by a vast explosion that took place there about a million years ago. Now revealed through new varieties of telescopes, these forces might well, according to Benford, support rich, complex life-forms unknown to humans in their distant corner of the galaxy. Benford believes that one more novel will be needed to complete the series.

Benford's work has been linked to the hard science-fiction tradition of Olaf Stapledon and Arthur C. Clarke, a tradition that highly prizes faithfulness to the physical facts of the universe while building new fictional worlds upon them. Like Stapledon's *Last and First Men* (1930), Benford's trilogy is the story of the human race from the present to its near-extinction. Like Stapledon's *Star Maker* (1937), its theme is not merely the story of humanity but also that of life and mind in the cosmos. It seeks to offer an explanation for the mystery of life and space-time consistent with contemporary biology, astronomy, and mathematics. Benfords vision of the beauty and awesome energies of stars at the galactic center, from early compressions to fiery deaths, characterizes the novels' most powerfully written passages. Like Stapledon and H. G. Wells, Benford imagines humanity not as the measure of all things but, rather, as a frail being caught in a brushfire, a brave theme in the larger music of storms and stars.

As a Southerner, Benford was familiar with William Faulkner's use of the history of Southern families as a principle of mythic storytelling, and he incorporates this idea with future history conventions drawn from Clarke and Wells to structure his trilogy. Critics characterize Benford's work as modernist: meticulously crafted, psychologically convincing, iconically familiar, and verbally skillful. Like many science-fiction writers, he finds that postmodernism may simply be a signature of exhaustion, its typical apparatus of self-reference, irony, self-conscious use of older genre devices, pastiche, and parody all signs of lack of invention. He distrusts the deconstructionists attack on science itself, attempting to reduce science to rhetoric rather than an order of nature or to the status of the ultimately arbitrary humanities. His work is therefore hostile to recent fashions in criticism, centering as it does on figures acting against a landscape of universal, scientific truths.

—*E. Laura Kleiner*

GREEN EYES

A woman and a reanimated man travel throughout Louisiana, doing good deeds and attempting to find a place for themselves and a way to keep him alive

Author: Lucius Shepard (1943–2014)
Genre: Science fiction—extrasensory powers
Type of work: Novel
Time of work: The present or the near future
Locale: Louisiana
First published: 1984

THE STORY

A research facility at Tulane University is conducting studies using recent corpses and dirt taken from a slave graveyard where, presumably, the bodies interacted with the soil. The research is an attempt to create a "Bacterially Induced Artificial Personality"—a "zombie." Zombies never have the personality of the person who died; they are helped by their "therapist" to realize and explain who they are. This help almost inevitably involves sex. The reanimated are all men, and therapists are chosen in part for their beauty.

Jocundra Verret, a therapist who studied voodoo cults before joining the facility, is assigned to the zombie Donnell Harrison. Harrison is a "slow burner," meaning that he is expected to live longer than many other zombies. Harrison demonstrates remarkable abilities and, with the aid of another "slow burner" named Magnusson, he comes to understand his situation exactly. Faced with the prospect of living in the facility until an inevitable, horrible death, Harrison—after Magnusson dies, leaving Harrison his notes—persuades Jocundra to leave with him. By this point they are, in most ways that count, in love with each other.

They escape with another zombie, a man named Richmond who causes some major contretemps before dying. After meeting a faith healer called Papa Salvatino, Harrison realizes that his enhanced vision enables him to see peoples auras and heal them. Jocundra and Harrison return to the Bayou area where she grew up, there realizing the truth of her statement that "This worl' she's full of supernatural creatures whose magic we deny."

Harrison, testing his powers and realizing that some of the methods and concepts of voodoo—most especially the *ti bon ange* (more or less the conscience) and the *gross bon ange* (the undying part, the immortal twin)—map exactly onto his current state. Throughout the final half of the novel, Harrison attempts to use the signs, symbols, and practices of voodoo to keep himself alive. With the assistance of Ms. Otille Rigaud, a wealthy patron with a shady past, he constructs a copper *veve* in order to focus the energies of his aura. The final third of the novel becomes increasingly convoluted as coincidences pile upon one another and matters that already stretched the readers credibility become conflated beyond all reason.

Ultimately, in a battle of zombies, Harrison dies. Jocundra is left to try to get on with her life, but the final scene of the novel makes it clear that her link to Harrison remains solidly intact well beyond his life.

ANALYSIS

As do many of Lucius Shepard's shorter works, *Green Eyes* features characters alienated from the world in which they live. No one is more alienated than Harrison, a zombie who wants to be able to live as normal a life as possible.

The various points at which Harrison's quest is interrupted highlight his being apart from the rest of the world. First there is his fellow zombie Richmond, who aspires to live what is essentially a version of the 1969 film *Easy Rider*, in which New Orleans plays a pivotal role. Richmond's adolescent desires—sex, drugs, and rock and roll—contrast with Harrison's even as Falstaff's clinging to the "chimes at midnight" alienates him from King Henry.

Harrison's initial encounter with Papa Salvatino also reveals his isolation. When Harrison sets up a faith healing practice, in an effort to strengthen and better understand his abilities, he encounters Herve Robichaux, whom he cures of "terminal lung cancer." Robichaux's heartless attitude after he is cured leaves Harrison questioning why he wants to help humanity.

Finally, there is the matter of Otille. Harrison compromises most of the principles by which he claims to abide (including having cuckolded Jocundra) to no positive effect. Harrison kills people both because he has to and because he can. By the time he dies, Harrison has become as human—in the sense of being vicious and evil—as anyone else on the plantation. He has followed the path to humanity, which in this novel is the path of pain, torture, cruelty, and death.

Ultimately it is Jocundra around whom the story resolves, and perhaps revolves. The first scene of the novel shows Jocundra "treating" a "short-termer," and the book closes on her ambivalence toward but ultimate recovery of a poem Harrison wrote for her. When she and Harrison have to flee, Jocundra takes them to Bayou Teche, to a man who reared—and, apparently, sexually assaulted her. Although she declares that "work has distanced me from friends and family," the reader will quickly apprehend that it is her attitude toward life, not the work itself, that led to that distancing and to Dr. Edman assigning her to Harrison.

Edman is aware of the possible consequences of his actions. His cold interpretation of Jocundra, in which he clinically notes that her first husband apparently misused her physically and declares a paternal interest in her, stands stark against the backdrop of the repeated patterns in her life. Although the end of *Green Eyes* makes it clear that Jocundra is not breaking out of the pattern into which she fell with Harrison, that pattern is arguably not as self-destructive as her previous choices.

Green Eyes is a novel of hopes and aspirations, two elements that made much of Shepard's early work seem so fresh and promising to the oft-moribund science-fiction genre. As a promise of things to come, *Green Eyes*, like Jocundra's final action, is a cautiously hopeful sign.

—Kenneth L. Houghton

THE GREEN ISLE OF THE GREAT DEEP

An old man and a young boy are transported into an afterworld run as a totalitarian state, and they become catalysts for its liberation

Author: Neil M. Gunn (1891–1973)
Genre: Fantasy—dystopia
Type of work: Novel

Time of work: The 1940s
Locale: The Green Isle of the Great Deep
First published: 1944

THE STORY

The Green Isle of the Great Deep is a sequel to *Young Art and Old Hector* (1942), one of Neil M. Gunn's many novels glorifying boyhood, set in the Scottish Highlands' crofting communities. Elements of both Christian and Celtic mysticism inform the earlier work, and in *The Green Isle of the Great Deep*, a young boy and old man decidedly enter a mythic realm. Through their efforts—and with last-minute assistance from God"—paradise is rescued from encroaching totalitarianism.

The novel begins naturalistically with a conversation among members of a small Highland community, gathered around a hearth during World War II. Provoked by newspaper reports touching on concentration camps, they anxiously discuss the idea of "breaking minds," that is, the forcible indoctrination to a set of beliefs known to later generations as brainwashing. The conflict that propels the plot is thus introduced.

That conflict is allegorized once the protagonists, Old Hector Macdonald and young Art Macrae, enter the Green Isle of the Great Deep (the name of the Celtic land of the dead). While initiating Art into the practice of poaching along the river, Hector plunges with him into the water, recapitulating Gunn's experience of nearly drowning, described in his autobiography as a "dream lying between life and death." The companions find themselves in an idyllic landscape whose inhabitants seem strangely hollow.

The newcomers are directed to report to the capital, the Seat on the Rock, and to stay at inns along the way. Guided by Art's intuition, they instead sleep in fields at night and eat the abundant fruit they find. They are befriended by a couple, Mary and Robert, who are disturbed by their eating the fruit. This fruit is revealed to be the fruit of the tree of knowledge, of enlightenment and moral awareness. It is withheld by the keepers of the Seat to "relieve" the Green Isle's inhabitants of the burden of freedom. Food manufactured for them makes the fruit poisonous and the people submissive to a mechanized existence.

When the companions arrive at the Seat and encounter the agents of the "Perfect Administration," Art instinctively flees. Hector, weary and confused, cooperates with the regime. This pattern repeats throughout the narrative: Art stubbornly resists the Administration's efforts to control him, and Hector increasingly breaks down under the remorseless probing of his thoughts and motives by its agent, Questioner. As Art, aided by the ever-nurturing Mary until her arrest, continues to elude his captors, he develops into a legendary figure. The boy's defiance and his ability to eat the forbidden fruit threaten the underpinnings of the Administrations programmed society.

When Art finally is caught, marking the story's culmination, his companion is an old man believed to be Hector. The old man is in fact God, summoned from his meditations by a desperate Hector, who insists on an audience. The Perfect Administration's sophistry fails to justify itself to true authority, but Hectors audience is far from the ordeal he had feared. The novel closes with the awakening of the inhabitants of the Green Isle from their spiritual deadness and also with the end of their collective "dream." Hector and Art are saved from drowning, and the last scene joins the first in bracketing the allegory in reality.

ANALYSIS

Critics generally find *The Green Isle of the Great Deep* inferior to other mystical-political, antitotalitarian parables that appeared in the 1930s and 1940s as hybrids of fantasy and reality. These works include Joseph ONeill's *Land Under England* (1935), Rex Warner's *The Aerodrome* (1941), and Ruthven Todd's *Over the Mountain* (1939). Many readers remain unconvinced of the success of Gunn's attempt in his novel to combine elements of Celtic folklore, Christian orthodoxy, and modern managerial society. Moreover, they find strained his use of Arts name to evoke not only Arthurian legend but also the creative powers of art and poetry.

Political allegory admittedly marked a departure for Gunn, who was generally known as a writer of sentimental regional novels of the Highlands. When a friend hinted that the loosely connected tales in *Young Art and Old Hector* verged on escapism, Gunn responded with *The Green Isle of the Great Deep*. Ironically, critics tend to consider the early work more profound in its simplicity as well as more successful in its implicit demonstration of values the sequel makes explicit.

Gunn's thoughts were clearly focused on the nature of despotic idealism and authoritarianism at the time he wrote *The Green Isle of the Great Deep*. Given the threat of fascism in the early 1940s, this preoccupation is not surprising. A contemporaneous work, *The Serpent* (1943; published in the United States as *Man Goes Alone*, 1944), develops an idea found in Gunn's "phantasy" (as he calls *The Green Isle of the Great Deep* in his dedication): the redemption of human nature by the individuals realization of what Gunn terms the "second self." Explained in his autobiography, the "second self" refers to the inner core of secret reality that makes a human free; it is this second self of Mary, Art, and ultimately Hector that resists the Dostoevskian Questioner.

In taking seriously the threat to freedom of the will from conditioning techniques, *The Green Isle of the Great Deep* is a forerunner to such novels as Anthony Burgess' *A Clockwork Orange* (1962). As such, it has a certain prophetic value. Although Gunn's evocation of dystopia is certainly less compelling than Burgess, or of Aldous Huxley's in *Brave New World* (1932) and George Orwell's in *Nineteen Eighty-four* (1949), critics generally credit *The Green Isle of the Great Deep* as a sincerely felt cautionary tale.

—Amy Adelstein

THE GREEN MAN

Maurice Allingham must overcome his own selfish drives to exorcise a demon intent on destroying his daughter

Author: Kingsley Amis (1922-1995)
Genre: Fantasy—high fantasy
Type of work: Novel
Time of work: The 1960's
Locale: A fictional village near Cambridge, England
First published: 1969

THE STORY

Cambridge University-educated Maurice Allingham owns an inn, The Green Man, which is haunted by a seventeenth century clergyman believed responsible for two horrible murders. The action takes place over four days, which Allingham recalls one year later.

He encounters a mysterious red-haired woman who disappears. No one else sees her. The same evening, Allingham's father, who seems to have seen something, dies of a stroke. Before falling asleep that night, Allingham hallucinates about a tree in the shape of a man and with the ability to walk. Allingham had earlier asked Diana, his best friend's wife, to meet him for a tryst the next day. Thus, the tone of the novel is set in this first chapter: the possible existence of ghosts, the foreboding of the Green Man, the intrusion of death, and the alcoholic Allingham's libidinous obsession.

The protagonist becomes increasingly aware of the ghostly presence of Dr. Thomas Underhill, whom only he can see. A trip to the fictional St. Michael's College at Cambridge produces Underhill's diary, which reveals the wizard's use of magical illusion to frighten very young village girls into submitting sexually. Later that night, Allingham and Diana dig up and open Underhill's casket, where they find a sheaf of papers. The following morning Allingham reads them and discovers precise instructions for how to achieve a meeting with Underhill.

Kingsley Amis leads the reader through a series of partial climaxes. Most immediate is Allingham's meeting with God as a well-dressed man of about twenty-eight. Despite Allingham having characterized himself as a hardened unbeliever, God directs him to eliminate Underhill, leaving the means up to Allingham but suggesting that he obtain help from the church. The next climax, the meeting with Underhill, involves the wizard producing a series of lewd and horrific illusions. Allingham, using a crucifix, breaks the spell in time to prevent the Green Man from destroying his daughter, which Underhill planned to do after realizing he could not ravish her. The final climax is seriocomic. Allingham persuades an unbelieving Anglican priest to exorcise Underhill from the inn.

ANALYSIS

Amis, one of the most prolific writers of his time, produced more than twenty novels, including *Colonel Sun: A James Bond Adventure* (1968, as by Robert Markham); a detective story, *The Riverside Villas Murder* (1973); and a science-fiction novel, *The Alteration* (1976). Other novels have elements of fantasy, but *The Green Man* focuses on the supernatural in the traditional sense. Not only do Underhill, appropriately dating from the era of witch trials, and his familiar, the Green Man, play crucial roles, but a literal divine intervention brings about the climaxes and resolution of the plot.

Amis professes to write a serious ghost story, so his first obligation is to establish realism. Thus, his fictional Fareham is off the A595 road and a few miles from the actual towns of Sardon and Mill End. St. Michael's College is near the corner of Silver Street in Cambridge. Allingham's interview with God lasts exactly twenty-four minutes, and readers know the prices on his menu as well as the source of produce for the kitchen. Most real, however, is Amis' characterization of Allingham.

Although scarcely likable, Maurice Allingham at fifty-three is completely credible. He admits to drinking a bottle of Scotch a day for twenty years, accounting for much of his behavior and such symptoms as convulsive twitches, hallucinations, and blackouts. Moreover, Allingham, a typical alcoholic, is preoccupied with his own needs to the exclusion of others. Even his success at getting Diana and his wife in the same bed with him results more from egotism than from desire. This near-misogyny attracts Underhill to a kindred spirit: Underhill was thought to have killed his wife, and Allingham feels guilt over the accidental death of his own first wife. Underhill has a record for terrifying young girls into sexual relations; Allingham seduces the wives of friends. For both, sex is a sport.

Although Allingham combines good and evil, Underhill, only evil, is a formidable antagonist, confident in his ability to manipulate Allingham. Almost a malicious alter ego, he understands Allingham's most serious weakness: his fixation on the possibility of life after death, which the ghost represents. A hypochondriac, Allingham constantly thinks about death. He is disgusted with his entire being: his drives, physical weakness, and intellectual restlessness. Thus, when the priest exorcises the evil spirit, Allingham is untouched by Underhill's temptations of wealth, women, or glory. Peace of mind comes close, but Allingham's clear duty takes charge.

In Underwood, Amis creates a creature of utter malevolence, in keeping with the seventeenth century idea of witches as servants of Satan. With his depiction of God, he has a greater challenge. In *The Anti-Death League* (1966), Amis seems to suggest that God lacks the traditional qualities of justice and mercy. In *The Green Man*, Allingham's cosmopolitan visitor offers an explanation of his role.

Immediately displaying his omnipotence, God suspends time for their interview. Although omniscient in the past and the present, God denies foreknowledge as being inconsistent with free will. He persuades Allingham to deal with Underwood because Underwood suggests human life beyond the grave. God also admits to having made "some fairly disputable decisions" right at the start, not having foreknowledge. The implication here is the presence of evil in Satan, whom God suggests is a part of Him, as Christ is. God permits Allingham one question, which he seizes upon: whether there is an afterlife. After assuring him that there is, God also tells Allingham that He will always be present and that they will meet again when God is in his "executive capacity." As a result of this meeting, incongruously enough, Allingham becomes the servant of God in a battle against evil.

Amis ends *The Green Man* ambiguously. Although Allingham saves his daughter and carries out the bidding of God, he appears surprisingly unchanged. Despite his wife leaving him and his promise to his daughter to sell the inn, he is still there a year later. Perhaps God's assurance of his immortality suffices.

—*James M. O'Neil*

THE GREEN MAN

A retelling of the Hamlet story in which a violent and heroic Amleth (Hamlet) meets both (King) Arthur and Beowulf, avenges his fathers murder, and is murdered by Beowulf

Author: Henry Treece (1912–1966)
Genre: Fantasy—mythological
Type of work: Novel
Time of work: The sixth century c.e.

Locale: Northern Europe and Great Britain
First published: 1966

THE STORY

This Green Man, Thenovel is framed by two letters from a man named Gilliberht. In the first letter, Gilliberht, a Christian, writes from France to his Italian patron asking help to go north and convert the northern barbarians. The novel ends with Gilliberht writing as a pagan to that former patron, telling him that the future belongs to the North. Gilliberhts statement tells what actually happened in history. In between, the novel proper tells a "history based on myth."

King Vendil of Jutland (Denmark) is murdered by his brother Feng while Vendils son Amleth (Hamlet) is off seeking service with the Geatish king, Beowulf. Rejected by Beowulf, the apparently doltish Amleth returns to Jutland to find Feng on the throne and married to Amleths mother, Gerutha. In this northern world, only violence gives honor and power, and sexual relations are almost without restraint.

The illiterate Feng decides to rid himself of Amleth by sending him to seek his fortune in Great Britain. Feng has a captured southerner, Gilliberht, write a letter to Duke Arthur of Britain, telling Arthur to kill Amleth. Gilliberht, resentful at his treatment, slyly changes the letter so that Fengs henchmen are executed instead. Afterward, Gilliberht, sold as a slave to Beowulf, becomes Beowulfs ruling adviser because he is educated and Beowulf desires to be remembered after his death in a poem only Gilliberht can write. Henry Treece even has Gilliberht compose some lines, which are the actual Anglo-Saxon text of the poem Beowulf, first transcribed about 1000 c.e..

In Great Britain, Amleth sets out to help Arthur fight the invading Saxons. Arthur is no king, only an old, tired, and crippled Celtic warlord defending Christian and Roman civilization, although there are no true Romans and little Christianity left. Medraut, Arthur's nephew by marriage, betrays Amleth, who is sold into slavery to the northern Picts. There Amleth, because of his size and violence, becomes king, married to the Pictish queen. They plan an invasion of the South in order to conquer not only Arthur but also the Saxons. Amleth, however, wants revenge on Feng first. He and his queen sail back to Jutland, where Feng has overthrown the old pagan order and imprisoned Amleths mother, Gerutha, in a basket hung from the castle walls. Feng is considering conversion to Christianity. Amleth kills his uncle and sets the castle on fire, unwittingly destroying his mother. It is at this moment that Beowulf makes a raid on the Jutlanders and, with the aid of Gilliberht, murders Amleth.

ANALYSIS

The Green Man was one of several historical novels that Treece wrote late in his career, works that embody a rather pessimistic worldview despite Treeces own professed Christian beliefs and Beowulfs suggestion that all religions have common roots. Treece points out in a note that the main plot of *The Green Man*, the Hamlet story, comes originally from Saxo Grammaticus, a Danish priest (c. 1150–1220). Treece has added a deliberately realistic and antiromantic version of the Arthur legend as well as the likely, but hardly heroic, tale of Beowulf.

Brought in as well are various elements of other European myths. The leaders of the Picts are a brother, Orest (Orestes), and his sister, Elekt (Elektra), who carry back their ancestry to the Greeks. Even the great labyrinth of Crete is reproduced in the Jutland maze, where the Danes dance in sexual abandon in order to cause the earth to produce. In short, the novel attempts to synthesize many of the violent and sexually charged myths of the Europeans in order to develop what Treece says is his theme: In real life, the meek do not inherit the earth.

Although Gilliberht himself is a minor character, his framing letters are the keys to this theme. The awful lives and terrible deaths of the main male characters are the proofs. Perhaps even more important is what happens to the "unimportant" and the weak, particularly the women. In a sense, Treece is criticizing patriarchy, but, more important, he is asserting that violence is inevitable. The women, not necessarily meek but certainly weaker than the men, almost all suffer brutal fates. Almost all, including Gerutha, have no real standing in the community, except to be fertile, although there is an apparent exception in Elekt, in that she selects Beowulf as her mate. She too must yield leadership in war to her brother, Orest, and then to Amleth. Sibbi, Geruthas illegitimate daughter, is the victim of mass rape and horrible torture; Elene, the young British princess whom Amleth marries, is crippled and enslaved. Even these women, however, can be vicious in their own right. This no doubt is part of their culture but also of their nature.

There is another theme, something more than Treece announces. Although the Christian message is rejected, Treece suggests that religion matters; however, it is the old pagan religions that are important. They emphasize fertility, sexuality, and the control of nature by magical acts. This control requires sacrifice by human beings—sometimes the sacrifice of other human beings. Gerutha is the Barley Queen, who must be dragged periodically across the ground in order to make it fertile. Kings are identified with trees, especially with the oak tree. The true king is therefore king of the wood, the green man, who brings the power of nature to the community. Most important, he also brings in the terrible threat of nature, uncontrolled by humans, or at least by human reason. In the end, the pagan belief does not save anyone. The final thematic statement then is that the meek do not inherit the earth, but neither do the strong.

—L. L. Lee

GREEN MANSIONS

In a dense forest of Guyana, Abel falls in love with Rima, a mysterious birdlike woman who is killed by natives who fear her as a supernatural being

Author: W. H. Hudson (1841–1922)
Genre: Fantasy—magical realism
Type of work: Novel
Time of work: About 1875
Locale: A tropical forest near the border of Guyana and Venezuela
First published: 1904

THE STORY

Abel Guevez de Argensola, a member of a wealthy Venezuelan family, joins a conspiracy to overthrow the government. When the plot is discovered, he is forced to flee into the wilderness of Guyana. After months of illness and misfortune, he settles in the village of an Indian chief named Runi. Near the village is a forest in which lives a supernatural creature who kills hunters.

Undaunted, Abel enters the forest and discovers abundant wildlife. A melodious, birdlike voice follows him as he explores. One day, he comes upon a young woman lying by a stream. Her small, delicate form and resplendent beauty captivate him. They meet when he hurls a stone at a snake and she comes to defend it. Her dark hair falls in a cloud on her shoulders and arms; her skin is pearly white, sometimes lustrous and iridescent. When he is bitten by the snake, he leaps off a precipice in a panic and falls unconscious. He wakes in the hut of an old man named Nuflo, who lives with the young woman. Abel learns that Rima, the luminescent creature with the mysterious voice, will not allow harm to come to any living creature in the forest.

Rima and Abel seal their mutual love by promising to do everything to please each other. She wants, most of all, to find her mother's people. Nuflo is persuaded to take Rima to Riolama, where her mother died. On the journey, he tells Abel the story of Rima's origin. Seventeen years earlier, Nuflo and other members of an outlaw band found a beautiful woman in the forest. In danger from the rest of the gang, Nuflo and the woman escaped to a Christian settlement, where she gave birth to Rima and soon after died. Nuflo took the child to the forest, where Rima grew to hate the natives for killing the animals and frustrated their attempts to hunt. When a native was killed chasing her, the Indians took her for an evil deity.

When the three find no one at Riolama, Abel persuades Rima that her mother was the sole survivor of a catastrophe that destroyed her people. After deciding to live with Abel in her forest, she returns alone to prepare for him. When Abel and Nuflo arrive, they find Rima gone. While the three of them journeyed to Riolama, the natives had returned to hunting in the forest. One day, Rima was seen, chased, and trapped in a tree. The natives set the tree on fire, and Rima fell into the flames. To avenge Rima's death, Abel destroys Runi and his people with the help of a rival chief.

In the forest, he finds that Nuflo has been killed by the Indians.

After months of near starvation, Abel leaves the forest, taking Rima's ashes with him in an earthen jar. He regains his mental and physical health by the time he reaches Georgetown, where he settles and finally achieves self-forgiveness and removal of the guilt he suffered as a result of killing God's creatures. Confident that Rima's ashes would mingle with his, Abel ends his days free of the sorrow that once darkened his life.

ANALYSIS

Green Mansions contains many elements found in W. H. Hudson's other books, both fiction and nonfiction. Both *The Purple Land That England Lost* (1885), Hudson's first novel, and *El Ombú* (1902), a collection, reveal Hudson's extraordinary talent for observing creatures in their natural habitat. His treatment of natural settings and wild creatures has been interpreted variously as pantheistic mysticism, mystical ecstasy, Wordsworthian romanticism, and primitive animism. His books on ornithology and the English countryside have been praised for their scientific accuracy and thoroughness.

As a romance, *Green Mansions* recalls William Shakespeare's *A Midsummer Night's Dream* (1595). That work contains a forest in which magical transformations occur and supernatural creatures abound. Hudson's novel differs from other romances in the attention it gives to the natural world. The novel's tropical forest, though idealized (Hudson claimed never to have seen a forest), is given so much detailed attention that it would be too real for romance were it not for the presence of Rima. In some respects, the novel resembles *Heart of Darkness* (1902) by Joseph Conrad, which recounts another journey into the interior of a tropical forest.

Green Mansions merits a place in fantasy literature by virtue of its treatment of Rima, the bird-woman whose mysterious presence gives the story a strangeness that realistic fiction cannot achieve. Rima's ability to disappear into the wood, reappear, climb high in the trees, trip along a limb, and communicate in some nonverbal way with the monkeys, snakes, and other creatures in the forest gives the novel a supernatural aura and arouses wonder. Wild creatures do her no harm, and rain and heat have no effect on her. Rima personifies nature's essential beauty and mystery as Hudson perceived them. She embodies the soul of nature.

Abel's reaction to Rima is a key element in how the reader responds to the novel's enchantment. Nowhere does Abel question or in any way disbelieve Rima's supernatural abilities. To him, they are as ordinary as the rain that gives the forest its resplendent beauty and life. To him, Rima represents perfection in a world that possesses too little of it in human form. The ease with which he accepts her birdlike nature, behavior, and appearance is communicated to the reader. Neither Rima nor Abel ever doubt their ability to be lovers in a physical sense, yet a part of her is not human. Her origin remains a mystery, her melodious language remains incomprehensible, and her ability to communicate with other forest creatures and her affection for them suggest a nature too pristine and spiritual to be entirely human. She is as elusive as fantasy itself.

—*Bernard E. Morris*

GREENMANTLE

A mother and daughter are caught between woodland magic and the Mafia

Author: Charles de Lint (1951–)
Genre: Fantasy—magical world
Type of work: Novel
Time of work: The late 1980s
Locale: Lanark County, Ontario, Canada
First published: 1988

THE STORY

Greenmantle is relatively unusual in its combination of high pastoral myth and violent crime fiction. Charles de Lint often writes what might be called urban fantasy, but this novel is set primarily in or alongside a Canadian forest.

Frances (Frankie) Treasure has won a large lottery and has moved to a family home in the country with her fourteen-year-old daughter, Alice

(Ali). Her former husband, Earl Shaw, a violent criminal who has worked with the Mafia, decides to take what money he can get from Frankie in order to finance a drug deal. Living next door to Frankie is a retired Mafia hitman, Tony Valenti, who is thought to be dead by everyone but a close older friend, Mario Papale.

In the neighboring forest is a mystery associated with a hidden village, New Wolding. The village piper's music sometimes calls to view a changeling figure, notably as a giant stag. Also in the woods is a secret, a wild girl called Maggy Mellan. People who hear the piping respond in various ways. A local man, Lance Maxwell, becomes violently lustful, but others seem nobler.

As the plot develops, various dangerous people threaten Frankie and Tony. Ali is in danger because Earl plans to use her to make ransom demands on Frankie. Meanwhile, Ali and Frankie become close friends of Tony. Ali develops a strong interest in the strange forest magic, forming a friendship with Maggy. She also becomes friends with a pair of people in New Wolding, the learned Lewis Datchery and his friend Lily. The stag intervenes to attack Earl in his car, and Earl's associate, Howie Peale, is shot by Tony. Earl and Tony recognize each other from former dealings.

In New York, one of the gangsters who framed Tony for murder, Broadway Joe Ricca, fails to honor a promise made to Mario that he will call off a hit against Tony. He has put his son Louie on the job. Louie is killed while attempting to murder Tony. Frankie is almost raped by Lance but is rescued by Howie and two young women from a nearby gangster's home. Ali is helped by the stag, whom she comes to call Greenmantle and who takes her into an alternate universe. She also is captured by "the Hunt of dogs," who become monks, and is violently interrogated. In the end, she must be rescued by Greenmantle, while Frankie and Tony are helped by the fast-moving Maggy.

ANALYSIS

To Ali and Frankie, the normal people in the story who have been untouched previously by supernatural experience or by violent crime, the fantastic elements and the gangsters that enter their lives are equally unreal; one belongs to magic and the other to B-films. The novel brings the worlds of fantasy and crime fiction together to shape the destinies of two ordinary, innocent people.

Ali, however, is not altogether ordinary, in that her inner fire and natural wisdom mark her as a person of importance to the mythic figures. That fire is shared, in a way, by Tony Valenti, who has behaved as a criminal all his life only because he was brought up within the "family." Valenti rejects his criminal life but is forced to use the violent techniques he has learned against his Mafia enemies. Ali comes to embrace mythic values, though her actions conflict with her desire to share her mothers suffering life.

The mystery and its piping, representative of religion, are related closely to Pan and to Jesus. De Lint seems to suggest that religion does not change people but rather reflects human desires. Accordingly, the Hunt is presented as a Christian group that would crucify Jesus again; its members associate the Greenmantle figure with Satan. Ali has to distinguish between their narrow truth and the full truth she has learned. The piping turns the relatively harmless Lance Maxwell into a rutting stag. He is prepared even to kill his own beloved dog, Dooker, when possessed by the music, and eventually he commits suicide.

The Mafia family, whose evil has overtaken its original moral functions, is destroyed by the actions of a betrayed hit man. The human family grows in moral strength, but Earl, breaker of that strength, must be destroyed. Justice therefore is achieved on both the mythical and the criminal levels.

The novel is unusual in naming several important writers of interest to the author. One of the writers, Caitlin Midhir, is a de Lint heroine featured in the novel *Yarrow: An Autumn Tale* (1986) and mentioned in other works. In his Author's Note, de Lint sets the roots of Greenmantle in Kenneth Grahame's *The Wind in the Willows* (1908) and also mentions Lord Dunsany's *The Blessing of Pan* (1927).

Greenmantle borrows characters and concepts from the Robin Hood legend. Lance Maxwell resembles in some ways the stag-headed Herne the Hunter featured in one televised version of the Robin Hood story. *Greenmantle* also adopts the greenwood, a place to which Robin Hood retreated from enemies. Tony is a "headman," and arrows are used in the action. Frankie and Ali share the Maid Marian persona, and Ali is almost executed by friars. Other works in de Lint's extensive and varied output explore the bigger mystery of which *Greenmantle* forms one part.

—*Michael J. Tolley*

GRENDEL

Grendel, the hideous monster slain by Beowulf in the first English epic, tells his own story while philosophizing about the meaning of life and the power of art and language

Author: John Gardner (1933-1982)
Genre: Fantasy—mythological
Type of work: Novel
Time of work: Probably the sixth century c.e.
Locale: Scandinavia
First published: 1971

THE STORY

Grendel, a young monster, lives with his mother in a vast cave under a marsh. Swimming through a pool of firesnakes, he finds a secret door leading to the world above. On the surface one night, he becomes stuck in a tree. Exhausted, he finally sleeps, awakening to find that a group of humans is trying to figure out what he is. Grendel understands their language, but they misinterpret everything he says and eventually try to kill him. Only his mother's arrival rescues him.

Grendel periodically visits the surface to observe these creatures who speak his language. They slowly evolve from small marauding groups, always fighting and bragging, into organized communities clustered around meadhalls; they begin planting crops and domesticating animals. Hrothgar gradually predominates, brutally subduing nearby tribes and building roads to consolidate his power. Despite these superficial changes, Hrothgar's actions merely change the scale, not the meaning, of the incessant strife. The arrival of a blind bard, whom Grendel dubs the Shaper, transforms everything. His poetic words turn violence into heroism for an ideal, and destruction into part of the glorious destiny of Hrothgar's people. Bloodshed, suffering, and sacrifice now have a historical context and transcendent meaning.

Grendel understands that the Shapers songs hide reality behind beautiful webs of words, but he still longs to believe the vision. He accepts the Shapers view that God divided humanity into two races, even if he himself is a member of the race that God cursed. Overwhelmed by emotion, he tries to make peace with the humans. Again, they misunderstand and attack him; when he defends himself, he inadvertently kills several of them and flees into the forest. Nevertheless, he begins to comprehend that, as the human's enemy, he helps to transform them into the creatures of the vision. A visit to the dragon who sees all of history reinforces this dawning realization.

Caught between despising humans and yearning to belong, Grendel begins his idiotic war. Rendered invulnerable to weapons by the dragon, he makes systematic, murderous raids on Hrothgar's meadhall. One thane, Unferth, understands Grendel's speech and tracks him down, seeking a hero's death; Grendel mockingly lets him live. Grendel has second thoughts, however, when he sees Wealtheow, the queen. Given to Hrothgar in a political marriage, she sacrifices her happiness for her people. Her beauty and sacrifice spur Grendel to greater violence. Confronting an old priest, Grendel pretends to be The Destroyer but slowly realizes that human society contains its own destruction, in the form of ambition, jealousy, and greed. As humans themselves recognize this, Grendel becomes obsolete.

In the twelfth year of Grendel's war, the Shaper dies, and strangers arrive from far away. One stranger fascinates Grendel with his mild voice, massive shoulders, beardless face, and empty eyes. Incredibly, he promises Hrothgar that he will destroy Grendel. That night, the stranger, wide awake and utterly fearless, awaits Grendel's raid. He grasps Grendel's arm in a merciless grip and whispers that his death is as inevitable as spring.

He tears off the monster's arm. Panic-stricken, Grendel flees to the forest and dies, protesting to the last.

ANALYSIS

Although most of the characters are familiar from the epic *Beowulf*, from about the eleventh century, they naturally play somewhat different roles in *Grendel*'s own retelling. Hardly a brute force of nature, this sophisticated monster asks philosophical questions and shows more self-awareness than his human foes. By contrast, whatever dignity Hrothgar has, he has gained from constantly confronting an enemy such as Grendel. Grendel does not even know the noble Beowulf's name; to him, the stranger's fearless heroism simply masks cold-blooded insanity.

This early work by John Gardner earned his first major critical acclaim. Like his other works, *Grendel* reveals Gardner's fascination with questions of morality and meaning, as well as his use of unexpected or alternating perspectives. Gardner strongly believed that literature should contribute positively to morality, as he wrote in *On Moral Fiction* (1978), by forcing readers to consider the moral premises of choices and by showing the consequences of evil. His novel *October Light* (1976) won the National Book Critics Circle Award.

Grendel recalls three types of fantasy literature. First, it resembles the works of J. R. R. Tolkien in its re-creation of a densely textured, premedieval world on the cusp between paganism and Christianity. Here readers find rituals from a distant past, fabulous creatures and characters who possess arcane powers, and a rich poetic language that animates the physical world. The resemblance to Tolkien's work should come as no surprise, for both Gardner and Tolkien were professors of early English literature, and Tolkien wrote influential works on *Beowulf*.

Like T. H. White's *The Once and Future King* (1958) and Marion Zimmer Bradley's *The Mists of Avalon* (1983), *Grendel* takes a familiar story and tells it from a different perspective. White introduces whimsical elements to the Arthurian legend, and Bradley considers it from the perspective of the women involved, producing fresh insights into tales that are now almost part of the collective unconscious. Gardner's reversal of perspective, from that of the hero to that of the monster, likewise reinvigorates an ancient story. Some might find *Grendel* even more powerful than modern renderings of the Arthurian legend, for fewer layers of romance separate modern readers from the brutal and primitive world of the original.

Finally, *Grendel* is an animal fantasy, like Richard Adams' *Watership Down* (1972). Such works teach readers to see the world from the perspective of nonhuman characters. This usually entails making the readers own human perspective appear foreign and strange. Gardner chose the even harder task of asking readers to empathize with a huge murderous monster, not with more vulnerable animals. This daring act of imagination, along with Gardner's teasing philosophical musings and gorgeous language, make *Grendel* a classic of modern fantasy literature.

—*Susan Wladaver-Morgan*

GREYBEARD

Following an accident involving nuclear weapons that leaves humanity sterile, a group of travelers navigates the Thames

Author: Brian W. Aldiss (1925–)
Genre: Science fiction—post-holocaust
Type of work: Novel
Time of work: 2029 and beyond
Locale: England and Washington, D.C.
First published: 1964

THE STORY

A plague of stoats convinces Greybeard and his wife, Martha, to leave the isolated English village of Sparcot. They take to the river Thames with their friend Charley Samuels and two other villagers, Becky and Towin Thomas. The group takes refuge downstream. Jeff Pitt, a poacher, finds them sheltering in the house of a man who committed suicide after the death of his wife.

In his late forties, Greybeard—born Algernon Timberlane—is one of the last people born before the nuclear experiments euphemistically called the Accident disrupted the Van Allen belts and made humanity sterile. Humans and domestic animals are becoming scarce as a childless, demoralized population allows civilization to collapse. Rumors abound concerning the long-term effects of the Accident, and there are reports that elves, gnomes, and little people with the faces of badgers lurk in the expanding English woodlands.

The first of three flashbacks shows a middle-aged Timberlane's near-fatal encounter with a local dictator. Even though both husband and wife were willing to cooperate, the strongman sent soldiers to kill them and confiscate Timberlanes recording equipment. Timberlane persuaded Captain Jeff Pitt, who was under orders to kill Timberlane, to join the couple. By forcing their van through a perimeter barricade, the three managed to escape.

Continuing down the Thames, the people from Sparcot come to bustling Swifford Fair, where charlatan Bunny Jingadangelow claims to have the secrets of youth and immortality. While Greybeard is bedazzled by the first interesting conversation he has had in years, the group is robbed. Becky and Thomas decide to remain at the fair, but Greybeard, Martha, Jeff, and Charley travel on toward the river's mouth.

The second flashback describes how Timberlane and Charley failed to save one of humanity's last children. Disheartened, Timberlane joined the Documentation of Universal Contemporary History project headquartered in Washington, D.C. After training, the young man married Martha and went home to England to record the end of the world.

Still further down the river, the party from Sparcot enters Oxford. Greybeard, who had sold his documentary van to a passing peddler for food, finds it garaged there. The would-be historian spends nearly two years trying to repurchase his equipment before he decides to renounce his mission. Greybeard and Martha resume their journey. Charley joins the couple at the last moment, but Pitt, off hunting, is left behind.

The third flashback describes the events that led to a compassionate doctor arranging that Algernon and Martha become companions as children. The boy's father, Arthur Timberlane, was unable to cope with the changes in his world, resulting indirectly from the Accident, including bankruptcy of his toy company and the restlessness of his wife, and killed himself in a single-car crash.

Jeff finds the three people from Sparcot lost on a newly formed freshwater sea in the Thames valley. They see a small excursion boat that has become a shrine to a religious figure, Jingadangelow under another name. Their old acquaintance Becky is among the charlatans attendants. She tells them that Towin has died. Despite the success of his pitch and the carnal company of a healthy fifteen-year-old girl, a bored Jingadangelow wants to abandon everything to travel with the four friends.

After Greybeard refuses, the captive girl's beast-faced companions appear and attack the charlatan. One of them is wounded and is discovered to be a normal boy camouflaged with animal masks and skins. So precious that their lives are in danger, humanity's feral children have hidden and cared for one another. Greybeard, his wife, and the boy, named Arthur, continue down the river, along with Jeff and Charley. Although her husband is eager to begin civilization again, wise Martha has her doubts.

Analysis

Readers should note that the British version of *Greybeard* restores material cut from the U.S. version. *Greybeard* is unusual among the many novels about the aftermath of a global holocaust because its tone is melancholy rather than horrific. People discover the scope and scale of the disaster very slowly. Most continue to strive to create comfortable day-to-day lives, more disturbed by the death of their own dreams than by the end of their species.

Civilization devolves stage by stage toward a pastoral existence as humanity begins to die out. The natural world flourishes. When people see half- and near-human beasts in the fields and forests, they are more than willing to believe. As rationality dies, the myths of a golden age are reborn; humanity hopes, however foolishly, for another chance.

Even Greybeard, always striving to be in command of himself and those around him, is joyful when he discovers that his rejection of hope as unreasonable is wrong and that humanity does have a future. The story ends on a note of optimism, although it is not clear whether a new age is beginning or an old one is being renewed.

In what is possibly his finest science-fiction novel, Brian Aldiss tells the story in a nonlinear way. The four sections in *Greybeard*'s present are linked by their setting on the river and move forward in time. The three flashbacks journey further and further into the novels past, establishing the history of a once-familiar world fatally disrupted. Each shift from present to past alters the readers perception of previous events. When humanity's last children discover the first members of the new generation, the resolution is logical and yet surprising.

Aldiss uses small scale, tight focus, and a long time span to personalize a common science-fiction theme. The book shows his characteristic interests in fertility, order versus chaos, and dislocations of perception. Fond of experimenting with literary techniques, Aldiss sometimes favors effects over a clear narrative; however, in *Greybeard* he is restrained. Although the telling becomes complicated by the changes in time from present to flashback, this is a simple tale, told in a satisfying manner.

—*Catherine Mintz*

GRIMUS

On an island of immortals controlled by his own double, Flapping Eagle searches for the secrets of identity, imagination, and consciousness

Author: Salman Rushdie (1947–)
Genre: Fantasy—magical realism
Type of work: Novel
Time of work: Undefined
Locale: An alternate dimension called Calf Island
First published: 1975

THE STORY

Salman Rushdie's first published novel, *Grimus*, follows Flapping Eagle, an immortal Axona Indian who searches an alternate dimension known as Calf Island for his missing sister, Bird-Dog. Guided by Virgil Jones—an exiled associate of Grimus, the dimensions creator—Flapping Eagle must climb Calf Mountain, survive the mind-altering dimension fever, and infiltrate the complex society of K, the town where others who have chosen immortality have come to live. By learning all he can about K, Flapping Eagle hopes to find the mysterious Grimus, uncover the secret of his sisters disappearance, and locate the source of Calf Islands shifting dimensions—the Stone Rose, an ancient instrument of imagination that controls dimensional space.

In K, Flapping Eagle is a guest in the house of Ignatius Quasimodo Gribb, a rationalist philosopher who has convinced the town's inhabitants that Grimus and the Stone Rose are meaningless myths. Gribb is the author of "The All-Purpose Quotable Philosophy," a book of clichés designed to spread his ideas among the people of K. While living with Gribb and his wife, Elfrida, Flapping Eagle also meets the town's leader, Count Alexsandr Cherkassov, a Russian aristocrat, and his wife, Irina. Both of the beautiful wives are mysteriously attracted to Flapping Eagle, but despite an affair with Irina Cherkassova, he falls in love with the more faithful Elfrida, who soon tells her husband that she loves the handsome Amerindian. His illusions about his marriage shattered, Gribb immediately loses his ability to conceptualize a rational world and dies as a result. The entire world of Calf Island begins to fall prey once again to the dimensional distortions of the Grimus Effect.

As the towns illusions begin to collapse, Bird-Dog appears and escorts Flapping Eagle to Grimus' house on the summit of Calf Mountain. There, Flapping Eagle discovers that he and Grimus resemble each other and that Grimus has lured him to the mountain to take his place as caretaker of the Stone Rose. Grimus—whose name is an anagram for Simurg, a mythical phoenix—may in fact already be a part of Flapping Eagle, a version of the Amerindians self that has created all reality. To convince Flapping Eagle to comply with his wishes, Grimus enters the Axonas mind; the two meld into a single split consciousness in which the I-Grimus and the I-Eagle fight to control the minds imagination. The struggle continues until the I-Eagle realizes the secret of conceptualizing a new dimension. He quickly re-creates Calf Island in his mind, but without the Stone Rose. At the same moment, the angry townspeople, deprived of their belief in a rational world, ransack the house and kill Grimus. With the destruction of the Stone Rose, however, all the islands inhabitants and the island itself begin to dissolve into unshaped conceptual energy.

ANALYSIS

Grimus belongs to a long tradition of intellectual fantasies that combine dreamlike, imaginative journeys with serious social or philosophical criticism. The novels use of a combined first-and third-person narration in which Flapping Eagle is both the protagonist and the principal narrative voice poses one of the works main questions: Does reality exist beyond the conceptual constructions of a single minds imagination? The failure of Ignatius Gribb's rationalist philosophy and the final dissolution of Calf Island suggest that imagination and reality are one and the same and that those human beings who ignore the powers of imagination and myth do so at their own peril.

Such fictional techniques and thematic concerns place the novel in a line that reaches back as far as François Rabelais' *Gargantua and Pantagruel* (1532–1564) and extends through Jonathan Swift's *Gullivers Travels* (1726), Lewis Carroll's *Alice's Adventures in Wonderland* (1865), and L. Frank Baum's *The Wonderful Wizard of Oz* (1900). In more recent terms, *Grimus* also bears some relation to the contemporary school of fiction known as Magical Realism, in which fantasy and reality continually intersect in ways that criticize or comment on history and politics.

Coming early in Rushdie's career, *Grimus* demonstrates some of the narrative and imaginative techniques developed in the novelists subsequent fiction, including *Midnight's Children* (1981), *Shame* (1983), and *The Satanic Verses* (1988). These more successful works, however, leave behind the earlier novels pervasive fantasy and offer instead versions of contemporary history in which fantasy and myth play a more limited but important role. The decision to ground his narratives more firmly in reality has brought Rushdie far greater success; critics have offered only mixed responses to *Grimus*, whereas his subsequent works were praised widely.

Grimus also initiates Rushdie's abiding concern with the clash of opposing cultures and the plight of the individual caught between alternative visions of reality and history. As an orphaned Amerindian at odds with his own people, Flapping Eagle represents the modern, divided individual both attracted to and alienated from two conflicting cultures. Like many of Rushdie's characters, he must learn to use his imaginative powers to reshape his world and so attempt to find a synthesis of the two halves of his culturally divided self. The vehicle for such transformations, as *Grimus* suggests, is myth or story, and much of Rushdie's writing examines the limits of narrative power to remake a divided world. This persistent theme, as well as Rushdie's skillful blend of Eastern and Western mythologies, has helped to foster a wider interest in multicultural fiction. These same concerns continue to develop in *East, West* (1994), a collection of short stories that investigate the continued tensions between contemporary and traditional cultures.

—*Clark Davis*

GULLIVER'S TRAVELS

Lemuel Gulliver goes on a series of sea voyages and has a variety of encounters in which his psychic deterioration as a human being is revealed

Author: Jonathan Swift (1667–1745)
Genre: Fantasy—cultural exploration
Type of work: Novel

Time of work: 1699–1715
Location: Various island communities
First published: 1726

THE STORY

Gulliver's Travels, as the book is now known, first appeared anonymously. Capitalizing on the lively interest in voyages at the time, Jonathan Swift called it *Travels into Several Remote Nations of the World* and ascribed it to "Lemuel Gulliver, First a Surgeon, and then a Captain of Several Ships." Swift published the book anonymously partly because of the occasional scatological references but more pressingly because of the thinly veiled political satire of England's powerful first prime minister, Whig party leader Sir Robert Walpole, whom Swift detested and whom contemporaries would have immediately recognized in the ridiculous figure of the tightrope dancer, Flimnap, the treasurer of Lilliput, in part 1.

The first two parts of *Gulliver's Travels* form a nicely balanced pair. In Lilliput, where Gulliver first is shipwrecked, he is twelve times as tall as the diminutive local inhabitants. Everything is kept to this scale except for their senseless warring and hypocrisy, which are out of all proportion to their size and therefore seem the more alarming; one, illogically perhaps, expects decent conduct from tiny people. Flimnap, however, so inflated is his ego, accuses Gulliver of having an affair with his six-inch-tall wife.

On the second island on which Gulliver is marooned, the natives are twelve times as tall as he is. He displays all the moral blindness of the Lilliputians in his dealings with the reasonable and generous Brobdingnagians. Gulliver, from his own over-inflated notion of his six-foot self, is offended that the local women do not cover themselves when undressing in front of him. Evidently, like Flimnap in part 1, Gulliver believes that he is at least their equal. After two years, Gulliver escapes to sea and returns to England.

Gulliver's third voyage, actually written by Swift after the fourth, is the most scattered in its focus. It is largely political and for this reason is usually not as well received by critics. Gulliver travels to Laputa and encounters scientists and intellectuals whose work is, for the pragmatic parish priest in Swift, altogether too far removed from real life. Attempting to distill sunlight from cucumbers is one of their projects. The Laputan Projectors, in their flying island, tyrannize the inhabitants of Balnibarbi and waste this fertile land. Visiting nearby Luggnagg, Gulliver for a moment envies the Struldbrugs, who live forever, though he quickly changes his mind when he discovers that the immortals do age in the normal way.

His fourth voyage, to the land of the Houyhnhnms (named after the whinnying sound horses make), is the climax of Gulliver's personal regression. That he cannot approach the level of rationality of the equine race who are in control drives him insane. His much closer resemblance to the bestial, greedy, bellicose, and irrational Yahoos, who are the other native inhabitants, depresses him severely. Viewing him as a possible subversive, the Houyhnhnms invite him to leave their rational world. Finally home again in England, he prefers the stable to his home and can no longer tolerate the company of other humans. Feeling oneself superior to the entire human race, as Gulliver does, is by most definitions a position of insane pride.

ANALYSIS

As a product of an age that celebrated reason and was then apt to think of life as a comedy, *Gulliver's Travels*, it should not go unsaid, is frequently funny. As an Irishman born in Dublin, Dean Swift of St. Patrick's Episcopal Cathedral was inclined to blame the Whig administration in London for Ireland's social ills. Satire is the outsider's mode, and Swift here uses and makes fun of the popular, first-person, sea voyage account. William Dampier's books of the late seventeenth century had been extremely successful in establishing the genre. Daniel Defoe had published the successful *Robinson Crusoe* in 1719, seven years before Swift's book appeared. Swift supported Irish aspirations for freedom from English domination and published his equally incendiary *The Drapier's Letters* anonymously in 1724. The Anglican clergyman in him also appreciated that some moral rearmament must accompany any political solution. It is this moral dimension, this focus on humankind's universal propensity to delude itself, that is the main appeal of the work for subsequent generations of readers, for whom the machinations of eighteenth century Westminster politicians mean very little. Swift deliberately sets up Gulliver's voyages in a realistic voyage framework. He provides maps of the voyages, complete with decorative, tiny, spouting whale drawings just like real maps. He also mixes actual places (Japan and Sumatra) with the imaginary.

Gulliver's level of pride is fairly stable in part 1, where he has the physical and moral advantage over the tiny Lilliputians. In part 2, however, he reveals himself to be suffering from their destructive, hubristic attitude. Having boasted of the political and social situation in England, and then having offered the king of Brobdingnag gunpowder, Gulliver is roundly deflated by that monarch, who informs him that he must represent "the most pernicious race of little odious vermin nature ever suffered to crawl upon the surface of the earth." In part 3, Gulliver's pride expands even further when for an instant he envies the Struldbrugs' immortality. His normal high level of this vice, the most damning in the Christian scheme of things, returns in part 4, where he resents being treated like a Yahoo and envies the superrational Houyhnhnms. Humankind exists, Swift suggests, between the animal world of the Yahoos and the rational world of the Houyhnhnms. Gulliver's recourse to living in the stable with his horses on his return to England is hardly a solution. To be out of step with the entire human race is to be insane; some kind of balance, however precarious, is Swift's proposal in this, his only trip into the world of fantasy voyages.

—Archibald E. Irwin

GUNNER CADE

A future soldier's world collapses when he learns at first hand the realities behind the interplanetary empire he defends

Author: Cyril Judd (C[yril] M. Kornbluth, 1923–1958, and Judith Merril [Juliet Grossman], 1923–1997)
Genre: Science fiction—future war
Type of work: Novel
Time of work: About c.e. 12,000
Locale: Earth, aboard a space flier, and Mars
First published: 1952 (serial form, *Astounding Science-Fiction*, March-May, 1952)

THE STORY

Although Cyril Kornbluth devised the initial outline of *Gunner Cade*, he and Judith Merril collaborated in a full sense in the actual writing, alternating rough drafts of chapters and revising each others work. The story follows the adventures and misadventures of Cade, a Gunner-ranked Armsman of the Realm of Man, from the time of his ignominious capture by a rebellious religious cult to his moment of victory, both personal and military, during the first battle between Earth's Armsmen and rebellious Mars forces.

Cade follows a path of discovery, seeking better understanding of himself and his world. The greatest obstacles on his path lie within himself. As a Brother in the Order of Armsmen, he has thoroughly assimilated the ascetic doctrines of Klin Philosophy, a set of verbal formulas that focus his mind on devoted service to a triumvirate: the Gunner Supreme, the Power Master, and the Emperor.

Shortly after his capture by the cult, Cade meets a woman who becomes his obsession. Constrained by his brainwashing, he can only equate her with the idealized woman who greets a Gunner at the point of honorable death. He later learns that she is Lady Jocelyn, niece of the Emperor. Believing that he has learned important secrets while with the cult and knowing no other course of action because he has been officially pronounced dead, Cade seeks out the Gunner Supreme and the Power Master. He obtains interviews but finds his life put in jeopardy each time.

Because of these treacheries, Cade opens himself to the teaching of Lady Jocelyn, who proves to be of vital assistance in his deprogramming. Jocelyn tells him the true history of the empire and convinces him of the importance of free thought. Cade also learns about seedier and more practical aspects of life from the thief Fledwick, whom he meets as a jailmate and who embodies values contrary to Cade's "clean" philosophy.

Ten thousand years before the story opens, the Realm of Man rose out of the ashes of global atomic warfare on Earth. One metaphoric fallout shapes the Realms attitudes and makes itself felt particularly in the petty and formalized warfare between the states of the empire, in which the Armsmen are employed: Everyone shares a deep-seated revulsion against attack from the air.

To even think of attacking an enemy from a flier marks one for disgrace.

Cade breaks completely from Klin Philosophy, even to the point of questioning his deep-seated disgust at firing a weapon from a spacecraft. He begins to see the Realm of Man as a static and sterile system in which creative thought and scientific curiosity are moribund. On Mars, however, the challenges of the frontier have helped liberate minds. Cade's decision to join the rebellion, when poised between Earth and Mars in a thoughtful free-fall moment, marks the beginning of his rebirth.

ANALYSIS

Gunner Cade fits in the mold of works that appeared under the editorship of John W. Campbell, Jr., who encouraged from his write'rs extrapolations that embraced not only technical matters but also social implications. The central speculation in *Gunner Cade* concerns social fallout from nuclear warfare, as experienced in a time so distant from the present that the nuclear weapons themselves have vanished from memory. Fear of attack from the sky becomes a building block for the Realm of Man, and that fear is not challenged for ten millennia.

Gunner Cade was the second and last novel collaboration between Kornbluth and Merril, preceded by *Outpost Mars* (1952; serial form as *Mars Child*, 1951; republished as *Sin in Space*, 1961). Although a success, with a long history of reprints, *Gunner Cade* has been overshadowed by the success of another Kornbluth collaboration, *The Space Merchants* (1953), with Frederik Pohl. Structurally, *Gunner Cade* anticipates the later novel.

Gunner Cade fits within Kornbluth's works in its strong thematic concern with the redemptive power of historical knowledge. In his 1949 short story "The Only Thing We Learn," Kornbluth similarly posits a decadent and static society being challenged by rebels from the frontier and portrays the situation as a cyclic occurrence in history. His 1952 short story "The Luckiest Man in Denv" not only echoes the notion that historical knowledge can renew a static society but also contains a scene that parallels the bedroom assassination attempt against Cade.

The plot moves through layers of masks and deception, a quality to be found in many Kornbluth works, including *Takeoff* (1952), *The Syndic* (1953), *Not This August* (1955), *The Man of Cold Rages* (1958), and "Two Dooms" (1958).

Strong female characters and the motif of sexual egalitarianism recur throughout the work of both collaborators. In *Gunner Cade*, Jocelyn plays a role considerably greater than that played by the typical love interest, initiating much of the action to which Cade reacts. Successive chapters of the novel reveal her as a complex and creative individual, for she appears to Cade under various guises and at one point speaks in riddlelike rhymes. By the time she makes clear her motives, she has emerged as a character more powerful and thoughtful than any other in the novel, including Cade. She gives way to Cade only in the area of military expertise. Cade's last vestiges of confusion about Jocelyn dissolve upon reaching Mars, where the sexes appear to be treated on a more egalitarian basis than on Earth.

The novels concern with the effects of nuclear warfare finds reflection in other solo works by the collaborators, including "The Remorseful" (1954) and "Two Dooms" (1958) by Kornbluth and "That Only a Mother" (1948) and *Shadow on the Hearth* (1950) by Merril.

—*Mark Rich*

HALF PAST HUMAN

The remnants of humanity struggle to survive in a regimented society determined to destroy any mutation or any rebellion against its power

Author: T. J. Bass (Thomas J. Bassler, 1932-2011)
Genre: Science fiction—future history
Type of work: Novels
Time of work: 2349 and an unspecified amount of time before and after that date
Locale: The Hive, various locations on Earth, and a new world
First published: *Half Past Human* (1971; brief extracts published as "Half Past Human" in *Galaxy*, 1969, and "G. I. T. A. R." in *If*, 1970) and *The Godwhale* (1974; brief extract published as "Rorqual Maru" in *Galaxy*, 1972)

The Story

T. J. Bass's *Half Past Human* and *The Godwhale* tell the story of humanity's struggle to survive in a world controlled by the regimented Big Earth Society, known as the Big ES or the Hive. The citizens of the Big ES are the weak descendants of humanity, known as Nebishes. Most of these beings cannot stand exposure to the sun and must live in underground cities. In both novels, a group of people who are genetically closer to humanity than the Nebishes rebel against the structured society of the Big ES. The rebels engage in a desperate struggle for survival and eventually succeed in gaining their independence. *Half Past Human* concludes with the humans who have rebelled being transported to a new world on a ship controlled by a computer known as Olga. In *The Godwhale*, the rebels succeed in taking control of the ocean and force the Hive to negotiate with them in order to ensure its continued survival.

Half Past Human begins with the discovery of Toothpick, a small robot known as a cyber, by Moon and Dan, an ancient man and dog, in the mountains. Moon agrees to take Toothpick with him when the cyber promises that it will help him and Dan find new teeth. Moon, Dan, and Toothpick eventually take shelter with a group of human outcasts, known as buckeyes, in the mountain village of Mount Tabulum.

Meanwhile, in the Hive, a Nebish who is a mechanical expert, Tinker, receives an order from the Big ES that he should mate. He meets a woman named Mu Ren, and they eventually have a child. Their son is declared to be an unauthorized child because of a prior miscarriage. Because the child is unauthorized, the Big ES eventually will put him to death. The threat to their child causes Tinker and Mu Ren to flee the Hive and take their chances in the hostile environment of the surface. Tinker and his family also find shelter in Mount Tabulum.

The Big ES begins a concentrated effort to eliminate the buckeyes and hunt down those who escaped the Hive. During the attempts to kill the buckeyes, one of the Nebishes, Moses Eppendorff, rebels against the Big ES and joins the buckeyes. The buckeyes eventually flee south in an effort to escape the reach of the Big ES. They hope to find salvation at the hands of a mysterious deity known as Olga. As the buckeyes travel south, they gain more members and eventually form an army. In response to this armed force, the Big ES gathers together an immense number of Hunters, Nebishes who go outside and kill buckeyes, to permanently eliminate those who rebel against it.

The buckeyes engage in a war that appears to be turning to the advantage of the Big ES until a meteor shower rains down on Earth. The meteors are actually sent by Olga in order to give it an opportunity to retrieve the buckeyes and other humans from Earth. Olga transports Moon, Dan, Mu Ren, Moses Eppendorff, and the other humans to a new world where they can start a new civilization and enjoy lives of freedom instead of regimentation. Olga also leaves a wandering robot, known as Gitar, to gather more Nebishes who possess human genes, in preparation for its return visit.

The story of *The Godwhale* starts before the events of *Half Past Human* with the account of an accident that cuts Larry Dever, a fully human male, in half. Rather than enduring life attached to a mannequin, a cyber that would act as his legs, Larry decides to be frozen until his lower half can be replaced. He wakes many years in the future and is given the opportunity to have his mind transferred to the body of a man who has been grown from his genes. He refuses to allow this to happen because he considers this man to be his son. He is frozen again rather than joining his descendants in their journey into space.

Larry wakes again in the time when the Big ES controls every aspect of society. He is rescued from death by Big Har, an unauthorized child who grew up in the sewers of the Hive with other unwanted citizens. They eventually escape from the Hive and make their way to an underwater civilization, known as the Benthics, who have fled from the Big Earth Society. They both fit into this new society, along with a cyber, known as Trilobite, who serves *Rorqual Maru*, an immense harvesting robot shaped like a whale. After centuries of inactivity, the whale wakes and falls into the service of the Hive. It breaks free along with its captain, ARNOLD, a genetically engineered human designed to serve the Hive. They eventually ally themselves with the Benthics against the Hive.

The Hive makes several attempts to destroy *Rorqual Maru* and the Benthics but ultimately fails. The Hive is forced to negotiate with the Benthics after the latter gain mastery over the oceans and devastate the Hive's central mind. At the novels conclusion, *Rorqual Maru* undertakes the mission of helping humanity repopulate the Earth.

ANALYSIS

As of 1995, *Half Past Human* and *The Godwhale* were T. J. Bass's only novels in the field of science fiction. Both received generally favorable reviews from critics. These two novels present a dark future in which the descendants of humanity live in a society that controls every aspect of their lives. There is little individual freedom, and anyone who attempts to deviate from the strictures of the Big ES must either be destroyed or flee to the outside world. In the midst of this dark future, Bass shows that there is hope; some individuals rebel and break free of the Big ES. These humans are willing to depend on their own abilities rather than on machines in their efforts to be free of a repressive society.

Bass's presentation of the Big Earth Society is a devastating condemnation of civilizations that attempt to stifle individual freedom. There appear to be certain benefits for citizens who live in the Big ES, such as having all their needs met, from living quarters to food. Under this pleasant surface, Bass reveals a hideous society. The Big ES destroys children for being born at the wrong time or because they may be deformed. There is no individual freedom because the Big ES does not allow its citizens to leave their regimented roles. It attempts to destroy those who rebel against its control. Furthermore, in this apparently perfect society, suicide and drug use are rampant, as seen in *Half Past Human*. Those conditions and the overcrowding evident in *The Godwhale* reveal the Big ES's hideous nature.

Along with his condemnation of this regimented society, Bass uses his novels to show the importance of individual freedom to human civilization. The society of the Big ES is stagnant and will never grow beyond its regimented form. There will be few, if any, new discoveries or attempts to explore space. Certain individuals refuse to live under this repressive regime. The efforts of Tinker, Mu Ren, Moses Eppendorff, Big Har, ARNOLD, and others to break free of the Big ES show how the human spirit cannot be crushed and will eventually rebel to gain freedom. At the end of both novels, these humans hold the potential to develop new civilizations that can grow and make better worlds for their descendants.

Another fascinating aspect of Bass's novels is his portrayal of the relationship of humanity to machines. In his account of Larry Dever's early life in *The Godwhale*, Bass shows how humans become progressively more dependent on machines for survival. Each time Larry wakes up, robots and machines have come to play a larger role in humanitys survival. During these early years, humanity still controls the machines. When

Larry wakes in the Big ES, however, the Nebishes depend on machines to provide for their every need and count on them for survival. In an indictment of dependence on technology, the individuals who escape the Big ES use primitive tools and only use technology when they can control it or can work in partnership with it.

—David A. Oakes

THE HAMPDENSHIRE WONDER

A mutant child develops great intelligence and other powers of the mind

Author: J(ohn) D(avys) Beresford (1873–1947)
Genre: Science fiction—superbeing
Type of work: Novel
Time of work: The early twentieth century
Locale: Hampdenshire, a village in the south of England
First published: 1911

THE STORY

The narrator is reading a book during a train journey when he is disturbed by the presence of a baby with an unusually large head and a disconcerting stare. He investigates the history of this remarkable infant, who turns out to be Victor Stott, the progeny of a marriage of convenience between a professional cricket player and an aging spinster. Following the fathers desertion, the mother and her son were given a new home by the local squire, Henry Challis, at the request of a clergyman, Percy Crashaw.

The narrator, who is a writer, is fascinated by Victor and begins a careful study of his burgeoning talents. By the time he is five years old, the boy has read through the contents of Challis library and has familiarized himself with the entire legacy of human knowledge. Victor's research leads him to deny the existence of God, which so offends Crashaw that the rector attempts to have him committed to an asylum. Challis thwarts this plan and also prevents the boy from being enrolled at a primary school where Crashaw might have the opportunity to indoctrinate him.

Victor treats all other humans with contempt but begins to form a relationship with the narrator, apparently hoping that he might find a sympathetic audience for the deductions and ruminations of his advanced intelligence. Unfortunately, the English language does not contain words for the concepts he wishes to express, and the child becomes frustrated with the narrators failure to make headway. The narrator does, however, save Victor from being pestered by the only human being who is not intimidated by his hypnotic gaze: a hydrocephalic idiot.

Eventually, the narrator becomes so discomfited by his failure to keep up with Victor intellectually, and by the subtle power that the boys stare exerts on him, that he begins to avoid him. When Victor is murdered, the narrator believes that his retreat allowed the crime to be committed, but he does not know whether the perpetrator of the crime was the idiot or the clergyman.

ANALYSIS

The Hampdenshire Wonder was not the first literary attempt to describe a being as far advanced above humankind as human beings are advanced above their apelike ancestors, but it was a significant improvement on earlier attempts. The man of the future in *The British Barbarians* (1895) by Grant Allen and the giants in *The Food of the Gods* (1904) by H. G. Wells are merely mouthpieces whose task is to lend support to the supposedly advanced intelligence of their creators, but J. D. Beresford tries to reach beyond that kind of self-flattery.

There is a sense in which the task is logically impossible, in that no author can transcend the limitations of his own intelligence, but Beresford found the method best fitted to the task in tracking the unnaturally rapid growth of intelligence in a child. Because Victor never grows to maturity, the full extent of his mental powers is never revealed and exists only as a series of delicate suggestions and half-formed impressions.

Physically, Victor bears some resemblance to the futuristic human being sketched in H. G. Wells's brief essay on "The Man of the Year Million" (1893): His brain is huge, but he is otherwise weak. This remained the stereotyped image of humanity's ultimate descendants for the greater part of the twentieth century. Victor's intellectual attainments are far more interesting than his physical form. Inevitably, these are stronger on the negative side than the positive side. Beresford found it easy to find follies that humanity's descendants would abandon, although he was well aware that many of his contemporary readers would reject Victors view on religion and used that as the main source of dramatic tension within the novels plot. Modern historians of the literary imagination are most interested in Victor's attitudes concerning philosophical issues.

The narrator's first encounter with Victor is juxtaposed with his struggle to understand a particularly challenging passage in the book he is reading. In the first edition of the novel, the book is Henri Bergson's *Time and Free Will: An Essay in the Immediate Data of Consciousness* (1910; *Essai sur les données immédiates de la conscience*, 1889) and the passage involves the equation of free will with irrationality—an opinion with which the narrator disagrees vehemently. In later editions, Beresford substituted a passage from G. W. F. Hegel's *The Phenomenology of Spirit* (1872; *Phänomenologie des Geistes*, 1807), which has to do with the nature of knowledge. The substitution was apt. Although the story of the Hampdenshire Wonder aspires to reveal an element of the irrational in human behavior that Beresford refuses to accept as a corollary of free will, its real argument is about the nature and limitations of human knowledge.

It is hardly surprising that Beresford's human characters cannot understand the insights of the superhuman child, who speaks at length only once, to Challis, who deliberately puts out of his mind whatever he has been told and refuses to repeat it to the narrator. The narrator is allowed to perceive the intellectual direction in which those discoveries lie. The essence of the intellectual triumph suggested by his name is that for Victor and his kind, there will be no more mysteries; everything that can be known will be known, and that which cannot be known will be deemed irrelevant. This is the endpoint of the philosophy of positivism, which was still gaining support when the novel was written.

The one book in Challis library that gives Victor cause for thought is Bergson's *Creative Evolution* (*L'Évolution créatrice*, first published in 1907 and translated into English in 1911), which presumably inspired the novel. Bergson sees evolution as the work of an élan vital that projects itself in material forms that constantly are being discarded, and this notion is central to the story. What the narrator must come to terms with—although Crashaw and Challis, in their different ways, refuse to do so—is the certainty that humankind eventually will be discarded by the creative process of evolution as a mere passing phase rather than a conclusive culmination of godly design. All subsequent science-fictional accounts of human evolution have had to confront this issue.

—*Brian Stableford*

THE HANDMAID'S TALE

Offred, a legal concubine in a totalitarian state, tells the story of her experiences and the adjustments she makes to survive

Author: Margaret Atwood (1939–)
Genre: Science fiction—feminist
Type of work: Novel
Time of work: The early twenty-first century
Location: Gilead, in what was once the United States
First published: 1985

THE STORY

In the late 1980's, an ultraconservative religious group toppled the U.S. government and established a totalitarian regime called Gilead. The leadership is strictly Christian in nature and ruthlessly fascist in practice. Using the former society's plummeting birth rates as an excuse, the Gilead leaders force women into restricted roles in society, with little freedom or power. Couples in the upper classes who are without children are assigned Handmaids, who essentially are legal concubines intended to bear their hosts' children. These Handmaids are fertile women who were politically unsafe, divorced, or in second marriages.

The narrator is a Handmaid assigned to the family of a high-ranking commander. She loses her identity and original family, and she is renamed "of Fred" (the commander's first name), or Offred. Offred is cared for by the family in exchange for having sex with the commander. In an elaborate ceremony required by the society, Offred lies between the legs of Fred's wife during the act, making her resemble a substitute womb for the wife. This ritual enacts a literal translation of the Old Testament, in which Rachel says to Jacob, "Behold my maid Bilhah, go in unto her; and she shall bear upon my knees, that I may also have children by her" (Genesis 30:1–3).

Even this tightly controlled society has hidden rebellions. The commander arranges clandestine meetings with Offred. They talk and play Scrabble. Such relationships of Handmaids and their hosts are forbidden, as Handmaids are meant solely for procreation. Offred's walking partner, Ofglen, reveals another rebellion, a resistance group called Mayday, of which she is a member.

The commander's wife arranges for Offred to have an affair with Nick, the chauffeur, so that she might become pregnant even if the commander is sterile. Offred begins to fall in love with Nick and loses all desire for the rebellion encouraged by her friends in Mayday. Offred's tenuous situation becomes more precarious when the commander's wife learns of Offred's secret meetings with the commander. Ofglen is discovered to be part of Mayday and is killed. Offred's story ends in a dramatic climax. The black death van of Gilead arrives at the house to take Offred. At that moment, it is unclear why the van came for her. To her surprise and dismay, Nick appears at her door with the military men and hands her over. As she passes him, he whispers in her ear to go with them because they are from Mayday and will take her outside Gilead. Offred goes into the van. Her ultimate fate, whether betrayal or salvation, is not revealed.

The final chapter of the novel is an epilogue set two hundred years after the story of Offred. The keynote speaker at a symposium on Gileadean studies is a professor who has been studying a document called "The Handmaid's Tale." He makes a few comments on the possible authenticity of this document, which was discovered shortly after the regime of Gilead fell. It remains unclear whether Offred escaped safely or, instead, that only her story survived.

ANALYSIS

The epilogue creates an interesting effect on building a possible future on top of a possible future. Margaret Atwood satirizes at two levels—modern society as a whole in the main story and the world of academia in the epilogue. Reminiscent of George Orwell, Atwood criticizes modern society by showing the horrible extent to which many current problems could advance. Like Orwell, Atwood presents criticism at the most obvious, political, level. She especially satirizes the workings of nations that impose strict control over their citizens.

Atwood has said that she borrowed every aspect of Gileadean oppression from something similar in known history. Some familiar tactics employed by Gilead include using religion to control people for the government's purposes; being constantly at war, as in Orwell's *Nineteen Eighty-Four* (1949), to keep people quiet in the name of national security (there are numerous hints that the war may be staged); and emphasizing the need for children and women's role as childbearers to keep women in limited roles. The novel focuses on the oppression of women, and it is commonly cited in the context of feminist criticism. Although men of lower classes also are shown to be limited in their choices, clearly the worst victims of the Gileadean regime are women. Even women higher up in the hierarchy, such as Aunts (who train the Handmaids) and Wives, are often as miserable as the others.

One of the most insidious tactics used to control Gilead's citizens, especially women, involves control over language. Atwood often addresses the role of language in human lives. In *The Handmaid's Tale*, language symbolizes power. All use of language is regulated by the regime. Handmaids are not allowed to write, read, or even carry on a free conversation. Only certain prescribed greetings are allowed, and even the signs on stores are pictorial symbols.

Against these kinds of limits, Offred's rebellion comes in strange forms, such as playing illicit games of Scrabble, speaking freely with her walking partner, and ultimately leaving behind a subversive record of her experiences for future scholars to discover. These rebellions are powerful because they involve the uninhibited use of language. Her name is symbolic of Offred's semantic rebellion. It could be read as "of Fred," or it could be "off-red," suggesting that she is not fully integrated into the role of the red-clad Handmaids.

The true effect of Offred's final document is uncertain, pointing to the ambiguous nature of language. Subversive words are powerful in this context but also problematic, because they are always subject to interpretation. In the epilogue to the novel, the professor working on Offred's story finds little evidence to support her statements and questions their authenticity. In a chatty, joking tone, he talks in general about Gilead and points to some discrepancies between the story and his own historical findings. The contrast between Offred's heartrending, urgent story and this skeptical, analytical conversation among scholars may present pain and frustration to the reader. Atwood frustrates her readers purposefully to make some pointed remarks about the world of academia.

—*Susan Hwang*

Hard to Be a God

Anton goes from a future communist Earth to an alternate, developing human world and learns that history is not easily engineered

Author: Arkady Strugatsky (1925–1991) and Boris Strugatsky (1933–2012)
Genre: Science fiction—alternate history
Type of work: Novel
Time of work: An indeterminate time in the future
Locale: Earth and the kingdom of Arkanar, on an unnamed planet
First published: *Trudno byt bogom* (1964; English translation, 1973)

The Story

The prologue introduces three children, Anton, Pashka, and Anka, who are on an outing in a Soviet forest. The bucolic mood of the afternoon is dampened by two events: A game of William Tell with a real crossbow and discovery of the skeleton of a Nazi soldier chained to a machine gun.

Action shifts, for the main narrative, to Arkanar, a kingdom on a distant planet. Its inhabitants are *Homo sapiens* and are developing along a path analogous to human history on Earth. Don Rumata is one of a team of specialists from the Institute of Experimental History on Earth. The team is charged with guiding historical change on this world so as to ensure an eventual peaceful transition to the classless, socialist society that developed on Earth. Feudal Arkanar seems about to become capitalist, but a power struggle led by Don Reba (and not predicted by Marxist science) threatens to take this society directly from feudal tyranny to state fascism. Don Reba is an enigma, a nobody, a man with no qualities, even in evil. He is an Adolf Hitler without the historical dynamic that produced Hitler, for he has no capitalist backing, yet he thrives. Rumata is revealed to be Anton, just as his fellow don Hug is Pashka. The Marxist guides find it impossible to play god in Arkanar. Their enemy, a human nature that is fundamentally unregenerate, is not in textbooks.

Rumata is at the climax of social upheaval, which is his moment of personal crisis as well. The Arkanar society experiences a coup and a countercoup. First, Reba unleashes the Gray forces (*sturmoviki*, or storm troops), petty shopkeepers and paid thugs, against intellectuals and cultivated and enlightened members of the bourgeoisie. This Hitler scenario (complete with book burnings and a Night of the Long Knives), however, is only a front. In a Reba double-cross, hooded soldiers of the Holy Order sweep down on the Gray troops and institute a reign of terror under a militant theocracy. Rumata has spent much money spiriting away noted intellectuals and scientists in order to preserve what he sees as agents of human progress. He has befriended courageous people on the planet, among them Baron Pampa (a Russian folk figure of prodigious appetite and strength) and Arata the rebel.

He takes a mistress, Kyra. Defending them, he becomes emotionally involved and increasingly unlike a god. He discovers that in his passion to bring about justice he is made of the same stuff as those he would judge. When Kyra is killed by a stray crossbow bolt in the final scene, Rumata goes berserk, using his superior weapons to kill monks and Reba. For this, he is repatriated to Earth to convalesce. An epilogue finds Anton, Anka, and Pashka again in the Soviet woods. Instead of finding a machine gunners skeleton, however, Anton returns to his friends with his hands stained by strawberries.

ANALYSIS

This novel bears the obvious marks of hasty collaboration. The English version is also a second-hand translation, from the German. Even so, the novel has great power. There is, first of all, the complexity of its treatment of historical dynamics. The novel recognizes, in most un-Marxian fashion, a fundamentally unregenerate and fallen nature for humankind, making all forms of engineered social progress impossible. Rumata's constant evocation of human baseness stymies all proposed movement toward progressive synthesis. Central is the dialogue between Rumata and the physician Budach. Ironically, the "god" Rumata shows less utopian imagination than this "primitive" specimen. Asked what he would do if he could change the decisions of the Supreme Power, Budach proposes to give food, shelter, and work to all. When Rumata counters that the strong will take from the weak, Budach offers to punish such cruelty. Rumata points out that punishment does no good: All people are born weak and grow strong only when challenged. There are only two solutions: All people must be held forcibly in check, or all of corrupt humanity must be eliminated and replaced. In the first solution, utopia is a prison; the second suggests that utopia is possible only by transcending humanity.

Hard to Be a God offers hope beyond this cosmic despair, but the solution is not completely satisfying. Rumata is sad because he lacks the power to save the race. In the eyes of Kyra, however, eyes filled with fear and hope, he sees that the race may save itself. Rumata has met future hope in great minds such as that of Budach and in dauntless dreamers such as the rebel Arata. He also has met helpless, selfless, and innocent victims, including Kyra. He realizes that "people like you have been born in every epoch in the bloody history of our planets." No matter how brutal the times, these gentle people abide, and if they can last, good may yet triumph at the end of history.

This organic sense of history may be the meaning of the enigmatic prologue and epilogue. Anton and his friends play god on other planets, but on Earth, they are simply human, playing games and growing up. They carry within themselves the violence they witness in Arkanar but do not realize it until they try to play god. As Don Kondor tells Rumata late in the novel, all the gods before him have reached the point where they must fight force with force. Anton's latent cruelty is seen in the William Tell scene, in which he torments Pashka by firing the real crossbow bolt. This is the bolt, fired on Earth, that later strikes Kyra on Arkanar. Anton, too, is playing god and finds, in the chained machine gunner, the violent source of human history. Meaning here may be simpler than critics have thought. It is easy to put directional signs on roads, to create a Communist Republic of Arkanar. Anton's discovery of his violence coincides with discovery of Kyras innocence, of the life force that, outlasting violence, fleshes out skeletons and allows the real, organic flow of history to advance. Anton's new journey up the down road in the epilogue is one of liberation, both from violence within the self and from the constraints of history. Casting off the chains of deadly passion, he emerges from the woods to reunion with childhood friend Anka. The blood on his hands has turned to the "innocent stain of strawberries."

—*George Slusser*

Hardwired

In a future United States defeated by orbiting megacorporations, a freedom-loving contraband runner and a reluctant hired assassin team up to battle their oppressors

Author: Walter Jon Williams (1953–)
Genre: Science fiction—cyberpunk
Type of work: Novel
Time of work: The twenty-first century
Locale: The United States
First published: 1986

THE STORY

Hardwired displays a future world similar to that of other cyberpunk fiction of the mid-1980s, most notably William Gibson's *Neuromancer* (1984). Political and military power are wielded by ruthless megacorporations, examples of capitalism run rampant. Courageous individuals, forced into illegal and ethically compromised positions, struggle for freedom. Computers and their worldwide networks are central to virtually all human activity, and bioengineering has made possible various human/computer linkups as well as certain bionic powers. Designer drugs, cosmetic surgery, and punkish hair and clothing styles are prominent features of the blighted urban scene. *Hardwired* also takes readers through a sparsely populated rural America.

In Walter Jon Williams novel, the Orbitals, an alliance of space satellites once serving Earth as manufacturing centers for pharmaceuticals and alloys, have become corporate powers that have conquered Earth via meteor bombardment. They continue to hold it in economic thralldom while plotting against one another. In a balkanized United States, states charge heavy tariffs for drugs and other goods crossing their borders. An elaborate black market has developed, with thirdmen (contractors) hiring smugglers. The latter, hardwired to their transports via head sockets, were at first deltajocks (jet pilots) until the states improved their combat technology; now they are panzerboys and-girls, operating armed, superfast hovercraft on their runs from the Rockies to the East Coast. Cowboy, one of the best pilots, revels in danger, in the thrill of being one with his machines, and in his belief that he is helping to foil the Orbitals.

Meanwhile, in the Florida Free State, Sarah is a former prostitute turned bodyguard and assassin for hire. She strives to earn enough for herself and her drug-addicted younger brother, Daud, a prostitute himself, to ride up the gravity well to live in the Orbitals, free of the dirt of earthly life. Cowboy and Sarah meet when she is assigned as bodyguard during a smuggling operation. They are betrayed by workers for the Tempel Corporation: Arkady, Cowboys thirdman, and Cunningham, Sarahs sinister former employer. Fleeing westward, on foot, Cowboy and Sarah become friends and lovers, though the bitterly experienced Sarah mistrusts all close involvements and finds Cowboys idealism naïve.

Eventually the two work together to unseat the rulers of Tempel, though to do so they must enlist the aid of the vile, pederastic Roon, a former Tempel chief executive. The scheme involves attacks on Orbital shuttles bringing Tempel drugs to Earth, thus causing Tempels stock to plummet in price. Betrayed by the drug-addicted and narcissistic Daud, Cowboys forces still manage to accomplish their mission, and Roon is incapacitated by Reno, a friend of Cowboy whose mind resides in the computer networks.

ANALYSIS

The beginning of *Hardwired* is like a verbal equivalent to a video game. Williams superheated prose describes Cowboy plugged into his Maserati, roaring along New Mexico mountain highways, his brain directly sensing the car and giving signals to it. Later episodes, such as the attack of the deltas on the Orbital convoy, also seem like video game sessions. Sarahs hand-to-hand combat with various attackers anticipates the Mortal Kombat type of martial arts game, especially with her wired body further boosted by a snakelike cyberextension. The novel, in fact, inspired a role-playing game. *Hardwired* is, however, much more than a simple action spectacle and a much finer novel than a list of its borrowings from other science fiction would suggest. Some critics consider the sequel, *Voice of the Whirlwind* (1987), to be a better novel.

Hardwired fits neatly into the cyberpunk category, from its sinister corporations, labyrinthine computer networks, tough-talking plugged-in heroes, drug dependencies, and punk hairstyles to such signature details as the heroines mirrorshades. The former deltajock Reno, now living in the worldwide computer matrix—a good position to foil villains—anticipates Max Headroom, the title character of a 1984 British cyberpunk television movie and 1987 American television series, though Reno surfaces only on audio.

Overall, *Hardwired* is a less visionary and unpredictable work than *Neuromancer* or Bruce Sterling's *Schismatrix* (1985), another cyberpunk classic. It has sparked far less literary criticism. It is not a mere trendy commercial exploitation; it vividly reimagines the cyberpunk milieu in its own rich detail and subtly differs from its peers. In one respect, *Hardwired* interestingly reverses *Neuromancer*, in that Cowboys hardwiring lets him interface with machines so that he can engage with the outside world more intensely than ordinary pilots could. Gibsons hero Case interfaces with the computer matrix to become absorbed in an inner universe.

Hardwired's tough, cynical view of the world, laced with hope that a brave couple might actually achieve love and at least some triumph, seems to derive from *Neuromancer* and Ridley Scott's film *Blade Runner* (1982), both of which appropriate, even flaunt, the sardonic yet poetically world-weary mood of Raymond Chandlers Philip Marlowe novels and 1940s film noir. *Hardwired* is not as Chandleresque in tone as *Neuromancer* and *Blade Runner*. It seems more a blend of the hard-boiled detachment of Dashiell Hammett and the lush romantic desolation of Jack Kerouac. Cowboy and Sarah, though familiar types in popular fiction, are memorably strong figures in their dark landscape.

Most impressive, perhaps, is *Hardwired*'s intricate plotting. A brief summary cannot cover the elaborate scheming and counterscheming among the various forces. Such elaboration is an artistic expression of the complexities of decision making in the worlds of high finance, war, and diplomacy. Williams offers a Machiavellian vision of political reality brought into the information age.

—*Joseph Milicia*

HASAN

Hasan, taken far from his home, tries to capture the love of a beautiful bird maiden, daughter of the king of the jinns

Author: Piers Anthony (1934–)
Genre: Fantasy—mythological
Type of work: Novel
Time of work: About 800 c.e.
Locale: Serendip (Sri Lanka), India, Tibet, Cathay (China), Indo-China, Malay, and Sumatra
First published: 1977 (serial form, Fantastic Stories, 1969–1970)

THE STORY

This novel has an unusual publishing history. After having the novel rejected twelve times because it did not seem to fit the type of fantasy many publishers were looking for in the mid-to late 1960's, Piers Anthony finally sent the novel to a fan reviewer, Richard Delap, who loved the book and published a favorable review of it in his fanzine. Ted White of Fantastic Stories saw the review and published the novel in two parts. After Anthony received two more rejections, Berkeley accepted the novel seventeen days after receiving it. A change of editors at Berkeley resulted in the novel not being published there. It finally was published in 1977, in a small press edition, then for Dell in 1979.

In the novel, Hasan, a young Muslim merchant, is lured from his home by a display of an alchemists magic of changing copper into gold. Hasans naïve yearning for adventure and riches, combined with his devotion to the ways and customs of his faith, causes him to disregard numerous clues to the Persian magicians evil nature. He winds up stolen from his home, trapped as a slave to the Persian, Bahram the Guebre, foremost magician of Persia.

When Hasan and the magician reach the base of a extremely tall mountain, Hasan is confined in a camels hide and carried by a Roc to the top, where he is supposed to find a precious herb the magician needs to create his elixir. When the magician leaves him to starve on the mountaintop, Hasan takes comfort in his faith and finds a chain descending down many ledges. The means of escape had not been discovered by the many people previously lured to the mountaintop.

Hasan makes his way to a beautiful palace and finds seven princesses, daughters of the mightiest king of Sind and enemies to Bahram. Hasan is adopted as their brother and lives with them in splendor and joy. The princesses leave one day to visit their father, and while they are away, Hasan finds a beautiful garden, upon which descend ten birds who shed their skins and reveal their nature as magnificently beautiful women.

Hasan is smitten immediately with the chief damsel and plots to have her. He eventually steals her feathered garment so she cannot change. When she finds that she cannot go home, she agrees to marry him. The woman, Sana, bears Hasan two sons and lives happily with him for several years but eventually discovers the hidden garment. With her sons, she flies back to her home, in the Isles of Wak. Hasan dedicates himself to bringing Sana back and travels through several lands, cultures, and adventures in order to do so.

Once he reaches the isles, Hasan convinces Shawahi, the leader of the Amazon army, of the importance of his quest. She travels with him to the palace of the eldest daughter of the Supreme King of Wak. This queen turns out to be Sanas sister, and she is not favorably disposed toward Hasan or his quest. Although Sana loves Hasan and wishes she had not left, Hasan must still face many trials to regain his wife, including obtaining a magical rod and cap and fighting in a war between the Amazons and the seven tribes of the jinn. In the end, however, Hasan's allies triumph, and Sana extends forgiveness to the queen who persecuted them both.

ANALYSIS
Anthony's retelling of this Arabian nights tale is his fourth novel. It reveals his love for fantasy and his wish to make this ancient tale accessible to modern readers. The novel also illustrates the extensive research he does for his works as well as his love for history and archaeology. These traits are illustrated in others of his works, including *Pretender* (1979, with Frances Hall) and *The Tatham Mound* (1991). Similar goals and research also can be seen in his collaboration with Mercedes Lackey, *If I Pay Thee Not in Gold* (1993).

Anthony's *Hasan* not only elaborates on the original tale but also provides an accurate historical basis for Hasan's travels throughout Asia. Anthony explains the cultures and lands Hasan visits, intertwining superstitious explanations that might have arisen from the people of the time. A tornado, for example, is viewed as an angry jinn, and a volcano as an awakening marid.

Although Anthony admits, in his autobiographical *Bio of an Ogre* (1988) and the authors notes in various versions of the novel, that the story is not originally his, his retelling brings a greater fullness and color to the tale. It is a celebration of the culture of the time and place in which the novel occurs. Anthony's attention to detail breathes new life into Hasan, providing an accurate portrayal of the language and cultural practices of the medieval Arabian people.

Hasan must face several important conflicts throughout the novel. His own devotion to Allah is tested, as well as his judgment and rationality in the face of his youthful enthusiasm and rashness. As the novel unfolds, Hasan less often rejects the advice of his elders, and through his adventures he becomes more the embodiment of the true believer he wishes to be.

—*Paul J. Baltes*

THE HAUNTING OF HILL HOUSE

A small group of people encounter a chilling and malevolent evil in the form of an isolated house

Author: Shirley Jackson (1919-1965)
Genre: Fantasy—extrasensory powers
Type of work: Novel
Time of work: The 1950s
Locale: Near Hillsdale, a fictional town in the United States
First published: 1959

The Story

In *The Haunting of Hill House*, a concealed evil is both psychically and physically aroused by the presence of a small group of people brought to a haunted house by a researcher of the paranormal, Dr. John Montague. Montague recruits three others to aid him in his analysis of what appears to be a genuine haunted house. The first, a lonely young woman named Eleanor Vance, had spent eleven years caring for an invalid mother whom she hated and who recently died. Theodora is an attractive artist with strong psychic gifts. Luke Sanderson, a cad with an instinct for self-preservation, is the nephew of Hill Houses current owner. Eleanor finds out that she was chosen by Montague because of a psychic experience she had when she was twelve years old: For three days, a shower of stones had fallen on her home.

As the first to arrive at Hill House, Eleanor immediately is struck by the vile and diseased nature of the mansion. Architecturally, Hill House is ruled by the principle of clashing disharmony; fractionally wrong in all of its dimensions, it is filled with dark woodwork, enclosed rooms, doors that swing shut, rickety staircases, and hideously monochromatic rooms. During the first evening there, Montague relates the story of the family feud and the string of mysterious deaths that constitute the eighty-year history of the house. Despite her clear sense of the pervasive evil emanating from the dwelling, Eleanor feels, for the first time, that she belongs both to a place and to a group of people. She and Theodora whimsically claim to be cousins.

Further investigation of the house reveals concrete evidence of the supernatural: a cold spot in front of the nursery, a deafening and prolonged hammering against a bedroom door, gloating laughter, and a fleeting glimpse of a mysterious animal. It becomes clear that the supernatural activities center on Eleanor when a message to her is written in chalk in the front hall. This cryptic message is repeated in blood on the walls of Theodora's room. One night, Eleanor is awakened by mysterious laughter and incomprehensible babble. She finds that the icy hand she has been gripping in fear could not have been human. She and Theodora witness a ghostly picnic.

Montague's wife and Arthur Parker arrive to undertake their own version of supernatural research. Insensitive to the house's true nature, they do not witness any manifestations, but during a séance they provide another opportunity for mysterious forces to send a message to Eleanor. She is singled out by the accelerating evil of the house, until she alone hears the messages it sends. Following them, she runs away mischievously, hiding from the others. At one point, she climbs a rotting staircase in the library, from which she must be rescued by Luke.

The others decide that, for her own safety, Eleanor must leave Hill House. In a final effort to remain in a place that she now perceives as both a home and an extension of herself, she deliberately crashes her car into the great tree at the curve of the driveway. Hill House can add another inexplicable death to its history.

Analysis

Shirley Jackson's work consistently reveals the strange and disturbing undercurrents that lurk beneath the mundane and the commonplace. *The Haunting of Hill House* concerns itself with the evil energies held within a number of structures, not only the upright walls of Hill House but also the social structure of the family and the fragile constructs that make up an individuals identity.

An acrimonious sense of social and family relationships permeates the novel. Eleanor's forced servitude to her controlling mother, her intense dislike of the sister with whom she now lives, and her own utter friendlessness mirror the stark history of the equally isolated Hill House, which was home to a morbid, oppressive patriarch, feuding sisters, and a suicidal companion, as well as other horrors. Montagues team becomes a de facto family, and Eleanor's relationship with Theodora, her "cousin," is replete with love, envy, and resentment. The house manifests physical evidence of Eleanor's complex array of affection and anger by splattering Theodora's room and belongings with blood, forcing the latter to share Eleanor's room and clothes. This sisterly proximity contrasts with Eleanor's emotional withdrawal from the others. She repeatedly is torn between her desire for connection with other people and for a normal life, on one hand, and the paranoia and suspicions that mark her desire for a life with those forces that reside in Hill House.

This novel is a psychological study as well as a literal ghost story. The ambiguities of Hill House's architecture parallel the ambiguities of the human mind, particularly Eleanor's mind. Closed doors, confusing hallways, and shifting perspectives represent the hidden feelings and contradictions within Eleanor. She repeatedly iterates her sense of connection with the mansion, seeing it as her home and wondering if she might be responsible for the vile activities taking place within its walls. In a novel that focuses not so much on plot as on a gradual unfolding of character, the animate house is as much a protagonist as Eleanor.

Eleanor's tenuous sense of closeness with the others shifts between isolation and rage. As her reactions to the others become progressively warier, her reactions to supernatural events become more matter of fact. Resolution remains elusive for the reader. It is uncertain whether the house wants Eleanor or she wants the house, and it is unclear whether she is responsible for the paranormal events. Is she mad, or possessed, or behaving rationally in the light of the supernatural events to which she is sensitive? Eleanor's final act is both self-destruction and self-realization: She irredeemably isolates herself and irrevocably fuses with the dark energies of the house.

—*Christina Sylka*

THE HAUNTING OF TOBY JUGG

A crippled young British fighter pilot, heir to millions, is secluded in a Welsh mansion by a Czech communist who intends to use his satanic powers to force him to sign away his fortune

Author: Dennis Wheatley (1897–1977)
Genre: Fantasy—occult
Type of work: Novel
Time of work: During World War II
Locale: Wales
First published: 1948

THE STORY

This novel concerns a struggle between the forces of God and Satan for the souls of a pair of young lovers. It has a political cast, with God on the side of British democracy and Satan helping the communists. The novel is one of a number by this author that involve Satanism and communism, along with brainwashing, hypnotism, and extrasensory perception (ESP).

Toby Jugg, soon to turn twenty-one and inherit the largest industrial fortune in Great Britain, lies paralyzed from the waist down in a bed in the library of an old mansion near the village of Llanferdrack in rural Wales. He was injured when his fighter plane crashed during the Battle of Britain. He is in the care of Dr. Helmuth Lisicky, who had been one of his teachers when Toby attended Weylands Abbey, a co-ed boarding school with Nietzschean principles embodied in its slogan: Do what thou wilt shall be the whole of the law. At Weylands Abbey, Toby was educated to become atheistic and amoral as part of Helmuths plans for him later in life.

Narration of the novel occurs through a secret journal Toby keeps in an attempt to rescue his sanity. He undergoes a series of hauntings by a maleficent force that finds embodiment as a giant spider that manifests when the moon is full. Toby assumes that this evil presence has some connection to the old, ruined castle onto which the mansion backs, or to the nearby lake. Toby slowly discovers that Helmuth is his mortal enemy and that his guardians, Julia and Paul, are under Helmuths satanic influence. He is to be driven mad deliberately so that his fortune will go to this cynical diabolist, whose communism is merely a front for his worship of evil.

Toby attempts to enlist various household servants, sometimes by use of hypnotic powers learned from a book in the library, to help him escape, but Helmuth thwarts all these efforts. When young Sally Cardew arrives as a replacement nurse, Toby finds both true love and the ally he needs to overthrow his captors. The satanic powers nearly prevail by using Toby and Sallys love for each other against them. Helmuth tells Sally that she must yield her virginity to him in the course of a Black Mass in order to spare Toby, and after Julia fakes death from a heart attack in the course of a struggle with Sally and Toby, Helmuth tells Toby that he will have Sally charged with murder unless he signs away his fortune.

Two events prove decisive. Divine intervention restores to Toby the use of his legs, and a *deus ex machina* comes in the form of an insane elderly relative. Trying to reunite with her lover who drowned in the lake, she digs a tunnel that fills with water and floods the Black Sabbath chapel, sweeping the satanists away. Toby, stretching forth his arm, telepathically zaps the Great Spider. The next day, the lovers find the document that Toby was forced to sign, and they destroy it. A postscript informs readers that Sally and Toby are the parents of twins and are living happily.

ANALYSIS

Dennis Wheatley's mother was Lady Newton, and his father, Albert, was in the family wine business. He was educated at Dulwich College, aboard HMS *Worcester*, and privately in Germany. He served in the British army from 1914 to 1919. In 1926, he inherited the family business, but he lost hundreds of thousands of pounds in the stock market crash and worldwide depression.

Wheatley was a prolific author, with more than sixty novels to his credit and translations into more than twenty languages. His literary output includes historical romances, police adventures, spy novels, and books involving satanism and the occult, along with nonfiction books. Political themes are common. Wheatley was what is now termed a wet conservative, basically in favor of the class system and private enterprise but in favor of a social safety net for the disadvantaged. He reveals a staunch anticommunist attitude, equating communism with the devil.

The supernatural often figures in his books, and those featuring the occult have proved to have the most lasting influence. He was interested in such matters as telepathy, hypnotism, and ESP. He was not above using sex to keep the reader engaged and displays a troublesome attitude toward it, as a conflict never quite resolved in himself. An uneasy mix of prurience and hypocrisy therefore stains the "sex is healthy" surface of some passages. *The Haunting of Toby Jugg*, for example, contains a scene with healthy, upright young Sally, a flower of English womanhood, spread-eagled and naked on a Black Mass altar as Helmuth, naked from the waist down, with a pair of female devotees kneeling on either side of him, prepares to have his way with her.

Wheatley is a master of suspense, his strong suit being plot. His characters seldom rise above the stock. In this book, Toby Jugg's situation is gripping in the extreme. He is in a paranoid nightmare, unable to move and tormented by mighty figures both natural and supernatural. No sooner does he persuade or entrance one or another servant into helping him escape than his antagonist discovers the scheme and thwarts the attempt. Readers identifying with Toby ride a roller coaster of hope and despair.

—*David Bromige*

THE HEADS OF CERBERUS

A mysterious dust propels three young persons from 1918 Philadelphia into the future, where they struggle against a brutal totalitarian regime

Author: Francis Stevens (Gertrude Barrows Bennett, 1884-1939?)

Genre: Science fiction—dystopia
Type of work: Novel
Time of work: 1918 and 2118
Locale: Philadelphia, Pennsylvania
First published: 1919 (serial form, *The Thrill Book*, 1919)

The Heads of Cerberus

THE STORY

Reduced to desperation by dishonest enemies, Robert Drayton attempts unsuccessfully to burglarize a house in Philadelphia. To his embarrassment, Drayton meets an old friend, Terence Trenmore, who by chance is staying in the house. Trenmore proves to be both understanding and compassionate, and soon he is showing Drayton an odd crystal vial filled with a strange dust reported to be from Purgatory. Trenmore accidentally inhales some of the dust and vanishes, followed soon by his lovely sister Viola and by a guilt-driven Drayton.

The three regain consciousness in a bizarre and shadowy realm named Ulithia, through which they make their way to a bright, moon-shaped gateway. They pass through the gateway only to find themselves in a transformed Philadelphia in the year 2118.

The three time travelers quickly find themselves in serious difficulties, as the civil liberties to which they are accustomed have been outlawed by a totalitarian government based on a twisted version of the history of the great Quaker statesman William Penn. At this point the focus of the novel changes, and character and drama move to the background in favor of social satire.

A series of confrontations with the Philadelphia au-thorities puts Drayton and the Trenmores, along with a blundering, time-traveling burglar they have met, on the verge of being put to death. Terence Trenmore heroically precipitates the destruction of the sacred temple which is the headquarters of the local government and plunges himself and his companions back to the place and time in which their adventures originated. Soon Drayton and Viola Trenmore become engaged to marry. The novel ends with the three making plans to repair Draytons fortunes in Cincinnati.

In the light of this conclusion and of the fact that the powerful dust has been stolen at the end of the novel, it seems likely that Francis Stevens intended to write a sequel to this work. That possibility is further supported by the enigmatic references within the text to Andrew Power, whose name recurs in several notable passages.

ANALYSIS

The novel is a notable combination of time travel and dystopian social satire. Although the coherence of the plot appears to suffer from a change of authorial plan during the composition of the work, several interesting features combine to establish Francis Stevens imaginative power. The complex account of time is one such feature. After the three protagonists return to their own era, a former associate of Andrew Power tells them "Time is not a dimension." It is a sequence, or rather a comparative sequence of vibrations. The novel also suggests that the dichotomy between subjectivity and objectivity is difficult to reconcile with the concept of time.

Another striking feature of the novel is its emphasis on the suffering that can result from human folly elevated to ideological status. The Philadelphia of 2118 is a dystopia in which the vocabulary of private ownership has been manipulated to the advantage of the ruling gangsters and to the disadvantage of the working class. Surely Stevens preoccupation with such a self-serving ideology reflects her reaction to the Bolshevik Revolution of 1917. One should in fairness also note that the unscrupulous capitalists who have reduced Robert Drayton to crime represent a similar depravity of human potential, but clearly a greater emphasis is placed on the dehumanizing effects of Communism, with its devastating brutality and its gross distortion of history. The hidden machine guns in the former City Hall of Philadelphia suggest the systematic terror of Bolshevism, and the sybaritic lives of the Superlatives point out the hypocrisy behind totalitarian ideology.

There are less somber dimensions of this work. The term "Ulithia," which is the middle realm through which the time travelers pass, echoes *Utopia* (1516), Sir Thomas More's fantasy of an idealized country, and other aspects of the work remind the reader of Lewis Carroll's *Alice's Adventures in Wonderland* (1865). At one point in the text, in fact, when confronted by the ironically allegorical characters Mr. Virtue and Mr. Mercy, Robert Drayton wonders whether he has blundered into John Bunyan's *The Pilgrim's Progress from This World to That Which Is to Come* (1678). Stevens clearly possesses a keen sense of self-location and individual identity within the Western tradition of fiction, and her satiric critique of the excesses of a contemporary political regime reflects an unusual combination of perspicuity and imagination.

On the other hand, the plot of the novel lacks full coherence and, perhaps more damaging, the main characters are not sufficiently developed for credibility. Their principal motive is cheap sentiment of the most predictable kind. When Drayton and the Trenmores are hauled before the Penn Service tribunal, the reader may half hope that they will be tossed into the execution pit, if only to test their sincerity. If plot and character development exhibit deficiencies, other dimensions of the work compensate substantially for such weaknesses.

Stevens published *The Heads of Cerberus* early in her brief period of professional writing. By 1919 she had already published *The Citadel of Fear* (1918 in serial form; book form 1970), and her novel *Claimed* (1920 in serial form; book form 1966) followed immediately after *The Heads of Cerberus*. By this time Stevens apparently had decided to give up her writing career, and works published later were either reprints or had been written but not published earlier.

—Robert W. Haynes

THE HEALER'S WAR

Lieutenant Kitty McCulley, an Army nurse in Vietnam, is given an amulet that enables her to see peoples auras as well as to heal them

Author: Elizabeth Ann Scarborough (1947–)
Genre: Fantasy—extrasensory powers
Type of work: Novel
Time of work: During the Vietnam War
Locale: Vietnam and the United States
First published: 1988

The Story

Lieutenant Kitty McCulley, a twenty-one-year-old Kansas girl, wants to provide good service as a U.S. Army nurse in Vietnam, but she has difficulty adjusting to military bureaucracy and the horrifying wounds of American soldiers and Vietnamese civilians. When she almost kills a young Vietnamese girl with an accidental overdose of medication, she is reassigned to a new hospital unit. She is much happier there because she has the opportunity to develop relationships with her patients.

Kitty meets a Vietnamese holy man named Xe. At first, she does not particularly care for Xe, but she notices that Vietnamese people and even some American soldiers treat him with great respect. Most Americans, however, including medical personnel, treat Xe like every other patient. When they operate on him, they insist that he remove his amulet. Xe does so only on the condition that Kitty will wear the amulet during his surgery.

The amulet enables Kitty to see peoples auras, but she does not understand what is happening, and she gladly returns the amulet to Xe when he comes back to the ward. Xe tries to help the wounded soldiers but is prevented from doing so by their ignorance and fear. He sinks into despair as Kitty's respect and compassion for him grows.

Xe dies and bequeaths his amulet to Kitty. A mutual friend explains to her that auras reveal information about the physical and mental well-being of people and that the amulet will help her use that information to heal. Soon afterward, her unit falls under the command of a racist officer who sends all Vietnamese patients to a filthy local hospital, where they certainly will die because of inadequate care and lack of cleanliness.

Kitty worries about the Vietnamese patients she has nursed for months, particularly a crippled orphan named Ahn. At the suggestion of a pilot friend, Kitty tries to save Ahn by flying him to his native village. The helicopter crashes, her pilot friend is killed, and Kitty and Ahn must make their way through a Vietcong jungle, aided only by the amulet. For a while, they travel with William, an American soldier who has become separated from his unit. William, however, has become psychotic; he frequently mistakes them for the enemy and tries to kill them. Fortunately, his aura betrays his intentions and gives Kitty and Ahn a chance to hide during his dangerous periods.

Kitty and Ahn eventually take shelter in a village, where Kitty learns of the amulets power to heal using the power of her (and others) life force. When Kitty is captured by the Vietcong, her amulet-given abilities convince them to spare her life. Her American rescuers" who easily are as brutal as her Vietcong captors—are convinced that she is a traitor; otherwise, they reason, she would be dead.

Kitty narrowly escapes a court-martial. When she returns home, she cannot readjust to American life. The amulet reveals only disappointing auras, her own included, and she no longer can use it to heal. She suffers from the same despair that Xe felt during the last days of his life. After a year of drifting, her postwar trauma is eased when she finds an opportunity to help Vietnamese refugees.

ANALYSIS

The Healer's War marks a turning point in Elizabeth Ann Scarborough's career. Her previous seven novels are humorous fantasy. In *The Healer's War*, Scarborough draws on her own experiences as an Army nurse in Vietnam to create a remarkably compelling story. Books that follow this one, such as *Nothing Sacred* (1991) and its sequel, *Last Refuge* (1992), also have a message in addition to offering entertainment. All of them are quite entertaining, filled with flashes of wit and humor, along with compassionate, interesting characters.

Kitty McCulley is a wonderful hero, compassionate and observant, yet not too quick to figure things out, as befits a sheltered girl from Kansas. It is refreshing to see a womans perspective on this war, and Kitty's confusion and pain go a long way toward explaining the feelings of all veterans and refugees. These people have learned in the most brutal manner possible that the best efforts toward creating peace can lead to disaster, and no matter what the political picture, nothing can soften the personal tragedies of homelessness, injury, and death.

Scarborough does a better job of writing about the war in this book than she does of creating the fantasy. The amulet is nicely mysterious at first, but it ceases to be significant. An aura is an aura is an aura, apparently. It is heartwarming to see Kitty healing people, and her ability to read others intentions is useful to the story, but for the most part, once Kitty figures out how to use the amulet, the book focuses on the ravages of war rather than on the effects of the magical device.

Scarborough reveals in the authors note to the Bantam Spectra edition that the amulet was useful mostly as a device to keep Kitty and Ahn alive. Realistically, a young nurse and a crippled orphan lost in the jungle would have been killed quickly. Furthermore, because the amulet gives Kitty insight into others, she is able to tell, convincingly, the stories of even non-English-speaking Vietnamese characters. Without the amulet, Scarborough would have had to employ different points of view in order to achieve such a balanced perspective without blurring Kitty's convincingly naïve personality.

The amulet is more than a means to longevity or an omniscient narrator. It comes to stand for the sense of purpose and connection to others that Xe felt before his country was torn apart by war and that Kitty ironically finds only in wartime and misses when she returns home. Everyone could benefit from such a touchstone.

—*Beth Rapp Young*

HEART OF A DOG

A renowned Soviet surgeon transplants the glands of a criminal into a dog, transforming the dog into a human being

Author: Mikhail Bulgakov (1891-1940)
Genre: Science fiction—cautionary
Type of work: Novel
Time of work: 1924-1925
Locale: Moscow, the Soviet Union
First published: Sobache serdtse, 1968; revised, 1969 (English translation, 1968)

THE STORY

Mikhail Bulgakov completed his satiric novel *Heart of a Dog* in 1925, but Soviet government censorship kept it from being published until after his death. The story opens from the canine point of view of a stray mongrel named Sharik that wanders the cold streets of Moscow in search of food and a warm place to sleep. The dog is puzzled by the harsh treatment he receives at the hands of the various shopkeepers from whom he begs scraps. He accepts the cruelty as a matter of course and is, therefore, puzzled when a well-dressed stranger offers him sausages and takes him home to a luxurious apartment.

The stranger is Philip Philippovich Preobrazhensky, a noted surgeon experimenting in organ transplants and sexual rejuvenation operations. Preobrazhensky treats the dog well. When a neighborhood petty criminal dies, the doctor has the opportunity to continue his experimentation. He promptly transplants the testes and pituitary gland of the deceased man into Sharik. The doctor does not make the purpose of the operation clear even to his assistant, Bormenthal. The results stun everyone involved. As Bormenthals log of the experiment records, Sharik's recovery is the evolution of a dog into a man. Surprisingly, he immediately is able to walk upright and speak, cursing and demanding liquor.

The short, hairy man promptly changes his name from Sharik to the more human Sharikov and adds Polygraph Polygraphovich, a first name and patronymic he reads on a calendar. It becomes clear to the doctor and his assistant that Sharikov retains the worst of the knowledge he picked up on the street both as a dog and as a criminal. He is slothful and petulant, reading Friedrich Engels and spouting revolutionary political aphorisms that the upper-class doctor finds objectionable. All attempts to extract calm, productive behavior from Sharikov leave him nonplussed, as though he cannot imagine any advantage in cooperating with his housemates. When Sharikov assaults the household help, he finds he is utterly unwelcome in the home and abruptly leaves. With the help of an officious bureaucrat he befriends, Sharikov finds a job he enjoys, working as the government-sanctioned director of a project to purge the city of cats.

Sharikov returns, bathed in self-important triumph and the fetid smell of cats, to Preobrazhensky's home. With him is a young woman whom he has deceived into becoming his secretary. When the doctor and Bormenthal realize the growing extent of his confidence and deception and again attempt to reason with him, Sharikov threatens to kill Bormenthal. In the end, Preobrazhensky finds no other way to rein in the unruly Sharikov and end his cruel and distasteful public behavior except to reverse the original operation. With Bormenthals help, he subdues Sharikov and completes the procedure. The story closes as it opened, from the dogs point of view, as Sharik watches the doctor use his mysterious tubes and dishes to prepare for another experiment.

ANALYSIS

Heart of a Dog was written midway through the most successful period of Bulgakov's literary life, a few years before he was banned from publication. In the novel, he advances his critique of science gone wrong found in earlier stories such as "The Fatal Eggs" and points to the sweeping, fantastic social critique of his classic novel, *The Master and Margarita* (1967). In The Heart of a Dog, Bulgakov capitalizes on the contemporary curiosity and speculation surrounding the possibility of organ transplantation to create a cautionary allegory on the dangers of transforming the world, a society, or an individual overnight by revolution.

Heart of a Dog is built on a premise similar to that of "The Fatal Eggs." The experiment of an overreaching scientist goes awry, wreaking havoc on the surrounding populace. Unlike the earlier story, the satire of *Heart of a Dog* is not directed solely at the mishaps and pretension of Soviet science. Instead, Preobrazhensky's inadvertent transformation of Sharik is a means of addressing the larger issues of what it means to be human and to live responsibly in the society of others. The doctor believes that he has scientifically proven the physical location of human nature when the addition of human sex and growth glands transforms the dog Sharik into a man, but the nature of Sharikov's behavior is clearly outside Preobrazhensky's scientific empiricism. Sharikov is a man with the heart of a dog as well as a dog with the heart of a man. He is the worst of each, and the doctors scientific knowledge does not equip him to reckon with the consequences. The resulting episodes provide ample opportunity for Bulgakov to comment on the workings of society in general and the relatively new Soviet society in particular.

Bulgakov's social satire works at several levels. Preobrazhensky is an ambitious technocrat in his own home and office but unable to control the physical, civic, or moral consequences of his creation.

Sharikov is at once an innocent creature at the mercy of those with power and scientific knowledge and a miscreant citizen of the society into which he has been introduced. Although both the doctor and the dog represent larger elements of the new Soviet nation, both characters live and work in tension with the absurdity and officiousness that Bulgakov found in the Muscovite bureaucracy he knew. Bulgakov's mockery of specific details of early Soviet life made him an easy target for censorship. It is in combination with an incisive view of human nature and motivation that the mockery in *Heart of a Dog* becomes a strong social and scientific satire.

—*Karsten Piper*

THE HEECHEE SERIES

A series of stories about human encounters with creatures called Heechee

Author: Frederik Pohl (1919–2013)
Genre: Science fiction—future history
Type of work: Novels and stories
Time of work: The twenty-first and twenty-second centuries
Locale: Throughout the solar system and the galaxy
First published: *Gateway* (1977), *Beyond the Blue Event Horizon* (1980), *Heechee Rendezvous* (1984), *The Annals of the Heechee* (1987), *The Gateway Trip* (1990), *and The Boy Who Would Live Forever* (2004)

THE STORY

These novels tell the story of human discovery of Heechee artifacts, eventual encounters with the mysterious Heechee, and subsequent encounters with a hostile race called the Assassins. When humans first explore the solar system, they discover an asteroid filled with tunnels that contain abandoned Heechee spacecraft, providing a gateway to the galaxy. Soon, the Gateway corporation trains prospectors in what little is known about the Heechee ships, then encourages them to ship out to random destinations in search of Heechee artifacts.

Because some of these artifacts provide valuable technological or scientific breakthroughs, the potential payoff to these missions is enormous. Many prospectors die on their missions and others do not return, but a lucky few discover Heechee artifacts or observe stellar phenomena and are richly rewarded.

In *Gateway*, Robinette Broadhead wins a lottery from the food mines on Earth and uses the money for a one-way ticket to Gateway. His first trips out are unsuccessful, and he watches many ships return with dead or dying crews. On his third trip, a black hole traps his ship and its companion. He escapes but leaves his lover, Gelle-Klara Moynlin, trapped in the event horizon. He returns to reap a fabulous science bonus.

In *Beyond the Blue Event Horizon*, some of the mysteries of the Heechee are resolved. Broadhead is now rich and happily married, but he still longs to see Klara. The plot centers on his recovery of two large Heechee artifacts, including a "food factory" that converts the basic elements of comets into food. These artifacts were inhabited by a feral boy named Wan, who had been born to a pregnant prospector who had landed there. Wan periodically had slept in a "dream couch" that allowed for two-way telepathic communications, and his dreams had wreaked havoc on the citizens of Earth who had been their unwilling recipients.

When Broadhead finally reaches the artifacts, he learns that the Heechee had observed Earth for some time using a dream couch and that they had captured some australopithecines and kept them on one of the artifacts. He also discovers that some of the prospectors who had never returned had in fact taken one-way trips to Heechee artifacts, from which their ships would not leave. The personalities and memories of some of these now-dead prospectors had been stored imperfectly in machine intelligence, a process that the Heechee practiced with their dead as well.

In *Heechee Rendezvous*, Wan inadvertently rescues Klara from the black hole while searching for his father, then heads for a huge collection of black holes outside the galaxy. Broadhead dies while chasing Klara and Wan, and he is stored as machine intelligence. The Heechee determine Wans path and intervene, capturing his ship. This book answers the question of why the Heechee disappeared: They had fled into a black hole because they feared a mysterious race known as the Assassins, who they believed had systematically destroyed all organic intelligence that they encountered. The Heechee believed that the Assassins systematically were adding mass to the universe in order to speed its eventual collapse. The Heechee feared that the Assassins sought to alter the initial conditions immediately after the Big Bang to make the emergence of organic life less likely and the conditions more favorable for life based on energy. With humans flitting around the galaxy broadcasting signals of life without fear, the Heechee decide to venture out and join the humans in watching for signs that "the Foe" is returning.

In *The Annals of the Heechee*, the Heechee and Broadhead encounter the Assassins, who turn out to be less fierce than the Heechee feared. Humanity and Heechee are saved when the Foe discovers that some humans are storing themselves voluntarily as electronic intelligence before their bodies wear out, because the quality of life is better in the computer than outside it. This encourages the Assassins to allow humans and Heechee to continue to evolve while the Foe continues to add mass to the universe. The collection of vignettes, *The Gateway Trip*, tells the tale of various explorers and prospectors who are mentioned briefly in the novels and ties them together with a brief recounting of the major events of the novels.

ANALYSIS

In the later books of this series, Frederik Pohl gradually develops a theme of the nature of cybernetic intelligence. In *Gateway*, Broadhead interacts with a somewhat limited psychiatric program called Sigfrid von Shrink, which projects a human image and creates the appearance of a personality. The story unfolds as a series of encounters between Broadhead and Sigfrid that ultimately result in Robin coming to terms with his guilt.

Beyond the Blue Event Horizon introduces a much more sophisticated program modeled on Albert Einstein. It serves as an information processor for Broadhead. Broadhead's wife continues to upgrade the Albert program, which eventually has a profound crisis when it is forced to accept the validity of quantum mechanics. In *Heechee Rendezvous*, Broadhead dies, and his wife reads his personality and memory into machine storage, where he is then free to interact with other, similarly stored individuals. In this cybernetic reality, Broadhead can simulate experiences such as skiing, drinking, or making love, and do so in conjunction with others. In *The Annals of the Heechee*, the Assassins are revealed to have far more in common with these machine-based entities than with organic life. The final two novels directly address the question of the nature of intelligence and life.

Gateway won the Hugo, Nebula, and John W. Campbell Memorial awards, and with good reason. The novel creates an interesting balance between the terrifying but exciting exploration of the galaxy on Heechee ships and Robinette Broadhead's painful and frightening exploration of his inner guilt in a series of sessions with a psychiatric computer program. *Gateway* effectively conveys both the terror that grips prospectors before they commit their fate to uncontrollable ships and the bleak alternatives to their quests. The book is filled with mysteries, especially the nature of the Heechee and why they disappeared, leaving behind such an eclectic collection of artifacts. Each of the remaining novels reveals new material on the Heechee; the series therefore progressively loses some of the original sense of mystery. Pohl introduces new elements throughout, however, and ultimately he creates a coherent and compelling future history.

The novels provide a consistent social, political, and economic critique, typical of Pohl's work. *Gateway* shows unskilled but brave prospectors who occasionally make unimaginable fortunes, in stark contrast to the bleak lives of most citizens of Earth. Those who strike it rich do so not because they are smarter or braver than other prospectors but rather because they are lucky. In later novels, it is clear that those who have full medical coverage can sometimes acquire necessary organs for transplant from those who are still using them, a theme that echoes the organ transplants in some of Larry Niven's work as well as actual events of the 1990s in some less-developed countries.

After the first novel, Broadhead is a very rich man and uses his wealth to manipulate the political system to achieve his often altruistic goals. In contrast, Pohl often portrays the desperation of poorer humans. In the final novel, the Heechee are puzzled by human ownership of private property and wide differences in wealth. Although the novels seem to constitute an indictment of capitalism, in fact Pohl shows Broadhead as a philanthropist millionaire and the Heechee as intrigued by the idea of money as a social mechanism to establish social value.

Pohl's exploration of the nature of intelligence and life in computer storage links this traditional future history to some of the themes explored by cyberpunk writers in the mid-1980s. Although he does not discuss it explicitly, it appears that the Albert program attains many of the characteristics of sentience, including mental problems. Most interesting is the nature of Broadhead, who appears to exist at the interstitial zone between computer program and sentient life. Although in the final novel Broadhead wheels and deals and acts like an independent agent, his wife does tinker with his program.

The Heechee novels are Pohl at his best, and Pohl has listed his address as Gateway, suggesting that they are his favorite among his creations. They have spawned two computer games that generally are faithful to the details of the novels. The final collection, however, is mostly for true fans, as the stories repeat material from the earlier novels. They do make a passing connection between the Gateway novels and the Merchants of Venus books.

—*Clyde Wilcox*

HEINRICH VON OFTERDINGEN

In search of the blue flower, Heinrich becomes a poet, and the novel itself becomes an apotheosis of poetry

Author: Novalis (Friedrich von Hardenberg, 1772–1801)
Genre: Fantasy—inner space
Type of work: Novel
Time of work: The Middle Ages
Locale: Germany
First published: 1802 (English translation, Henry of Ofterdingen, 1842)

THE STORY

Heinrich von Ofterdingen was published posthumously and remains a fragment. It is questionable whether Novalis could have taken the novel much further, for it progresses rapidly from the outer to the inner world, with associations increasing exponentially. Part 1 ends with Klingsohrs fairy tale, an extremely dense and complicated story that remains impervious to consistent interpretation. Some regard it as the epitome of a Romantic literary fairy tale. Others reject it because it does not make sense. The Germanist Emil Staiger omitted Klingsohrs fairy tale from his 1968 edition of Novalis works for that reason. To appreciate Novalis fully, the reader must be prepared to follow his flights of fancy.

At the beginning of the novel, Heinrich is twenty years old. He dreams of death and rebirth, of entering a cave and experiencing great longing, and of seeing a blue flower with a delicate face hovering in its center. Heinrich travels to Augsburg, in Swabia, to visit his grandfather Schwaning for the first time. As the coach heads into the distance, it seems as if he is actually going home. His traveling companions entertain him with the story of Atlantis. Novalis links this to Heinrichs dream of the blue flower, because when the kings daughter finds her future husband, a silent blue flame is burning in his fathers house.

Chapter 5 moves directly into the realm of fantasy. On an exploratory tour of caves, Heinrich encounters a hermit, Friedrich von Hohenzollern. In one of Friedrichs books, Heinrich is amazed to see pictures of himself with people he knows and people he does not yet know, including a man who seems to be of considerable importance to him. Friedrich explains that the book, written in Provençal, is a novel about the wonderful adventures of a poet and in praise of poetry itself in all of its diversity. The end of the novel is missing.

At his grandfathers house, Heinrich recognizes the important man from the book as Klingsohr the poet. Heinrich also immediately falls in love with Klingsohrs daughter Mathilde, whose face is the one that appeared to him in the blue flower. He dreams of being under a blue stream with her. She says a wonderful, secret word to him that rings through his entire being. His grandfather wakes him, and he cannot remember the word.

Klingsohr tells his fairy tale, a capricious condensation and combination of many fairy tales and myths. It takes place on three levels: the frozen world of Arcturus, the main world of the family, and the underworld where the three fates spin. Evil appears in the person of the rational family scribe, who plots to overthrow the family, but the child Fable outsmarts him and, together with Sophie (wisdom) and Eros, brings about the unfreezing and rebirth of the world. Eros dream of a flower floating on a blue stream provides the symbolic link to the main work.

Part 2 of the novel shows Heinrich in deep mourning after Mathildes death. Zyane, the daughter of Friedrich von Hohenzollern, appears to him, saying that her father is also his father. In answer to Heinrich's question "Where are we going?" she replies, "Always home."

ANALYSIS

Novalis wrote his Romantic novel *Heinrich von Ofterdingen* in reaction to Johann Wolfgang von Goethes classical novel and *Bildungsroman, Wilhelm Meisters Lehrjahre* (1795–1796; *Wilhelm Meisters Apprenticeship,* 1824), which he intended to transcend. *Heinrich von Ofterdingen* is written in keeping with the definition of Romantic poetry published by Novalis friend, Friedrich Schlegel, in the 116th fragment of his journal *Athenäum* (1798–1800). According to Schlegel, Romantic poetry is progressive, universal poetry that puts poetry in touch with philosophy and rhetoric. It should also mix poetry and prose, genius and criticism, and literary poetry and natural poetry. It recognizes that the capriciousness of the poet is subject to no laws.

This idea of Romantic poetry explains how Novalis could freely include theoretical commentary, poems, songs, legends, and Klingsohrs fairy tale within his work as well as how the work could well remain a fragment. Rules were there to be broken. Novalis could deviate from the *Bildungsroman* by turning the novel into a work about poetry instead of the poet. He could take Klingsohrs fairy tale beyond allegory by giving the metaphors so many meanings that they were no longer systematic.

Heinrich von Ofterdingen is one of the seminal works of early Romanticism. The vision that guided Heinrich, the blue flower, subsequently became the symbol for Romanticism per se.

Setting the trend for much of German Romantic literature, Novalis looked back to the Middle Ages as a golden age of high romance, and he derived the title for his novel from that period. The name Heinrich von Ofterdingen is that of a minnesinger to whom myth has ascribed the great ten thousand-verse anonymous heroic epic *The Nibelungenlied*, which was written around 1200. Likewise, the name Hohenzollern is that of a family of Swabian rulers originating in the eleventh or twelfth century.

Novalis works all were written in the span of a few years, between the death of his fiancée Sophie von Kühn in 1796 and his own early death from tuberculosis. Therefore, Heinrichs mourning in part 2 is quite autobiographical, and the reappearance of Friedrich von Hohenzollerns dead daughter reflects Novalis longing for the reappearance of his beloved Sophie. His love for her also explains the leading role given to Sophie in Klingsohrs fairy tale.

Critical response to *Heinrich von Ofterdingen* has been polarized from the start. As could be expected, Schlegel called it a "marvelous and thoroughly new phenomenon". Other Romantic authors were not impressed. A positive reception by author Hermann Hesse in 1900 brought the novel back into vogue, and it has been the subject of hundreds of studies in the twentieth century.

—*Jean M. Snook*

HELL HOUSE

A theory that links electromagnetic radiation with survival after death explains the mysterious haunting of a house

Author: Richard Matheson (1926–2013)
Genre: Science fiction—extrasensory powers
Type of work: Novel
Time of work: 1970
Locale: Maine
First published: 1971

THE STORY

The isolated Belasco House in Maine, otherwise known as Hell House, provides the gothic setting and atmosphere of this novel. Four persons visit the haunted house after it has been closed for thirty years. One visitor, Dr. Lionel Barrett, a physicist, brings his wife Edith, whose main reason for being there is that she fears being alone even for a few days. Dr. Barrett undertakes the visit because a wealthy, aging publisher, Rudolph Deutsch, offered him $100,000 to find proof one way or another about survival after death.

Barrett not only needs the money for his retirement but also finds the idea of dealing with a haunted house intriguing because it gives him an opportunity to test a machine he invented. Theoretically, his machine, which he calls a Reversor, could help him find the definitive proof about an afterlife that Deutsch requires. Barrett plans to find this proof by using electromagnetic radiation to demagnetize the house, dissipate the resonant negative energy, and thus end, through scientific means, the haunting of the house.

Florence Tanner and Benjamin Franklin Fischer, both psychics, are the two other visitors, also commissioned by Deutsch. They bring different perspectives. Tanner comes from a Spiritualist background and serves as a minister of the Temple of Spiritual Harmony. Her financial reward could provide a fine new building for her congregation. Fischer, a man of forty-five, had been an extraordinarily gifted medium in his early years and does not come as a stranger to Hell House, as Belasco's house came to be called in recognition of the former owners depravity. In fact, Fischer was the lone survivor of the second of two earlier attempts to investigate the haunted Belasco House. These investigations had resulted in the destruction of eight people through death, suicide, or insanity, and in the house being sealed off. Fischer himself has shunned any connection with parapsychology since his escape from the house, and since then he has led an aimless life. Despite his belief that the house intends to kill him and the other visitors, he is ready to face whatever he must to overcome his personal demons.

Each visitor to Hell House brings a distinctive point of view that proves important to the resolution. Although Barrett does not believe that personalities survive death, he does believe that psychic phenomena exist as manifestations of the human subconscious. Tanner firmly believes that personality survives after death.

Barrett's attempt to demagnetize the house with his electromagnetic radiation machine at first appears to rid it of all remnants of psychic energy and to break the curse pervading it. Terror returns, however, as subsequent events lead to Barrett's mysterious but violent death. Events also confirm Tanner's belief that personality survives after death. She dies because Belasco's surviving energy reasserts itself with enough evil and power to possess and then to destroy her.

Fischer recognizes that Barrett and Tanner each had been partially correct and realizes that one evil entity created what had seemed to be multiple hauntings. Fischer again risks being destroyed by Belasco's malign presence as he attempts to solve the puzzle of the evil remaining within the house. Tanner's surviving personality guides him to discover a lead shield that had protected Belasco's ego from the radiation. Edith Barrett and Fischer realize that Belasco no longer has the power to destroy them. Each of them has faced personal demons and survived the experience.

ANALYSIS

Unlike many stories of haunted houses, Richard Matheson's *Hell House* attempts to account scientifically for paranormal events, as remnants of psychic energy and manifestations of electromagnetism. A serious student of parapsychology for more than thirty years, Matheson believes in the paranormal. Near the beginning of *Hell House*, he provides a list of more than one hundred displays of psychic phenomena reportedly observed at the Belasco House on earlier occasions. Most, if not all, of these events manifest themselves again by the novel's conclusion and help create the tales terror.

At least two of Matheson's short stories anticipate events of *Hell House*. In "Mad House" (1953), remnants of the energy of a former occupants rages resonate in a house to the degree that the next occupant of the house commits suicide. An academic colleague explains this action, in theory, as a result of negative energy from the former occupants bad temper that lingered in the house.

Similarly, Matheson's "Slaughter House" (1953) creates a gothic atmosphere much like that of the Belasco House. A first-person narrator moves into an elegant old mansion where several people are believed to have died of arsenic poisoning. The narrator wakes one night to see his somnambulistic brother following a blue light. Within the light, he discerns a beautiful woman, whom he recognizes from a portrait as the deceased daughter of the houses original owner. Later, the apparition visits the narrator, who ultimately goes mad, sets fire to the curtains, and flees the house.

The imagery and atmosphere of both stories, as well as *Hell House*, echo the fiction of Edgar Allan Poe, as does much of Matheson's fiction and film work. Matheson wrote screenplays for several productions loosely based on tales by Poe and directed by Roger Corman: *House of Usher* (1960), *The Pit and the Pendulum* (1961), *Tales of Terror* (1962), and *The Raven* (1963).

Matheson based his screenplay for *The Legend of Hell House* (1973) on his own novel *Hell House*. As in Poes tale "The Fall of the House of Usher" (1839), the haunted house in Matheson's book and film comes complete with gothic trappings such as tarn and miasma. Like the sentient House of Usher, the windowless Belasco House creates terror that prompts visitors to flee aghast.

—*Roberta Sharp*

THE HELLICONIA TRILOGY

On Helliconia, the chief planet of a binary system, seasons are centuries long and winters are so severe that survivors must rediscover civilization as the planet emerges from its glacial ages

Author: Brian W. Aldiss (1925–)
Genre: Science fiction—alien civilization
Type of work: Novels
Time of work: Indeterminate future relative to Earth
First published: *Helliconia Spring* (1982), *Helliconia Summer* (1983), and *Helliconia Winter* (1985)

THE STORY

The first section of *Helliconia Spring* tells the story of Yuli, who finds an underworld where a perverted religion—the virtual worship of darkness— holds sway. He works his way back to the world of day and founds a city called Oldorando. There, as the planet emerges slowly from its centuries-long winter, the tribes of the equatorial continent emerge from their hiding places. They begin to do battle, not only for survival but also to dispute possession of the planet with the ferocious phagors. In the central city, all the appurtenances of civilization—love, trade, coinage, history, and science—are being rediscovered. Yuli's descendants hail him because he rejected his faith in favor of his people.

Other characters emerge in this episodic novel, which spans centuries. Helliconia eventually undergoes still another violent change as winter yields to a triumphant spring. Above the planet, five thousand astronauts from Earth orbit the planet in space station *Avernus*. They are prohibited from intervening in the affairs of Helliconia because some aspect of its atmosphere is poisonous to humans. They relay the day-today activities of Helliconia back to Earth, where Helliconian events have become a space opera on the "Eductainment Channel."

Helliconia Summer covers a time span of only a few months. Its plot events center on the king, Borlien, and his queen, MyrdemInggala. Borlien, for political reasons, decides to divorce his queen

543

The Helliconia Trilogy

and marry the princess of ancient Oldorando. The scene shifts rapidly from continent to continent until an Avernian Earthman, Billy Xiao Pin, attempts to intervene in the affairs of Helliconia, with predictably tragic and fatal results.

In *Helliconia Winter*, as Helliconia moves away from its larger sun, auguries of winter begin to haunt the planet. Snow falls, crops fail, and tyranny tightens under the sway of the Oligarch. On Helliconia, Luterin Shokerandt begins a pilgrimage of terror to the arctic regions of the planet. He enters the Great Wheel of Kharnabhar, where prisoners are supposed to row their planet back to light. This action has become almost a religious ritual, and all the trappings of the Darkness religion, first glimpsed in *Helliconia Spring*, are given new meaning. Coupled with the main story is the continuing saga of the observer space station, *Avernus*, and events on post-apocalyptic Earth that parallel those on Helliconia, separated by 1,500 light-years of time.

ANALYSIS

Little question exists that the Helliconia Trilogy is Brian Aldiss's epic masterpiece and one of the masterpieces of science fiction. The planet and binary sun system Aldiss created is one of the most complex ever to spring from the pages of science fiction. It is also one of the most human—and most humane—as well as the most germane. Readers seem to share the fascination with the planet that spurs the activities of the observers on *Avernus*. They can readily understand how Earth dwellers are virtually hypnotized by the long-running epic saga of Helliconia. The Helliconia Trilogy is far more than a science-fiction epic. It is a fully fleshed artistic creation in which Aldiss wishes not only to tell a series of loosely connected stores, both epic and miniature, but also to relate a parable about humanity's ability to ignore "reality" and revel in "eductainment." The three Helliconia novels are as much about Earth and its ways of approaching reality, its methods of ignoring the "shadow" side of itself, its headlong flight from unpleasantness, and its ability to revel in distancing itself from problems as it is about the multifaceted panorama of the Great Year and its effects on Helliconia.

Aldiss appears to ask if people could become so fascinated by distant drama, made unreal by distance and time, that they could fail to see the approaching apocalypse. Seeming to echo German physicist Werner Heisenberg, he asks if the very act of observing changes both the observer and the observed. Are the people of Earth changed by their ageslong observation of Helliconia? Can the five thousand exiled residents of *Avernus* remain unchanged because they can only observe but never interfere? What about the Helliconians themselves, unaware that they have provided "eductainment" to millions on a faraway planet? Is their climate so inexorable that change is forced upon them, albeit with glacial slowness?

Aldiss has returned in this trilogy to one of his most elemental themes, the question of change. The theme of awareness of change (or lack of awareness) pervades many of his novels and short stories, and he frequently explores the effects of change or the results of stasis. Rarely are these questions asked without some relevance to art. In these novels, the "art" is Helliconia itself as well as the interstellar space opera it has engendered.

Perhaps the most telling section of this remarkable series of novels occurs toward the end of *HelliconiaWinter*, in one of the italicized passages that concern Earth or *Avernus* rather than Helliconia. More than seven thousand Earth years have passed since the common era began, yet the memory of Helliconia still haunts the survivors of the apocalypse, and a new glacial age brought about by the overuse of fossil fuels stalks them. One character then advances the Gaia hypothesis: Earth itself may possess life, and humankind has to learn not to try to possess Earth or to ignore its needs.

Another major question raised by Aldiss is the nature of the ferocious phagors. Reminiscent of demoniac creatures, nightmarish minotaurs, and other hateful and hated monsters, they may provide some hideous balance with the humans they ceaselessly wage war against. Aldiss seems to ask if they are in some way the same as humans, merely in another guise or form.

Multiple meanings, all of them intended and many of them ironic, are found in the name of the planet Helliconia. The name draws upon the words halcyon, helix, and helios, as well as the flower helliconia itself. All give some hints of how Aldiss works: He provides questions rather than answers, and he suggests, hints, or alludes rather than being simplistic. Aldiss would be the first to insist that he is not in the business of writing to provide answers. He might maintain that there are no definitive answers to the questions he raises, that in fact the position of the artist is simply to question, to require the reader to think and to probe, not merely to be entertained. His requirement of careful thought is perhaps the best single reason to ponder—and be entertained by—the Helliconia Trilogy.

—*Willis E. McNelly*

HER SMOKE ROSE UP FOREVER

Stories of disease, love, sexuality, death, and alien contact illustrating human and alien biology and alienation both across and within species

Author: James Tiptree, Jr. (Alice Hastings Bradley Sheldon, 1915–1987)
Genre: Science fiction—alien civilization
Type of work: Stories
Time of work: Various times in the future
Location: Various locations on Earth and planets throughout the galaxy
First published: 1990

THE STORY

This collection of eighteen stories, published three years after her death, represents the best of James Tiptree, Jr.'s short fiction. The collection, subtitled *The Great Years of James Tiptree, Jr.*, was edited by James Turner and contains stories originally published between 1969 and 1981. Under the pen name of James Tiptree, Jr.—taken from the label of a marmalade jar—Alice Sheldon began publishing science fiction in 1968. She earned critical acclaim, and interest rose in the mystery of her identity, which was not revealed until 1977.

All the stories in this collection are about death as an inextricable part of the striving and dreams of living beings. In the title story, "Her Smoke Rose Up Forever" (1974), enigmatic alien visitors somehow cause moments of love, violence, and loss in the life of one man to be relived on the cinders of a dead Earth. In "Slow Music" (1980), two of the last people on Earth are betrayed by their love to follow the rest of humanity into a mysterious "River" of alien, bodiless sentience. In "The Man Who Walked Home" (1972), an experimental subject thrown into the far future "walks" back to the moment of the experiment by sheer willpower, appearing and reappearing on the post-apocalyptic Earth at the point of the civilization-destroying explosion caused by his return. In "The Last Flight of Dr. Ain" (1969), a biologist, in despair at the destruction of a "beautiful woman"—Earth—creates a humanity-destroying plague.

In many of the stories, the sex drive itself is a form of death. In "The Last Afternoon" (1972), a human colony is unable to stop waves of giant sea creatures who thrash ashore to mate in an orgy of sexual destruction. In "Love Is the Plan, the Plan Is Death" (1973), an alien being struggling toward sentience is trapped in a biological life cycle in which the females eat the males. The author also represents the human fascination with alien beings as itself a form of self-destruction. In "A Momentary Taste of Being" (1975), the first interstellar expedition, desperate to find new planets to relieve pressures on an overcrowded Earth, finds that humans are merely sperm for fertilizing the ovum of an unknown life-form. Tiptree's most famous stories deal with relations between the sexes in which the sexual aggression of men makes them deadly and alien to women. In "Houston, Houston, Do You Read?" (1976), a ship of NASA astronauts is thrown forward in time to an Earth sparsely populated by female survivors, all clones, of a plague that has destroyed humanity's ability to reproduce. The author represents the men as painfully driven by "alpha male" aggression and misogyny. In "The Girl Who Was Plugged In" (1973), a young man falls in love with a literally brainless, beautiful body that is animated by remote control by a woman whose own ugly body makes her a social outcast. In "The Women Men Don't See" (1973), a mother and a daughter leave Earth willingly on a thoroughly alien ship. The mother says to the shocked male narrator, "We survive by ones and twos in the chinks of your world-machine.... I'm used to aliens."

ANALYSIS

Tiptree's stories are a distinctive contribution to science fiction. In their settings and the way the plots are established, many of the stories evoke the "Golden Age" of science fiction in the early twentieth century. The author conjures up corrupt galactic empires, distant futures, amazing occurrences, bug-eyed and exotic aliens, and alien worlds with the stroke of a pen. Whereas older science fiction aimed at "amazing stories," Tiptree's work aims at unsettling and idiosyncratic explorations of the psychology and biology of love and death. Like the NewWave writers of the 1960's and 1970's, she uses her settings and plots metaphorically, occasionally experimenting with unusual narrative voices, as in "The Girl Who Was Plugged In," a Hugo Award winner. Unlike many of the New Wave writers, she pursues her themes with an expository directness. A strand of her work, composed of her most famous stories, can be identified clearly as feminist and therefore related to the feminist science fiction of the 1970's and 1980's. It is easy to read some of her fiction as representing a radical feminism. She consistently portrays the male sex drive as violent, most shockingly perhaps in "The Screwfly Solution" (1977, as Raccoona Sheldon), a Nebula Award winner. In that story, human males sprayed with an alien hormonal "pesticide" kill all women.

She evokes visions of women's societies as happily separate from men and of women as severely damaged by men, as in "Houston, Houston, Do You Read" (1977 Hugo Award and 1976 Nebula Award winner) and "Your Faces, O My Sisters! Your Faces Filled with Light!" (1976). She shows male culture as destructive of and contemptuous of women who do not fit male stereotypes of women, as in "With Delicate Mad Hands" (1981). Given all this, it is remarkable that the science-fiction community initially took Tiptree to be a male writer.

As angry and satirical as her representation of male and female differences is, it lacks the drive of most feminist writing to reform and enlighten ideologically. Most of her narrators are male, and woven in with the anger, sharp social satire, and even contempt of their portrayal is a strand of sympathy or understanding. Tiptree tends to present men and women, and all living beings, as trapped in their biology and mortality. "Love Is the Plan, the Plan Is Death" (Nebula Award winner) is perhaps the archetypal Tiptree story in this respect. Dark as her vision is, her fatalism allows space for appreciation of the doomed strivings of the spirit for love and transcendence.

—*D. Barrowman Park*

THE HERITAGE UNIVERSE SERIES

A motley group of humans and aliens attempts to discover the secrets of artifacts left behind millions of years ago and discovers that an alien race thought to be extinct has survived

Author: Charles Sheffield (1935–2002)
Type of work: Novels
Genre: Science fiction—galactic empire
Time of work: About c.e. 6200
Locale: Various planetary systems within the spiral arm of the galaxy occupied by Earth
First published: *Summertide* (1990), *Divergence* (1991), and *Transcendence* (1992)

THE STORY

The Heritage Universe series is a narrative about a group of humans and aliens seeking to solve the mystery of the disappearance of an ancient alien race (the Builders) millions of years ago. Humans and various alien races have formed empires throughout thousands of star systems in the galactic spiral arm and have discovered thousands of huge, mysterious Builder artifacts. One sector was formerly ruled by a ruthless race of aliens, the Zardalu, who made slaves of all other races.

In *Summertide*, troubleshooter Hans Rebka goes to the planet Opal to determine why Max Perry is refusing more challenging assignments. Opal has a twin planet, Quake, to which it is connected by a Builder artifact called the Umbilical, a sort of space elevator. The system is soon to reach summertide, a period of maximum tidal stress that occurs every 350,000 years. A number of individuals seek to visit Quake at summertide, including Darya Lang, an academic expert on Builder artifacts; Julius Graves, a Councilor from the galactic ethical authority; Louis Nenda, a fortune hunter with his fierce alien slave, Kallik; and Atvar Hsail, a mysterious insectoid Cecropian with his alien slave and translator, Jmerlia.

Lang and the two fortune hunters believe that events during summertide may help them discover why the Builders left and where they went. Despite being denied access, all those interested end up on Quake at summertide as tidal stresses nearly destroy both Quake and Opal. Nenda and Hsail, with their slaves, form an alliance and seek to kill all the others.

While leaving Quake, Lang sees two huge silver spheres, obviously of Builder origin, exit the core of Quake. One of the spheres heads toward extragalactic space and the other toward the gas giant planet Gargantua, taking with it the ship with the treacherous slave owners. As the book ends, Rebka learns Perry's secret: His girlfriend died on Quake at summertide. Lang and the two slaves decide to take a ship to Gargantua to look for the Builders and their masters, respectively.

In *Divergence*, E. C. Tally, an embodied computer, is sent to investigate. Lang, Rebka, Jmerlia, and Kallik have left for Gargantua. Birdie Kelly, assistant to Perry, must accompany Tally and Graves as they follow in their own ship. Lang and Rebka pick up a distress signal from Nenda and Hsails ship among the small moons and debris surrounding Gargantua, but they find the ship empty on a perfectly spherical small moon. As they approach, they are attacked by Phages, Builder artifacts of unknown purpose. After landing, Rebka and Lang enter the artificial hollow moon and find Nenda and Hsail trapped in a field. At the moons center, they are greeted by an intelligent emissary of the Builders, who puts them through a transfer node to a massive space station 30,000 light-years away. The others enter the moon, rescue Nenda and Hsail, and are eventually sent to the far-off space station. Rebka and Lang meet another Builder emissary. They explore the station, which is filled with thousands of inexplicable devices, and find stasis tanks that contain Zardalu. When Nenda and Hsail arrive, the threat of the Zardalu makes them join forces.

The Builder emissary tells them that the Builders evolved on Gargantua as huge floaters in the lower layers of the gas giant, later moving to higher layers and into space as they developed intelligence and technology. They explain that Phages are actually degenerated, unintelligent Builders, and that the Builders left to await the development of another intelligent species capable of helping them solve the great mystery of the purpose of life and the universe. The emissarys purpose is to allow the three primary intelligent species in the spiral arm (humans, Cecropians, and Zardalu) to fight to see who proves to be the most clever. Humans and Cecropians cooperate to overcome the huge, fierce Zardalu, making them fall into a transport node that sends them back to the spiral arm. The emissary asks the other two races to keep fighting, but they refuse. Nenda and Hsail agree to continue to fight if the others are returned.

In *Transcendence*, Graves and Tally are unable to convince the authorities that the fast-reproducing Zardalu exist. They join with Lang, Rebka, Jmerlia, and Kallik to seek the Zardalu. Nenda and Hsail return, having been banished by the Builder emissary for trying to steal artifacts. They join the rest on their quest for the Zardalu. Their search leads them to the long-avoided Torvil Anfract, a huge region of twisted space-time. They are aided by an alien pilot named Dulcimer, a Chism Polypheme who enjoys becoming inebriated from hard radiation.

After arriving outside the Anfract, Rebka, Nenda, Hsail, Jmerlia, and Kallik take a small ship to a candidate planet and find that it is indeed Genizee, the fabled home world of the Zardalu. As they approach the planet, a beam from the planets moon captures them and forces them to crash on Genizee. Jmerlia stays to repair the ship while the others explore. The scouting expedition soon finds Zardalu, from whom they flee into tunnels beneath the surface. Jmerlia sends a message to the main ship with directions to the planet, but his ship is captured by the beam and taken to the moon, where he talks to another Builder emissary, who is keeping the Zardalu grounded.

Back on the main ship, Lang has surmised that the Torvil Anfract is a huge Builder artifact. When they receive Jmerlia's message, Lang, Tally, and Dulcimer take another ship to Genizee, but they are captured by Zardalu. The group deep inside Genizee continues to explore, finding thousands of hungry baby Zardalu. Jmerlia mysteriously rejoins them but also shows up back on the main ship and with the group captured by Zardalu. Deeper within Genizee, Rebka's group finds that the low tunnels clearly were made by the Builders and guarded by another Builder emissary, from whom they learn that there are thousands of emissaries hidden throughout the spiral arm. Lang, Tally, and Dulcimer escape from the Zardalu into narrow air ducts and head for the surface, followed by thousands of starving Zardalu babies. Rebka and his group return to the main ship to find Graves unconscious, his mind disintegrating. Jmerlia arrives in another ship, also unconscious. Rebka and Nenda return to Genizee to rescue Lang, Tally, and Dulcimer.

All return to the main ship and figure out that macroscopic quantum states in the area explain both Jmerlia being in several places at once and Graves's mental problems. They also surmise that none of the emissaries actually had instructions from the Builders; each had manufactured reasons for their existence. Nenda and Hsail steal a small ship and return to Genizee, where they talk the Zardalu into surrendering and henceforth serving them.

ANALYSIS

Although he has proven capable of writing hard science fiction, in this series Charles Sheffield adopted the conventions of adventure fiction from the 1930s. The plot, characters, and milieu do not stand up to analysis within the boundaries of hard science fiction. Scientific advances are primarily in the physical sciences, with virtually none in the biological sciences. The protagonists, though interestingly diverse, are all competent adventurers who survive by savvy, quick wits, and instincts honed by experience. All the offstage galactic authorities are incompetent bureaucrats who maintain grossly inadequate official records and refuse to believe seven eyewitnesses who say that the Zardalu are alive, rather than extinct as previously believed.

In Sheffield's future, as in most early science-fiction adventures, problem-solving adventurers with competent scientific knowledge are the only ones who accomplish anything. Vast regions of space are known only by word of mouth and are officially uncharted. Scientific knowledge appears to have been at a standstill for millennia, despite the thousands of Builder artifacts being investigated. For example, a three-thousand-year-old spaceship is just as good as—maybe even better than—a newer model. Computers seem little advanced beyond 1960. Humans program them to solve problems, but there is no evidence of artificial intelligence, with the sole exception of E. C. Tally.

There are numerous examples of the space Western syndrome in these books; clichés from other adventure fiction genres are translated to science fiction. Dulcimer enjoys being inebriated (but from hard radiation rather than alcohol) and can pilot drunk better than most pilots who are sober. The Zardalu are physically fierce but do not seem technologically capable of ruling an intergalactic empire. Most of the alien races, despite their diverse morphology, biology, and evolution, are patterned on human archetypes. The human Nenda and the Cecropian Hsail think virtually alike, despite the fact that the insectoid alien is blind, seeing with sound and speaking with pheromonal emissions.

When viewed purely in the context of adventure science fiction, the Heritage Universe series is in many ways quite successful. The various alien species are interestingly diverse, and the Builder artifacts are even more so. The treatment of various aliens as slaves creatively skirts the bounds of political correctness, with the slave species being at least as intelligent as their masters but having little joy in free initiative. The plot moves quickly and clearly despite the numerous protagonists and subplots.

In this series, Sheffield has sought with considerable success to create a traditional, quick-moving science-fiction adventure. The formulas of adventure fiction are used with great creativity, and the result is an enjoyable tale eschewing the pretensions of both literature and hard science.

—*D. Douglas Fratz*

HEROVIT'S WORLD

The satirical chronicle of a pulp science-fiction writers descent into madness, at the end of which he assumes the persona of his fictional hero

Author: Barry N. Malzberg (1939–)
Genre: Science fiction—cautionary
Type of work: Novel
Time of work: 1973
Locale: New York City
First published: 1973

THE STORY

In *Herovit's World*, Barry Malzberg tells the grim tale of the last days of the books antihero, thirty-seven-year-old science-fiction writer Jonathan Herovit. Sitting at his desk in his crammed study in a rent-controlled apartment in New York City, Herovit finds himself unable to complete his ninety-third science-fiction novel. Beset by a severe case of writers block that comes from his justified feeling that his work is of poor literary quality, and plagued by ever-increasing personal problems, Herovit takes recourse in drinking and daydreaming. He attempts to assume a new, more self-assertive identity.

Under intense pressure by his strong-willed agent, Morton Mackenzie, to deliver his manuscript, Herovit furthermore has to face the disaffection of his wife, Janice, who quit her job when their baby, Natalie, was born, and resents her new role as housewife to an unproductive, alcoholic writer. A visit from his old friend Mitchell Wilk, who has escaped producing low-paid science-fiction manuscripts by accepting a college writing position, brings with it not only Wilks raid on Herovits Scotch but also a caustic condemnation of the awful text he is writing.

By graphically setting apart the typescript of Survey Sirius, the adventure Herovit is writing, Malzberg shows the reader plenty of the purple prose of classic science-fiction stories: Futuristic weaponry zaps alien life-forms while words tumble wildly in sentences haphazardly strung together.

Trouble with Janice, an overreliance on hard liquor, and a bitter self-realization of the miserable quality of his work lead Herovit to attempt to become another man. At first, he tries the character of Kirk Poland, who is based on what Herovit has imagined to be the suave, accomplished personality behind his own pen name. Since his start as a science-fiction writer, Herovit's editor has asked him to write his work under the more American-sounding name of Kirk Poland rather than using his own. Even as Kirk Poland, Herovit cannot avoid humiliation at the hand of Janice, who simply walks out of his life.

As Herovit continues his slide into despondence and madness, Malzberg uses his characters erratic actions, paranoid musings and sorrowful reflections to create a novel that paints a caustic, yet vividly realistic, picture of the living and working conditions of a burned out science-fiction writer.

The end comes as Herovit is visited again by Wilk, who arrives with Gloria, Herovits former mistress, with whom Wilk has spent the night. Unable to face reality even in his new incarnation as Kirk, Herovit suddenly believes himself to be his futuristic action hero Mack Miller, who is stranded on a world he has orders to destroy. Punching Wilk and running into the street, Herovit/Mack Miller assaults a few bystanders before being struck fatally by a car. Dying as a deluded man, the novel suggests, Herovit has become a victim of the gap between his violent fiction and his hopeless, shabby life.

ANALYSIS

The reception of Malzberg's sarcastic tale *Herovit's World* in the field of science fiction has been decidedly mixed. The text is a bitter and funny but also hard-hitting exploration of the often miserable circumstances of writers who are trapped writing subliterate fare for relatively little remuneration. Many of Herovit's musings about work in the field—the pay per word, the insularity of a genre in which most people know one another, the cultivation of ancient grudges, the infighting, and the interaction with less-than-generous fans at conventions and through the mail—ring true and have upset many readers who could detect unfavorable parallels to themselves in Malzberg's iconoclastic text.

Angry denunciations of Malzberg, however, were not the only responses. Among fellow writers, Harlan Ellison and Robert Silverberg have praised *Herovit's World* respectively as "long overdue" and "one of the most terrifying visions ever to come out of science fiction." Academic critics have found much to like in Malzberg's merciless satire of the genre, its working conditions, and the effect of strictly commercial work on writers with higher literary ambitions.

Science-fiction stories with science-fiction writers as characters predate the 1973 publication of *Herovit's World*, but none has been as unflinchingly deconstructive of the world they describe. Jonathan Herovit's world is light years apart, for example, from that of Jubal Harshaw, the avuncular part-time science-fiction writer, self-made entrepreneur, and millionaire of Robert A. Heinlein's *Stranger in a Strange Land* (1961). One of Harshaw's most devastating admissions is the claim that no science-fiction writer worth anything will ever pass up the opportunity to devour a free lunch.

Outside the field of science fiction, *Herovit's World* can stand proudly as a major literary achievement that focuses with exceptional clarity and brilliance of thought on a creative persons downfall in the harsh world of American capitalism. Many of the way stations Herovit passes on his descent into his private hell read like science fictions even sharper analysis of the forces that destroyed former stockbroker Tommy Wilhelm, the antihero of Saul Bellow's Nobel Prize-winning mainstream tale *Seize the Day* (1956).

In spite of the forecasts of some critics, *Herovit's World* has not marked the terminus of Malzberg's work in the field of science fiction. Instead, it can be seen as a critical moment of self-reflection in the middle of a career that, by the 1980's and 1990's, had also turned to critical analysis. Significantly, Malzberg concludes a collection of essays, *The Engines of the Night: Science Fiction in the Eighties* (1982), with a creative revision of Herovits world in which Herovit has survived after all. Although this later story has a cautiously optimistic tone, *Herovit's World* still convinces aesthetically. Its vision of the private hell of a creative mind forced to endure humiliation has a force rarely matched in the field of satire.

—R. C. Lutz

THE HIGH CRUSADE

When visited by aliens, a contingent of medieval soldiers and their leaders take control, launch themselves into space, fight the larger alien menace, and save Earth from future destruction

Author: Poul Anderson (1926–2001)
Genre: Fantasy—galactic empire
Type of work: Novel
Time of work: c.e. 1345 and the far future
Locale: England, a spaceship, and various locations through the universe
First published: 1960

THE STORY

A captain receives a translation of a thousand-year-old manuscript, written by Brother Parvus, telling of the exploits of his lord, Sir Roger de Tourneville, who established an English space empire based on the feudal system. The unexpectedness of the successes of the medieval British against aliens and advanced technology and the further irony of their tenacious independence helped this novel win a Hugo Award.

In c.e. 1345, when confronted by a scouting spaceship of the Wersgorxian Empire bent on conquest, Sir Roger and his men defeat the invaders, claim the spaceship, and take a single hostage, Branithar. Brother Parvus interrogates the alien, a short, blue-skinned, pig-snouted humanoid, learning his language and teaching him Latin. Sir Roger mounts an expedition against France and then the Holy Lands. He and his people board the spaceship and are launched toward the alien outpost by Branithar, who treacherously engages and locks the autopilot computer in an attempt to make them prisoners.

On arrival, the English defeat the three garrisons on the Wersgorxian outpost, partly through guile and brash strategy, partly through relying on difficulties of translating languages during negotiations, and most overtly by using the aliens own weapons against them. The aliens have become accustomed to terrorizing less technologically advanced species and therefore are unable to handle the brash English; they are overmatched in hand-to-hand combat. During this action, the route home is lost, and Sir Roger becomes increasingly estranged from his homesick wife, Lady Catherine, who is being courted by Sir Owain. Realizing that his battles constitute a war against the Wersgorxian Empire and that Earth might be in peril, Sir Roger seeks allies in alien worlds subjugated by his opponents.

While the alliance is forged, Sir Owain enlists Branithar in recovering the route home and persuades Catherine to search for Earth. Sir Owain forces Sir Roger to a parley and tries to take him prisoner. Sir Roger fights, defeats Sir Owain, and wins back Lady Catherine, but in the process, the data detailing the route home are sacrificed and the English are committed to an interplanetary existence. The epilogue reveals that the captain who is reading the transcript is an Earth man of the future who is preparing to meet the descendants of these English crusaders in their first encounter with Earth since 1345.

ANALYSIS
The outer frame of this story places the reader in the position of the man who is about to meet with an aggressive alien invasionary force. The irony is that this potential enemy is an accidentally exiled fragment of humanity taken from the medieval past. Although the cultural development of the homecoming English has been influenced by contact with other alien species, they have retained the essential patterns from their past, specifically the concepts of crusade, Christian religion (or at least the Catholic churchs administrative structure), and the heroic quest for adventure. Because of such anachronisms, the meeting of the English with the future Earth is one of vastly differing societies. By the time the English rediscover their home world, they have only a memorial interest in it. This outer frame provides a satisfying closure, and though separate from the events within the main plot, it seems a reasonable extrapolation from that inner story.

Within the outer frame, the narrative progresses partly as a record of events, roughly a chronicle. The narrative persona of Brother Parvus influences the tale by subjective moral and ethical biases. Nevertheless, he attempts to tell a tale as truthfully as possible and begs excuse when he must provide fictive reconstructions of conversations and events that he could not have observed directly. His humility smacks of Chaucerian disingenuousness and provides snatches of humor throughout the story, for example, when he verbally blushes at the English naming of new and perhaps erotic constellations.

Themes evident in the story include a strong sense of British patriotism and the tenacity of the English in the face of overwhelming odds. The story suggests that the structures of medieval society are superior to those of other cultures. This explains the otherwise incredible account of the failure of the Wersgorxian Empire to overpower the puny threat of the superstitious and technologically backward English. They have advanced beyond hand-to-hand combat and therefore are poorly matched against the mounted knights, English bowmen, and pike-wielding peasants.

Beyond the accidents of space conquest, the story of the interrelationships among Sir Roger, Lady Catherine, and Sir Owain is similar to that of Arthurian legend, advanced technology taking the role of Merlin. At one point, Sir Roger admits that his greatest error was in leaving his wife too much alone. It is thus no accident that the base for English operations is a planet they name New Avalon.

Having found their lost home at the end of the novel, the English are disappointed that the discovery offers them no new challenges. Instead, they launch themselves back into space, looking for new dragons to defeat.

The novel is a well crafted example of a what-if concept. Much of the implication is that the vibrancy and daring of the British are what have made them a powerful force. The alien species fails to defeat the crusading British because of having lost the urgency of survival and the inventiveness born of necessity. The British victories are as much attributable to the weaknesses of their foes as they are to the strengths of the British. The Wersgorix are analogous to the Romans overrun by rougher but more effective Goths.

—*Scott D. Vander Ploeg*

HIGH-RISE

The inhabitants of a high-rise apartment building turn against one another and dissolve into warring factions bent on mindless destruction and sexual perversion

Author: J. G. Ballard (1930-2009)
Genre: Science fiction—dystopia
Type of work: Novel
Time of work: The late twentieth century
Locale: A high-rise apartment building in London
First published: 1975

THE STORY

High-Rise begins as the last of the one thousand apartment units in a new forty-story high-rise building is filled. Parties are held every night in the fully occupied building. The first of many violent images in the book is a wine bottle falling from an upper balcony to a lower one, then shattering. Soon the building splits into three groups: the lower class, occupying the bottom ten floors, the middle class, on floors eleven through thirty-five, and the upper class, on the top five floors. The best unit of the top floor is reserved for Anthony Royal, the buildings architect. The people of the building become increasingly more vicious and destructive, tearing apart everything in the building and vandalizing it as they terrorize, violate, and kill one another.

Dr. Robert Laing moved into the high-rise to live in anonymity after his divorce. Throughout the book, he mostly manages to stay barricaded in his room, venturing out only occasionally to reflect on the destruction and the events outside his raid-proof door. He proves himself to be one of the strongest of the people in the building, exhibiting self-reliance and passivity. He personally does not engage in brutality. Laing appears in the beginning and ending chapters, holding the book together, but essentially slips out of the middle chapters, in which the other, more aggressive people are involved in their barbaric rites, rituals, and extreme acts of brutality.

The increasing violence is as interesting as any of the people involved. Violence begins because the people of the bottom floors believe that the people of the top floors are letting their dogs urinate in elevators that serve the bottom floors. The people of the top floors are supposed to take the high-speed elevators to their homes and never be on the other elevators.

Richard Wilder, inhabitant of a second-floor apartment, kills a dog. Soon thereafter, a neighbor of Wilder who regularly dined in the thirty-fifth story restaurant is found at the bottom of the building, on the floor of an elevator. He is barely conscious, with a severely bruised face and tattered clothes. The message is clear: The higher floors are off limits to the people of the lower floors. The war continues, but with little use of strategy. Clans form and dissipate, sexual abuse of women is rampant, and finally women learn to stay inside their enclaves or are kept by strong men who protect them.

The dilapidation of the building forms one element of the plot. The building begins as a state of the art, technological miracle. It has twenty elevators, a shopping mall, a grocery and restaurants, swimming pools, a bank, and a junior school. As its inhabitants become more degenerate, it naturally loses electricity and waste disposal systems. Soon it is little better as a living space than would be a cliff face pocked with caves.

As the battle for control of the building takes hold, Wilder realizes that he must reach the top floor in order to rule this world. He leads gangs and raiding parties on the lower floors for several chapters and finally ventures (with a hunting dog) up to the fortieth floor, where Royal is waiting, presiding over the balcony and his group of women there. Wilder shoots Royal with a pistol, firing the only gunshot in the entire book. It is indicative of the mood set in the book that all combat is hand to hand until this final blow.

ANALYSIS

J. G. Ballard is known as a leading author of catastrophic science fiction, and he is one of Britain's most highly esteemed science-fiction writers. His creative talents focus on the physical and psychological deterioration of people who are caught in extreme circumstances.

Empire of the Sun (1984) is Ballard's most acclaimed book. It is a somewhat autobiographical account, with elements similar to his experience as a child interned in a Civilian Assembly Center in China during World War II. To have witnessed the death, violence, disease, and human perversion there surely affected his writing.

In *High-Rise*, the building is a microcosm of the violent atrocities of which people are capable when left to their own devices. None of the residents move out of the building, even as the violence escalates toward and beyond absurd proportions. Many of the residents die, illustrating the books theme of survival of the fittest.

Ballard exposes technology as something that can destroy humanity. He writes, "the high-rise was a model of all that technology had done to make possible the expression of a truly free psychopathology." He indicates that the process of technology and subsequent civilization of people does great harm, in that natural instincts are repressed in order for the civilizing process to occur. As natural instincts are repressed, the inevitable outcome is violent and psychotic behavior. Ballard shows readers a world in which people can do absolutely anything they want and it makes no difference; they are not subjected to laws or punishment. Those who survive in *High-Rise* do so through personal fortitude and the ability to kill if necessary.

—*Beaird Glover*

THE HITCHHIKER'S GUIDE TO THE GALAXY SERIES

Arthur Dent, an ordinary Englishman, is drawn into an extraordinary galactic adventure involving personal danger and revelations about the meaning of life, the universe, and everything

Author: Douglas Adams (1952–2011)
Genre: Science fiction—cultural exploration
Type of work: Novels
Time of work: Before Earth existed to the end of time
Location: Throughout the universe
First published: *The Hitchhiker's Guide to the Galaxy* (1979), *The Restaurant at the End of the Universe* (1980), *Life, the Universe, and Everything* (1982; with the first two novels as *The Hitchhiker's Trilogy*, 1983), *So Long, and Thanks for All the Fish* (1984; with the first three novels as *The Hitchhiker's Guide to the Galaxy: A Trilogy in Four Parts*, 1986, in Great Britain and as *The Hitchhiker's Quartet*, 1986, in the United States), *The More than Complete Hitchhiker's Guide: Five Stories* (1987; contains the first four novels and a related short story, "Young Zaphod Plays It Safe"), *The Original Hitchhiker Radio Scripts* (1985), and *Mostly Harmless* (1992)

THE STORY

The Hitchhiker's Guide to the Galaxy series is a unique "trilogy," as it originally was called, in that by 1992 it consisted of five novels and a short story and still had yet to be concluded definitively. It began as a radio series broadcast by the British Broadcasting Company (BBC) beginning in 1978 and ending in 1980. Many fans of the story became acquainted with it through recordings of the old radio shows, the scripts of which were published as *The Original Hitchhiker Radio Scripts*. A television version of the series was broadcast by the BBC in 1981. There are, therefore, three versions of the Guide: radio, television, and print. Although all were written by Douglas Adams, these versions are not altogether consistent with one another. What follows is a summary of the five novels and the short story.

The Hitchhiker's Guide to the Galaxy begins with Arthur Dent, an ordinary young Englishman, waking to find that his home has been scheduled for demolition to allow construction of a new motorway bypass. In protest, Arthur lies prostrate between the bulldozer and his house. Arthur's friend, Ford Prefect, talks Arthur into giving up his protest (at least temporarily) and going to the local pub. There, Ford completely perplexes Arthur by claiming to be an alien and telling him that they must leave Earth immediately because it is about to be demolished to make way for an intergalactic bypass.

Thus begins Arthur's adventure. He and Ford, a researcher for and proud owner of the encyclopedic *Hitchhiker's Guide to the Galaxy*, manage to get on board a ship of the Volgon fleet, which has just demolished Earth. They are captured by the Volgons and expelled into the void of space. Fortunately, they are picked up by Ford's two-headed cousin, Zaphod Beeblebrox, and his companions, Trillian, an Earth woman Zaphod recently picked up, and Marvin, a chronically depressed robot. Zaphod's stolen ship, the *Heart of Gold*, is equipped with the prototype of an "improbability drive," which is what enabled them to rescue Arthur and Ford.

Zaphod is en route to Magrathea, a legendary planet that once was in the business of producing custom-made planets to order. After a brush with two deadly missiles, the travelers land on Magrathea. The planet seems to be shut down but is not. A new project is under way: the reconstruction of Earth.

As it turns out, Earth actually was a massive computer designed by advanced aliens from another dimension who took the form of laboratory mice on Earth. Its purpose was to determine the ultimate question of "life, the universe, and everything." The ultimate answer, the number forty-two, already had been derived by "Deep Thought," Earth's cybernetic predecessor, but the Volgons destroyed Earth five minutes before Deep Thought's main program was to be completed and the question delivered.

Upon discovering that Arthur is human, the mice cancel the order for another Earth, believing that they can get the answer they seek from an examination of Arthur's brain. Zaphod's pursuers arrive and are about to blast him and his companions when Marvin, the depressed robot, accidentally saves them all. The novel comes to a conclusion with the group back on the *Heart of Gold*, heading for the Restaurant at the End of the Universe.

The subsequent novels do not take this narrative forward systematically, although they occasionally present new variations on the theme. *The Restaurant at the End of the Universe* begins with the travelers being pursued by a Volgon fleet. The Volgons have been hired by Zaphod's psychoanalyst, who, it is revealed, arranged to have Earth destroyed. The answer to the riddle of life, the universe, and everything, he feared, would put psychoanalysts out of business, or at least drastically reduce their income.

With the help of one of Zaphod's long-dead ancestors, the travelers escape, but Zaphod disappears from the *Heart of Gold*. He finds himself drawn to a character named Zarniwoop, first experiencing the mindzapping "total perspective vortex." Zarniwoop wants the *Heart of Gold*. Zaphod manages to escape, and the travelers resume their journey to the restaurant.

After a hearty meal, during which they watch the destruction of the universe, the travelers leave on another stolen ship, one that is programmed to crash into the heart of a nearby sun. Fortunately, the ship has a transporter. Marvin stays behind to work the contraption (nevertheless appearing in future novels), and the others are transported off the ship.

Zaphod and Trillian are transported to a further adventure with Zarniwoop. More in line with the plot of the series, Arthur and Ford wind up on a spaceship containing human rejects—cosmeticians, hairdressers, telephone cleaners, and the like—from a planet called Golgafrincham. Their destination is prehistoric Earth. Once on Earth, Arthur and Ford find mates and settle down.

Life, the Universe, and Everything touches only peripherally on the main themes and plot line of the series. As the novel opens, Arthur and Ford are still on prehistoric Earth, but a time and space anomaly enables them to escape to a modern cricket match being played at Lord's. The universe is saved from disaster, and the fictional origin of cricket is revealed.

So Long, and Thanks for All the Fish is more closely connected to the primary plot of the series. In it, Arthur hitches a ride back to Earth, which somehow has been restored to its former condition, minus dolphins. In typically complicated fashion, Arthur finds Fenchurch, a young woman who also has been profoundly affected by the Earth's (alleged) demolition. The two fall in love, enjoying both mutual attraction and a shared cosmic consciousness. At the conclusion, it is revealed that dolphins saved Earth before departing, leaving the message contained in the book's title. Arthur and Fenchurch remain in a blissful state of uncertainty, tempered by love and companionship, as the novel closes.

For readers who like a happy ending, that would have been a good place to end the "trilogy." *Mostly Harmless* begins with Fenchurch already killed in an accident and Arthur adrift in the universe, searching for an Earth-like planet on which to settle. He finds one that is suitable and makes a home for himself. In short order, however, a mysterious daughter appears (and bolts), and Ford appears. Together, he and Arthur must rescue the universe from the new publishers of the *Hitchhiker's Guide to the Galaxy*, who are allowing different dimensions and universes to leak into one another, threatening the little meaning and stability left to the galaxies' inhabitants. The novel ends anticlimactically, allowing the possibility of further adventures.

ANALYSIS

The Hitchhiker's Guide to the Galaxy series is a unique experiment combining humor and science fiction. As humor, it lampoons everything from philosophers, psychoanalysts, and economists to the BBC, American television, and the publishing business. The trilogy also deals in high irony. For example, while the authorities are planning to demolish Arthur's house and coming up with all kinds of morally bankrupt reasons for doing so, they are about to have their habitat demolished, for equally vacuous reasons. Likewise, the rejects from Golgafrincham are portrayed as inept, useless idiots, but they survive while their fellow Golgafrinchams are wiped out by a plague contracted as a result of a dirty telephone.

As science fiction, the series creates a universe that becomes real to readers, although, again ironically, it is one in which reality is elusive, conditions constantly shift, and the meaning of life may be completely unknowable. Douglas Adams's universe is an existential one in which there is no knowable godhead to supply authoritative guidance and morals are relative. In the fourth novel, Adams offers love as an answer, but it is not a dominant theme in the work. As in Voltaire's *Candide* (1759), readers might draw the lesson that one should simply mind his or her own business, but Arthur is not allowed to do that. Trouble finds him, whether he is looking for it or not. Thus, Adams gives urgency to the questions he raises, though he gives no answers.

There is, in addition, an occasional environmental theme, as in the story "Young Zaphod Plays It Safe." As might be expected, no such crusade could long be sustained in this work, because environmentalists, like everyone else, must be lampooned. Their cause rests on the same flimsy philosophical foundations as all human ideals and principles.

—Ira Smolensky

THE HOBBIT

Bilbo Baggins, a hobbit, unwillingly accompanies the wizard Gandalf and thirteen dwarves on a quest for the treasure of the dragon Smaug

Author: J(ohn) R(onald) R(euel) Tolkien (1892–1973)
Genre: Fantasy—heroic fantasy
Type of work: Novel
Time of work: The Third Age
Location: Middle-earth, an imaginary land
First published: 1937 (2d ed., 1951; 3d ed., 1966)

THE STORY

Although J. R. R. Tolkien drew extensively from northern European myths in developing various inhabitants of his imaginary world, Middle-earth, *The Hobbit* (subtitled *Or, There and Back Again*) focuses on a new race of beings he created. His hobbit hero Bilbo Baggins likes the snug comforts of home with no adventures to interrupt his ordinary life. The wizard Gandalf draws Bilbo out of this sheltered and complacent life by sending him on an adventure—a quest with the dwarf Thorin and his twelve companions to recover the treasure that the dragon Smaug stole. Gandalf employs Bilbo as the dwarves' "burglar," engaging him against his will to steal back Smaug's hoard.

As the dwarves journey toward Smaug's lair in the Lonely Mountain, Bilbo learns to live up to Gandalf's expectations. He fails at first when he unsuccessfully tries to pick a troll's pocket, and Gandalf has to rescue the group. When they are captured again, this time by goblins, Bilbo is separated from his companions and must rescue himself. He finds a magic ring that makes the wearer invisible and uses it to escape first from Gollum, a threatening creature he encounters, and then from the goblins. He rejoins the dwarves and Gandalf, who have also escaped. Wolves (called "wargs") and goblins attack again, but the group is finally rescued by eagles and aided by Beorn, a man who can transform himself into a bear.

After Gandalf leaves the dwarves at the entrance to the forest of Mirkwood to pursue his own errand, Bilbo begins to lead the group, using his ring to save them from giant spiders and then from the dungeons of the Elvenking. When the dwarves arrive at the Lonely Mountain, Bilbo finds the secret door to Smaug's lair, then arouses the dragon's anger by stealing a cup. Seeking revenge, Smaug destroys nearby Lake-town, but he is killed by Bard the bowman, leader of the townsmen. Thorin refuses to share the treasure with the Lake-men and elves, despite their legitimate claim on part of it. Bilbo tries to prevent a war by offering Bard the Arkenstone, the fabulous gem Thorin values above all the rest of the hoard. Despite Bilbo's efforts, the competing races are about to fight when they are attacked by goblins and wargs. Working together, the dwarves, elves, and men defeat the enemy, although Thorin is killed in the battle. Bilbo refuses a large reward, desiring instead simply to go home. The book ends on a comic note as Bilbo returns to find that he has lost his reputation as an unadventurous and thus respectable hobbit.

ANALYSIS
Although many people read *The Hobbit* only as a precursor to Tolkien's masterpiece, *The Lord of the Rings* (1968 as omnibus; original volumes *The Fellowship of the Ring*, 1954; *The Two Towers*, 1955; and *The Return of the King*, 1955), the earlier book deserves discussion for its own considerable merits. The third edition, revised from the original, is considered the standard.

Tolkien is one of the preeminent fantasy writers of the twentieth century. For many readers, his books provide the standards by which to judge all other fantasy. Tolkien's success lies in his ability to "subcreate," a process he defines in his essay "On Fairy Stories" as the artist's ability to create a "Secondary World" that follows consistent internal rules. By describing in depth the peoples, geography, and history of his invented world, Tolkien offers an imaginary world so vividly portrayed in its complexity that readers do not so much "suspend disbelief" while reading as much as simply believe in Middle-earth.

One component of Tolkien's success as a "sub-creator" is his profound knowledge of Anglo-Saxon and Old Norse literature. He freely borrows its trolls, goblins, dwarves, elves, and dragons, as well as the quest motif. The quest is an archetypal pattern of fantasy literature present in fairy tales, romances, and epics; it provides structure for both the plot and character development in *The Hobbit*. Quest stories depict people, most often young, who leave home in search of some object. On the journey the protagonists pass a series of tests, often encountering evil and attempting to destroy it. At the end, the heroes return home fundamentally altered, with their identities reshaped.

Bilbo is a model quest hero. Readers easily identify with him. At the beginning of his travels he is not particularly imaginative, brave, or competent, but he develops these qualities as events demand them of him. Leaving his quiet, unchallenging home for the quest forces Bilbo to grow psychologically during his travels. One fundamental characteristic never changes: He remains good-hearted throughout the story, and much of his success comes from his best qualities of loyalty, perseverance, kindness, and unselfishness. In contrast with Bilbo, the dwarves, elves, and men lack these qualities; their greed over the dragon's treasure causes the clash among them that precedes the Battle of Five Armies.

The Hobbit has a reputation as a children's book, but it appeals to a broader audience because it is simultaneously amusing and serious. It deals with important themes in a humorous narrative style. The narrator is intrusive, addressing his audience directly to comment on the action or give information, a trait that younger readers enjoy but that some older readers may occasionally find tiresome. The novel reads aloud well to children, partly because of Tolkien's use of comic verse and onomatopoeic words.

The Lord of the Rings, the trilogy sequel to *The Hobbit*, differs vastly in its epic scope and thus is appropriate for adult readers rather than children. It tells the story of Bilbo's nephew Frodo, who must destroy the Ring of Power of Sauron, the Dark Lord. It explores the same themes of heroism and conflict between good and evil that are present in *The Hobbit*, but in far greater complexity and intricacy of detail. Although critics frequently favor the epic over its precursor, the two differ so much in aim that comparisons are unfair. *The Hobbit* furnishes an incomparable introduction to *The Lord of the Rings*, and its readers often wish to go on to the trilogy, but *The Hobbit* can stand alone as a rich fantasy experience.

—Kara K. Keeling

THE HOLY GROUND TRILOGY

An alien race, the Hefn, comes to Earth and makes humanity live in harmony with the planet

Author: Judith Moffett (1942–)
Genre: Science fiction—invasion story
Type of work: Novels
Time of work: 1990–2026
Locale: Earth
First published: *The Ragged World* (1991; chapters published separately as "Remembrance of Things Future," Isaac Asimov's *Science Fiction Magazine*, December, 1989; "The Hob," Isaac Asimov's *Science Fiction Magazine*, May, 1988; "Tiny Tango," Isaac Asimov's *Science Fiction Magazine*, February, 1989; "Final Tomte," *The Magazine of Fantasy and Science Fiction*, June, 1990; and "The Ragged Rock," Isaac Asimov's *Science Fiction Magazine*, December, 1990) and *Time, Like an Ever-Rolling Stream* (1992); *The Bird Shaman* (2008)

THE STORY

The Hefn are a race of hairy, gnomelike aliens who exist in some kind of relationship with an unseen race, the Gafr. Though never made explicit, this relationship has overtones of servitude, worship, symbiosis, sex-uality, and procreation. In the seventeenth century, some of the Hefn rebelled against the Gafr and were punished by being marooned on Earth in England and Sweden. Their furtive nocturnal existence reinforced the legends of the mythical Hobs in England and tomtes in Sweden.

In 2006, the Hefn return for their crewmates but, unable to locate any of them, leave without becoming involved in Earth's affairs. The aliens change their minds, however, and return four years later to issue an ultimatum to Earth: Clean up the planet by 2020 or face elimination as a species. In 2013, the Gafr, deciding that humans are not acting swiftly enough, use the Hefn's tremendous powers of suggestion to impose a reproductive ban on humanity: No children will be born until the directive is accomplished.

The interconnected stories in *The Ragged World* (subtitled *A Novel of the Hefn on Earth*) trace the fortunes of several groups of people during this era. Sandy Sandford is a college botany teacher who contracts AIDS and must wait until the Hefn can discover a cure. While doing so, she comes to grips with her condition by closely understanding how life operates on Earth. Frank Flinthof and Jenny Shepherd become involved with the last Hefn marooned on Earth, Elphi, who has one more rebellion to perform. Terry O'Hara and Carrie Sharpless become involved with the Hefn through the aliens' use of a time transceiver. Through a glimpse into the future, Terry is inspired to become a politician and devises an effective evacuation plan for a nuclear plant disaster that he knows will happen. The final main narrative strand deals with the deep friendship between Terry's son Liam and Jeff Carpenter. Each of these stories leads up to some kind of intimate involvement between humans and Hefn. Friendship, which at first seems impossible, especially on the aliens' part, becomes the basis for mutual understanding and for the possibility of the survival of humanity.

Time, Like an Ever-Rolling Stream, although beginning in 2026, mainly describes the events of the summer of 2014, when Liam O'Hara and Pam Pruitt, two young humans recruited into the Hefns' Bureau of Temporal Physics, vacation at Hurt Hollow, Kentucky, a place Pam particularly loves. On their riverboat journey to Hurt Hollow, they witness an abortive attack on a Hefn. They later learn about its extreme consequences: The attackers are "mindwiped" by the Hefn—all their memories back to the age of three are removed.

At Hurt Hollow some fifty years earlier, Orrin and Hanna Hubbell established a way of life based on self-sufficiency and deep connection to the land. Pam has severe emotional problems caused by her relationship with her father, and Liam is trying to work through the psychological abyss caused by the loss of his best friend. They are able to rescue the current owner of Hurt Hollow, Jesse Kellum, who has been bitten by a snake. His hospitalization means that Liam and Pam will have to perform the many tasks that life at Hurt Hollow entails. Even though they are successful at these, Liam feels the need for his Hefn friend, Humphrey, whose mental powers helped Liam get through his initial intense grief over his loss.

Unfortunately, at the time Humphrey arrives, a backwoods preacher, Otie Bemis, stirs up the nascent remnants of the Ku Klux Klan in the area against the Hefn and their directive. Bemis leads an attack on Humphrey and almost succeeds in killing him, but the main characters are providentially rescued. Humphrey learns an important lesson from this experience: that bonding and religious persuasion will work much more effectively than coercion or modeling in getting humans to change their habits.

By 2026, this realization has led to the formation of the Gaian Missionaries, human proselytizers for a way of life the Gafr will sanction. Liam also has devised mathematical formulas for discovering "Hot Spots," areas where humans are able to live in harmony with the environment much more easily. It seems certain that Hurt Hollow is one of these areas of "Holy Ground." In the concluding volume, flashbacks involving Pam's neurotic family history alternate with up-to-the-minute reconfigurations of the alien imperative and its reception by the humans, as well as long and thoughtful disquisitions on many aspects of human culture. A satisfying accommodation between humanity's best and worst traits is finally achieved.

Analysis

The ecological and political assumptions of Judith Moffett's Hefn novels—that Earth is so badly damaged that only the intervention of alien creatures can save it—are as firmly held as any of those on the opposite side of the political spectrum. *Fallen Angels* (1991) by Larry Niven, Jerry Pournelle, and Michael Flynn, for example, posits that ecological regulations will result in another Ice Age. The basic situation of the Hefn on Earth is reminiscent of Cold War alien intervention tales such as director Robert Wise's film *The Day the Earth Stood Still* (1951), in which aliens demand that humanity give up the self-destructive powers of atomic weapons.

The Hefn, though not as spectacularly destructive as the robot policeman Gort, are even more frightening in their suggestive powers and are more immune to human protestations of innocence than is the Christlike Klaatu. When Humphrey is almost killed, his first impulse is to kill his attacker. Moffett's aliens are truly alien, and one of the main thrusts of the story line is how humans and Hefns learn to understand, appreciate, and eventually love one another.

From the ecological premises it logically follows that any human resistance movement against the Hefn will not be represented as one would be in, say, John W. Campbell, Jr.'s *Astounding Science-Fiction*. That magazine's stories would have featured heroic, independent rebels dedicated to restoring humanity's freedom. Such rhetoric is ironically present in Moffett's novels, but most of the impetus for the resistance movement against the Hefn is bound up with some of the worst elements of American society, including the religious and ethnic bigotry of the Ku Klux Klan. Moffett does allow both sides to give their views by making Pam Pruitt a born-again Baptist and giving the explanations for human resistance to the admirable Jesse Kellum.

Moffett's depiction of the Hefn shows that the basic message of the novels is not monolithic. In appearance, the Hefn seem benevolent, but in their ruthless pursuit of their purposes they care nothing about human feelings, to say nothing of rights. Some of them, however, did rebel against the Gafr, and in forfeiting their relationship with the Gafr were in a sense cast out of heaven and onto Earth. Hefn such as Godfrey and Humphrey, those who become involved in helping and healing humans both physically and psychologically, are driven by similar impulses. They are the Hefn most able to bond with humans and to forge relationships. It is through this spirit of love, Moffett hints, that humanity will be saved. Bonding is only the aliens' means to their end of saving Earth, however, not an end in itself. It is perhaps ironic that all their human names end in a suffix that sounds like "free."

The narrative structures of both novels also reveal how far literary techniques have advanced in science fiction. A "fixup" novel—a novel constructed out of short stories published individually, not serially—usually moves in a straightforward chronological progression. *The Ragged World*, which is a fixup novel, is not told linearly, as indicated by the title of its first story, "Remembrance of Things Future." A time chart of the novel's events, provided at the end, is a necessary aid. Similarly, *Time, Like an Ever-Rolling Stream* contains narratives within narratives. The novel itself is a novel written by Pam Pruitt and annotated by Liam O'Hara. The character of Pam in her novel writes another novel about a visit of the Hefn to Hurt Hollow.

The basic message of the novels, that autarchy—economic self-sufficiency—is necessary to save the planet, is clear. What remains unsettled is why the Gafr and Hefn refuse to share any scientific advice with humanity to assist them in fulfilling the directive. Starfaring creatures must have come up with their own "green" technological solutions. Nevertheless, Moffett's Hefn novels are bold examples of what science fiction can say and do as the twentieth century draws to a close.

—William Laskowski

Homunculus and Lord Kelvin's Machine

Dr. Langston St. Ives, a Victorian English scientist, battles the evil Dr. Ignacio Narbondo in a series of adventures involving strange new machines and travels in time and space

Author: James P. Blaylock (1950–)
Genre: Science fiction—alternate history
Type of work: Novels
Time of work: The 1870s
Locale: England, principally London
First published: *Homunculus* (1986) and *Lord Kelvin's Machine* (1992; parts first appeared in different form, *Isaac Asimov's Science Fiction Magazine*, 1985)

The Story

Homunculus begins with a mysterious dirigible being sighted over London, piloted by an equally mysterious man named Birdlip. Dr. Langston St. Ives, a professor out of favor with the Royal Academy because of his unorthodox ideas, has constructed a spacecraft, for which he needs the services of a toymaker, William Keeble, who apparently has created a perpetual motion machine. St. Ives has elicited the help of Bill Kraken, a former assistant to Sebastian Owlesby, a deceased scientist who seems to have had some connection with the dirigible now belonging to Birdlip.

Gradually, two sides in a confrontation are sorted out. The protagonists are members of the Trismegistus Club, which meets in the tobacco shop of Captain Powers, a man with a wooden leg that can be used as a pipe and has a receptacle for liquor. This leg was built by Keeble, most of whose apparently magical inventions also serve as flasks. The other major member of the club is Jack Owlesby, son of the late scientist.

On the other side, Dr. Ignacio Narbondo apparently is in league with Kelso Drake, one of the worlds richest men, who is rumored to have hidden a spacecraft in one of his brothels. This was the original landing vessel of the homunculus, a humanlike creature a few inches high. Narbondo's primary allies are Billy Deener, a thief and probably a murderer, and Willis Pule, who is a wizard or scientist (the two types are never clearly differentiated) and who knows a lot about the homunculus.

The homunculus himself is suspected to be on board the dirigible with Birdlip, trapped in a box made by Keeble. At least two other almost identical boxes exist, one containing an emerald, the other an oxygenator Keeble built for use in St. Ives's ship.

Narbondo has been animating corpses by some mysterious means involving the use of carp glands and various chemicals. The Reverend Shiloh is a mad evangelist who has agreed to side with Narbondo in the hope of seeing his mother, Joanna Southcote, brought back to life. Narbondo tries to revive her because she was the first human to come in contact with the homunculus.

Homunculus ends as confusingly as it began. The dirigible lands, and Birdlip, the pilot, turns out to be a ghoul. The homunculus gets out of its box, enters its spaceship, which St. Ives has recovered, and departs into space. The dirigible explodes.

Lord Kelvin's Machine involves most of the same characters as *Homunculus*, the major addition being Hargreaves, an assistant to Narbondo. Hasbro, St. Ives's assistant, and Jack Owlesby play larger roles than in the first book. The story begins with a flashback to a coach chase in which St. Ives's lover, Alice, is killed by Narbondo.

The story proper begins with the approach of a comet that could hit Earth and cause widespread destruction. The Great Lord Kelvin has built a machine that will reverse Earths magnetic polarity. One scientific theory holds that during the changeover there will be no magnetic field at all around Earth, so the comet will not be attracted, assuming that gravity is a form of electromagnetic force.

Meanwhile, Narbondo is working on the basis of the hollow earth theory. He is formulating a plan to move Earth into the comets path by plugging up volcanoes in Norway, so that the pressure will be released in Peru, thereby making Earth move like a rocket in the proper direction. His plans are foiled by Kraken, under the direction of St. Ives. In Norway, Narbondo falls to his apparent death.

Lord Kelvin's machine is revealed to be under the North Sea. St. Ives retrieves it and discovers that it is actually a time machine. He decides that he will use the device to return to the incident involving Alice and Narbondo, then save the woman he loves. Before he accomplishes this, he experiments, beginning with a trip into the past, to London in 1835. There he finds Narbondo as a little boy and is surprised to see that the child is not a hunchback but apparently suffers from pneumonia. St. Ives decides that the boy also has meningitis as a complication of the disease and abandons his original idea of killing him. Instead, he travels forward to 1927, where he meets Alexander Fleming, the discoverer of penicillin. He takes some of that drug back to save the boys life.

St. Ives manages to save Alice, but in the process, he finds his memory fading. Narbondo, no longer a hunchback, is now an evangelist. Alice is St. Ives's wife, and the two have a baby boy. What becomes of the time machine is never made clear.

ANALYSIS

Homunculus and *Lord Kelvin's Machine* are very different in many ways, but they also have much in common. The first book is a wandering, deliberately confusing tale involving mysterious persons and devices with unknown functions and purposes. The second is a fairly straightforward narrative. Both are clearly satirical.

Both books, from the outset, blur the distinctions between fantasy and science fiction. Narbondo is described both as a scientist and as a wizard. Apparently, scientific principles are used to reanimate the dead. A man who makes his legitimate income constructing toys devises a perpetual motion machine. Lord Kelvin, a real historical figure of importance in the scientific world, creates a time machine.

Scientific principles that are patently ridiculous are brought into play, without any real explanation. The hollow earth theory was never taken seriously by scientists, and even if it were, the prospect of plugging volcanoes on one side of the earth to make others erupt is nonsensical because there are volcanoes all over the planet. In addition, there was no evidence in 1870, nor is there now, that gravity is a form of magnetic attraction.

The characters in both books are stereotyped. Narbondo, the mad scientist, is a hunchback. Shiloh, the evangelist, is an old man with a white beard and is hopelessly insane. Captain Powers seems to have stepped into *Homunculus* from Herman Melville's *Moby Dick* (1851), and Willis Pule is a villain who would make Charles Dickens proud.

The confusions in the first volume seem to be deliberate. The reader is carried along by the apparent mystery, which is never really solved. The second volume is clearer, but again the ending is far from satisfactory. "They all lived happily ever after" does not seem to be an appropriate ending for a story involving ghouls, time travelers, and murderers.

The treatment of time travel is particularly interesting. In most modern science fiction, the concept of time travel is treated either as a physical impossibility or as a joke. James Blaylock overcomes the problems of paradox by having multiple copies of St. Ives vanish and memories of previous versions of history fade.

Homunculus is among Blaylock's earliest works and is the first that clearly falls into the genre of science fiction. It followed the first two books of the Elfin fantasy series, *The Elfin Ship* (1982) and *The Disappearing Dwarf* (1983). There are significant stylistic differences between *Homunculus* and *Lord Kelvin's Machine*, but in both books the author seems more interested in poking fun at existing science-fictional themes than in proposing anything new. It is important that the themes being satirized are themes that most science-fiction writers of the 1980s had largely abandoned. It is equally significant that much of the science involved verges on magic, and many of the scientific principles were not taken very seriously even in 1870.

Both books seem as if they could have been written during the period in which the stories take place. Although Blaylock is an American of the late twentieth century, the settings primarily are in nineteenth century London. Even the time machine and the spacecraft are variations on devices present in 1870. In this sense, the story is realistic, in marked contrast to the ridiculous nature of the plot.

—*Marc Goldstein*

HOTHOUSE

At a time when Earth has ceased to revolve, a weakened human race struggles to survive amid ravenous plant life

Author: Brian W. Aldiss (1925–)
Genre: Science fiction—future history
Type of work: Novel
Time of work: About 2 billion c.e.
Locale: Various locations on Earth, and briefly the Moon
First published: 1962 (serial form, *The Magazine of Fantasy and Science Fiction*, February, April, July, September, and December, 1961; shortened American edition, also 1962, titled *The Long Afternoon of Earth*)

THE STORY

After Earth ceases to rotate, plant life—much of it mobile and carnivorous—flourishes on the sunny side. Humans have devolved and live in small tribes amid gigantic forest branches. *Hothouse* follows the adventures of Gren and others as they cross land and sea from the fecund tropics to the barren twilight region.

When Lily-yo, the leader of young Grens matriarchal tribe, comes to believe that she is past her prime, she makes the traditional choice to "Go Up," along with the other elders. On the topmost leaves of the jungle, mammoth spiderlike plants spin webs between Earth and the Moon. Attached to such "traversers," the elders are carried like pollen spores off to an "afterlife" that is in fact on the Moon, which now has an atmosphere and transplanted life-forms. The humans, exposed to radiation, develop leathery wings and become flymen who go back to Earth to bring younger humans to the "True World."

Tribal youths have trouble developing the discipline and wisdom for survival. The rebellious Gren is banished and is joined by Poyly, who loves him. An intelligent fungus called a morel falls on Grens head, merges its brain with his, and decides that it can use humans to conquer the planet for its own kind. Gren remains at the mercy of the clinging morel, which can torture him and make him threaten others.

Joined by Yattmur, a young woman from another tribe, Gren and Poyly escape the Siren-like Black Mouth and meet a tribe of half-humans, called Fishers or tummy-bellies, who are attached umbilically to large plants. Prodded by the morel, Gren cuts the cords of several, though they neither want freedom nor can flourish independently, and he seizes a fishing boat. Eventually Poyly is killed, Gren mates with Yattmur, and the boat takes them to an island where the cliffs literally have eyes. A cave tempts Gren toward mystic oblivion.

After further adventures, the voyagers find themselves in a cold twilight world inhabited by baboonlike sharp-furs. Yattmur bears Grens child but rightly fears that the morel wants to attach itself to the baby, Laren. Into their midst comes an intelligent dolphin, the Sodal Ye, borne by a male slave and guided by two "Arabler" women. Vain and full of apocalyptic warnings about the suns coming nova, the sodal tells Yattmur how to free Gren from the morel and offers to lead the group to a warmer climate. The tummy-bellies stay with the sharp-furs, who kill them. The morel manages to seize the sodal, and Lily-yo once again encounters Gren. As the novel ends, the morel plans to pilot a traverser to the stars, with Lily-yos group, while Gren, Yattmur, and Laren return to the forest.

ANALYSIS

Hothouse, Brian Aldiss' second science-fiction novel, harks back to classic British chronicles of afar distant future such as Olaf Stapledon's *Last and First Men* (1930) and especially H. G. Wells's *The Time Machine* (1895). In Wells's story, the devolved humans have nothing to fear but the Morlocks, while in Hothouse Nature has taken much more violent evolutionary turns. At the same time, in its gleefully bizarre inventiveness and mixture of mythic elements and scientific extrapolation, *Hothouse* foreshadows the 1960's New Wave, when Aldiss and others would conduct more radical experiments in applying techniques of modernist literature to science-fiction writing. The novel anticipates Aldiss' later work, such as the Helliconia series (1982–1985), in its epic sweep and its mix of science fiction and fantasy. The first American edition of the novel, retitled *The Long Afternoon of Earth*, cut more than ten thousand words, including episodes of the morel probing Gren's racial memories and the discovery of an ancient human dwelling and a propaganda machine.

Hothouse can be read as a gruesome comedy of puny humanitys helplessness in the face of a Nature "green in tooth and claw" or as a visionary work, awed by the universes mysteries and the role of humanity in the scheme of things. Freudian, Jungian, and feminist readers could all make much of Grens adventures: his breaking away from a matriarchal society, his narrow escapes from various devouring mouths of Nature, his ruthlessness while controlled by the masculine-seeming morel, the storys switch to the courageous and maternal Yattmurs viewpoint, and Grens final choice to take his family back to the jungle.

However one interprets this vivid, often grotesque saga, it is clear that Aldiss is pushing most definitions of science fiction to the limits. The book is traditional science fiction in its speculations on how the laws of evolution might cause new life-forms to develop, yet it makes no effort to account scientifically for some of its weirder features, such as the cliff of eyes, the mystic cave, or the jets of green energy shooting toward the sun near the novels end. To be sure, straight science fiction may have mythic or mystical elements, as in Arthur C. Clarke's *Childhood's End* (1953), but *Hothouse* also has much in common with the fantastic journeys of other kinds of literature. One important model is Homer's *The Odyssey* (transcribed sixth century b.c.e.). Gren may be a rather pathetic hero compared to Odysseus, but he does encounter his own Sirens and Lotus Eaters, not to mention assorted monsters, before he gets back to his jungle home. Another source is *Alice's Adventures in Wonderland* (1865). *Hothouse* has plants as whimsical as Lewis Carroll's and a character who fades in and out of visibility like the Cheshire cat. Aldiss also seems at times to indulge in allegory, another fantasy tradition, with the morel evidently representing a spirit of ruthless imperialism in humankind. Whether it is orthodox science fiction or not, *Hothouse* remains one of Aldiss most fascinating and disturbing works.

—*Joseph Milicia*

THE HOUSE NEXT DOOR

The comfortable lives of a complacent suburban couple are altered by the construction of a malevolent house next door

Author: Anne Rivers Siddons (1936–)
Genre: Fantasy—occult
Type of work: Novel
Time of work: The 1970s
Locale: An affluent neighborhood in a city of the New South
First published: 1978

The Story

"People like us don't appear in *People* magazine," Colquitt Kennedy asserts in the opening line of *The House Next Door*. Both she and her husband Walter find themselves in the full glare of publicity after they tell the world about the tragic events that have taken place in the house next door. Try as they might to preserve their insulated and privileged lifestyle, the Kennedys sacrifice everything to combat the nameless horror that comes to their cozy neighborhood after a new house is constructed on an adjacent lot.

The novels plot is divided into three main parts, each named for one of the three families that successively purchase the evil house: the Harralsons, the Sheehans, and the Greenes. With each new owner, the house escalates its reign of terror. The Harralsons, a fledgling tax lawyer named Buddy and his extroverted wife, Pie, encounter a string of catastrophes. Pie miscarries in her seventh month by falling down a flight of stairs; small animals, both domestic and wild, are found dismembered on the grounds; in front of a houseful of guests, Buddy and his law partner Lucas Abbott are caught in a naked embrace; and shocked by the assumed homosexual relationship, Pies father has a fatal stroke.

The next couple to move in are Buck Sheehan and his frail wife, Anita, who has only tentatively recovered from a nervous breakdown precipitated by her sons violent death in Vietnam and her husbands subsequent infidelity. The Sheehans are ripe for manipulation. War films are broadcast on Anitas television and nowhere else. When she eventually catches her alcohol-impaired husband and their neighbor Virginia Guthrie in the sexual act, Anita goes mad. During the Sheehan occupancy, even the Kennedys are directly affected. Inside the evil house, Walter discovers Colquitt and the young architect Kim Dougherty in each others arms; he is prevented from using a knife on both of them only by the swift intervention of Dougherty, who forces everyone outside, where passions cool and their situation is appraised. After asserting that Colquitt and he acted against their will, Dougherty theorizes that the house identifies the essence of each individual and then devises the means by which that person is deprived of the very thing that he or she needs to thrive. In the case of the Kennedys, it is their marriage.

The final homeowners are the Greenes, a perfectionist named Norman; his wife, Susan; and their daughter, Melissa. Normans professional and social ambitions are thwarted by his wifes disintegrating self-confidence and his daughters worsening health problems, both brought on largely by a proliferation of domestic mishaps. The crisis is reached after Norman is once again embarrassed by his wifes presumed absentmindedness. He publicly proclaims his stepdaughters illegitimacy. In response, Susan kills Norman and Melissa, then herself. The Kennedys hope to warn others away from the house under the premise that if there is something inside "feeding" on people, emptiness will starve it out.

When Dougherty, the architect who designed the house, decides that he will try to lift the curse by living in it himself, the Kennedys are forced to take immediate action. Their decision is further reinforced by their discovery that the architect designed two previous projects that proved equally disastrous to their owners. The Kennedys realize that Dougherty is a "terrible carrier" and that everything he touches will be similarly afflicted. The main plot ends after they murder Dougherty and while they wait for the lights to go out on the street before they commit arson.

In a short, open-ended epilogue, a young man and his bride rhapsodize over house plans designed by a recently deceased architect. The wife declares ominously, "It looks like its alive."

ANALYSIS

Much of the immediate inspiration for this novel seems to be derived from an even more famous account of a dream house turned nightmare abode, Jay Anson's *The Amityville Horror* (1977), which was published the year before *The House Next Door*. This self-described nonfiction work recounts the predicament of the real-life Lutz family, which buys a house despite the fact that it had been the scene of a mass murder. Although their residence in the place does not prove fatal to them, the Lutzes do experience personality changes, very much like the characters in Anne Siddons novel.

The House Next Door is part of a long tradition of haunted house narratives that subdivides roughly into two main categories. There are versions that stress the psychic interconnectedness between a haunted house and its haunted inhabitants. An example is Edgar Allan Poe's "The Fall of the House of Usher" (1839), wherein the troubled soul of the house is a mirror of the deteriorating mental condition of the main character, Roderick Usher. Other versions focus on the setting as an independent entity, as in the case of Shirley Jackson's *The Haunting of Hill House* (1959), wherein an actively evil dwelling exploits the flaws of four people for its own demoniac purposes.

Siddons' novel falls into the second category, with a focus on ordinary people confronting extraordinary events because of their occupancy of a sinister place. In this regard, some critics have objected not to the ordinariness of Siddons principal characters, the Kennedys, but to their self-satisfaction, which makes it difficult for some readers to sympathize with their problems. Other critics point to the strength of the novels first-person narrator, Colquitt Kennedy, who acknowledges that she and her husband perhaps have been too "involved with each other" and need to "give more to the world". Their campaign against the evil house may be their chance to balance the scales. The compelling voice of Colquitt Kennedy also gives evidence of the authors specialty—richly detailed accounts of the vicissitudes of spunky heroines in the American South. Siddons is essentially a local colorist. *The House Next Door* both reinforces and expands its authors canon. Although it features Southerners in a Southern locale, this third book by Siddons represents her first (and as of the mid-1990's, only) foray into fantasy literature.

—S. Thomas Mack

THE HOUSE ON THE BORDERLAND

A man defends his home against attacking monsters and travels far in time and space

Author: William Hope Hodgson (1877–1918)
Genre: Science fiction—cosmic voyage
Type of work: Novel
Time of work: The mid-1800s, with a journey to the end of time
Locale: Remote Ireland and the far reaches of the universe
First published: 1908

THE STORY

The story of *The House on the Borderland* is cast in the form of a manuscript written by an unnamed man, later referred to as the recluse, who lives in a large, ancient house with his sister and his dog. He writes the manuscript to document the strange events that he experiences, consisting of a mixture of visionary cosmic journeys and attacks by very real monsters.

The first such experience begins when the narrator sees a green glow at one end of his study and soon develops into a bizarre journey in which he floats over a vast "plain of silence" and into a mountain-ringed amphitheater in which sits a house identical to his own except that apparently it is made of green jade. The surrounding mountains are inhabited by strange and horrible monsters, many of whom are identified as the models for some of the gods and demons of human history. He watches as a swinelike creature attacks the green house, as though seeking a way in. He then is drawn into space, with a view of the solar system, before being returned to his study.

The next episode recounts a harrowing attack on the narrators home by swine-faced creatures that emerge from a cave in a nearby gorge. After several days of siege the narrator manages to drive them off. When the swine-things do not remount their attack, a peaceful period ensues during which the recluse explores the cave from which the monsters came. He finds that it leads to an enormous underground pit directly beneath the house and connected to it through a trapdoor in the cellar floor.

The longest episode in the novel begins with the narrator standing at his window, the swine-things apparently forgotten. He hears a strange whirring sound that turns out to be the clock running at high speed, signaling an acceleration of time. As time speeds up, readers are presented with a scientifically precise description of the flickering of the seasons, then the rhythmic pulsing of the suns path from north to south, and eventually the expansion of the sun until it swallows up Earth itself. By this time the recluse has left Earth. He floats bodiless in space for millions of years, eventually coming upon a great green star out of which come an endless series of white globes. In one of the globes he finds his long lost love on the shore of the beautiful "sea of sleep." Again out in space, he perceives another procession of globes, this time red and full of blind, tortured faces. After passing again through the amphitheater of his first vision and seeing the green replica of his house, with damage matching that resulting from the attack of the swine-things, he is deposited back in his chair in his study. Although the house apparently has not aged, a pile of dust that was once his dog paradoxically attests the reality of his journey through time.

A few days later, the house is attacked again by otherworldly creatures, though not necessarily the swine-things, that infect the narrator with a funguslike disease. The manuscript ends in mid-sentence, with the swine-things entering the house through the trapdoor in the cellar and climbing through the house to find the recluse in his study.

ANALYSIS

The nature of the plot of *The House on the Borderland* makes it nearly impossible to classify. Its mixture of monsters, science fiction, space and time travel, supernatural mystery, and allegorical fantasy make the novel unique.

The chapters of the story dealing with the attack of the swine-things from the pit beneath the house, coupled with the traditional haunted-house setting, place the novel between the ghost stories of M. R. James, in which the supernatural entities begin to assume physical form and do real damage, and the cosmic, tentacled monsters of H. P. Lovecraft. In fact, many of Lovecraft's ideas and themes can be traced to suggestions in *The House on the Borderland* and other works by William Hope Hodgson.

The other, contrasting plot of cosmic journeys through time and space develops the more modest ideas of H. G. Wells's *The Time Machine* (1895) and foreshadows the billion-year visions of Olaf Stapledon's *Last and First Men* (1930) and *Star Maker* (1937). Hodgson's descriptions of the future of the universe, extrapolated from the astronomical knowledge of the time, raise the novel above the more common "attack of the monsters" tale. The fact that the strange juxtapositions and allegorical suggestions in the novel are not spelled out or explained away adds depth and interest to the readers experience.

The House on the Borderland was written early in Hodgson's fiction career, which began in 1904 and continued until he was killed during World War I. It is a departure from the bulk of his work, which dealt with supernatural and monstrous horrors of the sea. It does, however, suggest the imaginative power of what was to become his most famous novel, *The Night Land* (1912), the story of a journey through the fantastic landscape of Earth millions of years in the future.

The contradictory plots and themes of *The House on the Borderland* did not seem to bother critics of the day, and the book received good reviews upon publication, with writers praising Hodgson's fertile imagination. Later critics have been more disturbed by the works faults, such as the seemingly unnecessary, sentimental love passages and the discordant counterpoint of the story lines. It is still considered by many to be a classic and an important milestone in the development of the genres of science fiction and horror.

—*Joseph W. Hinton*

THE HOUSE ON THE STRAND

Richard Young's experiments with hallucinogenic drugs enable him to travel back and forth in time to the mysteries of fourteenth century England

Author: Daphne du Maurier (1907-1989)
Genre: Fantasy—time travel
Type of work: Novel
Time of work: The 1960s, with flashbacks to the fourteenth century
Locale: Cornwall, England
First published: 1969

THE STORY

The House on the Strand takes place in Daphne du Maurier's six-hundred-year-old home, Kilmarth, on the rugged Cornish coast of southwestern England. Told from the first-person point of view, the novel relates the adventures of Richard Young, whose old school friend, Magnus, now a professor of biophysics, has lent him a house for a summer holiday. In the cellar, Magnus keeps some of his experimental drugs, hallucinogens that take Richard back and forth in time to Cornwall in the 1300's. Gradually, he becomes more involved in the lives of the medieval lords and ladies, and when his wife and two young stepsons join him, he finds his own life pale by comparison.

At Magnus' direction, Richard takes his first dose of the drug in the days before his family arrives. He finds himself transported back in time, able to move around the countryside without any sensation and to see everything without the participants being aware of his presence. Led by his guide, the steward Roger, who lives at Kilmarth, he meets the lords, ladies, and clergy embroiled in the political and romantic intrigue of early fourteenth century England.

The drug wears off, leaving only some nausea and vertigo. After obtaining further information in the next few days from Magnus, Richard takes several trips. He observes the romance between Lady Isolde and Sir Otto, both of whom are married to other people. After Otto is drowned by Isolde's husband, Richard becomes increasingly enthralled by her, so much so that on the arrival of his family, he has trouble keeping his mind anchored in the present. His wife and stepsons become increasingly upset with his peculiar behavior and sudden absences from the holiday activities.

When Magnus announces that he will visit, Richard eagerly looks forward to settling some of the mysterious details. Before he reaches Kilmarth, however, Magnus is killed by a train while trying to retrace history. In his will, he leaves the house to Richard, along with some instructions concerning the drug. Richard has become so enmeshed in the past that he feels more alive and more himself in that world than in his own.

Believing that he must find out what happened to Isolde, who has become an outcast cared for by Roger, Richard returns to the past. When Isolde is threatened, he steps in to help. The present returns with a jolt, however, as he finds his hands around the neck of his own wife. This action so devastates Richard that he consults a local doctor. Together, they manage to smooth things over, and the family decides to take a short vacation in Ireland while making plans for the house.

Richard, however, has not quite finished with the fourteenth century and manages to slip off from the airport waiting room to return to Kilmarth for one last trip. He finds Isolde dead and Roger dying, both struck down by the Black Death of 1348. Returning to the present, he sees a doctor by his side. Richard announces that with the situation resolved by death, at last he is free to join his family. The doctor warns him to wait, and he is right. Richard cannot feel any sensation in his fingers and hands, an ominous sign because use of the drug could lead eventually to death.

ANALYSIS

Fantasy developed from the gothic romance of the eighteenth century, and *The House on the Strand* is an excellent example of the connection between the two. Like Horace Walpole in *The Castle of Otranto* (1764), Ann Radcliffe in *The Mysteries of Udolpho* (1794), and numerous twentieth century paperback writers including Howard Batchelor, Daphne du Maurier uses a remote, mysterious setting with ancient estates that hold dark and romantic secrets of the past. To this gothic setting and cast of medieval characters she adds the essence of fantasy, the suspension of disbelief in the unreal. Actions that occurred more than six hundred years earlier recur in a nonexistent world side by side with the real one. The characters reach this world and operate within it by using scientific principles that are contrary to experience.

Richard enters the fourteenth century by taking a drink of Magnus liquid. When it takes effect, the past reappears instantaneously, as if nothing unusual has happened. In one case, after looking down at his watch, Richard finds the village as it was in the 1300's. Within this world, all senses except touch are heightened, and Richard can move wherever he wishes without contacting any other objects or people. Adding to the unreality is his sense of well-being and tranquillity, despite the unsettling events he observes.

The medieval characters with whom Richard becomes intrigued are enmeshed in a world of treachery and deceit. A monk who possesses medical knowledge is secretly administering poison to Sir Henry, Sir Oliver brutally murders Sir Otto on a night when the weather is equally wild and brutal, and Joanna schemes to exile Isolde to France, where she will be mistreated by evil monks. Adding to these characters is the sinister gothic setting. The weather is harsh and the landscape hostile. Even the villagers reveal their base instincts as they delight in skinning animals in the village square.

Elements of the gothic romance appear in most of du Maurier's work. She wrote *The House on the Strand* late in her career, after she became known for best-sellers such as *Rebecca* (1938), *My Cousin Rachel* (1951), and *The Scapegoat* (1957), all of which contain similar elements of character and setting. At the time *The House on the Strand* was published, critics noted its predictable gothic elements but added that du Maurier handled the characters and the time shifts well. Because she lived in Cornwall and was interested in its history, she created believable historical personages. As usual in her books, the plot is suspenseful up to the last line.

—Louise M. Stone

A House Boat on the Styx and The Pursuit of the House Boat

After their houseboat is stolen, a group of famous ghosts organize and attempt a rescue of their floating social club as well as those aboard it, only to have the hostages bring about the deliverance

Author: John Kendrick Bangs (1862–1922)
Genre: Fantasy—mythological
Type of work: Novels
Time of work: 1895
Locale: Hades
First published: *A House-Boat on the Styx: Being Some Account of the Divers Doings of the Associated Shades* (1896) and *The Pursuit of the House-Boat* (1897)

The Story

A House-Boat on the Styx proved to be so popular that John Kendrick Bangs quickly wrote a sequel, *The Pursuit of the House-Boat*. The stories concern the adventures and misadventures of the ghosts of a number of notable men and women from history, the Bible, and literature. The actions of all the characters center on a houseboat that accommodates an exclusive social club. Many people desire to become members, even going as far as stealing the boat to gain membership. The search for and recovery of the boat that follow its disappearance provide a series of hilarious and entertaining escapades that end happily.

The Associated Shades of Hades-on-Styx have acquired a houseboat in which to lodge their gentlemens social club. This fact upsets Charon, the ferryman, who transports the souls of the departed to the underworld. He is mollified somewhat when he is offered the position of janitor by the House Committee, which includes Sir Walter Raleigh, Confucius, Cassius, Demosthenes, and Sir William Blackstone. Charon accepts the position and thus comes into contact with an assortment of heroes and villains from every epoch as well as diverse characters from fiction.

Because he is in constant attendance, Charon is witness to a number of interesting events, not the least being a spirited discussion between William Shakespeare and Francis Bacon over the question of the authorship of the formers works. The one problem that seems to disturb the tranquillity of this otherworldly refuge for men is the desire of a host of female spirits to see the interior of the houseboat. To accommodate feminine curiosity, the members of the club decide to host a Ladies Day, but only after a spirited debate. Only Lucretia Borgia and Delilah are denied invitations, the former because of her reputation with poisons and the latter at the request of Samson.

As plans are advanced for this event, most of the members spend their time in conversation, playing billiards, and hosting a Story-Tellers Night when male shades who are not members are invited to enjoy the facilities of the houseboat. Poets and playwrights, promoters and politicians, and sculptors and scoundrels mingle in happy confusion while members and guests provide entertainment that ranges from the sublime to the boring.

Not willing to wait for Ladies Day, Elizabeth I, Ophelia, and Xanthippe decide to invade the male preserve one autumn afternoon when the houseboat is empty of members. Encountering the billiard room attendant, they discover that most of the men are attending a boxing match between Goliath and Samson. This suits their purposes. They overcome the protests of the servant and begin their tour of the vessel. Impressed by what they find, the three summon other female shades to join them. After some discussion, the women of Hades decide to appropriate the houseboat for their own use.

Their triumph is short-lived, because they soon discover that the houseboat is being towed from its moorings by a crew of ruffians under the command of Captain Kidd. This act of piracy is Kidds revenge for being rejected for membership in the club. The chance to kidnap the leading women of Hades adds to his satisfaction. When the membership returns to the place where their floating clubhouse lay at anchor, they discover their twin loss. Only Socrates seems undisturbed by this double act of piracy. At this point, *A House-Boat on the Styx* ends.

Captain Kidd quickly learns that a cargo of determined women is not the rich prize he originally thought. While the corsair captain tries to find a solution to his problem, the Associated Shades find help from an unexpected source, Sherlock Holmes, fresh from his encounter with Professor Moriarty at the Reichenbach Falls.

While the rescue party is busy chartering a ghost ship, the *Gehenna*, the women proceed to take matters into their own hands. After convincing the pirates that there are no provisions aboard the houseboat, the women persuade Kidd and his crew to go in search of food. While the buccaneers are so occupied, the women seize the houseboat and sail away with it.

Holmes and his fellows now give pursuit, only to have the *Gehenna* accidentally rammed by the houseboat. The women save their would-be rescuers, and all ends well. The Associated Shades admit their mistake and offer the women of Hades the right of full membership, which they graciously accept.

ANALYSIS

Bangs's rollicking tale of the adventures of the departed appears on the surface to be merely that, an amusing what-if narrative. Beneath the veneer of diverting anecdotes and imagined conversations, however, are several layers of meaning. Closer examination reveals a rather serious study of relations between the sexes as well as a subtle plea for female equality. The characters Bangs chooses, as well as the dialogue and action that he assigns them, disclose much about his own personality and prejudices.

Although Bangs was a popular humorist at the end of the nineteenth century, his reputation has been eclipsed in later generations by the subtler command of comedy found in the works of authors such as Mark Twain. Bangs was a respected journalist, and during his career he served as editor of *Harper's* as well as supervising the humor desk at *Harper's Bazaar*. He was a master of the joke, and in later life he became a favorite on the lecture circuit, where his brand of vocal humor proved extremely successful. Among his published works, *A House-Boat on the Styx* and *The Pursuit of the House-Boat*, which appeared at the midpoint of his career, have retained their popularity because they contain a message than transcends the merely amusing, a quality contemporary critics missed completely. Although they recognized his intelligent use of language and his sometimes infectious wit, they regarded his novels and essays as merely diverting.

Speculation about the nature of the afterlife has intrigued authors from Homer to Thornton Wilder. Bangs's two books are closer in spirit to the Topper novels of Thorne Smith, the ghost stories of Manning Coles, or Noël Cowards play *Blithe Spirit* (1941) than to the pathos of Virgil or Dante. Steve Allen, who is something of a modern Bangs, in a sense re-created the atmosphere of the stygian houseboat in his popular television series *Meeting of Minds*, a public television production that began airing in 1977. Those shows portrayed the great men and women of the past gathering for conversation and controversy. Bangs's ghosts frighten nobody, and when they attempt to engage in mischief, they resemble Edwardian college students planning a harmless prank.

Bangs's delineation of his characters is particularly fascinating. He obviously had his favorites among the men and women who peopled the past, and he does not hesitate to enjoy taking revenge on some others, such as Oliver Goldsmith, whose poetry must have bored him during his school days. The male characters often act and react to the various crises and situations in the novels like small boys. The females are more focused, facing their predicament with maturity and purpose. The reaction of the guests at George Washingtons birthday banquet to a serious discussion was to go haunt a vaudeville performance in London. Reacting to their kidnapping, the women organize themselves, examine several plans, work out a reasonable strategy, and then execute it with complete success, despite the inept interference of their would-be rescuers.

Those whom historians often condemn for their deeds are often forgiven by Bangs. Nero is discovered in the billiard room, happily playing a game with Shakespeare and Dr. Samuel Johnson. The women's Committee on Treachery suggests that Lucretia Borgia prepare a dish of lobster Newburg to serve to their pirates captors. This mixture of the sacred and the prophane, of saint and sinner, enhances rather than detracts from the enjoyment of the novels. Only when preconceived notions about the deeds and misdeeds of the departed are discarded does the reader truly appreciate these works.

Bangs's work was consistently underrated by critics in his own time and virtually is ignored by modern students of American humor. Devotees of fiction with a supernatural theme should find in these two books not only a new approach to their favorite literary genre but also fresh themes and departures in a form of literature that has been popular since antiquity.

—*Clifton W. Potter, Jr.*

Humour and Fantasy

A collection containing four novels exemplifying the authors distinctive approach to comic fantasy and seventeen of his short stories

Author: F. Anstey (Thomas Antsey Guthrie, 1856–1934)
Genre: Fantasy—magical realism
Type of work: Collected works
Time of work: The late nineteenth century
Locale: London, England
First published: 1931 (contains the novels *Vice Versa: Or, A Lesson to Fathers*, 1882; *The Tinted Venus*, 1885; *A Fallen Idol*, 1886; and *The Brass Bottle*, 1900; as well as the collection *Salted Almonds*, 1906; and two stories from *The Talking Horse*, 1891)

The Story

In *Vice Versa: Or, A Lesson to Fathers*, a magical stone allows schoolboy Dick Bultitude to exchange bodies with his father, Paul, a businessman fond of making pompous speeches about ones school days being the happiest of ones life. The parent trapped in the childs role learns the folly of this judgment, while the boy fails to find much enjoyment in adult life and responsibility. In the end, they are glad to switch back, suitably chastened and enlightened by their experience.

In *The Tinted Venus*, hairdresser Leander Tweddle places an engagement ring on the finger of a statue of Aphrodite to demonstrate the slimness of his fiancées finger. This tribute reanimates the goddess incarnate in the statue, who does not realize how much the world has changed since her last manifestation. Her directness in matters of sex contrasts sharply with Victorian prudishness. This embarrassment is compounded by her threats to destroy any and all rivals for Tweddle's affection. He is pursued by the thieves who had stolen the statue and by the police but finally contrives to set matters straight.

In *A Fallen Idol*, painter Ronald Campion acquires a Jain idol infused with the malevolent spirit of Chalanka, a fake holy man mistakenly promoted to a kind of godhood. The idols magical powers are limited, but their exercise casts a gradual blight upon Campion's personal and professional life until a Norwegian Theosophist identifies the source of his troubles and comes to his aid.

In *The Brass Bottle*, aspiring architect Horace Ventimore buys the eponymous object at an auction and discovers sealed within it the jinn Fakrash, imprisoned long ago with the rest of his kind by Suleyman. The jinn expresses his gratitude by heaping rewards on his savior in an absurdly flamboyant manner that causes the hapless young man excruciating embarrassment. Fakrashs gratitude soon begins to wear thin, and the jinns attitude is further transformed as he realizes the extent to which the world has changed since the time of his imprisonment. As in the famous story from *The Arabian Nights' Entertainments* of the fifteenth century, from which the central motif is borrowed, Ventimore must engage in a duel of wits with Fakrash in order to return the jinn to his bottle before serious damage is done.

ANALYSIS

These four novels are the principal deployments of a formula discovered by F. Anstey that subsequently was much imitated by other writers, most successfully by W. D. Darlington and the American Thorne Smith. In each story, the ultraconventional and morally rigid world of the Victorian middle classes is subject to severe disturbance by a magical intrusion. The subsequent chaos permitted contemporary readers temporary relief from the stern pressure of Victorian customs, allowing them to laugh at themselves (or, rather, at others not unlike themselves) without ever really undermining the values they held dear. In his introduction to the omnibus, Anstey observes apologetically that fashions in humor had changed and that the stories could not be expected to appeal to readers in a world that had discarded the smug censoriousness of the Victorians, but he was too cautious: The book sold well to a generation ready and willing to laugh at the absurdities of their parents hang-ups.

The underlying assumption of all four novels is that however artificial and constricting the order of things may be, it is an order well worth preserving. Although it was the least successful when first published, the strongest of the four novels is *A Fallen Idol*, in which the embarrassments suffered by the hero as a result of the idols mischievous influence occasionally tip over the edge of comedy into horror. Campion sees his whole life falling apart as a result of wrenches to its pattern that are so slight as to pass for mere coincidences. The readers participation in his tribulations conveys an impression of authentic unease. *The Brass Bottle*, however, is almost as powerful. It is less disturbing in an intimate sense" Ventimore is never really in mortal danger—but it provides a wider perspective in its climax, which carefully points out that if magic did work, the order and solidity of modern civilization would be quite frail. It is also the cleverest and slickest of the four narratives.

Although it is rather more rough-hewn, *Vice Versa* remained the most popular of the four novels while Anstey was alive, and it inspired new cinematic versions after his death. Victorian society may be long gone, but the generation gap will persist, and there always will be a special poignancy and propriety in stories that promote understanding between parents and children. The Tinted Venus had no chance of repeating the earlier novels success because it dealt with much more sensitive issues. It is, in essence, a parable about fidelity and sexual desire. Leander Tweddle gets into the mess only because he is uneasily keeping company with another young lady while his fiancée is away. This was a nettle that could not be grasped firmly at the time, and its evasion is painfully obvious. This is a pity, because the figure of Aphrodite is intrinsically more interesting than that of the jinn, who likewise fails to realize how profoundly the world has changed, and her observations on that subject might well have been fascinating had she been given the opportunity to develop them. Literary works no longer labor under the repressive notions of decency that constrained Anstey, but there is still a certain unease involved in addressing such matters, so the storys failure still seems frustrating rather than cowardly.

Anstey's fantasies are, in their own way, as revealing as the most earnest mundane novels as to the tenor and temper of Victorian manners. Their lightness and amiability was never quite captured by any of his imitators, perhaps because they could not achieve the remarkable innocence of his assumption that no sane human being could possibly aspire to be anything other than a Victorian gentleman.

—Brian Stableford

HYPERBOREA

A series of exotic fantasies set on a mythical polar continent

Author: Clark Ashton Smith (1893–1961)
Genre: Fantasy—magical world
Type of work: Stories
Time of work: About 15 million years ago
Location: Hyperborea
First published: 1971

THE STORY

In "The Tale of Satampra Zeiros" (1931), two thieves, unwisely undaunted by the evil reputation of a certain ruined city, attempt to plunder a shrine erected to the dark god Tsathoggua. The protagonist escapes, though badly maimed, after seeing his companion horribly killed. In "The Door to Saturn" (1932), the priest Morghi pursues the sorcerer Eibon through a doorway to another world. The two adversaries are forced to combine forces in order to survive in a wilderness of wonders until they find a place to settle.

"The Testament of Athammaus" (1932) is the tale of a hapless headsman appointed to execute a demoniac bandit. Every time his head is struck off, the bandit miraculously rises from the dead, becoming gradually more monstrous. In the end, the bandit degenerates to the point that further beheadings become impractical. In "Ubbo-Sathla" (1933), a modern occultist finds a magic lens that unites him with the personality of its wizard owner and allows him to share that owner's visionary quest to find the hideously repulsive mass of protoplasm that is parent to all Earthly life.

In "The Seven Geases" (1934), the vainglorious magistrate Ralibar Vooz falls prey, while out hunting, to the wrath of the sorcerer Ezdagor. Ezdagor places Vooz under a geas, which requires him to descend further into the Tartarean realm to present himself as a blood offering to Tsathoggua. Tsathoggua has no need of him and sends him deeper into the bowels of the earth. The pattern repeats as Vooz delivers himself in turn to the web of the spider-god Atlach-Natha, the palace of the "antehuman sorcerer" Haon-Dor, and the Cavern of the Archetypes. Finally, he arrives in the slimy gulf of Abhoth, "father and mother of all cosmic uncleanliness." By this time, he is in a realm so remote that his own ordered world is known only by ominous rumor, so Abhoth can think of no more awful place to send him than home. The journey back is fraught with far too many dangers for it to be made safely.

"The Weird of AvooslWuthoqquan" (1932), "The Ice-Demon" (1933), and "The Coming of the WhiteWorm" (1941) are all tales whose leading characters are drawn by avarice to some ironically bizarre end. The Hyperborean series also includes the sentimental extended prose-poem "The White Sybil" (1935) and the lackluster "The Theft of the Thirty- Nine Girdles" (1958). The collection also includes a group of prosepoems grouped under the heading "The World's Rim," including one extended account of "The Abominations of Yondo" (1926).

ANALYSIS

The balmy polar continent of Hyperborea, mentioned frequently in Greek mythology, was the third setting that Clark Ashton Smith set out to explore in some detail, following the imaginary French province of Averoigne and the legendary continent of Atlantis. Being even more remote in time than Atlantis (its obliterated civilizations flourished in the Miocene era, according to the occultist in "Ubbo-Sathla"), Hyperborea could more easily accommodate the kind of exotic landscapes, flora, and fauna that Smith earlier had attributed to the desert of Yondo near the world's rim.

Hyperborea retained one crucial limitation, by virtue of belonging to the past rather than the future: It was subject to the destiny of giving way to the mundane world of the present. For this reason, it was to be superseded by the far-future scenarios of Zothique when Smith wanted to push his vivid imagination to its most earnest limit, but it remained the location of choice for his lightest and most playful tales.

The characterization of the monsters and evil deities in these stories owes something to H. P. Lovecraft, to whose Cthulhu Mythos the god Tsathoggua sometimes is attached and to whose eccentric library of forbidden books Hyperborea contributed *The Book of Eibon*. Smith's handling of such material herein is, however, far more ironic than Lovecraft's ever was. Smith called these tales "Hyperborean grotesques," and they are indeed exercises in calculated grotesquerie, with a strong element of black comedy. The author's perennial fondness for tonguetwisting nomenclature is given its freest and most exuberant rein in "The Door to Saturn" and "The-Weird of AvooslWuthoqquan." The best of the Hyperborean tales, "The Testament of Athammaus" and the magnificently bizarre "The Seven Geases," are redolent with a macabre sarcasm no other writer ever matched.

Atheme that recurs in several of the stories is that of regression from order to chaos. In "The Testament of Athammaus," the sequence of the bandit's resurrections is from human being to a near-formless mass of primordial slime, a state of being highly reminiscent of that credited to the ultimate ancestor of all Earthly life in "Ubbo-Sathla." A similar degenerative sequence is provided, with more elaborate stages, in "The Seven Geases," but the endpoint is the same: Underlying all other notions of identity is an utterly loathsome, slimy mess.

The revelation that the ultimate reality is both degrading and disgusting is another echo of Lovecraft, but Smith's disgust at the concept of degradation is much less heartfelt than Lovecraft's. Smith's imagination agrees with Lovecraft's in reducing humankind to virtual insignificance in a vast and hostile universe, but Smith's vision is not straightforwardly horrific; it is extraordinarily lush and marvelously fecund.

Smith's imagined universe is by no means dismal; it is very colorful and full of bizarre life. Smith's is a universe in which there are not merely more things than are dreamed of in the dour Lovecraftian philosophy, but more things than are dreamed of in any philosophy. That is what makes Smith a uniquely precious writer.

—*Brian Stableford*

THE HYPERION CANTOS

Future humanity is caught in a conflict between rival groups of artificial intelligences seeking to control the universe

Author: Dan Simmons (1948–)
Genre: Science fiction—artificial intelligence
Type of work: Novels
Time of work: The distant future
Location: The planet Hyperion, cyberspace, and various unidentified planetary locations

First published: 1990 (previously published separately as *Hyperion*, 1989, and *The Fall of Hyperion*, 1990)

THE STORY
The two books of *The Hyperion Cantos* take their titles and themes from two unfinished poems by the Romantic poet John Keats (1795–1821) that deal with the displacement in Greek mythology of the old gods, the Titans, by the new gods, the Olympians. In Dan Simmons's work, Old Earth

has been destroyed by a black hole, and humans are spread across two hundred worlds and moons scattered throughout a thousand lightyears in space. Communication and travel are achieved through fatlines and farcasters, operated by Technocore Artificial Intelligences, who inhabit singularity environments and cyberspace. The artificial intelligences evolved in a symbiotic relationship with humankind but have decided that humans are no longer necessary.

There are three factions of artificial intelligences: the Volatiles, who want to remove humans altogether; the Ultimates, who are prepared to make way for a negotiated new order; and the Stables, who believe in continued coexistence. The fate of the universe depends on which of these groups is able to take control of the unforeseen variables occurring on the planet Hyperion. As the story opens, a number of futures theoretically are possible.

A cosmic conflict looms between the logically predestined Artificial Ultimate Intelligence and a newly evolved human Ultimate Intelligence, which is a triune god composed of Intellect, Empathy, and The Void Which Binds (or Quantum Reality). The Empathy part of this trinity has fled backward in time to avoid the conflict. To lure it back into the struggle, the artificial intelligences have accessed the worst nightmares of billions of humans to create an Avatar of Pain, called the Shrike. The idea is that the Shrike, which has impaled thousands of suffering humans on the branches of its Tree of Pain, will broadcast enough agony to drive Empathy out of hiding.

The Stable Artificial Intelligences also have constructed the perfect bodily trap for Empathy, a combination of a nearly divine human consciousness and an artificial imagination capable of spanning space and time. This body takes the form of cybrid (cyborg hybrid) personality retrieval projects based on John Keats. The Keats cybrids prove to be disinclined to accept godhood and prefer identification with humanity. Also involved in the conflict is a third group, the Ousters, a highly evolved branch of humanity that is interfering retroactively to favor humankind. They have modified the actions of the Shrike by creating Time Tombs on the planet Hyperion. They also have trained Rachel/Moneta to be the Shrike's companion, nemesis, and keeper, traveling backward in time with the Tombs and the Shrike toward the present of the text. Ordinary humans are caught in the crossfire of this conflict between gods and quasi gods. The human action begins when the Church of the Final Atonement decides to send a final group of seven pilgrims to the Time Tombs. These pilgrims represent the major human religious factions in the galaxy. Lenar Hoyt is a Catholic priest; Sol Weintraub is a Jewish philosopher; Fedmahn Kassad is a soldier of Islamic origin; Martin Silenus is a pagan poet; Het Masteen, the True Voice of the Tree, is a Templar conservationist; the nameless Consul is an atheist; and Brawne Lamia is a romantic agnostic.

The first book follows the model of Geoffrey Chaucer's *The Canterbury Tales* (1380–1390), with each of the pilgrims recounting a tale of relevant personal experiences. One of these, the Consul's tale, was published separately as "Remembering Siri" (1983). The pilgrims interact, but each has a separate role to play in the resolution of the conflict. Each of them is connected to the fate of humankind through the overriding motif of death and resurrection; each is approaching a form of apotheosis; and each apotheosis is controlled in some way by the Shrike, which functions as an agent of predestination.

The second book narrows the narrative focus to concentrate on the Keats cybrid. This part of the story is recounted by the Joseph Severn persona of Keats, who dreams much of the complicated action from his deathbed in a reconstructed cyberspace version of old Rome. The multiple story lines are drawn together through the agency of the Shrike. The political and philosophical actions eventually are united through an authorial suggestion that love is the reason for predeterminism in the universe. It is this love that links the imminent birth of Keats and Lamia's divine girlchild with the sacrifice of Weintraub's time-trapped daughter Rachel, which will enable her to be born into the future. The universal conflict is resolved by the humans with much help from the Ousters and the Keats cybrid. The TechnoCore is destroyed, and with it the farcaster system that had both aided and enslaved humanity.

Analysis

Simmons's early fiction was largely horror, with some fantasy, but *Hyperion*, which won the 1990

Hugo Award, is science fiction. *The Hyperion Cantos* might be described as metaphysical science fiction in that it deals with concepts relating to the universe as a whole. The two books are theological in that they offer a discourse on eschatology and predestination, as well as philosophical in their adaptation of the early Romantic concept of perfectibility as pure abstract process.

This work also falls within the category of recursive science fiction, which treats real people and the fictional worlds that they create as having equivalent reality. In placing a reconstructed John Keats persona at the center of the text, Simmons aligns this work with a number of other recursive texts, such as Tim Powers's *The Stress of Her Regard* (1989), that make extensive use of the already self-reflexive lives and works of the major late Romantic figures, particularly George Gordon, Lord Byron (1788–1824), Percy Bysshe Shelley (1792–1822), Mary Wollstonecraft Shelley (1797–1851), and John Keats. To these Romantic writers, the proper function of memory is to provide a path to the divine, using the mythopoeic powers of the imagination to transform base nature into transcendent reality. In postmodern fiction, especially in works dealing with cyberspace, the inspired order of memory has been reduced to the accumulation of data. This means that the inspired human memory is devalued as being less accurate than electronically recorded information that can be used to reconstruct "reality." The more humans rely on artificially recorded data, the less able they are to perform the romantic apotheosis. This problem is explored in *The Hyperion Cantos*, in which the role of the dreaming poet as creator has been usurped by the artificial intelligences.

The overall structure is a space opera on a grand scale, containing complexly interwoven strands of action. Simmons's technique is a self-consciously allusive postmodern collage of literary styles. His characters are drawn from a wide range of literary sources. Within the overtly Chaucerian framework of the first book, each of the pilgrim's tales is narrated in a completely different style, ranging from the romance of the Consul's tale, through the *Bildungsroman* of Silenus the poet's tale, to the tough, short-sentence detective form of Brawne Lamia's detective's tale. This technique is not sustained in the second book, which is more uniform in authorial tone, concentrating on the complexities of plot resolution.

There, Keats's notion of spiritual growth through creative suffering is given literal form in the multiple deaths, quasi deaths, and resurrections inflicted on the characters in their search for reconciliation between human and machine, creator and created. The emphasis rests, finally, on a metaphoric structure of birth and rebirth.

The Hyperion Cantos has given Simmons a prominent place in the science-fiction field. Simmons later resumed the Hyperion series with *Endymion* (1996), which follows the adventures of the hybrid girl Aenea and her lover and protector, Raul Endymion. Simmons concluded the series with *The Rise of Endymion* (1997), in which Raul and Aenea continue their journey in their search for the meaning of the universe. His other works include *The Hollow Man* (1992; a much expanded version of "Eyes I Dare Not Meet in Dreams," 1982) and the horror novel *Children of the Night* (1992). Neither of these works has received the acclaim accorded to *The Hyperion Cantos*.

—*Janeen Webb*